Medicare surtax on net investment income

200K (Single / HH)
250K (MFJ)
125K (MFS)

3.8% on net investment income
.9% on wages and compensation

TAXATION FOR DECISION MAKERS

2014 EDITION

Shirley Dennis-Escoffier

Karen A. Fortin

Wiley Custom Learning Solutions

Wiley Custom Learning Solutions

Taxation for Decision Makers, 2014 Edition
Shirley Dennis-Escoffier and Karen A. Fortin

Cover design by Rocky Buckley, Black Diamond Graphics.

Cover photo credits: Many dollars on the table: Denis Vrublevski/Shutterstock.

To order books or for customer service, please call 1 (800)-CALL-WILEY (225-5945).

This book was previously published by Pearson Education, Inc.

Printed in the United States of America.

ISBN 978-1-118-65454-5

Printed by Victor Graphics, Inc.

10 9 8 7 6 5 4 3 2 1

Brief Table of Contents

Table of Contents

Preface

Focus

This text is designed for a one-semester introductory tax course at either the undergraduate or graduate level. It is ideal for an MBA course or any program emphasizing a decision-making approach.

Comprehensive Yet Clear and Concise

This is the only text to introduce all topics on the CPA exam in only 12 chapters while striking the perfect balance between concepts and details. Tax concepts and applications are presented in a clear, concise, student-friendly writing style. It includes sufficient technical detail to provide a foundation for future practice in taxation and consulting while not overwhelming the student with seldom-encountered minutia.

Tax Planning

TAX PLANNING

The importance of tax planning is emphasized. It is woven into each chapter with margin icons highlighting planning opportunities. Tax planning strategies are introduced early in Chapter 2 along with the impact of taxes on cash flow.

Key Concepts

Each chapter begins with an introduction to the included topics, emphasizing why decision makers need to understand these topics. This is followed by a list of *Key Concepts* that provide an executive summary of the most important concepts students should master.

Setting the Stage—An Introductory Case

Each chapter-opening case introduces key issues while promoting critical analysis and decision-making skills. The case is then revisited at the end of the chapter.

Examples

Rigorous topics are tackled through numerous simple but realistic examples.

EXAMPLE 46

When Alex Rodriguez, the former Texas Rangers shortstop, lived in Texas (a state with no individual income tax), he owed more than $271,000 to California (which assesses a nonresident income tax) for games he played in that state during baseball season. It was estimated that if the Rangers had played all their games at home, A-Rod's state tax bill could have been reduced by more than half a million dollars a year. When A-Rod switched to the New York Yankees, his state and local tax burden increased dramatically. On the $155 million that A-Rod was to be paid over his seven-year contract, he was expected to owe $3.57 million to New York City and an additional $6.19 million to the State of New York for income taxes. His tax burden increased further when he renegotiated his contract in a deal worth $275 million over ten years.

Key Cases

Key Cases bring real world applications into the classroom.

KEY CASE *In 2008, actor Wesley Snipes was sentenced to 3 years in prison for willfully failing to file a tax return from 1999-2004, a period in which he earned more than $38 million. Following an unsuccessful appeal, he began serving his sentence in December 2010 in a medium-security prison in Pennsylvania.*

Expanded Topics

The *Expanded Topics* section included at the end of several chapters contains more advanced topics for instructors who wish to challenge their students. These advanced discussions relate to the other material within the chapters, but which our adopters and reviewers have indicated could be omitted to allow more time for the more critical material.

Summary

Each chapter closes with a *Summary* of the most important topics introduced in the chapter, reinforcing important concepts for students.

Key Terms

A list of *Key Terms* is included at the end of each chapter. They appear in bold print and are keyed to the first page on which the term is discussed.

Test Yourself

Each chapter includes a *Test Yourself* section of five multiple-choice questions for students to assess their understanding of topics covered in the chapter. Answers to these questions follow the end-of-chapter materials.

Problem Assignments

More than 60 problems are included at the end of each chapter. *Check Your Understanding* includes a wide variety of noncomputational questions that review the topics included in the chapter. *Crunch the Numbers* presents quantitative problems covering the computational aspects of chapter materials. Comprehensive problems integrate topics covered in several different chapters.

Think Outside the Text

For instructors wishing to challenge their students, *Think Outside the Text* questions develop critical thinking skills by requiring students to expand their thinking beyond the material covered in the chapter.

Identify the Issues

Identify the Issues includes short scenarios designed to challenge the students to identify issues and formulate research questions. These scenarios, however, do not provide enough information to enable students to develop definitive solutions but are designed to help students practice the issue-identification step in the research process, a step that many new tax students consider the most difficult.

Develop Research Skills

Develop Research Skills requires students to research the relevant authorities and present possible solutions. These can be solved using a subscription-based tax service such as Thompson Reuters RIA *Checkpoint*® (*for students at a school that subscribes to a tax service*) or free Internet sources. For most of these problems, citations to relevant Internal Revenue Code sections, cases, and rulings are included only with the separate Research Problem Solutions allowing each instructor to decide what, if any, hints should be given to students when a problem is assigned.

Develop Planning Skills

Develop Planning Skills problems give students the opportunity to test their knowledge in planning situations. The tax planning suggestions integrated throughout the text continually remind students of the importance of developing appropriate planning strategies.

Chapter Appendices

End-of-chapter appendices introduce topics not typically covered in a first tax course including corporate reorganizations, state and local taxation, and taxation of nonprofit entities. These materials are placed in chapter appendices to allow instructors the flexibility to include or omit them as deemed appropriate.

Tax Research Appendix

Appendix A at the end of the text provides a tutorial with screenshots of *Checkpoint*®, a subscription-based Internet tax service commonly used by tax practitioners. Students at schools that do not subscribe to Checkpoint® can gain a general understanding of how to research using subscription-only tax services by studying the screen captures.

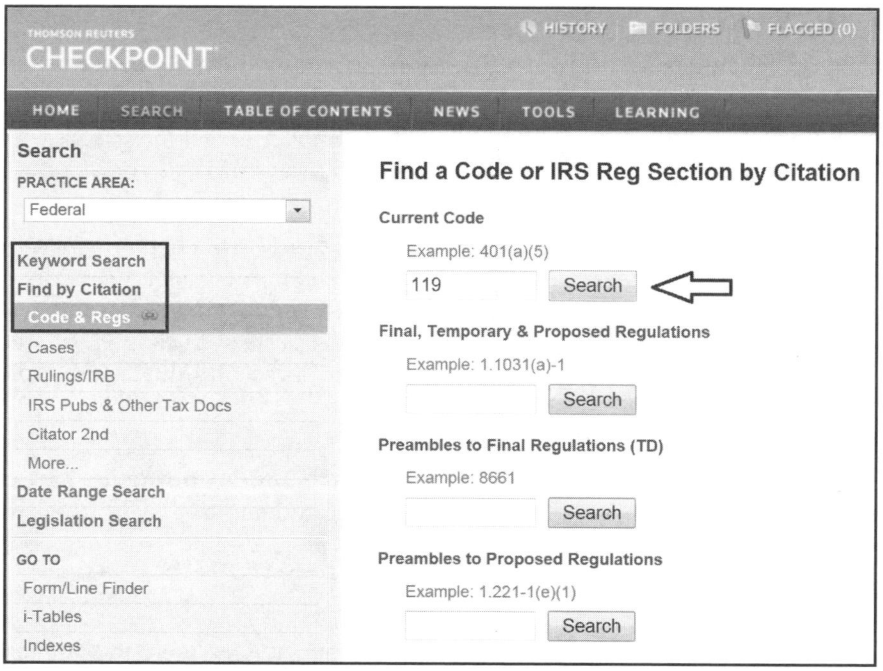

Sample Tax Returns

Sample Filled-In Tax Returns are included in Appendix C for a C corporation, S corporation, partnership, and a self-employed individual.

Tax Return Problems

Six ***Tax Return Problems***, covering the four types of business entities as well as individuals, are included in Appendix D. Using an appendix allows the instructor to assign an entire tax return problem or portion of a problem at whichever point in the term best suits a particular class.

Up-To-Date

This text has been completely updated for all recent legislation including the American Taxpayer Relief Act of 2012 and for all IRS pronouncements available as of April 2013, including the automobile ceiling limits. In addition, reference has been made to pending legislation that could affect text material where appropriate.

Organization

This text is ideal for schools with only one required tax course as it includes all the topics specified for the first course in the AICPA's Model Tax Curriculum. Its 12 chapters can be covered in one semester, with time for assessments, eliminating the need to omit chapters. The Model Tax Curriculum emphasizes tax planning to stimulate students' thinking in terms of the effect taxation has on decisions for entities as well as individuals. Although the text includes entity planning, it does not do so to the exclusion of individuals. An example of this dual planning orientation is illustrated in the discussion of employee compensation in Chapter 4. Most authors relegate compensation planning to the end of the text where, unfortunately, many students never see it. We chose this topics as an opportunity for students to view transactions from both the individual's perspective (minimizing taxable income) and the employer's perspective (maximizing deductions while providing a compensation plan that will attract valuable employees). This chapter is the bridge between the chapters on gross income and business expenses. This text maintains this planning orientation and integrates both entity and individual topics throughout Parts II and III as income, expense, and property transaction concepts are introduced.

Brief Contents

Your Course Your Way

Although this text is designed primarily for those who wish to provide an introduction to all entities before tackling the topics unique to individuals, the flexibility of this text makes it easy for those who wish to change the sequence of chapters. For example, sufficient notes and references to basic concepts in the preceding chapters are included within *Chapter 11: Income Taxation of Individuals* making it easy for instructors who wish to cover this chapter early in the term (such as after Chapter 4).

Supplements

Supplements include an author-prepared Solutions Manual, separate solutions to Research Problems, solutions to Appendix D Tax Return Problems, an extensive Test Bank, and PowerPoint slides. Also included are Reference Tables (with tax rate schedules and items indexed for inflation) so an instructor can easily choose which items to provide to students for an exam.

Comments and Suggestions

We realize that it is almost impossible for a text to be completely free of technical errors or to include every relevant topic. We welcome comments and suggestions on how we can improve the next edition. Please email your comments and suggestions to sdennis@miami.edu.

Acknowledgments

We wish to acknowledge and thank Joyce Middleton, Frostburg State University, Valerie Milliron, California State University in Chico, A. Blair Stanley, Bloomsburg University of Pennsylvania, Jacklyn Collins, University of Miami, and Diana Falsetta, University of Miami, for their suggestions. We are grateful to the entire Wiley team for their assistance, particularly Trista Waishkey, and Rocky Buckley for his special assistance in the production process.

Shirley Dennis-Escoffier and Karen A. Fortin

About the Authors

Shirley Dennis-Escoffier is an associate professor at the University of Miami, where she teaches both graduate and undergraduate tax classes. She received her Ph.D. from the University of Miami and returned to UM after teaching at the University of Hawaii and California State University in Hayward. She is a Certified Public Accountant licensed to practice in Florida. She is a Past President of the American Taxation Association and remains actively involved in the association receiving the Outstanding Service Award. She is also actively involved with the American Institute of Certified Public Accountants. She has received several teaching awards including the University of Miami Excellence in Teaching Award and the School of Business Alumni Association Excellence in Teaching Award. She has published numerous articles in tax and accounting journals and is the recipient of an Ernst and Young Foundation tax research grant.

Karen A. Fortin retired from her position as Professor of Accounting and Taxation at the University of Baltimore, where she had been Department Chair and taught graduate and undergraduate tax classes in both the Business School and the Law School. She received her Ph.D. from the University of South Carolina and held teaching positions at the University of Wisconsin–Milwaukee and the University of Miami. She is a Wisconsin Certified Public Accountant and a recipient of a Sells Award. During her teaching years, she was active in the American Taxation Association and the American Accounting Association as an editor, reviewer, and chairperson for numerous events. As a member of the AICPA she served on several committees and task forces. She has published numerous articles in tax and accounting journals and has co-authored and edited a number of textbooks. In between her extensive travels, she teaches part-time and volunteers in a local grade school tutoring students in mathematics.

To the memory of Marty Escoffier who was always ready with a willing hand to help, a word of encouragement as deadlines neared, and a sense of humor that never failed to make us laugh when we needed it most. His presence has been missed as we have worked on this revision.

—SHIRLEY DENNIS-ESCOFFIER AND KAREN A. FORTIN

part

I

INTRODUCTION TO TAXATION AND ITS ENVIRONMENT

chapter

1

An Introduction to Taxation

CHAPTER OUTLINE

This chapter presents an overview of the various types of taxation, several of the basic concepts important to the evaluation and understanding of taxation, and an introduction to taxable entities and alternate business forms. These serve as a backdrop to the more detailed provisions of income tax laws that follow in subsequent chapters. In reading this chapter, you should not be concerned with specific numbers or where they come from as the majority of these numbers change with each filing year and their origin will be discussed in subsequent chapters. Instead, you should focus on developing a broad understanding of how the U.S. income tax system works.

This chapter begins with some background information on the various forms of taxation (income, consumption, wealth, and wealth transfer taxes), the effects of various tax rate structures (progressive, proportional, and regressive), and a brief description of Adam Smith's Canons of Taxation (equity, economy, certainty, and convenience), which provide the framework that can be used to assess what constitutes a "good" tax. The chapter then specifically addresses income taxation, introducing taxable persons—individuals, C corporations, and fiduciaries—that are the ultimate payers of all income taxes.

Next, the concepts of gross income, taxable income, tax rates, gross tax liability, and tax credits are introduced in the context of both the corporate and individual tax models. The individual tax model includes several unique features, including adjusted gross income, deductions *for* adjusted gross income, deductions *from* adjusted gross income, and personal and dependency exemptions. Some of the basic concepts related to property transactions are also introduced.

The chapter ends with a discussion of the various types of business entities, including sole proprietorships, partnerships, C corporations, and S corporations. The individual owner of a sole proprietorship is taxed on the business's income. Partnerships and S corporations are conduits or flow-through entities because they do not pay income tax themselves but instead pass their income and loss items through to their owners for taxation at the owner level. A C corporation's income is subject to double taxation, once at the entity level when earned by the corporation and a second time at the shareholder level when distributed to shareholders as dividends. At the end, the basic attributes of these entities are compared.

KEY CONCEPTS

- ★ Taxes levied by governmental units include income taxes, sales or use taxes, wealth or property taxes, and wealth transfer taxes.
- ★ Tax rates may be progressive, proportional, or regressive.
- ★ Only individuals, C corporations, and fiduciaries pay income taxes.
- ★ In determining taxable income, individuals are allowed two sets of deductions from gross income—deductions *for* adjusted gross income (e.g. alimony and contributions to retirement plans) and deductions *from* adjusted gross

income (e.g. the greater of their itemized deductions or the standard deduction and their personal and dependency exemptions). Individual tax rates are progressive in that higher rates apply to increased levels of taxable income.

★ Sole proprietorships, partnerships, and S corporations are all business entities whose income and losses are passed through to owners and included in owners' tax returns for payment of income taxes.

★ Corporations are taxed on taxable income, which is the difference between gross income and deductions. The tax rates for corporations are made up of nominal rates and surtaxes that modify the basic nominal rates over certain ranges of taxable income.

Setting the Stage—An Introductory Case

Wing Hue, an engineer from China with U.S. residency status, recently obtained permanent employment with a U.S. consulting firm. Before coming to the United States, Hue developed a totally new system of gears for bicycles. He has obtained a patent on his gear design and plans to solicit some venture capitalists for funds to begin manufacturing and marketing the gears. He would like to sell the gears to both bicycle manufacturers and to repair shops as replacements for existing gears.

As a student in China, Hue never had sufficient income to pay taxes. He understands that as a U.S. resident, he will be subject to a variety of taxes. He is particularly interested in the potential taxation of his gear manufacturing enterprise. He asks you for a brief explanation of the tax landscape that he faces. We will return to this case at the end of this chapter.

An Introduction to Taxation

What Is a Tax?

A tax is a forced payment made to a governmental unit that is unrelated to the value of goods or services provided. Taxes are not voluntary. If we have income exceeding an allowable minimum, we are assessed income taxes on that income by the federal government and possibly state and local governments.[1] If we purchase certain goods or services, many of the states require sellers to collect sales taxes. Failure to pay or remit these taxes to the appropriate governmental unit, may subject persons to civil, or even criminal, penalties. If we own real estate, local governments place an assessed value on that property and send us a bill for property taxes. These taxes must be paid or the government may seize the property.

There are hidden taxes as well. Hidden taxes are those that are paid but that are not specifically itemized as part of the payment. When we buy gasoline for our automobiles, there are significant taxes imbedded in the price paid. The same is true for many other items, such as cigarettes and alcoholic beverages. Nevertheless, if we want that particular good (legally, that is), we pay the tax.

Taxes are not levied as punishment (as are fines for speeding), nor are they levied as payment for particular goods or services rendered by the government (such as a garbage collection fee). Although we may benefit from many governmental activities that are paid for by taxes, there is no direct connection between the benefit received by a taxpayer and the amount of tax the taxpayer must pay. Property taxes to support education are levied on the value of one's property, with no relationship to the number of children, if any, a person may have who are benefiting from free public school education. Thus, taxes are often termed forced extractions. You must pay them, but you may not necessarily derive any benefit from them.

[1] Individuals are assessed federal income taxes only if their income exceeds a certain minimum amount after their allowable deductions, including personal and dependency exemptions and the standard or itemized deductions.

TYPES OF TAXES

The Federal Income Tax

This text is primarily about the federal income tax—but what was an initially simple concept of taxing income has expanded over the years into an exceedingly complicated system. It is no longer a system with a primary goal of meeting the various revenue needs of the government to perform its basic functions, but has evolved into an engine for economic and social goals that lawmakers deem appropriate to foster. As our government has grown, so have the laws governing the determination of taxable income and taxes owed.

Over the last twenty or more years, there has been a realization that the current income tax system is no longer a workable system due to its complexity. Fewer than half the income tax filers actually prepare their own returns but are forced to pay tax preparers to perform this task. There have been many calls for simplifying the system but this cannot be done without having a basic understanding of other types of taxes that could be introduced as adjuncts to or in place of the current income tax system. So—before we begin an introductory study of the income tax system, certain basic concepts will be introduced including the various alternative types of taxes other than the income tax, the types of tax rates that can be applied to a taxable base, and Adam Smith's canons of taxation which were put forth many years ago as a foundation for the development of a good tax. Once these concepts are understood along with an understanding of the current income tax laws, one can intelligently participate in discussions about reforming our current tax system.

Wealth Taxes

Wealth taxes are based on the taxable entity's total wealth or the value of specific types of property. The most common wealth tax is the **real property tax**. This is the tax levied on individuals and businesses that own real property—that is, land and buildings. Local taxing jurisdictions rely heavily on the real property tax for the support of schools, police and fire protection, and other services furnished by the local municipality. The federal government generally does not levy any form of wealth tax, leaving the various forms of wealth taxes to the state or local governments.

To determine the real property tax to be levied, the municipality "works backward." The total budget is determined along with the total assessed valuation for all property subject to the tax. A mill levy (a "mill" is one-tenth of one cent) is then determined based on the total assessed value of the property that raises the revenue required by the budget. The mill levy is applied to each individual property within the district to determine its separate property tax.

EXAMPLE 1

The budget of the municipality is $1,000,000 and the total assessed value of all the property subject to the property tax is $200,000,000. To raise the required $1,000,000, a five-mill levy is required per $1 of assessed value ($1,000,000/$200,000,000 = $.005). When the mill levy is applied to a piece of property with an assessed value of $100,000, the owner would pay $500 ($.005 × $100,000) in real property taxes.

Other forms of wealth taxes include the personal property tax, the tangible property tax, and the intangible property tax. These taxes are collected annually on property owned as of a certain date based on a predetermined fixed rate applied to the fair market value of the property. Personal property or tangible property taxes are more likely to be levied on businesses. These taxes may take the form of inventory taxes or taxes on the value of a business's operating assets. Individuals do not always escape this tax, however, as a number of states base a part of the cost of obtaining automobile registrations or license plates on the value of the auto.

Some states may levy intangible taxes on businesses and individuals. Intangible assets are receivables, stocks, bonds, and other forms of investment instruments.

Intangible taxes are based on a fixed tax rate times the fair market value of the intangible assets owned as of a specific date.

Two major problems related to levying certain wealth taxes have lessened government reliance on them as a source of revenue: the difficulty in establishing fair market value annually and the taxpayer's ability to "hide" personal property. The value of many types of personal property (tangible or intangible) is not subject to verifiable market values. This can lead to significant undervaluation by the taxpayer. Moreover, the government may not know that a particular person owns a certain asset unless there is some way to trace or detect ownership. Thus, over the years, most local governments have begun to rely more heavily on real property taxes rather than on other types of personal property taxes. Real estate is much harder to hide—and through the assessment system, taxes are thought to be levied on a more uniform basis across the value of the properties.[2]

Based on the concept of ability to pay, wealth taxes would seem to be a sound source of tax revenue. However, many items such as a personal residence do not produce direct income. Thus, the owner may have little or no disposable income with which to pay the tax. This is often cited as a major problem for the elderly or others on fixed incomes when real property taxes increase.

Wealth Transfer Taxes

Wealth transfer taxes are levied when an individual transfers all or part of his or her wealth to another person. Since 1916, the United States has imposed an **estate tax**, a wealth transfer tax that applies to transfers of property as a result of the owner's death. A second wealth transfer tax, the **gift tax**, was enacted in 1932. The gift tax is imposed on a donor who makes a gratuitous lifetime transfer of property.[3] The recipient receives the property (whether as a gift or inheritance) free of tax.

In 1976, the federal estate and gift taxes were unified so that the wealth transfer tax would be levied based on the sum of a person's transfers during his or her lifetime and at death. The tax is assessed on the fair market value of the property transferred by the transferee. To ease the administrative burden, an *annual* gift exclusion (currently $14,000 per recipient per year) prevents smaller gifts from being subject to tax.[4] Additionally, an unlimited amount of transfers to spouses and qualified charities (during lifetime and at death) escape the tax entirely. A unified gift and estate *lifetime* credit assures that a certain base amount of wealth can be transferred to others (including children, grandchildren, other relatives, and friends) through lifetime gifts or transfers at death without tax

EXAMPLE 2

In 2013, Marleen gave $50,000 cash to a qualified charity. She also gave each of her five grandchildren 700 shares of stock valued at $10,000 on their birthdays. The charitable gift is not subject to the gift tax. The birthday gifts are free from gift tax due to the $14,000 annual gift tax exclusion for each grandchild. If any of the birthday gifts exceeded the annual exclusion, Marleen would still not have to pay any gift tax until she exhausted her unified credit equivalent of her lifetime exclusion. The receipt of a gift (no matter how large) is not subject to income tax so the grandchildren have no tax consequences on the receipt of the gifts; but any dividends received by the grandchildren on the stock or gains realized on a future sale may be subject to income tax.

---

[2]Ideally, this would be the result of an annual valuation process. In reality, property assessments may increase or decrease based on indices only and are otherwise revised only when a property is sold.

[3]Chapter 12 contains a more detailed discussion of wealth transfer taxes.

[4]If all gifts from a taxpayer to each recipient total less than $14,000 annually, then that taxpayer does need to file a gift tax return. The annual exclusion was $13,000 from 2009 through 2013 ($12,000 for 2006-2008, $11,000 for 2002-2005, and $10,000 prior to 2002). In addition, a husband and wife can effectively combine their $14,000 annual exclusions through gift splitting so that they can jointly give up to $28,000 to each recipient annually.

The gift and estate taxes are integrated so that any unified credit that has not been used for lifetime gifts is available to be used for transfers made by the decedent's estate. Thus, the decedent's estate escapes taxation unless his or her total lifetime taxable gifts and taxable transfers at death exceed the lifetime exclusion.[5]

A number of states levy inheritance taxes rather than estate taxes. The inheritance tax is based on a person's right to receive property upon the death of another. As such, the tax rates and amount excluded from taxation vary based on the relationship of the heir to the decedent and the value of the property received. The estate normally pays the inheritance tax, but the tax paid reduces the value of the property transferred to the heir. In addition to an inheritance or estate tax, many states also levy a gift tax.

Consumption Taxes

Consumption taxes may take many forms, but the **sales tax** is the most common form in the United States. Almost all states levy sales taxes on some or all of the goods and services purchased, although certain items considered necessities may be exempt from tax. For example, food, clothing, prescriptions, and many types of services may be excluded from a sales tax. Taxing services remains a controversial matter. A number of years ago, Florida attempted to levy sales taxes on many types of professional services, including banking and accounting services. The difficulties in determining the basis on which to levy the tax were considered so great that the tax was abandoned rather quickly. Other services, for which a base is readily determinable, such as dry cleaning or auto repair, may be fertile tax ground. As states need to raise revenue without an overt sales tax increase, they may add more items to the goods and services subject to the tax, or exemptions from the sales tax may be removed.

A second consumption tax, the **use tax**, is assessed on out-of -state purchases made by the purchaser's state of residence. The seller of goods that are shipped directly to an address in another state is not required to collect the seller's state's sales tax on that sale nor is the seller required to collect the sales tax for the state of residence for the purchaser. Instead, the purchaser is responsible for paying a use tax (usually at the same rate as the sales tax) to the state of residence. With the exception of commercial firms, few purchasers actually comply with the use tax provisions.

A major problem related to the use tax is that of the taxation of Internet sales. Most sales conducted over the Internet are free of sales taxes unless the Internet seller has a physical presence in the same state as the state of the purchaser. This leaves the responsibility of paying the use tax to the purchaser, something that is unlikely to occur. So far, the taxing authorities have not solved the problem of efficiently collecting the sales or use tax on these purchases, although discussion of this problem continues due to state budget deficits and the need to increase revenues.

One benefit of a consumption tax is that it encourages savings, which is considered a necessity for continued investment and economic growth. With a sales tax, a person can choose to avoid the tax by not purchasing certain goods for consumption; income that is not consumed is saved. Thus, to avoid this tax, the taxpayer saves part of his or her income. On the other hand, the income tax taxes not only income whether consumed or saved, but it taxes the income earned on savings, thus further discouraging savings.

Other types of consumption taxes include excise taxes, value-added taxes, and turnover taxes—although only the excise tax is in common use in this country. An excise tax is another form of sales tax and the only form of sales tax levied by the federal government. Excises are generally levied on taxable goods for which there is a low elasticity of demand or on goods whose use the government wishes to discourage, such as tobacco products and alcoholic beverages. This latter group of excises is generally referred to as "sin" taxes.[6] Because of their low elasticity of demand, many persons are

---

[5]The lifetime exclusion for taxable transfers is $5,250,000 for 2013 ($5,120,000 for 2012). Chapter 12 has a more complete discussion of the annual and lifetime exclusions for taxable transfers.

[6]The indirect costs incurred from the consumption of these products must be borne by the government; that is, treating persons for lung cancer and alcoholism is the justification for taxing these products at rates that are designed to discourage their use.

willing to pay any price to purchase and use these products. Other excises offset some of the costs incurred by the government for certain services to be provided—for example, the tax on airline tickets helps pay for the system of air traffic controllers.

The **value-added tax**, in use in most of the developed countries of the world, has not been adopted in the United States. It is a sales tax that is added to a product or service based on the value added at specific points in the production or service process. Although there are several methods for calculating the value-added tax, it basically works as described in the following example.

EXAMPLE 3

A business buys some parts from a manufacturer to assemble a widget. The parts cost $400, to which a 10 percent value-added tax was added by the manufacturer for a total cost of $440. The business assembles these parts into a widget and, in turn, sells the assembled widget for $800 plus a 10 percent value-added tax of $80 for a total selling price of $880 collected from the purchaser. However, when the business remits the tax to the government, the business remits only $40 of the tax—the additional 10 percent tax levied on the value added from the assembly-step (total $80 value added tax less the $40 valued added tax paid to the manufacturer for the parts purchased). The government collects the other $40 from the manufacturer of the parts for assembly. The consumer pays the full tax on the product to the last business in the business chain. The tax is collected at each step in the business chain, however, based on the difference in the price paid for the goods coming in to that step and the price received when they leave that step.

Some features of the value-added tax make it somewhat different from a sales tax. First, it generally is a hidden tax at the consumer level; that is, the tax is imbedded in the selling price. Second, the value-added tax is not levied on goods that are exported to other countries. Businesses that export goods to other countries apply for a refund of the value-added taxes paid on those goods that are exported.

In the United States, businesses are subject to the income tax on their profits from goods or services sold, regardless of where they are sold. Because its products must absorb the income tax if the business is to survive, export products must have higher prices than they would if subject instead to a value-added tax. When the United States exports goods to a foreign country in competition with another exporting country with a value-added tax (instead of a corporate income tax), the United States may be at a competitive disadvantage. All other costs being equal, the U.S. firm will have to charge more than the other exporter to make the same profit because the foreign exporter will receive a rebate of the value-added taxes paid. The U.S. firm must still pay income tax on the profit from the exported goods. Moreover, a foreign business shipping goods to this country receives a rebate of its value-added tax from the foreign government, making its costs lower than the costs for comparable goods produced here in the United States.[7]

The turnover tax, another consumption tax, is a sales tax levied at each step of a business chain—both wholesale and retail—but with no rebates for prior taxes paid. Thus, if one firm handles all the steps in a manufacturing process from raw materials to finished goods, the tax is levied only once, when the product is sold to the consumer. If, however, that same product's manufacturing process is handled by two or three firms, each handling one or more steps in the manufacturing process, the tax is levied and collected each time the items move from one manufacturer to the other. Thus, this latter item will have had the tax levied two or three times—driving up its costs relative to the manufacturer that is able to complete all the various manufacturing steps itself.

Tariffs and Duties

Tariffs are taxes levied on goods and materials brought into a country, usually for one of two reasons: (1) A foreign country is selling goods to the purchasers in the

[7]Foreign firms that sell goods within the United States may be subject to U.S. income taxes, but they may be levied at rates significantly different from those faced by comparable U.S. firms.

destination country at prices that are believed to be below the costs to produce in the country of origin; the foreign business may be attempting to capture a market and put the local operations out of business. (2) A local business's operating costs are higher than those costs for the same product produced in the foreign jurisdiction.[8]

Import duties are similar to tariffs as they are taxes on goods brought into a country and levied by the destination country. When persons travel abroad, they are permitted to purchase a certain amount of goods and bring them back "duty free." If the duty-free allowance is exceeded, then the government levies a tax on the excess brought back. This encourages the purchase of goods at home by making imported goods more expensive. Export duties are taxes levied on goods that are leaving the country of origin. These taxes discourage producers from selling their goods abroad by making their products more expensive. In this way, they are available for purchase in the country of origin at lower prices.

TYPES OF TAX RATE SYSTEMS

The Progressive Tax Rate System

The current income tax system is a **progressive tax system**—that is, one in which the tax rates on income increase as income increases. The progressive tax system is based on the fundamental belief that those taxpayers who enjoy a higher level of income should pay a greater proportion of the taxes necessary to support the government. This concept is known as the "ability to pay" or the "wherewithal to pay" concept. It is probably true that most taxpayers believe that a progressive system is a fair tax system in that they believe people who have more should contribute more to the country's welfare through taxes. There is, however, nothing that makes a progressive tax system inherently fairer—the fairness of a tax is a value judgment that varies from person to person.

The progressiveness of the U.S. income tax rate structure for individuals has varied over the years. In 1913, the rates ranged from a low of 1 percent to a high of 7 percent. As the nation sought greater revenue to finance the World War I effort, the top rate increased to 77 percent. In 1985, 15 tax brackets ranged from a low of 11 percent to a high of 50 percent. In an attempt to simplify the tax system, the Tax Reform Act of 1986 drastically reduced the number of brackets as well as the rates. However, the top rate and the number of rates continued to change either to raise revenue to balance the budget or to provide a tax cut when budget surpluses were predicted.

The Economic Growth and Tax Relief Reconciliation Act of 2001 (EGTRRA) introduced some of the lowest income tax rates that individuals enjoyed, the full implementation of which was accelerated by the 2003 Jobs and Growth Act. These Acts resulted in six rates from a low of 10 percent to a maximum rate of 35 percent. The rates, however, were to revert to the pre-EGTRRA rates for tax years after 2012. The potential return to these pre-2001 rates along with other specified spending cuts at the beginning of 2013 became known as the "fiscal cliff." President Obama was reelected for another term in 2012 and one of his campaign issues was to retain the tax rates for most individuals but raise rates on upper income taxpayers that he defined as individuals making $200,000 or more and married couples making $250,000 or more. This increase in rates, along with the budget deficit, was a major source of contention throughout the campaign and continued well after the election. It wasn't until January 2, 2013 that both houses of Congress passed the measure that kept the pre-2013 tax rates for most individuals but raised the top rate to 39.6 percent for taxable incomes of $400,000 for individuals (as shown in Table 1.1) and $450,000 for married couples filing jointly (MFJ). Postponed, however, was any real confrontation on the second part of that fiscal cliff–spending cuts and deficit reduction.

---

[8]The tariffs on foreign steel introduced by the George W. Bush administration are examples of taxes levied because of the concern that foreign countries were "dumping" steel here at prices below their costs.

TABLE 1.1 **2013 TAX RATES FOR SINGLE INDIVIDUALS**

TAXABLE INCOME	TAX RATE
0–$8,925	10%
$8,926–$36,250	15%
$36,251–$87,850	25%
$87,851–$183,250	28%
$183,251–$398,350	33%
$398,351–$400,000	35%
Over $400,000	39.6%

The range of income subject to a specific tax rate is known as a tax bracket. Thus, as a single individual's income exceeds a specific bracket amount, his or her income within that next bracket is subject to the increased income tax rate. Although the income ranges (or brackets) differ by filing status, the same set of progressive tax rates apply, with higher rates taking effect at different income levels as determined by filing status. The brackets to which these rates apply are adjusted annually for inflation.

The long-term capital gains of individuals are generally subject to alternative long-term capital gains tax rates but certain revisions have been made to these capital gains tax rates for tax years beginning after 2012. Prior to 2013, a majority of long-term capital gains were taxed at a flat rate of 15 percent with only those taxpayers whose taxable income did not exceed the 15 percent tax bracket paying no tax—a rate of 0 (zero) percent. Beginning in 2013, the long-term capital rate has been permanently increased to 20 percent for taxpayers whose taxable income exceeds $400,000 ($450,000 MFJ); however, a 3.8 percent surtax is added to the rates for all taxpayers on investment-type income when income exceeds $200,000 ($250,000 MFJ). The 0 and 15 percent rates remain for lower income taxpayers. Table 1.2 provides the base long-term capital gain tax rates (excluding the surtax) over all levels of income for a single person. Capital assets that do not meet the more-than-one-year holding period (short-term capital assets) are taxed at the individual's regular tax rates.[9]

TABLE 1.2 **LONG-TERM CAPITAL GAINS TAX RATES FOR SINGLE INDIVIDUALS IN 2013**

TOTAL TAXABLE INCOME	MAXIMUM ORDINARY INCOME TAX RATE	CAPITAL GAINS TAX RATE
$8.925 or less	10%	0%
$8,926–$36,250	15%	0%
$36,251–$87,850	25%	15%
$87,851–$183,250	28%	15%
$183,251–$200,000	33%	15%
$200,001–$398,350	33%	15%
$398,351–$400,000	35%	15%
Over $400,000	39.6%	20%

[9]A long-term capital gain results from the sale or exchange of a capital asset that has been held (the time from acquisition to disposition) for more than 12 months. Capital assets include investment assets and personal-use assets. Refer to Chapter 7 for a complete discussion of capital gains tax rates, including the surtax and higher base rates for certain assets. See Chapter 3 for investment income surtaxes.

Corporations also face a progressive tax system; however, the corporate rate structure consists of four nominal tax rates of 15%, 25%, 34% and 35% and two surtaxes applied at different income levels. A five percent surtax eliminates the benefit of the 15 percent and 25 percent brackets on income below $75,000 and a three percent surtax eliminates the benefit of the 34 percent rate on income below $10,000,000. The tax structure (brackets) for corporations, including both nominal rates and surtaxes, is shown in Table 1.3.

TABLE
1.3 CORPORATE TAX RATES

TAXABLE INCOME	TAX RATE
0–$50,000	15%
$50,001–$75,000	25%
$75,001–$100,000	34%
$100,001–$335,000	39% (34% nominal rate + 5% surtax)
$335,001–$10,000,000	34%
$10,000,001–$15,000,000	35%
$15,000,001–$18,333,333	38% (35% nominal rate + 3% surtax)
Over $18,333,333	35%

Corporations do not have special long-term capital gains rates. Their capital gains are taxed using the same nominal rates as their other ordinary income.

With a progressive tax system, several other tax rate concepts are important. The **average tax rate** is determined by dividing the taxpayer's tax liability by taxable income. For example, if a corporation has $75,000 of taxable income, the tax liability of the corporation is $13,750 [($50,000 × 15%) + ($25,000 × 25%)]. The average tax rate of the corporation is 18.33 percent ($13,750/$75,000). In comparing groups of taxpayers, the average tax rate is often used for comparison purposes.

The marginal tax rate is the tax rate to which the next dollar of taxable income is subject. If the above corporation's taxable income were to increase to $75,001, this extra dollar of income would be taxed at 34 percent. As a taxpayer moves from one tax bracket to another, the marginal tax rate moves from one nominal rate to the next. For decision purposes the **marginal tax rate** is the most relevant rate.[10]

In a purely progressive tax system, the marginal tax rate is always higher than the average tax rate. For individuals, the average rate may approach the highest marginal rate—but because there is always some income taxed at lower rates, average can never equal the marginal rate for individuals.

For two income ranges in the scheme of corporate taxation (with its structure of nominal rates and surtaxes), the marginal and average rates are identical. For corporate incomes between $335,000 and $10,000,000, the nominal rate is 34 percent, the marginal rate is 34 percent, and the average rate is 34 percent. The 5 percent surtax on incomes between $100,000 and $335,000 was designed to wipe out the benefit of the lower nominal tax rates of 15 and 25 percent. When the corporation's income reaches $18,333,333 or more, the nominal, marginal, and average rates are all 35 percent. Again, the 38 percent tax rate (including the 3 percent surtax) on income from $15,000,000 to $18,333,333 makes up for the lower 34 percent rate on income below $10,000,000.

[10]A third tax rate, the effective tax rate, divides the taxes paid by an individual's economic income (both taxable and nontaxable).

Proportional "Flat" Tax Rate

One alternative to a progressive system of taxation would be a proportional or flat tax system. A true **proportional tax system** would require all income to be taxed at the same rate regardless of the amount or type of income that the taxpayer has. Thus, marginal and average tax rates would be identical over all ranges of income.

Although we have had a number of flat tax proposals[11] over the past 25 or more years, none has been a true proportional tax. A true proportional tax would have no exempt income, no personal or dependency exemptions, and no standard or itemized deductions. The flat-tax proposals have all provided for a modified proportional tax system as certain income amounts are subject to a 0 (zero) percent tax rate due to limited exclusions and deductions. Only taxable income is subject to the flat-tax rate. Thus, the proposed flat taxes have been progressive taxes, but with only two rates—zero and some positive percent.

Regressive Taxes

A **regressive tax system** is one in which taxpayers pay a decreasing proportion of their income as their incomes increase. As the taxpayer's income goes from one bracket to another, his or her average tax on total income decreases, as does the marginal tax rate.

The only overtly regressive tax that taxpayers are subject to at the federal level is the Social Security portion of the FICA tax. The 6.2 percent Social Security tax applies to salaries and wages up to a maximum amount: $113,700 in 2013 ($110,100 in 2012 and $106,800 in 2011).The Tax Relief Act of 2010, however, temporarily reduced the Social Security portion of the FICA tax for 2011 and 2012 to 4.2 percent for the employee only in an attempt to stimulate the economy. The employer still paid the full 6.2 percent on wages up to the wage limit. The 1.45 percent Medicare portion of the FICA tax applies to all salary and wages without limit (so the Medicare tax is a proportional tax).[12] As a taxpayer's salary or wage exceeds the Social Security maximum, the rate drops to 0 (zero) percent for additional wages and the average tax rate begins to drop below the 6.2 percent reduced nominal rate for an employee as shown below based on year 2013 amounts:

Wages	Social Security Tax @ 6.2%	Average %
$75,000	$3,150.00	6.2%
$150,000	$7,049.40	4.7%

The Medicare portion, however, is proportional as illustrated below.

Wages	Medicare Tax @ 1.45%	Average %
$75,000	$1,087.50	1.45%
$150,000	$2,175.00	1.45%

Generally, the federal unemployment tax (FUTA) also is a regressive tax because the unemployment rate of 6 percent only applies to the first $7,000 of an employee's wages. When the employee's wages exceed this amount, no further unemployment taxes are collected from the employer. Federal unemployment taxes are levied on the

[11]The most widely publicized flat-tax proposal excluded investment income and capital gains from tax and allowed only standard and dependency deductions. Examples of recently proposed taxes include the 17 percent flat tax proposed as part of the *Tax Simplification Act of 2007* and the 20 percent flat tax proposed as part of the *Flat Tax Act of 2009*. Several of the potential Republican candidates for the 2012 Presidential election had also proposed alternative versions of a flat tax.

[12]Employers also pay the Federal Insurance Contributions Act (FICA) taxes in addition to that withheld from employees so that the total Social Security rate is 12.4 percent (6.2% employer rate + 6.2% employee rate) and the Medicare rate is 2.9 percent (1.45% x 2). Self-employed individuals, however, must pay both the employer's and employee's share (referred to as the *self-employment tax*), resulting in a combined rate of 15.3 percent on the first $113,700 for 2013 ($110,100 (in 2012) of self-employment income and 2.9 percent on the excess. The detailed computations are discussed in Chapter 4. To pay for expanded health care coverage, the Patient Protection and Affordable Care Act added two Medicare surtaxes beginning in 2013. The new 3.8 percent Medicare surtax on net investment income is discussed in Chapter 3 and the 0.9 percent Medicare surtax on earned income is discussed in Chapter 4.

employer only so individual taxpayers may not be aware of their regressive nature. A few states do levy unemployment taxes on the employee—not just the employer—and these are regressive because the tax applies only to wages up to some maximum level.

Consumption-type taxes, such as the sales and use taxes, are generally considered to be regressive taxes as shown in the following example:

EXAMPLE 4

Ted earns $15,000 in disposable income. He spends all $15,000 for basic living expenses subject to a 5 percent consumption tax and pays taxes of $750. The effective consumption tax rate for this consumer is 5 percent. Juan has $60,000 of disposable income. He saves $10,000 of his income and spends the rest on consumer goods subject to a 5 percent consumption tax. The tax that he pays is $2,500. Based on his income of $60,000, his effective consumption tax rate is only 4.2 percent. Because Juan's effective tax rate is lower than Ted's for a higher level of income, the tax is considered regressive.

This example illustrates the regressive nature of consumption taxes but highlights the beneficial features of a consumption tax: the encouragement of savings. While lower-income persons must spend all their income for day-to-day living expenses, higher-income persons can choose to save a portion of their income. If they invest the saved money, they avoid taxes on their investment income as well—until such time as they withdraw the investment income and/or principal for current consumption.

CHARACTERISTICS OF A GOOD TAX

If someone could come up with a universally acceptable definition of a "good" tax, he or she would probably become a political phenomenon. The problem with defining a good tax is that, like beauty, the definition is in the eye of the beholder. Most of us would like to assert that a good tax is one that applies to other persons and leaves us relatively unscathed—the NIMBY (not in my backyard) theory of taxation. In other words, a good tax is one that others pay—and that I do not. Unfortunately, whether we pay directly or indirectly, few of us escape taxation.

In 1776, Adam Smith proposed the concepts known as the four **canons of taxation**, *equity, convenience, certainty, and economy* in *The Wealth of Nations*.[13] To this day, these concepts are still valid for determining whether a tax should be considered a good tax. No one since Adam Smith has come up with a more widely accepted criteria for judging a tax, although other criteria have been added.

Equity

Equity is probably the most difficult of the four canons on which to achieve consensus. When is a tax equitable? How a person answers that question depends on that person's perspective, background, and view of society. If someone works very hard and, as a result, earns an extremely good living, it may not seem equitable to him or her that almost 40 percent or more of any additional income that could be earned is taken away in taxes. This person may not view the progressive tax system as equitable when it takes such a high percentage of this income. On the other hand, a person who is supporting a large family on a very meager income may not believe that paying any taxes, when basic necessities cannot be purchased, is an equitable tax.

The basic idea of equity is that persons with similar incomes will face similar taxes. There is a major problem in determining when persons have similar incomes. Do we look at similar gross incomes or similar taxable incomes? Consider that one person who is very wealthy may decide to invest in municipal bonds, the interest from which is exempt from tax. A working person's income may be no more than the wealthy person's interest from these bonds. In such a case, the working person may pay 25 to 30 percent of that equivalent income in taxes. Is this equitable? Both taxpayers have the same inflow of income, but one is able to avoid tax because of his or her wealth and ability to invest in tax-sheltered investments.

[13] *The Wealth of Nations*, Book V, Chapter II, Part II (New York: Dutton, 1910).

Various federal policies dictate why the taxes paid by the above taxpayers differ. It has been a long-standing policy of the federal government not to tax the income on debt instruments of municipalities. This permits a municipality to pay a much lower rate of interest on their bonds. These bonds, however, are generally only attractive to taxpayers with larger taxable incomes who pay taxes at the highest marginal tax rates. The untaxed, but lower, income that they earn from these bonds is still greater than the after-tax return that could be earned on taxable bonds because of their high marginal tax rate.

In the current U.S. system, most capital assets held more than 12 months by individuals are taxed at rates that are significantly lower than the maximum tax rate for salary or wages income. Consider two persons, both of whom are in the same marginal tax bracket because of equal salaries. Taxpayer A earns $20,000 in additional salary through a bonus arrangement, and Taxpayer B sells some bonds resulting in a $20,000 capital gain taxed at a lower capital gains tax rate. Taxpayer A will pay more tax than Taxpayer B because his additional income is in wages while Taxpayer B's extra income comes the sale of an investment asset. Again, is this equitable? These illustrations relate to the concept of **horizontal equity**, which dictates that equal incomes should be taxed equally.

Capital gains tax rates on the disposition of capital assets held for a substantial period of time have traditionally been taxed at rates that are lower than regular income tax rates for several reasons. First, there is no inflation adjustment for capital gains; yet often the capital gain is an inflation gain rather than a real gain. If inflation is very high, the taxpayer may indeed have a loss when constant dollars are considered, but he or she will still be subject to the capital gains tax. A lower capital gains rate also encourages investors to move their money from unprofitable investments into more profitable ones. When capital gains rates are high, taxpayers tend to keep their appreciated but no-longer-profitable assets to avoid the tax. (This is called the *lock-in effect* of capital gains taxes.) In each of the situations described above, arguments are made on both sides of the equity issue.

Equity has another side, however—**vertical equity**. Vertical equity would require higher-income persons to pay a greater proportion of their income than lower-income persons. Vertical equity is often referred to as *the ability to pay* concept. Vertical equity is the basis for a progressive tax system. As a person's income increases, he or she is assumed to need a smaller percentage of that income for basic living and other expenses and, thus, is in a better position to pay a greater share of that income in taxes. Difficulties arise with this concept of equity, however.

Consider a family with an income of $50,000 consisting of a husband and wife and one healthy child. Then consider another family consisting of a husband and wife with six children, two of whom have significant handicaps. They, however, have an income of $60,000. Vertical equity would tell us that the second family should pay a greater percentage of their income than the first. Which family is better able to pay taxes (has the ability to pay), however? Obviously, the U.S. tax system would help relieve some of the extra tax burden on the second family through the number of dependency exemptions that family would be allowed, the medical expense deduction, and child care credits, but this also complicates the system.

Each of us, however, will have to make up his or her own mind as to what truly constitutes an equitable tax system. As we try to make the tax system appear to be more equitable, we introduce more complexity into that system. The simplest system of all would be a single rate of tax applied to all increases in a person's wealth (including that used for consumption, the economists' definition of income); yet, this probably will never be considered because it would not be perceived as fair.

Economy

A tax meets the criterion of economy when the amount of revenue it raises is at an optimum level after the costs of administration and compliance are considered. The costs of a tax are not just limited to the costs incurred by the tax administration office in collecting the tax. Certain taxes impose an enormous burden on the taxpayer for compliance.

Consider that more than half the individual taxpayers in the United States use some form of tax preparer to assist in preparing their tax returns. Many businesses have their own tax departments with no other responsibility than to ensure that all federal, state, and local income, employment, and property taxes are paid in a timely manner.

Compare on economic grounds, for example, the state income tax to a state sales tax. A sales tax is collected at the point of retail purchase and remitted by the retailer to the state. The purchaser has only to pay the added tax to the retailer when the good or service is purchased. To comply with the state income tax, taxpayers normally cannot use the information from their federal tax returns without a number of adjustments. Thus, the taxpayer must pay a preparer or spend additional time preparing the state income tax return. The state must use procedures similar to the federal government to check for accuracy and compliance to the laws applicable to these returns. The state must conduct many more audits if they are to audit the same percentage of individual taxpayers' returns as they would retailers remitting sales taxes. Thus, administrative costs are also much higher for the income tax. Yet, in many states, the income tax is a revenue source secondary to the sales tax. Based on economy, a national sales tax has great appeal.

Economy is also related to the concept of simplicity. The simpler a tax system is, the less it costs to administer and comply with the tax. One of the major thrusts of the AICPA has been to simplify the tax system. There is a basic realization among tax professionals that the current system is so complex that even a reasonably well-educated person and his or her tax advisor can readily fall into tax traps because of obscure and obtuse provisions. When tax professionals make errors because of the complexity of the law, they may still be held liable for these mistakes—and the cost to the professional may be significant.

Certainty

Certainty is also a canon related to simplicity. Certainty would dictate that a taxpayer know with reasonable accuracy the tax consequences of a transaction at the time the transaction takes place. Unfortunately, U.S. tax laws are continually changing. The quest for a balanced budget has led to a hodgepodge of revenue-raising measures that have added complexity to the laws and reduced the certainty of the outcomes of various transactions. It is not uncommon today for a change in the tax laws to be effective from the date proposed, rather than from the date passed. This practice imposes a totally uncertain environment on the taxpayer who was contemplating a transaction that could be affected by a tax law change. He or she does not know if the law will be passed—thus, he or she cannot know if the transaction will be affected. Certainty would dictate that tax laws change as little as necessary so that the outcome of a particular transaction could be predicted with reasonable accuracy. The uncertainty regarding the extension of the 2001/2003 tax rate reductions beyond 2012 made planning future transactions more problematical than usual. Although most rates were ultimately extended beyond 2012 by the American Tax Relief Act of 2012, intelligent planning beyond 2012 became a nightmare because of the "fiscal cliff" and the inability of Washington to act in a timely manner. As a result, there are renewed discussions on simplifying the tax code or making major alterations in the income tax system.

Convenience

The last canon to be addressed is convenience. A convenient tax would be one that would be readily determined and paid with little effort. Again it may be helpful to think of the difference between a sales tax and an income tax. A sales tax is paid each time a taxed purchase is made. Most of us do not even think about the fact that we are paying a tax in addition to making a purchase of some good or service. Although the withholding of income taxes from salaries offers a measure of convenience, the myriad of forms and schedules that must be filed to reconcile the actual tax liability with withholding does not always meet the test of convenience. Consider the requirements for estimated tax payments for significant amounts of income other than salaries and wages subject to withholding. Persons must make estimated tax payments based on their anticipated tax liability, including the income that may be passed through from partnerships and S corporations. It may be impossible during the year for a partner or shareholder to obtain the information to accurately assess the anticipated tax liability. Having to make estimated payments based on unknown information places an enormous burden on the taxpayer.

INCOME TAXATION

Evolution of Income Taxation in the United States

Although there had been a federal income tax during the Civil War, the income tax system as we know it today did not begin until 1913 when the 16th Amendment to the U.S. Constitution was ratified. The 16th Amendment gave Congress the power to lay and collect taxes "on income, from whatever source derived," without the previous requirement that all direct taxes be imposed based on population. This first federal income tax law enacted in 1913 consisted of only 16 pages and required only a simple individual income tax return.

Each time the income tax statutes were revised between 1913 and 1939, an entire set of new provisions replaced the existing law. In 1939 this procedure changed, and the income tax laws were codified as the **Internal Revenue Code**. Amendments and revisions were then made to the specific sections of the Code, rather than replacing the old law with an entirely new set of statutes.

In 1954, there was another major overhaul of the tax laws. In this 1954 recodification, the income, estate, gift, and excise tax laws were incorporated into the *Internal Revenue Code of 1954*. There were many significant tax law changes between then and 1986, each amending the *Internal Revenue Code of 1954*. Because the Tax Reform Act of 1986 was so extensive, the Code was renamed the *Internal Revenue Code of 1986*. Any current changes to the tax laws are now amendments to the *Internal Revenue Code of 1986*; for example, both the Tax Relief, Unemployment Insurance Reauthorization, and Job Creation Act of 2010 (2010 Tax Relief Act) and the American Taxpayer Relief Act of 2012 (2012 Relief Act) amended the *Internal Revenue Code of 1986*.

Over the years, the tax rates have gone up and down numerous times, the exemptions and deductions have varied, additional filing statuses were added, multiple rate schedules were developed based on these added filing statuses, and the indexing of many provisions with specified numerical amounts was expanded. The 2012 tax year was unique, however, in that the stalemate in Congress right up to the end of 2012 over the potential reversion of certain tax provisions to pre-2001 levels, including that basic individual tax rates and capital gain taxes, had a major effect on the markets and business growth. This uncertainty totally violated one of Adam Smith's basic tenets of a good tax system and made future planning for tax years no better than a guess.

The complexity of business taxation has also expanded at an ever-increasing pace. It is now almost impossible for one person to be familiar with all areas of the federal tax law. In addition, as the United States has developed a greater presence in the global economy, the necessity to understand the tax laws of other countries has become more apparent. Add to this the tax laws of the 50 states, which often differ from one another and from federal law, and it is obvious that the tax profession will continue to grow and to need well-trained professionals to assist both businesses and individuals.

Objectives of Taxation

Raising revenue is only one of the many goals of taxation. The tax laws foster many economic and social goals such as wealth redistribution, price stability, economic growth, full employment, home ownership, charitable activities, and environmental preservation. For example, the government encourages contributions to charities through the charitable contribution deduction. If the charitable organizations did not exist, the government would have to undertake many of the activities the charities provide. Thus, the tax law is used to achieve this social objective.

Tax policy struggles to achieve fairness. Differing notions of fairness, however, guarantee that this goal remains elusive. The fairness debate revolves around two very different concepts of what is fair. Horizontal equity, one of the key principles of tax fairness, asserts that persons in similar circumstances should face similar tax burdens. The difficult part is determining when different taxpayers are in similar circumstances.

EXAMPLE 5

Susan rents a condominium for $2,500 per month. Barry pays $2,500 per month on the mortgage for his condominium in the same building. Both Susan and Barry are single, have no dependents, and have annual incomes of $75,000. Susan cannot deduct any portion of her rent, but Barry can deduct the interest portion of his mortgage payment. In this case, the goal of horizontal equity gives way to the objective of encouraging home ownership.

The other major fairness concept is vertical equity. Vertical equity asserts that persons with higher incomes should pay not only more tax but also higher percentages of their income as tax. Underlying this is the economic theory that income has diminishing marginal utility. In other words, as a person's income rises, each dollar is worth less to that person. As a result, higher rates are necessary to obtain approximately comparable sacrifices from all taxpayers. Although this has long been a feature of the U.S. tax system (as evidenced by the progressive tax rates), it remains controversial, especially among those subject to the higher tax rates.

EXAMPLE 6

Bill and Susan are married and have two children. They have taxable income of $75,000. Shelly and John are married and also have two children but their taxable income is $150,000. Because they have income that is twice times that of Bill and Susan, vertical equity would demand that Shelley and John pay more than twice the income tax that Bill and Susan pay. For example, if Bill and Susan were required to pay $12,500 tax on their taxable income, Shelley and John would have to pay more than $25,000 of tax on their income to satisfy vertical equity.

Fairness also underlies the preferential treatment given to a married taxpayer who supports a spouse. The married taxpayer will pay less tax than a single individual with the same taxable income because of the differences in tax rate schedules applicable to their taxable income.

EXAMPLE 7

John and Laura each have $50,000 in taxable income. John is married and files a joint return, but his wife attends college and has no income. Laura, however, is unmarried and must file as a single person. Even though they have identical taxable incomes, John's tax liability will be significantly less than Laura's as the tax rate schedule for married persons is less progressive than that of a single person.

On the other hand, two married persons each with moderately high incomes will pay more taxes than two single persons with the same incomes. This is commonly called the marriage penalty. The marriage penalty exists because of the make-up of the rate structure for single individuals versus a married couple filing jointly. Although the standard deduction for a married couple is twice that of the single person, only the 10 and 15 percent brackets in the tax rate schedules are exactly twice the width of those for a single person with half the income. Thus, two single persons who each have equal incomes and are taxed at upper income levels will pay less in combined taxes than a married couple with the same total combined income as their brackets are no longer double the width of the brackets for single persons. As a result, upper income married couples with similar incomes face a marriage penalty.

Alternatively, when one of the spouses earns all or a greater portion of their combined income, the couple can benefit from a marriage bonus by filing jointly. They will now pay less tax than they would pay if they were single individuals paying taxes on their separate, but widely differing, incomes.[14]

EXAMPLE 8

Barbara is single and has taxable income of $90,000 in 2013. As a single individual, she will pay taxes of $18,493.25. Shelly and John are married and have $180,000 in taxable income, one-half earned equally by each of them. They pay $37,865.50 in taxes. This is $879 [$37,865.50 – (2 × $18,493.25)] more than they would pay if each of them was taxed separately as a single individual. The $879 is their marriage penalty.

Alternatively, if John's taxable income is $155,000 and Shelly's is $25,000 as single persons, John's tax would be $36,693.25 and Shelly's would be 3,303.75, a combined total of $39,997, or $2,131.50 [($36,693.25 + $3,303.75) – $37,865.50] more than they would pay as married filing jointly. The $2,131.50 is their marriage bonus.

The complete schedule of tax rates appears in Table 1.6 on page 27.

Current Influences on the Tax Law

A number of factors influence the tax laws, but probably the makeup of Congress is the most important. The political parties have different views of the level of taxation relative to the services that should be provided by the federal government. In general, the Democratic party believes that the federal government is best able to service the public, while the Republicans would leave far more in the hands of the states and local governments. (The debate over a government health care option as part of health care reform was one of the reasons that the passage of the Patient Protection and Affordable Care Act took over a year.) Individual states or regions have particular interests that their elected representatives espouse and bargain to achieve. This often leads to rather strange results. Although the federal government successfully sued the tobacco industry for the harm done by cigarette smoking, it still has subsidy programs for tobacco farmers.

Washington is full of lobbyists who try to influence representatives and senators to sponsor or vote for legislation favorable to their particular industries. This influence is manifested in two ways. First, industries contribute substantial monies to election campaigns. They will generally pour the greatest amount of money into the campaigns of persons they believe will support their positions—whether incumbent or not. Campaign finance reform sought to address some of the perceived abuses of the unlimited amount of "soft money" that could be contributed to various campaign organizations. Second, however, is the fact that many of the lobbyists and political action committees (PACs) have extremely large staffs available to research various technical issues. They can funnel this research, which is often slanted in their desired direction, to the various members of Congress. It is not unusual for a lobbyist to provide the basic text of a tax law to be introduced to Congress.

The attempt to satisfy the many constituencies of our elected representatives has led to a collection of tax laws that are becoming more and more complex for the taxpayer to comply with and the Internal Revenue Service (IRS) to administer effectively. In spite of many calls for simplification, each tax law adds complexity to the system. For example, the 2003 Act reduced tax rates on certain long-term capital gains depending on the taxpayer's marginal tax rate. This change, however, was only effective for capital assets sold after May 5, 2003. Assets sold before May 6, 2003 were taxed under the prior long-term capital gains rate schedule. Thus, a taxpayer with asset sales before and after the change date faced a daunting task in calculating his or her 2003 tax liability.

The 2003 Act made numerous temporary changes that were to revert to prior law after a specified time period. Uncertainty surrounding the extension of some of

[14]Refer to the material in Chapter 11 for the calculation of individual income taxes and a detailed comparison of tax rates by filling status including single and joint filers.

these provisions made tax planning increasingly difficult for tax years beyond 2004. Congress did not pass the Working Families Tax Relief Act of 2004 until late September 2004 to extend many of the expiring provisions to the 2005 tax year. It is probably not by coincidence that these changes were passed shortly before the presidential and congressional elections of November 2004. In 2006, however, the potential changes in the makeup of Congress due to the increasing controversy over the war in Iraq delayed the passage of another bill to extend these provisions until the lame duck session after the general elections. Many of the expiring provisions were then made effective retroactively to 2006 and extended through 2007. The bill extending various provisions for 2008 through 2009 was not passed until the latter part of 2008 as the presidential elections approached. At the end of 2009, all legislative energies began to be focused on healthcare overhaul legislation while popular tax provisions expired. With the healthcare legislation taking up most of the first part of 2010, an extension of the expired tax provisions did not materialize until late in the year. The 2010 Tax Relief Act passed during the lame duck Congressional session (after the November elections) contained certain retroactive extenders for 2010 and future years. Its main focus, however, was the extension of many of the "Bush era" tax cuts through 2012 that had been in effect since 2001. With a divided Congress after the 2010 elections, the subsequent rancor between the parties created gridlock in Washington effectively stymieing most of the 2011-2012 legislative initiatives. This led to what has now been known as the "fiscal cliff." The Budget Control Act of 2011 was passed only by including a provision that imposed "sequestration"—10 percent across-the-board spending cuts on January 1, 2013 if Congress and the President could not come to an agreement prior to that time. Given the state of the weak economy that remained throughout 2012, there were many dire predictions of return to recession if there was not corrective legislation to continue the majority of the Bush tax cuts and to rein in spending. The debate continued until January 2, 2013 when the Taxpayer Relief Act was approved by both houses of Congress retroactively extending most provisions. While tax rates were continued for most lower-income taxpayers, Congress put off for two months addressing deficit reduction. With sequestration becoming a reality in March 2013 and the debt ceiling a continuing problem, it should be another "interesting" tax year.

THE TAXING UNITS AND THE BASIC INCOME TAX MODELS

There are only three types of persons[15] subject to income taxation in the United States: the individual, the C corporation,[16] and the fiduciary. An individual is a male or female person subject to the tax. A **C corporation** is a business entity formed under state law on which the income tax is levied directly. A fiduciary is either an estate or a trust; it may be subject to income taxes, but in most cases the income is passed through to the income beneficiaries and is included in the beneficiaries' income for taxation. The **fiduciary** is a modified "flow-through" entity because the tax may be levied on income retained by either the estate or the trust, or it may be levied on the recipients to whom the income is distributed. Partnerships, limited liability companies not electing corporate status, and S corporations are flow-through entities.

Individual and corporate taxpayers pay the bulk of all income taxes collected. The corporation is the basic business unit, but it is only one of the forms in which a business can operate. In addition to the C or regular corporate form, a business may be

[15]Any entity subject to the income tax is a taxable person; the term "individual" is reserved exclusively for a man, woman, or child subject to an income tax.

[16]The term "C" or "regular corporation" (called "C" corporation because its governing tax rules are contained in Internal Revenue Code subchapter C) is used to distinguish it from a Subchapter S (or simply "S") corporation (whose rules are contained in IRC subchapter S), which is a flow-through entity.

organized as a sole proprietorship, a partnership, a limited liability company (LLC), or an S corporation. The income taxes on these businesses are not levied or paid by the businesses (except for LLCs electing to be taxed as C corporations); instead, at the end of the tax year their income flows through to the owners and the owners pay the taxes.[17] If one flow-through entity is an owner of all or part of another flow-through entity, the income continues to flow through to the owners until it finally reaches an individual, a C corporation, or a fiduciary, which then pays the tax.

EXAMPLE 9

The BST partnership is owned one-third by Bob (an individual); one-third by S, an S corporation (owned 100 percent by Jane); and one-third by T (a trust fiduciary). The partnership reports $300 of income at the end of the current tax year. One hundred dollars of income flows through to each of the owners: Bob, S, and T. T distributes only $50 of its $100 income to its beneficiary, Sarah. Bob includes all $100 of income along with his other income and pays taxes on the total. S does not pay taxes on the $100. This $100 is combined with its other income; the total then flows through to Jane, the owner of all of the S corporation stock. Jane includes all of this income on her personal tax return. T pays taxes on the $50 retained in the trust; the remaining $50 is taxed to Sarah on her individual tax return, along with her other sources of income.

The income of C corporations is subject to double taxation: once at the corporate level and again at the owner level when the income is distributed as dividends to the owners. The flow-through entities avoid double taxation because their income is passed through at the end of the year to the owners and taxed once only (at that time) at the owner level. The income of a sole proprietorship is reported and taxed annually along with the individual taxpayer owner's other income. The advantages and disadvantages of each of these forms of business will be explored later in this chapter. At this point, it is not necessary to have a detailed understanding of taxable and flow-through entities. It is, however, important to understand that individuals and C corporations are the primary taxpaying entities. The primary focus of the text is on tax planning for individuals, C corporations, and flow-through entities because of the latter's effects on the taxation of individuals and C corporations.

The fiduciary has a vastly different role than a business. A trust is established for a specific purpose, such as managing the assets for beneficiaries who are unable or unwilling to manage the assets themselves and must follow the dictates of the person establishing the trust. An estate is created at the death of an individual, and its primary purpose is to manage the decedent's assets until they can be distributed to his or her heirs. Income tax planning opportunities are limited for estates and trusts.

The final chapter of this text addresses the basics of estate and trust taxation, along with the estate and gift transfer tax. The first eleven chapters are devoted to the two primary tax-paying entities and the related flow-through businesses, although the basic principles of income, deduction, gain, and loss discussed throughout this text also apply to fiduciary entities.

The Individual and Corporate Tax Models

It is important to get an overall sense of the basic taxing units before studying the details of the tax laws. This will aid in understanding how the terms and concepts referred to throughout our study of tax fit into the scheme of the basic tax models. The corporate and individual tax models are shown in Figure 1.1 and should be referenced throughout the following discussions.

[17] An S corporation that was previously a C corporation may be subject to tax on specific types of income. The corporate tax model also applies to limited liability companies that elect taxation as regular corporations. The references to partnerships include those limited liability companies taxed as partnerships.

FIGURE 1.1 **THE CORPORATE AND INDIVIDUAL TAX MODELS**

	Corporate Tax Model
	Gross revenue
Less	Cost of goods sold
Equals	Gross income
Plus	Other includible income items
Equals	Total income
Less	Deductions
Equals	Taxable income (loss)
Times	Applicable tax rate
Equals	Gross income tax liability
Plus	Additions to tax
Less	Tax credits and prepayments
Equals	Tax liability owed or refund due

	Individual Tax Model
	Gross income
Less	Deductions *for* adjusted gross income
Equals	Adjusted gross income
Less	Deductions *from* adjusted gross income (greater of itemized or standard deduction)
Less	Personal and dependency exemptions
Equals	Taxable income (loss)
Times	Applicable tax rate
Equals	Gross income tax liability
Plus	Additions to tax
Less	Tax credits and prepayments
Equals	Tax liability owed or refund due

Gross Income

The term *gross income* is used in slightly different contexts for individual and corporate taxpayers. *Gross revenue* and *gross income* have different meanings for businesses under the tax laws. **Gross revenue** is the title given to a business's total receipts that result from the sale of its goods and services. **Gross income** denotes a business's gross receipts reduced by its cost of goods sold. (This is similar to its use for financial accounting.) The term **total income** is used by the corporation to designate its gross income (gross revenue less cost of goods sold) plus all other income items subject to tax. It does not include those items that are excluded from taxable income, however.

For an individual, gross income is an all-inclusive term that includes not only net business income (or loss) from a sole proprietorship and income (or loss) passed through from a partnership or S corporation. It also includes all other items of income not specifically excluded.[18] Certain "income" items may, however, be negative amounts or losses. They reduce other positive income items in determining corporate total income or individual gross income. For example, the capital gain on a stock sale increases income while the sale of business assets at a loss reduces income. In general, however, only realized losses from business or property transactions are recognized and reduce other income. Figure 1.2 provides examples of the types of income and loss items included in gross income. Gross income inclusions are examined in detail in Chapter 3.

[18] An individual reports his or her gross income to the Internal Revenue Service on Form 1040: *U.S. Individual Income Tax Return*. A sample filled-in tax return is included in Appendix C.

FIGURE 1.2 ITEMS INCLUDED IN GROSS INCOME (TOTAL INCOME FOR THE CORPORATION)

Corporations	**Individuals**
Gross income from the sale of goods and services	Wages and salary
Taxable interest	Taxable interest
Dividends	Tax refunds (to the extent of prior tax benefit)
Tax refunds	Gains and losses (subject to limitation) on capital assets
Gains on capital assets (losses in excess of gains are not deductible)	Gains and losses on other property transactions
Gains and losses on other property transactions	Income and loss from sole proprietorships, partnerships, and S corporations
Income and loss from interests in partnerships	Income and loss from rental real estate
Income and loss from rental real estate	Taxable pension plan distributions
	Unemployment compensation
	Alimony received
	Taxable portion of Social Security benefits

EXAMPLE 10

The Brogan Corporation has gross income from the sales of shoes of $4,500,000. In addition, it has taxable interest income of $50,000 and a loss of $400,000 from a partnership in which it has an 80 percent interest that it deducts from its positive income. As a result, it has total income of $4,150,000 ($4,500,000 + $50,000 – $400,000).

Losses (negative income) can be grouped into three broad categories: business losses, investment losses, and personal losses.[19] Losses are normally deducted from positive income items, except that most personal losses are not deductible by individuals.[20] Losses incurred as part of an active business are deductible in full against ordinary income. Most investment losses, however, are subject to limitations on their deductibility because they are capital losses. Individuals can deduct only $3,000 of capital losses in excess of capital gains annually. Capital losses that are not deductible in the current year may be carried forward indefinitely by individuals. Corporations can only offset capital losses against capital gains; they are not permitted to deduct capital losses against other income. Corporate capital losses in excess of those that offset capital gains can be carried back three years and then forward five years to offset gains realized in those years.

EXAMPLE 11

John incurred a $17,000 net capital loss in the current year. He is permitted to deduct only $3,000 against other income; however, the remaining $14,000 can be carried forward and deducted in future years subject to the $3,000 annual limitation.

[19]Losses are distinguished from deductions for which there must be a specific provision in the Code that allows a reduction in corporate or individual taxable income.

[20]Casualty and theft losses of personal property are deductible as itemized deductions to the extent that they exceed 10 percent of the individual's adjusted gross income.

EXAMPLE 12

Classic Corporation incurred a net capital loss of $5,000 in 2013. Classic may not deduct any of this loss currently; instead, the corporation may carry it back first to 2010, then to 2011 and 2012. If it is not offset by capital gains completely in those years then it may be carried forward sequentially to years 2014 through 2018. If this had been an individual, he or she would have been able to deduct $3,000 of the loss currently and carry the remaining $2,000 forward to the next year as illustrated in the previous example.

Over the years, certain items have been excluded from gross income. These excluded items may not even be reported anywhere on the tax return. Only in those instances in which the excluded item may affect some other reporting provision is it required to be reported along with taxable items. For example, interest on tax-exempt municipal bonds is excluded from income. An individual taxpayer must report it, however, because it is used to determine if part of a taxpayer's Social Security benefits will be subject to tax. On the other hand, an individual who is a beneficiary of life insurance proceeds excluded from income does not report these proceeds anywhere on the tax return. Figure 1.3 provides examples of the types of items excluded from income. Exclusions from gross income are examined in detail in Chapter 3.

FIGURE 1.3 EXCLUSIONS FROM GROSS INCOME

Corporate and Individual Taxpayers	Individual Taxpayers Only
Tax-exempt interest Nontaxable stock dividends Nontaxable stock rights Proceeds of life insurance policies Tax refunds to the extent no prior tax benefit was received Gains and losses on property transactions subject to disallowance or nonrecognition provisions Unrealized gains and losses	Nontaxable portion of pension plan distributions Nontaxable portion of Social Security benefits Damages awarded for physical injury Gifts and inheritances Welfare benefits including food stamps, workman's compensation, and family aid Up to $250,000 gain on the sale of personal residence ($500,000 if married filing jointly) Scholarships Qualified employee fringe benefits

EXAMPLE 13

Brogan Corporation (example 10) had $4,150,000 of total income. If it had also received $100,000 of tax-exempt interest, collected $1,000,000 from the life insurance policy on the life of its controller who was killed in an auto accident, and had unrealized[21] appreciation in its assets of $300,000, its total income would remain $4,150,000 as each of these items can be excluded from income.

Property Transactions

The **recognized gains and losses** from sales or exchanges of assets are included in the gross income of both a corporation and an individual. The gain or loss is determined by subtracting the **adjusted basis** of the asset from the amount realized on the disposition of the assets. The amount the taxpayer realizes on the disposition is the sum of the cash and fair market value of property received.

[21]Income is taxed (recognized) only when realized. Thus, if securities have appreciated in value from $5,000 to $9,000, the $4,000 in unrealized appreciation will not be taxed until realized when the securities are sold.

EXAMPLE 14

John received $10,000 cash and property with a fair market value of $5,000 in exchange for an asset. The amount realized for the asset is $15,000.

A property's adjusted basis is similar to book value. When an asset is purchased, its beginning basis is its cost. If the asset is a business asset, it may be subject to depreciation. As the asset is depreciated, its basis is reduced for allowable depreciation. If a capital improvement is made, its basis is increased. The original cost less reductions for depreciation plus increases for improvements determine the asset's adjusted basis.

EXAMPLE 15

John bought an asset for $30,000 for his sole proprietorship. He claimed $13,000 of depreciation deductions and made a major addition to the asset valued at $7,000. His adjusted basis in the asset is $24,000 ($30,000 – $13,000 + $7,000).

When the asset is sold, the **realized gain** is the excess of the amount realized over the adjusted basis of the property sold. The realized loss is the excess of the adjusted basis of the property sold over the amount realized on the transaction.

EXAMPLE 16

John receives $24,000 for an asset that has an adjusted basis of $15,000. John has a realized gain on the transaction of $9,000 ($24,000 – $15,000). If John receives only $12,000 for the asset, he has a $3,000 realized loss ($12,000 – $15,000 = – $3,000).

After the realized gain or loss is determined, the taxpayer must determine if all or part of the realized gain or loss will be recognized. If a gain is recognized, it is included in income; if a loss is recognized, it is deducted from other income. Not all realized gains or losses are recognized when realized, however. There are a number of provisions applicable to realized gains and losses that either defer gain or loss recognition to a later period or provide for nonrecognition entirely. These provisions are discussed later in the text. There is never recognition, however, unless there is an event or transaction that results in the realization of the gain or loss.

EXAMPLE 17

John will recognize (include in income) the $9,000 gain (or $3,000 loss) realized in the preceding example unless there is a specific provision that either defers recognition to a later period or provides for nonrecognition.

The details of property transactions are examined in Chapter 7 and nontaxable exchanges are examined in Chapter 8.

Deductions

After the corporation determines its total income and the individual determines his or her gross income, certain deductions are permitted. For an item to be deductible by either an individual or business, there must be either a specific provision or a general category in the Internal Revenue Code that permits the deduction. If no provision can be found that allows an item as a deduction, then it cannot be deducted. In addition, certain items might fall into one of the categories for which a deduction has specifically been disallowed.

For a corporation, its allowable expenses are simply deductions from its total income. In general, all businesses, regardless of their form of operation, are allowed deductions for business expenses that are ordinary, reasonable, and necessary. There is a general presumption that all expenses of a business are deductible unless there is a gross violation of the ordinary, necessary, and reasonable criteria. The tax laws do, however, include several disallowance provisions that render certain items nondeductible; for example fines, bribes, and expenses related to tax-exempt income are not deductible expenses.[22]

EXAMPLE 18

After determining its $4,150,000 of total income, Brogan Corporation (example 10) calculates $2,300,000 of ordinary and necessary business expenses. As a result, its taxable income is $1,850,000 ($4,150,000 – $2,300,000).

Individual taxpayers have two sets of deductions, the **deductions *for* adjusted gross income** (or the above-the-line deductions) and **deductions *from* adjusted gross income** (the below-the-line deductions). The relationship between these two sets of deductions in computing taxable income is illustrated in Figure 1.4.

FIGURE 1.4 **DEDUCTIONS *FOR* VERSUS *FROM* AGI**

	Gross Income
Less	Deductions *for* adjusted gross income
Equals	Adjusted gross income (AGI)
Less	Deductions *from* adjusted gross income (1) the greater of itemized deductions *or* the standard deduction (based on filing status) (2) personal and dependency exemptions
Equals	Taxable income (loss)

Deductions *for* adjusted gross income consist of a number of adjustments to gross income, including educator expenses, health savings account contributions, moving expenses, one-half of the self-employment tax, contributions to retirement plans, and alimony. Subtracting these deductions *for* adjusted gross income results in an intermediate subtotal between gross income and taxable income called **adjusted gross income (AGI)**, a subtotal unique to individual taxpayers.

Once AGI has been determined, the taxpayer is permitted two additional deductions classified as deductions *from* adjusted gross income and these are then subtracted from AGI to determine taxable income. These two deductions *from* adjusted gross income are (1) the greater of the taxpayer's standard deduction (based on the taxpayer's filing status as discussed later) *or* his or her itemized deductions (based on the taxpayer's actual expenditures for such items as medical expenses, taxes, and interest) and (2) the sum of the taxpayer's personal and dependency exemptions. If the taxpayer itemizes deductions, they are reported on Schedule A of an individual's Form 1040. Figure 1.5 provides a list of the more common deductions *for* AGI and an individual's itemized deductions.

It is important to accurately determine an individual's AGI—this intermediate income figure—before determining whether to itemize deductions or claim the standard deduction because certain itemized deductions are subject to limitations or thresholds based on AGI. For example, an individual's actual expenditures for medical and dental expenses are itemized deductions, but they are deductible, only to the extent they exceed 10 percent of AGI in 2013 (7.5 percent for taxpayers age 65 and over and for all taxpayer prior to 2013). Thus, AGI is used as a measure of a person's ability to absorb personal expenses by placing certain limits on or thresholds for their deductibility. Only those amounts in excess of a threshold or less than a limit are allowable as itemized deductions. Individuals who do not choose to itemize their deductions and retain supporting documentation for their actual expenditures, can instead claim the

[22]The latter is an example of the matching principle.

FIGURE 1.5 DEDUCTIONS OF INDIVIDUAL TAXPAYERS

Deductions *for* Adjusted Gross Income	Itemized Deductions (Deductions *from* AGI)
Contributions to certain pension or retirement plans (including IRAs) Health savings account contributions Moving expenses One-half of self-employment taxes Self-employed health insurance premiums Penalty on early withdrawal of savings Alimony paid Tuition and fees[23] Qualified student loan interest[24]	Medical and dental expenses (in excess of 10% of AGI) Taxes (state, local, and foreign income and property taxes) Interest (mortgage interest and investment interest expense) Charitable contributions (up to 50% of AGI) Casualty and theft losses (in excess of 10% of AGI) Unreimbursed employee business expenses, investment expenses, and tax preparation fees (in excess of 2% of AGI) Gambling losses (to extent of gambling winnings)

standard deduction based on their filing status (for example, $6,100 for a single individual or $12,200 for a married couple filing jointly) regardless of actual expenditures.

Deductions *for* AGI have two advantages over itemized deductions. First, they are deductible and reduce gross income (before adjusted gross income is calculated) independent of the taxpayer's choice to use the standard deduction or itemize his or her deductions. Second, they do not have to exceed a certain percentage based on AGI before the excess can be deducted. Deductions *for* AGI related to employee expenses are examined in Chapter 4; the other deductions *for* AGI are examined in Chapter 11 along with the information necessary to determine an individual's itemized deductions or claim the standard deduction.

EXAMPLE 19

In 2013, James, who is single, was paid a salary of $62,000. He also had a $4,000 deductible loss from a partnership in which he is a material participant. He paid alimony to his former spouse of $6,000 and made a deductible contribution to his IRA of $3,000, both of which are deductions *for* AGI. His itemized deductions (including mortgage interest, property taxes, and charitable deductions) total $12,000, which is greater than his allowable standard deduction of $6,100 as a single individual. James has gross income of $58,000 ($62,000 – $4,000) because the business loss reduces his salary income. His adjusted gross income is $49,000 ($58,000 – $6,000 – $3,000). His taxable income before deducting his personal exemption is $37,000 ($49,000 – $12,000).

To reduce record keeping for taxpayers and the administrative burden on the IRS, all individuals are permitted a **standard deduction** allowance, a minimum deduction *from* adjusted gross income. Individuals will only itemize their deductions if their total deductions exceed their standard deduction allowance. This standard deduction varies by the **filing status** of the taxpayer; that is, if a taxpayer is single, his or her standard deduction is less than the deduction allowed a married couple filing a joint return as shown in Table 1.4.[25] Thus, an individual may always deduct some amount from his or her adjusted gross income—either the standard deduction *or* his or her itemized deductions—*but not both.*

[23]The $4,000 deduction for AGI for qualified higher education expenses expired at the end of 2011 but was retroactively extended through 2013 by the 2012 Taxpayer Relief Act.

[24]The maximum deductible interest is $2,500 for 2013, the same that it has been for a number of years.

[25]Additions to the standard deductions are made for taxpayers who are blind and/or age 65 or over.

TABLE
1.4 STANDARD DEDUCTION BY FILING STATUS

FILING STATUS	2013	2012
Married filing jointly	$12,200	$11,900
Married filing separately	6,100	5,950
Head of household	8,950	8,700
Single	6,100	5,950
Dependent	1,000*	950*

*If larger, a dependent's standard deduction is earned income plus $350 in 2013 ($300 in 2012) up to their otherwise allowable standard deduction.

EXAMPLE 20

Assume James in the preceding example qualifies as head of household as a single parent but has only $3,000 of itemized deductions. James would now have taxable income before his personal and dependency exemptions of $40,050 ($49,000 AGI – $8,950 standard deduction).

The standard deduction varies by filing status because of the assumption that single persons have fewer personal expenses than married couples or those who qualify as heads of household.[26] Thus, a single person who owns a home and pays mortgage interest and property taxes is more likely to itemize than a married couple paying the same amount of interest and taxes. Similarly, individuals claimed as dependents on another taxpayer's return are not viewed as needing a large standard deduction and are only permitted to claim a modified standard deduction of $1,000 ($950 in 2012); if, however, a dependent is employed and has earned income exceeding $1,000, the standard deduction is increased to the total of their earned income plus $350 up to their allowable standard deduction.

Individuals are permitted to take another deduction called the exemption deduction. For 2013, the exemption amount is $3,900 ($3,800 in 2012). Only one exemption deduction is permitted per individual. If the taxpayer claims the exemption on his or her tax return, it is called a personal exemption; thus married persons filing a joint tax return are permitted two personal exemptions on the joint return. Taxpayers may also deduct an exemption amount for each person claimed as a dependent (a dependency exemption). A person claimed as a dependent on another taxpayer's return, however, *cannot* take a personal exemption deduction for him- or herself even if he or she files a tax return.

Between the standard deduction allowance (based on the person's filing status) and the exemptions allowed (based on the taxpayer's personal and dependency exemptions), the taxpayer can receive a significant amount of income free of income tax. These basic allowances exempt a substantial number of low-income taxpayers from filing annual tax returns. For example, a married couple's taxable income would need to exceed $20,000 ($12,200 + $3,900 + $3,900) before they would be required to file an income tax return for 2013. Corporations, on the other hand, do not have any such personal or dependency exemptions. They must file returns annually regardless of whether they report net income or loss for the tax year.

[26]To qualify for head of household status, the taxpayer must be a single individual and maintain a home for a child or qualified dependent. A single parent with a dependent child could qualify for head of household status.

EXAMPLE 21

Assume James in the previous examples is a single parent caring for his two small children. James's taxable income after his personal exemption and two dependency exemptions is $28,350 [$40,050 – ($3,900 × 3 exemptions)].

After a corporation has taken all of its deductions from total income or an individual has reduced his or her gross income by the allowable deductions *for* and *from* adjusted gross income, taxable income is reached.

Determining the Gross Tax Liability

A corporation uses the corporate rate schedule to determine its tax once taxable income is determined. The corporate tax rates and the income levels at which they are applied are given in Table 1.5.

TABLE 1.5 CORPORATE TAX RATES

TAXABLE INCOME	TAX RATE
0–$50,000	15%
$50,001–$75,000	25%
$75,001–$100,000	34%
$100,001–$335,000	39%
$335,001–$10,000,000	34%
$10,000,001–$15,000,000	35%
$15,000,001–$18,333,333	38%
Over $18,333,333	35%

EXAMPLE 22

Waldo Corporation has $125,000 of taxable income for the current year. Its gross tax is $32,000 [($50,000 × 15%) + ($25,000 × 25%) + ($25,000 × 34%) + ($25,000 × 39%)].

The individual determines his or her tax due using the appropriate individual tax rate schedule or table. The tax rate schedule the individual uses corresponds to the taxpayer's filing status; therefore, there are schedules for single individuals, married couples filing jointly, married couples filing separately, and heads of household. Although the actual tax rates are the same for each filing status, they do not apply to the same amount of income—that is, the income level at which each higher rate applies varies by the taxpayer's filing status as shown in Table 1.6.

TABLE 1.6 2013 TAX RATES FOR INDIVIDUAL TAXPAYERS BY FILING STATUS

TAX RATES	MARRIED FILING JOINTLY	MARRIED FILING SEPARATELY	HEAD OF HOUSEHOLD	SINGLE INDIVIDUAL
10%	0–$17,850	0–$8,925	0–$12,750	0–$8,925
15%	$17,851–$72,500	$8,926–$36,250	$12,751–$48,600	$8,926–$36,250
25%	$72,501–$146,400	$36,251–$73,200	$48,601–$125,400	$36,251–$87,850
28%	$146,401–$223,050	$73,201–$111,525	$125,401–$203,150	$87,851–$183,250
33%	$223,051–$398,350	$111,526–$199,175	$203,151–$398,350	$183,251–$398,350
35%	$398,351–$450,000	$199,176–$225,000	$398,351–$425,000	$398,351–$400,000
39.6%	Over $450,000	Over $225,000	Over $425,000	Over $400,000

EXAMPLE 23

Patricia has taxable income in 2013 of $38,000 and is single. Her tax liability is $5,428.75 [(10% × $8,925) + (15% × $27,325) + (25% × $1,750)].

The 2003 Act altered the tax rates applicable to long-term capital gains and introduced lower tax rates on dividends for individual taxpayers. The sale of personal or investment assets owned by an individual for longer than one year for more than their purchase price typically results in a long-term capital gain. Dividends, normally paid from after-tax corporate profits, are not deductible as an expense by the corporation; thus, the lower tax rate compensates for the double taxation of dividends.

For individuals whose total taxable income does not exceed the upper limit of the 15 percent tax bracket, long-term capital gains and dividends are taxed at 0 percent (5 percent for years prior to 2008). If taxable income exceeds the 15 percent income tax bracket but is less than $400,000 ($450,000 MFJ), the long-term capital gain and dividend portion of that income is taxed at 15 percent. The capital gain and dividend portion of taxable income that exceeds $400,000 ($450,000 MFJ) are taxed at the highest capital tax rate of 20 percent.[27]

Corporate taxpayers, however, are not allowed to use these alternate tax rates for long-term capital gains or dividends.[28]

Tax Losses

Taxpayers do not always show positive taxable income when they subtract all of their deductions from their income items. For corporate taxpayers, their negative income is a net operating loss (NOL) that the corporation may carry back to the two prior tax years to receive a refund of taxes paid in those years, or it may carry the net operating loss forward for 20 years.[29]

EXAMPLE 24

Baba Corporation had the following five-year history of income and loss:

Year	Income (Loss)
2009	$3,000
2010	$8,000
2011	($12,000)
2012	($2,000)
2013	$12,000

Baba carries its 2011 loss back first to 2009 to offset $3,000 of income and then carries $8,000 of its remaining $9,000 loss to 2010 to offset that year's $8,000 income and receives a refund of $1,650 ($11,000 × 15%) in total. In 2013, it can carry the reminaing $1,000 loss from 2011 and the $2,000 loss in 2012 forward to reduce that year's taxable income to $9,000.

A business that carries back an NOL to a prior profitable year can obtain a quick refund from the IRS of that prior year's taxes that the business can use to pay current expenses and make new investments. Due to the time value of money, however, losses that are carried forward do not provide the same tax relief as losses that are carried back.

[27]This rate excludes the 3.8% Medicare surtax on investment-type income and gains on taxpayers whose modified AGI exceeds $200,000 ($250,000 MFJ). Refer to Chapter 3 for more details.

[28]Corporations, however, are permitted a dividend received deduction for all or part of a dividend received from another corporation, as discussed in Chapter 9, but the taxable portion of the dividend and net capital gains are subject to the regular corporate tax rates.

[29]An expanded election was available for NOLs incurred in 2008 or 2009 allowing businesses to carry back those NOLs for up to five years.

EXAMPLE 25

Gee Corporation has a $10,000 net operating loss in the current year. If it had $10,000 of taxable income in the previous year, it could carry the $10,000 loss back and receive an immediate refund of $1,500 ($10,000 × 15%) of prior taxes. If, however, Gee has never been profitable and does not expect $10,000 in profits until 10 years in the future, the present value of a $1,500 tax refund to be received in 10 years is only $762 ($1,500 × 0.508) at a 7 percent discount rate.[30]

Individuals are also permitted to carry their net operating losses back two years and forward 20 years, but their NOLs must be adjusted to reflect business-related losses only (as discussed in Chapter 11).

Additions to the Tax Liability

Both corporate and individual taxpayers may be liable for an *addition* to the regular tax called the **alternative minimum tax** or AMT. If the taxpayer takes what is considered to be "excess" advantage of certain benefits built into the tax laws, the taxpayer may be subject to the alternative minimum tax, which is almost a "flat" tax.[31] Corporations and individuals determine this tax by (1) including certain items[32] that were excluded from regular taxable income, (2) reducing or eliminating deductions for other items, (3) changing the timing of the recognition of certain income and deductible items, and (4) deducting any allowable AMT exemption to calculate an expanded tax base called alternative minimum taxable income.[33] The appropriate alternative tax rate is then applied to this expanded tax base resulting in a tentative minimum tax. Corporations are subject to a single 20 percent alternative tax rate; individuals are subject to two rates—26 percent on alternative taxable income up to $175,000 and 28 percent on income in excess of $175,000. If the tentative minimum tax does not exceed the regular tax, there is no alternative minimum tax. Only the amount of the tentative minimum tax that *exceeds* the regular tax is the alternative minimum tax. The taxpayer then pays the total of the regular tax plus the increment of alternative minimum tax.

EXAMPLE 26

The Z Corporation owes a regular tax of $43,000. It has alternative taxable income of $340,000. It has a tentative minimum tax of $68,000 ($340,000 × 20%). Its alternative minimum tax is $25,000 ($68,000 – $43,000 regular tax). It pays a total tax of $68,000 consisting of the $43,000 regular tax and the $25,000 alternative minimum tax.

In addition to the alternative minimum tax, individuals must include self-employment taxes (Social Security and Medicare taxes) that must be paid on self-employment income[34] in their tax liability. Other items added here include the penalty for premature withdrawal from a pension plan and the employment taxes due for wages paid to household help.

Tax Prepayments and Credits

After determining the tax liability, an individual or corporation deducts certain items of prepayment and credit from the tax owing. The most common credit (which is not

---

[30]Present value concepts are discussed in Chapter 2.

[31]A tax that defines income very broadly, allows few deductions, and has a single tax rate applicable to all taxpayers is normally considered a flat tax.

[32]Tax-exempt interest income from private activity bonds (municipal bonds whose proceeds benefit private businesses) is an example of an item that is not taxable for regular tax purposes but is subject to the alternative minimum tax.

[33]For example, the depreciation adjustment is the difference between depreciation calculated for regular tax purposes and depreciation calculated under an alternative set of rules using longer lives and less accelerated methods. The alternative minimum tax computation for corporations is discussed in Chapter 9 and for individuals is discussed in Chapter 11.

[34]Self-employment income includes income from sole proprietorships and most income passed through from partnerships to their general partners.

really a credit at all, but a prepayment of the tax) is for the taxes withheld and for estimated tax payments. Taxpayers are required to make some form of prepayment of the anticipated tax liability. For corporations, this takes the form of estimated tax payments. For most individuals, prepayments take the form of withholding on salary or wages. If, however, the taxpayer has self-employment income or transactions resulting in significant income on which there is no withholding (such as gain on sale of investments), then the individual must also make estimated tax payments. Failure to make the appropriate amount of tax prepayments subjects the taxpayer to penalties and interest.

EXAMPLE 27

Z Corporation in the previous example paid $67,500 in estimated tax payments. It now only owes $500 in tax because its estimated tax payments offset the remaining tax liability determined for the year.

Taxpayers may be entitled to other credits for certain activities such as the investment tax credit for investing in business equipment or for having made certain qualifying expenditures, such as paying for child care. Credits are a direct reduction in the tax liability of the taxpayer. If the taxpayer's tax liability exceeds the credits, then the taxpayer must pay the additional tax. If the taxpayer's credits are greater than the tax liability, only a limited number of tax credits allow for a refund after the tax is reduced to zero, except for those taxes withheld or prepaid through estimated tax payments.[35] If other credits exceed the tax liability, some credits may be carried to other years to offset a tax liability in the carryover year (for example, the general business credit), but other credits are lost entirely (for example, the dependent care credit). Figure 1.6 provides examples of credits.

FIGURE 1.6 **TAX CREDITS**

Credits Applicable to All Taxpayers	Credits Applicable to Individual Taxpayers Only
Alternative minimum tax credit	Earned income credit
Foreign tax credit	Education credits
Investment tax credit	Child tax credit
Other general business credits including:	Dependent care credit
Low-income housing credit	Adoption credit
Enhanced oil recovery credit	Credit for elderly or disabled
Orphan drug credit	Credit for excess payroll tax withheld
Renewable electricity production credit	

Other Entities

A business operated as a sole proprietorship, partnership, limited liability company, or S corporation follows the corporate tax model, except the model ends at taxable income or loss. This taxable income or loss is reported directly to the business owners (except for LLCs taxed as C corporations) who then include their share of this income or loss in their tax returns.

The third type of taxable entity, the fiduciary entity, is either a trust or an estate. Trusts and estates are nonbusiness legal entities that hold assets and may have income. An estate is created when a person who has any assets dies. An executor or personal representative manages the estate assets until they can be distributed to the

[35] There are several refundable credits—that is, credits that will result in a payment to the taxpayer even if there is no tax liability. One such refundable credit is the earned income credit applicable to low-income taxpayers. This credit acts like a negative income tax and is discussed in Chapter 11.

heirs or beneficiaries. A trust is created by a person (called a grantor) placing assets in the hands of a trustee for the benefit of a third party (called a beneficiary). Because trusts and estates may hold assets that earn income, they are subject to income taxes. Their tax formula has characteristics of both the individual tax model and the flow-through entity. Income is generally taxed at the entity level to the extent the income remains in the entity. However, to the extent that the income flows through to the beneficiary, that income is taxed only to the beneficiary. The tax rates for estates and trusts for 2013 are shown in Table 1.7.

TABLE 1.7 **2013 INCOME TAX RATES FOR TRUSTS AND ESTATES**

TAXABLE INCOME	TAX RATE
0–$2,450	15%
$2,451–$5,700	25%
$5,701–$8,750	28%
$8,751–$11,950	33%
Over $11,950	39.6%

The tax brackets for estates and trusts are much more compact than the individual tax brackets. They reach the highest tax bracket at taxable income of more than $11,950 and there are no 10 or 35 percent tax brackets. Because the beneficiaries are usually in lower marginal tax brackets, distributing the income annually to the beneficiaries usually results in lower taxes overall.

EXAMPLE 28

A trust has $1,850 of taxable interest that it receives in the current year. It can retain the income or distribute it to the beneficiary, Craig, who is 22 years old and a college student with no other income, and is claimed as a dependent on his parents' tax return. The trust's taxable income is $1,750 ($1,850-$100 exemption allowed the trust) and it will pay a tax of $262.50 (15% × $1,750). Craig has a standard deduction of only $1,000 because he is claimed on his parents' tax return and he is permitted no personal exemption. If the $1,850 is distributed to Craig, he has taxable income of $850, all taxed at 10 percent—a tax of $85. Thus, distributing the income to Craig saves $177.50 in taxes ($262.50 – $85).

CHOICE OF BUSINESS ENTITY

Businesses are normally operated as sole proprietorships, partnerships, or corporations. Corporations can be divided into C or regular corporations and S corporations. There is a newer type of entity called the limited liability company (LLC). This entity combines the advantages of a partnership (primarily taxing income at the owner level) with the advantages of a corporation (primarily limited liability). Additionally, other special variations on the partnership form include the limited liability partnership (LLP) and the professional limited liability partnership (PLLP). The differences among these special forms revolve around the liability protection afforded the owners. For tax *return* purposes, however, there are only four types of business entities:[36]

1. Sole proprietorships
2. Partnerships

[36]There is no separate tax return for an LLC. Most multi-owner LLCs file partnership tax returns but can instead elect to file as corporations. An LLC choosing to file as an S corporation would have to comply with all of the S corporation rules. A single-owner LLC would usually file as a sole proprietorship.

3. C corporations
4. S corporations

Regardless of their form, all businesses must report their results of operations following the tax rules for one of these four entities. Of these, only the C corporation and limited liability companies electing to be treated as C corporations actually pay income taxes. A sole proprietorship passes its income directly to the sole proprietor using a Schedule C that is included in the sole proprietor's individual tax return. Partnerships, limited liability companies treated as partnerships, and S corporations also pass their income through to their owners, who are then taxed on that income. These businesses, however, must file information tax returns (Form 1065 for partnerships and limited liability companies taxed as partnerships and Form 1120S for S corporations) with the IRS.[37]

Sole Proprietorships

A one-owner business can operate as a sole proprietorship or a corporation. If the one owner is an individual who chooses no other form in which to operate the business, it is a sole proprietorship and the proprietor has *unlimited* liability. Most limited liability companies are taxed as partnerships and must have at least two co-owners. Some states with limited liability company statutes do not allow one-person limited liability companies. In those states, the limited liability company is not available to a sole owner. In those states that do allow a limited liability company to have one owner, the business will be taxed as a sole proprietorship but with the benefit of limited liability. The only other way for one individual to obtain the benefits of limited liability and a single level of taxation is to incorporate and then elect S corporation status. Most individuals who do business as independent contractors, however, simply operate as sole proprietors, accepting the liability risk.

There are both advantages and disadvantages of a **sole proprietorship**. A sole proprietorship requires no formal filing with the state, which a corporation is required to do. In other words, nothing extra must be done to form a sole proprietorship.

A sole proprietorship may have no employees or it can be a large business with many employees. It can operate any type of business—manufacturing, distribution, retail, or service. However, the owner of a sole proprietorship is considered a self-employed individual, so self-employment tax[38] must be paid on the net profit of the business. Also, because the sole proprietor is not considered an employee, he or she is not eligible for the tax-free employee fringe benefits for which a corporate employee is eligible.[39]

Income and expenses for a sole proprietorship are reported on Schedule C: *Profit or Loss from Business (Sole Proprietorship)* of the individual's Form 1040 and self-employment tax is computed on Schedule SE: *Self-Employment Tax*. No separate business tax return is due. The sole proprietor reports all of the net profits from the business as income regardless of how much he or she withdrew from the business during the year.

[37]An information return is a tax return that reports each owner's share of profits or losses to the IRS. No tax is paid with this return; instead any tax owed is paid by the owners with their tax returns.

[38]Self-employed individuals pay both the employer's and employee's share of Social Security and Medicare taxes resulting in a combined rate of 15.3% on the first $113,700 of self-employment income for 2013 and 2.9% on the excess. Social Security was assessed on the first $110,100 and $106,800 of self-employment income in 2012 and 2011, respectively. In addition, the 2010 Tax Relief Act provided a 2% reduction in the Social Security tax for 2011 and 2012 resulting in a reduced combined rate of 13.3% for those years only. For years prior to 2011, the combined rate was 15.3%. If a business has a loss, no self-employment tax is owed that year. See Chapter 4 for a detailed discussion of employment taxes.

[39]Employee fringe benefits are discussed in Chapter 4. Examples include health insurance, life insurance, moving expenses, and parking benefits.

EXAMPLE 29

Gary is the sole proprietor of Gary's Garage. Gross income for the business is \$100,000 and operating expenses are \$40,000 for the year. During the year Gary withdraws \$50,000 from the business for his living expenses. Gary reports the operating income and expenses on Schedule C, resulting in a net profit of \$60,000 (\$100,000 – \$40,000). Gary must report all of the \$60,000 net profit from his business on his Form 1040, where he computes taxable income for the year, even though he withdrew only \$50,000. Gary must also pay self-employment tax on the \$60,000 net business profits.

A tax advantage for a sole proprietorship is that a business loss can reduce or *shelter* the taxpayer's other income in calculating taxable income for the individual.

EXAMPLE 30

Christina owns a sole proprietorship that has a net loss of \$10,000. Christina also works as an employee for another business from which she receives a salary of \$30,000. Christina will be able to use her \$10,000 sole proprietorship loss to shelter part of her salary from taxation, reducing her adjusted gross income to \$20,000.

The tax savings realized from the flow through of a business loss depends on the marginal tax rate of the individual. The individual's marginal tax rate is dependent on his or her other taxable income.

EXAMPLE 31

Joshua, a single individual, owns a sole proprietorship that has a net loss of \$20,000. Joshua's taxable income before deducting this loss is \$480,000, placing him in the 39.6% marginal tax bracket (determined by the tax bracket for \$480,000 on the tax rate schedule for a single individual). His tax savings from deducting the \$20,000 loss are \$7,920 (\$20,000 × 39.6%). If, instead, Joshua's taxable income is only \$30,000 before deducting the loss, he would be in the 15% marginal tax bracket and his tax savings from deducting the \$20,000 loss would be only \$3,000 (\$20,000 × 15%).

The primary disadvantage of the sole proprietorship is that the owner is fully liable for all the debts of the business and could lose all of his or her personal assets to satisfy a judgment against the business. A sole proprietorship is simply not considered an entity separate from its owner.

EXAMPLE 32

Jason owns a small bicycle shop that he operates as a sole proprietorship. He recently assembled a bicycle and sold it to a customer. Unfortunately when Jason assembled the bicycle, he failed to tighten the lug nuts that secure the front tire. The customer was riding her new bicycle when the front wheel came off and she was thrown off the bike, breaking her collarbone and injuring her neck. She filed a lawsuit against the bicycle shop for negligence. Assuming that Jason loses this lawsuit, he would have to use his personal assets to cover any judgment if his insurance is not sufficient to cover his liability for damages. Jason can lose more than he has invested in his business activity.

Partnerships

A **partnership** consists of two or more individuals (or other entities) who join together to carry on a business. One advantage of the partnership form is the absence of restrictions on who can be a partner. A partner can be an individual or any type of entity, including another partnership, a corporation, an estate, or a trust. Similar to sole proprietors, however, general partners have unlimited liability for partnership debts and cannot be employees of the partnership or participate in most tax-free employee fringe benefits.

A partnership is referred to as a "conduit" because the income, gains, losses, deductions, and credits flow through to its owners to be taxed on their individual returns. The partnership itself pays no income tax. Although a partnership must file a separate tax return (Form 1065: *U.S. Partnership Return of Income*, which is due by April 15 for calendar-year partnerships), it is only an informational return that reports each partner's share of the profits or losses to the IRS so that the IRS knows how much each partner should be reporting on his or her individual tax return. Most of the items of income or deduction that flow through to the partners retain their individual character. For example, a partnership's long-term capital gain will be taxed as a long-term capital gain to the partners receiving it.

One disadvantage of conduit taxation is that the owners are taxed on their share of the profits, regardless of whether they receive any distributions from the business. Similar to a sole proprietor, a general partner must also pay self-employment taxes on his or her share of partnership profits. Thus, if profits are retained in the business, the partners must pay taxes on these retained profits, even though they receive no cash distributions. These profits can be distributed at a later date, however, without incurring a second tax.

EXAMPLE 33

Ginny owns a one-third interest in the PEP Partnership. The partnership reports $21,000 of income for the current tax year but makes no distributions to the partners. In spite of receiving no distribution, Ginny includes $7,000 ($21,000 × 1/3) of partnership income in her gross income for the tax year. The $7,000 is subject to self-employment taxes and if she is in the 25 percent marginal tax bracket she will also pay $1,750 income tax on her $7,000 share of the partnership profits this year. In the future, however, Ginny can withdraw $7,000 from the partnership without being subject to additional tax.

If a partnership incurs a loss, the loss also flows through to the partners and may be deductible from the partner's other income effectively *sheltering* that other income from tax. The total loss that an owner may deduct from an investment in a partnership is limited to the partner's basis in the partnership interest.[40]

Partner's Basis Account

The partner's basis account is a measure of a partner's investment in the partnership at any given time. It ensures that the partnership's income is taxed only once and is the upper limit on the amount a partner may receive as a tax-free distribution, as well as the limit on the amount of loss that can be deducted. A partner's beginning basis is the cash and basis of any property that is contributed to the partnership. The partner's basis is then increased by any income or gains that flow through to the partner and is decreased by any losses and distributions. The deduction for losses that flow through is limited to the partner's basis in the partnership interest (after all adjustments for gains, income, and distributions) because the partner's basis can never be negative. Once a partner's basis is reduced to zero, no additional loss can be deducted. This excess loss is carried forward until the partner again has positive basis.

EXAMPLE 34

Jennifer is an active 40 percent partner in ABC partnership. Her basis in the partnership is $200 at the beginning of year 1. During this year, the partnership has $2,000 of ordinary income. The partnership distributes $500 in cash to Jennifer. Jennifer must recognize $800 (40% × $2,000) of income that flows through to her increasing her basis to $1,000 ($200 beginning basis + $800 income passed through). Her basis is then reduced to $500 by the $500 distribution ($1,000 - $500). Jennifer has other income that puts her in the 28% tax bracket so she will pay $224 ($800 x 28%) in income taxes on her share of the partnership profits.

In year 2, the partnership reports a $2,500 loss and $1,000 ($2,500 × 40%) of this again flows through to Jennifer. Her loss deduction, however, is limited to her $500 basis and Jennifer carries the remaining $500 loss ($1,000 loss – $500 deducted) forward because she cannot have a negative basis in her partnership interest.[41] Jennifer now has tax savings from the $500 deductible loss of $140 ($500 × 28%).

[40]The passive income and at-risk rules may also prevent the deduction unless the partner materially participates in the partnership and his or her investment is at risk. These rules are discussed in Chapter 10.

[41]Jennifer can increase her basis by contributing cash or other property to the partnership. Her basis will also be increased when the partnership earns a profit and allocates Jennifer's share of that profit to her basis account.

In year 3, the partnership has $5,000 of income and $2,000 ($5,000 × 40%) of this flows through to Jennifer. Jennifer reports the $2,000 as income, increasing her basis to $2,000. She is now able to deduct the $500 loss carried over from the prior year. Her basis at the end of the third year is $1,500 ($0 + $2,000 - $500). Jennifer will only pay $420 ($1,500 × 28%) in income taxes as her $2,000 share of the profit is also reduced for the deductible loss carried forward from the prior year.

A unique feature of the partnership form is the increase in the partners' bases for their share of partnership liabilities. If the partnership defaults on its debts, the general partners would be held liable for them. Because of this potential liability, the partners can increase their basis accounts by their share of partnership liabilities. A partner in a partnership with liabilities can deduct a greater share of losses as a result of the increased basis than one without. When the liabilities are repaid, however, partners must also reduce their bases for their share of discharged debt.

EXAMPLE 35

Assume the partnership in example 34 borrows $5,000 at the beginning of year 2. As a 40 percent partner, Jennifer's basis increases to $2,500 [$500 beginning basis + (40% × $5,000 liability)] as a result of the debt. She is now able to deduct the entire second-year loss of $1,000, reducing her basis to $1,500 ($2,500 – $1,000 loss). If the partnership then repays $2,000 of the loan at the beginning of year 3, Jennifer must reduce her basis by $800 (40% × $2,000) to $700 ($1,500 – $800).

Limited Liability Companies

The newest form of business entity generally recognized is the limited liability company (LLC). Similar to the corporation, the limited liability is a "creature of the state;" that is, the owners, who are called members, must apply to the state to form a limited liability company. The limited liability company files articles of organization and must have an operating agreement.

A limited liability company will be treated as a partnership for tax purposes unless the company affirmatively elects to be taxed as a corporation. (If it complies with all S corporation requirements, it could then also elect S corporation status.) If a limited liability company with a single owner-member fails to elect corporate status, it cannot be treated as a partnership for tax purposes as the partnership form requires at least two owners. In those states that allow single member limited liability companies, a non-electing single member limited liability company with a corporate owner will be treated as a division of the owning corporation for tax purposes. If the single member-owner is an individual, the limited liability company will be treated as a sole proprietorship for tax purposes.

Most multi-member limited liability companies are treated as partnerships for tax purposes, filing the Form 1065: *U.S. Return of Partnership Income*. Thus, they are conduits in the same manner as partnerships; that is, the income or loss flows through to their members who are then taxed on this income and the income retains its character when it flows through. Active members in an LLC must also pay self-employment tax on their share of profits in the same manner as general partners or sole proprietors.

Corporations

Corporations must file articles of incorporation with the state in which their principal office is located. A corporation sells its stock and the shareholders are only at risk for their capital investment. If the corporation fails, the shareholders are not liable for the outstanding debts of the corporation. If a shareholder desires to withdraw from the corporation, he or she need only find a buyer for the stock.

A corporation facilitates centralized management so that day-to-day operations do not require the input of all the owners. Additionally, the corporation's life is not restricted. The death of an owner or a transfer of stock ownership does not end the corporation's legal existence.

The owners of a corporation are also allowed to be employees subject to the same payroll taxes as all other employees. Shareholder-employees, however, are able to benefit from fringe benefits (for example, employees' health insurance premiums paid by the corporation are fully deductible by the corporation and tax-free benefits to the employees) denied the working-owners of other business forms. In addition, when the corporate tax rates are lower than individual tax rates, the owners have increased capital for reinvestment and business expansion.

The main disadvantage of the corporate form is that corporate income can be subject to taxation twice—first, the corporation pays tax on its net income when it is earned; then when the after-tax income is distributed to the shareholders as dividends, most shareholders pay tax on this dividend income. (Generally, the other forms of business avoid this double level of tax.) The impact of this double taxation on individual shareholders is somewhat mitigated by the fact that their dividend income is generally taxed at a lower rate than their regular marginal tax rate.

EXAMPLE 36

Tom, a taxpayer in the 25 percent tax bracket, owns the Big Creek Corporation. Big Creek earns $50,000 taxable income in the current year and pays tax of $7,500 on these earnings. If Big Creek distributes the $42,500 of after-tax earnings to Tom as a dividend, he may pay up to $6,375 ($42,500 × 15%) in federal income taxes on the distribution. In total, a tax of up to $13,875 ($7,500 + $6,375) may have been paid on the $50,000 earned by the corporation, or almost 28 percent of the pretax earnings.

Another disadvantage of a C corporation is that losses do not flow through to the shareholders. Corporate losses can only offset corporate profits. Although net operating losses can generally be carried back two years and forward twenty years, there are no tax savings from corporate losses until there are corporate profits.

EXAMPLE 37

Newborn Corporation, a new C corporation, has a loss of $40,000 in its first tax year, a $30,000 loss in its second year, a $20,000 loss in its third year, and finally a $100,000 profit in its fourth year. The shareholders of Newborn Corporation are not permitted to deduct any of the losses on their individual tax returns. Newborn Corporation receives no tax benefit from its losses until its fourth year when it can offset the $90,000 in accumulated losses from the first three years against its $100,000 profit, reducing its taxable income in the fourth year to $10,000. It has tax savings in the fourth year of $20,750, the difference between the $22,250 corporate tax on $100,000 [($50,000 × 15%) + ($25,000 × 25%) + ($25,000 × 34%)] and the $1,500 corporate tax on $10,000 ($10,000 × 15%).

The tax return of a C corporation, Form 1120: *U.S. Corporate Income Tax Return*, is due two-and-one-half months after year-end (March 15 for calendar-year corporations). C corporations can adopt either a calendar-year or fiscal-year accounting period, while other entities are frequently restricted to only calendar years.

S Corporations

S corporations are formed the same as C corporations and revert to being taxed as C corporations if they cease to qualify for S status. S corporation shareholders have the same limited liability protection that C corporation shareholders possess; however, S corporations avoid the principal disadvantage of the C corporation form—double taxation—by being taxed in a manner similar to partnerships with both profits and losses flowing through to its shareholders. To elect S corporation status, the corporation must qualify as a "small business corporation" as defined under Internal Revenue Code Section 1361 and its shareholders must consent to this election. A small business corporation is a domestic corporation that may have no more than 100 shareholders who, with limited exception, must be individuals who are not nonresident aliens, and it may have only one class of common stock outstanding. If a corporation violates any one of the above requirements at any time, the S corporation status will be revoked and it will be taxed as a regular C corporation.

To become an S corporation, the corporation must file Form 2553: *Election by a Small Business Corporation*, along with consent statements signed by all shareholders of record at the time the election is made. The election can be made at any time during the preceding year or before the 15th day of the third month of the tax year for which the corporation wishes to have S corporation status.

Qualifying corporations that elect S corporation status use the conduit concept of taxation, passing their profits and losses through to their individual owners, thus avoiding a double tax on corporate profits. S corporations file an information tax return, Form 1120S: *U.S. Income Tax Return for an S Corporation*, due two-and-one-half months after year-end (March 15 for calendar-year corporations). The shareholders are taxed on their share of profits, whether they are actually distributed to them or they are retained in the corporation. So a conduit entity is usually appropriate if the profits are distributed to the owners rather than reinvested in the business, because such profits can be distributed without the owners incurring any additional tax. Personal-service business activities (such as accounting or engineering) usually fall into this category.

S corporation shareholders can be employees of an S corporation for employment tax purposes and pay the same payroll taxes as other employees on their salary or wages. Similar to partners, however, shareholders who own more than 2 percent of the corporation's stock, cannot participate in most employee fringe benefit programs on a tax-free basis. For example, the payment of health insurance premiums by the corporation for shareholders owning more than a 2-percent interest in the corporation, results in additional salary rather than a tax-free benefit.[42]

Similar to partnerships, a shareholder's basis is a measure of the shareholder's investment in the corporation's stock. A shareholder's beginning basis is the cash and adjusted basis of any property contributed to the corporation (or the price paid for the corporate stock). The shareholder's basis is then increased by the shareholder's share of the corporation's income or gain and decreased by any distributions or losses. The deduction of losses by the shareholder is limited to the shareholder's basis in his or her stock, similar to the limit on a partner's loss deduction to his or her basis in the partnership interest. Unlike a partnership, however, a shareholder in an S corporation cannot increase his or her basis for debts undertaken by the corporation because an S corporation shareholder has no personal liability for the debts of the corporation. Thus, if the entity in examples 34 and 35 were an S corporation, Jennifer could not have increased her basis for the corporation's debt.

EXAMPLE 38

Assume the same facts as examples 34 and 35 except that the business is an S corporation instead of a partnership. Jennifer's basis adjustments are the same shown in example 34 as an S corporation. When the S corporation borrows $5,000 (example 35), however, Jennifer cannot increase her basis; it will remain $500. Jennifer's second-year deduction is limited to her $500 basis, reducing it to zero, and she must carry the remaining $500 loss forward to year 3 when she again has basis in her S corporation stock. Similarly, the loan repayment has no effect on Jennifer's stock basis.

S corporations and partnerships also differ in that a shareholder's share of S corporation profits are not subject to self-employment tax while general partners must pay self-employment tax on their share of the partnership profits. This provides an incentive for S corporation shareholders to take lower salaries (which are subject to employment taxes) and a higher distribution of profits (which are not subject to self-employment taxes). If the IRS deems the salary paid to a shareholder-employee to be unreasonably low on audit, it may reclassify some or all of a cash distribution of profits as salary and assess additional employment taxes on both the shareholder and the corporation.

[42]Some of the benefits that greater-than-2-percent S corporation shareholders and partners cannot receive on a tax-free basis include health and accident insurance, group term life insurance, on-premises lodging, employee achievement awards, moving expenses, transit passes, and parking benefits. To mitigate the difference in this treatment of employer-provided health insurance for employees and the self-employed, self-employed individuals, S corporation shareholders, and general partners may deduct the cost of health insurance *for* AGI. See Chapters 4 and 11.

As conduit entities, partnerships, limited liability companies, and S corporations are especially attractive in the early years of a business activity when operating losses are likely to occur. In the case of a C corporation, such losses are locked inside the corporation. The losses do not provide a tax benefit until the corporation becomes profitable. Losses from a conduit entity flow through to the owners and benefit the owners in the same year that the loss occurs (assuming the owners are able to deduct the losses). When conduit entity owners have high marginal tax rates, the benefit of loss flow-through is especially attractive.

At first glance, conduit entities may appear to be superior to C corporations from a purely tax perspective. Such a conclusion is shortsighted. C corporations have some favorable tax characteristics that are not available to any conduit entity. In cases in which these characteristics can be exploited (such as the ability of owners to be treated as employees and to benefit from tax-free employee fringe benefits), they can more than compensate for double taxation.

Comparing Business Entity Attributes

Choosing the best legal entity to use for the operation of a business activity is an extremely difficult decision. The future needs of both the business and its owners must be estimated and evaluated as part of this decision. Once a decision is implemented it will have long-lasting effects. Changing from one entity type to another can be difficult and expensive. Federal and state income taxes are an important component of the legal entity decision; however, taxes alone are insufficient criteria for making a decision. Figure 1.7 presents a basic comparison of partnerships, S corporations, and C corporations across some of the tax and nontax attributes that should be considered when evaluating the choice of entity for the conduct of business activity. These various attributes will be explored in more detail in the later chapters of this text.

REVISITING THE INTRODUCTORY CASE

Wing Hue is a resident of the United States and is subject to its tax laws as if he were a citizen. Thus, as an employee of the consulting firm, Hue will be required to pay employment taxes (his share of FICA taxes) through withholding by his employer. His employer will also withhold a certain percentage of his gross income for his income tax liability. His income tax rates will range from 10 to 39.6 percent of his taxable income. He will be able to deduct either his itemized deductions or his standard deduction in addition to his personal exemption in determining his personal income tax liability.

In trying to obtain backing from venture capitalists, they may stipulate the type of entity that Hue will have to establish for his manufacturing business. To limit their liability, the venture capitalists may require that Hue establish a regular corporation. If so, Hue can own a certain percentage of the corporation and can be an employee, fully participating in the corporation's fringe benefits. (If the venture is successful, he will most likely leave his consulting position.) Hue needs to be aware that as an owner-employee he can take profits out of the corporation as a salary. The salary will be subject to FICA taxes and income tax withholding, but will be paid with the before-tax income of the corporation due to the corporation's salary deduction. Any additional corporate profits taken out as dividends will be paid with the after-tax income of the corporation and will be subject to additional taxes when received by Hue and his backers.

Wing Hue could operate the manufacturing business in several other entity forms, if his financial backers permit him. It is unlikely he will be allowed to operate as a sole proprietorship (the lenders would have to lend the money directly to Hue), but if he is, he will be taxed on all of the profits from the business and will have to pay self-employment taxes on the total. He will, however, be able to deduct his losses against other income. It is more likely that the backers would permit the business to operate as either a partnership or an S corporation. They can limit their liability either through a limited liability company that elects partnership taxation or through the S corporation. Either of these entities will pass income directly through to the owners for taxation, eliminating the double taxation of earnings. As a general partner, Hue would be responsible for self-employment taxes on his share of income passed through, in addition to income taxes. He cannot be an employee of the partnership and participate in tax-free

FIGURE 1.7 COMPARISON OF BUSINESS ENTITY ATTRIBUTES

Attribute	Partnership	S Corporation	C Corporation
Limited liability protection	Limited partners have limited liability protection. General partners have unlimited liability with respect to partnership debts.	Yes	Yes
Owner identity restrictions	None; any person or entity may be an owner.	Substantial restrictions: corporations, partnerships, certain trusts, and non-resident aliens not permitted.	None; any person or entity may be an owner.
Number of permitted owners	Minimum 2; maximum unlimited	Minimum 1; maximum 100 (family members treated as one)	Minimum 1; maximum unlimited
Differences in ownership rights permitted between owners	Flexible; economic and management rights can vary between general and limited partners.	Generally fixed; only common stock is permitted, but voting rights may vary.	Flexible; no limit on different classes of stock that may be created.
Excludible employee fringe benefits for employee owners	Generally not available.	Generally not available for greater than 2% owners.	Available to all employees.
Tax treatment of capital gains and losses	Gains flow through to partners and are taxed at partner's capital gains tax rate. Losses deductible by partner subject to capital loss limits.	Gains flow through to shareholders and are taxed at owner's capital gains tax rate. Losses deductible by shareholder subject to capital loss limits.	Gains taxed to corporation at same marginal rate as ordinary income. Capital losses are carried back 3 years and forward 5 years.
Marginal tax rate structure applied to ordinary income	Flow through to owner and taxed at owner's marginal tax rate.	Flow through to owner and taxed at owner's marginal tax rate.	Taxed using progressive rate structure for corporations. Substantial power to shelter first $100,000 of income due to low rates.
Allocation of entity income and loss	Allocations made under partnership agreement.	Fixed; all allocations based on ownership of stock.	N/A; not a conduit entity.
Self-employment taxes	Imposed on ordinary income share of general partners.	Not imposed.	N/A; not a conduit entity.
Overall capacity of owner to derive tax benefit from entity losses	Very good for partners who participate in management and receive basis for entity debts.	Good for shareholders who are material participants in the business; however, basis may be limited because no basis is available for entity debts.	Not a conduit entity. Corporate net operating losses collect within corporation and are carried back 2 years and forward 20 years for eventual corporate tax benefit.

employee fringe benefits. Although he can be an employee of an S corporation (with FICA taxes and income tax withholding on his salary), ownership of more than 2 percent of the stock limits his ability to benefit from tax-free employee fringe benefits.

SUMMARY

Taxes are payments to a governmental unit unrelated to the benefits received. Besides raising revenues, taxes are used to redistribute wealth, to foster price stability and economic growth, and to meet social goals.

A major source of revenue for many jurisdictions is income tax, but there are many other forms of taxation. Various governmental units levy consumption taxes (sales and use taxes), wealth taxes (property taxes), and wealth transfer taxes (estate and gift taxes). These taxes may be proportional, progressive, or regressive. Adam Smith's four canons of taxation of equity, economy, certainty, and convenience can be used to evaluate a tax.

The income tax is the primary source of revenue for the federal government, but only individuals, corporations, and fiduciaries pay income taxes. Other business entities, such as sole proprietorships, partnerships, and S corporations pass their incomes through to their owners until they reach one of the three types of income tax-paying persons. This income is then included with the other income of the individual, corporation, or fiduciary and taxed to such persons.

The corporate and individual tax models have certain items in common—that is, they both have income and deductions, and the tax is levied on taxable income. Individual taxes are more complex, however, as individuals have both deductions *for* adjusted gross income and deductions *from* adjusted gross income. The intermediate income subtotal of adjusted gross income is used to limit certain itemized deductions. As an alternative to itemizing, individuals are also permitted a standard deduction. They may also deduct personal and dependency exemptions. The standard deduction and exemption amounts exempt many low-income taxpayers from filing income tax returns.

In addition to the income tax, many things must be considered when deciding in which form to operate a business. S corporations and limited liability companies can limit the owner's liability for corporate acts. Sole proprietors and partners may have to surrender personal assets to satisfy judgments against the business. Other variations include, but are not limited to, the treatment of employment taxes, participation in fringe benefit programs, and the ability to sell an interest in the business. These and more must be considered when determining in which form to operate a business.

KEY TERMS

Adjusted basis 22
Adjusted gross income (AGI) 24
Alternative minimum tax 29
Average tax rate 10
C corporation 18
Canons of taxation 12
Deductions *for* adjusted gross income 24
Deductions *from* adjusted gross income 24
Estate tax 5
Fiduciary 18
Filing status 25
Gift tax 5
Gross income 20
Gross revenue 20
Horizontal equity 13
Internal Revenue Code 15
Losses 21
Marginal tax rate 10
Partnership 33
Progressive tax system 8
Proportional tax system 10
Real property tax 4
Realized gain 23
Recognized gains and losses 22
Regressive tax system 11
S corporations 36
Sales tax 6
Sole proprietorship 32
Standard deduction 25
Total income 20
Use tax 6
Value-added tax 7
Vertical equity 13

TEST YOURSELF

ANSWERS APPEAR AFTER THE PROBLEM ASSIGNMENTS

1. Which of the following is correctly categorized as a tax?
   - **a.** The dog license fee
   - **b.** The annual property tax on your home
   - **c.** An assessment for putting streetlights in front of your home that increases the home's value
   - **d.** The bond a person must post to get out of jail

2. Which of the following applies only to individual taxpayers?
   a. Taxable income
   b. Estimated tax payments
   c. Total income
   d. Standard deduction
3. Which of the following entities does not pass its income directly through to its owners?
   a. Sole proprietorship
   b. Partnership
   c. C corporation
   d. S corporation
4. What type of tax is a sales tax?
   a. Income tax
   b. Consumption tax
   c. Wealth transfer tax
   d. Turnover tax
5. What characteristic of a tax states that taxpayers with equal incomes should pay equivalent amounts of taxes?
   a. Horizontal equity
   b. Vertical equity
   c. Certainty
   d. Convenience

PROBLEM ASSIGNMENTS

CHECK YOUR UNDERSTANDING

1. When was the constitutional amendment permitting an income tax ratified?
2. What is a sin tax?
3. What are three objectives of income taxation?
4. What are the three taxable persons that pay all of the income taxes?
5. What is the difference between gross revenue and gross income for a business?
6. What are at least three unique features of the individual tax model when compared to the corporate tax model? What are three similarities between these models?
7. What is the purpose of adjusted gross income for an individual?
8. What are the four filing statuses for which there are standard deductions?
9. Differentiate the personal exemption from the dependency exemption.
10. How is gain or loss on the disposition of business or investment property determined?
11. What is the difference between a deduction from income and a credit against a tax liability? Illustrate your answer.
12. What are three characteristics of a sole proprietorship? Are these characteristics the same as or different from those of a partnership? What are three characteristics of a limited liability company that differ from those of a partnership?
13. Compare a C corporation to an S corporation.

14. What are consumption taxes?

15. Differentiate horizontal from vertical equity.

CRUNCH THE NUMBERS

16. Determine Amy's taxable income for 2013 if she has $40,000 of salary income, is single, and uses the standard deduction.

17. Marlee is a single parent with three dependent children and qualifies as head of household in 2013. Determine her taxable income if she has salary income of $71,000 and interest income of $1,500.

18. Determine a corporation's taxable income if it has $450,000 of gross receipts, $145,000 cost of goods sold, $276,000 of deductible business expenses, $20,000 of gain on the sale of machinery, and $500 of interest income from State of New York bonds.

19. The Warner Corporation has gross income of $560,000. It has business expenses of $325,000, a capital loss of $20,000, and $2,500 of interest income on temporary investments. What is the corporation's taxable income?

20. Determine George and Mary's taxable income for 2013 if George has $65,000 of salary income and Mary has $45,000 of salary income and they file a joint tax return. They have two dependent children and $20,000 of itemized deductions.

21. Refer to the information in problem 16. Determine Amy's income tax liability for 2013.

22. Refer to the information in problem 17. Determine Marlee's income tax liability for 2013.

23. Refer to the information in problem 18. Determine the corporation's income tax liability.

24. Refer to the information in problem 19. Determine Warner Corporation's income tax liability.

25. Refer to the information in problem 20. Determine George and Mary's income tax liability for 2013. How much tax do they save by itemizing their deductions rather than taking the standard deduction?

26. Sally and Jim are married and have taxable income in 2013 of $160,000. If they could file their income tax as single individuals, each of them would have taxable income of $80,000. Do they have a marriage penalty when they file their joint return? If so, what is the amount of the penalty?

27. Conrad and Anita (a college student with no income) plan to marry on December 21, 2013. Filing jointly, they expect to have $180,000 of taxable income for the year. If they wait until January of 2014 to marry, Conrad will file as a single person and report the $180,000 of taxable income on his separate return. Will it be to their advantage to marry before the end of 2013 or should they wait until 2014? How much in tax will they save or have to pay extra if they marry in 2013? How would your answers change if Conrad and Anita each expect $90,000 of taxable income in 2013?

28. John has taxable income of $30,000. William has taxable income of $60,000. Determine their 2013 income taxes if they are both single individuals. Compare their incomes and their income taxes. What does this illustrate?

29. Lilikoi Corporation began business in 2011. Lilikoi earned taxable income of $40,000 in 2011 and $120,000 in 2012. For 2013, Lilikoi Corporation has a net operating loss of $50,000 and decides to carry the loss back, filing a refund claim. Compute the amount of corporate income tax that

Lilikoi paid for 2011 and 2012 and then determine the amount of tax that will be refunded from carrying back the 2013 NOL.

30. Hunter Corporation has $250,000 in gross income, $125,000 in deductible business expenses, and a $12,000 business tax credit. Determine the corporation's net tax liability.

31. Carrie and Stephen have gross salary and wages of $76,000 in 2013 and file a joint return. They have one dependent child, itemized deductions of $13,200, and a $240 child care credit. Determine their taxable income and their tax liability.

32. The Pigalle Corporation has taxable income of $450,000. Determine its tax liability. If the corporation's alternative minimum taxable income is $902,000, what is its alternative minimum tax?

33. Betty, a single woman, has $140,000 of taxable income in 2013. Her alternative minimum taxable income is $195,000. What is her alternative minimum tax?

34. An estate has $20,000 of taxable income in 2013. What amount of tax will the estate pay if it fails to distribute the income to the beneficiaries?

35. Carolyn has a 50 percent interest in a partnership that has a $14,000 loss for the year. She materially participates in the partnership, but she also has salary from other employment of $46,000. If she is single with no dependents, what is her taxable income in 2013 and what is her tax liability?

36. June and John decide to form a business. They each plan to contribute $20,000 in exchange for a 50 percent interest in the business. They will then take out a bank loan for $30,000 to cover the balance of their working capital needs. They expect that the business will make a profit of $64,000 in the first year and that it will not make any cash distributions that year. Excluding the business income, June, who files as head of household, has $480,000 of salary income and $450,000 of taxable income. John is married and files a joint return; he and his wife have $120,000 of combined salary income and $100,000 of taxable income. They want to know how much tax the business will pay and how much additional tax they will personally pay in 2013 if they form the business as a partnership, S corporation, or C corporation. Consider only income taxes.

37. Assume the same facts as in the previous problem, except that the business expects to make a cash distribution of $28,000 each to June and John the first year. Determine how much tax the business will pay and how much additional tax they will personally pay if they form the business as a partnership, S corporation, or C corporation. Consider only income taxes.

38. Assume the same facts as problem 36, except that John and June expect the business will have a $44,000 loss in the first year (instead of a $64,000 profit) and will not make any cash distributions. Determine the income tax savings in the current year for the business and for them personally if they form the business as a partnership, S corporation, or C corporation. (They both materially participate in the business and their marginal tax bracket will not change because of the business loss.)

39. Clara and Charles decide to form a business. They each plan to contribute $15,000 in exchange for a 50 percent interest. The business will borrow $20,000 to cover the balance of its working capital needs. In their business plan, Clara and Charles show that the business will have a loss of $54,000 in its first year. In the second year, however, the business will have a profit of $60,000 and they will each be able to withdraw $5,000 from the business. Clara is in the 28 percent marginal tax bracket and Charles is in the 25 percent marginal tax bracket.

a. Determine the taxes paid by the business (if any) in the first and second year if they organize the business as (1) a partnership, (2) an S corporation and (3) a C corporation.

b. Determine Clara's and Charles's income tax savings in the first year and their bases in the business at year-end if they organize the business as (1) a partnership, (2) an S corporation, and (3) a C corporation.

c. Determine the income tax Clara and Charles will pay in the second year from business operations and their bases in the business at year-end if they organize the business as (1) a partnership, (2) an S corporation, and (3) a C corporation.

40. Carl is a 30 percent partner in the CCF Partnership. At the beginning of the year, his basis in the partnership is $4,000. The partnership reports $7,000 of ordinary income and distributes $3,000 to the partners. What is Carl's basis at the end of the year?

41. Dane City's total assessed valuation for all of the property in its jurisdiction is $4,000,000,000. It needs $20,000,000 in revenue for the services it provides its citizens. Joe owns property that is assessed at $150,000. How much will he pay in property taxes?

42. Perform the calculations to prove that the 5 percent surtax on corporate income between $100,000 and $335,000 equals the benefit that the corporation enjoys on income of no more than $100,000.

43. Perform the calculation to prove that the 3 percent surtax on corporate income between $15,000,000 and $18,333,333 equals the benefit of the 34 percent tax rate on income of no more than $10,000,000.

44. **a.** Differentiate a wealth tax from a wealth transfer tax and give examples of each.

b. Differentiate a tax based on consumption from an income tax and illustrate with an example.

c. Over what ranges of taxable income in 2013 would the income tax liability be equal for two persons with equal incomes who file as single individuals or who file jointly as a married couple?

45. If a taxpayer has $40,000 of employee salary in 2013, how much will be withheld for the Social Security and Medicare taxes? How would your answer change if the year had been 2012?

46. If a taxpayer has $130,000 of employee salary, how much will be withheld for the Social Security and Medicare taxes in 2013? How much less Social Security and Medicare taxes would the taxpayer have paid in 2012 on his $130,000 of wages?

THINK OUTSIDE THE TEXT

These questions require answers that are beyond the material that is covered in this chapter.

47. Evaluate the sales tax and the income tax using Adam Smith's four canons of taxation.

48. Compare the benefits of a $4,000 deduction and a $4,000 tax credit for two single taxpayers, one with taxable income of $40,000 and the other with taxable income of $200,000.

49. If the Congress were to enact a flat tax, do you believe that there should be any exclusions or deductions from income before the single tax rate is applied? Explain.

50. Evaluate allowing married individuals with dual incomes to choose to file a joint tax return or to file as two single individuals as a remedy for the marriage penalty.

51. Do you believe that a progressive, proportional, or regressive tax is the most fair? Explain your answer.

52. What is the after-tax cost in 2013 of deductible interest expense of $9,000 and property taxes of $2,500 for a single taxpayer with gross income of $80,000? The taxpayer's only other itemized deduction is a $2,000 charitable contribution.

53. What is the after-tax interest rate that a corporation in the 38 percent tax bracket pays on a loan of $100,000 at 7 percent interest?

54. Is a property tax generally a progressive, proportional, or a regressive tax? Explain.

55. Refer to the information in problem 36 and assume modified AGI is equal to salary income. Complete the solution to this problem considering both income and employment taxes. (Employment taxes are discussed in Chapter 4 and investment income surtaxes in Chapter 3.)

56. Refer to the information in problem 37 and assume modified AGI is equal to salary income. Complete the solution to this problem considering both income and employment taxes. (Employment taxes are discussed in Chapter 4 and investment income surtaxes in Chapter 3.) How would your answers change if the distributions made by the S and C corporations were salary payments subject to employment taxes?

IDENTIFY THE ISSUES

Identify the issues or problems suggested by the following situations. State each issue as a question.

57. John and Mary filed for divorce in November of the current year. The divorce will not become final until May of the following year.

58. William, age 25, left his studies for the priesthood and moved back into his parents' home and has lived there this entire year. He had only $4,000 in income from a part-time job that he used to purchase a used auto. His parents provided all of the other money necessary for his support.

59. DEE is an S corporation with 100 shareholders. John, one of these shareholders, gives half of his shares of stock to his new wife as a wedding gift.

60. Clifford owns 75 percent of AFK, a C corporation. He spends little time in the business, but takes a salary of $750,000.

SEARCH THE INTERNET

For the following four problems, consult the IRS Web site (www.irs.gov).

61. Briefly describe the statistical information available when you search for statistics.

62. How do you make a comment or ask a question about the tax statistics provided by the IRS?

63. What subheadings appear under the "Statistics of Income"?

64. Where would you find information about the IRS history and structure?

65. Go to *www.taxfoundation.org* (the Web site for the Tax Foundation).
    - **a.** What is Tax Freedom Day?
    - **b.** When were Tax Freedom Days in 2011 and 2012?

DEVELOP PLANNING SKILLS

66. John and Martha are planning to be married. Both are professionals each with gross incomes of $100,000 annually. They are deciding on a wedding date. They have two dates to choose from: December 14, 2013, or January 11, 2014. If they marry on December 14, 2013, they will have to choose between married filing separately and married filing jointly. They will both claim the standard deduction. Is there an advantage to either method of filing? If they postpone their wedding until the January date and file as single persons, will they reduce their tax bill for 2013?

67. Jeremy is setting up a service business. He can either operate the business as a sole proprietorship or he can incorporate as a regular C corporation. He expects that the business will have gross income of $60,000 in the first year with expenses of $12,000 excluding the following: He plans to take $30,000 from the business for living expenses as a salary.

a. Compare his tax costs for 2013 considering only income taxes if he is single and he has no other income. Which option do you recommend based solely on these tax costs?

b. Refer to the information in Chapter 4 on employment taxes for employees and self-employed individuals. Complete the analysis of this problem considering both income and employment taxes.

68. Marla and Joe are a married couple who are very thrifty and generous, donating 10 percent of their income to various charities. They have no itemized deductions except their charitable contributions and normally file a joint income tax return. In 2013 their income is $100,000 and it is expected to increase to $105,000 in 2014. By the end of 2013, their savings are $25,000 and they want to know how they should distribute the money to their chosen charities. Can you suggest a strategy to minimize their taxes? Assume that the standard deduction and tax rates schedules do not change in 2014.

69. A corporation is in the 34 percent tax bracket. It has $1,000,000 in excess cash that it plans to hold and invest for future expansion of its facilities. It can invest in tax-exempt bonds that pay 4.5 percent interest or it can invest in taxable bonds that pay 6 percent interest. Which investment should the corporation make?

70. Carol has recently incorporated her sole proprietorship and is considering making an S election. The corporation has $200,000 of gross revenue and expenses of $75,000 before Carol's salary. She plans to take a gross salary of $60,000 from the business and this will be her only income for the year. Compare the total tax burden for Carol and the corporation with and without the S election. Consider both income and employment taxes. Carol is single and does not itemize her deductions. She plans to reinvest all of the corporation's net income after taxes into the business. Based on tax burden alone for 2013, should Carol make the S election?

ANSWERS TO TEST YOURSELF

1. **b. The annual property tax on your home**
2. **d. Standard deduction**
3. **c. C corporation**
4. **b. Consumption tax**
5. **a. Horizontal equity**

chapter 2

The Tax Practice Environment

Tax practice involves tax compliance and tax research and planning. A practitioner involved in compliance must understand all the laws regulating how and when to file a client's tax return, as well as all the laws that govern how and what items are reported on the return. Practitioners who do not meet acceptable levels of competence and fail in their responsibilities to their clients and to the tax system may be subject to severe penalties.

Tax researchers function in two areas. First, they must defend the actions of clients who have completed certain transactions so that the client receives the best possible tax outcome. Second, they assist clients who are contemplating one or more potential tax transactions. Researchers must determine all the relevant facts and with their knowledge and experience present their clients with the best alternative based on a complete analysis of relevant issues and outcomes, including present value determinations of net cash flows. The suggested alternatives must be communicated to the client in an acceptable form that includes the practitioner's reasoning and conclusions.

Tax professionals must be conversant with all of the tools at their disposal for solving tax problems. They may consult the actual tax laws, as well as interpretations of the laws by both the Treasury Department and the judiciary. Numerous other print and electronic media resources are available for learning about tax law.

All tax practitioners must abide by rules set forth by the Internal Revenue Service. CPAs are subject to additional regulations that have been promulgated by the AICPA. Moreover, practitioners should have a well-developed sense of personal and professional ethics so that they can carry out their responsibilities in spite of client pressures.

CHAPTER OUTLINE

KEY CONCEPTS

- ★ Tax compliance involves filing tax returns and representing clients at audit.
- ★ Tax research involves closed-fact transactions in which the result is fixed and open-fact transactions in which the practitioner can influence the form of the transaction.
- ★ Net present value procedures can be used to select the alternative that provides the optimum tax result.
- ★ Primary sources of tax law include the Internal Revenue Code, Treasury Regulations, revenue rulings, and judicial decisions.
- ★ The steps in tax research are (1) gather the facts and identify the issues, (2) locate and evaluate the relevant authority, and (3) communicate the recommendations. The most challenging of these are issue identification and locating the relevant authority.
- ★ A taxpayer's tax returns may be subject to correspondence, office, or field audits. If additional taxes are due, administrative appeal procedures are available to settle disagreements prior to taking them to the Tax or District Courts or the Court of Federal Claims.
- ★ Taxpayers who fail to comply with the tax laws are subject to a variety of penalties and interest charges. Practitioners can also be subject to penalties if they are not scrupulous in assisting their clients in complying with the tax laws.

Setting the Stage—An Introductory Case

Your friend, Kevin, has come to you for advice. He was recently audited by the IRS and received a notice stating that they were reclassifying his part-time dog training business as a hobby. They disallowed his deductions relating to this part-time business resulting in a tax deficiency of $3,000. Kevin does not believe he owes the additional tax (and really cannot afford to pay it). He would like your advice regarding his appeal options. We will return to this case at the end of this chapter.

An Introduction to Tax Practice

Accountants have many opportunities to specialize in tax compliance, tax planning, or a combination of both. More than 50 percent of all taxpayers pay someone else to prepare their tax returns. Tax preparation is generally referred to as tax compliance. **Tax compliance** consists of gathering relevant information, evaluating and classifying the information, and filing the tax returns. Tax compliance also includes representing clients at an Internal Revenue Service (IRS) audit.

Commercial tax return preparers, attorneys, and certified public accountants (CPAs) all perform tax compliance to some extent. Commercial tax return preparers (such as H&R Block) often complete only the more basic individual and business tax returns. CPAs and attorneys usually prepare more complex tax returns, represent their clients before the IRS, and provide extensive tax planning services. Many businesses employ their own internal tax advisers. The largest U.S. corporate tax departments employ up to 400 tax professionals on a full time basis who spend much of their time complying with state and local tax provisions, as well as those of the federal government. The top tax executive in these corporations typically has a title such as Vice President of Taxation and usually reports to the Chief Financial Officer (CFO). Individuals working for large corporations frequently develop industry specializations, and many accountants hired by private industry have prior tax experience in either public practice or in government.

The largest single employer of tax professionals is the Treasury Department, of which the IRS is a part. The Justice Department, the Tax Court, the Office of Management and Budget, and various congressional committees, as well as state and local governments, employ numerous tax professionals.

Although much of the work done by tax professionals can be described as compliance oriented, the most challenging assignments often involve tax planning. **Tax planning** is the process of evaluating the tax consequences associated with a transaction and making recommendations that will achieve the desired objective at a minimal tax cost. Effective tax planning generally requires extensive tax research.

Tax research can be divided into two major categories: closed-fact transactions and open-fact transactions. In a closed-fact transaction, all of the relevant transactions have been completed; therefore, research usually consists of finding support for the action that the client has already taken. Issues in a closed-fact tax research problem often arise from a conflict with the IRS. In an open-fact transaction, however, the tax practitioner maintains some degree of control over the tax liability because the transaction is not yet complete. If all the facts have not been established, there is an opportunity to plan anticipated facts carefully. Good tax planning establishes an optimal set of facts from the standpoint of tax results. The procedures followed in making such a determination differ significantly from the procedures used in compliance work.

Tax planning allows a practitioner to exercise a higher degree of creativity than possible in any other area of practice. A good tax planner spends a considerable amount of time simply thinking about alternatives to achieve the client's objectives. A common tendency of new tax students is to rush too quickly into a search for authority, often overlooking the best alternative.

TAXES AND CASH FLOW

Every business generates transactions designed to produce a profit for its owners. Some business transactions result in cash inflows, others in cash outflows. Many transactions involve both inflows and outflows. Net cash flow is cash inflows less cash outflows. When faced with alternatives, managers should choose the alternative that generates the greatest positive net cash flow (or minimizes cash outflows if only considering costs).

The net cash flow calculated must include any tax cost or tax savings from the transaction. The **tax cost** is the increase in tax for the period and is a cash outflow. When a profit is generated from the sale of a product, any income tax paid is a cash outflow that reduces the net cash flow. A **tax savings** is a decrease in tax for a period and is a cash inflow. When a deductible expense is incurred, the expense generates an outflow but the tax deduction generates a tax reduction. The tax savings are a cash inflow that increases the net cash flow.

EXAMPLE 1

Widget Corporation sells its merchandise for $5,000. Widget's cost for the merchandise is $3,000, resulting in $2,000 of taxable income. If Widget is subject to a 35 percent income tax, the tax cost of this sale transaction is $700 ($2,000 × 35%), which is a cash outflow. This sale transaction results in a positive net cash flow of $1,300 ($5,000 – $3,000 – $700).

Widget also paid $3,000 in wages to its employees. Wages can be deducted in computing taxable income, resulting in a tax savings of $1,050 ($3,000 × 35%). The after-tax cost of the wages is $1,950 ($3,000 – $1,050).

The federal income tax is very different from most other business expenses in its impact on cash flow. Federal income taxes are not deducted in determining taxable income. Thus, reducing the income taxes paid (tax savings) is a pure cash inflow; that is, the increased cash flow does not trigger any additional increase in tax, as tax savings are not taxable income. The exemption from income tax for tax savings differentiates tax planning from most other profit-motivated activities.

EXAMPLE 2

A corporation, with a 39 percent marginal tax rate, can pay $10,000 to a marketing consultant who claims he can generate $50,000 in new revenue. Alternatively, the corporation can pay $10,000 to a tax consultant who claims he can save the corporation $50,000 in taxes through tax planning. The $10,000 paid to either consultant is deductible, so its after-tax cost is $6,100 [$10,000 – ($10,000 × 39%)]. The after-tax cash inflow from the marketing plan is $30,500 [$50,000 – ($50,000 × 39%)] resulting in a net after-tax cash flow of $24,400 ($30,500 – $6,100). Because tax savings are not subject to income tax, the after-tax cash inflow from the alternative plan is $50,000 resulting in a net after-tax cash flow of $43,900 ($50,000 – $6,100).

Cash Flows and Present Value

When cash inflows or outflows continue beyond the current year, it is important to reduce the net cash flows to their net present value (that is, cash flows in future years are discounted to their present value so they can be compared using comparable dollars).[1]

[1]Present value = future value/(1 + interest [discount] rate). If you will receive $1,000 in one year, it will only be worth $926 to you currently if the interest rate for your investments is 8 percent ($1,000/1.08 = $926). Alternatively, future value = present value × (1 + interest rate). If you invest $926 in a bond that pays 8 percent interest, after one year the value of the investment has grown to $1,000 ($926 × 1.08 = $1,000).

Present value concepts dictate that a dollar received in a future year is worth less than a dollar received in the current year. Table 2.1 shows how much $1 to be paid at a future date is worth today at the discount rate indicated.[2]

EXAMPLE 3

HomeBuild Construction must decide between two mutually exclusive construction projects. Both projects would take two years to complete, but the company has sufficient workers to complete only one of them. The first job will generate $510,000 of revenues in the current year and $130,000 of revenues in the next year. HomeBuild estimates that this job will incur $310,000 of expenses in the current year and $80,000 of expenses in the next year. The second job will generate $320,000 of revenues and $195,000 of expenses in each of the two years. Assuming an 8 percent discount rate and a 25 percent tax rate, the net present value of these jobs is as follows:

	JOB 1		JOB 2	
Current year				
Revenues		$510,000		$320,000
Expenses		(310,000)		(195,000)
Before-tax cash flow		$200,000		$125,000
Income tax @ 25%		(50,000)		(31,250)
After-tax cash flow		$150,000		$93,750
Next year				
Revenues	$130,000		$320,000	
Expenses	(80,000)		(195,000)	
Before-tax cash flow	$50,000		$125,000	
Income tax @ 25%	(12,500)		(31,250)	
After-tax cash flow	$37,500		$93,750	
Present value				
(after-tax cash flow × 0.926)		34,725		86,813
Net present value		$184,725		$180,563

HomeBuild should select Job 1 because its net present value is $4,162 greater ($184,725 – $180,563).

TABLE 2.1 **PRESENT VALUE OF A SINGLE PAYMENT**

YEAR	5%	6%	7%	8%	9%	10%	12%
1	0.952	0.943	0.935	0.926	0.917	0.909	0.893
2	0.907	0.890	0.873	0.857	0.842	0.826	0.797
3	0.864	0.840	0.816	0.794	0.772	0.751	0.712
4	0.823	0.792	0.763	0.735	0.708	0.683	0.636
5	0.784	0.747	0.713	0.681	0.650	0.621	0.567
6	0.746	0.705	0.666	0.630	0.596	0.564	0.507
7	0.711	0.665	0.623	0.583	0.547	0.513	0.452
8	0.677	0.627	0.582	0.540	0.502	0.467	0.404
9	0.645	0.592	0.544	0.500	0.460	0.424	0.361
10	0.614	0.558	0.508	0.463	0.422	0.386	0.322

[2]Additional present value tables are included in Appendix B at the end of this textbook.

Significance of the Marginal Tax Rate

The marginal tax rate is the rate that applies to the next dollar of income. This rate should be used when evaluating transactions that increase or decrease taxable income. If a corporation's marginal tax rate changes from one year to the next, the company's tax costs and savings also fluctuate. The previous example assumed a fixed marginal tax rate.[3] If the corporation in the previous problem has no other taxable income, then the actual corporate tax rates of 15 percent on the first $50,000 of taxable income, 25 percent on the next $25,000, 34 percent on the next $25,000, and 39 percent on taxable income over $100,000 up to $335,000 should be used and the revised problem is as follows.

EXAMPLE 4

The current year's before-tax cash flow (taxable income) from Job 1 was $200,000. Income tax on this taxable income is $61,250 [($50,000 × 15%) + ($25,000 × 25%) + ($25,000 × 34%) + ($100,000 × 39%)]. Income tax on the $50,000 taxable income in the next year is $7,500 ($50,000 × 15%). The income tax for Job 2 on $125,000 taxable income is $32,000 [($50,000 × 15%) + ($25,000 × 25%) + ($25,000 × 34%) + ($25,000 × 39%)] in each year. The revised net present value calculation using the actual tax rates is as follows:

	JOB 1		JOB 2	
Current year				
Revenues		$510,000		$320,000
Expenses		(310,000)		(195,000)
Before-tax cash flow		$200,000		$125,000
Income tax		(61,250)		(32,000)
After-tax cash flow		$138,750		$93,000
Next year				
Revenues	$130,000		$320,000	
Expenses	(80,000)		(195,000)	
Before-tax cash flow	$50,000		$125,000	
Income tax	(7,500)		(32,000)	
After-tax cash flow	$42,500		$93,000	
Present value				
(after-tax cash flow × 0.926)		39,355		86,118
Net present value		$178,105		$179,118

Job 2 now has the higher net present value because so much of Job 1's first year income is taxed at 39 percent.

When marginal tax rates are expected to change from one year to the next, the timing of the transaction should be controlled to the extent possible to minimize tax costs and maximize tax savings.

TAX PLANNING STRATEGIES

Tax planning strategies include timing, income shifting, and changing the character of income. These strategies are introduced in this chapter. These and other strategies will be discussed and applied in later chapters.

Timing Income and Deductions

Timing involves the question of when income and deductions should be claimed. One traditional technique defers the recognition of income and accelerates the recognition of deductions. This technique relies on savings achieved due to the time value of

[3]Fixed marginal rates are often assumed for simplicity. The structure of the corporate tax, however, includes fixed marginal tax rates of 34 percent for income between $335,000 and $10,000,000 and 35 percent for incomes above $18,333,333.

money by delaying tax payments on deferred income or accelerating tax savings by taking deductions in an earlier period. Changing marginal tax rates also impacts the year that income or deductions should be taken. Good tax plans recognize income in the years with the lowest anticipated marginal tax rates and deduct expenses in years with the highest marginal tax rates.

EXAMPLE 5

Ronco Corporation, a cash-basis calendar-year taxpayer, is in the 25 percent marginal tax bracket. Depending on when it bills its customers, it will receive $10,000 of income in December of year 1 or in January of year 2. If Ronco is in the same 25 percent marginal tax bracket in both years, the only factor to consider is the time value of money because its after-tax cash inflow is $7,500 [$10,000 – ($10,000 × 25%)] in both years. If, however, Ronco expects its marginal tax rates to change, it should try to report the income in the year with the lowest expected marginal tax rate. What are the tax effects if Ronco defers income to year 2 when its marginal tax rate is 15 percent, 25 percent, or 34 percent in that year, using an 8 percent discount factor?

	Year 2 Marginal Tax Rates		
	15%	25%	34%
Tax paid in year 2 ($10,000 × tax rate)	$1,500	$2,500	$3,400
Present value factor	×0.926	×0.926	×0.926
Present value if tax paid in year 2	$1,389	$2,315	$3,148
Present value if tax paid in year 1	2,500	2,500	2,500
Net tax savings by deferring income	$1,111	$185	
Net tax cost of deferring income			$648

If Ronco expects that its marginal tax rate will be either 15 or 25 percent in year 2, it should defer recognition of the income. If, however, Ronco expects that its marginal tax rate will increase to 34 percent in year 2, it should recognize the income in year 1 because it would cost $648 to defer income until year 2.

The same approach can be used to determine the optimal year in which to take a deduction to maximize the after-tax savings in taxes paid.

EXAMPLE 6

Carbonnaire Corporation, a cash-basis taxpayer, owes a $20,000 expense that may be paid and deducted in either year 1 or year 2. Carbonnaire's marginal tax rate is 25 percent. If it pays the expense in year 1, its after-tax cost is $15,000 [$20,000 – ($20,000 × 25%)]. What happens if the deduction is deferred to year 2 and Carbonnaire's marginal tax rate is 15 percent, 25 percent, or 34 percent in that year and it uses an 8 percent discount factor?

	Year 2 Marginal Tax Rates		
	15%	25%	34%
Tax savings from deduction ($20,000 × tax rate)	$3,000	$5,000	$6,800
Present value factor	×0.926	×0.926	×0.926
Present value of tax savings if deducted in year 2	$2,778	$4,630	$6,297
Present value of tax savings if deducted in year 1	5,000	5,000	5,000
Tax savings by deducting in year 1	$2,222	$370	
Tax cost of deducting in year 1			$1,297

Carbonnaire Corporation should claim the deduction in year 1 if it expects the marginal tax rate to decrease to 15 percent or to remain at 25 percent to maximize its tax savings. If the corporation expects its marginal rate to increase to 34 percent, it should defer the deduction to year 2.

Income Shifting

The purpose of income shifting is to lower the total tax paid by splitting income among two or more taxpayers in the same family or between different entities that are owned by the same individual. The total tax paid is lower because of the progressive tax rate system.

EXAMPLE 7

Vivian and Troy, married taxpayers filing a joint return, have $150,000 in taxable income in 2013. They have 3 children (ages 2 to 12) who have no taxable income. If they can legally shift $2,000 in taxable income to each child, they can save $1,308 in taxes for the family as follows:

Tax on $150,000 for a married couple filing a joint return	$29,465.50
Tax on $144,000 ($150,000 – $6,000 shifted to children)	(27,857.50)
Tax savings to parents	$1,608
Tax paid by children ($100 × 3)[4]	(300)
Net tax savings to family from income shifting	$1,308

To legally shift income to family members, the parents will need to transfer ownership of income-producing property to the children; a mere assignment of income will not result in the desired tax shifting.[5]

Another popular income-shifting technique used by owner-employees of a corporation is to split income between themselves and the corporation by paying themselves salaries, which are deductible by the corporation, to take advantage of the progressive tax rates for individuals and corporations.

EXAMPLE 8

Vivian and Troy have $150,000 in taxable income from a sole proprietorship run by Troy. In a typical year, Troy withdraws only half of the profits from the business, leaving the other half in the business for expansion. If Troy incorporates the business and pays himself a salary of $75,000, he will be taxed on only $75,000, with the other $75,000 taxed at the corporation's rates (the corporation can deduct the salary paid to Troy as a business expense). The corporate tax is $13,750 (15 percent on the first $50,000, and 25 percent on the next $25,000). Splitting the income between the taxpayer and a corporation in 2013 results in a tax savings of $5,108.

Tax on $150,000 for a married couple	$29,465.50
Tax on $75,000 for a married couple	(10,607.50)
Tax saving on the couple's tax return	$18,858
Tax on $75,000 for a corporation	(13,750)
Net tax savings	$5,108[6]

Other strategies include employing children and maximizing the use of tax-free employee fringe benefits. These techniques are discussed in Chapter 4.

Changing the Character of Income

The character of income is determined by tax law and is ultimately characterized as either ordinary income or capital gain. Income from sale of merchandise to customers is characterized as ordinary income and is subject to tax using the regular tax rates.

[4]Each child is allowed a $1,000 standard deduction, reducing taxable income to $1,000. This is then subject to tax at a 10 percent rate, resulting in a tax liability of $100 per child. The income tax rates were introduced in Chapter 1. See Chapter 11 for more details.

[5]Even if a valid transfer of property is made, if the child is younger than nineteen (twenty-four, if a full-time student), the kiddie tax rules reduce much of the marginal rate advantage of such a shift by taxing unearned income (such as interest and dividend income) in excess of $2,000 at the parents' marginal tax rate. See Chapter 12.

[6]This example does not consider the impact of employment taxes. Employment taxes are discussed in Chapter 4. The computation of income tax liability for individuals (including married couples) is discussed in detail in Chapter 11. This example assumes that they have other income that offsets their deductions and exemptions so the income from the business is their taxable income. The income tax rates were introduced in Chapter 1.

Capital assets enjoy favorable tax treatment with most gains on capital assets held (the time from acquisition to disposition) for more than 12 months taxed to individuals at a maximum 20 percent rate, compared to the top current individual tax rate of 39.6 percent (plus surtaxes).

EXAMPLE 9

John owns 10,000 shares of XYZ stock that he purchased 11 months ago at a cost of $10 per share that is now trading at $18 per share. John's regular marginal tax rate is 25 percent and his tax rate for long-term capital gains is 15 percent. If John sells the stock now, the gain will not qualify for the special long-term capital gain tax rates and his 25 percent ordinary rate would apply. If John waits another month before selling the stock, he can change the character of the income from income taxed at his regular rates to income taxed at the favorable 15 percent long-term capital gains rate, thus significantly increasing his after-tax cash flow:

	25% Tax Rate	15% Tax Rate
Sales proceeds ($18 × 10,000)	$180,000	$180,000
Cost ($10 × 10,000)	(100,000)	(100,000)
Net before-tax cash flow	$80,000	$80,000
Tax cost ($80,000 × tax rate)	(20,000)	(12,000)
Net after-tax cash flow	$60,000	$68,000

John saves $8,000 ($20,000 – $12,000) in taxes, increasing his cash flow by the same amount, by changing the character of the income to long-term capital gain.

There are several tax policy reasons for providing a preferential tax rate for long-term capital gains. First, individuals do not pay tax on any unrealized gains as they are earned, but are taxed only in the year the gain is realized. Recognizing several years' gains in one year can cause the gain to be taxed at a higher marginal rate than if the gain were taxed annually. Second, a lower rate mitigates the effects of inflation. Some or all of the gain realized on an asset held for a number of years may be due to inflation. Finally, the preferential rate helps compensate for the risks associated with long-term investments. By offering a preferential rate to capital assets held for more than one year, the government uses tax policy to encourage investors to invest for the long-term rather than churning their investments.

Other Factors Affecting Tax Planning

A number of factors affect the estimates of net cash flow used in evaluating projects, such as the discount rate, inflation, and uncertainty.[7] Good tax planning requires non-tax factors to be considered as well.

Cash Flow

The discount rate used for project evaluation is an after-tax rate of interest that must be earned on invested funds over the period. The discount rate that is used by a firm in evaluating a project is normally its cost of capital (the required return on the firm's invested funds), a composite based on the cost of retained earnings, other equity, and the after-tax cost of debt financing. Financing of a specific project is not traced to any specific financing source. This discount rate factors in the after-tax cost of debt. Thus, in evaluating projects, the after-tax interest costs are not considered as part of the cash flow as this would double count after-tax interest costs.

To avoid changing discount rates, many firms use an ideal cost of capital as their discount rate. They may, however, calculate discount rates based on changes in the cost of debt and equity financing from year to year, leading to different problem solutions than a static rate. Moreover, two firms may have different discount rates. Thus, one firm would accept a project that another firm would reject. If one firm's discount rate is lower relative to another firm's, the net present value of future cash flows will

[7]Most introductory finance texts provide a complete discussion of cost of capital, inflation, and uncertainty in determining cash flows for any project.

be higher. Conversely, the higher a firm's discount rate, the lower the present value of its future cash flows.

EXAMPLE 10

Wilson and Meyers, two competing firms, can each undertake a project that will cost $10,500. The expected net cash inflow from the project is $6,000 at the end of years 1 and 2. Wilson uses a 6 percent discount rate to evaluate projects and Meyers uses a 12 percent rate.

	Wilson	Meyers
Year 1	$6,000 × .943 = $5,658	$6,000 × .893 = $5,358
Year 2	$6,000 × .890 = $5,340	$6,000 × .797 = $4,782
Total	$10,998	$10,140
Cost	(10,500)	(10,500)
Net cash inflow (outflow)	$498	$(360)

Wilson would accept the project, but Meyers would reject it because of their differing discount rates.

Inflation can be factored into present value calculations in one of two ways: either by increasing the discount rate for expected inflation or by actually factoring inflation-adjusted cash flows into the present value calculations. Although neither method usually produces a completely satisfactory result, ignoring inflation may skew the cash flow and lead to poor decisions.

EXAMPLE 11

Assume in the previous example that Meyers uses a 12 percent discount rate because the costs factored into its net cash flow ($6,000) in years 1 and 2 are expected to rise by at least 6 percent. Alternatively, Wilson decides to reduce its estimates of net cash flows so that its net cash flow in year 1 is only $5,640 and $5,302 in year 2. Its net present value is now a negative $462 [($5,640 × .943 = $5,319) + (5,302 × .890 = $4,719) – $10,500 = ($462)] and it, too, would reject the project.

All of the project evaluations presented have been based on projections or estimates of the future cash inflows and outflows. Thus, every evaluation has uncertainty built in. Because the net present value is generally calculated on uncertain cash flows, they are worth less than the present value of a guaranteed cash flow (such as U.S. government bond interest). Thus, a higher discount rate would be used to evaluate risky cash flows than used for guaranteed cash flows. As shown previously, the higher the discount rate used for analysis, the greater the required net cash flows in future years for project acceptance. Alternatively, a probability can be assigned to a cash flow or, if there are several estimates of cash flow, each estimate can be assigned a probability and an expected value determined.

EXAMPLE 12

Assume that Meyers in the previous examples received estimates of the net cash flow from its project manager of $7,000 with a 40 percent probability and $5,350 with a 60 percent probability for each of the two years. The expected value is $6,010 [(.4 × $7,000 = $2,800) + (.6 × $5,350 = $3,210)]. It would then use the $6,010 expected value of the cash flow in both years to determine if it should accept the project.

Nontax Considerations and Judicial Doctrines

The goal of tax planning is to minimize the tax costs of a transaction while meeting the nontax objectives of the client. Saving taxes is not always the most important consideration for a client. For example, a tax planner may come up with the best possible tax plan for a wealthy grandmother to avoid any estate tax upon her death by transferring title of all assets to her grandchildren while she is still alive. She, however, is not willing to give up control of all of her property to ensure that her grandchildren will still come to visit her in the nursing home. In this situation, the amount of tax saved by the plan may be irrelevant because the nontax factor of continued control over the property outweighs any tax savings. Effective tax planning must consider both tax and nontax factors.

Another factor that must be considered is the cost of implementation. The cost of implementing a sophisticated plan may exceed the potential tax savings, so it is imperative to consider all of the costs of a plan before beginning implementation.

Tax planners must consider three legal doctrines that the IRS can invoke when a taxpayer seems to be taking excessive advantage of the tax law. The federal courts and the IRS require taxpayers to adhere not only to the letter of the law but the spirit of the law as well.

The **business purpose doctrine** holds that a transaction will be recognized for tax purposes only if it is made for some business or economic purpose other than a tax avoidance motive.[8]

EXAMPLE 13

Mega Corporation has $10,000,000 in taxable income and is looking for a way to avoid paying taxes. Loser Corporation has $9,000,000 of tax losses that it cannot use because it has no prospect of profits. Mega Corporation acquires Loser Corporation in a tax-free merger. If Mega Corporation has no business purpose for the merger other than to acquire Loser's tax losses, the IRS can prevent Mega from using the tax losses.

In 2010, Section 7701(o) codified the economic substance doctrine. This new code section specifically requires taxpayers to establish the presence of both economic substance (measured objectively in terms of pre-tax profit potential) and business purpose. This new law also enacted a minimum penalty of 20 percent of the underpayment attributable to any disallowed tax benefits for a transaction lacking economic substance and increases that penalty to 40 percent of the disallowed benefits if they were not adequately disclosed in the tax return.

Taxpayers attempting to avoid taxation sometimes carefully craft transactions that are completely unrealistic. Although the courts have consistently held that taxpayers are under no legal obligation to pay more tax than the law prescribes, the courts have also said that the form of the transaction cannot be used to disguise its actual substance. This judicially created concept is referred to as the **substance-over-form doctrine** and states that the taxability of a transaction is determined by the reality of the transaction, rather than its appearance.[9]

EXAMPLE 14

A profitable corporation that has never paid dividends pays a huge bonus to its sole owner-manager, who earned a more-than-generous salary. The IRS can recharacterize all or part of the bonus as a dividend. Under the circumstances, although the payment is in the form of a bonus, its substance is that of a dividend. Dividends are not deductible by corporations so recharacterizing the bonus as a dividend increases the corporation's taxable income and tax liability.

The IRS has successfully used the substance-over-form doctrine to attack tax shelters.

KEY CASE *One significant tax shelter case involves Long Term Capital Management, a well known hedge fund run by Myron Scholes (Nobel laureate and co-author of the Black-Scholes pricing model). The U.S. District Court found that structured partnership transactions resulting in a $106 million capital loss deduction on the sale of preferred stock lacked economic substance. It disallowed the loss and assessed a $40 million tax deficiency along with up to $16 million in penalties.*[10]

Under the **step transaction doctrine**, the IRS can collapse a series of intermediate transactions into a single transaction to determine the tax consequences.[11] This doctrine is usually applied to transactions that are so interdependent that the taxpayers

[8]*Gregory v. Helvering*, 293 US 465 (1935) held that the transaction in question had no business purpose and therefore the applicable tax law did not apply, establishing the business purpose doctrine.

[9]*U.S. v. Phellis*, 257 US 156 (1921) made the first application of the substance-over-form doctrine when it held that the substance of a transaction should be considered and the form of a transaction can be disregarded in applying the provision of the tax law.

[10]*Long Term Capital Holdings v. U.S.*, 330 F.Supp.2d 122; 94 AFTR2d 2004-5666; 2004-2 USTC ¶50351 (DC Conn. 2004), affd. 96 AFTR2d 2005-6344, 2005-2 USTC ¶50575 (CA-2, 2005).

[11]Helvering v. Alabama Asphaltic Limestone Co., 316 US 179 (1942).

would probably have not completed the first transaction without anticipating that the entire series would take place. The IRS most frequently invokes this doctrine for a series of transactions occurring within a short period of time. The taxpayer should have a bona fide business purpose for each individual step of the transaction to prevent the IRS from negating what seems to be a good tax plan.

Example 15

Jim, the sole shareholder of a corporation, needs money for another investment. To obtain the funds, he sells a large block of the corporation's stock to a friend at a huge profit. Jim then has the corporation redeem the stock from his friend for the purchase price. The IRS can collapse the steps and treat this as a redemption of Jim's stock by the corporation, ignoring the sale involving his friend. The entire sale proceeds could be taxed to Jim as if they were a dividend distribution by the corporation.

Tax planners need to be aware of these doctrines when crafting a creative tax plan, making sure it complies not just with the letter of the law but also with the spirit of the law.

Sources of Authority

The tax treatment of any particular transaction normally must be based on supporting authority. Thus, mastery of taxation requires an understanding of how and where the rules of taxation originate. The tax rules contained in each of the chapters in this textbook all have their origin in some source of authority.

Tax authority is generally classified as primary or secondary authority. **Primary authority** comes from statutory, administrative, and judicial sources. **Secondary authority** is used to assist in the location and interpretation of the primary sources of authority. Secondary authority consists of tax services (also called reference services), books, journals, and newsletters.

Statutory sources include the U.S. Constitution, tax treaties, and tax laws passed by Congress and are the basis for all tax provisions. The Constitution is the source of all federal laws, both tax and nontax; however, it is the 16th Amendment (ratified in 1913) that specifically gives Congress the power to impose a federal income tax.

Tax treaties (sometimes referred to as tax conventions) are agreements negotiated between countries concerning the treatment of individuals and other entities subject to tax in both countries. The purpose of these treaties is to eliminate the double taxation that taxpayers would face if their income were subject to tax in both countries.

The source most tax practitioners are concerned with is the result of the legislative process—the Internal Revenue Code. To develop an understanding of how the primary sources of authority can help clarify the way a transaction should be treated for tax purposes, one needs to understand the legislative process, the means by which tax bills are enacted, and how to determine the legislative intent of Congress.

The Legislative Process

The legislative process is the procedure by which a legislative proposal becomes part of our tax law. Tax legislation arises from various sources. The president's economic report and budget message, studies made by the IRS, and bills introduced by individual representatives who are either acting on their own or reacting to pressures exerted by various special interest groups give rise to the legislation.

The Constitution vests the House of Representatives of the U.S. Congress with the basic responsibility for initiating revenue bills. Before there can be a federal law on any subject, there must be general agreement on the matter both in the House of Representatives and in the Senate. Congress operates through committees, however, that act both as drafters and gatekeepers for legislative proposals. Each house has its own committees, and each committee is concerned only with its own legislative proposals that fall into certain categories. The two standing committees concerned with federal tax legislation are the Ways and Means Committee of the House of Representatives and the Finance Committee of the Senate.

Each new bill introduced in Congress is given a number that it retains throughout its congressional journey. A House bill number has the prefix *H.R.* and a Senate bill number has the prefix *S.* A new series of numbers starts in each house with each new Congress.[12]

EXAMPLE 16

The American Taxpayer Relief Act of 2012 is numbered H.R. 8. After passage by Congress, H.R. 8 became P.L. 112-240 and was signed into law by the President on January 2, 2013. The prefix of the public law number (112) refers to the session of Congress that passed the law. The suffix of the public law number (240) indicates that this was the 240th bill adopted during this congressional session.

After a tax bill introduced in the House is assigned a number, it is ordinarily referred to the House Ways and Means Committee. This committee usually holds public hearings on the bill. Thereafter, the committee will decide either to kill the bill by tabling it (postponing action on it indefinitely) or to submit the bill to the full House for its consideration, usually with amendments made by the committee. The committee sends a report containing a general and technical discussion of the bill's provisions to the floor of the House. This **committee report**, which may provide important authoritative support by indicating the legislative intent of the bill, is often considered in court cases to help resolve disputes between taxpayers and the IRS.

The bill is debated on the floor of the House, typically under *closed rule*, which limits debate and allows no amendments. If the bill fails on the floor of the House, it may go back to the committee; if it passes, the bill is sent to the Senate, where it is referred to the Senate Finance Committee.

The Senate Finance Committee, like its counterpart in the House, also provides an analysis of the bill in its report. After public hearings, the Senate Finance Committee sends its report, along with proposed amendments to the House bill, to the Senate floor. There the bill is debated under *open rule* with unlimited debate and amendments, and often under intense lobbying pressure. Amendments made during consideration of a bill by the full House or Senate are commonly called floor amendments to distinguish them from committee amendments. Thus, the bill passed by the Senate is usually different from the version passed by the House. The bills are then referred to a Joint Conference Committee to work out the differences between the two versions.

The Joint Conference Committee is established to settle the differences between the House and the Senate on a particular bill. The committee members are ordinarily members of the House Ways and Means Committee and of the Senate Finance Committee, though other members of the two houses also can participate in the Joint Conference Committee.

The Joint Conference Committee reviews each provision of the bill on which the two houses disagree. In most instances, the Joint Conference Committee agrees with either the Senate version or the House version. In other instances it may agree with the Senate version but add amendments or it may propose a compromise version. The Joint Conference Committee also prepares a report explaining its proposed amendments and compromise provisions; it also indicates which house defers to the other in the case of the remaining conflicting provisions of the House and Senate versions of the bill. The report is sent back to the House and then to the Senate for a vote on the Joint Conference Committee's compromise bill. Upon approval of both houses, the bill is sent to the president for signature or veto.

Once members of the Joint Conference Committee reach a compromise, the rest of the process may move very quickly.

[12]Each session of Congress lasts for two years to coincide with the biannual elections of the congressional representatives. The 112th congressional session extended from 2011 through 2012; the 113th congressional session extends from 2013 through 2014.

EXAMPLE 17

H.R. 4462, which allowed an income tax deduction on 2009 income tax returns for charitable contributions of cash made in 2010 for the relief of earthquake victims in Haiti (P.L. 111–126), sailed through Congress in less than 24 hours. It was passed by the House on January 20, 2010 and passed by the Senate on January 21. President Obama then signed it into law on January 22, 2010.

A tax bill passed by Congress is usually enacted as a revenue act that amends the existing Internal Revenue Code. The most recent exception to this practice occurred in 1986, when the Tax Reform Act of 1986 also created the Internal Revenue Code of 1986. From 1954 to 1986, tax legislation simply amended the Internal Revenue Code of 1954.

Shortly after each new revenue act, the major tax services issue explanations of the new tax law that cite or quote the relevant congressional committee reports. Debates and other statements made on the floor of the House or Senate are published in the *Congressional Record* for each day that Congress is in session. The reports from the various committees are published in the *Congressional Record* and the *Cumulative Bulletin*.

Internal Revenue Code

The **Internal Revenue Code** is considered the most important source of tax law. The Internal Revenue Code is usually cited simply as *Code* or *IRC*. The latter distinguishes the Internal Revenue Code from other Codes, such as the United States Code and the Code of Federal Regulations. The Internal Revenue Code of 1986 is divided into the following subtitles and related chapters:

Subtitles		Chapters
A	Income Taxes	1–6
B	Estate and Gift Taxes	11–15
C	Employment Taxes and Collection of Income Tax	21–25
D	Miscellaneous Excise Taxes	31–50
E.	Alcohol, Tobacco, and Certain Other Excise Taxes	51–55
F	Procedure and Administration	61–80
G	The Joint Committee on Taxation	91–92
H	Financing of Presidential Election Campaigns	95–96
I	Trust Fund Code	98
J	Coal Industry Health Benefits	99
K	Group Health Plan Requirements	100

The majority of the income tax provisions are included in Chapter 1. Chapter 1 contains twenty-five subchapters (A to Y). The subchapters divide the Code by income tax topics, and each subchapter is further divided into sections. Chapter 1 of Subtitle A includes the following:

SUBTITLE A. INCOME TAXES

Chapter 1. Normal Taxes and Surtaxes

Subchapter		Sections
A	Determination of Tax Liability	1–59B
B	Computation of Taxable Income	61–291
C	Corporate Distributions and Adjustments	301–385
D	Deferred Compensation, etc.	401–436
E	Accounting Periods and Methods of Accounting	441–483
F	Exempt Organizations	501–530
G	Corporations Used to Avoid Income Tax on Shareholders	531–565
H	Banking Institutions	581–597
I	Natural Resources	611–638
J	Estates, Trusts, Beneficiaries, and Decedents	641–692
K	Partners and Partnerships	701–777

L	Insurance Companies	801–848
M	Regulated Investment Companies and Real Estate Investment Trusts	851–860G
N	Tax Based on Income from Sources from Within or Without the U.S.	861–999
O	Gain or Loss on Disposition of Property	1001–1092
P	Capital Gains and Losses	1201–1298
Q	Readjustment of Tax Between Years and Special Limitations	1301–1351
R	Election to Determine Corporate Tax on Certain International Shipping Activities Using Per Ton Rate	1352–1359
S	Tax Treatment of S Corporations and Their Shareholders	1361–1379
T	Cooperatives and Their Patrons	1381–1388
U	Designation of Treatment of Empowerment Zones, Enterprise Communities, and Rural Development Investment Areas	1391–1397F
V	Title 11 Cases	1398–1399
W	District of Columbia Enterprise Zone	1400–1400C
X	Designation of Renewal Communities	1400E–1400J
Y	Short-Term Regional Benefits	1400L–1400U-3

Citations to provisions of the Internal Revenue Code usually are to sections (often abbreviated as Sec. or §) of the Code. This is the most convenient designation because sections are uniquely numbered in a consecutive manner. In other words, each section number is used only once. If a section has several subdivisions, the citation is usually to the lowest subdivision that supports the point for which the section is cited.

Administrative Sources of Authority

Laws are usually written in general language, as it is impossible to anticipate all the situations to which a particular provision of the law may apply. The general rules of most laws are usually clear. It is the application of those rules to particular facts that most frequently is uncertain.

Example 18

It is clear that, under the Internal Revenue Code, business expenses are deductible from gross income. However, it is not always clear whether a particular item incurred at a given time in a particular factual setting is a qualified business expense. In example 14, the bonus is really a disguised dividend and is not deductible.

The Treasury Department has the responsibility of implementing the tax statutes passed by Congress. It is authorized to explain and interpret the law as part of its duties. The Internal Revenue Service division of the Treasury Department specifically carries out this function.

Treasury Regulations

Treasury Regulations provide explanations, definitions, examples, and rules that explain the language in the Code. Frequently, there is a considerable delay between the addition to or amendment of a particular Code section and the issuance of Treasury Regulations. In this situation, taxpayers must rely on the committee reports for guidance until regulations are released.

Most income tax regulations (or *regs*) are interpretative regulations that provide examples and detailed explanations to help interpret the Code. A Code section may, however, specifically authorize regulations to provide the details of the meaning and rules for that particular Code section. Regulations issued under this authority are called *legislative regulations*. These regulations are considered to have the same level of authority as the Code.

There are three classes of regulations: (1) proposed, (2) temporary, and (3) final. The proposed regulations provide taxpayers with an advance indication of the likely IRS position and signal areas of potential disagreement. Comments and criticisms by interested parties can then be made either in writing or at hearings. Because proposed regulations are just proposals, they cannot be relied upon. Consequently, when a major tax law is enacted, the Treasury Department may skip the proposal step and issue temporary regulations to provide operating rules in the interim before the issuance of final regulations. The current practice is to issue regulations that are both proposed and temporary. The final regulations are issued after the public comments on the proposed regulations are evaluated; they then supersede the temporary regulations.

Treasury Regulations relating to all federal taxes are printed in Title 26 of the Code of Federal Regulations, which is divided into major subdivisions called *parts.* Part 1 contains the regulations dealing with the income tax provisions of the Internal Revenue Code; part 20 contains the regulations dealing with the estate tax provisions; part 25 contains the regulations dealing with the gift tax provisions; and part 301 contains administrative and procedural rules. Other parts contain temporary regulations and other regulations dealing with employment and excise taxes.

The regulations are arranged in the same sequence as the Code. Each part of the regulations is divided into sections with the same root number as the corresponding section of the Internal Revenue Code. Each section number consists of the following three elements:

1. *A prefix number to the left of the decimal point* indicates the part of Title 26 of the Code of Federal Regulations in which the section will be found. Thus, an income tax section of the regulations has the prefix number 1.
2. *A root number to the right of the decimal* (and before the hyphen) indicates the Code section the regulation is interpreting.
3. *A suffix number (and letter) to the right of the hyphen following the root number* indicates the subdivision of the section of the regulations. It is not, however, the same as the number of any related subdivision of the Internal Revenue Code.

EXAMPLE 19

Reg. Section 1.61–7(a) is an income tax regulation that deals with interest income addressed in Section 61(a)(4) of the Internal Revenue Code.

Because the root elements of the regulation section numbers correspond to the related sections of the Internal Revenue Code, regulations pertaining to a particular section of the Internal Revenue Code are readily ascertainable.

Other IRS Rulings

The IRS issues several types of rulings. These rulings are issued for three reasons: (1) to inform taxpayers how the Code and the regulations have been applied to a particular set of facts; (2) to indicate the government's interpretation of a certain point of tax law and thus establish guidelines that the Treasury will follow; and (3) to outline those procedures that affect the taxpayer's rights or duties.

Taxpayers who are uncertain about the correct tax treatment of a prospective transaction can ask the IRS for a **letter ruling** (also called a private letter ruling) that provides guidance on how the transaction will be taxed. The IRS charges a fee for these rulings. Many taxpayers feel that obtaining a ruling is well worth its cost as a favorable ruling reduces the risk of an IRS challenge to their tax treatment in a subsequent audit.

Each year the IRS publishes **revenue rulings** that clarify ambiguous tax situations for which the public needs administrative guidance. Many of these situations have been the subject of letter rulings. The facts of published revenue rulings are highly individualized, but other taxpayers with similar situations may rely on these rulings. The IRS also issues **revenue procedures**, which explain procedures and the duties of the taxpayer.

Judicial Sources of Authority

Judicial interpretations are the result of litigation. If the IRS and the taxpayer cannot settle the controversy regarding a tax liability between them, either of them may ask a court to decide.

When a tax controversy is litigated, it is first heard and decided by a trial court. That court decides the question according to its interpretation and understanding of the law. If either party is dissatisfied with the trial court's decision, that party may ask an appellate court to review that decision. Ultimately, the controversy may be appealed to and decided by the U.S. Supreme Court. The judicial decision of each court reflects that particular court's interpretation of the law. Although Congress sets forth the words of law and the administrative branch of government is charged with enforcing those words, it is the judiciary that has the final say with respect to what the words really mean. Under our legal system, every word in the law means whatever the Supreme Court says it means. Thus, one can seldom determine the practical impact of any area of law on a given set of facts without investigating what those words of law have been held to mean under similar factual circumstances. The court's role as the final interpreter of language cannot be overemphasized.

KEY CASE *Shortly after the 16th Amendment to the Constitution was passed, giving Congress the power to tax income, Congress declared stock dividends (a distribution of a corporation's own stock) to be taxable income. In the landmark case of* Eisner v. Macomber *the U.S. Supreme Court held that stock dividends are not taxable on the grounds that they do not fall within the meaning of the word* income *as used in the 16th Amendment.*[13] *Although the Constitution contains no definition of the term income, Congress declared that the term includes stock dividends, but the Court held to the contrary. Under current law, stock dividends are generally not taxed.*

Under the doctrine of *stare decisis*, each case has precedential value for future cases with the same fact pattern.[14] By consistently treating similar cases in a similar way, the courts establish their interpretations of the statutes as laws in themselves. It is through this use of precedent that the courts build stability and order into the judicial system. Decisions concerning prior similar cases are used as guides when deciding current cases. The process of finding analogous cases from the past and convincing the tax authorities of the precedential value of those cases is a principal focus of research in the judicial area.

Figure 2.1 shows the primary sources of tax authority. Note that the inner circle (Internal Revenue Code, Regulations, and Supreme Court) represents the highest level of authority for each branch of government.

Tax Research

The purpose of tax research is to find solutions to tax problems. The researcher must locate the authority, evaluate the usefulness of that authority, and then apply that authority to a specific situation. Frequently, tax professionals are called upon to provide quick solutions to their clients' problems. The average client may feel that the tax adviser is a walking encyclopedia of facts on taxation. Sometimes the answer is obvious to the trained observer; if it is not or when the wrong answer may be costly to a client, research is necessary. Reliance on memory for even the most obvious answer can often be a mistake. The importance of tax research cannot be overemphasized.

Typically federal tax research is required in the following instances:

---

[13] *Eisner v. Macomber*, 252 US 189, 3 AFTR 3020; 1 USTC ¶32 (1920).

[14] The judicial doctrine of *stare decisis* means to let the decision stand on settled points of law so that a court views its own prior decision as precedents to be followed.

FIGURE 2.1 PRIMARY SOURCES OF TAX AUTHORITY

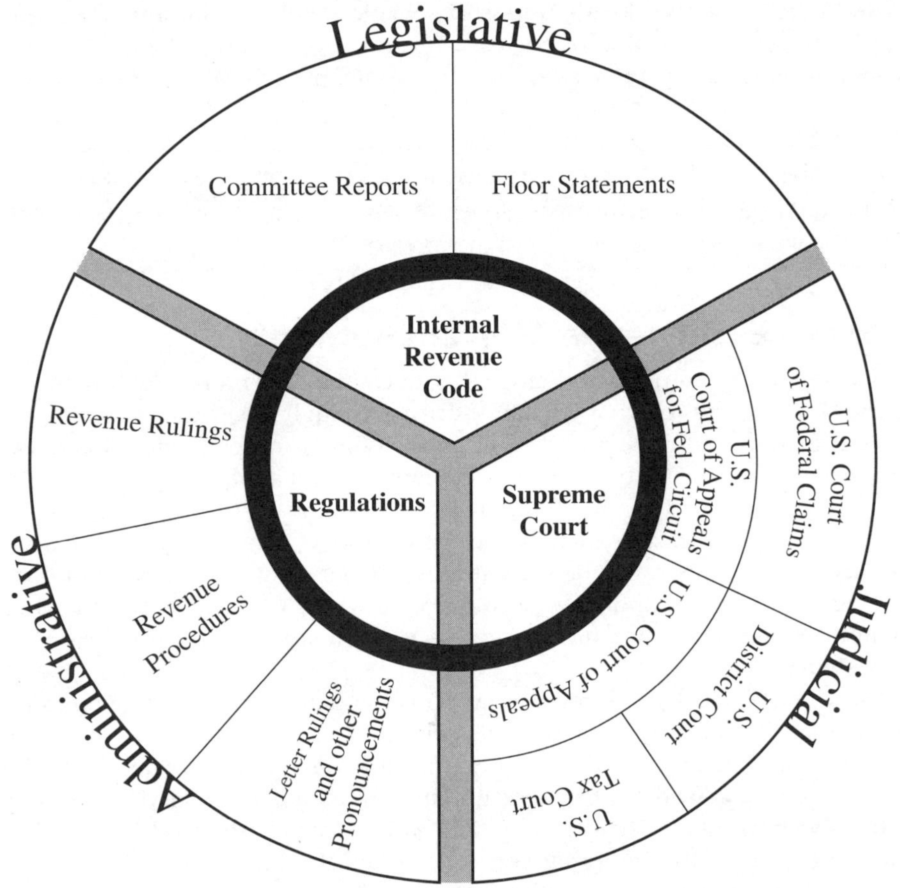

- During the preparation of a client's return if the tax consequences of a transaction are not clear.
- When the IRS raises a question during an audit of a client's tax return.
- In preparation of a claim for refund if it appears that a client may have overpaid his or her taxes.
- When recommending whether or not a client should consider litigation.
- If the government raises issues after a client starts litigation.
- When a client wants to know the tax consequences of a proposed transaction.

Each time a taxpayer consults a tax practitioner, the practitioner is presented with a new problem. Although many basic questions may be nearly identical, each case may involve a slightly different set of facts. Despite the uniqueness of each case, tax research always involves the same key steps:

1. Gather the relevant facts and identify the issues.
2. Locate and evaluate the relevant authorities.
3. Communicate the recommendations.

Gather the Facts and Identify the Issues

Once the facts have been gathered, the tax issues or questions need to be identified. Learning to identify and phrase the critical tax question implicit in any set of facts is often difficult because the most important issues may not be obvious. A combination of training and experience enables the researcher to successfully identify all of the issues in a tax problem. Many beginning researchers find this step to be the most difficult element of the research process.

Typically, new tax students can state a tax question in only broad terms. As a tax professional gains a greater level of technical competence, he or she can review a situation and state the relevant questions in terms of specific statutory authority. Their questions frequently suggest the location of answers. If a researcher knows which Code sections apply to a given situation, the task of locating pertinent authority is greatly simplified.

EXAMPLE 20

Sharon sold her home and wishes to know if the gain on the sale is taxable. A beginning tax student may question whether gross income is recognized in these circumstances. A more experienced tax professional might ask if Sharon qualifies for gain exclusion under Section 121.

Locate and Evaluate the Relevant Authority

Once facts have been gathered and the questions or issues identified, the tax researcher must locate relevant legal authority. Although government publications are available regarding statutory laws, regulations, rulings, and court decisions, these references are found in a variety of places. The number and complexity of the tax statutes make it impossible for any individual to understand all of the rules and regulations relevant to tax practice. Fortunately, tax practitioners have a variety of secondary authorities at their disposal to help locate the official answers to tax questions in the ever-changing primary authorities. Secondary authority consists of unofficial sources of tax information; examples include tax services, textbooks, magazines or journals, and newsletters.

Tax service (also called reference service) is the name commonly given to comprehensive tax-law research publications. Historically, these services were comprehensive, multivolume, loose-leaf sets of reference information relating to tax problems. The loose-leaf feature allowed for frequent updating. Most of these services are now also published electronically.[15] Most leading tax services include the Code, regulations, rulings, and cases, as well as editorial comment to aid the practitioner in understanding the tax law. A researcher can usually locate the relevant discussion in a tax service by using its topical index or by performing a key-word search when using an electronic service. Appendix A on tax research at the end of this textbook shows step-by-step screen captures of Thomson Reuters RIA Checkpoint®, a subscription-based Internet tax service commonly used by tax practitioners.[16]

Figure 2.2 lists Web sites for locating primary sources of authority that can be accessed free of charge.

After the authorities applicable to the client's facts have been located, the researcher must determine if the authorities apply to the client's case and analyze their inherent strengths or weaknesses as precedents. The researcher will compare the facts of the case to the authorities located, evaluate each authority by applying the reasoning of the authority to the client's facts, and draw a conclusion.

Communicate the Recommendations

The final step in the research process is to communicate the results and recommendations of the research, usually by summarizing them in a memorandum to the client file and in a letter to the client. Both the memo and the client letter usually contain a restatement of the relevant facts, any assumptions the researcher made, the issues addressed, the applicable authority, and the researcher's recommendations. The memo to the file usually contains more detail than the client letter, however. The appendix at

[15] Several of these services are still available in paper; however, some are converting to electronic (CD or Internet) subscriptions only.

[16] Students who do not have access to Thomson Reuters RIA Checkpoint® can gain a general understanding of how to research using subscription-only tax services by studying the screen captures in the appendix.

FIGURE 2.2 TAX SOURCES ON THE INTERNET

SOURCE	INTERNET ADDRESS (URL)
Internal Revenue Code	*http://uscode.house.gov/download/title_26.shtml*
Treasury Regulations	*http://www.gpo.gov/fdsys/*
IRS Revenue Rulings, Revenue Procedures, Announcements, Notices, and tax cases	*http://www.legalbitstream.com*
Revenue Rulings	*http://www.taxlinks.com*
Internal Revenue Bulletins	*http://www.irs.gov/irb/*
Court Decisions	*http://www.legalbitstream.com*
Tax Court Decisions	*http://www.ustaxcourt.gov*
Internal Revenue Service	*http://www.irs.gov*
Tax and Accounting Sites Directory	*http://www.taxsites.com*

the end of this chapter includes a more detailed description of the research process and includes a sample memo to the file and client letter.

Keeping Up-To-Date

Every accountant engaged in tax practice needs to keep up-to-date with the ever-changing federal tax law. Keeping up-to-date does not require the same exhaustive research as a specific tax problem. Numerous tax newsletters, including the following, cover the more significant tax law developments:

Tax Notes published by Tax Analysis
Daily Tax Report published by Bureau of National Affairs

Tax magazines or journals contain a variety of articles that may be helpful in researching new or developing areas of tax law. These articles might provide an in-depth review of a recent court decision or an analysis of the impact of a recent change in a tax law on the overall economy. A researcher can use these articles to optimize research time by using the author's expert judgment and bibliography of a relevant topic to quickly get to pertinent primary sources of authority.

TAX COMPLIANCE

Under the U.S. system of voluntary compliance, taxpayers self-assess their tax liabilities on an annual basis. Taxpayers must file on a timely basis using the appropriate tax forms.

Filing a Tax Return

Returns for individuals, partnerships, estates, and trusts must be filed on or before the fifteenth day of the fourth month following the close of the taxpayer's tax year (April 15 for calendar-year taxpayers). Corporate tax returns are due on or before the fifteenth day of the third month following the close of a corporation's tax year (March 15 for calendar-year corporate taxpayers). When the legal due date for a return falls on a weekend or legal holiday, the due date is the next weekday.[17] For example, if April 15 is a Saturday, the due date for individual tax returns is the following Monday, April 17. Taxpayers can apply for an automatic six-month extension of time to file their tax returns.[18] Filing an extension does not, however, extend the time for paying the tax. Applications for automatic extensions must include payment of any tax owed based on the taxpayer's reasonable estimate of his or her final tax liability.

Taxpayers who overpay their income tax through excess withholding or large quarterly estimated installment payments effectively loan money to the federal government. The government is not required to pay interest on any tax overpayment that is refunded within 45 days after the due date for the return.[19] This is why the IRS tries to process refund requests quickly. It pays interest to a taxpayer only if it fails to mail a refund within the 45-day grace period.[20]

Late Filing and Late Payment Penalties

The IRS may impose a *failure-to-file penalty* on taxpayers who fail to file an income tax return on a timely basis. The IRS can also impose a *failure-to-pay penalty*, in addition to charging interest, on taxpayers who fail to pay the tax on time.[21] The failure-to-pay penalty is 0.5 percent of the tax liability for each month (or part of a month) that the payment is late. The maximum penalty is 25 percent of the tax liability.

EXAMPLE 21

Kyle filed his tax return on April 15 and his tax return showed that he owed $5,000. Due to some bad planning, Kyle could not pay his taxes when filing his tax return. Kyle finally made his payment in full on June 6. Kyle's penalty amounts to 1 percent of the balance due (0.5 percent for each month or part of a month). Although Kyle was less than two months late, his penalty is 0.5 percent for two months; one full month and one partial month. Kyle's late payment penalty is $50 (1% × $5,000).

The failure-to-pay penalty will not be applied during the six-month automatic extension of the filing period if at least 90 percent of the actual tax liability is paid by the original due date and any balance due is paid when the return is filed at the end of the extension period.

The failure-to-file penalty is 5 percent per month (or partial month) that the return is late, to a maximum of 25 percent, also based on the taxpayer's tax liability. If the 0.5 percent failure-to-pay penalty and the failure-to-file penalty both apply, the failure-to-file penalty drops to 4.5 percent per month (or part month), so the total combined penalty remains 5 percent of the tax liability. The maximum combined penalty for the first five months is 25 percent. Thereafter, the failure to pay penalty continues at 0.5 percent per month for 45 more months (an additional 22.5 percent) so that the combined penalties can reach a total of 47.5 percent of the tax liability over time. In abusive situations involving a fraudulent failure-to-file, the late-filing penalty can increase to 15 percent a month, up to a 75 percent maximum of the tax liability.

EXAMPLE 22

Kyle decided not to file his return on April 15 because he knew that he could not pay the balance due. Kyle files his return on June 5 and pays the full $5,000 balance at that time. He can expect to receive a notice from the IRS charging an additional $500 in late payment/late filing penalties ($5,000 × 10%), 5 percent

[17]§7503.

[18]Reg. §1.6081-4T. Individuals must file Form 4868 no later than the original due date of the return to obtain an automatic six-month extension. Corporations receive an automatic six-month extension by filing Form 7004; partnerships also use Form 7004 but can receive no more than a five-month extension. Prior to 2005, individuals could only request a four-month extension using Form 4868 and had to use Form 2688 to request an additional two-month extension.

[19]§6611(e)(1).

[20]The interest rate for individuals is the federal short-term interest rate plus three percentage points. The interest rate for corporations is generally the short-term rate plus two percentage points. §6611(a) and §6621(a)(1).

[21]The interest rate for tax underpayments is determined by adding three percentage points to the short-term federal rate that is calculated each quarter. §7206.

for each of two months. Kyle could have saved $450 in penalties by filing the forms on April 15 even if he could not pay the tax in full at that time.

If a taxpayer files a return more than 60 days late, there is a minimum failure-to-file penalty equal to the smaller of $135 or 100 percent of the tax due on the return. If no tax is owed on an individual's return, however, there is no penalty. As flow-through entities, partnerships and S corporations normally pay no tax on which to base a penalty. Thus, they are assessed a late filing penalty based on the number of owners. The penalty is $195 for each month or partial month (up to 12 months) the return is late multiplied by the total number of partners or shareholders during the year.

If a taxpayer cannot pay the full tax with the return, the taxpayer can request an installment agreement with the IRS.[22] Generally, the IRS will accept an installment agreement if the tax owed is less than $10,000 and the balance due will be paid within three years. The taxpayer must pay a user fee to obtain the installment agreement and is also charged interest and late payment penalties.

Statute of Limitations

Some taxpayers feel a sense of relief when they receive their refund check for an overpayment of tax, erroneously assuming that once their refund is processed they will not be audited. Although the IRS usually does not audit an individual's return more than two years after the date the return was filed, the general statute of limitations allows up to three years. The **statute of limitations** is the period of time beyond which legal actions or changes to the tax return cannot be made by either the taxpayer or the government. The general statute of limitations is three years from the date a return is filed or its due date, whichever is later.[23] Filing a return early does not start the clock on the statute of limitations.

Example 23

Maureen, a calendar-year taxpayer, files her income tax return for 2013 on March 31, 2014. The return is treated as filed on April 15, 2014 , its due date. The statute of limitations expires on April 15, 2017.

If instead of filing her return in March, Maureen requests an automatic six-month extension of time and files her return on October 15, 2014, the statute of limitations for Maureen's 2013 return expires on October 15, 2017.

There are some exceptions to the general three-year statute of limitations. If a taxpayer inadvertently omits gross income in excess of 25 percent of the gross income reported, the statute of limitations increases to six years. The six-year statute of limitations only applies to omitted income and not excess deductions. Therefore, claiming excess deductions inadvertently will not increase the statute of limitations to six years.

Example 24

John filed his 2011 return on April 2, 2012. His tax return showed salary of $30,000. He failed to include an $8,000 capital gain on an early January stock transaction. As the omitted $8,000 capital gain exceeds 25 percent of the gross income stated on the return (25% × $30,000 = $7,500), the statute of limitations is extended until April 15, 2018.

As part of the government's war on tax shelters, the Treasury instituted disclosure rules that require taxpayers who participate in tax shelters to disclose these transactions (referred to as listed transactions) on their tax returns or face significant penalties. Congress extended the statute of limitations for tax returns that have not

[22]Form 9465: *Installment Agreement Request* can be filed separately or can be attached to the tax return.

[23]§6501(a) and (b)(1).

complied with these disclosure requirements until one year after the date the required information is provided to the IRS.

Filing a fraudulent return triggers an unlimited assessment period; that is, there is no statute of limitations for fraud. The government can bring charges of fraud against a taxpayer at any time, but the burden of proof is on the IRS to prove that the return was fraudulent.[24] When a taxpayer fails to file a complete return or no return at all, the statute of limitations does not begin to run until a complete return has been filed.

Refund claims can be initiated by a taxpayer within three years of the filing date for the return or two years from the date the tax is paid, whichever is later.

EXAMPLE 25

Joyce filed her 2010 return on April 15, 2011, and paid a tax of $3,000 at that time. An audit in May 2013 results in a deficiency of $400 that Joyce pays on May 18. Upon reviewing the return, Joyce discovers a $700 tax credit that she did not claim. If Joyce files a claim for a refund by April 15, 2014, she can recover $700. However, if Joyce fails to file a refund claim until after April 15, 2014 (but before May 19, 2015), she can only recover the $400 deficiency payment. If Joyce waits until May 19, 2015 to file her claim, she will not be entitled to any refund.

Selecting Returns for Audit

Over one million individual returns are audited annually. Although that may sound like a large number, the audit rate is one percent of the approximately 144 million individual returns filed annually. This examination percentage is misleading, however, as over half of the returns filed are subjected to a computerized matching in which the IRS compares the tax return information to the information on documents (such as Form W-2 or Form 1099) submitted by employers and other payers.[25]

Because only a small number of tax returns can be audited each year, the IRS attempts to select those returns that will generate additional revenue for the U.S. Treasury. It primarily relies upon a sophisticated computer model to identify returns that possess the greatest potential revenue for the IRS's investment of audit resources. In addition to this computer selection process, a number of returns are manually selected for examination at an examiner's discretion.

All individual and business tax returns are routinely reviewed by IRS personnel for obvious errors, such as the omission of required signatures and Social Security numbers, at one of the IRS service centers. After this initial review, the tax returns are processed through the IRS computer program. One of the most important functions performed by this program is the matching of information recorded on a return with corresponding data received from third parties (for example, a Form W-2 from an employer). This procedure, the Information Document Matching Program, has uncovered millions of cases of discrepancies between the income that recipients report on tax returns and the corresponding deductions or other information reported by the payers.

This computer program also executes the IRS's Mathematical/Clerical Error Program, designed to uncover relatively simple and readily identifiable problems that can be resolved easily through the mail. When a mathematical or clerical error is identified by the service center, the IRS mails the taxpayer a corrected tax computation and requests that he or she pay the additional tax within ten days of the date of the notice. If the deficiency is paid within this period, no interest is charged on the underpayment. When an error results in a taxpayer overpayment, the IRS usually sends a corrected computation of the tax, together with a brief explanation of the error, and refunds the excess payment.

[24] *Burden of proof* is a legal concept requiring the party who is subject to carrying the burden of proof to demonstrate, by appropriate evidence, that the particular requirement has been met.

[25] Form W-2 reports employees' salaries and withholding tax and Form 1099 reports income such as interest and dividends.

The IRS also conducts a similar program, the Unallowable Items Program, at each service center. If a return is identified as including an unallowable item, the IRS computes the adjustment in taxes and the taxpayer is notified by mail. If the taxpayer is able to explain the questioned item adequately, the assessment is abated. However, the case is continued as a correspondence or office audit if the taxpayer's response is deemed unsatisfactory.

Once a return has been processed through the above programs, each return is rated for its audit potential by means of computer scoring using the discriminant inventory function (DIF) formula. This formula assigns numeric weights to certain return items, generating a score for the return. When the computer selects a return that has a high DIF score, the potential that an examination of that return will result in a change to the income tax liability is also high. Attempts have been made by several taxpayers to obtain the actual DIF formula under the Freedom of Information Act. The courts have refused to require the IRS to disclose detailed information, however, stating that it would undermine the program.

In addition to the previously discussed computerized methods for identification of returns for IRS examination, returns may be selected manually for a variety of reasons. An examination may be initiated from information provided by an informant. The IRS Whistleblower Office processes tips it receives from individuals. A reward of between 15 and 30 percent of the total proceeds that the IRS collects can be paid if the IRS moves ahead based on the information provided.[26] All rewards, of course, are fully taxable.[27]

EXAMPLE 26

The highest whistleblower award ever paid was $104 million to a former employee of Swiss bank UBS for revealing schemes used by the Swiss bank to help American citizens dodge taxes. UBS paid more than $780 million to avoid criminal prosecution and turned over account information on more than 4,500 American clients.[28]

The government may also conduct undercover operations. Each district performs criminal investigations by special agents whose job is to look for fraud. Revenue agents suspend work whenever fraud is detected and refer the case to special agents in the Criminal Enforcement Division.

KEY CASE *The courts have upheld the legality of evidence that the IRS obtained through a special agent who posed as an investor interested in businesses with substantial cash flow subject to skimming. The owner and his wife disclosed their skimmed invoices to the undercover agent who noted the location of the records in their home. A few days later the IRS agents executed a search warrant and seized the records.*[29]

Types of Audits

Frequently, IRS personnel question only one or two items on a selected return. In these cases, an examination is typically conducted as a **correspondence audit**. The IRS auditor requests that the taxpayer verify the questioned item by mailing copies of receipts, canceled checks, or other documentation to the IRS.[30] If the taxpayer requests an interview or the issues become too complex, the case is referred to an office or field audit for resolution.

Office audits usually involve one or more issues that require some analysis and the exercise of the IRS auditor's judgment, rather than a mere verification of

[26]§7623. The reward may be limited to 10% if the whistleblower's contribution is not considered substantial. The IRS Whistleblower's Office will determine the extent to which the whistleblower's information contributed to the administrative or judicial action and the amount of the reward.

[27]To claim a reward, use Form 211: *Application for Reward for Original Information*.

[28]David Kocieniewski, "Whistle-Blower Awarded $104 Million by I.R.S." *New York Times*, 9/11/12.

[29]*Jones v. Berry*, 722 F.2d 443; 83-2 USTC ¶9653; 52 AFTR 2d 6188 (9th Circ, 1983), cert. denied, 466 US 971 (1984).

[30]*The Internal Revenue Manual* suggests that this type of audit is limited to certain types of issues, such as minor business expenses, interest deductions, and charitable contributions.

the item. The taxpayer is asked to come to the district office for an interview and to bring any records and documents that support the questioned items.

Field audits are more comprehensive than office audits and are usually limited to an examination of business returns. Field audits are usually conducted on the taxpayer's premises and generally involve a complete review of the entire financial operations of the business. This type of audit is usually used for corporations.

When the IRS has audited the taxpayer's return for the same item in at least one of the two previous years and the earlier audit resulted in no change to the tax liability, the taxpayer can request that the IRS suspend the audit and review whether it should proceed.

Example 27

In August 2013, the IRS notified Diana that it plans to audit her 2011 interest expense deduction. Two years ago, the IRS audited Diana's 2009 interest expense deduction but did not assess any additional tax. Diana may request that the IRS suspend the audit of her 2011 interest expense deduction.

If, however, the IRS had audited Diana's 2009 charitable contributions (instead of interest expense), then Diana could not request a suspension of her 2011 return audit because the previous audit was for a different deduction.

The Appeals Procedure

When an audit is complete, there are three possible outcomes. First, the agent may find that the return is correct as filed. If the agent proposes adjustments, which may either increase or decrease the tax, the taxpayer may agree or disagree.

If the taxpayer does not agree with the agent's proposed adjustments, the agent submits a report of the findings to the review staff. After review, the revenue agent's report is mailed to the taxpayer. The cover letter, called the **30-day letter**, notifies the taxpayer of the proposed deficiency and normally gives the taxpayer 30 days to request a conference with an agent from the **IRS Appeals Division**.[31]

The purpose of the Appeals Division is to resolve tax controversies without litigation, to the extent possible. The appeals officer has full authority to consider the hazards of litigation. The term "hazards of litigation" refers to factors that may affect the outcome of the case if it is litigated. This includes ambiguous facts, uncertain application of the law to known facts, credibility of witnesses, and ability to meet the required burden of proof. The great majority of cases are settled at the appellate conference.

If the taxpayer still does not agree with the IRS after an appeals conference or fails to request a conference, a **90-day letter** (statutory notice of deficiency) is mailed to the taxpayer by certified or registered mail. Once this formal assessment has been made, the IRS is entitled to collect the tax. This notice gives the taxpayer three options:

1. File a petition with the U.S. Tax Court within 90 days of receiving the notice.
2. Pay the tax; the taxpayer may then go to a U.S. District Court or the U.S. Court of Federal Claims to sue for refund.
3. Take no action and be subject to IRS-enforced collection procedures.

All litigation begins in one of three trial courts: the U.S. Tax Court, the U.S. District Courts, or the U.S. Court of Federal Claims. The Tax Court is the only court that does not require the taxpayer to pay the tax and then sue for refund. The District Court and Court of Federal Claims cannot hear the taxpayer's case unless he or she is suing for a refund.[32] Consequently, the taxpayer first must pay the disputed tax and then file an unsuccessful claim for refund to obtain a judicial review in either of these latter two courts.

[31] If the additional tax due is more than $10,000, the taxpayer must include a written response to the agent's finding, called a *protest letter*; however, for an office audit an oral request is acceptable. Reg. §601.106(a)(1)(iii).

[32] The District Court is the only court in which a jury trial can be obtained.

If the amount in dispute (including interest and penalties) does not exceed $50,000 for a tax year, the taxpayer may use the Small Tax Case Division of the Tax Court.[33] Its procedures are less formal than regular Tax Court procedures, and taxpayers may appear without an attorney. This alternative is not available in other courts, but the decision in this division cannot be appealed.

Regardless of the judicial route chosen, the unsuccessful party has the right to appeal the decision (except for the Small Case Division of the Tax Court) to a Circuit Court of Appeals. Cases decided in the Tax Court and District Court can be appealed to the appropriate Circuit Court of Appeals. Appeals from the Court of Federal Claims are decided by the Court of Appeals for the Federal Circuit. Decisions from either appellate court can be appealed to the U.S. Supreme Court. The Supreme Court chooses the cases it will agree to hear on the basis of their significance or because of a conflict in the lower courts. Therefore, the Supreme Court accepts very few tax cases for review.

One should not consider tax litigation lightly. The additional costs to the taxpayer for attorney and accountant fees, in addition to filing and processing fees and the time involved in gathering supporting documentation for the taxpayer's position, make litigation a costly prospect.

Taxpayer Noncompliance Penalties

Our self-assessment system requires all individuals subject to tax to file a tax return that accurately reports their income and deductions. Taxpayers who fail to meet their self-assessment obligations are subject to a variety of penalties. Many new penalties have been imposed in response to taxpayers who play the audit lottery; that is, taxpayers take very aggressive positions on their tax returns, gambling that their returns will not be audited. Some view the potential penalties for an unfavorable audit as small enough to be worth the risk. In reaction to this, many penalties were enacted to address this problem.

The most important taxpayer penalties are for negligence and fraud. The negligence penalty is 20 percent of any tax underpayment caused by the taxpayer's intentional disregard of rules and regulations or failure to make a reasonable attempt to comply with the law.[34] The most severe administrative penalty is for civil fraud. This penalty is 75 percent of the portion of the tax underpayment attributable to the fraud.[35] Fraud involves the deliberate intention to cheat the government by understating the tax. Due to the severity of the penalty, the burden of proof rests with the IRS to establish by *clear and convincing evidence* that the taxpayer committed fraud.[36] An even more severe penalty applies to criminal fraud, otherwise known as tax evasion. Tax evasion is punishable by imprisonment, in addition to significant fines.[37] The burden of proof is on the IRS to establish, *beyond a reasonable doubt*, that the taxpayer committed fraud.

KEY CASES *In 2006, Richard Hatch was sentenced to 51 months in federal prison for failing to report $1 million in income won from the first "Survivor" television series along with income from some other sources. He was also ordered to pay almost $475,000 in taxes, interest and penalties.*[38]

In 2008, actor Wesley Snipes was sentenced to 3 years in prison for willfully failing to file a tax return from 1999-2004, a period in which he earned more than $38 million. Following an unsuccessful appeal, he began serving his sentence in December 2010 in a medium-security prison in Pennsylvania.[39]

---

[33]Sec. 7463. The limitation was increased from $10,000 to $50,000 in 1998.

[34]§6662(a) and (b)(1). §6662A increases the penalty to 30% for listed and other nondisclosed avoidance transactions and §6707A imposes a penalty of up to $200,000 for failure to report information on "listed" tax shelter transactions.

[35]§6663.

[36]§7454(a).

[37]§7201. Penalties of up to $100,000 ($500,000 for corporations) and/or up to five years in prison may be assessed.

[38]"Tax Report," *Wall Street Journal*, May 17, 2006, Section D, Column 5, page 2 and "FY2006 Examples of General Tax Fraud Investigations," IRS Web site, *www.irs.gov*.

[39]Dave Itzkoff, "Wesley Snipes Surrenders to Begin Sentence on Tax Convictions," *New York Times*, 12/9/10.

Collection Procedures

Collection of an unpaid tax liability begins with the IRS mailing a bill to the taxpayer requesting payment. If the taxpayer does not respond, the IRS sends a letter demanding payment within 10 days. If the taxpayer still does not respond, the IRS can impose a lien on the taxpayer's property or seize other assets.[40]

Offer in Compromise

If the IRS believes that it will be unable to collect the full tax liability, it may accept payment of less than the assessed amount. These compromises occur when there is either doubt about the liability or its collectibility. The IRS is more inclined to settle a delinquent account as long as criminal proceedings are not pending or contemplated. A taxpayer wishing to make an offer in compromise files a Form 656 along with a detailed financial statement specifying the hardship the taxpayer would suffer if the entire tax were paid. Any offer in compromise consisting of five or fewer installment payments must be accompanied by an initial payment of 20 percent of the total amount offered the IRS. All other offers must include the first proposed installment. If the offer is not rejected within 24 months of the date of submission, it is deemed to have been accepted.[41]

Innocent Spouse Relief

When a married couple files a joint tax return, they become joint and severally liable for any tax deficiency related to that return; that is, the IRS can assess either spouse for the entire deficiency if the return is audited.[42] In some situations (such as a now-divorced couple), the IRS assesses the one spouse it can locate but who may know nothing about the disputed income. Section 6015(b)(1) provides that the innocent spouse can be relieved of any tax liability if all of the following requirements are met:

1. The return contains an understatement of tax attributable to erroneous items of one individual filing the return.
2. The other individual filing the return establishes that in signing the return he or she did not know, and had no reason to know, that there was such an understatement.
3. Taking into account all the facts and circumstances, it is inequitable to hold the individual liable for the deficiency attributable to such understatement.
4. The individual elects innocent spouse relief within the time period that the statute of limitations is open for collection activities.

EXAMPLE 28

Gillian and Steven filed a joint tax return three years ago but have since divorced. Gillian has no contact with Steven and does not know where he lives. At the time the return was filed, Gillian knew that Steven failed to report $5,000 of gambling winnings. On audit, Steven's actual unreported gambling winnings were found to be $25,000. Because Steven cannot be located, Gillian is assessed for the full tax due. If Gillian establishes that she did not know about, and had no reason to know about, the additional $20,000 of gambling winnings, the understatement of tax attributable to the $20,000 of additional gambling winnings qualifies for innocent spouse relief. The $5,000 of winnings that Gillian knew about does not.

Professional Responsibilities and Ethics

Avoidance versus Evasion

Any discussion of a tax professional's responsibilities necessitates a discussion of the difference between tax avoidance and tax evasion. There is nothing illegal or immoral

[40] §§6621 and 6331.
[41] §7122.
[42] §6013(d)(3).

in the avoidance of tax according to the tax system's rules. Judge Learned Hand best expressed this doctrine in *Commissioner v. Newman*:

> *Over and over again, courts have said that there is nothing sinister in so arranging one's affairs as to keep taxes as low as possible. Everybody does so, rich or poor; and all do right, for nobody owes any public duty to pay more than the law demands: taxes are enforced extractions, not voluntary contributions. To demand more in the name of morals is mere cant.*[43]

Tax avoidance is the minimization of the tax burden by using acceptable, legal alternatives. *Tax evasion*, however, describes illegal means of reducing taxes and is not acceptable. Any practitioner who is contemplating participation in some form of tax evasion should first study the penalties that are assessed for civil and criminal tax fraud

Tax Preparer Registration

In 2011, the IRS began requiring all tax return preparers to obtain a **preparer tax identification number (PTIN)**. Section 7701(a)(36)(A) defines a tax return preparer as any person who is paid for, or who employs one or more persons who are paid for, the preparation of all or a substantial portion of a federal tax return or claim for refund. Preparers obtain a PTIN by submitting Form W-12 *IRS Paid Preparer Tax Identification Number (PTIN) Application* to the IRS.

Tax Preparer Penalties

Code Section 6694 imposes penalties on preparers when clients' tax deficiencies appear to be the result of an "unreasonable position" on the return that the preparer knew or should have known was a departure from the rules or regulations. The penalty, the greater of $1,000 or 50 percent of the fees for the work, is imposed if the position was not properly disclosed. The Emergency Economic Stabilization Act of 2008 clarified that a reasonable position requires the preparer to have "substantial authority" upholding a "realistic possibility of success" for nonabusive, undisclosed tax return positions. Substantial authority exists if the weight of authorities (including the Internal Revenue Code, regulations, court cases, committee reports, revenue rulings, revenue procedures, and similar documents) supporting the reported tax treatment is substantial in relation to the weight of those authorities taking a contrary position. A return preparer who does not have substantial authority for a position taken on a tax return would be subject to a penalty unless the position was adequately disclosed. Disclosure is typically accomplished by using Form 8275; however, filing the form would probably raise a red flag with the IRS.

If the position taken on the tax return involves a tax shelter (or similar abusive transaction called a "listed transaction"), however, a higher "more-likely-than-not" (greater than 50 percent) standard applies. Thus, under current law, a tax return preparer can avoid this penalty if the position:

1. Is supported by substantial authority and does not involve a tax shelter
2. Has a reasonable basis and is adequately disclosed or
3. Involves a tax shelter, as defined in Code Section 6662(d)(2)(C)(ii), but the preparer reasonably believes the position is more likely than not correct.

If a preparer takes an unreasonable position in a "willful" attempt to understate the taxpayer's liability or if the preparer is guilty of "reckless or intentional disregard" of rules or regulations, the penalty increases to the greater of $5,000 or 50 percent of the preparer's fees. This type of penalty frequently becomes the subject of an investigation that culminates in the withdrawal of the right to practice.

Preparer penalties are of special importance because of the following:

1. Penalties on the preparer may not be covered by malpractice insurance.
2. Penalties are not deductible.
3. Preparer penalties may result in an IRS review of the preparer's entire practice.

[43]*Commissioner v. Newman*, 159 F.2d 848, 850–851; 47-1 USTC ¶9175; 35 AFTR 857 (CA-2, 1947)

If a preparer is convicted of criminal tax evasion, the penalty can consist of a fine of up to $100,000 ($500,000 in the case of a corporation) and imprisonment.

KEY CASES *Raymond Scott Stevenson, the former Vice President of Taxation for Tyco, was sentenced to 3 years in federal prison for failing to report $170 million in company income. Prosecutors claimed that he backdated documents to reduce the company's tax liability. If the correct amount had been reported, Tyco would have faced an additional tax liability of up to $60 million.*[44]

Adrian Dicker, a former BDO Seidman LLP manager, pleaded guilty to tax evasion. He admitted assisting clients engage in tax-shelter transactions that created more than $1 billion in fraudulent tax losses. He faced up to five years in prison for each count of tax evasion.[45]

To strengthen the government's attack on tax shelters, tax shelter promoters and advisors who fail to file required information returns (or provide false or incomplete information) for listed tax shelter transactions face fines up to the greater of $200,000 or 50 percent of gross income received that is attributable to advice on the transaction. Advisors who fail to maintain required investor lists or fail to provide those lists to the government when requested, can be assessed a penalty of $10,000 per day.

Tax Professionals' Dual Responsibilities

Tax professionals have duties to two parties: the tax system and their clients. In many situations, the duties to these two parties are in conflict. The conflict is most apparent in areas in which the law is not clear or in situations in which the facts are subject to more than one legitimate interpretation. In those cases, the tax professional must make decisions that benefit one party at the expense of the other. In those cases, the question arises as to whom the tax professional owes his or her primary responsibility.

Tax practitioners and the IRS view the role of tax practitioners differently. Tax practitioners, especially CPAs and attorneys, see themselves as client advocates. The IRS, however, wants tax practitioners to take an active enforcement role by checking client documentation and probing for other sources of income.

The IRS's position is that the tax practitioner's primary responsibility is to the tax system. The IRS Director of Practice stated the following:

> *While it is generally agreed that a tax practitioner owes a client competence, loyalty and confidentiality, it also is recognized that the practitioner has responsibilities to the tax system as well. The latter responsibility is of pervasive importance. . . .In the normal practitioner–client relationship, both duties are recognized and carried out. However, there are situations in which this is difficult. In those situations, the practitioner is required to decide which obligation prevails and, in so doing, may correctly conclude that the obligation to the tax system is paramount. . . .The IRS relies on tax practitioners to assist it in administering the tax laws by being fair and honest in their dealings with the Service and by fostering confidence by their clients in the integrity of the tax system and in complying with it.*[46]

The American Institute of Certified Public Accountants (AICPA) takes the position that a taxpayer is under no obligation to pay more taxes than are legally due, and the CPA has a duty to the client to assist in achieving that result. Thus, the tax system is best served by professionals who act with honesty and who do not give in to client pressure to do otherwise. At the same time, they best serve the public good by helping their clients determine their minimum tax liability under the law. To resolve honest doubts in favor of one's client does not, by itself, impair the CPA's integrity.

---

[44] "Former Tyco VP gets three years in prison," *The Miami Herald*, November 30, 2006, page 3C.

[45] Chad Bray, "Guilty Plea in Bogus Tax Shelters," *The Wall Street Journal*, March 18, 2009, Section D, Column 1, page 3

[46] Leslie Shapiro, "Professional Responsibilities in the Eyes of the IRS," *The Tax Adviser* (March 1986) p. 139.

Sources of Guidance

Literature dealing with the ethical responsibilities of a tax practitioner can be found in various publications. All tax practitioners are regulated by *Treasury Circular 230: Regulations Governing Practice before the Internal Revenue Service*. The ethical conduct of a CPA who is a member of the AICPA must follow its *Code of Professional Conduct* and any other rules generated by state boards of accountancy. The AICPA has also produced a series of *Statements on Standards for Tax Services (SSTS)* that contain guidelines for CPAs who prepare tax returns.

Circular 230 To effectively serve a client's tax needs, the tax practitioner must maintain the privilege to appear before the IRS on behalf of clients. The regulations governing such representation are found in *Circular 230*. *Circular 230* protects the IRS and taxpayers by requiring tax preparers to be technically competent and to adhere to ethical standards. *Circular 230* identifies who may practice before the IRS, including representing clients during audit procedures. Tax return preparation or furnishing information in response to an IRS request is not considered practice before the IRS.

If a tax practitioner violates the rules contained within *Circular 230*, he or she may be suspended or disbarred from practice before the IRS for incompetence, disreputable conduct, refusal to comply with the rules and regulations of *Circular 230*, or willfully and knowingly deceiving, misleading, or threatening the IRS.

AICPA Code of Professional Conduct In addition to the regulations imposed by the Treasury Department, CPAs in tax practice are guided by pronouncements of the accounting profession. Members of the AICPA are subject to the *AICPA Code of Professional Conduct*, which consists of two integral sections: the principles and the rules. The principles provide a foundation upon which the rules are based and discuss the CPA's responsibilities to the public, clients, and colleagues. The principles state that a CPA should strive for behavior above the minimal level of acceptable conduct required by the law and regulations. Members are expected to perform professional services with integrity, objectivity, and independence. Integrity is measured in terms of what is right and just. Integrity requires a professional to observe both the form and spirit of technical and ethical standards. Objectivity and independence require the professional to be impartial, intellectually honest, and have no conflict of interest.

The rules consist of a set of enforceable ethical standards that have been approved by a majority of the members of the AICPA. These rules are broad in nature and apply to all of the professional services that a CPA performs. Any failure to follow the rules under the *Code of Professional Conduct* may result in the offender receiving admonishment, suspension, or expulsion from membership in the AICPA. The rules apply not only to the CPA, but also to those employees who are under his or her supervision.

Statements on Standards for Tax Services (SSTS) To help delineate the extent of the tax practitioner's responsibility to his or her client, the public, the government, and his or her profession, the AICPA Federal Taxation Executive Committee issued a series of statements defining what constitutes appropriate standards of tax practice.[47] These statements are intended to address specific problems inherent in the tax practitioner's dual role of serving both the client and the public.

SSTS No. 1—Tax Return Positions The CPA should recommend a tax return position to his or her client only if there is a "realistic possibility" of success if challenged either on appeal with the IRS or in court. A CPA should not prepare or sign as preparer a return that he or she knows takes a position that does not meet the realistic possibility standard. A CPA may recommend a specific return position if there is a reasonable basis for that position, and the position is adequately disclosed on the tax return.

SSTS No. 2—Answers to Questions on Returns This statement requires a CPA, before signing as a preparer, to make a reasonable effort to obtain and provide appro-

---

[47]The *Statements on Responsibilities in Tax Practice* (*SRTP*) were issued between 1964 and 1977. The *SSTS* replaced the *SRTP* as of October 31, 2000. The revised *SSTS* that became effective on January 1, 2010 combined *SSTS* 6 and *SSTS* 7, reducing the total number of statements from eight to seven.

priate answers from the client to all questions on a tax return. The fact that an answer might prove disadvantageous is not a valid reason for omitting a response.

SSTS No. 3—Procedural Aspects of Preparing Returns This statement examines the CPA's responsibility regarding examination of supporting data, use of prior years' returns, and consideration of relevant information known to the CPA from tax returns of other clients. It sets forth guidelines as to the extent CPAs may rely on information furnished by clients and other third parties; for example, it specifies that although a CPA may in good faith rely upon information furnished by the client or other third parties without verification, blind reliance is unacceptable. If the information furnished appears to be incorrect, incomplete, or inconsistent either on its face or on the basis of other facts known to the CPA, the CPA should make additional inquiries.

SSTS No. 4—Use of Estimates This statement defines those situations in which the use of estimates is acceptable on a taxpayer's return (for example, a fire or computer failure destroyed relevant records) and discusses whether disclosure is appropriate. Estimates also may be necessary when records are missing or precise information is not available at the time of filing. If a CPA uses a taxpayer's estimates, however, the estimates should not imply greater accuracy than exists or present misleading facts.

SSTS No. 5—Departure from a Previous Position An administrative proceeding or court decision does not bind the CPA to use the same treatment of an item in a later year's return unless there is a binding contract. Otherwise, the CPA may recommend a more advantageous tax treatment for a later year's tax return. Subsequent court decisions and revenue rulings may place the taxpayer in a more favorable position. The recommendation for the tax treatment of an item in a tax return should be based on the facts and the law as they are evaluated at the time the return is prepared.

SSTS No. 6—Knowledge of Error: Return Preparation and Administrative Proceedings If a CPA discovers an error in a client's previously filed tax return, an error in a return that is the subject of an administrative proceeding (such as an examination), or a taxpayer's failure to file a return, the CPA is obligated to inform the client of the problem and to recommend appropriate action. Once the taxpayer has been adequately informed, the course of action is the client's decision. The CPA cannot inform the IRS without the client's permission, except if required by law. If the CPA is preparing the current year's return and the client refuses to correct an error in a prior year's return, SSTS No. 6 indicates that the CPA should consider withdrawing from the preparation of the taxpayer's current year return or from representing the client in the administrative proceeding and should consider severing any professional relationship with the client. If the CPA does prepare the current year's return, the CPA should take reasonable steps to ensure that the error is not repeated.

SSTS No. 7—Form and Content of Advice to Clients This statement recognizes that changes in the tax laws and the development of new interpretations may affect past tax advice. It addresses the circumstances under which a CPA has a responsibility to update a client when subsequent developments affect previously provided advice. SSTS No. 7 indicates that the CPA has no duty to update the advice unless the CPA is implementing it or the obligation is specifically provided for in the client's contract. CPAs should state that their advice is based on authorities that are subject to change and that subsequent developments could affect previous professional advice. Thus, the communication of significant developments affecting previous advice is an additional service, rather than an implied obligation in the normal client relationship.

Other Moral Standards There is more to ethical behavior than just following the rules of conduct of the AICPA. The tax professional must deal with different standards of personal morality. All individuals do not use the same level of moral standards in determining whether something is morally right or wrong. Some people feel that cheating on their tax return is morally acceptable because "Everyone does it." Professional fees generated from a client who gets too aggressive seldom justify the cost (in dollars or mental anguish) of defending violations of professional standards or Treasury Department rules.

If a tax professional does not agree with the client's views on what is morally acceptable, the practitioner risks losing the client. Alternatively, both the client and tax practitioner could face fines and penalties or even risk going to jail. A tax professional must be ready to deal with clients with varying views on acceptable moral behavior and be willing to accept the consequences for the decisions made.

To be prepared to make these ethical decisions, a tax professional must develop two skills:

1. The ability to recognize ethical dilemmas when confronted by them.
2. The ability to evaluate the alternatives.

A CPA must raise his or her awareness to the level that he or she can easily spot a potential ethical problem arising from business situations. In evaluating the alternatives, most practitioners find that real world problems usually do not involve a clear choice between right and wrong. Instead, a decision frequently must be made between what appears to be two goods or two evils. The true professional must evaluate all the alternatives in light of the competing interests of all parties involved and attempt to predict the consequences of each alternative before making a decision.

Revisiting the Introductory Case

Kevin should request an appeals conference with the IRS where he can present the reasons why he believes his part-time dog training operation is a business and not a hobby. Most disputes with the IRS are settled at this level. If he cannot reach a satisfactory agreement with the IRS, then he could take the case to the Small Case Division of the Tax Court where he can represent himself. (There is no appeal from this court, however.) If he wants to take his case to any other court, he will probably need to hire an attorney. This expense may not be warranted, however, given the size of the tax deficiency. If he wants to take his case to Tax Court, he must file within 90 days of receiving a Notice of Deficiency. To take his case to either District Court or the U.S. Court of Federal Claims, he will have to first pay the tax and then sue for refund. His final option would be to do nothing and wait for the IRS to begin collection procedures, but this is not advisable.

Summary

Tax practice involves compliance, research, and planning. Tax return preparation and client representation at audit are the primary compliance activities. Tax research on closed-fact situations usually involves presenting a completed transaction in the best light relative to the tax consequences. In open-fact situations, the practitioner can affect the form and outcome of a transaction that has yet to be completed. Open-fact planning situations most often involve two or more alternatives that can be evaluated using net present value concepts to find the optimum strategy. Tax planning strategies include timing, income shifting, and changing the character of income. Good tax planning requires consideration of nontax factors as well as the legal doctrines that the IRS can invoke when a taxpayer takes excessive advantage of the tax law.

Tax research involves gathering the relevant facts, identifying issues, locating and evaluating relevant authorities, and communicating recommendations to the client. Both education and experience are necessary to identify the issues in a complex planning situation. The practitioner has both primary sources and secondary sources to aid in solving a tax research problem, but only primary sources should be cited. Primary sources include the Internal Revenue Code, Treasury Regulations, revenue rulings, and judicial opinions. Additional information can be found in congressional committee reports and the *Congressional Record*. Secondary sources include tax services, journal articles, and tax newsletters.

Tax practitioners must maintain an acceptable level of competence by keeping up with the ever-changing tax laws. There are many sources for studying new developments in both print and electronic media.

Taxpayers must file their annual tax returns by specific due dates, with allowable extensions, or numerous penalties along with interest charges can be levied. Extensions of time to file do not permit the taxpayer to extend payment of taxes. Failure to pay the tax due on time can also subject the taxpayer to penalties and interest.

To maintain the integrity of the tax system, the Internal Revenue Service first makes a computerized mathematical check of all tax returns and checks for unallowable items. Many discrepancies are settled through correspondence with the taxpayer. The IRS also selects numerous tax returns for more extensive office and field audits. The latter, however, are usually reserved for business audits. Taxpayers who owe additional taxes after an audit can pay the tax, appeal to an appeals officer, or initiate court action to settle the dispute. The Tax Court is the only court in which the taxpayer can file suit without previously having paid the disputed tax. A Small Tax Case Division of the Tax Court handles disputes that do not exceed $50,000; there is no appeal to a higher court, however, for a Small Tax Case Division decision.

Tax professionals have a responsibility to both their clients and the tax system; at times, these responsibilities may appear to be in conflict. All tax preparers are subject to the government's regulations in *Circular 230*; they may be subject to penalties if they recommend unrealistic positions to their clients. CPAs are subject to both the *Code of Professional Conduct* and the *Statements on Standards for Tax Services*, both products of the AICPA. The tax service standards provide guidance specific to the problems faced by tax practitioners. Practitioners who fail in their responsibilities face serious consequences.

KEY TERMS

Business purpose doctrine 56
Committee report 58
Correspondence audit 69
Field audit 70
Golsen rule 90
Internal Revenue Code 59
IRS Appeals Division 70
Letter ruling 61
90-day letter 70
Office audit 69
Preparer tax identification number (PTIN) 73
Primary authority 57
Revenue procedure 62
Revenue ruling 61
Secondary authority 57
Statute of limitations 67
Step transaction doctrine 56
Substance-over-form doctrine 56
Tax compliance 48
Tax cost 49
Tax planning 48
Tax savings 49
30-day letter 70
Treasury Regulations 60

TEST YOURSELF

ANSWERS APPEAR AFTER THE PROBLEM ASSIGNMENTS

1. George owns 1,000 shares of ABC stock that he purchased a little more than 11 months ago at a cost of $5 per share. The stock is now trading for $40 per share. George's tax advisor suggested that he wait another month before selling the stock. This is an example of which tax planning strategy?

a. Avoiding income recognition
b. Deferring income recognition
c. Shifting income
d. Changing the character of income

2. The primary purpose of effective tax planning is:
   a. Minimizing tax liability
   b. Repealing all federal taxes
   c. Converting capital gain into ordinary income
   d. Deferring deductions and accelerating income
3. Primary sources of authority include all of the following except:
   a. Treasury Regulations
   b. Tax Court decisions
   c. Internal Revenue Code
   d. Tax journals
4. Regarding the Small Case Division of the Tax Court, which of the following statements is correct?
   a. The IRS (but not the taxpayer) can appeal an adverse judgment.
   b. The taxpayer (but not the IRS) can appeal an adverse judgment.
   c. Either the IRS or the taxpayer can appeal an adverse judgment.
   d. Neither the IRS nor the taxpayer can appeal an adverse judgment.
5. While preparing this year's tax return, a CPA discovers that the client has underpaid his income taxes due to an omission on last year's tax return, which was prepared by another accountant. According to the Statement on Standards for Tax Services, the CPA preparing this year's tax return:
   a. Must report it immediately to the IRS.
   b. Must advise the client of the omission and recommend appropriate action.
   c. Should refuse to sign the current tax return.
   d. Is not expected to address issues that relate to previous tax returns.

PROBLEM ASSIGNMENTS

CHECK YOUR UNDERSTANDING

1. Distinguish tax planning from tax compliance.
2. For each of the following independent situations, identify whether the item would be primarily a tax or a nontax factor in performing tax planning.
   a. The taxpayer lost a quarter of her net worth when the dot-com bubble burst and does not want to own any investments with risk such as stocks.
   b. The taxpayer hates to pay any federal income taxes and would rather pay an equal amount of money to an accountant or attorney than pay taxes to the federal government.
   c. The taxpayer has a large capital loss carryforward from last year.
3. Beta Corporation anticipates $800,000 of taxable income for the year before considering additional projects. What marginal tax rate should it use in evaluating a project that may generate $200,000 of additional income?
4. Maria is a single individual with taxable income of $75,000 in 2013. What marginal tax rate should she use to determine the tax savings from a $2,000 deductible expense?
5. Identify three tax planning strategies.
6. Explain the business purpose doctrine.

7. What is the difference between primary authority and secondary authority?
8. As a bill proceeds through Congress, various committee reports are generated. What three committee reports typically are generated as a result of this process?
9. Why are committee reports useful to a tax researcher?
10. What uniquely numbered part of the Internal Revenue Code does a tax researcher usually cite?
11. In the citation Reg. §1.247-3, what do the 1 and the 247 indicate?
12. What is the difference between a legislative regulation and an interpretative regulation?
13. What is the difference between proposed and temporary regulations? What weight do they carry?
14. What is the difference between a letter ruling and a revenue ruling?
15. What is a tax service?
16. What is the purpose of the DIF formula? What happens if someone has a high DIF score?
17. Describe the various types of audits.
18. If the taxpayer does not agree with proposed adjustments, what alternative is available to a taxpayer who receives a 30-day letter?
19. What alternatives are available to a taxpayer who receives a 90-day letter?
20. Explain the meaning of hazards of litigation.
21. In which three courts may a taxpayer initiate tax litigation to settle a dispute with the IRS? Can all adverse decisions from these courts be appealed to a higher court?
22. Your client, Teresa, claimed a dependency exemption for her elderly father. Upon audit, the IRS agent disallowed the dependency exemption. Teresa received a 30-day letter notifying her of the proposed additional tax liability of $1,050. Teresa is very upset by this assessment and tells you that she refuses to pay "another dime" and she wants to take this "all the way to the Supreme Court, if necessary." What advice should you give Teresa?
23. Do taxpayer penalties consist of only monetary fines or can a taxpayer be sentenced to jail?
24. What is a statute of limitations? What is its significance to taxpayers?
25. What is the difference between tax avoidance and tax evasion?
26. Can tax return preparers be assessed penalties?
27. Name three sources of guidance for tax professionals.
28. What are the *Statements on Standards for Tax Services*? Who issues them?
29. What guidelines are provided by the *Statement on Standards for Tax Services No. 3* regarding a CPA's reliance on information supplied by the client for use in preparing the client's tax return?
30. *Statement on Standards for Tax Services No. 4* states that a CPA may use estimates in completing a tax return. When would using estimates be appropriate in tax return preparation?

CRUNCH THE NUMBERS

31. Monico Corporation, a cash basis calendar-year taxpayer, is in the 25 percent marginal tax bracket this year. If it bills its customers at the beginning

of December, it will receive $5,000 of income prior to year-end. If it bills its customers at the end of December, it will not receive the $5,000 until January of next year.

a. If it expects its marginal tax rate to remain 25 percent next year, when should it bill its customers? Use a 6 percent discount factor to explain your answer.

b. How would your answer change if Monico's marginal tax rate next year is only 15 percent? Explain.

c. How would your answer change if Monico's marginal tax rate next year is 34 percent? Explain.

32. Kimo Corporation, a cash basis calendar-year taxpayer, is in the 25 percent marginal tax bracket this year. Kimo owes a $15,000 expense that it may pay before the end of this year or in January of next year.

a. If it expects its marginal tax rate to be 25 percent next year, should it pay the expense this year or next? Use a 7 percent discount factor to explain your answer.

b. How would your answer change if Kimo's expected marginal tax rate next year is only 15 percent? Explain.

c. How would your answer change if Kimo's expected marginal tax rate next year is 34 percent? Explain.

33. Cynthia and Howard, married taxpayers filing a joint return, have $100,000 in taxable income in 2013. They have 4 children (ages 4 through 12) who have no taxable income. If they can legally shift $2,000 in taxable income to each child, how much does the family save in taxes?

34. The 4,000 shares of Medco stock that Diana purchased 11½ months ago for $12 per share are now trading at $19 per share. Diana's regular marginal tax rate is 28 percent and her tax rate for long-term capital gains is 15 percent.

a. What is Diana's after-tax net cash flow from the sale if she sells the stock now?

b. What is Diana's after-tax net cash flow from the sale if she waits one month before selling the stock for $19 per share?

c. What do you recommend?

35. Adam files his tax return on April 15 and his tax return shows that he owes $3,000. Due to some bad planning, Adam could not pay his taxes when filing his tax return. Adam finally made his payment in full on July 10. How much is the late payment penalty that will be assessed against Adam?

36. Robert decided not to file his return on April 15 because he knew that he could not pay the balance due. Robert files his return on August 3, paying the full $4,000 balance. How much can Robert expect to be charged for late-payment/late-filing penalties?

37. Denise files her 2013 tax return on February 4, 2014. If there is no material understatement of income on her return and the return is properly signed and filed, when will the statute of limitations expire for Denise's 2013 tax return?

38. Kevin deliberately omitted $40,000 of gross income from the restaurant that he owned on his 2013 tax return. The return indicated gross income of $200,000 when it was filed it on April 14, 2014. As of what date can the IRS no longer pursue Kevin with the threat of collection of the related tax, interest, and penalties?

39. Alison accidentally omitted $40,000 of gross income from the restaurant she owned on her 2012 tax return. The return indicated gross income of $150,000 when it was filed on October 15, 2013. As of what date can the IRS no longer pursue Alison with the threat of collection of the related tax, interest, and penalties?

40. Thomas received $30,000 in a legal settlement in 2013. The tax treatment of the item is not certain. Thomas's research results were ambiguous so he is not sure if the income is taxable. Because some doubt remained and because he did not think he would be audited, Thomas took the position that the income was not taxable and did not include it on his tax return filed on April 14, 2014. His gross income, excluding the $30,000 in question, was $50,000.
    a. When does the statute of limitations expire for Tom's 2013 tax return?
    b. Would your answer change if Thomas were certain the amount was taxable but decided to exclude it from his return anyway?

THINK OUTSIDE THE TEXT

These questions require answers that are beyond the material that is covered in this chapter.

41. Tax law provisions change over time. Explain how this might affect tax planning and tax research.

42. When Keith created a new corporation as the sole shareholder, he was advised by his accountant to treat 50 percent of the amount invested as a loan and 50 percent as a purchase of stock. What are the advantages and disadvantages of this structure as compared with treating the entire investment as a purchase of stock?

43. Revenue-raising bills (such as tax bills) are supposed to originate in the House of Representatives. How could a senator initiate a tax bill?

44. How do rulings issued by the IRS benefit both the IRS and taxpayers?

45. From the perspective of both the taxpayer and the IRS, what are the advantages and disadvantages of the statute of limitations?

46. What type of penalty or incentive provision do you think would significantly improve compliance with the Internal Revenue Code? Do you think such a provision could be passed?

IDENTIFY THE ISSUES

Identify the tax issues or problems suggested by the following situations. State each issue as a question.

47. Your client, Barry Backache, suffers from a pain in the neck caused by arthritis. He installed a hot tub in his backyard. His doctor advised him that daily periods in the hot tub would relieve his pain in the neck.

48. Two months before the due date for his tax return, Simon provides his accountant with all the information necessary for filing his return. The accountant was overworked during tax season and filed the return after its due date.

49. Jennifer did not file a tax return for 2004 because she honestly believed that no tax was due. In 2013, the IRS audits Jennifer and the agent proposes a deficiency of $500.

50. On his 2008 tax return, Stewart inadvertently overstates deductions in excess of 25 percent of the adjusted gross income on his return. In 2013, the IRS audits Stewart and the agent proposes a deficiency of $1,000.

51. Georgia researched a major tax plan for a client. She discovered a case in a circuit that is not in the client's circuit that is unfavorable to the client. She has also found a revenue ruling that appears to have facts similar to her client's that sanctions the preferred alternative.

52. Bert has developed a position for a client on a potential tax transaction that he believes has approximately a 25 percent chance of surviving in a judicial proceeding.

53. In preparing the client's tax return, Verne must use a number of estimates supplied by his client because the client's computer records were corrupted and the client has not been able to retrieve the correct numbers in time to file the return by its due date. The client's tax returns have always included cents as well as dollars.

54. Jim was reviewing several of a client's prior tax returns in preparation for completing the current year's return. Jim discovered a serious error on the return filed almost three years earlier that would subject the client to $40,000 in additional taxes.

55. Last year, the IRS disallowed a deduction on a client's tax return when it was audited. The client wants you to deduct a similar item on this year's tax return.

DEVELOP RESEARCH SKILLS

56. Your client, Ms. I. M. Gorgeous, is an aspiring actress. She has managed to earn a living doing television commercials but was unable to get the acting parts she really wanted. She decided to have botox injections in her forehead and collagen enhancements to her lips. After these procedures, her career improved dramatically and she received several movie offers. Ms. Gorgeous is sure that she should be able to deduct the cost of the cosmetic enhancements because she read about another actress having a face lift in 1988 and deducting the cost on her tax return as a medical expense. Can Ms. Gorgeous deduct the cost of these procedures?

    Research Aid: Section 213(d)(9)

57. Last year your client, Barney Bumluck, worked part-time for Timely Tax Return Preparation Service. Barney was promised an hourly wage plus a commission. He worked under this arrangement from early February until April 15. His accrued pay amounted to $900 plus $120 of commissions. When he went to collect his pay, however, he found only a vacant office with a sign on the door reading "Nothing is sure but death and taxes." Can Barney take a bad debt deduction for the wages and commission he was unable to collect?

    Research Aid: Reg. Section 1.166–1(e)

58. Your clients, Sonny and his wife, Honey, believe in worshiping Ta-Ra, the Sun God. To practice their religious beliefs, they take a weeklong trip to Hawaii to worship Ta-Ra. The cost of this pilgrimage (including airfare, hotel, and meals) is $2,800. Sonny wants to know if he can deduct the cost of this trip as a charitable contribution to his religion.

    Research Aid: *Kessler*, 87 TC 1285 (1986)

59. Fred Fisher is a licensed scuba diver who lives in Key Largo. He is employed full-time as an engineer. Five years ago he had been employed as a professional diver for a salvage company. While working for the salvage company, he became interested in marine archaeology and treasure

hunting. Until last year he gave diving lessons on weekends and trained individuals in the sport of treasure hunting under the name of "Fred's Diving School." Three of the diving students he taught subsequently found shipwrecks. Fred generally did not engage in recreational diving.

Last year, Fred began a treasure-hunting business named "Treasure Seekers Company." He bought a boat specifically designed for treasure hunting and did extensive research on potential locations of shipwrecks. Fred located several shipwrecks, but none were of substantial value. He did retrieve several artifacts but has not sold any yet. Although these artifacts may have some historical significance, they have a limited marketability. Thus, Fred has not yet had any gross income from his treasure hunting activities.

Other than retaining check stubs and receipts for his expenses and an encoded log, Fred did not maintain formal records for Treasure Seekers Company. Fred maintains as few written records as possible because he fears for his safety. He took steps to keep his boat and equipment from public view and took precautionary measures to maintain the secrecy of his search areas. Fred incurred $5,000 of expenses relating to his treasure-hunting activities last year. Can Fred deduct the expenses of his treasure-hunting business, or will the IRS claim it is a hobby and disallow the expenses?

Research Aid: Randy R. Reed, III, TC Memo 1988-470, 56 TCM 363, PH TC Memo ¶88,470

60. Locate and read *Greg McIntosh*, TC Memo 2001-144, 81 TCM 1772, RIA TC Memo ¶2001-144 (6/19/2001). Answer the following questions.

   a. What requirements must be met for a taxpayer to recover litigation costs from the IRS?

   b. Was the taxpayer in this case able to recover his attorney fees from the IRS? Why or why not?

61. Locate and read the following two cases:

J.B.S. Enterprises, Inc., TC Memo 1991-254, 61 TCM 2829, 1991 PH TC Memo ¶91,254

Summit Publishing Company, Inc., TC Memo 1990-288, 59 TCM 833, 1990 PH TC Memo ¶90,288

List those facts that you feel most influenced the judges to reach different conclusions in these two cases.

SEARCH THE INTERNET

62. Go to *www.irs.gov* (the IRS Web site) and click on Careers under Work at IRS. Look under Students & Recent Grads, then under Opportunities, and finally look under Accounting, Budget & Finance to learn more about Internal Revenue Agent positions.

   a. What are the basic requirements to work for the IRS as an Internal Revenue Agent at level GS-5?

   b. What are the additional requirements to qualify for a senior-level Internal Revenue Agent in the Large Business and International Division?

63. Go to *www.ustaxcourt.gov* (the Tax Court site). What is the filing fee to file a small tax case?

64. Go to *www.irs.gov/irb/* (the IRS site containing Internal Revenue Bulletins). Locate the Definition of Terms section in a recent IRB. Differentiate between the following terms as used by the IRS in its rulings: amplified, modified, clarified, and distinguished.

65. Go to *www.irs.gov* (the IRS Web site) and locate Publication 971: Innocent Spouse Relief. What form must be filed to request innocent spouse relief?

66. Go to *www.irs.gov* (the IRS Web site) and locate Form 656: *Offer in Compromise*. What does the IRS need to process an offer in compromise?

67. Go to *www.irs.gov/irb/* (the IRS site containing Internal Revenue Bulletins). Locate and read IRS Notice 2008-14, 2008-4 IRB 310 and answer the following questions.

a. What is the penalty for filing a frivolous tax return?

b. What are the first three broad categories cited in this notice as examples of frivolous positions?

68. Go to *www.irs.gov/pub/irs-utl/pcir230.pdf* or to the general IRS site (*www.irs.gov*) and under tax Professionals locate "Circular No. 230." Download a copy of *Treasury Circular 230: Regulations Governing Practice before the Internal Revenue Service*.

a. Read §10.33 and then list four best practices for tax advisors.

b. Read §10.35 regarding opinions that fail to reach a more likely than not conclusion. What must be disclosed?

69. Go to *www.aicpa.org* (the AICPA's Web site) and search for *Statements on Standards for Tax Services*. Read the history section of the most recent version of the *Statements on Standards for Tax Services*. What reasons were provided for revising the SSTS?

DEVELOP PLANNING SKILLS

70. Jessica plans to invest $150,000 in a second business. She expects to generate a 12 percent before-tax return on her investment the first year. Her marginal tax rate is 25 percent due to the income from her other business. She needs to decide whether to establish this second business as a sole proprietorship or a C corporation.

a. Compute the after-tax cash flow from a sole proprietorship if she withdraws 50 percent of the profits from the business the first year. (Ignore employment taxes.)

b. Compute the after-tax cash flow from a C corporation if she receives a dividend equal to 50 percent of the before-tax profits from the business the first year.

c. What nontax factors should Jessica consider in making this decision?

d. What do you recommend?

71. Richard plans to invest $100,000 for a 50 percent interest in a small business. His friend Jack will also invest $100,000 for the remaining 50 percent interest. They expect to generate a 10 percent before-tax return on their investment the first year. Richard's marginal tax rate is 25 percent, and Jack's marginal tax rate is 28 percent. They need to decide whether to establish the business as a partnership or a C corporation.

a. If they establish a partnership, compute the after-tax cash flow for each partner if each of them withdraws $4,000 of the profits from the business the first year. What is the amount of cash that remains in the partnership? (Ignore employment taxes.)

b. If they establish a C corporation, compute the after-tax cash flow for each shareholder if each of them receives a dividend of $4,000 from the profits of the business the first year. What is the amount of cash that remains in the C corporation?

c. What nontax factors should Richard and Jack consider in making this decision?

d. What you do recommend?

e. Discuss how your answers would change if you consider the impact of employment taxes in your solutions? (Employment taxes for employees, employers, and self-employed partners are discussed in Chapter 4.)

72. Norman is considering the purchase of some investment land from his neighbor, Robin, a high school math teacher. Robin purchased the land 10 years ago for $6,000. They have agreed on the overall terms of payment of $800 every month for the next three years for a total of $28,800. They have not agreed on how much of each payment is interest and how much is principal. Norman thought that a fair interest rate would be 8 percent, with the rest of each payment allocated to principal. Robin, however, said that he wanted to "give his neighbor a break" and have only 4 percent designated as interest with the rest of each payment allocated to principal. What difference does it make to Norman and to Robin how much is allocated to interest versus principal if the total of the cash payments will not change? Which interest rate would be better for Norman?

73. Debbie owns some investment land that she purchased 10 years ago for $12,000. The land consists of two adjoining lots recently appraised at $80,000. She needs $40,000 cash for another investment opportunity and is considering two alternatives: (1) sell half of the land for $40,000 or (2) borrow the $40,000 by taking out a mortgage on the land. Discuss the advantages and disadvantages of each alternative. What do you think Debbie should do?

74. The manager at Striker Corporation can hire only one student for the summer. She can hire Ken, a marketing student, who will do research on a marketing plan, or Lisa, a tax student, who will research tax strategies to reduce corporate taxes. If she hires Ken, his wages and benefits will total $5,600 (all tax-deductible expenses). Ken's marketing plan is expected to generate $6,000 in new revenues with a probability of success estimated at 80 percent. If she hires Lisa, her wages and benefits will be $6,000 (also fully tax-deductible). Lisa's tax plan is expected to save Striker $5,600 in federal income taxes. The probability of success for this plan is estimated to be 75 percent. Striker's marginal tax rate is 39 percent. Who should the manager hire?

75. Marlin Corporation must decide between two mutually exclusive projects because it lacks sufficient employees to complete both projects. Each project will take two years to complete and the project selected will be Marlin's only source of taxable income for the two years. The first job would generate $360,000 of revenues in the first year and $80,000 in the second year. Marlin estimates that this job will incur $200,000 of expenses in the first year and $40,000 of expenses in the second year. The second job will generate $220,000 of revenues and $120,000 of expenses in each of the two years. Assuming a 7 percent discount rate, which project should Marlin accept?

ANSWERS TO TEST YOURSELF

1. **d. Changing the character of income**
2. **a. Minimizing tax liability**
3. **d. Tax journals**
4. **d. Neither the IRS nor the taxpayer can appeal an adverse judgment.**
5. **b. Must advise the client of the omission and recommend appropriate action.**

APPENDIX 2A

TAX RESEARCH

The purpose of tax research is to find solutions to tax problems. The process of doing tax research involves three key steps:

1. Gather the relevant facts and identify the issues.
2. Locate and evaluate the relevant authorities.
3. Communicate the recommendations.

Gather the Facts and Identify the Issues

To begin the research process, the researcher must gather all the relevant facts. The following example presents a set of sample facts from hypothetical client Royal Trump, Inc.

EXAMPLE 2A.1

Royal Trump plans to open a new hotel and casino in Atlantic City. Royal Trump plans to require its employees to stay on the business premises during their working hours and has decided to provide free meals to those employees in an on-premises employee cafeteria for two reasons. First, if employees ate off-premises, they would have to go through two security checks each day (one when they went to lunch and another at the end of their shifts). Second, the number of fast-food eating establishments within a reasonable distance of the casino is insufficient to accommodate the large number of employees who would go for meals at one time. Royal Trump would like your advice regarding the correct tax treatment of these meals.

Once the relevant facts are known, the tax issues or questions must be identified. A combination of training and experience is necessary to enable the researcher to successfully identify all of the issues of a tax problem.

EXAMPLE 2A.2

Royal Trump's situation appears to have two separate issues: (1) are the meals tax free to employees and (2) are the costs of the employee cafeteria deductible by Royal Trump?

Locate and Evaluate the Relevant Authorities

After gathering the facts and identifying the issues, the researcher must locate relevant legal authority. Appendix A at the end of this textbook shows step-by-step screen captures of Thomson Reuters RIA Checkpoint®, a major internet subscription-based tax service commonly used by tax practitioners, illustrating how to locate tax authorities. Free materials available on the Internet do not have the same search features and indexes that are included in this subscription-based tax service.

Tax services provide two major tools for researchers: (1) explanations and (2) citations to primary sources of authority. Explanations may include discussions of the key issues of an Internal Revenue Code section and provide summaries of recent cases or rulings. Anything included in an explanation section of a tax service is a secondary authority because it is only another person's opinion about the tax law. Even though that person may be an expert about that area of tax law, a good researcher should not rely on another person's opinion, but should go to the underlying source of authority. Thus, the principal purpose of a tax service should be to provide citations to primary sources of authority.

A researcher wants to locate authorities with similar facts that specifically address the client's issues. Research usually starts with the relevant Code section, followed by reading the appropriate congressional committee reports and regulations, and finally expanding to include relevant rulings and court cases. Reading the text of each applicable authority carefully is necessary to complete this step.

Reading the Code

The provisions of the Internal Revenue Code frequently are long and consist of many subdivisions. In researching a tax question, it is important to read every Code section that may be applicable to the client's case in its entirety. A mere sentence or phrase at the very end of a section may include or exclude the client's case from the application of that section.

Language that indicates quantities or time periods must be carefully noted and accurately stated. Carelessness in reading such language may lead to incorrect conclusions. For example, "50 percent or more" is not the same as "over 50 percent," and "not more than 50 percent" is not the same as "less than 50 percent."

Committee Reports

The congressional committee reports and debates contain statements indicating the intent of Congress with respect to some provision of the law. They apply, however, only if that provision was enacted into law in the same form as when the particular committee wrote its report or when it was debated on the floor of the House or Senate. For example, a statement in the House Ways and Means Committee report does not indicate the intent of Congress if the Senate's version or the Joint Conference Committee's version of the particular provision was finally enacted.

When examining committee reports for indications of congressional intent, it is generally best to start with the Joint Conference Committee report. This will indicate whether the provision enacted is the conference version or the Senate or House version as amended in conference. If the Senate version was enacted, the explanation will be in the Senate Finance Committee report unless the Senate version was introduced through a floor amendment. In the latter event, the only committee explanation will be in the Joint Conference Committee report.

Regulations

Treasury Regulations, published as Treasury Decisions, are the highest level of administrative interpretations of the Internal Revenue Code. The publication date of the latest Treasury Decision amending a regulation should be compared to the date of the latest amendment of the corresponding provision of the Internal Revenue Code. Regulations often do not reflect Code amendments until as much as a year or more after the Code was amended. The old regulations continue to apply to any part of the Code provision not affected by the amendment. The publication date of the latest amending Treasury Decision is usually indicated at the end or the beginning of each regulation provision in the major tax services. Some tax services also note when a regulation provision does not reflect the latest amendments to the corresponding Code provision.

Proposed regulations have no force or effect. Nevertheless, they should not be ignored in researching a tax question that deals with a prospective transaction to which the proposals could apply. If they would have an adverse tax effect on the client's transaction, the tax advisor may wish to recommend completion of the transaction before the proposed regulations are finalized. If this is not practical, the advisor may wish to recommend postponing the transaction until final regulations are adopted, as they may clarify their effect on the taxpayer.

Revenue Rulings and Letter Rulings

A revenue ruling is an application of the law or regulations to a particular set of facts stated in the ruling. It usually discusses other rulings and court decisions as well as the Code and regulations pertinent to the legal questions raised by the facts. The significance of revenue rulings lies in the fact that they reflect current IRS policy. Because agents of the IRS are usually reluctant to vary from that policy, revenue rulings carry considerable weight.

Soon after a revenue ruling is issued, it appears in the weekly Internal Revenue Bulletin (cited as IRB), published by the U.S. Government Printing Office (GPO). Revenue rulings later appear in the *Cumulative Bulletin* (cited as CB) that is issued semiannually by the GPO. Revenue rulings have hyphenated numbers. The number to the left of the hyphen indicates the year in which the ruling was published and the number to the right is the number of the ruling for that year.

EXAMPLE 2A.3

An example of a revenue ruling citation is Rev. Rul. 75-320, 1975-2 CB 105. This is the 320th ruling issued in 1975 and appears on page 105 in volume 2 of the 1975 *Cumulative Bulletin.*

Revenue procedures are issued in the same manner as revenue rulings but explain procedures and other duties of the taxpayer. Revenue procedures are cited in the same manner as revenue rulings except that Rev. Proc. is substituted for Rev. Rul.

Letter rulings, also called private letter rulings, are interpretations of the Internal Revenue Code and Regulations by the National Office of the Internal Revenue Service. They are similar to revenue rulings except that each letter ruling is issued to a particular taxpayer in response to his or her specific question. Although a letter ruling applies only to the particular taxpayer to whom it was issued, such a ruling could prove helpful to any other taxpayer faced with a substantially identical fact pattern. Letter rulings are not officially published by the government, but are published by several major tax services (after any confidential information has been deleted).

Acquiescence Policy

In some instances, the Commissioner of Internal Revenue will publicly *acquiesce* or *nonacquiesce* to a court decision in which the court has disallowed a deficiency asserted by the IRS. The acquiescence or nonacquiescence relates only to the issues decided against the government. In announcing an acquiescence, the commissioner publicly declares agreement with a conclusion reached by the court. This does not necessarily mean that the commissioner agrees with the reasoning used by the court in reaching the conclusion. It only indicates that the IRS will dispose of similar disputes in a manner consistent with that established in the acquiesced case. Nonacquiescence is a clear signal that the IRS will not follow the decision, even though it may choose not to appeal it.

All acquiescences and nonacquiescences are announced in the Internal Revenue Bulletin. Citations for them are usually shown next to the citations of the related court decision in the tax services and citators.

Other Pronouncements

The IRS also issues information releases to newspapers throughout the United States for issues that it thinks will be of interest to the general public. For example, an information release is used to announce the standard mileage rate allowed for business use of an automobile.

Announcements are information releases that are more technical in nature and are generally aimed at tax practitioners instead of the general public. They are used to summarize new tax law or procedural matters and can be considered equivalent to revenue rulings and revenue procedures.

The IRS also publishes tax return instructions and other materials for the guidance of taxpayers, such as *Pub. 17: Your Federal Income Tax.* None of the statements in these publications are ordinarily supported by citations to the Code, regulations, or any other authority. Additionally, because these publications are generally revised only once a year, they are not always up-to-date. For these reasons, the IRS does not consider itself bound by the information in these publications.

Court Decisions

The parties in a tax case are generally the taxpayer and the Internal Revenue Service. Cases arising because a taxpayer contests a tax deficiency claimed by the IRS are identified as *Taxpayer v. Commissioner of Internal Revenue*, while those that arise because a taxpayer seeks to recover an overpayment of tax he or she claims to have made are indicated as *Taxpayer v. United States.*[48]

A case between a taxpayer and the IRS may involve a single question, called an issue, or it may involve a number of questions or issues. When a number of issues are involved in a case, the court will decide each issue separately. Although it renders only a single decision in the case, that decision indicates how each separate issue was decided. A court's decision on an issue is its determination of who wins that issue. In a two-issue case, for example, one issue may be decided for the taxpayer and the other for the government or both may be decided for the taxpayer or both for the government.

The party who raises an issue generally has the burden of convincing the court that his or her contention with respect to that issue is correct. Thus, a taxpayer who contests a deficiency or claims a refund must convince the court that he or she is entitled to the relief asked for in the petition. If the court consists of more than one judge, a majority of them must be convinced.

This burden of convincing the court is usually, but not always, on the taxpayer. However, the Internal Revenue Code places the burden of proof on the government in a few special instances, such as proof of fraud with intent to evade taxes.[49]

The *opinion*, the court's statement of the reasons for its decision, is generally the largest part of the published case report. It usually consists of a discussion and explanation of the applicable law and of prior court decisions on the same point of law. In contrast to the opinion, the decision may consist of only a few lines at the end of the court's statement.

There are two types of courts: courts of original jurisdiction or trial courts in which cases are first heard, and courts of appeal in which the decisions of the trial courts are reviewed. Courts of original jurisdiction include the U.S. Tax Court, U.S. District Courts, and the U.S. Court of Federal Claims. The Tax Court hears only tax cases and the presiding judge is more familiar with the tax law than is the typical judge presiding in the other courts. Jury trials are available only in district courts.

If either the taxpayer or the government is dissatisfied with the decision of the trial court on any issue, it can appeal to or ask a higher court to review that decision. Sometimes both parties appeal. The taxpayer appeals on those issues decided against him or her, and the government appeals on those issues decided against it. Figure 2A.1 lists the 13 Circuit Courts of Appeal (numbered 1 through 11 plus the District of Columbia and the Federal Circuit Court).

Appellate courts frequently issue decisions without opinions. This ordinarily means that the appellate court is satisfied with the decision and opinion of the court below. If it is not satisfied, the appellate court may simply refer to its opinion in a prior decision, or it may write its opinion to accompany its decision.

The appellate court separately decides each question of fact or of law raised on the appeal by either party. It may affirm the decision of the lower court on certain issues and reverse it on other issues. A reversal means that the party who won in the lower court now loses and the other party becomes the winner on that particular issue. The lower court's decision on issues from which neither party appeals is not disturbed because the appellate court has no jurisdiction over those issues.

EXAMPLE 2A.4

Jane wins in the Tax Court and the IRS appeals. The Court of Appeals reverses the Tax Court's decision. This means that the IRS has now won at the appellate level. Jane then appeals the appellate court's decision to the U.S. Supreme Court. The Supreme Court reverses the decision of the appellate court. This means that the case is now finally settled in favor of Jane (the same result as the original Tax Court decision).

Sometimes reversal by an appellate court does not resolve the controversy between the parties without further proceedings. In such instances, the appellate court reverses and remands (returns) the case to the lower court for further consideration in accordance with the appellate court's opinion. The lower court then renders a new decision.

A party who is dissatisfied with a decision of any of the appellate courts may ask the U.S. Supreme Court to review that decision by filing a petition for a *writ of certiorari*. If the Supreme Court denies the writ, its refusal does not mean that the Supreme Court agrees with the decision of the lower court; it merely means that it does not feel the case warrants its attention. Because the Supreme Court rarely agrees to hear tax cases, appeals seldom go higher than the Circuit Court of Appeals or the Court of Appeals for the Federal Circuit.

[48]Before 1954, a taxpayer suing to recover an overpayment usually brought the suit against the particular Collector of Internal Revenue (an office since abolished) into whose office the payment had been made. In that event the case was denominated *Taxpayer v. the particular collector by name.*

[49]The IRS Restructuring and Reform Act of 1998 shifts the burden of proof for factual issues to the IRS *only* for court proceedings if the taxpayer introduces credible evidence regarding the facts that apply to a tax liability. Note that the burden of proof still falls to the taxpayer at the audit level.

FIGURE
2A.1 FEDERAL CIRCUIT COURTS OF APPEAL

Circuit	Circuit Court Jurisdiction
First	Maine, Massachusetts, New Hampshire, Puerto Rico, Rhode Island
Second	Connecticut, New York, Vermont
Third	Delaware, New Jersey, Pennsylvania, Virgin Islands
Fourth	Maryland, North Carolina, South Carolina, Virginia, West Virginia
Fifth	Louisiana, Mississippi, Texas
Sixth	Kentucky, Michigan, Ohio, Tennessee
Seventh	Illinois, Indiana, Wisconsin
Eighth	Arkansas, Iowa, Minnesota, Missouri, Nebraska, North Dakota, South Dakota
Ninth	Alaska, Arizona, California, Guam, Hawaii, Idaho, Montana, Nevada, Oregon, Washington
Tenth	Colorado, Kansas, New Mexico, Oklahoma, Utah, Wyoming
Eleventh	Alabama, Florida, Georgia
DC	Washington, DC
Federal	US Court of Federal Claims

Legal Precedents When a court decides a particular issue, a legal precedent is set for future cases involving the same issue. Legal precedents, however, are circuit-specific; that is, different circuits can hand down different decisions based on identical facts. Cases in which there is disagreement between the different circuit courts of appeal are the types of tax cases the Supreme Court will usually agree to hear to provide uniformity of treatment throughout the country.

After the Tax Court decided the *Golsen* case, it agreed to follow the Court of Appeals that has direct jurisdiction over the taxpayer in question.[50] If the applicable appellate court has not yet ruled on that issue, the Tax Court is free to decide the case on the basis of its own interpretation of the issue. This **Golsen rule** allows the Tax Court to reach opposite decisions for taxpayers in different geographical areas of the country, even though their cases have identical facts. Thus, the Tax Court will not follow a decision of a prior Tax Court case in the same circuit if it was reversed by the Court of Appeals. The Tax Court may continue to follow the prior Tax Court decision in any circuit in which the Court of Appeals has not yet considered the issue or a circuit in which the Court of Appeals has sustained the Tax Court's position. In judging the precedential authority of a Tax Court decision, the researcher must always note whether the Tax Court reached its decision independently or merely followed the holding of the Court of Appeals to which its decision would have been appealed, without necessarily agreeing with it.

[50]*Jack E.* Golsen, 54 TC 742 (1970).

Some Tax Court transcripts disclose that a "decision has been entered under Rule 155" (prior to 1974, known as Rule 50). This notation signifies that the court has reached a conclusion regarding the facts and issues of the case but leaves the computational aspects of the decision to the opposing parties. Both parties subsequently submit to the court their versions of the refund or deficiency computation. If both parties agree on the computation, no further argument is necessary. In the event of disagreement, the court will reach its decision on the basis of the data presented by each party.

Tax services and other secondary authorities provide citations for the court decisions they cite as supporting authorities. Figure 2A.2 presents sample citations for decisions from several different courts. In each of these, the name of the case appears first, followed by the volume number and name of reporter service in which the case is located, and then the page or paragraph number where the case begins. The date may appear at the end, in parenthesis, along with the district in which it was heard.

Example 2A.5

Golsen, 54 TC 742, means that a decision involving a taxpayer whose name was Golsen is reported in volume 54 of the *Tax Court of the United States Reports* starting on page 742.

If there are differences between facts in the research problem and the facts of a case the researcher has located, the researcher needs to determine whether the court would rule differently regarding the client's facts. If there

FIGURE
2A.2 CITATION EXAMPLES

Internal Revenue Code	§213(d)(9)
Treasury Regulation	Reg. §1.166-1(e)
Revenue Ruling	Rev. Rul. 2003-102, 2003-2 C.B. 559
Letter Ruling	Ltr. Rul. 200517024
Revenue Procedure	Rev. Proc. 2006-1, 2006-1 IRB 1
IRS Announcement	Ann. 99-77, 199-2 C.B. 243
Tax Court Regular Case	*Golsen*, 54 T.C. 742 (1970)
Tax Court Memorandum Case	*McIntosh,* TC Memo 2001-144; RIA TC Memo ¶2001-144; 81 TCM 1772 (2001)
District Court Case	*Long Term Capital Holdings v. U.S.*, 330 F. Supp.2d 122; 94 AFTR2d 2004-5666; 2004-2 USTC ¶50351 (D. Conn, 2004)
Appeals Court Case	*Long Term Capital Holdings v. U.S.*, 96 AFTR2d 2005-6344; 2005-2 USTC ¶50575 (CA-2, 2005)
Supreme Court Case	*Comm. v. Groetzinger*, 480 U.S. 23; 107 S.Ct. 980; 59 AFTR2d 532; 87 USTC ¶9191 (1987)

is more than one case on point, the researcher needs to decide which one is the most authoritative. A researcher must citate every case and ruling to ensure that the authority located has not been overruled, modified, or otherwise lost its authoritative validity.

Using a Citator

A citator contains an alphabetical list of tax cases and a numerical list of revenue rulings and some other IRS rulings. A citator allows a researcher to find out two things about a court case: the decision's history and what the other courts may have said about it. There is a list of other decisions that cite or refer to the same court decision after the name of each case. The validity of a particular decision may be assessed by examining how the subsequent cases viewed the cited decision. By reading the authorities listed, a researcher can learn whether other courts and the IRS agree or disagree with the decision. Additionally, a case located by the citator that disagrees with an earlier case, but provides a higher level of authority, may provide a more appropriate answer to your question.

EXAMPLE 2A.6

In researching for our hypothetical client, Royal Trump, Inc., we found that the Ninth Circuit Court of Appeals reversed the Tax Court's decision in *Boyd Gaming et al. v. Commissioner* by ruling that a casino with a stay-on-premises policy was permitted to deduct 100 percent of the meals furnished to employees. In Announcement 99-77, IRS subsequently issued an acquiescence indicating they will no longer fight this issue.

For revenue rulings, historical citations consist of related rulings. There may be later revenue rulings that modify, supersede, or revoke the cited revenue ruling or earlier rulings that were modified or revoked by the cited ruling.

When to Stop Searching

An area many researchers wrestle with is knowing when to stop researching. Ideally, the tax researcher would like to find a favorable authority *on all fours* with the client's situation. The term *on all fours* refers to finding a situation in relevant tax authority that is factually similar in all legally pertinent ways to the situation being researched. Such perfect results are seldom achieved. Thus, the researcher must look for a tax authority in which the critical facts are similar to those of the client.

In determining whether to continue searching, the researcher should consider several items. First, what is the level of the relevant authority located? The higher the level of authority, the better. Second, does the IRS say anything about the issue? Some degree of comfort is provided when the client's position is supported in IRS rulings. However, an adverse IRS position may prompt the researcher to continue the search for additional authority. Third, do different sources of authority cite the same tax authority? If several different tax services and primary authorities cite the same authority in reaching their answer, this may make the researcher feel more comfortable that the best possible results have been obtained.

After evaluating the authorities, the researcher should be able to reach a conclusion on each issue. The conclusions sum up the state of the law on the issue as indicated by the primary authorities. Occasionally, the research will not offer a clear solution to the client's tax problems. There may be unresolved issues of law. If unresolved issues exist, the researcher might inform the client about alternative possible outcomes for each disputed transaction, and give the best recommendation for each.

Communicating the Recommendations

The final step in the research process is to communicate the results and recommendations of the research. The results of the research usually are summarized in a memorandum to the client file and in a letter to the client. Both the memo and the client letter usually contain a restatement of the relevant facts, any assumptions the researcher made, the issues addressed, the applicable authority, and the researcher's recommendations. The memo to the file usually contains more detail than does the letter to the client.

The memo to the file can take different forms. One simple format contains the following four sections:

1. *Facts*: a statement of the relevant facts
2. *Issues*: the tax questions or issues involved
3. *Conclusions*: the researcher's conclusions to the issues
4. *Discussion*: a discussion of the reasoning and authorities upon which the conclusions are based

The *facts* section should include all facts necessary to answer the tax questions or issues raised, with events stated in chronological order and dates given for each event.

Following the facts, the *issues* should be numbered as separate questions. The issues should be arranged in logical order, particularly when the answer to one question raises another question. Tax questions should be as specific as possible, including dates, amounts, and any other relevant information. Over-generalization should be avoided.

The *conclusions* are short answers to each issue. A separate conclusion should be stated for each numbered issue, ensuring that conclusion number 2 answers the question raised in issue number 2.

The *discussion* section is the longest. The reasoning and authorities underlying each conclusion should be presented separately, along with a concise summary of the facts and findings, plus a complete citation for each authority mentioned. Also noted should be the relative strength of each authority, such as whether the IRS expressed acquiescence, nonacquiescence, or neither, and whether the cited authority has been upheld in subsequent decisions. A detailed, logical analysis should be provided to support each of the conclusions using the primary authorities cited.

The client letter typically is structured as follows, allowing approximately one paragraph for each topic:

- Salutations and general conclusions
- Summary of the research results
- Presentation of the area researched
- Summary of the most important sources of law that lead to the results
- Implications of the results

A sample memo and client letter follow for hypothetical client Royal Trump, Inc.

Memo to File

Client:	Royal Trump, Inc.
Subject:	Employee Cafeteria Meals
For:	Pam Partner
Researched by:	Steven Staff
Date:	October 1, 2013

Facts

Royal Trump, Inc. plans to open a new hotel and casino in Atlantic City. It plans to require its employees to stay on the business premises during their working hours for security and logistic reasons and to provide free meals to those employees in an on-premises employee cafeteria. If employees ate off-premises, they would have to go through two security checks a day (one when they went to lunch and another when their shifts end). Additionally, the number of fast-food eating establishments is insufficient to accommodate the large number of employees that would go for meals at one time.

Issues

1. Are the meals tax-free to employees?
2. Are the costs of the employee cafeteria deductible?

Conclusions

1. Meals provided for the convenience of the employer where employees are confined to the premises during mealtimes are tax free under Section 119.
2. The cafeteria will qualify as a de minimis fringe benefit under Section 132, permitting a 100 percent deduction for its costs.

Discussion of Reasoning and Authorities

1. Section 119 provides that the value of meals is excludible from an employee's income if the meals are furnished on the business premises for the convenience of the employer. Under Regulation Section 1.119-1, a meal is considered furnished "for the convenience of the employer" if it is furnished for a "substantial noncompensatory business reason." A substantial noncompensatory business reason includes meals furnished because the employee could not otherwise secure proper meals within a reasonable meal period because there are insufficient eating facilities in the vicinity. Reg. Section 1.119-1 also defines business premises of the employer as the place of employment of the employee. Under Section 119(b)(4), if more than half the employees satisfy the "for the convenience of the employer" test, then all employees will be considered as satisfying the test.
2. As a general rule, Section 274(n) permits a taxpayer to deduct only 50 percent of the otherwise allowable cost of business meals. However, meals provided to employees are 100 percent deductible in certain circumstances. The two most important are (1) meals treated as compensation and (2) meals that are tax-free de minimis fringe benefits under Section 132(e).

   Section 132(e) provides exclusion for de minimis fringe benefits for which accounting would be an unnecessary hassle. Included within these de minimis benefits are subsidized cafeterias for employees.

To qualify under Section 132(e)(2), a cafeteria must be located on or near the business premises, must not favor executives, and must generate revenue that normally equals or exceeds its direct operating costs. However, if all employees' meals are excluded under Section 119, the employees are treated under Section 132(e)(2) as having paid an amount equal to the direct operating costs of the facility attributable to meals. This in turn causes the employer-operated cafeteria to qualify as a de minimis fringe benefit under Section 132(e)(2). Under Section 274(n)(2)(B), an employer may fully deduct the cost of meals that are tax-free de minimis fringe benefits under Section 132(e)(2).

In Boyd Gaming Corp., et al. v. Commissioner (177 F. 3d 1096; 99-1 USTC ¶50,530; 83 AFTR 2d 99-2354), the Ninth Circuit reversed the Tax Court by ruling that a casino with a stay-on-premises policy was permitted to deduct 100 percent of the meals furnished to employees. The court held that once the stay-on-premises policy was adopted, the affected employees had no choice but to eat on the premises and that the furnished meals thus were indispensable to the proper discharge of their duties. The IRS has since acquiesced (Ann. 99-77, 1999-32 IRB 1) to this decision, indicating that it will not challenge similar businesses that have valid business reasons for a stay-on-premises policy. The security concerns of Boyd Gaming appear to be the same as the security concerns of Royal Trump, so this should meet the valid business reason test.

Client Letter

October 1, 2013
Mr. R. Trump
Royal Trump, Inc.
123 Park Place
Atlantic City, New Jersey

Dear Mr. Trump:

Thanks again for requesting my advice concerning the tax treatment of your proposed employee cafeteria. I have good news for you. The meals will be tax-free to your employees, and you will be able to deduct 100 percent of the costs of the cafeteria.

In reaching this conclusion, we consulted relevant provision of the Internal Revenue Code, related Treasury Regulations, and pertinent case law.

The facts as we understand them are as follows:

Royal Trump plans to require its casino employees to stay on the business premises during their working hours for security and logistic reasons and has decided to provide free meals to those employees in an on-premises employee cafeteria.

Generally, a taxpayer is permitted to deduct only 50 percent of the otherwise allowable cost of business meals. However, meals provided to employees are 100 percent deductible when they qualify as tax-free de minimis fringe benefits under Section 132(e). To qualify, the cafeteria must be located on or near your business premises and must not favor executives. You must also have valid business reasons for a stay-on-premises policy for the cafeteria to qualify.

Section 119 provides that the value of meals is excludible from an employee's income if the meals are furnished on the business premises for the convenience of the employer. The convenience-of-employer test is met if the meals are provided for a "substantial noncompensatory business reason." Your business reasons were due to security and logistical concerns. First, if employees ate off-premises, they would have to go through two security checks a day (one when they went to lunch and another at the end of their shifts). Additionally, the number of fast-food eating establishments within a reasonable distance of the casino is insufficient to accommodate the employees when they go for meals.

My research has uncovered a recent case similar to your situation in which a casino was permitted to deduct 100 percent of its costs while employees were permitted tax-free treatment as well. It required its employees to remain on-premises during their entire shifts for security and logistic reasons. The IRS has acquiesced with the decision and indicated that it will not challenge other businesses in similar situations that have valid business reasons for a stay-on-premises policy. This is good news for you.

Please call me at 661-1234 so that we may discuss any questions you have concerning this conclusion.

Sincerely,

Pam Partner

Pam Partner

PROBLEM ASSIGNMENTS

CHECK YOUR UNDERSTANDING

1. What signal does the IRS give taxpayers to indicate that a court decision will not be followed?
2. Explain the Golsen rule.
3. What information is found in a citator?
4. What does it mean when a Tax Court decision says that the decision has been entered under Rule 155?
5. What are the four sections of a memo to the file? Explain what each section should include.

INCOME AND EXPENSE DETERMINATION

p

CHAPTER

DETERMIN
GROSS INC

CHAPTER 4
EMPLOYEE
COMPENSAT

CHAPTER 5
BUSINESS
EXPENSES

chapter

3

Determining Gross Income

CHAPTER OUTLINE

Gross income includes income from all sources unless a specific provision in the tax law excludes it. Certain types of income may be excluded from gross income for social, economic, or political reasons. Taxes, however, are not levied on gross income but on taxable income, which is gross income (net of exclusions) less allowable deductions. This chapter focuses on determination of those items included in gross income and identification of the period in which they are included (recognized).

Income for tax purposes is not the same as financial statement income, because tax policy has different objectives than generally accepted accounting principles. A number of basic tax principles affect the determination of gross income, including the realization principle, the return of capital principle, the doctrine of constructive receipt, and the claim of right. In addition, the period in which income is recognized is determined by the taxpayer's method of accounting. Identifying the period in which income is recognized is important because a taxpayer's marginal tax rate may change, the tax laws may change, and the time value of money may affect the value of a dollar paid in taxes.

This chapter discusses interest, dividends, annuities, government transfer payments, legal settlements, and prizes. Each of these items normally results in taxable income to the recipient, but exceptions may render some or all of what is received nontaxable. We also look at the most common exclusions from income and several provisions by which income recognition is postponed to a later period.

At the completion of this chapter, you should be able to determine gross income for the most frequently encountered situations and understand the situations over which taxpayers can control the timing or taxability of the income.

KEY CONCEPTS

- ★ Taxable income is the base against which tax rates are applied to compute the taxpayer's tax liability. Taxable income is gross income less allowable deductions.
- ★ There are many differences between income for tax purposes and income for financial accounting purposes because they have different goals.
- ★ All forms of income must be included in gross income unless they are specifically excluded. For various social, economic, and political reasons, certain income items are excluded from gross income and thus, not subject to income tax.
- ★ Under the return of capital principle, a taxpayer's investment (basis) can be recovered tax free; that is, excluded from gross income.

SETTING THE STAGE—AN INTRODUCTORY CASE

Steven, an individual taxpayer, has his ordinary income taxed at the 39.6 percent marginal tax rate; however, his long-term capital gains are subject to the 20 percent capital gains tax rate. He has $50,000 that he wants to invest for the next five years, at which time he will liquidate his investment to start his own consulting business. He is considering three investment alternatives: (1) corporate bonds yielding 6 percent before tax with the interest reinvested at 6 percent before tax; (2) general revenue bonds issued by his municipality yielding 4 percent, and the interest can be reinvested at 4 percent; (3) land that is expected to increase in value by 6 percent each year. Which investment alternative should Steven choose? We will return to this case at the end of this chapter.

What is Income?

The Internal Revenue Code's definition of *income* is extremely broad. The opening phrase of Section 61(a) provides a general all-inclusive definition of **gross income** by stating "[e]xcept as otherwise provided in this subtitle, gross income means all income from whatever source derived. . . ." Although the section lists a number of included items, such as rents, interest, and dividends, two things have happened to provide a more definitive explanation of those items that must be included in income. First, the courts adopted the accounting concept that measures income only when a realization event occurs for tax purposes. This is known as the **realization principle**, which states that no income is recognized (included in gross income) until it is realized by the taxpayer. Realization usually takes place when an arm's-length transaction occurs, such as the sale of goods or the rendering of services.[1] Fluctuations in value are not income unless that change is realized through some transaction.[2]

Example 1

Ambler Company purchased 500 shares of XYZ Company stock at a cost of $5 per share. At the end of the year, XYZ stock was trading at $12 per share. Although Ambler's wealth increased by $3,500 ($7 per share), it has no taxable income from this increase in wealth until the stock is sold.

Second, the tax laws themselves have been refined and amended to add a number of other specific items that are either included or excluded from income. For example, although Section 61 specifically mentions interest as taxable, Section 103 excludes from gross income interest earned on bonds issued by a state or a local municipality.

Taxable versus Gross Income

Taxable income is the base against which tax rates are applied to compute the taxpayer's tax liability. Taxable income is gross income less allowable deductions.[3] The determination of what is included in gross income does not vary by taxpayer. The Internal Revenue Code applies uniformly, regardless of whether the taxpayer is a business or an individual.[4] Deductions from gross income differ for individuals and businesses, however. Businesses are generally allowed to deduct all ordinary and necessary expenses of operating the business. Individuals are also allowed to deduct their business expenses, but their deductions may be limited. In addition, individuals are permitted to deduct a limited amount of personal expenses or take a standard deduction. Regardless of the taxpayer, the starting point is always gross income. Unless the taxpayer can find some tax law that states that an income item can be excluded from gross income, it is taxable. This chapter presents not only an explanation of the items most commonly included in income but also discusses some specific exclusions, such as municipal bond interest income, gifts, inheritances, and life insurance proceeds.

Tax versus Financial Accounting

Although many similarities exist between the income reported for financial accounting purposes and the income that is included on a tax return, there are also many differences. The U.S. Supreme Court has indicated three reasons for disallowing generally accepted accounting principles (GAAP) for tax purposes. First, the goals of

[1]An arm's-length transaction is one in which both the buyer and seller have bargained in good faith and for their own benefit.

[2]*Eisner v. Macomber*, 252 US 189 (1920).

[3]§63(a).

[4]The few special provisions that apply only to corporations are discussed in Chapter 9.

financial accounting and tax reporting are very different. The former seeks to provide information that decision makers, such as shareholders and creditors, find useful. The latter seeks to collect revenue equitably. Second, financial accounting often relies on the principle of conservatism, which tends to understate income when uncertainty exists. In contrast, the income tax system would be greatly hampered in its collection of revenue if taxpayers were allowed the freedom of reporting income conservatively. Third, financial accounting often relies on estimates and probabilities. The tax system would not function very efficiently or equitably if taxpayers were allowed to estimate income or base their reported income on probabilities.

EXAMPLE 2

For tax purposes, a corporation wrote down its excess inventory to net realizable value in accordance with GAAP. The Supreme Court indicated that this treatment was inappropriate because it did not clearly reflect taxable income.[5]

The differences between financial accounting income and taxable income fall into two general categories:

1. Income is taxed in a different period than it is accrued for accounting purposes. For example, prepaid rent generally is taxable when received but is included in financial accounting income only as it is earned. These differences are temporary or timing differences.
2. Income that is not taxed but is included in financial accounting income. For example, municipal bond interest generally is not taxed but it is recorded as income on the financial statements. These differences are permanent differences.

Financial statements prepared in accordance with GAAP report income tax expense based on the current-year financial statement income, not the current-year taxable income. Thus, the tax expense reported in the financial statements matches the transactions reported in that period on the financial statements, regardless of when the tax is actually paid. As a result, timing differences cause a difference between income tax expense shown on the books and the actual tax shown on the tax return. These differences are accounted for on financial statements as *deferred tax assets* or *deferred tax liabilities*.[6]

Most businesses do not maintain separate books and records for financial and tax reporting. They simply make the appropriate adjustments so that financial statements and tax returns can be prepared from the same basic data and the different concepts of income reconciled.

Return of Capital Principle

One of the basic tax principles is that gross income excludes the return of capital, referred to as cost recovery.[7] A **return of capital** is the recovery of a prior investment. The amount invested in an asset is referred to as its **basis**. If a taxpayer's return is more than basis, gain results; if less than basis, the taxpayer has a loss.

EXAMPLE 3

Ambler sells 500 shares of XYZ stock for $11 per share that were purchased for $5 per share. Ambler has a taxable gain of $3,000 [($11 selling price -$5 basis) × 500 shares]. If Ambler had sold the stock for only $4 per share, it would have a $500 loss [($4 selling price - $5 basis) × 500 shares] because the capital it invested in the stock was not completely recovered.

[5] *Thor Power Tool Co. v. Comm.*, 439 US 522 (1979), 43 AFTR 2d 79-362, 79-1 USTC ¶9139.

[6] Differences in expense recognition can also result in timing and permanent differences. See Chapter 5 for a discussion of accounting for book/tax differences.

[7] *Doyle v. Mitchell Bros. Co.*, 247 US 179 (1918).

Tax law favors investments that yield appreciation rather than annual interest income because tax is deferred until a gain has been recognized and the gain is frequently taxed at lower long-term capital gains rates.[8] The current income tax rates on ordinary income (which includes interest income) and long-term capital gains are summarized in Table 3.1.

TAX PLANNING

EXAMPLE 4

Anne's marginal tax bracket is 33 percent for ordinary income and 15 percent for long-term capital gains. She has $20,000 to invest for eight years, at which time the investment will be liquidated. She is considering two investment alternatives: (1) corporate bonds yielding 5 percent before tax with the interest reinvested at 5 percent before tax; (2) land that will increase in value by 5 percent each year. The value of the tax deferral that results from investing in the land rather than the bonds is $1,711 ($8,109 - $6,398), determined as follows:

	CORPORATE BONDS	INVESTMENT LAND
Annual interest income		
$20,000 × 5%	$1,000	
Income tax @ 33%	($330)	
After-tax cash flow	$670	
Reinvested @ 5% for 8 years*	× 9.549	
After-tax cash flow from interest for 8 years	$6,398	
Original investment in land		$20,000
5% factor		× 1.477
Land value in 8 years		$29,540
Return of capital		(20,000)
Pretax gain		$9,540
Tax on gain @ 15%		(1,431)
After-tax value		$8,109

**Future value tables are in Appendix B at the end of this textbook.*

TABLE 3.1 **INDIVIDUAL TAX RATES FOR ORDINARY INCOME AND LONG-TERM CAPITAL GAINS**

TAXABLE INCOME BRACKET FOR SINGLE INDIVIDUALS	TAXABLE INCOME BRACKET FOR MARRIED FILING JOINT RETURNS	TAX RATES FOR ORDINARY INCOME	TAX RATES FOR LONG-TERM CAPITAL GAINS
$0–$8,925	$0–$17,850	10%	0
$8,926–$36,250	$17,851–$72,500	15%	0
$36,251–$87,850	$72,501–$146,400	25%	15%
$87,851–$183,250	$146,401–$223,050	28%	15%
$183,251–$398,350	$223,051–$398,350	33%	15%
$398,351–$400,000	$398,351–$450,000	35%	15%
$400,001 and above	$450,001 and above	39.6%	20%

[8]Individuals qualify for lower long-term capital gains rates when an investment has been held for more than a year. If the investment has been held for one year or less, it is a short-term capital gain and ordinary income tax rates apply. Capital gains are discussed in Chapter 7. Corporations do not have special tax rates for long-term capital gains.

Under this principle, a taxpayer who receives an amount that must be paid back, through a loan or other form of indebtedness, does not have income. This transaction increases both the recipient's assets and liabilities, resulting in no net change in equity or wealth.

When is Income Recognized?

Taxable income is measured and reported based on the tax year. Determining the period in which income is taxed is important for several reasons:

1. The taxpayer's marginal tax rate may differ from one year to the next. Changes in marginal rates can result from fluctuations in the taxpayer's taxable income, legislative changes to the tax rate structure, or a combination of both.
2. The tax law may change the treatment of some items. For example, income that previously was taxed may no longer be taxable; thus, the taxpayer prefers to report the income in the later year.
3. Because of the time value of money, a dollar of tax paid in year 1 actually costs more than a dollar of tax paid in year 2. Thus, taxpayers generally prefer to have income taxed in a later tax year and to deduct expenses in an earlier tax year.

Deferring taxable income from one year to the next produces tax savings, as discussed in the previous chapter. By controlling the timing of a transaction, taxpayers can reduce their tax cost or increase their tax savings. Thus, determining the end of a tax year is critical for decision makers. Tax laws restrict the selection of accounting periods and methods to prevent taxpayers from abusing the tax system. Without these restrictions, taxpayers could manipulate income so that it falls into whichever tax year minimizes their tax liability.

The Tax Year

A business's tax year corresponds to its annual accounting period for financial statement purposes. If a business keeps its financial records on a **calendar year**, it measures income from January 1 through December 31. If adequate books and records are maintained to measure taxable income, a taxpayer can use a fiscal year over an acceptable annual period. Any 12-month period ending the last day of any month other than December is a **fiscal year**. The choice of a calendar year or fiscal year is usually determined by the organization's operating cycle. For example, a ski resort may select an April 30 fiscal year-end so it can close its books and calculate its profit at the end of its natural business cycle.

TAX PLANNING

Businesses can also choose to use a 52-to-53-week fiscal year that ends in any calendar month (including December) but ends on the same day of the week each year. The ending day selected must be either the last time that day occurs in the month or the day closest to the end of the month.[9] For example, a fiscal year that ends on either the last Friday in January or the Friday that is closest to January 31 is an acceptable 52-to-53-week year. Companies that are closed for business on weekends often select Friday to end their fiscal year because this permits inventory to be taken during the weekend without disrupting regular business operations.

Most individual taxpayers use the calendar year as their taxable year because they do not keep adequate books and records and because of the publicity surrounding the April 15 tax deadline for filing calendar-year individual tax returns.[10] The calendar year is also more convenient for individuals because most information reporting,

---

[9]§441(f).

[10]When an individual taxpayer files his or her first return on a calendar year, the calendar year automatically becomes the taxpayer's tax year.

for example W-2 forms for wages and 1099 forms for interest and dividends, is based on the calendar year.

Corporations generally maintain extensive financial records and often adopt fiscal years. Flow-through entities, such as S corporations and partnerships, as well as personal service corporations (PSCs), face restrictions that usually force them to adopt tax years ending September 30 through December 31, with most adopting a calendar year.[11] These restrictions prevent their owners from enjoying significant tax deferrals.

A new business usually chooses its tax year when it files its initial tax return.[12] This return reports operating results from the date the business begins operations until the end of its first tax year. As a result, the initial tax return is usually for a year of less than 12 months. Once a tax year is established, a taxpayer (including an individual) cannot change its tax year unless it receives permission to do so from the IRS.[13]

EXAMPLE 5

Jim begins a new business as a sole proprietorship. Jim would like to use a fiscal year, but the business must report its operating results on Jim's tax return and Jim has always filed his tax return on a calendar-year basis. Although the sole proprietorship is new, Jim has already established himself as a calendar-year taxpayer. Therefore, Jim must request permission from the IRS to change to a fiscal year to accommodate his sole proprietorship's accounting records.

The IRS will usually grant permission for the business to change its taxable year if a taxpayer has a valid business reason for changing its annual accounting period.[14] When the IRS does grant permission to change, the taxpayer has a **short tax year** and files a short-year tax return.

A short-year tax return reports less than 12 months of operating results. Because of the progressive tax rate structure, the tax liability of a short-year tax return might be unusually low and the short tax year could result in permanent savings in tax dollars. To prevent this, taxable income reported on a short-year return (except for the first or last tax return of an individual or a business) must be **annualized**; that is, it must be adjusted to reflect 12 months of operations.[15] This is accomplished by dividing the actual income by the number of months in the short tax year and then multiplying this average monthly income by 12 to gross up the taxable income to an annualized amount. The tax liability is then computed on this annualized number; it is reduced proportionately for the short period by multiplying by the number of months in the short tax year divided by 12.

EXAMPLE 6

Marvel Corporation requests and receives permission to change from a calendar year to a fiscal year ending on June 30. To make the change, the corporation must file a return for the period January 1 through June 30 (a short tax year consisting of only six months). Marvel has taxable income of $54,000 for the period January 1 through June 30. Marvel must gross up its income by first computing average monthly income of $9,000 ($54,000/6 months) and then multiplying this average monthly income by 12 to get an annualized taxable income of $108,000 ($9,000 × 12). The tax liability is then computed on this annualized taxable income using the regular corporate tax rates as follows:

[11]A PSC is a service corporation whose employees own substantially all of the stock. Examples include engineering, law, accounting, and consulting corporations.

[12]Reg. §1.441-1T(b)(2).

[13]§442.

[14]One valid purpose is to change to a tax year that coincides with the natural business year. To have a natural business year, at least 25 percent of the company's gross receipts for the 12-month period must be realized in the final 2 months of the 12-month period for 3 consecutive years. Usually only seasonal businesses qualify under this test.

[15]§443(b).

Tax on first \$50,000 × 15%	=	\$7,500
Tax on next \$25,000 × 25%	=	6,250
Tax on next \$25,000 × 34%	=	8,500
Tax on next \$8,000 × 39%	=	3,120
Total 12-month tax liability		\$25,370

This annual tax liability is then multiplied by 6/12 to reduce it to a tax of \$12,685 (6/12 × \$25,370) for the short tax year. Without this annualization rule, Marvel Corporation would pay only \$8,500 [(\$50,000 × 15%) + (\$4,000 × 25%)], resulting in a permanent tax savings of \$4,185 (\$12,685 – \$8,500) due to a change in tax year. For all future returns, Marvel Corporation will file tax returns reflecting operating results for a 12-month year beginning on July 1 and ending on June 30.

This annualization requirement does not apply to an entity that either begins or ends business in the tax year (its first or its last return). It applies solely to businesses that make a change in their tax year. As a result, short-period income reported on the first or final business return may be taxed at a favorable rate.

Accounting Methods

The method of accounting identifies the year within which income falls for tax purposes. Taxpayers can use the cash, accrual, or hybrid (a combination of cash and accrual) accounting methods for tax purposes as long as the method chosen clearly reflects income.[16] In many cases, taxpayers use the same accounting method for both tax and financial accounting purposes. They can use different accounting methods as long as they keep a separate set of records that allows them to convert financial accounting data into the information necessary for the tax return. Taxpayers must use the same accounting method from one year to the next, however, unless they receive permission from the IRS to change accounting methods.

A taxpayer can use different tax accounting methods for different activities. For example, a taxpayer engaged in two sole proprietorships can use the accrual method for one and the cash method for the other or the accrual method for business and the cash method for personal activities.[17]

Cash Method

The **cash method** requires the taxpayer to recognize income during the tax year in which cash or a cash equivalent is received and permits deductions during the tax year in which cash or its equivalent is paid.[18] A cash equivalent is defined broadly here as anything with a market value, including most noncash property and services.[19] Cash equivalents are included in income at their fair market value.

Example 7

Ted, a cash-basis, calendar-year sole proprietor, prepares a tax return for his dentist, sending a bill for \$400 in year 1. On December 31, year 1, the bill is unpaid and Ted shows a \$400 account receivable in his ledger. In year 2, Ted agrees to accept dental work worth \$350 in full settlement of the bill. Ted has \$350 of gross income in year 2. This type of exchange of services is a barter transaction.

The **constructive receipt doctrine** modifies the requirement that cash-basis taxpayers must actually receive cash (or cash equivalents) before income is recognized. This doctrine requires the cash-basis taxpayer to recognize income when it is credited to the taxpayer's account, set apart for the taxpayer, or made available in some other way to the taxpayer. In effect, the constructive receipt doctrine prevents cash-

[16] § 446(b), (c).

[17] Reg. § 1.446-1(c)(1)(iv)(b).

[18] Reg. § 1.446-1(c)(1)(i).

[19] The mere recording of an account receivable, however, is not considered a cash equivalent.

basis taxpayers from turning their backs on income and, as a result, arbitrarily shifting gross income between tax years.

Income is not constructively received in three situations: (1) The taxpayer is not yet entitled to the income; the fact that the taxpayer could have contracted to receive the income earlier is irrelevant.[20] (2) The payor has insufficient funds from which to make payment (such as a bounced check). (3) There are substantial limitations or restrictions placed on actual receipt.[21]

EXAMPLE 8

Bongo Company, a cash-basis, calendar-year taxpayer, received a check at noon on December 31, year 1. It was too late to deposit the check in the bank that day, so it was not deposited until January 2, year 2. Bongo must recognize the $12,000 in income in year 1 because it was made available and therefore was constructively received in year 1. If, however, the check was postdated to January 3, year 2, because the payor will not deposit sufficient funds to cover the check until January 2, year 2, Bongo does not recognize the income until year 2.

TAX PLANNING

Professional athletes and other highly compensated individuals can avoid the application of the constructive receipt doctrine through the careful wording of their employment contracts. If the contract language legally defers their right to some portion of their compensation until a later taxable year, the compensation is not gross income until that time (or until actually received, if earlier).[22]

EXAMPLE 9

Calusa Construction Company is a cash-basis taxpayer. Big Developers offers to pay Calusa $15,000 in advance for building a retaining wall during December, year 1. Calusa expects to be in a lower tax bracket in year 2 and counter offers to build the wall in December, year 1, for $15,100 to be paid in January, year 2. The final written contract reflects this counteroffer, and the payment is made according to the contract. Calusa does not have constructive receipt in year 1 because it is not entitled to the income until year 2. It does not matter that the company could have contracted for the money earlier. Calusa reports gross income of $15,100 from this job in year 2.

Limits on Use of Cash Method

Congress was concerned that taxpayers could manipulate their taxable income under the cash method by deferring income and accelerating payment of expenses. (Cash-basis taxpayers can easily defer income by delaying billing their customers at year-end.) Therefore, it put some restrictions on the use of the cash method. Businesses that carry inventory and sell merchandise to their customers must use the accrual method to account for sales and purchases.[23] Under the **hybrid method**, the accrual method is used for recording sales of inventory and determining cost of goods sold, but the cash method is used for all other income and expense items.

EXAMPLE 10

Appliance Depot, Inc., sells and services appliances. It keeps an inventory of appliances on hand for sale but purchases parts only as needed for repairs. Appliance Depot must use the accrual method to record sales of appliances and to determine the cost of appliances sold. As long as it clearly reflects income, it can use the cash method for the service portion of the business and for expenses relating to either sales or services (other than cost of goods sold). Alternatively, Appliance Depot can use the accrual method for its entire business.

[20] *Amend*, 13 T.C. 178 (1949).

[21] Reg. §1.451-2.

[22] Deferred compensation is discussed in Chapter 4.

[23] Reg. §1.446-1 and §1.471-1.

TAX PLANNING

Businesses with average annual gross receipts of $10 million or less qualify for a special variation of the cash method, under which they account for the cost of merchandise inventory at year-end as an asset but are permitted to account for their sales on the cash basis.[24] This special method is much more favorable than the hybrid method because it allows the business to defer recognition of income until payment is received.

In addition to meeting the average annual gross receipts test, a business cannot be one that is prohibited from using the cash method under Section 448. This section prohibits C corporations with average annual gross receipts of more than $5 million, from using the cash method for tax purposes.[25] This prohibition does not extend to personal service corporations, so no matter how large a personal services corporation is, it can use the cash method.

Accrual Method

Generally accepted accounting principles require the use of the accrual method. Under the **accrual method**, gross income is recognized in the tax year in which it is earned rather than the year in which it is received. Income is earned when all events have occurred that establish the right to the income and the income amount can be determined with reasonable accuracy. These criteria are known as the **all events test** and are generally satisfied when goods are delivered or services are performed.

EXAMPLE 11

Hightec Computers (a calendar-year, accrual-basis corporation) sold a computer system to a customer for $18,000 on account on December 18, year 1, and delivered the computer system to the customer on December 22. The first week of January, year 2, Hightec billed the customer and the customer paid the bill on February 1, year 2. The $18,000 is gross income in year 1. All events have occurred that establish the corporation's right to the $18,000 as of December 31, year 1, and the amount of income is known with reasonable accuracy.

If the liability for payment is in dispute, the all events test is not satisfied; resolution of the dispute is a relevant event in establishing the taxpayer's right to the income. If the taxpayer has already received payment, however, the claim of right doctrine modifies the normal rules for accrual-basis taxpayers. The **claim of right doctrine** requires the taxpayer to recognize income when payment is received as long as the taxpayer's use of the money is unrestricted, regardless of whether the money may have to be repaid later.[26] If the taxpayer must return all or part of the income later, a deduction is allowed in the repayment year.[27] When the deductible portion of the repayment exceeds $3,000, the taxpayer can either (1) deduct the repayment in the year repaid or (2) reduce the current year's tax by the amount of tax paid in the prior year on the disputed income.[28] The optimal choice depends primarily on the taxpayer's marginal tax rates in the two taxable years.

EXAMPLE 12

In November, year 1, Computer Training Services (CTS), an accrual-basis, calendar-year taxpayer, was hired by Lowtech Company to provide a five-week computer training program for its employees. CTS was paid its full training fee of $20,000 on the first day of training. After four weeks of training sessions, Lowtech cancelled the last week of training and demanded a refund of $4,000 because its employees felt they were not learning anything useful. In January, year 2, CTS refunded $4,000 to Lowtech. CTS's marginal tax rate for year 1 is 34 percent.

---

[24] Rev. Proc. 2002-28, 2002-1 CB 815.

[25] § 448. This prohibition of the cash method extends to partnerships with corporate partners.

[26] *North American Oil Consolidated v. Burnet*, 286 US 417 (1932), 11 AFTR 16, 3 USTC ¶943.

[27] *U.S. v. Lewis*, 340 US 590 (1951), 40 AFTR 258, 51-1 USTC ¶9211.

[28] § 1341.

Because the repayment exceeds $3,000, CTS can either deduct the $4,000 repayment in year 2 or reduce its year-2 tax liability by $1,360 ($4,000 × 34%), the amount by which its tax would have decreased in year 1 if the refunded $4,000 had not been included in gross income. If CTS's marginal tax rate in year 2 is 35 percent, the company should deduct the $4,000 (rather than reduce its tax by $1,360) because the tax savings from the deduction is $1,400 ($4,000 × 35%). If CTS has a lower marginal tax rate in year 2, then it should select the $1,360 credit.

The rationale behind the claim of right doctrine is the concept of **wherewithal to pay**, which asserts that a taxpayer should be taxed on income at the time that the taxpayer is best able to pay the tax.[29] The government does not wait for the settlement of a dispute before taxing income. Instead, it chooses to tax the income while the taxpayer has the wherewithal to pay. A delay in taxing income increases the risk that the taxes will be uncollectible later. The claim of right doctrine does not apply to contested amounts that the taxpayer has not yet received.

Accrual-basis taxpayers are often treated as cash-basis taxpayers if they receive prepaid income. Once again, the reason for taxing prepaid income is the wherewithal to pay concept. Prepaid income items that are taxed when received include rent, royalties, and interest.[30]

Landlords often require tenants to pay the last month's rent in advance. As prepaid rent, it is taxable currently. Instead of prepaid rent, landlords should require a refundable security deposit in the same amount. The tax on a deposit is deferred because the landlord is obligated to return it if all rent is paid and no damage is done to the apartment.

TAX PLANNING

Special exceptions allow accrual-basis taxpayers to defer recognition of some prepaid items. Recognition of deposits for the purchase of goods as income generally can be deferred if the taxpayer's method used to account for the sale is the same for both accounting and tax purposes.[31] Similarly, prepayments for services to be performed beyond the current year can be deferred until the tax year following the prepayment year. Generally, deferral to a tax year later than the next succeeding year is not allowed.[32]

EXAMPLE 13

On November 1, 2013, Flamingo Dance Studios, a calendar-year, accrual-basis taxpayer, receives advance payment for a two-year contract for 96 one-hour lessons. Flamingo provides 8 lessons in 2013, 48 lessons in 2014, and 40 lessons in 2015. On its financial statement, Flamingo recognizes 1/12 of the revenue in 2013, 6/12 in 2014, and 5/12 in 2015. On its tax return, Flamingo must include 1/12 of the payment in 2013 and 11/12 in gross income for 2014.[33]

WHO RECOGNIZES THE INCOME?

Assignment of Income Doctrine

Congress recognized that significant tax revenue can be lost through income shifting between taxpayers and has restricted income-shifting techniques through the **assignment of income doctrine**. An assignment involves the transfer of rights from one party to another. The assignment of income doctrine precludes the taxpayer from shifting personal service income to another.[34]

[29]One reason for reliance on the cash method for income tax purposes, in addition to its simplicity, is that it imposes the tax at the same time that the taxpayer receives the resources with which to pay the tax.

[30]Reg. §1.61-8(b).

[31]Reg. §1.451-5(b).

[32]Rev. Proc. 2004-34, 2004-22 IRB 991. A limited exception exists when the next year is a short tax year.

[33]Ibid.

[34]*Lucas v. Earl*, 281 US 111 (1930), 2 USTC ¶496, 8 AFTR 10,287. In its now-famous fruit-and-tree analogy, the court explained that fruit (personal service income) must be attributed to (taxed to) the tree on which it grew (the individual who earned it).

Example 14

Karim is a professional basketball player earning more than $1 million in annual compensation. Karim requested that $200,000 of his salary be paid to his girlfriend, Crystal. Karim's employer paid the $200,000 directly to Crystal. According to the assignment of income doctrine, the $200,000 is gross income to Karim because he is the taxpayer who earned it. For tax purposes, it will be treated as if Karim received the income and then made a gift to Crystal.

The doctrine also applies to the assignment of income from property, unless the ownership of the underlying property is transferred.[35]

Example 15

Samuel gives his son, Harry, corporate bonds. Interest accruing up to the date of the gift is taxable to Samuel. Interest accruing after the gift is taxable to Harry because the bonds were transferred to Harry, not just the interest from the bonds.

Community Property Laws

Community property laws affect the allocation of income between spouses. The states that follow a community property system are Arizona, California, Idaho, Louisiana, Nevada, New Mexico, Texas, Washington, and Wisconsin.[36] All other states are common law states. Under common law, income is usually taxed to the individual who earns the income. In most community property states, community income is the sum of personal service income and income from community property. However, in Idaho, Louisiana, Texas, and Wisconsin, community income also includes income from separate property. In other words, all income in these four states is considered community income.[37]

For tax purposes, community income is split evenly between spouses who file separate returns. Spouses who are separated must still report half of the community income on their separate returns until such time as they divorce and the divorce becomes final. (The filing of joint returns by a married couple effectively allows spouses to be taxed as if each earned half of the couple's combined income.)

Sources of Income

The two most common sources of gross income for a business are from sale of goods and performance of services. Corporations report their gross income on their corporate income tax return and pay tax based on their taxable income. If the business is a flow-through entity (such as a partnership or S corporation), the gross income is reported first on the entity's information tax return (but not taxed); income is then allocated to the owners and included on the owners' returns as income, where it is then taxed. For employees, common sources of income include salaries, wages, commissions, bonuses, and tips; employee compensation is discussed in the next chapter. The remainder of this chapter focuses on the tax treatment of other sources of income. The sample filled-in tax returns in Appendix C contain illustrations of how the various sources of income are reported.

Interest Income

Individuals and businesses receiving interest income generally must report these amounts as gross income. Thus, interest income from savings accounts, certificates of deposit, corporate bonds, and Treasury bills is included in gross income. The primary exception is interest received on state and local bonds.

[35] *Helvering v. Horst*, 311 US 112 (1940), 40-2 USTC ¶9787, 24 AFTR 1058.

[36] In Alaska, spouses can choose to have community property rules apply.

[37] Personal service income is not considered community income in any of the nine states if the couple lives apart the entire year, does not file a joint return, and does not transfer earned income (such as alimony) between them. §66(a).

Interest on Municipal Bonds

The term **municipal bonds** (or munis) is frequently used to describe all tax-exempt bonds issued by any city, county, state, or other governmental entity to raise money for projects such as building schools, highways, hospitals and sewer systems. The exclusion from gross income of interest income on municipal bonds used to finance government operations has existed since 1913.[38] It was thought that the authority for this exclusion was rooted in the U.S. Constitution's intergovernmental tax immunity doctrine and that taxing such interest would impair the ability of state and municipal governments to finance their basic operations.[39] Although the Supreme Court has since determined there is no constitutional prohibition,[40] the law remains unchanged and the exclusion continues to provide state and local governments with low-interest financing.

The exclusion does not extend to the gain realized on the disposition of state and municipal bonds, however. If a municipal bond is sold at a gain, the gain is taxable (and if sold at a loss, the loss is deductible). Only interest income is tax free. Interest is included in financial accounting income, however, providing a permanent difference between tax and accounting income.

EXAMPLE 16

Bill paid $20,000 to the City of Miami for general revenue bonds. During the current year, he receives $600 interest from the bonds. Market interest rates drop, causing the value of the bonds to increase. Bill sells the bonds for $22,000. The $600 interest is excluded, but Bill reports the $2,000 ($22,000 – $20,000) gain as gross income.

TAX PLANNING

Taxpayers in high tax brackets should consider investing in tax-exempt state or local bonds. Although offering a lower interest rate than taxable bonds, the after-tax investment yield may be higher.

EXAMPLE 17

Two taxpayers each have $50,000 to invest. Taxpayer A is in the 33 percent marginal tax bracket and taxpayer B is in the 15 percent marginal tax bracket. They are considering two alternative investments: corporate bonds with a stated interest rate of 6 percent or tax-exempt municipal bonds issued for government activities with a stated interest rate of 4.5 percent.

TAXPAYER A	CORPORATE BONDS	TAX-EXEMPT BONDS
Interest income		
$50,000 × 6%	$3,000	
$50,000 × 4.5%		$2,250
Income tax @ 33%	(990)	0
After-tax cash flow	$2,010	$2,250

TAXPAYER B		
Interest income	$3,000	$2,250
Income tax @ 15%	(450)	0
After-tax cash flow	$2,550	$2,250

Taxpayer A will have $240 ($2,250 – $2,010) more in after-tax cash flow by investing in tax-exempt municipal bonds, while taxpayer B will have $300 ($2,550 – $2,250) more in after-tax cash flow by investing in the taxable corporate bonds.

A taxpayer with a 33 percent marginal tax rate requires only a 6.7 percent yield on a tax-exempt bond to obtain the same after-tax income as a taxable bond paying 10 percent interest [6.7% / (1 – .33)].

---

[38] § 103(a).

[39] *Pollack v. Farmer's Loan & Trust Co.*, 3 AFTR 2602, 158 US 601 (1895).

[40] *South Carolina v. Baker III*, 61 AFTR 2d 88–995, 88-1 USTC ¶9284, 485 US 505 (1988).

To maximize these benefits, cash-basis taxpayers may purchase zero-coupon bonds; these bonds pay interest only at maturity. Zero-coupon bonds are particularly attractive for taxpayers who would otherwise reinvest the interest each year. Zero-coupon bonds save on broker fees and the hassle of finding a suitable investment for the interest earned each year.

Over the years, the use of municipal bonds has expanded to include bonds issued to finance certain private activities (such as construction of sport facilities) that do not meet essential public needs and these bonds are not completely tax exempt.[41] The interest from tax-exempt bonds issued for qualified private activities (usually called AMT bonds) is not subject to the regular income tax but it is subject to the federal alternative minimum tax (AMT).[42] The yield on these AMT bonds is typically higher than fully tax-exempt municipal bonds. Investors who are not subject to the AMT can achieve higher returns by investing in these AMT bonds rather than municipal bonds not subject to the AMT.

Original Issue Discount

Federal tax law generally does not permit investors to defer the recognition of interest income. When debt instruments are issued at a price below their stated maturity value, they are said to be issued at an original issue discount. **Original issue discount (OID)** is the excess of a debt instrument's stated maturity value over its issue price.[43] The OID is essentially interest paid at maturity rather than periodically over the life of the debt instrument. All debt instruments that pay no interest before maturity are presumed to be issued at a discount; zero coupon bonds are one example. With some exceptions, Section 1272 requires cash-basis taxpayers to recognize OID as it accrues as if they were accrual-basis taxpayers. Without this provision, cash-basis taxpayers could defer interest income (OID) until the debt instrument's maturity.

Example 18

Xenon Corporation, a small cash-basis corporation, issues $1,000,000 of 10-year bonds with a stated interest rate of 4 percent for $920,000. Under normal cash-basis rules, Xenon would recognize the entire $80,000 of discount as a loss in year 10 when the bonds mature. The OID rules, however, require accrual of the discount as part of interest expense annually.

Frederico purchased $20,000 of Xenon Corporation bonds for $18,400. Frederico's return on this investment consists of an $800 ($20,000 × 4%) annual interest payment plus the $1,600 ($20,000 – $18,400) OID that he will collect at maturity. Each year Frederico will receive a Form 1099 from Xenon Corporation that reports (to him and to the IRS) the $800 interest payment and the portion of the discount Frederico must recognize as additional interest income that year.[44] Frederico increases his basis for the bonds by the amount of OID he reports as income each year. When the bonds mature, Frederico's basis will then be $20,000 and he can receive the $20,000 maturity value as tax-free return of capital.

The OID is zero for relatively small discounts; that is, discounts that are less than ¼ percent times the number of full years to maturity.[45] Additionally, the OID rules do not apply in two situations. First, OID can be deferred until received on any debt instru-

[41] § 103(b). Interest exclusions are also not allowed for unregistered bonds, bonds guaranteed by the federal government, and arbitrage bonds.

[42] § 57(a)(5). AMT income is broader than ordinary taxable income. It differs from taxable income in its treatment of certain deductions and also in its inclusion of income from preference items such as interest from private activity bonds. Taxpayers compute their tax under both the regular tax rules and the AMT rules and then pay whichever tax is higher. Refer to Chapter 11 for a more complete discussion. The American Recovery and Reinvestment Tax Act of 2009 provided that tax-exempt interest on private activity bonds issued in 2009 or 2010 only would not be considered an AMT preference item.

[43] § 1273(a)(1).

[44] The amortization of the discount is calculated using the constant interest rate method. The total amount of the interest is calculated by multiplying the interest yield to maturity by the adjusted issue price. Under this method, the amount of OID amortization increases each year the bond is held.

[45] § 1273(a)(3).

ment if its maturity date is one year or less from the date of issue. Second, government savings bonds (Series EE and I bonds) are generally issued as OID bonds with all interest paid at maturity.[46] The taxpayer is not required to report the interest until the bonds mature (or are cashed in prior to maturity). Electively, however, the taxpayer may report the interest income on an annual basis. If such an election is made, the OID on any other similar government bonds purchased in the future must also be amortized.

TAX PLANNING

Parents frequently give their children U.S. government savings bonds as planned savings for college or other future expenses. If a child is in a low tax bracket or has insufficient income to be subject to taxation currently, it may be preferable to recognize the OID from these bonds each year as it accrues rather than later when the child's annual income may be greater and he or she is in a higher tax bracket. If elected, the children can recognize the OID as gross income each year.[47]

Another favorable provision allows exclusion of the interest if parents use the redemption proceeds of Series EE or Series I bonds to pay for tuition and fees of qualified higher education. Only a limited group of taxpayers can benefit from this provision, however, due to income limits.[48]

Market Discount

TAX PLANNING

Investors who purchase bonds later in the open or secondary market at a price lower than the bond's stated maturity value are not required to accrue the discount as interest income over the life of the bond, although they may elect to do so.[49] If they do not elect to recognize the discount over the life of the bond, they must recognize the excess of the redemption proceeds over the cost as interest income in the year of redemption.[50] Most taxpayers prefer to defer the recognition of the discount until the year of redemption due to the time value of money.

EXAMPLE 19

Sandra purchased corporate bonds with a maturity value of $50,000 from her broker for $46,000. The bonds were trading at a discount because their interest rate is below the market rate. Sandra includes only the cash interest payments in income each year. When she redeems the bonds at maturity, Sandra will recognize the $4,000 discount ($50,000 – $46,000) as interest income in the year of redemption.

Below-Market-Rate and Interest-Free Loans

Interest-free or below-market-rate loans are frequently made between related parties. In these cases, the interest income that is not actually received or accrued is imputed (treated as received or accrued) at a predefined federal rate of interest. Otherwise, a taxpayer with excess cash could shift investment income to another taxpayer through these low or no-interest loans.

EXAMPLE 20

Gary (who is in the 33 percent marginal tax bracket) loans $50,000 to his oldest son, Mark (who is in the 15 percent marginal tax bracket). The loan is interest-free for a term of one year. Mark invests the $50,000 in corporate bonds that yield 8 percent. Because Gary forgoes investment earnings on his $50,000 during this year, $4,000 of income has been shifted, in effect, from Gary to Mark. If Gary invested the $50,000 at the same earnings rate, he would have had to pay $1,320 in tax ($4,000 × 33%) while Mark only pays $600 in tax ($4,000 × 15%), resulting in a tax savings of $720 ($1,320 – $600).

---

[46] Series EE bonds are issued at a discount and provide a constant rate of return. Series I bonds provide a return that is indexed for inflation.

[47] § 454(a).

[48] § 135. The exclusion begins to phase out when modified adjusted gross income is $74,700 ($112,050 for a married couple filing jointly) in 2013 and is completely phased out over the next $15,000 ($30,000 if married). Additionally, to be eligible for exclusion, the taxpayer must be at least age 24 when the bonds are issued.

[49] § 1278(a) and (b).

[50] § 1276.

Congress curtailed some advantages of interest-free loans by enacting provisions that turn such loans into multi-step transactions. Section 7872 recharacterizes an interest-free or below-market-rate loan as a loan requiring the payment of interest at a predefined federal rate. The lender is deemed to have received interest income (imputed interest) at the current applicable federal rate of interest.[51] The lender is then treated as returning the imputed interest to the borrower (because the interest was not actually paid). Thus, below-market-rate and interest-free loans are recharacterized as arm's length transactions in which the lender is treated as having made a loan to the borrower in exchange for a note that requires the borrower to pay hypothetical interest at the applicable federal rate to the lender and the lender then makes a hypothetical payment to the borrower equal to the interest not charged. The hypothetical payment to the borrower is treated as a gift, payment of compensation, or dividend depending on the circumstances of the loan and the relationship between the lender and the borrower.

Interest-free and below-market-rate loans fall into three basic categories: (1) gift loans, (2) employment-related loans, and (3) shareholder loans. In each case the lender has interest income. It is the characterization of the return of the hypothetical interest to the borrower that differs, as summarized in Table 3.2.

A loan made between family members or friends is a gift loan. The return of the imputed interest on these loans is considered a gift from the lender to the borrower.

Example 21

Michael loans his daughter Sarah $200,000 interest-free for one year. Assume that the applicable federal rate of interest is 5 percent. The imputed interest that Sarah is deemed to have paid to Michael is $10,000 ($200,000 × 5%), and Michael is deemed to have earned $10,000 in interest on the loan and Sarah has $10,000 of imputed interest expense. Michael is then deemed to have given the $10,000 back to Sarah. Michael must include the $10,000 interest in his gross income. Sarah has interest expense of $10,000 that may or may not be deductible, depending on how she uses the money.

TABLE 3.2 **BELOW-MARKET-RATE LOANS**

TYPE OF LOAN	EFFECT ON LENDER	EFFECT ON BORROWER	EXCEPTIONS
Gift	Interest income followed by gift to borrower	Interest expense followed by gift from lender	(1) $10,000 exception (2) Interest limited to net investment income for loans of $100,000 or less (zero if income $1,000 or less)
Employee	Interest income followed by compensation expense	Interest expense followed by compensation income	$10,000 exception if no tax avoidance purpose
Shareholder	Interest income followed by dividend paid	Interest expense followed by dividend income	$10,000 exception if no tax avoidance purpose

[51] The applicable federal rate (AFR) changes on a monthly basis and is tied to the yield on Treasury securities. The IRS publishes AFRs each month on its Web site.

TAX PLANNING

There are two exceptions to the rules for interest-free loans between individuals. First, any loan of $10,000 or less is exempt from the imputed interest rules (as long as the total amount of loans outstanding between the borrower and lender is $10,000 or less).[52] This exception is for administrative convenience; it would be very costly to keep track of all small loans that people make to friends and relatives. Therefore, a small amount of income can still be shifted through the use of $10,000 interest-free loans.

The second exception, for gift loans of $100,000 or less, states that the imputed interest on the loan cannot exceed the borrower's net investment income for the year.[53] Further, if the borrower's net investment income for the year does not exceed $1,000, the imputed interest is deemed to be zero and the loan has no tax effect.[54] Therefore, small gift loans that do not produce much income for the borrower or that are used for personal expenses escape the imputed interest rules.

EXAMPLE 22

Justin makes interest-free loans to his four children: Joshua, Holly, Dave, and Ben. Joshua borrowed $150,000 to purchase a new home. Joshua has unrelated net investment income of $500 for the year. Holly borrowed $30,000 to invest in stock and she has net investment income of $1,200 for the year. Dave borrowed $35,000 to invest in land and his net investment income is $800 for the year. Ben borrowed $8,500 to buy a new car and his net investment income for the year is $900.

The loan to Ben is exempt because it is for less than $10,000 and the loan to Dave is exempt because he has less than $1,000 of net investment income. If the applicable federal rate is 5 percent, the imputed interest on the $30,000 loan to Holly would be $1,500 ($30,000 x 5%) but is limited to her net investment income of $1,200. Interest income of $7,500 ($150,000 x 5%) is imputed on the loan to Joshua; it is not limited to his net investment income because the loan is for more than $100,000. Justin must report imputed interest income of $8,700 ($1,200 + $7,500) for the year.

When an employer makes an interest-free or below-market-rate loan to an employee, the return of the imputed interest is deemed to be compensation, taxable to the employee and deductible by the employer. When an interest-free loan is made to a shareholder of a corporation, the return of the imputed interest is deemed to be a taxable dividend, but the corporation is not allowed a deduction for the imputed dividend.

EXAMPLE 23

Roofers-R-Us Corporation loans $50,000 interest-free for one year to Carl, an employee. The applicable federal rate of interest is 4 percent. Carl is assumed to pay the corporation $2,000 ($50,000 × 4%) in interest, and the corporation is assumed to have received interest income of $2,000. The imputed interest payment is then assumed to be returned to Carl as compensation that is taxable to Carl and deductible by the corporation. Note that the net effect of this arrangement for the corporation is zero; that is, it has an increase in its income of $2,000 because of the imputed interest income that is offset by the compensation payment deduction of $2,000. If Carl cannot deduct the interest, he would have an increase in taxable income for the $2,000 in imputed compensation.

If Carl is a shareholder, rather than an employee, of Roofers-R-Us Corporation, the $2,000 in interest is still imputed to the corporation and Carl, but the $2,000 imputed interest payment is deemed to be returned to Carl as a dividend. It is taxable to Carl as dividend income, but the corporation is allowed no deduction for the dividend paid.

[52]§7872(c)(2).

[53]Net investment income includes interest, dividends, and short-term capital gains, less any investment expenses.

[54]§7872(d)(1)(E)(ii).

For employee and shareholder loans, the $10,000 exception does not apply if tax avoidance is one of the principal purposes of the loan.[55] This tax avoidance rule means that only a few shareholder and employee loans, such as employee-relocation loans, will qualify for the $10,000 exception.

Dividend Income

A corporate distribution to shareholders out of earnings and profits is an ordinary **dividend** and is included in the recipient's gross income. Distributions that are in excess of corporate earnings and profits are nontaxable dividends that reduce the basis of the shareholder's stock.[56] Dividends can be received as cash, property, or stock.

The 2003 Tax Act reduced the tax rates for most corporate dividends to the same tax rates as long-term capital gains. This change did not convert dividend income into capital gains but merely applied the same 15 percent rate to qualified dividend income for individuals (corporations are not eligible for the reduced rates).[57] Prior to this change in law, dividend income was taxed using the taxpayer's ordinary marginal tax rates. The rate reductions introduced by the 2003 Act provided a 5 percent tax rate for taxpayers with income in the 10 or 15 percent tax brackets through 2007 and zero rate for 2008-2010, while the 15 percent dividend rate remained unchanged. The 2010 Tax Relief Act extended the zero and 15 percent dividend tax rates through 2012.[58] This change was made permanent for most taxpayers in 2013, except for taxpayers in the top bracket who are subject to a 20 percent dividend tax rate.

Qualified dividends are ordinary dividends that are eligible for the reduced tax rates and include most dividends received from domestic corporations and qualified foreign corporations.[59] Dividends from most tax-exempt organizations are not eligible for the lower rates.[60] Additionally, day traders are not eligible for the reduced rates. To prevent individuals from purchasing stock immediately prior to the ex-dividend date to collect low-tax-rate dividends and then quickly selling the stock generating a short-term capital loss, the rules disallow the low dividend tax rates unless the stock is held at least 60 days during the 120-day period surrounding the ex-dividend date.[61]

Investors in stock and mutual funds are frequently offered a dividend reinvestment option in which dividend income is used to purchase additional shares. Although the taxpayers choosing shares have not received a cash payment, they are in constructive receipt of the reinvested dividends, resulting in taxable income. They are treated as if they received a cash dividend and then used the cash to purchase additional shares.

Some receipts that are called dividends are actually other types of income. Dividends that credit unions and savings-and-loan associations pay on deposits are actually interest. Similarly, mutual funds often pay dividends from the gains they realize on the sale of investment assets. These dividends are actually net long-term capital gains to the mutual fund shareholders and are called *capital gains distributions.*

---

[55]§7872(c)(3).

[56]If the distribution is in excess of the shareholder's stock basis, the excess is taxed as a capital gain.

[57]Corporations, however, are permitted a dividend received deduction for all or part of a dividend received from another corporation to minimize triple taxation. This is discussed in Chapter 9.

[58]The zero rate that applies to individuals in the 10 and 15 percent marginal brackets appears to provide a perfect planning opportunity for parents to transfer stock to their children and allow the dividend income to be tax-free if the children's tax rates fall within the two lowest tax brackets. To close this loophole, Congress increased the age at which the kiddie tax rules apply to all children under age 19 as well as most full time students under age 24. Refer to Chapter 12 for a detailed discussion of the kiddie tax.

[59]Qualified foreign corporations include U.S. possessions corporations, foreign corporations whose stock is traded on an established U.S. securities market, and foreign corporations eligible for income tax treaty benefits.

[60]Dividends are also not eligible if they are payments in lieu of dividends (payments received by a person who lends stock in a short sale), distributions on trust-preferred stock (as this really represents interest income rather than dividends), and most distributions by a real estate investment trust (REIT).

[61]The ex-dividend date is the day following the record date on which the corporation finalizes the list of shareholders who will receive the dividend.

Shareholders do not report these distributions as dividend income but instead report these distributions with their other capital gains.[62]

EXAMPLE 24

Carol owns 10,000 shares of XYZ common stock and 5,000 shares of Leadership mutual fund. Carol elects to participate in Leadership's dividend reinvestment plan, reinvesting her annual dividends and capital gains distributions in additional Leadership shares. Carol receives an $11,000 distribution from XYZ and receives a statement (Form 1099-DIV) indicating that $10,000 of the distribution is a dividend and $1,000 is a nontaxable distribution. She receives another statement (Form 1099-DIV) from Leadership mutual fund indicating that she has a dividend of $5,000 and a capital gains distribution of $2,000 for a gross distribution of $7,000. This $7,000 distribution was used to purchase 140 additional shares of Leadership mutual fund through the reinvestment plan, increasing her total shares of Leadership to 5,140.

Carol includes $15,000 ($10,000 from XYZ and $5,000 from Leadership) in gross income as dividend income and $2,000 as a long-term capital gain (from Leadership). Carol is in the 28 percent marginal income tax bracket so both the dividend income and long-term capital gains distribution are eligible for the 15 percent tax rate. Carol reduces the basis of her XYZ shares by $1,000 for the nontaxable portion of the distribution.

TAX PLANNING

The reduced tax rates for dividend income make stock a more attractive investment than interest income from corporate bonds that is taxed at the individual's ordinary marginal tax rate. But dividends taxed at the reduced rates will not be treated as investment income when computing the investment interest expense deduction limit (discussed in Chapter 11). Taxpayers may elect to forgo the reduced tax rates and have their dividends taxed as ordinary income so that it can be considered investment income when computing this deduction limit. Before making this election, taxpayers should calculate the tax savings from the investment interest expense deduction to ensure that this will provide a greater after-tax benefit than the reduced tax rates on the dividend income.

Stock Dividends

A simple common **stock dividend** (shares of the company's own stock) that is paid on a common stock investment is generally nontaxable. A stock dividend is treated the same as a *stock split* for tax purposes. The recipient shareholder realizes no increase in wealth from a stock split or a stock dividend.[63] He or she simply has more shares of stock indicating the same ownership percentage. Shareholders who receive a nontaxable stock dividend allocate their capital investment in pre-dividend shares to all shares they own after the stock dividend.

EXAMPLE 25

The Board of Directors of ABC Corporation votes to issue a stock dividend to the shareholders of one share of stock for each share held (commonly known as a *2-for-1 stock split*). Just prior to the dividend, Susan owned 1,000 shares of ABC stock she purchased for $30 per share ($30 × 1,000 = $30,000 total basis). Susan receives 1,000 new shares, so after the dividend she owns 2,000 shares of ABC. The additional 1,000 shares she receives are not income to her. Her basis in each share after the dividend is $15 ($30,000 original cost of 1,000 shares/2,000 shares).

More complex stock dividends may or may not be taxable.[64] For example, if one class of common stock receives a stock dividend while another class of common

[62]Some mutual funds and real estate investment trusts (REITs) keep their long-term capital gains and pay tax on them. These gains are reported on Form 2439 *Notice to Shareholder of Undistributed Long-Term Capital Gains* and are currently taxable to the individual investors even though not actually distributed to them. The investors get credit for the tax paid and then increase their basis in the mutual fund or REIT by the difference between the taxable gain they report and the tax credit they claim. See Chapter 7 for a discussion of the tax treatment of capital gains and losses.

[63]*Eisner v. Macomber*, 252 US 189 (1920). The shareholder must sell the shares to realize income.

[64]See Chapter 9 for a discussion of dividends.

stock receives a cash dividend, both the stock and cash dividends are taxable. The shareholders who receive the stock dividend have increased their percentage ownership in the corporation relative to those shareholders receiving cash. They have an increase in their wealth (their share of company assets) and have income equal to the value of the stock received.

Annuity Income

People usually purchase annuity contracts to provide a fixed stream of income in future years. The purchase amount is invested and returned as an **annuity**, a series of periodic payments that consist of two components. One is a nontaxable recovery of cost and the other represents interest earned that must be included in gross income. The following formula is used to calculate the nontaxable portion of each payment that represents the annuitant's return of capital;[65] the residual portion of each payment is the interest that is included in gross income.

$$\frac{\text{Investment in Annuity Contract}}{\text{Expected Return from the Contract}} \times \text{Annuity Received} = \text{Nontaxable Portion}$$

The fraction's denominator (expected return from the contract) depends on the term of the annuity, that is, the number of payments and the amount of each payment. If the annuity is payable over a specific period of time, such as 10 years, the annual receipts under the contract are multiplied by 10 to obtain the expected return. If the annuity is payable over the lives of one or more annuitants, an *expected return multiple*, obtained from Treasury Department tables, is multiplied by the annual amount received.[66] For a single-life annuity, the expected return multiple is the estimate of the individual's remaining life.[67]

The amount an annuitant ultimately receives may be more or less than the expected return; that is, the annuitant may live more or less than his or her expected life. If the annuitant lives longer than expected and recovers his or her full investment before death, additional payments are all gross income, as cost has been fully recovered. If the annuitant dies prematurely, the unrecovered cost is deducted on the annuitant's final tax return.[68]

EXAMPLE 26

Cindy pays $150,000 for a single-life annuity that pays her $10,000 a year for life. Treasury Department tables estimate her remaining life to be 20 years. Thus, the expected return under the contract is $200,000 ($10,000 payments × 20 years). Of each $10,000 payment, Cindy reports $2,500 as gross income; $7,500 is a nontaxable return of investment determined as follows:

$$\frac{\$150{,}000 \text{ Investment}}{\$200{,}000 \text{ Expected Return}} \times \$10{,}000 \text{ Receipt} = \$7{,}500 \text{ Nontaxable Portion}$$

If Cindy lives for 25 years and receives total annuity payments of $250,000, she will be taxed fully on each of the $10,000 payments received in the last five years as her investment will have been fully recovered. If Cindy dies after receiving annuity payments totaling only $150,000 over 15 years, three-fourths of these payments, or $112,500, were recoveries of cost. Thus, $37,500 remains unrecovered when Cindy dies; this amount can be deducted on her final tax return.

If retirement benefits are received as an annuity, any portion that represents the return of the employee's *after*-tax investment goes into the numerator of the annuity formula, ensuring that this amount will not be taxed a second time. If, however, the employer made all of the contributions to the retirement plan or the employee made

[65] §72(b)(1).

[66] The tables are found in Reg. §1.72-9.

[67] If the annuity is paid over lives of more than one annuitant, the denominator is based on the expected return for all annuitants. The Small Business Jobs Act of 2010 allows part of a nonqualified annuity to be paid out over 10 or more years as a separate annuity while the remainder continues to earn interest.

[68] §72(b)(2) and (3).

the contributions on a *pretax* basis, the after-tax investment would be zero and all amounts collected would be taxable.[69]

Transfers from Others

Prizes and Awards

Cash and the fair market value of noncash prizes and awards (such as cars or vacations) are included in a recipient's gross income[70] and cannot be excluded as gifts. Thus, the value of prizes received from lotteries, game shows, contests, sweepstakes, raffles, and gambling activities must be included in gross income.[71] Similarly, treasure that a taxpayer finds or discovers is included in gross income once the taxpayer establishes undisputed ownership in the property.[72]

EXAMPLE 27

Michael wins his state's $9 million lottery, payable over 20 years. In years 1 through 5 he receives annual installments of $450,000. At the beginning of year 6, Michael sells his right to receive the remaining 15 payments to a third party for a lump-sum payment of $3,950,000. As a cash-basis taxpayer, Michael includes $450,000 in income each year for years 1 through 5. In year 6, Michael must include $3,950,000 in gross income.[73]

TAX PLANNING

A taxpayer who shares winnings with others may have to pay tax on the entire amount, depending on the sharing arrangement. If the taxpayer wins and then gives away part of the winnings, the taxpayer will be taxed on the full amount and will be treated as making a separate gift (which could be subject to gift tax). If the sharing agreement is made before the ticket turns out to be a winner, then each individual reports only his or her share in gross income. The key is when the sharing arrangement (assignment) of the lottery ticket took place, before or after the taxpayer won the lottery.

Government Transfer Payments

NEED-BASED PAYMENTS Individuals who receive need-based payments from a federal, state, or local government agency exclude the payments from gross income.[74] Therefore, welfare payments, school lunches, and food stamps are nontaxable.

UNEMPLOYMENT COMPENSATION Unemployment compensation is a payment from either a government or employer-financed program to provide for an individual's basic living costs during a period of unemployment. At one time, all or part of such income was excluded from income. Since 1987, all unemployment compensation has been included in gross income.[75] The rationale for taxing unemployment compensation is that it is a substitute for taxable salary or wages.

SOCIAL SECURITY BENEFITS The Social Security system is a federal program that imposes a tax on employees, employers, and self-employed persons. The tax revenue is pooled in a trust fund and used to provide monthly Social Security benefits to retirees, disabled individuals, and surviving family members of deceased workers.

Before 1984, Social Security benefits were completely excluded from gross income, as they provided for a person's general welfare. From 1984 and through 1993, a maximum of one-half of the benefits could be included in income.[76] Since 1993, however,

---

[69]Retirement plans are discussed in Chapter 4.

[70]§74.

[71]A limited exception for employee length of service and safety awards is discussed in Chapter 4.

[72]Regulation §1.61-14(a).

[73]*Maginnis*, 89 AFTR 2d 2002-3028. The sale of the right to receive future payments of ordinary income is taxed as ordinary income, not as capital gain.

[74]Rev. Rul. 71-425, 1971-2 CB 76.

[75]§85. The American Recovery and Reinvestment Tax Act of 2009 provided a temporary exception that excluded from income the first $2,400 of unemployment benefits received in 2009. The exclusion for $2,400 of unemployment benefits was not extended beyond 2009.

[76]Because the employer's half of the contributions to the system had never been subject to federal income tax, it was decided that beneficiaries should pay a federal income tax on up to that half of the Social Security benefits received.

as much as 85 percent of an individual's Social Security benefits received may be included in income. Eighty-five percent of total payments represents the untaxed employer contributions and the income on those contributions. The 15 percent that escapes taxation represents the employee contributions that have already been taxed.[77]

The government devised a plan that taxes up to 85 percent of the benefits of taxpayers who have significant other income while leaving Social Security benefits completely tax free for those taxpayers who have little or no other income. To ensure that untaxed economic income is considered in determining the individual's ability to pay tax on their Social Security benefits, tax-exempt interest income along with one-half of Social Security benefits are added to the taxpayer's other adjusted gross income (for purposes of this test only).[78] This modified adjusted gross income is then compared with fixed base amounts established by Congress as follows:

- Single individuals with less than $25,000 and married couples with less than $32,000 of modified adjusted gross income are not taxed on any of their Social Security benefits.
- Single individuals with modified adjusted gross income between $25,000 and $34,000 and married couples with between $32,000 and $44,000 may be taxed on up to 50 percent of their benefits.[79]
- Single individuals with more than $34,000 and married couples with more than $44,000 of modified adjusted gross income may be taxed on up to 85 percent of their benefits.[80]

EXAMPLE 28

Silvia, a single individual, receives $17,000 of dividend income, $40,000 of interest income from tax-exempt bonds, and Social Security benefits of $15,000 in the current year. Because of the magnitude of her modified adjusted gross income (which includes her tax-exempt interest income), 85 percent of Silvia's benefits are taxable. Thus, $12,750 ($15,000 × 85%) of Silvia's Social Security benefits must be included in her gross income along with her dividend income. (Her interest income from tax-exempt bonds is excluded from her gross income, however.) Silvia's brother, John, also receives Social Security benefits of $15,000, but he has no additional income. John can exclude all of his Social Security benefits from his gross income and pays no income tax.[81]

MILITARY BENEFITS Members of the Armed Forces receive many different types of pay and allowances. Basic pay, most bonuses, and incentive pay must be included in gross income. Many allowances, however, are excluded. The following is a list of the most common exclusions:

- Combat zone pay
- Living allowances (such as a basic allowance for housing, basic allowance for subsistence, and overseas housing allowance)
- Moving allowances (such as military base realignment and closure benefits, storage, and temporary lodging)
- Travel allowances (such as an annual round trip for dependent students, leave between consecutive overseas tours, and per diems)

---

[77]The 85 percent and 15 percent were actuarially determined.

[78]§86. Modified adjusted gross income also includes any foreign earned income exclusion (discussed in Chapter 4) and interest from qualified U.S. savings bonds.

[79]The taxable portion of Social Security is equal to the lesser of (1) 50 percent of Social Security benefits or (2) 50 percent of the amount that modified adjusted gross income exceeds the base amount of $25,000 if single or $32,000 if married filing jointly.

[80]The taxable portion of Social Security is equal to the lesser of (1) 85 percent of Social Security benefits or (2) the sum of 85 percent of the amount that modified adjusted gross income exceeds the base amount ($34,000 single or $44,000 married), plus the smaller of Social Security included in income under the 50 percent formula (see previous footnote) or a fixed amount ($4,500 if single or $6,000 if married filing jointly).

[81]IRS Publication 915 contains filled-in worksheets showing the details of the complex calculations for taxpayers with modified adjusted gross income in between those shown in this example. This publication can be downloaded from the IRS Web site at *www.irs.gov*.

- Family allowances (such as educational expenses for dependents, for emergencies, and evacuation to a place of safety)
- Death allowances (including burial services and travel of dependents to burial site)
- Uniform allowances
- Disability payments

Legal Settlements

Legal settlements must be included in taxable income unless a provision in the tax law specifically excludes them. Awards for lost business income are taxable income because they are substitutes for income that would be taxable. Similarly, awards for injury to reputation are taxable. Recoveries for damages to property are also included in income to the extent they exceed the property's basis because property damage recoveries are treated as if they are proceeds from the sale of the property.

Damage Payments for Physical Injuries Compensatory damages paid for physical injuries to an individual's person are excluded from gross income.[82] The underlying theory is that a compensatory damage recovery is a tax-free return of human capital under the cost recovery principle. Punitive damages are awarded to the victim to punish the party who caused the harm. They must be included in income because punitive damages may improve the victim's pre-injury economic situation. Damages awarded for emotional distress are not considered received for physical injury and are included in gross income (except for any amount paid for medical care).

Example 29

Albert, an attorney operating as a sole proprietor, represented Eddie's ex-wife in a dispute that resulted in a $1,000,000 award against Eddie. Eddie goes to Albert's office and slanders Albert in front of several of Albert's important clients. Then he throws an ashtray at Albert, hitting him in the head. Albert sustains a large gash on his forehead that requires treatment at the hospital emergency room. In an out-of-court settlement, Albert receives $4,000 for his physical injury, $1,800 for emotional distress, and $4,800 for lost income due to damage to his business reputation. Albert paid $3,100 in medical expenses for the treatment of the wound but was able to recover from his emotional distress without medical care. The $4,000 for physical injury is excluded, but the $1,800 is included in gross income as it relates to a nonphysical injury. The $4,800 is taxable because it is a substitute for business income.

Payments received from a state-sponsored workers' compensation plan for an occupational injury are also exempt from tax.[83]

Divorce Married couples who divorce or separate usually enter into legal agreements affecting the financial aspects of breaking up the family unit. Common financial arrangements include property settlements, alimony, and child support payments. The tax implications for each of these arrangements differ. A property settlement divides the assets of divorcing spouses between them. This division of marital property is generally a nontaxable event.[84] Neither party recognizes gross income, and neither is entitled to a deduction. Property received in the settlement takes the same tax basis as the property had before the settlement.[85]

TAX PLANNING

Property settlements should take into consideration the after-tax value of an asset, not just its fair market value. For example, assume a taxpayer has a choice between receiving $100,000 cash or $110,000 in stock that has a cost basis of $10,000. Assuming a 15 percent capital gains rate, the $110,000 in stock has an inherent tax cost of $15,000 [($110,000 – $10,000) × 15%] so the after-tax value is only $95,000 ($110,000 - $15,000 tax due upon sale).

[82] § 104(a)(2).

[83] § 104(a)(1).

[84] For income tax purposes, this is treated as a nontaxable gift. Additionally, this transfer is not subject to gift tax.

[85] § 1041.

Alimony is a cash transfer from one former spouse to the other for support.[86] The recipient includes alimony in gross income.[87] The individual who pays the alimony is allowed a deduction for the amount that is included in the recipient's gross income to prevent double taxation of the income.[88] In essence, alimony is a legal shifting of taxable income between former spouses. To qualify as alimony, the payment must be made in cash, according to a divorce or written separation agreement, and the payor's obligation to make payment must terminate at the recipient's death.[89]

Child support is an amount paid for the support of the children of divorced or separated parents. Generally, the noncustodial parent pays child support to the custodial parent. Child support does not result in gross income to the recipient parent because the funds are intended to provide for the children's support. Similarly, no deduction is allowed the payor because that parent is fulfilling a legal obligation to care for his or her children.

EXAMPLE 30

Kathy and Mark divorce after 12 years of marriage. Under the divorce decree, Kathy receives investment land that had been held jointly while they were married. The land was acquired 9 years ago for $100,000 but is worth $180,000 today. Kathy also receives $18,000 cash in return for her half-interest in some stock they owned jointly. The stock was purchased 8 years ago for $50,000. Additionally, Mark is required to pay Kathy $1,800 per month; $1,000 is for alimony and $800 is for child support for their five-year-old daughter who lives with Kathy.

Mark recognizes no gross income from transferring his half-interest in the land to Kathy. If Kathy later sells the land for $180,000, she will recognize the entire $80,000 gain in her gross income at that time. Kathy is not allowed to deduct any loss on the transfer of stock to Mark. If Mark later sells the stock for $40,000, he will be entitled to deduct the entire $10,000 loss. Kathy includes $1,000 per month in her gross income for the alimony and Mark deducts the same amount in determining his adjusted gross income. The child support is neither taxable nor deductible.

TAX PLANNING

The person making periodic payments prefers to have them classified as alimony so they will be deductible; the recipient, however, does not want the payments to be classified as alimony, but rather as child support, so they are tax free. If the person paying the alimony is in a higher marginal tax bracket than the recipient, both parties may benefit by negotiating an increased payment if that amount will qualify as alimony.

EXAMPLE 31

Roberto and Miriam are negotiating a divorce settlement. Roberto is in the 39.6 percent marginal tax bracket and Miriam is in the 15 percent marginal tax bracket. Roberto has offered to pay Miriam $11,000 each year for 10 years, with payments ceasing if Miriam dies before the end of the 10-year period. Miriam is willing to settle for that amount only if the payments are a tax free property settlement because she needs at least $11,000 after tax to meet her expenses. Roberto's accountant suggests an alternative in which Roberto will pay Miriam $13,500 alimony each year. This compromise improves the after-tax cash flow for both parties.

	ROBERTO	MIRIAM
Original property settlement offer	($11,000)	$11,000
Revised alimony payment	($13,500)	$13,500
Tax savings @ 39.6%	5,346	
Tax @ 15%		(2,025)
After-tax cash flow	($8,154)	$11,475
Benefit from alimony alternative	$2,846	$475

[86]§71(b)(1). Payments will only be classified as alimony if the payments do not continue after death of the recipient, the payor and recipient are not members of the same household, and the divorce decree does not specify that the payments are not alimony.

[87]§71.

[88]§215.

[89]§71(b).

Some divorce agreements provide for large payments in the early post-separation years that level off in later years. These large up-front payments resemble property settlements even though the agreement might refer to them as alimony. The tax law treats the excess portion of large payments in the first two years as property settlements, regardless of what they are called. To prevent large alimony payments from being reclassified as nondeductible property settlements, alimony payments during the first three years should not decrease by more than $15,000 between years.

TAX PLANNING

Discharge of Indebtedness

No gross income is recognized when a taxpayer borrows money. The increase in cash is offset by an increased liability. Similarly, there is no income when the debt is repaid. If a taxpayer repays a debt with appreciated property, however, the taxpayer realizes a taxable gain as if the property had been sold for its fair market value and the debt repaid with the sale proceeds.[90]

EXAMPLE 32

Davila Corporation owes a creditor $70,000. Davila transfers investment land to the creditor to satisfy the debt. Davila purchased the land five years ago for $50,000, but it is currently worth $70,000. Davila must report a taxable gain of $20,000 ($70,000 – $50,000). It is treated as if Davila sold the land for $70,000 using the proceeds to repay the debt.

Creditors sometimes forgive debt for many different reasons. Foreclosing could leave the creditor with property that it cannot manage or sell; collecting the amount owed is difficult or expensive; or demanding payment may create a negative public image. If a taxpayer can satisfy a legal obligation for an amount less than the outstanding debt, the amount of debt that the creditor forgives represents an increase in the taxpayer's wealth and must be included in gross income.[91]

EXAMPLE 33

Jessica borrowed $100,000 from her bank to begin a business. She agreed to make monthly payments for 12 years. The interest on the note was 5%. Several years later, when the principal balance had been reduced to $60,000 through monthly payments, the bank offers to accept $58,000 in full settlement of the note because interest rates increased to 10%. If Jessica accepts the bank's offer, she will recognize $2,000 ($60,000 - $58,000) of gross income.

Exceptions are provided for debtors in some situations, particularly if hardship is involved. For example, bankrupt and insolvent taxpayers whose debts are forgiven do not recognize gross income. Instead, they must reduce tax attributes, including basis in the property, for the debt forgiven.[92] The reduction in tax attributes, in many cases, defers the tax liability for the forgiven debt to some future tax year.

To address the subprime lending crisis, the Mortgage Forgiveness Debt Relief Act of 2007 provided relief for homeowners whose mortgage debts were forgiven. For home mortgage debts discharged from 2007 through 2009, gross income did not include forgiveness of up to $2 million of qualified debt on a principal residence. This provision was extended through 2013 for debt forgiven on the homeowner's principal residence. The basis of the residence is reduced (but not below zero) by the amount excluded under this provision.

This exclusion also applies to mortgage debt reduced through restructuring (known as a mortgage workout) as well as a short sale or deed-in-lieu-of foreclosure

---

[90]*Kenan v. Comm.*, 25 AFTR 607, 40-2 USTC ¶9635, 114 F.2d 217 (CA-2, 1940). Generally, loss would also be recognized on depreciated property unless it was a personal-use asset or the transfer is between related parties.

[91]§ 108.

[92]§§ 108(a) and (b). The Katrina Emergency Tax Relief Act of 2005 allows individuals who suffered damage due to Hurricane Katrina to reduce tax attributes instead of recognizing income from a discharge of nonbusiness bad debt. These tax attributes include net operating losses, general business credits, capital losses, adjusted bases of properties, suspended passive activity losses and credits, and foreign tax credits.

as long as the debt qualifies as acquisition debt on the taxpayer's principal residence. If, however, a taxpayer sells property for less than the mortgage that secures it, but that property is *not* his or her principal residence, the lender will usually issue a Form 1099-C, *Cancellation of Debt* to the taxpayer for the amount of the unpaid debt that is discharged as part of the sale.

Some student loans have a provision that the loan will be forgiven if the student works in a certain profession upon completion of his or her education. The amount of the student loan forgiven under these conditions is excluded from gross income.[93]

Tax Benefit Rule

If a taxpayer claims a deduction for an item in one year and in a later year recovers all or part of the amount previously deducted, the recovery is included in income in the year received. Under Section 111, the amount that must be included in income is limited to the extent of tax benefit received from the tax deduction.

Example 34

Mayor Corporation, an accrual-basis, calendar-year taxpayer, sold $8,000 of its product on account to Ted in December, year 1. In year 2, Ted declares bankruptcy, so Mayor takes a bad-debt deduction in year 2 for the $8,000. In year 3, Ted wins a lottery and repays some of his previous debts, including $5,000 to Mayor. Because Mayor took a bad-debt deduction in year 2, the tax benefit rule requires it to include the $5,000 in income in year 3. Note that Mayor does not change its prior year's tax return.

Medicare Surtax on Net Investment Income

Starting in 2013, the Patient Protection and Affordable Care Act (PPACA) requires taxpayers to pay one of two potential Medicare surtaxes on specific types of income if certain income thresholds are exceeded. The thresholds are $200,000 for single individuals (and heads of household), $250,000 for married taxpayers filing a joint return, and $125,000 for married taxpayers filing separately. The Medicare surtax rates and the type of income to which each applies are:

- 3.8 percent on net investment income (NII)
- 0.9 percent on wages and other taxable compensation

It is important to note that the additional 3.8 percent NII surtax and 0.9 percent surtax on wages are mutually exclusive; that is, they do not apply to the same types of income; thus, income can only be subject to one or the other of the Medicare surtaxes, but not both. The 0.9 percent additional Medicare surtax applies only to earned income such as wages, salaries, self-employment income, and other taxable compensation and is discussed in Chapter 4.

Investment income is broadly defined to include dividends, interest, capital gains (whether long-term or short-term), and royalties, as well as rental income and profits from a passive investment such as limited partnership interest. Although investment income does not include income from a business (such as a partnership or S corporation) in which the taxpayer is actively involved, business owners could be affected if they are considered passive investors such as limited partners (as discussed in Chapter 10). Some common types of income that are not considered investment income for this tax include: operating income from a non-passive business, unemployment compensation, social security benefits, alimony, and tax-exempt interest income.

Investment income is reduced by investment expenses to get net investment income (NII). Examples of common investment expenses include investment interest expense, investment advisory and brokerage fees, expenses related to rental and royalty income, and state and local income taxes allocated to investment income. This tax is based on the lesser of NII or modified adjusted gross income in excess of the threshold. This is discussed further in Chapter 11.

[93] § 108(f)

EXAMPLE 35

Andrew, a single individual has salary income of $175,000, $5,000 dividend income, and $19,000 net long-term capital gains. Andrew's modified adjusted gross income is less than the $200,000 threshold so he is not subject to the Medicare surtax on net investment income.

Lenora, a single individual, has $190,000 of salary income and also received $5,000 dividend income, $20,000 interest income from corporate bonds, $10,000 interest income from tax-exempt municipal bonds, and $60,000 net long-term capital gains. Lenora's modified adjusted gross income is $275,000 which exceeds the threshold of $200,000 by $75,000. Lenora's NII tax is based on the lesser of $75,000 (the excess income over the $200,000 threshold) or $85,000 (net investment income). Lenora owes Medicare NII tax of $2,850 ($75,000 x 3.8%).

When this NII Medicare surtax is added to the maximum income tax or capital gains tax rates, the effective combined rate for many higher-income taxpayers becomes 23.8 percent for long-term capital gains and dividend income, and 43.4 percent for short-term capital gains and interest income as illustrated in Table 3.3.

System for Reporting Income

Employers, banks, and other entities that make income payments (for example, salaries, interest, and dividends) are required to report the payments they make to the recipients along with the payee's identification number (social security number for individuals). The IRS then matches much of this reported information with the payees' tax returns to ensure that income is properly reported. Some of the principal reporting forms are listed in Table 3.4.

EXCLUSIONS

For various social, economic, and political reasons certain income items are excluded from gross income and, thus, are not subject to federal income tax.

Gifts and Inheritances

Since its inception in 1913, the tax law has excluded gifts of property from the donee's gross income.[94] A **gift** is a voluntary property transfer from one party to

TABLE 3.3 **COMBINED INCOME AND SURTAX RATES FOR INDIVIDUAL INCOMES ABOVE $400,000 SINGLE AND $450,000 JOINT RETURNS**

	INCOME FROM INTEREST, RENTS, AND PASSIVE INVESTMENTS	SHORT-TERM CAPITAL GAINS	LONG-TERM CAPITAL GAINS	DIVIDEND INCOME
2013 Maximum Income Tax Rate	39.6%	39.6%	20.0%	20.0%
NII Medicare Surtax Rate	3.8%	3.8%	3.8%	3.8%
2013 Combined Maximum Rates	43.4%	43.4%	23.8%	23.8%

[94] § 102(a). If the value of gifts received by a U.S. person from a nonresident alien or foreign estate exceeds $100,000 (or $15,102 from a foreign corporation or partnership in 2013), the U.S. person must report each foreign gift to the IRS. §6039F(a).

TABLE
3.4 FORMS REPORTING PAYMENTS

FORM	TYPE OF PAYMENT
W-2	Salaries and wages
W-2G	Gambling winnings
1099-B	Sale of a security
1099-C	Cancellation of debt
1099-DIV	Dividends
1099-G	Government payments including unemployment compensation and tax refunds
1099-INT	Interest
1099-MISC	Miscellaneous income include nonemployee compensation and royalties
1099-OID	Original issue discount
1099-R	Distributions from retirement plans

another without full and adequate consideration received in return. Whether a transfer of property is intended to be a gift or compensation by the donor depends on all the facts and circumstances.[95] The absence of legal or moral obligation or the fact that the donee does not expect to receive anything do not necessarily mean that the property received is a gift.

EXAMPLE 36

John owns a plumbing business. Stan is an electrical contractor. John knows Stan does excellent electrical work, and when any of his customers needs an electrician, John always refers them to Stan. John believes he only enhances his own reputation by referring his clients to another reputable service person. During the last year, almost one-quarter of Stan's business came from referrals from John. As a result, he sent John a Rolex watch valued at $4,000. John must include the value of the watch in income. The watch does not meet the gift requirement of proceeding from "detached and disinterested generosity" made "out of affection, respect, admiration, charity, or like impulses."[96]

Cash and other property that an employer gives to an employee are usually considered compensation, not a gift.[97] However, a transfer that clearly has no direct connection to the employment relationship, such as a wedding gift, may be treated as a gift.[98]

TAX PLANNING

Stocks, bonds, and other investment instruments given to family members in lower tax brackets allow future earnings such as dividends and interest to be taxed at lower rates. Additionally, any gain on sale or other disposition of such properties is taxable to the donee, even if all or a portion of the gain accumulated while the donor possessed the asset.

[95] Although the recipient of a gift can exclude an unlimited amount of gifts from taxable income that does not mean that there are no tax consequences from making a gift. The donor (the person who made the gift) may be subject to a transfer tax on gifts in excess of $14,000. The federal gift tax is discussed in Chapter 12.

[96] *Comm. v. Duberstein*, 363 US 278 (1960), 60-2 USTC ¶9515, 5 AFTR 2d 1626.

[97] § 102(c).

[98] Prop. Reg. § 1.102-1(f)(2).

EXAMPLE 37

Joseph gives his 24-year-old daughter, Sara, 400 shares of RapidGrowth stock. Joseph purchased the stock nine months ago at $30 per share. On the gift date, the stock is worth $40 per share. Joseph and Sara are in the 39.6 and 15 percent marginal tax brackets, respectively, When the Medicare surtax is included, Joseph's effective rate is 43.4 percent for short-term capital gains and 23.8% for dividend income. After the gift, RapidGrowth declares and pays a $100 cash dividend that is income to Sara because she now owns the stock. One month later, Sara sells her 400 shares for $45 per share. The entire $6,000 short-term capital gain [400 × ($45 – $30)] increases Sara's gross income. Thus, $6,100 of income is shifted from Joseph to Sara. The family tax savings from shifting the income is $1,728 ([$6,000 gain × (43.4% – 15%)] + [$100 dividend × (23.8% – 0%)]).

Inheritances are gifts taking place at a donor's death and are excluded from gross income.[99] As with gifts, any income an heir derives from the property after its receipt is gross income.[100] A bequest that is actually compensation for past or future services, however, must be included in gross income.[101]

EXAMPLE 38

Miguel dies and bequeaths $100,000 to his son, Mike. Miguel's will also specifies a payment of $9,000 to his attorney, Simon, for acting as the executor of his estate. If Simon fails to serve as executor, the will specifies that he forfeits all rights to the $9,000. Mike excludes his $100,000 inheritance. Simon, however, must include the $9,000 he receives as gross income because it represents compensation for services.

Insurance Proceeds

Life Insurance

Since 1913, life insurance proceeds paid because of the insured party's death have been excluded from the beneficiary's gross income.[102] Congress apparently saw little difference between inheritances and life insurance proceeds as both are received as a result of death.[103]

The proceeds are excluded from the beneficiaries' gross income, regardless of whether the policy was provided by the decedent's employer or purchased with the decedent's own funds.[104] If the beneficiaries receive the proceeds over time in installments, the interest element in each installment is taxable.[105] The amount excluded from each installment (nontaxable amount) is determined by dividing the face value of the policy by the number of installments over which the payments will be received. Any amount received in excess of each installment's excluded amount is interest income and is fully taxable.

EXAMPLE 39

Peggy's husband dies this year and she is the sole beneficiary of a $200,000 life insurance policy. She has two options: (1) she can receive the entire $200,000 in one lump-sum payment or (2) she can receive annual installments of $24,000 for 10 years. If Peggy takes the lump-sum option, the entire $200,000 is

[99] § 102(a). While the receipt of inherited property is not subject to income tax, the receipt of income in respect of a decedent (IRD) is taxable. IRD is gross income that the decedent earned before death but was not includible in the decedent's final tax return. Examples include salary or interest earned by the decedent but not received before death and income from tax-deferred retirement accounts. The income tax on IRD is paid by the estate or the beneficiary receiving it. See Chapter 12 for details.

[100] § 102(b)(1).

[101] *Wolder v. Comm.*, 493 F.2d 608 (CA-2, 1974), 74-1 USTC ¶9266, 33 AFTR 2d 74-813.

[102] § 101(a).

[103] The owner of the insurance policy must have an insurable interest in the insured either through a personal or business relationship.

[104] § 101(a). However, proceeds paid because of death might be subject to federal or state estate tax. Estate taxes are discussed in Chapter 12.

[105] § 101(d). Beneficiaries generally may choose to receive the proceeds as annuities. The annuity rules are used to determine the taxable amount with the face value of the policy considered the invested capital.

excludable. If instead she elects the installment option, she must include $4,000 [$24,000 – ($200,000/10)] as interest in gross income each year.

Many businesses insure their officers and managers with the business as the beneficiary to protect against business disruption if an essential person dies. When the insured employee dies and the business receives the life insurance proceeds, the payment is not taxable income but is recorded as revenue for financial statement purposes.[106]

Some life insurance policies provide not only proceeds upon death but also have an investment element called the *cash surrender value.* The cash surrender value increases every year that the policy remains in effect; the annual increase in value is called the *inside buildup.* This inside buildup is not considered taxable income unless the taxpayer decides to liquidate the policy for its cash surrender value. If the owner of the policy decides that the life insurance is no longer needed and cashes in the policy for its cash surrender value, the excess of cash surrender value over the total premiums paid is taxed as ordinary income.[107]

EXAMPLE 40

Gary purchased an insurance policy on his own life that provided a $500,000 death benefit payable to his wife. After divorcing his wife, Gary decided to liquidate the policy for its $56,000 cash surrender value. He paid $40,000 in premiums for this policy. Gary has $16,000 ($56,000 – $40,000) in ordinary income from surrendering the policy.

TAX PLANNING

Many taxpayers view life insurance as a good investment due to the dual benefits of tax deferral on the inside buildup while providing for beneficiaries in the event of premature death. By borrowing against the policy's cash surrender value, the owner can receive the policy's increase in value in cash without recognizing income.

Owners of closely held businesses often enter into **buy–sell agreements** to buy the shares (or the partnership interest) of another owner who dies. Without such advance planning, the surviving owners could find themselves doing business with the deceased owner's heirs, who may be undesirable as business associates. Even if the owners agree that surviving owners (or the business itself) will have the first opportunity to buy a deceased owner's interest, funds may not be available to make the purchase. One popular means of financing such buy–sell agreements is through life insurance. The swap of life insurance policies between shareholders or partners or the transfer of life insurance policies to a controlled corporation or a partnership are nontaxable exchanges.[108]

EXAMPLE 41

Maria and Martin each own half of a business worth $500,000. Both Maria and Martin would like to run the entire business if the other dies. Neither, however, has sufficient funds to buy the other's share upon his or her death. As one solution, Maria and Martin can enter into a buy–sell agreement funded through life insurance. Each can purchase a $250,000 policy on his or her own life, transfer the policy to the corporation, and agree to have the corporation redeem the decedent's shares. The collection of insurance proceeds upon either Maria's or Martin's death is not taxable.

---

[106]Premiums paid on life insurance policies for which the company is the beneficiary are not deductible because the proceeds are not taxable. This limitation is discussed in Chapter 5. The life insurance proceeds and premium payments result in permanent differences between tax and accounting income.

[107]§72(e)(2). There is an exception for certain terminally ill patients who receive accelerated death benefits. Accelerated death benefits include the proceeds from the assignment or sale of life insurance to a viatical settlement provider (a company licensed to be in the business of purchasing life insurance from the terminally ill). §101(g).

[108]The transfer of a life insurance policy for valuable consideration, such as the payment of a loan, makes the life insurance proceeds in excess of basis (the amount paid, plus any additional premiums paid by the transferee) taxable upon the death of the insured.

Accident and Health Insurance

Health and accident insurance benefits received by individuals for themselves, their spouses, or their dependents are excluded from gross income to the extent they pay or reimburse for qualified medical or dental expenses.[109] Congress wants to encourage this type of insurance coverage so individuals do not look to the government for assistance when they are sick or injured. It is irrelevant whether an employer or employee pays the cost of this coverage.[110] If the employee receives benefits in excess of qualified medical or dental expenses, however, and the benefit is employer provided, all excess benefits are taxable to the employee. If the employee pays part of the cost of the insurance, a ratable portion of the excess payments equivalent to the employee contribution is excluded from income.[111]

Disability insurance, for which many individuals pay part or the entire premium, provides income if an individual cannot work because of a serious illness or injury. If the employer pays the premiums for disability insurance to replace the employee's lost income, all payments collected are fully taxable because they are a substitute for income from the employer. If, however, the employee pays for the disability insurance, none of the payments collected are taxable. If the employer and employee share the costs, a ratable portion equivalent to the employer contribution is gross income to the employee.

EXAMPLE 42

Jessica's employer pays for 60 percent of the premiums for a disability insurance policy and Jessica pays the other 40 percent. The policy pays Jessica 70 percent of her normal salary in the event she is injured and cannot return to work for an extended period. Jessica severely injures her back and is unable to work for several months. During the current year, Jessica collects \$20,000 under her disability policy. Jessica must include \$12,000 (\$20,000 × 60%) in gross income for the portion paid for by her employer; she can exclude the other \$8,000 (\$20,000 × 40%) that represents the portion of the policy for which she pays.

Benefits paid for the permanent loss (or loss of use) of a bodily function or body part by an individual are excluded. Similarly, benefits collected by an individual because of injury or sickness that result in permanent disfigurement are excluded.[112]

Scholarships

Scholarships are amounts paid to enable individuals to pursue research or study. Congress encourages education by making these funds tax free. Scholarships, fellowships, and need-based grants, such as Pell grants, are usually excluded from gross income when (1) the recipient is a candidate for a degree, (2) the amount received is not a payment for services, and (3) the amount received is used to pay for tuition, books, and other similar educational expenses.[113] Personal living expenses (such as lodging, meals, and laundry), are not qualified expenses and any portion of the scholarship funds designated for them cannot be excluded from gross income. This limitation provides equity with nonstudents who are effectively taxed on income they spend for personal living expenses. Similarly, if excess scholarship funds are used to pay nonqualified expenses, the amounts used for nonqualified expenses must be included in gross income.[114]

---

[109] Medical expenses are discussed in Chapter 11.

[110] Excluded benefits from long-term care insurance are limited to the greater of \$320 (in 2013) per day or the actual cost of care, whether the employer or employee pays the premiums. The limit was \$310 for 2012.

[111] Reg. §§1.105-1(c), (d), (e).

[112] §105(c).

[113] §117. Payments for books, supplies, and equipment are tax free only if they are required for all students in the course.

[114] Funds that are included in gross income are treated as earned income, and may increase a student's standard deduction. Prop. Reg. §1.117-6(h).

Any grant received in return for past, present, or future services must be included in gross income.[115] Funds received by graduate assistants in return for teaching or research activities are taxable, even if all degree candidates are required to render similar services.[116]

EXAMPLE 43

Laura is awarded an $8,000 per year scholarship to attend the state university. For the current year, Laura spends $7,000 on tution and required textbooks and $1,000 for room and board. Laura also works part-time on campus and earns $6,000 which covers the rest of her room and board and other expenses. Laura must include in her gross income $1,000 from the scholarship spent for room and board and the $6,000 she earned from her part-time job.

Sometimes an academic year's scholarship payments are received in one taxable year, even though some of the expenses will not be incurred until the following taxable year. When this occurs, the nontaxable portion of the scholarship may not be known until the academic year has ended. This timing difficulty is resolved by keeping the transaction open and including any taxable portion of the scholarship in gross income for the taxable year in which the academic year ends.[117]

EXAMPLE 44

Marah receives a scholarship to attend the local university. The scholarship terms provide $10,000 for tuition, books, and related expenses for the academic year. Marah only spends $4,900 for tuition, books, and qualifying supplies from September through December of year 1 and $4,600 from January through April of year 2. She includes the $500 in excess of her qualified expenses in her gross income on her year-2 tax return.

Employees of nonprofit educational institutions are allowed to exclude tuition waivers from gross income.[118] This exclusion applies to the employee, the employee's spouse, and dependent children, but is usually limited to undergraduate tuition.[119] This and many other fringe benefits provided by employers are very important components of employee compensations packages and are discussed in detail in Chapter 4.

Other Exclusions

When a lease expires, the landlord regains control of the property, including any improvements made to the property by the tenant. Improvements made to leased property are excluded from the landlord's gross income unless the improvement is made in lieu of rent.[120] Effectively, the tax on the value of the improvements is deferred until the property is sold.

As a matter of public policy, Congress favors home ownership. To promote home ownership, Congress provides an exclusion of up to $250,000 of gain realized on the sale of a principal residence. If the taxpayers are married and file a joint return, the exclusion is increased to $500,000. Taxpayers must have owned and occupied the home as their principal residence for at least two years to qualify. This very beneficial provision is discussed in detail in Chapter 7.

---

[115]Students receiving athletic scholarships are usually viewed as "voluntarily" participating in sports without participation being a "requirement" for their scholarships; for this reason, athletic scholarships are usually viewed as tax free if they continue even if the student can no longer participate. Specific exclusions also apply for National Health Service Corps Scholarships and the Armed Forces Scholarship Program. See IRS Publication 970: *Tax Benefits for Education* for more details.

[116]Prop. Reg. §1.117-6(d)(2).

[117]Prop. Reg. §1.117-6(b)(2).

[118]§117(d).

[119]Graduate teaching and research assistants may qualify for exclusion of graduate tuition waivers. §117(d)(5).

[120]§109.

Jurisdictional Issues

Jurisdictional issues arise at both the state and the international level. Two principles are normally used to guide the determination of who will be taxed by a specific jurisdiction: the residency of the earning party (the residency principle) and the jurisdiction in which the income is earned (the source principle). Under the residency principle, if individuals or corporations meet a jurisdiction's rules for residency, then they will be subject to that jurisdiction's tax rules. Under the source principle, many jurisdictions also claim the right to tax nonresident individuals and corporations if they are earning income in that jurisdiction. Thus, the jurisdiction in which the activity producing the taxable event takes place claims the right to tax the income involved.

International Issues

Most countries follow the source principle with regard to foreign persons and corporations by taxing income earned within their borders but exclude income from activities taking place (sourced) in other countries. Most countries, however, apply the residency principle to resident citizens and corporations by claiming the right to tax their worldwide income. Individuals and corporations that are residents in one country, but earn income in another country, face the prospect of double taxation.

Example 45

Corporation A has its home office and one of its manufacturing facilities in Country X. It has a second manufacturing facility in Country Y and sells many of its products in Country Y. Under the residency principle, Country X claims the right to tax all of the profits from A's sales in both Countries X and Y. Under the source principle, Country Y claims the right to tax all the profits from the sales in Country Y.

Most countries address this issue of double taxation through tax treaties. A **tax treaty** is an agreement between two countries that explains how a taxpayer of one country is taxed when conducting business in the second country. The objective of the treaty is to minimize double taxation. Under a typical treaty, a corporation's income is taxed only by the country of residence unless the business maintains a permanent establishment (such as an office or factory) in the second country. If such a permanent establishment exists, the treaty allows the source country to tax income earned within its boundaries. The resident country then allows its citizens and corporations to offset the domestic tax on this foreign income with a foreign tax credit up to the amount of tax paid to the source country. The result is that the taxpayer who earned the income pays only one level of tax. The net tax paid will usually be the greater of the taxes imposed by the two countries claiming jurisdiction over the income.

Example 46

Continuing example 45, Corporation A also sells some of its products in Country Z through mail or Internet orders, but maintains no offices or manufacturing facilities in Country Z. Country X has typical tax treaties in force with Countries Y and Z. Country Y would tax the profits of sales made in Country Y only. Country Z would not tax any of the profits on sales in Country Z. Country X would tax the profits from A's sales in Countries X, Y, and Z, but Corporation A would be permitted to take a tax credit for taxes paid to Country Y up to the lesser of the actual taxes paid to Country Y or the taxes it paid on that income to Country X.

Taxpayers Subject to U.S. Taxation

United States citizens, resident aliens, and U.S. corporations are subject to U.S. tax on their worldwide income. A **resident alien** is an individual who is not a U.S. citizen but who has established a legal residence in the United States either by obtaining a permanent resident card (called a green card) or meeting the substantial presence test that requires residency in the United States for 183 days.[121] An individual who is not a U.S. citizen and does not satisfy the tests to be a resident alien is considered a **nonresident alien**.

Income earned by nonresident aliens and foreign corporations is divided into three categories: U.S. business income (called effectively connected income), non-U.S. business income, and U.S. investment income. Nonresident aliens and foreign corporations are taxed similar to U.S. citizens and U.S. corporations on their effectively connected business income (for example, from sales of goods manufactured in the United States or from personal services performed in the United States). Business income that is not effectively connected with the United States is usually not subject to U.S. tax. U.S. investment income includes interest, dividends, and royalties and is usually taxed at a flat 30 percent rate (or treaty rate if lower).

TAX PLANNING

When a nonresident alien is married to a U.S. citizen or resident alien, and they both have taxable income, they normally must file their tax returns as married persons filing separately. The nonresident alien can, however, elect to be taxed as a resident alien if both individuals agree to be taxed on their worldwide income and provide all information necessary to determine both spouses' tax liability.[122] This election permits a nonresident alien to file a joint tax return with his or her spouse to take advantage of the lower tax rates for joint returns.

A U.S. corporation can establish a presence in a foreign country by opening either a foreign branch or creating a foreign subsidiary. A branch is simply considered an extension of the U.S. firm. Its profits or losses are combined with the income and loss of the corporation's other business operations, and, if the branch is profitable, its income is subject to U.S. tax.

Alternatively, a U.S. corporation may establish a subsidiary to operate its foreign business. A **controlled foreign corporation (CFC)** is a corporation incorporated outside the United States that is more than 50 percent owned by U.S. shareholders. The U.S. parent corporation generally is not taxed on the earnings of the foreign subsidiary until the earnings are repatriated (brought back) to the United States as dividends. When the U.S. parent receives a dividend, the dividend is included in its income.[123] The parent is entitled to a foreign tax credit at this time based on the income tax paid by the foreign corporation. If the U.S. parent does not need cash from its overseas operations, it can direct its subsidiary to withhold dividends, and by doing so, the parent can postpone the payment of taxes. As long as the parent receives no repatriated earnings as dividends from the foreign corporation, the U.S. parent generally can avoid paying taxes on this income indefinitely.

EXAMPLE 47

Beagle Corporation (a U.S. corporation) forms Pup Corporation in a foreign country. Beagle owns 80% of Pup Corporation's stock and the remaining stock is owned by citizens of the country in which Pup is located. Pup Corporation earns $3 million of taxable income from its manufacturing operations and pays $600,000 in taxes to the foreign country in which it is located. Because Pup Corporation does not make any dividend distributions, Pup's $3 million is not subject to U.S. taxes. When the earnings are repatriated, Beagle Corporation will be able to claim a foreign tax credit for the taxes Pup paid to the foreign country on the income it recognizes.

---

[121]§7701(b). The substantial presence test requires presence in the United States for 31 or more days during the current calendar year and presence in the United States for a total of 183 or more days during the current tax year and the two preceding tax years when using a weighted-average calculation. This calculation counts each day in the current year as one, each day in the immediately preceding year as one-third, and each day in the year before that as one-sixth. Some individuals are exempt from this substantial presence test including diplomats, teachers, students, and certain professional athletes.

[122]§6013(g). A social security number (SSN) must be furnished on all tax returns. If an individual is not eligible to get a SSN, then he or she must apply for an individual taxpayer identification number.

[123]Dividends received from domestic corporations are eligible for the dividend received deduction so that only a portion of the dividend income is subject to U.S. tax (see Chapter 9). Dividends from a foreign corporation are not eligible for the dividend received deduction and this can result in double taxation.

Certain foreign source income earned by a CFC does not have to be repatriated to its U.S. shareholders to be taxed, however. A type of income (called **Subpart F income**) is treated as a constructive dividend and taxed even if it is not paid to the parent. Subpart F income is taxed when earned similar to the way earnings of a flow-through entity (a partnership or S corporation) are taxed. Subpart F income consists of interest, dividends, rents, royalties, and foreign base company income.[124] Because the parent is taxed on the Subpart F income when it is earned, the parent is not taxed a second time when the subsidiary pays a dividend.

State and Local Taxation

Jurisdictional issues arise not only in international taxation but at the state level as well. Most states (and some local governments) impose both corporate and personal (individual) income taxes on both residents and nonresidents.[125] States can generally tax nonresidents only on income derived from business activity within that state or income from property located in that state.

Example 48

When Alex Rodriguez, the former Texas Rangers shortstop, lived in Texas (a state with no individual income tax), he owed more than $271,000 to California (which assesses a nonresident income tax) for games he played in that state during baseball season. It was estimated that if the Rangers had played all their games at home, A-Rod's state tax bill could have been reduced by more than half a million dollars a year.[126] When A-Rod switched to the New York Yankees, his state and local tax burden increased dramatically. On the $155 million that A-Rod was to be paid over his seven-year contract, he was expected to owe $3.57 million to New York City and an additional $6.19 million to the State of New York for income taxes.[127] His tax burden increased further when he renegotiated his contract in a deal worth $275 million over ten years.

If a resident of one state derives income from another state, double taxation can result. To minimize this, states that charge an income tax usually allow their residents to claim a credit for some or all of the income taxes paid to other states.

The state in which a corporation is organized has the right to impose an income tax on that corporation (the residency principle). Additionally, whenever a business has an economic connection, such as deriving income from assets or activities located in a state, the state has the right to tax the business (the source principle). The type and degree of connection between a business and a state necessary for the state to have the right to impose a tax is referred to as **nexus**.

Example 49

Corian Corporation manufactures equipment for sale nationwide. Corian's corporate headquarters and production facilities are located in Florida. Corian has regional sales offices in New York, Illinois, and California. Corian has nexus in Florida, New York, Illinois, and California due to the presence of employees and business property in those states.

[124]The definition of foreign base company income is very complex and beyond this introductory discussion.

[125]States that do not impose some type of corporate income tax or some form of business tax are Nevada, South Dakota, and Wyoming. Alaska, Florida, Nevada, South Dakota, Texas, Washington, and Wyoming do not impose individual income taxes. Additionally, some states only tax certain types of interest and dividend income.

[126]Mark Hyman, "Why the 'Jock Tax' Doesn't Play Fair," *Business Week*, July 7, 2003, p. 37.

[127]Dan Kadison, "$10M is Ballpark for Taxman," *The New York Post*, February 17, 2004, p. 4.

Although some double taxation may be unavoidable when engaging in multi-jurisdictional transactions, minimizing this double taxation is the key tax-planning goal. Multi-state businesses may be able to reduce their overall tax cost by shifting income from a high-tax state to a low-tax state. This is discussed further in Appendix 9B (Chapter 9).

For federal tax purposes, state income tax is deductible in computing taxable income.[128] The tax savings from this deduction reduce the cost of the state tax.

EXAMPLE 50

Carson Corporation paid $20,000 in state income tax this year. If its federal tax rate is 35 percent, the after-tax cost of its state income tax payment is only $13,000 [($20,000 – ($20,000 × 35%)].

When a taxpayer must pay income tax at both the federal and state level, it increases the total effective tax rate and decreases the after-tax cash flow.

EXAMPLE 51

Yanney Corporation has before-tax income of $500,000 and is subject to a state income tax of 6 percent. Yanney's total effective tax rate for the current year is 37.96 percent, computed as follows:

State income tax ($500,000 × 6%)	$30,000
Federal income tax [($500,000 – $30,000) × 34%]	159,800
Total income tax	$189,800

$189,800/$500,000 income = 37.96%
Yanney's after-tax cash flow = $310,200 ($500,000 – $189,800).

EXPANDED TOPICS—SPECIAL METHODS

Installment Method

The installment method of reporting gain on certain transactions is a taxpayer-friendly application of the wherewithal to pay concept. Under the **installment method**, gain is recognized as proceeds from the sale are received rather than recognizing the entire gain in the year of sale.[129] A transaction in which one or more payments are to be received in any tax year other than the year of sale may be eligible for installment sale treatment.[130]

EXAMPLE 52

Todd sells a parcel of land for $100,000 that he purchased 10 years ago for $40,000. Todd's long-term capital gain is $60,000 ($100,000 – $40,000). Todd is to receive the $100,000 at the rate of $25,000 per year for four years, plus interest on the unpaid balance. Because 60 percent of the principal payments that Todd will receive represent gain ($60,000 gain/$100,000 payments to be received), 60 percent of each payment is recognized as gain in the year it is received. Thus, each payment of $25,000 triggers recognition of $15,000 ($25,000 × 60%) gain. After all four payments are received, Todd will have recognized a total of $60,000 of gain.

If Todd is in the 28 percent marginal tax bracket with a 15 percent capital gains tax rate, the present value of his tax savings from using the installment method is $846 using a discount rate of 7 percent.

[128] State income taxes are an itemized deduction for individual taxpayers.

[129] The installment method is not available for a transaction in which a loss rather than a gain results.

[130] § 453(b)(1).

	YEAR OF SALE	YEAR 1	YEAR 2	YEAR 3	TOTAL
Regular Sale					
Gain	$60,000				
Tax rate	× 15%				
Tax	$9,000				$9,000
Installment Sale					
Gain	$15,000	$15,000	$15,000	$15,000	
Tax rate	× 15%	× 15%	× 15%	× 15%	
Tax	$2,250	$2,250	$2,250	$2,250	
Discount factor	× 1.0	× .935	× .873	× .816	
Discounted tax cost	$2,250	$2,104	$1,964	$1,836	8,154
Present value of tax savings					$846

The installment method also has a number of restrictions on its use and is generally available only for what might be termed casual sales by a taxpayer. It cannot be used by a taxpayer for the sale of (1) inventory,[131] (2) personal property regularly sold on the installment plan (revolving charge accounts),[132] (3) depreciable property between a taxpayer and a controlled entity,[133] (4) the sale of stock or securities traded on an established securities market,[134] and certain other transactions. The installment method cannot be used for financial accounting resulting in a difference between financial and taxable income.[135]

TAX PLANNING

If a transaction qualifies for installment reporting, the taxpayer must use the installment method unless the taxpayer elects not to use it.[136] A taxpayer might want to report the gain in the year of sale if the taxpayer's marginal tax rate is expected to increase in future years when the payments will be received. The taxpayer might also elect to accelerate the recognition of the gain if the taxpayer has unused net operating losses or if the gain involved is a capital gain and the taxpayer has unused capital losses. A taxpayer makes the election by reporting the entire gain in the year of sale.

Long-Term Contracts

A long-term contract is a contract for the manufacture, building, installation, or construction of property that will not be completed in the year the contract is executed.[137] Two methods are used to account for long-term contracts for tax purposes. Under the **completed contract method**, no income is recognized (and no deductions taken) until the contract is complete. Costs simply accumulate until completion of the contract. At that time, the gross contract price is included in income and all the related costs are deducted to determine the net income from the contract.[138] Under the **percentage-of completion method**, income is recognized each year the contract progresses.[139] The

[131]Exceptions exist for the sale of farm property, timeshares, and unimproved residential lots. §453(l)(2)(A), (B).

[132]§453(l)(1)(A).

[133]§453(g).

[134]§453(k)(2)(A).

[135]Financial accounting standards authorize the use of the installment method only for the sale of real property where the collectability of the payments is in doubt or other special conditions exist.

[136]§453(a), d(1). Any §1245 depreciation recapture must be recognized in year of sale.

[137]§460(f)(1). A manufacturing contract will only be considered long term if it is for an item that takes more than 12 months to complete or is a unique item not usually included in the taxpayer's finished goods inventory. §460(f)(2).

[138]Reg. §1.451-4(d)(1).

[139]Under a de minimis rule, if less than 10 percent of the estimated contract costs have been incurred by the end of the taxable year, a taxpayer using the percentage-of-completion method can elect to defer the recognition of income and the related costs until the tax year in which cumulative contract costs are at least 10 percent of estimated contract costs.§460(b)(5).

income recognized annually is based on an estimate of actual costs incurred to total projected costs for the contract. In the final year of the contract, a final calculation is made and any previously unrecognized income is recognized.[140]

EXAMPLE 53

Acme Construction begins construction in October of year 1 on a building that is to be completed in June of year 3. The contract price is $1,000,000 and Acme estimates its total costs at $860,000. Actual costs incurred are $215,000 in year 1, $387,000 in year 2, and $283,000 in year 3. Under the completed contract method, the $1,000,000 contract price is recognized as income and the total costs of $885,000 are deducted in year 3. No income is recognized and no costs deducted in years 1 or 2. Thus, the total gain of $115,000 on the contract is recognized in year 3, the year of completion.

Under the percentage-of-completion method, Acme recognizes the following:

Year 1: Income of $250,000 [($215,000/$860,000 = 25%) × $1,000,000] and costs of $215,000.

Year 2: The costs incurred of $602,000 ($215,000 + $387,000) out of a total cost of $860,000 indicate the project is 70 percent complete. Income of $450,000 ($700,000 - $250,000) is recognized along with costs of $387,000 ($602,000 - $215,000).

Year 3: The remaining $300,000 of the contract price is recognized and actual costs of $283,000 are deducted. The total profit recognized is $115,000 ($35,000 + $63,000 + $17,000), the same as under the completed contract method.

If Acme has a marginal tax rate of 34 percent and uses a 7 percent discount rate, the present value of its tax saving from using the completed contract method is $2,637.

	YEAR 1	YEAR 2	YEAR 3	TOTAL
Percentage-of-Completion Method				
Income	$250,000	$450,000	$300,000	
Deductible costs	(215,000)	(387,000)	(283,000)	
Taxable profit	$35,000	$63,000	$17,000	
Income tax @ 34%	$11,900	$21,420	$5,780	
Discount factor	× .935	× .873	× .816	
Discounted tax cost	$11,127	$18,700	$4,716	$34,543
Completed Contract Method				
Income	0	0	$1,000,000	
Deductible costs	0	0	(885,000)	
Taxable profit	0	0	($115,000)	
Income tax @ 34%	0	0	$39,100	
Discount factor			× .816	
Discounted tax cost			$31,906	$31,906
Present value of tax savings				$2,637

TAX PLANNING

Given the choice, taxpayers would prefer to use the completed contract method because it defers taxes and is simpler. It can, however, lead to a problem of bunching of income into a single tax year that could be a disadvantage because of the progressive tax rates. The use of the completed contract method is restricted, however, to certain construction contracts.[141]

[140] Reg. § 1.451-3(c).

[141] § 460(e). The completed contract method can only be used for certain home construction contracts and construction contracts that will be completed within a two-year period by a taxpayer whose average annual gross receipts do not exceed $10,000,000.

Revisiting the Introductory Case

The municipal bonds yield a higher after-tax return because the interest income earned on the municipal bonds is tax free and the interest earned on the corporate bonds is taxable. Because Steven is subject to the net investment income Medicare surtax, his effective tax rate is 43.4% (39.6 % + 3.8%) for interest income and 23.8% (20% + 3.8%) for long-capital gains. The investment land yields an even better return because the increase in value is not taxed until the end of five years when the land is sold. Additionally, the gain on the sale of land is taxed at a lower capital gains rate than the rate that applies to the interest income. Steven should invest in the land.

	Corporate Bonds	Tax-Exempt Bonds	Investment Land
Annual interest income			
\$50,000 × 6%	\$3,000		
\$50,000 × 4%		\$2,000	
Income tax @ 43.4%	(\$1,302)	0	
After-tax cash flow	\$1,698	\$2,000	
Reinvested for 5 years			
6% annuity factor	× 5.637		
4% annuity factor		× 5.416	
After-tax cash flow			
from interest for 5 years	\$9,572	\$10,832	
Original investment			
in land			\$50,000
6% factor			× 1.338
Land value in 5 years			\$66,900
Return of capital			(50,000)
Pre-tax gain			\$16,900
Tax on gain @ 23.8%			(4,022)
After tax-value	\$9,572	\$10,832	\$12,878

Summary

The Internal Revenue Code states that all forms of income are taxable unless specifically excluded. Congress has chosen to exclude certain items from income due to social, economic, and political reasons. A taxpayer can also use certain provisions to defer income recognition. The difference between the two is that excluded income is never taxed, while deferred income is taxed in some future period.

Several key principles govern the determination of gross income. The realization principle states that no income is recognized (included in gross income) until the taxpayer realizes it. Under the return of capital principle, a taxpayer's investment (basis) can be recovered tax free and is not included in gross income. The assignment of income doctrine prevents taxpayers who earn income or own property on which income is earned from shifting that income to a lower-income individual for taxation.

The period in which income is recognized is determined by the method of accounting. Cash-basis taxpayers generally recognize income when cash or a cash equivalent is received. Accrual-basis taxpayers generally recognize income when the earnings process is complete and the all-events test has been met. The constructive receipt doctrine modifies the cash method by requiring taxpayers to recognize income when it is set aside for them or otherwise made available to them. The claim of right doctrine requires accrual-basis taxpayers to recognize income when it is received as long as the taxpayer's use of the income is unrestricted, even if some or all of the income may have to be repaid at a later date. Because generally accepted accounting principles have different objectives than does tax reporting, income may be recognized in different periods for tax and financial accounting.

You should be able to determine gross income for the most frequently encountered situations and understand the situations over which taxpayers can control the timing or taxability of the income. The most common sources of income (other than property transactions) are salaries and wages, interest, dividends, annuities, and government transfer payments. Although interest and dividends are normally taxable, exceptions exist for state and local bonds and stock dividends. Only the part of an annuity that represents income rather than annuity investment is taxed. Government transfers that are in the form of welfare payments escape taxation, but federal unemployment insurance is fully taxable. Up to 85 percent of a taxpayer's Social Security payments may be taxed, depending on the amount and type of the taxpayer's income. As a matter of law, however, unless the taxpayer can find a specific provision that excludes an item of income from taxation, that item will be taxed.

KEY TERMS

Accrual method 104
Alimony 118
All events test 104
Annualized 101
Annuity 114
Assignment of income doctrine 105
Basis 98
Buy–sell agreement 124
Calendar year 100
Cash method 102
Child support 118
Claim of right doctrine 104
Completed contract method 131
Constructive receipt doctrine 102
Controlled foreign corporation (CFC) 128
Dividend 112
Fiscal year 100
Gift 121
Gross income 97
Hybrid method 103
Inheritance 123
Installment method 130
Municipal bonds 107
Nexus 129
Nonresident alien 128
Original issue discount (OID) 108
Percentage-of-completion method 131
Realization principle 97
Resident alien 127
Return of capital 98
Scholarship 125
Short tax year 101
Stock dividend 113
Subpart F income 129
Tax treaty 127
Taxable income 97
Wherewithal to pay 105

TEST YOURSELF

ANSWERS APPEAR AFTER THE PROBLEM ASSIGNMENTS

1. Jason receives semiannual annuity checks of $4,500. Jason purchased the annuity five years ago for $110,000 when his expected return under the annuity was $200,000. How much of Jason's total annual payment is a nontaxable return of capital?
   - **a.** $9,000
   - **b.** $4,950
   - **c.** $4,050
   - **d.** Zero
2. Kevin owes his gardener $100. After several unsuccessful attempts to collect the debt, the gardener notifies Kevin that the debt is forgiven and that he will continue as gardener only if he is paid in cash in advance. How much of the $100 forgiveness should Kevin report as gross income?
   - **a.** $100
   - **b.** $50
   - **c.** $20
   - **d.** $0

3. Elio (age 66) is retired. His wife, Mary (age 64) still works part-time. They have income from the following sources and plan to file a joint tax return.

Mary's salary	$10,000
Elio's retirement annuity (all contributions made by his employer)	15,000
Elio's Social Security benefits	5,000
Interest income from their municipality's general revenue bonds	1,000
Cash dividend from Ford Motor Company	500
Lottery prize	50

What is their gross income?

a. $31,550
b. $30,500
c. $25,550
d. $10,000

4. Cindy was awarded a $6,000 scholarship to attend the state university. She spent $4,000 for tuition, $500 for required textbooks, and $1,500 for room and board. She works part-time on campus earning $5,000 which covers the balance of her room and board and other expenses. How much of these amounts must Cindy include in her gross income?

a. $0
b. $5,000
c. $6,500
d. $7,000

5. Marcus sells a parcel of land that he has held for investment purposes. His basis in the land is $16,000 and the selling price is $20,000. Marcus is to receive the $20,000 at the rate of $5,000 per year for four years, plus interest on the unpaid balance. How much of each payment will be recognized as gain in the year received under the installment method?

a. $6,000
b. $4,000
c. $3,000
d. $1,000

PROBLEM ASSIGNMENTS

CHECK YOUR UNDERSTANDING

1. Michelle (a calendar-year individual) begins a new business as a sole proprietorship. She would like to use an October 31 fiscal year-end for her business because the calendar year ends during her busy season. Can Michelle use a fiscal tax year?

2. Jabba Company uses the cash method of accounting. Jabba received a computer from a customer as payment for a $2,000 bill. Can Jabba avoid recognizing income because it received payment in a noncash form? Explain.

3. Murphy Company, a cash-basis, calendar-year taxpayer, received a call on December 28, year 1, from a client stating that a check for $9,000 as payment in full for their services could be picked up at their offices, two blocks away, any weekday afternoon between 1:00 and 6:00 P.M. Murphy

does not pick up the check until January 3, year 2. In which year does Murphy recognize the income?

4. Are there any restrictions on which businesses can use the cash method of accounting? Explain.
5. Explain why accrual-method taxpayers treat prepaid income differently for GAAP and tax purposes.
6. Ryan's annual salary is $120,000 per year. He asked his employer to pay $20,000 of his salary to his elderly grandmother who is in a nursing home. The employer makes the $20,000 payment directly to the grandmother and pays the balance to Ryan. What is Ryan's gross income?
7. Virginia gives her 14-year-old grandson, Tommy, $10,000 in common stock. One month later, a $100 dividend is paid to Tommy on the stock. How much income is taxed to Tommy and how much is taxed to Virginia?
8. Why is interest income on state and local bonds tax-exempt?
9. In year 1, Lauderhill Corporation issues three-year bonds. Martha, a cash-basis taxpayer, purchased a $10,000 bond at its issue price of $7,000. In year 1, $840 of interest accrues. How much income does Martha report in year 1?
10. While walking through the park, Jane finds a $100 bill. No one is around to claim it, so she keeps it. Does Jane have any gross income as a result of this?
11. What is the rationale for taxing unemployment compensation?
12. Are the recipients of gifts and inheritances subject to double taxation?
13. What is a buy–sell agreement, and how does life insurance facilitate it?
14. Compare how the United States taxes a U.S. citizen and a nonresident alien.
15. What is the purpose of the United States establishing a tax treaty with a foreign country?
16. What is the purpose of the foreign tax credit?
17. What is nexus?
18. What is an installment sale? If a transaction qualifies for installment sale treatment, when will the taxpayer be taxed on the sale? What does a taxpayer do if the taxpayer does not want to use the installment method?
19. What is a long-term contract? Briefly describe the two possible accounting treatments for long-term contracts.

CRUNCH THE NUMBERS

20. Beta Corporation received permission to change its tax year from a calendar year to a year ending August 31. Its income for the eight months ending August 31 is $96,000. What is Beta Corporation's tax liability for its short tax year?
21. At the end of October, year 1, Specialty Training, an accrual-basis, calendar-year taxpayer, was hired by Dunbar Company to provide a six-week training program for its employees. Specialty was paid its full training fee of $30,000 on the first day of training. After five weeks of training sessions, Dunbar cancelled the last week of training and demanded a refund of $5,000 because its employees felt the training was misrepresented in that it did not provide the in-depth coverage of the topics they desired. In

January, year 2, Specialty refunded $5,000 to Dunbar. Specialty's marginal tax rate for year 1 is 34 percent.

a. What choices does Specialty Training have as to how to account for the $5,000 refund?

b. If Specialty's marginal tax rate in year 2 is 39 percent, how should the company account for the refund for tax purposes?

c. If Specialty's marginal tax rate in year 2 is 25 percent, how should the company account for the refund for tax purposes?

22. Realty Corporation, an accrual-basis, calendar-year corporation, agrees to rent office space to Tenant Company for $3,000 per month beginning on January 1, year 2. On December 15, year 1, Tenant gives Realty Corporation a $3,000 deposit in addition to rent for the months of January and February. In year 2, Tenant pays rent for the months of March and April. On May 15 Tenant closes its business and vacates the office. Realty withholds $1,500 from the deposit for unpaid rent and $1,000 for damages. Realty Corporation refunds the balance of the deposit to Tenant on May 20, year 2.

a. How much income should Realty Corporation report in year 1 from the above transactions for tax and financial accounting?

b. How much income should Realty Corporation report in year 2?

23. On December 1, year 1, Peak Advertising (a calendar-year, accrual-basis taxpayer) receives a $24,000 retainer fee for a two-year service contract.

a. How much income should Peak report in year 1 for tax and financial accounting?

b. How much income should Peak report in year 2 for tax and financial accounting?

c. How much income should Peak report in year 3 for tax and financial accounting?

24. Carl paid $40,000 to the City of Hollywood for general revenue bonds. During the current year, he receives $2,300 interest income from the bonds. Market interest rates drop, causing the value of the bonds to increase so Carl sells the bonds for $43,000. How much gross income must Carl report for the year?

25. Jessica has $10,000 invested in corporate bonds with a stated interest rate of 7 percent and $10,000 in tax-exempt municipal bonds issued for governmental activities with a stated interest rate of 7 percent. Calculate her after-tax cash flow from each investment if:

a. her marginal tax rate is 15 percent.

b. her marginal tax rate is 39.6 percent.

26. Joshua loans his son, Seth, $100,000 interest free for five years. Seth uses the money for a down payment on his home. Assume that the applicable federal rate of interest is 4 percent.

a. What are the tax consequences of this loan to Joshua and to Seth?

b. How would your answer change if Seth uses the money to invest in corporate bonds paying 8 percent annual interest?

27. Sheldon Corporation loans $80,000 interest free for one year to Lynn, an employee. Assume that the applicable federal rate of interest is 4 percent. Lynn uses the loan to pay for personal debts. What are the tax consequences of this loan to Sheldon and to Lynn? How would your answer change if Lynn is a shareholder of Sheldon Corporation?

28. George owns 1,000 shares of ABC common stock and 3,000 shares of Brightstar mutual fund. George elects to participate in Brightstar's dividend reinvestment plan, reinvesting his annual dividends and capital gains distributions in additional Brightstar shares. George receives a $5,000 distribution from ABC and a Form 1099-DIV indicating that $4,000 of the distribution is a dividend and $1,000 is a nontaxable distribution. He also receives a Form 1099-DIV from Brightstar mutual fund indicating that he has a dividend of $6,500 and a capital gains distribution of $1,300 for a gross distribution of $7,800 that is reinvested in 90 additional shares of Brightstar mutual fund. How much does George include in his gross income for the year?

29. The Board of Directors of CYZ Corporation votes to issue two shares of stock for each share held as a stock dividend to shareholders. Just prior to the dividend, Cheryl owns 100 shares of CYZ Corporation stock that she purchased for $10 per share. She receives 200 new shares as a result of the dividend. How much gross income must Cheryl report as a result of the dividend and what is the basis of her stock after the dividend?

30. Charles pays $120,000 for a single-life annuity that pays him $11,000 a year for life. Treasury Department tables estimate his remaining life to be 15 years.
    a. How much of each $11,000 payment must Charles report as gross income?
    b. If Charles dies after receiving annuity payments totaling $77,000 over seven years, what happens to the unrecovered cost?

31. Barney retired from the Marlin Corporation where he worked for 25 years. Barney elects to receive his retirement benefits as an annuity over his remaining life, resulting in annual payments of $15,000. His plan balance consists of $70,000 employer contributions, $20,000 after-tax employee contributions, $10,000 pretax employee contributions, and $22,000 investment earnings. Based on Barney's life expectancy, his expected return is $240,000. Of each $15,000 payment, how much must Barney report as gross income?

32. Julie wins $15 million in the lottery payable over 30 years. In years 1 through 4, she receives annual installments of $500,000. At the beginning of year 5, Julie sells her right to receive the remaining 26 payments to a third party for a lump-sum payment of $8,900,000. How much does Julie include in income each year?

33. Vera, a single individual, receives $18,000 of dividend income and $38,000 of interest income from tax-exempt bonds. Vera also receives Social Security benefits of $16,000. What is Vera's gross income?

34. Jeff, a single individual, receives $5,000 interest income from Treasury bills and $18,000 in Social Security benefits. What is Jeff's gross income?

35. Mike was shopping in Produce Market when it was robbed. Mike suffered some injuries during the robbery and filed suit against Produce Market for not maintaining a secure environment for its customers. In an out-of-court settlement, Mike receives $12,000 for his physical injuries, $2,000 for emotional distress, and $3,000 for lost wages while he recovered from his injuries. Mike paid $11,000 in medical expenses attributable to treatment for his injuries but was able to recover from his emotional distress without medical care. How much gross income does Mike have as a result of this settlement?

36. Stu and Harriett divorce on January 2 of the current year after eight years of marriage. Under the divorce decree, Harriett receives a vacation home that had been held jointly with Stu while they were married. The vacation home was acquired seven years ago for $90,000 but is worth $170,000 today. Additionally, Stu is required to pay Harriett $2,000 per month beginning in January; $1,300 is for alimony and $700 is for child support for their six-year-old son who lives with Harriett.

a. How much gross income does Harriett recognize in the current year?

b. Will Stu get a tax deduction for any of these payments?

37. Markum Corporation owes a creditor $60,000. Markum transfers property to the creditor to satisfy the debt. Markum purchased the property four years ago for $45,000 and it is currently worth $60,000. Does Markum have any gross income as a result of this transaction?

38. Sandle Corporation, an accrual-basis, calendar-year taxpayer, sold $15,000 of its products on account to Jim in November, year 1. In year 2, Jim declares bankruptcy and Sandle writes off the account as a bad debt. In year 3, Jim unexpectedly inherits a large sum of money and uses part of it to repay his creditors, including a $12,000 payment to Sandle Corporation.

a. What does Sandle Corporation report on its tax returns for years 1, 2, and 3?

b. How would your answers change if Sandle is a cash-basis taxpayer?

39. Mac's 24-year-old daughter, Alana, is a full-time student. In 2013, Mac gives Alana 600 shares of Highgrowth stock. Mac purchased the stock 10 months ago at $20 per share. On the gift date, the stock is worth $35 per share. After the gift, Highgrowth declares and pays a $170 dividend to Alana. The next month, Alana sells her 600 shares for $38 per share. Mac and Alana are in the 39.6 and 15 percent marginal tax brackets, respectively.

a. How much must Alana and Mac include in gross income in 2013?

b. What family tax savings are achieved through this gift?

40. Myra receives a $20,000 gift from her cousin and inherits $80,000 in corporate bonds from her aunt at the beginning of the current year. Myra receives $7,000 in interest income from the bonds at the end of the current year. How much does Myra include in gross income?

41. Linda's husband dies, naming her the sole beneficiary of a $500,000 life insurance policy. The insurance company informs her that she has two options: (1) she can receive the entire $500,000 in one lump-sum payment or (2) she can receive annual installments of $58,000 for 10 years.

a. How much does Linda include in gross income if she takes the lump-sum payment?

b. How much does Linda include in gross income each year if she elects the installment payments?

42. Mark's employer pays 55 percent of the premiums for a disability insurance policy and Mark pays for the other 45 percent. The policy pays Mark 65 percent of his normal salary in the event he is injured and cannot return to work for an extended period. Mark is hit by a truck and is unable to work for several months. During the current year, Mark collects $30,000 under his disability policy. How much does Mark include in his gross income?

43. Sara receives a $5,500 per year scholarship to attend the state university. Sara spends $4,000 for tuition, $500 for required textbooks and $1,000 for room and board. Sara also has a part-time job on campus earning $3,000 which covered the balance of her room and board and supply expenses. How much does Sara include in her gross income?

44. Larry receives a scholarship to attend the local college. The scholarship terms provide $7,000 for tuition, books, and related expenses for the academic year. Larry only spends $3,200 for tuition, books, and related supplies from August through December of year 1 and $3,400 from January through April of year 2. Does Larry have any income from this scholarship and if so, in which year is it recognized?

45. Giant Corporation (a U.S. corporation) forms Small Corporation in a foreign country. Giant owns 70% of Small Corporation's stock and the remaining stock is owned by citizens of the country in which Small is located. This year Small Corporation earns $1,500,000 of taxable income from its manufacturing operations and pays $200,000 in taxes to the foreign country in which it is located. Small does not make any dividend distributions. How much of Small Corporation's taxable income will be subject to U.S. income tax this year?

46. Mango Corporation has before-tax income of $450,000 and is subject to a state income tax of 5 percent in addition to the federal income tax. What is Mango's after-tax cash flow?

47. On January 2, year 1, Randy sold a parcel of land that he held as an investment for a number of years. The land has a basis to Randy of $8,500. The buyer made a $6,000 down payment on the date of sale and made $7,000 payments on January 2 in both year 2 and year 3. In addition, an 8 percent rate of interest was charged on the unpaid balance. How much income should Randy have recognized in years 1, 2, and 3, assuming that he used the installment method? What is the result if Randy elects out of the installment method for this sale?

48. In year 1, Highrise Company contracts to manufacture a piece of customized equipment for a customer. The contract will take two years to complete. The contract price is $250,000 and the company estimates its total costs at $220,000. Actual costs incurred are as follows:

Year 1	$121,000
Year 2	105,000
	$226,000

What amount of gross income and deductions does the company recognize in each of the two years, assuming the company uses (1) the completed contract method and (2) the percentage-of-completion method of accounting for long-term contracts?

49. Marco and Lisa are married and file a joint tax return. Lisa has salary income of $260,000 and Marco has salary income of $400,000. They also have the following items of investment income: $60,000 net long-term capital gain on sale of stock, $8,000 dividend income, $6,000 interest income from corporate bonds, and $5,000 interest income from tax-exempt municipal bonds. Compute their net investment income (NII) Medicare surtax.

50. Raymond, a single individual, received a salary of $196,000. He also had the following items of investment income: $40,000 net short-term capital gain on sale of stock, $7,000 dividend income, $5,000 interest income from corporate bonds, and $4,000 interest income from tax-exempt municipal bonds. Compute Raymond's net investment income (NII) Medicare surtax.

THINK OUTSIDE THE TEXT

These questions require answers that are beyond the material that is covered in this chapter.

51. Some politicians have proposed changing the way Social Security benefits are taxed. One proposal would increase the amount of Social Security benefits included in gross income to 100 percent. A tax rate of 100 percent would then apply for some high-income individuals, effectively preventing them from receiving benefits. What do you think about this proposal?

52. Congress has the power to tax income "from whatever source derived." Do you believe that this allows Congress the discretion to tax municipal bond interest (or other tax-exempt income) earned throughout a tax year retroactively if the law to make this income taxable is not enacted until the very end of the tax year? (Note: The Tax Relief Act of 2010 retroactively reinstated the estate tax for decedents dying in 2010 late in the year after it had been scheduled to be repealed in 2010.)

53. John and Mary are divorcing. John is demanding that Mary pay him $75,000 of alimony in the first year after the divorce, $50,000 in the second year, and $25,000 in the third and all subsequent years until he dies or remarries. What are the income tax ramifications of alimony structured in this manner?

54. Joe owes Willy $5,000 from an old gambling debt. Joe knows that there is no way he can repay the debt in the near future. He asks Joe if he will take a $25,000 life insurance policy that has a cash surrender value of $4,200 and release him from the debt. Willy agrees to take the insurance policy and cancels Joe's debt. Willy makes only one premium payment on the insurance policy of $50 when Joe is killed in an auto accident. Willy collects the $25,000. Explain all the tax consequences of these events for both Joe and Willy.

55. Walter used the cash method to account for income from his cattle ranch. During an audit in year 3, the IRS auditor discovered a document from a customer indicating that Walter sold 115 head of cattle to the customer two years earlier for $77,000. The document appeared to be a tear slip, the top half of a document that normally includes a business check. Walter's bank records for year 1 showed no such deposit, and a conversation with the customer revealed that its check for $77,000 had never been cashed. A new check was issued in year 3. Walter included the $77,000 as income on his year 3 tax return. The IRS then issued an audit report contending that the income was taxable in year 1 under the doctrine of constructive receipt. If you were a tax court judge hearing this case, how would you rule?

56. On O's Favorite Giveaway Show, the host gives 100 audience members debit cards, each one for $15,000, with the stipulation that the audience members donate the money to their favorite charitable cause (they cannot keep the money for themselves or give it to their relatives). The debit cards are sponsored by the Bank of America. Each audience member is also given a DVD recorder to record their stories for a future show. Identify all of the possible tax implications of this giveaway and explain what you think the tax treatment is for each.

IDENTIFY THE ISSUES

Identify the issues or problems suggested by the following situations. State each issue as a question.

57. Jason owns a computer repair shop. Jason needs some repair work done on his company car, so he agrees to repair the computer at Bob's Auto Repairs in exchange for fixing the car.

58. A landlord requires tenants to pay at the beginning of their lease an amount equal to 3 months of rent. He informs the tenants that this is for the first month's rent, the last month's rent, and a refundable security deposit equal to one month's rent.

59. In December, year 1, Sid's Body Shop (an accrual-basis taxpayer) did repair work on Lisa's car and was to be paid $2,000 by her insurance company. Lisa was not satisfied with the repair job but finally agreed that her insurance company should pay $1,700 for the repair work, subject to approval by the insurance company adjuster. In March, year 2, the insurance company paid $1,700 to Sid's Body Shop.

60. Ken receives interest income from Province of Ontario (Canada) bonds.

61. While diving in the Florida Keys on vacation, Gillian finds a gold bar from a sunken ship.

62. Bill and Susan are planning to divorce. Their daughter, Melissa, will live with Susan. Bill has offered to pay Susan $1,000 per month for eight years.

63. Sharp Corporation has $250,000 in assets and $300,000 in liabilities. Sharp negotiates a deal with one of its creditors to write off $20,000 of the $60,000 owed to the creditor.

DEVELOP RESEARCH SKILLS

64. Thomas ran for Congress, raising $2 million for his campaign. Six months after losing the election, auditors discovered that Thomas kept $160,000 of the campaign funds and used the money to purchase a vacation home. What are the tax consequences of this use of campaign funds?

65. Samantha has been unemployed for some time and is very short of money. She learned that the local blood bank has a severe shortage of her type of blood and is therefore willing to pay $120 for each blood donation. Samantha gives blood twice a week for 12 weeks and receives $120 for each donation. Are these funds includable in Samantha's gross income?

66. Alice and Manny agree to divorce. Alice proposes that Manny purchase and assign to her a life insurance policy on his life as part of the divorce agreement. She wants Manny to continue paying the premiums on this policy for the next 10 years. Manny wants to know if the premium payments will be treated as alimony.

67. A minister receives an annual salary of $16,000 in addition to the use of a church parsonage with an annual rental value of $6,000. The minister accepted this minimal salary because he felt that was all the church could afford to pay. He plans to report these amounts on his income tax return but he is uncertain how to treat the cash gifts he receives from the members of his congregation. These gifts were made out of love and admiration for him. During the year the congregation developed a regular procedure for making gifts on special occasions. Approximately two weeks before each special occasion when the minister was not present, the associate pastor announced before the service that those who wished to contribute to the special occasion gifts could do so by placing cash in envelopes and giving them to the associate who would give them to the minister. Only cash was accepted to preserve anonymity. The church did not keep a record of the amounts given nor the contributors, but the minister estimates that these gifts amount to about $10,000 in the current year. How should he treat these gifts?

SEARCH THE INTERNET

68. Go to the IRS Web site (*www.irs.gov*) and locate Publication 537: *Installment Sales*. Which form is used to report an installment sale?

69. Go to the IRS Web site (*www.irs.gov*) and locate Publication 915: *Social Security and Equivalent Railroad Retirement Benefits*. Determine how much of the Social Security benefits must be included in income for a single individual who had $20,000 in dividend income and $5,000 in interest from tax-exempt bonds, in addition to receiving $10,000 in Social Security benefits.

70. Go to the IRS Web site (*www.irs.gov*) and print the first page of Form 1040. Compute Pierre Lappin's adjusted gross income by entering the following information on Form 1040: $60,000 salary, $5,000 qualified dividend income, $3,000 interest income from corporate bonds, $2,000 interest income from municipal general revenue bonds, $4,000 in long-term capital gains, and $10,000 income from an S corporation. In addition, Pierre paid his ex-wife $5,000 for alimony and $6,000 for child support. Pierre remarried prior to the end of the year and files a joint return with his new wife, Jeanie Lappin. Jeanie earned $10,000 from her part-time job for the year. The Lappins live at 123 Cottontail Lane, Houston, TX and have no dependents. Pierre's social security number is 123-45-6789 and Jeannie's social security number is 445-67-9876. Pierre's ex-wife's social security number is 345-67-8899.

71. Go to *www.legalbitstream.com* (or *www.irs.gov/irb/* and start with IRB 2011–37) and locate Notice 2011–64. Read the appendix of Notice 2011–64 and determine if dividend income received from foreign corporations located in the following four jurisdictions will be treated as qualified dividends eligible for the reduced dividend (i.e., 0, 15 or 20 percent) tax rate: Bermuda, China, Jamaica, and the Netherland Antilles.

72. Go to *www.legalbitstream.com* and locate Announcement 2002–18. What is the IRS's policy on taxing frequent flyer miles?

DEVELOP PLANNING SKILLS

73. Robert plans to start a new business that he expects will experience steady growth in profits for the next 15 years. He needs to select a method of accounting to use: cash or accrual. He would like to select the method that will provide the higher net present value for the company's cash flows. Which method should he choose and why?

74. Sandra, a single taxpayer in the 39.6 percent marginal tax bracket, has $60,000 she can invest in either corporate bonds with a stated interest rate of 9 percent or general revenue bonds issued by her municipality with a stated interest rate of 6 percent. What do you recommend she do? Would your answer change if her marginal tax rate is only 28 percent?

75. Palace Company (an accrual-basis taxpayer) is writing the lease agreements for its new apartment complex, Palace Apartments, which will rent for a minimum of $2,000 per month. Palace wants tenants to pay $6,000 when they sign the lease and is considering two alternatives. Under the first alternative, $4,000 would be rent for the final two months of the lease, with $2,000 for the damage deposit. Under the second alternative, $2,000 would be for the last month's rent and $4,000 would be for the damage deposit. Discuss the tax implication of each alternative and recommend one.

76. Kevin and Elizabeth are negotiating a divorce settlement. Kevin is in the 33 percent marginal tax bracket and Elizabeth is in the 15 percent marginal tax bracket. Kevin has offered to pay Elizabeth $15,000 each year for 10 years; payments would cease if Elizabeth dies before the end of the 10-year period. Elizabeth is willing to settle for that amount only if the payments qualify as a tax-free property settlement because she needs at least $15,000 after tax to meet her expenses.

a. How much would Elizabeth have to receive in taxable alimony payments from Kevin to have the equivalent of a $15,000 tax-free payment?

b. If Kevin agrees to an $18,500 alimony payment, what is the after-tax cash flow for Kevin and Elizabeth? By how much does their cash flow improve over the proposed $15,000 property settlement payment?

ANSWERS TO TEST YOURSELF

1. **b. $4,950**. ($110,000/$200,000)($4,500 × 2 payments) = $4,950.

2. **a. $100.**

3. **c. $25,550.** ($10,000 salary + $15,000 employer's provided retirement annuity + $500 dividend + $50 lottery prize). The interest is not taxable because it is from municipal bonds, and the Social Security benefits are not taxable because their modified adjusted gross income is less than $32,000.

4. **c. $6,500.** The $4,500 portion of the scholarship that is used for tuition and required textbooks is tax exempt. The $1,500 of scholarship that is used for room and board and the entire $5,000 salary from the part-time job is taxable.

5. **d. $1,000.** Marcus's gain is $4,000 ($20,000 – $16,000). Because 20 percent of the principal payments that Marcus will receive represent gain ($4,000 gain/$20,000 payments to be received), 20 percent of each payment will be recognized as gain in the year it is received. Thus, each payment of $5,000 will trigger the recognition of $1,000 ($5,000 × 20%) of gain.

Employee Compensation

chapter 4

In this chapter, we look at compensation from both the employee's and employer's perspective. It includes the basic information necessary to design a compensation package that offers tax savings to both.

Employees can significantly increase the after-tax value of compensation by taking some of their compensation as tax-exempt fringe benefits. The cost of tax-exempt fringe benefits is deductible by the employer, even though the value of such benefits is not taxable income to the employee, providing a win-win situation for both employer and employee. To prevent abuse, however, most of the tax-free benefits have significant limitations. An awareness of these limitations is important to maximize the tax savings that can be achieved through the best use of these tax-free fringe benefits.

Stock and stock options are popular compensation tools and are used as incentives to both recruit and retain employees, while requiring no cash outlay by the employer. Stock options offer employees an opportunity to acquire stock at a bargain price and can provide the dual tax advantages of deferring income to a future year and converting what would otherwise be ordinary compensation income into long-term capital gains taxed at favorable rates.

Deferred compensation plans are key to retirement planning and are important components of most compensation packages. Qualified plans provide an immediate deduction for contributions by the employer but defer the taxation of benefits until the employee retires. The amount of compensation that can be offered on a tax-deferred basis under qualified plans is limited; as a result, many employers have established nonqualified plans that can provide unlimited deferred compensation only to key or highly compensated executives.

Whether you are an employer trying to attract and retain talented employees or an employee looking to maximize the value of your compensation, knowledge of the tax impact on compensation is critical.

KEY CONCEPTS

- ★ Most forms of employee compensation are fully taxable to the employee as income and fully deductible by the employer as a business expense.
- ★ Fringe benefits are taxable as income to employees unless they fit into one of the specific categories of tax-exempt fringe benefits. Tax-exempt fringe benefits are deductible by the employer even though they are not taxable income to the employee.
- ★ Most tax-exempt fringe benefits have some dollar limit. Benefits paid in excess of these limits are compensation, taxable to the employee and deductible by the employer.
- ★ Qualified stock options allow employees to defer income recognition and require no cash outlay by the employer.
- ★ Qualified deferred compensation is deductible by the employer when the contribution is made to the trust fund, but employees are not taxed until they receive the funds. Income on the contributed funds accrues tax free until it is withdrawn.
- ★ Employers can offer unlimited deferred compensation to key and highly paid employees through nonqualified deferred compensation plans.

CHAPTER OUTLINE

Setting the Stage—An Introductory Case

Your friend Bob has received two job offers. Alpha Corporation would like to hire him as an employee at a salary of $73,000 and would also provide him with several fringe benefits. Beta Corporation would like to hire him as an independent contractor. Although Beta provides no fringe benefits, Bob would earn $85,000 annually in consulting fees.

Bob is married to Julie, who works part-time at a company that provides no benefits for its part-time employees. Bob is very concerned that he and his family have medical insurance. Alpha Corporation pays the premiums for comprehensive medical insurance for all its employees and their immediate families. Under its group plan, Alpha Corporation would pay $5,000 per year for Bob's family medical coverage. If Bob works for Beta Corporation, he could purchase similar health insurance for himself and his family at an annual cost of $7,000.

Alpha also provides free on-premise athletic facilities and free parking for its employees. These benefits have an annual cost to Alpha of $300 and $600, respectively, per employee. If Bob works for Beta Corporation, renewing his current athletic club membership would cost $600 per year. Parking would cost $600 annually.

Bob asks you to evaluate the after-tax cash flow generated by each job. Assume Bob is in the 25 percent marginal tax bracket. Next, determine the after-tax cost of each compensation package provided by Alpha and Beta Corporations, assuming each is in the 34 percent marginal tax bracket. Is it possible to provide a compensation package that will both maximize the after-tax value to the individual while minimizing the after-tax cost to the employer? We will return to this case at the end of this chapter.

Employee Compensation

This chapter bridges the topics of gross income and deductible business expenses. Salaries and wages are a major deductible expense for most businesses, particularly service organizations. **Compensation** includes not only base salaries and wages but also bonuses, vacation pay, employer-provided sick pay, and other fringe and economic benefits received by employees. All forms of compensation are taxable income to the employee unless excluded by a specific provision of the Internal Revenue Code.

Payroll Taxes

Employers are assessed payroll taxes on employee wages. Both the wages and taxes are deductible business expenses. Taxes include those specified under the Federal Insurance Contributions Act (FICA) tax along with federal and state unemployment taxes. The **FICA tax** has two components. The employer's tax rate for the old age, survivors and disability insurance (OASDI), commonly referred to as Social Security, portion of this tax is 6.2 percent of wages up to a maximum of $113,700 for 2013 ($110,100 for 2012).[1] The Medicare hospital insurance (HI) portion of the FICA tax is 1.45 percent of total compensation so an employer pays 7.65 percent FICA tax on each employee's wages up to $113,700 and 1.45 percent on compensation above $113,700.[2]

---

[1]The ceiling was $106,800 for 2009-2011 and $102,000 for 2008.

[2]As an incentive to hire unemployed workers, the 2010 Hiring Incentives to Restore Employment Act allowed employers who hired qualified new employees after February 3, 2010 and before January 1, 2011 to elect to be exempt from the Social Security portion of their payroll taxes for these employees. To qualify, an employee had to sign an affidavit stating that he or she had not been employed for more than 40 hours in the last 60 days prior to beginning the new job. The employer could not be replacing another employee unless that employee left voluntarily; the employee could not be related to the employer; and the employee could not be one for which the employer claims the work opportunity credit. The employer still paid the Medicare tax of 1.45 percent of employee wages. Employees who met the above criteria also qualified the employer for the employee retention credit if they worked for 52 consecutive weeks (see Chapter 9 for retention credit).

In addition to the tax on employers, employees have traditionally paid a matching, but nondeductible, FICA tax; however, for 2011 and 2012, the employee's rate on the Social Security portion of the tax was reduced from 6.2 percent to 4.2 percent on employee wages up to the Social Security limit. Congress reduced the rate paid by employees in an attempt to stimulate the economy. The rate returned to 6.2 percent for 2013. Employees also pay a 1.45 percent tax rate on total compensation for Medicare.[3] Employers withhold this employee FICA tax from their employees' compensation, along with the employees' federal income tax.[4] In states that levy an income tax, employers also withhold state income tax. Self-employed individuals, including independent contractors, pay their own Social Security and Medicare taxes (discussed in detail later in this chapter) and must make their own quarterly estimated tax payments for their self-employment and income taxes.

Employers also pay federal unemployment taxes (FUTA) in addition to state unemployment taxes. The current **FUTA tax** rate is 6 percent on the first $7,000 of covered wages paid during the year to each employee; however, employers are allowed to claim a credit against FUTA for their state unemployment taxes. The FUTA tax is paid entirely by the employer.[5]

EXAMPLE 1

Jennifer is an employee of Moneybags Corporation. In 2013, Jennifer received a salary of $100,000 and a bonus of $20,000 (total taxable compensation of $120,000). Moneybags Corporation paid a Social Security tax of $7,049.40 ($113,700 limit × 6.2%) plus a Medicare tax of $1,740 ($120,000 × 1.45%) for a total FICA tax of $8,789.40. Jennifer's share of payroll taxes is also $7,049.40 for her Social Security tax plus a Medicare tax of $1,740 for her total employee FICA tax of $8,789.40 for 2013. Moneybags Corporation withheld $21,720 of federal income tax (determined from IRS-issued tables based on Jennifer's marital status and number of exemptions) and $8,789.40 FICA tax from Jennifer's $120,000 compensation. Therefore, Jennifer's net pay was $89,490.60 ($120,000 – $21,720 withholding – $8,789.40 employee's FICA taxes) for 2013.

Moneybags Corporation will also pay unemployment tax of $420 ($7,000 × 6%) in 2013. Moneybags can deduct $120,000 as employee compensation expense and it also deducts $9,209 ($8,789 + $420) as payroll tax expense for 2013.

Starting in 2013, the Patient Protection and Affordable Care Act (PPACA) requires taxpayers to pay a Medicare surtax if certain income thresholds are exceeded. The thresholds are $200,000 for single individuals (and heads of household), $250,000 for married taxpayers filing a joint return, and $125,000 for married taxpayers filing separately. The additional tax rate is 0.9 percent on taxable compensation income. (This Medicare surtax is discussed further in Chapter 11.)

[3]§3101. The employee's share of FICA is not deductible by anyone for federal income tax purposes. To pay for expanded health care coverage, the Patient Protection and Affordable Care Act expands the Medicare tax. As discussed in this chapter, an additional 0.9 percent Medicare tax applies to the earned income of employees and self-employed persons with earnings and wages in excess of $200,000 ($250,000 if married filing a joint return); this new rate applies only to individuals and a matching amount is *not* assessed on businesses. Additionally, a new Medicare tax is levied on the net investment income (including taxable interest, dividends, capital gains, annuities, royalties, and certain rents) of individuals with AGI in excess of $200,000 ($250,000 if married filing a joint return) at a rate of 3.8 percent. The Medicare tax on net investment income was discussed in Chapter 3. Additional details in computing both of these Medicare surtaxes are provided in Chapter 11.

[4]Withholding is based on information (including marital status and exemptions) provided by the employee to the employer on Form W–4. Supplemental payments (such as bonuses) may be subject to an alternative 25% withholding rate. See IRS *Publication 15 (Circular E) Employer's Tax Guide*.

[5]Employers can claim a credit against FUTA tax for state unemployment taxes up to a maximum rate of 5.4% effectively reducing the FUTA rate to 0.6%. The FUTA rate was 6.2% (an effective 0.8% after the state credit) prior to July 1, 2011. A few states assess employees for a special unemployment tax to provide for supplemental unemployment compensation or disability benefits.

Employers are required to withhold the additional Medicare tax from salary, wages, or other compensation (including commissions, bonuses, tips, and any benefits subject to the regular Medicare tax) they pay to employees in excess of $200,000 in a calendar year, without regard to the employee's filing status or wages paid by another employer. An employee may owe more than the amount withheld by the employer, depending on the individual's filing status, wages, other compensation, and self-employment income. Employees cannot request that their employer withhold the additional Medicare tax on wages of less than $200,000. Instead, employees who want more tax withheld should request additional income tax withholding using Form W-4: *Employee's Withholding Allowance Certificate* or make estimated tax payments.

EXAMPLE 2

Marco is an employee of Moneybags Corporation. In 2013, Marco received a salary of $180,000 and a bonus of $40,000 (total taxable compensation of $220,000). Moneybags Corporation paid a Social Security tax of $7,049.40 ($113,700 limit × 6.2%) plus a Medicare tax of $3,190 ($220,000 × 1.45%) for a total FICA tax of $10,239.40 on Marco. Marco's share of payroll taxes is also $7,049.40 for his Social Security tax plus a Medicare tax of $3,190 but he also is subject to an additional Medicare surtax of $180 ($220,000 total compensation - $200,000 threshold) × 0.9%] for total employee payroll taxes of $10,419.40 for 2013. Moneybags Corporation withheld $51,020 of federal income tax (determined from IRS-issued tables based on Marco's marital status and number of exemptions) and $10,419.40 payroll tax from Marco's $220,000 compensation. Therefore, Marco's net pay was $158,560.60 ($220,000 – $51,020 withholding – $10,419.40 employee's payroll taxes) for 2013.

Moneybags Corporation will also pay unemployment tax of $420 ($7,000 × 6%) in 2013 on Marco. Moneybags can deduct $220,000 as employee compensation expense and it also deducts $10,659 ($10,239 + $420) as payroll tax expense for Marco for 2013.

Within 31 days following the end of the year, the employer reports the taxable compensation paid to an employee and the taxes withheld for the year on Form W-2: *Wages and Tax Statement*. A copy is sent to the government to verify the income the employee reports on his or her individual tax return.

Employers pay payroll taxes for employees only, not for independent contractors. Instead, independent contractors pay their own Social Security and Medicare taxes both as the employee and employer as self-employed individuals. Therefore, the distinction between employee and independent contractor has significant payroll tax consequences.

Employee versus Independent Contractor

Working individuals are either self-employed or employees. Self-employed individuals include partners, sole proprietors, and independent contractors. An **independent contractor** is a worker who is subject to the direction of another only as to the result of the work accomplished, not the means to accomplish it.[6] Most consultants are independent contractors.

The determination of employee or self-employed status is a very controversial area. Businesses try to increase the use of self-employed individuals to eliminate FICA and FUTA taxes and to exclude them from most employee fringe benefit programs.

Workers who incur significant unreimbursed business expenses have an incentive to be treated as independent contractors rather than employees because they deduct their business expenses directly from their gross self-employment income, paying self-employment taxes only on their net self-employment income. As employees, they would pay FICA taxes on their gross earnings and their unreimbursed business expenses might be of only limited benefit as miscellaneous itemized deductions.[7]

[6]Revenue Ruling 87-41, 1987-1 CB 296 provides a 20-factor test that is frequently used to determine whether an individual is an independent contractor or employee.

[7]These itemized deductions are only deductible to the extent they exceed 2 percent of adjusted gross income. Itemized deductions are discussed in Chapter 11.

An employer may attempt to avoid paying employment taxes and providing fringe benefits for persons who perform work for them by deliberately misclassifying the workers as independent contractors instead of employees. A person who is anxious to be employed may be willing to accept independent contractor status simply to obtain the work. The IRS is aware of this and has audited businesses looking for such misclassifications, billing businesses for back taxes and penalties.

KEY CASE *Microsoft hired software testers, production editors, proofreaders, formatters, and indexers as independent contractors. Microsoft employees supervised them, they performed functions also performed by Microsoft employees, and they worked the same hours. Rather than being paid through the Microsoft payroll department, these workers submitted invoices for their services to the accounts payable department. The IRS determined that they were misclassified and were in fact employees. Microsoft agreed to pay back employment taxes and issue retroactive W-2 forms to allow these employees to recover Microsoft's share of FICA taxes, which they had been required to pay. These reclassified employees then sued Microsoft for fringe benefits paid to other employees, including the right to participate in the company's stock purchase and 401(k) plans. The Ninth Circuit ruled against Microsoft and in favor of the workers.*[8]

Incorrectly classifying an employee as an independent contractor can not only result in additional taxes, interest, and penalties, but in some cases, it can also affect careers.

EXAMPLE 3

The nanny tax affected the careers of three individuals whom President Clinton nominated to his cabinet.[9] Zoe Baird and Kimba Wood (both Attorney General nominees) and retired Admiral Bobby Inman (Secretary of Defense nominee) withdrew from consideration when the press revealed that they had failed to pay employment taxes on the wages of household employees because they had improperly treated these employees as independent contractors. Bernard Kerik, President Bush's nominee to head Homeland Security, had a similar problem and also withdrew his name from consideration.

Individuals reclassified as employees may have significant additional taxes assessed, even if they properly reported their incomes and paid self-employment taxes. For example, deductions for home office expenses can be lost.[10] Frequently, the refund due for self-employment taxes paid is less than employee FICA taxes plus additional income taxes on the lost deductions, leaving the worker with a net tax liability.[11]

Determining whether an individual is self-employed or an employee can be very difficult because there is no unequivocal definition of an independent contractor. Revenue Ruling 87-41 provides a 20-factor test that is frequently used to determine an individual's work status under common law rules.[12] No one factor is decisive, but five of these factors have been found to be most important.[13]

1. *Instructions*. Employers usually have the right to specify how, when, and where their employees are to perform their jobs. Independent contractors decide how to achieve the end result.
2. *Payment*. Employees are usually compensated on a regular schedule (by the hour, week, or month). Independent contractors are usually paid by the job.

---

[8] *Vizcaino et al. v. Microsoft Corp.*, 97 F.3d 1187; 96-2 USTC ¶50,533; 78 AFTR 2d. 96-6690, aff'd. 120 F.3d 1006; 80 AFTR 2d 97-5594 (CA-9, 1997).

[9] The nanny tax refers to employment taxes that individual taxpayers must pay for household employees, including nannies, baby-sitters, health aides, maids, yard workers, and other domestic workers. The threshold for paying employment taxes is reached when a household employee is paid wages of $1,800 or more in 2012 and 2013.

[10] The limitations on home office expense deductions are discussed in Chapter 5.

[11] The IRS can assess the employer for the individual's share of FICA taxes if they cannot be collected from the individual.

[12] Rev. Rul. 87-41, 1987-1 CB 296.

[13] Reg. §31.3401(c)-1(b). Jane O. Burns and Tracy A. Freeman, "Avoiding IRS Reclassification of Workers as Employees," *The Tax Adviser*, February 1996, p. 105.

3. *Tools and Materials*. Employers usually furnish employees with any necessary materials, tools, and supplies. Independent contractors generally supply their own.
4. *Significant Investment*. Employees usually use the employer's office space. Independent contractors frequently invest in their own office facilities.
5. *Realization of Profit or Loss*. An independent contractor bears the risk of realizing a profit or loss.

Example 4

Jamie is hired to perform laboratory tests for a medical doctor. Jamie works at the doctor's office, uses the doctor's equipment, and performs the tests by the methods prescribed by the doctor, entering the results in the patients' charts. Marie has a small laboratory in her home. She receives samples forwarded from doctors' offices and performs tests with her own equipment, using methods she determines to be appropriate for the desired analyses. She provides the doctor with a written report of the test results only. Jamie is an employee while Marie is self-employed.

Timing of Compensation Deduction

A business's method of accounting affects the timing of a compensation deduction.[14] A cash-basis business takes the deduction in the year the compensation is paid. An accrual-basis business usually takes the deduction in the year the liability is incurred. If, however, an accrual-basis corporation accrues an obligation to pay compensation, the payment must be made within 2½ months after the close of the corporation's tax year or it cannot be deducted until the year of payment.

A more restrictive provision prevents a related taxpayer and a business in which the taxpayer owns more than a 50 percent interest from engaging in tax avoidance schemes in which one party uses the accrual method of accounting and the other uses the cash method.[15] If an accrual-basis corporation accrues a payment to a related cash-basis taxpayer (such as an employee-shareholder who owns more than 50 percent of the corporation), the deduction for the payment is deferred until the related party recognizes the income in the year of payment.

Example 5

Black Inc., an accrual-basis, calendar-year corporation, is owned 100 percent by its president, Bill Black, a cash-basis, calendar-year individual. On December 15, year 1, Black Inc. accrues a $90,000 bonus to Bill and a $60,000 bonus to its top sales representative, Steve, but does not pay these bonuses until January, year 2. Black Inc. can deduct Steve's $60,000 bonus on its year 1 tax return but cannot deduct Bill's $90,000 bonus until year 2. Both Bill and Steve will include the bonuses as income on their year 2 tax returns. If Black Inc. does not pay the bonuses by March 15, year 2, then it cannot deduct either bonus until the year paid.

To preserve the deduction for bonuses to related taxpayers in the year accrued, the corporation should ensure those bonus payments are paid before year-end. It should be noted that this deferral provision does not apply if the related taxpayers both use either the cash method or the accrual method or if the taxpayer receiving the income uses the accrual method and the related party taking the deduction uses the cash method. (There is no tax deferral benefit in this situation.)

Reasonable Compensation

To be deductible, employee compensation must be reasonable. **Reasonable compensation** is the amount that a similar business would pay for the services under similar

[14]Although most salaries and wages are currently deductible, some compensation must be capitalized—for example, direct labor costs are capitalized as part of finished goods inventory.

[15]Related taxpayers include family members (spouse, parents, grandparents, children, brothers, and sisters), as well as a corporation owned more than 50 percent (either directly owned or indirectly owned through other related parties) by the taxpayer.

circumstances. Reasonableness is applied on a per employee basis and frequently arises in closely-held corporations in which employees are also shareholders. Because dividends are not deductible by a corporation, the business has an incentive to inflate shareholder-employees' salaries instead of paying dividends. If a shareholder-employee's salary is unreasonable, only the reasonable part is deductible and the IRS reclassifies the excess as a nondeductible dividend distribution by the corporation.

EXAMPLE 6

Lynn owns 100 percent of Lowry Corporation. The Lowry Corporation has been very profitable but has not paid any dividends for several years. Lynn's salary is $700,000. Similar businesses ordinarily pay only $400,000 to persons performing services comparable to Lynn's. If the $300,000 excess compensation is reclassified as a dividend, Lynn will still be taxed on the full $700,000 ($400,000 as salary and $300,000 as dividend income), but the dividend will be taxed at only a 20 percent rate while the excess $300,000 salary would have been taxed as ordinary income at a 39.6 percent rate saving $58,800 [$300,000 × (39.6% - 20%)] in income taxes. Lynn will also save $4,350 ($300,000 x 1.45%) in regular Medicare taxes that are not imposed on dividend income but will pay an $8,700 higher Medicare surtax [(3.8% NII - 0.9%) × $300,000)] resulting in a tax savings to Lynn of $54,450 ($58,800 + $4,350 - $8,700). Lowry Corporation can deduct only the $400,000 salary, however. If Lowry is in the 34 percent tax bracket, the reclassification of salary to dividend costs the corporation an additional $102,000 ($300,000 nondeductible dividend × 34%) in corporate income taxes. Lowry will save $4,350 in Medicare taxes but then loses tax savings of $1,479 ($4,350 × 34%) from deducting the Medicare taxes, resulting in a net corporate tax increase of $99,129 ($102,000 - $4,350 + $1,479). The net effect will be an increase in overall taxes of $44,679 ($99,129 - $54,450).

The IRS can also reclassify any excessive salary paid to a party related to the shareholder (for example, a child or parent) as a nondeductible dividend.

Code Section 162(m) limits the amount of deductible compensation paid to top executives of publicly traded companies to $1 million annually.[16] Employees covered by the provision include the chief executive officer and the next four most highly compensated officers. Compensation subject to the limitation includes all cash and noncash benefits except:

- Compensation based on individual performance goals (if these goals were approved in advance by certain outside directors and shareholders)[17]
- Compensation paid on a commission basis
- Employer contributions to a qualified retirement plan
- Tax-free employee benefits (described later in this chapter)

EXAMPLE 7

Star Corporation's stock is traded on the New York Stock Exchange. During the current year, Jane, the chief executive officer, receives the following compensation: $1,100,000 salary, $170,000 commissions based on sales she generated, $24,000 employer contributions to a qualified pension plan, and $9,000 tax-free fringe benefits. Only $1,000,000 of the $1,100,000 salary is deductible by Star Corporation. The commissions, retirement plan contributions, and fringe benefits are not subject to the $1 million annual deduction limit (so the corporation can deduct them in full). Jane is still taxed on the entire $1,100,000 salary as well as on the $170,000 sales commission. (As explained later in this chapter, Jane will not be taxed on the contribution to the pension plan or the tax-free fringe benefits.)

[16]A $500,000 deduction limit applies to covered executives (CEO, CFO, and the other 3 highest paid officers) for any entity that received Troubled Asset Relief Program (TARP) financial assistance. The $500,000 limit remains in effect as long as any obligation arising from TARP assistance is outstanding. Since 2012, a $500,000 limit applies to all officers, employees, directors, and other persons working at or providing services for health insurance companies that derive at least 25% of their gross premium income from health insurance plans that meet the minimum essential coverage requirements of the Patient Protection and Affordable Care Act of 2010.

[17]See Reg. §1.162-27 for specific requirements on performance goals.

TAX PLANNING

Some corporations protect themselves by having highly compensated employees agree to repay any compensation for which a deduction is disallowed. The employee may then deduct the taxable income in the year of repayment if the payback agreement meets two conditions. First, the parties must have entered into it before the compensation is paid. Second, the employee must be legally obligated to repay the excess amount.[18]

S Corporations and Unreasonably Low Salaries

When an individual is a controlling shareholder-employee of an S corporation, IRS auditors look for an unreasonably low salary because salaries are subject to employment taxes while distributions of profits are not. An S corporation can minimize its costs for payroll taxes by paying a low salary and making income distributions.[19] If an employee-shareholder's salary is unreasonably low, however, the IRS can reclassify some of the S corporation's distribution as salary, requiring the payment of additional employment taxes (and possibly penalties).

KEY CASE *David Watson, a CPA with 20 years' experience, formed an S corporation that became a partner in his accounting firm. Watson was employed by his S corporation and in each of the two years involved in the case, Watson received a salary of $24,000 from the S corporation. Walton also received distributions from the S corporation of $203,651 in one year and $175,470 in the other year that were not subject to payroll taxes. The IRS determined that his $24,000 salary was not reasonable compensation and that his salary should have been $91,044. The District Court agreed with the IRS that an additional $67,044 was subject to FICA tax and the decision was affirmed by the Eighth Circuit Court of Appeals.*[20]

Employing Children

TAX PLANNING

Closely-held businesses frequently hire family members as employees. Owners who employ their children can effectively shift income to their children (and have that income taxed on the children's tax returns) if the compensation paid to the children is reasonable for the services performed. The income is usually taxed at the child's lower income tax rates, and the owners benefit from savings in payroll taxes because wages paid to an employer's child under age 18 are not subject to employment taxes if the business is not a corporation.[21]

EXAMPLE 8

Harry, an individual in the 28 percent tax bracket, owns a sole proprietorship for which his 16-year-old daughter, Sarah, works after school. Harry pays Sarah a reasonable wage of $6,100 for the work performed for the business. Harry deducts the $6,100 in wages paid to Sarah, resulting in a tax saving of $1,708 ($6,100 × 28%).[22] This also reduces Harry's net earnings subject to the self-employment tax, resulting in additional income and employment tax savings.

---

[18]See Rev. Rul. 69-115, 1969-1 CB 50 and *Oswald*, 49 TC 645.

[19]An S corporation's income is taxed to the shareholders when earned, even if not distributed to them. Thus, a distribution incurs no additional tax.

[20]*Watson v. U.S.*, 757 F. Supp. 2d 877; 107 AFTR 2d 2011-311; 2011-1 USTC ¶50,443 (DC IA, 2010), affd. No. 11-1589 (8th Cir. 2/21/12). Also see *Spicer Accounting, Inc. v. U.S. 66* AFTR 2d 90-5806, 918 F.2d 90, 91-1 USTC ¶50,103 (CA-9, 1990).

[21]§3121(b)(3)(A). Payments for the services of a child under age 18 who works for his or her parents are not subject to Social Security and Medicare taxes if the business is a sole proprietorship or a partnership in which each partner is a parent of the child. Payments for the services of a child under age 21 who works for his or her parents are not subject to FUTA tax. Wages for the services of a child are subject to Social Security, Medicare, and FUTA taxes if he or she works for a corporation, even if it is controlled by the child's parent.

[22]Sarah will not pay any income taxes herself because her taxable income is less than the standard deduction. The standard deduction for a single individual in 2013 is $6,100. Refer to Chapter 11 for a discussion of the standard deduction. Because wages paid to a sole proprietor's child under age 18 are not subject to payroll taxes, the wage payment to Sarah is not subject to any payroll taxes.

Employee Fringe Benefits

Employees may receive **fringe benefits** in addition to base salary or wages. Congress encourages employers to offer employee fringe benefits by providing tax incentives that allow deductions for their cost. Unlike wages, however, the value of certain fringe benefits is excluded from the employee's income. For some types of benefits, such as insurance, the employer is able to buy the coverage on a group basis for much less than individual policies purchased directly by employees. The use of qualified fringe benefits can greatly increase the employee's effective after-tax pay.

Example 9

Alistar Corporation offers its employees the option to participate in the company's health insurance plan (a tax-exempt fringe benefit) or take \$2,000 per year in cash. An employee who takes the cash is taxed on the receipt of \$2,000. Assuming a 28 percent marginal tax rate, the employee has only \$1,440 [\$2,000 – (28% × \$2,000)] after taxes to purchase alternative insurance. In most situations, an employee cannot purchase a comparable insurance plan for this amount, leaving the employee with fewer after-tax dollars.

TAX PLANNING

Tax-exempt fringe benefits increase employees' real after-tax compensation without increasing the employer's cash outflow. The employer's income tax savings are the same for the payment of a tax-free benefit as for payment of wages, but tax-free fringe benefits generally are not subject to FICA or FUTA taxes, further reducing the cost of employee compensation.

Example 10

Sam is negotiating an employment contract with Friendly Corporation. Sam's tax rate is 25 percent and Friendly's tax rate is 34 percent. Friendly offers Sam a salary of \$80,000. The after-tax value to Sam and after-tax cost to Friendly are as follows:

	SAM	FRIENDLY CORP.
Salary	\$80,000	(\$80,000)
FICA (\$80,000 × 7.65%)	(6,120)	(6,120)
FUTA (\$7,000 × 6%)		(420)
Income tax (\$80,000 × 25%)	(20,000)	
Tax Savings:		
Salary deduction (\$80,000 × 34%)		27,200
Payroll tax deduction (\$6,540 × 34%)		2,224
After-tax value (cost)	\$53,880	(\$57,116)

Sam states that he would prefer to take \$20,000 of his compensation in tax-free fringe benefits and be paid a salary of \$61,000. The after-tax value to Sam and after-tax cost to Friendly of this \$81,000 compensation package is as follows:

	SAM	FRIENDLY CORP.
Salary	\$61,000	(\$61,000)
Fringe benefit value (cost)	20,000	(20,000)
FICA (\$61,000 × 7.65%)	(4,667)	(4,667)
FUTA (\$7,000 × 6%)		(420)
Income tax (\$61,000 × 25%)	(15,250)	
Tax Savings:		
Salary deduction (\$61,000 × 34%)		20,740
Fringe benefit deduction (\$20,000 × 34%)		6,800
Payroll tax deduction (\$5,087 × 34%)		1,730
After-tax value (cost)	\$61,083	(\$56,817)

By taking a significant portion of his salary in tax-free fringe benefits, Sam is \$7,203 (\$61,083 – \$53,880) better off than just taking salary. Friendly Corporation also saves almost \$300 while providing a larger total compensation package.

TABLE 4.1 **EMPLOYEE FRINGE BENEFITS**

BENEFIT	EXCLUDED AMOUNT
Group Term Life Insurance	Premiums for up to $50,000 coverage
Health and Accident Insurance	Premiums and most benefits received
Child and Dependent Care	Annual exclusion of $5,000 ($2,500 if married and filing separately)
Meals and Lodging	Value provided in-kind
No-Additional-Cost Services	Value of excess capacity services
Employee Discounts	Bargain element on property up to normal gross profit and up to 20% on services
De Minimis Fringes	Employer-provided items of small value
Transportation and Parking	Value of services received within certain dollar limits
Athletic Facilities	Value of use
Working Condition Fringes	Employer-provided items related to job
Relocation Reimbursements	Any reimbursed amount that employee could otherwise deduct if not reimbursed. No dollar limit.
Educational Assistance	Annual exclusion of $5,250. No dollar limit if job related.

Source: IRS Publication 17: *Your Federal Income Tax*.

To prevent abuse of tax-free benefits, significant limitations are built in to prevent the conversion of excess taxable compensation into tax-free income. If an employer provides nonqualifying employee benefits or benefits in excess of the allowable limits, the employee has additional income, although the employer can still deduct the excess benefits. The primary benefits are summarized in Table 4.1.

To encourage businesses to provide benefits to all employees and not just top executives, many of these benefit programs cannot discriminate in favor of highly compensated employees.[23] Do not get bogged down in the details of these limitations as they change as inflation adjustments take effect or by congressional action. A tax practitioner can research the specifics in effect at any point in time.[24]

Group Term Life Insurance Premiums

Premiums on employer-provided life insurance are included in the employee's gross income, except for limited coverage under a group term life insurance policy. **Term life insurance** has no cash surrender value and covers the insured individual for a specific period of time. An employee's gross income excludes the cost of annual premiums for up to $50,000 of group term life insurance coverage provided by the employer. Life insurance premiums in excess of $50,000 paid by the employer are

[23]A highly compensated employee is any of the following employees: (1) an officer, (2) a greater than 5% shareholder, (3) an employee who is highly compensated based on the facts and circumstances, and (4) a spouse or dependent of any of the above.

[24]This is one of the reasons why it is important to be able to do tax research. The specifics of how to do tax research are addressed in Chapter 2.

TABLE 4.2 **UNIFORM MONTHLY PREMIUMS FOR $1,000 OF GROUP TERM LIFE INSURANCE COVERAGE**

EMPLOYEE'S AGE	MONTHLY AMOUNT
Under 25	$.05
25 to 29	.06
30 to 34	.08
35 to 39	.09
40 to 44	.10
45 to 49	.15
50 to 54	.23
55 to 59	.43
60 to 64	.66
65 to 69	1.27
70 and above	2.06

income to the employee. To simplify the income computations, the IRS provides a table of premiums paid based on the employee's age to determine the taxable amount in excess of the $50,000 exclusion. Table 4.2 provides the monthly amount for each $1,000 of taxable coverage.[25]

If the employer's group term life insurance plan discriminates in favor of key employees, each key employee must report gross income equal to the greater of (1) the employer's actual premiums paid or (2) the benefit determined from the table without excluding the first $50,000 of coverage.[26] If the plan is nondiscriminatory, key employees use the table to determine their gross income from excess coverage and exclude the cost of the first $50,000 in coverage.

EXAMPLE 11

Gloria, a 46-year-old employee, receives $80,000 of group term life insurance from her employer for the year, for which the employer pays $300. Gloria must include $54 in her gross income (30 increments of $1,000 above the $50,000 threshold × $.15 × 12 months). If Gloria is a key employee and the insurance plan is discriminatory, Gloria must include $300 in her gross income, the greater of the actual premiums paid ($300) or the $144 computed from the table without excluding the first $50,000 of coverage (80 × $.15 × 12 months). If Gloria is a key employee but the plan is not discriminatory, she includes $54 in gross income.

The group term life insurance exclusion applies only to coverage for an employee or former employee. The cost of coverage for the employee's spouse or other dependents paid by the employer must be included in income. No other types of life insurance (such as whole life) qualify for the exclusion.

Health and Accident Insurance Premiums

To encourage employers to provide for the health insurance needs of employees and their families, the cost of health and accident plan premiums paid by an employer is

[25] Reg. §1.79-3(d)(2).

[26] §79(d)(1). A key employee is an employee who is (1) an officer with annual pay of more than $165,000, (2) a 1% owner whose annual pay is more than $150,000, or (3) a 5% owner.

a tax-free fringe benefit.[27] Because many employees rely on their employers for insurance protection, this fringe benefit has a significant impact on the U.S. labor force. All employees can exclude the value of both employer-paid premiums and benefits received from their health and accident plans from income, even if the plans discriminate in favor of key employees.[28] This exclusion also applies to employer-provided benefits for the employee's dependent children and spouse.

EXAMPLE 12

Kenneth is the president of Sterling Corporation, which pays the premiums on a group health insurance policy for all its employees. The annual premiums for Kenneth and his family are $25,000. Kenneth excludes this benefit from gross income.

Some businesses choose to self-insure their health plans under which the employees receive reimbursements directly from the business rather than through insurance or other prepaid plans such as a health maintenance organization (HMO). Under health reimbursement arrangements (HRAs), the employer makes payments to the plan and the plan reimburses the employees for qualified medical expenses. The reimbursements are usually excluded from income. Highly compensated employees, however, can exclude all reimbursements for medical care only when the self-insured medical plan is nondiscriminatory. If the plan is discriminatory, highly compensated employees must recognize gross income for any medical reimbursement that is not available to all other participants.[29] Employees who are not highly compensated, however, can exclude all reimbursements for medical care, even if the plan is discriminatory.[30]

EXAMPLE 13

Wayne is chief financial officer of Sonesta Corporation, which has a self-insured health plan that covers only its top executives. During the current year, Wayne incurs $11,000 in medical expenses, all of which are reimbursed by the plan. Because the plan discriminates in favor of highly compensated employees (as only executive officers are covered), all payments are taxable to Wayne. Thus, Wayne must include the $11,000 reimbursement in his gross income.

Child and Dependent Care Programs

An employee can exclude up to $5,000 ($2,500 if the taxpayer is married filing separately) annually of the value received from an employer-financed program for child or dependent care. The child or dependent care can be provided at either an on-site

[27]Beginning in 2014, the Patient Protection and Affordable Care Act of 2010 (PPACA) requires most individuals not eligible for Medicare, Medicaid, or another government plan to maintain minimum essential health care coverage. To help finance the cost of health care coverage, the PPACA provides that large employers (businesses with 50 or more full-time employees) that fail to offer qualifying health care coverage for their employees will be subject to a tax of up to $2,000 per full-time employee (assessed only on the excess number of employees above a 30-employee threshold) also beginning in 2014. Small employers (businesses with no more than 25 employees and average annual wages of less than $50,000) may qualify for a tax credit of up to 35 percent of their contributions towards the employee's health insurance premiums in 2010 through 2013. Starting in 2014, eligible employers who purchase coverage through a state exchange may qualify for a credit of up to 50 percent of their contribution for two years. Beginning in 2018, a 40 percent excise tax will be imposed on insurance companies if annual premium payments for group plans exceed $10,200 for individual coverage and $27,500 for family plans (as adjusted for inflation) with higher premium levels allowed for retirees and employees in high-risk professions. Employers will be required to disclose the value of employer-provided health insurance on each employee's Form W-2.

[28]§106. Payments received for medical benefits that do not qualify as tax-deductible medical expenses will result in taxable income (see Chapter 11 for a discussion of deductible medical expenses).

[29]§105(h)(1), (7).

[30]Reg. §1.105-11(a).

or off-site facility.[31] Benefits in excess of the limit are included in gross income.[32] Excluded benefits cannot exceed the employee's earned income for the year or, if less, the earned income of a spouse.[33]

The program must benefit employees exclusively and be nondiscriminatory. Highly compensated employees cannot exclude the value of services received if the plan discriminates in their favor. All other employees continue their eligibility for the exclusion, however.[34]

Cafeteria Plans

One reason fringe benefit plans are so popular is that the employer's cost of providing a benefit is usually less than the benefit's value to the employee. Employers can usually provide health insurance or on-site child care for less cost than an employee would pay for comparable services. Every employee, however, does not derive the maximum benefit from every type of fringe benefit. For example, a single individual with no dependents receives no benefit from employer-provided child care. Some employees even prefer cash to fringe benefits. If an employee is offered a choice of a fringe benefit or cash, the doctrine of constructive receipt would cause the fringe benefit to be taxed.

Cafeteria plans are an exception to the doctrine of constructive receipt. A **cafeteria plan** is a nondiscriminatory, written agreement that allows employees to choose benefits from a menu of options up to a certain dollar amount or to take cash. The menu of available benefits may include both qualified nontaxable benefits (including health insurance, dependent care assistance, adoption assistance, and group-term life insurance) and taxable cash.[35] Participants can exclude the nontaxable benefits they choose, but they are taxed on the cash or other taxable benefits selected. With a cafeteria plan, employees can combine both taxable and nontaxable benefits to yield the greatest after-tax compensation based on the employee's individual needs.

EXAMPLE 14

Marco Corporation allows its employees to choose from a variety of benefits up to an amount equal to six percent of their annual salary. During the year, Sara chose $8,000 of health insurance coverage for herself and her family, $3,000 of child care assistance, $500 for a health club membership, and $600 in cash. The $500 for the health club membership and the $600 cash are taxable while the health insurance and child care assistance are tax free.

To qualify for this favorable treatment, the plan must be available to all employees on a nondiscriminatory basis. If the plan discriminates in favor of highly compensated employees, those employees include all benefits received in their gross income.[36]

One of the most useful plan options offered is a flexible spending arrangement (FSA). A **flexible spending arrangement** allows employees to reduce their salaries for the cost

TAX PLANNING

[31]§129(e)(8). A tax credit initiated in 2002 provides an incentive for employers to establish these facilities. The credit equals 25 percent of qualified expenses for employee child care and 10 percent of qualified expenses for child care resource and referral services, up to a maximum credit of $150,000 per year. §45F.

[32]§129(a). Generally, the type of assistance that qualifies for the dependent care credit when paid by an employee can be excluded when provided by an employer.

[33]§129(b).

[34]§129(d)(1)-(3).

[35]§137. Only up to $50,000 value of group term life insurance is tax free.

[36]A highly compensated employee for this purpose includes the following: (1) an officer, (2) a shareholder who owns more than 5% of the voting power or value of all classes of the employer's stock, (3) an employee who is highly compensated based on the facts and circumstances, and (4) a spouse or dependent of a person described in (1), (2), or (3). Since 2011, small employers (with 100 or fewer employees) can establish a Simple Cafeteria Plan that has a safe harbor exception from the nondiscrimination requirements to encourage more small employers to offer tax-free benefits to their employees. This plan would also include self-employed individuals as qualified employees.

of certain nontaxable fringe benefits not provided by their employers, such as dental expenses or co-payments required by their medical insurance. FSAs can be offered for medical and dependent care. Under an FSA, a participant decides in advance how much to set aside for costs not covered by the employer or insurance. In 2013, the maximum annual contribution to a health FSA is $2,500. The designated amount is withheld by the employer, deposited with the employer's FSA plan administrator, and excluded from the employee's taxable compensation. The participant then applies for a nontaxable reimbursement from the plan administrator as qualified expenses are incurred. If the employee's reimbursements are less than contributions made, the excess contributions are lost. Employees should carefully estimate their anticipated expenses and set aside only an amount they are certain they will spend for qualified expenses during that year.[37]

Example 15

Carl's employer pays $7,000 of the $8,000 cost of health insurance for him and his family. Carl elects to reduce his $50,000 salary to $49,000, using the foregone $1,000 to pay for his cost of the health insurance. Carl also elects to set aside $1,000 in an FSA for unreimbursed dental expenses. During the year, Carl incurs $970 of otherwise unreimbursed dental expenses. Carl is paid $970 from the funds set aside in his FSA. Although he lost the remaining $30, he was able to pay for $1,970 of medical insurance and dental expenses with the pretax $2,000 that reduced his taxable salary to $48,000.

Meals and Lodging

If meals and lodging provided employees meet certain conditions, the employees can exclude their value from their gross income. Meals must be provided on the employer's business premises for the employer's convenience.

Employees can exclude the value of lodging (for themselves and their family) only if it, too, is provided on the business premises for the employer's convenience. In addition, the lodging must be accepted as a condition of employment. (Employees cannot choose whether or not to accept employer-provided lodging.) If the lodging is a condition of employment, then it should be specified in an employment agreement to ensure the tax-free treatment.

Example 16

Richard manages a bed-and-breakfast business. The owner requires Richard to live in one of the rooms at no charge so he can be available if a problem should arise. The owner also wants Richard to eat his meals, at no charge, in the dining room so that he can respond quickly to guest needs. Richard excludes the value of the lodging and meals from his gross income.

If an employee can choose between meals and lodging or additional compensation, the value of any meals and lodging selected is taxable. Additionally, cash allowances for meals or lodging are usually included in the employee's gross income.[38]

Employees can also exclude reimbursements for business-related meals and travel expenses. The limitations that apply to deductibility of these expenses are discussed in the next chapter.

No-Additional-Cost Services

When an employer provides free "excess capacity" services to employees without incurring substantial additional costs, the employees can exclude the value of the services from gross income; for example, the value of unsold seats on an airplane or train is

[37]The IRS has somewhat eased this rule by permitting employers to allow a grace period of up to 2½ months following the end of the year. Notice 2005-42, 2005-23 IRB 1204. Beginning in 2011, the definition of medical expenses eligible for payment through an FSA no longer includes over-the-counter medicines. Beginning in 2013, the maximum annual contribution to a health FSA is limited to $2,500.

[38]Reg. §1.119-1(e). An exception exists for persons who work a significant amount of overtime. They are permitted to exclude "supper money" received.

excluded.[39] Only services (not property) that the employer offers in the ordinary course of its business qualify for the exclusion. Employees must be employed in a business rendering similar services or at an affiliated corporation to qualify for the exclusion.[40] For example, an employee of a corporation that performs baggage handling for an airline is considered to be in the same business as the airline and qualifies for the exclusion.[41]

Example 17

Gary, an employee of the Empty Arms hotel chain, may stay in any of its hotels for 10 nights a year without charge. Gary uses the chain's unreserved hotel rooms for six nights during the year at no charge. Gary excludes the value of the rooms. If, however, Gary reserved rooms that would have been sold to paying guests, he could not exclude their value as a no-additional-cost service. (As discussed below, a portion of the benefit might be excludable as an employee discount.)

In addition to current employees, a spouse and dependent children of current employees, retired employees, and parents of airline employees may benefit from this exclusion.[42] Highly compensated employees and their families, however, cannot exclude the value of any benefits received on a discriminatory basis.[43] Partners who perform services for the partnership are eligible for this exclusion.[44]

Employee Purchase Discounts

The sale of property or services to employees at below fair market value results in taxable income unless it qualifies as an employee discount. To qualify, the discounted service or property (excluding real estate and investment property) must be offered to customers in the ordinary course of business.[45]

The excludable discount on merchandise is limited to the gross profit percentage times the price charged to customers, effectively preventing employees from purchasing property below the employer's cost without recognizing taxable income. The gross profit percentage is based on sales data from the immediate preceding tax year computed by dividing the excess of total sales over the cost of property sold by total sales. The excludable discount for services (other than the no-additional-cost services) cannot exceed 20 percent of the price normally charged customers for the services.[46] Any additional discount is taxable income.

Example 18

Fine Furnishings Corporation's gross profit percentage last year was 25 percent allowing its employees to buy its products at a 25 percent discount. Mack, an employee, pays \$450 for furniture that normally retails for \$600. Mack excludes the \$150 discount from income. Mack also pays \$600 for some used office equipment valued at \$1,000; because this equipment is not normally sold in Fine's business, Mack is taxed on the \$400 discount.

Example 19

Linda works for Speedy Carwash Company. Its normal charge for car washes is \$10, but employees pay only \$5. During the current year, Linda has her car washed 12 times, paying a total of \$60 (\$5 × 12) for her car washes. Because the maximum discount allowed for service is 20 percent, any discount in excess of \$2 (\$10 × 20%) is income. Linda must report \$36 as income (\$5 discount - \$2 maximum discount allowed = \$3 excess × 12 car washes).

[39] §132(b)(2) and Reg. §1.132-2(a)(2). To determine if substantial additional costs are incurred, lost revenues count as a cost; however, any employee payments for services are ignored and do not reduce the costs incurred. Reg. §1.132-2(a)(5)(i).

[40] §132(b)(1).

[41] §132(j)(5).

[42] §132(h).

[43] §132(j)(1).

[44] Reg. §1.132-2(b)(1).

[45] §132(c)(4).

[46] §132(c)(2).

Only employees who work in the same line of business that sells the property or renders the services to nonemployee customers can exclude their discounts.[47] Highly compensated employees can exclude their discounts only if such discounts are nondiscriminatory.[48] **Bargain purchases** are essentially employee discounts that are made available only to select employees and are taxable.

Employee Achievement Awards

The value of most awards and prizes is included in gross income, except for employee awards for length of service or safety achievement. To qualify for exclusion, the award must be made in the form of tangible personal property (such as a watch) rather than as cash or a gift certificate.[49] Under a nondiscriminatory qualified plan, a single award can be valued as high as $1,600 in any year, if the average value for all achievement awards does not exceed $400. If the award is not made under a qualified plan, exclusions are limited to $400 per employee per year.[50]

De Minimis Fringe Benefits

Employees can exclude from income the value of **de minimis benefits** (small in value) provided by their employers. Property and services are de minimis when their value is so small that accounting for them is unreasonable or impractical.[51] Examples of de minimis fringe benefits include coffee and doughnuts, limited personal use of photocopy machines or computers, use of business phones for local personal calls, occasional tickets to sporting or cultural events, noncash holiday gifts with minimal value such as turkeys, nominal birthday gifts, occasional company picnics or cocktail parties, and flowers sent to an employee because of illness.[52] If an employee receives cash or an item easily exchanged for cash, the employee has taxable compensation.[53]

KEY RULING

In prior years, an employer provided employees with a ham, turkey, or gift basket as an annual holiday gift. These items qualified as excludable de minimis benefits. To satisfy employees with religious or dietary limitations, the employer began distributing gift certificates. The gift certificates had a face value of $35 (equal to the value of holiday gifts previously provided) and were redeemable for groceries at several local markets during a 2½-month period. They could not, however, be exchanged for cash. The IRS determined that the coupons were not excludable as de minimis benefits because the certificates had a value that was readily ascertainable and, therefore, accounting for them was not impractical.[54]

Food service employees can exclude meals furnished by their employer during, immediately before, or immediately after their working hours. An employer can also provide subsidized meals for employees as a de minimis fringe benefit if the dining facility is on or near the employer's business premises and employees are charged an

---

[47]§132(c)(4). The employee discount exclusion also is available to certain individuals other than employees who qualify for no-additional-cost exclusions. §132(h).

[48]§132(j)(1).

[49]This exclusion does not apply to awards of cash, cash equivalents, gift certificates, or other intangible property such as vacations, meals, lodging, tickets to theater or sporting events, stock, bonds, and other securities.

[50]§74(c).

[51]The frequency with which similar benefits are provided to employees is one factor in determining whether property or services are de minimis. §132(e)(1). If an employer provides a benefit that is not de minimis because of either its value or its frequency, no portion of the benefit can be considered de minimis. Reg. §1.132-6(d)(4).

[52]De minimis fringes do not include season tickets to sporting or cultural events, commuting use of employer vehicles more than one day a month, memberships in social or athletic clubs, and weekend use of an employer's boat or hunting lodge. Reg. §1.132-6(e). Fringe benefits that are not considered de minimis might be excludable under other provisions, such as no-additional-cost services or working condition fringe benefits.

[53]Occasional meals or "supper money" provided to an employee who works overtime can be excluded if the supper money is not calculated based on the hours worked.

[54]TAM 200437030 (9/10/2004).

amount that equals or exceeds the facility's direct operating costs. De minimis fringe benefits, except subsidized meals, can be provided on a discriminatory basis.[55]

Employees can also exclude employer-provided qualified transportation benefits from gross income. Mass transit passes (valued up to $245 per month for 2013) and free or discounted parking on or near the employer's business premises (valued up to $245 per month for 2013) can be excluded.[56] Employees who commute to work by bicycle can receive up to $20 per month from their employers to cover the cost of the bicycle purchase, improvements, repairs, and storage. Benefits in excess of these amounts must be included in income.

Employees who use qualified employer-provided athletic facilities operated by the employer and located on premises the employer owns or leases (such as tennis courts, gymnasiums, and swimming pools) can exclude the value of this benefit from gross income. To qualify for exclusion, substantially all of the use of the athletic facility during the tax year must be by employees, their spouses, and their dependent children.

Working Condition Fringe Benefits

If an employer pays ordinary and necessary business expenses on behalf of its employees, the employees can exclude their value from gross income as **working condition fringe benefits**.[57] Excludable working condition fringes include job-related education, professional membership dues, subscriptions to professional journals, bodyguards, use of an employer-provided cellphone, and use of the company car or plane for business.[58]

EXAMPLE 20

Alan is a CPA employed by a public accounting firm. The firm pays Alan's annual professional dues to the AICPA. Alan excludes the payment from gross income because he could have deducted the dues as an employee business expense if he paid for it himself.

TAX PLANNING

This rule benefits employees whose business expenses cannot be deducted due to the limits on miscellaneous itemized deductions.[59] Highly compensated employees can exclude working condition fringes, even if made on a discriminatory basis.[60]

The use of a company-owned car for business purposes is a tax-free working condition fringe benefit; however, the value of an employee's personal use of a company car is taxable as compensation. The employer may use one of three optional valuation methods to determine the value of an employee's personal use of an employer's vehicle: the lease-value, the cents-per-mile, or the commuting method. To determine the annual lease value, multiply the annual lease value from a table in the regulations by the ratio of the employee's annual personal mileage to the total annual mileage.[61] A portion of this table is reproduced as Table 4.3.[62]

[55] Reg. §1.132-6(f) and §1.132-7.

[56] §132(f)(2). Both the parking exclusion and transit pass exclusion were $230 for 2011. The American Recovery and Reinvestment Act of 2009 increased the monthly transit pass exclusion from $120 to $230 as of March 1, 2009 but this provision providing parity with the parking exclusion expired at the end of 2011. Congress increased the transit pass exclusion retroactively to the same $240 amount allowed for parking in 2012.

[57] §132(d). The key is whether the employee is entitled to a tax deduction if he or she pays the expense. If an employer pays for or reimburses an employee for a nonqualified expense, the employee has income as if it were wages, and it is subject to payroll taxes as well.

[58] Business expense deductions are discussed in Chapter 5.

[59] See Chapter 11 for a discussion of the 2 percent of AGI limitation on miscellaneous itemized deductions.

[60] Reg. §1.132-1(b)(2). Independent contractors, partners, and corporate directors can receive qualifying working condition fringe benefits tax free.

[61] See Reg. § 1.61-21(d)(2)(iii) for a list of the five specific requirements that must be met to use this method.

[62] The complete table can be found at Reg. §1.61-21(d)(2)(iii). For vehicles valued at $60,000 or more, the annual lease value = [(25% × fair market value) + $500]. The annual lease value does not include the value of fuel provided to an employee so the fair market value of fuel is separately added to the employee's compensation. Fuel can be valued at 5.5 cents per mile or the actual amount paid or reimbursed.

TABLE 4.3 **PARTIAL TABLE OF ANNUAL LEASE-VALUE AMOUNTS FOR PERSONAL USE OF EMPLOYER-PROVIDED AUTOMOBILES**

FAIR MARKET VALUE OF AUTO	ANNUAL LEASE VALUE
\$ 0–\$ 999	\$ 600
1,000–1,999	850
10,000–10,999	3,100
15,000–15,999	4,350
20,000–20,999	5,600
30,000–31,999	8,250
40,000–41,999	10,750
50,000–51,999	13,250

Under the vehicle cents-per-mile method, the employer taxes the employee at the rate of 56.5 cents per mile for personal use in 2013.[63] Under the special unsafe conditions commuting valuation method, the employer includes a value of only \$1.50 per one-way commute in the employee's income.[64]

EXAMPLE 21

LMN Corporation purchased cars for use by its president and two employees, Will and Sara. The president's car has a fair market value of \$40,000. If 50 percent of the miles the president drives are for personal trips, under the lease-value method, the president has \$5,375 of taxable compensation for his personal use of the car (\$10,750 table value × 50% personal use).

Will drives 12,000 personal miles in his company-owned car that cost \$15,000. Using the standard mileage rate, the LMN includes \$6,780 (12,000 miles × 56.5¢) in Will's income in 2013 due to his personal use of the car.

Sara uses a company-owned car for commuting. LMN Corporation provides Sara with a company-owned car when she works the night shift because she lives in a high-crime neighborhood and commuting via public transit late at night would not be safe. The LMN Corporation prohibits Sara from using the auto for personal purposes other than commuting. Sara used the car to commute to work 220 days during the year. Sara has \$660 in taxable fringe benefit compensation (220 days × \$1.50 each way × 2 one-way trips each day).

The employer cannot deduct this noncash compensation, however. Instead, the employer deducts depreciation (or lease payments), gasoline, insurance, repairs, and other expenses of operating the vehicle.[65]

[63]Notice 2012-72, 2012-50 IRB 673. The rate was 55.5 cents for 7/1/11-12/31/12, 51 cents for 1/1/11-6/30/11, 50 cents for 2010, 55 cents per mile for 2009, 58.5 cents per mile for 7/1/08-12/31/08, and 50.5 cents per mile for 1/1/08-6/30/08.

[64]Reg. §1.61-21(f)(1). The employee would ordinarily walk or use public transportation for commuting; (2) the employer has a written policy that transportation for personal purposes is not allowed other than commuting because of unsafe conditions; and (3) the employee does not use the vehicle for personal purposes other than commuting because of unsafe conditions. One factor indicating whether it is unsafe for the employee to walk or use public transportation is the history of crime in the area surrounding the home or work place during the time of day he or she must commute. To qualify, the employee must be paid on an hourly basis for services and receive pay of not more than \$115,000 during the year.

[65]As long as the value of all personal use is taxed as employee income, the auto is considered used 100 percent for business, regardless of the actual business use. The employer's depreciation deduction is discussed in Chapter 6.

Employee Relocation Expenses

An employee does not have income if the employer reimburses qualified relocation or moving expenses. If the employer reimburses or pays directly nonqualified relocation costs, the employee has taxable compensation.

Qualified moving expenses include the reasonable costs of the following:

- Packing, crating, and transporting household goods and personal belongings (including personal vehicles and household pets) from the old home to the new home
- 30 days of storage and insurance while in transit and before delivery to the new home
- Travel expenses for all family members from the old home to the new home

Travel expenses include the cost of transportation and lodging en route for the taxpayer and members of the taxpayer's household but exclude the cost of meals.[66] Reasonable moving expenses implies that the move is made by the shortest and most direct route over the shortest period of time required to travel the distance. A member of the household is anyone who lives in the taxpayer's home before and after the move.[67] Travel expenses are limited to one trip for each household member, but the family does not have to travel together.[68]

If the taxpayer uses his or her own automobile as transportation for the move, an auto expense deduction can be computed in one of two ways: (1) total all actual expenses for gasoline and oil (depreciation and insurance cannot be deducted) or (2) deduct a flat rate of 24 cents per mile in 2013 (plus parking and tolls).[69]

A qualified move includes a transfer by a current employer, hiring by a new employer, and obtaining employment after the move. A move in any of these situations qualifies, as long as the distance and time requirements are met.

Distance Test

To meet the distance test, the distance between the old residence and the new principal place of work (the new commuting distance if the taxpayer does not move) must be at least 50 miles greater than the distance between the old place of work and the old residence (the old commuting distance). These distances are measured by the shortest commonly traveled routes.[70]

Example 22

Karen lives in Oldtown and works at Oldjob. Her employer transfers her to Newjob. Karen moves 51 miles to Newtown. The relevant distances are:

Old residence to Newjob = 53 miles

Old residence to Oldjob = 4 miles

Karen does not meet the distance test because the distance from the old residence to Newjob is only 49 miles greater than the old commuting distance (53 miles – 4 miles).

Time Test

To meet the time test, a taxpayer must have full-time employment for any 39 weeks during the 12 months following the move.[71] A self-employed individual must work full-time at the new location for at least 78 weeks during the 24 months following the move. Of the 78 weeks, the individual must work 39 weeks within the first 12 months.[72]

---

[66]§217(b).

[67]§217(b)(3)(C). Moving expenses for tenants or employees (such as a servant, governess, chauffeur, or nurse) do not qualify. Reg. §1.217-1(b)(6).

[68]Reg. §1.217-1(b)(4).

[69]Notice 2012-72, 2012-50 IRB 673. The rate was 24 cents for 2012, 23.5 cents for 7/1/11-12/31/11, 19 cents for 1/1/11-6/30/11, 16.5 cents per mile for 2010, 24 cents per mile for 2009, 27 cents per mile for 7/1/08-12/31/08 and 19 cents per mile for 1/1/08-6/30/08.

[70]Reg. §217(c).

[71]Reg. §1.217-2(c)(4)(iii).

[72]Reg. §1.217-2(c)(4)(i)(b).

Semi-retired persons, part-time students, and other individuals who work only a few hours each week do not meet this test.[73]

EXAMPLE 23

Caroline had severe allergies. On her doctor's advice, she quit her job and moved to Arizona. After six weeks she became a consultant for an accounting firm. She quit after six months when she eloped and moved to California with her new husband. She immediately began full-time work as a consultant, developing a thriving business over the next several years. Caroline's Arizona moving expenses do not qualify because she did not meet the time test. The expenses of her move to California qualify, however.

The time tests do not apply if the individual dies or becomes disabled, is terminated from full-time employment for other than willful misconduct, or is transferred again by the employer for reasons other than the employee's convenience.[74] An individual who has not met the time test and would like to request a transfer should consider postponing the transfer until the time test can be met.

If an employee is not reimbursed for qualified moving expenses, the costs are deductible *for* adjusted gross income (AGI).[75] If an employee has paid for his or her own moving expenses but the time requirement is not satisfied by the due date for filing the tax return, the employee may deduct the moving expenses currently or wait until the time requirement is satisfied and file an amended return for the year in which the moving expenses were paid. If the employee deducted moving expenses but does not satisfy the time requirement, the employee must either include the amount previously deducted for moving expenses as other income in the current year or file an amended return excluding the previously deducted moving expenses.

TAX PLANNING

The taxpayer should calculate the taxes owed under both options and select the method of reporting the disallowance of the moving expense deduction that results in the least tax cost.

No moving expense deductions are allowed for relocation to a temporary place of employment. An assignment is considered temporary unless it is for more than one year. If the employment is temporary, there is no change in tax home and expenses for travel away from home are deductible.[76]

Education Expenses

An employer can reimburse employees for their job-related education expenses or establish a qualified educational assistance plan. Under the latter, the education does not have to be job related, but reimbursements are limited. An educational assistance program is a separate written plan that provides educational assistance only to employees. It cannot favor highly-compensated employees and cannot provide more than 5 percent of its benefits for the year to shareholders or owners of more than 5 percent of the business.

Employees can exclude up to $5,250 in educational assistance plan reimbursements annually. Reimbursements for tuition, fees, books, supplies, and equipment qualify and the education does not have to relate directly to employment.[77]

An unlimited amount of reimbursements or direct payments by employers for employee's education expenses to maintain or improve skills required in the taxpayer's

---

[73]Reg. §1.217-2(f)(1).

[74]Rev. Rul. 88-47, 1988-1 CB 111.

[75]When a deduction is taken *for* AGI, it means that the deduction is subtracted before calculating adjusted gross income. One advantage of a deduction *for* AGI is that taxpayers who take the standard deduction instead of itemizing their deductions may still benefit from a deduction *for* AGI. Refer to Chapter 11 for a more detailed discussion.

[76]Deductible travel expenses are discussed in Chapter 5.

[77]§127(c)(1). The value of instruction for sports, games, or hobbies must be included in income unless it is part of the required course of instruction. Excludable educational assistance does not include: meals, lodging, transportation or supplies that the employee can retain after the course ends (other than textbooks).

business are excluded from income. Qualified educational expenses include books, tuition, fees, and transportation from the workplace to school. Expenses for education that (1) meet the minimum educational requirements for the taxpayer's job or (2) qualify the taxpayer for a new trade or profession do not qualify for exclusion. Continuing professional education (CPE) requirements imposed by states on professionals (such as CPAs, attorneys, and physicians) as a condition for retaining a license to practice are considered qualifying education expenses. Fees incurred for professional qualification exams (such as the bar exam or CPA exam) and fees for review courses (such as a CPA review course) do not qualify.[78]

EXAMPLE 24

Cherie, an accountant with a bachelor's degree in accounting, was hired when a bachelor's degree was her employer's minimum educational requirement. Recently, her employer changed these minimum educational requirements for all current and newly hired accountants to a master's degree, and Cherie must now take graduate classes to keep her job. Because Cherie satisfied the minimum requirements at the date she was hired, the expenses related to completing a master's degree qualify as job related and reimbursements for these expenses are not taxable. Tom, a newly hired accountant, has not completed a master's degree. Any reimbursement by the employer for expenses related to his completion of the master's degree is taxable income to him because the master's degree is now needed to satisfy the minimum educational requirements for his position.

Figure 4.1 illustrates the steps necessary to determine if education expenses qualify as work related. Employees who pay for their own job-related education and are not reimbursed may deduct these expenses as miscellaneous itemized deductions.

Educational institutions frequently provide qualified tuition reduction plans to employees and their family members. These benefits are excluded from income if the tuition is for education below the graduate level; graduate tuition waivers are taxable.[79]

Employees who pay for their own tuition, and are not eligible to deduct it as job-related education, may be eligible for the American Opportunity or Lifetime Learning tax credit for eligible expenses.[80] Alternatively, the taxpayer may be eligible for a deduction of up to $4,000 *for* AGI.[81] Qualified expenses are limited to tuition and fees paid to qualified higher education institutions. Education expenses cannot create a double tax benefit; that is, if a taxpayer deducts them as a business expense or excludes them from income, the taxpayer cannot also claim a tax credit for the same expenses. Table 4.4 summarizes the possible tax benefits that may be derived from education expenses.

Substantiating Business Expenses

Most employers require some form of accounting for business expenditures to support reimbursement requests. If the employer has an **accountable plan**, the employee must provide a record of the amount, date, place of expenditure, and business pur-

[78]Reg. §1.212-1(f) and Rev. Rul. 69-292, 1969-1 CB 84.

[79]§117(d). A special provision allows tuition reduction benefits paid to graduate teaching and research assistants employed by education institutions to be excluded from gross income. This exclusion is limited to the value of the tuition benefit in excess of reasonable compensation for services. Prop. Reg. §1.117-6(d). Free or discounted tuition provided to employees of an educational institution cannot qualify as a no-additional-cost benefit or working condition fringe benefit.

[80]For 2013, the Lifetime learning credit is phased out for single taxpayers with modified AGI of $53,000 to $63,000 ($107,000 to $127,000 for married taxpayers filing joint returns). The American opportunity tax credit (formerly called the Hope credit) is phased out for single taxpayers with modified AGI of $80,000 to $90,000 ($160,000 to $180,000 for married taxpayers filing joint return) as discussed in Chapter 11.

[81]To qualify for this $4,000 deduction the taxpayer must have an adjusted gross income of less than $65,000 ($130,000 for a married couple filing a joint return) as discussed in Chapter 11. A deduction of $2,000 is available for taxpayers whose adjusted gross income does not exceed $80,000 ($160,000 for a married couple filing a joint return). These deductions are scheduled to expire at the end of 2013 but could be extended by Congress.

FIGURE 4.1 **WHEN DO EDUCATION EXPENSES QUALIFY AS WORK RELATED?**

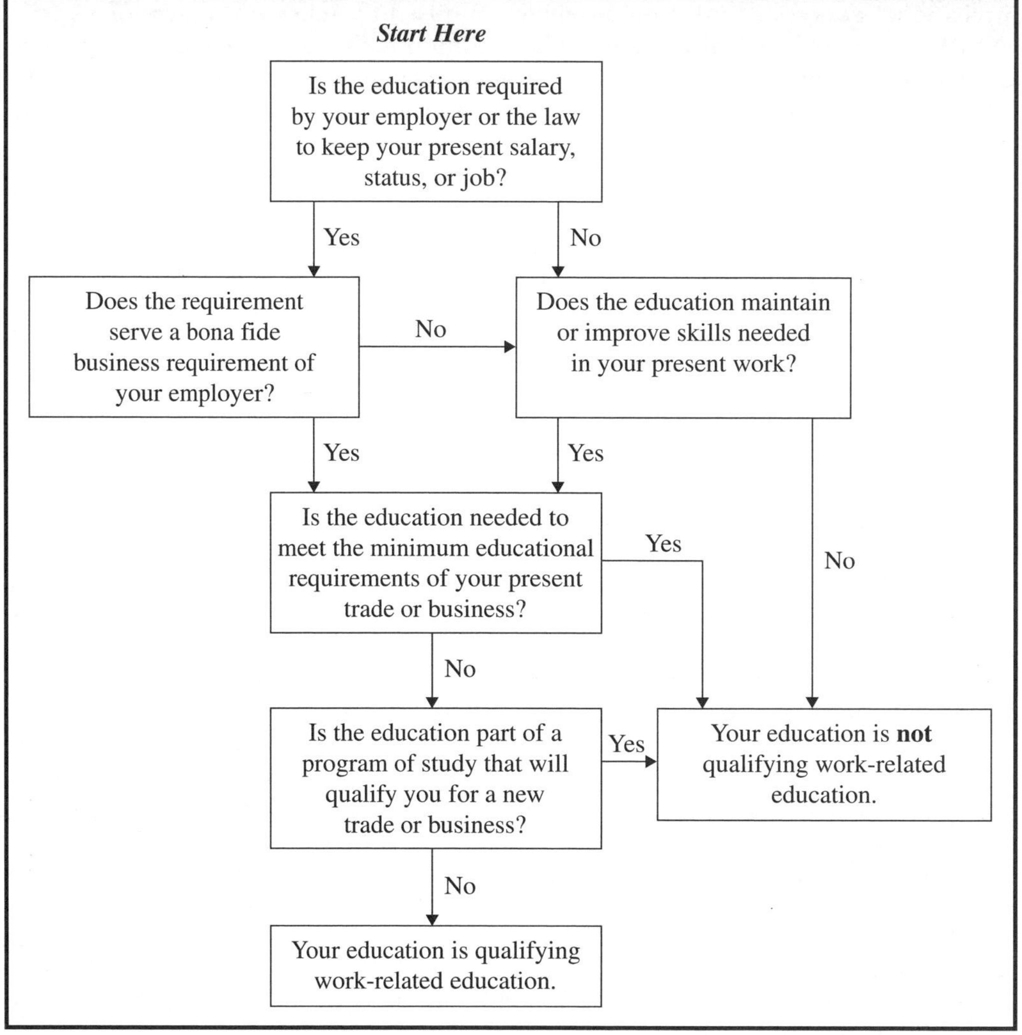

Source: IRS Publication 17: *Your Federal Income Tax*.

pose, along with all appropriate receipts.[82] Receipts are required to support any expenditure for lodging (regardless of cost) while traveling away from home and for any other expenditure of $75 or more.

With an accountable plan:

- If the reimbursement equals the business expenses, the employee excludes the reimbursement from income and the employer deducts the expenses.
- If the reimbursement exceeds the expenses, the excess reimbursement is income.[83]
- If the expenses exceed the reimbursement, the employee deducts the unreimbursed expenses as miscellaneous itemized deductions.[84]

[82]Effectively, the employee should maintain a diary or account book in which this information is recorded at the time the expense is incurred.

[83]If the reimbursement equals or exceeds the expenses and is included in the employee's income, the employee takes an offsetting deduction for the expenses.

[84]Some of the deductions may be lost due to the limit on the deductibility of miscellaneous itemized deductions in excess of 2 percent of AGI. See Chapter 11 for the discussion of itemized deductions.

TABLE
4.4 TAX BENEFITS FROM EDUCATION EXPENSES

PROVISION	TYPE OF BENEFIT	MUST BE WORK RELATED?	TYPE OF QUALIFYING EXPENSES
Business Expense Deduction	No dollar limit on amount of deduction	Yes	Tuition, fees, books, supplies, equipment, transportation, meals, and lodging
Working Condition Fringe Benefit	No dollar limit on exclusion from income	Yes	Tuition, fees, books, supplies, equipment, transportation, meals, and lodging
Educational Assistance Program	Maximum exclusion from income of $5,250 per year	No	Tuition, fees, books, supplies, and equipment
Qualified Tuition Reduction	No dollar limit on exclusion from income of employee	No	Tuition for undergraduate courses only
Qualified Scholarship	No dollar limit on exclusion from income	No, but will not qualify if for past, present or future services	Tuition, fees, books, supplies, and equipment
Tuition Deduction *for* AGI	Maximum deduction of $4,000 per year	No	Tuition and fees
American Opportunity Credit	Maximum credit of $2,500 per year per student	No	Tuition, fees, and books for first four years of undergraduate courses
Lifetime Learning Credit	Maximum credit of $2,000 per year per taxpayer	No	Tuition and fees

If an employee does not make an adequate accounting, the employer has a **nonaccountable plan** and the employee includes reimbursements in income. The employee then deducts the allowable business expenses as miscellaneous itemized deductions.

Some employers reduce their paperwork by using a **per diem allowance**. This is a flat dollar allowance per day of business travel. When a per diem allowance is used, expenses are deemed substantiated to the extent of the lesser of the per diem allowance or the federal per diem rate.[85] The per diem method only substantiates the amount of expense; the other substantiation requirements must still be met, including the place, date, and business purpose for the expense.

Employee Stock and Stock Options

From the employer's perspective, the use of its stock as compensation is attractive because it requires no cash outflow and encourages employees to work for the success of the company as they become stockholders and are able to share in that success. To avoid diluting existing shareholders' control, however, employers frequently issue nonvoting stock to employees. When a corporation uses stock as payment for services, the employee recognizes ordinary income equal to the stock's fair market value when received. The employer is permitted to take a corresponding compensation deduction, but cannot recognize any gain or loss on the transaction.

Example 25

Todd Corporation paid Randy $80,000 salary plus 2,500 shares of Todd stock valued at $25,000. Todd deducts $105,000 as compensation expense and Randy must pay taxes on $105,000 of ordinary income. When Randy sells the stock, he will recognize a capital gain or loss equal to the difference between his $25,000 basis in the stock and the sales price.

[85]The federal per diem rates differ by location. These amounts may be found at http://www.gsa.gov/portal/content/104877 or by searching the GSA website for per diem rates.

Restricted Stock

Stock that is transferred to an employee as compensation for services but is subject to a vesting schedule is referred to as restricted stock. Normally, the employee is not required to pay for the stock. Restricted stock plans are usually established to retain key employees who otherwise might leave the company. Employees cannot sell the restricted stock issued to them until some future date because the employee's right to the stock is nontransferable or is subject to a substantial risk of forfeiture when received. Employees are normally required to forfeit their shares (return them to the employer) if they leave the company before the stock vests (that is, becomes unrestricted, typically within a two- to five-year period). In some cases, the shares are tied to the company's performance and the shares are forfeited if certain financial targets are not met.

The value of restricted stock received generally is not taxed until it vests; at that time, the employee recognizes ordinary income equal to the fair market value of the stock and the employer receives a corresponding compensation deduction.[86] The income recognized is ordinary income because the employee received the restricted stock in return for services. Note, however, that restricted stock shares have value when granted and that their value can vary between the grant date and the vesting date. This differs from stock options (discussed later) that generally have no value to the employee (the option price generally must be equal to or greater than the current market price) unless the stock appreciates in value after the option is granted. As a result, a share of restricted stock has more value than an option to acquire a share of stock. Thus, employers who issue restricted stock rather than stock options are able to use fewer shares to provide the same value to employees.

Shareholders usually are entitled to receive any dividend payments on their shares of restricted stock, even before the stock has vested, but these dividends are taxed as ordinary income and deductible by the employer as compensation expense. After vesting, any dividends received are eligible for the maximum 15 percent dividend tax rate (20 percent for high-income taxpayers).

Example 26

On July 1, year 1, Maria received 300 shares of her employer's stock as a bonus. If she leaves the company before July 1, year 5, she must return the stock to the company. If she is still working for the company after July 1, year 5, the risk of forfeiture lapses, and she will be vested in the stock (that is, have an unrestricted right to the shares). If the shares are worth $60,000 when the risk of forfeiture lapses, Maria will have $60,000 of ordinary income in year 5. The employer also takes a $60,000 compensation deduction in year 5. Any dividends Maria received on the stock prior to vesting were taxable as ordinary income. Dividends received after vesting are eligible for the reduced dividend tax rates of 0/15/20 percent based on her other taxable income.

Employees may elect to accelerate the recognition of income on restricted stock by recognizing the fair market value as income in the year of receipt.[87] Any appreciation in the stock after receipt will be taxed at capital gains rates when it is sold. There is a significant amount of risk associated with the income acceleration election if, at a later date, the employee must forfeit the stock. The employee is allowed no deduction for the loss on the stock forfeited, nor is he or she allowed a refund of any taxes paid as a result of the prior income recognition.[88]

Example 27

Continuing the previous example, assume that the fair market value of the stock at the time it was issued was $12,000. If Maria elects income acceleration, she will recognize only $12,000 ordinary income in year 1 and no additional income in year 5 when the restrictions lapse. Her basis for the shares is $12,000. When she sells the shares, the difference between the $12,000 and the selling price is taxable at capital gains

[86] §83(a).

[87] §83(b). The employee has only 30 days after receipt to make the election.

[88] A capital loss would only be allowed for any amount the employee paid for the stock.

rates. The employer's compensation deduction matches Maria's income recognition, so it is entitled to a $12,000 deduction in year 1. It will have no additional deduction when the restrictions lapse.

If Maria elects to recognize the $12,000 of ordinary income in year 1 but quits her job in year 3, she may not deduct her $12,000 basis in the stock and she would have paid tax on income never received. Additionally, the employer must repay any taxes saved by the compensation deduction in year 1.[89] If she had not made the election, she would have recognized no income and had no basis in the forfeited stock.

Most employees do not make the income acceleration election because it results in immediate recognition of ordinary income (with no cash flow with which to pay the tax as no stock can be sold) and potential adverse consequences from forfeiture. The election could be considered under the following circumstances, however; the value of the stock is initially low, substantial appreciation is expected, there is a very high probability that the stock will vest, and the tax on the current fair market value will be less than the discounted present value of the tax on the fair market value in the year the restrictions lapse.

TAX PLANNING

Stock Options

Stock options, the right to acquire employer stock, are granted to corporate employees as part of a compensation package or as an incentive to forego seeking employment elsewhere. A corporate **stock option** is a right to purchase a certain number of shares of the corporation's stock for a stated price (called the *strike price* or exercise price) for a specified period of time. The grant date is the date on which the option is first offered to the individual. An employee *exercises* an option when he or she purchases the stock from the company. An employee has no obligation to exercise an option and would normally do so only when it is beneficial to exercise it; that is, when the stock's value has appreciated beyond the strike price between the grant date and the exercise date The employee usually recognizes no income when the option is granted; instead, income is deferred to a future year when the option is exercised or the stock is sold. Options provide employees another opportunity to have an investment in their employer's company without requiring an immediate cash outlay. Unlike actual stock ownership, if the value of the stock declines, the employee does not suffer a direct loss as the employee can simply allow the option to lapse. Employees also like the inherent leverage in options because the increase in the value of the options is proportionately greater than the increase in the value of the company stock.

EXAMPLE 28

Adam receives 3,000 shares of restricted stock worth $20 per share. If the price increases to $50, the shares would be worth $150,000. Alternatively, assume Adam receives 10,000 stock options with a strike price of $20. When the stock price reaches $50, the options will be worth $300,000 [($50 – $20) × 10,000].

Employers favor stock options because they require no cash outlay by the employer when they are granted and can result in cash inflow for the employer when the employee exercises the options. Employers also receive a tax benefit from the compensation deduction equal to the employee's compensation income in the year the income is recognized.

Nonqualified Stock Options

A majority of stock options issued to employees are nonqualified stock options. A **nonqualified stock option (NQSO)** allows the employee to purchase employer stock at a strike price that is usually set at or above its current selling price.[90] If the

[89]Reg. §§1.83-6(c) and 2(a).

[90]If an employee receives a stock option that is currently exercisable with a strike price below the current market value, then that option has an ascertainable value and is taxed as compensation at the grant date.

employee exercises the option because the fair market value of the stock now exceeds the strike price (the cost to the employee), the employee recognizes income equal to this unrealized gain—the difference between the strike price and the fair market value of the stock on the exercise date (called the *bargain element*). The employer claims a matching compensation deduction when the employee recognizes income. If the fair market value of the stock is lower than the strike price (referred to as *out-of-the-money*), the option should not be exercised. When the employee sells the stock acquired by exercising the option, a gain or loss is recognized on the difference between the employee's basis (the strike price plus the bargain element) and the sales price of the stock.

EXAMPLE 29

In year 1, Kam Corporation grants Janis, an employee, an option to buy 1,000 shares of Kam stock for $32 per share at any time during the next seven years. On the grant date, Kam stock is selling for $30 per share. Because the strike price exceeds the market price, the option has no ascertainable value and Janis recognizes no income on receipt of the option. If the stock price does not rise above $32 per share over the seven-year term of the option, Janis will let the option lapse or expire. She has no income and Kam Corporation has no deduction.

If Kam Corporation stock is selling for $82 per share in year 7, Janis will pay $32,000 ($32 strike price × 1,000 shares) cash to the corporation to exercise her option for the 1,000 shares of stock with a fair market value of $82,000 ($82 FMV × 1,000 shares). Janis must recognize the $50,000 bargain element ($82,000 FMV – $32,000 cost) as ordinary income in year 7 and Kam Corporation deducts the $50,000 bargain element as compensation paid in year 7. Janis has a negative cash flow in year 7 because she pays $32,000 for the stock plus taxes on the $50,000 that is treated as compensation; so she may wish to generate cash by selling some of her shares of stock. Janis recognizes no gain on the sale of the stock unless she sells it for a price greater than her $82 per share basis.

Some employers allow employees to exercise their stock options under a cashless program. Under this program, the employee exercises the stock options and immediately sells some or all of the shares at the prevailing market price. The employee receives the proceeds of the sale after deducting the strike price, withholding taxes, and any brokerage commissions.

For financial statement purposes, a corporation must record the estimated value of stock options as a compensation expense in the year the option is granted,[91] but the corporation is not allowed a tax deduction until the year the options are exercised. This causes a book/tax difference in the year the options are granted that reverses in the year they are exercised.

Incentive Stock Options

Incentive stock options (ISO), also known as qualified or statutory stock options, receive more favorable tax treatment from the perspective of the employee because they do not trigger income recognition at either the grant date or at exercise. Instead, the employee recognizes income when the stock is sold and the employee recognizes long-term capital gain rather than ordinary income. To qualify for this favorable tax treatment, the employee cannot sell the stock for one year after exercising the option or two years after the grant date, whichever is later. Failure to hold the stock for the required time disqualifies the ISO changing the tax treatment for the employer and employee so that it is taxed like an NQSO.

A significant negative feature of ISOs is that the employer receives no compensation deduction at any time for the option. Similar to the NQSO, the corporation must record the estimated value of qualified stock options as compensation expense for financial statement purposes in the year the options are granted. This also causes a book/tax difference, but it is a permanent book/tax difference because the

[91]FASB ASC 718 Stock Compensation (formerly 123R Share-Based Payment).

corporation never gets a tax deduction. An ISO also has more requirements and restrictions than an NQSO.[92]

EXAMPLE 30

Assume the facts of the previous example except that Janis's option qualifies as an ISO. Now Janis recognizes no income when she purchases the 1,000 shares of stock worth $82,000 for $32,000 in year 7. Janis holds these shares until year 13, when she sells them for $200,000. Her capital gain on the sale is $168,000 ($200,000 selling price – $32,000 cost basis), $50,000 of which represents the untaxed bargain element on exercise of the option. Thus, Janis's ISO has two advantages over an NQSO: (1) the taxes are deferred until the year of sale and (2) the option's bargain element ($50,000) is converted from ordinary income to capital gain. Because this option is an ISO, Kam Corporation receives no tax deduction and thus derives no tax benefit from the option. Kam's only benefit is the $32,000 cash it receives from Janis when the shares of stock are issued.

TAX PLANNING

Individuals who are planning to exercise ISOs should be aware that the untaxed bargain element is an individual alternative minimum tax (AMT) adjustment. Individuals may wish to avoid exercising ISOs in a year in which they may be subject to the AMT.[93]

Phantom Stock and Stock Appreciation Rights

A drawback of stock options is that employees must have cash to exercise their options. To address this problem, corporations have developed alternative forms of deferred compensation that capture the appreciation of company stock without requiring the employee to actually buy the stock. In a **phantom stock** plan, the employee's deferred compensation is hypothetically invested in shares of the company's stock. At the end of the deferral period, the employer pays the employee the full fair market value of the phantom shares.

In a **stock appreciation right (SAR)** plan, employees receive a cash payment equal to the appreciation only in their assumed shares of the employer's stock over a certain period of time. The employees receive these payments and recognize the related income when they exercise their SARs. SARS differ from phantom stock plans in the amount received from the employer. In a SARs plan only the appreciation over a period of time is received, but under a phantom stock plan the full value of a share of stock is received.

EXAMPLE 31

Horizon Corporation granted 400 SARs to Lillian in year 1, when its stock was selling for $10 per share. Lillian can exercise the rights at any time during the next eight years. In year 7, when the stock is selling for $40 per share, Lillian exercises the 400 SARs, receiving $12,000 [400 SARs × ($40 – $10)] from Horizon Corporation. Lillian has $12,000 of compensation income and Horizon deducts $12,000 as compensation expense in year 7. (If this had been a phantom stock plan, Lillian would have received $16,000 (400 hypothetical shares x $40).

TAX PLANNING

Plans that provide the advantages of stock options without the employees owning stock can be particularly useful to S corporations that are limited to 100 shareholders and closely-held corporations that do not want their employees to become shareholders.

[92]The option price cannot be less than the fair market value of the stock at the date the option is granted, the option cannot be exercised more than 10 years after the date of grant, the option must be granted to an individual who owns less than 10% of the employer (unless the strike price is at least 110% of the fair market value and it is not exercisable for more than 5 years), and the option is not transferable. Employees can purchase no more than $100,000 through ISOs annually. §422(d).

[93]§56(b)(3). See Chapter 11 for a discussion of the AMT.

Deferred Compensation and Retirement Planning

Deferred compensation plans are agreements under which an employer makes a promise to pay benefits to its employees in future years. The most common deferred compensation plan is the retirement plan. Retirement plans may be qualified or non-qualified.

Qualified Retirement Plans

Deferred compensation plans that meet the requirements of the Internal Revenue Code and the Employee Retirement Income Security Act of 1974 (ERISA) are referred to as **qualified deferred compensation plans**; those not meeting the requirements are referred to as *nonqualified plans*. Qualified deferred compensation plans are funded arrangements that receive the following favorable tax treatment:

- The employer deducts contributions as they are paid into a trust administered by an independent trustee.
- The earnings on these contributions accumulate tax free.
- The employee is not taxed on the benefits until they are actually received.[94]

Thus, the employer gets an immediate tax deduction while the employee's tax is deferred until income is received in a future year. Employees may also make contributions to a qualified pension plan and defer taxation of these contributions until they are withdrawn. This deferral is in addition to the tax deferral of employer contributions.

Example 32

Cindy is an employee of Xtra Corporation. Xtra contributes 7 percent of each employee's salary annually to a qualified pension plan. Cindy's current year salary of $50,000 results in a pension plan contribution of $3,500 (7% × $50,000). Because Xtra Corporation's plan is qualified, the $3,500 payment is deductible by the corporation but is not taxed to Cindy currently. Assume Xtra Corporation's employees can also contribute up to 7 percent of their annual salary to its pension plan. Cindy contributes the maximum $3,500 (7% × $50,000) to the plan. This contribution reduces Cindy's gross salary from Xtra Corporation from $50,000 to $46,500 for her $3,500 contribution to the plan. Cindy will not be taxed on her contribution (or on her employer's contribution) until she withdraws the funds from the plan.

Nondiscrimination rules ensure that qualified deferred compensation plans provide benefits in an equitable manner to all participating employees. Additional rules require that employees vest fully (have a nonforfeitable right to the retirement benefits) after they have worked for the employer for a certain number of years. Gradual vesting allows an employee to vest a specified percentage for each year of employment; for example the employee could vest 20 percent per year starting with the second year and be fully vested at the end of the sixth year. An alternate method is cliff vesting in which an employee is fully (100%) vested at the completion of three full years of employment, but until that point the employee would not be vested in any employer contribution. Vesting requirements are intended to ensure that a significant percentage of employees will eventually receive retirement benefits. In all cases, any employee contributions vest immediately.

The IRS imposes a 10 percent penalty (in addition to the regular income tax) on **premature withdrawals** (generally a withdrawal before age 59½) to discourage employees from withdrawing funds before retirement. Exceptions to the penalty exist, however, for the disability or death of the employee.[95] To ensure that the

[94]In many cases, employees can further delay taxation by transferring these amounts into another tax-deferred plan, such as an IRA.

[95]The penalty is also waived if the employee is age 55 or over and has terminated employment with the plan sponsor. The penalty is also waived for certain qualified withdrawals made due to Hurricanes Katrina, Rita, or Wilma.

income in a retirement plan is eventually taxed, the IRS requires participants to begin minimum distributions from their plan after they reach age 70½[96] The distributions are taxed in the year received.

A taxpayer who receives a premature lump-sum distribution may roll over all or part of the distribution into another qualified plan or an individual retirement account within 60 days of its receipt without paying any tax or penalty on that part of the distribution. The plan trustee must withhold 20 percent of any lump-sum distribution, however, unless the distribution is transferred directly into another plan (a trustee-to-trustee transfer). Thus, if the taxpayer receives a lump-sum distribution, the withheld 20 percent is a tax prepayment that is not available for rollover into the new plan.[97]

EXAMPLE 33

Ellen, age 35, has $50,000 in her employer-sponsored retirement plan. She takes the maximum distribution of $40,000 ($50,000 less 20 percent withheld in taxes) when she changes jobs. If she fails to roll over the entire $50,000 into another qualified plan, she must pay a $5,000 (10% × $50,000) penalty on the premature withdrawal. If she rolls over only $40,000 into a new plan within the required 60 days, her penalty tax on the premature distribution is $1,000 (10% × $10,000) for the withheld taxes and $10,000 is also included in income. Ellen should have requested a direct rollover (trustee-to-trustee transfer); no withholding would be required and no taxes would be due. It may, however, be possible for her to borrow money to replace the withheld taxes until she receives her tax refund. Her interest expense on the borrowed amount will generally be far less than the penalty and taxes on the premature distribution.

Types of Retirement Plans

There are two basic types of qualified retirement plans: defined benefit plans and defined contribution plans. A **defined benefit plan** provides for a fixed benefit at retirement based on the employee's years of service and compensation. These plans are funded entirely by the employer. Contributions are actuarially calculated to provide the promised benefits. For example, a defined benefit plan might provide a retirement benefit equal to 40 percent of an employee's average salary for the five years before retirement. The employer has a compensation expense deduction for the contributions, even though the employees do not recognize income until the benefits are received. Companies must meet the minimum funding standards that may require contributions even in years when there are operating losses.[98]

A **defined contribution plan** is a qualified plan in which the contribution is specified (such as a fixed percentage of compensation) but the future benefit to be paid is not. Each plan participant has an individual account with benefits based solely on the amount contributed to the participant's account and any allocated investment income, gains, and losses. The employer receives a deduction when it makes a contribution into the employee trust account, but the employee does not recognize income until benefits are received.

EXAMPLE 34

Sara, a manager for Soho Corporation earning $100,000 annual salary, is a participant in Soho's qualified defined contribution plan. Soho contributes $25,000 to its defined contribution plan for Sara. Soho

[96]§401(a)(9) and §408(a)(6). A 50 percent excise tax is assessed on the undistributed amount if a participant does not receive the minimum required distribution by April 1 of the year following the year in which he or she reaches age 70½. Employees who continue to work after age 70½ may postpone distributions from their employer-sponsored plans until they retire. The Worker, Retiree, and Employer Recovery Act of 2008 provided a one year suspension of the required minimum distribution rules so that no minimum distributions were required for calendar year 2009.

[97]For qualified individuals in the Hurricane Katrina disaster area, the rollover period extended to three years and the 20 percent mandatory withholding did not apply.

[98]§412.

Corporation deducts Sara's $100,000 salary and the $25,000 retirement plan contribution as compensation expense for the year. Sara is taxed only on the $100,000 currently. The $25,000 retirement plan contribution remains untaxed until she withdraws the funds from the plan.

The two most common defined contribution plans are the *money purchase plan* and the *profit sharing plan*. In a money purchase plan, the company (and the employee if it is a contributory plan) contributes a fixed percentage of the employee's salary to the plan. Because the employer's annual contribution is fixed, this may not be an attractive plan for a new or growing business.

TAX PLANNING

Profit-sharing plans are very popular with start-up companies because employer contributions are based on earnings. In profitable years, the business contributes a percentage of the profits to an employee trust account. In unprofitable years, no contributions are required.

One difference between defined benefit and defined contribution plans is which party bears the risk of investment losses. In a defined benefit plan, investment gains or losses do not affect the ultimate benefits promised the employees. Rather, gains and losses affect the employer's contributions to the plan. Thus, the employer bears the risk of investment gain or loss. In a defined contribution plan, investment gains or losses increase or decrease the value of the employee's account. Thus, the employee bears the risk of investment gain or loss.

A **401(k) plan**, also called a *cash or deferred arrangement (CODA)* or a salary reduction plan, is a defined contribution plan that permits an employee to defer a certain amount of pay that is then contributed to the 401(k) plan by the employer on his or her behalf. These contributions are usually made on a pretax basis so the contributions and all earnings remain untaxed until the employee withdraws them from the plan.[99] The employer is still entitled to a current deduction when funds are put into the plan.[100] For this type of plan, the employer has little cost beyond the costs of administering the plan.[101]

The popularity of 401(k) plans is due primarily to their flexibility.[102] Within plan limits, each year each employee can contribute a different amount, or no amount, from his or her salary to the plan. Nondiscrimination rules make the contributions of highly compensated employees depend on the level of nonhighly compensated employee participation and contributions. Some employers make matching contributions to these plans to provide an incentive for lower-paid employees to join the plan.[103]

EXAMPLE 35

Under the Boulder Company 401(k) plan, employees may direct Boulder to contribute up to 10 percent of their salaries to the plan rather than receiving it in cash. Boulder will match 50 percent of the employee's contribution up to a maximum of 5 percent of compensation. Charlie, whose salary is $45,000, elects to have Boulder contribute the maximum allowable amount of $4,500 (10% × $45,000), and Boulder makes a matching con-

[99]Funds usually cannot be withdrawn until the employee reaches age 59½, retires, becomes disabled, leaves the employer, or dies. The plan may also provide for loans and hardship withdrawals. Since 2005, a 401(k) plan may allow participants to elect to have all or part of their contributions treated as Roth contributions. As discussed later in this chapter, Roth contributions are not deductible (that is, they are includible in the employee's income) but both the contributions and related earnings may be withdrawn at a later date tax free. Unlike a Roth IRA, a Roth 401(k) has no income limitations so high-income individuals who may be ineligible to contribute to a Roth IRA could contribute to a Roth 401(k).

[100]This compensation is subject to FICA tax in the year contributed. §3121(v)(1)(A).

[101]Employees of tax-exempt educational, charitable, and religious organizations can qualify for similar benefits under a 403(b) plan also known as a tax-sheltered or tax-deferred annuity program.

[102]Participants can direct their contributions to a broad range of investment options, including self-directed brokerage accounts.

[103]Even with employer matching, few low-income wage earners contribute to retirement plans because they spend almost all their disposable income. To encourage greater participation, the Tax Reform Act of 2001 added a tax credit for low-income employees, which is discussed in Chapter 11.

tribution of $2,250 (5% × $45,000). Charlie's current salary subject to income taxation is $40,500 ($45,000 – $4,500), but Boulder deducts the entire $45,000 salary plus its matching contribution of $2,250.

Other plans within these general categories include the following:

1. *Employee stock ownership plans (ESOPs)*—shares of employer stock are purchased to fund the plan.[104]
2. *Simplified employee pension (SEP) plans*—small businesses make contributions to SEP individual retirement accounts on behalf of employees and receive tax advantages similar to qualified plans.
3. *Savings incentive match plan for employees (SIMPLE) retirement plans*—an employer with 100 or fewer employees establishes an individual retirement account for each employee and makes matching contributions based on contributions elected by participating employees under a qualified salary reduction arrangement. It is not subject to complex nondiscrimination requirements so administrative and legal costs are minimized.
4. *SIMPLE 401(k) plans*—these plans are similar to SIMPLE plans but are deemed to meet the complex nondiscrimination tests for 401(k) plans.

TAX PLANNING

Employers should consider the demographics and incomes of their workforce when selecting a particular type of pension plan. If most workers earn at or near minimum wage, it is highly unlikely that they would make contributions to any type of contributory plan. The more highly educated and older the workforce, the more likely they are to welcome a contributory plan that allows them to make significant contributions to their accounts in addition to the employer's contributions.

Contribution Limits

All qualified plans limit the amount of employee compensation that can be tax deferred through an employer-sponsored retirement plan. For defined benefit plans, the maximum pension benefit that a plan can fund is 100 percent of a participating employee's average compensation for the three highest-paid years, subject to a $205,000 cap.[105]

Two important annual limits affect defined contribution plans. One limits the maximum contribution (by employer and employee combined) to each participant's account to 100 percent of compensation up to a maximum of $51,000.[106] The other restricts the maximum deductible contribution to 25 percent of compensation paid to all employees covered by the plan.[107]

EXAMPLE 36

Tom, an engineer, owns an incorporated engineering practice that maintains a profit-sharing plan. Tom is the only employee and his annual compensation is $120,000. The business may contribute up to $51,000 to Tom's account, but its deduction is limited to $30,000 (25% × $120,000).

For 401(k) plans, the maximum pretax compensation that can be deferred is $17,500 in 2013.[108] If an employer matches an employee's contribution, the maximum deduction is 25 percent of covered employee compensation.

[104]Employees who participate in ESOPs become shareholders. When employees retire, they receive distributions of stock held in the ESOP accounts so the value of their retirement benefits is dependent upon the market value of the stock. These distributions are taxable only to the extent of the ESOP's aggregate basis in the stock with any gain on the unrealized appreciation deferred until the shares are sold.

[105]§415(b). The maximum dollar amount is indexed for inflation.

[106]§415(c). The maximum dollar amount will increase for inflation in future years in $1,000 increments.

[107]Since 2002, elective deferrals as well as employees' elective set-asides in cafeteria plans are treated as compensation.

[108]The maximum compensation deferral was $13,000 in 2004, $14,000 in 2005, $15,000 in 2006, $15,500 for 2007-2008, $16,500 in 2009-2011, and $17,000 in 2012. This limit also applies to 403(b) annuities and salary reduction SEPs. The maximum annual elective deferral that may be made to a SIMPLE plan was $10,500 in 2007-2008, $11,500 for 2009-2012, and $12,000 in 2013.

TAX PLANNING

Catch-up contributions allow employees age 50 or older at year-end to make additional contributions to certain pension plans as they approach their retirement years. The maximum catch-up contribution for 401(k) plans is $5,500.[109] These catch-up contributions provide a significant tax-deferral opportunity for highly compensated employees age 50 and over because the catch-up contributions are not subject to the plan's nondiscrimination rules.

EXAMPLE 37

Employees of Baker Corporation may contribute up to 10 percent of compensation or the annual dollar limit, whichever is less, to its 401(k) plan. Bill, a 52-year-old employee of Baker Corporation, earns $90,000 annually. In 2013, Bill defers $9,000 plus an additional elective catch-up contribution of $5,500. Bill's taxable income is $75,500 ($90,000 – $14,500), while Baker Corporation deducts the entire $90,000.

Nonqualified Deferred Compensation Plans

A **nonqualified deferred compensation plan** is one that does not meet the requirements of the Internal Revenue Code or ERISA. Under a nonqualified plan, an employer can defer an unlimited amount of compensation for highly compensated executives without extending the plan benefits to other employees. The employer and the employee usually have a contract that provides for the payment of part of the employee's compensation for his or her present employment to be delayed until sometime in the future (for example, after a specified number of years, at retirement, or on the occurrence of a specific event, such as a corporate take-over). The employer accrues its liability but sets aside no assets to secure the liability. The employer has no tax deduction until the year in which the deferred compensation is actually paid to the employee and the employee is usually taxed when the funds are received. If the employer's business fails and it is unable to pay its liabilities for deferred compensation, the employee becomes an unsecured creditor.

EXAMPLE 38

In year 1, David, the chief executive officer of Arco, Inc. receives a bonus of $280,000 to be paid in four annual installments, beginning when David retires in three years. Arco accrues a $280,000 liability for the deferred compensation on its financial statements but sets aside no cash or other property to fund David's deferred compensation. In year 1, David recognizes no income and Arco is not permitted to take a tax deduction for the bonus. When David receives the first $70,000 installment in year 4, he will recognize $70,000 as income and Arco will deduct $70,000 as compensation. David will recognize income and Arco will take a deduction over the remaining years as the compensation is actually paid. If Arco declares bankruptcy prior to paying the entire $280,000, David may collect little or none of the remaining compensation. He is merely another unsecured Arco creditor.

TAX PLANNING

The employee's risk can be somewhat reduced by using an arrangement called a *rabbi trust.*[110] In this situation, the employer funds the deferred compensation by transferring property or cash into a trust. Although the employer is legally prohibited from reclaiming the trust assets, these assets are subject to claim by the employer's creditors. The employee has no interest in the assets and does not recognize income until the trust pays the compensation.

Individual Retirement Accounts

An **individual retirement account (IRA)** is a personal retirement plan available to anyone with earned income during the year.[111] The maximum each individual may contribute

[109]These catch-up limits also apply to 403(b) annuities and salary reduction SEPs.

[110]This is referred to as a rabbi trust because one of the first plans that received IRS approval involved a rabbi.

[111]Earned income includes all wages, salaries, commissions, tips, bonuses, and self-employment income.

is the lesser of $5,500 ($6,500 if age 50 or older) or earned income.[112] A married taxpayer can also contribute a maximum of an additional $5,500 to a spousal IRA for a nonworking spouse or a spouse whose earned income is less than $5,500, if together they have at least $11,000 of earned income. All earnings accumulate tax free until withdrawn.

EXAMPLE 39

Sharon (single and age 28) earned a salary of $34,000. She can contribute up to $5,500 to her IRA.

Jim (age 51) and Olga (age 48) are married and file a joint return. Jim earned a salary of $50,000 and Olga earned $2,000 working at a part-time job. Jim may contribute up to $6,500 to his IRA and up to $5,500 may be contributed to Olga's IRA.

If the taxpayer is not an active participant in any other qualified retirement plan, the contribution to a traditional IRA is fully deductible *for* AGI (the contributions are pretax contributions). Employees who are active participants in employer-sponsored qualified retirement plans may have their deductions limited. Table 4.5 shows the adjusted gross income (AGI) ranges over which the deductibility of contributions to traditional IRAs declines to zero. For example, if the taxpayer is married and files a joint return in 2013, AGI must exceed $95,000 before the deduction begins to decrease; the deduction is completely eliminated if AGI equals or exceeds $115,000.

The nondeductible portion of the contribution is determined as follows:

$$\frac{\text{(AGI – Beginning of phase-out range)}}{\text{Amount in phase-out range}} = \text{Percentage phased out}$$

$$\text{Maximum contribution} \times (1 - \text{Percentage phased out}) = \text{Maximum IRA deduction}$$

Taxpayers who are not covered by an employer's retirement plan but whose spouses are active participants in an employer's plan may make a fully deductible contribution to an IRA if their AGI is $178,000 or less. The deduction phases out, however, over an AGI range of $178,000 to $188,000.[114] High-income individuals who do not get a deduction for their IRA contributions, can still benefit from the tax deferral on the earnings in their IRA.

EXAMPLE 40

In 2013, Cindy and David (both age 38), a married couple with AGI of $107,000, file a joint tax return. Both are active participants in qualified retirement plans and they each contribute the $5,500 maximum to

TABLE 4.5 **AGI PHASE-OUT LIMITS FOR DEDUCTIBLE IRAS**

	PHASE-OUT RANGE	
TAX YEARS	**SINGLE**	**MARRIED FILING JOINTLY[113]**
2013	$59,000–$69,000	$95,000–$115,000
2012	$58,000–$68,000	$92,000–$112,000
2011	$56,000–$66,000	$90,000–$110,000

[112] The 2001 Tax Act increased the maximum annual IRA contribution, which had been set at $2,000 for the previous 20 years. The limit was raised to $3,000 for 2002–2004, $4,000 for 2005–2007, and $5,000 as of 2008-2012. Individuals age 50 and over are permitted to make an additional catch-up contribution of $500 for 2002–2005 and $1,000 for 2006 and thereafter.

[113] The AGI phase-out threshold for a married person filing separately remains at zero for all years so that otherwise deductible contributions phase out ratably between zero and $10,000.

[114] These deductions phased out in 2012 over an AGI range of $173,000 to $183,000.

their IRAs. Due to the phase-out rules, they cannot deduct 60 percent [($107,000 – $95,000)/$20,000 = 60%] or $3,300 of the contribution. Although they can each contribute $5,500 to their IRAs, only $2,200 ($5,500 – $3,300) of that amount could be deducted by each of them.

If Cindy is not an active participant in a qualified retirement plan, she can deduct her entire $5,500 contribution, while David would still be limited to a $2,200 deduction.

If their AGI is $188,000 or more, neither spouse's contribution would be deductible, as their AGI exceeds the income limit.

The taxpayer must set up the IRA and make the contribution by the *unextended* due date of the tax return. Thus, a calendar-year taxpayer has until April 15, 2014, to establish and make a contribution into an IRA and deduct the contribution on his or her 2013 tax return. Care should be taken that the contribution limit is not exceeded because a 6 percent nondeductible excise tax penalty applies to any excess contributions to an IRA during the year (including any contributions after age 70½).

Earnings on IRA contributions accumulate tax free, but taxes must be paid on the earnings and all pretax (deductible) contributions when the funds are withdrawn. On funds withdrawn before age 59½, taxpayers must pay a 10 percent penalty in addition to the regular tax.[115] Taxpayers must begin taking minimum distributions from IRAs no later than age 70½.[116]

TAX PLANNING

A traditional IRA may also be set up by an individual to receive a rollover distribution from a qualified retirement plan, as discussed previously. Distributions rolled over into an IRA are not subject to any contribution limits.

Roth IRAs

An individual may make a nondeductible contribution of up to $5,500 ($6,500 if age 50 or over) per year to a **Roth IRA**, but the aggregate amount of contributions to both the traditional and Roth IRAs cannot exceed $5,500 ($6,500 if 50 or over).[117] With a traditional IRA, the money is contributed on a pretax basis (the contribution is deductible), but both contributions and earnings are taxed when withdrawn. Although taxpayers make contributions to a Roth IRA with after-tax dollars (there is no deduction), they withdraw earnings tax free along with the contributions that were already taxed. Qualified distributions generally cannot begin until five tax years after the year for which the first contribution is made and the taxpayer must be at least age 59½[118]

Contributions to Roth IRAs phase out for single individuals with AGIs between $112,000 and $127,000 and for joint filers with AGIs between $178,000 and $188,000.[119] These phase-out limits apply whether or not the individual is an active participant in an employer-sponsored plan.

Individuals still working after age 70½ may continue to make contributions to their Roth IRAs. There are no minimum distribution requirements during the owner's

[115]There are exceptions to the 10 percent penalty for certain qualified distributions, such as the death or disability of the taxpayer, payment of medical expenses, payment of education expenses, or first-time home-buyer expenses.

[116]Taxpayers who do not take minimum distributions are subject to a penalty tax of 50 percent of the amount by which the minimum required distribution exceeds the actual distribution. The Worker, Retiree, and Employer Recovery Act of 2008 provided a one year suspension of the required minimum distribution rules so that no minimum distributions were required for calendar year 2009.

[117]The Roth IRA is named after Senator William Roth, who was its primary advocate. The maximum annual contribution limits (including catch-up provisions) are the same for both traditional and Roth IRAs.

[118]Exceptions apply for death, disability, and for first-time home buyers (subject to a $10,000 maximum).

[119]For 2012, contributions to a Roth IRA for single individuals were phased out at AGIs between $110,000 and $125,000 ($107,000 and $122,000 for 2011 and $105,000 and $120,000 for 2009-2010). For joint return filers the contributions phased out at AGIs between $166,000 and $176,000 for 2009, $167,000 to $177,000 for 2010, $169,000 to $179,000 for 2011, and $173,000 - $183,000 for 2012.

lifetime, so funds can be left in the account to continue to grow tax free. This can be used as an estate-planning tool for passing funds to beneficiaries.[120]

TAX PLANNING

Individuals who can make either a nondeductible contribution to a traditional IRA or a nondeductible contribution to a Roth IRA should contribute to the Roth IRA to take advantage of the tax-exempt treatment of earnings upon withdrawal.[121]

EXAMPLE 41

Martha (single and age 51) is an active participant in her employer's qualified retirement plan. Her AGI is $40,000 and she would like to contribute the maximum to an IRA for 2013. Martha can make a $6,500 fully deductible contribution to a traditional IRA or a nondeductible contribution to a Roth IRA.

If Martha's AGI is $90,000, she can make a $6,500 *nondeductible* contribution to a traditional IRA or a $6,500 nondeductible contribution to a Roth IRA.

If Martha's AGI is $130,000, she can only make a nondeductible contribution to a traditional IRA.

Prior to 2010, an individual's AGI could be no more than $100,000 to convert a traditional IRA into a Roth IRA. Since 2010, the $100,000 AGI limit has been eliminated, allowing high-income taxpayers to transfer all or part of the funds in a traditional IRA to a Roth IRA. There is a tax cost to do this, however. The earnings and deductible contributions transferred from a traditional IRA to a Roth IRA are taxed as ordinary income, but no penalty tax is assessed. To make this conversion more attractive, taxpayers who converted in 2010 could spread the income (and related tax payments) over 2011 and 2012. The tax cost when converted may be small if there are substantial losses on IRA investments; this is one of the few ways to benefit from such losses.

TAX PLANNING

SELF-EMPLOYED INDIVIDUALS

Self-employed individuals include independent contractors, sole proprietors, partners, and LLC managing members. Shareholders of both C and S corporations can be employees of a corporation, but shareholder-employees of S corporations are not eligible for many fringe benefits.

Employment Tax Consequences

Similar to the FICA tax on employers and employees, self-employed individuals are subject to the Self-Employment Contributions Act (SECA) tax but they are responsible for paying **self-employment taxes** on their self-employment net income at a rate that is equal to the combined employer and employee FICA tax rates for Social Security and Medicare.[122] Thus, self-employed persons pay Social Security and Medicare taxes as if they are both the employer and employee. Self-employment taxes are calculated on Schedule SE: *Self-Employment Tax* and are paid along with the individual's regular income tax. For 2013 the SECA tax rate is 15.3 percent, 12.4 percent for the Social Security portion (to up a maximum income of $113,700), and 2.9 percent for the Medicare portion with no maximum. For 2011 and 2012, the Social Security SECA rate was temporarily decreased to 10.4 percent (4.2 percent employee's portion + 6.2 percent employer's portion) while the 2.9 percent Medicare rate remained the same. Starting in 2013, the Medicare surtax on salaries, wages, and other compensation of high-income individuals also applies to self-employment income if certain income thresholds are exceeded. The thresholds are $200,000 for single individuals (and heads of household), $250,000 for married taxpayers filing a

[120]See Chapter 12 for a discussion of wealth transfer planning.

[121]Deciding between a deductible contribution to a traditional IRA and a nondeductible Roth IRA is a complex matter and depends upon the individual's tax rates in retirement, as well as upon current rates and other investment issues.

[122]The deduction for qualified U.S. production activities (discussed in Chapter 10) is not allowed when computing income subject to self-employment tax.

TABLE 4.6 FICA AND SECA TAX RATES AND LIMITS

	2013	2012
FICA Social Security tax rate	6.2%	4.2%
SECA Social Security tax rate	12.4%	10.4%
FICA Medicare tax rate	1.45%	1.45%
SECA Medicare tax rate	2.9%	2.9%
Social Security income limit	$113,700	$110,100
Medicare income limit	None	None
Total SECA rate below SS income limit	15.3%	13.3%
Deductible SECA rate below SS income limit	7.65%	7.65%
Medicare surtax	0.9%	None

joint return, and $125,000 for married taxpayers filing separately. These rates are summarized in Table 4.6.

To provide tax relief for self-employed individuals similar to that provided other businesses (that can claim a deduction for the 7.65 percent employer's share of FICA taxes they pay), Congress enacted two deductions for the employer's portion of SECA that are allowed in computing two different types of taxes. The first deduction affects the computation of income subject to the SECA tax while the second deduction affects the computation of income subject to the federal income tax.

To compute self-employment income subject to self-employment tax, a deduction is allowed for the employer's 7.65 percent share of tax. Note that this is effectively the same as taxing only 92.35 percent (100% - 7.65%) of net earnings from self-employment.[123] Thus, to compute the Medicare portion of the SECA tax, self-employment income is first multiplied by 92.35 percent and then by the 2.9 percent Medicare rate. Because the Social Security portion of the tax is imposed on no more than $113,700 of income, the SECA Social Security tax rate is applied to the lesser of (a) self-employment income × 92.35 percent or (b) $113,700.[124] Once total SECA tax is computed, the individual is allowed a deduction for the employer's half of the self-employment taxes *for* AGI on his or her individual income tax return, reducing the income subject to the federal income tax.[125]

EXAMPLE 42

Steven, a single individual, has $130,000 of net income from his sole proprietorship in 2013. Steven's self-employment taxes on $130,000 of self-employment income are $17,581 as computed on Schedule SE:

[123]To simplify this computation, the deduction is allowed for the full 7.65% even when the income is in excess of the Social Security ceiling limit. The instructions on *Schedule SE* state that the self-employment income should be multiplied by 92.35% before the tax is computed.

[124]The ceiling for the Social Security portion was $110,100 for 2012, $106,800 for 2009-2011, and $102,000 for 2008, resulting in a $13,652.40, $13,243.20, and $12,648 maximum, respectively. To pay for expanded health care coverage, the Patient Protection and Affordable Care Act expands the Medicare tax in 2013 by levying an additional 0.9 percent Medicare surtax on the earned income of self-employed persons with earnings in excess of $200,000 ($250,000 if married filing a joint return and $125,000 if married filing separately). This increase also applies to the earned income of employees but is not assessed on the employer.

[125]An individual taxpayer's deductions *for* AGI are discussed in depth in Chapter 11.

Self-Employment Tax. He reports $130,000 in income from his sole proprietorship on Schedule C: *Profit or Loss from Business (Sole Proprietorship)*[126] and takes an $8,791 deduction *for* AGI. Steven's after-tax income from his business is $87,987.

DETERMINING SELF-EMPLOYMENT TAX		AFTER-TAX NET INCOME
Sole-proprietorship income	$130,000	$130,000
Less SECA deduction (7.65% × $130,000)	(9,945)	
Amount subject to self-employment tax (can also be computed as $130,000 × 92.35%)	$120,055	
Medicare tax ($120,055 × 2.9%)	$ 3,482	
Social Security tax (lesser of $120,055 or $113,700 income limit) × 12.4%	14,099	
Self-employment tax liability	$17,581	(17,581)
DETERMINING FEDERAL INCOME TAX		
Sole-proprietorship income	$130,000	
Deduction for employer's portion of self-employment tax ($17,581 × 50% employer's share)[127]	(8,791)	
Adjusted gross income	$121,209	
Standard deduction	(6,100)	
Personal exemption	(3,900)	
Taxable income	$111,209	
Income tax liability [$17,891.25 + 28% ($111,209 - $87,850)]	$24,432	(24,432)
After-tax net income		$87,987

An individual with income both as an employee and as a self-employed individual first considers employment taxes paid as an employee. Any employee compensation on which FICA taxes are paid reduces the ceiling for Social Security taxes imposed on self-employment earnings.

EXAMPLE 43

Juan earns $50,000 of income as an employee and $70,000 of self-employment income in 2013. Juan's employer withheld $3,825 ($50,000 × 7.65%) from his salary for Social Security and Medicare taxes and also paid the employer's $3,825 ($50,000 x 7.65%) share of these taxes. To determine his self-employment tax, Juan first multiplies his $70,000 self-employment income by 92.35% ($70,000 × 92.35% = $64,645). Juan then reduces the $113,700 ceiling by the $50,000 of employee earnings on which Social Security tax has already been paid. Only $63,700 ($113,700 – $50,000) of his self-employment earnings is subject to the Social Security tax; however, his entire $64,645 of self-employment earnings is subject to the Medicare tax (because there is no limit on Medicare taxes). Juan's self-employment taxes are $9,773.51 [($63,700 × 12.4% = $7,898.80) + ($64,645 × 2.9% = $1,874.71)].

Sample filled-in tax returns are included in Appendix C at the end of this textbook.

Higher-income taxpayers calculate their self-employment tax in the same manner but also have to calculate their Medicare surtax. As discussed earlier in this chapter, employers are required to withhold the additional Medicare tax when they pay an employee more than $200,000 in salaries, wages, or other compensation in a calendar

[126] Schedule C or C-EZ is the form on which an individual's sole-proprietorship income and expenses are reported. It is attached to the individual's income tax return as is Schedule SE.

[127] If Steven's income had been above the threshold for the Medicare surtax he would owe an additional 0.9% Medicare tax on the excess.

year, without regard to the employee's filing status, wages paid by another employer, or any self-employment income the employee may have. When a taxpayer has both wage income and self-employment income, there are three steps necessary to calculate the additional Medicare surtax that is owed:

1. Calculate the Medicare surtax on wages or salary from all employers in excess of the threshold for the filing status.
2. Reduce the threshold by the total amount of wages received, but not below zero.
3. Calculate the additional Medicare surtax on self-employment income in excess of the reduced threshold and add the surtax in (1) for the total owed.

The following examples illustrate the computation of this 0.9 percent Medicare surtax.

EXAMPLE 44

Maria and Jose are married and file a joint tax return. Maria has $150,000 in salary and Jose has $175,000 in self-employment income from his medical practice. Maria's salary does not exceed the $250,000 threshold for joint filers, so there is no additional Medicare tax on Maria's salary. Before calculating the additional Medicare tax on Jose's self-employment income, the $250,000 threshold is reduced by Maria's $150,000 salary resulting in a reduced income threshold of $100,000. Maria and Jose must pay a $675 (0.9% x $75,000) Medicare surtax on $75,000 of self-employment income ($175,000 in self-employment income minus the reduced threshold of $100,000) on their individual tax return.

John, a single individual, has $225,000 in salary and $50,000 in self-employment income. John's employer withheld the Medicare surtax on $25,000 ($225,000 salary minus the $200,000 withholding threshold) as part of his FICA taxes. Before calculating the Medicare surtax on his self-employment income, the $200,000 threshold is reduced to zero by John's $225,000 in salary (note that the threshold cannot be reduced below zero). John is liable for the additional Medicare surtax on all $50,000 of self-employment income ($50,000 self-employment income minus the reduced threshold of $0). In total, John is liable for Medicare surtax of $675 [($25,000 of his salary + $50,000 self-employment income) x 0.9%] on both the salary and self-employment income. Since John's salary exceeded $200,000, his employer withheld the Medicare surtax of $225 (at a rate of .9%) on the excess $25,000 salary over the $200,000 threshold. This is applied against all taxes shown on his individual income tax return, including his Medicare surtax liability.

If John's $225,000 salary had been from two different employers, neither of which paid him over $200,000, he would have had no additional Medicare surtax withheld and he would have to pay the additional $225.

Fringe Benefits Limited

Self-employed individuals cannot participate in many of the fringe benefits provided on a tax-free basis to employees. Self-employed individuals must use after-tax dollars for many of the benefits that employees can obtain with before-tax dollars.[128] Some of the benefits that self-employed individuals cannot receive on a tax-free basis include health and accident insurance, group term life insurance, on-premises lodging, employee achievement awards, moving expenses, transit passes, and parking benefits. To mitigate the difference in this treatment of employer-provided health

[128]For this rule, self-employed individuals also include shareholders of S corporations who own more than 2 percent of the S corporation's outstanding stock. When a partnership pays a partner's health insurance premiums, it is treated as a guaranteed payment (salary). When an S corporation pays a greater-than-2 percent shareholder's health insurance premiums, it is treated as wages subject to withholding but is not subject to employment taxes.

insurance for employees and the self-employed, self-employed individuals may deduct the cost of health insurance *for* AGI.[129]

EXAMPLE 45

Jordan operates an electrical contracting business as a sole proprietorship. He employs three electricians who are eligible to participate in the company-sponsored health insurance plan in which Jordan also participates. The premium for each employee is $2,100 per year. Jordan deducts $6,300 from business revenue for the cost of the health insurance for the three employees on Schedule C. Jordan deducts $2,100 for his own health insurance as a deduction *for* AGI.

Self-employed individuals can participate on a tax-favored basis in certain benefits including educational assistance plans, no-additional-cost benefits, dependent care assistance, employee discounts, on-premises meals, athletic facilities, de minimis benefits, and working condition fringe benefits.

Retirement Plans

Self-employed individuals can provide for their retirement on a tax-deferred basis by establishing a **Keogh plan** (or HR 10).[130] Payments into Keogh plans are deductible *for* AGI. Funding sources for Keogh plans include mutual funds, annuities, real estate shares, certificates of deposit, commodities, securities, debt instruments, and personal properties, but exclude collectibles, such as coins or works of art.

TAX PLANNING

Keogh plans are subject to the same basic plan qualifications, contribution limits, and nondiscrimination rules that apply to qualified corporate retirement plans. Thus, a sole proprietor who establishes a Keogh plan for himself or herself must also provide similar retirement benefits for all eligible employees. Due to this requirement, a Keogh plan offers the greatest tax savings when used by a self-employed person with no employees.

The business deducts contributions to the employees' retirement accounts in determining its net income. The limit on contributions to the sole proprietor's retirement account is determined on the net income from the business after the deduction for the contributions to the employees' accounts and is a deduction *for* AGI. The firm cannot determine the contribution limit to the sole proprietor's retirement account until after the deduction for the contributions to the employees' account.

Keogh plans may be either defined benefit or defined contribution plans. Because of actuarial costs, most Keogh plans are defined contribution plans. The maximum contribution under a defined contribution plan is the lesser of $51,000 or 20 percent of net earnings from self-employment, calculated after subtracting the deduction for self-employment taxes.[131]

EXAMPLE 46

Mac's sole proprietorship has a net profit of $57,000 in 2013. He pays self-employment tax of $8,054 ($57,000 × 92.35% × 15.3%). He deducts $4,027 ($57,000 × 92.35% × 7.65% employer's portion of tax) *for* AGI. His eligible self-employment income is $52,973. Mac can contribute a maximum of $10,595 to his defined contribution profit-sharing Keogh plan. His contribution is limited to the lesser of $51,000 or 20 percent of his eligible self-employment income ($52,973 × 20% = $10,595).

TAX PLANNING

A sole proprietor must establish a Keogh plan before the end of the tax year to deduct the current year's contribution, but the contribution is not due until the extended

[129]For 2010 only, self-employed individuals' health insurance premiums that were deductible for income tax purposes for AGI were deductible in determining net earnings from self-employment when calculating self-employment taxes. If the taxpayer or spouse was otherwise eligible to participate in an employer-sponsored health insurance plan, this deduction for AGI was lost; the entire expense was then deducted as a medical expense.

[130]The Keogh plan is named after the congressman who sponsored the legislation that created this plan.

[131]This amount will increase in future years for inflation in $1,000 increments. The contribution percentage is actually 25% for a profit-sharing or stock bonus plan but it is based on earned income after the contribution effectively reducing the percentage to 20% as follows: 25%/(100% + 25%) = 20%.

due date for his or her tax return. If a taxpayer cannot fund a Keogh contribution by April 15, he or she can request an automatic extension of time to file the individual tax return. This extension applies to the due date for making the Keogh contribution, as well as to the date for filing the tax return.

A sole proprietor's contributions to the Keogh plan are made with before-tax dollars; thus, they are fully taxed when withdrawn. With limited exceptions, contributions may not be withdrawn before age 59½ without a penalty for premature withdrawal.[132]

A self-employed individual may also contribute to an IRA. If the sole proprietorship has a net loss, the taxpayer must have earned income from other sources to make an IRA contribution. The net loss does not reduce this other earned income, however, in determining the amount eligible to be contributed to the IRA.

EXAMPLE 47

Jorge is an architect in a small firm that provides no retirement benefits. His salary is $42,000. Additionally, Jorge operates a small cleaning service as a sole proprietorship that lost $2,100 this past year. He has $600 of net income from a rental property and $1,340 in interest income. Jorge has $42,000 of earned income for determining the amount he is eligible to contribute to an IRA. He does not reduce his salary for the loss from his sole proprietorship. If Jorge had no salary income, he could not make any IRA contribution for the year because the cleaning business had a loss and neither the rental nor the interest income is earned income.

EXPANDED TOPICS—FOREIGN ASSIGNMENTS

All income of United States citizens is subject to federal income taxation regardless of how or where that income is earned. As a result, individuals who work in foreign countries (referred to as **expatriates)** may be subject to double taxation when those foreign countries also tax the income earned within their borders. To lessen the burden of potential double taxation, qualifying individuals may (1) elect to exclude up to $97,600 for 2013 ($95,100 for 2012) of their foreign earned income or (2) include the foreign income when computing U.S. taxable income and then claim a credit for foreign taxes paid.[133] Expatriates working in foreign countries that either impose no income tax or have effective rates lower than those in the United States should elect the foreign earned income exclusion, if eligible, instead of the credit.

TAX PLANNING

Foreign Earned Income Exclusion

The **foreign earned income** exclusion applies to salaries, bonuses, allowances, and noncash benefits earned in a foreign country for the individual's personal services (other than as an employee of the United States government).[134] Earned income is excludable only if it is considered foreign source income, with income normally sourced according to where the services are performed.[135]

To be eligible for the foreign earned income exclusion, an individual must have a tax home in a foreign country[136] and meet either the bona fide foreign resident test

[132]The exceptions and the 10 percent penalty for premature withdrawals are similar to those for employer-sponsored qualified retirement plans.

[133]Taxpayers may deduct the foreign taxes paid instead, but claiming the credit usually results in greater tax savings.

[134]The denial of the foreign earned income exclusion to government employees, including diplomats and members of the U.S. armed forces, is justified on the basis that they are typically exempt from tax by a host country. Additionally, members of the armed services are entitled to many other tax benefits such as exclusions for combat zone pay, living allowances, moving allowances, travel allowances, family allowances, and other payments (as discussed in Chapter 3).

[135]Reg. §1.911-3(a) states that the location where the money is received is irrelevant as long as the services for which the income is earned are performed in a foreign country.

[136]Reg. §1.911-2(g) states that the term foreign country does not include United States possessions and territories such as Puerto Rico, Guam, the Northern Mariana Islands, the Virgin Islands, American Samoa, Wake, and the Midways Islands.

or physical presence test. The bona fide resident test requires a U.S. citizen to be a bona fide resident of one or more foreign countries for an uninterrupted period of at least one tax year.[137] The physical presence test requires that a U.S. citizen or resident be physically present in a foreign country (or countries) for 330 full days during a period of 12 consecutive months.

Some factors used to decide if an individual is a bona fide resident of a foreign country include:[138]

- Intention of the taxpayer with regard to the length and nature of the stay;
- Establishment of the taxpayer's home in the foreign country for an indefinite period;
- Status of resident and payment of taxes to the foreign country;
- Marital status and residence of his or her family; and
- Reason and length of temporary absences from his or her foreign home.

Once a taxpayer establishes bona fide residency in a foreign country, this status can extend backward to a prior partial year beginning with the date that the residency actually began and forward to any subsequent partial year ending with the date of return to the United States. The exclusion, however, must be prorated based on the actual number of residency days in the partial period. When both spouses work in a foreign country, the exclusion limit applies separately to each spouse.[139]

EXAMPLE 48

Jim and Christina, husband and wife, became bona fide residents and worked in New Zealand for the last 78 days of 2012 (a leap year) and all of 2013. Jim has foreign earned income of $17,000 for 2012 and $84,000 for 2013. Christina has foreign earned income of $25,000 for 2012 and $99,000 for 2013. Because they are bona fide residents of New Zealand for all of 2013, they are each eligible to exclude up to $97,600 of their foreign earned income for that year. They can also qualify for a partial exclusion in 2012 for the 78 days that they were bona fide residents of up to $20,267 (78/366 × $95,100). Jim can exclude all $17,000 of his 2012 income and all $84,000 of his 2013 income. Christina can exclude only $20,267 of her 2012 income and $97,600 of her 2013 income. Unused exclusions of one spouse cannot be applied to the other spouse's income.

The tax on income in excess of the exclusion is computed using the marginal tax rate that would apply if the foreign income were still included (that is, at the taxpayer's highest marginal rate).

If doubt exists about a taxpayer's ability to satisfy the bona fide foreign resident test, detailed records should be kept to establish that the 330-day physical *presence* test was met. The days do not need to be consecutive[140] and this rule only requires physical presence in a foreign country, whether that day is a work or nonwork day.[141] If the 330-day physical presence requirement is met, but the taxpayer is in the foreign country for less than one full tax year, the exclusion must be prorated for the number of qualifying days present that tax year.

Persons working abroad for less than 330 days should consider the tax advantages of extending their assignments (if the option is available), particularly if the foreign country does not tax the individual's compensation. TAX PLANNING

Excess Housing Cost Exclusion

When working in foreign countries, many expatriates incur additional costs to maintain the same standard of living they enjoyed in the United States. Normally, personal

[137] §911(d)(1)(A).

[138] *Sochurek v. Comm.*, 300 F.2d 34 (CA-7, 1962), 9 AFTR 2d 883, 62-1 USTC ¶9293, rev'g 36 T.C. 131 (1961).

[139] Reg. §1.911-5(a).

[140] Reg. §1.911-2(d)(2) requires 330 full days with full days defined as beginning at midnight of one day and ending the following midnight. Partial days within a foreign country (such as the day of departure or arrival) are not included in the 330 days.

[141] Rev. Rul. 57-570, 1957-2 CB 458.

housing costs paid or reimbursed by an employer must be included in taxable income. Section 911(c)(1)(B), however, allows an individual who qualifies for the foreign earned income exclusion to exclude housing costs paid or reimbursed by an employer in *excess* of a base amount equal to 16 percent of the foreign earned income exclusion, or $15,616 ($97,600 × 16%) for 2013. Reimbursements equal to or less than the base amount are subject to tax as the minimum costs taxpayers would incur for housing regardless of where they lived.

The exclusion for excess foreign housing cost reimbursements is capped at 30 percent of the foreign earned income exclusion less the base amount resulting in a maximum excess housing exclusion for 2013 of $13,664.[142] This amount must also be prorated for the number of days in the tax year that the individual's tax home is in a foreign country. The sum of the foreign earned income exclusion and the housing cost exclusion cannot exceed the individual's foreign earned income for the tax year. The foreign earned income and housing cost exclusion elections are made separately on Form 2555.[143]

Credit for Foreign Taxes

Individuals who do not qualify for the foreign earned income exclusion (or who choose to forego it) are allowed a **foreign tax credit** for the taxes paid to the foreign government. To prevent taxpayers from using the foreign tax credit to reduce taxes on income earned in the United States, the foreign tax credit cannot exceed what the tax would be if the foreign income were earned in the United States.[144] To compute this limit, the taxpayer's total U.S. tax liability is multiplied by the ratio of the taxpayer's taxable income from all foreign countries divided by his or her total worldwide taxable income. The foreign tax credit equals the lesser of the computed foreign tax credit limit or the taxes paid to all foreign countries. Taxpayers who qualify for the income exclusion and the credit should calculate both, selecting the option with the lower net tax payable.

EXAMPLE 49

Roger, who is single, works in Europe for all of 2013. His salary is $90,000 and he pays $20,500 in tax to the foreign government. His other taxable income (from U.S. sources) after allowable deductions is $20,000. If he claims the foreign earned income exclusion, Roger excludes the $90,000 salary, leaving only the $20,000 of taxable income on which he will pay a U.S. tax of $5,600 using the 28 percent rate that applies to income from $90,000 to $110,000. If he does not claim the foreign earned income exclusion, Roger's taxable income is $110,000 ($90,000 foreign salary plus $20,000 other taxable income). The U.S. tax on income of $110,000 is $24,093.[145] Roger's foreign tax credit is limited to the equivalent U.S. tax on his foreign income of $19,712 [$24,093 × ($90,000/$110,000)], as this is less than the $20,500 of foreign taxes paid. Roger's tax is reduced to $4,381 ($24,093 – $19,712). Roger's remaining $788 ($20,500 – $19,712) foreign tax credit may be carried back one year and forward ten years subject to the foreign credit limitation. Taking the tax credit instead of the income exclusion results in a tax savings of $1,219 ($5,600 – $4,381).

[142]§911(c)(2)(A). This maximum exclusion is calculated as 30% of the foreign earned income exclusion over the base amount of 16% of the exclusion or $13,664. [(30% – 16%) x $97,600]. In recognition of the large variation in international housing costs, §911(c)(2)(B) allows the Treasury Secretary to increase the 30 percent limit for locations with very high housing costs. See Notice 2012-19, 2012-10 IRB. Self-employed individuals are not eligible to exclude excess housing expenses, but can instead elect to deduct these expenses in computing adjusted gross income. §911(c)(4)(A).

[143]A taxpayer may use Form 2555-EZ if no housing exclusion (or deduction) is claimed, foreign earned income does not exceed the maximum earned income exclusion, and the taxpayer has no self-employment income, business expenses, or moving expenses for the year. If a husband and wife each qualify for the exclusion, each must file a separate form. Once made, an election remains in effect for all subsequent years unless the taxpayer revokes it. Once revoked, the election cannot be made for the next five years without IRS approval. §911(e) and Reg. §1.911-7.

[144]§904(a).

[145]This tax on $110,000 is calculated using the tax rate schedule for a single individual as in Chapter 11 as follows: [($110,000 – $87,850) x 28%] + $17,891.25 = $24,093.25.

A key factor in deciding whether to elect the exclusion or the foreign tax credit is the foreign tax rate on the foreign earned income as compared to the U.S. tax rate. In a country with a low tax rate (or no income tax), taxpayers will usually benefit by electing the exclusion. In foreign countries whose rates are higher than those of the United States, however, taxpayers are usually better off claiming the foreign tax credit instead of the exclusion. Not only do the higher foreign taxes offset the U.S. tax on the foreign earned income, but excess foreign taxes can be carried back one year and forward 10 years to offset foreign income in those other years.

TAX PLANNING

Taxpayers with foreign earned income in excess of the exclusion may also qualify for a partial foreign tax credit, but only for the taxes on income in excess of the excluded foreign income. The amount of foreign taxes ineligible for the credit is computed by multiplying total foreign taxes by:

$$\frac{\text{Excluded foreign income less deductible expenses allocated to excluded income}}{\text{Total foreign income less deductible expenses related to this income}}$$

Total foreign taxes less this ineligible amount are the allowable *creditable* taxes.

EXAMPLE 50

Olga is a U.S. citizen living and working in a foreign country. Her total foreign earned income is \$135,000 of which she excludes \$111,264 under the foreign earned income and housing exclusions (\$97,600 + \$13,664). She paid \$30,000 in foreign income taxes and \$28,000 for unreimbursed business expenses. She allocates \$23,077 (\$28,000 × \$111,264/\$135,000) of her business expenses to the excluded income. Of her \$30,000 in foreign taxes, \$24,725 is related to her excluded income determined as follows:

$$\frac{(\$111,264 - \$23,077)}{(\$135,000 - \$28,000)} \times \$30,000 \text{ taxes paid} = \$24,725$$

Olga's creditable taxes are \$5,275 (\$30,000 – \$24,725).

Moving Expenses

Employer reimbursements for allowable moving expenses (the cost of moving household goods, as well as transportation and lodging expenses incurred in traveling to the new residence) for the employee and family members are usually excluded from the employee's gross income. The unreimbursed portion of allowable moving expenses is deductible *for* AGI. For foreign moves, reasonable costs of storing household goods while the taxpayer's tax home is outside the United States also qualify as moving expenses.[146]

Indirect expenses, such as pre-move house-hunting trips and temporary living expenses, are not deductible. The employee has taxable compensation income if the employer reimburses the employee or pays directly for these or other nonqualifying relocations costs, unless they can be properly classified as reimbursable business travel expenses.

Tax Reimbursement Plans

To encourage employees to accept foreign assignments, some companies agree to include payment of the employees' taxes as part of their compensation packages in addition to housing allowances. If an employer pays an employee's taxes, the employee has additional taxable compensation. The two most common types of tax reimbursement arrangements are tax protection and tax equalization plans.

A **tax protection plan** reimburses an individual for any U.S. or foreign taxes paid in excess of the liability he or she would have incurred in U.S. tax if the individual had remained in the United States. If actual taxes are lower than the assumed tax liability, the employee benefits from the foreign assignment because only the actual U.S. and foreign taxes are paid; the employee keeps any tax savings. Thus, under a tax protection plan,

[146]§217(h)(3).

an employee may realize significant tax savings in a move to a low-tax country. From an employer's perspective, however, employees may be reluctant to accept assignments in high-tax countries in which actual taxes exceed the assumed U.S. tax.

Under a **tax equalization plan**, an employee working in a foreign country has the same net tax liability he or she would have paid had the employee remained in the United States. To achieve this balance, the employee's salary is reduced by the hypothetical U.S. tax, but the employee is then reimbursed for the actual U.S. and foreign taxes on the covered income. Under this plan, the employer pays any excess tax but keeps any tax benefit from having employees in low-tax countries. This helps offset the tax costs of having employees in high-tax countries and also prevents employees from preferring one foreign assignment over another merely due to tax differences. Although the objectives of tax protection and equalization plans are similar, a tax equalization plan is usually considered less costly for the employer. Any amounts excluded under foreign earned income or housing cost exclusions reduce the cost of protection or equalization plans to employers because the company does not have to reimburse the employee for U.S. tax on those amounts.

TAX PLANNING

Tax Treaties

The United States has income tax treaties with many countries. Although no two treaties are exactly alike, they generally provide tax exemptions to residents of one treaty country on short-term assignments to the other country. If an American employer maintains its employee on the U.S. payroll, physical presence in the other treaty country for a short period usually exempts that personal service income from foreign income tax. A typical treaty allows no more than 183 days presence in a year. Thus, an assignment for the last 183 days in one year and the first 183 days in the next year may comply with the typical treaty. Some treaties, however, use a shorter period of time and others have monetary limits. Treaties also frequently exempt teachers and students from foreign income tax. Thus, it is important to know the specific provisions of the treaty for any country where the taxpayer plans to conduct business.

Revisiting the Introductory Case

If Bob accepts the position with Alpha Corporation, he will be taxed on the $73,000 salary. Alpha Corporation will deduct FICA of 7.65 percent from his gross pay and the corporation will pay a matching amount. Alpha will also have to pay unemployment tax on the first $7,000 of wages at a rate of 6 percent. The benefits of medical insurance, athletic facilities, and free parking will be tax free to Bob and deductible by Alpha Corporation.

If Bob works as an independent contractor for Beta Corporation, he will receive $85,000 in consulting fees on which he will have to pay self-employment taxes of 15.3 percent. He can, however, deduct half his self-employment tax. He will also have to pay $7,000 for his own medical insurance, but he can deduct the health insurance premiums. From his remaining net income, Bob must pay $600 for athletic club dues and $600 for parking with after-tax dollars to maintain the same lifestyle. The after-tax values to Bob are computed as follows:

	EMPLOYEE	INDEPENDENT CONTRACTOR
Salary	$73,000	
Consulting fees		$85,000
Income tax on salary ($73,000 × 25%)	(18,250)	
Income tax on consulting fees ($85,000 × 25%)		(21,250)
Employee FICA tax ($73,000 × 7.65%)	(5,585)	
Self-employment tax ($85,000 × 92.35% × 15.3%)		(12,010)
Tax savings from self-employment tax deduction ($12,010 × 50% × 25% tax rate)		1,501

Medical insurance cost		(7,000)
Tax savings from medical insurance deduction ($7,000 × 25% tax rate)		1,750
Athletic club cost		(600)
Parking cost		(600)
After-tax value	$49,165	$46,791

As shown above, accepting the job with Alpha Corporation results in a $2,374 ($49,165 - $46,791) higher after-tax value for Bob. It is also important to note that Alpha Corporation provides this higher value to Bob at approximately the same cost as Beta Corporation would spend for its compensation package. Thus, it is possible to develop a compensation package that maximizes the value to the employee at no additional cost to the employer—a win-win situation. The after-tax costs to Alpha and Beta Corporations are computed as follows:

	ALPHA CORPORATION	BETA CORPORATION
Salary payment	$(73,000)	
Consulting fees paid		$(85,000)
Employer FICA tax ($73,000 × 7.65%)	(5,585)	
Unemployment tax ($7,000 × 6%)	(420)	
Medical insurance cost	(5,000)	
Athletic club facilities cost	(300)	
Parking cost	(600)	
Income Tax Savings:		
Salary deduction ($73,000 × 34%)	24,820	
Consulting fee deduction ($85,000 × 34%)		28,900
FICA tax deduction ($5,585 × 34%)	1,899	
Unemployment tax deduction ($420 × 34%)	143	
Medical insurance deduction ($5,000 × 34%)	1,700	
Athletic facilities deduction ($300 × 34%)	102	
Parking expense deduction ($600 × 34%)	204	
After-tax cost	$(56,037)	$(56,100)

SUMMARY

Businesses can deduct the gross amount of current compensation paid to their employees. Compensation includes not only base salaries and wages but bonuses, vacation pay, fringe benefits, and any other economic benefits received for services rendered in the course of employment. All these forms of compensation are income taxable to the employee unless a specific provision of the Internal Revenue Code excludes them.

Employee fringe benefits are taxable income unless the benefits fit into one of the tax-exempt categories. The cost of tax-exempt fringe benefits is deductible by the employer even though their values are not taxable income to the employee. To prevent the abuse of tax-free benefits and attempts to convert excess taxable compensation into tax-free benefits, most of the tax-free benefits have significant limitations. Benefits in excess of these limits are taxable compensation, fully taxable to the employee but still deductible by the employer.

Public corporations frequently offer their executives some form of stock or stock options as part of their total compensation package. Stock-based incentive plans offer employees an opportunity to acquire stock at a bargain price and can provide the dual tax advantages of deferring income to a future year and converting what would otherwise be ordinary compensation income into long-term capital gain. Employers view stock options as a form of compensation with no cash outlay. They may also receive cash if the option is exercised. Because employees may require significant amounts of cash to exercise their options, corporations have developed alternative forms of deferred compensation that are tied to the stock's fair market value at a future date but do not require the employee to actually buy the stock. Both phantom stock plans and stock appreciation rights capture appreciation in a company's stock that can be used to compensate employees.

Under a deferred compensation plan, an employer makes a promise to pay benefits to the employee in a future year. The most common deferred compensation plan is the retirement plan. Contributions to qualified plans are deductible by the employer, but the benefits paid to employees are not taxable until received. The employer's contributions, along with any taxpayer contributions made with before-tax dollars and all income earned on the contributions, are fully taxed when withdrawn. Distributions from the taxpayer's after-tax contribution are exempt from tax (including Roth IRAs, which are completely excludable).

There are limitations on the amount of compensation that can be offered on a tax-deferred basis under qualified plans, and such plans are subject to complex nondiscrimination requirements. As a result, many employers have established nonqualified plans. Under these plans, employers can offer unlimited deferred compensation to key or highly compensated executives without extending the benefits to other employees. The employee has no income and the employer no deduction until the employer makes the actual payment.

Americans who work outside the United States may be eligible for a foreign earned income exclusion of up to $97,600 (for 2013) or a foreign tax credit. They may also be eligible to exclude excess foreign housing costs.

KEY TERMS

401(k) plan 174
Accountable plan 165
Bargain purchase 160
Cafeteria plan 157
Catch-up contribution 176
Compensation 146
De minimis benefits 160
Defined benefit plan 173
Defined contribution plan 173
Expatriates 184
FICA tax 146
Flexible spending arrangement 157
Foreign earned income 184
Foreign tax credit 186
Fringe benefits 153
FUTA tax 147
Incentive stock options (ISO) 170
Independent contractor 148
Individual retirement account (IRA) 176
Keogh plan 183
Nonaccountable plan 167
Nondiscrimination rules 172
Nonqualified deferred compensation plan 176
Nonqualified stock option (NQSO) 169
Per diem allowance 167
Phantom stock 171
Premature withdrawals 172
Qualified deferred compensation plans 172
Reasonable compensation 150
Roth IRA 178
Self-employment taxes 179
Stock appreciation right (SAR) 171
Stock option 169
Tax equalization plan 188
Tax protection plan 187
Term life insurance 154
Working condition fringe benefit 161

TEST YOURSELF

ANSWERS APPEAR AFTER THE PROBLEM ASSIGNMENTS

1. Sarah, a cash-basis, calendar-year individual, is president and owns 80 percent of SRS Corporation's stock. SRS is an accrual-basis, calendar-year C corporation. In December year 1, SRS Corporation accrued a $50,000 bonus payable to Sarah and $120,000 in bonuses payable to other employees. The bonuses were all paid on March 1, year 2. How much of the bonuses can SRS deduct in year 1?

a. 0
b. $50,000
c. $120,000
d. $170,000

2. Martha, an employee of Beneficial Corporation, receives an annual salary of $60,000. Beneficial has a cafeteria plan that allows all employees to select an amount equal to 7 percent of their annual salary from a menu of nontaxable fringe benefits or receive the cash. Martha selects $45,000 of group term life insurance that costs the company $400 and also selects health insurance that costs the company $1,600; she takes the remaining $2,200 in cash. How much income does Martha recognize from Beneficial Corporation?
   a. $60,000
   b. $62,200
   c. $63,800
   d. $64,200

3. Mike received two job offers. Friendly Corporation would like to hire him as an employee at a salary of $50,000 and would pay the premiums for comprehensive medical insurance. Micro Corporation would like to hire him as an independent contractor. Mike would earn $55,000 annually in consulting fees working for Micro but would have to pay for his own medical insurance coverage at an annual cost of $5,000. Assume Mike is in the 25 percent tax bracket. Calculate the after-tax cash flow generated by each job.
   a. $33,675 from Friendly and $30,700 from Micro
   b. $35,000 from Friendly and $36,250 from Micro
   c. $37,500 from Friendly and $31,950 from Micro
   d. $42,350 from Friendly and $33,479 from Micro

4. In year 1, Incentive Corporation grants Jessica, an employee, an ISO to buy 1,000 shares of Incentive stock for $28 per share at any time during the next seven years. On the grant date, Incentive stock is selling for $26 per share. In year 5, when the stock is selling for $38 per share, Jessica exercises the option by paying $28,000 ($28 strike price × 1,000 shares) cash to the corporation to exercise her option for the 1,000 shares of stock. Jessica holds these shares until year 8, when she sells them for $128,000. How much income does Jessica recognize and how much can Incentive Corporation deduct, respectively?
   a. No income and no deduction
   b. $26,000 ordinary income at date of grant and $26,000 deduction at date of grant
   c. $10,000 ordinary income when options are exercised and $10,000 deduction when options are exercised
   d. $100,000 capital gain when options are sold and no deduction

5. During 2013, Robin has net income from his sole proprietorship of $25,000. He also earned $91,700 as an employee in 2013. How much must Robin pay for self-employment tax?
   a. $1,913
   b. $3,366
   c. $3,398
   d. $3,825

PROBLEM ASSIGNMENTS

CHECK YOUR UNDERSTANDING

1. Ricardo is a professional football player. In negotiating his contract for the upcoming season, Ricardo is given two options. He can receive (1) 12 monthly checks of $325,000 with no deferred payments or (2) $250,000 monthly with the $900,000 balance placed in escrow and payable to him (with interest) after he retires from professional sports. What are the tax implications of these two alternatives?

2. Gaudy Gift Gallery Corporation (owned 100 percent by Barbara) operates a gift shop. Barbara employs her daughter, Jenny, after school and on weekends. Other employees with similar responsibilities are paid $7 per hour while Jenny is paid $15 per hour. Jenny earned $15,000 in the current year from the store. Is Jenny's salary fully deductible by the corporation? Explain.

3. John is a single individual who works for Auto Rental Cars in Japan during the entire calendar year. His salary is $100,000. How much of this salary can he exclude?

4. Anne is an employee of Marvel Corporation. Marvel provides its employees with an educational assistance plan that pays for up to $5,000 in tuition for any work-related courses. Marvel Corporation also provides free on-premises parking (valued at $50 per month) and free child care (valued at $300 per month). Does Anne have any taxable income as a result of these benefits?

5. What is the difference between a qualified employee discount and a bargain purchase by an employee?

6. In which of the following cases should the employees report the benefit received as gross income?
   a. The employer provides an annual picnic for employees and their families to celebrate Independence Day.
   b. Employees can use the company photocopier for small amounts of personal copying as long as the privilege is not abused.
   c. Employees receive a free ticket to watch the Dolphins play the Raiders.
   d. Each employee receives a $50 check on his or her birthday.

7. A taxpayer moves from Atlanta to Chicago on December 3, year 1, to accept a new job. She would like to deduct $3,000 in unreimbursed direct moving expenses. As she will not meet the time test by the due date for her year 1 tax return, what are her options?

8. What is the difference between an NQSO and an ISO?

9. Gabor Family Enterprises, a closely-held family corporation, would like to offer a stock option plan as an incentive to its employees, but it does not want its stock owned by anyone who is not a member of the Gabor family. What type of plan should Gabor consider?

10. High-Tec Corporation offers a stock option plan as an incentive to its employees. Few employees participate in the plan because they do not have the cash necessary to exercise the options. What type of incentive plan can High-Tec offer the employees who do not have the cash to exercise stock options?

11. What are the advantages of a qualified retirement plan?

12. Discuss why corporations frequently offer both qualified and nonqualified retirement plans to their employees.

13. Your friend Mark suggested that you should open an Individual Retirement Account. He said that an IRA is a great way to save because you do not have to pay tax on the income from the investment and you get a tax deduction for your contribution. Is Mark correct? Explain.

14. Identify the type of IRA (Roth or traditional) that would be best for a taxpayer in each of the following circumstances:
   a. Sharon believes she will be in a higher tax bracket when she withdraws the money in retirement.
   b. Ken believes he will be in the same or a lower tax bracket in retirement.
   c. Susan wants to use her retirement savings for building her estate to pass on to her children.

15. James and Dean plan to start a new business and have not yet decided whether to organize as a partnership, an S corporation, or a C corporation. They are interested in taking advantage of any tax-free fringe benefits that may be available to them. Discuss the advantages and disadvantages from a fringe-benefit perspective of each form of business entity.

16. Explain the difference between a tax protection plan and a tax equalization plan. Which one is usually less costly to the employer?

CRUNCH THE NUMBERS

17. Charlie, who is in the 39.6 percent marginal tax bracket, is the president and sole owner of Charlie Corporation (a C corporation in the 34 percent tax bracket). His current salary is $700,000 per year. What are the income and FICA tax consequences if the IRS determines that $200,000 of his salary is unreasonable compensation?

18. Amy, a cash-basis taxpayer, received a salary of $100,000 during year 1, year 2, and year 3. Amy also was awarded a bonus of $30,000 that was accrued by Amy's employer, Vargus Corporation (an accrual-basis, calendar-year C corporation), in December of year 1 but the bonus was not paid until March 31 of year 2. In December of year 2, Vargus accrued an additional $32,000 bonus that was paid to Amy in January of year 3.
   a. How much income does Amy recognize in year 1, year 2, and year 3?
   b. How much can Vargus Corporation take as a compensation deduction in year 1, year 2, and year 3?

19. Tom is 68 years old. His employer pays the premiums for group term life insurance coverage of $110,000. The cost to the company for Tom's coverage is $3,000.
   a. If the plan providing this coverage is nondiscriminatory and Tom is not a key employee, how much gross income does Tom have?
   b. How does your answer to (a) change if Tom is a key employee?
   c. If the plan is discriminatory, but Tom is not a key employee, what is Tom's gross income?
   d. How does your answer to (c) change if Tom is a key employee?

20. Priscilla, an employee of Choice Corporation, receives an annual salary of $70,000. Choice has a cafeteria plan that allows all employees to choose an amount equal to 8 percent of their annual salary from a menu of nontaxable fringe benefits or to take cash. Priscilla selects $50,000 of group term life insurance that costs the company $900 and also selects health insurance that costs the company $2,000; she takes the remaining $2,700 in cash. How much compensation income does Priscilla recognize from Choice Corporation?

21. Jennifer elects to reduce her salary by $2,500 so she can participate in her employer's flexible spending arrangement. Her salary reduction is allocated as follows: $1,700 for medical and dental expenses and $800 for child care expenses. During the year, Jennifer uses $1,500 of her salary reduction for medical and dental care and $700 for child care assistance.
    a. How much of the $2,500 set aside in the FSA is included in Jennifer's gross income?
    b. How much of the $2,200 reimbursed from the FSA is included in Jennifer's gross income?
    c. What happens to the remaining $300?

22. Clark works all year at the front desk of the Dew Drop Inn and earns a salary of $30,000. He is offered the option of a $400-per-month living allowance or rent-free use of a room at the Dew Drop Inn. Clark chooses to live at the inn in a room that normally rents for $400 per month. How much gross income does Clark have from the Dew Drop Inn?

23. Kevin is an employee of One Hour Dry Cleaners, Inc. All employees of One Hour are eligible for a 40 percent discount on their dry cleaning. During the year, Kevin paid $300 for cleaning that normally would have cost $500. Does Kevin have any taxable income as a result of this discount?

24. Betsy receives a salary of $50,000 from her employer (a retail clothing store) and several fringe benefits. Her employer pays premiums of $300 for her $40,000 group term life insurance coverage and pays $3,200 for medical insurance premiums. Her employer provides dependent care facilities (where she places her young children while she is at work) valued at $4,500 per year. Her employer also allows employees to purchase clothing (the employer's inventory) at 50 percent off the retail sales price (which is 5 percent more than the employer's cost). During the year, Betsy purchases clothing with a retail value of $10,000 for $5,000. In addition to her salary, how much must Betsy include in gross income?

25. Jill worked for a business in Denver. She took a new job with a different company in Colorado Springs, 90 miles away. Her commuting distance from her old home to her old employer in Denver was 15 miles. If she does not move to Colorado Springs, her commuting distance from her old home near Denver to her new place of employment in Colorado Springs would be 70 miles. She decides to move to Colorado Springs. The commuting distance from her new home in Colorado Springs to her new place of employment is 10 miles.
    a. Which commuting distances are important in meeting the mileage test for deductibility of moving expenses?
    b. By how many miles does Jill's commute exceed the minimum necessary to pass the mileage test?

26. In January, Susan's employer transferred her from Chicago to Houston (where she continues to work for the remainder of the year). Her expenses are as follows:

Transportation for household goods	$2,300
Airfare from Chicago to Houston	200
Pre-move house-hunting travel	700
Temporary living expenses in Houston	400
Apartment lease cancellation fee	1,200
Total moving expenses paid	$4,800

a. If Susan is not reimbursed for any of these expenses, how much of her moving expenses can she deduct?

b. If Susan's employer reimburses her $3,600 for all of these moving expenses except the lease cancellation fee, will she have any taxable income?

27. Luis received 400 shares of his employer's stock as a bonus. He must return the stock to the company if he leaves before the 5-year vesting period ends. The fair market value of the stock at the time it was issued was $20,000. After five years, the stock vests when it has a fair market value of $75,000. Two years after vesting, Luis sells the stock for $100,000.

a. If Luis makes no election, how much income or gain does he recognize (1) when the stock is issued, (2) when the stock vests, and (3) when the stock is sold?

b. If Luis makes an election to accelerate the recognition of income, how much income or gain does he recognize (1) when the stock is issued, (2) when the stock vests, and (3) when the stock is sold?

c. If Luis makes an election to accelerate the recognition of income but he leaves the company after three years, is he eligible for a refund of taxes paid?

28. Five years ago, Cargo Corporation granted a nonqualified stock option to Mark to buy 3,000 shares of Cargo common stock at $10 per share exercisable for five years. At the date of the grant, Cargo stock was selling for $9 per share. This year, Mark exercises the option when the price is $50 per share.

a. How much income should Mark have recognized in the year the option was granted?

b. How much income does Mark recognize when he exercises the option?

c. What are the tax consequences for Cargo from the NQSO in the year of grant and in the year of exercise?

29. Three years ago, Netcom granted an ISO to Karen to buy 2,000 shares of Netcom stock at $6 per share exercisable for five years. At the date of the grant, Netcom stock was selling for $5 per share. This year, Karen exercises the ISO when the price is $30 per share.

a. How much income should Karen have recognized in the year the ISO was granted?

b. How much income does Karen recognize when she exercises the ISO?

c. What are the tax consequences for Netcom from the ISO in the year of grant and in the year of exercise?

d. What are the tax consequences to Karen and Netcom if Karen sells all of the stock for $50 per share two years after exercising the options?

30. Four years ago, Handcock Corporation granted 300 SARs to Maria as a bonus. Handcock's stock was worth $20 a share on the date of grant. Maria exercises her SARs this year when the stock is worth $60 a share.

a. How much income should Maria have recognized in the year she received the SARs?

b. How much income does Maria recognize when she exercises the SARs?

c. If Maria is single and in the 28 percent marginal tax bracket, what is her after-tax cash flow from the exercise of the SARs?

d. Does Handcock Corporation get a tax deduction for the SARs and if yes, when and in what amount?

31. Larry, age 32, works for Horizon Corporation. His annual salary is $60,000. Horizon provides the following benefits to all employees:
- Group term life insurance (each employee is provided with $80,000 worth of coverage that costs Horizon $120 per employee)
- Medical insurance (the cost of Larry's policy is $3,900)
- Qualified pension plan (Horizon matches employee contributions up to $2,500. Larry contributes 7 percent of his salary to the plan.)
- Qualified award program (Larry received a watch Horizon purchased for $100 to recognize his 5 years of service with Horizon.)

How much income must Larry recognize and how much can Horizon Corporation deduct in the current year?

32. Nick, age 53, is single and has AGI of $61,000. He contributes $5,000 to his IRA in 2013.

a. How much can Nick deduct if he is not covered by an employer-sponsored qualified retirement plan?

b. How much can Nick deduct if he is covered by an employer-sponsored qualified retirement plan?

33. Jennifer, age 35, is single and is an active participant in her employer's qualified retirement plan. Compute the maximum Roth IRA contribution that she can make in 2013 if

a. her adjusted gross income is $130,000.

b. her adjusted gross income is $59,000.

c. her adjusted gross income is $38,000 and she makes a $2,000 contribution to a traditional IRA.

34. Carrie owns a business that she operates as a sole proprietorship. The business had a net profit of $25,000 in 2013. This is Carrie's only earned income.

a. How much must she pay for self-employment taxes?

b. How much can she deduct on her tax return?

c. If the business had a net loss of $10,000 (instead of a $25,000 profit), how much in self-employment taxes must Carrie pay?

35. George has $78,200 in salary from his full-time position and $43,000 in net income in 2013 from his sole proprietorship. What must he pay for self-employment tax? What portion of this can he deduct?

36. Andrew, a single individual, has $220,000 in salary and $60,000 in self-employment income in 2013. What must he pay for self-employment tax? What portion of this can he deduct? How much must he pay in total for the Medicare surtax?

37. Lisa and Marco are married and file a joint tax return. Lisa has $180,000 in salary and Marco has $190,000 in self-employment income in 2013. What must they pay for self-employment tax? What portion of this can they deduct? How much must they pay in total for the Medicare surtax?

38. Luis operates a bakery as a sole proprietorship. He has four bakers whom he employs on a full-time basis and who participate in a company-paid health insurance plan. Luis is also covered by this same plan. The annual premiums are $2,300 per person. The business paid $11,500 for health insurance premiums for 2013. Are these insurance premiums deductible? If they are, where should Luis deduct them on his tax return?

39. Alexander works as an electrician at a small company that provides no retirement benefits. He receives a salary of $45,000. In addition, Alexander operates a small roof repair service as a sole proprietorship; this business has a net loss of $2,500. In addition, Alexander realizes $800 of net income from rental property and $1,500 in interest income. What is Alexander's earned income for determining the amount he is eligible to contribute to an IRA?

40. Wendy is a single individual who works for MTP, Inc. During the entire calendar year, she works in France and pays French taxes of $8,000 on her $95,000 salary. Her taxable income without considering her salary from MTP is $10,000. Should Wendy claim the income exclusion or tax credit and how much tax does she save using the alternative selected?

41. Mark works in a foreign country for the entire calendar year. His salary is $120,000 and he pays $18,000 in tax to the foreign government. His other taxable income (from U.S. sources) after all deductions is $30,000. If he claims the foreign earned income exclusion, how much are his creditable foreign taxes?

THINK OUTSIDE THE TEXT

These questions require answers that are beyond the material that is covered in this chapter.

42. Evan is setting up a new business. He can operate the business as a sole proprietorship or he can incorporate as a regular C corporation or as an S corporation. He expects that the business will have gross income of $130,000 in the first year with expenses of $25,000 excluding the following. He plans to take $35,000 from the business for living expenses as a salary and will have the business pay $3,000 annually for his health insurance premiums.

a. Compute the total tax cost in 2013 for each alternative if Evan is single and this is his only source of income.

b. Which alternative business form do you recommend based solely on the first year tax costs?

c. What are some of the other factors Evan should consider in deciding between a C corporation and an S corporation for his business?

43. Cindy is president and sole shareholder of Chipsmart Corporation. Through her hard work (frequently putting in 70 hours per week), she has managed to triple the number of clients and revenue in the past year. Chipsmart has never paid a dividend to Cindy, although it does have retained earnings. Last year, Cindy's salary was $200,000; this year, due to her success, she would like to pay herself a $600,000 salary. As Chipsmart's tax adviser, prepare a list of questions you would like to ask Cindy when you meet her to discuss the salary increase.

44. What tax planning should be done before exercising incentive stock options?

45. Construct a scenario in which the tax treatment of stock options is very unfavorable for the employee.

46. The scandal on backdating stock options introduced new terminology to describe these controversial practices. Describe what you think each of these terms means.

a. Backdating

b. Repricing

c. Reloading

d. Spring-loading

e. Bullet-dodging

47. Would an employee who first becomes a participant in a pension plan at age 52 generally prefer to have a defined benefit plan or a defined contribution plan? Explain.

48. What do you think the effect would be if Congress changes the law so that retirement plan contributions are included in taxable income at the time they are made rather than taxing the payment when received in retirement?

IDENTIFY THE ISSUES

Identify the issues or problems suggested by the following situations. State each issue as a question.

49. Susan is the second-highest-paid executive for Sanibel Corporation, a publicly traded corporation. Her salary is $1,600,000.

50. Virginia is the president and founder of VT Corporation. She is extremely devoted to the business, frequently working 70-hour weeks. She did not take any salary from the business for its first two years of operations. She is now receiving a salary that is 150 percent of what comparable businesses pay their presidents.

51. George just accepted a job as an apartment manager and is paid a salary of $28,000 per year. In addition to the salary, he is offered the choice of rent-free use of an apartment or a $500 per month housing allowance. George decides to accept the rent-free apartment.

52. Victor has the full-time use of a company-owned Jaguar automobile. This year Victor drove 24,000 miles for business and 10,000 personal miles. His employer does not require him to report his personal mileage but, instead, includes the lease value of the full-time use of the automobile as additional compensation on his Form W-2.

53. In February, Margaret's employer asked her to move from the Miami office to the Atlanta office. In March, Margaret spent $900 on a house-hunting trip to Atlanta. She located a home and moved into it in April. Margaret's employer reimbursed her for all direct costs of moving to Atlanta and also for the cost of the house-hunting trip.

54. Sarah is single and earns $60,000 in salary. She wants to invest $2,500 per year in an IRA but is not sure which type she qualifies for and whether this would be a better investment than investing the money in preferred stock paying a 6 percent annual dividend.

55. Ken is single and earns a salary of $60,000 per year. He also receives $4,000 a year in taxable interest and dividend income. Ken would like to contribute the maximum allowable to his company's qualified pension plan.

DEVELOP RESEARCH SKILLS

56. Martin Martindale, the 40-year-old founder and president of Martindale Corporation (an accrual-basis, calendar-year C corporation), owns 60 percent of the stock and receives a salary of $600,000. Four unrelated shareholders own the rest of the stock equally. The corporation has paid dividends regularly to the shareholders and plans to continue to do so in the future. Martin plans to recommend that the board of directors authorize the payment of a bonus to himself and two other employees (all cash-basis, calendar-year individuals). The first employee is the vice president, who owns 10 percent of the corporation and receives a salary of $400,000. The other employee is the controller, who is not currently a shareholder in the corporation and receives a salary of $200,000. Martin would like the bonus to equal 75 percent of each recipient's current salary. Martin believes that the annual salaries are probably a little high when compared to the corporation's competitors. Martin asks you, as the corporation's tax advisor, to recommend what the corporation needs to do so that it gets a deduction for the planned bonuses. Martin would prefer that the bonuses be paid next year but deducted by the business this year.

a. Locate and read *Mayson Manufacturing Co.*, 178 F.2d 115, 38 AFTR 1028, 49–2 USTC ¶9467 (CA6, 1949) and then summarize the important points of this case as it relates to Martindale.

b. Prepare a summary of the relevant Code and regulations sections as they apply to Martindale.

c. Prepare a one-paragraph summary for Martin on what the corporation needs to do to qualify for a deduction for the planned bonuses.

57. McGuire Corporation is planning to acquire a corporate jet to increase the efficiency and security of its executives who will use the jet for both business trips and personal vacations. McGuire Corporation wants to know how it should determine the amount that is taxed to its employees when they use the corporate jet for personal travel.

58. Robert, age 35, has accumulated $36,000 in his traditional IRA. He recently married and would like to withdraw $25,000 from his IRA for a down payment on his first house. Write a letter to Robert stating the tax implications of his proposed withdrawal.

59. Jennifer, age 40, has accumulated $40,000 in her traditional IRA. She would like to withdraw $22,000 from her IRA to pay for her daughter's college expenses. She plans to use $15,000 for tuition and $7,000 for room and board. Write a letter to Jennifer stating the tax implications of her proposed withdrawal.

SEARCH THE INTERNET

60. Go to *www.legalbitstream.com*. Locate and read Regulation Section 1.62–2(j), example 6. If an employer has an otherwise accountable plan but reimburses employees at 60 cents per mile, how is the reimbursement treated?

61. Go to *www.legalbitstream.com*. Locate and read Revenue Ruling 2003–102. What type of medicines and drugs can be reimbursed through a flexible spending arrangement (FSA) according to this ruling? What change took effect in 2011?

62. Go to *www.irs.gov* and print Form 1040 and Schedule SE for 2012.

a. Complete the first page of Form 1040 and Schedule SE for Angelina, a single individual, who reports $75,000 of net profit on her Schedule C from her sole proprietorship for 2012.

b. What would Angelina's adjusted gross income be for 2013?

c. What would Angelina's self-employment tax be for 2013?

63. Find an article on the Internet that describes how a traditional IRA can be converted into a Roth IRA. Summarize the process explaining any tax costs associated with the conversion. Include the URL for the article.

DEVELOP PLANNING SKILLS

64. Jorge, a single individual, agrees to accept an assignment in Saudi Arabia, a country that imposes no income tax on compensation, beginning on January 1. Jorge will be paid his normal monthly salary of $5,000, plus an additional $1,400 per month for each month he works in Saudi Arabia.

His employer requires him to remain in Saudi Arabia for at least six months; however, he can elect to continue working there for up to six additional months if he wishes or return to work in the U.S. office. Advise Jorge of the tax ramifications if he stays in Saudi Arabia only six months and if he stays there an additional six months.

65. Sherry just received a big promotion at Barcardo Corporation. Last year her salary was $100,000, but due to her promotion she expects to earn $180,000 this year. She expects that she will be able to save about $60,000 of her pay raise and is interested in exploring ways to minimize her federal tax liability. List some of the tax-planning opportunities with respect to her salary.

66. Maria, age 42, just resigned from Bygone Corporation to accept a new job with Future, Inc. Bygone informed Maria that she has a $38,000 balance in its qualified retirement plan and wants to know if she plans to roll over this balance into another plan or prefers to receive a lump-sum payment. Maria is in the 28 percent marginal tax bracket and would like to buy a new car with the funds although the local car dealer is currently offering very attractive low-interest financing. Determine the amount of after-tax funds Maria would have available to pay for the car if she takes a lump-sum distribution, and make a recommendation regarding what you think she should do.

67. William, an employee for Williamson Corporation, receives an annual salary of $120,000 and is in the 28 percent marginal tax bracket. He is eligible to contribute to Williamson's 401(k) plan and could contribute the pretax amount of $12,000. Alternatively, he could contribute only $6,000 to the plan and use the remaining $6,000 to purchase municipal bonds paying 6 percent interest. Evaluate the tax savings and after-tax cash-flow effect of each of these investment choices. State which option you recommend for William and explain why.

68. Robert, age 55, plans to retire when he reaches age 65. He is not currently an active participant in any qualified retirement plan. His budget will allow him to contribute no more than $3,000 of his income before taxes to either a traditional IRA or a Roth IRA to provide retirement income. His marginal tax rate will be 28 percent until he retires, at which time it will drop to 15 percent. He anticipates a rate of return on either type of IRA of 7 percent before considering any tax effects. Prepare an analysis for Robert comparing the tax effects of investing in a traditional IRA and in a Roth IRA.

69. Melinda has been offered two competing employment contracts for the next two years. Argus Corporation will pay her a $75,000 salary in both years 1 and 2. Dynamic Corporation will pay Melinda a $100,000 salary in year 1 and a $49,000 salary in year 2. Melinda expects to be in the 25 percent marginal tax bracket in year 1 and in the 33 percent marginal tax bracket in year 2 (due to a significant amount of income from new rental properties). She does not expect either offer to change her marginal tax bracket for either year. Both Argus Corporation and Dynamic Corporation expect their marginal tax brackets to remain at 34 percent over the two-year period and expect that employment tax rates will remain the same.

a. Compute the net present value of the after-tax cash flow for Melinda and after-tax cost for Argus and Dynamic for each of the proposed employment contracts using a 6 percent discount rate.

b. Which alternative is better for Melinda and which is better from the corporation's perspective?

ANSWERS TO TEST YOURSELF

1. c. **$120,000**. Compensation accrued to employees must be paid within 2½ months after the close of the corporation's tax year or the payment is considered deferred compensation and cannot be deducted until the year of payment (so the $120,000 accrued for employee bonuses is deductible in year 1). A more restrictive provision applies to related taxpayers who own more than 50 percent of the corporation; the deduction for the president's bonus is deferred until the year the president recognizes the income (so the $50,000 bonus will not be deductible until year 2).

2. b. **$62,200**. The $60,000 salary and the $2,200 cash are taxable. The non-cash benefits of life insurance premiums (not in excess of $50,000 insurance value) and health insurance premiums are tax free.

3. a. **$33,675 from Friendly and $30,700 from Micro**.

	Friendly	Micro
Salary	$50,000	
Consulting fees		$55,000
Income tax on salary ($50,000 × 25%)	(12,500)	
Income tax on consulting fees ($55,000 × 25%)		(13,750)
Employee FICA tax ($50,000 × 7.65%)	(3,825)	
Self-employment tax ($55,000 × 92.35% × 15.3%)		(7,771)
Tax savings from self-employment tax deduction ($7,771 × 50% × 25% tax rate)		971
Medical insurance cost		(5,000)
Tax savings from medical insurance deduction ($5,000 × 25% tax rate)		1,250
After-tax value	$33,675	$30,700

4. d. **$100,000 capital gain when options are sold and no deduction**. Jessica recognizes a $100,000 ($128,000 selling price - $28,000 basis) capital gain when the stock is sold. However, because this option is an ISO, Incentive Corporation receives no tax deduction and thus derives no tax benefit from the option.

5. c. **$3,398**. Robin first multiplies his $25,000 self-employment income by 92.35% ($25,000 × 92.35% = $23,087.50). Robin then reduces the $113,700 ceiling by the $91,700 of employee earnings on which Social Security tax has already been paid. Only $22,000 ($113,700 - $91,700) of his self-employment earnings is subject to the Social Security tax; however, his entire $23,087.50 of self-employment earnings is subject to the Medicare tax. Robin's self-employment taxes are $3,397.54 [($22,000 × 12.4% = $2,728) + ($23,087.50 × 2.9% = $669.54)].

chapter

5 Business Expenses

CHAPTER OUTLINE

The treatment of many business expenses differs for tax and financial accounting. No tax deduction is allowed for expenses unless a specific provision in the Internal Revenue Code grants it. Additionally, a number of restrictions limit the current year's deduction. For example, expenses such as start-up costs may need to be amortized over several years, expenses such as meals and entertainment are only partially deductible, and expenses such as fines are not deductible at all.

The taxpayer's method of accounting determines the year in which a deduction is taken. An accrual-basis taxpayer deducts expenses when the all-events test is met and economic performance has occurred. A cash-basis taxpayer usually deducts expenses in the year paid. Cash-basis taxpayers may be able to make early payments of expenses at year-end to accelerate their tax deductions. Before making early payments, however, taxpayers should consider their tax rates for each year. Usually the time value of money dictates taking the deduction as soon as possible. If the tax rate is higher in the later year, however, the time value of money may not be enough to offset the tax savings that can be achieved by deferring the expense.

Taxpayers should not fall into the trap of making unnecessary expenditures solely to obtain a tax deduction. The best strategy for maximizing after-tax income is to avoid expenses whenever possible. If an expense is desirable or necessary, however, then every possibility should be explored to make it deductible. That is the essence of good tax planning.

KEY CONCEPTS

- ★ Trade or business expenses must be ordinary, necessary, and reasonable in amount to be deductible.
- ★ Accrual-basis taxpayers deduct their expenses when the all-events test is met and there is economic performance. Cash-basis taxpayers generally deduct expenses when paid; however, prepaid expenses that benefit future years may have to be capitalized.
- ★ Business travel expenses are only deductible when the taxpayer is away from home. Deductible transportation expenses do not include commuting to and from work.
- ★ Deductions for business expenses require proper documentation and the deductions for certain expenses may be limited.
- ★ The income tax expense reported on financial statements is based on financial statement income, which can differ from income shown on the tax return. Temporary book/tax differences are accounted for as deferred tax assets or deferred tax liabilities.

Setting the Stage—An Introductory Case

Mark has a great idea for a new business, but he decides to spend both time and money to properly investigate before jumping into the business. He spends $2,000 for a market survey and $2,200 for a feasibility study. After this investigative work, Mark proceeds to establish the business. He will operate the business as a sole proprietorship, using a room in his home as an office and living off of his substantial savings until the business becomes profitable.

Mark spends $1,500 for pre-opening advertising and will begin his business operations on July 1. For the balance of the first year he anticipates incurring the following expenses. He expects to spend $2,500 for business travel ($500 for meals, $900 for hotels, and $1,100 for airfare), $5,000 for supplies, and $1,800 for advertising. He plans to pay $2,400 for dues to join the local country club where he can entertain potential customers, and he expects to spend $800 for business meals there with his clients. Mark will use his Toyota Celica to drive approximately 4,500 miles on business this year; he will also use the car for personal travel, putting about 8,000 personal miles on the car. This morning he received a speeding ticket while rushing to meet a potential customer and paid a $60 fine.

Mark plans to use one room in his home exclusively and regularly as his office. The room occupies 400 of the 2,000 square feet in his house. Annual expenses for his home include $8,000 for mortgage interest, $3,000 for real property taxes, $1,600 in utility bills, and $600 for homeowner's insurance. Depreciation for the portion of the home used as an office is $500.

Mark expects that first-year gross receipts will be only $19,700, but he anticipates a much better second year. Mark assumes that all expenses incurred for his new business are fully deductible this year. Is he correct? We will return to this case at the end of the chapter.

Criteria for Deductibility

The previous chapters explained that all income is taxable unless there is a specific provision in the Internal Revenue Code excluding it. In contrast, no deductions are allowed for expenses unless a specific provision in the Internal Revenue Code grants them. Although this may not seem fair, the tax laws define income very broadly while deductions are defined narrowly. Tax deductions have been described as a matter of "legislative grace," meaning that Congress can decide from year to year which expenses are deductible.[1]

General Provisions for Trade or Business Expenses

Section 162 governs the deductibility of expenses by corporations, partnerships, sole proprietorships, and all other forms of business organizations, and reads as follows:

> *There shall be allowed as a deduction all the ordinary and necessary expenses paid or incurred during the taxable year in carrying on any trade or business. . . .*

Although this appears to suggest that every business expense is deductible, problems arise from differing interpretations of the terms *ordinary, necessary*, and *trade or business*. The term **trade or business** is used many times throughout the Internal Revenue Code but is never precisely defined. As a result, determining trade or business status depends on the facts and circumstances surrounding each business activity. Several criteria have been developed as a result of hundreds of cases litigated over the years. The first criterion of profit motive requires the activity be entered into with the expectation of revenues exceeding expenses. This issue is critical in determining whether a particular activity is a trade or business rather than a hobby. When a taxpayer consistently reports losses, the IRS may assert that the real motivation is personal enjoyment rather than the conduct of a profitable business. If the taxpayer cannot establish that an activity is a trade or business, many deductions may be lost. The tax law limits the deductions attributable to hobbies to the income from the hobby in any year; thus a hobby cannot generate a deductible tax loss, as discussed later in this chapter.

---

[1]*New Colonial Ice Co. v. Helvering*, 13 AFTR 1180, 292 US 435, 4 USTC ¶1292 (1934)

The second criterion for a trade or business is the taxpayer's involvement on a regular and continuous basis. If a taxpayer enters into an activity with the intention of making a profit but does not spend the necessary time and effort required to elevate it to trade or business status, it may be considered only an investment activity. **Production of income** or **investment activities** consist of the ownership of income-producing assets or assets held for long-term appreciation in value. Generally, owners have a passive role in their investment activities, and it is this passivity that distinguishes an investment activity from a business activity.

EXAMPLE 1

Kay and Larry are partners in the Office Supply Company. When they started the business three years ago, Larry provided start-up capital and set up the accounting system. Larry has had no involvement in the business since then; instead he works full-time in his accounting practice. Kay invested some of her own money in the business and also serves as manager for the company. She spends 45 hours per week overseeing daily operations and has no other employment. Kay's unreimbursed expenses are business expenses; Larry's unreimbursed expenses are investment related.

Section 212 allows deductions for expenses paid or incurred during the taxable year (1) for the production or collection of income; (2) for the management, conservation, or maintenance of the property held for the production of income; and (3) in connection with the determination, collection, or refund of any tax, even though these expenses are not incurred in a trade or business.

EXAMPLE 2

Jill is an investor in marketable securities. She subscribes to the *Wall Street Journal* to monitor the performance of specific stocks. She also rents a safe deposit box in which she keeps stock certificates and other investment-related documents, and she pays a fee to an investment counselor for advice. All these expenses would qualify as deductible under Section 212 because they relate to her activity as an investor in marketable securities.

Although Section 212 authorizes a deduction for investment expenses, the deduction may be limited. Investment expenses of individuals are deductible only as miscellaneous itemized deductions (deductible only to the extent they exceed 2 percent of adjusted gross income).[2] Because of this limitation, many individuals receive no tax benefit from their investment expenses.

EXAMPLE 3

Roger has an adjusted gross income (AGI) of $60,000 and incurs $900 of investment expenses during the year. The investment expenses are his only *miscellaneous* itemized deduction. Roger cannot deduct any of the investment expenses because the $900 is less than the 2 percent of AGI threshold of $1,200 ($60,000 × 2%).

Ordinary and Necessary

A deductible expense must be ordinary, necessary, and reasonable. An **ordinary** expense is one that is common and accepted in that type of business, but it does not have to occur on a regular basis during the life of that business. A **necessary** expense is one that is appropriate and helpful to the production of revenues. The expense does not have to be indispensable to be necessary. The courts generally do not second-guess taxpayers on the necessity of making expenditures. The expense merely needs to appear necessary when incurred.

In addition to being ordinary and necessary, the amount of a deductible expense must also be **reasonable**. Technically, this requirement is included in Section 162(a)(1)

[2]Individuals' miscellaneous itemized deductions are discussed in Chapter 11.

as it relates to compensation only. The courts, however, have found that the element of reasonableness was inherent in the ordinary and necessary tests.[3] There is no limit on the size of a deduction if the amount is reasonable. If the deductions are large enough to create a net loss, however, the expenses may be limited.[4] For example, the deductions for home office expenses and hobby expenses of individuals are limited. These limitations are discussed later in this chapter.

In addition to the above criteria, an expenditure cannot be deducted as a current expense if it is

- contrary to public policy
- related to tax-exempt income
- accrued to a related party
- the obligation of another taxpayer

Contrary to Public Policy

Section 162 disallows deductions for several types of expenses that are considered contrary to public policy to avoid subsidizing the taxpayer's undesirable activity. Examples include fines and penalties for speeding, for violating city housing codes, and for violating federal laws regarding safety standards.[5]

EXAMPLE 4

Heavy Freight, Inc. is a trucking company that carries freight across the country. Because certain states have more stringent weight restrictions than others, the company is regularly fined for overweight trucks. To follow the strictest weight limitations would cost the company more than the overweight penalties. Although the fines are a necessary business expense, they are not deductible because the violations are considered contrary to public policy.

The same code section disallows a deduction for expenses incurred for political contributions and lobbying. Political contributions paid to a political party or candidate, or by extension to a political action group or committee, as well as expenditures to influence public opinion about legislation or how to vote in an election, are not deductible.[6] The nondeductible contributions include direct or indirect payments of cash, payments for attendance at a convention or admission to a dinner, and gifts of any other property.[7]

Related to Tax-Exempt Income

The taxpayer cannot deduct interest or any other expense incurred in earning tax-exempt income.[8] Without this provision, a taxpayer in an upper marginal tax bracket might be able to obtain a positive cash flow by borrowing higher-interest money and investing it in lower-interest tax-exempt municipal bonds.

EXAMPLE 5

Tim, a taxpayer in the 35 percent marginal tax bracket, borrows $1 million at 11 percent and invests the proceeds in 8 percent tax-exempt municipal bonds. Annual interest expense is $110,000. Without Section 265, Tim could reduce his tax liability by $38,500 (35% × $110,000). The tax-exempt interest earned on

[3]*Comm. v. Lincoln Electric Co.*, 38 AFTR 411, 176 F.2d 815, 49-2 USTC ¶9388 (CA-6, 1949).

[4]Deductions can also be limited by the at-risk and passive loss rules discussed in Chapter 10.

[5]Additionally, bribes and kickbacks (payments for referring customers) are not deductible if they are made directly or indirectly to an official or employee of any government in violation of the law.

[6]§ 162(e).

[7]§ 276. Only direct lobbying expenses at the local level (such as city and county governments) are deductible. Taxpayers incur direct lobbying expenses only if they have a *direct* interest in specific legislation affecting their businesses.

[8]§ 265.

the bonds is $80,000, producing a net positive cash flow of $8,500 per year ($80,000 income + $38,500 tax savings – $110,000 interest expense). Section 265 prevents this by disallowing a deduction for the interest expense.

Similarly, no deduction is allowed for premiums paid on life insurance policies for which the business is the beneficiary as the proceeds are tax exempt.

EXAMPLE 6

Mega Corporation takes out a $1 million insurance policy on its president for which Mega Corporation is the beneficiary. If the president dies, the $1 million in insurance proceeds are not taxable to Mega Corporation. Therefore, Mega Corporation is not permitted to deduct the premiums it pays on this life insurance policy.

Accrued to Related Party

If two taxpayers are related but one is on the accrual basis of accounting and the other is on the cash basis, an expense cannot be deducted by the accrual-basis taxpayer until the revenue is recognized by the cash-basis taxpayer.[9] This provision prevents an accrual-basis taxpayer from recognizing an expense prior to the related party recognizing the income. The government tolerates this type of mismatch only when it involves unrelated parties.

EXAMPLE 7

Bigcom, an accrual-basis, calendar-year corporation, hires Littlecom, a cash-basis, calendar-year corporation, to provide services for it. Bigcom receives the bill in December of year 1 and pays it in January of year 2. If Littlecom and Bigcom are not related, then Bigcom can deduct the expense on its year 1 tax return. If, however, Bigcom owns more than 50 percent of Littlecom, they are related taxpayers and Bigcom cannot deduct the expense until year 2 when Littlecom includes it in income.

Obligation of Another Taxpayer

An expense must be incurred for the taxpayer's benefit or arise from the taxpayer's obligation to be deductible. If one taxpayer pays the obligation of another taxpayer, the payment is usually not deductible.

EXAMPLE 8

Ted does not have the money to make his monthly interest payment on a business loan, so his mother, Sara, makes the payment for him. Neither Sara nor Ted can take a deduction for the loan interest expense. Sara is not entitled to a deduction because the loan is not her obligation. Ted is not entitled to a deduction because he did not make the payment.

TAX PLANNING

The tax result would have been more favorable if Sara made either a cash gift or loan to Ted and Ted made the loan payment; then Ted could have deducted the interest. This would have preserved the deduction with no cash difference to the family.

Substantiation

All taxpayers must maintain records that substantiate their expense deductions. In the absence of adequate records, the IRS usually prevails over the taxpayer if a dispute arises. Because the taxpayer can usually control the transaction, it seems reasonable to require the taxpayer to properly document the transaction to obtain a deduction.

[9]§ 267. Related parties include brothers, sisters, spouse, parents, grandparents, children, and grandchildren of the taxpayer; a corporation owned more than 50 percent by the taxpayer; and several other relationships.

Substantiation can take the form of receipts, canceled checks, and paid bills.[10] Because it is frequently several years after the expenditure has been made before the IRS conducts an audit, taxpayers must be prepared to retain these records for several years.[11] If substantiation is not available at the time of an audit, the courts have sometimes allowed an unsubstantiated deduction if it is clear that the taxpayer made the expenditure. In this case, the taxpayer estimates the expense based on facts and circumstances.[12]

Stringent substantiation requirements must be followed for travel, entertainment, gifts, and automobile expenses.[13] The substantiation may consist of diaries, trip sheets, travel logs, paid bills and receipts, account books, expense reports, and statements of witnesses.[14] Items that need to be documented for these expenses include

- Amount of expenditure
- Time and place of expenditure, or date and description of gift
- Business purpose of expenditure
- Business relationship of person being entertained or receiving a gift[15]

Timing of Deductions

The taxpayer's method of accounting determines when an expense is deductible. The Internal Revenue Code frequently uses the phrase "paid or incurred" in determining when an expense is deductible. A cash-basis taxpayer is allowed to deduct an expense only when the expense is paid. An accrual-basis taxpayer can take the deduction when the liability for the expense is incurred (the amount and liability are certain) whether or not it is paid for in the same period.

Accrual Method

Taxpayers who use the accrual method deduct their business expenses when both of the following conditions are met:

1. The **all-events test** is met—that is, when all events have occurred that fix the fact of liability and the liability can be determined with reasonable accuracy.
2. There is economic performance.

Economic performance occurs when the property or services are provided or the property is used.[16]

Example 9

Elizabeth, a sole proprietor, had some repair work done at her business in late November of year 1. She received the bill in December of year 1 and paid it in January of year 2. If Elizabeth uses the accrual method, she deducts the expense on her year 1 tax return because all events have occurred establishing the liability and there was economic performance in that year. If Elizabeth uses the cash method, she deducts the expense on her year 2 tax return when she actually pays the bill.

Generally accepted accounting principles frequently require establishing reserves for estimated expenses. Such reserves are usually not deductible for tax purposes

[10]Rev. Proc. 92-71, 1992-2 CB 437 discusses procedures to use when a bank does not return checks to a taxpayer.

[11]See Chapter 2 for a discussion of the statute of limitations.

[12]*Cohan v. Comm.*, 8 AFTR 10552, 39 F.2d 540, 2 USTC ¶489 (CA-2, 1930).

[13]§ 274(d) and § 280F(d)(4).

[14]Temp. Reg. § 1.274-5T(b).

[15]§ 274(d).

[16]The recurring item exception allows a current deduction even if economic performance has not yet occurred. To qualify, economic performance must occur within 8½ months after the close of the year and the expense either is not material or the accrual of the expense results in a better matching of income and expenses. Reg. § 1.461-4.

because the economic performance test is not satisfied. This is one of many examples of differences between financial statement (book) income and taxable income. At the end of this chapter we will examine how to account for these differences.

Cash Method

Taxpayers using the cash method of accounting are allowed to deduct an expense when the expense is paid. An expense paid by check is deductible when the check is mailed, not at the time the check is received. If a check is not honored because the taxpayer has insufficient funds to pay the check (the check bounces), the deduction is not allowed until there are sufficient funds for the check to clear. When a taxpayer pays an expense with a credit card (or borrows from another source), the expenditure and the borrowing of funds occur simultaneously. Therefore, an expense charged on a credit card is deductible in the year charged, even if the credit card payment is made in another tax year.[17] Simply promising to pay or issuing a promissory note does not constitute payment, however.[18]

EXAMPLE 10

Stu, a cash-basis sole proprietor, purchased $500 of office supplies for his business on December 12 of year 1 by using his business credit card. The charge for these office supplies appeared on the January statement in year 2, and Stu paid the credit card bill on February 1 of year 2. The purchase is deductible in year 1.

If an expense is paid with property or services, payment occurs when the taxpayer surrenders the property or renders the services. The deduction is generally the fair market value of the property or services provided. When appreciated property is used to pay an expense, the taxpayer usually must recognize gain on the excess of the property's fair market value over its cost basis.[19] When a cash-basis taxpayer pays an expense by providing services, he or she can deduct the expense but must recognize the fair market value of the services as income.

EXAMPLE 11

Ken does computer programming for a local newspaper in exchange for weekly ads for his computer programming business. During the year, Ken receives $2,800 worth of newspaper advertising for his services. Ken reports $2,800 as business income and deducts $2,800 as advertising expense.

Not all payments by a cash-basis taxpayer result in a current deduction. The regulations require the cost of assets with useful lives extending substantially beyond the end of the year to be capitalized with their cost recovered through depreciation, amortization, or depletion, regardless of the taxpayer's method of accounting.[20] Cost recovery methods for these assets are discussed in the next chapter.

TAX PLANNING

Cash-basis taxpayers sometimes have the ability to make early payments for their expenses at year-end. Examples of business expenses that are candidates for acceleration include replenishment of supplies that are not part of inventory, advertising, and travel expenses. A tax deduction in the current year may be worth more than the same deduction in the next year due to the time value of money. Before taxpayers pay their expenses early, they should consider their tax rates for both years. Additionally, an early payment may not be wise if it will cause a cash-flow problem.

EXAMPLE 12

Logo, a cash-basis corporation, is considering paying $20,000 of expenses at the end of this year rather than waiting until their due date on January 10 of the next year. Logo's marginal tax rate for the current

[17]Rev. Rul. 78-39, 1978-1 CB 73.

[18]*Page v. Rhode Island Trust Co.*, 19 AFTR 105, 88 F.2d 192, 37-1 USTC ¶9138 (CA-1, 1937).

[19]Effectively the transaction is treated as if the taxpayer sold the property for its fair market value, recognized the gain (resulting in a tax liability on the gain), and then used the cash proceeds from the sale to pay for the expense.

[20]Reg. §1.461-1(a).

year is 34 percent, and it expects to be in the same marginal tax bracket next year. Logo will save $6,800 ($20,000 × 34%) in taxes when it deducts the expenses on its tax return. Logo uses a 6 percent discount rate for evaluation purposes. If Logo waits until next year to pay the expenses, the present value of the $6,800 tax savings is $6,412 ($6,800 × .943). Logo will save $388 ($6,800 – $6,412) more in taxes by paying the expenses this year due to the time value of money. If Logo's tax rate is only 25 percent in the current year but is expected to increase to 34 percent next year, waiting to deduct the expenses until next year produces greater tax savings [($20,000 × 34% × .943 = $6,412) – ($20,000 × 25% = $5,000) = $1,412 additional tax savings].

Businesses that sell merchandise to their customers must use the accrual method to account for purchases and sales of inventory because the cash method can be manipulated to accelerate deductions (and defer income).[21] Although inventory and cost of goods sold must be kept on the accrual basis, the cash method may be used for other transactions. Many businesses with average annual gross receipts of $10 million or less qualify for a special variation of the cash method under which they account for the cost of merchandise inventory at year-end as an asset, but are permitted to account for their other expenses on the cash basis.[22] Large corporations, however, defined as those with average annual gross receipts of more than $5 million, are prohibited from using the cash method for tax purposes.[23] This prohibition does not extend to personal service corporations, so no matter how large a personal service corporation is, it may use the cash method.[24]

Restrictions on Prepaid Expenses

A **prepaid expense** is the current period payment for future benefits. Generally, an expenditure that benefits a future period should be capitalized. Payments for assets to be consumed by the close of the following year are fully deductible in the year of payment, however.[25]

EXAMPLE 13

On December 20, Lowkey Corporation (a calendar-year, cash-basis corporation) spent $3,000 for office supplies for the next five months and $6,000 for an insurance policy covering its office building for the next three calendar years. Lowkey Corporation can deduct the $3,000 payment for office supplies because the supplies will be consumed by the end of the next year. Lowkey must capitalize the $6,000 insurance premium and deduct one-third ($2,000) of the cost in each of the next three taxable years.

Prepaid rents are deductible in the period they are paid only if the prepaid period does not exceed one year and the taxpayer has a contractual obligation to prepay rent beyond the current tax year.[26] If prepaid rents do not meet both of these requirements, they must be capitalized as if the taxpayer was on the accrual method of accounting.

EXAMPLE 14

On November 1, Carlton Company (a cash-basis, calendar-year taxpayer) signs a lease with Realty Corporation to rent office space for 36 months. Carlton is able to obtain a favorable monthly rent of $700 by agreeing to prepay the rent for the entire 36-month period. Only $1,400 ($700 x 2 months) of the total payment is deductible in the current year. The balance must be capitalized and amortized over the life of

[21] Reg. §1.446-1(a)(4)(i) and §1.471-1.

[22] Rev. Proc. 2001-10, 2001-1 CB 272 and Notice 2001-76, 2001-52 CB 613.

[23] §448. This prohibition of the cash method extends to partnerships with corporate partners.

[24] A *personal service corporation* is a corporation that provides services in the field of accounting, actuarial science, architecture, consulting, engineering, health, law, or the performing arts and whose employees own substantially all of the corporation. §448(d)(2).

[25] *Zaninovich v. Comm.*, 45 AFTR 2d 80-1442, 616 F.2d 429, 80-1 USTC ¶9342 (CA9-1980).

[26] Ibid.

the lease. If the lease terms require Carlton to prepay $8,400 for each 12-month rental period on November 1 for the next 12 months of rent, it could deduct $8,400 annually because each prepayment does not exceed one year.

Section 461(g) requires prepaid interest to be allocated to the time period over which the interest accrues. Thus, prepaid interest is deductible in the same period for both cash- and accrual-basis taxpayers.

EXAMPLE 15

On November 1, Taxatron (a cash-basis, calendar-year corporation) borrows $100,000 from the bank at 12 percent annual interest. On December 29, Taxatron pays $12,000 to the bank for the first year's interest on the loan. Even though Taxatron is a cash-basis taxpayer, it can deduct only $2,000 interest expense (the interest charged for November and December of the current year). The $10,000 interest charged for the period from January 1 through October 31 of the following year is deductible by Taxatron in the following year.

Original issue discount (OID) is a form of prepaid interest. The original issue discount is the difference between the stated redemption price at maturity (principal) and the issue price (proceeds) of the loan. OID must be amortized over the term of the loan.[27]

EXAMPLE 16

RiteMart Corporation borrowed $100,000 on January 1, year 1, and received $98,500 in proceeds. The loan matures in 10 years, and the $100,000 principal is due on that date. Interest of $10,000 is payable on January 1 of each year beginning January 1, year 2. The $1,500 OID ($100,000 – $98,500) is deductible at the rate of $150 each year for 10 years. The $10,000 interest is also deductible each year as it is paid.

The term *points* refers to the interest prepaid when a borrower takes out a loan or mortgage. Points are also called *loan origination fees*. Points are usually treated in the same manner as OID, described above.[28] Individuals' deductions for interest expense on personal loans are limited to home mortgage interest or student loan interest, as discussed in Chapter 11.

Disputed Liabilities

TAX PLANNING

If a taxpayer contests a liability, the deduction usually cannot be taken until the dispute is settled by compromise or court decision. A taxpayer may, however, claim a deduction for a contested liability by paying the disputed amount or placing that amount in escrow until the dispute is settled, allowing the taxpayer to get an immediate deduction. When the dispute is finally settled, any adjustment to the deduction adjusts income in the year of settlement.

COSTS OF STARTING A BUSINESS

Once business operations have begun, the ordinary and necessary expenses of operating the business are deductible under Section 162. Expenses incurred before business operations begin cannot be deducted as ongoing business expenses; instead, the costs of starting a business are capital expenditures. These costs may need to be amortized rather than deducted currently. Examples include expenses of investigating a new business, start-up costs, and organization costs.

[27]The OID can be deducted on a straight-line basis if it is de minimis. OID is considered de minimis if it is less than one-fourth of 1 percent of the stated redemption price of the loan at maturity multiplied by the number of full years from the date of original issue to maturity. If the OID is not de minimis, the constant-yield method must be used.

[28]An exemption exists for points paid on a home mortgage. Details are discussed in Chapter 11.

Business Investigation and Start-up Expenses

Business investigation expenses are expenses incurred before a decision to enter into a new business has been made. They include expenses for travel, market surveys, feasibility studies, and engineering reports while preparing to enter a business. The deductibility of business investigation expenses depends on the nature of the taxpayer's current business activities, if any, and the nature of the business being investigated.

For taxpayers who are investigating a new business of the same nature as the taxpayer's *existing* business, all business investigation expenses are deductible in the current period, whether or not the new business is actually acquired, as these expenses relate to the expansion of its ongoing business activities.[29]

For taxpayers who have no current business, or who are investigating a new business different in nature from the taxpayer's existing business, one of the following applies:

- If the new business is not acquired, the investigation expenses cannot be deducted.[30]
- If the new business is acquired, all investigation expenses are included as part of start-up expenses.[31]

EXAMPLE 17

Pam, president and sole shareholder of Southbay Construction, Inc., incurs $3,000 in expenses to travel to New York to investigate the feasibility of Southbay acquiring a restaurant in New York. Southbay Construction is currently in the business of building townhouses. If no acquisition takes place, Southbay may not deduct any of the expenses. If the restaurant is acquired, the $3,000 will be included with any start-up expenses incurred. If Southbay already operates a chain of restaurants and it is thinking of adding the New York restaurant to its chain, expenses could be deducted in the current year, even if it did not acquire the restaurant.

Start-up expenses are incurred before the beginning of actual operations and include employee training, advertising, professional services, and development of distributors and customers. Business investigation expenses are included as part of start-up costs and qualifying taxpayers can elect to deduct up to $5,000 of these combined costs with the balance amortized over 15 years (180 months).[32] If total start-up costs exceed $50,000, however, the $5,000 expensing allowance is reduced for each dollar total start-up expenses exceed $50,000. Thus, a company with $55,000 or more of start-up costs can only amortize these costs over 15 years. Start-up costs to expand an existing business are deductible as a cost of continuing operations.[33]

EXAMPLE 18

Continuing example 17, Pam directs Southbay to invest in the New York restaurant, a new business for the construction company. Southbay incurs $5,600 of start-up expenses for advertising and training of the staff. The business investigation expenses of $3,000 are included with the start-up expenses for a total of $8,600. Southbay can expense $5,000 of these expenses; the remaining $3,600 ($8,600 – $5,000) must be amortized at a rate of $20 per month ($3,600/180), beginning with the first month of actual operations. If this had not been a new business for Southbay, it would have been able to expense the entire $8,600 immediately as an expense relating to the continuation of an existing business.

---

[29] *York v. Comm.*, 2 AFTR 2d 6178, 261 F.2d 421, 58-2 USTC ¶9952 (CA4-1958).

[30] Rev. Rul. 57-418, 1957-2 CB 143.

[31] § 195(b).

[32] Prior to October 2004, start-up expenses were capitalized and amortized over 60 or more months with amortization beginning the month operations actually began. The 2010 Small Business Jobs Act increased the deductible amount from $5,000 to $10,000 for start-up expenses incurred in 2010 and also increased the deduction phase-out threshold to $60,000 for tax years beginning in 2010 only. A proposal is pending in Congress that would permanently increase the deductible amount to $10,000.

[33] § 195(c)(1)(B).

Organization Costs

When a corporation is formed, its **organization costs** include fees for legal and accounting services incident to the formation process; fees paid to the state of incorporation for the corporate charter; and expenses for organization meetings of directors and stockholders. These expenditures create an intangible asset (the corporate form) that lasts for the life of the entity and must be capitalized rather than currently deducted. Similar to start-up expenses, taxpayers can elect to deduct up to $5,000 of organizational costs and amortize the balance over 15 years (180 months). If organizational costs exceed $50,000, the $5,000 expensing allowance is reduced ratably and is completely phased out when organizational costs reach $55,000.[34]

EXAMPLE 19

Newborn Corporation, a calendar-year taxpayer, incorporates and begins its business operations on July 1. It incurs $54,000 of organization costs and $20,000 of start-up expenses. Newborn can expense $1,000 of the organization costs and $5,000 of its start-up costs. It will amortize the remaining $53,000 of organizational costs and $15,000 of its start-up costs over 15 years [($53,000 + $15,000)/180 months = $377.78 per month] resulting in a first year deduction of $8,267 [$6,000 + ($377.78 × 6 months)].

OPERATING EXPENSES

Most of the operating expenses shown on an income statement prepared under generally accepted accounting principles (GAAP) are also deductible on a business tax return. Examples include advertising, bank charges, commissions, depletion, depreciation, employee benefit programs, insurance, interest, legal fees, licenses, pension and profit sharing plans, rent or lease payments, repairs and maintenance, salaries and wages, supplies, taxes, travel, and utilities. Nevertheless, some current financial expenses are not deductible in computing taxable income, and not all tax-deductible expenses can be expensed under GAAP. In dealing with these inconsistencies, the general rule is that tax deductions are more narrowly defined than accounting expenses.

Business Meals and Entertainment

In 1986, Congress first tightened the rules on deductions for business meals and entertainment by imposing an 80 percent limit on the deductible amount. Among the principal targets of this tax reform were extravagant business luncheons where little business was discussed. In 1993, Congress further reduced the deductible portion of business meals and entertainment to only 50 percent. Since then, Section 274(n)(1) has limited the deduction for business meals and entertainment expenses to 50 percent of qualified expenses.[35] This limit applies to all business meals and includes the cost of food, beverages, taxes, and tips and any type of activity that is considered entertainment.[36]

This 50 percent limit applies to either the employer or the employee, whoever ultimately pays the cost of the meal or entertainment. If the employer pays the expense directly or reimburses the employee, the 50 percent limit applies to the employer. If the employee is not reimbursed, he or she can only deduct 50 percent of the expense.

---

[34]§ 248. An election to expense or amortize start-up or organization costs is made by attaching Form 4562: *Depreciation and Amortization* to the business's first tax return. Prior to October 2004, an election could be made to amortize organization costs over a period of 60 or more months beginning with the month in which the corporation began its business.

[35]Under § 274(n)(3)(B), a higher deduction limit (70% for 2005, 75% for 2006 and 2007, 80% for 2008 and thereafter) applies to individuals subject to the hours of service limitations of the Department of Transportation, including airline personnel, interstate truck and bus drivers, and railroad employees.

[36]§ 274(n)(1)(B). Transportation expenses, such as taxi fares for getting to and from a restaurant, are 100 percent deductible.

The 50 percent disallowance rule does not apply in the following situations:[37]

- Any meal or entertainment that is treated as compensation to the recipient.
- Meals that are furnished to employees on the business premises if all of the meals are excluded from the employees' wages because they were furnished for the convenience of the employer (for example, meals provided by a restaurant to its wait staff required to work during meal hours).
- A business meal that qualifies as a de minimis fringe benefit (for example, food and beverages provided by an employer for an annual holiday party for employees and their families) that is not taxable to the employee.

Directly Related to or Associated with Entertainment

Expenses to entertain current and potential clients or customers must be either directly related to or associated with the active conduct of the taxpayer's trade or business to be deductible. To be **directly related** to the taxpayer's business, an active discussion related to that business must take place in a clear business setting.[38] Thus, entertainment at certain events at which the noise level would preclude a meaningful discussion does not meet this requirement.

Events that are not directly related may meet the **associated with** test if the event precedes or follows a meaningful business discussion. There must be a clear business purpose for the discussion, it must be substantial in relation to the entertainment, and the taxpayer must expect a clear business benefit.[39] Entertainment tickets are not only subject to the 50 percent limit, but the 50 percent limit applies to the face value of the tickets.

Example 20

Mark takes a customer to see a new Broadway show. Although the face value of each ticket is $100, the only way he can get tickets is by paying a scalper $500 for each ticket. After leaving the theater, the two discuss a new product that Mark would like to sell to the customer. Because it is unlikely that the two discussed business during the show, it is not directly related entertainment. However, the cost of the tickets is deductible because the business discussion following the show qualifies it as associated with the conduct of Mark's business. Mark's deduction is limited to $50 for each ticket ($100 face value × 50%). If, however, there is no business discussion, then none of the costs are deductible as entertainment.

Restrictions on Deductions

No deduction is allowed for the costs of owning and maintaining recreation facilities, such as hunting lodges and yachts, nor for membership dues and fees (including initiation fees) paid to social, athletic, or sporting clubs. This prohibition does not apply to dues for professional organizations (such as bar associations and medical associations), public service organizations (such as Rotary, Kiwanis, and Lions), or trade associations (including business leagues and chambers of commerce).

Example 21

Jack is a CPA. He pays $5,000 annual membership dues to the local country club where he spends $1,800 for business lunches entertaining his clients. Jack also pays $125 per year for dues to the American Institute of Certified Public Accountants (AICPA). Jack can deduct the $125 AICPA dues and $900 ($1,800 × 50%) for the business lunches, but he cannot deduct the country club dues.

---

[37] § 274(n)(2). Samples and promotional activities available to the general public as advertising are not affected by this limit.

[38] Reg. § 1.274-2(c)(3).

[39] Costs of including the customer's or the taxpayer's spouse are normally considered part of the active conduct of business and are deductible. Reg. § 1.274-2(d)(4).

Business gifts are deductible only to the extent of $25 per donee per year.[40] Gifts costing $4 or less with the company's name on them or other promotional materials are not counted in the $25 limit. Samples given to customers or potential customers to elicit business are not treated as business gifts subject to the $25 limitation.

EXAMPLE 22

Chandon Corporation gives each of its best 100 customers a $70 bottle of champagne. It also distributes 500 pens (costing $2 each) with the company's name on them. Chandon can deduct the first $25 of each champagne gift for a total of $2,500 ($25 × 100) and can also deduct the full $1,000 (500 × $2) cost of the pens.

Travel and Transportation Expenses

Congress imposes numerous restrictions and limitations on the deductibility of travel expenses because of the potential for taxpayer abuse. Taxpayers can easily bend the rules, so IRS agents pay particular attention to these deductions, scrutinizing a taxpayer's records for any unsubstantiated or suspicious expenses.[41]

Travel Away from Home

Travel expenses include amounts spent for lodging and meals while temporarily away from home on business, the cost of transportation to the destination and back, and incidental expenses. The expenses must be reasonable, necessary, and directly attributable to the taxpayer's business.[42] To qualify as travel, taxpayers must be away from home overnight or for substantially longer than an ordinary workday so that sleep or rest is required.

EXAMPLE 23

Dan is a truck driver who leaves his home terminal on a regularly scheduled round-trip run between two cities and returns home 18 hours later. During the run, he has 6 hours off at the turnaround point where he eats two meals and rents a hotel room to sleep before starting the return trip. He is away from home and can deduct his travel expenses. If his trip took only 9 hours, with only 1 hour for a meal, Dan would not be away from home and could not deduct the meal.

To determine if a taxpayer is away from home, home must be defined. A **tax home** is identified by the IRS as the location of the taxpayer's principal place of employment, regardless of where the family residence is maintained.

EXAMPLE 24

Linda and her husband maintain a home in Red Bank, New Jersey. Linda teaches at a university in New York City, where she rents a room and eats in restaurants four days during the week. She returns to New Jersey the other days. New York City, where she works, is Linda's tax home. She cannot deduct any expenses for lodging or meals in New York City, as she is not away from home. Her transportation between New Jersey and New York is a personal nondeductible expense.

Temporary Assignments

The away-from-home test requires a **temporary absence** from the home. If the employment away from home in a single location is expected to last (and does in fact

[40]§ 274(b)(1). Incidental costs such as engraving or nominal charges for gift wrapping are not included in the cost of the gift in applying this limitation. Additionally, business gifts are not subject to the 50 percent limitation that applies to meals and entertainment.

[41]An employer's reimbursement of an employee's personal travel expenses does not convert them to business travel expenses. The payment is income to the employee.

[42]Reg. § 1.162-2(a).

last) for no more than one year, it is temporary.[43] Assignments of more than one year are not temporary; the individual's tax home shifts to the new location and travel expenses and living costs there are not deductible.[44] If the expected length of temporary employment later increases to more than one year, the employment is temporary *until* the date the taxpayer's expectation changes.

EXAMPLE 25

Alan, who is employed in Fort Pierce, Florida, accepts work in Jacksonville, 250 miles away. Alan expects the work in Jacksonville to last no more than six months. Although he is employed for 10 months before returning to Fort Pierce, Alan's employment in Jacksonville is temporary, and his travel expenses are deductible.[45] If after six months, Alan agrees to stay for 7 more months (a total of 13 months), his employment is no longer temporary. Travel expenses for the additional 7-month period are not deductible.[46]

Transportation Expenses

Transportation expenses are the costs of traveling from one place to another when the taxpayer is not away from home, and they include automobile expenses, tolls, parking, and taxi fares. When the taxpayer uses his or her personal automobile for business transportation, either the actual expenses for the business-use portion or a standard mileage allowance may be deducted. Actual expenses include depreciation or lease payments, gas and oil, tires, repairs, insurance, registration fees, parking, and tolls.[47] The standard mileage allowance is 56.5 cents per mile in 2013.[48] Parking and tolls are allowed in addition to the mileage allowance.[49] The actual cost method for automobile expenses usually results in a larger deduction than the standard mileage allowance. The principal disadvantage of using the actual cost method is the additional record keeping necessary to substantiate the actual costs.

TAX PLANNING

Qualifying transportation expenses include expenses between home and a temporary work location (*temporary* is defined as one year or less), if the taxpayer has a regular place of business[50] and expenses for travel from one job to another on the same day. The deduction is the same whether the taxpayer travels between two job sites for the same employer or two different employers. Transportation expenses do not include the cost of commuting to and from work as this is considered a nondeductible personal expense.[51]

EXAMPLE 26

Carl, an accountant employed by a Houston CPA firm, travels 60 miles round-trip from his home to an audit client located in the Houston metropolitan area. Carl eats lunch on his own at a restaurant near the client's office and returns home in time for dinner. Carl's employer reimburses him \$33.90 (60 miles × 56.5 cents per mile). The employer deducts the \$33.90 as a business expense on its tax return. If Carl's employer did not reimburse him, Carl could deduct \$33.90 as an unreimbursed employee business expense on his own tax return as a miscellaneous itemized deduction. No deduction is allowed for Carl's lunch because he is not traveling away from home. Carl cannot deduct the cost of his regular commuting to his employer's office.

---

[43]Rev. Rul. 93-86, 1993-2 CB 71.

[44]§ 162(a).

[45]Rev. Rul. 93-86, Situation 1, 1993-2 CB 71.

[46]Rev. Rul. 93-86, Situation 3, 1993-2 CB 71.

[47]Deprciation limits are discussed in the next chapter.

[48]Notice 2012-72, 2012-50 IRB 673. The standard mileage allowance was 55.5 cents for 7/1/11-12/31/12, 51 cents for 1/1/11-6/30/11, 50 cents for 2010, 55 cents for 2009, 58.5 cents for 7/1/08-12/31/08, 50.5 cents for 1/1/08-6/30/08, and 48.5 cents for 2007.

[49]A self-employed individual may also deduct the business part of interest on the car loan.

[50]Rev. Rul. 90-23, 1990-1 CB 29. It is not necessary for the individual to report to his or her office first before going to the temporary work site to deduct these transportation expenses.

[51]Reg. § 1.162-1(e).

Combining Business with Pleasure Travel

If the primary purpose of combined business and pleasure travel within the United States is business, then the transportation costs to and from the destination are deductible. If the primary purpose is pleasure, however, none of the transportation expense is deductible. For travel within the United States, if the number of days on business exceeds those on pleasure, the primary purpose is business; if not, the trip is a pleasure trip. Travel days, however, are considered business days along with any days on which business is conducted. Meals and lodging are deductible only for business days.

EXAMPLE 27

Carol flies from Atlanta to San Diego for business. She spends four days conducting business in San Diego and then stays an additional day to do some sightseeing. Because the primary purpose of her trip is for business, she can deduct her entire round-trip airfare between Atlanta and San Diego, along with her lodging and meals for the four business days. She cannot deduct her lodging or meals for the day she spent sightseeing, as they are considered nondeductible personal expenses. If she spends more than four days on pleasure, her airfare would not be deductible.

Bryan takes a one-week vacation trip to San Diego. While in San Diego he meets with a client for six hours one day. The rest of the week he spends sightseeing and relaxing. Because the primary purpose of Bryan's trip is a vacation, none of the airfare to San Diego is deductible. Bryan can deduct his travel expenses associated with his one business day (meals and lodging). His other travel expenses are considered nondeductible personal expenses.

The IRS has accepted Saturday meal and lodging expenses as qualified business travel expenses when an employer requests that an employee extend the business trip to take advantage of a low-priced airfare requiring a Saturday night stay. The savings in airfare must be greater than the cost of the weekend meals and lodging.[52]

TAX PLANNING

If a taxpayer's presence is required for business both on a Friday and the following Monday, the intervening weekend expenses are deductible if staying for the weekend is cheaper than returning home. Thus, scheduling business on both a Friday and the following Monday turns the weekend into business days for allocation purposes.

No deduction is permitted for travel expenses of a spouse, dependent, or other person accompanying the taxpayer unless that person is also an employee (or owner) of the business, the travel is for a bona fide business purpose, and the expenses otherwise would be deductible.[53] Expenses incurred to attend a convention, seminar, or meeting related to the taxpayer's business are allowable travel expenses; however, attendance at the convention or other meeting must be for the benefit of the taxpayer's trade or business, rather than for social, political, or similar purposes unrelated to the business.[54] Travel deductions are disallowed if the travel is for general education only.[55]

Different rules apply to travel outside the United States.[56] If the entire time outside the United States is spent on business activities, all allowable travel expenses are deductible as if the travel had been entirely in the United States. If personal activities are combined with foreign business travel, transportation expenses must be allocated between business and personal days unless (1) the travel does not exceed one week or (2) less than 25 percent of the total time is spent for personal purposes.[57] If a foreign trip is primarily personal, the travel expenses to and from the

[52]LTR 9237014.

[53]§ 274(m)(3).

[54]Reg. § 1.162-2(d). Travel to attend investment seminars is generally disallowed if the travel relates only to an income-producing activity (under Section 212) instead of the taxpayer's trade or business. § 274(h)(7).

[55]§ 274(m)(2).

[56]Foreign travel is travel outside the geographical United States, defined as the 50 states and the District of Columbia only. Reg. § 1.274-4(a).

[57]§ 274(c)(2).

destination are not deductible (even if the traveler engages in limited business activities at the destination).[58]

EXAMPLE 28

Joan flies to Paris from Cincinnati. She spends three days in Paris on business, stays over in Paris for a two-day vacation, and returns to Cincinnati. The full cost of transportation and 50 percent of meals while traveling to and from Paris are deductible. No allocation of the transportation cost to personal activities is required because the travel does not exceed one week. The cost of meals and lodging for the two days of vacation are nondeductible, however. If Joan spends seven days in Paris on business and four days on vacation, she is gone for more than one week and spends more than 25 percent of the time on vacation. She must allocate 4/11 of her transportation costs to nondeductible personal expenses. If Joan spent only four days on business and seven were spent on vacation, none of the transportation would be deductible.

Expenses of attending conventions, seminars, or other meetings aboard cruise ships are not deductible unless the cruise ship is a vessel registered in the United States and all ports of call are in the United States or its possessions. Because most cruise ships are registered in foreign countries, this requirement effectively prevents most cruises from qualifying.[59]

Bad Debt Expenses

According to generally accepted accounting principles, businesses should use the allowance method to account for bad debts.[60] Congress, however, does not allow businesses to claim a tax deduction based on the expectation of a future event. Thus, businesses must use the **specific charge-off method** for tax purposes, under which they deduct accounts receivable or other business debts only when actually written off as uncollectible during the year.

EXAMPLE 29

Marlin, Inc. (an accrual-basis corporation) began the year with a $50,000 balance in its allowance for bad debts. During the year, the controller concluded that $40,000 of Marlin's accounts receivable were worthless and should be written off against this allowance. Based on Marlin's year-end accounts receivable, the independent auditor determines that a $48,000 addition to the bad debt reserve is necessary. As a result, the year-end balance in the reserve increases to $58,000 ($50,000 + $48,000 – $40,000). Although Marlin's financial statement shows a bad debt expense of $48,000, Marlin deducts only $40,000 on its tax return.

No deduction is allowed for a bad debt unless the receivable was included in income. So cash-basis taxpayers are not allowed a bad debt deduction because they have not recognized the revenue and the inability to collect income is a nondeductible loss.

EXAMPLE 30

Bob (a cash-basis individual) did some consulting work for FlyByNight Company. He sent a bill to FlyByNight for $2,000 for work he had done, but he received no response. When he went to the office to collect his $2,000, he found that FlyByNight had moved and left no forwarding address. Thus, Bob is unable to collect the $2,000 he is owed. Bob is a cash-basis taxpayer and had not previously included the $2,000 in taxable income. He is not allowed a bad debt deduction.

[58]Reg. §1.274-4(f)(5)(ii).

[59]Even when all the requirements are met, the maximum deduction allowed is $2,000 per individual per year. §274(h)(2).

[60]Under this method, businesses estimate the portion of their accounts receivable that are uncollectible. An annual addition is made to the allowance account to bring the total up to the amount of the current year's receivables expected to be uncollectible.

Substantial restrictions apply to the deductibility of nonbusiness bad debts.[61] First, the taxpayer must be able to substantiate that the loan is, in fact, a valid debt. This may present a problem for loans between friends or related parties because the transaction often resembles a gift rather than a loan. For these loans, the taxpayer needs to provide evidence that *both parties* intended the transaction to be a loan. If at all possible, taxpayers should obtain written documentation, signed by both parties, that provides for a specific due date for repayment of the debt, and for payment of interest at a reasonable rate. If the taxpayer can substantiate the debt, a nonbusiness bad debt is deductible only as a capital loss.[62]

EXAMPLE 31

Jerry loaned $1,000 to his brother, Gary, to invest in the stock market. Jerry did not establish a specific due date for repayment of the debt, nor did he charge Gary interest on the loan. There is no documentation of any sort indicating that the transaction was a loan rather than a gift. Gary never repaid the money. Accordingly, Jerry is not allowed a bad debt deduction.

Insurance Premiums

Insurance premiums for fire, casualty, and theft coverage on business property are deductible as business expenses. If a business self-insures, however, payments into the self-insurance reserve are not deductible for tax purposes; only actual losses are deductible. Life insurance premiums paid by a business as employee fringe benefits are deductible, but premiums paid on key-person life insurance policies are not deductible if the business is the beneficiary.[63]

Legal Expenses

Legal expenses are deductible only if the taxpayer can show that the origin and character of the claim are directly related to a trade or business, such as legal fees to protect an existing business or its reputation.[64] Personal legal expenses (such as the preparation of a will) are not deductible; however, legal fees incurred for the determination, collection or refund of any taxes are deductible. Legal fees incurred in the acquisition of property or to defend title to property are added to the asset's basis. If a taxpayer incurs legal fees in connection with the defense of a criminal charge, these fees are deductible only if the legal action has a direct relationship to a profit-seeking activity.[65]

EXAMPLE 32

Miguel owns a tabloid newspaper. A famous talk show host featured in his paper sued Miguel for libel. Miguel paid $50,000 in legal fees for his defense but was found guilty. Miguel also paid his attorney $500 for preparation of his personal will. Because the $50,000 in legal fees is related to Miguel's business, it is deductible. The $500 for preparation of a personal will is a nondeductible personal expense.

Taxes

Taxes paid by most businesses are deductible with one exception—federal income taxes. Deductible taxes include the following:

---

[61]Investment and personal loans made by taxpayers are considered nonbusiness loans.

[62]§ 166(d)(1)(B). Nonbusiness bad debts are always treated as short-term capital losses. The capital loss deduction for individuals is limited to $3,000 in excess of capital gains (that is, capital losses first offset capital gains). Capital losses not deductible due to the $3,000 limit are carried forward to future years.

[63]§ 165. See example 6 in this chapter.

[64]Legal fees paid by individuals for producing or collecting taxable income or for tax advice may be deductible as itemized deductions. Itemized deductions are discussed in Chapter 11.

[65]The legal fees are deductible even if the taxpayer is convicted.

1. State, local, and foreign real property taxes
2. State and local personal property taxes
3. State, local, and foreign income taxes[66]
4. Employer's payroll taxes (employer's share of FICA and unemployment taxes)
5. Other federal, state, local, and foreign taxes that are incurred in a business or other income-producing activity

Sales taxes paid on a service or for the purchase or use of property are part of the cost of the service or property. If the property is depreciable, the sales tax is added to the cost of the property to be depreciated.

When the real estate is sold, the real estate taxes for the entire year must be apportioned between the buyer and seller based on the number of days the property is held by each during the tax year. The seller's portion of the taxes begins on the first day of the year and ends on the day before the date of sale. A taxpayer must also distinguish between the payment of real property taxes and the payment of assessments that fund improvements specifically benefiting the taxpayer's property. Examples include assessments for streets, sidewalks, water mains, sewer lines, and public parking facilities. Assessments generally are not deductible but instead increase the cost basis of the property by the amount of the assessment.[67]

LIMITED EXPENSE DEDUCTIONS

Expenses for the rental of residential property, the use of part of the home as an office, or for an activity classified as a hobby are limited to prevent taxpayers from generating tax losses when the activity does not produce sufficient gross income.

Residential Rental Property

The rental of real estate is usually treated as a trade or business. All income is included and all expenses are deductible, even if they exceed income.[68] Expenses typically include advertising, cleaning, maintenance, utilities, insurance, taxes, interest, commissions for the collections of rent, and travel to collect rental income or to manage or maintain the rental property.

Most expenses for the personal use of residential property are not deductible except for property taxes and mortgage interest, which are deductible as itemized deductions. This provision encourages home ownership but limits the taxpayer's deduction for mortgage interest to the interest incurred for a principal residence and one other residence.[69] There are two situations in which a taxpayer must allocate expenses between the personal and rental use of residential property: when the personal residence is converted from (to) personal use to (from) rental real estate, and when the real estate is used for both rental and personal purposes.

EXAMPLE 33

Ken moves out of his home in May and rents it starting on June 1. He deducts 7/12 of the annual expenses, such as mortgage interest, property taxes, and insurance, against the rental income. Starting in June, he also deducts the monthly expenses, such as utilities and maintenance. Ken deducts the mortgage interest and property taxes for the first five months of the year as itemized deductions. He cannot deduct insurance for the first five months while the home was personal-use property.

---

[66]Either a deduction may be taken for foreign income taxes or a foreign tax credit may be claimed, but not both.

[67]If, however, the assessments are for maintenance, repairs, or current interest on financed improvements, they are deductible.

[68]The deductibility of these losses may be limited by the at-risk and passive loss rules. These rules are discussed in Chapter 10.

[69]The interest deduction is generally limited to mortgages with a principle balance of $1 million or less as discussed in Chapter 11.

When a home is rented to others for part of the year but is not converted to or from rental property (for example, a vacation home) the expenses must be allocated between rental use and the owner's personal use. Expenses directly related to the rental of the property, such as advertising and real estate fees to obtain tenants, are fully deductible against rental income. The rental portion of mixed-use expenses is deductible against rental income, subject to limitations discussed below. Property taxes and mortgage interest related to the personal use of a residence are deductible as itemized deductions.

De Minimis Exception

Rental payments are usually included in gross income, but for administrative convenience a de minimis exception applies if a taxpayer's home is rented for less than 15 days during the year. Under this exception, the home is not considered rental property. The rental income is excluded from gross income and no deduction is allowed for the expenses related to the rental of the property, except for the mortgage interest and property taxes otherwise allowed as itemized deductions. This provision allows taxpayers to rent their home for a short period of time (such as a major sporting event) without paying tax on the rental income.

TAX PLANNING

Nominal Number of Personal Days

When property is rented for more than two weeks during the year but the owner's use *does not exceed* the greater of 14 days or 10 percent of the rental days the property is considered *primarily* rental property. All rent received must be included in income and all expenses related to the rental use are deductible even if they exceed rental income. Certain expenses must be allocated between personal-use and rental days, however, using the following allocation formula:[70]

$$\frac{\text{Number of rental days}}{\text{Total number of days used}} \times \text{Total expense} = \text{Rental-use expense}$$

Both the rental income and rental expenses are reported on Schedule E: *Supplemental Income and Loss*. The net rental profit or loss is then combined with the taxpayer's other income.

Nominal Number of Rental Days

If the property is rented for more than two weeks but the taxpayer's personal use exceeds the greater of 14 days or 10 percent of rental days, special rules apply to prevent a loss deduction. The property is now treated as both a residence and a rental unit and the deductible expenses for the rental portion are limited to the rental income.[71] The mortgage interest and taxes on the personal-use portion, and any portion of these expenses disallowed against rental income due to the limitations, are deductible as itemized deductions.[72] Figure 5.1 summarizes the tax treatment of residential rental property.

---

[70]Personal use includes use by family members or use under a home-swapping arrangement, but it does not include days spent on maintenance of the property. An alternative to this formula substitutes the total number of days in the year for the total number of days used and is sanctioned by several courts, but not the IRS. See *Bolton v. Comm.*, 51 AFTR2d 82-305, 82 USTC ¶9699 (9th Cir., 1982) and *McKinney v. Comm.*, 52 AFTR 2d 83-6281, 83-2 USTC ¶9655 (10th Cir., 1983). This method allocates a smaller portion of the taxes and interest to the rental use and allows a greater portion of other expenses to be deducted against the income. This method only applies to taxes and interest, not to other expenses.

[71]There are specific provisions in §280A that prevent the temporary rental of the taxpayer's primary residence (for example, when the taxpayer moves and temporarily rents the home until it is sold) from being subject to these rules.

[72]As discussed in Chapter 11, individuals are allowed to deduct the mortgage interest expense for their principal residence plus only one additional home as an itemized deduction. For any of the mortgage interest on a property that has been rented to qualify as an itemized deduction, the taxpayer must have personally used the home more than the greater of 14 days or 10 percent of the rental days during the year. §280A(d)(1).

FIGURE 5.1 **TAX TREATMENT OF RESIDENTIAL RENTAL PROPERTY**

Rental Period	Personal Use	Tax Treatment
All occupied days	None	Report all rental income and deduct all expenses for the property.
Less than 15 days	Balance of year	No rental income reported and no rental expenses deducted. Mortgage interest and property taxes are deducted as itemized deductions.
More than 14 days	Does not exceed the greater of 14 days or 10% of rental days	Rental income reported and all rental expenses deducted on rental schedule. Property taxes for personal use are deducted as itemized deductions.
More than 14 days	Exceeds the greater of 14 days or 10% of rental days	Rental income reported and rental expenses deducted on rental schedule but expenses are limited to rental income (cannot create a rental loss). Mortgage interest and property taxes for personal use are deducted as itemized deductions.

EXAMPLE 34

John has a vacation home in Maui that he rents to some friends for 12 days for $1,200. Although John is unable to use the home himself this year, under the de minimis exception the $1,200 is not income and he cannot deduct any of the related expenses. He can, however, deduct his mortgage interest and property taxes that would be deductible as if the home had not been rented.

In the next year John uses the home in Maui for 10 days and rents it for 190 days during the year. In this case, John apportions 95 percent (190/200) of the expenses to the rental of the home. All rental income and the rental portion of all the expenses are reported on Schedule E: *Supplemental Income and Loss.* He can deduct all rental expenses even if they exceed rental income as the property is considered *primarily* rental property.

The next year John takes a leave from his job and uses the home on Maui for 100 days and rents it out for 100 days. The home is now treated as both a personal residence and a rental unit. John must apportion the expenses between his personal and rental use. The apportioned rental expenses are deductible only to the extent that there is income from the property. He can, however, deduct as itemized deductions both the personal portion of the mortgage interest and property taxes and any portion of these expenses disallowed as a rental expense deduction due to the income limitation.

TAX PLANNING

Although the term *vacation home* is usually used, the term is broader than what is normally considered a home because Section 280A refers to dwelling units. A dwelling unit is one that provides shelter for living and sleeping and cooking facilities.[73] Thus, campers, motor homes, trailers, and houseboats that provide these facilities qualify as vacation homes.

[73]Reg. §1.163-10T(p)(3)(ii).

Home Office Expenses

A home office of a sole proprietor or independent contractor must be used exclusively and on a regular basis and meet *one of the following three tests* for its costs to be deductible:[74]

1. It is the principal place of business for any business of the taxpayer.
2. It is used as a place to meet clients or customers regularly in the normal course of business.
3. It is located in a structure separate from the home.

The term **principal place of business** includes a place of business used by the taxpayer for the administrative or management activities of his or her trade or business if there is no other fixed location where the taxpayer conducts substantial administrative or management activities. Costs of a home office that is not the taxpayer's principal place of business may still be deductible if it is a place at which he or she meets patients, clients, or customers on a regular and continuous basis.[75]

Example 35

Dr. George, a dentist, has an office in a nearby city. He also maintains an office in his home as he lives in an area that does not have another dentist. He sees patients at his home one and one-half days per week and four days per week at his city office. The costs of the office in the home are deductible because he regularly meets patients there, even though it is not the principal location of his business.

TAX PLANNING

If the home office occupies a separate structure (such as a detached garage), the structure only needs to be used exclusively and regularly in one of the taxpayer's businesses. A sole proprietor whose home office does not meet the principal-place-of-business requirement (or the meeting of clients, patients, and customers) should consider moving the office to a detached garage or building a small separate structure to house the office.

Exclusive use does not require that the office occupy a separate room; however, the room(s) or portion of a room used for business purposes must be used only for those business activities. Any personal use of the home office space by the taxpayer makes the home office expenses nondeductible.

An employee can deduct the cost of a home office only if the home office meets the requirements applicable to all home offices (discussed above) *and* it is *for the convenience of the employer*. If the employer provides an adequate workplace outside the home for the employee, no home office deduction is allowed, even if the employee uses the area exclusively and on a regular basis.

Deductible home office expenses include a portion of rent or mortgage interest, property taxes, insurance, utilities, and repairs related to the office space.[76] Depreciation is allowed on the part of the home used as the office. The IRS and courts prefer an allocation of household expenses based on relative square footage.

Home office expenses are deductible only to the extent of the income generated by the business use of the home and are deductible in the following order:

1. Expenses directly related to the business other than home office expenses (such as supplies)

---

[74]There are two exceptions: (1) if a part of the home is used on a regular basis to store inventory or product samples, a deduction is permitted for that part of the home; (2) if the home is used on a regular basis as a daycare facility, the allocation of expenses must be made both on space and amount of time used.

[75]Occasional meetings with such people in the home office are not sufficient. The physical presence of a client is also necessary to satisfy this standard. Thus, the mere phoning of clients from the home office is not sufficient.

[76]If a home office qualifies as the individual's principal place of business, daily transportation expenses incurred in traveling between the taxpayer's residence and other work sites are deductible.

2. The allocated portion of expenses that would otherwise be deductible as itemized deductions (mortgage interest and property taxes)[77]
3. Operating expenses including utilities, insurance, and maintenance
4.. Depreciation

This limitation prevents taxpayers from creating a tax loss with home office deductions if the business does not produce sufficient gross income.

If income is insufficient to deduct all of the expenses, the mortgage interest and property taxes are still deductible as itemized deductions by the individual. Other expenses that cannot be deducted due to the income limitation can be carried forward and deducted in future years, subject to the same limitations. Nondeductible depreciation expense does not reduce the basis of the property.

EXAMPLE 36

Holly, a self-employed artist, uses two rooms in her home exclusively and regularly for her home office. This office space consists of 400 square feet of the home's total 2,000 square feet or 20 percent of the floor space of her home. She has gross income from her business of $7,000 and her expenses (other than home office expenses) are $4,500. Holly has the following household expenses:

Mortgage interest on her home	$5,000
Real property taxes on her home	2,400
Utility bills for her home	1,900
Homeowner's insurance	1,800
Depreciation (for the 20 percent used as an office)	$600

Holly first deducts the $4,500 nonhome office expenses, reducing available income from $7,000 to $2,500. Next she deducts $1,000 of her mortgage interest ($5,000 × 20%) and $480 of property taxes ($2,400 × 20%) for a total of $1,480 that otherwise would be allowable as itemized deductions. This leaves only $1,020 of income against which the remaining expenses can be deducted. She deducts $380 ($1,900 × 20%) for utilities, and $360 ($1,800 × 20%) for insurance, and $280 of depreciation. The remaining $320 of depreciation expense is carried to the next year; Holly does not reduce her basis in the home for this disallowed amount.

Beginning in 2013, IRS has provided a simplified option that taxpayer can elect to use to determine the amount of deductible home office expenses. As an alternative to the calculation and allocation of actual expenses, a taxpayer can deduct $5 per square foot for up to 300 square feet of qualified use providing a maximum deduction of $1,500 for a full year home office deduction without requiring any allocation of mortgage interest or property taxes.[78] This means that taxpayers will be able to deduct 100 percent of mortgage interest and 100 percent of property taxes as itemized deductions in addition to deducting $1,500 for other home office expenses. The home office must still be used regularly and exclusively for business to qualify for this simplified provision. Taxpayers with higher home office expenses can choose to use the regular provision.

A self-employed individual files Form 8829: *Expenses for Business Use of Your Home* to claim a home office deduction. An employee's home office expenses are deductible as miscellaneous itemized deductions.

Hobby Expenses

Taxpayer activities that earn income and incur expenses but do not meet the requirements of a business or investment are classified as personal hobbies. If the activity is

[77]Home mortgage interest, property taxes, and other itemized deductions are discussed in Chapter 11.
[78]Rev. Proc. 2013-13, 2013-6 IRB 478.

classified as a **hobby**, the deductibility of some or all of the expenses incurred in the activity may be disallowed.

The regulations list a number of factors to consider in determining whether an activity should be classified as a hobby, including the following:[79]

1. The manner in which the taxpayer carries on the activity
2. The expertise of the taxpayer and/or the taxpayer's consultants
3. The time and effort spent by the taxpayer in the activity
4. The taxpayer's history of profits or losses for this activity
5. The success of the taxpayer in similar activities
6. The overall financial status of the taxpayer
7. The elements of pleasure or recreation that are part of the activity

All the facts and circumstances surrounding the activity must be considered in determining if the taxpayer's activity is a hobby or if it has the requisite profit motive.

The burden of proof normally rests upon the taxpayer to establish that the activity meets the requirements of a trade or business. If, however, the activity shows a profit in at least three out of five years of operation (two out of seven for activities involving breeding or racing horses), the burden of proof shifts to the IRS.[80] The IRS must then prove that the activity is a hobby.

If the activity does not result in a profit in three out of five consecutive tax years, the burden of proof remains with the taxpayer to show that the activity is a legitimate business. The taxpayer could accomplish this by showing that the activity was run in a businesslike manner, good business records were maintained, and there was intent to make a profit.[81]

If the activity is a hobby, all income from the hobby is included in gross income, but expenses are deductible only to the extent of the gross profit from the hobby and must be deducted in the following order:[82]

1. Expenses that would otherwise be deductible as itemized deductions (home mortgage interest, property taxes, and casualty losses)
2. Other business-type expenses (advertising, insurance, utilities, and maintenance)
3. Depreciation and amortization expense

Expenses in categories 2 and 3 in excess of income are simply lost because there are no carryover provisions for any nondeductible expense. (The basis of assets is not reduced for disallowed cost recovery deductions, however.)[83]

EXAMPLE 37

Chet is an orthodontist whose hobby is making cabinetry in his spare time. He uses a workshop that occupies 10 percent of his home for the woodworking. Chet has the following expenses from the activity:

Solid woods and veneers	$ 4,000
Other supplies	600
Workshop expenses:	
Property taxes and interest on home	10,000
Utilities and maintenance on home	4,000
Depreciation (10% of home)	500

[79]Reg. §1.183-(2)(b)(1)-(9).

[80]§183(d).

[81]Reg. §1.183-2(b).

[82]Reg. §1.183-1(b). These expenses are deductible as miscellaneous itemized deductions.

[83]If only a portion of the depreciation expense can be deducted, the allowable depreciation should be apportioned across all the depreciable assets, based on the ratio of allowed depreciation to total depreciation for all the assets. Reg. §1.183-1(b).

Chet sold four pieces of cabinetry for $6,200. He is able to deduct expenses from the $1,600 gross profit ($6,200 revenue – $4,600 for wood and other supplies) as follows:

Taxes and interest (10%)	$1,000
Utilities and maintenance (10%)	400
Depreciation	200
Total	$1,600

Chet cannot deduct the remaining $300 of depreciation, but he does not have to reduce the basis of the home for the nondeductible amount.

TAX PLANNING

A taxpayer may elect to use straight-line depreciation to reduce the expenses chargeable to an activity.[84] Additionally, deferring year-end expenses and accelerating income are effective strategies for moving an activity from loss to profit for a year. With a good business plan, the taxpayer may have a greater likelihood of showing a profit in three of five years, shifting the burden of proof to the IRS to prove that the activity is not an active trade or business.

Expanded Topics—Book/Tax Differences

Accounting for Income Tax Expense

A corporation's income tax expense is frequently the largest expense item on its income statement. Thus, a good understanding of how tax expense is determined is critical for all readers of financial statements. In addition, a company's chief executive officer and chief financial officer must certify that financial reports filed with the Securities and Exchange Commission fairly present the company's financial position (including the adequacy of the tax-related accounts), since the passage of the *Sarbanes-Oxley Act* in 2002. These corporate executives as well as tax professionals must understand how the tax expense and deferred taxes (commonly termed the tax provision) are determined. Failure of this required executive oversight can lead to significant personal penalties.

Financial statements that are prepared in accordance with generally accepted accounting principles (GAAP) must follow the provisions of Statement of Financial Accounting Standards No. 109, *Accounting for Income Taxes* **(FAS 109)** which has been incorporated into the Accounting Standards Codification (ASC) Section 740-10-05.[85] According to **ASC 740**, the income tax expense reported on the current-year financial statements must be based on financial statement income rather than taxable income. Thus, the tax expense on the income statement matches financial accounting income, even though the taxes actually paid are substantially more or less than the recognized expense. The taxes paid are determined on taxable income and taxable income can differ dramatically from accounting income due to the differences in the rules followed in their determination.

These differences in the principles used to determine taxable versus financial income are divided into permanent differences and temporary differences. A **permanent difference** results from an expense that can never be deducted on the tax return (such as fines and political contributions), expenses that have limited deductibility (such as the nondeductible portion of meals and entertainment), or income that will never be subject to tax (such as tax-exempt bond interest). A **temporary difference** occurs because an income or expense item is reported in one year for accounting income and in a different year for taxable income. Temporary differences include depreciation on fixed assets (such as accelerated

[84]Depreciation is discussed in Chapter 6.

[85]The accounting standards were codified in 2009 with FAS 109 included under ASC 740. The Financial Accounting Standards Board issued FAS 109 in February 1992. FAS 109 was preceded by FAS 96, which replaced Accounting Principles Board Opinion No. 11.

depreciation used for tax but straight-line used for book purposes), accrued expenses (such as warranty expenses and bad debt expenses accrued for book purposes but not deductible for tax purposes until incurred), and accrued income (such as sales reported under the percentage-of-completion method for book purposes but reported under the completed contract method for tax purposes). These items will be fully recognized in both types of income statements, but the timing of the recognition differs. Because of this, timing differences occurring between statements in one period (for example, tax depreciation that exceeds financial depreciation) will *reverse* when recognized in a later period (when financial depreciation exceeds tax depreciation). Figure 5.2 provides examples of temporary and permanent book/tax differences.

Schedule M-1 of Form 1120: *U.S. Corporate Income Tax Return* (see Appendix C for sample filled-in tax returns) reconciles accounting (book) income to the taxable income reported on the tax return by accounting for the permanent and temporary differences occurring in that tax year.

EXAMPLE 38

Targo Corporation has income per books before tax of $4,000,000. Permanent differences are: $10,000 interest income from tax-exempt municipal bonds and $500,000 of life insurance proceeds from the death of a corporation officer included in book income; the nondeductible portion of the $60,000 for meals and entertainment expenses and $5,000 for premiums on officers' life insurance policies (the corporation is the beneficiary of these policies) are deductible for book income. Temporary differences include the differences in straight-line depreciation of $80,000 on its financial statements and the $120,000 of accelerated depreciation claimed on its tax return, and the $30,000 accrued for bad debt expense on its financial statements (using the allowance method), while it actually wrote off only $10,000 in bad debts this year. Targo reconciles its book income to taxable income as follows:

Income per books before tax	$4,000,000
Interest income from tax-exempt municipal bonds	(10,000)
Life insurance proceeds	(500,000)
Nondeductible portion of meals and entertainment	30,000
Nondeductible premiums on officers' life insurance policies	5,000
Excess of tax accelerated depreciation over book straight-line	(40,000)
Excess of addition to bad debt allowance over direct write off	20,000
Taxable income	$3,505,000

Targo computes its income tax liability (the actual amount paid) on its tax return as $1,191,700 ($3,505,000 × 34%). It must now calculate its tax expense, however, based on its financial accounting income, following the principles of ASC 740.

FIGURE 5.2 **EXAMPLES OF BOOK/TAX DIFFERENCES**

Temporary Differences	Permanent Differences
Amortization of organization & start-up costs	Fines and penalties
Bad debts	Interest on state & local bonds
Depreciation	Life insurance proceeds
Installment sales	Meals & entertainment expenses
Inventory costs capitalized under UNICAP	Premiums on key-person life insurance
Long-term construction contracts	Political contributions & lobbying expenses
Prepaid income	Dividend received deduction (see Chapter 9)
Related party transactions	U.S. production activities deduction (see Chapter 9)
Warranty expenses	

Since 2004, large corporations with assets of $10 million or more must file a Schedule M-3 instead of Schedule M-1. The Schedule M-3 requires corporations to separately disclose each item of income, gain, loss, deduction, or credit for book-tax differences greater than $10 million with temporary differences reported separately from permanent differences. The IRS is particularly interested in the disclosure of permanent differences because many abusive tax shelters are structured either to reduce the amount of taxes paid without reporting any corresponding decrease in book income or to increase book income without a corresponding increase in tax liability.

Calculating Tax Expense

If a corporation has permanent tax differences, it must modify its book income by adding back expenses that are not tax deductible and by subtracting income that is tax exempt. If it has only permanent differences (that is, there are no temporary differences to consider), it will determine its book tax expense based on this modified income at its current tax rates.

EXAMPLE 39

Refer to the information in the previous example but exclude all temporary differences. Targo Corporation will subtract the $10,000 tax-exempt interest and $500,000 life insurance proceeds and add $30,000 for one-half of the meals and entertainment expense and $5,000 for the life insurance premiums. Targo's modified income is $3,525,000. At 34 percent, its book tax expense is $1,198,500 ($3,525,000 × 34%). Due to these adjustments, its effective tax rate is only 30 percent ($1,198,500/$4,000,000).

If a corporation has both permanent and temporary differences, the permanent differences are first accounted for as described. Accounting for the temporary differences is far more complex (as will be explained) because temporary differences cause the income tax expense per books to differ from the tax expense shown on the tax return. This difference in tax expenses must be accounted for using deferred tax accounts. Although permanent differences have no effect on these deferred taxes, they do cause the effective tax rate for the period to differ from the statutory tax rate. As a consequence, in the notes to the financial statements, the company must reconcile the statutory rate to the effective rate so that the reader can determine the significance of any permanent differences.

In accounting for temporary differences, ASC 740 uses a balance sheet approach to account for deferred taxes by using a deferred tax asset or deferred tax liability account. The deferred tax asset account represents future tax savings while the deferred tax liability account represents future tax costs. Although a student may think of assets as good news and liabilities as bad news, the reverse is true for the deferred tax asset and liability accounts. A deferred tax liability is essentially an interest-free loan from the government, allowing the business to invest the savings until the taxes are paid at a later date. The longer the taxes are deferred, the greater the value of the tax savings. Deferred tax assets, however, are prepayments of taxes, the benefit of which may not be realized until many years in the future.

A **deferred tax liability** is a current tax savings that will have to be paid in a future year when temporary differences reverse. It is created when (1) an expense is deductible for tax in the current period but not deductible on the books until some future period or (2) income is includible currently on the books but is not includible in taxable income until a future period. If the deferred tax expense is not accrued, a corporation's current-year financial statement income and retained earnings are overstated to the extent the taxes will have to be paid when the differences reverse.

EXAMPLE 40

Cargo, a corporation in the 34 percent marginal tax bracket, recognizes tax depreciation expense of $60,000 in year 1 and $20,000 in year 2. On its financial statements, Cargo reports depreciation expense of $40,000 in year 1 and $40,000 in year 2. In year 1, the tax depreciation is $20,000 greater than the book depreciation and the adjusted basis of the assets is $20,000 greater for book purposes than for tax purposes. The deferred tax liability is credited (increased) for $6,800 ($20,000 × 34%) accounting for the favorable temporary difference between the provision for income tax expense in the financial statements and the income tax payable per the tax return. In year 2, the difference reverses and the book depreciation is $20,000 greater than the tax depreciation. The deferred tax liability account is debited (reduced) for the $6,800 ($20,000 × 34%) that the income tax payable exceeds the provision for income tax expense in the financial statements, eliminating the deferred tax liability account.

A **deferred tax asset** is a prepayment of tax that will be refunded in a future year when temporary differences reverse. It is created when (1) an expense is deductible on the books in the current year but is not deductible for tax until some future period or (2) income is includible in taxable income currently but is not includible in income per books until a future period. Book tax expense is based only on the reported financial statement net income; it does not include any of the tax prepayments related to these nondeductible expenses or includible income for tax purposes. Instead, the prepayment is a deferred tax asset (a receivable).

EXAMPLE 41

Warwick, a corporation in the 34 percent marginal tax bracket, accrues $40,000 in warranty expense on its year 1 financial statements for expected warranty repairs. This warranty expense is not deductible for tax purposes until actually incurred. If the $40,000 of warranty expense is not actually incurred until year 2, in year 1 a temporary difference is created. In year 1, a deferred tax asset is debited (increased) for $13,600 ($40,000 × 34%) accounting for the difference between the provision for income tax expense on the financial statements and the income tax payable per the tax return. In year 2, when the the warranty expense is incurred, the book tax warranty difference reverses and the deferred tax asset is credited (reduced) for $13,600, eliminating that account.

Figure 5.3 shows when temporary differences are reported as deferred tax assets or deferred tax liabilities.

Effects of NOL Carryovers

When a corporation's[86] deductible expenses exceed its gross income, it has a net operating loss (NOL). Because there is no taxable income, there is no income tax liability for that year. Corporations are allowed to carry these NOLs back two years (filing a claim for refund of the previous years' taxes) and forward up to 20 years. For financial statement purposes, the corporation reports the tax benefit of a NOL carryback by debiting a tax refund receivable on its balance sheet and crediting a benefit due to loss carryback (negative tax expense) on its income statement.

EXAMPLE 42

Milor Corporation, a calendar-year, accrual-basis corporation, has a $20,000 NOL for both book and tax purposes for 2013. Milor carries the loss back to 2011 when its taxable income was $75,000 and is entitled to

FIGURE 5.3 **REPORTING TEMPORARY DIFFERENCES**

	Revenues	Expenses
Reported on tax return before books	Deferred tax asset	Deferred tax liability
Reported on books before tax return	Deferred tax liability	Deferred tax asset

[86]This discussion is based solely on corporate businesses as they are not flow-through entities. The owners of flow-through entities with NOLs would also be allowed carryovers of these losses subject to possible adjustments based on the type of owner.

a $5,000 refund ($20,000 × 25% tax rate for 2011) of 2011 taxes. Milor accounts for the tax effect of the NOL on its financial statements by debiting a tax refund receivable (an asset) on its 2013 balance sheet for $5,000 and crediting a tax benefit due to loss carryback (negative tax expense) on its 2013 income statement for the same amount.

If the corporation elects not to carry the NOL back, the tax benefit can only be realized in a future year or years to which the corporation carries forward the NOL. For financial accounting purposes, the future tax savings *expected* from the loss carry forward is reported as a deferred tax asset in the year the loss occurs.

EXAMPLE 43

Assume the same facts as the previous example except that Milor does not carry the 2013 NOL back but elects to carry it forward because it expects sufficient income to be in the 34% marginal tax bracket in 2014. For 2013 financial accounting, however, Milor debits a deferred tax asset account for $6,800 for the *expected* tax effect of the NOL on its 2013 balance sheet and credits a tax benefit due to loss carryforward (negative tax expense) for the same amount on its 2013 income statement. In 2014, Milor has $400,000 of taxable income before deducting the NOL; when it deducts the $20,000 NOL, it realizes tax savings of $6,800 ($20,000 × 34%). Milor recognizes tax expense on its income statement of $136,000 ($400,000 × 34%) and its income tax payable is $129,200 [($400,000 – $20,000) × 34%]. In 2014 Milor accounts for the difference between the two amounts by crediting (reducing) the deferred tax asset created in 2013.

Realizing Deferred Tax Assets

To benefit from a deferred tax asset, the business must have future income (and the related taxes) to realize the benefit of a deferred tax asset (tax prepayment). Determining whether the tax benefit should be recognized currently or modified using a valuation allowance is based on a more-likely-than-not test (greater than 50 percent probability). If it is determined to be more likely than not that the benefits can be realized, the adjustment is included in the current tax provision. If not, the adjustment is deferred by use of a valuation allowance. The valuation allowance is a contra-asset account that offsets all or a portion of the deferred tax asset. The existence of net operating loss carryforwards[87] and excess foreign tax credits[88] most often give rise to problems surrounding the realization of the deferred tax benefit.

EXAMPLE 44

Carson Corporation reports income per books and taxable income of $1 million. Its current income tax liability is $340,000 ($1 million × 34%). During the current year it paid $50,000 in foreign income taxes that cannot be used as a credit against the current tax liability due to the foreign tax credit limitation. If its auditors believe that Carson will only be able to use $30,000 of the foreign tax credit before it expires, the $50,000 future tax benefit recorded in the deferred tax asset account should be reduced to $30,000 by use of a valuation allowance. The net income tax expense should be recorded at $310,000 ($340,000 – $30,000 benefit from foreign tax credit). This is recorded on Carson's books through the following journal entry:

	Debit	Credit
Income tax expense	340,000	
Deferred tax asset	50,000	
Valuation allowance		20,000
Benefit from foreign tax credit		30,000
Income tax payable		340,000

[87]If there are insufficient profits in the carryback and carryforward years to offset the losses, then the excess losses expire unused and the related deferred tax asset becomes worthless.

[88]The allowable foreign tax credit in any year is limited to the U.S. tax imposed on the foreign source income included on the U.S. tax return. The foreign tax credit limitation can prevent the total amount of foreign taxes paid in high-tax jurisdictions from being credited, thereby reducing the value of the related deferred tax asset.

The valuation allowance increases Carson's current effective book tax rate from 29 percent [($340,000 tax payable – $50,000 deferred tax asset)/$1 million] to 31 percent ($310,000/$1 million). If Carson can satisfy its auditors in a later year that the adoption of a new tax planning strategy will allow use of the entire foreign tax credit carryforward, the valuation account will be released and the company allowed to recognize the expected tax benefit. The release eliminates the valuation allowance, reduces the provision for income tax expense, and reduces the effective tax rate for the release year.

The determination of whether the more-likely-than-not test is met can have a significant impact on book tax expense and the reported book net income. Without a careful review of the allowance by the auditors, it would be possible for companies to smooth their earnings by adjusting the valuation allowance up or down as needed, possibly misleading readers of the financial statements.

Accounting for Uncertainty in Income Taxes

In an attempt to improve transparency and accountability of companies and restore investor confidence after the Enron and WorldCom scandals, the Financial Accounting Standards Board (FASB) issued an interpretation of FAS 109 called FASB Interpretation No. 48, *Accounting for Uncertainty in Income Taxes* (**FIN 48**) which was incorporated into ASC 740-10-55. It applies to flow-through and nontaxable entities, as well as taxable corporations.

ACS 740 does not provide any specific guidance on accounting for deferred taxes when a business takes an uncertain tax position. The term tax position refers to the manner of recognition of a transaction in a current or previously filed tax return that will result in a current or deferred income tax asset or liability. Examples of **uncertain tax positions** include: a deduction taken on a tax return for a current expenditure that the IRS may assert should be capitalized and amortized over future periods, the determination of the amount of taxable income to report on intercompany transfers between subsidiaries in different tax jurisdictions, or a decision to classify a particular transaction as tax exempt.

Prior to the issuance of FIN 48, businesses used diverse criteria to determine whether tax return benefits should be recognized in their financial statements. Many companies simply assumed that amounts reported on their tax returns would be allowed except for a few very aggressive and material positions that were considered so uncertain that it was likely that the IRS would successfully challenge them on audit and that the company's tax liability would be increased. FIN 48 no longer allowed this approach. Instead, any tax benefit from an uncertain tax position that reduces a business's current or future income tax liability can only be reported in its financial statements to the extent each benefit is recognized and measured under a two-step approach.

Step 1: The business must evaluate each tax position to assess whether it is more likely than not (greater than 50 percent) that the position would be sustained upon examination (including the administrative appeals and litigation process). The business must base its assessment on an analysis of the relevant tax authorities (such as the Code, regulations, rulings, and court cases) and it must assume that the tax authorities have full knowledge of all relevant information (including access to work papers and legal opinions from outside tax advisors). This requirement must be met even if the business believes the possibility of audit or discovery of the matter is remote. Additionally, each tax position must stand on its own technical merits so that a business may not consider one position as a bargaining chip against another tax position.

Step 2: If a tax position satisfies the first step, the business can then proceed to measure the tax benefit that can be recognized in the financial statements from its uncertain position. If no single amount is more likely than not to be realized, then a cumulative probability analysis of the possible outcomes is required. The business records the largest tax benefit that meets a greater than 50 percent cumulative probability of realization upon ultimate settlement.

EXAMPLE 45

Solaris Corporation claims a $10,000 deduction in its current year tax return and has determined that this tax position meets the recognition threshold of more likely than not. Having met the requirements of the first step, Solaris must now measure the benefit. As there is no single amount that can be recognized, Solaris must determine the benefit using the possible range of outcomes from $10,000 (complete success in litigation or settlement with IRS) to zero (total loss) and the cumulative probability. The possible outcomes and their probabilities are as follows:

POSSIBLE OUTCOME	PROBABILITY OF OCCURRING	CUMULATIVE PROBABILITY OF OCCURRING
$10,000	25%	25%
$7,500	20%	45%
$5,000	25%	70%
$2,500	20%	90%
0	10%	100%
	100%	

Solaris will recognize a $5,000 deduction in its financial statements because it is the largest amount of benefit that is more than 50 percent likely to be sustained based on the outcome's cumulative probability.

After the initial two-step evaluation, a business must review the information available at each subsequent financial reporting date to determine if there should be a reassessment of its prior uncertain tax positions. This reassessment must be based on new information rather than a new evaluation or interpretation of information that was available on the earlier reporting date. If a tax position that previously failed to meet the more-likely-than-not threshold subsequently meets that threshold, the business may recognize a tax benefit in its financial statements in the first interim period in which it meets the more-likely-than-not standard, is settled through negotiation or litigation, or upon the expiration of the statute of limitations. If a business subsequently determines that a tax position no longer meets the more-likely-than-not threshold of being sustained, then the business must derecognize all or a portion of the tax benefit previously recognized for the uncertain tax position. FIN 48 prohibited the use of a valuation allowance as a substitute for derecognition of the tax benefit.

One of the more controversial aspects of financial reporting for uncertain tax positions is an expanded disclosure requirement. Companies must include a table that identifies their beginning and ending unrecognized tax benefits, and they must provide the details related to tax uncertainties for which it is reasonably possible that the amount of unrecognized tax benefit will significantly increase or decrease within the next year. Previously, many companies bundled together their various uncertain positions and provided one general reserve to account for the possibility of losing some of the tax positions upon audit. Now, companies must disclose the nature of the uncertainty and the nature of the event that could cause a change in the next twelve months.

Some managers expressed concern that IRS will use these new disclosures as a roadmap for identifying tax positions to audit. It appears that this concern is well founded. In 2010 the IRS announced that it would require any corporation with total assets in excess of $10 million that has any uncertain tax positions to file a new schedule with its tax return.[89] To reduce the burden on businesses, the IRS agreed to a phase-in of this new reporting requirement based on a corporation's asset size. Corporations that have total assets equal to or exceeding $100 million must file Form 1120, Schedule UTP starting with their 2010 tax returns. The asset threshold is reduced to $50 million in 2012 and to $10 million in 2014.[90]

[89]Ann. 2010-9, 2010-7 IRB 408.

[90]Ann. 2010-75, 2010-41 IRB 428.

EXAMPLE 46

Beta, a U.S. corporation with more than $100 million in assets, claims a deduction for the entire amount of a specific expenditure on its 2013 tax return. In reviewing its tax positions for its 2013 audited financial statements, Beta determines that it is uncertain whether this expenditure should have been amortized over 5 years instead of expensed and records a reserve on its financial statements. The tax position taken on the return (that is, that the expenditure could be fully deducted in 2013 rather than amortized) must be reported on Schedule UTP filed with its 2013 tax return.

Schedule UTP requires a corporation to describe each uncertain tax position for which the corporation has recorded a reserve in its audited financial statements and then rank all of these tax positions based on the U.S. federal income tax reserve recorded for them. Although the actual amount of reserve for each position does not need to be reported, the corporation must identify the positions for which the reserve exceeds 10 percent of the aggregate amount of the reserves for all of the reported positions. This information could then assist the IRS in identifying those uncertain tax positions that are large enough to warrant IRS inquiry so that its audit can be focused on those areas.

Traditionally, understanding the complex provisions of accounting for income taxes typically was left to corporate accountants and their independent auditors. Now it is essential that tax professionals, in both private industry and public practice, have a good understanding of how uncertain tax positions are recognized, measured, and disclosed.

Exception for Foreign Earnings

Multinational corporations can significantly reduce their reported effective tax rate if they have one or more foreign subsidiaries. For federal income tax purposes, the income of foreign subsidiaries cannot be included in the consolidated tax return (although this income will be included in the corporation's financial statements). This allows the foreign subsidiary's income to escape U.S. taxation until it is repatriated back to the United States (for example, through dividend payments). As a result, the income tax liability on the federal income tax return is computed on U.S. income only.[91] A U.S. corporation with one or more foreign subsidiaries located in jurisdictions with lower tax rates than the United States, defers any U.S. tax on their foreign income that is not repatriated, reducing their worldwide tax cost.

Under ASC 740, the income tax expense reported on the consolidated financial statement should include the total of all federal, state, local, and foreign income taxes, including both current and deferred income taxes. An exception under Accounting Principles Board Opinion No. 23, *Accounting for Income Taxes—Special Areas* (APB 23), also incorporated into ASC 740, allows the parent corporation to exclude the future U.S. income tax on foreign subsidiary income from the determination of the deferred tax liability (and tax expense) if these earnings are permanently reinvested outside the United States. Thus the U.S. corporation can report higher financial statement income because its income statement can include the foreign income, but can exclude the deferred U.S. tax that could eventually be due on this income. This also allows the corporation to report higher earnings per share.

EXAMPLE 47

Grand, a U.S. corporation, owns 100 percent of Subsidiary, a foreign corporation. Grand's U.S. tax rate is 35 percent and the foreign country's tax rate is 15 percent. Grand has $20 million in taxable income and pays $7 million in U.S. income taxes. (It has no temporary book-tax differences.) Subsidiary has $10 million in taxable income and pays $1.5 million in foreign income taxes. None of Subsidiary's income has been repatriated back to Grand, so Grand is not taxed on any of the profits of Subsidiary. Grand can use APB 23 to avoid recording any deferred U.S. income tax expense. On its financial statements, it will report $30 million ($20 million + $10 million) of worldwide income but only $8.5 million of total income tax

[91]Any state and local income taxes paid are reported as deductions on the federal tax return.

expense ($7 million current U.S. tax + $1.5 million current foreign tax). Its effective tax rate on worldwide income is 28.33 percent ($8.5 million tax expense/$30 million net income). This enables Grand to report higher after-tax book income and higher earnings per share than if it were required to record the additional $2 million [$10 million × (35% – 15%)] in deferred U.S. taxes.

The permanent reinvestment exception should not be used unless the corporation expects to leave its foreign earnings outside the United States indefinitely. Using APB 23 and then later repatriating the foreign earnings can cause a spike in the corporation's effective tax rate for the year of repatriation as book income will not include the repatriated income (as it was previously recorded in income) but must include the tax on this income in the year's tax expense.

UNICAP Rules and Inventory

The cost of merchandise purchased is its invoice price, less discounts, plus incidental costs such as shipping and handling.[92] Under the **uniform capitalization (UNICAP) rules**, indirect costs must also be capitalized as part of inventory by businesses whose average annual gross receipts for the preceding three years exceed $10 million.[93] The UNICAP rules require the value of inventory to include all direct costs of manufacturing, purchasing, or storing inventory and the following overhead items:

- Factory repairs, maintenance, utilities, insurance, rent, and depreciation (including the excess of tax depreciation over financial depreciation)
- Rework, scrap, and spoilage
- Factory administration and officers' salaries related to production
- Taxes (other than income tax)
- Quality control and inspection
- Profit sharing and pension plans, for both current and past service costs
- Service support such as payroll, purchasing, and warehousing

Nonmanufacturing costs (such as research, selling, advertising, and distribution expenses) are not required to be included in inventory. The UNICAP rules require the inclusion of indirect costs typically not included in the traditional full absorption costing used for financial accounting, creating temporary differences. For example, personnel and data processing costs are usually not included in manufacturing overhead. UNICAP rules, however, require the allocation of costs associated with these departments between manufacturing and nonmanufacturing functions.[94]

EXAMPLE 48

Leather Works Corporation manufactures leather furniture in a factory with 50 employees. The office staff consists of 5 employees who handle personnel, accounting, and other office responsibilities. The sales staff includes 7 employees who travel extensively selling the furniture to retail outlets. The remaining 38 employees work in the factory. Under the UNICAP rules, manufacturing costs include the wages of the 38 factory workers and all other factory costs, plus a portion of the salaries for the 5 office employees. The costs for the sales staff are not manufacturing costs and can be deducted with selling expenses. Any reasonable method can be used to allocate the cost of the office staff between manufacturing overhead and deductible expenses. If the allocation is made based on the number of employees, 84 percent (38/45) of the office costs are treated as manufacturing overhead and allocated to inventory, while 16 percent (7/45) are deductible as expenses.

The allocation of costs between ending inventory and cost of goods sold is determined by the method of accounting selected. A number of methods are acceptable,

[92]Reg. §1.471-3.

[93]§263A.

[94]Wholesalers and retailers must also capitalize certain storage costs, purchasing costs, and handling, processing, assembly, and repackaging costs.

including specific identification, FIFO (first-in-first-out), LIFO (last-in-first-out), or the average cost methods. The choice of method may have a significant effect on taxable income and the resulting income tax liability. As in financial accounting, the FIFO method assumes that most recently acquired items remain in ending inventory. LIFO assumes the opposite; that is, ending inventory consists of the oldest items. The weighted average (average cost) method usually yields an inventory valuation somewhere between FIFO and LIFO. In periods of rising prices, LIFO results in a smaller ending inventory than FIFO.

TAX PLANNING

An incentive exists to value inventory as low as possible for tax purposes because a low valuation results in tax savings through a higher cost of goods sold deduction.[95] Although the tax benefit is from a deferral, the deferral is of indefinite duration. As inventories increase with business expansion, more taxable income is deferred.

EXAMPLE 49

Adams Corporation, a new business, decides to use the FIFO method for valuing its inventory because this method reflects the true physical flow of goods. At the end of its first year, its ending inventory using FIFO is $200,000. If Adams had used LIFO, its ending inventory would have been $150,000. Adams is in the 34 percent marginal tax bracket. If Adams had used LIFO, it would have increased cost of goods sold and decreased taxable income by $50,000 ($200,000 − $150,000), producing a tax savings of $17,000 ($50,000 × 34%).[96]

In general, there is no requirement to use the same accounting method for both financial accounting and tax purposes, with one exception: a taxpayer who wants to use the LIFO method for tax purposes must also use it for any report or statement to owners or to obtain credit.[97] This is referred to as the **LIFO conformity rule**. A taxpayer can use an alternative inventory method as a supplement to or in an explanation of the financial statements, but the supplemental information cannot be presented on the face of the income statement.[98] The use of LIFO can reduce the perceived performance of the company and can affect the compensation (or even job security) of management if the compensation level of managers of the business is tied to net income. The use of LIFO has thus become a two-edged sword.

The potential adoption of International Financial Reporting Standards (IFRS) is a major issue for businesses using LIFO as LIFO is not permitted under IFRS. Unless the LIFO conformity rule is changed, businesses currently using LIFO will face a tax cost when they change their inventory valuation method to meet IFRS for financial reporting. Under current law, the impact of a change from LIFO to FIFO may be spread over four years; however, Congress is considering repealing the use of the LIFO method of inventory valuation for tax purposes. If it does, it may allow a longer period (one proposal would allow up to 8 years) over which to spread the income and resulting tax effect. Businesses using LIFO should monitor progress on the adoption of IFRS as well as pending tax legislation.

REVISITING THE INTRODUCTORY CASE

The $2,000 for a market survey and the $2,200 for a feasibility study are investigation expenses that are combined with the start-up expenses of $1,500 for pre-opening advertising. The first $5,000 is expensed and the remaining $700 is amortized over

---

[95]A lower ending inventory means a smaller reduction in cost of goods sold.

[96]A taxpayer can change to the LIFO method by attaching Form 970: *Application to Use LIFO Inventory Method* with the tax return for the year of change. A change from LIFO to any other method requires IRS approval.

[97]§472(c), (e)(2).

[98]Presentation in the footnotes, appendixes, or supplements to the financial statements is acceptable. Reg.§1.472-2(e).

180 months beginning on July 1. The club dues are not deductible and only 50 percent of Mark's meals are deductible. Mark can use the standard mileage rate of 56.5 cents per mile (and deduct any parking and tolls in addition to that rate) but can take no deduction for the speeding ticket. Mark must allocate his home expenses based on the square footage (400/2,000 = 20%) of his home office. The home office expenses are only deductible to the extent of income and must be deducted in a specific order (interest and taxes first, utilities and insurance next, and depreciation last). Only $44 of his $500 depreciation expense can be deducted this year due to the income limit (his home office expenses must be deducted last and cannot create a loss). Mark's cash outflow and deductible expenses are as follows:

Cash Outflow	Deductible Expenses	
$2,000	$2,000	Market survey
2,200	2,200	Feasibility study
1,500	823	Pre-opening advertising [$800 + ($700/180 months × 6)]
2,400	0	Club dues (club dues are not deductible)
1,300	650	Meals [($500 + $800) × 50%]
900	900	Hotels
1,100	1,100	Airfare
5,000	5,000	Supplies
1,800	1,800	Advertising
2,543	2,543	Automobile mileage (4,500 miles @ 56.5 cents per mile)[99]
60	0	Speeding ticket (fines are not deductible)
1,600	1,600	Mortgage interest for home office ($8,000 × 20%)
600	600	Real property taxes for home office ($3,000 × 20%)
320	320	Utilities for home office ($1,600 × 20%)
120	120	Insurance for home office ($600 × 20%)
0	44	Depreciation for home office ($500 but limited to remaining income)[100]
$23,668	$19,700	Total deductible expenses

Mark can carry forward the $456 unused depreciation expense and use it in a future year in which he has sufficient net income from his business. Alternatively, he could elect the simplified option and deduct $1,500 for utilities, insurance, and depreciation (deducting 100% of the interest and taxes as itemized deductions).

Mark may wish to rethink his plans to join the country club, as these dues will not be deductible. Unless he feels that club membership is essential to his business, these dollars may be better spent elsewhere. The business meals with clients will be 50 percent deductible whether at the club or in restaurants. Additionally, Mark should keep track of all of his automobile expenses so that he can deduct the greater of his actual expense or the standard mileage allowance.

If Mark changes his mind and decides not to continue with the business, none of his pre-opening or investigation expenses would be deductible.

---

[99]For simplicity, in this example we assume that cash outflows for actual expenses are the same as the standard mileage allowance.

[100]Depreciation is a non-cash expenditure. Depreciation is discussed in Chapter 6.

SUMMARY

Expenses incurred in a trade or business can be deducted from gross income if they are ordinary, necessary, and reasonable in amount. An activity is a trade or business if the taxpayer is regularly involved and intends to make a profit. Expenses incurred in activities that are contrary to public policy or related to tax-exempt income are not deductible.

The method of accounting determines the year in which a taxpayer takes a deduction. An accrual-basis taxpayer deducts expenses when the all-events test is met and economic performance has occurred. A cash-basis taxpayer usually deducts expenses in the year paid; however, prepaid expenses that benefit future years may have to be capitalized.

After the limited expensing provisions are considered, start-up and organizational costs associated with a new business must be capitalized and amortized over a period of 180 months. If a taxpayer is in a similar business, business investigation expenses can be deducted currently. The expenses are nondeductible if a taxpayer is not in a similar business and abandons starting the new business after investigation.

Deductions for business expenses, particularly travel, entertainment, or gift expenses, require proper documentation. Taxpayers who lack adequate substantiation may lose the deduction for these expenses.

The taxpayer must be away from home to deduct travel expenses. When combining business and personal travel, careful planning is required to keep all the costs of getting to and from the destination deductible. If the taxpayer is not away from home, only business-related transportation can be deducted; meals are not deductible. The actual cost of the business use of the car or a standard mileage rate can be used to compute automobile expenses. The cost of commuting to and from work is a personal, nondeductible expense.

Limits apply to the deductions for expenses incurred in hobby activities, the renting of vacation homes, and home offices. In general, deductible expenses cannot exceed the income earned from the activity, and they must be deducted in a specific order.

There are both temporary and permanent differences between the determination of financial accounting (book) income and taxable income resulting from the differences in income and expense recognition for book and tax purposes. Temporary differences will reverse, requiring a deferred tax account. Permanent differences do not reverse, so the tax expense in the financial statements must be adjusted.

KEY TERMS

ASC 740 225
All-events test 207
Associated with 213
Business investigation expenses 211
Deferred tax asset 228
Deferred tax liability 227
Directly related 213
Economic performance 207
FAS 109 225
FIN 48 230
Hobby 224
Investment activities 204
LIFO conformity rule 234
Necessary 204
Ordinary 204
Organization costs 212
Original issue discount (OID) 210
Permanent difference 225
Prepaid expense 209
Principal place of business 222
Production of income 204
Reasonable 204
Specific charge-off method 217
Start-up expenses 211
Tax home 214
Temporary absence 214
Temporary difference 225
Trade or business 203
Uncertain tax positions (UTPs) 230
Uniform capitalization (UNICAP) rules 233

TEST YOURSELF

ANSWERS APPEAR AFTER THE PROBLEM ASSIGNMENTS

1. On October 1, Pembroke Inc. (a cash-basis, calendar-year corporation) borrows $60,000 from the bank at 12 percent annual interest. On December 30, Pembroke pays $7,200 to the bank for the first year's interest on the loan. How much can Pembroke deduct for interest expense in the current year?

a. 0
b. $600
c. $1,800
d. $5,400
e. $7,200

2. Which of the following items is *not* deductible?
   a. Dues for club used solely for business meetings
   b. Directly related business entertainment
   c. Business gift of less than $25 in value
   d. Dues for professional association

3. Howard, a self-employed consultant, uses one room in his home exclusively and regularly for his home office. This office space constitutes 360 square feet of the floor space of his 2,400 square foot home. Howard's wife works at a bank and is paid an annual salary of $80,000. Howard has gross income from his business of $10,000. Expenses of his business (other than home office expenses) are $7,400. Howard has the following home-use expenses:

Total mortgage interest on the home	$8,000
Total real property taxes on the home	3,000
Utility bills for the home	2,000
Homeowner's insurance	2,000
Depreciation (only for the 15% used as an office)	400

   How much of these home-use expenses can Howard deduct as home office expenses (if he does not elect the simplified option)?
   a. $15,400
   b. $10,000
   c. $3,080
   d. $2,600

4. Esslinger Corporation has income per books before tax of $300,000. Included in the income per books is $4,000 interest income from tax-exempt municipal bonds. Esslinger also deducted $20,000 for meals and entertainment expenses, $3,000 for premiums on officers' life insurance policies (the corporation is the beneficiary for these policies), and $100 for fines. What is Esslinger Corporation's taxable income?
   a. $296,100
   b. $299,100
   c. $306,100
   d. $309,100
   e. $313,100

5. Stadler Corporation pays federal income tax at a 34 percent rate. Stadler Corporation reports $100,000 depreciation expense on its financial statements and deducts $140,000 depreciation expense on its tax return. How will Stadler account for the difference between its federal tax liability and its book tax expense on its financial statements?
   a. $13,600 deferred tax liability
   b. $13,600 deferred tax asset
   c. $40,000 deferred tax liability
   d. $40,000 deferred tax asset

PROBLEM ASSIGNMENTS

CHECK YOUR UNDERSTANDING

1. What are the characteristics of a qualified trade or business?
2. What is an investment activity and how are its expenses deducted?
3. Marvin, an attorney, is a cash-basis, calendar-year taxpayer. Marvin's two daughters each own 50 percent of the stock of Marvil Corporation, a calendar-year, accrual-basis corporation. During year 1, Marvin completes some legal work for Marvil Corporation on December 18 and earns a $20,000 fee. In which year should Marvil Corporation deduct the legal expense if
   a. payment is made to Marvin on December 30, year 1?
   b. payment is made to Marvin on January 6, year 2?
4. What records can the IRS require from a taxpayer to substantiate a tax deduction?
5. Aloha Airlines is required by law to have its aircraft engines tested and recertified after 5,000 flight hours. Molokai Maintenance performs the engine tests and recertification for $2,200 per aircraft. For financial accounting purposes, Aloha establishes a reserve account and accrues a maintenance expense of 44 cents per flight hour. When the maintenance is done, the amount paid for the maintenance is deducted from the reserve account. For tax purposes, when can the maintenance expense be deducted?
6. Diane owns and manages a successful clothing store in Dallas. Just prior to the graduation of her brother, Cameron, they investigated the possibility of opening another store in Atlanta for Cameron to manage. Diane and Cameron each paid $1,600 in travel costs while looking for sites for the store. Each paid $300 in legal fees for a lawyer to compile a list of zoning regulations and other relevant city ordinances. They decide that it is not feasible to open a new store at the present time. Can Diane and Cameron deduct their business investigation expenses? Explain.
7. In its first year of operations, Bell Corporation paid its attorney $4,000 and its accountant $2,000 for services related to the organization of the corporation. In its second year of operations, Bell paid the attorney $700 to handle contract negotiations with a new customer. Which expenses are immediately deductible and which ones must Bell Corporation amortize?
8. Randy gave one of his best customers a $150 bottle of wine. How much can he deduct for this business gift?
9. Explain the differences between the rules governing travel within the United States and those governing travel outside the United States.
10. How are deductions for expenses of rental property limited if the taxpayer also uses the property as a vacation home?
11. What are the requirements for a self-employed person to claim a deduction for an office in the home? What are the additional requirements for an employee to take a home office deduction?
12. What factors differentiate a hobby from an active business?
13. Differentiate permanent differences and temporary differences. Provide examples of each.
14. Which corporations are required to file Schedule M-3? What is the purpose of this schedule?

15. Explain the two-step evaluation process of FIN 48.

16. What are the UNICAP rules, and which businesses do they affect?

17. Which of the following costs must be included in inventory by a manufacturer under the UNICAP rules?

a. Factory insurance

b. Advertising

c. Payroll taxes for factory employees

d. Research and experimentation costs

e. Repairs to factory equipment

18. Explain the advantages and disadvantages of a publicly held company using LIFO for inventory valuation.

CRUNCH THE NUMBERS

19. Mary, a taxpayer in the 33 percent marginal tax bracket, borrows $500,000 at 10 percent interest to invest in 7 percent tax-exempt municipal bonds. The annual interest expense on the loan is $50,000. Mary earns $35,000 interest income on the bonds. What is Mary's interest expense deduction?

20. On October 1, Bender Company (a calendar-year, cash-basis taxpayer) signs a lease with Realco Corporation to rent office space for 36 months. Bender obtains favorable monthly payments of $600 by agreeing to prepay the rent for the entire 36-month period.

a. If Bender Company pays the entire $21,600 on October 1, how much can it deduct in the current year?

b. Assume the same facts above except that the lease requires Bender Company to make three annual payments of $7,200 each on October 1 of each year for the next 12 months rent. On October 1 of the current year, Bender Company pays $7,200 for the first 12-month rental period. How much can Bender Company deduct in the current year?

21. On December 15, Simon Corporation (a cash-basis, calendar-year corporation) paid $5,000 for five months of supplies and $9,000 for an insurance policy covering its office building for the next three calendar years. How much can Simon deduct this year for these expenses?

22. Foster Corporation, a cash-basis taxpayer, borrowed $100,000 on January 1, year 1, and received $98,000 in proceeds. The loan matures in 10 years and the $100,000 principal is due on that date. Interest of $10,000 is payable on January 1 of each year beginning January 1, year 2. How much interest is deductible in year 1 and in year 2?

23. When Kelley couldn't make several monthly payments on a business loan, her brother Mike made three of the monthly payments of $700 each, a total of $2,100 ($1,950 for interest expense and $150 for principal) for Kelley's loan. Kelley makes the other nine monthly payments herself ($5,850 for interest expense and $450 for principal).

a. What is Mike's deduction for interest expense?

b. What is Kelley's deduction for interest expense?

c. What could they have done to preserve the tax deductions? Explain.

24. Elisa spends $1,000 on business lunches to entertain her customers at the local country club. The club charges an annual membership fee of $800. Elisa uses the facility 80 percent of the time for business. Her employer does not reimburse her for any of these expenses. What is her deductible expense?

25. Jim, a self-employed individual, takes an important customer to the hockey playoffs. Although the face value of a ticket is only $70, he pays a scalper $400 for each ticket. Assuming all other requirements are met, how much can Jim deduct for the two tickets?

26. Martha lives with her husband in Los Angeles but works in San Diego. During the week she stays in a hotel in San Diego and eats in nearby restaurants. On weekends, she flies home to Los Angeles. During the year, Martha spent $5,000 for the hotel, and $2,000 for meals while in San Diego. Her airfare for travel between San Diego and Los Angeles was $2,500. What is Martha's deduction for travel expenses?

27. Mark flew from Baltimore to Phoenix on business. He spent four days on business and visited friends for two days before returning home. He stayed at a hotel for the four business days but he stayed at his friend's home the last two days. He paid the following expenses:

Airfare	$420
Hotel	500
Meals for 4 business days	200
Meals for 2 days visiting friends	80
Gift for customer in Phoenix	80
Gift for friends	30
Rental car for 6 days at $20 per day	120

How much qualifies as deductible travel expenses?

28. Tim accepts a temporary assignment that is 500 miles away from his office. The assignment is expected to last 7 months. Tim spends $7,000 for lodging and transportation and $3,000 for meals during these 7 months. At the end of the 7 months, Tim is notified that the assignment is extended for another 10 months. Tim incurs $13,000 in travel expenses ($4,000 of which is for meals) during months 8 through 17. What qualifies as deductible travel expenses?

29. Dan's employer assigned him to the New York office for 18 months. During this 18-month assignment, Dan spent $18,000 for apartment rent and $8,500 for meals. During this time, Dan's family remained in St. Louis. At the end of the 18-month assignment, Dan returns to St. Louis. Dan's employer paid for his airfare from St. Louis to New York and back to St. Louis, but did not reimburse him for his other temporary living expenses. What expenses can Dan deduct for travel away from home?

30. John is a teacher at a local high school. During 2013, he travels three days per week to a school in the next county to work with gifted children in an after-school program that does not end until 6:30 P.M. He normally eats dinner before driving home. If he drives 75 miles each way on 90 days to the gifted program, his meal expense is $900, and he maintains adequate records, how much may John deduct for these trips?

31. Luis, a self-employed individual, flies from New York to Rome. He spends seven days in Rome on business and stays over in Rome for an additional three days to vacation. Transportation costs incurred were $1,400; his hotel cost $200 per day for a total of $2,000; and his meals cost $100 per day for a total of $1,000. What expenses can Luis deduct?

32. Maria earns $50,000 from consulting contracts during the year. She collects only $48,000 from her clients and expects the $2,000 will remain uncollectible.

a. If Maria's business is on the accrual basis, what is her gross income for the year and how much can she deduct for bad debt expense?

b. If Maria's business is on the cash basis, what is her gross income for the year and how much can she deduct for bad debt expense?

33. In the current year, Melbourne Corporation pays the $2,000 annual premium for a life insurance policy on its president, for which Melbourne Corporation is the beneficiary. Melbourne also pays $20,000 in annual premiums for group term life insurance for its employees as an employee benefit; the employees designate the beneficiaries. Additionally, Melbourne pays $16,000 in annual premiums for business fire, casualty, and theft insurance. How much can Melbourne deduct as business expenses?

34. Jim, the owner of a tabloid magazine, is sued by an actor for libel and pays $15,000 in legal fees. Jim is found guilty. Jim also received many parking tickets while attending various business meetings in areas where legal parking spaces are extremely difficult to find. The tickets totaled $1,000. What is Jim's deduction for these business expenses?

35. Maureen operates a cosmetics sales business from her home. She uses 400 of 1,600 square feet of the home as an office. If her income before her home office deduction is $3,400, how much of the following unapportioned expenses for the home are deductible? If any of the expenses are not deductible currently, how are they treated for tax purposes?

Mortgage interest	$5,000
Property taxes	1,400
Utilities	1,200
Repairs and maintenance	600
Depreciation for entire home	6,000

36. Teresa is an accomplished actress. During the summer, she rented a vacant store to stage productions of four plays, using the local townspeople as actors and stagehands. She sold $24,000 of tickets to the various plays. Her expenses included $10,000 for copyright fees, $3,000 store rental, $8,000 for costume purchases and rentals, $2,000 for props and other supplies, and $4,000 for all other miscellaneous expenses related to producing the series of plays.

a. How does Teresa treat the revenue and expenses if the activity is deemed a business?

b. How does Teresa treat the revenue and expenses if the activity is considered a hobby?

c. What are some of the factors that should be considered in deciding if this constitutes a business or a hobby?

37. Neil owns a ski lodge in Aspen. His use of this lodge varies from year to year. The annual expenses for the lodge are as follows:

Mortgage interest	$24,000
Property taxes	12,000
Snow removal	1,000
Yard maintenance	800
Utilities	2,000
Repairs and other maintenance	1,200
Annual depreciation	12,000

How does Neil treat the income and expense if

a. he uses the lodge for 100 days and rents it out for 10 days at a rate of $150 per day?

b. he uses the lodge for 10 days and rents it out for 100 days at $150 per day?

c. he uses the lodge for 50 days and rents it out for 60 days at $150 per day?

38. Maxwell Corporation has income per books before tax of $400,000. Included in the income per books is $8,000 interest income from tax-exempt municipal bonds. In computing income per books, Maxwell deducted $22,000 for meals and entertainment expenses, $3,300 for premiums on officers' life insurance policies (the corporation is the beneficiary for these policies), and $200 for fines.

a. What is Maxwell Corporation's taxable income?

b. What should Maxwell Corporation report as its income tax expense on its financial statements, assuming it uses a 34 percent tax rate?

39. Sorbon Corporation pays federal income tax at a 34 percent rate. In year 1, Sorbon deducts $80,000 as bad debt expense in computing its book income but deducts only $70,000 for bad debt expense on its tax return.

a. What is the difference between Sorbon's book tax expense and its federal tax liability?

b. How does Sorbon account for this difference on its financial statements?

c. In year 2, Sorbon reports $50,000 for bad debt expense on its books and $60,000 bad debt expense in computing taxable income. How does Sorbon account for this difference on its financial statements?

40. Arnold Corporation (a calendar-year, accrual-basis taxpayer) reported $500,000 pre-tax income on its financial statements for the year. In examining its records, you find the following:

- $3,000 of interest income from municipal bonds
- $200 of expenses incurred in earning the interest income from the municipal bonds
- Arnold wrote off $900 of accounts receivable as uncollectible and added $3,000 to its allowance for bad debts this year.
- Arnold deducted $4,000 for meals and entertainment expenses on its financial statements.
- Straight-line depreciation for financial reporting is $7,000; MACRS tax depreciation is $11,000
- Arnold paid $2,800 in premiums on key officer life insurance policies for which it is the beneficiary
- Arnold collected $50,000 from a life insurance policy due to the death of a key officer
- Arnold paid $2,500 in fines for violating Environmental Protection Agency anti-pollution regulations.

a. Identify Arnold's permanent and temporary book/tax differences.

b. Compute Arnold's taxable income and income tax payable.

41. Refer to the information in problem 40 for Arnold Corporation.

a. Identify which of Arnold Corporation's book/tax differences result in a deferred tax asset or a deferred tax liability.

b. Prepare the journal entry to record the federal tax expense and federal tax liability for Arnold Corporation.

42. Makai Corporation has a potential deduction of up to $1,000 that it would like to claim on its current-year tax return. Its tax position meets the recognition threshold of more likely than not, but the deduction cannot be measured by a single amount. The possible outcomes and their probabilities determined by Makai are as follows:

POSSIBLE OUTCOME	PROBABILITY OF OCCURRING	CUMULATIVE PROBABILITY OF OCCURRING
$1,000	10%	10%
$750	30%	40%
$600	25%	65%
$500	15%	80%
$200	10%	90%
$100	5%	95%
0	5%	100%

What amount should Makai recognize as a deduction for its financial statements according to FIN 48?

43. Tropical Patios Corporation manufactures patio furniture in a factory with 24 employees. The office staff consists of 4 employees who handle personnel, accounting, and other office responsibilities. The sales staff includes 6 employees who travel extensively selling the furniture to retail outlets. The remaining 14 employees work in the factory. If the allocation for UNICAP purposes is based on the number of employees, what percentage of the office costs should be allocated to inventory?

44. Barley Corporation decides to use the FIFO method for inventory valuation when it begins operations because this reflects the true physical flow of inventory. Its inventory under FIFO is valued at $375,000 at the end of its first year of operations. If Barley instead used LIFO, its ending inventory would be valued at $75,000. Due to its first-year profitability, Barley is in the 34 percent marginal tax bracket. For the next several years, Barley expects to see a steady increase in the cost of its products. Barley expects that its inventory will probably remain at about the same quantity for the next several years.

a. Is Barley Corporation required to use the inventory method that matches its actual physical flow?

b. If Barley Corporation had used LIFO instead of FIFO, how much income tax could it have saved for the current year?

c. If Barley changes from FIFO to LIFO for tax purposes, does this have any impact on what it reports on its financial statements?

45. Comprehensive Problem for Chapters 4 and 5. Martin, the sole proprietor of a consulting business, has gross receipts of $45,000 in 2013. Expenses paid by his business are

Advertising	$ 500
Supplies	2,900
Taxes and licenses	500
Travel (other than meals)	600
Meals and entertainment	400
Health insurance premiums (for Martin)	1,400
Individual retirement account contribution	2,500

During the year, Martin drives his car a total of 15,000 miles (700 business miles and 550 personal miles per month). He paid $100 for business-related parking and tolls. He paid $120 in fines for speeding tickets when he was late for appointments with clients. Martin's office is located in his home. His office occupies 500 of the 2,000 square feet in his home. His total (unallocated) expenses for his home are

Mortgage interest	$6,000
Property taxes	1,700
Insurance	700
Repairs and maintenance	300
Utilities	1,600

Depreciation for the business portion of his home is $1,364.

a. What is Martin's net income (loss) from his business?

b. How much self-employment tax must Martin pay?

c. Based on this information, are there any other deductions that Martin can claim on his individual tax return other than those reported on his Schedule C?

THINK OUTSIDE THE TEXT

These questions require answers that are beyond the material that is covered in this chapter.

46. Orlando purchased a time-share property in Hawaii that he can use for five weeks each year. If Orlando uses this property for his vacations during the year and rents the property to others when he chooses not to use it, can he deduct any expenses related to this property? Explain.

47. Michael's friend suggests that he file Form 5213: *Election to Postpone Determination To Whether the Presumption Applies That An Activity Is Engaged in for Profit* if he expects to incur losses in his new activity. If he files this form within the first three years, the IRS cannot question whether it is a hobby for 5 years after beginning operations. What do you think are the possible advantages and disadvantage of filing this form with the IRS?

48. List three types of expenses or allowances that can cause temporary differences between book and taxable income and explain how their financial accounting treatment differs from their tax treatment. Why do you think the treatments differ?

49. Your friend recently read a newspaper article that said the largest of the Fortune 500 companies do not pay the federal income tax expense reported on their financial statements. The tax they pay is frequently a lower number. Your friend asks you to explain how this is possible. Do you believe this is good public policy?

50. If Congress reduces the corporate income tax rates, how would this affect deferred tax liabilities and deferred tax assets?

51. AAA Airlines, an accrual-basis taxpayer, frequently issues travel vouchers to customers who voluntarily surrender their reserved seats on overbooked flights. The vouchers are for a specific dollar amount that customers can use to reduce the purchase price of future tickets. The vouchers are valid for one year and many expire unused. Explain how AAA Airlines should account for these vouchers for both financial accounting and tax purposes.

IDENTIFY THE ISSUES

Identify the issues or problems suggested by the following situations. State each issue as a question.

52. Ken is a high school history teacher. Each summer he travels to a different location to further his knowledge of American history. This summer he plans to attend a four-day conference for high school history teachers in Philadelphia. Immediately following the conference he plans to spend a week exploring the battlefield area at Gettysburg. He plans to incorporate the information he learns from his trip into the classes he teaches.

53. In year 1, Sharon loaned her friend Christina $10,000 to start a new business. The loan was documented by a signed note, at market interest rate, and required repayment in two years. Christina appeared successful at first but her office manager embezzled a large amount of money, causing Christina to declare bankruptcy in year 2. In year 3 Sharon recovers only $1,000 of the $10,000 she loaned to Christina.

54. Ace Builders begins construction on a building in January. Its contract specifies that the building must be completed by July 1 or it must pay a penalty of $100 for each day the building is delayed. Ace Builders completes the building on July 31 and pays a penalty of $3,000.

55. You rent your beach house to your friend, Sarah. Sarah rents her condo in Aspen to you. You each pay a fair rental price.

56. Carl is the president of Carlton Corporation. He spends three days testifying before Congress on the impact that proposed legislation has on his industry. In his testimony he states that if the legislation passes, he will have to lay off 20 percent of his workforce. He spent $1,000 for airfare, $700 for the hotel, and $310 for meals.

57. Scott is the CEO of a large corporation in Chicago. He spends the month of August in Wisconsin at his vacation home, where he has a separate structure furnished as an office. Scott uses the office each August for long-range corporate planning because he can avoid the interruptions that occur in Chicago and he finds the isolation he needs to concentrate. The rest of the year the office is not used.

58. Anne operates a dog-training business out of her home. She started the business four years ago but has not yet made a profit. She gets all of her business by word-of-mouth and thinks that she might try running some ads in the newspaper to increase her business.

DEVELOP RESEARCH SKILLS

59. Gary Sanders owns his own real estate business. He has developed a reputation within the community for honesty and integrity. He believes that this is one of the reasons his firm has been so successful. Gary was a 30 percent shareholder in an unsuccessful fast-food restaurant, Escargot-to-Go. Although he personally thought the business had great food and was well run, escargot never appealed to the local community. Early this year the corporation filed for bankruptcy.

Many of the creditors of Escargot-to-Go were also clients of Gary's real estate business. After Escargot declared bankruptcy, Gary's real estate business began to suffer. Gary felt that the decline in his real estate business was related to the bankruptcy of Escargot, so Gary used the earnings of his real estate business to repay all the creditors of Escargot-to-Go. Within a few months, Gary's real estate business began to pick up. Gary has asked you to determine if his real estate business can deduct the expenses of repaying Escargot-to-Go's creditors.

60. Ben is the chief executive officer of a restaurant chain based in Maine. Ben began the business 15 years ago and it has grown into a multimillion-dollar company, franchising restaurants all over the country. Ben has a new interest, however, in horse breeding. He previously raised horses with some success over the years but has only recently decided to pursue this new business with the same intensity with which he originally pursued the restaurant business. Ben likes South Florida and sets up his new horse breeding business there. He purchased a fully operating breeding farm and leased a nearby condominium for six months so he can oversee the business. Ben plans to spend about six months each year in Florida for the next three years overseeing his horse business, which should provide about 30 percent of his total income. Ultimately, Ben wants to sell his interest in his restaurant business and retire to Florida to devote all of his time to his horses. Ben wants to know if he can deduct any of the costs associated with his travel to Florida.

61. Marino Corporation pays $6,500 to rent a 10-seat skybox for three football games to use for business entertainment at each game. The price for a regular nonluxury box seat at each game is $45. How much can Marino Corporation deduct for this entertainment expense?

62. Suzanne owns a vacation home at the beach in which she lived for 30 days and rented out for 61 days during the current year. Her gross rental income is $2,600. Her total expenses for the vacation home are as follows:

Mortgage interest	$1,500
Property taxes	900
Utilities	700
Maintenance	300
Depreciation for entire house	1,100

a. Compute Suzanne's net rental income using the IRS method for allocating expenses.

b. Compute Suzanne's net rental income using the Tax Court method (also known as the Bolton method) for allocating expenses.

c. Which method results in less taxable income? Explain.

SEARCH THE INTERNET

63. Go to the IRS Web site *(www.irs.gov)* and locate the publication on travel, entertainment, and gifts. Julie plans to attend a business convention in Costa Rica. Her friend told her that she cannot deduct expenses for attending a convention outside of North America. Does Costa Rica qualify as part of North America?

64. Go to the IRS Web site *(www.irs.gov)* and print Form 2106: *Employee Business Expenses*. Use the following information to complete this form.

Carl is an employee of Intelligent Devices, Inc. in San Jose. In a typical week, Carl spends a lot of time on the road showing products to prospective customers. He also frequently takes customers out to lunch to discuss new products. Carl purchased his car on January 1, 2012. Carl's wife has her own automobile that is used for most of their personal driving. Carl uses the standard mileage rate for his automobile expenses. He keeps a written log of his mileage that shows he drove a total of 30,000 miles during the year of which 24,000 miles (2,000 per month) were for business. His records also show that he spent $300 for business parking and tolls, $2,800 for business meals, $1,200 for business entertainment, and $1,100 for hotel expenses while traveling away from home on business. He also paid $250 for a business-related seminar. He was not reimbursed for any of these expenses.

65. Go to the IRS Web site *(www.irs.gov)* and print Schedule E: *Supplemental Income and Loss.* Use the following information to complete this form.

Gillian rented her vacation home for 60 days during the year receiving $6,900 in rental income. She used the property herself for 15 days. Her total expenses include: $4,000 mortgage interest, $2,000 property taxes, $500 utilities, $400 insurance, $200 cleaning, $700 annual depreciation, and a $600 rental commission paid to the real estate agent who found the tenant.

66. Go to the IRS Web site *(www.irs.gov)* and print Schedule C: *Profit or Loss for Business (Sole Proprietorship)*, Schedule SE: *Self-Employment Tax*, and Form 8829: *Expenses for Business Use of Your Home.* Use the information in problem 45 to complete these forms and assume the simplified option is not elected.

67. Go to the IRS Web site *(www.irs.gov)* and print the page of Form 1120: *U.S. Corporate Income Tax Return* that includes Schedule M-1. Use the information in example 38 to complete Schedule M-1.

68. Go to Gap Inc.'s Web site *(www.gapinc.com)* and locate its annual report. Find the note on income taxes.

a. What was Gap's effective tax rate for its two most recent fiscal years?

b. How much was Gap's valuation allowance for its two most recent fiscal years?

c. How much does Gap have in NOL carryovers and when will they begin to expire?

DEVELOP PLANNING SKILLS

69. Kondex, a cash-basis corporation, is considering paying $50,000 of expenses at the end of this year rather than waiting until next year. Kondex's marginal tax rate for the current year is 25 percent but it expects to be in the 34 percent marginal tax bracket next year. Kondex uses a 7 percent discount rate for evaluation purposes. Should Kondex pay the expenses at the end of the current year?

70. Bob lives in Atlanta and needs to set up three days of business meetings with customers in San Francisco. While he is in California, he would like to spend two days sightseeing in the wine country. Bob's customers are willing to meet any weekday with him, so the scheduling is totally up to him. Bob wants to maximize the deductible portion of his travel expenses. What should he consider in scheduling his business meetings?

71. Ken, owner of Kendrick Corporation, realizes that he needs to send an employee to a temporary assignment at a plant in another state. He can either send one employee for an 18-month assignment or two employees for 9-month assignments. Kendrick Corporation will pay for all the meal and lodging expenses while the employees are on their out-of-town assignments. Does it make any difference from a tax perspective to Kendrick and to the employees which option Ken chooses?

72. John has a vacation condo in the Florida Keys that he has rented out for two weeks in December for $250 a day. John has used this vacation home himself for a total of three weeks during the year. His total (unallocated) expenses for the condo are

Taxes	$1,500
Insurance	2,000
Repairs and maintenance	1,100
Interest	4,500
Depreciation for year	1,000

John received a call from his tenants who want to extend their rental of the condo for another week. John is in the 33 percent marginal tax bracket. What tax factors should John consider in making the decision to extend the rental of the condo?

ANSWERS TO TEST YOURSELF

1. c. **$1,800**. $7,200/12 months = $600 per month × 3 months = $1,800.
2. a. **Dues for club used solely for business meetings**. All of the other items are deductible.
3. d. **$2,600**. Home office expenses are only deductible to the extent of the income from the business after first deducting the other expenses ($10,000 – $7,400 = $2,600). Howard first deducts 15 percent of his mortgage interest ($8,000 × 15% = $1,200) and property taxes ($3,000 × 15% = $450) for a total of $1,650 otherwise allowable itemized deductions. This leaves only $950 ($2,600 – $1,650) of income against which the remaining expenses can be deducted. He deducts $300 ($2,000 × 15%) for utilities $300 ($2,000 × 15%) for insurance, and $350 for depreciation. The remaining $50 of depreciation expense is carried forward to the next year; Howard does not reduce his basis in the home for this disallowed amount.
4. d. **$309,100**. $300,000 income per books – $4,000 tax-exempt interest + $10,000 disallowed 50% of meals and entertainment + $3,000 insurance premiums + $100 fines.
5. a. **$13,600 deferred tax liability**. ($140,000 – $100,000) × 34% = $13,600.

part

II

Property Concepts and Transactions

chapter

6

Property Acquisitions And Cost Recovery Deductions

The cost of a long-lived asset is usually recovered over the accounting periods in which it produces income through depreciation (for most tangible property), depletion (for natural resources), or amortization (for intangible assets). The method and timing of the cost recovery deductions used for tax reporting affect the after-tax cost of the asset. The earlier a taxpayer can recover the cost of an asset through depreciation deductions, the greater the present value of the tax savings and the lower the net after-tax cost of the asset.

The choice of method and useful life for cost recovery are restricted for tax purposes. The current Modified Accelerated Cost Recovery System (MACRS) dictates the recovery life and the averaging convention and restricts the choice of method to a predetermined accelerated method or an alternative straight-line method.

There are significant limits on tax depreciation deductions for certain assets that are often used for both business and personal purposes, such as automobiles and computers. Incentive tax provisions, including Section 179 expensing and bonus depreciation, encourage investment in long-lived assets. It is important to understand these incentive and limitation provisions and their interplay with regular MACRS depreciation deductions to maximize the value of tax savings from cost recovery deductions.

CHAPTER OUTLINE

KEY CONCEPTS

- ★ Basis is a taxpayer's unrecovered investment in an asset. Taxpayers can recover their basis in an asset without tax cost; any excess recovered beyond basis results in realized gain that may be subject to taxation.
- ★ Depreciation, depletion, and amortization are ways an asset's cost is recovered. Adjusted basis is basis that is reduced for cost recovery deductions.
- ★ Annual cost recovery deductions provide tax savings and reduce the effective after-tax cost of an asset. The shorter an asset's recovery period, the lower the after-tax cost.
- ★ Section 179 allows immediate expensing of up to $500,000 of qualified personalty. The expensed amount reduces an asset's basis; the remaining basis is depreciated using regular MACRS depreciation. Bonus depreciation allows a higher write off in the first year for new assets, but does not apply to used property.
- ★ The cost of natural resources is recovered through depletion. For certain natural resources, taxpayers annually can elect the greater of cost depletion or percentage depletion.
- ★ The cost of intangible assets acquired in the purchase of a business is recovered using the straight-line method over 15 years.

Setting the Stage—An Introductory Case

Windom Corporation, a calendar-year taxpayer, purchased and placed the following business assets in service during 2013:

Asset	Date Placed in Service	Initial Cost
New automobile	March 10	$48,000
New computer equipment	June 12	300,000
Used office furniture	July 18	652,000
Used office fixtures	October 5	1,000,000

Windom Corporation is also considering the purchase of $500,000 of additional used office furniture. It could wait until early next year to make the purchase, or it could buy the furniture and place it in service in December to try to increase its current-year tax depreciation deduction. What impact would this proposed purchase have on Windom's current tax year depreciation deduction? At the end of the chapter, we will return to this case.

Capital Expenditures

Businesses make many capital expenditures to purchase long-lived assets (or to significantly improve the efficiency or useful life of an existing asset) and these costs are treated in one of three ways: (1) deducted currently, (2) capitalized until disposal, or (3) capitalized, but with the cost allocated to the years the asset's use benefits the taxpayer (the cost recovery period).[1]

In the first category is immediate expensing under Section 179 that allows taxpayers to elect to expense up to $500,000 of the cost of qualifying depreciable business property. (The details of this provision are discussed later in this chapter.) In the second category are costs of nonwasting assets, such as land and works of art, that cannot be recovered until the assets are sold. Most capital expenditures fall into the third category with their cost recovered over several years through depreciation, amortization, or depletion deductions. This applies to cash basis as well as accrual basis taxpayers.

Example 1

Kilgo Corporation made the following capital expenditures during the current year: $10,000 for new computer equipment, $100,000 for a mineral interest in a coal mine, and $300,000 for a new office building ($100,000 for the land and $200,000 for the building). The computer equipment is eligible to be expensed immediately (under Section 179) or depreciated. The interest in the coal mine is recovered through annual depletion allowances. The cost of the office building is recovered through annual depreciation allowances. The cost of the land on which the office building is located is capitalized and remains on the company's books until its cost is recovered in the year of disposition.

Before 1981, tax depreciation was based on the useful life of the property, similar to financial accounting depreciation. As part of the Economic Recovery Tax Act of 1981, Congress enacted the Accelerated Cost Recovery System (ACRS) to replace the depreciation rules. ACRS used very short lives for depreciation and greatly accelerated depreciation deductions to stimulate capital investment. ACRS also attempted to simplify the law by establishing only a few class lives, standardizing the averaging conventions, and ignoring estimated salvage value in determining an asset's depreciable basis.

In 1986, ACRS was replaced by the **Modified Accelerated Cost Recovery System (MACRS)**, which lengthened the recovery periods over which depreciation deductions were taken. Congress made this change when it became more focused

[1]The cost of personal-use assets cannot be recovered until they are sold. When a cost is capitalized, it is added to an asset account rather than an expense account.

on raising tax revenue than on stimulating the economy. Neither ACRS nor MACRS require a business to estimate actual useful life, as is required for financial accounting. As a result, the depreciation deductions are very different on the business's tax return and in its financial statements, creating deferred tax accounts for these differences.

EXAMPLE 2

Biltmore Corporation pays federal income tax at a 34 percent rate. Biltmore Corporation reports $100,000 depreciation expense on its financial statements and deducts $150,000 depreciation expense on its tax return, resulting in a favorable temporary difference. Biltmore's book income is $50,000 more than its taxable income, and its book tax expense is $17,000 ($50,000 × 34%) more than its federal tax payable. Biltmore records the extra $17,000 tax expense as a deferred tax liability. In future years when the depreciation expense difference reverses, the corporation's taxable income will be $50,000 more than its book income, its tax payable will be $17,000 more than its tax expense, and the $17,000 deferred tax liability will be eliminated.

Cost recovery deductions begin the year an asset is placed in service, that is, when it is set up and ready to be used for its intended business purpose.[2] This may not be the same as the year an asset is purchased.

EXAMPLE 3

Ratronic Corporation (a calendar-year taxpayer) purchased $90,000 of equipment on December 28, year 1. It installs and places the equipment in service on January 4, year 2. Ratronic will not begin depreciating the equipment until year 2.

The tax rules that apply when an asset is placed in service must continue to be used over the asset's entire life until its basis is fully recovered or the asset is disposed of or is no longer used in the business. As a result, a business that places two identical assets into service in two different years may be required to use different methods to compute their tax depreciation.

Capitalize or Expense

Incidental materials and supplies with an acquisition cost of $100 or less can be deducted at the time of purchase. Other, more costly, materials and supplies are usually expensed to the extent they are expected to be consumed in the operation of the business during the current year or have an expected useful life of not more than 12 months. The purchase price of any other asset with a useful life of more than 12 months, however, is usually capitalized with the cost recovered through depreciation or amortization.

The treatment of the expenditures for repairs or maintenance is more complicated. Section 162(a) states that expenditures are currently deductible if they are incidental repair expenses; Section 263(a) states that expenditures are required to be capitalized, however, if they are for permanent improvements or betterments that increase the value of the property, restore its value or use, substantially prolong its useful life, or adapt it to a new or different use. Thus, it is up to a business to determine if the costs of repairs or the refurbishing of existing equipment are simply "incidental" and merely serve to maintain current functionality. If so, they should be treated as an ordinary repair expense. If, however, the costs incurred are sufficiently significant that they meet the one of the criteria of Section 263(a), then they must be capitalized and depreciated. Often the answer to this may require input from someone in the maintenance department of the business. But for tax purposes, the issue is one of timing; that is, whether the expenditure should be recovered currently or over a longer period of time through depreciation.

---

[2]Reg. §1.167(a)-2.

Basis of Property

Basis is the taxpayer's unrecovered investment in an asset that can be recovered without tax cost. Basis is reduced as the taxpayer recovers part of the asset's basis (through depreciation or depletion deductions); this reduced basis is called **adjusted basis**.

The original basis of an asset includes the following:[3]

1. The amount of cash and the fair market value of the property given up by the purchaser
2. Money borrowed and used to pay for the property acquired[4]
3. Liabilities of the seller assumed or taken "subject to" by the purchaser
4. Expenses of making the purchase, such as attorney fees and brokerage commissions

Example 4

Katleen Corporation purchases a storage building for $18,000 cash and a mortgage of $22,000. It also assumes the seller's property tax liability of $2,000 and pays attorney's fees of $1,800 to complete the purchase. Katleen's original basis is $43,800, because all of these amounts are part of the cost of the purchased property.

If more than one asset is acquired in a single transaction (such as land, buildings, and equipment), the cost must be apportioned to each of the individual items to determine their original bases using their relative fair market values (FMV).[5] The original basis of each asset is equal to its FMV divided by the FMV of all of the assets acquired multiplied by the cost of all of the assets, as summarized in the following formula:

$$\text{Total Purchase Price} \times \frac{\text{FMV of Specific Asset}}{\text{FMV of All Assets Acquired}} = \text{Original Basis of Specific Asset}$$

If the purchase price exceeds the sum of the value of the individual assets, the excess price is considered goodwill (an intangible asset discussed later in this chapter).

Example 5

Maryco Corporation purchases land, an office building, and furniture for $400,000. An appraiser determines that the land has a value of $200,000, the building $270,000, and the furniture $30,000. Maryco's original basis for each asset under the relative FMV method is

$$\$400{,}000 \times \frac{\$200{,}000}{\$500{,}000} = \$160{,}000 \text{ for the land}$$

$$\$400{,}000 \times \frac{\$270{,}000}{\$500{,}000} = \$216{,}000 \text{ for the building}$$

$$\$400{,}000 \times \frac{\$30{,}000}{\$500{,}000} = \$24{,}000 \text{ for the furniture}$$

If Maryco instead had paid $550,000, the basis would be $200,000 for the land, $270,000 for the building, $30,000 for the furniture, and $50,000 for goodwill.

TAX PLANNING

Instead of this allocation method, the buyer and seller can agree to a written allocation of the purchase price to individual assets.[6] Taxpayers should allocate as much of the

[3]See §1012, Reg. §1.1012-1 and *Crane vs. Comm.*, 35 AFTR 776, 331 US 1, 47-1 USTC ¶9217, (USSC, 1947).

[4]Payments on debt used to finance the acquisition of property do not affect the basis because these payments affect only the liability and cash accounts.

[5]Reg. §1.61-6(a).

[6]§1060.

purchase price as possible to assets that are subject to some form of capital recovery and as little as possible to those assets whose bases cannot be recovered until they are sold.

After acquisition, a taxpayer increases the basis of an asset for nondeductible capital expenditures that prolong its useful life or enhance its usefulness. Cost recoveries (such as depreciation) reduce the property's basis to avoid a double tax benefit. Without a basis reduction for cost recoveries, gains would be smaller or losses larger on the subsequent sale or other disposition of the property. Other recoveries, such as casualty losses, also reduce original basis for similar reasons.

Example 6

At the beginning of year 1, Marino Corporation bought some equipment for $80,000 cash and a $30,000 loan. Later that year it made a major improvement to the equipment that cost $25,000. In years 1 through 3, it took annual depreciation deductions of $18,000 on the equipment and paid $14,000 on the debt. Marino's adjusted basis at the end of year 3 is $81,000 ($80,000 + $30,000 + $25,000 – $18,000 – $18,000 – $18,000). The payment on the debt does not affect the asset's adjusted basis.

Cost recovery deductions are allowed only on property that is used in a trade or business or in an income-producing activity. If an asset is used for both business and personal purposes, generally depreciation is based on the relative amount of time that the asset is used for business purposes.

Example 7

Mark purchased a computer for $1,000 that he uses 80 percent for business and 20 percent for personal purposes. Mark's basis for depreciation is $800 ($1,000 × 80%). He cannot depreciate the portion that he uses for personal purposes.

If the property is converted from personal use to business use, the basis for depreciation is the lesser of the property's adjusted basis or fair market value at the date of conversion, preventing taxpayers from depreciating the loss in value during the time it was used for personal purposes.

Example 8

On October 4 of year 3, Roger starts using a computer entirely for business. Prior to that time, the computer was used entirely for personal purposes. The computer cost Roger $2,200 in year 1 and has a fair market value of $1,000 on the date of its conversion to business use. The basis of the computer for depreciation purposes is $1,000.

If a taxpayer fails to claim a depreciation deduction on an asset in any year, the basis of the asset is still reduced by the allowable depreciation the taxpayer should have claimed. The allowable depreciation is the amount of depreciation that the taxpayer is entitled to deduct for the property based on the applicable depreciation method.[7]

Example 9

Last year, Ray purchased a computer costing $5,000 for use in his business. The computer has an estimated useful life of five years. Ray forgot to claim the depreciation deduction last year. He must still reduce the computer's basis for the unclaimed depreciation because he was entitled to the deduction. Ray may not claim a double depreciation deduction in a later year.[8]

Acquisition in a Taxable Exchange

Sometimes assets are acquired in exchange for services or for property other than cash. In these situations, the basis of the acquired asset equals the fair market value

---

[7] § 167(a) and Reg. § 1.167(a)-1.

[8] Ray should amend the previous year's tax return to claim the depreciation deduction.

of the property given up or the services performed. Unless an exchange of properties qualifies as a tax-deferred exchange, the parties recognize gain or loss as if cash had been exchanged, and the basis of the property acquired is its fair market value.[9]

EXAMPLE 10

Gilpin Corporation exchanges $50,000 in equipment for Developer Corporation's tract of undeveloped land in a taxable exchange. The land's basis is $50,000, the fair market value of the equipment Gilpin gave up to acquire the land.

John, an attorney, performed legal services for New Corporation and billed the corporation $20,000 for these services. New Corporation issued 2,000 shares of its own common stock to John to pay the bill. John recognizes $20,000 income and has a basis of $20,000 in the stock.

Acquisition by Gift

Section 1015 provides that a donee (the gift recipient) takes the donor's adjusted basis in appreciated property as his or her basis. If the donor pays a gift tax on appreciated property, the donee increases the donor's adjusted basis by the amount of the gift tax attributable to the net increase in value of the gift property up to the date of the gift.[10] This net increase is calculated as follows:

$$\text{Gift tax paid by donor} \times \frac{\text{FMV at date of gift} - \text{donor's adjusted basis}}{\text{FMV at date of gift}}$$

EXAMPLE 11

Larry receives appreciated property as a gift from Gene worth $24,000. Gene's basis is $18,000, and he pays $2,000 in gift taxes on the transfer to Larry. Larry's basis is $18,500 (after the $500 basis increase for a portion of the gift tax), determined as follows:

$$\$18{,}000 + \left[\$2{,}000 \times \left(\frac{\$24{,}000 - \$18{,}000}{\$24{,}000}\right)\right] = \$18{,}500$$

If the fair market value of the gift is less than the donor's basis at the time of the gift and the gift property is subsequently sold at a loss, the donee uses the lower fair market value as basis. This prevents donors from shifting their losses to other taxpayers through gifts. The donor's higher basis is used, however, to determine gain. This rule means that donees who receive a gift of loss property must keep track of its dual basis until the property is sold. If the asset is sold at a price between the lower fair market value and the donor's basis, the donee has neither gain nor loss on the disposition. Additionally, if the property's fair market value at the date of the gift does not exceed the donor's basis, no gift taxes are added to the donor's basis.

EXAMPLE 12

Sherry receives a gift of stock from Helen worth $18,000. Helen purchased the stock three years ago for $20,000 and paid $1,000 in gift taxes on the transfer to Sherry. If Sherry sells the stock for $14,000, she uses the $18,000 fair market value as basis for determining loss and she has a $4,000 loss. This prevents Helen from shifting her $2,000 loss ($18,000 – $20,000) to Sherry. If Sherry sells the stock for $23,000, she can use Helen's $20,000 basis to determine gain; thus, her gain is only $3,000. If she sells the stock at any price between $18,000 and $20,000, Sherry has neither gain nor loss. None of the gift tax can be added to the basis because the stock's fair market value when given is lower than the donor's basis. If Helen had sold the stock (an investment asset) for its fair market value and then gifted the proceeds from the sale to Sherry, Helen would have been able to claim the tax loss.

[9]Tax-deferred exchanges are discussed in Chapter 8.

[10]For gifts before 1977, the entire gift tax was added to basis.

Acquisition by Inheritance

Under Section 1014, beneficiaries use fair market value for their basis in inherited property.[11] This favorable treatment of inherited property may be due to administrative convenience because in many cases it is difficult to determine the decedent's basis in property due to lack of records. Congress briefly created a carryover basis rule for inherited property in 1976 that was repealed very quickly due to its complexity.[12]

EXAMPLE 13

Sam inherits two assets from his mother in the current year. The first asset was worth $50,000 when she died, and the second asset was worth $45,000. She paid $40,000 for the first asset five years earlier, and she paid $47,000 for the second asset last year. Sam's basis for the first asset is $50,000, and his basis for the second asset is $45,000, their fair market values.

TAX PLANNING

The differences in bases between appreciated property that is inherited versus property that is received by gift forms one of the major considerations for persons wishing to reduce the total tax burden when passing property to younger generations. If the property is gifted, the donee must pay income tax on all the appreciation (while owned by both the donor and the donee), but the property is removed from the donor's estate, reducing potential estate taxes. If appreciated property is inherited, the heir has the higher fair market value as basis in the property, reducing taxable gain on a future sale. Potential estate taxes will be higher, however, as the asset's fair market value is included in the decedent's estate.[13]

CASH FLOW AND AFTER-TAX COST

Unlike many other expenses, depreciation deductions do not require a cash outflow, nor are they intended to represent true reductions in the fair market value of an asset. The tax savings from annual depreciation or other cost recovery deductions, however, reduce the effective after-tax cost of an asset. The annual tax savings equal the deduction multiplied by the marginal tax rate.

EXAMPLE 14

Corbin Corporation purchases an asset for $10,000. Assume for simplicity that it is allowed to recover the entire cost of this asset over five years using a straight-line method for tax purposes. Corbin deducts $2,000 each year and reduces the asset's basis by this deduction. At the end of the five years, the asset's adjusted basis is zero. If Corbin's marginal tax rate is 35 percent, the cost recovery deductions result in a $700 annual tax savings. Using a 6 percent discount rate, the net present value of the tax savings is $2,948. Corbin's after-tax cost of the $10,000 asset is $7,052 ($10,000 – $2,948).

YEAR	COST RECOVERY DEDUCTIONS	TAX RATE	TAX SAVINGS	DISCOUNT FACTOR	PRESENT VALUE
1	$2,000	35%	$700	.943	$660
2	2,000	35%	700	.890	623
3	2,000	35%	700	.840	588
4	2,000	35%	700	.792	554
5	2,000	35%	700	.747	523
			$3,500		$2,948

[11]Usually, fair market value is determined as of the date of death. If the executor elects to value assets in the estate at the alternate valuation date (six months after the date of death), the valuation at that alternate date will be used instead of the date of death.

[12] The Tax Relief Act of 2010 gave executors of estates for decedents dying in 2010 the option to elect to pay no estate tax and use the carryover basis rules instead of receiving a stepped-up basis for inherited property and paying the estate tax (with a $5 million exemption and a 35% tax rate on taxable estates above that amount).

[13]See Chapter 12 for a discussion of wealth transfer planning.

The basis of an asset is the same regardless of whether it is purchased for cash or the purchase is financed. The use of borrowed funds to create basis can reduce the after-tax cost of acquiring an asset, however, and is referred to as leverage.

EXAMPLE 15

Refer to the facts in the previous example, except Corbin Corporation pays only $2,000 cash for the asset and finances the $8,000 balance at a 6 percent interest rate. Interest payments of $480 are due at the end of each year, and the $8,000 principal balance is due at the end of the fifth year. Deductions for both the interest payments and cost recovery result in $868 [($480 interest expense deduction + $2,000 cost recovery deduction) × 35% tax rate] of annual tax savings. The after-tax cost of the $10,000 asset is now $6,342.

YEAR	INITIAL CASH PAYMENT	PRINCIPAL REPAYMENT	INTEREST PAYMENTS	TAX SAVINGS	NET CASH FLOW	DISCOUNT FACTOR	NET PRESENT VALUE
0	$(2,000)				$(2,000)		$(2,000)
1			$(480)	$868	388	.943	366
2			(480)	868	388	.890	345
3			(480)	868	388	.840	326
4			(480)	868	388	.792	307
5		$(8,000)	(480)	868	(7,612)	.747	(5,686)
							$(6,342)

Even though Corbin incurred additional net annual interest cost of $312 [$480 interest payment – ($480 × 35% = $168 tax savings)], it is still able to save an additional $710 ($7,052 – $6,342) through leverage.

Recovering an asset's basis over a shorter time period also reduces the after-tax cost of the asset.

EXAMPLE 16

Assume the same facts as example 14, except that Corbin recovers the cost of the asset over three years (instead of five years) for tax purposes. Annual cost recovery deductions are now $3,333 ($10,000/3 years). Its annual tax savings for the cost recovery deduction is $1,167 ($3,333 × 35%). Corbin's after-tax cost for the asset is $6,881.

YEAR	INITIAL CASH PAYMENT	TAX SAVINGS	NET CASH FLOW	DISCOUNT FACTOR	NET PRESENT VALUE
0	$(10,000)		$(10,000)		$(10,000)
1		$1,167	1,167	.943	1,100
2		1,167	1,167	.890	1,039
3		1,167	1,167	.840	980
					$(6,881)

The shorter life results in an additional $171 ($7,052 – $6,881) reduction in the after-tax cost for the asset.

Taxpayers usually prefer to write off assets over the shortest time for tax purposes; however, the choices are limited because the IRS predetermines the life for most assets. For financial purposes, taxpayers can choose the appropriate useful life for their assets.

MACRS

Assets are divided into two broad categories: realty (real property) and personalty (personal property). **Realty** includes land and buildings (although the cost of land cannot be depreciated). **Personalty** is defined as any tangible asset that is not realty and includes machinery, equipment, furniture, and many other types of assets. It is important not to confuse personalty (or personal property) with personal-use property.

Personal-use property is any property (personalty or realty) that is used for personal purposes rather than in a trade, business, or in an income-producing activity. Depreciation is not allowed for personal-use assets.

Assets eligible for depreciation under MACRS are assigned to a class with a predetermined recovery period. Table 6.1 lists the recovery periods, averaging conventions, and examples of assets assigned to each recovery period for the assets most commonly encountered in business.

There are two depreciation methods used for these MACRS properties: the 200 percent declining-balance method with a switch to straight line to maximize deductions and the straight-line method. The 200 percent declining-balance method applies to MACRS property in the 5-year and 7-year classes. The straight-line method must be used for all property in the 27½-year and 39-year classes.[14]

Taxpayers acquiring property to which the accelerated depreciation method applies, can elect the straight-line method, but they must use the recovery period and averaging convention for its class. The election to use the straight-line method is made annually on a class-by-class basis.[15] For example, if the taxpayer elects to depreciate 5-year class property on a straight-line basis in the current year, all 5-year class property acquired in this year must be depreciated using the straight-line method. Taxpayers can choose different methods for different classes, however; therefore, the

TABLE
6.1 MACRS RECOVERY PERIODS AND AVERAGING CONVENTIONS

RECOVERY PERIOD	AVERAGING CONVENTION	EXAMPLES OF ASSETS
5 years	Half-year or mid-quarter	Automobiles, taxis, trucks, buses, computers and peripheral equipment, typewriters, calculators, and duplicating equipment.
7 years	Half-year or mid-quarter	Office furniture and fixtures (such as files and safes) and most other machinery.
27½ years	Mid-month	Residential rental property that includes buildings or structures if 80 percent or more of the gross rental income is from dwelling units. This does not include a unit in a hotel, motel, or similar establishment where more than 50 percent of the units are used on a transient basis.
39 years[a]	Mid-month	Commercial and industrial buildings and other realty that is not residential rental property.

[a]Nonresidential realty placed in service after December 31, 1986, but before May 13, 1993, was subject to a 31½-year MACRS recovery period.

[14]Examples of other classes include 3 years for certain horses, 10 years for barges, 15 years for land improvements, and 20 years for water utilities. A special 15-year, straight-line class applies to qualified leasehold improvements and certain improvements to restaurant buildings.

[15]§ 167(j)(2)(B).

taxpayer can depreciate 7-year class property on an accelerated basis and 5-year property on the straight-line basis, even though they were purchased in the same year.

Averaging Conventions

To minimize the difficulty of computing depreciation for a fraction of a year, Congress adopted three averaging conventions: half-year, mid-quarter, and mid-month. All the IRS depreciation tables incorporate the appropriate averaging convention. Use of these conventions means that the exact date of acquisition is not needed to compute depreciation.

Half-Year Averaging Convention

Under MACRS, property in the 5-year and 7-year classes is treated as placed in service exactly halfway through the year. The **half-year averaging convention** allows only one half-year of depreciation in the first year of an asset's recovery period, regardless of whether the asset is placed in service on the first day or the last day of the year. The same rule applies to a year in which an asset is sold.

The IRS tables incorporate these averaging rules and consist of a series of annual percentages that are multiplied by the original cost basis of the asset to determine the depreciation deduction for the year. Because most business assets are in the 5-year or 7-year classes, these are the only classes of personalty included here. Table 6.2 contains the MACRS rates for 5-year and 7-year personalty.[16] These rates are computed using the 200 percent declining-balance method with a switchover to straight-line depreciation when the latter yields a larger depreciation deduction.

EXAMPLE 17

Funco Corporation purchases a $4,000 computer (5-year personalty) on January 15 and $20,000 of office furniture (7-year personalty) on July 30. Funco's first-year depreciation expense for these assets is $800 ($4,000 × 20%) for the computer and $2,858 ($20,000 × 14.29%) for the office furniture, for a total of $3,658. Funco's second-year depreciation expense for these assets is $1,280 ($4,000 × 32%) for the computer and $4,898 ($20,000 × 24.49%) for the office furniture, for a total of $6,178.

TABLE **6.2** **MACRS RATES FOR 5-YEAR AND 7-YEAR PERSONALTY USING THE HALF-YEAR AVERAGING CONVENTION**

RECOVERY YEAR	5-YEAR	7-YEAR
1	20.00%	14.29%
2	32.00	24.49
3	19.20	17.49
4	11.52[a]	12.49
5	11.52	8.93[a]
6	5.76	8.92
7		8.93
8		4.46

[a]*Switchover to straight line*

[16]Complete tables for all recovery periods are included in IRS Publication 946: *How to Depreciate Property*. IRS publications can be downloaded from the IRS Web site at *www.irs.gov*.

The use of the half-year averaging convention[17] causes the write-off to extend an additional year to recover the last half-year depreciation.[18] Thus, 5-year property is really depreciated over six years and 7-year property is depreciated over eight years.

Example 18

Juan purchases 5-year class equipment for $10,000 on April 2 in year 1. Juan is allowed a depreciation deduction of $2,000 for year 1, $3,200 for year 2, $1,920 for year 3, $1,152 for year 4, $1,152 for year 5, and $576 for year 6. The half-year averaging convention extends the recovery period one year longer than the class-life for the property.

Mid-Quarter Averaging Convention

To discourage taxpayers from waiting until the end of the year to make their purchases, Congress introduced a generally less beneficial averaging convention, the **mid-quarter convention**, under which depreciation is computed from the midpoint of the quarter in which the property is placed in service. If more than 40 percent of all personalty purchased during the year is placed in service in the last quarter (three months) of the tax year, the mid-quarter convention method must be used; this is not an elective provision. When calculating if the 40 percent test is met, any personalty expensed under Section 179 and all realty are excluded from the computation. If the taxpayer must use the mid-quarter convention, *all* personalty placed in service during the year (except expensed personalty) is subject to the mid-quarter convention rules. Property acquisitions are grouped into the quarter in which they are acquired, based on the taxpayer's taxable year. The mid-quarter convention tables must then be used throughout the life of these assets.

Under the mid-quarter convention, the tax year is divided into four quarters. An asset acquired in any quarter is depreciated from the midpoint of that quarter. Thus, an asset acquired anytime during the first quarter of the tax year is allowed 10½ months/12 months times a full year's depreciation. The IRS provides tables that have this averaging convention already built in, so the principal problem is in identifying when the mid-quarter convention must be used. Table 6.3 shows the mid-quarter depreciation rates for 5-year and 7-year property.

Example 19

Bigbucks Corporation, a June 30 fiscal year-end taxpayer, purchases a small machine (7-year property) for its business on November 15, at a cost of $30,000. On May 2, Bigbucks purchases a larger machine for $50,000. These are the only two personalty purchases in the current year. (The company does not use Section 179 expensing or bonus depreciation.) Because more than 40 percent [$50,000/($30,000 + $50,000) = 62.5%] of total purchases occur in the last quarter of Bigbucks's tax year, the mid-quarter convention must be used. Depreciation on the smaller machine (the one purchased in the second quarter) is $5,355 ($30,000 × 17.85%), and the depreciation on the larger machine (the one purchased in the fourth quarter) is only $1,785 ($50,000 × 3.57%). Depreciation for the second year is $7,041 ($30,000 × 23.47%) for the smaller machine and $13,775 ($50,000 × 27.55%) for the larger machine.

TAX PLANNING

As a general rule, the total depreciation deduction using the mid-quarter convention is smaller than the half-year convention when acquisitions are spaced throughout the year, because of the small first-year depreciation allowed for fourth-quarter acquisitions. Thus, most taxpayers who want to maximize their depreciation deductions for the year plan their acquisitions so no more than 40 percent of personalty is placed in service in

[17]The 200 percent declining-balance rate is double the straight-line rate or 40 percent for five-year property. When the half-year averaging convention is applied to the 40 percent rate, it results in a 20 percent rate for the first year, extending depreciation into the sixth year.

[18]The sixth-year deduction (5.76%) for five-year personalty is one-half of the previous year's deduction (11.52%).

TABLE
6.3 MACRS RATES FOR 5-YEAR AND 7-YEAR PERSONALTY USING THE MID-QUARTER AVERAGING CONVENTION

5-YEAR PROPERTY

RECOVERY YEAR	FIRST QUARTER	SECOND QUARTER	THIRD QUARTER	FOURTH QUARTER
1	35.00%	25.00%	15.00%	5.00%
2	26.00	30.00	34.00	38.00
3	15.60	18.00	20.40	22.80
4	11.01	11.37	12.24	13.68
5	11.01	11.37	11.30	10.94
6	1.38	4.26	7.06	9.58

7-YEAR PROPERTY

RECOVERY YEAR	FIRST QUARTER	SECOND QUARTER	THIRD QUARTER	FOURTH QUARTER
1	25.00%	17.85%	10.71%	3.57%
2	21.43	23.47	25.51	27.55
3	15.31	16.76	18.22	19.68
4	10.93	11.97	13.02	14.06
5	8.75	8.87	9.30	10.04
6	8.74	8.87	8.85	8.73
7	8.75	8.87	8.86	8.73
8	1.09	3.33	5.53	7.64

the last three months of the tax year.[19] There are, however, situations in which the mid-quarter convention results in a larger depreciation deduction. If most assets are acquired in the first and fourth quarters, the mid-quarter convention may be beneficial.

EXAMPLE 20

ABC, a calendar-year corporation, acquires $50,000 of 5-year property in the first quarter and $40,000 of 7-year property in the fourth quarter. ABC must use the mid-quarter convention because over 40 percent ($40,000/$90,000 = 44%) of the property is placed in service in the fourth quarter. Using the mid-quarter convention, total depreciation is $18,928 [($40,000 × 3.57%) + ($50,000 × 35%)]. The half-year convention depreciation deduction would have been only $15,716 [($40,000 × 14.29%) + ($50,000 × 20%)]. The mid-quarter convention increased the depreciation deduction by $3,212.

Careful planning of asset acquisitions allows taxpayers to use the conventions to their advantage.

Mid-Month Averaging Convention for Realty

Realty (buildings) must be depreciated using the straight-line method based on the month in which the property is placed in service.[20] Under the **mid-month convention**,

[19]Refer to the discussion of Section 179 later in this chapter.
[20]§ 168(b)(3).

depreciation is calculated from the midpoint of the month in which the property is placed in service; that is, one-half month depreciation is allowed for the first month of use. Table 6.4 shows the MACRS table for residential rental property. The rate is selected from the table according to the month in the taxpayer's tax year in which the property is placed in service.

EXAMPLE 21

Construction Corporation (a calendar-year taxpayer) purchases a rental apartment building on July 10 for \$120,000. Of this purchase price, \$20,000 is for the land and the remaining \$100,000 is for the building that is depreciated over 27½ years. As July is the seventh month of the taxpayer's year, the first-year depreciation rate is 1.667 percent. The depreciation deduction for the first year is \$1,667 (\$100,000 × 1.667%). The depreciation deduction is \$3,636 (\$100,000 × 3.636%) in the second year. The building will be completely depreciated in year 29 after the final year's depreciation of \$152 (\$100,000 × 0.152%) is claimed.

Table 6.5 shows the MACRS table for nonresidential real property.[21]

EXAMPLE 22

Crane Corporation (a calendar-year taxpayer) purchases a warehouse on December 6 for \$250,000. The value of the land is \$50,000. The remaining \$200,000 is for the building that is depreciated over 39 years. As December is the twelfth month of the taxpayer's year, the first-year depreciation rate is 0.107 percent. The first-year depreciation is \$214 (\$200,000 × 0.107%). The depreciation deduction is \$5,128 (\$200,000 × 2.564%) in the second year.

Similar to the half-year convention, the depreciation deduction for realty under the mid-month convention extends beyond 27½ and 39 tax years.

TABLE 6.4 **MACRS RATES FOR 27½-YEAR RESIDENTIAL RENTAL PROPERTY**[a]

MONTH	YEAR 1	YEARS 2–18	YEARS 19–27	YEAR 28	YEAR 29
1	3.485%	3.636%	3.637%	1.970%	0
2	3.182	3.636	3.637	2.273	0
3	2.879	3.636	3.637	2.576	0
4	2.576	3.636	3.637	2.879	0
5	2.273	3.636	3.637	3.182	0
6	1.970	3.636	3.637	3.485	0
7	1.667	3.636	3.637	3.636	0.152%
8	1.364	3.636	3.637	3.636	0.455
9	1.061	3.636	3.637	3.636	0.758
10	0.758	3.636	3.637	3.636	1.061
11	0.455	3.636	3.637	3.636	1.364
12	0.152	3.636	3.637	3.636	1.667

[a]*This table groups years 2–18 and 19–27 for simplicity in presentation. In some cases, this produces a rounding difference of .001 when compared with the official table.*

[21]Nonresidential real property placed in service before May 13, 1993, was depreciated over a 31½-year life.

TABLE 6.5 MACRS RATES FOR 39-YEAR NONRESIDENTIAL REAL PROPERTY

MONTH	YEAR 1	YEARS 2–39	YEAR 40
1	2.461%	2.564%	0.107%
2	2.247	2.564	0.321
3	2.033	2.564	0.535
4	1.819	2.564	0.749
5	1.605	2.564	0.963
6	1.391	2.564	1.177
7	1.177	2.564	1.391
8	0.963	2.564	1.605
9	0.749	2.564	1.819
10	0.535	2.564	2.033
11	0.321	2.564	2.247
12	0.107	2.564	2.461

Year of Disposition

Under MACRS, taxpayers must use the same averaging convention that applied at acquisition when an asset is not fully depreciated in the year of sale or disposition. When using the half-year convention, the cost recovery rate at disposition is one-half the annual rate. For the mid-quarter convention, depreciation is allowed only from the beginning of the year until the midpoint of the quarter in which the asset disposition takes place. For example, if a corporation disposes of mid-quarter property during its first quarter, depreciation is allowed only from the beginning of the year to the mid-point of the first quarter; only 1½ months/12 months depreciation of the total normal annual depreciation is allowed that year. For assets disposed of in the second, third, or fourth quarter, only 4½, 7½, or 10½ months depreciation is allowed, respectively.

Example 23

Ryan Corporation (a calendar-year taxpayer) purchased one asset, a computer, on June 1, year 1, for $20,000. Ryan uses the MACRS half-year averaging convention and claims $4,000 ($20,000 × 20%) depreciation in year 1 and $6,400 ($20,000 × 32%) depreciation in year 2. If Ryan sells the computer in year 3, it would be allowed a year-3 depreciation deduction of only $1,920 ($20,000 cost × 19.2% × ½). Alternatively, assume Ryan Corporation purchased the computer on December 7, year 1, and must use the mid-quarter convention. If Ryan sells the computer on July 17, year 3, its year-3 depreciation deduction is $2,850 ($20,000 cost × 22.8% year-3 mid-quarter rate × 7½ months/12 months). Depreciation is computed from the beginning of the tax year (January 1) to the midpoint of the quarter of disposition (August 15).

Similarly, for the mid-month convention for realty, the month in which a building is sold determines the percentage of the annual depreciation rate. Thus, depreciation is taken from the beginning of the year until the midpoint of the month in which the disposition takes place.

Example 24

Dylan Corporation (a calendar-year taxpayer) purchased an office building on April 25, year 1, for $1,200,000 of which $200,000 is for the cost of the land. If it sells the building on March 2, year 3, it claims a depreciation deduction in year 3 of $5,342 ($1,000,000 building cost × 2.564% year-3 mid-month rate × 2½ months/12 months). Depreciation is computed from the beginning of the tax year (January 1) to the midpoint of the month of disposition (March 15).

Alternative Depreciation System (ADS)

The **alternative depreciation system (ADS)** is computed using the straight-line method and applying the appropriate averaging convention. Although the recovery period for computers and automobiles is the same under ADS as under MACRS (5 years), the recovery periods for many other assets are longer than the MACRS recovery periods. For example, buses are assigned a 9-year life and realty (both residential and nonresidential) is assigned a 40-year life. Table 6.6 provides the straight-line depreciation percentages under ADS for 5- and 7-year property using the half-year convention.

The alternative depreciation system must be used for the following:[22]

- For certain *listed* property (listed property is discussed later in this chapter)
- In computing earnings and profits[23]
- For property financed with tax-exempt bonds
- For property used outside the United States
- For property used by a tax-exempt entity
- To compute the portion of depreciation treated as an alternative minimum tax (AMT) adjustment[24]

TAX PLANNING

Taxpayers with net operating losses may prefer using the straight-line method with a longer recovery period to reduce their losses; thus they may elect to use ADS.

Section 179 Expensing Election

Section 179 immediate expensing has a long history as an incentive specifically targeting small businesses. Prior to the passage of the Jobs and Growth Tax Relief and Reconciliation Act of 2003, the maximum annual amount that could be expensed by

TABLE **6.6** **ADS STRAIGHT-LINE (HALF-YEAR CONVENTION) FOR 5-YEAR AND 7-YEAR PERSONALTY**

RECOVERY YEAR	5-YEAR	7-YEAR
1	10.00%	7.14%
2	20.00	14.29
3	20.00	14.29
4	20.00	14.28
5	20.00	14.29
6	10.00	14.28
7		14.29
8		7.14

[22] § 168(g).

[23] If the ADS straight-line method is elected, separate depreciation records are not required for earnings and profits calculations. Refer to Chapter 9 for a discussion of earnings and profits.

[24] This AMT adjustment applies to personalty placed in service after December 31, 1998, if the 200 percent declining-balance method is used for regular tax purposes.

a taxpayer was $25,000. As part of a package of temporary incentives intended to stimulate a sluggish U.S. economy, the annual expensing limit was increased to $100,000 for 2003, $102,000 for 2004, $105,000 for 2005, $108,000 for 2006 and $125,000 for 2007.The Economic Stimulus Act of 2008 doubled that limit to $250,000 for 2008 where it remained through 2009. The Small Business Jobs Act of 2010 doubled that limit to $500,000 for 2010 and 2011 but the Tax Relief Act of 2010 reduced the limit to $139,000 for 2012. Then the American Taxpayer Relief Act of 2012 retroactively reinstated the $500,000 limit for 2012 and extended it through 2013. It is now scheduled to return to the pre-2003 level of $25,000 in 2014; however, it is possible that Congress will increase the 2014 limit.

Property eligible for immediate expensing includes both new and used tangible personalty and computer software; it does not apply to real property.[25] Each year, the taxpayer can elect to apply this provision to the acquisition cost of eligible property placed in service during that year. Property basis remaining after reducing it for the Section 179 deduction is subject to regular MACRS depreciation.

EXAMPLE 25

Sampson Corporation purchased $548,000 of used 5-year equipment in March 2013. Sampson can elect to expense $500,000 under Section 179. Regular MACRS depreciation on the balance will be $9,600 [($548,000 – $500,000 expensed) × 20% regular MACRS rate] resulting in total 2013 depreciation of $509,600. Sampson's 2014 depreciation expense for this equipment will be $15,360 [($548,000 – $500,000 expensed) × 32% regular MACRS rate]. Depreciation expense in 2015 will be $9,216 [($548,000 – $500,000 expensed) × 19.2% regular MACRS rate]; $5,530 [($548,000 – $500,000 expensed) × 11.52% regular MACRS rate] in 2016; $5,530 [($548,000 – $500,000 expensed) × 11.52% regular MACRS rate] in 2017; and $2,764 [($548,000 – $500,000 expensed) × 5.76% regular MACRS rate] in 2018.

For 2010 through 2013, taxpayers may elect to expense up to $250,000 of qualified leasehold improvements, qualified restaurant property, and qualified retail improvements.[26] After 2013, these types of property are no longer eligible for expensing under Section 179. Any property expensed under this provision must be included in the overall $500,000 expensing limit. No carryforward is allowed to years after 2013 for any unused special expensing of these properties.

EXAMPLE 26

In 2013, Alpha Corporation places in service $280,000 of equipment and $300,000 of qualified leasehold improvements. Alpha can expense no more than $250,000 of the cost of the leasehold improvements. For example, Alpha could elect to expense $250,000 of the leasehold improvements and $250,000 of the equipment. Alternatively, Alpha could expense all $280,000 of the equipment and use the remaining $220,000 of the Section 179 limit to expense the leasehold improvements. The basis remaining after Section 179 expensing can be depreciated using the regular MACRS depreciation rules applicable to that property.

Two other limitations, one based on cost and the other taxable income, may further restrict the amount expensed under Section 179 beyond the basic limitation. Because the expensing provision is intended to benefit only small businesses, a taxpayer that acquires over $2,000,000 of *qualifying* assets in 2013, must reduce the maximum annual limitation on a dollar-for-dollar basis for each dollar in excess of $2,000,000. If a taxpayer acquires and places in service more than $2,500,000 ($2,000,000 threshold + $500,000 Section 179 limit) of eligible assets, no Section 179 expensing is allowed. In determining this limitation, only assets eligible for

[25]Expensing is not available for assets used in investment activities, nor is it available for property acquired by gift, inheritance, or from a related party as defined in § 267. § 179(d)(1) and (2).

[26]Qualified leasehold improvement property is described in § 168(e)(6), qualified restaurant property is described in § 168(e)(7), and qualified retail improvement property is described in § 168(e)(8).

Section 179 expensing are considered; thus, buildings are left out of the computation. Any amount disallowed due to this cost limitation cannot be carried over to a future year. The annual Section 179 limits and phase-out ranges are summarized in Table 6.7.

EXAMPLE 27

Barnard Corporation purchases $2,300,000 used equipment in 2013. Its Section 179 expensing limitation for 2013 is reduced to $200,000 [$500,000 – ($2,300,000 – $2,000,000)]. If Barnard had purchased $2,500,000 or more equipment in 2013, it could not claim any Section 179 expensing for the year.

The amount expensed under Section 179 is also limited to the taxable income from the taxpayer's business, determined before the Section 179 expensing deduction (but after all regular depreciation).[27] If the taxpayer's taxable income limits the Section 179 deduction, the currently nondeductible portion may be carried to future taxable years; however, any carryforward does not increase the dollar expensing limit in the carryover year.

EXAMPLE 28

In 2013, Rocko Company had income of $10,000 before the Section 179 deduction. It purchased used equipment (7-year class) for $25,000. Rocko claimed $25,000 as a Section 179 deduction but deducted only $10,000 in 2013 due to the income limit. Rocko carries the excess $15,000 to 2014. The $15,000 carryover and any additional Section 179 expensing items will be subject to the 2014 expensing limit, however.

A taxpayer may choose to use all, part, or none of the annual Section 179 deduction. By electing to expense less than the maximum for a tax year, the taxpayer can avoid a Section 179 carryforward.

EXAMPLE 29

In August, Makai Corporation purchases $25,000 of used equipment in the 5-year class. Makai's income before considering the Section 179 deduction is $20,000. If Makai elects to expense only $18,750 under Section 179, it will depreciate the remaining $6,250 ($25,000 – $18,750) using regular MACRS depreciation ($6,250 × 20% = $1,250). Makai's total depreciation deduction is $20,000 ($18,750 under Section 179 + $1,250 regular MACRS depreciation), which equals its prededuction taxable income for the year. In the next year, Makai will claim regular MACRS depreciation of $2,000 ($6,250 × 32%) and it will be allowed the full expensing deduction for other equipment acquired in that year.

The $500,000 limit applies separately to each business entity (C corporation, S corporation, partnership) and to individual taxpayers. As flow-through entities, a portion

TABLE 6.7 **SECTION 179 ANNUAL LIMITS AND PHASE-OUT RANGES**

	ANNUAL LIMIT	PHASE-OUT RANGE
2009	$250,000	$800,000 - $1,050,000
2010-2013	$500,000	$2,000,000 - $2,500,000
2014	$25,000*	$200,000 - $225,000*

May be adjusted for inflation

[27] § 179(b)(3). A self-employed individual's taxable income is computed without regard to the deduction for one-half of self-employment taxes paid; if he or she is also an employee, wages and salary may be included in determining taxable income for purposes of this limitation.

of any Section 179 expensing deduction elected by an S corporation or partnership flows through to its owners and is deducted on the owner's tax return. This Section 179 deduction plus the individual's Section 179 deductions from all other sources cannot exceed the annual taxpayer limit. Any excess Section 179 deduction carries forward and can be deducted in future years (subject to the annual limits).

TAX PLANNING

An important consideration in maximizing the benefit of expensing occurs when multiple qualifying Section 179 assets are placed in service during the year. Generally, taxpayers try to maximize current deductions based on the time value of money. Expensing the asset with the longest class life generally maximizes the value of the Section 179 deduction. The use of Section 179 expensing can also alter the application of the mid-quarter convention, because amounts expensed under Section 179 are excluded from the test to determine if more than 40 percent of assets are placed in service in the last quarter of the year.

EXAMPLE 30

Tara Corporation (a calendar-year corporation) purchases two assets in 2013. The first is 5-year class used property purchased on September 23 for $500,000 and the second is 7-year class used property purchased on November 4 for $500,000. Both assets are eligible for Section 179 expensing. Tara would be better off expensing the 7-year class property rather than the 5-year class property because of the time value of money. Additionally, by expensing the 7-year class asset, it is eliminated from the 40 percent mid-quarter convention test and Tara avoids the application of the mid-quarter convention.

TAX PLANNING

When comparing the use of Section 179 to accelerate depreciation of 7-year property with its use to avoid the mid-quarter convention, preference should usually be given to avoiding the mid-quarter convention.

EXAMPLE 31

Assume the facts of the previous example, except that the 7-year class property was acquired in September and the 5-year property was acquired in November. Tara should expense just enough of the 5-year property to avoid application of the mid-quarter convention, using the balance to expense property with the 7-year life. $1,000,000 total assets acquired − $500,000 Section 179 expensing = $500,000 × 40% = $200,000 so less than $200,000 must be placed in service in the last quarter to avoid the mid-quarter convention. If $300,001 of the 5-year property and $199,999 ($500,000 − $300,001) of the 7-year property are expensed under Section 179, less than 40 percent [($500,000 − $300,001)/($1,000,000 − $300,001 − $199,999) = 39.99%] of acquired property is placed in service during the last quarter of the year, and the mid-quarter convention is not required. Thus, the maximum Section 179 expense deduction is claimed while avoiding the mid-quarter convention.

Bonus Depreciation

First-year **bonus depreciation** was introduced by the Job Creation and Worker Assistance Act of 2002 as an incentive for businesses to purchase *new* equipment to stimulate the economy after September 11, 2001. Initially, the bonus depreciation rate was 30 percent. The 2003 Act increased the bonus depreciation rate to 50 percent for property acquired after May 5, 2003 and extended its expiration date to qualifying property placed in service by December 31, 2004. With a few exceptions, bonus depreciation was not available from 2004 until the 2008 Economic Stimulus Act reinstated 50 percent bonus depreciation for one year.[28] The American Recovery and

[28]As an incentive to encourage rebuilding in areas hit by Hurricanes Katrina, Rita, and Wilma, the Gulf Opportunity Zone Act of 2005 allowed 50 percent bonus depreciation for assets acquired and placed in service after August 27, 2005 and before January 1, 2012. To qualify, the assets must have been used in the Gulf Opportunity Zone (the core disaster area) in the active conduct of the taxpayer's business. This version of bonus depreciation was much broader than the other versions in that nonresidential real property and residential rental property was eligible.

Reinvestment Act of 2009 extended bonus depreciation through 2009 and the Small Business Jobs Act of 2010 extended bonus depreciation into 2010. The Tax Relief Act of 2010 significantly modified bonus depreciation by temporarily increasing it to 100 percent for assets acquired after September 8, 2010 and before January 1, 2012 effectively allowing full expensing for eligible assets acquired during this period. The 100 percent bonus depreciation reverted to 50 percent bonus depreciation for 2012 and the American Taxation Relief Act of 2012 extended 50 percent bonus depreciation through 2013.[29]

Bonus depreciation applies only to new (not used) tangible personalty, software, and leasehold improvements. Any basis remaining after the reduction for the bonus depreciation is subject to regular MACRS depreciation. Realty and other assets with recovery periods greater than 20 years are not eligible for any bonus depreciation.[30] Unlike Section 179 expensing, bonus depreciation is not limited to small businesses, so there is no phase-out provision (or taxable income limitation). Regular MACRS depreciation can be claimed on the balance remaining after claiming the 50 percent bonus depreciation.

Example 32

On September 15, 2013, Menlo Corporation, a calendar-year corporation, purchases $3,000,000 of 7-year equipment. If this is used equipment, the allowable depreciation will be $428,700 ($3,000,000 × 14.29% regular MACRS rate) for 2013. If Menlo purchases new equipment, its allowable depreciation expense for 2013 will be $1,714,350, consisting of $1,500,000 for the 50 percent bonus depreciation ($3,000,000 × 50%) and $214,350 [($3,000,000 – $1,500,000 bonus) × 14.29%)] from regular MACRS.

When Section 179 expensing is elected, the expensed amount is deducted first before the bonus depreciation is computed; thus, the 50 percent bonus depreciation is sandwiched between the Section 179 expensing deduction and the regular MACRS depreciation deduction.

Example 33

On September 1, 2013, Molokai Corporation, a calendar-year corporation, purchased $1,800,000 of 5-year equipment and elected to expense $500,000 under Section 179. If this was used equipment, the maximum allowable depreciation would have been $760,000 consisting of $500,000 Section 179 expensing and $260,000 [($1,800,000 – $500,000) × 20%] regular MACRS for 2013; the 2014 depreciation would be $416,000 [($1,800,000 – $500,000) × 32%]. If Molokai purchased new equipment, its allowable depreciation expense for 2013 would be $1,280,000, consisting of $500,000 Section 179 expense, $650,000 [($1,800,000 – $500,000) × 50%] bonus depreciation and $130,000 [($1,800,000 – $500,000 – $650,000) × 20%] regular MACRS depreciation. Molokai's 2014 depreciation for this equipment would be $208,000 [($1,800,000 – $500,000 – $650,000) × 32%].

If the mid-quarter averaging convention is required for depreciation (because more than 40 percent of personalty is placed in service in the last quarter of the year), bonus depreciation can still be claimed.

Example 34

On November 23, 2013, Merlin Corporation, a calendar-year corporation, purchases $2,500,000 of new 7-year equipment. This is the only asset Merlin acquires during the year, so it is required to use the

[29] Under § 168(k)(4), corporations can elect to use ADS depreciation and forego bonus depreciation and accelerated depreciation in exchange for the current allowance, as refundable tax credits, of otherwise deferred research tax credits and alternative minimum tax (AMT) credits. For property placed in service after December 31, 2010, a corporation may elect to increase the AMT credit limitation (but not the research credit limitation) by bonus depreciation for purchases placed in service in 2011-2013.

[30] Property required to be depreciated using ADS is ineligible, but property for which ADS is elected could be eligible. Restaurant property and retail improvements are not eligible for bonus depreciation.

mid-quarter convention. Merlin's 2013 depreciation expense will be $1,294,625, consisting of $1,250,000 ($2,500,000 × 50%) bonus depreciation and $44,625 [($2,500,000 – $1,250,000) × 3.57%] regular MACRS depreciation. Merlin's 2014 depreciation will be $344,375 [($2,500,000 – $1,250,000) × 27.55%].

Unlike Section 179 expensing, there are no income limits for bonus depreciation; thus bonus depreciation can be claimed even in years when businesses have losses (similar to regular MACRS depreciation). Bonus depreciation applies to all eligible property unless the taxpayer elects to forego the deduction. A taxpayer might elect to forego the additional depreciation for one or more classes of assets in two situations: (1) when a business expects to be in a higher marginal tax bracket in future years and (2) when a business has expiring net operating losses.

Table 6.8 compares the types of property eligible for Section 179 expensing and bonus depreciation. Because bonus depreciation does not apply to used property, taxpayers are better off expensing used property before expensing new assets.

TAX PLANNING

Provisions Limiting Depreciation

Mixed-Use Assets

If an asset is used for both business and personal purposes, depreciation is permitted for the business-use or investment-use portion only.

Example 35

Julio purchases a computer for $5,000 on March 1. He uses the computer as follows: 70 percent for business, 20 percent for managing investments, and 10 percent for personal use. Julio will use a basis of $3,500 ($5,000 × 70% business use) for computing business depreciation and an investment basis of $1,000 ($5,000 × 20% investment use) for computing depreciation on the investment portion of the asset. No depreciation is allowed for the $500 ($5,000 × 10%) personal-use portion.

No depreciation deductions are permitted beyond the end of the cost recovery period even though there is unrecovered basis related to the personal use of the asset. For business purposes, the asset is considered fully depreciated.[31]

Limitations are imposed on MACRS deductions for listed properties readily used for both business and personal purposes, including passenger automobiles, comput-

TABLE 6.8 **COMPARISON OF SECTION 179 AND BONUS DEPRECIATION**

	SECTION 179 EXPENSING	BONUS DEPRECIATION
Eligible purchased property	Both new and used	Only new
Property that must use ADS	Ineligible	Ineligible
Property acquired after 2013	Eligible	Ineligible
Elective	Must elect to claim	Elect out if not claiming
Phase-out limits	Yes	No

[31] § 280F(d)(2); Temp. Regs. § 1.280F-4T(a)(1).

ers and peripheral equipment, and other personal and business-use property used for entertainment, amusement, or recreation.[32] The **listed property** rules require the taxpayer to substantiate the percentage of time an asset is used for business. If the property is used predominantly for business (more than 50 percent is business use), the taxpayer uses the MACRS tables to determine depreciation expense for the business portion of the property's use. If, however, business use is 50 percent or less, the ADS straight-line depreciation method is required and neither Section 179 expensing nor bonus depreciation may be claimed. The portion of time that the property is used for investment purposes rather than in a trade or business does not count toward meeting the more-than-50 percent threshold, and the actual depreciation claimed must reflect a reduction for nonbusiness use. Once a taxpayer is required to use ADS depreciation because business use does not exceed 50 percent, ADS depreciation must continue to be used in all future years, even if business use subsequently exceeds 50 percent.

EXAMPLE 36

Elisa purchases a computer for $8,000 on July 24. If Elisa uses the computer 40 percent of the time for business, 25 percent to manage her portfolio of investments, and 35 percent of the time for personal use, she must use the ADS straight-line method to calculate her depreciation because her business use does not exceed 50 percent. Elisa's first-year depreciation deduction is $520 ($8,000 × 10% ADS rate × 65% business and investment use). In the second year, Elisa increases her business use of the computer to 70 percent, decreasing personal use to only 5 percent. Elisa must continue computing her depreciation using the ADS straight-line method for that asset. Elisa's second-year depreciation deduction is $1,520 ($8,000 × 20% ADS rate × 95% business and investment use).

TAX PLANNING

Any computer or peripheral equipment used exclusively at a regular business and owned or leased by the person or entity operating the establishment is exempt from classification as listed property. This means that taxpayers who use computers exclusively at a business office, including a qualifying home office, do not have to keep documentation to meet the substantiation requirements because those requirements are automatically assumed to be met.

KEY CASES *A taxpayer claimed a deduction for his home office and depreciated the computer he kept in that office. The home office deduction was disallowed because he did not meet the necessary requirements. The Tax Court then disallowed the depreciation deduction for the computer because the taxpayer failed to maintain records as to the time and business purpose of the computer use.*[33]

In another case, however, the taxpayers were exempted from the substantiation requirements for their computer because the home office requirements were met.[34]

Reduction in Business Use

If the business use decreases to 50 percent or less, a portion of the depreciation previously claimed must be *recaptured* (included in ordinary income). The amount that must be recaptured is the excess of depreciation deducted (including any Section 179 expensing) over the alternative straight-line depreciation deduction.[35]

EXAMPLE 37

Martina purchased a computer on April 29, year 1, for $10,000. She used the computer 90 percent of the time for business in years 1 and 2 and claimed only regular MACRS depreciation. In year 3, she uses the computer only 45 percent for business. Because the business-use percentage is only 45 percent in year 3, Martina must add (recapture) $1,980 to ordinary income in year 3. The $1,980 is the difference between the $4,680 MACRS

[32]§ 280F(d)(4).

[33]Verma, TC Memo 2001-132, RIA TC Memo ¶2001-132, 81 CCH TCM 1720.

[34]Zeidler, TC Memo 1996-157, RIA TC Memo ¶96157, 71 CCH TCM 2603.

[35]§ 280F(b)(3).

depreciation she claimed [$1,800 in year 1 ($10,000 × 90% × 20%) and $2,880 in year 2 ($10,000 × 90% × 32%)] and the alternative straight-line depreciation of $2,700 [$900 for year 1 ($10,000 × 90% × 10%) and $1,800 for year 2 ($10,000 × 90% × 20%)] for those years. She deducts straight-line depreciation of $900 (10,000 × 45% × 20%) in year 3 and continues straight-line depreciation in years 4, 5, and 6, even if the business use again exceeds 50 percent.

If Martina had expensed the computer under Section 179 in year 1, in year 3 she would have to recapture the $6,300 ($9,000 Section 179 expensing for the 90% business use less the $2,700 ADS depreciation) excess expensed over the alternative straight-line depreciation for the first two years and then would claim ADS straight-line depreciation each year it continued to be used for business.

Additional Requirements for Employees

Employee-owned property that is used for business cannot be depreciated unless it satisfies two tests. First, the use of the employee's property must be for the convenience of the employer and, second, the use of the property must be required as a condition of employment. Generally, these tests are interpreted to mean that a deduction is allowed only when the employee relieves the employer of providing an asset that is required to perform his or her job.

EXAMPLE 38

Carol owns a personal computer that is compatible with the computers used at work. Her employer has hired additional staff but does not have sufficient space and computers for all of them. Because Carol is a trusted employee with a compatible computer, her employer asks her to work out of her home on her own computer. Carol can depreciate the computer because its use in her job is for her employer's convenience. If Carol had a computer available but asked her employer if she could work at home, she would have no deduction because working at home is for her convenience.

Limits for Passenger Vehicles

Automobiles are subject to more restrictive rules than those that apply to other depreciable assets.[36] The Economic Stimulus Act of 2008 increased the ceiling limits by $8,000 for new vehicles eligible for the 50 percent bonus depreciation; used vehicles were only eligible for the base limits. The additional $8,000 for bonus depreciation has been extended by the Tax Relief Act through 2013 for new vehicles. Note that taxpayers cannot circumvent these automobile ceiling limits through either Section 179 expensing or 50 percent bonus depreciation. The ceiling limits shown in Table 6.9 cap

TABLE **6.9** **CEILING LIMITS FOR AUTOMOBILES**

YEAR	WITHOUT BONUS DEPRECIATION	WITH BONUS DEPRECIATION
1	$3,160	$11,160
2	5,100	5,100
3	3,050	3,050
4 and thereafter	1,875	1,875

Note: All limits assume 100% business use. Limits must be reduced by any personal use.

[36]A passenger automobile is any four-wheeled vehicle that is manufactured primarily for use on public streets, roads, and highways, and which is rated at 6,000 pounds unloaded gross vehicle weight or less. § 280F(d)(5).

the total depreciation (including Section 179 expensing) that can be claimed on passenger vehicles.[37] A used automobile can cost up to $15,800 before the $3,160 ceiling limit takes effect.

Example 39

Kendrick, a calendar-year corporation, purchased two automobiles in June: one is a used car costing $14,500 and the other is a new car costing $60,000. Both cars are used exclusively for business. The first year's depreciation for the used car is $2,900, the lesser of the regular MACRS depreciation of $2,900 ($14,500 × 20%) and the ceiling limit of $3,160. The first year's depreciation for the new car is $11,160 due to the bonus depreciation. By electing Section 179 expensing, the first year's depreciation for the used car could be increased by $160 (from $2,900 to the $3,160 ceiling); however, electing Section 179 for the new car would not increase depreciation. If Kendrick has other assets that qualify for Section 179 expensing, it should elect to expense those other assets up to the allowable limit rather than waste it on the automobiles.

In future years, depreciation for the cars will continue to be determined using the lesser of regular MACRS depreciation and the ceiling limit. At the end of 6 years, the $14,500 car will be fully depreciated while it will take an additional 19 years (at the rate of $1,875 per year) to fully depreciate the $60,000 car.

Separate higher ceiling limits apply to trucks and vans that weigh no more than 6,000 pounds. These limits are shown in Table 6.10.

TAX PLANNING

Vehicles, such as heavy sport utility vehicles (SUVs) weighing more than 6,000 pounds, were originally excluded from the ceiling limits, allowing their cost to be fully expensed in the year of purchase by electing Section 179.[38] In 2004, Congress partially closed this loophole by limiting Section 179 expensing to $25,000 for SUVs weighing up to 14,000 pounds with any excess depreciated using the regular MACRS rates. SUVs weighing 6,000 pounds or less continue to be subject to the vehicle ceiling limits.

Example 40

On August 28, 2013 Beta Corporation purchased a new heavy SUV for $40,000. Beta can expense only the first $25,000 under Section 179 and can then claim $7,500 [($40,000 – $25,000) × 50%] for bonus depreciation and $1,500 [($40,000 – $25,000 – $7,500) × 20%] for regular MACRS depreciation for a total depreciation deduction of $34,000.

If the car is used less than 100 percent in a trade or business, the annual limitations must be reduced accordingly.

TABLE 6.10 **CEILING LIMITS FOR TRUCKS AND VANS**

YEAR	WITHOUT BONUS DEPRECIATION	WITH BONUS DEPRECIATION
1	$3,360	$11,360
2	5,400	5,400
3	3,250	3,250
4 and thereafter	1,975	1,975

Note: All limits assume 100% business use. Limits must be reduced by any personal use.

[37] Rev. Proc. 2013-21, 2013-12 IRB 660. The limits for automobiles placed in service in 2012 were the same.

[38] Other vehicles excluded from the Section 280F restrictions include taxicabs, rental trucks, ambulances, and hearses used in a trade or business.

EXAMPLE 41

In April, Julie purchases a new automobile for $30,000 to use primarily in her sole proprietorship. In the first year, she drives 70 percent of the miles for business and 90 percent of the miles she drives in the second year are for business. Julie's depreciation deduction for the first year is $7,812 ($11,160 limit × 70%) and for the second year is $4,590 ($5,100 × 90%).The personal-use portion of the car's cost will never be depreciated.

If an employee uses an employer's auto for personal use but the employee is taxed on the value of that use as income, the employer's qualified business use is considered 100 percent of total use and the employer is entitled to claim 100 percent of the allowable depreciation deduction.[39]

EXAMPLE 42

Sara, a salesperson for Monitor Corporation, purchases a used car for $22,000 that she uses 80 percent for business and 20 percent for personal purposes. Her first-year depreciation is limited to $2,528, the lesser of regular MACRS depreciation [($22,000 × 80% business use × 20% = $3,520 regular MACRS depreciation) or the ceiling limit ($3,160 × 80% business use = $2,528)]. If Monitor purchases the car for Sara and treats her personal use as taxable fringe benefit income, Monitor's qualified business use of the car is 100 percent and it can claim a full first-year depreciation allowance of $3,160.

Figure 6.1 illustrates the steps for computing the amount of basis eligible for claiming the various types of depreciation. Note, however, that when calculating the income limit for Section 179 expensing, all other depreciation, except the Section 179 expensing, must be deducted first to determine this income limitation.

Automobile Leasing

Taxpayers who lease autos can deduct the business portion of their lease payments. To prevent taxpayers from taking advantage of the difference between lease payments and the limit on depreciation deductions for automobiles, taxpayers must add a **lease inclusion** amount determined from IRS tables to their income.[40] The dollar amount of the inclusion is based on the fair market value of the automobile and is prorated for the number of days the automobile is leased. This lease inclusion factor replaces the depreciation ceiling limits that apply to car buyers. Table 6.11 shows a portion of this lease inclusion table.

FIGURE 6.1 **STEPS FOR COMPUTING DEPRECIATION**

1. Determine basis
2. Multiply basis by business-use percentage to determine depreciable basis
3. Subtract Section 179 expensing (if elected) from depreciable basis
4. Calculate bonus depreciation on adjusted basis (after Section 179 expensing) and subtract from adjusted basis (or elect not to claim)
5. Calculate regular MACRS depreciation on remaining basis
6. If a passenger vehicle, compare to applicable ceiling limit (adjusted for any personal use) and deduct the lesser of depreciation or ceiling limit.

[39]Personal use of a company car by a more-than-5 percent owner of a business or someone related to the owner is never qualified business use for MACRS depreciation.

[40]Reg. §1.280T (a). The complete lease inclusion tables for leases commencing in 2013 are included in Rev. Proc. 2013-21, 2013-12 IRB 660.

TABLE
6.11 PARTIAL TABLE OF LEASE INCLUSION AMOUNTS FOR AUTOMOBILES

FAIR MARKET VALUE OF AUTO	YEAR 1	YEAR 2	YEAR 3	YEAR 4	YEAR 5 AND LATER YEARS
Up to $19,000	0	0	0	0	0
$19,001–$19,500	$2	$4	$6	$7	$8
$19,501-$20,000	2	5	6	9	9
$24,001-$25,000	5	10	15	18	21
$29,001-$30,000	7	16	24	29	33
$39,001-$40,000	13	28	42	49	58
$49,001-$50,000	18	40	59	71	82
$59,001-$60,000	24	52	76	92	106
$78,001-$80,000	34	75	111	133	154
$95,001-$100,000	44	97	144	172	199

EXAMPLE 43

On April 12, Carrie leases an automobile worth $80,000. The lease period is five years. During the first year, Carrie uses the automobile 70 percent for business and 30 percent for personal use. The IRS lease inclusion table amount is $34 for the first year and $75 for the second year. Carrie must include $17 [$34 × (263 days leased/365 days in year) × 70% business use] in income for the first year and can deduct 70 percent of the lease payments. If Carrie continues to use the automobile 70 percent for business, she includes $53 ($75 × 70% business use) in income for the second year and deducts 70 percent of the lease payments.

TAX PLANNING

The lease inclusion amount is relatively small in early years and increases in the later years of the lease. This makes short-term leases potentially more attractive than longer leases. Using present value concepts, taxpayers can compare the after-tax cost of leasing versus buying.

EXAMPLE 44

A corporation can buy a new car for business use for $25,000 (including tax, license, and title fees) or it can lease an identical car for $250 per month, paying $2,000 up front for tax, license, and title fees. (This $2,000 must be amortized over the term of the lease.) The corporation normally keeps its cars for three years and, if purchased, expects that it will be able to sell the car at the end of three years for $8,000. At that time, its adjusted basis will be $5,690 ($25,000 – $19,310 depreciation deductions), so the sale will result in a $2,310 taxable gain. The corporation is in the 35 percent tax bracket and uses a 6 percent discount rate for evaluation purposes. (For simplicity, the monthly rental fees are assumed to be paid at the end of years 1, 2, and 3.)

If purchased, the after-tax cost of the car is $12,790.

YEAR	DEPRECIATION DEDUCTIONS	TAXABLE GAIN ON SALE	TOTAL DEDUCTIONS	TAX RATE	TAX SAVINGS
1	$11,160		$11,160	35%	$3,906
2	5,100		5,100	35%	1,785
3	3,050	$2,310	740	35%	259
	$19,310				$5,950

YEAR	PAYMENT AND SALES PROCEEDS	TAX SAVINGS	CASH FLOW	DISCOUNT FACTOR	PRESENT VALUE
0	$(25,000)		$(25,000)		$(25,000)
1		$3,906	3,906	.943	3,683
2		1,785	1,785	.890	1,589
3	8,000	259	8,259	.840	6,938
					$(12,790)

If leased, the after-tax cost is only $6,597.

YEAR	DEDUCTION FOR PAYMENTS	LEASE INCLUSION	NET TAX DEDUCTION	TAX RATE	TAX SAVINGS
1	$3,667*	$(5)	$3,662	35%	$1,282
2	3,667*	(10)	3,657	35%	1,280
3	3,667*	(15)	3,652	35%	1,278
					$3,840

**$3,000 + (⅓ × $2,000)*

YEAR	PAYMENTS	TAX SAVINGS	CASH FLOW	DISCOUNT FACTOR	PRESENT VALUE
0	$(2,000)		$(2,000)		$(2,000)
1	(3,000)	$1,282	(1,718)	.943	(1,620)
2	(3,000)	1,280	(1,720)	.890	(1,531)
3	(3,000)	1,278	(1,722)	.840	(1,446)
					$(6,597)

It will cost the corporation $6,193 less to lease than to purchase ($12,790 – $6,597).

DEPLETION

The cost of minerals, other natural resources, and timber are recovered through **depletion**. Depletion deductions on certain natural resources are calculated using either cost depletion or percentage depletion, and taxpayers claim the greater of the two amounts for qualifying property. The choice between cost and percentage depletion is an annual election. Thus, cost depletion may be used in one year and percentage depletion may be used in the following year.

The **cost depletion** method is similar to the units-of-production method of depreciation. Depletion per unit is calculated by dividing the adjusted basis of the asset by the estimated recoverable units of the asset (such as tons or barrels). Cost depletion is determined by multiplying the depletion per unit by the number of units sold (not the units produced) during the year. Under cost depletion, total deductions cannot exceed the taxpayer's cost basis in the property.

EXAMPLE 45

On January 1, year 1, Striker Oil Company purchases the mineral rights to an oil well for $100,000. At the date of purchase, the well is expected to produce 20,000 barrels of oil. The depletion per unit is $5/barrel ($100,000 cost/20,000 estimated recoverable barrels). During year 1, 6,000 barrels of oil are produced and sold. The cost depletion deduction for year 1 is $30,000 (6,000 barrels × $5 per barrel). During year 2, 6,000 barrels of oil are produced, but only 3,000 are sold. The cost depletion for year 2 is $15,000 (3,000 barrels sold × $5 per barrel).

Percentage depletion uses percentage rates specified in the Internal Revenue Code. These rates vary from 5 to 22 percent, depending on the type of resource being mined or refined. Following are some examples:

Uranium and sulphur	22%
Copper, gold, silver, oil, and gas	15%
Limestone, marble, slate	14%
Coal	10%
Gravel, sand	5%

TAX PLANNING

Percentage depletion is calculated as a specified percentage of gross income from the property and is unrelated to the property's cost. Percentage depletion continues as long as revenue is generated, even if the costs of acquiring and developing the property have been fully recovered. Thus, when percentage depletion is used, it is possible to deduct more than the original cost of the property, but the adjusted basis of the property is only reduced to zero. The percentage depletion deduction in any year cannot exceed the net income from the property before the deduction, however.[41] By permitting deductions far in excess of their actual investment, the government provides an incentive for companies to continue to make the investment necessary to extract essential natural resources.

Example 46

Kevin purchases a royalty interest in an oil well for $112,000. Kevin's share of the gross income from the sale of oil for the year is $35,000. His share of the expenses related to the production of the oil is $10,000. His share of the taxable income before considering the depletion deduction is $25,000 ($35,000 gross income – $10,000 expenses). The percentage depletion deduction is $5,250 (15% × $35,000), which is less than his taxable income. The adjusted basis of Kevin's investment is reduced to $106,750 ($112,000 cost – $5,250 depletion expense).

Intangible drilling and development costs (IDC) are costs associated with the development of oil and gas properties such as the cost of labor to clear the property, erect derricks, and drill the well. These costs generally have no salvage value and are lost if the well is dry. At the taxpayer's option, the IDCs can be deducted fully as an expense in the year incurred, or they can be capitalized and deducted through depletion.

TAX PLANNING

If the percentage depletion deduction exceeds cost depletion, capitalization of the IDC does not provide a benefit to the taxpayer because percentage depletion is not calculated on the property's basis; thus, a deduction for the IDCs could be lost if they are capitalized. Expensing IDCs permits the taxpayer to deduct them entirely in the current year plus claim the percentage depletion.[42] By allowing an immediate deduction for IDCs, the government in effect reduces the cost of dry holes and provides an incentive for oil producers to drill for new oil wells.

Amortization

The cost of intangible assets generally is recovered through **amortization** if the intangible asset has a determinable life that can be established with reasonable accuracy.[43] As a result of the determinable life requirement, intangible assets are grouped into three categories: (1) intangibles with a perpetual life that cannot be amortized, (2) 15-year intangibles acquired as part of a business purchase (called Section 197

[41]The percentage depletion deduction cannot be more than 50 percent (100 percent for oil and gas property) of taxable income from the property computed without the depletion deductions.

[42]The taxpayer makes the election in the first year the expenditures are incurred by either taking a deduction on the tax return or by adding them to the basis for depletion. Whichever option the taxpayer chooses, it is binding on the taxpayer for similar future expenditures.

[43]Reg. §1.167(a)-3.

assets), and (3) intangibles amortizable over a life other than 15 years. Assets in the first category include equity investments such as stock and partnership interests, and they are not amortizable. Basis is recovered only upon disposition of the asset. The rest of this discussion focuses on the other two categories.

When a business is purchased, the purchase price frequently is more than the value of the separate assets. Fair market value is allocated to and becomes the basis for each asset. The purchase price in excess of value allocated to the tangible assets is an intangible asset, most often classified as goodwill. Prior to 1993, disputes frequently arose over whether an intangible asset such as a covenant-not-to-compete (an amortizable asset) was separate and distinct from goodwill and going-concern value (at that time a non-amortizable asset). In 1993, Congress added Section 197, which treats most intangible assets (including franchise rights) acquired in connection with the purchase of a business as amortizable over a 15-year period using the straight-line method. The 15-year recovery period applies regardless of the actual useful life of the Section 197 intangible asset.

EXAMPLE 47

ABC Company acquires all the assets of XYZ Company for $3 million. On the purchase date, the appraisal values of the assets acquired by ABC were:

ASSET	APPRAISED VALUE
Supplies	$ 50,000
Inventory	950,000
Furniture and fixtures	1,400,000
Covenant-not-to-compete for 5 years	200,000
	$2,600,000

ABC will use the appraised value as its basis for each asset. The $400,000 difference between the purchase price and the fair market value of the appraised assets is considered goodwill. ABC will recover its basis in these assets as follows:

ASSET	BASIS RECOVERY
Supplies	Deducted as consumed
Inventory	Deducted through cost of goods sold
Furniture and fixtures	Deducted through MACRS depreciation
Covenant-not-to-compete	Deducted through amortization over 15 years
Goodwill	Deducted through amortization over 15 years

Note that the covenant-not-to-compete, which prohibits the former owner from establishing a similar business in the same area for 5 years, must be amortized over 15 years (not the 5-year duration of the agreement not to compete).

Patents and copyrights acquired separately rather than as part of the purchase of an entire business are amortized over the expected legal life of the asset instead of the 15-year statutory amortization period. Other intangibles, acquired independently of the purchase of a complete trade or business (for example, a customer list), can be amortized if a definite and limited life can be established.

EXAMPLE 48

Blazing Computers Corporation purchases a patent on a computer chip from Smartchip Corporation. Blazing pays $600,000 for the patent. No other assets of Smartchip Corporation are included in the purchase. Because the patent has a remaining legal life of 17 years, the annual amortization deduction for the patent is $35,294 ($600,000/17 years).

Research and Experimentation Expenditures

Regulation Section 1.174–2(a) defines research and experimentation expenditures as costs incident to obtaining a patent, and costs for development of an experimental or pilot model, formula, invention, or similar property. Research and experimentation expenditures do not include expenditures for the ordinary testing or inspection of products for quality control or those for efficiency surveys, management studies, consumer surveys, advertising, or promotions.

Three alternatives are available for handling research and experimentation expenditures:

1. Expense them in full in the year paid or incurred.
2. Amortize them over a period of not less than 60 months.
3. Capitalize them.

TAX PLANNING

If the costs are capitalized, a deduction is not allowed until the research project becomes worthless or is abandoned. Because many products resulting from research projects do not have a definite useful life, either of the first two choices is usually preferable to the third. Usually a taxpayer will elect to immediately expense the research expenditures because of the time value of money. By allowing an immediate deduction, the government provides an incentive for businesses to conduct basic research.

EXAMPLE 49

Medtronics Corporation began work on a new experimental project in year 1. It incurred $10,000 in qualifying research expenses in year 1 and $12,000 in year 2. The benefits from the project are realized beginning June 1 of year 3. If Medtronics Corporation elects a 60-month amortization period, there is no deduction prior to June of year 3. The deduction for year 3 is $2,567 ($22,000 research expenditures × 7 months/60 months). If Medtronics Corporation elects to expense the research expenditures, it deducts $10,000 in year 1 and $12,000 in year 2.

Software

The cost of acquiring off-the-shelf software is deducted on a straight-line basis over 36 months, beginning in the month the software is placed in service.[44] It is also eligible for Section 179 expensing and bonus depreciation.

EXAMPLE 50

In June 2013, JM Corporation purchased $130,000 of off-the-shelf software. If none of its cost is expensed, the first year's deduction is $25,278 [($130,000/36 months) × 7 months]. Alternatively, the entire amount could be expensed under Section 179.

TAX PLANNING

If software is purchased with hardware (bundled software), the cost of the software is depreciated as part of the hardware cost unless the software cost is separately stated.[45] Thus, making sure that the cost of bundled software is separately stated can provide a faster write off.

If software is leased, the lessee can deduct the lease payment as a business expense. If the cost of developing computer software is considered research and development, then it can be either expensed in the year the costs are incurred or amortized over 60 months beginning with the month in which the taxpayer first realizes benefits from the expenditure.

REVISITING THE INTRODUCTORY CASE

If the proposed additional used furniture purchase is made in December, Windom Corporation's depreciation for the current year will *decrease* by $533,742. Thus, the proposed purchase should be deferred until January.

[44]Off-the-shelf software is software that is readily available to the general public, subject to a nonexclusive license and not substantially modified.

[45]Rev. Proc. 2000-50, 2000-2 CB 601.

If the proposed furniture purchase is postponed until the next year, (that is, not made in December), the total depreciation deduction for the current year is $855,781 computed as follows:

New automobile	limited to $3,160 base + $8,000 bonus	$ 11,160
New computer equipment	($300,000 × 50% bonus depreciation = $150,000) + [($300,000 – $150,000 bonus) × 20% = $30,000] =	180,000
Used office furniture	$652,000 × 14.29% =	93,171
Used office fixtures	$500,000 Sec. 179 expense + [($1,000,000 – $500,000) × 14.29% = $71,450] =	571,450
Total depreciation		$855,781

By electing to expense $500,000 of the used office fixtures under Section 179, the mid-quarter convention can be avoided.

Total depreciation will decrease if the additional used office furniture is placed in service in December. Windom will not be eligible for Section 179 expensing because its asset purchases now total $2,500,000. The mid-quarter convention will be required because more than 40 percent of personalty will be placed in service in the last quarter of the year [($500,000 additional furniture + $1,000,000 used fixtures)/$2,500,000 total assets = 60%].

If the proposed purchase of used furniture were made in December, the depreciation for the assets using the mid-quarter convention would be as follows:

New automobile	limited to $3,160 base amount + $8,000 bonus	$ 11,160
New computer equipment	($300,000 × 50% bonus depreciation = $150,000) + [($300,000 – $150,000 bonus) × 25% = $37,500] =	187,500
Used office furniture	$652,000 × 10.71% =	69,829
Used office fixtures	$1,000,000 × 3.57% =	35,700
Subtotal		$304,189
Proposed additional used office furniture	$500,000 × 3.57%	17,850
Total depreciation		$322,039

The $322,039 total depreciation is $533,742 less than the amount ($855,781) that would be allowed under the regular half-year convention with Section 179 expensing. Therefore, Windom Corporation should postpone the purchase of the additional used office furniture until January. Additionally, some of the furniture purchased next year may be eligible for Section 179 expensing depending on the value of other assets purchased in that year.

SUMMARY

The method and timing of the cost recovery deductions used for tax reporting affect the after-tax cost of an asset. As a general rule, the earlier the taxpayer can recover the cost of an asset through depreciation deductions, the greater the present value of the tax savings and the lower the net after-tax cost of the asset.

MACRS assigns assets to a class with a predetermined recovery period. The 5-year and 7-year classes are the most common for personalty, and the 27½-year and 39-year classes are the most common for realty. Most personalty is depreciated using the 200 percent declining-balance method, while realty is depreciated using the straight-line method. A half-year convention applies to personalty; however, if more than 40 percent of all personalty placed in service during the year enters service in the last quarter of the tax year, the mid-quarter convention must be used. A mid-month convention applies to depreciable realty.

Bonus depreciation allows the immediate expensing of 50 percent of qualifying new personalty for 2013. The Section 179 incentive tax provision allows immediate expensing of up to $500,000 of qualified new or used personalty with the remaining basis deductible using regular MACRS depreciation. It is important to understand the limitations of any incentive provisions and their interplay with regular MACRS depreciation deductions to maximize the value of tax savings from cost recovery deductions.

Significant limits apply to tax depreciation deductions for certain assets that are most likely to be used for both business and personal purposes, such as automobiles and computers. Depreciation deductions for automobiles are subject to ceiling limits, and assets that are not used more than 50 percent for business can only be depreciated using the straight-line method. It is important to be aware of these limitations and to make the best use of allowable depreciation deductions within these limits.

The cost of intangible assets is recovered through amortization deductions using the straight-line method over 15 years for most intangibles acquired in connection with the purchase of a business. The cost of natural resources is recovered through depletion. Taxpayers can claim the greater of cost depletion or percentage depletion; the choice is an annual election. Percentage depletion, under which it is possible to deduct more than the original investment, is one way the government provides an incentive for companies to continue to make the investment necessary to extract essential natural resources.

KEY TERMS

TEST YOURSELF

ANSWERS APPEAR AFTER THE PROBLEM ASSIGNMENTS

1. Maria received some Mega Corporation stock as a gift from her Uncle Glen two years ago when it had a fair market value of $90,000. Glen paid $60,000 for the stock five years ago, and he paid $3,000 in gift taxes when he made the gift to Maria. What is Maria's basis for the stock?
   - **a.** $60,000
   - **b.** $61,000
   - **c.** $63,000
   - **d.** $90,000
   - **e.** $93,000
2. Ricardo purchased a personal computer for $3,000 two years ago. He used the computer exclusively for personal use until this year. In the

current year, when the computer is worth $1,000, Ricardo begins using it exclusively in his sole proprietorship. What basis must Ricardo use in calculating his depreciation on the computer?

a. $3,000
b. $2,000
c. $1,000
d. $0

3. Probest Corporation (a calendar-year corporation) purchased and placed in service the following assets during 2013:

DATE	ASSET	COST
March 4	New automobile	$39,000
May 23	Warehouse	$900,000
October 1	Used office furniture	$525,000

All assets are used 100 percent for business use. $100,000 of the cost of the warehouse property is allocated to the cost of the land. The corporation has $1,000,000 in income from operations before calculating depreciation deductions. Probest is willing to make any necessary elections to claim the maximum depreciation. What is Probest's total depreciation for the year?

a. $163,793
b. $527,573
c. $577,186
d. $584,105

4. On October 2, 2013, Bedrock Corporation (a calendar-year corporation) acquires and places into service 7-year used business equipment costing $880,000. No other acquisitions are made during the year. The depreciation for 2013 (rounded to the nearest dollar) is

a. $513,566
b. $555,366
c. $696,783
d. $717,683

5. In May 2012, Jose purchased a used automobile for $12,000 and used it 75 percent for business. No Section 179 election was made for this asset. In 2013, Jose's business use of the automobile decreases to 45 percent. As a result of this change in business use

a. there is no change in the way Jose computes his 2013 depreciation.
b. Jose's depreciation in 2013 is $2,250.
c. Jose must recapture $900 as ordinary income in 2013.
d. Jose must amend the 2012 tax return and recompute depreciation.

PROBLEM ASSIGNMENTS

CHECK YOUR UNDERSTANDING

1. Linda inherited a car from her Uncle Ted. Ted purchased the car two years ago for $38,000. The car had a value of $30,000 at the date of Ted's death. What is Linda's basis for the car? Linda's basis is $30,000, the fair market value at the date of death.

2. Cynthia, a sole proprietor, has incurred a loss this year and would like to claim no depreciation this year and then take double depreciation next year. Can she elect to do this?

3. What limits are placed on the amount and type of property that can be expensed under Section 179? Compare the characteristics of Section 179 expensing to bonus depreciation.

4. What averaging conventions exist under MACRS? How does a taxpayer determine which averaging convention should be used?

5. Delta Corporation purchased three assets during 2013: a new automobile costing $60,000, used office furniture costing $600,000, and a warehouse costing $850,000 (of which $100,000 is for the land). Which asset(s) should Delta Corporation elect Section 179 expensing for and why?

6. Carl purchases a Jaguar automobile for $60,000. Carl plans to use the automobile exclusively in his business and boasts that he intends to recover his cost through MACRS depreciation deductions over five years. What restrictions have been imposed to reduce the tax benefits of purchasing a luxury automobile for business use? Explain how the restrictions work. Will he be able to circumvent these restrictions by leasing the vehicle?

7. An employee uses her employer's auto 75 percent for business use and 25 percent for personal use. The personal use is taxed to her as income. What percentage of the auto can the employer consider used for business and depreciate? Will your answer change if the employee's business use decreases to only 35 percent?

8. Why would a business elect to use the ADS straight-line method to compute regular income tax depreciation rather than the 200 percent declining-balance method allowed under MACRS?

9. Indicate whether a taxpayer could claim deductions for depreciation or amortization for the following:
   a. Land used in the taxpayer's ranching business.
   b. An automobile used in business. The taxpayer accounts for the deductible car expenses using the standard mileage rate.
   c. The costs attributable to goodwill and a covenant-not-to-compete.

10. Why is the Section 179 expensing election more valuable to a small business than to a large business?

11. What additional tests must employee-owned property satisfy before it is eligible for depreciation?

12. RCL Corporation is negotiating with Royal Corporation to acquire a patent that has nine years remaining on its legal life. RCL can either purchase the patent for $50,000 or purchase all of the assets for Royal Corporation for $500,000, including the patent. Discuss how amortization of the patent will be handled under each alternative.

13. Explain the difference between cost depletion and percentage depletion.

14. What are IDCs and how are they treated for tax purposes?

15. What are research and experimentation expenditures and how are they usually treated for tax purposes?

CRUNCH THE NUMBERS

16. Two years ago, Warren purchased a computer for $4,000. Until this year, he used it exclusively for personal purposes. At the beginning of the cur-

rent year, Warren opened a consulting business and began using the computer solely for business purposes. At the time he began his business, Warren's computer was worth $600. What basis must Warren use in calculating his depreciation on the computer?

17. Last year, Anne purchased a condo unit for $125,000. She used the condo as her personal residence. In the current year, when the condo unit appraises at $132,000, Anne moves out and converts the condo to rental property. What basis can Anne use when computing her depreciation on the rental condo unit?

18. In 2008, Sharon purchased her principal residence for $500,000. In 2013, she converts the property to rental use because she has been unable to sell it due to the depressed real estate market. The property's current fair market value is $400,000 (of which $100,000 is for the land). What basis does Sharon use when computing depreciation on her rental property?

19. David received a gift of stock from Ted this year when the stock was worth $24,000. Ted purchased the stock for $18,000 five years ago and paid $2,000 of gift taxes on the gift. What is David's basis for the stock?

20. Ellen received a gift of stock from Gisela this year when the stock was worth $50,000. Gisela purchased the stock for $60,000 four years ago. Calculate Ellen's basis for the stock if she sells it

a. for $65,000

b. for $45,000

c. for $55,000

21. Blanco Corporation (a calendar-year taxpayer) purchased $10,000,000 of new equipment in July 2013. Compute Blanco's depreciation deduction for 2013.

22. Azona Corporation (a calendar-year taxpayer) purchased only one business asset during 2013, used 7-year property that cost $2,600,000. Compute Azona's depreciation for 2013 assuming that

a. the asset was purchased and placed in service on September 30, 2013.

b. the asset was purchased and placed in service on October 1, 2013.

23. In July 2013, Lenux Corporation (a calendar-year taxpayer) purchased $2,100,000 of new office furniture. Lenux claimed the maximum allowable depreciation deduction (including having made any allowable elections). Calculate Lenux's total depreciation deduction for 2013 and 2014.

24. Kondar Corporation (a calendar-year taxpayer) spent $2,050,000 to purchase used machinery in early 2013.

a. What is the maximum that Kondar may elect to expense under Section 179 for the year?

b. What is the basis for calculating regular MACRS depreciation on this machinery if the maximum Section 179 deduction is elected?

c. What is Kondar's maximum depreciation deduction for 2013?

25. Corando Corporation (a calendar-year taxpayer) purchased $840,000 of new factory equipment at the beginning of 2013. Determine the maximum depreciation deduction for the equipment for 2013.

26. Kensington Corporation, Inc. (an October 31 fiscal year-end corporation) plans to purchase $2,700,000 of used office fixtures (7-year property). This will be Kensington's only personalty acquired during the year.

Kensington's management is willing to purchase and place the property in service anytime during the year to maximize its depreciation deductions.

a. Compute the depreciation expense for the first year, assuming all of the property is purchased and placed in service on June 19, 2013.

b. Compute the depreciation expense for the first year, assuming all of the property is purchased and placed in service on September 19, 2013.

c. What course of action do you recommend for Kensington?

27. Tatum Corporation (a calendar-year corporation) purchases a building on June 6 of the current year for $300,000, of which $60,000 is for the land. What is the depreciation for the first year if the building is

a. a warehouse?

b. a rental apartment building?

28. At the beginning of 2013, AB Corporation (a calendar-year corporation) owned the following assets:

	OFFICE FURNITURE	COMPUTER EQUIPMENT
Date placed in service	11/15/10	4/15/09
Initial cost	$20,000	$10,000
Accumulated depreciation	$10,160	$8,272
Recovery period	7-year	5-year
Averaging convention	Mid-quarter	Half-year

On February 1, 2013, AB sold its office furniture. On March 15, 2013, AB sold its computer equipment. Compute AB Corporation's depreciation deduction for 2013 for these two assets.

29. On March 1, 2013, Harry Corporation (a calendar-year taxpayer) purchased and placed in service office furniture costing $550,000. Compute the maximum amount Harry Corporation could elect to expense under Section 179 and claim as bonus depreciation for this furniture in 2013 if

a. this is new furniture and it is the only asset placed in service this year by Harry Corporation.

b. in addition to the $550,000 of new office furniture, Harry Corporation also acquired and placed in service $980,000 of new factory equipment during the year.

c. this is used furniture and in addition to this $550,000 of used office furniture, Harry Corporation also acquired and placed in service $1,850,000 of new factory equipment during the year.

d. What is Harry Corporation's total depreciation expense deduction for 2013 for each of the above scenarios?

30. David operates his business as a sole proprietorship. In 2013, he spends $20,000 for a used machine (7-year property). His business income, before consideration of any Section 179 deduction, is $17,000. David elects to expense $20,000 under Section 179. Calculate his total depreciation deduction for 2013.

31. In 2013, McDowell Corporation (a calendar-year corporation) purchased and placed in service a new $25,000 automobile on August 15, $300,000 of new furniture on September 1, and a $680,000 warehouse (of which $100,000 is for the land) on November 8. Compute the depreciation deductions for the first two years of these assets' lives.

32. Craig Corporation (a calendar-year corporation) purchased $3,000,000 of used office furniture in April 2013. It would like to know how much less the depreciation would be for the first three years if it elects to use ADS to compute its depreciation instead of regular MACRS accelerated depreciation.

33. In August, Jimbo Corporation (a calendar-year corporation) purchased new computers for $655,000. These are the only assets Jimbo purchased this year. Jimbo Corporation is in the 34 percent marginal tax bracket and uses a discount rate of 6 percent for evaluation. Assuming that Jimbo makes any necessary elections to maximize the depreciation deduction, what is the after-tax cost of the computers if they are placed in service in

a. 2013

b. 2014.

34. On June 26, 2011, Elaine purchased and placed into service a new computer system costing $8,000. The computer system was used 80 percent for business and 20 percent for personal use in both 2011 and 2012. Elaine claimed only regular MACRS depreciation. In 2013, the computer system was used 45 percent for business and 55 percent for personal use.

a. Compute the depreciation deduction for the computer system in 2013 and the cost recovery recapture.

b. Assume that Elaine had instead expensed the cost of the computer system under Section 179 in 2011. Compute the cost recovery recapture in 2013.

35. Trish entered into a 36-month lease of an automobile on January 1. She uses it 90 percent for business use and 10 percent for personal use. The fair market value of the automobile at the inception of the lease is $50,000. She made 12 monthly lease payments of $650 during the year.

a. What is Trish's deduction for the lease payments made during the year?

b. What is the lease inclusion amount that Trish must include in her gross income this year?

c. How would your answer to (b) change if the fair market value of the automobile was only $15,000?

36. Byron entered into a 36-month lease of an automobile on March 1, year 1. He used it 80 percent for business and 20 percent for personal use. In year 2 he used it 90 percent for business and 10 percent for personal use. The fair market value of the automobile at the inception of the lease was $60,000. Byron made 10 monthly lease payments of $660 in year 1 and 12 monthly payments in year 2.

a. What is Byron's deduction for lease payments made during year 1? What is his deduction for year 2?

b. What is the lease inclusion amount that Byron must include in his gross income for year 1? What amount must he include in income for year 2?

37. Orange Corporation acquires all of the assets of Apple Company for $10,000,000. The fair market value of the tangible assets totaled $8,000,000. The $2,000,000 difference is considered goodwill. Orange Corporation expects to continue its business operations for at least 40 years. What is the annual amount of amortization for the goodwill?

38. Zenon Corporation (a calendar-year corporation) began work on a new experimental project in 2012. It incurred $8,000 in qualifying research expenses in 2012 and $11,000 in 2013. The benefits from the project will be realized beginning in February 2014.

a. If Zenon elects a 60-month amortization period, how much will it deduct in 2012, in 2013, and in 2014?

b. If Zenon elects to expense the research expenditures, how much will it deduct in 2012, in 2013, and in 2014?

39. Goldrush Corporation bought a mine in year 1 for $90,000 and estimated that there were 100,000 tons of ore to be extracted. In year 1, it mined 8,000 tons and sold 7,000 tons. In year 2, it mined 7,000 and sold the remaining 1,000 tons from year 1 and 6,500 of the ore mined in year 2. At the end of year 2, Goldrush Corporation estimated that, including the ore extracted but unsold, there were 160,000 tons of ore remaining. Compute the allowable cost depletion for year 1 and year 2.

40. Striker Corporation bought a mine in year 1 for $100,000 and estimated that there were 100,000 tons of ore to be extracted. In year 1, it mined 10,000 tons and sold 8,000 tons. In year 2, it mined 9,000 and sold the remaining 2,000 tons from year 1 and 6,000 of the ore mined in year 2. At the end of year 2, Striker Corporation estimated that, including the ore extracted but unsold, there were 150,000 tons of ore remaining. Compute the allowable cost depletion for year 1 and year 2.

41. Paul purchases a royalty interest in an oil well for $125,000. Paul's share of the gross income from the sale of oil for the year is $40,000. His share of the expenses related to the production of the oil is $13,000. What is Paul's percentage depletion deduction for the year? What is the adjusted basis of Paul's investment after deducting the depletion allowed?

42. Nicko Corporation (a calendar-year corporation) purchased a new machine (7-year property) in July 2013 for $20,000. Nicko did not elect Section 179 for this asset but did claim 50 percent bonus depreciation. In November 2016, Nicko sells the machine. What is the adjusted basis of the machine at the date of sale?

43. Karen is an employee of KF Corporation (a calendar-year taxpayer). In February 2013, KF purchased a new $40,000 car for Karen's use. During 2013, 2014, and 2015, 60 percent of Karen's mileage on the car was business related and 40 percent was for her personal driving. Her personal use was properly treated as taxable fringe benefit income.

a. Compute KF Corporation's depreciation deductions for 2013, 2014, and 2015 if the maximum depreciation was claimed.

b. How would your answers change if Karen had used the car for only 45 percent business use and 55 percent personal use?

44. **Comprehensive Problem for Chapters 4, 5, and 6**. Robert, the sole proprietor of a consulting business, has gross receipts of $600,000 in 2013. Expenses paid by his business are

Advertising	$ 2,500
Employee salaries	150,000
Office rent	24,000
Supplies	18,000
Taxes and licenses	17,000
Travel (other than meals)	3,800
Meals and entertainment	2,400
Utilities	3,800
Employee health insurance premiums	6,600
Health insurance premiums for Robert	2,200

Robert purchased a new car for his business on May 15 at a cost of $28,000. He also purchased $50,000 of new 5-year equipment and $238,000 of used 7-year fixtures on August 1. Robert drove the new car 10,000 miles (8,000 for business and 2,000 personal miles). He paid $200 for business-related parking and tolls. He also paid $1,000 for insurance and $1,200 for gasoline and oil for the new car. He would like to maximize his deductions.

a. What is Robert's net income (loss) from his business?

b. How much self-employment tax must Robert pay?

c. If this is Robert's only source of income, what is his adjusted gross income?

THINK OUTSIDE THE TEXT

These questions require answers that are beyond the material that is covered in this chapter.

45. How do you think assets that are acquired and disposed of in the same tax year are handled for depreciation purposes?

46. You are a self-employed individual thinking about buying or leasing a car to use in your business. What information is needed to properly evaluate this lease versus purchase decision?

47. Your friend is thinking about starting up a new Internet business and would like to know how Web site development costs are treated for tax purposes. What are some of the costs involved in Web site development, and what are the issues involved in determining their tax treatment?

48. When a business rents tangible property for use in its business, it may incur up-front costs to acquire the lease on the property. How do you think these leasehold costs are treated for tax purposes?

49. Is the treatment of purchased goodwill the same for tax and for GAAP? Explain.

IDENTIFY THE ISSUES

Identify the issues or problems suggested by the following situations. State each issue as a question.

50. James Corporation had a net operating loss of $30,000 before claiming any depreciation deductions. James purchased $26,000 in equipment in 2013 but claimed no depreciation on its 2013 tax return.

51. Demark Corporation took delivery of a new machine on December 31, 2013. Due to the high number of employees out for the holidays, the machine was not set up for use until January 3, 2014.

52. Marble Corporation purchased 300-year-old marble statutes that it displays in the entrance hall of its main office building.

53. Monicon Corporation purchased a $24,000 computer in 2010 and elected to expense it under Section 179. In 2013, the IRS audited Monicon and determined that its taxable income was incorrectly calculated and was only $20,000 before considering Section 179 expensing instead of the $24,000 reported on its 2010 tax return.

DEVELOP RESEARCH SKILLS

54. Robert owns some investment land that has a basis of $1,000 and a fair market value of $22,000. He expects that it will continue to appreciate in value. Robert's uncle, Mike, has a terminal illness and is expected to survive no more than six months. Robert would like to increase the basis of the land and has devised a scheme in which he gifts the land to Mike. When Mike dies, Robert will inherit the land. Mike has agreed to participate in the plan; however, Robert wants you to confirm what his basis will be when he inherits the land from Mike.

55. Jessica, a professional violinist with the Lincoln Symphony Orchestra, purchased a 100-year-old antique violin at a cost of $180,000. She thinks that it is a good investment because she knows that it will continue to appreciate in value as a treasured work of art. She plays this violin in concerts and wants to know if she can depreciate it as a business-use asset.

56. Juan owns 40 percent and Mario owns 60 percent of Crispy Donuts, Inc. (CDI). Juan wants to buy out Mario's interest in CDI, so he arranges a stock sale agreement under which CDI will redeem (purchase) all of Mario's shares for $900,000. This will then make Juan the sole shareholder of CDI. Juan wants to ensure that Mario does not open a competing donut business nearby so he also has a covenant-not-to-compete drawn up at the same time as the stock sale agreement. Under the terms of the covenant-not-to-compete, Mario cannot open another donut business within a 10-mile radius for a period of five years. During this 60-month period, CDI will pay Mario $9,000 per month in return for his agreement not to compete. CDI wants to know over what time period it should amortize the covenant-not-to-compete.

SEARCH THE INTERNET

57. Go to the IRS Web site at *www.irs.gov* and locate Publication 946: *How to Depreciate Property*. Locate the depreciation tables at the end of the publication and calculate the regular first-year depreciation for the following assets, all placed in service in the third month of the year:

a. Sidewalks costing $6,000

b. Dairy milking barn costing $120,000

c. Tugboat costing $85,000

58. Go to the IRS Web site at *www.irs.gov* and locate Publication 946: *How to Depreciate Property.* Locate the depreciation tables at the end of the publication and calculate the first-year depreciation for a $60,000 bus using ADS.

59. Go to the IRS Web site at *www.irs.gov* and print Form 4562, Schedule C, Schedule SE, and the first page of Form 1040. Using the information in problem 44, complete these forms to the extent possible with the information given.

DEVELOP PLANNING SKILLS

60. Roman Corporation (a calendar-year corporation) purchased and placed in service the following new assets during 2013:

DATE PLACED IN SERVICE	ASSET DESCRIPTION	COST
5/8/13	New automobile	$30,000
5/15/13	Used equipment	$700,000
10/1/13	Used office furniture	$800,000
11/3/13	Warehouse	$260,000

$60,000 of the cost of the warehouse property is for the land.

a. Roman Corporation wants to maximize its depreciation deduction for 2013. Which asset(s) should it elect to expense under Section 179 and why?

b. What is Roman's total depreciation deduction for 2013 assuming that it follows your recommendation?

61. Herald Corporation, a calendar-year taxpayer, purchased and placed the following business assets in service during 2013:

ASSET	DATE PLACED IN SERVICE	INITIAL COST
New computer equipment	April 3	$50,000
Used office furniture	July 14	940,000
Used office fixtures	October 29	1,060,000

Herald Corporation is also considering the purchase of $450,000 of additional office furniture. It could wait until January to make the purchase, or it could buy the furniture and place it in service in December to try to increase its current-year tax depreciation deduction. What impact would this proposed purchase have on Herald's depreciation deduction for its year ending December 31, 2013 if the additional office furniture is (a) new or (b) used?

62. In March 2014, Arco Corporation decides to acquire some heavy equipment (this is in addition to the $2,500,000 in equipment purchased in January of this year). The new equipment is 7-year class property, but Arco expects that it will be able to use the equipment for 8 years. It could purchase the equipment for $120,000 cash, and at the end of 8 years it would have no salvage value. Alternatively, Arco could lease the equipment for 8 years for $22,000 annually. Arco is in the 35 percent marginal tax bracket and uses a 6 percent discount rate for evaluation. Should Arco purchase or lease the equipment? Prepare a schedule showing your calculations to support your recommendation.

63. Bing Corporation can buy a car for business use for $40,000 (including tax, license, and title fees) or it can lease an identical car for $450 per month, paying $2,100 up front for tax, license, and title fees. The corporation normally keeps its cars for three years and, if the car has been purchased, expects that it will be able to sell the car at the end of three years for $18,000. The corporation is in the 35 percent tax bracket and uses a 6 percent discount rate for evaluation purposes. (For simplicity, the monthly rental fees are assumed to be paid at the end of years 1, 2, and 3.) Should Bing purchase or lease the automobile? Prepare a schedule showing your calculations to support your recommendation.

ANSWERS TO TEST YOURSELF

1. b. **$61,000**. Maria adds $1,000 of the gift tax onto her uncle's cost of $60,000 to get a basis of $61,000. The portion of the gift tax added is the portion due to appreciation [($90,000 – $60,000)/$90,000 × $3,000 = $1,000].

2. c. **$1,000**. When property is converted from personal use to business use, the lower of basis or fair market value at the date of conversion is used as basis for depreciation.

3. b. **$527,573**. Depreciation on the automobile is limited to the ceiling limit of $11,160. Depreciation for the warehouse (39-year property) is

$12,840 ($800,000 × 1.605%). The warehouse is not eligible for Section 179 expensing. By electing to use the Section 179 expensing on the used office furniture, the mid-quarter convention can be avoided. After expensing $500,000 of the furniture, regular MACRS depreciation of $3,573 is computed on the remaining basis [($525,000 – $500,000) × 14.29%]. Neither realty nor used property is eligible for bonus depreciation.

4. a. **$513,566**. $500,000 Section 179 expense + [3.57% × ($880,000 – $500,000)] MACRS depreciation using the mid-quarter convention. Used property is not eligible for bonus depreciation.

5. c. **Jose must recapture $900 as ordinary income in 2013**. MACRS depreciation was $12,000 × 20% × 75% = $1,800. Straight-line depreciation would have been $12,000 × 10% × 75% = $900. The $900 difference ($1,800 – $900) must be recaptured. The 2013 depreciation will be $1,080 ($12,000 × 45% × 20%).

Ch.7 know 291 - middle of 317

and pg. 320 - sale of principle residence

chapter 7

Property Dispositions

Determining the final treatment of a property disposition requires navigating a complex set of definitions, netting procedures, and potential alternative tax rates. It starts with identifying the three types of gain (income) or loss that can be recognized on property dispositions: ordinary gains and losses, Section 1231 gains and losses, and capital gains and losses, each corresponding to asset classifications as ordinary, Section 1231, and capital. Gains (income) or losses classified as ordinary are included in operating income. Section 1231 gains and losses are first netted against each other. Net losses are deducted directly from ordinary income, but net gains are included in the netting of capital gains and losses. After these gains are netted with all other capital gains and losses, the net capital gains may be included directly in income or taxed at more favorable rates, depending on the taxpayer and the length of time the property had been held prior to disposition. Similarly, all or part of the net capital loss may not be deductible from current income, depending on the taxpayer. Carryover features may allow these losses to be deducted against gains in other years, however.

Careful planning of property dispositions may allow taxpayers to reduce taxes. To take full advantage of the opportunities to time asset dispositions, the taxpayer must understand the gain and loss classifications, their treatment (whether they are included in income directly or go through a netting process), the ultimate disposition based on whether the taxpayer is a corporation or an individual, and the applicable tax rates.

Several provisions encourage taxpayers to invest in specific assets by either changing the character of the loss (Section 1244 stock) or excluding gain from income (sales of qualified small business stock and personal residences). These provisions do not apply to all taxpayers, and they are subject to limitations. The details of these provisions must be understood to plan for and take advantage of their benefits.

KEY CONCEPTS

★ The character of assets, classified first as business, investment, or personal-use assets, and then as Section 1231, capital, or ordinary income assets, determines the taxation of gains and losses.

★ Section 1231 assets are depreciable assets and nondepreciable realty used in a trade or business. Net Section 1231 gains are taxed as long-term capital gains, while net Section 1231 losses are fully deductible as ordinary losses.

★ Section 1245 full recapture (applicable primarily to personalty), Section 1250 partial recapture (applicable to realty), and Section 1231 look-back rules convert all or part of Section 1231 gain into ordinary income.

★ Corporate capital gains are included in ordinary income; corporate capital losses can only offset capital gains in the current or specified carryover years. Individuals include short-term capital gains in ordinary income; their long-term capital gains are usually taxed at reduced tax rates, but their deductions for capital losses are limited to $3,000 annually. Individuals can carry unused losses forward indefinitely.

CHAPTER OUTLINE

- ★ Section 1244 allows taxpayers to deduct capital losses on small business corporation stock as ordinary losses, and Section 1202 allows taxpayers to exclude up to one hundred percent of their gains on qualified small business corporation stock.
- ★ Section 121 allows qualifying taxpayers to avoid gain recognition of up to $250,000 ($500,000 if married filing jointly) on the sale of their personal residences.

SETTING THE STAGE—AN INTRODUCTORY CASE

In addition to its service revenue, the Manhattan Corporation generated revenue from a number of property transactions during the year. The company sold 100 shares of ADC stock for $63,000 that it purchased four months ago as a temporary investment for $65,000. It sold land it acquired two years ago for future plant expansion that was used as a temporary parking lot when expansion plans were abandoned. The land cost $180,000 and was sold for $240,000. It sold four machines that represented excess capacity for $120,000. The machines originally cost $140,000, and the company had taken $80,000 of depreciation deductions on them. The corporation also sold a small building that it had used for storage for $125,000, $25,000 of which was for the land. It had acquired the building and land on which it sat in 1988 for $150,000. The land was assigned a basis of $30,000. The company had taken $45,000 in depreciation deductions on the building.

Several months ago, a tornado wiped out a distribution warehouse the corporation owned in Kansas. The warehouse building originally cost $450,000 in 1990 and had a basis of $220,000 (exclusive of the land) when it was destroyed. The corporation was self-insured and received no insurance payment. Because the corporation was downsizing, it did not replace the warehouse. Instead, it sold the land that remained at a $10,000 gain.

As the newest accountant on Manhattan's staff, you have been asked to develop a complete schedule of the gains and losses on the property transactions by amount and type and to determine the effect they will have on Manhattan's taxable income. At the end of the chapter, we will return to this case.

DETERMINING GAIN OR LOSS ON DISPOSITIONS

This chapter continues the discussion of property transactions by focusing on taxable property dispositions. To accurately determine the amount of the realized gain or loss on an asset disposition, two attributes must be identified: the amount realized on the disposition and the adjusted basis of the property. To determine the character of the realized gain or loss on a disposition, the taxpayer must identify the asset as a business, investment, or personal-use asset, determine the owner's holding period for the asset, and then, using this information, determine if the disposition generates ordinary, Section 1231, or capital gain or loss. Finally, applying the applicable tax laws, the taxpayer determines if any or all of the realized gains or losses must be recognized currently or deferred to a future period.

Property Dispositions and Cash Flow

When property is disposed of in a taxable transaction, the gain or loss realized is the difference between the amount realized on the sale and the adjusted basis of the property sold. The cash flow equals the cash received on the sale and the tax effect of any gain or loss recognized.[1] Taxes on a recognized gain reduce the taxpayer's cash flow, while a recognized loss increases cash flow due to the tax savings generated by the loss.

---

[1]For simplicity, our cash flow examples assume only cash is received. If property other than cash is received, the cash flow analysis would require the assumption that the property is sold for cash; its net realizable value would then be included as cash received.

EXAMPLE 1

Mega Corporation sells an asset with an adjusted basis of $150,000 for $180,000 cash. Mega's marginal tax rate is 34 percent, and it pays $10,200 [($180,000 – $150,000) × 34%] in tax for a net cash flow of $169,800 ($180,000 cash received – $10,200 tax). If, however, Mega sells the asset for only $125,000, its $25,000 loss ($125,000 – $150,000 adjusted basis) reduces its taxes by $8,500 ($25,000 × 34%). Its net cash flow is now $133,500 ($125,000 cash received + $8,500 tax savings). If Mega Corporation sells the asset for $150,000, it would recognize no gain or loss, and its cash flow would be $150,000.

It is the tax cost of a gain or tax reduction of a loss on the sale that affects the cash flow on an asset disposition.

The type of taxpayer (corporation or individual), the taxpayer's marginal tax rate, and the type of asset disposed of all affect the cash flow. Depending on the asset type, income and capital gains of an individual are taxed at rates ranging from zero percent to 39.6 percent in 2013 (zero to 35 percent in 2008 through 2012 and 5 to 35 percent in 2003 through 2007). Long-term capital gains of individuals have basic tax rates of zero, 15 percent or 20 percent with short-term capital gains taxed at ordinary income rates. Both long- and short-term capital gains are potentially subject to an additional Medicare surtax of 3.8 percent based on the taxpayer's other taxable income.[2] The deductibility of individuals' capital losses is limited to $3,000 annually, however, while ordinary and net Section 1231 losses can be deducted in full against ordinary income.

Corporate taxpayers' basic marginal tax rates vary from 15 to 35 percent (excluding surtaxes) and apply to ordinary income and Section 1231 and capital gains. Corporations deduct ordinary and Section 1231 losses in full against ordinary income but their capital losses can only be deducted against capital gains.[3]

EXAMPLE 2

Jim has income from many different sources and is in the 25 percent marginal tax bracket. During the year, he sold some stock and realized a $25,000 long-term capital gain. He also earned $25,000 of ordinary income from his sole proprietorship. Jim pays $3,750 ($25,000 × 15%) tax on the long-term capital gain and $6,250 ($25,000 × 25%) tax on the ordinary income. If Jim were a corporation, both the ordinary income and long-term capital gain would be taxed at the corporation's marginal tax rate.

EXAMPLE 3

Assume the facts of the previous example except that Jim's stock sale results in a $25,000 capital loss and he has a $25,000 ordinary loss from his sole proprietorship. Jim deducts the entire $25,000 ordinary loss against his other income, resulting in immediate tax savings of $6,250 ($25,000 × 25%). He deducts $3,000 of the capital loss for additional tax savings of $750 ($3,000 × 25%). Although Jim can carry the remaining $22,000 capital loss forward, the time value of money reduces the value of this loss.

These examples illustrate the importance of understanding the basic requirements of property dispositions. Misapplication can result in unfavorable tax consequences and reduced cash flows.

Types of Dispositions

Asset dispositions may take several forms: sale, exchange, involuntary conversion, or abandonment. By far the most common disposition, however, is the simple sale. A sale is a transaction in which the seller receives cash or cash equivalents in return for one or more of his or her properties or assets.[4] The assumption of a seller's liability

[2]The basic maximum long-term capital gains tax rate returned to the 20 percent rate in effect for individuals prior to 2003 for individuals in the top marginal tax bracket. Capital gains of higher income taxpayers may be subject to a 23.8 percent rate due to the Medicare surtax on capital gain income, however. Very specific types of long-term capital gains may be subject to maximum capital gains tax rates of 25 or 28 percent in addition to the potential 3.8 percent Medicare surtax.

[3]Corporations carry capital losses back three years and forward five years to offset capital gains in those years.

[4]Reg. §1.1002-1(d).

by a buyer is a cash equivalent. An **exchange** is a transaction in which the taxpayer receives property other than cash or cash equivalents in return for property (other than money) transferred to the other party.[5]

Involuntary conversions include "destruction in whole or in part, theft or seizure, or requisition or condemnation."[6] Involuntary conversions are events that are not under the control of the taxpayer and, as a result, gains and losses may receive favorable tax treatment.[7]

Abandonments are not sales or exchanges. Nevertheless, an abandonment can result in a recognized loss on business or investment property. A taxpayer abandons property by permanently withdrawing it from use in the taxpayer's trade or business or activity operated for profit.

EXAMPLE 4

Tom and his sole proprietorship have a number of dispositions in the current year. He sells his auto to Jerry for $1,000 cash, and Jerry assumes the $6,000 balance on the car loan. Tom has received cash and cash equivalents of $7,000 on this sale. Next, Tom exchanges a pool table valued at $1,200 for Lenny's motorcycle valued at $1,100 and $100 cash. Depending on their bases in these properties, Tom and Lenny will have either gain or loss on this exchange transaction. Tom then has an investment painting destroyed in a fire at the museum where it was displayed and had computers stolen from his business. Both of these events qualify as involuntary conversions. Finally, the business discards a machine because it was obsolete and producing defective goods. The abandonment loss is equal to the machine's basis.

The steps required to determine the tax impact of a property disposition are: (1) determine the amount realized on the disposition and the property's adjusted basis, (2) calculate the gain or loss realized, (3) determine the character of the gain or loss, and (4) analyze the applicable tax laws to determine if all, part, or none of the realized gain or loss is recognized currently and the amount of any gain or loss that is deferred.

Realized gains on sales and exchanges are generally recognized and taxable unless a specific provision provides for nonrecognition or postpones recognition to a later time. Realized losses on sales, exchanges, and abandonments are recognized and deducted only if the property involved is used in a trade or business or held for investment. The character of a recognized gain or loss refers to how a gain or loss is classified for tax purposes. Gains and losses are characterized as (1) ordinary gains and losses, (2) capital gains and losses, and (3) Section 1231 gains and losses.

Amount Realized

The **amount realized** on a transaction equals the sum of the following:[8]

1. The amount of money received
2. The fair market value of property received
3. Seller's liabilities that are assumed by the buyer

Minus the sum of the following:

1. The selling or exchange expenses
2. Buyer's liabilities assumed by the seller

The **fair market value** of property received is the price at which the property would change hands between a willing buyer and a willing seller.[9] In some cases, valuation by a qualified appraiser may be necessary to determine fair market value. If property such as stock is sold on an established market, market quotations can be used. If the

---

[5]Reg. §1.1002-1(d). An exchange can also involve money paid or received, and either the property exchanged or the property received may be subject to a mortgage or other liability.

[6]§1231(a)(4)(B).

[7]Involuntary conversions are discussed in the next chapter.

[8]§1001(b) and Reg. §§1.1001 and 1.1002.

[9]See *Comm. vs. Marshman*, 60-2 USTC ¶9484, 5 AFTR 2d 1528 (CA-6, 1960).

property's fair market value cannot be determined readily, the fair market value of the property given up in the exchange can be used.[10] Liabilities assumed by the buyer are equivalent to giving cash to the seller to pay off the liability. Property taxes owed by the seller are a liability assumed by the buyer if the seller does not pay them.

EXAMPLE 5

Charlie sold land for $5,000 cash and gold coins with a fair market value of $10,000. The buyer also assumed Charlie's mortgage on the land of $40,000. Charlie paid attorney's fees of $2,000 and broker's fees of $3,000 on the sale. Charlie's amount realized on the sale is $50,000 ($5,000 cash + $10,000 gold coins + $40,000 mortgage assumed by the buyer - $2,000 attorney's fees – $3,000 broker's fees).

Realized versus Recognized Gain or Loss

The realized gain or loss on an asset disposition is the mathematical difference between the amount realized on the transaction and the asset's adjusted basis.[11] A **realized gain** occurs when the amount realized from the asset's disposition is larger than the asset's adjusted basis. There is a **realized loss** if the asset's adjusted basis is greater than the amount realized.[12]

EXAMPLE 6

Cart Corporation exchanged a truck with an adjusted basis of $5,000 for a machine worth $3,000 and cash of $500. Cart has a realized loss of $1,500 (the amount realized of $3,500 is less than the $5,000 adjusted basis of the truck). If Cart had also received cash of $3,000 instead of $500, it would have a gain of $1,000 ($6,000 – $5,000).

After determining the realized gain or loss, the taxpayer must determine the recognized gain or loss. A **recognized gain** is the amount of a realized gain that is includible in the taxpayer's gross income.[13] A **recognized loss** is the amount of a realized loss that is deductible by the taxpayer.[14]

The sale or other disposition of an asset with no applicable nonrecognition provision (such as the like-kind exchange provision) requires the recognition of the realized gain or loss. Recognition of losses is generally limited to business, investment, and casualty and theft losses, however. With very limited exceptions, taxpayers cannot deduct realized losses on personal-use property.[15]

Holding Period

For certain types of assets, it is important to know the holding period (the period of time the taxpayer is credited with owning the property) to determine how a gain or loss is taxed. For example, both capital assets and Section 1231 assets (discussed later) must be held for "more than one year" to receive tax-favored treatment.[16]

EXAMPLE 7

Gilpin Corporation, an equipment manufacturer, purchases a $50,000 parcel of land from Goodwin Corporation on July 15, year 1, to expand its outlet store (a Section 1231 asset). Gilpin's holding period for the land begins on the date of the purchase. If Gilpin later decides not to expand the store, it must hold the land until July 16, year 2, for it to meet the more-than-one-year holding period.

[10]*U.S. vs. Davis*, 82 S Ct. 1190, 62-2 USTC ¶9509, 9 AFTR 2d 1625 (USSC, 1962).

[11]The asset's adjusted basis is its original basis increased by any capital expenditures and reduced by any capital recoveries, as discussed in Chapter 6.

[12]§ 1001(a).

[13]See § 61(a)(3) and Reg. § 1.61-6(a).

[14]See § 165(a) and Reg. § 1.165-1(a).

[15]§ 165(c)(3) permits deductions for losses arising from theft, storm, or other casualty on personal-use property.

[16]A worthless security (a capital asset) is deemed to be sold on the last day of the tax year. Its holding period is determined by the date acquired and the date of deemed sale. § 165(g)(1).

An asset's holding period normally begins on the date acquired. If, however, an asset's basis carries over from another asset (a carryover basis) or takes its basis by reference to another asset (a substituted basis), then the holding period normally carries over (is added to) the holding period of the acquired asset.

EXAMPLE 8

The Venus Corporation acquired a piece of land in exchange for a warehouse building. This exchange of properties qualifies as a like-kind exchange on which no gain or loss is recognized. The land that Venus acquires takes the same basis as the land that it exchanged (a substituted basis) under the like-kind exchange provisions.[17] Thus, Venus's holding period includes the time that it owned the warehouse because its basis in the land is determined by its basis in the warehouse. If, however, Venus acquired the land for cash, it would be a purchase and the holding period would begin on the date of acquisition.

The holding period of a gift derives from the basis used by the donee on the subsequent sale of the gift. If the donee's basis carries over from the donor, the holding period carries over as well. If, however, the donee uses the gift's lower fair market value at the time of the gift as the basis, the holding period begins on the date the donee received the gift.[18]

EXAMPLE 9

Sherry received a gift of stock from her friend Helen, who had purchased the stock eight months earlier for $20,000. If Sherry sells the stock for $23,000 five months after she receives it, she uses Helen's $20,000 basis to determine gain and adds Helen's holding period to hers; thus, Sherry's gain is $3,000 and her holding period is 13 months (8 months + 5 months). If the stock's fair market value at the date of the gift was only $18,000 and Sherry sells it five months later for $14,000, she must use $18,000 (the lower fair market value) as her basis for loss. Sherry has a $4,000 loss, and her holding period is only five months.

The holding period of any asset acquired by inheritance is always long term (more than one year) regardless of the amount of time the decedent held the asset before it passed to the heir.

TAX PLANNING

The basis rules for gifts and inheritances that require the use of a fair market value that is lower than basis by the recipient effectively prevents recognition of any loss in value that accrued during the time the donor or decedent held the property. Thus, property with a fair market value below basis on which the owner could recognize the realized loss should be sold rather than given away or kept as part of a future estate, as neither the donee nor heir will be able to benefit from the loss in value.[19]

Character of Gains and Losses

The character of the gain or loss recognized depends on the type of property sold. The three types of property that determine this character are Section 1231 assets, capital assets, and ordinary income assets. Taxpayers must classify their gains and losses on business, investment, and personal-use property into one of these three categories to determine how the gain or loss on asset dispositions will be taxed.

Section 1231 Assets

The current tax treatment of Section 1231 assets evolved before and during World War II. Initially, all business assets were afforded capital treatment on disposition. With the longer lives for depreciation at that time, assets' bases often exceeded their fair market value. The limited deductibility of capital losses on disposal discouraged businesses from investing in new assets. To stimulate investment, business assets became ordinary income assets. This treatment, however, caused gains on business

[17] The like-kind provisions are discussed in Chapter 8.

[18] See Chapter 6 for a discussion of gift basis.

[19] Gifts and inheritances are discussed in Chapter 12. Their holding periods are included here to complete the discussion of holding period.

assets to be taxed as ordinary income. During World War II, gains became far more common due to inflation. Moreover, the government often acquired business property for the war effort through condemnation. Although adequately compensated, businesses could not take advantage of the nonrecognition provisions for involuntary conversions because no qualified replacement property was available.[20] As a result, capital gain treatment was reinstated for the gains on business property while leaving ordinary loss treatment for losses—today's Section 1231 asset treatment. To ensure this treatment, however, the gains and losses on the disposal of Section 1231 assets must go through a complex netting process.

The principal **Section 1231 assets** include depreciable realty and personalty used in a trade or business, nondepreciable trade or business realty, and long-term capital gain property held for the production of income that is involuntarily converted by theft, casualty, seizure, or condemnation. Section 1231 property also includes the land from which wasting assets are taken and some amortizable intangible assets.[21] To qualify as Section 1231 assets, however, these assets must be held for *more than one year*.

EXAMPLE 10

Forge Company owns the land and the buildings used in its cement and cement product manufacturing operations in addition to all the necessary machinery and equipment. As long as all these assets have been owned for more than one year, they are Section 1231 assets because they are used in a trade or business. Forge also owns the gravel pit from which materials for making cement are extracted and a patent on a special cement curing process that will not expire for eight more years. Both of these assets are subject to allowances—depletion and amortization, respectively—similar to depreciation and are Section 1231 assets.

It is important to correctly identify trade or business and investment assets because Section 165 specifically *disallows* the recognition of losses on personal-use property, except for losses resulting from casualties and thefts.[22]

TAX PLANNING

Capital Assets

The sale or exchange of a capital asset results in capital gain or loss. Thus, it is necessary to differentiate capital assets from ordinary and Section 1231 assets. Section 1221 states that **capital assets** are any assets other than the following:

1. Inventory or stock in trade held for sale in the ordinary course of business to customers
2. Real and depreciable property used in a trade or business
3. Accounts and notes receivable from the performance of services or sale of inventory in the ordinary course of business
4. Copyrights and artistic and literary compositions created by the taxpayer or acquired by gift or nontaxable exchange from the creator (except the creator or gift recipient of a musical composition or copyright for a musical work can elect to treat its sale as the sale of a capital asset)

In general, capital assets are restricted to investment properties and personal-use assets. Capital assets held for investment include securities, investment property, and collectibles. Personal-use assets include jewelry, clothing, personal autos, furniture, and personal residences. Artistic creations of the taxpayer, assets used in a trade or business, and inventory and receivables arising from a business are not capital assets.

EXAMPLE 11

Wilma owns a painting acquired at an auction two years ago, some land purchased three months ago as an investment, and a rental apartment building purchased five years ago. The painting and the land are capital assets, but the apartment building is Section 1231 rental property. She also owns two automobiles. One

[20]To avoid recognition of gain, qualified replacement property must be acquired.

[21]Patents and franchises are subject to capital asset treatment under specific circumstances.

[22]§ 165(h) limits the deductibility of personal casualty and theft losses, however.

is a minivan used solely for her accounting business. The other is a convertible that she uses for nonbusiness transportation. Both autos have been owned for more than one year. The convertible is a capital asset because it is a personal-use asset. The minivan is a Section 1231 business asset.

Ordinary Income Assets

The Internal Revenue Code does not define ordinary income assets—it only includes definitions of capital and Section 1231 assets. Because there are only three differing tax treatments based on the type of asset—ordinary income, capital, and Section 1231—any asset not categorized as either of the latter two types, must be an **ordinary income asset**. The most common ordinary income assets are business inventory, accounts receivable, and those assets used in a trade or business that do not meet the more-than-one-year holding period requirement to be classified as Section 1231 assets.

Generally, only business-use assets, other than Section 1231 or business capital assets, can be ordinary income assets as they are assets that form an integral part of the income generation process from normal business operations. Although most Section 1231 assets are depreciable—with depreciation expense considered an ordinary expense—unless held for no more than 12 months, these assets are given their own special classification as Section 1231 assets to provide favorable tax treatment upon disposition.

EXAMPLE 12

Meghan sold a machine that she purchased six months ago for her manufacturing business at a loss. The asset was used in Meghan's business so it cannot be a capital asset. She did not own it for more than one year, so it cannot be a Section 1231 asset. Thus, it must be an ordinary income asset and the loss is an ordinary loss. In addition, the business's inventory and accounts receivable are both ordinary income assets.

Mixed-Use Assets

Property that is used both for business and personal purposes is a mixed-use asset. The consequences of any transaction affecting the asset must be partitioned according to the business and personal-use portions.

EXAMPLE 13

Alma owns a beauty salon that occupies 40 percent of her home. She depreciates only 40 percent of the home's basis. If she sells the home, 40 percent of the home qualifies as the sale of property used in a trade or business; the other 60 percent qualifies as a sale of a personal-use asset.

DISPOSITION OF SECTION 1231 PROPERTY

Section 1231 property includes all depreciable realty and personalty, all nondepreciable realty used in a trade or business, and all capital assets held by a trade or business or for the production of income that are involuntarily converted, as long as the property is held for more than one year.[23] When Section 1231 property is disposed of, the taxpayer must do the following:

1. Determine the gains and losses on the individual Section 1231 assets.
2. Reduce the gain on assets with realized gain for depreciation recapture. Depreciation recapture is included in ordinary income.
3. Net the remaining gains and losses following a two-step netting procedure (netting requires offsetting losses against gains).
4. If the result is a net loss, deduct it from ordinary income.

[23]§ 1231(a)(3). This section also specifically mentions the inclusion of property used in a trade or business as § 1231 property even though it is included under the general definition of § 1231 assets.

5. If the result is a net gain, apply the five-year look-back procedure. Include any gains in ordinary income that are subject to the look-back rule.
6. The balance of the net gain is treated as a long-term capital gain and is included in the netting process for long-term and short-term capital gains.

If a corporation has no capital gains or losses to offset with the net Section 1231 gain, it simply includes the net Section 1231 gain in ordinary income. An individual with no capital gains or losses treats the net Section 1231 gain as a long-term capital gain, generally taxed at the basic zero, 15, or 20 percent alternative capital gains tax rate (excluding the surtax).[24] Depreciation recapture, the Section 1231 netting process, the look-back rules, and the capital asset netting process are all explained in sequence below.

Depreciation Recapture

Depreciation deductions on rental realty and related personalty, and realty and personalty used in a trade or business, offset ordinary income. These deductions result in tax savings based on the taxpayer's marginal tax rate. The deductions also reduce an asset's basis. When the taxpayer disposes of the asset, some or all of the gain realized may be a result of this reduced basis. The net tax savings could be significant if this gain is then taxed at reduced capital gains rates. As a result, taxpayers may not receive tax-favored Section 1231 gain treatment for the gain realized on subsequent dispositions of depreciable assets. The recapture provisions convert all or part of the Section 1231 gain to ordinary income.[25]

EXAMPLE 14

Jack is single and owns Sims Appliances, a sole proprietorship. He is in the 33% percent marginal tax bracket. Two-and-a-half years ago, Sims purchased depreciable equipment at a cost of $100,000. Sims claimed $61,600 in depreciation deductions, reducing the asset's adjusted basis to $38,400. Jack deducted these expenses from the sole proprietorship income, resulting in a $20,328 ($61,600 × 33%) tax savings to him. Because of a shortage of this equipment, Sims is able to resell it for $100,000. The gain on the sale of this equipment is $61,600 ($100,000 sales price − $38,400 adjusted basis), all of which is attributable to the depreciation claimed. If the recapture rules did not apply, Jack would be taxed on the gain at the 15 percent long-term capital gain rate, resulting in $9,240 ($61,600 × 15%) tax. Jack would have saved $11,088 ($20,328 − $9,240) in taxes due to the rate differential between ordinary income and capital gains. The recapture provisions change this result. Jack will pay tax on the gain at his 33 percent ordinary income tax rate, resulting in $20,328 ($61,600 × 33%) in taxes—the same amount that he saved over the past two-and-a-half years because of the depreciation deductions. Thus, there is no net tax savings generated by the equipment after the depreciation is recaptured at ordinary income tax rates.

The two most important points to remember about property subject to recapture are these

1. The property's basis must have been reduced through depreciation deductions.
2. Gain is realized on the disposition.

There is no recapture on property sold at a loss. The recapture provisions have no effect on the determination of the *amount* of gain or loss realized on an asset's disposition. The recapture rules operate solely to recharacterize all or part of the Section 1231 gain as ordinary income.

TAX PLANNING

A good time to dispose of Section 1231 assets on which there will be depreciation recapture is a year in which (1) other operating income is very low (or there is a loss)

[24]With surtaxes, long-term capital gains can be taxed at 18.6 percent or 23.6 percent based on the taxpayers other income as explained later. Unrecaptured § 1250 gains are taxed at a 25 percent rate while gains on § 1202 stock and collectibles are taxed at 28 percent; with surtaxes these special rates can be as high as 28.6 percent and 31.6 percent, respectively.

[25]The recapture provisions under § 1245 and § 1250 are the ones most commonly encountered by taxpayers. While other recapture provisions exist (see, for instance, § 1252 and § 1254), they apply to other specialized property and their treatment is beyond the scope of this text, but the principles explained here would apply to these other types of recapture provisions.

to take advantage of lower income tax brackets or (2) there are expiring net operating loss carryovers.

Section 1245 Full Recapture

The **Section 1245 full recapture** provision requires ordinary income tax treatment for the gain realized on the disposition of specific Section 1231 assets up to the total of all previously allowed depreciation deductions. Although depreciation methods have changed over the years, the provisions for determining Section 1245 recapture have changed very little. Depreciable property subject to the Section 1245 recapture rules includes[26]

1. Machinery, equipment, furniture, and fixtures
2. Property (except buildings and their structural components) used as an integral part of manufacturing, production, or extraction or to furnish transportation, communications, electrical energy, gas, water, or sewage disposal services[27]

Buildings and their structural components are generally excluded from Section 1245 recapture.[28]

The method of depreciation used by the taxpayer to depreciate the property subject to Section 1245 recapture is irrelevant. The taxpayer recognizes ordinary income in an amount equal to the lesser of the gain realized or prior depreciation deductions.[29] Any realized gain in excess of prior depreciation deductions is Section 1231 gain.

Example 15

Harmon Corporation sells a machine tool for $6,000 that cost $10,000 and has an adjusted basis of $3,000. Because the $3,000 gain on the sale is less than the $7,000 prior depreciation deductions, the entire $3,000 is treated as Section 1245 recapture and is taxed as ordinary income. None of the gain is Section 1231 gain. Assume instead that Harmon Corporation sells the machine tool for $11,000; the $8,000 gain is made up of $7,000 of Section 1245 recapture income and $1,000 of Section 1231 gain. The $7,000 maximum recapture is ordinary income and the remaining $1,000 is Section 1231 gain.

Under Section 179, taxpayers can expense up to $500,000 in 2013 of qualifying tangible personalty used in a trade or business in lieu of the normal depreciation deduction.[30] Section 1245 recapture applies to property for which this expensing election is made and equals the lesser of the amount expensed or the gain recognized on the disposition.[31]

Example 16

Moldov, Inc. purchased a new machine for $16,000, expensing the entire purchase price under Section 179. Moldov has a gain of $11,500 (the selling price) when it sells the machine two years later, all of which is Section 1245 recapture. If Moldov sold the machine for an $18,000 gain, its Section 1245 recapture would be limited to $16,000; the amount it expensed under Section 179. The remaining $2,000 gain would be Section 1231 gain.

Section 1250 Partial Recapture

Section 1250 recapture of Section 1231 gains differs from Section 1245 recapture because it applies only to realty and only part of the gain realized from prior depreciation deductions is recaptured. **Section 1250 recapture** applies to the "excess"

[26]§ 1245(a)(3).

[27]Certain other specialized equipment and facilities also are subject to Section 1245 recapture.

[28]Nonresidential realty put into service during 1981 through 1986 on which accelerated ACRS depreciation was taken is subject to Section 1245 recapture.

[29]§ 1245(a).

[30]§ 179(b)(1). The maximum amount that could be expensed in 2010 through 2012 was also $500,000.

[31]§ 1245(a)(3)(C).

depreciation on certain real property assets. Excess depreciation is that portion of an accelerated depreciation deduction that exceeds the alternative straight-line depreciation deduction.[32]

Under current MACRS rules (applicable to realty acquired after 1986 tax years), realty is depreciated only on a straight-line basis.[33] Thus, for realty placed in service after 1986, there is no excess depreciation recapture for either residential or nonresidential realty depreciated under MACRS. Only realty placed in service prior to 1987 could have any accelerated depreciation affected by Section 1250 recapture. Corporations, however, are subject to an additional amount of recapture under Section 291 as an alternative to the original Section 1250 recapture, as explained in the following section.

Additional Section 291 Corporate Recapture

Corporate taxpayers that dispose of realty that would have been subject to Section 1250 recapture provisions (if acquired prior to 1987) must convert a percentage of their Section 1231 gain to ordinary income under the Section 291 recapture rules. This additional recapture is 20 percent of the excess of the Section 1245 recapture (as if Section 1245 recapture applied) over Section 1250 recapture. As Section 1250 recapture is zero for acquisitions after 1986 under MACRS, the corporate recapture increment is simply 20 percent of the Section 1245 recapture.[34]

EXAMPLE 17

The Wanyu Corporation sells a factory building for $1,025,000. The building cost $1,010,000 when purchased eleven years ago. The corporation claimed $260,000 of MACRS depreciation, and the building has an adjusted basis of $750,000. The total recapture is as follows:

Step 1. Determine the Section 1250 recapture.

There is no Section 1250 recapture as the building was depreciated using the straight-line method under MACRS.

Step 2. Determine the Section 1245 recapture.

Amount realized	$1,025,000
Less adjusted basis	(750,000)
Total gain	$275,000

Section 1245 recapture is $260,000, the lesser of the total gain realized ($275,000) and the prior depreciation deductions ($260,000).

Step 3. Determine the additional recapture.

Section 1245 recapture	$260,000
Less Section 1250 recapture	(0)
	$260,000
Step 4. Multiply by 20 percent	× 20%
Additional recapture	$52,000

Step 5. The total Section 1250 recapture required is $52,000.

The remaining $223,000 ($275,000 – $52,000) gain is Section 1231 gain.

This provision applies only to corporate taxpayers and creates Section 1250 recapture on real property dispositions that otherwise would have no recapture. This corporate recapture rule eliminates some of the capital gains that would otherwise

[32]§ 1250(a).

[33]MACRS depreciation for realty is discussed in the preceding chapter.

[34]§ 291(a)(1). On a pre-1987 asset subject to Section 1250 recapture, the corporation adds the actual Section 1250 recapture to 20 percent of the excess of Section 1245 recapture over the actual Section 1250 recapture to determine the total Section 291 recapture.

be available to offset capital losses, as corporations can only offset capital losses with capital gains.

Unrecaptured Section 1250 Gains for Individuals

Individuals who have realized and recognized gains on depreciable real property (that previously would have been classified as Section 1250 gain) may be subject to a higher capital gains tax rate on gain up to the amount of the straight-line depreciation deductions taken.[35] As these gains are no longer subject to recapture, they are called the unrecaptured Section 1250 gain, and individuals are subject to a maximum 25 percent tax rate (28.8 percent if the Medicare surtax is included) on the gain.

EXAMPLE 18

Judy sold an apartment building for $1,400,000. She had purchased the building 12 years ago for $1,200,000 and had taken $300,000 of MACRS straight-line depreciation deductions on the building. Judy has $500,000 realized gain ($1,400,000 – $900,000) on the apartment building, $300,000 of which is classified as unrecaptured Section 1250 gain (the lesser of the gain realized or the prior depreciation deductions) subject to the maximum 25 percent tax rate. The remaining $200,000 of Section 1231 gain is subject to the lower 20 percent basic capital gains tax rate (rates exclude Medicare surtax). Table 7.1 summarizes the tax treatment of gains and losses by asset type.

Section 1231 Netting

After all Section 1231 gains have been adjusted for Section 1245 and Section 1250 recapture, the remaining gains and the Section 1231 losses enter the two-step Section 1231 netting process. Both corporate and individual taxpayers must separate these gains and losses into two baskets. The first basket contains gains and losses resulting from involuntary conversions specifically defined as *casualties* or *thefts* of Section 1231 and investment properties held for more than one year.[36] The second basket contains the gains and losses from all other types of involuntary conversions (for example, condemnations) of Section 1231 and investment properties held for more than one year and gains and losses from all other dispositions of Section 1231 properties. The basic netting procedure for both corporate and individual taxpayers is as follows:

> **Step 1.** Net all gains and losses on assets in the first basket (casualty and theft gains and losses on Section 1231 and investment property held more than one year.). Only a net *gain* continues to Step 2. The treatment of a net loss is explained later.
>
> **Step 2.** Net all the gains and losses from the assets in the second basket (all other involuntary conversions of Section 1231 and investment property and all other Section 1231 dispositions) with the *net gain* only from Step 1.

The treatment of a net loss at either Step 1 or Step 2 and a net gain at Step 2 differs depending on whether the taxpayer is a corporation or an individual.

Corporate Taxpayers

A corporation with a net loss at the end of either Steps 1 or 2 in the Section 1231 netting process simply deducts the net loss directly from ordinary income at the end of either step; that is, a net loss does not carry forward to the next step but provides an immediate deduction.[37] A net gain at the end of Step 1, however, is included in Step 2

[35]If the real estate was acquired prior to 1987, the unrecaptured Section 1250 gain would be the lesser of the gain realized or depreciation deductions reduced by the actual Section 1250 recapture.

[36]The determination of recognized gain and loss on casualties, thefts, and other involuntary conversions is covered in the following chapter. Section 1231 property includes properties held for the production of rents and royalties.

[37]Technically, the corporation includes all gain items as ordinary income and deducts all loss items from ordinary income.

TABLE
7.1 TAX TREATMENT OF GAINS AND LOSSES

ASSET TYPE	EXAMPLE	TREATMENT OF GAIN	TREATMENT OF LOSS
Nondepreciable Section 1231 asset	Business-use land	Section 1231 gain	Ordinary loss
Section 1245 recapture	Equipment	Prior depreciation (not exceeding realized gain) recaptured as ordinary income; excess is Section 1231 gain	Ordinary loss
Section 1250 recapture	Office building	Corporations: 20% of prior depreciation (not exceeding realized gain) recaptured as ordinary income; excess is Section 1231 gain Individuals: 25% maximum tax rate applies to gain equal to or less than prior depreciation; excess is Section 1231 gain	Ordinary loss
Capital asset	Investment land	Capital gain	Capital loss
Ordinary asset	Inventory	Ordinary income	Ordinary loss

for further netting as explained above. If Step 2 results in a net gain, the corporation first applies the five-year look-back rule (discussed later) to this gain; any remaining gain enters the capital asset netting process (also discussed later).

EXAMPLE 19

Bobbitt Corporation has a \$400,000 casualty loss on a factory building, a \$50,000 casualty gain on machinery (after deducting depreciation recapture), a \$200,000 Section 1231 gain on the condemnation of land, a \$150,000 Section 1231 loss, a \$210,000 Section 1231 loss, and a \$120,000 Section 1231 gain.

Step 1. Netting the \$400,000 casualty loss with the \$50,000 casualty gain = \$350,000 net casualty loss that is deducted directly from ordinary income.

Step 2. Netting the remaining gains and losses (\$200,000 – \$150,000 – \$210,000 + \$120,000) = a net \$40,000 Section 1231 loss that is deducted directly from ordinary income.

Thus, Bobbitt has a total deduction of \$390,000 for net Section 1231 losses. If Step 2 had resulted in a net Section 1231 gain instead of a loss, the corporation would treat the net gain as a long-term capital gain after applying the Section 1231 look-back rule.

Individual Taxpayers

The Section 1231 netting process for individual taxpayers is the same as that for corporate taxpayers *unless* the individual has losses from the involuntary conversion of *investment* assets held for more than one year. Thus, if the individual's gains or losses from involuntary conversions are from business property only, the procedure is the same as that for corporations. That is, if there is a net loss at the end of either Step 1 or Step 2, the individual deducts the net loss directly from income; a net gain at the end of Step 1 is included in Step 2 for further netting; and a net gain at the end of Step 2 is subject to the 5-year look-back rule with any remaining gain entering the capital asset netting process (both discussed later). If Bobbitt Corporation (Example 19) had been Mary Bobbitt's sole proprietorship, the Section 1231 netting process would not have changed as there were no involuntary conversions of investment property of the individual-owner included in the netting process.

If the Section 1231 netting process includes *any* losses from involuntary conversions of investment property (through theft, casualty or other involuntary conversion), the process is altered for the individual only if there is a net loss at the end of either Step 1 or Step 2. If this is the case, the *losses* on the involuntarily converted assets are removed from the net loss total at the end of either Step 1 or Step 2 and must be deducted separately as itemized deductions.[38] The net loss (or in unusual cases, net gain) remaining after removing and deducting separately the loss on the investment assets, is included directly in ordinary income.

Figure 7.1 illustrates the Section 1231 netting process.

FIGURE 7.1 SECTION 1231 NETTING PROCESS

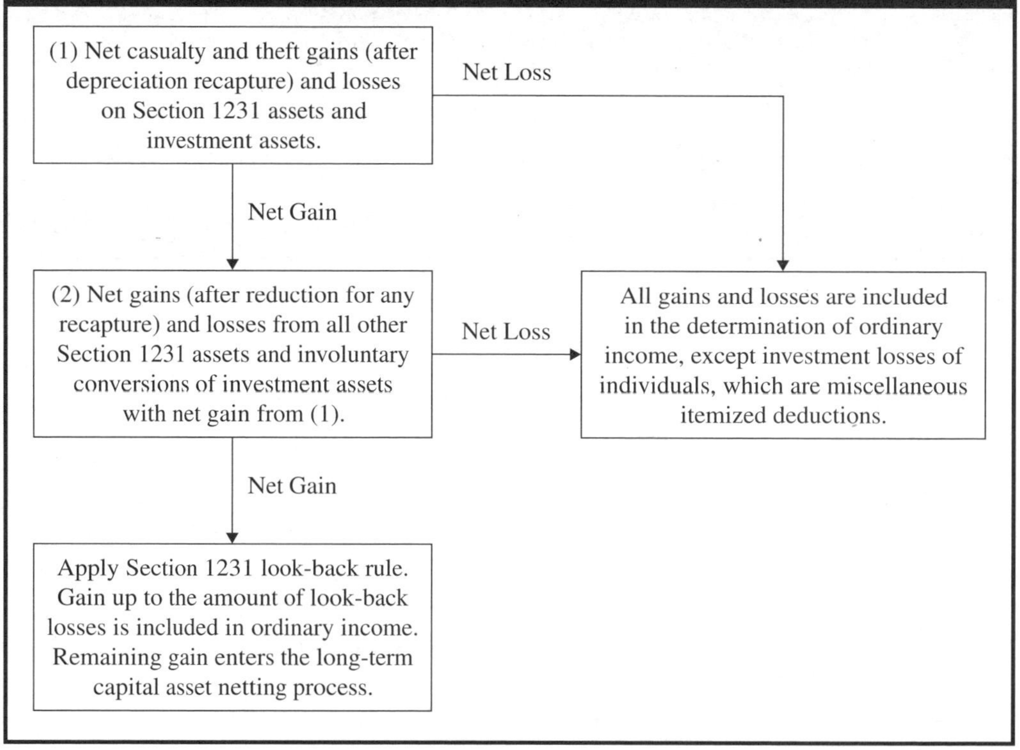

[38]In this case, an individual's loss on the involuntary conversion of an investment asset is not subject to the 2 percent floor as are other miscellaneous itemized deductions. See Chapter 11.

EXAMPLE 20

Joe has a $10,000 casualty loss on an investment asset and a $5,000 casualty gain on a Section 1231 asset used in his sole proprietorship. He has a $25,000 condemnation loss on some investment land and a $40,000 Section 1231 gain and a $20,000 Section 1231 loss.

Step 1. Net the casualty loss and gain: – $10,000 + $5,000 = $5,000 net casualty loss. Joe includes the $5,000 Section 1231 gain in ordinary income but must deduct the $10,000 casualty loss as a miscellaneous itemized deduction. (The $5,000 gain is not included in Step 2 because the results of netting were a net loss.)

Step 2. Net the remaining gains and losses: – $25,000 + $40,000 – $20,000 = $5,000 net loss. Joe only includes the $20,000 net Section 1231 gain from the $40,000 Section 1231 gain and the $20,000 Section 1231 loss in ordinary income; the $25,000 condemnation loss on the investment land must also be treated as a miscellaneous itemized deduction.

TAX PLANNING

Taxpayers generally have no control over the timing of the realized gains and losses from involuntary conversions, but they can control dispositions of other Section 1231 assets. If gains must be recognized from involuntary conversions in high marginal tax years, the taxpayer should consider disposing of loss assets to offset these gains. If losses occur in high marginal tax years, however, the taxpayer may benefit by postponing planned dispositions of appreciated property so the losses can be recognized.

Section 1231 Look-Back Rules

The Section 1231 look-back rules prevent taxpayers from generating tax savings by bunching their Section 1231 gains into one year (to receive the tax-favored long-term capital gain treatment for gains) and losses into alternate years (deducting the Section 1231 losses against ordinary income).[39]

EXAMPLE 21

Dave, who is in the 33 percent marginal tax bracket, was able to deduct a $50,000 net Section 1231 loss last year. In the current year, Dave has a $50,000 net Section 1231 gain. Last year Dave's tax savings from the loss deduction were $16,500 ($50,000 × 33%). If the look-back rules did not apply, the current gain would be taxed at 15 percent ($50,000 × 15% = $7,500). Dave would have a net tax savings of $9,000 ($16,500 – $7,500) due to his net Section 1231 gains being taxed at favorable capital gains tax rates.

To limit this maneuver, Congress enacted Section 1231(c), which requires taxpayers to recapture any of the current year's net Section 1231 gains as ordinary income to the extent of any net Section 1231 losses deducted during the previous five tax years.

To determine the amount of the Section 1231 gain that must be recognized as ordinary income in the current year:

1. Total all Section 1231 losses deducted in the previous five years.
2. Total all Section 1231 gains already recaptured as ordinary income due to those losses deducted in the previous five years.
3. Determine the excess of total Section 1231 losses in the five previous years over the previously recaptured Section 1231 gains [(1) – (2)]. These are the current year's unrecaptured Section 1231 losses.
4. The look-back recapture is the lesser of the current year's unrecaptured Section 1231 losses (3) and the current year's net Section 1231 gain; this is taxed as ordinary income.

[39]Although a corporation has no tax-favored capital gains rates, the look-back rules reduce the amount of Section 1231 gain that can be treated as capital gain; this, in turn, reduces the amount of capital gain available to offset capital losses. Excess capital losses cannot be deducted in the current year but instead must be carried back 3 years and forward 5 years.

5. The excess of the current year's net Section 1231 gain over the amount recaptured as ordinary income (4) is a long-term capital gain and enters into the capital asset netting process.

Figure 7.2 is a diagram of the Section 1231 look-back process.

EXAMPLE 22

In the current year, George sells several business properties with the following results:

Property A	$10,000	Section 1231 loss
Property B	25,000	Section 1231 gain
Property C	5,000	Section 1231 loss

George recognized a Section 1231 loss of $22,000 two years ago. George first nets the Section 1231 gain on Property B with the Section 1231 losses on Properties A and C. He has a net Section 1231 gain of $10,000 (– $10,000 + $25,000 – $5,000). He treats this entire gain as ordinary income due to the Section 1231 look-back rules, and he has $12,000 ($22,000 – $10,000) of unrecaptured Section 1231 losses remaining.

FIGURE 7.2 THE SECTION 1231 LOOK-BACK RULES

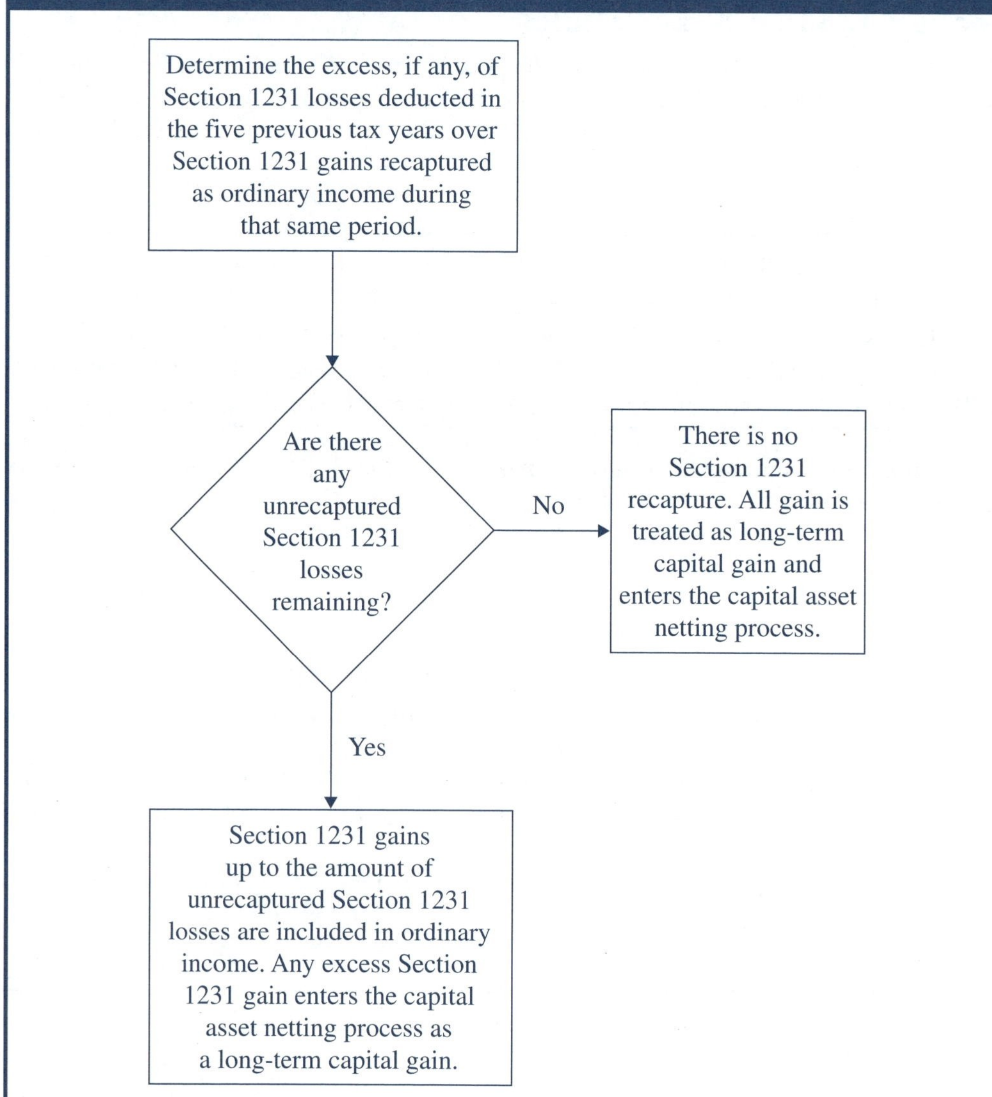

If George has a net Section 1231 gain of $16,000 in the following year, he would recapture only $12,000 (the current year's unrecaptured Section 1231 loss) of this gain. The remaining $4,000 ($16,000 – $12,000) would receive long-term capital gain treatment.

If the taxpayer has not deducted any net Section 1231 losses in the five preceding tax years, the look-back rules are inoperative.[40] If the taxpayer is a corporation, the look-back rules do not affect the taxation of the gain. As discussed in the next sections, corporate net capital gains are included in ordinary income as corporations have no reduced capital gains tax rates.

TAX PLANNING

Individual taxpayers still may be able to benefit from timing their Section 1231 gains and losses, however. A net Section 1231 loss deducted in one or more of the five prior years causes a current net Section 1231 gain to be treated as ordinary income. A net Section 1231 gain realized in a year prior to a net Section 1231 loss has no effect on the deductibility of the loss. Thus, to the extent possible, individuals can benefit by realizing net Section 1231 gains in years prior to Section 1231 loss years. The net gain can be taxed at the individual's lower capital gains rate, but the loss is deducted against ordinary income taxed at the taxpayer's marginal tax rate.

Disposition of Capital Assets

The majority of assets held by individual taxpayers are capital assets; businesses, however, may also hold capital assets for investment purposes rather than for business use. Outside of personal-use assets such as personal residences, personal automobiles, clothing, and home furnishings, the major category of capital assets held by individual taxpayers is investment assets. These assets include stocks, bonds, land held for appreciation, and collectibles such as coins, works of art, and other rare objects. The majority of capital assets held by businesses are stocks or securities, although investment in other types of assets is possible.

If a taxpayer disposes of a capital asset, the taxpayer's holding period at the time of disposition is important. Subject to certain exceptions, a capital asset held for more than one year is a **long-term capital asset**. Capital assets held one year or less are **short-term capital assets**.[41]

The Capital Gain and Loss Netting Process

Neither corporate nor individual taxpayers include their separate capital gains and losses directly in income. Instead, they must complete a two-step netting process of capital gains and losses to determine their final disposition.

To begin the two-part netting process, the taxpayer (1) determines the recognized gain or loss on each short-term and long-term capital asset, separating the long term from the short term and (2) separately nets short-term capital gains with short-term capital losses and long-term capital gains with long-term capital losses. (Long-term capital gains include the net Section 1231 gain from the final step in the Section 1231 netting process.) If this separate netting results in only net capital gains or net capital losses, no further netting is required. The net gains or net losses are taxed based on the type of taxpayer, as explained later. If the separate netting process yields both a net capital gain and a net capital loss, the net gain and net loss are then offset against each other. The result is either a short-term or long-term gain or loss based on the larger of the two items (for example, if the net long-term capital loss is larger than the net short-term capital gain, the difference is a long-term capital loss). Again, the taxation of the resulting short-term or long-term gain or loss is dependent upon the taxpayer. Figure 7.3 illustrates this netting process.

---

[40]§ 1231(c).

[41]§ 1222.

FIGURE 7.3 **CAPITAL GAIN AND LOSS NETTING PROCEDURE**

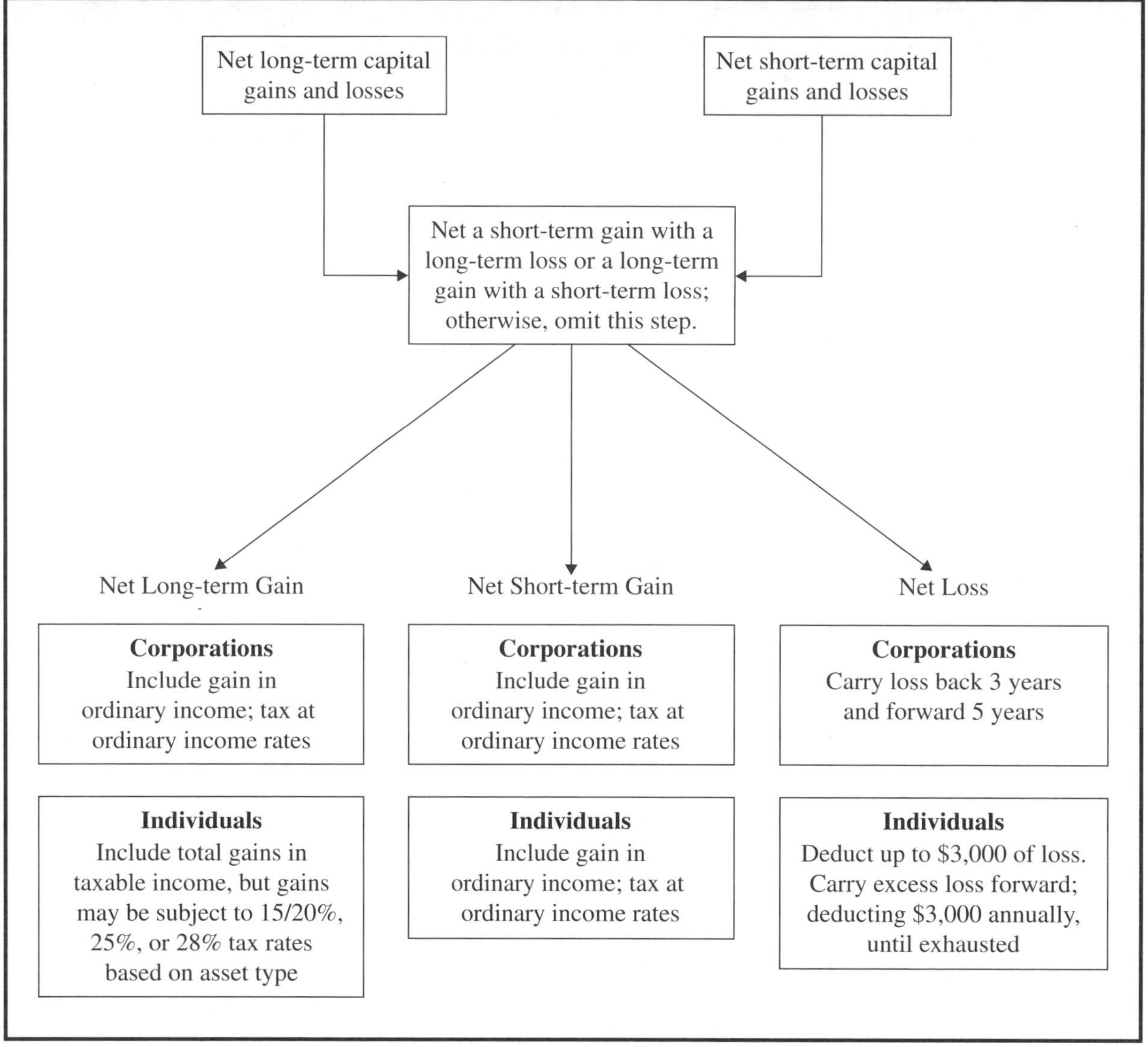

EXAMPLE 23

The Buck Company disposed of a number of securities as follows:

Asset	Date Acquired	Date of Disposition	Gain or Loss
100 shares A	2/2/year 1	5/5/year 5	$200
200 shares B	2/6/year 2	5/5/year 5	(800)
400 bonds	8/8/year 5	11/1/year 5	(200)
200 shares C	5/4/year 5	11/1/year 5	500

Buck also has a $200 net Section 1231 gain for the year.

Stocks A and B, held more than one year, are long term. Stock C and the bonds, held less than one year, are short term. Buck has a $400 long-term capital gain ($200 from Stock A plus the $200 net Section 1231 gain), an $800 long-term capital loss, a $200 short-term capital loss, and a $500 short-term capital gain. Following the above procedure, Buck nets the gains and losses.

(a) The $400 long-term capital gain is netted with the $800 long-term capital loss; the result is a net $400 long-term capital loss.

(b) The $200 short-term capital loss is netted with the $500 short-term capital gain; the result is a net $300 short-term capital gain.

As there is both a net loss and a net gain, further netting is required.

(c) The $400 long-term capital loss offsets the $300 short-term capital gain; the result is a net $100 long-term capital loss.

Tax Treatment of Net Capital Gains and Losses

The taxation of net capital gains and losses depends on whether the taxpayer reporting the result of the capital asset netting process is a corporation or an individual, with corporate taxpayers following one set of rules and individual taxpayers following another set. Flow-through entities, such as partnerships and S corporations, report their capital gains and losses to their partners and shareholders for inclusion in their respective tax returns.

Corporate Taxpayers

After completing the netting process, corporations include their net short-term and long-term capital gains in ordinary income for taxation at the regular corporate tax rate. No special tax provisions apply to the long-term capital gains of corporations.[42]

A corporation with net capital losses (whether short term or long term) cannot deduct the losses currently. Corporations can only carry net losses to other tax years to offset capital gains realized in those years. Corporations can carry capital losses back three years and then forward five years. The carryback must begin with the third year prior to the current year. If the corporation doesn't have a net capital gain in the third prior year, or the net gain in that year cannot absorb the entire loss, the remaining net loss carries over to the second prior year, then to the first prior year. If unabsorbed losses remain, the corporation must wait and carry these losses forward in turn to the next five tax years after the current year.[43] Regardless of whether the current year's net capital losses are short term or long term, they are considered short-term capital losses when carried to another year, where they will enter that year's netting process.[44] Figure 7.4 illustrates this carryover provision. The longer it takes to use a carryover, the less valuable that carryover is to the taxpayer.

FIGURE 7.4 CORPORATE CAPITAL LOSS CARRYOVERS

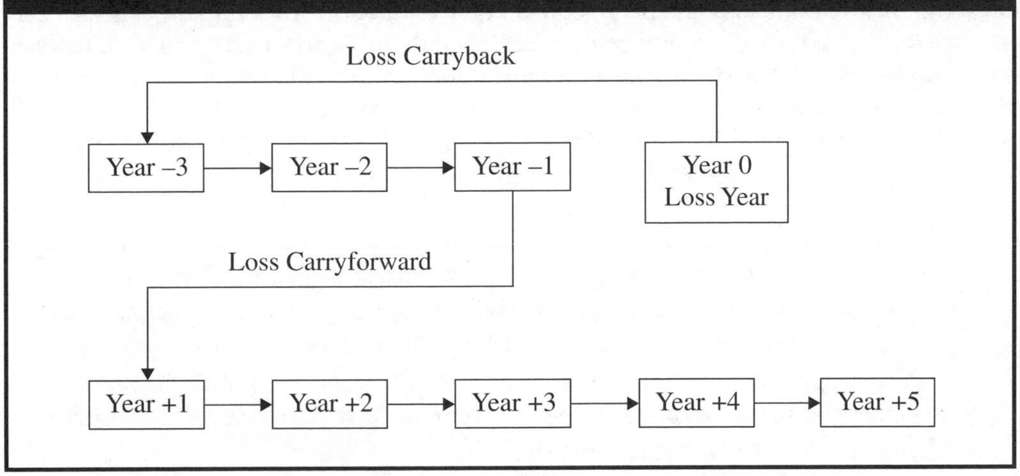

[42]§ 1201(a). Technically, an alternative 35 percent tax rate applies to corporate capital gains, but this rate is equal to the maximum corporate tax rate; thus, there is no tax break for corporations.

[43]§ 1212(a).

[44]For all practical purposes, it is irrelevant whether they are carried over as long term or short term under current law; under prior law, however, it was an important distinction.

EXAMPLE 24

Corporation C is in the 34 percent tax bracket. It has a capital loss in the current year of $400,000 that it cannot deduct or carry back to offset a gain. It does not expect to have an offsetting gain for four years. Thus, it cannot use the $136,000 tax savings ($400,000 × 34%) that deducting the loss in the current year would allow. If the corporation uses a 6 percent discount rate for present value evaluations, the present value of the tax effect of the loss that is deferred for four years is $107,712 ($136,000 × .792).

TAX PLANNING

If losses remain after the five-year carryforward, the losses are lost. As a result, a corporation may want to accelerate disposing of some assets that will yield net capital gains if it has a net capital loss carryover that is about to expire.

EXAMPLE 25

Masten Corporation had a net short-term capital loss of $18,000 and a net long-term capital loss of $15,000 in year 4. None of the losses are deductible. The losses ($33,000) are carried back as a short-term capital loss to year 1 in which Masten reported a net short-term capital gain of $12,000 and a net long-term capital gain of $8,000, both of which were taxed at a rate of 34 percent. Masten claims a tax refund of $6,800 [($12,000 + $8,000) × 34%] and carries the remaining $13,000 ($33,000 – $12,000 – $8,000) short-term capital loss to year 2. Masten has no capital gains in years 2 and 3. It must wait until years 5 through 9, in turn, to offset the remaining $13,000 of capital losses. If Masten has no capital gains in years 5 or 6, the $13,000 ($33,000 – $20,000) would be carried forward to year 7. If any loss remains after year 9, Masten loses the benefit of the loss deduction.

The treatment of capital gains and losses is not as favorable for corporations as it is for individuals. This significantly limits corporate tax savings generated by a capital loss and tax planning opportunities.

Individual Taxpayers

The taxation of an individual's net capital gains and losses is more complex than a corporation's, but the netting process is identical. When the netting process is complete, the individual will have either a net long-term and/or short-term capital loss or a net long-term and/or short-term capital gain.

Individuals with net capital losses (either short- or long-term or both) at the end of the netting process have a $3,000 annual deduction for capital losses in excess of capital gains. The individual deducts up to $3,000 of the net short-term capital loss first. If the net short-term capital loss is less than $3,000, the individual deducts the net long-term capital loss up to a total $3,000 deduction. Individuals cannot carry excess capital losses back to any prior year. Instead, they carry their capital losses forward indefinitely. The losses carried forward maintain their character as short term or long term and enter the netting process in the carryover year. The $3,000 limit on the deduction for net capital losses applies to all capital losses in a year, whether arising from transactions in that year or as carryovers from a prior year.

EXAMPLE 26

Betty has a $12,000 long-term capital loss, an $8,000 short-term capital loss, a $9,000 long-term capital gain, and a $6,000 short-term capital gain in year 1. The result of netting the long-term capital loss and long-term capital gain is a $3,000 net long-term capital loss. After netting the short-term capital loss and the short-term capital gain, a $2,000 net short-term capital loss results. Betty deducts the $2,000 net short-term capital loss and $1,000 of the net long-term capital loss. The remaining $2,000 of the net long-term capital loss is carried forward to the next year.

In year 2 Betty has the following gains and losses exclusive of her $2,000 long-term capital loss carryover:

Long-term capital gain	$1,000
Long-term capital loss	$900
Short-term capital gain	$900
Short-term capital loss	$700

The long-term capital loss carryover is treated as another long-term capital loss incurred in year 2, so Betty has total long-term capital losses of $2,900 ($900 + $2,000 carryover). Netting the year-2 short-term and long-term capital gains and losses yields a $1,900 net long-term capital loss ($2,900 – $1,000) and a $200 ($900 – $700) net short-term capital gain. After netting this gain and loss, Betty deducts the $1,700 net long-term capital loss ($1,900 loss + $200 gain) that remains. No carryover to year 3 remains.

An individual with a net short-term capital gain (with or without a net long-term capital gain) includes this short-term gain in ordinary income to be taxed at ordinary income tax rates. Net long-term capital gains are subject to alternative capital gains tax rates that are generally less than ordinary income rates. The majority of long-term capital gains of individuals are subject to three basic tax rates—0 percent, 15 percent, and 20 percent based on the ordinary income tax rate otherwise applicable to the individual's taxable income. A 3.8 percent Medicare surtax rate on net investment-type income (which includes capital gains) may be added to the basic rate when modified adjusted gross income exceeds a specific threshold based on the taxpayer's filing status. There are also two additional long-term capital gains rates of 25 and 28 percent that may also apply to certain limited types of long-term capital gains based on the individual's taxable income. They, too, may be subject to the Medicare surtax.

The total of an individual's *ordinary* taxable income (including short-term capital gain) must be determined first before an individual's *long-term capital gains* are added to determine the individual's *total taxable income*. The applicable long-term capital gains tax rates cannot be determined until total taxable income is first computed. The long-term capital gains of taxpayers whose total taxable income does not exceed the 15 percent tax bracket are subject to a 0 percent tax rate on long-term capital gains that would otherwise be taxed at 10 or 15 percent—the same as prior law. A taxpayer with taxable income subject to tax rates greater than 15 percent but less than 39.6 percent will have their long-term capital gains taxed a rate of 15 percent to the extent that total taxable income does not exceed the threshold for the 39.6 percent ordinary income tax rate. Taxpayers with total taxable income that exceeds the threshold for the 39.6 tax rate will have their long-term capital gains that exceed this threshold taxed at the 20 percent rate. Long-term capital gains below this threshold remain subject to the 15 percent tax rate. The 3.8 percent Medicare surtax, however, increases both the 15 and 20 percent rates to 18.8 and 23.8 percent, respectively, for taxpayers with modified adjusted gross incomes in excess of $250,000 (MFJ), $125,000 (MFS), $200,000 (Single) or $225,000 (HOH). These rates and applicable income and rate levels are shown in Table 7.2. The increased rate applies to the lesser of net investment income or the excess of modified adjusted gross income over the threshold amount.

EXAMPLE 27

In 2013, John, who is single, has $21,000 of ordinary income and a $6,000 of long-term capital gain. John's $27,000 of total taxable income is less than the maximum income in the 15% tax bracket for single individuals and his capital gains will escape taxation due to the 0% tax rate.

EXAMPLE 28

In 2013, Mary and Steven file a joint return and report $168,000 of total taxable income that includes $40,000 of long-term capital gains. Their $128,000 of ordinary income is taxed at a maximum tax rate of 25%; as a result, their long-term capital gains are taxed at 15%.

EXAMPLE 29

In 2013, Sheryl qualifies as a head of household and has $323,000 of taxable income that includes $80,000 of long-term capital gains. Her $243,000 of ordinary income is taxed at a maximum tax rate of 33% and her long-term capital gains are taxed at 18.8%, made up of the capital gain's rate of 15% and the 3.8% Medicare surtax.

Alternatively, if Sheryl is married but files a separate return, her ordinary income is taxed at the maximum rate of 39.6 % and her long-term capital gains are now taxed at a 23.8% rate, the 20% capital gains tax rate plus the 3.8% Medicare surtax.

TABLE
7.2 CAPITAL GAINS TAX RATES FOR INDIVIDUALS

MAXIMUM TAX RATE BASED ON TOTAL TAXABLE INCOME	TAX RATE ON LONG-TERM CAPITAL GAINS (WITHIN APPLICABLE TAX BRACKET)	MEDICARE SURTAX ON NET INVESTMENT INCOME	MAXIMUM TAX RATE ON LONG-TERM CAPITAL GAINS
10%, 15%	0%	0%	0%
25%, 28%	15%	0%	15%
33%, 35%	15%	3.8% on lesser of net investment income or income exceeding threshold amount*	18.8%
39.6%	20%	3.8% on lesser of net investment income or income exceeding threshold amount*	23.8%

**Thresholds for applying the 3.8% Medicare surtax are $200,000 for single filers, $225,000 for Heads of Household, $250,000 for married persons filing jointly, and $125,000 for married persons filing separately.*

Although the majority of long-term gains are taxed at 15 or 20 percent, the 25 percent tax rate applies to unrecaptured Section 1250 gains, and the 28 percent rate applies to collectibles such as antiques, art objects and rare coins and to Section 1202 gains.[45] To determine the tax, an individual includes the net long-term capital gain in taxable income, but completes a worksheet to calculate the tax liability on taxable income.

EXAMPLE 30

Cletus, who is single, has $185,000 of ordinary taxable income excluding his capital gains and is in the 33 percent marginal tax bracket. He sold stock purchased for $40,000 several years ago for $65,000 and a Salvador Dali pencil sketch purchased for $5,000 twenty years ago for $125,000. These are his only capital transactions for the year. Cletus has total taxable income of $330,000 that includes a $25,000 long-term capital gain on the stock taxed at 15% and a $120,000 long-term capital gain on the pencil sketch taxed at 28%. He will also be subject to the 3.8% Medicare surtax on the $130,000 of net investment income that exceeds the $200,000 threshold. His remaining $185,000 of ordinary taxable income is taxed using the regular tax rate schedule.

The last section of the chapter provides additional information on the taxation of the different classes of assets when the taxpayer has both capital gains and losses along with the modification of the rates for taxpayers subject to ordinary income tax rates that are less than the capital gains tax rates.

TAX PLANNING

STRATEGIES Individuals should look for opportunities to take advantage of the capital asset disposal provisions. Although an individual has an unlimited capital loss carryover, the value of the $3,000 annual capital loss deduction becomes smaller and smaller the further into the future the loss is carried. Thus, an individual should consider accelerating disposal of assets on which gains are realized, as effectively there

[45]Section 1202 gains are the includible portion of gains on qualifying small business corporation stock and are explained later in this chapter.

is no current tax cost to the extent they offset losses. Similarly, accelerating the disposal of loss assets into years in which gains are realized can reduce or eliminate the tax cost. The individual may also be able to plan dispositions to use the tax rates on capital gains to his or her advantage by estimating ordinary income prior to the end of the year. They could accelerate capital gains into years in which ordinary income is expected to be low and avoid the 20 percent capital gains tax rate or the Medicare surtax. If income is expected to be high, postponing dispositions of capital gain assets to a lower tax rate year may be possible. Additionally, a capital loss on a 15 percent taxed asset offsets a gain on a 28 percent taxed asset. Thus, accelerating a gain on a 28 percent asset is more advantageous than accelerating a gain on a 15 percent asset to offset a loss. Assets should not be disposed of simply for the tax effect, however, if the disposition does not make economic sense.

EXAMPLE 31

Jason expects to have some expensive dental work done in early January before he begins a new job at a much higher salary. He needs to sell an asset with a $6,000 gain to pay for the dental work. He estmated that his taxable income this year will not exceed the 15% tax bracket but believes it will be significantly higher next year. He should sell his capital asset close to the end of year so that his $6,000 gain will escape taxation. If he waits until next year, his gain may be subject to a 15% capital gains tax. He saves $900 by selling before the end of the year.

EXAMPLE 32

Greg is in the 33 percent marginal tax bracket and recently sold a collectible at a $10,000 long-term capital gain that will be taxed at a 28 percent capital gains tax rate. He has two stocks that he plans to sell next year. He expects a $10,000 long-term capital gain on one and a $10,000 capital loss on the other. (Gains on stocks are generally taxed at 15 percent.) Unless Greg does some planning, he will pay a tax of $2,800 on the gain in this year and have no taxable gain next year. If he accelerates the sale of the loss stock to the current year, his $10,000 loss offsets this year's gain. He will have no taxable gain this year and his tax on the $10,000 gain next year will be only $1,500. Thus, by accelerating the loss, he reduces his total tax by $1,300. (Because he defers paying the tax for one year, he will have an even greater savings due to the time value of money.)

EXAMPLE 33

Davis, who is in the 33 percent marginal tax bracket, sells some stock early in the current year resulting in a $40,000 short-term capital gain. He also holds some other stock that has declined in value by $48,000. Davis should consider selling enough of this other stock in the current year to realize a $43,000 capital loss. That capital loss will offset the $40,000 short-term capital gain and $3,000 of ordinary income. As a result, Davis will save $14,190 in taxes ($43,000 × 33%) in the current year. If he doesn't sell the stock this year but sells it at a $48,000 loss next year, he will pay $14,190 in taxes in the current year. Assuming no future capital gains, he will save $990 of taxes per year ($3,000 × 33%) over the next 16 years. By timing the loss sale with the gains, Davis's present value of tax savings is far greater.

EXAMPLE 34

Ted is single, is in the 33 percent marginal tax bracket, but is below the threshold for the Medicare surtax on capital gains. As of June 1, he has some Marco stock that if sold would result in a $10,000 short-term capital gain. He would have to hold the stock until September 28 to meet the more-than-one-year holding period to have the gain treated as a long-term capital gain. If the price of the stock is expected to hold steady or increase, the stock should be held at least until September 28. Holding the stock until then increases his after-tax profit by $1,800 [$10,000 × (33% – 15%)]. Of course, if the price is expected to increase, holding the stock would be even more worthwhile. If Ted needs cash immediately, he could borrow the needed money using the stock as collateral, selling the stock after the required long-term holding period has been reached to pay off the loan. His net gain would be the tax savings less the interest on the loan. If the stock's price is declining, however, a current sale may be warranted as the tax savings of holding the stock until September 28 may not offset the potential reduced selling price.

TAX PLANNING

If an individual has already realized net short-term or long-term capital losses during a given year of less than $3,000, additional loss property could be sold up to $3,000 in total to take advantage of this offset against ordinary income. If capital losses already exceed $3,000, the taxpayer may find it advantageous to sell appreciated assets to generate gains to offset the excess capital losses.

EXAMPLE 35

Shelli sold capital assets in the current year, generating a $4,000 short-term capital loss and a $5,000 long-term capital loss. If she sells no more capital assets during the current year, she can deduct $3,000 of the short-term capital loss only and carry the remaining $1,000 short-term and $5,000 long-term losses over to next year and beyond. If she has some disposable capital assets, she may want to consider selling them to generate enough short-term or long-term capital gains to offset the remaining $6,000 of capital losses as the tax benefit will be greater in the current year. In making the decision, she should consider the expected future price performance of the assets she considers selling and the investment potential for the proceeds.

TAX PLANNING

In planning for asset dispositions, individuals must also consider those gains and losses that flow through to them from partnerships and S corporations.[46] The net Section 1231 gains and losses and net long-term and/or short-term capital gains and losses are included in the determination of the individual's taxable income. These gains and losses are combined with the individual's own gains and losses that must be recognized. The results of the netting processes are taxed or deducted on the individual owners' returns.

EXAMPLE 36

Jim is a shareholder in an S corporation. The corporation sold a long-term capital asset and Jim's share of the gain will be $20,000. Jim has a significant amount of other income (salary, interest, and dividends) and his marginal tax rate is 33 percent with investment income subject to the Medicare surtax. If Jim does nothing, he will pay $3,760 in taxes ($20,000 × 18.8%) on the long-term capital gain. Jim sells enough stock that has declined in value to generate a $20,000 loss. Jim offsets the gain with $20,000 of the loss and saves the $3,760 in taxes. In addition, he has the cash flow from the sale of the loss asset that he can now invest in a more profitable asset.

If, instead of selling the asset at a gain, the corporation sells the asset at a loss and passes through a $20,000 capital loss to Jim, Jim can only deduct $3,000 of the capital loss this year against his ordinary income, resulting in tax savings of only $990 ($3,000 × 33%). If Jim sells an unwanted asset that will generate at least a $17,000 short-term capital gain, he can get an immediate tax benefit from the corporation's capital loss of $7,246 that is made up of the $990 tax savings from $3,000 of the loss that is deductible and the $6,256 ($17,000 × 36.8%) tax saved by offsetting the $17,000 gain.

These examples show why taxpayers receive maximum benefit from their capital losses in years in which they have sufficient capital gains to offset against them. This is even more critical for corporate taxpayers because they are permitted no deduction for capital losses and their capital gains are taxed at ordinary income rates.

Both individuals and corporations file a Schedule D to report their current capital transactions along with any capital loss carryovers and capital gains and losses passed through from partnerships or S corporations. To encourage accurate reporting of property transactions, brokers must by law report the gross proceeds on sales and exchanges of stocks and securities on Form 1099-B and real estate transactions on Form 1099-B to the government and to taxpayers.[47]

[46]The flow-through nature of partnerships and S corporations is discussed in Chapter 10.

[47]§6045(a)-(c).

Disposition of Ordinary Income Property

Any asset that is not a capital asset or a Section 1231 asset must be ordinary income property. The most commonly encountered ordinary income assets are the following:

1. Trade or business assets that do not meet the more-than-one-year holding period to qualify as Section 1231 assets
2. Property held for sale to customers in the ordinary course of business (inventories)
3. Accounts and notes receivable arising from the sale of goods or services by a business

Any other asset that cannot be identified as a capital or Section 1231 asset must also be an ordinary income asset. A recognized gain or loss on the disposition of an ordinary income asset is included directly in operating income.

In addition to the ordinary income or loss on the disposition of the ordinary assets mentioned above, part or all of the gain on the sale of Section 1231 assets that is subject to recapture under Section 1245 and 1250 is ordinary income.[48] If, however, a Section 1231 asset is sold at a loss, the entire loss is a Section 1231 loss. There are no special provisions whatsoever for ordinary income or loss in the process of determining taxable income; the gain or loss on these items is simply calculated and included directly in taxable income.

Example 37

The Marywood Corporation, an accrual-basis taxpayer, manufactures various types of household linens. During the current year, its total revenue from linen sales is $5,200,000. Its cost of goods sold is $2,800,000, and all other deductible expenses are $1,700,000. Marywood has net income of $700,000 from the sale of its linens. The entire amount is ordinary income because it results from the sale of goods (inventory) in the course of its normal operations.

Marywood sold a truck that it had purchased for use in the business only three months ago. The truck cost $14,000 and was sold for $12,500. The company has a $1,500 ordinary loss on the sale of the truck; if the truck had been held for more than one year, it would have been a Section 1231 asset and the loss would have been a Section 1231 loss. Because it was sold in such a short time and does not meet the Section 1231 holding period, the truck must be an ordinary asset and the loss is ordinary.

Lastly, Marywood made sales of $500,000 on account during the last week of December. Due to a year-end cash shortage, the company sells the receivables to a factor at 80 cents on the dollar. Marywood recognizes $500,000 of sales revenue because of the sales on account. When it factors the receivables for $400,000, it has a $100,000 ordinary loss. Assuming no other taxable transactions, Marywood's operating income is $598,500 ($700,000 – $100,000 – $1,500).

Mixed-Use Property

Realty and personalty that are used partly for business and partly for personal use must be divided into business-use (Section 1231) property and personal-use property. Any gain or loss on the disposition is determined separately for the business and personal-use parts, and the character of that part dictates the treatment for each part.

Example 38

Wanda uses her automobile 60 percent for business and 40 percent for personal use. Wanda is only able to depreciate 60 percent of the cost of the automobile. Only 60 percent of the auto is classified as Section

[48] The gain on the sale or exchange of an asset that will be depreciated by the purchaser will be ordinary if the transaction is between related parties. §1239(a).

1231 property, and only the gain or loss on the disposition of that 60 percent is classified as gain or loss on the disposition of Section 1231 property, subject to Section 1245 recapture. The other 40 percent is subject to the rules for personal-use property. If Wanda purchased the auto for $15,000, her beginning basis in the business-use part is $9,000 ($15,000 × 60%) and the personal-use part is $6,000 ($15,000 × 40%). If she sells the auto for $4,000 after taking $7,000 in depreciation deductions, she has a $400 Section 1231 gain on the business portion [($4,000 × 60%) – ($9,000 – $7,000)] that must be recaptured as ordinary income under Section 1245. She has a nondeductible loss of $4,400 [($4,000 × 40%) – $6,000] on the personal-use portion.

Tables 7.2 and 7.3 summarize the tax treatment of gains and losses on ordinary, capital, and Section 1231 assets for individual and corporate taxpayers.

TABLE

7.2 SUMMARY OF PROPERTY TRANSACTION TAXATION FOR INDIVIDUALS

TYPE OF PROPERTY	TREATMENT OF GAINS	TREATMENT OF LOSSES
Ordinary	Taxed at ordinary income rates up to 39.6%.	Deductible against other ordinary income taxed at rates up to 39.6%.
Short-term capital assets	Net short-term capital gain taxed at ordinary income rates up to 39.6%.*	Maximum $3,000 of net short-term capital losses deductible annually against ordinary income. Excess losses may be carried forward indefinitely.
Long-term capital assets	Most net long-term capital gains taxed at a maximum rate of 20%; Section 1250 unrecaptured gain and collectibles gain taxed at a maximum 25% and 28% rate, respectively.*	Maximum $3,000 of net long-term capital losses deductible annually against ordinary income; deduction for net short-term and long-term losses combined cannot exceed $3,000. Excess losses may be carried forward indefinitely.
Section 1231	Net Section 1231 gain taxed as a long-term capital gain at a maximum rate of 20%, except Section 1250 unrecaptured gain taxed at 25%.*	Net loss deductible against other ordinary income taxed at rates up to 39.6%.

Excludes 3.8% Medicare surtax.

TABLE
7.3 SUMMARY OF PROPERTY TRANSACTION TAXATION FOR CORPORATIONS

TYPE OF PROPERTY	TREATMENT OF GAINS	TREATMENT OF LOSSES
Ordinary	Taxed at ordinary income rates up to 35%.*	Deductible against other ordinary income taxed at rates up to 35%.*
Short- and long-term capital assets	Net short-term or long-term gain taxed at ordinary income rates up to 35%.*	Net short-term or long-term loss not deductible in the year realized. May be carried back three and forward five years to offset capital gains in those years.
Section 1231	Net gain taxed at ordinary income rates up to 35%*	Net losses fully deductible against ordinary income taxed at rates up to 35%.*

**Nominal rates excluding surtaxes.*

Special Rules for Small Business Stock

Although the alternative capital gain tax rates are designed to encourage investment in capital assets (including stock and securities), two additional provisions—Section 1244 and Section 1202—encourage investment in new corporations.

Losses on Section 1244 Stock

The $3,000 limit on the deductibility of capital losses discourages investment in risky capital assets. Individuals who invest in a small business company whose stock qualifies as Section 1244 stock may be able to deduct all or part of their losses on the stock as ordinary losses. To encourage investment in new corporations, up to $50,000 of the losses on qualifying Section 1244 stock can be deducted as an ordinary loss annually.[49] Any loss in excess of the $50,000 is a capital loss and is subject to all the capital loss provisions discussed earlier. This provision applies only to individuals and partnerships that are the original purchasers of the stock.[50] There is no lifetime limit on the total loss a taxpayer may deduct, but the annual limit is $50,000 of ordinary loss.[51]

[49]If the taxpayer files a joint return, the eligible ordinary loss is increased to $100,000 whether the stock is owned by one spouse or both spouses. Joint returns are discussed in Chapter 11.

[50]Individuals who are partners when a partnership acquires Section 1244 stock are also eligible for this treatment when the *partnership* sells the stock. If the partnership distributes the stock to the partners, it no longer qualifies as Section 1244 stock.

[51]Because of the $1,000,000 capitalization limit, the Section 1244 losses of all individuals are effectively limited to $1,000,000.

To be **Section 1244 stock,** it must be stock in a domestic small business corporation issued in exchange for money or property.[52] A small business corporation is one whose total capitalization does not exceed $1,000,000; however, the corporation must be an operating company at the time the shareholder disposes of the stock. To meet the definition of an **operating company,** 50 percent or more of the corporation's gross revenues must be from the sales of goods or services (operations) for the five years preceding the year in which the Section 1244 stock is sold. Income from rents, royalties, dividends, interest, annuities, and gains on the sales of securities (generally, investment income) is limited to 50 percent or less in the five years preceding the sale year.

EXAMPLE 39

In year 4, John sells one-half of his 40 percent interest in JBC Corporation for $25,000. He originally contributed $120,000 cash for his 40 percent interest; all the stock qualified as Section 1244 at the time it was issued. The corporation currently qualifies as an operating company. John has a $35,000 loss ($25,000 – $60,000) on the sale of the stock, all of which is deductible as an ordinary loss as it does not exceed the $50,000 maximum. In year 6, John sells his remaining stock to another shareholder for $5,000. John has a $55,000 loss ($5,000 – $60,000) on the sale. He can only deduct $50,000 from ordinary income. The other $5,000 loss is a capital loss and must be included in the capital loss netting process. If John has no other capital gains or losses, he can deduct $3,000 of the $5,000 capital loss in the current year. The remaining $2,000 loss carries forward to the next year as a capital loss.

Section 1202 Gains on Qualified Small Business Stock

Another provision that is intended to make investment in small corporations more attractive is the reduction in recognized taxable gain on the sale of qualified small business stock (QSBS or Section 1202 stock) that a noncorporate taxpayer has held for more than five years. The reduction in recognized gain is 100 percent for qualifying stock acquired after September 27, 2010 and before January 1, 2014; 75 percent for stock acquired after February 17, 2009 and before September 28, 2010; and 50 percent for stock acquired before February 18, 2009 and after December 31, 2013. The requirements for a corporation to be a **qualified small business corporation** are far more restrictive than those for small business corporations under Section 1244.

A corporation must meet the following criteria to be a qualified small business corporation:

1. It must be a domestic C corporation (and cannot be an S corporation).[53]
2. The gross value of the corporation's assets cannot exceed $50,000,000.
3. The seller of the stock must be the original owner who acquired the stock in exchange for money, property, or services.
4. The corporation is an active trade or business engaged in manufacturing, retailing, or wholesaling.[54]

When a stockholder disposes of qualifying Section 1202 stock that has been held for more than five years, 50, 75, or 100 percent of the capital gain may be excluded from capital gain and loss determination based on its *purchase* date. Gain eligible for the exclusion, however, cannot exceed the greater of (1) 10 times the adjusted basis of the qualifying stock sold in the tax year or (2) $10,000,000 less any eligible gain on qualifying stock taken into consideration in the preceding tax years by the

[52] A domestic corporation is a corporation incorporated in one of the 50 states.

[53] C and S corporations are discussed in Chapters 9 and 10.

[54] The corporation cannot be a personal service corporation, a banking or other financing-type business, a farm corporation, a mining corporation, or a motel, hotel, or restaurant. It cannot own rental realty or securities that exceed 10 percent of its total assets.

taxpayer. The remaining capital gain on the Section 1202 stock (purchased before September 28, 2010 and after December 31, 2013) that is recognized is included in the capital gain netting process. Because of the tax benefit from the exclusion, the included gain is taxed at the 28 percent capital gains tax rate along with gains on assets characterized as collectibles. Note that the 3.8 percent Medicare surtax can increase the effective rate to 31.8 percent.

EXAMPLE 40

In 2013, Jonas sells one-quarter of his qualifying Section 1202 stock in Magnum Corporation for \$4,000,000. He originally purchased the stock in 2005 for \$300,000. He has a gain of \$3,700,000. He can exclude \$1,850,000 (50% × \$3,700,000) of the gain. The remaining \$1,850,000 of gain is part of the capital asset netting process and is taxed at a maximum 31.8 percent tax rate (28% + 3.8% Medicare surtax). (The stock is not eligible for either the 75% or 100% gain reductions as it was not purchased between February 17, 2009 and January 1, 2014.)

In 2014, Jonas sells his remaining 75 percent interest with a basis of \$900,000 in Magnum Corporation for \$12,000,000. He has a total gain on the sale of \$11,100,000. His gain exclusion now is limited \$4,500,000. This is 50 percent of the greater of \$9,000,000 (10 times the \$900,000 adjusted basis of the stock and \$6,300,000 (the maximum \$10,000,000 eligible gain exclusion less the \$3,700,000 eligible gain on the previous sale). His remaining \$4,500,000 gain is taxed at the maximum 31.8% rate (28% + 3.8% Medicare surtax).

A taxpayer that sells Section 1202 stock held for at least six months and reinvests all the proceeds in another qualified small business corporation's stock may avoid all gain recognition.[55] If only a portion of the proceeds are reinvested, only the gain proportionate to the reinvested proceeds may be excluded. If the stock meets the five-year holding period, the remaining gain is subject to the 50, 75, or 100 percent exclusion based on its purchase date.

EXAMPLE 41

Carolyn sells Section 1202 stock that she has held for nine months for \$750,000. The stock has a basis of \$600,000. She reinvests \$500,000 of the proceeds in other qualifying Section 1202 stock. Carolyn has a gain of \$150,000 on the sale. As she reinvested two-thirds of the proceeds, she may defer two-thirds of her gain on the sale or \$100,000. She cannot exclude any of the remaining \$50,000 gain, however, as she has not held the stock for more than five years. Carolyn has a \$50,000 short-term capital gain and her basis in the stock acquired is \$400,000 (\$500,000 – \$100,000 deferred gain).

Comparison of Sections 1244 and 1202

TAX PLANNING

The Section 1244 stock and Section 1202 stock provisions are both designed to encourage new investment, but there are major differences in the two provisions. Table 7.4 provides a comparison of these provisions. The Section 1244 designation applies to a potentially far smaller corporation than does the Section 1202 designation, but the activities of the QSB are far more limited than the small business corporation. A more important distinction, however, relates to the investor's risk tolerance. An investor who assesses loss as a greater possibility, knowing that the losses would offset other ordinary income, would prefer the stock to be Section 1244 stock. An investor with confidence in the success of a business would be attracted to the gain exclusion of Section 1202 stock.

[55]The basis of the qualified stock acquired with the proceeds is reduced for the excluded gains. Seven percent of the 50 percent or 75 percent excluded gains (but not the 100 percent) are a preference item for the AMT.

TABLE 7.4 A COMPARISON OF SECTIONS 1244 AND 1202

SECTION 1244 STOCK PROVISIONS	SECTION 1202 STOCK PROVISIONS
• Applies only to shareholders that are individuals or partnerships.	• Applies to all noncorporate shareholders that own the stock for five or more years.
• Applies to stock of C and S corporations.	• Applies to C corporation stock only.
• Only stock issued for the first $1,000,000 of capital is eligible.	• Only stock issued when the corporation's gross assets do not exceed $50,000,000 qualifies.
• Allows ordinary loss treatment for a shareholder's losses of up to $50,000 annually.	• Excludes 50% (on stock acquired before February 18, 2009 and after December 31, 2013), 75% (on stock acquired after February 17, 2009 and before September 28, 2010) and 100% (on stock acquired after September 27, 2010 and before January 1, 2014) of the capital gain held more than five years. Total gain eligible for the exclusion is generally $10,000,000 over all years. Eligible gain is limited annually to 10 times the basis of the stock sold if it is greater than the balance of overall exclusion.
• As little as 50 percent of the corporation's income must be from operations for the five years preceding the year of the sale.	• Rental and investment securities are limited to 10 percent of total assets at time of sale. Numerous restrictions apply to the corporation's business activities. Generally, the corporation must be a manufacturer, retailer, or wholesaler.

SALE OF PRINCIPAL RESIDENCE—SECTION 121

Know this paragraph

Investing in a personal residence can be one of the best ways to avoid taxes. Taxpayers who meet the quite liberal qualification provisions that apply to the sale of a personal residence can elect to exclude up to $250,000 of gain realized ($500,000 if married filing jointly) from income. This elective provision applies to all taxpayers regardless of their age and does not require a purchase of a new residence.[56] Any gain in excess of the allowable exclusion of $250,000 ($500,000) is capital gain and is subject to the capital gain treatment for individuals discussed previously. Losses, however, on the sale of a personal residence are personal losses and remain nondeductible.

[56]Under the laws in effect for sales prior to May 6, 1997, persons under 55 could only exclude gain to the extent the proceeds of the sale were reinvested in a new residence. Persons age 55 or over could exclude gain of up to $125,000 if certain conditions were met.

The taxpayer's realized gain is the difference between the amount realized on the sale and the adjusted basis of the residence. The amount realized is the selling price less the selling expenses. In the case of a home, there is a high probability that the adjusted basis is not the same as the home's original purchase price. Basis of the home is adjusted upward for capital improvements, such as room additions and major remodeling of the existing structure, and the addition of landscaping, driveways, and fencing. Normal repairs, however, do not increase the home's basis. The basis must also be reduced for deductible casualty losses or insurance recoveries that are not reinvested in the property.

The amount realized on the sale of the home can require complex calculations as the selling costs can be significant, depending on the state in which the property is located. In general, anything that the seller must pay as part of the sale reduces the amount realized. There is an exception, however. If the taxpayer can deduct part of the expenses, the deductible expense does not reduce the amount realized.[57]

EXAMPLE 42

William, a bachelor, sold his condominium for $325,000. He purchased the condominium five years ago for $189,000. Since then, he made a number of capital improvements to the home at a cost of $47,000, increasing his basis in the property to $236,000 ($189,000 + $47,000). William paid a realtor's commission of $18,000, a $3,250 tax on the transfer of the deed, and other selling expenses of $400. William's amount realized on the sale is $303,350 ($325,000 – $18,000 – $3,250 – $400). William's realized gain on the sale is $67,350 ($303,350 – $236,000). He recognizes none of the gain because it is less than $250,000. If William deducts the transfer taxes as an itemized deduction, the amount realized is $306,600 ($325,000 – $18,000 – $400).

The amount realized on the sale of a home may require an adjustment for the property tax levied in the year of sale. Property taxes must be prorated based on the date of sale. If there is no proration, the selling price must be adjusted to reflect the required split.

EXAMPLE 43

Barton sells his home for $300,000 on July 15 of the current year. Barton agreed to the sales price (which was $20,000 less than his asking price) only after the purchaser agreed to pay the property taxes for the entire year. The property taxes for the year of the sale were $3,650. Barton's apportioned share is $1,960 ($3,650 × 196/365).[58] Barton must increase his amount realized on the sale to $301,960. Alternatively, if Barton had paid the property taxes for the entire year and they were not apportioned between him and the buyer, he would have reduced his amount realized by $1,690 ($3,650 × 169/365), the buyer's share for the time after the sale.

To qualify for nonrecognition of gain on the sale of the taxpayer's principal residence, the taxpayer must meet ownership and use tests. The ownership test requires the taxpayer or the taxpayer's spouse to have owned the residence for at least two of the previous five years.[59] The taxpayer must also have occupied the residence for two of the last five years prior to the date of sale. For a married couple filing jointly to qualify for the $500,000 exclusion, they both must meet the use test, but only one of them must meet the ownership test.[60]

Prior to 2008, if a home was sold after the year of a spouse's death (when a joint return could no longer be filed), the surviving spouse was eligible for a maximum exclusion of $250,000 only. The Mortgage Forgiveness Debt Relief Act of 2007 modified

---

[57]States often levy an ad valorem tax on the deed transfer that is paid by the seller; as an ad valorem tax, it is deductible as an itemized deduction.

[58]The day of the sale is attributed to the seller.

[59]Ownership by a divorced or deceased spouse is included.

[60]§ 121(a) and (b). Neither of them may have sold or exchanged a personal residence within two years of the sale to claim the $500,000 exclusion.

this rule for sales and exchanges after December 31, 2007 to allow the surviving single spouse to qualify for the maximum $500,000 exclusion as long as the sale occurs no later than two years after the spouse's death and the requirements for the $500,000 exclusion were met immediately before the spouse's death.

Under normal circumstances, owners who fail to meet the two-year ownership and use test or who have sold another principal residence within two years of the sale of the current principal residence cannot claim the gain exclusion. If, however, the sale is due to a change in health, employment, or other circumstances beyond the control of the taxpayer, a portion of the gain may be excluded.[61] The allowable excluded portion equals the $250,000 exclusion times a ratio, that has a denominator of 24 months and a numerator that is the shorter of the following:[62]

1. The time period the ownership and use tests were met in the previous five years
2. The time period since the exclusion was last claimed

EXAMPLE 44

Bob bought a new personal residence on June 1 of year 1. In December of year 2, he was laid off from his job and found a new job in a city 200 miles away. He sold his house on February 1, year 3, at a gain of $230,000. Because Bob's move was necessitated by a change of employment, he can exclude a portion of the gain. He owned the house for 20 months, up to the date of the sale. He can exclude $208,333 of the gain (20/24 of the $250,000). He will be taxed on the remaining $21,667 capital gain that cannot be excluded.

The exclusion is determined on an individual basis and increases to $500,000 only if both spouses meet the use test and neither has claimed the exclusion in the previous two years.

TAX PLANNING

There may be problems surrounding the determination of a taxpayer's principal residence, particularly if the taxpayer owns two or more homes. It is possible for a taxpayer to own two homes that are used on a regular basis and to meet the occupancy requirement of two out of five years on each. Under these circumstances the home that is occupied the greater amount of time would be considered the **principal residence**. If a taxpayer contemplates selling one of the homes in the future, care should be taken to establish that home as the permanent residence. Some other relevant factors in determining which home is the principal residence include the taxpayer's place of employment, the principal abode of the taxpayer's family, and the address on the taxpayer's state and federal tax returns, driver's license, car registration, and voter registration.[63]

A vacation home or rental property does not qualify for this exclusion because it is not the taxpayer's principal residence. The Housing Assistance Tax Act of 2008 closed a loophole that had allowed taxpayers to readily convert a vacation home into a principal residence qualifying for the exclusion if it met the two-year ownership and use tests at the time of sale. For sales or exchanges after December 31, 2008, however, the realized gain that is eligible for the exclusion must be reduced based on nonqualified use. The reduction is computed as a percentage by dividing the period of nonqualified use after 2008 by the period of ownership.[64] Nonqualified use is any period after December 31, 2008 during which the house is not used as the principal residence of the taxpayer or spouse.

EXAMPLE 45

Robert and Sarah, a married couple, bought a vacation home on January 1, 2007 for $400,000. They used it as a vacation home until January 1, 2011 when it became their principal residence. It continues to be

[61]Reg. §1.121-3T(e). Examples of unforeseen circumstances include death of a spouse or co-owner, divorce, unemployment, disasters, and involuntary conversion of residence.

[62]§121(c).

[63]Reg. §1.121-1(b)(2) includes factors to be considered in determining if a home is a taxpayer's principal residence.

[64]§121(b)(4).

their principal residence until January 1, 2014 when they sell the home for $700,000. Their realized gain is $300,000 ($700,000 – $400,000). Because they did not use the home as their principal residence for 2 years (2009 and 2010) of their 7 years of ownership (2007 through 2013) $85,714 (2/7 × $300,000) of the gain is ineligible for the exclusion. They can exclude $214,286 ($300,000 – $85,714) of the gain under Section 121 resulting in a recognized gain of $85,714 ($300,000 – $214,286). If Robert and Sarah had used the home as their principal residence for the entire time they owned it, they would have been able to exclude the entire $300,000 gain.

If a taxpayer has claimed depreciation for a portion of the home used as a home office, any gain related to the depreciated portion of the home is not eligible for this exclusion and must be recognized as gain on the sale of business property.[65]

Debt Reductions, Short Sales, and Foreclosures

Normally, when all or part of a taxpayer's debt is reduced or forgiven, the taxpayer has income from this cancellation of debt regardless of whether the cancellation is a result of modification of mortgage loan terms or the taxpayer disposes of the property in a short sale, abandons the property, or the property is taken in foreclosure proceedings. Fortunately for taxpayers, Congress addressed the problem initially in the Mortgage Forgiveness Debt Relief Act of 2007 by excluding from income the discharge or forgiveness of qualified principal residence debt occurring after 2006 and before 2010. With the continued problems in the housing market, this exclusion was extended an additional three years, through 2012, by the Emergency Economic Stabilization Act of 2008 and was extended through 2013 by the Taxpayer Relief Act of 2012. This provision allows taxpayers to exclude the cancellation of up to $2 million of qualified principal residence debt from income.[66]

Qualified principal residence indebtedness is defined as acquisition debt[67] on the taxpayers' principal residence but with a limit of $2 million ($1 million for married individuals filing separately).[68] The taxpayer's principal residence is determined under Section 121 rules for excluding the gain on the sale of the principal residence. Acquisition indebtedness includes debt secured by that residence and incurred in the acquisition, construction, or substantial improvement of the residence. If qualifying acquisition debt is refinanced, none of the refinancing debt that exceeds the amount of refinanced debt (immediately before refinancing) qualifies as acquisition debt. The income exclusion applies only to that part of the loan that represents qualified principal residence indebtedness. In the event the taxpayer continues to own the home after debt cancellation, the basis of that home must be reduced by the amount of the cancelled debt, but not below zero.

Example 46

Willis purchased his home in 1996 for $150,000 paying $20,000 down and undertaking a $130,000 mortgage secured by the home. In 2009, he refinanced the home for $200,000 taking the $120,000 cash over the balance of the existing mortgage of $80,000 to invest in a friend's restaurant. In 2012, the restaurant went bankrupt and Willis lost his job. In 2013, after being unemployed for almost a year, Willis worked out a mortgage reduction on the home with his bank after obtaining a new, but lower paying job. The bank forgave $90,000 of the existing $190,000 balance on the mortgage and revised the terms for the remaining $100,000 mortgage. Willis has $10,000 of income from the forgiveness on the loan because the $90,000 of debt forgiven is $10,000 greater than his original qualifying residential indebtedness of $80,000. None of the additional $120,000 debt included at the time of refinancing is qualified acquisition

[65] Reg. § 1.121-1(e)(4), Ex. 5. Any gain due to depreciation is unrecaptured Section 1250 gain taxed at a 25 percent rate.

[66] § 108(a)(1)(E).

[67] § 163(h)(3)(B)

[68] § 108(h)(2)

indebtedness. In addition, Willis must reduce the basis of his house to $70,000 ($150,000 purchase price – $80,000 acquisition debt) for the amount of the qualifying acquisition debt forgiven.

Losses on Related Party Sales

Sometimes taxpayers sell assets to family members or other related buyers (such as family-owned corporations), hoping to trigger a loss for tax purposes without fully relinquishing control of the asset. Though there is no prohibition against selling property to **related parties,** Section 267 disallows loss recognition on a sale or exchange of property between related parties, even though the selling price can be validated as fair market value at the time of the sale. This provision only applies to losses; gains on sales to related parties are recognized.

An individual is directly related to his or her spouse, brothers and sisters, ancestors, and lineal descendants. A taxpayer is related to a corporation if the taxpayer owns more than 50 percent of the stock in a corporation. If an individual owns more than 50 percent in each of a corporation and a partnership, the entities are considered related parties under the attribution rules.[69]

The related buyer's basis is the price actually paid, even though the seller's loss is not deductible. If the buyer later sells the property at or below the purchase price, any deductible loss is measured from that purchase price. The net effect is that the original seller's loss is never deducted.

If the buyer sells the asset at a gain, however, no gain is recognized unless the purchase price exceeds the related-party's original basis. In effect, the *seller's* unrecognized loss is allowed to offset all or part of the buyer's gain on a subsequent sale.

EXAMPLE 47

Gerry had a $2,000 capital gain on which he did not want to pay taxes. To avoid the tax, he sold 100 shares of stock to his brother for $3,000 that he had purchased for $5,000. Gerry has a realized loss of $2,000, but he is unable to recognize (deduct) the loss to offset the gain because of the loss disallowance provisions for related party sales.

If Gerry's brother then sells the stock for a price between $3,000 and $5,000, he will recognize no gain because Gerry's unrecognized loss can be used to offset his gain. He will only recognize gain if he sells the stock for more than $5,000 (the price at which Gerry purchased the shares). If he sells the stock for $3,000 or less, the tax benefit of Gerry's $2,000 loss is never recognized.

Individual Capital Gains Tax Rates

Determining tax liability and tax planning for individuals is complicated by the different long-term capital gains tax rates that apply to individuals based on their ordinary income tax rates and types of long-term assets. Although most capital gains are taxed at 15 (20 percent for upper income taxpayers only), unrecaptured Section 1250 gains (due to depreciation on realty) are taxed at a maximum 25 percent, and collectibles such as antiques and art objects along with Section 1202 gains (from sales of qualified small business stock) are taxed at a maximum 28 percent.[70] The existence of capital losses and capital loss carryovers further complicates the determination of the tax liability. In addition, individuals whose total taxable income does not exceed the 15 percent tax bracket have all of their long-term capital gains taxed at a zero percent rate. Other taxpayers whose marginal ordinary income tax rates are less than the 25 or 28 percent tax rate also have these capital gains tax rates modified. Finally,

[69]There are also rules covering relationships between controlled corporations and the parties involved in estates and trusts that are beyond the scope of this brief discussion.

[70]Note that the 25 percent tax rate only applies to gains resulting from depreciation deductions on Section 1231 real property that are not recaptured at ordinary income tax rates .

higher income taxpayers may be subject to a 20 percent capital gains tax rate and/or the Medicare surtax.

Determining the Long-Term Capital Gains Tax Rate

If the result of the capital asset netting process is a net long-term capital gain, the net long-term capital gains are separated into three groups based on the asset type and maximum tax rates (15/20, 25, and 28 percent). Gains first offset losses in each of the three categories. Next, if there is a net loss in the 28 percent category, it first offsets a net gain in the 25 percent category and any remaining loss offsets a net gain in the 15/20 percent category. If there was no net loss in the 28 percent category, then a net loss in the 15/20 percent category offsets the net gain in the 28 percent category before a net gain in the 25 percent category. (There are no losses in the 25 percent rate to offset other gains as it only has unrecaptured Section 1250 gains.) If the taxpayer has a net short-term capital loss, it offsets any remaining net long-term capital gains only after losses in other categories have offset the gains. This net short-term loss offsets the highest taxed long-term gain first—the 28 percent, then the 25 percent, and finally the 15/20 percent. Long- and short-term capital losses that are carried over from other years follow a similar pattern to offset any remaining gains.

If a taxpayer has no short-term or long-term capital losses or capital loss carryovers included in the netting process, the taxpayer simply separates the gains into their proper categories and applies the appropriate tax rates.

Example 48

Toby is in the 28 percent income tax bracket after considering his ordinary income and a number of transactions involving several types of capital assets held more than one year: a $6,800 long-term capital gain and a $4,300 long-term capital loss on some stock investments; a $2,000 Section 1250 unrecaptured gain on property; a $4,200 gain on the sale of his gun collection, a $3,100 loss on the sale of an antique automobile, and a $1,500 loss on a painting (collectibles).

He first nets all of his long-term gains and losses (regardless of their type or tax rate) to determine if he has a net long-term capital gain or loss. Because he has a net $4,100 long-term capital gain ($6,800 − $4,300 + $2,000 + $4,200 − $3,100 − $1,500), Toby must separate his long-term gains and losses into their proper categories to determine which rates apply to the net gain. He has a $2,500 ($6,800 − $4,300) net long-term gain on his investments (15/20 percent category), a $2,000 Section 1250 gain (taxed at 25 percent); and a $400 ($4,200 − $3,100 − $1,500) net loss on the collectibles (28 percent assets). The $400 net loss on the 28 percent assets offset $400 of the $2,000 Section 1250 gain. As a result, Toby has a $1,600 net capital gain taxed at 25 percent and a $2,500 net gain taxed at 15 percent. (Neither the Medicare surtax nor the 20 percent capital gains tax rate apply.)

Example 49

An individual taxpayer is in the 33 percent tax bracket with ordinary income of $220,000. In addition he has a $15,000 net capital gain that consists of a $20,000 collectible gain (28 percent), a $30,000 long-term gain (15/20 percent), and a $35,000 net short-term loss. The taxpayer first offsets $20,000 of the collectible gain with $20,000 of the net short-term loss; the remaining $15,000 net short-term loss offsets $15,000 of the long-term gain. The taxpayer's remaining $15,000 long-term gain is taxed at the maximum capital gain rate of 15 percent to which he must add the 3.8 percent Medicare surtax for a total rate of 18.8 percent because the taxpayer's taxable income exceeds the $200,000 threshold.

While this process is extremely cumbersome, it is necessary only when the net result of the final netting process is a long-term capital gain.[71] If the final result is only a net capital loss, whether short term or long term, or a net short-term capital gain

[71]In addition, if the long-term capital gains are all in one category, any resulting net capital gain is simply taxed at that category's tax rate.

only, the losses are deducted up to $3,000 and the short-term gain is included as ordinary income. The determination of different tax rates is unnecessary.

Modified Capital Gains Rates

The 15, 25, and 28 percent capital gains tax rates are all modified for taxpayers in the lower income tax brackets. (The 20 percent capital gains tax rate only applies to higher income taxpayers.) Long-term capital gains subject to the 15 percent capital gains tax rate are eligible for a zero tax rate for taxpayers whose taxable income, including their capital gains, does not exceed the maximum taxable income in the 15 percent tax rate bracket. Most capital gains that exceed these bracket limits are taxed at the normal 15 percent capital gains rate.

EXAMPLE 50

Sally is single and has $30,000 of taxable income excluding an $8,000 long-term capital gain on some investments for total taxable income of $38,000. Sally's tax liability is calculated as follows: ($8,925 × 10%) + [($30,000 – $8,925) × 15%] + [($36,250 – $30,000) × 0%] + [($38,000 – $36,250) × 15%] = $892.50 + $3,161.25 + $0 + $262.50 = $4,316.25. Only $30,000 of Sally's taxable income is taxed using the tax rate schedule and is the sum of the first two calculations. Only $6,250 of her long-term capital gains are eligible for the zero tax rate as the limit of the 15 percent tax bracket is $36,250. The capital gains in excess of $36,250 are taxed at 15 percent. The tax on her capital gains is the sum of her capital gains taxed at zero percent and 15 percent.

If Sally's ordinary taxable income had been more than $36,250, all of her long-term capital gains would have been taxed at 15 percent. If her total taxable income had been below $36,250, all of the portion representing long-term capital gains would have been tax free.

Taxpayers with the type of capital gains subject to the maximum 25 or 28 percent tax rate, have these capital gains taxed at a lower tax rate to the extent that their taxable income including these gains does not exceed the maximum income subject to the 15 percent tax rate. Thus, the gains on 25 and 28 percent assets are taxed at 10 or 15 percent to the extent all or part of these gains do not exceed the 10 or 15 percent tax bracket when combined with ordinary taxable income. Any gains attributed to these 25 and 28 percent assets that exceed the 15 percent bracket are taxed at 25 and 28 percent, respectively.

EXAMPLE 51

Tony, who is single, has $30,000 of taxable salary income and a $10,000 long-term capital gain on the sale of his coin collection (a 28 percent asset). In 2013, the 15 percent bracket applies to incomes between $8,925 and $36,250. The 15 percent rate applies to Tony's $30,000 taxable salary income above $8,925 and to $6,250 ($36,250 – $30,000) of his long-term capital gain. The remaining $3,750 ($10,000 – $6,250) of his capital gain is taxed at 28 percent.

Because these modifications to the rates apply to different types of long-term capital gains, a person with more than one type of capital gain has to include them in taxable income in a specific order: 25 percent gains are included first, then 28 percent gains, and 15 percent gains included last. (If taxable income exceeds the threshold for the 39.6 percent bracket, the rate on capital gains taxed at 15 percent increases to 20 percent as discussed previously.)

EXAMPLE 52

A single taxpayer has $9,000 of ordinary taxable income in 2013, a $18,000 long-term capital gain on the sale of some antiques (28 percent assets), a $12,000 unrecaptured Section 1250 gain on realty (25 percent assets), and a $4,000 gain on the sale of bonds (15 percent assets), for total taxable income of $43,000. Using 2013 rates:

a. The tax on the $9,000 of ordinary taxable income determined first is: ($8,925 × 10%) + [($9,000 – $8,925) × 15%] = $903.75

b. The $12,000 Section 1250 gain is taxed next at 15 percent ($1,800 tax) as it falls entirely within the 15 percent tax bracket.

c. Next, the $18,000 collectible gain causes taxable income to exceed the 15 percent tax bracket and is taxed as follows: [($36,250 – $9,000 – $12,000) × 15%] + [($39,000 – $36,250) × 28%] = $2,287.50 + $770 = $3,057.50

d. The taxpayer's final $4,000 of gain on the sale of the bonds is taxed at 15 percent ($600 tax). Her total income tax is $6,361.25 ($903.75 + $1,800 + $3,057.50 + $600).

The rate reductions introduced by the 2003 Act were made effective for sales and exchanges made after May 5, 2003, and provided a 5 percent long-term capital gains tax rate for taxpayers with income in the 10 or 15 percent tax brackets through 2007. This act also replaced the 5 percent rate with a zero rate for the years 2008 through 2010, and the 2010 Job Creation Act extended the zero and 15 percent long-term capital gains rates through 2012. In the first days of 2013, Congress passed the 2012 Taxpayer Relief Act that continued the zero and 15 percent tax rates except for taxpayer's whose taxable income exceeded $400,000 to $450,000 based on filing status. Long-term capital gains exceeding this threshold are now taxed at 20 percent.[72] The 2012 Taxpayer Relief Act did not change the 25 percent or 28 percent special tax rates for certain long-term capital gains.

Planning

The zero long-term capital gains tax rate that applies to individuals in the 10 or 15 percent marginal tax brackets initially appears to provide a perfect planning opportunity for parents to gift appreciated stock to their children and then have the children sell the securities tax-free if the children's tax rates are in the two lowest tax brackets. To close this loophole, Congress increased the age at which the kiddie tax rules apply to all children under age 19 as well as most full time students under age 24. These kiddie tax rules tax unearned income (including capital gains) of a "child" in excess of a fixed amount at the parents' tax rates, effectively allowing only a small amount of gain to escape taxation.[73]

Individuals can benefit from the difference in the tax rates on gains for specific long-term capital asset dispositions if alternative asset dispositions are available. For example, a loss on a 15 percent long-term capital asset can offset gains on both 25 and 28 percent assets. A long-term capital loss can offset a short-term capital gain and a long-term capital loss carryover offsets gains in the 28 and 25 percent asset categories before a gain taxed at 15 percent. These rate differences and the order in which they are imposed offer planning opportunities for individuals.

EXAMPLE 53

George (who is in the 33 percent marginal tax bracket) has a long-term capital gain of $20,000 on some artwork that he sold. As a collectible, the gain will be taxed at 28 percent. He has 100,000 shares of CDC stock that have decreased in value by $22,000 since he bought them five years ago. If George sells the stock before the end of the tax year, he will realize the $22,000 long-term capital loss and he will be able to offset the entire $20,000 gain taxed at 28 percent and an additional $2,000 of ordinary income taxed at 33 percent. Instead of paying an additional $5,600 ($20,000 × 28%) in taxes from the sale, he will save $660 ($2,000 × 33%) on his regular tax bill. (His savings would be even greater if the gain would have been subject to the 3.8% Medicare surtax.)

---

[72]The 3.8 percent Medicare surtax increases this 20 percent top rate to 23.8 percent for upper income taxpayers.

[73]Since 2009, a child is subject to the kiddie tax rules if he or she has not attained age 19 before the close of the tax year or is a full time student under age 24 and the child's earned income does not exceed one-half of his or her own support. A child subject to the kiddie tax pays tax at his or her parents' marginal rate on the child's unearned income over $2,000 if that tax is higher than the tax the child would otherwise pay. See Chapter 12 for a more complete discussion of the kiddie tax.

Example 54

Christian, who is in the 33 percent tax bracket, has a $12,000 short-term capital loss on ABC stock purchased earlier in the year. He also has an unrealized gain of $18,000 on XYZ stock that he purchased several years ago. He deals with a discount broker who charges only $20 per transaction. If Christian sells half of his XYZ stock, he will realize a $9,000 gain and reduce his net loss for the year to a fully deductible $3,000 loss. He can then repurchase identical XYZ shares to replace those sold at a cost of $40 for the two trades. (The wash sale rules only affect loss recognition, not gain, as explained in Chapter 8.) By realizing the $9,000 gain, he accelerates an additional $9,000 loss deduction that would normally have to be deducted at a rate of $3,000 per year over the next three years. At a discount rate of 8 percent, he is better off by $379 [($9,000 × 33%) – ($3,000 × 33% × .926) – ($3,000 × 33% × .857) – ($3,000 × 33% × .794) – $40].

Revisiting the Introductory Case

The following is the schedule of gains and losses and their type:

Asset	Gain/Loss and Type	Calculation
ADC Stock	$2,000 capital loss	($63,000 – $65,000)
Expansion land	$60,000 Section 1231 gain	($240,000 – $180,000)
Machines	$60,000 Section 1245 gain	($120,000 – $60,000)
Storage building	$20,000 Section 1231 gain and	($100,000 – $75,000)
	$5,000 additional Section 291 recapture	($25,000 × 20%)
Storage building land	$5,000 Section 1231 loss	($25,000 – $30,000)
Warehouse	$220,000 Section 1231 casualty loss	(0 - $220,000)
Warehouse land	$10,000 Section 1231 gain	

The $60,000 Section 1245 gain on the machines and the $5,000 Section 291 additional recapture on the storage building are included in ordinary income. The $220,000 Section 1231 loss on the warehouse is the only casualty loss in the first step of the Section 1231 netting process and is deducted directly from ordinary income. The $60,000 gain on the expansion land is netted with the $5,000 Section 1231 loss on the storage building land, the $20,000 Section 1231 gain on the storage building, and the $10,000 Section 1231 gain on the warehouse land. The net Section 1231 gain is $85,000. This net gain is treated now as a long-term capital gain. As it is the only long-term gain or loss, it is netted with the $2,000 short-term capital loss on the ADC stock. The corporation has a net long-term capital gain of $83,000 that is included directly in ordinary income. The net effect of these transactions is to decrease the corporation's taxable income by $72,000 ($65,000 depreciation recapture – $220,000 casualty loss + $83,000 net capital gain).

Summary

Two important ways to classify assets for tax purposes are: (1) business, investment, or personal use and (2) ordinary, capital, or Section 1231. Together, these classifications determine the tax treatment of all asset dispositions. The most common asset disposition is a sale; other dispositions include exchanges, abandonments, and involuntary conversions.

Section 1231 property includes all depreciable property and all nondepreciable realty used in a trade or business and rental realty and related property held for more than one year. Section 1231 also includes assets held for the production of income that are subject to involuntary conversions. Section 1231 gains and losses must go through a two-step netting process to determine their final disposition. Generally, net Section 1231 gains are included in the capital asset netting process as long-term capital gains. Net Section 1231 losses are deducted immediately from ordinary income.

Several provisions impact the treatment of Section 1231 gains, requiring all or part of the gain to be treated as ordinary income. The Sections 1245 and 1250 recapture provisions reduce Section 1231 gains for all or part of the prior depreciation deductions on assets. This portion of the gain is taxed as ordinary income. Section 291 requires corporations to recapture an extra increment of Section 1250 gain as ordinary income. The Section 1231 look-back rule provisions require Section 1231 gains to be treated as ordinary income to the extent of Section 1231 loss deductions in the prior five years.

Capital assets include personal-use property and most investment assets. Gains and losses on capital assets must also go through a netting process after they are separated into long term and short term. The treatment of capital gains and losses for individuals and corporations differs widely. Corporations include all net capital gains directly in income and are only allowed to deduct net capital losses against capital gains in the three carryback and five carryforward years.

Individuals may deduct a maximum of $3,000 of net capital losses annually, but they may carry forward remaining net losses indefinitely. A net short-term capital gain is included directly in income. Net long-term capital gains of individuals are subject to multiple tax rates varying from zero to 28 percent based on the specific type of capital gain and the taxpayer's tax rate bracket. Individuals' net investment income, which generally includes capital gains, is also subject to the Medicare surtax of 3.8% if their taxable income exceeds a specified threshold based on filing status.

The primary ordinary assets are inventory, accounts receivable, and business-use assets that fail to meet the more-than-one-year holding period for Section 1231 status. Gains and losses on ordinary income assets are included directly in the taxpayer's income along with ordinary income from business operations. Two provisions encourage taxpayers to invest in smaller corporations. The first allows taxpayers to deduct up to $50,000 in losses annually on Section 1244 stock as ordinary losses, rather than capital losses. The second excludes up to 50, 75, or 100 percent of the gain on qualified small business stock from taxation based on purchase date.

Section 121 allows individuals who have owned and occupied their personal residences to exclude up to $250,000 ($500,000 if filing jointly) of the gain from income. This provision is available once every two years to all individuals who meet the ownership and occupancy requirements.

KEY TERMS

Abandonments 294
Amount realized 294
Capital assets 297
Exchange 294
Fair market value 294
Involuntary conversions 294
Long-term capital asset 307
Operating company 318
Ordinary income asset 298
Principal residence 322
Qualified small business corporation 318
Realized gain 295
Realized loss 295
Recognized gain 295
Recognized loss 295
Related parties 324
Section 1231 assets 297
Section 1244 stock 318
Section 1245 full recapture 300
Section 1250 recapture 300
Short-term capital asset 307

TEST YOURSELF

ANSWERS APPEAR AFTER THE PROBLEM ASSIGNMENTS

1. Vera has three assets she plans to sell. The first is her personal automobile that is seven years old; the second is a truck used in her business for 11 months; and the third is some land that she bought four years ago for expansion of her business. What types of assets are they: capital, Section 1231, or ordinary income?
   a. car = capital; truck = Section 1231; land = capital
   b. car = capital; truck = ordinary; land = Section 1231
   c. car = ordinary; truck = ordinary; land = capital
   d. car = ordinary; truck = Section 1231; land = capital

2. A taxpayer has the following gains and losses from property transactions in the current year:

$40,000	Section 1231 gain
$25,000	Section 1231 loss
$12,000	Long-term capital gain
$9,000	Short-term capital loss

How are these transactions treated for tax purposes if the taxpayer recognized an $8,000 Section 1231 loss in the previous tax year?

a. $18,000 long-term capital gain
b. $15,000 Section 1231 gain; $3,000 short-term capital loss
c. $8,000 ordinary income from look-back; $10,000 long-term capital gain
d. $8,000 ordinary income from look-back; $7,000 Section 1231 gain; $3,000 long-term capital gain

3. Trendy Corporation has a net short-term capital loss of $9,000 and a net long-term capital loss of $14,000 in year 5. Trendy Corporation can

a. deduct $3,000 of the short-term capital loss from its ordinary income and carry the remaining losses back to year 2.
b. deduct $3,000 of the long-term capital loss from its ordinary income and carry the remaining losses forward indefinitely.
c. deduct all $23,000 of the capital losses from its ordinary income.
d. deduct none of the capital losses. The corporation must carry back the entire net capital loss as a short-term capital loss to year 2.

4. Jonathon sells the computer that he has used 75 percent for business use and 25 percent for personal use for $1,200. The computer cost $4,000 and the allowable depreciation on the computer is $2,200. How much Section 1231 gain or loss does Jonathon recognize?

a. $800 gain
b. $400 gain
c. $100 gain
d. $800 loss

5. Mason is an original shareholder of 1,000 shares of Section 1244 stock in Miles Corporation that he acquired four years ago. He has a basis of $65,000 in the stock. The stock has significantly declined in value so he sells it in the current year for $5,000. Identify the amount and type of gain or loss that Mason has on this sale.

a. $50,000 ordinary loss and a $10,000 capital loss
b. $60,000 capital loss
c. $53,000 ordinary loss and a $12,000 capital loss
d. $60,000 ordinary loss

PROBLEM ASSIGNMENTS

CHECK YOUR UNDERSTANDING

1. How are assets classified to determine their tax treatment on disposition? What are other ways to classify assets? What events qualify as asset dispositions?

2. How is the amount realized on a sale or exchange determined?

3. Explain the difference between a realized gain and a recognized gain.

4. What type of assets are Section 1231 assets? What type of assets are capital assets? What type of assets are ordinary income assets? Give several examples of each type of asset.

5. Why do taxpayers have to recapture depreciation on depreciable assets sold at a gain? To which assets do the Section 1245 and 1250 recapture provisions apply?

6. Explain the look-back procedure for Section 1231 assets. Why did this particular provision evolve?

7. What is Section 291 recapture? Compare this to unrecaptured Section 1250 gains.

8. How are net losses treated in the Section 1231 netting process? How is a net Section 1231 gain taxed?

9. How are capital assets classified as short-term and long-term? How are long-term gains and losses and short-term gains and losses treated in the capital asset netting process?

10. How are net short-term capital gains of individuals treated? How are net short-term capital gains of corporations treated?

11. How are net capital losses of individuals treated for tax purposes? How are net capital losses of corporations treated for tax purposes?

12. What is the significance of having stock qualify as Section 1244 stock?

13. Why could it be very advantageous to have a substantial investment in stock in a qualified small business corporation?

14. What are the ownership and use tests for excluding the maximum gain on the sale of a personal residence? Under what circumstances may the owner of a personal residence exclude gain if the required ownership and use tests are not met?

15. What are the maximum tax rates that would apply to a single individual's $20,000 long-term capital gain on corporate stocks if total taxable income is
   a. $35,000?
   b. $230,000?
   c. $430,000?
   d. How would your answers change for (a), (b), and (c), if the $20,000 gain was from the sale of an Egyptian statue?
   e. How would your answers change for (a), (b), and (c), if the $20,000 was an unrecaptured Section 1250 gain?

16. If a married couple who file jointly have a $10,000 net long-term capital gain, what are the maximum tax rates applicable to that gain if their total taxable income would otherwise be taxed at 15 percent, 25 percent, 33 percent, or 39.6 percent and the gain is from
   a. an investment bond?
   b. a stamp collection?
   c. an unrecaptured Section 1250 gain?

CRUNCH THE NUMBERS

17. Charlie sold Whiteacre for $40,000 cash and the buyer assumed Charlie's $19,000 mortgage on the property. Charlie paid a realtor commission of $2,000 on the sale. What is his realized gain or loss if Whiteacre has an adjusted basis of
   a. $47,000?
   b. $67,000?

18. Allan received $5,000 cash and an auto worth $15,000 in exchange for land that was encumbered by a $13,000 liability that the buyer assumed.

a. What is the amount realized on this sale?

b. If Allan had a basis of $34,000 in the land, what is his gain or loss on the sale?

c. If Allan has owned the land for five years as an investment, what is the character of the gain or loss?

d. How would your answer to (c) change if the land had been used by Allan's business as a parking lot?

19. Corgill Corporation sold land that it had used for storing old equipment. Corgill owned the land for seven years and it had a basis of $234,000. Corgill received $50,000 cash and a note for $100,000 and the purchaser assumed Corgill's $150,000 mortgage on the property. Corgill also paid a realtor's fee of $15,000 and other selling expenses of $2,000.

a. What is Corgill's gain or loss on the sale and what is its character?

b. If Corgill had held the land as an investment, how would your answer change?

20. Bernadette sold her home. She received cash of $40,000, the buyer assumed her mortgage of $180,000, and she paid closing costs of $2,300 and a broker's commission of $7,000.

a. What is the amount realized on the sale?

b. If she has a basis in the home of $138,000, what is her gain or loss on the sale?

c. What is the character of the gain or loss?

d. How would your answer to (c) change if Bernadette sold a building used by her sole proprietorship rather than her personal residence?

21. DDF Corporation sold land it had used for parking and storage for 20 years for $575,000. Its basis in the land was $68,000. It also sold some manufacturing equipment for $125,000 that it replaced with more modern equipment. The equipment sold had a basis of $760,000.

a. Determine the amount and character of DDF's gains or losses on these sales.

b. If DDF has no other property transactions, how is the net gain or loss treated?

22. Barry Corporation sold a machine used in its business for two years for $27,000. The machine originally cost $24,000 and it had an adjusted basis at the time of the sale of $17,000. Determine the amount and type of gain realized on the sale.

23. The Grid Corporation owns a bank of boring machines. They regularly replace two machines each year. In the current year, the company sold Machine 8 for $12,000. It was purchased six years earlier for $40,000, and its adjusted basis was $14,000. Machine 6 was sold for $24,000. It was purchased four years ago for $45,000 and had an adjusted basis of $19,000.

a. How much gain or loss is realized on each asset?

b. What is the character of the gain or loss?

c. If the company disposed of no other assets during the year, how are the results of these sales treated for tax purposes?

24. Jonas, an individual, acquired a building nine years ago for $650,000. He sold it in the current year for $680,000 when its adjusted basis was

$500,000. Determine the amount and type of gain or loss realized on the sale

a. if the building is a factory.
b. if the building is an apartment complex.
c. if Jonas is a corporation rather than an individual.

25. Barbara sold two assets during year 5. How much and what kind of gain or loss does she have from each sale?
 a. On February 25 of year 5, she sold 200 shares of XYZ stock for $19,000. She bought that stock for $16,000 on February 23 of year 4.
 b. On July 20 of year 5, she sold an antique automobile for $30,000. She purchased the automobile for $31,000 on July 21 of year 4.

26. Barbara had the following Section 1231 gains and losses in the previous four years:

YEAR	SECTION 1231 GAIN (LOSS)
1	$50,000
2	($45,000)
3	$20,000
4	$15,000

 a. How will Barbara treat a $25,000 gain in year 5?
 b. Is there any unrecaptured Section 1231 loss remaining?

27. The Angel Corporation acquired an office building for $600,000 12 years ago. The corporation claimed $80,000 of cost recovery deductions before it sold the building for $700,000.
 a. Determine the amount and type of gain or loss that Angel Corporation must recognize on the sale of the building.
 b. Would your answer change if Angel were a sole proprietorship?
 c. Would your answer change if Angel Corporation incurred $43,000 of Section 1231 losses in the prior year?

28. Performance Industries, Inc. sold three pieces of equipment and a small building on March 1, year 6. Data on these disposals are as follows:

MACHINE	COST	DATE ACQUIRED	DEPRECIATION	SELLING PRICE
1	$45,000	April 24, year 2	$35,000	$19,000
2	$105,000	May 2, year 1	$90,000	$24,000
3	$63,000	June 4, year 4	$12,000	$66,000
Building	$400,000	April 30, year 1	$45,000	$425,000

 a. Determine the amount and character of the gain or loss on each of these assets.
 b. Determine the sum of each type of gain or loss and the net effect these gains/losses have on Performance Industries' net income.
 c. How would your answers change if Performance Industries had $6,000 of Section 1231 losses in year 3?

29. Determine the amount of the capital gain or loss in each of the following transactions and state whether the gain or loss is long term or short term.
 a. 100 shares of Bilco stock bought for $8,000 on January 22 of year 3 and sold for $10,000 on January 22 of year 4.
 b. 20 acres of investment land bought for $8,000 on January 31 of year 3 and sold for $7,000 on February 2 of year 4.
 c. 150 shares of Dantron stock bought for $15,000 on April 1 of year 3 and sold for $17,000 on May 28 of year 5.

30. Late in the current year, Brad Corporation's factory was destroyed by a tornado. Brad determined that it had a $200,000 unreimbursed loss on the building built ten years ago and a $75,000 gain on ten-year-old machinery (cost $100,000). Prior to the tornado, Brad had a condemnation gain on land of $100,000, a Section 1231 loss of $150,000, and a $25,000 Section 1231 gain.

   a. Determine the results of both Step 1 and Step 2 of the Section 1231 netting process and the effect of these occurrences on Brad's net income.

   b. How would your answers change if Brad was a sole proprietorship instead of a corporation?

31. In the current year, Serena sold investment land for $105,000 that she purchased six years ago for $61,000; a diamond engagement ring for $1,800 that her ex-fiancée had given her nine months ago (purchased for $2,500 a week before giving it to her); 2,000 shares of stock for $14,000 that had been purchased two years ago for $18,000; and a personal auto for $12,000 purchased two months ago for $10,900. Determine the capital gain or loss on each sale, if it is short or long term, and the result of the capital asset netting process.

32. Sharon has salary income of $68,000, a net short-term capital gain of $15,000, and a net long-term capital loss of $24,000. What is Sharon's adjusted gross income if she has no other income items?

33. Wilma had a loss of $25,000 on some bearer bonds that were stolen and never recovered. She suffered a $20,000 loss when a piece of land she had held as an investment was condemned to make way for a new city park. She also had a Section 1231 gain of $60,000 and a Section 1231 loss of $15,000 from asset sales by her sole proprietorship.

   a. Determine the result of both Step 1 and Step 2 of the Section 1231 netting process and explain the treatment of the resulting gains or losses.

   b. How would your answer change if Wilma had a Section 1231 loss of $12,000 two years ago?

34. Chester provides you with the following income information for years 1 through 3, exclusive of capital loss carryovers:

	SHORT-TERM CAPITAL GAIN	SHORT-TERM CAPITAL LOSS	LONG-TERM CAPITAL GAIN	LONG-TERM CAPITAL LOSS
Year 1	0	$2,400	$400	$3,500
Year 2	$500	$1,700	$900	$1,000
Year 3	$2,000	$400	$300	$500

Determine the amount and type of capital loss deduction each year, if any, and the carryover to the following year.

35. An individual taxpayer has the following gains and losses from property transactions. What is the effect on the taxpayer's taxable income?

$4,000	Long-term capital gain
7,000	Long-term capital loss
10,000	Section 1231 gain
6,000	Section 1231 loss
3,000	Short-term capital gain
6,000	Short-term capital loss

36. Juno Corporation had ordinary taxable income of $127,000 in the current year before consideration of any of the following property transactions. It sold two blocks of stock held for investment. One yielded a short-term capital gain of $8,000 and the other a long-term capital loss of $14,000. In addition, Juno sold four pieces of machinery for $30,000. It purchased the machines three years ago for $80,000 and claimed $35,000 of depreciation deductions. Juno also sold a building for $400,000 that it had purchased fifteen years ago for $390,000. The depreciation deductions up to the date of sale for the building were $108,000. Determine the amount and character of each gain or loss from the property transactions and Juno Corporation's taxable income for the current year.

37. Eight years ago, Daniel bought some qualified small business stock for $2,000,000. In the current year, he sells that stock for $13,000,000. How much and what kind of gain or loss does he have? How would your answer change if Daniel sold the stock for $25,000,000?

38. Vanessa bought 2,000 shares of Barbco stock when the company was formed for $107,000. The company had $900,000 of total capital upon formation; thus, it qualified as Section 1244 stock. Vanessa sold the stock three years later for $3,000. If Vanessa is single, how much and what kind of gain or loss does she have?

39. Taylor bought 10,000 shares of qualifying Section 1202 stock from a start-up company A on May 1, 2009 for $1,000,000 and 5,000 shares of start-up company B on June 1, 2012 for $200,000. In February 2013, she sold 1,000 shares of A for $500,000; in December she also sold 2,000 shares of B for $300,000 but immediately invested $150,000 in qualifying Section 1202 stock of a third start-up company.

a. What are the tax effects on Taylor's income for these sales in 2013?

b. How would your answers change if Taylor had purchased the stock of start-up company A in 2006?

40. George bought 6,000 shares of Section 1244 stock from Dorado Corporation six years ago for $160,000. The company has not done well so this year George sold all of his stock for $45,000.

a. Determine the amount and type of George's loss if he is single.

b. How would your answer change if George is married and files a joint return?

41. Wilma does secretarial work out of her home. She purchased her own computer that she uses 2,250 hours for her work during the year; her children, however, also use the computer for 250 hours to do their homework. She paid $4,000 for the computer and had claimed $2,200 of depreciation on it when she sold it for $1,100. Determine the amount and type of her gain or loss realized on the sale of the computer.

42. Tina and Tony, a married couple, have owned and lived in their house for 20 years. They want to sell it now and move to a smaller place. They purchased the home for $56,000 and put $30,000 of improvements into the home over the years. If they sell the house for $387,000, what is their realized and recognized gain?

43. Carlotta moved into a smaller home nine months ago, after her husband died. She sold the home that they had lived in together for fifteen years and elected Section 121 so she would not have to recognize the $150,000 of gain on that home. She then purchased the smaller home for $210,000. She is unhappy in the neighborhood after living there for 10 months and wants to move again. If she sells the home for $235,000, what is her realized and recognized gain? How would your answer change if Carlotta were forced to move into a nursing home because of her health?

44. Marilyn owned 500 shares of Ibis stock that she purchased several years ago for $25,000. This year, she sold 200 of the shares to her brother for $7,000, its fair market value, when she wanted money for some plastic surgery. Determine Marilyn's realized and recognized gain or loss on the sale and her basis in the 300 shares remaining. Determine her brother's basis in the purchased stock and his realized and recognized gain or loss if he sells the shares for $12,000 the following year.

45. William bought 1,000 shares of Bevo stock three years ago for $100 per share. This year he has a $20,000 short-term capital gain from the sale of his shares of an initial public offering of GBD Company stock. To offset the gain, William sells his shares of Bevo to his grandfather for $80,000, its current fair market value. The next month, William's grandfather sells the stock for $85,000 to his neighbor. Determine William's realized and recognized gain or loss on the sale of Bevo stock. Determine the grandfather's basis in the stock purchased from William and his realized and recognized gain or loss when he sells the stock to his neighbor.

46. Bill had the following gains and losses on asset sales: $500 gain on stock held 11 months; a $2,300 gain on land held two years; $1,900 loss on gold coins held two years; $1,200 gain on antique toys held three years; and a $1,300 loss on investment land held six months. Determine Bill's net capital gain or loss, the capital gains rate that applies to each asset sale, and the capital gain rate(s) that would apply to the final net capital gain assuming Bill is in the 25 percent marginal tax bracket.

47. Clarice became very ill in February of 2013 and was unable to work the rest of the year. She had only $12,000 of income from her sole proprietorship for the time she worked and was forced to sell the following investments to pay for her living expenses. She sold 10,000 shares of BBC stock purchased two years ago for $34,000 (basis = $16,000) and a coin collection she inherited from her grandfather many years ago for $55,000 (basis = $30,000). If Clarice is single and has no dependents, determine her taxable income and her income tax liability for 2013.

48. Al Shalou, a single individual, had only $14,000 of salary income in 2013, but he had a number of property transactions during the year with the following results:

a. $26,000 Section 1202 gain on ABC stock
b. $5,000 short-term capital loss on Zephyr bonds
c. $24,000 long-term capital loss on Magnum stock
d. $13,000 Section 1245 recapture and $3,000 Section 1231 gain on equipment
e. $8,000 long-term capital loss on a coin collection
f. $6,000 Section 1231 loss on a machine
g. $20,000 long-term capital gain on Jobe stock

Calculate Shalou's taxable income and his income tax liability for 2013.

49. Geraldine's ordinary income places her in the 28 percent income tax bracket after a number of transactions involving several types of capital assets held more than one year, including several collectibles: a $10,200 gain on a stamp collection, a $5,000 loss on the sale of antique jewelry, and a $2,500 loss on an original oil painting. She also had a $15,000 long-term capital gain, an $11,300 long-term capital loss on some stock investments, and a $5,000 Section 1250 unrecaptured gain on some real property. Determine the result of the netting process for these transactions and the tax rates that would apply.

50. A single taxpayer has $15,000 of ordinary taxable income in 2013, a $9,000 long-term capital gain on the sale of an antique painting, a $10,000 unrecaptured Section 1250 gain on realty, and a $25,000 gain on the sale of bonds.

a. What is his 2013 tax liability?

b. How would your answer change if his ordinary taxable income was $225,000?

c. How would your answer change if his ordinary taxable income was $380,000?

51. Comprehensive Problem for Chapters 6 and 7. Sam Johnson started a small machine shop, Machines, Inc., in his garage and incorporated it in March of 2010 as a calendar-year corporation. At that time, he began using his personal computer and tools solely for the business as part of his contribution to the corporation. The computer cost $2,700 but had a fair market value of only $900 at conversion and the tools, which had cost $1,500, were valued at $1,100. During 2010, Machines, Inc. purchased two machines: Machine A, purchased on May 2, cost $24,000; Machine B, purchased on June 5, cost $40,000.

The corporation expensed Machine A under Section 179. The computer, tools, and Machine B were depreciated using accelerated MACRS only. The corporation did not take any depreciation on the garage nor did Sam charge the business rent because the business moved to a building the business purchased for $125,000 on January 5, 2011. On January 20, 2011, Machines purchased $4,000 of office furniture and on July 7, it purchased Machine C for $48,000. It depreciated these assets under MACRS (including allowable bonus depreciation), but did not use Section 179 expensing. Machines acquired no new assets in 2012.

On February 4, 2013, Machines bought a new computer system for $5,100. It sold the old computer the same day for $300. On March 15, it sold Machine A for $6,000 and purchased a more versatile machine for $58,000. On August 15, Machines sold bonds it had purchased with $9,800 of the cash Sam had originally contributed to the corporation for $10,400 to pay creditors. The business takes the maximum allowable depreciation deduction on assets purchased in 2013 but does not use Section 179 expensing.

a. Determine Machines, Inc.'s depreciation expense deductions for 2010 through 2013.

b. Determine the realized and recognized gains or losses on the property transactions in 2013.

THINK OUTSIDE THE TEXT

These questions require answers that are beyond the material that is covered in this chapter.

52. Beth had been using an automobile for personal purposes. In year 2, when she started a business, she began to use the car exclusively for this business at a time when it was worth $12,000. She had purchased the auto in year 1 for $16,000.

a. Assuming that she takes $3,000 of depreciation on the auto and then sells it, how much gain or loss does she have and what is its character if the amount realized is $8,000?

b. How would your answer change if she realizes $14,000?

53. Mary had the following transactions involving BMN stock:

DATE	SHARES PURCHASED	SHARES SOLD	PRICE PER SHARE	TOTAL PRICE
July 2, year 2	150		$5.00	$750
April 9, year 3	250		6.00	1,500
May 4, year 3		200	7.00	1,400
November 5, year 3	200		6.50	1,300
April 12, year 4		150	4.00	600

a. Determine Mary's gain or loss on each sale, assuming the shares are not specifically identified.

b. Determine Mary's gain or loss on the second sale if she specifically identifies the shares as coming from the November 5 of year 3 purchase.

54. If the netting process for capital gains really has no impact on corporations, why do you think it still remains as part of the tax law?

55. In 2013, Gregory, a single person, had $375,000 of ordinary taxable income. He sold Section 1202 stock at a taxable gain of $45,000, his art collection at a taxable gain of $102,000, and stock at a taxable gain of $55,000. Compare the tax result if Congress would simplify the capital gains tax provisions by having a single 20 percent capital gains rate versus the current capital gains tax provisions now in effect for 2013.

56. What are the policy reasons for allowing a portion of the gain on a personal residence to escape taxation?

IDENTIFY THE ISSUES

Identify the issues or problems suggested by the following situations. State each issue as a question.

57. Kwan Lu bought 100 shares of Duchco stock on July 25, year 3, for $1,000. The company declared bankruptcy on July 8 of year 5, and his stock became worthless.

58. The Gallagher Farms has been in business for a number of years. During the peak planting and harvesting season, it hired a number of temporary workers. To house the temporary workers, it built three buildings that were essentially dormitories that had bathing and sleeping facilities. It provided meals in a central kitchen with an attached dining area. The dormitories were built in 1983 and depreciated under ACRS accelerated methods. Recently, the state declared that the buildings were inadequate for the workers. Gallagher Farms has decided to sell the buildings and the portion of the land on which they sit. It expects to have a $100,000 gain on the land and a $75,000 gain on the sale of the buildings.

59. Martco, a manufacturer and seller of eyeglasses and contact lenses, purchased all the stock of Fetco, a manufacturer of hearing aids. Management of Martco quickly had second thoughts about keeping Fetco in business and liquidated the company. Martco was unsuccessful selling the hearing aids to customers, although a few small lots were sold to several retail outlets before the balance was sold to one distributor at $100,000 profit.

60. Geralyn and Marco sold their home and moved into a smaller home. They used their Section 121 election to exclude their $20,000 gain on the sale of the larger home. Six months after they moved into the smaller home, Geralyn died. Two months later Marco had a stroke and was in the hospital for one month and in a rehabilitation center for another seven months. At the end of that time, Marco moved back to his home. Three months later, he put the home up for sale and sold it within one month at a gain of $185,000 and moved out.

DEVELOP RESEARCH SKILLS

61. A number of specific transactions do not necessarily follow the general tax provisions applicable to property transactions. Following are a group of transactions that are subject to specific tax provisions. For each of the situations, you are to answer the questions and cite the source for your answer.

- **a.** Martin, a securities dealer, bought 100 shares of Datacard stock on April 5 of year 5 for $10,500. Before the end of that day, he identified the stock as being held for investment purposes.
  1. Never having held the stock for sale to customers, he sold the stock on May 22 of year 6 for $11,500. How much and what kind of gain or loss does he have?
  2. Assume that later in year 5 he starts trying to sell the stock to customers and succeeds in selling it on May 1 of year 6 for $9,000. How much and what kind of gain or loss does he have?
- **b.** Ruth subdivided a piece of real estate she had owned for seven years into 12 lots. Each lot was apportioned a $10,000 basis. In year 2, she sold four lots for $15,000 apiece with selling expenses of $500 per lot.
  1. How much and what kind of gain or loss does Ruth have?
  2. If in year 3 she sold two more lots for $20,000 apiece and incurred selling expenses of $500 per lot, how much and what kind of gain or loss does she have?
- **c.** For 60 years, Shakia owned 1,000 acres of land in Kentucky on which coal was being mined under a royalty arrangement. Shakia received $164,000 in the current tax year in royalties. The coal's adjusted basis for depletion was $37,000. Determine the amount and type of gain Shakia realizes on the income.
- **d.** Howard owned a large farm on which he raised a variety of farm animals. Determine the type of gain or loss he would realize on the following sales:
  1. a six-month-old calf
  2. a one-and-one-half-year-old foal
  3. six-week-old chickens
  4. a 6-year-old bull
  5. a 12-year-old mare
  6. six-month-old lambs
  7. a 2-year-old ram

62. A subsidiary of Corporation A, an electrical utility located in Springfield, and a subsidiary of Corporation B, a diversified manufacturer also located in Springfield, formed a joint venture under the general partnership laws of their state. The partnership was formed to construct and ultimately operate another electrical generating plant. Sufficient excess space was provided at the plant site to accommodate substantial future additions to the initial generating equipment. Three years after construction of the generating equipment had been started and was 50 percent complete, the partnership on the advice of its financial counselors, began negotiations with a consortium of businessmen for the possible sale and leaseback of the generating equipment. Thirteen months later, when the plant was complete, the deal was finalized with the consortium for the sale and leaseback of the generating equipment. The sale resulted in a gain of $500,000 that the partnership treated as $250,000 of Section 1231 gain and $250,000 as ordinary income. Was the partnership correct in its determination of the type of gain recognized?

63. Sheralyn was in the wholesale distribution business for pecans and peanuts grown in Georgia. She and her brother owned and operated several warehouses. Seven years ago, they purchased property for another warehouse in the eastern part of Georgia because the nut crop had been getting progressively larger over the past several years. Early last year, they had plans drawn up for the warehouse and had gotten several bids from contractors. Unfortunately, Sheralyn's brother was killed in an auto accident just days before they were to sign papers to begin the construction. Sheralyn knew that she would not be able to manage their existing warehouses and oversee the construction of this new facility. She abandoned plans to construct the warehouse and put the property up for sale. It was sold early this year at a $125,000 loss. How should Sheralyn treat the loss on the sale?

SEARCH THE INTERNET

64. Locate at least one article that comments on the tax provisions for capital gains that were included as part of the 2012 Taxpayer Relief Act. Summarize the comments and provide a citation for your article.

65. Locate the Schedule D and the accompanying instructions for both an individual and a corporation on the IRS Web site, *www.irs.gov*. Compare the length of the two forms and the instructions as they appear on the Web site. Summarize your findings.

66. Go to the IRS Web site *(www.irs.gov)* and print Form 4797: *Sales of Business Property*. Complete Form 4797 for the following sales of machinery on December 20, year 6:

MACHINE	COST	DATE ACQUIRED	COST RECOVERY	SELLING PRICE
A	$45,000	April 24, year 2	$25,000	$25,000
B	$75,000	March 5, year 1	$67,000	$18,000
C	$63,000	June 18, year 4	$21,000	$51,000
D	$87,000	Nov. 10, year 5	$18,000	$93,000

67. Go to the IRS Web site *(www.irs.gov)* and print Schedule D for Form 1040 and Form 8949. Compute the net effect of the following asset sales on Gineen Tibeau's taxable income using Form 8949 and Schedule D:

a. 100 shares of ABC stock; original cost = $4,000; selling price = $6,000
b. $5,000 in CDF bonds; original cost = $5,100; selling price = $4,950
c. Original Dali drawing; cost = $23,000; selling price = $31,000
d. 200 shares of GHI stock; original cost = $8,000; selling price = $6,400
e. 5,000 shares of XYZ stock; original cost = $20,000; selling price = $12,000

All assets except the CDF bonds have been held for more than one year.

68. Using the IRS Web site, *www.irs.gov,* locate the information and instructions for reporting the sale of a personal residence. Write a summary of what the taxpayer needs to do to elect Section 121 gain exclusion and how the sale is reported.

DEVELOP PLANNING SKILLS

69. Natalie expects to be in the 28 percent tax bracket with respect to her ordinary income for this year. So far this year, she has a $5,000 short-term capital loss. As of June 1, she is holding 1,000 shares of Dritco stock purchased on June 15 of last year for $15,000. The market value of the stock as of May 21 is $27,000. Lately the value of the stock has been decreasing and Natalie feels it may go down by $1,000 or so in the next month and probably stabilize thereafter. Advise Natalie as to the various courses of action she might take.

70. George has a short-term capital loss of $42,000 this year. His brother wants to buy a piece of land that George has owned as an investment for $60,000. The land's basis is only $20,000. George also knows that the land is appreciating in value every year, and he is not sure he should sell it now. He thinks if he holds on to the land for three more years, he will be able to sell it for $66,000 net of expenses. If George's combined state and federal tax rate is 40 percent and he uses a 6 percent discount rate for all decisions, should he sell the land now?

71. Wilma had a number of stock transactions during the year that resulted in an $18,000 capital loss. She has one stock remaining in her portfolio that would give her a $16,000 capital gain if she sold it now. She believes this stock is going to increase more in value, so she does not really want to sell it. What do you suggest that Wilma do?

72. Betty is a real estate dealer and has numerous properties for sale, many of which she owns. Her son is finishing his education and plans to go into the consulting business. Betty has committed to providing him with at least $25,000 to help out until the business becomes self-sufficient. Betty plans to dispose of one of the properties but wants to know if there is any way the gain on the property can be taxed at capital gains rates rather than as ordinary income.

73. Monique is planning to increase the size of the manufacturing business that she operates as a sole proprietorship. She has a number of older assets that she will replace as part of the expansion. In addition, to finance this expansion she will have to sell some of her personal assets. Because it is close to the end of the tax year, she can time the sales of the assets to take the greatest advantage of the tax laws. Monique is currently in the 39.6 percent tax bracket.

Following are the assets that Monique plans to sell; assume that she will realize their fair market value on the sales.

BUSINESS ASSETS	ACQUISITION DATE	FAIR MARKET VALUE	DEPRECIATION METHOD	ADJUSTED BASIS	ORIGINAL COST
Truck	1997	$3,000	MACRS	$0	$20,000
Office building	1992	300,000	MACRS	160,000	285,000
Machine 1	2006	10,000	MACRS	25,000	80,000
Machine 2	2007	60,000	MACRS	55,000	95,000

PERSONAL ASSETS	ACQUISITION DATE	FAIR MARKET VALUE	ORIGINAL COST
Sculpture	1993	$400,000	$260,000
Painting	2000	400,000	525,000
100,000 shares ACC	2007	800,000	1,050,000
10,000 shares of BBL	2012	400,000	350,000

In addition to the proceeds from the sales of the business assets, Monique needs a minimum of an additional $800,000 for her planned expansion. What assets should Monique sell to minimize her tax liability on the sales of the business and personal assets?

74. Joy purchased a home in Maine on December 15, 1996 for $250,000 and lived in it full-time until she purchased a second home in Florida on October 1, 2008 for $380,000. In 2008 and 2009 she continued to have her primary residence in Maine. On December 1, 2010, however, she changed her primary residence to Florida. She needs to sell one of these home before the end of 2013 as she needs cash for an investment opportunity. If she expects a minimum gain of $200,000 on either home, which home do you recommend she sell?

ANSWERS TO TEST YOURSELF

1. **b. car = capital; truck = ordinary; land = Section 1231.** The car is a personal-use asset; the truck cannot be a Section 1231 asset as it has not been held for more than one year; the land was to be used in the business and is not an investment.

2. **c. $8,000 ordinary income from look-back; $10,000 long-term capital gain.** Only $7,000 of the net Section 1231 gain becomes long-term capital gain. $8,000 must be treated as ordinary income due to the Section 1231 look-back rules.

3. **d. deduct none of the capital losses. The corporation must carry back the entire net capital loss as a short-term capital loss to year 2.**

4. **c. $100 gain.** ($1,200 × 75%) – [($4,000 × 75%) – $2,200] = $100 gain; the depreciation applies to the 75 percent business portion only and only 75 percent of the proceeds apply to that portion.

5. **a. $50,000 ordinary loss and a $10,000 capital loss.** $50,000 of the loss is an ordinary loss under Section 1244. The remaining loss is a long-term capital loss; he can deduct $3,000 of this loss from ordinary income in the current year but that does not change its character.

chapter

8

Tax-Deferred Exchanges

Most taxpayers would like to arrange their property transactions so they can recognize their losses and avoid recognizing their gains. Absent the complete nonrecognition of gain, the deferral of gain recognition reduces taxes due to the time value of money. This chapter focuses on provisions that defer gains such as like-kind exchanges, involuntary conversions, and transfers to businesses by their owners. Taxpayers must follow specific rules, however, to take advantage of gain deferral.

Some of these transactions, such as like-kind exchanges and asset transfers to businesses by their owners, defer losses as well as gains. If the taxpayer wants to recognize the loss rather than deferring it, the relevant provisions must be understood so that a transaction will *not* qualify for loss deferral.

An important set of deferral provisions allows taxpayers to transfer assets to sole proprietorships, partnerships, or controlled corporations in exchange for an ownership interest in the business. These provisions allow the tax laws to remain neutral in relation to the selection of business form by taxpayers.

Complex tax laws affect the reorganization of corporations through mergers and acquisitions. Adherence to the specific provisions applicable to all parties involved in a reorganization is necessary to defer gains. A basic explanation of reorganizations is provided in the appendix to this chapter.

The purpose of this chapter is to familiarize the reader with the basics of these tax-deferred transactions so that they can be used to advantage when planning asset transfers.

KEY CONCEPTS

- ★ A tax-deferred sale or exchange postpones gain or loss recognition to a future transaction by adjusting the basis of the asset acquired; a deferred gain causes a reduction in an asset's basis while a deferred loss causes an increase in an asset's basis.
- ★ Boot received in an otherwise tax-deferred exchange may cause all or part of the realized gain to be recognized.
- ★ Like-kind exchanges of real property are very flexible, allowing exchanges of business and investment realty, but like-kind exchanges of personalty are greatly restricted to exchanges between properties within the same class.
- ★ Losses on involuntary conversions are deductible, while gains may be deferred if qualifying replacement property is obtained within the required replacement period.
- ★ Taxpayers may transfer property to sole proprietorships, corporations, or partnerships on a tax-deferred basis.
- ★ One corporation may acquire another corporation in a qualifying reorganization. All parties to a qualifying reorganization may defer gain and loss recognition.

CHAPTER OUTLINE

Setting the Stage—An Introductory Case

Perry Winkle Corporation owns a large tract of land on which its manufacturing facility is located. It has held the land for a number of years so it would be available for expansion. On November 12 of last year, the state condemned 30 percent of the total land area for a highway and access ramps, leaving the corporation with very little land for expansion. The state paid Perry Winkle $500,000, the fair market value of the land, which has a basis of $100,000.

This year, one of Perry Winkle's products became far more successful than anticipated and the corporation needs to expand as soon as possible. The company has received an offer from one of its suppliers to purchase its facilities at a fair price, but the sale would result in a large gain in addition to the gain on the condemned property. The corporation's effective state and federal tax rate on the gain is expected to be 40 percent, and the corporation needs to conserve its cash for the expansion. What plan(s) can you devise for the corporation so it can defer as much gain as possible? We will return to this case at the end of this chapter.

Basics of Tax-Deferred Exchanges

A **tax-deferred exchange** is a transaction in which all or part of the gain or loss realized currently is not recognized. A number of events may give rise to the deferral of gain or loss, such as like-kind exchanges, casualty losses, condemnations, and wash sales. In some cases, both gains and losses are deferred (for example, like-kind exchanges), but in others only gains (condemnations) or losses (wash sales) are deferred. In each case, recognition is deferred, that is, excluded from current income. In a tax-deferred exchange, the expectation is that the gain or loss will be recognized at some point in the future.

The ability to postpone gain recognition has tax advantages due to the time value of money.

Example 1

Jordan, a single taxpayer in the 39.6 percent tax bracket, wants to dispose of 20 acres of investment land. If he sells it, he will have a long-term capital gain of $400,000 on which he will pay a tax of $95,200 ($400,000 × 23.8% capital gains rate as a higher income taxpayer). If Jordan can arrange a qualifying like-kind exchange and postpone gain recognition for 10 years, the present value of the $60,000 tax paid in 10 years at a 6 percent discount rate is $53,122 ($95,200 × .558). If his discount rate is 10 percent, the present value is now only $36,747 ($95,200 × .386). If he can postpone the gain for 20 years at 6 percent, the present value is $29,702 ($95,200 × .312).[1]

This example demonstrates that the longer gain recognition can be postponed and the higher the taxpayer's discount rate, the greater the tax savings. By similar reasoning, the longer a loss is postponed and the higher the discount rate, the less valuable a loss is.

The previous chapter explained the nonrecognition of gain on the sale of certain property, for example, the exclusion of a portion of the gain on qualified small business stock under Section 1202 and the exclusion for up to $250,000 ($500,000 if married filing jointly) on the sale of a personal residence. Table 8.1 provides a list of some of the more common nonrecognition and tax-deferral provisions. The nonrecognition provisions were presented in the preceding chapter, and the tax-deferral provisions are discussed in this chapter. (The Section 1244 provision discussed in the preceding chapter is neither a deferral nor a nonrecognition provision, but a change in the type of loss recognized.)

The at-risk rules and the passive loss rules may postpone the deductibility of losses by the shareholders and partners of S corporations and partnerships. A basic explanation of the at-risk and passive loss deferral rules is included in Chapter 10.

[1]This problem includes the 3.8% Medicare surtax and assumes that tax rates remain constant.

TABLE 8.1 **COMMON NONRECOGNITION AND TAX-DEFERRAL PROVISIONS**

NONRECOGNITION PROVISION	TAX DEFERRAL GAIN	TAX DEFERRAL LOSS	NONRECOGNITION GAIN	NONRECOGNITION LOSS
Wash sales		×		
Related party sales		×*		
Rollover of qualified small business stock into another qualified small business stock	×			
Sales of qualified small business stock			×	
Sales of personal-use assets				×
Like-kind exchanges	×	×		
Involuntary conversions	×			
Sales of personal residence			Limited	×
Exchanges of property between divorcing spouses	×	×		
Exchanges of qualifying insurance policies	×	×		
Exchanges of common stock for common stock in the same corporation	×	×		
Transfers to corporations and partnerships by owners	×	×		
Reorganizations of corporations	×	×		

**The loss may offset gain realized on a subsequent sale of the property by the related party.*

Basis Adjustments

In tax-deferred property transactions the **basis adjustment** is the mechanism that allows gains and losses to be deferred and then recognized at a later date on the subsequent disposition of the assets. When a gain is deferred, the basis of the asset acquired is reduced by the deferred gain.[2] This downward basis adjustment increases the gain on a subsequent disposition. Similarly, a deferred loss increases the basis of the acquired asset.[3] When the asset is sold at a later date, this increased basis then causes loss or a reduced gain to be realized on a subsequent sale.[4]

EXAMPLE 2

Peter exchanges land with a basis of $20,000 for other realty valued at $30,000 in a qualified like-kind exchange, a gain and loss deferral provision. Peter has $10,000 realized gain on the land that is not

[2] § 1031(d).

[3] Ibid.

[4] The loss disallowance on related party transactions is an exception to the usual basis adjustment on a deferral transaction as explained in the preceding chapter.

recognized ($30,000 – $20,000 = $10,000 gain). He reduces the basis of the realty received by the deferred gain; thus, its basis is now $20,000 ($30,000 price paid – $10,000 deferred gain), rather than its fair market value. This basis adjustment builds a $10,000 gain into the basis of the realty that may be recognized on a future transaction. If the realty is sold the next year for $35,000, Peter will recognize a gain of $15,000 ($35,000 – $20,000 adjusted basis). This $15,000 gain is made up of the $10,000 gain that was built in due to the gain deferral, plus the $5,000 gain from additional appreciation.

In several types of deferral transactions, the basis of the original asset follows the asset to the new owner (the carryover basis), and the basis of the original asset is substituted for the basis of the asset acquired (the substituted basis).

EXAMPLE 3

James joins with three friends in forming a new corporation. The formation of a corporation is a tax-deferral provision. James contributes an asset valued at $400,000 to the corporation in exchange for stock valued at $400,000. James's basis in the asset is $250,000 at the time of its contribution to the corporation. James does not recognize the $150,000 gain on the transfer of the asset, so he substitutes his $250,000 basis in the asset for the basis in the corporate stock received. The corporation carries over James's basis and has a $250,000 basis in the asset contributed. If James later sells the stock for its $400,000 value, he will recognize a $150,000 ($400,000 – $250,000) gain at the time of sale. If the corporation sells the asset it received for its $400,000 value, it will recognize a $150,000 ($400,000 – $250,000) gain on the sale.

Holding Period

When an asset's basis is determined by reference to the basis of another asset (either through carryover, substitution, or basis adjustment), the holding period of the old asset is added to the holding period of the new asset.[5]

LIKE-KIND EXCHANGES—SECTION 1031

A **like-kind exchange** is an effective planning tool to defer recognition of gain on the disposition of business or investment property. A number of requirements must be met however, to qualify a transaction as a like-kind exchange. The most important requirement is that the transaction must be an exchange of noncash qualifying properties.[6] If nothing but qualifying properties are exchanged, none of the parties to the exchange recognize either gain or loss. This provision is not elective; if the transaction qualifies as a like-kind exchange, nonrecognition of gain and loss is required.

EXAMPLE 4

PRT Corporation exchanges a piece of land for an office building in a qualifying like-kind exchange. If PRT sold the land, it would have to recognize a $200,000 gain on the sale. PRT expects to use the office building for at least 15 years before it will be sold. By participating in a like-kind exchange, PRT has postponed recognizing the $200,000 gain for at least 15 years. If PRT is in the 34 percent marginal tax bracket, it saved $68,000 ($200,000 × 34%) in taxes this year. The present value of the $68,000 of tax paid in 15 years, assuming no change in the tax rate and a discount rate of 6 percent, is $28,356 ($68,000 × .417). Thus, the company has saved almost $40,000 in taxes by arranging a trade rather than selling the land.

The inclusion of cash or other nonqualifying property may not defeat the like-kind exchange provision, but the parties may not be able to defer the entire gain realized. Cash and other nonqualifying property received as part of the exchange is **boot**, and gain must be recognized to the extent of the lesser of the gain realized or the fair market value of the boot received.[7]

---

[5]There is a more complete discussion of holding period in the preceding chapter.

[6]§ 1031(a)(1).

[7]§ 1031(b).

Boot only affects recognition of a realized gain; it has no effect on a realized loss.

EXAMPLE 5

The Kilgore Corporation has a small airplane that it uses to transport its executives between plant locations. The corporation needs a larger plane due to recent growth. One of its suppliers has a larger plane that it is willing to trade for Kilgore's plane and $200,000 cash. The exchange of the planes qualifies as a like-kind exchange. The payment of $200,000 cash by Kilgore is boot. Kilgore recognizes no gain or loss on the exchange but the supplier must recognize gain up to the lesser of the gain realized or the $200,000 value of the boot received. If the supplier realized loss on the exchange, neither Kilgore nor the supplier would have any current gain or loss recognition as the receipt of boot triggers only gain recognition.

TAX PLANNING

A person wanting to recognize loss should avoid qualifying for this nonrecognition provision by making sure the properties exchanged fail to qualify as like-kind or by structuring the transaction as a sale.

Qualifying Properties

The nonrecognition provisions of Section 1031 apply to business or investment property only, not to personal-use property. In addition, exchanges of stock or other securities, inventory, and limited or general partnership interests do not qualify for nonrecognition.[8] Beyond these exclusions, two sets of rules determine if an exchange qualifies for nonrecognition as like-kind. The first applies to the exchange of realty and is very flexible. Almost any type of business or investment realty can be exchanged for any other type of business or investment realty as long as both properties are situated in the United States; for example, the exchanges of a factory building (including land) in Michigan for undeveloped land held for investment in Hawaii and a rental apartment building (including land) in Ohio for a shopping mall (including land) in New Jersey both qualify as like-kind exchanges.[9]

The second rule applies to personalty and is extremely rigid. Under this rule only personalties of the same "class" may be exchanged. This effectively requires the exchange of almost identical types of property. Thus, machines must be exchanged for similar machines; a light truck must be exchanged for a light truck; and an airplane would have to be exchanged for an airplane. The regulations under Section 1031 require tangible personalty subject to depreciation to be of the same general business asset classification, such as the following:[10]

1. Airplanes
2. Automobiles and taxis
3. Buses
4. General-purpose light trucks
5. General-purpose heavy trucks
6. Computers and related information systems equipment
7. Furniture, fixtures, and equipment generally found in an office

EXAMPLE 6

The Barber Company exchanges a computer for a duplicating machine, a new pickup truck for an old tractor trailer, and several small machines from its factory for one with much larger capacity in the same class. The first two exchanges do not qualify as like-kind exchanges. Computers are in a separate class of equipment related to information systems. A duplicating machine would be part of the office equipment class and can only be exchanged tax free for another asset in that same class. A pickup truck is a light-duty truck and a tractor trailer is a heavy-duty vehicle. Only the exchange of the machines qualifies as a like-kind exchange.

---

[8] § 1031(a)(2).

[9] An improvement to land (e.g., a building) cannot be exchanged for land under the like-kind provision unless the land to which the improvement is attached is also exchanged as part of the exchange.

[10] Reg. § 1.1031(a)-2(b).

Determining Realized Gain or Loss and the Effect of Boot

Realized gain on an exchange is the amount realized less the adjusted basis of the property surrendered. The **amount realized** is the total of the cash, fair market value of the like-kind and any nonlike-kind property received, and the liabilities assumed by the purchaser less the costs incurred and the liabilities assumed by the seller. If only qualifying like-kind property is received, neither party recognizes gain or loss. If boot is received in the exchange, gain may be recognized.[11] The recognized gain is the lesser of the realized gain or the value of the boot received. The deferred gain equals the difference between realized and recognized gain.

EXAMPLE 7

Joann exchanges land with a small apartment building that has an adjusted basis of $46,000 for a piece of undeveloped land valued at $60,000 and $5,000 cash. She paid fees related to the exchange of $7,000. Joann has an amount realized of $58,000 ($60,000 + $5,000 – $7,000) and a realized gain of $12,000 ($58,000 – $46,000). Joann must recognize $5,000 gain on the exchange because that is the lesser of the boot received ($5,000) and the realized gain ($12,000). She defers $7,000 ($12,000 – $5,000) of the gain.

The *giving of boot does* not affect the gain recognition on the qualifying property exchanged. If the boot given has a fair market value greater or smaller than its basis, gain or loss is recognized. Boot, by definition, is not like-kind property and does not qualify for nonrecognition of gain or loss.

EXAMPLE 8

Porter exchanges a business auto valued at $10,000 and a forklift valued at $2,000 for another auto worth $12,000 (of which $10,000 is apportioned to the exchanged auto and $2,000 to the folklift). The auto has a basis of $5,000 and the forklift a basis of $1,000 to Porter. Porter has a realized gain of $5,000 ($10,000 – $5,000) on the exchange of the auto, none of which is recognized. He recognizes the $1,000 gain realized ($2,000 – $1,000) on the sale of the forklift because it is not like-kind property.

In the context of a like-kind exchange, the assumption of liabilities is treated as boot and can lead to gain recognition. The liability relief is treated as cash (boot) received, with the cash used to satisfy the liability.[12]

EXAMPLE 9

The Grunt Corporation exchanges an office building that is encumbered by a $125,000 mortgage for some land valued at $325,000 that is owned by Tug Corporation. In addition, Tug assumes Grunt's $125,000 mortgage. The office building has a basis and fair market value of $230,000 and $450,000, respectively. The amount realized by Grunt is $450,000 ($325,000 + $125,000) and its gain realized is $220,000 ($450,000 – $230,000). The mortgage relief is considered cash (boot) received. Grunt must recognize $125,000 of gain on the transaction, but defers the remaining $95,000 ($220,000 – $125,000) of gain.

If each party assumes a mortgage of the other party, the liabilities offset each other and only the net amount of liabilities is considered as boot given or received. Actual cash received, however, cannot offset any part of the mortgage assumed by that party on the exchange.

EXAMPLE 10

Assume that the land received by Grunt Corporation from Tug Corporation in the previous example has a fair market value of $400,000, but that it is encumbered by a $75,000 mortgage that Grunt assumes. The amount realized by Grunt is still $450,000 and consists of $400,000 fair market value of land plus $50,000 ($125,000 – $75,000) net liability relief. Grunt's realized gain remains $220,000 ($450,000 – $230,000).

[11] § 1031(b).

[12] § 1031(d).

Grunt has net mortgage relief of only $50,000, which is the limit of the gain that it must recognize; Grunt defers $170,000 ($220,000 – $50,000) of gain.

If Grunt had received $125,000 cash instead of the mortgage relief, it could not offset any portion of the mortgage it assumed against the cash received. The cash received would be boot. Grunt would recognize gain of $125,000 and could defer only $95,000 ($220,000 – $125,000) of the gain.

Several points are important to remember with like-kind exchanges:

1. There must be an exchange of qualifying business or investment properties with realty and personalty following separate rules for qualification.
2. No gain is recognized unless boot is received.
3. The amount of gain recognized is the lesser of the fair market value of the boot received or the gain realized.
4. The receipt of boot only causes realized gain recognition; loss is never recognized.
5. Net liability relief is considered boot.

Basis and Holding Period of Like-Kind Property

The basis of the like-kind property received in a qualifying exchange is its fair market value less the unrecognized (deferred) gain or plus the unrecognized loss. If no boot is involved in the exchange, the basis of the property given simply carries over to the basis of the property received.[13] If boot is received, the basis of the like-kind property remains its fair market value, adjusted for deferred gain or loss. Basis of any boot received is always its fair market value.

The **holding period** for like-kind property received in a qualifying exchange includes the holding period of the property surrendered. The holding period for boot always begins on the date of the like-kind exchange.[14]

Example 11

Nomad Corporation exchanges a small building it acquired on January 4, year 1, for a parking lot that ABC Corporation owned for 20 years and a bond with a fair market value of $20,000. The building has a basis of $50,000 and a fair market value of $75,000. The parking lot has a fair market value of $55,000 and a basis of $40,000. Nomad Corporation has a $25,000 ($55,000 + $20,000 – $50,000) gain realized on the exchange. It must recognize $20,000 of gain due to the bond (boot) received and $5,000 of the gain is deferred. The basis of the parking lot is $50,000 ($55,000 – $5,000 deferred gain) and its holding period begins on January 4, year 1. The bond's basis is its $20,000 fair market value and its holding period begins on the date of the exchange.

ABC has a $15,000 gain realized ($75,000 – $40,000 – $20,000) on the exchange, all of which is deferred because it did not receive boot. Its basis in the building is $60,000 ($75,000 – $15,000 deferred gain), and the parking lot's 20-year holding period tacks on to the building. If the basis of the bond that ABC transferred was more (or less) than its $20,000 fair market value, ABC would recognize the loss (or gain) on its transfer to Nomad.

There is an alternative basis calculation provided in the Code. Under this method, basis of the property received is the basis of the property surrendered, plus the adjusted basis of boot *given* plus gain recognized less the fair market value of boot received.[15]

[13] Ibid.

[14] § 1223 and Reg. § 1223-1(a).

[15] § 1031(d). The Code also includes a subtraction for loss recognized, but loss is not recognized on a like-kind exchange.

Example 12

Using the information in the previous example, Nomad's basis in the land is equal to the following:

	$50,000	basis of building surrendered
Plus	0	boot given
Plus	$20,000	gain recognized
Minus	$20,000	fair market value of the boot received
Equals	$50,000	basis of land received

ABC's basis in the building is as follows:

	$40,000	basis of parking lot surrendered
Plus	$20,000	boot given
Plus	0	gain recognized
Minus	0	fair market value of boot received
Equals	$60,000	basis of the building received

These are the same bases calculated by the first formula.

When loss is deferred, the basis of the new property is its fair market value increased by the deferred loss.[16]

Indirect Exchanges

A direct exchange of properties may not be possible if two or more parties who are willing to exchange properties cannot be found. Taxpayers do not have to give up on an exchange transaction that allows gain deferral, however. This dilemma can be solved in two ways, but both involve third parties and some additional costs. In the first scenario, the taxpayer hires a third party to purchase the desired property; the third party then exchanges the just-purchased property for the taxpayer's property. The taxpayer has a qualifying exchange, but the seller of the property and the third party must treat the transactions as taxable events.

Example 13

Corrine has some investment land that was recently rezoned residential, which she wants to trade for land on which she can build a factory. She locates a piece of land owned by Billie that she wants, but Billie refuses to exchange properties because their families had been involved in a business dispute years ago. Corrine asks Sam, a licensed real estate broker, to purchase the property from Billie. After he purchases the property, Corrine exchanges her land for the property. Sam then sells Corrine's land. Corrine has a qualifying like-kind exchange because she exchanged investment land for business property, but Billie and Sam have taxable transactions.

The second way to structure a like-kind exchange is through a **nonsimultaneous exchange.** In a nonsimultaneous exchange, a taxpayer can sell his or her property, but a third party must hold all proceeds so that the taxpayer has no access to any cash or other property received in the sale. The taxpayer has 45 days from the date the property is given up to identify like-kind property to be exchanged and 180 days to complete acquisition of the identified property.

Example 14

Fianola's neighbor offered to purchase her entire farm at a very good price, but Fianola did not want to recognize the substantial gain on the sale. Instead, she hired an escrow agent to close the sale and hold all the proceeds until she located suitable investment land. The sale closed on May 25. Fianola

[16]The alternative formula can also be used for deferred-loss situations by inserting zero for gain recognized.

has until July 9 to locate the property she wants and until November 21 for the escrow agent to close the purchase of the desired property in Fianola's name, using the escrowed proceeds from the sale of the farm.

TAX PLANNING

In either of these indirect exchanges, the taxpayer must weigh the costs of using a third party with the tax savings, but with multimillion-dollar properties and significant gains to defer, these savings normally far outweigh the costs.

Although gain deferral is usually desirable, a few situations occur in which the immediate recognition of gain may be preferable, for example, when taxpayers have net operating or capital loss carryovers or if they expect to be in significantly higher marginal tax brackets in future years.

EXAMPLE 15

Sag Corporation can sell an auto used in its business for \$10,000 and purchase a new auto for \$26,000. Alternatively, it can trade in the auto on a new one from a different dealer. This dealer will allow \$11,000 on the trade-in of the old car but requires an additional \$16,000 payment. The old auto has a basis of \$6,000, and Sag Corporation is in the 35 percent marginal tax bracket. Which alternative should Sag choose if it generally uses its cars for only three years?

If Sag sells the auto, it will have a \$4,000 gain on the sale and pay a tax of \$1,400. It will have a basis in the new auto of \$26,000. If it trades in the auto, it will not have to recognize any gain, but the new auto will have only a basis of \$22,000 [(\$11,000 + \$16,000) cost – (\$11,000 – \$6,000) unrealized gain]. Sag should trade in the auto and avoid the gain recognition. Even though it has a lower basis in the new auto, its depreciation deductions will be the same for a number of years, regardless of which alternative is chosen, due to the depreciation limits on listed property.[17]

EXAMPLE 16

Quorum Corporation can sell an office building for \$4,000,000 that has a basis of \$2,500,000 and can purchase replacement property for \$4,000,000. Alternatively, it can exchange the building for property with a fair market value of \$3,500,000. Both buildings are equally attractive to Quorum. The owner of this building is unwilling to pay Quorum anything additional to make up for the difference in appraisals. Should Quorum sell the building at its fair market value and purchase the \$4,000,000 property, or should it make the exchange? Assume Quorum has a 35 percent marginal tax rate in all years and assume depreciation evenly over 40 years and a 6 percent discount rate.

If Quorum sells the building, it will have a recognized gain of \$1,500,000 and a tax of \$525,000 (\$1,500,000 × 35%) on that gain. Its basis in the purchased building will be \$4,000,000. If it exchanges the buildings, it will have no recognized gain, but its basis in the building will be only \$2,500,000 (\$3,500,000 – \$1,000,000 deferred gain). It will have increased depreciation deductions of \$37,500 annually on the sale option over the 40 years, which will reduce its taxes by \$13,125 (\$37,500 × 35%). This is equivalent to an annuity of \$13,125 per year for 40 years. At a 6 percent discount rate the annuity has a value of \$197,479 (\$13,125 × 15.046). Thus, if Quorum exchanges the building, it has tax savings of \$327,521 (\$525,000 – \$197,479).

Alternatively, if Quorum Corporation has a \$1,200,000 net operating loss that will expire at the end of the current year, it will be able to offset all but \$300,000 of the gain on the sale with this loss. Its tax liability of \$105,000 (35% × \$300,000) in the current year is \$92,479 (\$197,479 – \$105,000) less than the tax savings over the next 40 years for the increased depreciation deductions.

---

[17]Automobile ceiling limits for depreciation are discussed in Chapter 6.

Other Tax-Deferred Exchanges

Under Section 1035, a life insurance contract can be exchanged for a life insurance contract, an endowment contract, or another annuity contract.[18] In addition, an annuity contract can be exchanged for either an endowment or an annuity contract, and an endowment contract can be converted (exchanged) to an annuity contract. Realized gain or loss, recognized gain on the receipt of boot, and the basis of the policy received are all determined under the like-kind exchange provisions.[19]

TAX PLANNING

A taxpayer recognizes no gain or loss on the transfer of property to an ex-spouse if the transfer is part of a divorce settlement. The actual property transfer must occur no later than one year after the date of the final divorce decree.[20] The basis of the property received carries over to the ex-spouse. The structuring of the property settlement as part of divorce proceedings is one reason divorcing parties should consult separate tax practitioners as well as attorneys to avoid any unpleasant tax surprises.

Exchanges of stock between a corporation and its shareholders and between shareholders of the same corporation are tax-deferred exchanges if common stock is exchanged for substantially similar common stock and preferred stock is exchanged for substantially similar preferred stock.[21] If stocks of the same class have significant differences, the exchange is taxable. Similarly, common stock exchanged for preferred and preferred stock exchanged for common are normally taxable exchanges (except for the exercise of a preferred stock conversion feature).

Wash Sales

Whenever a seller of stock or securities acquires substantially identical stock or securities within 30 days, either before or after, the sale or exchange of stock, the taxpayer has a **wash sale**. A loss realized on a wash sale is not recognized. The sale is treated as a nontaxable exchange and loss recognition is deferred. Wash sale rules do not affect gain recognition, however. The deferred loss increases the basis of the substantially identical stock that is acquired, and the holding period of the stock includes the holding period of the stock that is sold.[22] Loss is deferred, even if tax avoidance is not the motive and the taxpayer is unaware that the prohibited sale took place. If the taxpayer sells more stock than is purchased within the 61-day window (the day of sale, 30 days before, and 30 days after), only a portion of the loss representing the repurchased stock is deferred.

Example 17

Barker purchased 100 shares of ABC stock for $4,000 on June 10 and 200 shares of MNO stock on June 30 for $3,000 through the Internet. Without consulting Barker, his broker sold 100 shares of ABC for $3,800 and 200 shares of MNO stock for $3,300 on June 28. Two years ago, the broker had purchased the ABC shares for $4,100 and MNO shares for $3,100 and had been holding them in Barker's account until the sale. Both purchases were made within 30 days of the sale of identical stock. Barker has a realized loss on the ABC stock of $300 ($4,100 – $3,800) and a realized gain on the MNO stock of $200 ($3,300 – $3,100). Barker cannot recognize the loss on the sale of the ABC stock, but he must recognize the gain on the MNO stock. The basis of the ABC stock acquired on June 10 is adjusted for the deferred loss to $4,300 ($4,000 + $300), and has a

[18] An endowment contract is a contract with an insurance company that depends in part on the life expectancy of the insured but may be payable in full in a single payment during life. An annuity contract is a contract sold by an insurance company that pays a monthly (quarterly, semiannual, or annual) income benefit for the life of one or more persons or for a specified period of time.

[19] § 1035(a) and (d).

[20] The transfer is treated as a gift from the taxpayer to the ex-spouse, but no gift taxes are due.

[21] § 1236.

[22] A "substantially identical stock or security" is open to interpretation. Common and preferred stock of the same company would not be similar nor would common stock and bonds, but preferred stock and bonds could be substantially similar if they are both convertible into common stock. Rev. Rul. 56-496, 1956-2 CB 523.

two-year holding period. The basis of the MNO stock is the purchase price of $3,000, and its holding period begins on the purchase date of June 30.

If the broker sold 200 shares of ABC stock for $7,600 that had a basis of $8,200, Barker would have a $600 realized loss. He would defer only $300 ($600 × 100/200) of the loss because he only purchased 100 shares of ABC; the $300 remaining loss would be recognized.

The wash sale rules also apply to losses on options to acquire or sell stock and short sales.

Involuntary Conversions

Involuntary conversions take a variety of forms such as thefts, casualties, and condemnations. A **theft** loss includes embezzlement, larceny, and robbery but does not include simply losing items. A **casualty** requires some form of sudden, unexpected, and unusual event that affects the taxpayer's property, such as fires, floods, hurricanes, tornadoes, vandalism, and mine disasters. The event must be identifiable, and it must directly affect the taxpayer's property. The erosion or destruction of property that takes place over a period of time, such as damage from mold or termites, does not meet the requirement of suddenness. Events that indirectly affect value, such as an area becoming flood prone due to excessive development of nearby areas, are not casualties. A **condemnation** is the lawful taking of property for its fair market value by a governmental unit under the right of eminent domain.

When insured property is subject to a casualty or theft, the difference between the insurance proceeds and the amount of damage or loss results in a net gain or loss. Gain is deferred if all insurance proceeds are used to repair the damaged property or to obtain qualified replacement property. If the property is uninsured, only loss is realized. Casualties and thefts are much more likely than condemnations to result in losses, even if insured, due to insurance policy deductibles.

Casualty and Theft Losses

Gains and losses sustained on casualties and thefts are not under a taxpayer's control and receive special tax treatment. Allowable losses from thefts and casualties are immediately deductible, but realized gains may be deferred if qualifying replacement property is acquired. Business and investment casualty losses and nondeferred gains are included as Section 1231 gains and losses.[23] Although most personal losses are not deductible, a limited deduction applies to casualty and theft losses of personal-use property.

Measuring the Loss

To measure the loss on casualties and thefts, business and investment property must be separated from personal-use property. The loss on business or investment property that is stolen or totally destroyed is always its adjusted basis at the time of the loss, regardless of the property's fair market value.[24] If the business or investment property is only partially destroyed, the loss is the lesser of its adjusted basis at the time of the loss or the difference in the property's fair market value immediately before and after the loss occurrence.[25]

Example 18

A fire destroyed part of the building the Cairn Corporation used for manufacturing and all of the equipment inside. The building had a basis of $450,000 and an estimated fair market value of $750,000 before the fire.

[23]Business property includes rental realty and property producing royalties. The taxation of Section 1231 gains and losses is discussed in the preceding chapter.

[24]Taxpayers can recover their investment (basis) in an asset under the capital recovery doctrine.

[25]Reg. §1.165-7(a).

Its fair market value after the fire was $400,000. The machinery had a basis of $320,000 and an estimated fair market value of $400,000 before the fire. Cairn has a loss of $350,000 on the partial destruction of the building (the lesser of the basis of $450,000 or the $350,000 difference in its fair market value before and after) and a loss of $320,000 (its basis) on the complete destruction of the machinery.

The loss on personal-use property, whether stolen or completely or partially destroyed, is always the lesser of its adjusted basis at the time of the loss or the difference in the property's fair market value before and after the casualty. The loss on mixed-use property must be determined separately for the personal-use and business portions. Often, the difference in fair market value before and after a loss is not available.[26] In this case, the costs to restore the property may be a substitute for the amount of the loss if the repairs do not improve the property beyond its pre-loss condition and the value of the property after repairs does not exceed its pre-loss value.[27]

EXAMPLE 19

An uninsured motorist hit Georgette's car. The loss was not insured because Georgette had forgotten to pay her insurance premium. The car cost $23,000; its value before the accident was $15,000 and $6,000 after the accident. Georgette's loss is $9,000, the difference between the car's value before and after the accident. If Georgette could not establish the fair market value of the car before and after the accident, she could use the $8,000 repair cost as an alternative estimate of her loss.

Insurance and Basis Considerations

If property that is subject to a casualty or theft loss is covered by insurance, the insurance proceeds reduce the amount of the loss.[28] If the insurance proceeds are less than the loss, the excess of the total loss over the insurance proceeds is the maximum deductible loss. If the insurance proceeds exceed the loss, the taxpayer has a gain from the casualty.

EXAMPLE 20

GDG Corporation had a computer stolen and a car that was totally destroyed when a truck hit it. The computer had a basis of $1,200 and a fair market value of $800. Insurance paid $600 for this loss. The car had a basis of $6,000 and a fair market value of $7,000. GDG recovered $6,500 from the insurance company for the car. GDG has a $600 loss on the computer ($1,200 basis – $600 insurance recovery) and a $500 gain on the car ($6,500 insurance recovery – $6,000 basis).

The expectation of insurance recovery affects the timing of the loss deduction. If the taxpayer expects to receive full payment for the loss, no deduction is allowed in the year of the loss. If the taxpayer expects only partial recovery, only the loss less the expected insurance recovery is deductible in the loss year. If the final settlement is less (more) than the amount expected, the taxpayer has a loss (income) in the settlement year.

EXAMPLE 21

Cordero Corporation had $40,000 damage to its manufacturing plant from a hurricane last year. It anticipated receiving a settlement from its insurance company of $36,000 because it had a deductible of 10 percent of the loss. It deducted the $4,000 loss that the insurance was not expected to cover on last year's return. This year Cordero learned that there was a specific provision for hurricanes that stated the first $5,000 of loss was not covered at all and a 20 percent deductible applied to the balance. Thus, its

[26] Appraisals are readily available for the after-loss fair market value, but it may not be possible to obtain a valid pre-loss fair market value after the fact.

[27] Reg. § 1.165-7(a)(2).

[28] § 165(h)(4)(E). If covered, a taxpayer must file an insurance claim for damage to personal-use property.

insurance reimbursement was only $28,000 [$40,000 – $5,000 – (20% × $35,000)]. It can deduct the additional $8,000 loss in the current year.

A taxpayer reduces the basis of property subject to a casualty for a deductible loss. If the insurance recovery covers all or part of the loss, the basis is reduced for the insurance recovery and any remaining deductible loss. If the taxpayer uses the insurance proceeds or other funds to repair the damaged property, the amount spent on repairs increases the property's basis.

EXAMPLE 22

Crup Corporation's home office suffered a $600,000 loss from a fire in its home office building. It received $500,000 from its insurance company and deducts the remaining $100,000 loss. The building had a basis of $750,000 at the time of the loss. The basis of the property is reduced to $150,000 ($750,000 – $100,000 deduction – $500,000 insurance proceeds) because $600,000 of its basis is recovered through the $100,000 casualty loss deduction and the $500,000 of insurance proceeds. The company spends $800,000 repairing and upgrading the building. The basis of the building after repairs are complete is $950,000 ($150,000 + $800,000). If the building had not been insured, the result would be the same except that Crup would deduct the entire $600,000 loss.

Deductible Amount

To determine the **deductible loss** and the tax treatment for casualty and theft losses, business and individual taxpayers follow similar, but not identical, procedures. First, individuals are required to separate their gains and losses from casualties and thefts of personal-use property from those of business and investment property. The deductible loss and its treatment are determined as discussed later. The casualty and theft gains and losses from business and investment property of both businesses and individuals enter the Section 1231 asset netting process as described in the previous chapter. When this netting results in a net loss, the business includes all the gains and losses in ordinary income. This results in the net loss reducing the business's ordinary income. The individual, however, includes all gains and losses except losses on investment property in ordinary income. These investment losses are deductible only as a miscellaneous itemized deduction.[29]

EXAMPLE 23

Walter owns a sole proprietorship. One of his business computers and some bearer bonds were stolen from the business by an employee and were not recovered. The computer cost $2,400 and had a basis of $1,100 and a fair market value of $900. The bearer bonds cost $4,800 but were currently valued at $5,200. Walter has a business casualty loss on the theft of the computer of $1,100 and $4,800 on the bonds for a total casualty loss of $5,900. He deducts the $1,100 loss directly from income as it is a business loss, but he must deduct the $4,800 loss on the bonds as a miscellaneous itemized deduction because it is a theft loss of investment property.[30]

If Walter's business had been incorporated, the corporation could have deducted the entire $5,900 loss from ordinary income.

A separate netting procedure applies to the casualty and theft gains and losses on an individual's personal-use property. Before entering this netting process, however, the value of each casualty or theft loss occurrence must first be reduced for a basic floor amount of $100.[31] This $100 floor is applied to *each* loss occurrence (but has no

[29]See Chapter 7 for a more complete explanation of these netting processes.

[30]Property transactions of a sole proprietorship are treated as incurred by the sole proprietor.

[31] The floor amount of $100 was increased to $500 for 2009 only by the National Disaster Relief Act of 2008. It was $100 for years both prior and subsequent to 2009.

effect on casualty gains) by reducing the total loss for each separate event by $100.[32] Then all of the individual taxpayer's gains and losses (net of the $100 floor) on personal casualties and thefts are netted against each other. If the result is a net gain, the separate gains and losses on the involuntarily converted items enter the capital gain netting process as short-term or long-term capital gains and losses based on the length of time the taxpayer held the asset subject to the casualty. If the result of netting gains and losses is a net loss, there is a second limit on the deductibility of the loss; the individual must reduce the total of all losses by 10 percent of adjusted gross income. The loss amount, after applying these limitations, is an itemized deduction.[33] The $100 loss reduction per event removes small losses from deductibility for individuals (similar to the deductible on an insurance policy). The 10 percent threshold for all losses requires the net loss to be fairly large relative to income for a portion to be deductible.

EXAMPLE 24

In 2013, Cheryl's personal auto was stolen and never recovered. Its fair market value prior to the theft was $7,800. She received only $6,800 from her insurance company, however, after her $1,000 deductible. Later that same year, her apartment was broken into and a personal computer and jewelry were stolen. She did not carry insurance on any of this property. The computer cost $2,100 and had a fair market value of $850 at the time of the theft; the jewelry cost $5,500 and had a fair market value of $7,800. Cheryl has a $1,000 loss on her auto that must be reduced by the $100 floor to $900. She has a total loss of $6,350 ($850 + $5,500) on the computer and jewelry (considered one occurrence) that must be reduced by the $100 floor to $6,250. Together, she has a $7,150 ($900 + $6,250) loss that can only be deducted to the extent it exceeds 10 percent of her adjusted gross income because these are losses on personal-use assets. If Cheryl is single and her adjusted gross income is $50,000, her deductible loss is limited to $2,150 [$7,150 – ($50,000 × 10%)], and it must be treated as an itemized deduction.She would not have any tax benefit from the loss unless the total of her itemized deductions exceeded her standard deduction of $6,100 in 2013.

Taxable Year of Deduction

Taxpayers deduct a theft loss in the year the theft is discovered, even if the theft occurred in a different tax year. Casualty losses, however, must be deducted in the year the casualty occurs since a casualty is usually the result of a specific, identifiable event such as a fire or storm. If a casualty is discovered after the taxpayer has filed a tax return for the year of the casualty, an amended return must be filed to claim the loss.

EXAMPLE 25

In year 5, Bob discovers that his bookkeeper has been taking most of the money that customers have paid for cash sales over the past three years. Through a reconstruction of his sales of goods over the past three years, Bob establishes that the bookkeeper stole $45,000. Bob also owns a cabin on a lake in the Ozarks. He was unable to visit the cabin for almost two years because of business pressures. When he visited the cabin late in year 5, he discovered that the roof and one of the walls had been severely damaged in a storm. Through contact with neighbors, he learned that the storm took place in the early part of the preceding year. Bob can claim the entire $45,000 theft loss in year 5, but he must file an amended return for year 4 to claim the storm damage on the cabin as a personal casualty loss.

[32]This $100 floor applies only to the casualty losses of individual taxpayers and does not apply to casualty gains. The 2005 Gulf Opportunity Zone Act removed the two limitations on personal casualty and theft losses described above (the $100 floor and 10 percent threshold) for losses related to Hurricanes Katrina, Rita, and Wilma. The National Disaster Relief Act (part of the Emergency Economic Stabilization Act of 2008) removed the 10% of AGI threshold for persons suffering losses in presidentially declared disaster areas eligible for federal assistance for 2008 and 2009. Disasters in the Midwest from May 20, 2008 through July 31, 2008 are covered by alternative provisions.

[33]If an individual uses the standard deduction (does not itemize), the casualty or theft loss cannot be deducted, except for casualties in presidentially declared disaster areas in 2008 and 2009.

If the casualty occurs in an area that the president declares a disaster area, the taxpayer may elect to deduct the allowable amount of the casualty loss in the year prior to the year of occurrence. This allows the taxpayer to file an original or an amended return for the prior year to obtain a refund as soon as possible to assist in recovery from the casualty. If the election is made, however, the taxpayer treats the casualty as having occurred in the year the deduction is claimed. A **presidentially declared disaster** is one that occurs in an area that warrants federal assistance under the Disaster Relief and Emergency Assistance Act.[34]

TAX PLANNING

A business taxpayer generally is better off taking an eligible casualty deduction that occurs in a presidentially declared disaster area in the year prior to the casualty. An individual, however, should carefully consider which year would be more advantageous due to the reduction in the loss (after the deduction for the $100 floor) for 10 percent of adjusted gross income. The year with the lower adjusted gross income would normally provide the greater deduction.

EXAMPLE 26

Jamie's home was severely damaged by fire September, 2013. She sustained a $40,000 loss on the property. If her adjusted gross income for 2013 was $50,000, she could claim a $34,900 ($40,000 – $100 – $5,000) loss as an itemized deduction on her 2013 tax return. If the loss occurred due to a wildfire in a presidentially declared disaster area, she would have the option of deducting the allowable loss when she files her return for the current year (2013) or deducting it on her return for the prior year (2012) to obtain a refund of taxes already paid. If Jamie's 2012 adjusted gross income had been only $24,000, she should claim $37,500 ($40,000 – $100 – $2,400) as part of her itemized deductions on her 2012 tax return due to her lower income.

Gains on Involuntary Conversions—Section 1033

Section 1033 allows all or part of the gain on an involuntary conversion to be deferred if the taxpayer acquires qualifying property within the prescribed time limits. Gains are most likely to result from condemnations because the proceeds received in a condemnation are normally the fair market value of the property. Although it is less likely that insurance recoveries on thefts and casualties will exceed the affected property's basis, gains are deferred on all types of involuntary conversions as long as the taxpayer acquires qualifying property within the required time period.

A condemnation or requisition is the taking of a person's property involuntarily by the exercise of the power of eminent domain by a governmental unit. The benefits of this tax provision extend to property owners whose property is under threat of condemnation that can be objectively verified. The owners can even sell the property to a third party rather than a governmental unit, as long as there is a real threat of condemnation. In addition, the provisions apply even if later the condemnation does not take place.[35]

Tax Deferral on Involuntary Conversions

Involuntary conversions are events that taxpayers cannot avoid by planning. The tax consequences are moderated, however, by specific provisions in the tax law that are designed to help those persons who are the victims of involuntary conversions. The key word here is *involuntary*. If the taxpayer is deliberately responsible for the conversion (for example, hiring an arsonist to set fire to a property), it is not involuntary and the provisions do not apply.[36]

If a taxpayer realizes a gain on the involuntary conversion of his or her property, the gain may be deferred if qualifying property is acquired within the required time period for replacement.

[34]Special rules were enacted for disasters in presidentially declared disaster areas that occurred in 2008 and 2009—the 10% of AGI threshold for deducting a casualty loss was not applied and nonitemizing taxpayers could add their deductible casualty loss to their standard deduction.

[35]Rev. Rul. 81-180, 1981-2 CB 161.

[36]Rev. Rul. 69-654, 1969-2 CB 162.

- This provision defers gain only; qualifying losses are recognized.[37]
- This provision defers gain on business, investment, and personal-use property subject to an involuntary conversion.[38]
- The taxpayer may receive cash (or nonqualifying replacement property) with which to acquire qualifying replacement property.
- The taxpayer generally has an extended period of time in which to acquire qualifying replacement property.

To defer the entire gain, the cost of the qualifying replacement property must equal or exceed the amount realized from the conversion. If the entire proceeds are not reinvested, the taxpayer must recognize gain equal to the lesser of the gain realized or the amount of proceeds that are retained and not invested in qualifying replacement property.[39] When gain is deferred, the deferral mechanism is the basis adjustment. The fair market value of the qualifying replacement property is reduced for the deferred gain. If gain is recognized, the character of the property that was involuntarily converted determines the character of the gain recognized.

EXAMPLE 27

Byron Corporation's parking lot was condemned by the city for an expansion of a highway interchange. Byron was paid $400,000 for the property that had a basis to Byron of $290,000. Byron purchased property for $425,000 a block away from the office as a replacement parking lot. Byron has a realized gain of $110,000 ($400,000 – $290,000) on the condemnation. Because it paid more than the $400,000 condemnation proceeds for the replacement property, it recognizes no gain; the entire gain is deferred. The basis of the new property is $315,000 ($425,000 – $110,000 deferred gain).

If Byron reinvests only $350,000 in the replacement parking lot, it would have to recognize $50,000 of Section 1231 gain because that was the amount of the proceeds that Byron failed to reinvest. The basis of the replacement property would be $290,000 ($350,000 – $60,000 deferred gain).

If Byron reinvests only $250,000, it must recognize the entire $110,000 gain (the lesser of the gain of $110,000 or the unreinvested proceeds of $150,000) as Section 1231 gain. The basis of the property would be its cost of $250,000 as there is no deferred gain.

TAX PLANNING

Under most circumstances, the deferral of gain is optional. In those rare instances that the taxpayer receives replacement property directly, then gain deferral is mandatory.[40] A business might choose to recognize gain in the year of the conversion if it is currently in a lower tax bracket than it expects to be in future years. The higher depreciation deductions on replacement property would offset income in those higher tax years. If the taxpayer has capital loss carryovers that are about to expire, recognizing the gain may have little or no tax cost.

EXAMPLE 28

The Clyde Corporation has a $30,000 realized loss from the sale of a capital asset. A painting in its corporate offices was stolen during the year, and the company received $40,000 from the insurance company for the loss. The painting had a basis of $20,000. A replacement painting cost $45,000. The company has no other property transactions during the year. The corporation had a net capital gain two years ago of $10,000. The corporation's tax rate on that gain was 25 percent. Its expected marginal tax rate this year is 34 percent. Should the corporation elect to defer the gain on the painting this year? If it defers the $20,000 gain on the theft of the painting, it will be able to carry the $30,000 capital loss back two years

[37]§ 165(b). For personal-use property, only casualty and theft losses are deductible. Losses on condemnations of personal-use property are not deductible.

[38]Like-kind exchange provisions are not applicable to personal-use property.

[39]§ 1033(a)(2)(A).

[40]§ 1033(a). An insurance company could find a substantially similar automobile to replace one that is totaled rather than paying out cash, or a governmental unit might replace one piece of condemned land with a satisfactory substitute.

and apply for an immediate refund of \$2,500 (\$10,000 × 25%). It will have a \$20,000 loss carryover for future years.

If Clyde recognizes the \$20,000 gain in the current year, the \$20,000 loss on the capital asset offsets it and Clyde will still have a \$10,000 capital loss remaining that it can carry back to offset the prior loss. It will have the \$2,500 refund, and there will be no loss carryover. The corporation now has a basis of \$45,000 in the replacement painting for any future disposition. This latter strategy is sound if there are few asset dispositions planned for future years. If, however, the corporation expects to have other significant gains on assets in future years, it may still decide to defer gain recognition to preserve the loss carryover for those gains. The higher the expected tax rate in those future years, the more the taxes that could be saved by deferring gain recognition. (This must be balanced against the loss in value due to the time value of money.) If it does not expect additional capital gains, however, it must remember that capital loss carryovers expire in five years.

Qualifying Replacement Property

Two differing rules determine qualifying replacement property depending on the taxpayer's use of the converted property. The first, the **functional-use test**, requires the replacement property to provide the same function as converted property that was owned and used by the taxpayer. This is the most restrictive of all the replacement tests and is narrowly interpreted. Thus, a bowling alley replaced with a billiards center could not meet the functional-use test.[41]

The second test, the **taxpayer-use test**, is far less restrictive but applies only to investment real estate that is rented and not used by the owners. The owner of the converted property is only obligated to replace it with property that can be leased. The use that the tenant makes of the replacement property is irrelevant.[42]

EXAMPLE 29

Harvey owns a strip mall and a small office building that were destroyed by a tornado. All the property in the strip mall was entirely leased to others. Harvey used the other building for his offices. Harvey decided to build a high-rise apartment complex on the land previously occupied by the strip mall, using the insurance proceeds from both the mall and the office building. Harvey realized a \$3,000,000 gain on the conversion of the mall and a \$50,000 gain on the conversion of the office building. Harvey can defer all the gain on the mall (rental property) because he has replaced it with an apartment complex (also rental property) that qualifies as replacement property under the taxpayer-use test. He cannot defer the \$50,000 gain on the office building, however, because the apartment complex does not meet the functional-use test.

An exception to these two rules allows the replacement property for business or investment real property that is condemned to follow the replacement rules for like-kind property.[43] Thus, investment property can replace property used in a business or raw land can replace improved property.

Time Limits for Replacement

The last requirement for gain deferral on involuntarily converted property is the time limit for replacement. The replacement property must be acquired within "two tax years after the close of the first taxable year in which any part of the gain upon the conversion is realized," unless it is business or investment real property that is condemned.[44] For condemned realty, the replacement period is extended for one additional year, that is, until three years after the close of the year in which any gain is realized.

---

[41]Rev. Rul. 76-319, 1976-2 CB 242.

[42]Rev. Rul. 64-237, 1964-2 CB 319.

[43]If converted business or investment property is located in a presidentially declared disaster area, any tangible property that is used in a productive trade or business is qualified replacement property.

[44]§ 1033(a)(2)(B). The replacement period was extended to five years for Hurricane Katrina-related damage or destruction to property located in the Hurricane Katrina disaster area.

EXAMPLE 30

Lotic Corporation, a calendar-year corporation, lost a manufacturing facility due to a hurricane on November 12, year 1. Its insurance company claimed that it had not received the premium payment for November or December and it took until early January to locate their clerical error. They issued a check to Lotic for the damage on February 1, year 2. Lotic has until the end of year 4 to replace the plant because the insurance proceeds were not received and the gain realized until the year following the hurricane. If Lotic Corporation's manufacturing facility had been condemned, it would have until the end of year 5 to find replacement property.

Involuntary Conversion of a Principal Residence

A taxpayer whose principal residence is involuntarily converted may exclude gain under the sale provisions discussed in the previous chapter, under the involuntary conversion provisions discussed above, or under a combination of both provisions. The involuntary conversion is considered a sale; thus, a taxpayer may exclude up to \$250,000 (\$500,000 if both spouses qualify) of gain on the sale. Using **Section 121** to exclude gain does not require the taxpayer to purchase a replacement residence. If the taxpayer acquires a replacement residence using all the proceeds received on the conversion, the gain can be deferred under Section 1033. If the taxpayer replaces a residence and the gain exceeds \$250,000 (\$500,000), the taxpayer first excludes \$250,000 (\$500,000) of gain under Section 121, if eligible. The required investment in replacement property must equal or exceed the total proceeds less the Section 121 exclusion to exclude the remaining gain using Section 1033.

EXAMPLE 31

Monica and Steve, a married couple filing a joint return, lost their home of 30 years in a wildfire. Fortunately, they had replacement-value insurance on the home, and they received a \$1,200,000 settlement from the insurance company. Their basis in the home was \$350,000. They constructed a smaller replacement home on their same land at a cost of \$800,000. They have a realized gain of \$850,000 (\$1,200,000 – \$350,000) from the insurance settlement. As a married couple filing jointly, they can exclude \$500,000 of the gain under Section 121. They are required to invest \$700,000 (\$1,200,000 – \$500,000) in a replacement residence to exclude the remaining \$350,000 (\$850,000 – \$500,000) gain. As they exceeded this reinvestment, they recognize no gain on the conversion. Their basis in the new residence is \$450,000 (\$800,000 – \$350,000 deferred gain). Because Section 121 is a nonrecognition provision, they do not adjust the basis of the new home by the gain exclusion. They only reduce the basis for the \$350,000 gain deferred under Section 1033.

ASSET TRANSFERS TO BUSINESSES

The deferral of gains and losses is the hallmark of transfers of assets to businesses. An individual can transfer personal assets to his or her sole proprietorship, partners can transfer assets to a partnership, and shareholders can transfer assets to corporations with no gain or loss recognition as long as some basic requirements are met.

Transfers to Sole Proprietorships

Many sole proprietors transfer assets other than money to a sole proprietorship. Often, the sole proprietor will have used these assets personally, and no gain or loss is recognized on the transfer. Instead, the basis of these transferred assets is the lesser of their adjusted bases as personal-use assets or fair market values at the date of conversion.[45]

[45]If fair market value is below basis, the basis for depreciation and a loss on a subsequent sale is the lower fair market value; the basis for gain, however, is the carryover basis reduced for any depreciation.

Transfers to Controlled Corporations—Section 351

Potential and existing shareholders can transfer money and other property to a corporation in exchange for its stock and defer any gain or loss if they follow the requirements of **Section 351**. To be a fully nontaxable event, the transfers must meet three requirements:

- The transfer must be of property (including money) only (not services).
- The transferor(s) must receive only stock in exchange for the property transferred.
- The transferor(s) must be in control of the corporation immediately after the transfer.

If any of these requirements is not met, either the entire transaction is treated as a taxable sale or exchange or one or more of the transferors may be required to recognize gain or income. Generally, only the failure to meet the control requirement renders the entire transaction taxable to all transferors. The transfer of services for stock or the receipt of property other than stock causes gain (income) recognition only to the parties involved, leaving the remaining transferors with recognition deferral.

The Control Requirement

Control is defined as owning 80 percent of all outstanding voting stock and 80 percent of each separate type of nonvoting stock, measured immediately after the transfer.[46] After the transfer of property in exchange for stock, transferors are free to dispose of their stock as long as there is no prearranged plan for disposal.[47]

EXAMPLE 32

Sara transfers property with a fair market value of $35,000 and a basis of $18,000 for 70 shares of Denton Corporation stock. Dan transfers property valued at $15,000 and a basis of $18,000 for the remaining 30 shares. The transfer qualifies for nonrecognition because Sara and Dan, the transferors, receive 100 percent of the outstanding stock and this exceeds the required 80 percent.

Property Other Than Stock Received

If a transferor receives property other than stock (for example, cash, stock rights, stock warrants, and any short-term or long-term corporate debt) in exchange for the property transferred to the corporation, the other property is considered boot and the transferor must recognize gain to the extent of the lesser of gain realized or boot received.[48] If the transferor has a loss on the transfer of depreciated assets (assets with basis greater than fair market value) to a controlled corporation, the loss is not recognized even if boot is received.[49] To recognize the loss, either the transaction must fail the Section 351 requirements (usually by failing to meet the 80 percent control test) or the shareholder could sell the property and transfer the proceeds to the corporation.

TAX PLANNING

If a corporation transfers appreciated property as boot to the shareholders in a qualifying Section 351 exchange, the corporation must recognize gain. If the boot is depreciated property, however, the corporation cannot recognize the loss. If the corporation has a depreciated asset to transfer to the shareholder, it would be better off selling the depreciated asset, recognizing the loss, and transferring the proceeds to the shareholder. If an outside sale is not available, the transfer of property on which loss would be realized allows the shareholder to extract something of value from the corporation without corporate income tax consequences.

---

[46]§ 368(c).

[47]Immediate sale of the stock after the transfer may give the appearance of a prearranged plan and should be avoided.

[48]§ 351(b).

[49]This boot rule is similar to the boot rule for like-kind exchanges.

EXAMPLE 33

The three equal shareholders of Baby Corporation transfer the following cash and property to the corporation for common stock and other property in a qualifying Section 351 transaction:

1. *Shareholder A*: Transfers a building; fair market value = \$800,000; basis = \$850,000. He receives 70 shares of common stock and \$100,000 cash.
2. *Shareholder B*: Transfers \$800,000 cash. She receives 70 shares of common stock and a machine valued at \$100,000 that has a basis of \$150,000.
3. *Shareholder C*: Transfers land; fair market value = \$700,000; basis = \$400,000. He receives 60 shares of common stock and 100 Baby Corporation bonds with a face value of \$1,000 each.

Shareholder A has a realized loss of \$50,000 (\$800,000 – \$850,000); none of the loss is recognized even though he receives \$100,000 boot.

Shareholder B realizes no gain or loss on the transfer of cash.

Shareholder C has a realized gain of \$300,000 (\$700,000 – \$400,000) on the land; he recognizes only \$100,000, however, the value of the boot received (the lesser of gain realized or boot received).

Baby Corporation has a \$50,000 (\$100,000 – \$150,000) realized loss that it cannot recognize on the transfer of the machine to Shareholder B.

Shareholder A and Baby Corporation could have recognized their losses if they had sold their depreciated assets to outsiders and used the proceeds to complete the transaction.

Transferred Services

In some cases, a person with particular expertise is given stock in exchange for past or future services as part of a corporate formation. If the person receives stock solely for services, the stock is excluded from control determination.[50] If the service provider transfers property in addition to performing services, all of the stock received is included in meeting the control requirement as long as the value of the property transferred equals 10 percent or more of the value of services provided. A person who receives stock in exchange for services recognizes income for the value of the services regardless of the tax consequences to the other transferors.

EXAMPLE 34

Claudia performed \$10,000 worth of accounting services in exchange for 1,000 shares of stock when her friends formed FGH Corporation. Claudia must recognize \$10,000 income. If she transfers no property, the other owners cannot include her 1,000 shares in determining if together they meet the 80 percent control requirement for a qualifying Section 351 corporate formation. Claudia would have to contribute at least \$1,000 in cash or property along with her services for all of the shares she received to be included in the control determination.

Basis and Holding Period

In a qualifying Section 351 transaction, under most circumstances the transferor's basis in the stock received is:[51]

	Basis of property transferred
Plus	Gain recognized
Less	Fair market value of the boot received
Equals	Basis of stock received

[50]§351(d)(1). If the person receives more than 20 percent of the stock solely for services, the corporation will fail the control requirement.

[51]§358(a)(1). If the aggregate basis of property transferred is greater than its aggregate fair market value, the transferor's stock basis cannot exceed the property's fair market value if the corporation takes the carryover basis in the transferred property. §362(e)(2).

If no boot is received, the stock has the same basis as the property transferred (a substituted basis).

The corporation's basis in property received is normally equal to the shareholder's basis (a carryover basis), unless the transferor recognizes gain. The corporation increases its basis in the property by the gain recognized by the shareholder to prevent the corporation from being taxed on the same gain in the future.[52] The shareholder uses the fair market value as basis in any boot received.[53] If the shareholder receives more than one class of stock, basis is apportioned using relative fair market values.

These basis provisions may be altered, however, if the aggregate bases of the property transferred to a corporation by a transferor exceeds the property's fair market value. In this unlikely case, the aggregate basis the corporation takes in the transferred property cannot exceed their aggregate fair market value unless the transferor-shareholder agrees to reduce the stock basis by this excess fair market value.[54]

EXAMPLE 35

Zoar transfers land with a basis of \$200,000 and a fair market value of \$400,000 to Cory Corporation in exchange for 200 shares of common stock. Yara transfers machines with a basis of \$150,000 and a fair market value of \$260,000 to Cory in exchange for 200 shares of stock and \$60,000 cash. The transfers are qualified Section 351 transfers. Zoar has a \$200,000 (\$400,000 – \$200,000) realized gain that is deferred and has a \$200,000 basis in her stock. The corporation has a \$200,000 basis in the land. Yara has a realized gain of \$110,000 (\$260,000 – \$150,000) and must recognize \$60,000 of the gain, the lesser of her realized gain (\$110,000) and the boot received (\$60,000 cash). The basis in her stock is \$150,000 (\$150,000 + \$60,000 gain recognized – \$60,000 boot received). The corporation's basis in the machines is \$210,000 (\$150,000 basis of the machines + \$60,000 gain recognized by Yara).

If Zoar's basis in the land transferred is \$450,000 rather than \$200,000, the corporation's basis cannot exceed the land's \$400,000 fair market value unless Zoar elects to reduce her basis in the stock received to \$400,000.

The holding period of stock a shareholder receives in exchange for capital or Section 1231 property includes the property's holding period. The holding period for stock exchanged for ordinary income property (such as inventory) begins on the date of the exchange. The holding period for all property received by a corporation in exchange for its stock in a Section 351 transaction includes the shareholder's holding period.[55] A shareholder who receives stock in exchange for services has a basis in the stock equal to the income recognized. The holding period begins on the date of the exchange. The corporation either expenses or capitalizes the value of the services as appropriate.[56] If capitalized, the asset's holding period begins on the date of the exchange.

Effect of Liabilities

Liabilities encumbering assets transferred to a corporation as part of a Section 351 transfer have no effect on the transferor's nonrecognition of gain and loss or the amount of gain recognized when boot is received. The value of liabilities assumed does reduce the transferor's basis in the stock received, however. The liability assumption has value separate from the stock and cannot become part of the stock basis. Thus, the transferor's stock basis formula is modified to

---

[52]§ 362(a).

[53]§ 358(a)(2).

[54]§ 362(e)(2).

[55]§§ 1223(1) and (2). Because the holding periods are combined, the corporation is responsible for any depreciation recapture associated with the disposal of the assets transferred.

[56]Rev. Rul. 74-503, 1974-2 CB 117.

	Basis of property transferred
Plus	Gain recognized
Less	Fair market value of the boot received and liabilities assumed by the corporation[57]
Equals	Basis of stock received

If the liabilities assumed by a corporation on the transfer of assets in a qualifying Section 351 transfer exceed the transferor's bases in the properties transferred, gain must be recognized to the extent of the excess liability to avoid a negative basis in the stock received.[58]

EXAMPLE 36

As part of a qualifying Section 351 transaction, Gene transfers a building with a fair market value of \$750,000 (basis = \$500,000) in exchange for \$500,000 in corporate of stock and the assumption of the \$250,000 mortgage on the building by the corporation. Although Gene has a \$250,000 realized gain, he has no recognized gain on the transfer. His basis in the stock received is \$250,000 (\$500,000 basis – \$250,000 liability). If the liability assumed exceeded the \$500,000 basis of the building, Gene would have to recognize gain equal to the excess liability.

Transfers to Existing Corporations

The tax-deferral provisions of Section 351 apply anytime money or property is transferred to a corporation in exchange for stock and the control requirement is met. This allows existing shareholders to make tax-free transfers of additional property to the corporation in exchange for stock, and it allows the tax-free entry of new shareholders as long as existing shareholders make transfers and together they control the corporation after the transfer.[59]

Existing shareholders can also make contributions to a corporation's capital account with no gain or loss recognized by the corporation or the shareholder receiving additional stock. The corporation takes a carryover basis in the property contributed, and its holding period includes that of the shareholder. The shareholder increases the basis of his or her existing stock holding for the basis of the property contributed.[60]

The transfer provisions discussed above apply equally to C corporations and S corporations. No separate Code provisions cover the transfer of property to an S corporation at formation or at a later time.

Transfers of Property to a Partnership

No gain or loss is recognized when a partner transfers property to a partnership in exchange for a partnership interest. Any gain or loss is deferred through the carryover or substitution of basis from the property surrendered. Unlike a corporation, however, the transferring partners are not required to have any minimum level of ownership for gain deferral, making the partnership provision more flexible. Taxes are deferred on transfers whether the property is transferred at formation or during the life of the partnership.

If a partner receives property from the partnership in addition to a partnership interest, the property is *not* considered boot. Instead, the transaction is separated into a *transfer* of part of the assets for a partnership interest and a *sale* of the remaining part of the assets for the property received from the partnership.

[57]If liabilities are assumed and the motive is tax avoidance, all liabilities assumed are considered boot. §357(b).

[58]When gain is recognized because liabilities are assumed in excess of basis, the basis of the stock acquired is always zero. §357(c).

[59]Existing shareholders must transfer property equal to at least 10 percent of their current holdings, or their transfer is disregarded in determining control.

[60]If a nonshareholder contributes money or property, the corporation has no income but the corporation's basis in the contributed property and property acquired with contributed money is zero.

EXAMPLE 37

Myron transfers an asset valued at $100,000 (basis equal to $50,000) for a partnership interest valued at $90,000 and $10,000 cash. The acquisition of the $100,000 asset must be recognized as part nontaxable transfer (for the $90,000 partnership interest) and part sale (for the $10,000 cash received). Myron has a $45,000 ($90,000 – [.90 × $50,000] apportioned basis) deferred gain on the transfer of $90,000 of the asset for the partnership interest and a recognized gain of $5,000 ($10,000 – [.10 × $50,000] apportioned basis) on the sale of the remaining 10 percent of the property.

If a partner transfers services in exchange for a partnership interest, the partner has taxable income equal to the fair market value of the partnership interest because the definition of property excludes services.[61] The value of a partnership interest received is determined at the time the service provider has unconditional control of the partnership interest. The partnership recognizes either a deductible expense or a capitalized asset on the transfer of services.

TAX PLANNING

A partner may either sell or lease assets to a partnership if for some reason he or she does not want to exchange them for a partnership interest. Leasing allows the partner to avoid gain or loss recognition while allowing the partnership to have use of the assets for the rental period.[62]

Basis and Holding Period of a Partnership Interest

One of the most important concepts at formation and throughout the life of a partnership is that of the **partner's basis** in his or her partnership interest. At formation, the basis of a partner's interest in a partnership is determined by the basis of the property (including money) transferred to the partnership and the income recognized on the transfer of services. In this case, the partner takes a substituted basis in the partnership interest.

If the partner transfers Section 1231 or capital assets to the partnership, his or her holding period for the partnership interest includes the period of time the assets were held prior to contribution. If cash or ordinary income assets are transferred, the holding period for the partnership interest begins on the date of transfer.[63]

EXAMPLE 38

X, Y, and Z form the XYZ Partnership. X transfers materials and machines with a fair market value of $45,000 (basis equal to $35,000) to the partnership. Y transfers land valued at $35,000 (basis equal to $40,000) and $10,000 cash to the partnership; Z transfers services valued at $5,000 and $5,000 cash to the partnership. X and Y each receive a 45 percent interest in the partnership, and Z receives the other 10 percent. X has a realized gain of $10,000 ($45,000 – $35,000) and Y a realized loss of $5,000 ($35,000 + $10,000 – $35,000) on their transfers; neither, however, has a recognized gain or loss. Z, however, must recognize $5,000 of income when she has unrestricted right to her 10 percent partnership interest. X has a basis of $35,000 in his partnership interest (the adjusted basis of the material and machines), Y has a basis of $50,000 in her interest (the adjusted basis of the land plus the cash), and Z has a basis of $10,000 ($5,000 cash plus the $5,000 income recognized on the value of services) when she has an unrestricted right to her partnership interest.

Partnership Basis and Holding Period in Contributed Property

The partnership takes a carryover basis in the property acquired in a tax-deferred transfer; that is, the partnership "steps into the shoes" of the partners with respect to the bases of contributed assets. The partnership uses this carryover basis for computing depreciation, if applicable, and for determining gain or loss on subsequent dispositions of the assets.[64]

---

[61]Reg. §1.1721-1(b)(2).

[62]The entity theory of partnership allows both the sale and the rental because the partner and the partnership are considered separate taxpayers as discussed in Chapter 10.

[63]The partnership interest's holding period is partitioned to reflect different holding periods for contributed assets.

[64]The partnership's basis in the contributed assets is termed its *inside* basis to differentiate it from partners' outside bases in their partnership interests.

EXAMPLE 39

Using the facts in the previous example, the XYZ Partnership will have a $35,000 basis in the materials and the machines from X, a $40,000 basis in the land and a $10,000 basis in the cash from Y, and a $5,000 basis in the cash from Z. It will either have a $5,000 asset or a $5,000 expense for the services provided by Z.

Because they have a carryover basis, the partnership's holding periods for the materials, machines, and land include the time they were held by the various partners. If Z's services are capitalized, the asset's holding period begins when Z recognizes the income.

Effect of Liabilities

The effect of liabilities assumed by a partnership on assets transferred by a partner can be very complex. The assumed liabilities reduce the partner's basis in the assets transferred, but a portion of the liability may also increase basis. Partners who may be held personally responsible for payment of a partnership's liabilities have basis in their partnership interest for their share of these potential payments.[65] Thus, a 30 percent partner who could be held liable for $100,000 partnership debt increases his or her partnership interest basis by $30,000 ($100,000 × 30%).

This provision affects the determination of the liabilities in excess of basis when a partner transfers assets that have liabilities assumed by the partnership. Gain is recognized to the extent the liabilities assumed exceed basis, but basis must first be increased for the partner's share of the liability assumed by the partnership before the excess liabilities can be determined. The formula for determining the basis of the partnership interest received is as follows:

	Basis of the property transferred
Less	Liabilities assumed by the partnership
Plus	Partner's share of partnership liabilities
Plus	Gain recognized
Equals	Basis of partnership interest received

Gain must be recognized to the extent that the combination of the first three items is a negative number.

EXAMPLE 40

Joe transfers a building to a partnership in exchange for a 20 percent interest in the partnership valued at $50,000. The building has a fair market value of $100,000, a basis of $45,000, and a liability of $50,000 that the partnership assumes. Joe's realized gain is $55,000 ($100,000 – $45,000). His basis in the partnership interest after the transfer is $5,000 [$45,000 – $50,000 liability assumed + his $10,000 ($50,000 × 20%) share of the liability]. Joe's gain is deferred because he does not have a liability assumed in excess of basis.

Now assume that Joe's basis in the building is only $20,000. His realized gain is $80,000 ($100,000 – $20,000), and he must recognize a gain of $20,000 ($20,000 basis – $50,000 liability assumed + his $10,000 share of the liability = negative $20,000) to avoid a negative basis in his partnership interest. His basis in his partnership interest is zero.

A comparison of asset transfers by owners to corporations and partnerships is illustrated in Table 8.2.

Formation of a Limited Liability Company

When a limited liability company is formed, for tax purposes, its members may elect to treat the limited liability company as a corporation or it will be treated as a partnership by default. Most limited liability companies are treated as partnerships for tax purposes because it provides its members with limited liability along with the single level of taxation as a conduit or flow-through entity. There are no separate rules for the formation of the limited liability company. If it is a partnership for tax purposes,

[65]The effect of liabilities on a partner's basis in the partnership interest is discussed in more detail in Chapter 10.

TABLE
8.2 COMPARISON OF ASSET TRANSFERS BY OWNERS TO CORPORATIONS AND PARTNERSHIPS

	PARTNERSHIP	CORPORATION
Control required by owner	No	Yes; 80 percent by transferors
Loss recognized	No	No
Gain recognized	1. Liabilities assumed in excess of basis (basis must be adjusted for partner's share of liabilities assumed)	1. If gain realized and boot received
	2. Services exchanged for partnership interest	2. Liabilities assumed in excess of basis of all properties transferred
	3. Boot not a factor; any property, other than a partnership interest received, treated as a separate sale	3. Services exchanged for stock
Basis of partnership interest or stock	Basis of property transferred plus gain recognized minus net liabilities assumed	Basis of property transferred plus gain recognized minus liabilities assumed
Holding period in partnership interest or stock	1. Carries over on Section 1231 and capital assets	1. Carries over on Section 1231 and capital assets
	2. Starts at transaction date for ordinary income assets and partnership interest for services rendered	2. Starts at transaction date for ordinary income assets and stock received for services rendered

then the members follow the tax provisions related to the formation of a partnership. If an election is made to treat the limited liability company as a corporation, then the members will follow the tax consequences of corporate formations.

Corporate Reorganizations

Over the past several decades, numerous businesses have restructured to increase their opportunity to grow and survive in an increasingly competitive business environment. They have acquired new businesses, disposed of unwanted enterprises, and merged with other firms to ensure remaining competitive. Legal and accounting firms have specialists who handle these complex mergers and acquisitions. Hollywood has even produced movies that portray the less flattering side of the mega-mergers and their architects. Although the pace of mergers and acquisitions has slowed, corporate reorganizations play a major role in business restructuring because these provisions provide the blueprint for acquiring or disposing of entire corporations or their assets at little or no tax cost.

A tax-deferred **corporate reorganization** involves the transfer of all or part of one corporation's assets or stock to a second corporation over which it has control in a transaction that qualifies as a reorganization under Section 368. A reorganization may be an acquisitive reorganization in which one corporation acquires the assets or stock of another corporation; it can be a divisive reorganization in which one corporation splits into two or more corporations; or it can involve a recapitalization or reincorporation that makes minimal changes in an existing corporation.

Corporations and their shareholders that participate in a qualified reorganization may exchange stock for property and stock for stock on a tax-deferred basis. As with most other tax-deferred transactions, the property or stock received will have a carryover or substituted basis to ensure that gain or loss is built into a future disposition. Boot received will also cause part or all of a realized gain to be recognized.

EXAMPLE 41

Pam owns 1,400 shares of Target Corporation when Target is merged into Giant Corporation. Pam receives 700 shares in Giant Corporation (fair market value $23,000) and $1,000 cash in exchange for her Target Corporation stock. Pam's Target stock had a basis of $20,000 and a $24,000 fair market value. Although Pam has a $4,000 realized gain ($23,000 + $1,000 – $20,000), she recognizes only $1,000 gain. The gain recognized is the lesser of the realized gain ($4,000) or the boot received ($1,000 cash). Pam's basis in the Giant stock is $20,000 ($20,000 basis of Target stock + $1,000 gain recognized – $1,000 boot received).

A more complete discussion of corporate reorganizations is included in the appendix to this chapter.

REVISITING THE INTRODUCTORY CASE

The most advantageous solution for Perry Winkle Corporation would be for it to combine the like-kind provisions with those applicable to the condemnation of the land. To do so, it may have to use an indirect acquisition, although it may be possible to find a property that is suitable and for which the owner is willing to make a direct exchange. Because time is important, and there is a buyer waiting for the property, the indirect exchange seems more practical. Perry Winkle needs to engage an escrow agent to hold the proceeds of the sale while it locates property that it wants. To avoid all gain, the property purchased should have a price of at least $500,000 in excess of the selling price of its facilities. As they are looking to expand their current facilities, the purchase price will most likely be well in excess of the $500,000 plus sale proceeds. Winkle will trade its land and give boot of $500,000 from the condemnation proceedings to complete the transaction. The corporation needs to pay close attention to the time requirements for the like-kind exchange: the 45 days to identify property and 180 days to closing. If the corporation does not use the entire $500,000 from the condemnation, it has more than two years to acquire additional real property and avoid gain recognition. (Alternatively, Perry Winkle could contact the supplier and have the supplier purchase a large section of the property that Winkle could then exchange for its property. Winkle could purchase adjacent or other property with the condemnation proceeds.)

SUMMARY

In a tax-deferred exchange, the taxpayer postpones recognizing gain or loss until a future event triggers recognition. Deferral is accomplished by decreasing basis for unrecognized gains and increasing it for unrecognized losses. The holding period of the asset received includes the holding period of the asset surrendered in a tax-deferred exchange.

One of the most important deferral provisions is the like-kind exchange that allows business or investment property to be exchanged for other business or investment property under certain conditions. To qualify, personalty must be exchanged for personalty of the same class. For realty, any investment or business realty may be exchanged for other investment or business realty. If property other than like-kind property is received as part of a qualifying like-kind exchange, gain must be recognized to the extent of the boot received or the gain realized, if smaller. Exchanges may involve more than two parties, and third-party intermediaries may be used to arrange a qualifying exchange.

Dispositions include involuntary conversions by theft, casualty, and condemnation. Deductible losses on involuntary conversions are reduced by insurance recoveries. Involuntary conversions of business and investment property are deductible as Section 1231 losses. Casualty and theft losses of individuals' personal-use property can be deducted only to the extent they exceed a $100 floor per occurrence and 10 percent of adjusted gross income.

Gains on involuntary conversions may be deferred if the taxpayer acquires qualifying replacement property. If the taxpayer owns and uses the property, the replacement property must have the same function as the converted property. If the taxpayer owns and leases the converted property to another, the taxpayer is only required to replace the converted property with other property that can be leased.

Individuals may transfer property to a sole proprietorship without tax effects. Gains and losses on transfers of property to a controlled corporation in exchange for stock in the corporation, and gains and losses on transfers of property to a partnership in exchange for a partnership interest, are deferred. Corporations may acquire the stock or property of another corporation in a qualified reorganization without tax consequences.

KEY TERMS

Amount realized 348
Basis adjustment 345
Boot 346
Casualty 353
Condemnation 353
Control 361
Corporate reorganization 367
Deductible loss 355
Functional-use test 359
Holding period 349
Involuntary conversions 353
Like-kind exchange 346
Nonsimultaneous exchange 350
Partner's basis 365
Presidentially declared disaster 357
Realized gain 348
Section 121 360
Section 351 361
Tax-deferred exchange 344
Taxpayer-use test 359
Theft 353
Wash sale 352

TEST YOURSELF

ANSWERS APPEAR AFTER THE PROBLEM ASSIGNMENTS

1. JB Manufacturing and BP Company exchange two pieces of land. JB's land has a basis of $800,000 and a fair market value of $750,000. BP's land has a basis of $560,000 and a fair market value of only $700,000 so BP gives JB an additional $50,000 cash. What are JB's and BP's deferred gain or loss on this exchange?

a. JB $50,000 deferred loss; BP $140,000 deferred gain
b. JB $50,000 deferred gain; BP $140,000 deferred gain
c. JB $50,000 deferred loss; BP $90,000 deferred gain
d. JB $50,000 deferred gain; BP $90,000 deferred gain

2. Cragin's manufacturing facility had an adjusted basis of $7,600,000: $2,000,000 for the land and $5,600,000 for the building when destroyed by fire. It received $7,000,000 from its insurance company to replace the building, and it sold the land for $2,800,000. How much must Cragin invest in a new facility to defer all of its gain?

a. $7,000,000
b. $7,600,000
c. $9,000,000
d. $9,800,000

3. The Joneses' home that they had owned and lived in for 12 years was destroyed in a flood. Fortunately, they had flood insurance that paid replacement value of $280,000 for their loss. The home had a basis of $223,000. How much gain must they récognize if they purchase a new home for only $268,000?

a. 0
b. $12,000
c. $45,000
d. $57,000

4. Marylou transfers $220,000 of equipment (basis = $170,000) to her wholly owned corporation in exchange for all the authorized nonvoting stock and $20,000 cash. How much gain or loss does Marylou recognize on the transfer, and what is her basis in the stock?

a. gain = 0; basis = $150,000
b. gain = $20,000; basis = $150,000
c. gain = $20,000; basis = $170,000
d. gain = $50,000; basis = $220,000

5. Mark, Nancy, and Carl form a partnership with each partner having an equal share in profits and losses. Mark and Carl each contribute $40,000 in cash to the partnership. Nancy contributes land valued at $100,000. The land has a basis of $90,000 and is encumbered by a $60,000 mortgage that the partnership assumes. What basis does Nancy have in her partnership interest immediately after the contribution of land to the partnership?

a. $50,000
b. $90,000
c. $100,000
d. $110,000

PROBLEM ASSIGNMENTS

CHECK YOUR UNDERSTANDING

1 How are gain and loss deferral usually accomplished? How is holding period affected by gain or loss deferral?

2. What types of realty qualify for like-kind exchange treatment? What kinds of personalty qualify for like-kind exchange treatment?

3. What is boot? What effect does boot have on a like-kind exchange?

4. What is a nonsimultaneous exchange? What are the critical factors in qualifying a nonsimultaneous exchange for tax deferral?

5. How is a casualty loss that completely destroys personal-use property measured? How is a casualty loss that partially destroys personal-use property measured?

6. How is a casualty loss that completely destroys business or investment property measured? How is a casualty loss that partially destroys business or investment property measured?

7. What limits are placed on the deductibility of casualty and theft losses of personal-use property in 2013?

8. In what year are casualty losses deducted? What choices are available if the casualty occurs in a presidentially declared disaster area?

9. Explain the functional-use test. Explain the taxpayer-use test.

10. What provisions apply to a personal residence that is subject to an involuntary conversion?

11. What is the critical requirement of a corporate formation to ensure tax-deferred property transfers to all participants?

12. How do liabilities assumed by a corporation affect a shareholder transferring property to it in a qualifying Section 351 transfer?

13. Explain the general provisions applicable to a partner transferring property to a partnership in exchange for a partnership interest.

14. Explain the tax treatment of services transferred to a partnership in exchange for a partnership interest.

15. What is a corporate reorganization?

CRUNCH THE NUMBERS

16. Peter exchanges a building valued at $400,000 for land also valued at $400,000 in a qualifying like-kind exchange. The building has a basis of $230,000. What are Peter's realized gain or loss and the basis of the land?

17. Shawn exchanges a factory building for an apartment building in a qualifying like-kind exchange. The factory has a basis of $350,000 and the apartment building has a fair market value of $320,000.

- **a.** What is Shawn's realized gain or loss and the basis of the apartment building?
- **b.** What alternative could you suggest to Shawn?

18. Wilma trades a fully depreciated computer used in her business for a new computer with a selling price of $3,200. Wilma pays only $2,500 for the computer because she receives a $200 discount as a favored customer and a $500 allowance for trading in the old computer.

- **a.** Does Wilma recognize any gain or loss on the exchange?
- **b.** What is the deferred gain or loss?
- **c.** What is Wilma's basis in the new computer?

19. The Taylor Corporation acquires a large boring machine in exchange for two of its smaller boring machines. The large machine has a fair market value of $108,000. The smaller machines are valued at $92,000, so Taylor pays an additional $16,000 on the exchange.

- **a.** If the basis of the smaller machines is $69,000, what is Taylor's realized and recognized gain or loss on the exchange?
- **b.** What is the deferred gain or loss?
- **c.** What is its basis in the large machine?

20. Whipple Corporation exchanges several pieces of office furniture for 10 file cabinets that the Go-Along Corporation no longer needs. Go-Along also gives Whipple a pair of season tickets for the local hockey team. The file cabinets have a value of $2,500 and a basis of $3,000. Go-Along paid the $400 face value for the tickets. The office furniture has a basis of $1,250 and value of $2,900.

- **a.** What are Whipple's and Go-Along's realized and recognized gains or losses?
- **b.** What are their deferred gains or losses?
- **c.** What are their bases in the properties acquired?
- **d.** What alternative transaction would you suggest to Whipple?

21. Delta Airlines trades two of its short-range jets to one of its regional commuter partners for a newer medium-range jet. Delta's jets have a fair market value of $4,000,000 and a basis of $2,250,000. The newer jet has a fair market value of $3,750,000, so Delta received $250,000 cash from the regional airline to complete the exchange.

a. What is Delta's realized and recognized gain or loss on the exchange?
b. What is its deferred gain or loss?
c. What is its basis in the airplane acquired?
d. How would your answers change if Delta's basis in the two short-range planes was $3,900,000?
e. How would your answers change if its basis in the planes was $4,150,000?

22. Lab Kennels, Inc. and Wolman Developers have agreed to exchange two parcels of land and each will assume the other's mortgage on the parcel acquired. Lab owns 500 acres within city limits that has a value of $750,000 and a basis of $300,000. It is encumbered by a $200,000 mortgage. Wolman's property is raw land outside the city that has a value of $900,000, a basis of $400,000, and is encumbered by a $350,000 mortgage.
    a. What are Lab Kennels, Inc. and Wolman Developer's realized and recognized gains or losses on the exchange?
    b. What are their deferred gains or losses?
    c. What are their bases in the land acquired?

23. DDD Corporation has agreed to exchange $50,000 and some raw land for a building owned by Jason Briggs. DDD Corporation's land has a value of $600,000, a basis of $200,000 and is encumbered by a $200,000 mortgage that Briggs has agreed to assume. Briggs's building is valued at $450,000 and has a basis of $125,000.
    a. What are DDD Corporation and Briggs's realized and recognized gains or losses on the exchange?
    b. What are their deferred gains or losses?
    c. What are their bases in the properties acquired?

24. The Clover Corporation wants to exchange land it has held for expansion for a building that will provide additional office space to avoid gain recognition. The land has a value of $1,200,000 and a basis of $800,000. What alternative can you suggest to Clover to accomplish its goal?

25. A tornado destroyed part of the offices of Heywood Corporation. The building had a fair market value of $500,000 before and $200,000 after the tornado. The basis of the building is $320,000.
    a. What is Heywood's casualty loss from the tornado?
    b. What is its remaining basis in the property, assuming it deducts its loss?
    c. What is Heywood's gain or loss if it receives $250,000 from its insurance company as compensation for its loss?
    d. What is its basis in the property if it spends $150,000 to repair the property?

26. Jewel's home was completely destroyed by fire in 2013. The home itself had an appraised value of $185,000 before the fire. Four years ago Jewel paid $160,000 for the house and the land, with $25,000 of the price allocated to the land.
    a. What is Jewel's loss on the fire, assuming no insurance?
    b. What is her deductible loss if her adjusted gross income is $40,000?
    c. What is Jewel's realized gain or loss if she receives $190,000 from the insurance company to rebuild the home?
    d. What is her recognized gain if she uses only $130,000 of the insurance proceeds to rebuild a smaller replacement residence on the same land?

27. Danny's living room furniture and his flat screen television were damaged in a fire in his home in January 2013. In March 2013, his golf cart was damaged in a flood. He was able to establish the following information to determine his losses on these assets.

ASSET	FMV BEFORE CASUALTY	FMV AFTER CASUALTY	INSURANCE RECOVERY	COST	DATE PURCHASED
Television	$4,600	$1,100	$2,000	$5,000	10 months ago
Furniture	5,500	1,500	3,200	3,000	11 years ago
Golf Cart	6,500	2,000	1,500	7,000	8 months ago

Danny's AGI is $37,000 before considering these casualties and he has $10,000 of other itemized deductions. Determine Danny's deductible casualty loss for 2013.

28. Cora was in Europe from Thanksgiving of 2012 until early January of 2013. When she returned to her home, she found it had been broken into and jewelry with a fair market value of $40,000 and a basis of $54,000 was missing. Her adjusted gross incomes in 2012 and 2013 are $56,000 and $72,000, respectively. If she is a calendar-year taxpayer, what is the amount of her theft deduction, and in what year is the deduction taken?

29. Clayton Corporation owns business realty that the county condemns on July 15, year 1. The county pays Clayton $400,000 for the property that has an allocated basis of $235,000.

- **a.** What is Clayton's realized and recognized gain, assuming it does not replace the property?
- **b.** What is its recognized gain, assuming it spends $350,000 on replacement property?
- **c.** What is its basis in the replacement property?
- **d.** What is its recognized gain, assuming it spends $500,000 on replacement property?
- **e.** What is its basis in the replacement property?
- **f.** If the corporation has a June 30 fiscal year-end, what is the last date that it can acquire qualifying replacement property?

30. Coronado Corporation owns business realty that was destroyed by fire on March 15, year 1. Its insurance company pays Coronado $325,000 for the property, which has an allocated basis of $275,000.

- **a.** What is Coronado's realized and recognized gain, assuming it does not replace the property? 325,000 - 275,000 = 50,000 realized and recognized gain
- **b.** What is its recognized gain, assuming it spends $300,000 on replacement property? 325,000 - 300,000 = 25,000 recognized gain
  50,000 - 25,000 recognized = 25,000 deferred gain
- **c.** What is its basis in the replacement property? 300,000 - 25,000 deferred gain = 275,000
- **d.** What is its recognized gain, assuming it spends $350,000 on replacement property? If 350,000 is spent on replacement property, there is no recognized gain; 50,000 gain is deferred
- **e.** What is its basis in the replacement property? 350,000 - 50,000 deferred gain = 300,000
- **f.** If the corporation has an April 30 year-end, what is the last date on which it can acquire qualifying replacement property? April 30th year 3 (2 years from April 30 year 1

31. Xenon Corporation can sell an auto used in its business for $4,000 and purchase a new auto for $20,000. Alternatively, it can trade in the auto on a new one from a different dealer. This dealer will allow $4,000 on the trade-in of the old car but requires an additional $17,000 payment. The old auto has a basis of $500 and Xenon Corporation is in the 25 percent marginal tax bracket. It generally uses its cars for only three years. Which alternative should Xenon choose?

32. Bently Corporation can sell a warehouse for $800,000 that has a basis of $300,000. It has two replacement alternatives. It can purchase a replacement warehouse for $800,000 or it can make a direct exchange for another suitable warehouse. This property has a fair market value of only $725,000, but the owner will not pay anything additional for Bently's warehouse. Assume Bently uses a 40 percent combined federal and state marginal tax rate and an 8 percent discount rate for all asset decisions. Assume either property would be depreciated evenly over 40 years. Should Bently sell the building at its fair market value and purchase the $800,000 property, or should it make the exchange?

33. Moore bought 2,000 shares of VBT stock over the Internet on January 2 of year 4 for $50,000. On December 28 of year 3, his broker sold 3,000 shares of VBT for $85,000 that she had been holding in Moore's account. This stock had been purchased in year 1 for $100,000. What is Moore's realized and recognized gain or loss? What is his basis in the stock purchased on January 2?

34. Monroe Corporation's chief financial officer sold 2,000 shares of TNC stock that the corporation was holding as a temporary investment on July 3 at a $4,000 loss. On July 30, the controller of Monroe purchased 1,000 shares of TNC for the corporation at $8 per share as the stock had received a favorable recommendation from the corporation's financial advisor. What are the tax consequences of these transactions?

35. Kelly was active in the market, buying and selling stocks for her own account. Below are a series of transactions Kelly initiated during the last quarter of 2013:

DATE OF TRANSACTION	TRANSACTION	NUMBER OF SHARES	STOCK	PRICE PER SHARE
10/15	Bought	1,000	ABC	$25
10/29	Bought	500	DEF	$20
11/01	Sold	800	XYZ	$15
11/04	Sold	500	DEF	$22
11/07	Bought	1,000	GHI	$16
11/18	Bought	2,000	XYZ	$12
11/20	Sold	500	ABC	$22
11/22	Bought	500	DEF	$18
12/02	Bought	1,000	ABC	$21

The XYZ stock sold on 11/01 had been purchased two years earlier for $18 per share. What is Kelly's realized and recognized gain or loss on each of the sale transactions? (Use FIFO for determining which stocks were sold.) What is Kelly's basis in each of the stocks remaining in her portfolio?

36. Jim and Cindy form JC Corporation, with each receiving 50 percent of the shares issued. Jim transfers land valued at $50,000 with a $40,000 basis for his stock, and Cindy transfers property valued at $45,000 with a basis of $50,000 for her stock. In addition, Cindy provides $5,000 of legal and accounting services in establishing the corporation. What are the tax consequences of the incorporation? What are Jim and Cindy's bases in their stock?

37. Wilbur transfers property valued at $100,000 (basis = $70,000) to the Debold Corporation in exchange for 100 percent of its stock.

a. What is Wilbur's realized gain or loss on the transfer and his recognized gain or loss?

b. What is his basis in the stock received?

c. What is the corporation's basis in the property transferred?

38. Arleta transfers property valued at $210,000 (basis = $190,000) to BCD Corporation in exchange for 70 percent of its stock. Georgia transfers property valued at $85,000 (basis = $75,000) and performs $5,000 in accounting services in exchange for the other 30 percent of BCD's stock.

a. What are Arleta and Georgia's gains/income or losses realized?

b. What are Arleta and Georgia's gains/income or losses recognized?

c. What are their bases in BCD's stock?

d. What is BCD's basis in the property received?

39. Carol decides to transfer her rental apartment building to a wholly owned corporation to insulate herself from tenant liabilities. The apartment building is valued at $1,250,000 and has a basis of $1,350,000 due to $400,000 of recent improvements made to the building. The new corporation also assumes the $200,000 remaining on Carol's mortgage on the building.

a. What is the value of the stock Carol receives from the corporation?

b. What is Carol's realized and recognized gain or loss on the transfer?

c. What are Carol's basis in her stock and the corporation's basis in the building? Explain your answer.

40. Cornelia transfers property valued at $400 (basis = $350) to Wayside Corporation (an existing corporation) in exchange for 50 percent of its stock. Ferdinand transfers property valued at $450 (basis = $260) in exchange for the other 50 percent of Wayside's stock and property valued at $50 (basis = $20).

a. What are Cornelia's and Ferdinand's realized gains or losses?

b. What are their recognized gains or losses?

c. What are their bases in Wayside's stock?

d. What is Wayside's basis in the property received?

e. Does Wayside have any other tax consequences?

41. Tinker incorporates his sole proprietorship by transferring a building, equipment, and inventory to the Tinker Corporation in exchange for all its stock. The building has a value of $750,000 and a basis of $800,000, the equipment has a value of $400,000 and a basis of $375,000, and the inventory has both a value and basis of $50,000.

a. What is Tinker's gain or loss realized on the transfer?

b. What is Tinker's gain or loss recognized on the transfer?

c. What is his basis in the stock received and the corporation's basis in the property transferred? Explain your answer.

42. Jim and Angie form the JAZ Partnership with Zoe by contributing $75,000 each to partnership equity. Zoe, the third partner, contributes property with a basis of $50,000 and fair market value of $75,000. The three are equal partners in the partnership. Determine the tax consequences to Zoe for the contribution of property to the partnership. What are the partnership's tax consequences? What is each partner's basis in the partnership interest? What is the partnership's basis in the property?

43. Moe, Larry, and Curly form a partnership with each partner having an equal share in profits and losses. Moe and Curly each contribute $50,000 in cash to the partnership. Larry contributes a piece of land valued at $170,000. The land has a basis of $125,000 and is encumbered by a $120,000 mortgage (non-recourse debt). What basis does each of the partners have in their partnership interest immediately after the contribution of money and land to the partnership?

44. X, Y, and Z form XYZ Partnership by contributing cash and property as follows: X contributes $40,000 cash for a 20 percent interest. Y contributes property valued at $80,000 for a 40 percent interest. This property has a basis in Y's hands of $50,000. For the remaining 40 percent interest, Z develops the partnership agreement and performs other services that are valued at $5,000. In addition, he contributes property with a fair market value of $100,000 with a $25,000 mortgage that the partnership guarantees. The property has a basis of $70,000 in Z's hands. Determine X, Y, and Z's basis in their partnership interests. Determine the partnership's basis in the assets contributed.

45. Comprehensive Problem for Chapters 5, 6, 7, and 8. Columbo Corporation, a calendar-year corporation, began business in 2010. With the initial capital contributions from its sole shareholder, it purchased a building on March 12 for $250,000. It also purchased the following items, all used, for use in the business:

ITEM	PURCHASE DATE	ACQUISITION COST
Office Furniture	April 1	$8,000
Computer	April 15	$4,000
Machine A	May 2	$15,000
Machine B	August 4	$21,000
Machine C	August 12	$31,000

Columbo did not elect bonus depreciation in 2010 but used MACRS accelerated depreciation on all the assets except Machine B, which it expensed under the Section 179 election.

On January 5, 2013, Columbo sold Machine A for $7,000. It purchased an upgraded Machine D for $45,000 on January 20. On May 5, its computer was completely destroyed by a power surge and had to be replaced. The new computer equipment cost $6,000. In October, their building was condemned by the city and Columbo had to move. The city paid Columbo $275,000 for the building and it purchased a new building for $310,000 and moved in on October 30. Also in October, the sole shareholder purchased the office furniture for $100 (fair market value = $2,000) and Columbo purchased new furniture for the new building for $15,000. Rather than move Machine B (fair market value = $6,000), it traded it in on new Machine E paying an additional $28,000 cash for the machine.

a. Determine Columbo Corporation's depreciation expense in years 2010 through 2013 if it did not elect bonus depreciation or Section 179 expensing (except for Machine B).

b. Determine the amount and type of realized and recognized gain or loss on each of the property dispositions in 2013.

c. Determine the net effect of the property transactions on Columbo's taxable income in 2013.

d. Columbo used straight-line depreciation with a 10-year life for the office furniture and machines and a 5-year life for the computer, taking a full year's depreciation in the year of acquisition and none in the year of disposal, for financial accounting purposes.

1. Determine its financial accounting depreciation deductions for years 2010 through 2013.
2. Determine its gains and losses on property transactions for financial accounting in 2013.
3. For 2010 through 2013, determine if the differences between financial accounting and tax accounting depreciation and property transactions would result in a deferred tax asset or a deferred tax liability for the corporation (consider each year separately).

THINK OUTSIDE THE TEXT

These questions require answers that are beyond the material that is covered in this chapter.

46. Why do you think the specifications for like-kind properties are so different for real property and for personalty?

47. What policy reason do you think explains why losses on the personal-use property of individuals are nondeductible except for a limited amount of loss from involuntary conversions?

48. Why do you think businesses are allowed an additional year to find qualifying replacement real estate for realty that is condemned?

49. What is a possible reason for allowing persons to use the provision that allows the deferral of gain or loss for involuntary conversions on property that is sold under the threat of condemnation only?

50. What is the rationale behind a corporation's increasing its basis in property received in a Section 351 transaction for the gain recognized by the transferor shareholder?

51. A shareholder receives stock valued at $500,000 and $50,000 cash for two pieces of equipment as part of a Section 351 transaction. He transfers (1) Machine A with a fair market value of $330,000 and a basis of $300,000 and (2) Machine B with a fair market value of $220,000 and a basis of $250,000. How do you think the shareholder should determine if he should recognize any gain on the transfer of the equipment? Comment on the result.

IDENTIFY THE ISSUES

Identify the issues or problems suggested by the following situations. State each issue as a question.

52. The Westlawn Corporation is located in a flood plain. Twelve years ago, its offices were flooded when the nearby river overflowed. Six years ago, the area received 12 inches of rain in a six-hour period, the river overflowed, and the offices flooded again. This year, excessive runoff from melting snow in the nearby mountains caused the river to overflow again and flood the company's offices.

53. Karen purchased her personal auto two years ago from a local new car dealer. Since purchasing the car, she took it into the dealer for major warranty repairs five different times and minor repairs a total of fourteen times. She is so unhappy with the car that one day she just drove the car into a bridge abutment at 20 miles per hour, which was sufficient to have the car declared as a total loss.

54. The Timmins Corporation has three acres of land on which its warehouse and offices are located. The state condemned two acres of the land for an extension of a highway frontage road. The strip that was condemned took the warehouse and parking area, leaving only the small office building. The corporation received $3,000,000 for the property that was condemned and $1,000,000 in severance damages due to the separation of the office property from the rest of the facility. The warehouse and parking area have a basis of $425,000 and the office area a basis of $250,000. Timmins plans to replace the entire warehouse and office facility.

55. Claiborne, Inc. has received an offer to purchase its manufacturing facilities for $7,500,000. If sold, it would have a gain of $5,000,000 on the property. Claiborne has found an ideal location for a new facility, but the only available property is three times as large as it needs. It can, however, acquire a one-third interest in the property and move its operations into that area. The purchaser of its property is willing to cooperate in an indirect exchange.

56. Barry owned a number of rental properties. One of the rental properties was located next to his personal residence. Both properties were condemned by the state. Barry found a perfect residence to replace the rental property almost immediately but not one to replace the personal residence. As a result, Barry moved into the replacement rental unit for five months until he found a suitable home to replace the residence.

57. Carlson Manufacturing's plant was condemned by the federal government to allow for expansion of one of its secured locations for government employees. The government paid the company $6,800,000 for the property that had a basis of $2,500,000 and it moved out in December of year 1. In March of year 2, Carlson contracted with a construction company to build new facilities in West Virginia. The construction was to take two years with occupancy planned for June of year 4. Severe floods followed extraordinary rains in the spring of year 4. The construction company was forced to halt construction for six months until a bridge into the property could be replaced. As a result, construction was not completed until February of year 5. Carlson occupied the building in March of that year.

DEVELOP RESEARCH SKILLS

58. Barry is very dedicated to the arts and has made a career of purchasing copyrights to various art forms. Once purchased, he publicizes these works to capitalize on the copyrights and has been very successful. Last year, he acquired a book manuscript that he believes would be better suited to a mainstream publisher. He approaches a publisher about trading the book copyright for the copyright on the words and music for a new musical comedy that he heard the publisher had acquired. Will the exchange qualify as like-kind exchange?

59. Cheryl owned six horses that she and her family used for riding and occasionally showing in hunter-jumper competitions. At the beginning of May, one of the horses showed signs of severe illness and was diagnosed with equine encephalitis. She was required to destroy all of her horses, none of which was insured. The horses had been purchased for $23,000 but had a current value of $45,000. What type of a loss does Cheryl have on these horses?

60. Joe, June, and Jim—coworkers—decide that they want to start their own business. Joe has $200,000 to contribute, June has equipment valued at $100,000 (basis = $90,000), and Jim has real estate suitable for the business valued at $200,000 (basis = $110,000). Joe and Jim are each to receive 40 percent of the corporate stock, and June is to receive 20 percent. Joe and June transfer title to their property to the corporation immediately. When Jim tries to transfer title to the real estate to the corporation, several legal errors in the title are discovered, and he is unable to transfer title until the errors are corrected. Correcting the errors takes more than 14 months. In the meantime, the corporation begins operating, renting the building from Jim. In the 15th month, Jim is able to transfer title and receive his stock. Is Jim eligible to use the nonrecognition provisions of Section 351 on this transfer?

SEARCH THE INTERNET

For the following problems, consult the IRS Web site (www.irs.gov).

61. Locate and read Publication 550: Investment Income and Expenses. How do you report a wash sale?

62. Locate and read Publication 544: *Sales and Other Disposition of Assets.* How is a like-kind exchange reported? If there is a recognized gain, how is that reported?

63. Locate and read Publication 547: *Casualties, Disasters, and Thefts*. Where is a casualty loss on a personal-use asset reported? Where is a casualty gain on personal-use property reported?

64. Locate and print Form 4684 *(Casualties and Thefts)*. Enter the following information and complete the form to the extent possible: Howser Corporation, a calendar-year corporation, discovered in January that its bookkeeper (who was fired late last year) had embezzled $45,000 from the company. The theft was not covered by insurance. In October, a hurricane damaged its warehouse building in the Florida Keys. The building's fair market values before and after the hurricane were $425,000 and $150,000, respectively. The basis of the building at the time of the damage was $235,000. Howser received only $200,000 from its insurance company due to its limited hurricane coverage.

DEVELOP PLANNING SKILLS

65. The Glades Corporation has located a building that it would like to have for its new warehouse. The corporation has contacted the owner about making a trade for its existing property. The owner of the desired property is only willing to sell the building for cash as he will have little gain on the sale and has no use for the Glades property. Glades, however, has an extremely low basis in its property and is unwilling to sell it in order to purchase the new property. Is there an alternative that will satisfy Glades and the owner of the warehouse property?

66. The Timberlake Corporation has an opportunity to sell its manufacturing facility to Carroll Corporation for $4,500,000. The property has a basis of $2,000,000, and the prospective purchaser is willing to wait up to six months for occupancy to allow Timberlake time to locate and purchase new facilities. Timberlake's marginal tax rate is 35 percent. What alternatives should Timberlake consider, and what are the tax consequences of the alternatives?

67. Refer to the material in the preceding problem. Timberlake locates suitable property that the owner would sell for $4,800,000 although the property appraises at only $4,250,000. Carroll Corporation is willing to purchase this property for the $4,800,000 asking price. It would then trade this property to Timberlake for its property, but Timberlake would have to pay it $300,000 in addition to transferring the property. What are the tax consequences?

68. William, Wally, and Wilma want to form a corporation. William has cash of $100,000; Wally has property valued at $100,000 with a basis of $80,000; and Wilma has property valued at $50,000 that has a $70,000 basis. Wally doesn't want to recognize his gain, but Wilma wants to recognize her loss because she has capital gains to offset the loss. As their tax advisor, develop several alternatives from which they can choose that would allow Wally to avoid gain recognition but allow Wilma to recognize her loss.

ANSWERS TO TEST YOURSELF

1. **a. JB $50,000 deferred loss** ($750,000 – $800,000); **BP $140,000 deferred gain** ($750,000 – $610,000)

2. **d. $9,800,000**; even though the proceeds were obtained from two sources, all must be reinvested to defer the entire gain.

3. **a. $0**; they recognize no gain under Section 121 because this is considered a sale.

4. c. **gain = $20,000; basis = $170,000**. Marylou must recognize gain equal to the lesser of gain realized or boot received. Her basis = $170,000 + $20,000 gain – $20,000 boot received.

5. a. **$50,000**. $90,000 carryover basis – $60,000 liability + ($60,000 × 1/3)

Appendix 8A

REORGANIZATIONS

Seven types of reorganizations, commonly referred to as Types A through G, are presented in Section 368(a)(1)(A) to (G). Types A, B, and C are acquisitive reorganizations. Types E and F involve only one corporation making technical changes. The Type D reorganization can be either a divisive reorganization or an acquisitive reorganization. A Type G reorganization is similar to the Type D reorganization but applies only to a corporation that is in bankruptcy.

Acquisitive Reorganizations

An acquisitive reorganization generally involves (1) the acquisition of one corporation's assets (the target) by a second corporation (the acquirer), after which the target ceases to operate or (2) the acquisition of the target corporation's stock for stock of the acquirer, after which the target becomes a subsidiary of the acquiring corporation. Types A (the statutory merger or consolidation), C (a stock for asset acquisition), and acquisitive D reorganizations follow this asset acquisition pattern, while Type B is the stock for stock acquisition.

Figures 8A.1 and 8A.2 illustrate the asset and stock acquisitive reorganizations.

FIGURE 8A.1 ACQUISITIVE REORGANIZATION ASSET ACQUISITION

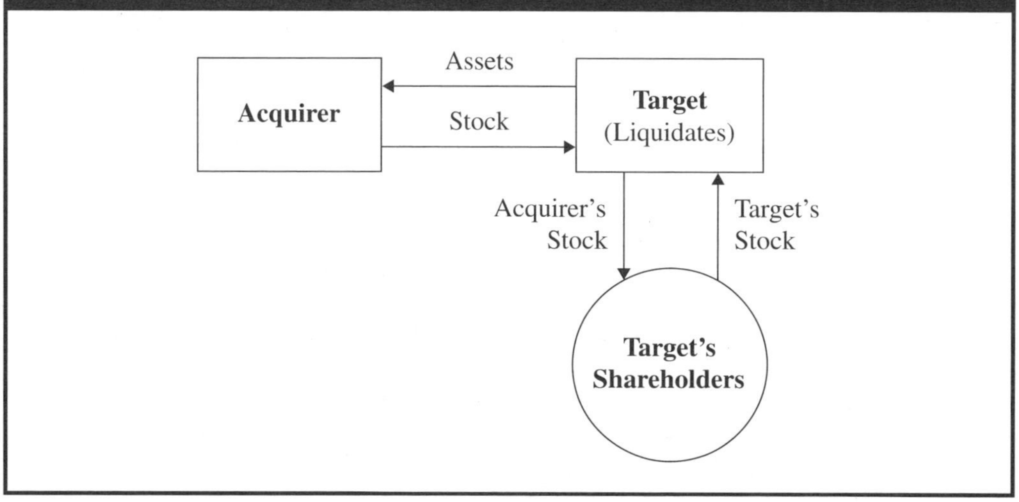

FIGURE 8A.2 TYPE B ACQUISITIVE REORGANIZATION STOCK ACQUISITION

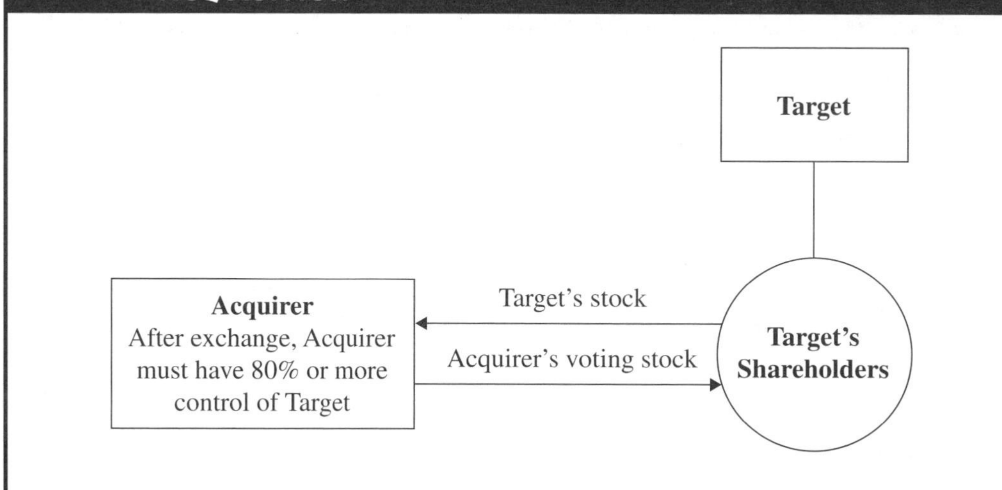

FIGURE 8A.3 GENERAL TAX CONSEQUENCES FOR CORPORATIONS THAT ARE PART OF AN ASSET ACQUISITION REORGANIZATION

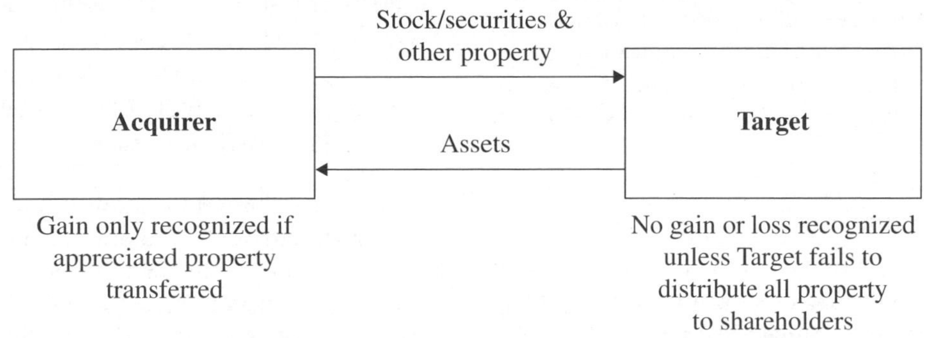

FIGURE 8A.4 TARGET SHAREHOLDER'S GENERAL TAX CONSEQUENCES IN AN ASSET ACQUISITION REORGANIZATION

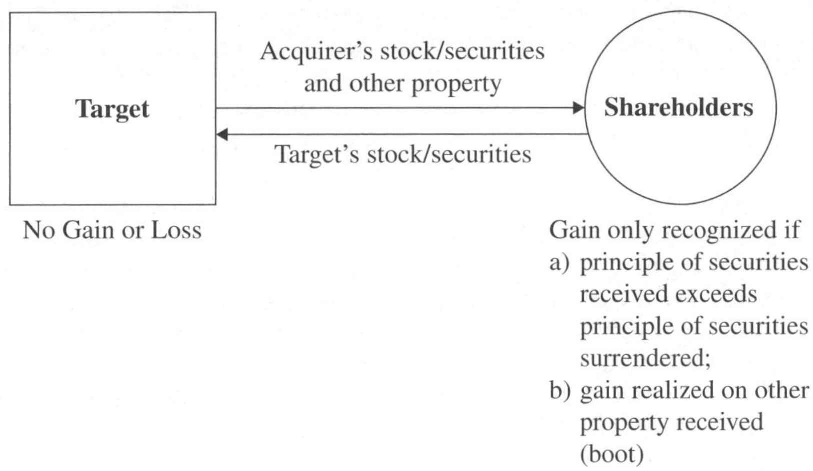

Basic Tax Consequences

In an asset acquisition, when Acquirer transfers stock and securities to Target in exchange for Target's assets in a qualifying reorganization, neither Acquirer nor Target recognizes gain or loss on this transfer. Acquirer takes the same basis in the assets as their basis in Target's hands. Target recognizes no gain or loss on the receipt of stock or securities; it recognizes no gain on the receipt of any other property as long as that property is distributed to its shareholders. Gain is recognized only by Acquirer if it transfers appreciated property other than stock or securities to Target, in which case Target uses fair market value for its basis in the property retained. (No loss is recognized on depreciated property transferred.) Figure 8A.3 illustrates the asset transfers between the corporations and the tax consequences.

Target's shareholders recognize no gain or loss on the receipt of stock in exchange for their stock in Target; they may be required to recognize gain on the receipt of securities if the principal of the securities received exceeds the principal of the securities surrendered.[66] If Target distributes cash or property other than stock or securities, the shareholders have received boot and must recognize gain to the extent of the lesser of the fair market value of the boot received or the gain realized. The boot received may be assets that Target did not transfer to Acquirer, or it may be property that Acquirer transferred to Target as part of the acquisition. Target's shareholders have the same basis in the stock and securities received as they had in the stock surrendered, decreased for the boot received and increased by any gain recognized. They use fair market value for the basis of the boot received. Figure 8A.4 illustrates the shareholder's consequences on a Type A reorganization.

[66]Technically, gain is recognized only if the fair market value of the excess principal on securities received exceeds the fair market value of the excess principal of securities surrendered.

In a Type B stock-for-stock reorganization, the acquiring corporation acquires Target's stock from its shareholders in exchange solely for stock of Acquirer. This is an acquisition that involves Target's shareholders and Acquirer only, not Target's management. Acquirer can use nothing but its own voting stock to acquire Target's stock; thus, neither Acquirer nor Target's shareholders recognize gain or loss on this exchange. Figure 8A.2 illustrates the Type B reorganization.

Type A Reorganization

A basic Type A reorganization, a statutory merger or consolidation, is the most flexible of all reorganizations. A merger is the acquisition of the assets of a target corporation; the target liquidates and the acquiring corporation continues. A consolidation is the transfer of assets by two or more corporations to a new corporation; the transferring corporations liquidate and the new corporation survives.

To qualify as a Type A reorganization, the reorganization must follow the provision of law in the state in which the corporation reorganizes. The acquiring corporation can acquire the assets of the target corporation using both its stock and securities, but the reorganization must meet the judicial doctrine of continuity of interest. To meet this doctrine (as interpreted by the IRS), at least 50 percent of the shareholders of the target corporation must become shareholders of the acquired corporation.[67] The basic Type A reorganization has disadvantages, however. In most states, the shareholders of both the acquiring corporation and the target corporation must approve the merger. In addition, the acquiring corporation becomes liable for all the liabilities (including contingent liabilities) of the target.

Example 8A.1

Corporation A exchanges its stock valued at $20,000,000 for all the assets of target Corporation T, which have a basis of $12,000,000, in a Type A reorganization. Corporation T distributes Corporation A's stock to its sole shareholder and receives all of her stock with a basis of $7,500,000 in return. Corporation T does not recognize its $8,000,000 realized gain; Corporation A takes a carryover basis of $12,000,000 in the transferred assets. The sole shareholder recognizes none of her $12,500,000 realized gain on the exchange of T's stock for A's stock. Her basis in Corporation A's stock is $7,500,000.[68]

Alternatively, Corporation A acquires the assets of Corporation T for $8,000,000 cash and $12,000,000 stock, distributing both the cash and stock to the sole shareholder. Corporation T does not recognize its $8,000,000 realized gain because all of the cash (other property) is distributed to its sole shareholder. The sole shareholder must recognize $8,000,000 gain, the lesser of the realized gain of $12,500,000 or the value of other property received, and defers gain recognition of $4,500,000 ($12,500,000 – $8,000,000). The shareholder has a basis in the distributed stock of $7,500,000 ($7,500,000 – $8,000,000 boot + $8,000,000 gain recognized).

The Type A reorganization has a variety of permissible alternative formulations: (1) the acquiring corporation may transfer the assets of the target to a subsidiary corporation; (2) a subsidiary could be the acquiring corporation with the target shareholders becoming minority shareholders of the target; (3) a subsidiary may acquire the assets of the target corporation using the stock of the parent corporation. These latter two are called forward triangular mergers. Using the subsidiary to acquire Target may avoid the requirement of having parent's shareholders approve the acquisition. This also has the advantage of insulating the parent-acquiring corporation from the target corporation's liabilities.

If the target cannot liquidate (for example, it has nontransferable licenses or patents), the parent can transfer the assets of the subsidiary (which will include the parent's stock) to the target, after which the subsidiary will liquidate and the target will become a new subsidiary of the parent. In this form, the parent has effected a reverse triangular merger.[69] The triangular merger using the parent's stock and the reverse triangular merger impose additional requirements to qualify as a tax-free reorganization.[70]

Type B Reorganization

An acquisition of the target corporation's stock in exchange for voting stock of the acquiring corporation is a Type B (the stock for voting stock) reorganization. After the reorganization, the shareholders of the target corporation are shareholders of the acquiring corporation and the acquiring corporation controls the target. Control is defined as owning 80 percent of the voting stock and 80 percent of all other stock of the acquired corporation. A parent corporation may also use a subsidiary as the acquiring corporation using stock solely of the parent, or it may

[67]The IRS will not issue advance rulings on a Type A reorganization unless the 50 percent continuity of interest is met.

[68]This reorganization could also qualify as a C reorganization. In a Type C reorganization, the target corporation must liquidate.

[69]§§368(a)(1)(c) and 368(a)(2)(C), (D), and (E).

[70]In a forward triangular merger, only stock of the parent can be used and substantially all of the target's assets must be acquired. In a reverse triangular merger, only voting stock of the parent can be used to acquire control (80 percent voting and 80 percent of all other stock) of the target; additionally, the target must have substantially all of its assets and the assets of the subsidiary, except for parent stock, after the merger.

drop the stock of the target corporation into a subsidiary as part of the reorganization.[71]

The Type B reorganization has several advantages. First, if the acquiring corporation has acquired stock in the target for cash in transactions prior to establishing a plan of reorganization, the prior purchases will not taint the acquisition as long as they took place a reasonable time period prior to filing the reorganization plan. Second, the acquiring corporation has a period of up to one year after establishing a plan of reorganization to complete the acquisition of control of the target.[72] Moreover, control does not have to be acquired as part of the reorganization. Thus, a parent already owning 82 percent of the target may acquire 10 percent more in a tax-free reorganization.

EXAMPLE 8A.2

Three years ago, Corporation B acquired 15 percent of Corporation T's stock for cash. It filed a plan of reorganization on January 3 that spelled out its intention to acquire a controlling interest in T. Corporation B transfers 200,000 shares of its voting stock to the shareholders of Corporation T in exchange for 75 percent of their stock in T, completing the exchange on December 14 of the same year. This is a qualifying Type B reorganization. The previous purchase does not taint the stock acquisition because it took place substantially before the corporation filed its plan of reorganization and acquired the control of T.

Type C Reorganization

The Type C reorganization looks like the basic Type A reorganization, but specific requirements must be met to qualify as a tax-free reorganization. The acquiring corporation must acquire substantially all the assets of Target solely for voting stock of Acquirer. It must distribute any remaining assets and the stock of Acquirer to its shareholders and then liquidate. Generally, the assets acquired must permit Acquirer to continue Target's historic business. The acquiring corporation may assume an unlimited amount of Target's liabilities if only the acquirer's voting stock is used in the acquisition. A limited amount of boot is permitted in the acquisition, but the combination of boot and liabilities assumed cannot exceed 20 percent of the value of the consideration used to acquire Target's assets. Only Target's shareholders must approve the merger and liquidation of the target.

The acquiring corporation in a C reorganization may drop the assets acquired from Target into a subsidiary, or a subsidiary may use the parent stock to acquire the Target in a forward triangular merger. The Type C reorganization does not include a reverse triangular merger, however.

Type D Acquisitive Reorganization

In a Type D acquisitive reorganization, the acquiring corporation transfers substantially all of its assets to Target in exchange for the stock of the Target. Target corporation then holds its own assets, as well as those of the acquiring corporation. Target stock is then distributed to the acquiring corporation's shareholders, and they receive sufficient stock to control the target corporation; control for this type of reorganization is only 50 percent of the voting stock or 50 percent of the value of all stock. The acquiring corporation in a Type D acquisitive reorganization may not transfer the assets to a subsidiary nor may it use a subsidiary to acquire the target corporation.

Type D Divisive Reorganization

The Type D divisive reorganization can take three forms commonly known as a *spin off, split off,* and *split up.* In a spin off and a split off, some (but not all) of the original corporation's assets are transferred to a subsidiary and the subsidiary's stock is then distributed to shareholders of the original corporation. If the original shareholders generally receive a pro rata distribution of stock and do not surrender stock of the original corporation, it is a spin off. If the stock of the new corporation is distributed to some of the shareholders in exchange for their stock in the original corporation, it is a split off. Figure 8A.5 illustrates these divisions.

If all of the assets of the original corporation are split between two or more new companies and the stock of each company is distributed to the shareholders in exchange for their stock in the original corporation (with the original corporation going out of business), it is a split up. Both the split off and split up allow a division of shareholder groups when differences among shareholders hamper continued operations.

The transfer of assets to a new corporation normally is not taxable if it meets the requirements of Section 351. As a reorganization, however, the stock of the transferee corporation can be distributed to (spin off) or exchanged by (split off and split up) the shareholders tax free.[73]

To qualify for nonrecognition, the divisive D reorganization must meet several requirements. First, the transfer of assets must result in at least two corporations, each of which must conduct an active business immediately after the transfer. These active businesses must have been conducted for at least five

[71]§§368(a)(1)(B) and 368(a)(2)(B).

[72]The Type B reorganization is often called a creeping consolidation for this reason.

[73]§354(a).

FIGURE
8A.5 SPIN OFF AND SPLIT OFF

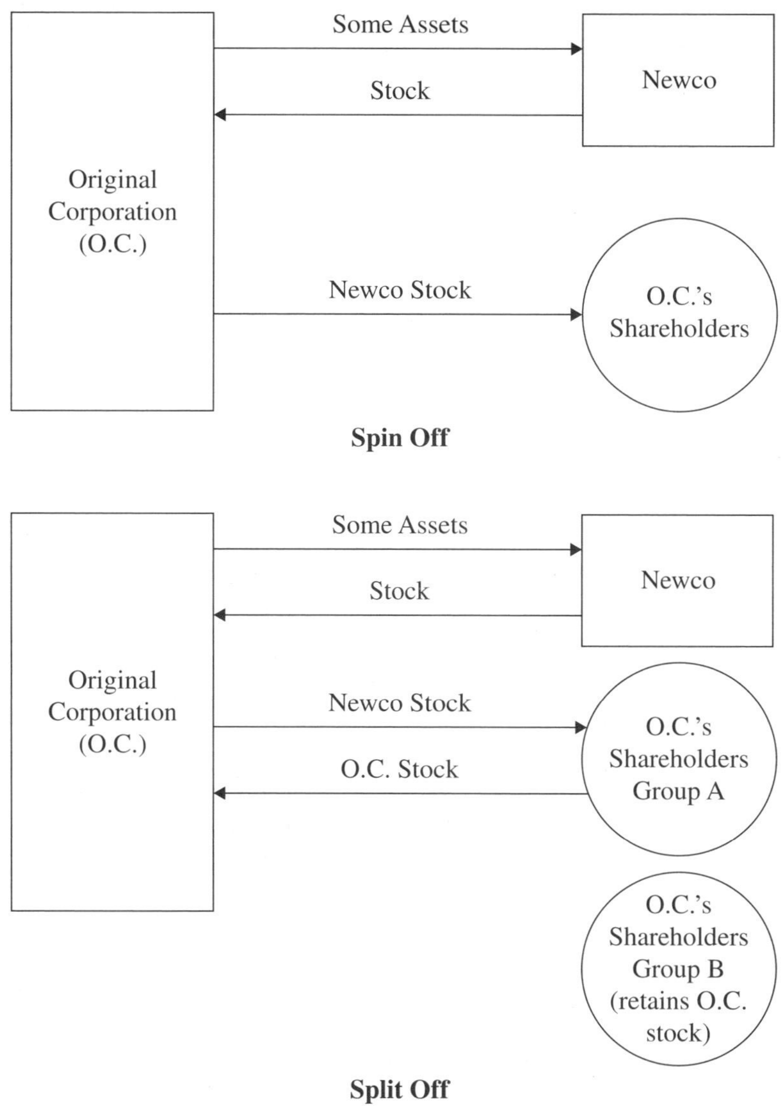

years prior to the separation. Second, sufficient stock and securities of the new corporation(s) must be distributed to the shareholders so that they have at least 80 percent control of the corporation(s). Any other property distributed to the shareholders is boot and causes all or part of a realized gain to be recognized. Finally, the reorganization may not be a device to distribute a corporation's earnings without tax.

If the division fails to qualify as a reorganization, a spin off will be taxed as a dividend distribution; a split off will be treated as a redemption of the stock of those shareholders surrendering their stock in the old corporation; the split up will be treated as a liquidation of the old corporation in exchange for the stock received in the new corporation. The basic taxation of dividend distributions, redemptions, and liquidations are discussed in the following chapter.

Other Reorganizations

The Type E reorganization is a recapitalization of an existing corporation. This allows the tax-free exchange of common or preferred stock for other common or preferred stock, bonds for other bonds, and bonds for stock. Stock, however, may not be exchanged tax free for bonds as that upgrades a shareholder to the status of a creditor.

A Type F reorganization is effected when a corporation simply changes its name, its place of incorporation, or its status from profit to nonprofit or vice versa. The shareholders of the original corporation must continue as shareholders of the reorganized corporation for this to qualify as a tax-free reorganization.

The Type G reorganization allows the transfer of assets to a new corporation as part of bankruptcy proceedings. The stock or securities are distributed to the shareholders in a manner resembling the D reorganization. The federal bankruptcy provisions may impact the form in which a G reorganization is carried out.

Other Considerations

The corporations involved in a reorganization must establish a plan of reorganization, following the tax rules specific to the type of reorganization desired.[74] It is advisable for the acquiring corporation to make a request for an advance ruling on the tax consequences of the reorganization to ensure the tax-deferred nature of the transaction if the plan is followed as set forth in the ruling request. The reorganization must have a sound business purpose; that is, there must be a nontax business reason. Acquiring an unprofitable corporation primarily to take advantage of its tax attributes, such as net operating loss or capital loss carryovers, does not meet this requirement.[75] There must be a continuity of ownership by shareholders of the participating corporations; that is, a majority of the target corporation's shareholders must continue to have a financial interest in the reorganized corporation.[76] There must be continuity of business enterprise.[77] The acquiring corporation must continue the historic business of the acquired corporation or use a significant part of the assets acquired. Thus, it cannot acquire a corporation and immediately sell off its assets. Failure to take these factors into consideration can doom a reorganization to failure.

[74]Reg. §1.368-3(a).

[75]Reg. §1.355-2(b).

[76]The continuity of interest applies primarily to Type A reorganizations. The tax law only requires that the merger or consolidation meet the requirements of the law in the state in which it is effected; if it does not meet the continuity of interest doctrine, however, it will not qualify as a tax-deferred reorganization in spite of meeting state law.

[77]Reg. §368-1(d).

In addition, a reorganization should not be entered into unless consideration has been given to factors other than the taxation of the actual transfers. The acquiring corporation must consider the status of the target corporation's net operating losses and applicable limitations, capital loss carryovers, the earnings and profits of the combined corporations, the other attributes that follow the target corporation, the provisions affecting built-in gains on acquired assets, the change in tax years for the acquired corporation, and other effects of filing a consolidated return. The applicable Code sections, related regulations, and interpretive rulings related to these other factors are much too extensive to include with this introductory material, but they must be consulted to achieve the best tax result for all parties to the reorganization.

PROBLEM ASSIGNMENTS

CHECK YOUR UNDERSTANDING

1. If a corporation wants to change its name, what type of reorganization does it undertake?
2. What types of reorganizations allow the shareholders to divide one corporation into two or more corporations?
3. What types of reorganizations entail asset acquisitions?
4. What types of reorganizations may use a subsidiary to acquire the assets or stock of another corporation?
5. When would the acquiring corporation in a reorganization recognize gain?
6. When does a shareholder recognize gain if he or she participates in a reorganization?
7. Describe the three types of divisive reorganizations.
8. What does the continuity of interest mean?

BUSINESS TAXATION

part

I

CHAPTER 9

TAXATION O
CORPORAT

CHAPTER 10

SOLE PROPRIETO
AND FLOW-THR
ENTITIES

chapter

9

Taxation of Corporations

CHAPTER OUTLINE

The choice of entity type in which to operate a business is one of the most important decisions owners of businesses can make. Owners generally can form a sole proprietorship, a partnership, or a corporation without tax consequences, but the formation of a business is only a small part of what must be considered in determining the type of entity.

It is extremely important to consider the day-to-day operations of the business and any applicable legal or tax restrictions on a particular business form. What are permissible tax years and methods of accounting? How will its income be taxed? How will the business be able to raise additional capital if it is to grow? Who bears the liability if the business fails? How will owners be compensated? Can an owner easily divest himself or herself of the ownership interest? How easily are new owners able to join the business? What are the tax consequences to the business and its owners if the business ceases operations?

This chapter begins to answer these questions for a regular C corporation. The following chapter answers these questions for sole proprietorships, partnerships, and S corporations. At the end of these two chapters, a basic comparison of the operating characteristics of these types of entities will be possible.

No one entity generally satisfies all characteristics that owners desire. Selecting the entity usually involves determining a priority for the desirable characteristics and selecting the form that satisfies the most important characteristics. To make these compromises, it is necessary to understand an entity's characteristics from formation through dissolution.

Shareholders can have unexpected problems if they attempt to use the corporate form to avoid taxes through excess salary, low-interest loans, or bargain purchases. The IRS can disallow any deductions taken for these disguised dividends. In addition, profitable corporations that fail to pay dividends to shield shareholders from the tax on dividend distributions may be assessed penalty taxes that must be paid in addition to the regular corporate tax.

KEY CONCEPTS

- ★ A corporation can obtain funds by issuing debt and equity securities. The flexibility to issue common and preferred stock with different dividend and voting rights is unique to a corporation.
- ★ A corporation's taxable income and financial accounting income generally differ because they are calculated using different income and expense determination rules.
- ★ A corporation's net income is taxed when earned, and taxed again when shareholders receive dividend income.
- ★ If a corporation liquidates, the corporation recognizes gain and loss on the sale or distribution of its assets. The shareholders recognize gain or loss on the surrender of their stock to the corporation.
- ★ Closely held corporations are subject to additional scrutiny by the IRS for disguised dividends due to the close relationship between the corporation and its limited number of shareholders.

★ Corporations that withhold paying dividends to their shareholders may be subject to the personal holding company tax or the accumulated earnings tax in addition to the regular corporate tax.

SETTING THE STAGE—AN INTRODUCTORY CASE

John Williams has owned and managed a manufacturing business for seven years. During that time, the business has grown from a shop in his garage with revenues of $25,000 during its first full year of operations to a facility on two acres of land with revenues of $2.3 million and profits in excess of $200,000. Three years ago John incorporated the business, which he had operated as a sole proprietorship up to that time.

John manufactures a unique product on which he holds the patent. The demand for his product has grown, and he needs to further expand the business. To do this, he must have a significant infusion of cash because internal growth will not be sufficient. He has considered trying to go public, but discussions with investment bankers indicated that he would have to give up control of the business to have a successful initial public offering (IPO). He also discussed loans with the local banks, and the interest rates they quoted were excessive. John would have to accept personal liability for the loan due to the relatively short time the corporation has been in business, something John is unwilling to do.

Several parties are interested in investing in the corporation. John's chief engineer has a minimum amount of money that he can invest in the corporation, but he is willing to work out an arrangement whereby a significant portion of his salary is in company stock and stock options based on profitability. One of his suppliers (another corporation) will invest cash, but it wants at least 20 percent of the voting stock to ensure that it remains one of the major suppliers. John's father-in-law has $500,000 that he would like to invest if he can be guaranteed a return of $30,000 per year for 10 years with the return of his investment at the end of the 10-year period. John's brother recently received $2,000,000 in settlement of a lawsuit for injuries received in an auto accident. He wants to invest $1,000,000 of the settlement in John's company as he worked in the business for 5 years prior to the accident and believes John is an excellent businessman and manager. He wants an annual return on this investment but plans to leave the stock to his heirs when he dies. John plans to continue reinvesting as much of the corporation's income as possible to sustain its growth.

John needs a steady income from the business as he has a wife and four children, ages 12 to 19. His wife has recently taken a number of courses in computer operations, database management, and network administration, but she is not employed outside the home. His two older sons are both going to college while living at home. They have part-time jobs in the fast-food industry.

John was not fully aware of how the income from the corporation would be subject to double taxes when he incorporated. He knows if all of the potential investors receive common stock the corporation will have to pay large dividends to satisfy some of the investors. Suggest ways John could minimize taxes while obtaining the cash infusion that the corporation needs. Can John save on taxes in other ways? We will return to this case at the end of this chapter.

INTRODUCTION TO CORPORATIONS

A corporation is a business entity created under the laws of the state in which it is incorporated. The corporation owns property in its own name and can be sued directly. The shareholders own a part of the corporation as a whole but do not own an interest in the corporation's individual assets. Except in unusual circumstances, shareholders' liability is limited to their investment in the corporation.[1] This feature

[1]In certain circumstances, the corporate veil is pierced and a shareholder is held liable for corporate acts. This generally happens when the corporation is a sham; that is, it has no real business purpose but to protect the owner.

is commonly referred to as limited liability.[2] The corporation's charter allows a corporation to carry on business indefinitely. Thus, a corporation has unlimited life. Corporate stock is freely traded on the open market or through private sales, and the corporation must have a board of directors that oversees general management and approves the corporate officers. Thus, the corporate form allows free transferability of interest and provides for centralized management.

These four characteristics, along with associates and a profit motive, defined a corporation for tax purposes prior to 1997.[3] A business entity that possessed three of these four characteristics was taxed as a corporation regardless of its legal form. This led to numerous disagreements with the IRS in determining whether certain unincorporated entities (for example, limited liability companies) would be taxed as corporations or partnerships. Since 1997, most partnerships and limited liability companies can elect taxation as a partnership or a corporation.[4] Any entity with a corporate charter under state law, however, is always taxed as a corporation.

These four characteristics apply to both regular corporations (also referred to as C corporations) and S corporations, corporations whose income flows through to its shareholders. The operating characteristics of the S corporation are addressed in the following chapter.

Corporate Advantages

A C corporation has the flexibility to sell both common and preferred stock with different voting and dividend rights, along with an ability to sell corporate bonds. As a result, it generally finds it easier to raise capital than other business forms. The major stock exchanges list these corporations, and this facilitates the exchange of their stock in the secondary market.

Prior to the 2013 tax year, the maximum tax rate for individuals (35%) was the same as the maximum tax rate for C corporations (excluding surtaxes). The Taxpayer Relief Act of 2012 increased the maximum individual tax rate to 39.6 percent, however. Due to the difference in the graduated rate structures, corporations that reinvest their income rather than pay dividends can have a lower tax bill than flow-through entities with equivalent income taxed at the shareholders' marginal rates. It is possible to lower an overall tax bill (corporation and shareholder) by splitting income. Because a shareholder can be an employee of the corporation, the shareholder can take income out of the corporation in the form of salary that is deductible by the corporation and taxed only to the shareholder; as a result, both may be able to take advantage of the lower tax rates for incomes under certain levels.[5]

Example 1

A corporation has taxable income of \$75,000 after deducting its sole shareholder-employee's salary of \$75,000. The corporation pays a tax of \$13,750 [(\$50,000 × 15%) + (\$25,000 × 25%)] on this income. The shareholder with a 20 percent average tax rate (after all deductions, exemptions, and credits) pays a tax of \$15,000 (\$75,000 × 20%) on her income. Their combined tax is \$28,750 (\$13,750 + \$15,000). If the corporation did not pay the salary, it would be taxed on \$150,000 of income and its total tax would be \$41,750 [(\$50,000 × 15%) + (\$25,000 × 25%) + (\$25,000 × 34%) + (\$50,000 × 39%)]. A tax savings of \$13,000 (\$41,750 – \$28,750) is obtained by employing the shareholder.[6]

[2]The shareholders of new or closely held corporations may have to provide personal guarantees on any loans to the corporation, but their liability is limited to the amount of the loan.

[3]Reg. §301.7701-2, effective prior to January 1, 1997.

[4]A limited partnership, organized after December 17, 1987, that is traded on the securities market is a publicly traded partnership (PTP) and is taxed as a corporation.

[5]Technically, corporations have a regular maximum tax rate of 35%; surtaxes, however, increase a corporation's rates to 39% on incomes between \$100,000 and \$340,000 and 38% on incomes between \$10 and \$15 million. Corporate and individual tax rates are compared in Chapter 1.

[6]Although an average rate is used for the individual, the tax is not significantly different from that of a single individual in the current year. This example ignores the effect of employment taxes, however.

An often overlooked advantage of the corporate form is the ability of a shareholder-employee to participate in tax-free employee fringe benefits that are deductible by the corporation.[7] Corporations are also the only entities that can offer employees stock options and other stock-based plans designed to share corporate ownership as an employee incentive.[8]

A corporation is free to select either a calendar or fiscal year as its tax year. Thus, it can select the tax year that best fits its natural business cycle. For example, retail department stores often choose a January 31 year-end because inventories are low from post-holiday sales.

Disadvantages of the Corporate Form

The corporate disadvantage most often cited is the double taxation of income; that is, income is taxed once as earned by the C corporation and taxed a second time when the after-tax income is distributed to shareholders in the form of dividends.[9] The effective tax rate for this income can far exceed the maximum rate applied to individuals or corporations separately. Shareholders of closely held corporations (corporations with few shareholders) often reduce some of the effects of double taxation by becoming employees of the corporation or renting property to it.[10]

EXAMPLE 2

ABC Corporation earned $100,000 of income in the current year. It pays a tax of $22,250 [($50,000 × 15%) + ($25,000 × 25%) + ($25,000 × 34%)] on that income. It distributes the balance of $77,750 to its sole shareholder who has other income of $90,000 and is in the 28 percent marginal tax bracket. The shareholder pays a tax of $11,662.50 ($77,750 × 15%) on the dividend. Total taxes are $33,912.50 for an effective tax rate of 34 percent. As both the corporate and individual incomes increase, their tax rates increase. Effective rates can approach 50 percent.

Assume the corporation earned $500,000 of income and pays a tax of $170,000 ($500,000 x .34) and distributes the remaining $330,000 as a dividend to the shareholder who has $450,000 of other income. The dividend is now taxed at the highest rate of 20% and is also subject to a 3.8% Medicare surtax for a tax of $78,540 ($330,000 × .238). Total taxes are $248,540–an effective tax rate of 49.71%.

Unlike flow-through entities, the shareholders of a C corporation cannot deduct losses of the corporation. A corporation can only deduct its operating and net capital losses against its operating income and its capital gains, respectively, recognized in other years.

Establishing and maintaining a corporation can be costly in time and money. Normally, a lawyer handles the filing of the articles of incorporation and states charge for issuing corporate charters. In addition, yearly fees must be paid to maintain the corporation's charter and conduct its business. The corporation must maintain a list of all the shareholders, and generally it will conduct at least one shareholder meeting per year, adding to its corporate expenses.

Capital Structure

A corporation's capital structure may include both **equity** (stock) and **debt** (bonds and other long-term securities). When a corporation is established, its board of directors determines the types and number of shares of common and preferred stock to be issued. The board also authorizes additional shares as the company grows. A cor-

---

[7] More than 2 percent S corporation shareholders, partners, and LLC members do not qualify for most tax-free fringe benefits as discussed in Chapter 4.

[8] Chapter 4 contains a more complete discussion of employee compensation and stock option plans.

[9] Lower income taxpayers may have all or a portion of their corporate dividends taxed at a zero percent rate. Stock appreciation due to corporate earnings is also taxed a second time when the shareholder sells the stock, but lower income taxpayers may also have all or a part of their capital gains taxed at a zero percent rate.

[10] Both rents and salaries must be reasonable, or they can be recharacterized as dividends.

poration may have a single class of common stock only or may have multiple classes of common and preferred stock.

A corporation must have **common stock**. Common shareholders have the last claim on the corporation's income and its assets in liquidation. There is no limit, however, on the income the common shareholders may share when a corporation is successful. Consistent with the financial risk–reward relationship, common shareholders take the risk that they could lose everything invested in the corporation for the opportunity to share in its unlimited income potential. When a corporation fails, however, the value of limited liability protection becomes apparent. Although shareholders can lose all their investment in the stock, corporate creditors cannot seize their personal assets.

Preferred stock is preferred because the owners' claims to dividends and assets in liquidation take precedence over the claims of the common stockholders. Preferred stock generally carries a stated dividend rate based on its par value. A corporation cannot pay a dividend on its common stock until it first pays dividends on the preferred stock. If the preferred stock is cumulative, the corporation must also pay all preferred stock dividends in arrears in addition to the current dividend before it can pay any common stock dividends.

Corporations may also issue bonds to obtain funds. From the shareholder's perspective, the receipt of both interest on debt and dividends on stock is taxable income (although dividends are currently subject to a tax rate not exceeding 20 percent, excluding the Medicare surtax). Corporations have a significant incentive to issue debt rather than equity, as interest is deductible but dividends are not. This makes the after-tax cost of debt less than its stated interest rate.

EXAMPLE 3

Crayton Corporation issues $100,000 in bonds at a 7 percent interest rate. Its marginal tax rate is 34 percent on its income. Its after-tax cost of the debt is only 4.62 percent [(100% – 34%) × 7%].

Corporate debt must be structured as legitimate debt, with a stated interest rate, interest paid at least annually, and a reasonable maturity date specified. Although bonds can be convertible into stock, the conversion provision cannot be so attractive that most creditors are likely to exercise the conversion feature. These restrictions can satisfy the IRS that the debt is legitimate and not stock disguised as debt.

Corporations whose shareholders are also creditors must be wary of an excessive debt-to-equity ratio (the corporation is *thinly capitalized*). The IRS can assert that the debt is disguised equity and that the interest and principal payments are dividends (taxable to the shareholder but nondeductible by the corporation). A *safe* debt-to-equity ratio is two or three to one. Debt issued to the shareholders in the same proportion as equity is the most likely to be reclassified as equity.[11]

EXAMPLE 4

The Wing Corporation issued $10,000 in common stock and $20,000 in debt securities to its sole shareholder at formation. The stated interest rate on the debt is 5 percent, but no maturity date is specified. For the first seven years, the corporation pays no interest to the shareholder. The IRS could recharacterize the debt as equity and reclassify interest and principal payments as dividends.

TAXATION OF C CORPORATIONS

A corporation calculates **taxable net income** and financial accounting net income by subtracting its relevant expenses from its relevant revenues.[12] Significant differences exist between items that constitute taxable income and expenses and items that constitute accounting income and expenses.

[11]§385 lists factors that may indicate that debt is disguised equity and gives the IRS the authority to make this reclassification.

[12]The following discussion of corporate taxation applies solely to C corporations.

A corporation uses its selected method of accounting to determine those revenues and gains that must be included in the current tax year's income. Corporations with more than $5 million in average annual gross receipts must use the accrual method.[13] Other corporations may choose between the cash or the accrual method of accounting.

The sale of goods or services is the primary source of revenue for most businesses, but they may also have dividend, interest, and rental income, as well as gains and losses on property transactions. Gross income for tax purposes is an all-inclusive concept that applies equally to corporations and individuals. Unless an item is specifically excluded from income, the corporation must include it. Determining a corporation's gross income follows the concepts discussed in Chapter 3. Gains and losses on property transactions are discussed in Chapters 7 and 8.

EXAMPLE 5

A C corporation has $100,000 of revenue from services it performs, $10,000 gain on the sale of property, and $5,000 interest from municipal bonds. The corporation has $110,000 of gross income. The $5,000 tax-exempt bond interest is excluded from taxable income. It is included in financial accounting income, however.

The corporation also follows the general tax rules for deducting expenses and losses; that is, unless there is a specific provision that allows a deduction, it is nondeductible. Chapters 4 through 6 explain the deductions for employee compensation and other business expenses, including depreciation and amortization. Several deductions are modified for corporations, however, and the American Jobs Creation Act of 2004 added the corporate deduction for qualified U.S. production activities as explained later.

EXAMPLE 6

TiBo Corporation has gross revenues from sales of $200,000, cost of sales of $100,000, a Section 179 expense deduction of $20,000, and other expenses of $45,000, including fines of $2,000 for failing to dispose of hazardous waste materials properly. TiBo's taxable income is $37,000 ($200,000 – $100,000 – $20,000 – $43,000). If financial accounting depreciation on the expensed item is $4,000, TiBo's pretax accounting (book) income is $51,000 ($200,000 – $100,000 – $4,000 – $45,000). Immediate expensing of a long-term asset is not permitted for financial accounting, but a deduction is allowed for the fines.

Dividend Received Deduction

To relieve some of the burden of multiple taxation on corporate income, a corporate shareholder is granted a **dividend received deduction (DRD)** based on its percentage ownership in the distributing corporation.[14]

Corporate Shareholder Ownership	Dividend Received Deduction
80% or more (must be an affiliated corporation)[15]	100%
20% up to 80%	80%
Less than 20%	70%

EXAMPLE 7

JF Corporation owns 65 percent of JN Corporation and has operating income of $30,000. JF receives a $100,000 dividend from JN and has total income of $130,000 before its dividend received deduction. JF has an $80,000 ($100,000 × 80%) dividend received deduction and only the net $20,000 of the distribution increases its income. JF's taxable income is $50,000.

[13]§ 448.

[14]When a corporate shareholder receives a dividend, it could be taxed at least three times by the time an individual shareholder benefits from it. Dividends from foreign corporations are not eligible for the dividend received deduction.

[15]Affiliated corporations are corporations eligible to file a consolidated return as explained later.

There are two other factors that affect the determination of a dividend received deduction. First, the dividend received deduction may be limited to 70% (80%) of taxable income (before the deduction) if this amount is less than the normally deductible dividend received deduction. If, however, the normal dividend received deduction either creates or increases a net operating loss, this limitation does not apply and the corporation may take the full dividend received deduction.[16]

EXAMPLE 8

Assume the same facts as the preceding example, except that JF has a loss from operations of \$10,000. Its income including the dividend but before the dividend received deduction is \$90,000 (\$100,000 – \$10,000). Its dividend received deduction is limited now to \$72,000 (\$90,000 × 80%), as this is less than the \$80,000 that would normally be allowed as a deduction. Its taxable income is \$18,000 (\$90,000 – \$72,000). If, however, JF has an operating loss of \$30,000 before the dividend, its income, including the dividend but before the dividend received deduction, is \$70,000 (\$100,000 – \$30,000). JF may now take the full \$80,000 dividend received deduction because it will have a net operating loss of \$10,000 (\$70,000 – \$80,000) and the income limitation on the deduction does not apply.[17]

TAX PLANNING

A corporation that may lose part of its dividend received deduction due to the income limitation should accelerate deductions or postpone income if possible to take advantage of the exception for the creation of a net operating loss. Alternatively, it could try to accelerate income or postpone deductions to ensure income exceeds the dividend received deduction. There is no carryover permitted for the part of a dividend received deduction that is lost due to the income limitation.

Charitable Contribution Deduction

Corporations are subject to an overall **charitable contribution deduction limitation** of 10 percent of taxable income before the charitable contribution deduction and the dividend received deduction, but after any net operating or capital loss *carryforwards*.[18] (Loss carrybacks are excluded as they originate in a future year and inclusion would require amending prior years' returns.) Contributions in excess of the limit can be carried forward up to five years.

EXAMPLE 9

The Bama Corporation has net income of \$600,000 before its \$55,000 charitable contribution and its \$100,000 net operating loss carryover from a prior year. The corporation's charitable contribution deduction is limited to \$50,000 [(\$600,000 – \$100,000) × 10%]. A net operating or capital loss carried back to this year from a subsequent year would not cause the charitable contribution deduction limitation to be recomputed and thus would not reduce the amount of the contribution that could be deducted.

The deduction for ordinary income property is generally limited to its basis, while the deduction for most long-term capital gain property is its fair market value. If a corporation donates inventory to a charitable organization solely for the care of infants, the poor, or the ill, the deduction is increased by 50 percent of the difference between basis and fair market value, but the deduction cannot exceed twice the property's basis.[19] A similar exception applies to gifts of scientific property given to universities and certain other research organizations for research purposes.[20]

---

[16]These provisions do not apply to the 100 percent dividend received deduction.

[17]The income limitation applies if the corporation's net income, including the dividend but before the dividend received and the U.S. production activities deductions, is less than the dividend but more than the dividend received deduction. In the example, if JF's income before the dividend received deduction is between \$80,000 and \$100,000, the income limitation applies.

[18]§ 170(b).

[19]§ 170(e)(3). The general rules for the deductibility of property contributions are discussed in Chapter 11.

[20]§ 170(e)(4).

EXAMPLE 10

The Cody Corporation donates a large supply of measles vaccine to the local health department to be used to vaccinate babies as part of their well-baby initiative. The vaccine's fair market value is $25,000, but its basis is only $9,000. The corporation's charitable contribution is $17,000 [$9,000 + ($25,000 – $9,000) × 50%]. If the basis of the vaccine is only $3,000, the deduction would be limited to $6,000 (2 × $3,000) as this is less than the alternate deduction of $14,000 [$3,000 + ($25,000 - $3,000) × 50%].

A corporation normally deducts the contribution in the year made, but an accrual-basis corporation may deduct a charitable contribution in the year it is accrued if (1) payment is authorized by the board of directors prior to year-end and (2) payment is actually made by the 15th day of the third month following the close of the tax year in which it is accrued.

Capital Gains and Losses

Corporations must follow the netting process outlined in Chapter 7 for short-term and long-term capital gains and losses. A net capital gain, whether short-term or long-term, is included in and taxed as ordinary income by corporations. A net capital loss must be carried back three years as a short-term capital loss, starting with the earliest year; if the loss is not completely absorbed in the three carryback years, it is carried forward five years in sequence from the loss year.[21] If the loss is not used within this period, it is lost.

EXAMPLE 11

The Jeans Corporation has a $50,000 net capital loss in year 4. In year 1 it had a $4,000 net capital gain, and in year 3 it had a $20,000 net capital gain. The corporation must first carry the $50,000 loss back to year 1 to offset the $4,000 net capital gain. Next, it carries the $46,000 remaining net capital loss to year 3, offsetting the $20,000 gain. The remaining $26,000 loss will be carried in sequence to years 5, 6, 7, 8, and 9 to offset any capital gains in those years. Any loss remaining after year 9 is lost.

TAX PLANNING

Corporations need to keep track of expiring capital losses. They can avoid paying taxes in later years if they accelerate the realization of capital gains to offset expiring capital losses. Similarly, corporations that have included capital gains in income in prior years can realize losses in a current year and carry the loss back for a refund of taxes paid in previous years.[22]

Deduction for Qualified U.S. Production Activities

In response to the World Trade Organization's increasing tariffs due to U.S. export subsidies they ruled illegal, as part of the American Jobs Creation Act of 2004 Congress eliminated these subsidies and replaced them with a deduction that effectively decreased the corporate tax rate for manufacturers by three percentage points.[23] For tax years 2005 and 2006, corporations were allowed a deduction in computing taxable income of 3 percent of the lesser of qualified production activities income or taxable income without consideration of this deduction (an effective tax rate reduction of approximately one percent) This deduction increased to 6 percent for tax years 2007 through 2009 (an effective tax rate reduction of 2 percent) and then increased to 9 percent for tax years after 2009 (an effective rate reduction of 3 percent). At no time, however, may the deduction exceed 50 percent of the wages paid during the year.[24]

[21]The short-term loss is netted with the corporation's other capital gains and losses in the carryover year.

[22]See examples in Chapter 7 that illustrate the timing of capital gains and losses.

[23]A 9% deduction for a corporation in the 35% tax bracket decreases the corporation's marginal tax rate by about 3% (35% × 9% = 3.15%).

[24]The 50% wage limit is based on wages paid (including elective deferred compensation) in the calendar year that ends in the corporation's tax year.

Qualified production activities income is equal to domestic production gross receipts less the sum of (1) cost of goods sold, other deductions, expenses, and losses directly related to these gross receipts and (2) a ratable share of other deductions, expenses, and losses not directly related to this or other income classes.[25] Domestic production gross receipts is broadly defined to include most manufacturing, leasing, construction, and architectural or engineering activities that take place within the United States. Gross receipts from the sale of food or beverages prepared by the taxpayer at a retail establishment are specifically excluded, but gross receipts from food processing will qualify.

EXAMPLE 12

Calabrese Company manufactures shoes in its New Jersey plant. In 2013, its total gross receipts were \$4,000,000, \$3,250,000 of which is related to sales within the United States. Expenses related to these sales were \$3,100,000 in total of which \$2,600,000 is for U.S. sales. Total net income is \$900,000 with \$650,000 attributed solely to U.S sales. Its deduction for qualified production activities is \$58,500, the lesser of nine percent of qualified production activities income (\$650,000 × 9% = \$58,500) or taxable income (\$900,000 × 9% = \$81,000).

Net Operating Losses

A corporation reports its taxable income on an annual basis. If it has income in one year and a loss the next, it must pay taxes in the income year. If the corporation could combine the two years, it might have little or no income on which to pay taxes. The **net operating loss (NOL)** carryovers simulate the combining of income in some years with the losses in other years to reduce the corporation's taxes. Corporations can carry back net operating losses to the two previous tax years.[26] If the corporation cannot use the entire NOL in carryback years, it may carry the remaining NOL forward 20 years. When using the carryback, the corporation must carry the NOL back to the earliest eligible year and then carry it forward in sequence. It cannot choose the year to which to carry the NOL.

TAX PLANNING

The corporation can elect to forego the carryback period and carry the NOL forward only. In making this decision, a corporation should look at its pattern of income, taxes, and credits in the available carryback years. It may choose to forego the carryback period if, for example, it had nonrefundable credits that offset taxes in the carryback year. The credits could be lost if the NOL is used in the carryback year, and the corporation could gain nothing by the carryback.

EXAMPLE 13

Hightec Corporation has an operating loss of \$80,000 in 2013. In 2011 Hightec Corporation reported taxable income of \$50,000 and paid income taxes of \$7,500 (\$50,000 × 15%). In 2012 it reported taxable income of \$20,000 and paid income taxes of \$3,000 (\$20,000 × 15%). Thus, Hightec will be entitled to receive a refund of \$10,500 (\$7,500 + \$3,000) from the NOL carryback and has a \$10,000 carryforward (\$80,000 – \$70,000) remaining.

[25] IRS developed rules for proper allocation similar to §263A UNICAP rules (as discussed in Chapter 5).

[26] For the 2008 tax year, the American Recovery and Reinvestment Act of 2009 allowed an eligible small business (one with less than \$15 million average annual gross receipts for its last three years) to carry its net operating loss back for 3, 4, or 5 years. The Worker, Homeownership, and Business Assistance Act of 2009 expanded this election to all U.S. businesses for either 2008 or 2009 (but not both, except for eligible small businesses) and imposed a 50-percent income limit on the NOL in the fifth year; any remaining NOL could fully offset taxable income in the remaining four carryback years. The 50 percent limit did not apply to an eligible small business that elected to carry back its 2008 NOL; however the 50-percent limit applied to its 2009 NOLs. This 5-year carryback election was not available to corporations that received assistance under the Troubled Asset Relief Program (TARP) if the federal government acquired stock in the corporation and was not extended to any post 2009 tax year.

Assume that Hightec Corporation expects to have $500,000 of taxable income in 2014 and be in the 34 percent marginal tax bracket. The $10,000 carryforward results in a $3,400 tax savings in 2014. The total benefit Hightec receives from the NOL is $13,900 ($10,500 for the carryback years and $3,400 in 2014). Hightec could achieve a greater tax savings by electing to waive the carryback. If it uses the entire $80,000 NOL in 2014, its tax savings will be $27,200 ($80,000 × 34%). Although Hightec will have to wait until it files its 2014 tax return to receive any tax benefit from the NOL, waiving the carryback results in an additional $13,300 ($27,200 – $13,900) tax savings.

Computing the Corporate Income Tax

The formula to compute the regular **corporate income tax** is as follows:

	Taxable revenues
Less	Deductible expenses
Equals	Taxable income
Times	Corporate tax rate
Equals	Corporate gross tax liability
Plus	Additions to tax
Less	Tax credits
Equals	Net corporate tax

The relevant tax laws dictate taxable revenues and deductible expenses that must be included in this formula, as discussed in earlier chapters. The excess of taxable revenues over deductible expenses is taxable income to which the corporate tax rate is applied to determine the corporation's gross tax liability.

The **corporate tax rate** follows a progressive rate schedule, with rates that increase as taxable income increases, as shown in Table 9.1.[27] Technically, the 34 percent bracket extends from $100,000 to $10,000,000, and the 35 percent bracket applies to all income over $10,000,000. To eliminate the benefit of the lower rates on incomes up to $100,000 and then up to $10,000,000, a surtax of 5 percent is added to the tax rate on incomes of $100,000 to $335,000; then a 3 percent surtax is added to the tax rate on incomes of $15,000,000 to $18,333,333. Thus, for income of $335,000 to $10,000,000, a flat tax rate of 34 percent applies, and for income over $18,333,333, a flat tax rate of 35 percent applies.

TABLE 9.1 CORPORATE TAX RATE SCHEDULE

CORPORATE INCOME		
OVER	BUT NOT OVER	TAX RATE
$0	$50,000	15%
$50,000	$75,000	25%
$75,000	$100,000	34%
$100,000	$335,000	39%[a]
$335,000	$10,000,000	34%
$10,000,000	$15,000,000	35%
$15,000,000	$18,333,333	38%[b]
$18,333,333		35%

[a]The 34 percent rate plus a 5 percent surtax.
[b]The 35 percent rate plus a 3 percent surtax.

[27]§11(b). As discussed later, a single rate of 35% applies to personal service corporations.

EXAMPLE 14

Corporation	Income	Tax	Calculation
A	$40,000	$6,000	$40,000 × 15%
B	$225,000	$71,000	($50,000 × 15%) + ($25,000 × 25%) + ($25,000 × 34%) + ($125,000 × 39%)
C	$400,000	$136,000	$400,000 × 34%
D	$11,000,000	$3,750,000	($10,000,000 × 34%) + ($1,000,000 × 35%)
E	$20,000,000	$7,000,000	$20,000,000 × 35%

A qualified personal service corporation (PSC) is a corporation that provides service in the fields of accounting, actuarial science, architecture, consulting, engineering, health, law, or the performing arts and whose employees own substantially all of the corporation.[28] A qualified PSC pays a flat 35 percent tax (the maximum individual tax rate) on its entire income.

TAX PLANNING

The flat 35 percent tax rate encourages owner-employees to take earnings out of the corporation as salary. When all the income of the business is paid out as salary, the total tax liability is similar to that of a flow-through entity.

EXAMPLE 15

James, the owner of BuildRite Architectural Consulting and Designing, Inc., provides all the company's architectural designs and performs all its consulting. The corporation's net income for the year is $68,000. Its corporate tax is $23,800 ($68,000 × 35%) because it is a personal service corporation. If James increases his salary by approximately $68,000, the corporation would pay no income tax. It would have to pay payroll taxes, however, and James would be taxed on the increased salary at his marginal tax rate.

Reconciling Book and Taxable Income

A corporation uses **Form 1120**, the **corporate tax return**, to determine its taxable income. A sample filled-in Form 1120 is included in Appendix C at the end of this textbook. It must complete a number of schedules including **Schedule L**, the corporation's beginning and ending financial accounting balance sheet, Schedule M-2, and either Schedule M-1 or M-3.[29] **Schedule M-1** is a basic reconciliation of after-tax net income (or loss) on the financial accounting books with taxable income (or loss) before the dividends received deduction and net operating loss carryovers. For tax years ending December 31, 2004 or later, only corporations with assets less than $10 million may use the Schedule M-1. (Larger corporations must complete Schedule M-3.)

The left column of the M-1 schedule starts with after-tax book income; to this the corporation first adds its federal income tax liability. A number of additions are then made for items that are deductible for book purposes but are not deductible in calculating taxable income. The right side of the Schedule M-1 contains all the reductions in book income in arriving at taxable income for income items excluded from taxable income and expense items excluded from book income. A number of these additions and subtractions are listed in Table 9.2.

EXAMPLE 16

Corporation BDC reports financial accounting income of $250,000, including $5,000 of tax-exempt bond interest income. Its federal income tax expense per books is $80,000. Its tax depreciation is $40,000 but financial accounting depreciation is only $30,000. Its total meals and entertainment expense is $30,000, and its net capital losses are $20,000. Its book income is reconciled to taxable income on Schedule M-1 as follows:

[28]§ 448(d) (2).

[29]Prior to 2007, Form 1120-A could be used by small corporations; this form only required the balance sheet and the equivalent of the Schedule M-1.

Schedule M-1 **Reconciliation of Income (Loss) per Books With Income per Return**
Note: Schedule M-3 required instead of Schedule M-1 if total assets are $10 million or more—see instructions

1	Net income (loss) per books	250,000	7	Income recorded on books this year not included on this return (itemize): Tax-exempt interest $ 5,000	5,000
2	Federal income tax per books	80,000			
3	Excess of capital losses over capital gains	20,000			
4	Income subject to tax not recorded on books this year (itemize):		8	Deductions on this return not charged against book income this year (itemize):	
5	Expenses recorded on books this year not deducted on this return (itemize):		a	Depreciation $ 10,000	
a	Depreciation $		b	Charitable contributions $	
b	Charitable contributions $				10,000
c	Travel and entertainment $ 15,000	15,000	9	Add lines 7 and 8	15,000
6	Add lines 1 through 5	365,000	10	Income (page 1, line 28)—line 6 less line 9	350,000

Schedule M-2 provides details of the changes in the corporation's unappropriated retained earnings from the beginning to the end of the tax year and should tie into the change in unappropriated retained earnings reported in the comparative balance sheets. Beginning retained earnings is increased for net income and reduced by dividend payments. Changes in appropriations of retained earnings, as well as other changes as a result of retiring stock and accounting provisions that require a direct addition or reduction to retained earnings (for example, certain changes in value of marketable securities), must be shown here.

Example 17

The Babco Company had retained earnings of $51,000 at the beginning of the year. Its net income after taxes is $21,000, and it paid $15,000 in dividends to its shareholders. Its end-of-year retained earnings is $57,000 ($51,000 + $21,000 – $15,000).

TABLE 9.2 **ADDITIONS TO AND SUBTRACTIONS FROM BOOK INCOME TO CALCULATE TAXABLE INCOME ON SCHEDULE M-1**

ADDITIONS TO BOOK INCOME Left Side of Schedule M-1	SUBTRACTIONS FROM BOOK INCOME Right Side of Schedule M-1
Federal income tax	
Capital losses that exceed capital gains	Tax-exempt bond interest
Excess of book depreciation over tax depreciation	Tax depreciation in excess of book depreciation
Contributions in excess of the contributions limit	Carryover of contributions from prior tax years
The excess of completed contract income in this year over income recorded on the books under the percentage-of-completion method	Percentage-of-completion income recognized prior to the year of completion when the completed contract method is used for tax purposes
Insurance premiums on key-person life insurance policies	Increase in the cash value of key-person life insurance
Bad debt reserve deductions in excess of actual bad debt expense	Bad debt expense in excess of the addition to bad debt reserves
The nondeductible portion of meals and entertainment expense	Life insurance proceeds
Fines and bribes	
Expenses related to tax-exempt income	

For tax years ending on or after December 31, 2004, corporations with at least $10 million in assets must complete a **Schedule M-3** instead of the M-1. The first part of the Schedule M-3 reconciles the corporation's worldwide book income reported on its consolidated financial statements with book income for entities included in its consolidated tax return.[30] Corporations must then itemize book-tax differences for each item of income, gain, loss, deduction, or credit that is greater than $10 million. This schedule requires much more detailed information on book-tax differences than Schedule M-1 with temporary and permanent differences reported separately.[31] The IRS hopes that this expanded book-tax reconciliation will identify as audit targets those corporations with large tax shelter transactions.

Tax Credits

A corporation can reduce its tax liability, but not below zero, by tax credits for which it is eligible. The tax credit most useful to corporations is the **general business credit**, which is actually an extensive list of credits, not just one.[32] Each credit in the group is calculated separately according to its specific provisions. The separate credits are then aggregated into one general business credit to which a specific overall limit applies. The allowable credit cannot exceed $25,000 plus 75 percent of the corporation's tax liability in excess of $25,000.[33]

EXAMPLE 18

Behan Corporation has a regular tax liability of $205,000. It has a general business credit available of $190,000. The general business credit offsets only $160,000 of the corporation's regular tax [$25,000 + ($205,000 – $25,000) × 75%]. The corporation pays a net tax of $45,000, and it has $30,000 of general business credit remaining.

Unused general business credits are not lost but are carried back one year to reduce taxes in that year (subject to the same limitation as above) and then forward 20 years. If a corporation has carryover business credits from more than one year, the credits arising in the earliest years are used first (a FIFO basis). The following is a list of some of the credits that make up the general business credit and their related Code sections:[34]

1. Investment credit, which itself is made up of three credits: the rehabilitation credit, the energy credit, and the reforestation credit (Section 46)
2. Credit for increasing research activities (Section 41) (Expires 12/31/13)
3. Low-income housing credit (Section 42)
4. Disabled access credit (Section 44)
5. Orphan drug credit (Section 45C)[35]
6. Small-employer pension plan startup credit (Section 45E)

[30]For financial accounting purposes, the consolidated reporting group usually includes the parent corporation and all subsidiaries (both domestic and foreign) in which the parent has a greater than 50% ownership interest. For tax purposes, a consolidated group consists of only the domestic parent corporation and its domestic subsidiaries in which it owns at least an 80% interest. All foreign subsidiaries are excluded because the U.S. tax system does not usually tax foreign-sourced income until repatriated as dividends to the U.S. parent corporation.

[31]Temporary and permanent book-tax differences are discussed in Chapter 5.

[32]Corporations are also eligible for the foreign tax credit and the alternative minimum tax credit.

[33]§38(c). As originally enacted, the general business credit could not exceed the corporation's regular tax liability less its gross alternative minimum tax, as the general business credit could not reduce a corporation's alternative minimum tax liability. A number of targeted credits, however, have been allowed to reduce the AMT; for example, eligible small businesses could offset the AMT liability in tax years beginning in 2010. The alternative minimum tax is discussed later.

[34]§§43 and 45 contain a description of other credits that make up the general business credit.

[35]For tax years beginning in 2009 and 2010, the Healthcare Reconciliation Act of 2010 includes a credit equal to 50% of qualified investment in qualifying therapeutic discovery projects by qualifying taxpayers. This expands the credits available for healthcare research beyond the orphan drug credit. §48(D).

7. Credit for employer-provided child care (Section 45F)
8. Empowerment zone employment credit (Section 1396)
9. Work opportunity credit (Section 51) (Expires 12/31/13)

The credits contained within the general business credit have not remained static overtime. Credits have been added and credits have been allowed to expire. Often credits that have expired are reinstated on a retroactive basis.[36] Credits numbered 6, 7, and 8 are credits that were first effective for tax years beginning after 2001. The addition, expiration, and retroactive reinstatement add significant complexity for the taxpayer; for example, a credit may not be carried back to a year before its addition to the general business credit.

The 2010 health care legislation included a credit equal to 35 percent of the required contribution to employees' health insurance coverage by eligible small employers for tax years beginning in 2010 through 2013. Eligible small employers are defined as employers with no more than 25 full-time equivalent employees with average annual salaries not exceeding $50,000 during the year. Certain owners (for example, self-employed persons and 2% corporate shareholders) are excluded from the employee and salary limit calculations. For tax years beginning after 2013, the credit is increased to 50 percent for health insurance purchased through a state exchange for two years only. The credit is reduced for employers with between 10 and 25 employees and average annual wages between $25,000 and $50,000. This credit is also part of the general business credit.[37]

The 2010 Hiring Incentives to Restore Employment Act had added an employee retention credit as an increase in Section 38(b) of the general business credit. Under this provision, the employer could claim a credit of the lesser of $1,000 or 6.2 percent of wages paid for retaining an employee for at least 52 consecutive weeks. In addition, the employer had to pay wages during the last 26 week period equal to at least 80 percent of wages paid during the first 26 week period. The employer could only claim the credit for employees who qualified the employer for payroll tax forgiveness for 2010; as a result, most employers could only have claimed this credit in 2011.

TAX PLANNING

Corporations should make sure to recognize and take advantage of all allowable business credits. Credits are far more valuable than a deduction of equal amount as credits are a direct reduction in taxes.

A further discussion of these credits is beyond the scope of this text as each of these credits is calculated under a specific set of guidelines. The relevant Code sections should be consulted.

Alternative Minimum Tax

Many corporations with significant accounting income substantially reduce their taxable income by the judicious use of allowable deductions and income exemptions. To ensure that most corporations pay some taxes, Congress instituted a second parallel tax system aptly named the **alternative minimum tax (AMT)**, which applies to all corporations except those that are exempt as *small* corporations. A small corporation is one whose average annual gross receipts are less than $5,000,000 in each of its prior taxable years. Once qualified, a small corporation remains exempt from the AMT until its average annual gross receipts for the previous three years exceed $7,500,000.[38] Once this threshold is exceeded, a corporation is no longer exempt from AMT, even if its receipts decline in future years.

[36]The general provisions of the work opportunity credit were extended to workers employed through 2011 and to qualified veterans through 2012. After expiring, the research credit was first extended by the American Recovery and Reinvestment Act through 2009, and then reinstated retroactively and extended through 2011 by the 2010 Tax Relief Act. Due to Hurricane Katrina, certain provisions of the work opportunity credit extend beyond 2011 for certain employers and employees in affected areas.

[37]§ 45R

[38]§ 55.

To determine the AMT, the regular income tax base is broadened by a series of positive and negative adjustments and positive preference items to arrive at alternative minimum taxable income (AMTI). Next the corporation deducts an exemption amount (subject to limitation) to determine its AMTI base, to which it then applies the flat alternative minimum tax rate of 20 percent to calculate gross AMT.[39] The corporation's regular tax liability and foreign tax credit reduce the gross AMT to the net AMT that the corporation must pay. The formula for the AMT is as follows:

	Corporate taxable income
Plus or minus	AMT adjustments
Plus	Preference items
Equals	AMT income
Less	Exemption
Equals	AMTI base
Times	AMT rate
Equals	Gross AMT
Less	Regular corporate tax
Equals	Alternative minimum tax
Less	Credits
Equals	Net AMT

Because the corporation's regular tax must be subtracted from its AMT, the corporation only pays an AMT if the gross AMT is greater than its regular corporate income tax.

EXAMPLE 19

Corporation LP's taxable income is $400,000, on which it pays a regular income tax of $136,000. Its AMTI base is $800,000, and its gross AMT is $160,000. Its AMT is $24,000 ($160,000 – $136,000).

AMT adjustments represent timing differences only; that is, in earlier years any adjustments that increase (decrease) taxable income reverse in later years and reduce (increase) taxable income.[40] Adjustments include the following:[41]

1. The difference between regular tax depreciation and AMT depreciation[42]
2. The difference between gain reported for AMT by the percentage-of-completion method over gain reported on the completed contract method for regular tax.
3. 75 percent of the difference between adjusted current earnings (ACE) and AMT income before this adjustment and any allowable exemption.[43]

A corporation has an exemption of $40,000 if its AMT income is $150,000 or less. The exemption is phased out at a rate of $1 for every $4 AMT income exceeds $150,000. When AMT income reaches $310,000 ($310,000 – $150,000 = $160,000; $160,000/4 = $40,000), the exemption is completely phased out and the AMT income equals the AMTI base.

EXAMPLE 20

Corporation Z has AMT income of $250,000. Its AMT exemption is $15,000 [$40,000 – ($250,000 – $150,000) × 25%]. Its AMTI base is $235,000 ($250,000 – $15,000), and its gross AMT is $47,000 ($235,000 × 20%).

---

[39]§§55(a)(2) and (3).

[40]This is an example of how the government takes advantage of the time value of money.

[41]§§56(a) and (c) list the adjustment items applicable to corporations.

[42]Applies to property placed in service after 1986.

[43]The ACE adjustment includes tax-exempt bond interest, life insurance proceeds, and 100 percent of the gain on an installment contract. Disallowed deductions include the 70 percent dividend received deduction and the amortization of organization expenses.

EXAMPLE 21

The Baylor Corporation has $100,000 of taxable income on which it pays a regular tax of $22,500. It has $150,000 of net positive adjustments and a $10,000 preference item. Its AMT is as follows:

	$100,000	Taxable income
Plus	150,000	Positive adjustments
Plus	10,000	Preferences
Equals	$260,000	AMT income
Minus	12,500	Exemption[(1)]
Equals	$247,500	AMTI base
Times	20%	AMT rate
Equals	$49,500	Gross AMT
Minus	22,500	Regular Tax
Equals	$27,000	AMT

	[(1)]Exemption	
	$260,000	
Minus	150,000	
Equals	$110,000	
Times	25%	
Equals	$27,500	Exemption reduction
	$40,000	Maximum exemption
Minus	27,500	Exemption reduction
Equals	$12,500	Exemption allowed

Because the adjustments to regular taxable income are the result of timing differences, the corporation is allowed an AMT credit against the regular tax. The AMT credit is equal to the AMT paid in prior years. The AMT credits are carried forward indefinitely, but they can only offset the regular tax in excess of the AMT.

EXAMPLE 22

Continuing the previous example, assume the following year that Baylor Corporation pays a regular tax of $230,000. Its gross AMT in that year is only $210,000. The corporation may use $20,000 ($230,000 – $210,000) of its $27,000 AMT from the previous year as a credit against its regular tax. It may continue to carry the remaining $7,000 AMT forward as a credit against its regular tax liability in excess of its AMT until it is used up.

Corporations must pay any AMT due with their regular tax by the due date for their income tax returns.

Filing and Payment Requirements

Corporations file Form 1120: *U.S. Corporate Income Tax Return*. The return is due on the 15th day of the third month following the close of its tax year.[44] Corporations may obtain an automatic six-month extension for filing the return by filing Form 7004: *Application for Automatic Extension of Time to File Corporation Income Tax Return* by the unextended due date.[45] **Estimated taxes** due must be paid with this extension request. The IRS can terminate the six-month extension with 10 days notice.

[44]§ 6072(b). Corporations are permitted to use calendar or fiscal years for tax purposes.

[45]§ 6081(a) allows a maximum extension of six months. Because Form 7004 provides for an automatic extension of six months, no additional extension is normally allowed.

Example 23

CBC is a June 30 fiscal year-end corporation. Its unextended due date for its fiscal year ending June 30, 2013 return is September 15, 2013; its six-month extended due date is March 15, 2014.

Corporations must make estimated payments throughout the tax year equal to one-quarter of their tax liability for the year on the 15th day of the 4th, 6th, 9th, and 12th months of the corporation's tax year.[46] For a calendar-year corporation, these dates are April 15, June 15, September 15, and December 15. An underpayment penalty is assessed if a corporation's tax liability is at least $500 more than its estimated payments.[47] Corporations whose taxable income is less than $1,000,000 in each of the preceding three years can avoid the underpayment penalty if each of their estimated tax payments equals 25 percent of their prior year's tax liability.[48]

Consolidated Returns

The consolidated return regulations recognize that one corporation can exert substantial control over a second corporation in which it has substantial ownership. It allows the controlling corporation to file a consolidated return with the controlled corporation as if it were a division of the controlling corporation for tax purposes. To be treated in this manner, the corporations must be affiliated. To form an **affiliated group**, a **parent corporation** (Corporation P) must directly own 80 percent or more of the stock of another corporation—the **subsidiary** (Corporation S)—measured both by voting rights and the value of all the stock outstanding. In addition, the affiliated group can have more than two corporations if each of the other included corporations meets the ownership requirements. In this case, 80 percent of the corporation's stock must be owned by one or more corporations that are part of the affiliated group, measured both by voting rights and the total value of outstanding stock.

Example 24

Corporation P owns 90 percent of the voting stock of Corporation S and 85 percent of the value of all its outstanding stock. Corporation S owns 95 percent of the stock of Corporation S1, which has only one class of stock outstanding: voting common stock. Corporation P is the common parent; Corporation S is the subsidiary of Corporation P; and Corporation S1 is a subsidiary of Corporation S. The three corporations form an affiliated group.[49]

Tax-exempt corporations, insurance companies,[50] foreign corporations, DISCs (domestic international sales corporations), REITs (real estate investment trusts), and RICs (real estate investment corporations) are not permitted to be part of an affiliated group.[51] Includible corporations that meet the ownership requirements are eligible to join in filing a consolidated return. A **consolidated return** reports the combined results of the operations of all corporations in the group.

The parent corporation must elect to file a consolidated return, and all of the subsidiaries must consent to the election. This election is generally binding on the

[46] §6655(b). The Patient Protection and Affordable Care Act requires corporations with assets of at least $1 billion to increase their estimated tax payments due in July, August or September of 2014 by 74.25 percent.

[47] §6655(f).

[48] §§6655(d) and (e). This exception only applies to the first estimated payment for a corporation with taxable income exceeding $1,000,000; otherwise it can only avoid a penalty by annualizing its income.

[49] An affiliated group is also a parent-subsidiary controlled group, but not all parent-subsidiary controlled groups (discussed later) are affiliated groups eligible to file consolidated returns.

[50] Affiliated groups consisting only of insurance companies are permitted.

[51] §1504(b).

affiliated group as long as there is at least the one parent and one subsidiary at all times during the tax year.[52]

All corporations joining in a consolidated return must either have or change to the parent's tax year. Subsidiaries changing to the parent's tax year must generally file short-period returns for the period before the change by closing their books as of the date of consolidation.

Consolidated Net Income

To determine consolidated net income, each corporation first computes separate taxable income, the corporation's taxable income after modification for intercompany transactions, and certain items that must be determined on a consolidated basis.[53] Two of the required modifications for deferred intercompany transactions and intercompany dividends are the result of looking at the affiliated corporations simply as divisions of the parent corporation.

EXAMPLE 25

Corporation P owns 100 percent of Corporation S and files a consolidated return for them. P sells land to S for $50,000 that had a basis of $25,000. S pays $5,000 of dividends to P. On their separate books, P recognizes a $25,000 gain on the sale of the land and $5,000 of dividend income. S recognizes the dividend paid of $5,000 and records the land at its cost of $50,000. When S is viewed as a division of P, P cannot recognize gain on a sale to itself, nor can S pay dividends to itself. Thus, separate taxable income excludes both the $25,000 gain on the sale of land and the dividends received and paid.[54] They are eliminated in the determination of consolidated income.

Items that are subject to limitations and netting must be determined on a consolidated basis because these items are subject to limitations and netting for the group as a whole. These items include capital gains and losses, Section 1231 gains and losses, and the charitable contributions deduction. After determining separate taxable income and the items subject to limitations or netting on a consolidated basis, the parent can complete the consolidated return based on consolidated net income.

EXAMPLE 26

Corporations P and S file a consolidated return. P has $50 of separate taxable income and a capital gain of $40. S has $25 of separate taxable income, a capital loss of $30, and a charitable contribution of $5. P and S have a combined capital gain of only $10 that is included in their regular income. Consolidated taxable income before the charitable contribution deduction is $85 ($50 + $25 + $10) for the year and $80 ($85 – $5) after the contribution deduction. If S had filed a separate return, it would not have been able to deduct its $30 capital loss, and its charitable contribution deduction would have been limited to $2.50.

From the preceding brief discussion, some of the advantages of filing consolidated returns become apparent:

1. Intercompany dividends are eliminated.
2. Gains on intercompany transactions are eliminated.

---

[52] The members at the beginning of the year may be completely different than at the end of the year as long as the parent corporation has direct ownership of one subsidiary at all times during the tax year. The affiliated group must show good cause to receive permission from the IRS to discontinue filing consolidated returns unless the IRS grants blanket permission to all affiliated groups to discontinue filing consolidated returns for a change in law or regulation.

[53] §1502. Intercompany transactions include deferred intercompany transactions, intercompany distributions, built-in deductions, initial inventory adjustments, recapture of excess loss accounts, and income or loss due to changes in accounting methods. Only deferred intercompany transactions and dividend distributions are discussed here.

[54] The gain on the sale is eliminated by reducing the basis of the land to S by $25,000.

3. Deductions that are disallowed on a separate corporation basis due to limitations may be deductible when the limitations are applied to the consolidated group.
4. The losses of one corporation can offset the gains of another corporation.
5. Income from one corporation can offset losses from another corporation.
6. Limitations based on the consolidated return income or taxes may permit greater use of deductions or credits.

A number of disadvantages also must be considered when electing to file consolidated returns, such as the complex issues that result when corporations enter and leave the consolidated group; the tax-year change of subsidiaries to conform to the tax year of the parent; and that the combining of separate income may not always benefit the consolidated group.[55]

Corporate Distributions

The most common corporate distribution is a **dividend**, the distribution of corporate **earnings and profits (E&P)** that is taxable income to shareholders but not deductible by the corporation. Dividends are paid from the after-tax profits of the corporation and are taxed a second time when received by the shareholder. Most corporate distributions come only from E&P. Corporations whose distributions exceed E&P invade corporate capital. A return of capital is a return of some or all of the shareholders' original investment in the corporation. It is tax free to the shareholders to the extent of their stock bases, and it reduces the shareholders' bases. If a distribution exceeds a shareholder's basis, the excess distribution is treated as proceeds from the sale of the stock and is taxed as capital gain.

Example 27

Alexander receives a $5,000 cash distribution from his 100 percent owned corporation that is a $2,000 dividend and a $3,000 return of capital because the corporation only has $2,000 in earnings and profits. Alexander's basis in his stock is only $1,000. Thus, only $1,000 of the $3,000 return of capital is tax free, and the remaining $2,000 is taxed as gain on sale. Alexander has a total of $4,000 of income ($2,000 dividend and $2,000 capital gain).

The majority of corporations do not distribute dividends unless there are sufficient earnings and profits to ensure dividend treatment. The determination of earnings and profits along with the procedures necessary to determine the tax treatment of a distribution are included in *Expanded Topics* at the end of this chapter.

Property Distributions

Although most corporate distributions are in cash, a corporation may make a property distribution, a distribution of something other than cash or the corporation's own stock. The preceding discussion was based on cash distributions, but the same rules apply to property distributions (except nontaxable stock dividends) to determine the shareholder's taxable income. However, several questions arise:

1. What is the value of a property distribution?
2. What is the property's basis in the recipient's hands?
3. Does the distributing corporation have any tax consequences?

The value of a property distribution is its net fair market value at the date of distribution.[56] If the property is encumbered by a liability, the value of the distribution is reduced by the liability. The basis of the property the shareholder receives is its fair market value (unreduced by any liability assumed).

[55] A discussion of these issues is generally postponed until an advanced course in corporate tax.
[56] § 301.

A corporation that distributes appreciated property as a dividend recognizes gain equal to the difference in its fair market value and its basis when distributed.[57] If depreciated property is distributed, however, the corporation is not permitted to recognize the loss.[58]

EXAMPLE 28

When Howel Corporation has E&P of $100,000, it distributes a piece of land valued at $40,000 with a basis of $25,000 to Lynn and some machinery valued at $40,000 with a basis of $45,000 to Dave. Howel Corporation recognizes the $15,000 gain on the distribution of the land but cannot recognize the loss on the distribution of the machinery. Lynn and Dave both recognize a taxable dividend of $40,000. Lynn's basis for the land is $40,000 and Dave's basis for the machine is $40,000.

Stock Dividends

The most common form of **stock dividend**, a distribution of common stock on common stock, does nothing more than give a shareholder a greater number of shares of stock. The shares have a proportionately smaller value per share and the shareholder has no income, but he or she apportions the stock's original basis over all the shares now owned.[59] From the shareholder's perspective, the net effect is similar to a stock split.

EXAMPLE 29

B has 10 shares of stock that cost $60 per share. The corporation issues a 20 percent stock dividend when the stock's value is $120 per share. After the dividend, the price of a share falls to $100 per share (1 share at $120 now equals 1.2 shares valued at $120 or $100 per share), and B allocates her $600 basis in the 10 shares to the 12 shares ($50 per share).

If common shareholders receive a pro rata distribution of stock or **stock rights** on common stock, the distribution is tax free.[60] Basis of the shares of stock on which the stock dividend or stock rights are distributed is apportioned to the property received using relative fair market value. If the value of the rights is less than 15 percent of the value of the stock on which they were issued, the shareholder may ignore the allocation and assign a zero basis to the rights.[61]

EXAMPLE 30

Joanna receives one stock right to purchase one additional share of stock in V Corporation at $20 for each of the 200 shares of stock that she currently owns. V stock is currently selling for $25 per share. Her basis in the 200 shares is $3,000. The value of the stock rights is $5 ($25 – $20) per right. That is more than 15 percent of the value of the stock (5/25 = 20%), and Joanna must allocate part of her basis to the rights. The total value of the shares is $5,000. The total value of the rights is $1,000. Her basis in the stock rights is $500 [$1,000/($5,000 + $1,000) × $3,000]. She reduces the basis in her stock to $2,500 ($3,000 – $500).

In several instances, however, a shareholder will have tax consequences on a stock dividend. If a shareholder can choose between cash and a stock dividend (the usual

[57]§ 311. If the property is encumbered by a liability in excess of its fair market value, the fair market value is assumed to be no less than the liability.

[58]If the distributed property is appreciated, the corporation first increases its E&P for the gain realized and then reduces it for the fair market value of the property; on depreciated property, however, the corporation only reduces E&P by the property's basis.

[59]§§ 305(a) and 307(a).

[60]§ 305.

[61]§ 307(b).

stock reinvestment plan), the dividend is taxable under the doctrine of constructive receipt regardless of which alternative is selected. In general, if a distribution of stock or stock rights increases the percentage ownership of some shareholders relative to others, the distribution is taxable.[62] If a distribution of stock or stock rights is taxable, the shareholder recognizes income equal to the property's fair market value.

EXAMPLE 31

Shareholders of Class A common stock receive a 10 percent stock dividend while shareholders of Class B common stock receive a cash dividend. As a result, Class A shareholders now own a greater proportion of the stock of the corporation due to the stock dividend and both the stock (valued at fair market value) and the cash dividends are taxable. The basis of the stock received by the shareholders is its fair market value.

Corporate Redemptions

A **redemption** of stock is the sale of stock by a shareholder back to the issuing corporation. In a qualifying redemption, the shareholder surrenders all or part of his or her stock in exchange for cash or property from the corporation, recognizing capital gain or loss equal to the difference between the amount realized and the basis of the stock surrendered. A redemption could be used by the shareholder, however, to extract assets from a continuing corporation to avoid dividend income.[63] As a result, Congress enacted a complex set of rules designed to prevent taxpayers from disguising dividends as redemptions.

To qualify for sale treatment, a redemption must result in a significant reduction in the shareholder's equity ownership. This can be achieved by showing the redemption is either (1) substantially disproportionate or (2) a complete termination of a shareholder's interest in the corporation.[64]

The requirement for the redemption to be substantially disproportionate has specific numerical guidelines:[65]

1. The shareholder must own less than 50 percent of the voting power after the redemption.
2. The shareholder's percentage ownership of voting stock and common stock must be less than 80 percent of the ownership percentage before the redemption.

EXAMPLE 32

Al and Barbara each own 30 of the 100 outstanding shares of ABC Corporation's common stock; Carrie owns 40 shares. The corporation redeems 25 shares from Al and 5 shares from Barbara, paying each shareholder $1,000 cash for each share redeemed. The corporation has $100,000 in earnings and profits. The corporation's outstanding stock before and after these transactions is as follows:

[62] Stock rights are rights to acquire additional shares of stock at a set price (similar to stock options).

[63] Although the tax rates for dividend income and long-term capital gains are similar a shareholder recovers stock basis tax free in a qualifying redemption while the entire dividend distribution is taxed if the corporation has sufficient earnings and profits.

[64] There is a third test, "not essentially equivalent to a dividend," which must result in a "meaningful reduction in the shareholder's interest." *US v. Maclin P. Davis*, 70-1 USTC ¶998, 25 AFTR 2d 70-287, 397 US 301 (USSC, 1970). Because "meaningful reduction" is a term of art and open to several interpretations, it should be used only as a last resort (if neither of the other two specific provisions can be met). Relevant case law can provide some guidance on its use, however. See *William F. Wright v. US*, 73-2 USTC ¶9583, 32AFTR 2d 73-5490, 482 F.2d 600 (CA-8, 1973). Also see Rev. Rul. 75-502, 1975-2 CB 111.

[65] §302(b)(2). Such numerical guidelines are often referred to as *bright lines*.

	Before Redemption			After Redemption	
	(A)	(A) / 100	(B)	(A)–(B)	[(A)–(B)]/70
Shareholder	Shares Owned	Percentage Ownership	Shares Redeemed	Shares Owned	Percentage Ownership
Al	30	30%	25	5	7.1%
Barbara	30	30%	5	25	35.7%
Carrie	40	40%	0	40	57.2%
Total	100	100%	30	70	100.0%

Al's redemption is substantially disproportionate because he owns less than 50 percent of the stock after the redemption and his post-redemption ownership (7.1 percent) is less than 80 percent of his pre-redemption ownership (30% × 80% = 24%). Barbara's redemption is not substantially disproportionate because she does not have the necessary reduction in her stock ownership. Although she owns less than 50 percent, Barbara's post-redemption ownership (35.7 percent) is not less than 80 percent of her pre-redemption stock ownership (30% × 80% = 24%). Al receives sale treatment and recognizes capital gain equal to the difference between the $25,000 cash received and his basis for the 25 shares redeemed. Barbara is taxed as if she received a $5,000 dividend.

A complete termination of interest means the shareholder must divest himself or herself of all shares of the stock in the corporation. Under normal circumstances, a complete termination of interest also qualifies as a substantially disproportionate redemption, but the attribution rules may make it difficult to completely terminate all interest in the corporation when the redeeming shareholder is related to continuing shareholders.

Related persons have common interests and can be expected to act for mutual benefit of all related persons. The attribution rules are based on this assumption and provide that stock owned by one related party is considered to be indirectly owned by the other related party.

Relationships include the following:[66]

1. **Family Attribution** — An individual owns stock owned by a spouse, parent, child, and grandchild.
2. **Entity to Owner**
   - **a.** Stock owned by a partnership is owned proportionately by the partners.
   - **b.** Stock owned by a corporation is attributed proportionately only to a 50 percent or more shareholder.
   - **c.** Stock owned by an estate or trust is attributed proportionately to the beneficiaries.
3. **Owner to Entity**
   - **a.** Stock owned by a partner is attributed in full to the partnership.
   - **b.** Stock owned by a 50 percent or more shareholder is attributed in full to the corporation.
   - **c.** Stock owned by a beneficiary is attributed in full to the estate or trust.

These attribution rules are applied when calculating the ownership tests to determine whether a redemption really is a significant reduction in ownership to qualify for sale treatment. For a complete termination of interest, an individual is allowed to waive only the family attribution rules.[67]

[66]§318(a). These rules differ somewhat from the rules applicable to transactions between related parties.

[67]§302(b)(3). When attribution is waived, the only interest a shareholder may maintain in the corporation is that of a creditor (that is, the shareholder may still own corporate bonds). §302(c).

EXAMPLE 33

John and Jackie, husband and wife, own 100 percent of the outstanding stock of J & J Corporation. John has other business interests and wants to leave the running of the business completely to Jackie. J & J redeems all of John's stock. Because John and Jackie are closely related, John is assumed to have influence over Jackie, and her shares are attributed to him. This influence could deny him redemption as a complete termination of interest. If he waives the family attribution rules, however, the transaction qualifies as a complete termination of interest.

If the sale fails to qualify as a redemption, the proceeds that the shareholder receives are dividends to the extent of the corporation's earnings and profits. The shareholder's basis transfers to the other shares still owned. If the shareholder owns no other shares, the basis transfers to the related party's shares.[68]

If the corporation distributes appreciated property to redeem the shareholder's stock, the corporation must recognize the gain; it is prohibited from recognizing loss on depreciated property that is distributed.[69]

TAX PLANNING

If a corporation has little or no earnings and profits, a nonqualifying stock redemption may result in little or no dividend income before the shareholder begins to recover basis. If the shareholder is a corporation, dividend treatment may be preferable to sale treatment, due to the dividend received deduction.

Partial Liquidation

A partial corporate liquidation resembles a redemption except that qualifying depends on the corporation rather than the shareholder. A distribution of cash or property by a corporation qualifies as a **partial liquidation** if the corporation significantly reduces its operations or terminates one of its qualifying businesses.[70] The treatment of the distributing corporation's corporate and noncorporate shareholders differs, however. Noncorporate shareholders receive sale treatment for the distributions on the surrender of their shares in a partial liquidation, while corporate shareholders usually treat the distributions as dividends.[71] The distributing corporation recognizes gain (but not loss) on the distribution of appreciated (depreciated) property in a partial liquidation.

Liquidating Distributions

When a corporation adopts a plan of liquidation, ceases operations, distributes its assets to its shareholders in exchange for all of their stock, and cancels the stock, the corporation is liquidated. While the corporation is liquidating, it no longer is a going concern and its activities are directed at the closing of the business. The corporation's treatment in liquidation differs from that of other distributions, however, because the corporation not only recognizes gain on the distribution of appreciated assets but also recognizes losses on depreciated property distributed.[72]

EXAMPLE 34

BH Corporation decides to liquidate. It sold most of its assets for cash but distributed its only two remaining assets to its sole shareholder—a car valued at $3,100 (basis = $2,000) and a machine valued at $6,800 (basis = $9,000)—in exchange for her stock, along with the cash. The corporation recognizes the $1,100 gain on the car and the $2,200 loss on the machine.

[68]§302(d).

[69]§311. These gain/loss rules are the same as those that apply to dividend distributions.

[70]The corporation must abandon one of its qualifying businesses and continue to operate another qualifying business; both must be active businesses operated for at least five years and neither of these businesses were acquired in a taxable transaction within the preceding five years. §302(e)(3).

[71]Because of the dividends received deduction, this treatment may be advantageous to a corporation.

[72]Losses may not be recognized on certain distributions to controlling shareholders or on recently acquired assets.

All shareholders of a liquidating corporation recognize gain or loss on the distribution of assets exchanged for their stock based on the cash and fair market value of the property received and the basis of the stock surrendered.[73] If the shareholder receives the liquidation proceeds over several years, loss cannot be recognized until the final distribution is received. The shareholder recognizes gain, however, on any current (and subsequent) distribution after basis is fully recovered.

EXAMPLE 35

Green Corporation distributes $20,000 cash plus other property having a $12,000 fair market value to Jennifer as part of its plan of liquidation. Jennifer's basis in her Green stock is $16,000. Jennifer recognizes a $16,000 gain ($20,000 + $12,000 – $16,000) on the liquidation. If Jennifer received the $20,000 cash in the first year and the $12,000 of property in a subsequent year, she would recognize $4,000 gain ($20,000 – $16,000) in the first year and the remaining $12,000 gain in the subsequent year. If she received less than $16,000 total on the distributions, she could recognize no loss until the final year of distributions.

A parent corporation that liquidates a subsidiary corporation is subject to separate liquidation provisions.[74] Neither the subsidiary nor the parent recognizes gain or loss on the distribution of property from the subsidiary to the parent. The parent takes a carryover basis in the assets, effectively postponing any gain or loss until the parent disposes of the assets.

Dividend and Redemption Planning Issues

The Taxpayer Relief Act of 2012 increased the maximum basic tax rate for dividends and capital gains to 20 percent for taxpayers with incomes in excess of $450,000 MFJ, The basic tax rates on dividends and long-term capital gains for the lower-income taxpayers remained at zero percent for taxpayers in the 10 and 15 percent tax brackets and 15 percent for those taxpayers with taxable income not exceeding $450,000 MFJ. A surtax was introduced of 3.8 percent that is added to the capital gains and dividends of taxpayers whose AGI is greater than $250,000 MFJ. The potential 8.8% increase in the maximum rate for upper income taxpayers ($450,000 MFJ), however, makes extracting cash or property from a corporation less attractive. Although dividend payments remain nondeductible by a corporation, distributing dividends to shareholders in higher tax brackets is no longer as attractive as it was prior to 2013. The top rate for dividends remains almost 16 percent less than the top rate on individual income of 39.6 percent, however.

EXAMPLE 36

A corporation with $1,000,000 taxable income decides to distribute all of its after-tax income as a dividend to its sole shareholder who is in the 39.6 marginal tax bracket. The corporation will pay $340,000 of tax on the $1,000,000 of income; prior to the 2013 increase in the dividend tax rate, the shareholder would pay an additional $99,000 [($1,000,000 – $340,000) × 15%] tax on the dividend for a total of $439,000 in taxes. At 23.8%, the shareholder's tax is now $157,080 ($660,000 × 23.8%); total taxes are now $497,080, an increase of $58,080 ($497,080 – $439,000) in total taxes.

The recharacterization of excessive salary or rental payments as dividends poses a greater threat than when the dividend rate was 15%, but may still not be prohibitive at current rates, particularly if the corporation reports a loss or very low income for the year.

EXAMPLE 37

ABC Corporation reports a $100,000 loss for the year while raising its owner's salary from $650,000 to $850,000. If the $200,000 raise is considered excessive compensation and is recharacterized as a div-

[73]Gain and loss is determined separately for different blocks of stock. Loss is not recognized until the final distribution is received.

[74]The parent corporation must own directly at least 80 percent of the voting power or at least 80 percent of the value of all the subsidiary's stock.

idend, the corporation will lose the $200,000 deduction and will now have $100,000 of taxable income on which it will pay a tax of $22,250. The owner's tax rate on the $200,000, however, will only increase from 15% to 23.8% and he will save $31,600 [(39.6% – 23.8%) $200,000] in taxes. In addition, both ABC and the owner will each receive a refund of employment taxes on the $200,000 recharacterized as dividend.

Although the corporation could have made the $200,000 dividend payment directly to the owner with the same result, it would have been required to make similar proportionate dividend payments to the other shareholders holding that same class of stock as the owner.

TAX PLANNING

Shareholders with loans from the corporation should still have the corporation distribute sufficient cash as a dividend to pay off the loan directly even though it could be taxed at a maximum rate of 23.8 percent (rather than the pre-2013 rate of 15 percent). If the debt had been forgiven, the shareholder would have been taxed at ordinary income rates (up to 39.6 percent) for the discharge of indebtedness income.

With the current dividend rates, shareholders who want some or all of their stock redeemed may still benefit from dividend treatment for the proceeds of a redemption. Family members who want to redeem only a portion of their stock may still do so generally with less tax cost. Family members can only qualify for sale treatment if they dispose of all of their stock and waive the family attribution rules. This waiver requires the shareholder to cease all interest in the corporation except as a creditor. This prevents a family member from remaining an employee or consultant of the corporation if they want to receive sale treatment.

EXAMPLE 38

Frank wants to redeem all 10,000 shares of his stock in a family corporation while remaining as a consultant on future projects. Beverly, Frank's sister, wants to redeem only a portion of her shares for her son's college expenses. Neither Frank nor Beverly will have sufficient other taxable income that would result in dividend income at a rate geater than 15 percent of the total proceeds. Although sale treatment may have resulted in less tax (only the gain on sale would be subject to tax), neither would be able to receive sale treatment due to their circumstances.

Shareholders with a relatively high basis in their stock may still prefer to receive sale treatment if they qualify. It may make little difference, however, to shareholders with very low stock basis if they receive sale or dividend treatment.

EXAMPLE 39

Shelly has a basis of $20,000 in the 2,000 shares of stock she wants ABC to redeem; Carol has a basis of only $2,000 in her 2,000 shares. Both Shelly and Carol are in the 28% marginal tax bracket (15% dividend and capital gains tax rates) and the corporation pays each of them $40,000 for their shares. If Shelly has sale treatment, her tax is $3,000 [($40,000 – $20,000 basis) × 15%] but her tax doubles to $6,000 (15% × $40,000) if it is a dividend. Carol, however, will pay $6,000 tax as a dividend but only $5,700 [($40,000 – $2,000) × 15%] tax as a sale. If Shelly had held her stock for less than one year, however, she would prefer dividend treatment. At ordinary income rates, her $20,000 of short-term capital gain would result in a tax of $5,600 ($20,000 × 28%).

There are several other situations in which sale treatment remains preferable to dividend treatment. For example, a shareholder with capital loss carryforwards would prefer the capital gain from sale treatment to offset these capital losses. In addition, sale treatment is preferable on a redemption if the taxpayer is going to be paid the proceeds over more than one year. The installment method would not be available for sale proceeds recharacterized as dividend.[75]

[75]See Andrew R. Lee, "New Dividend Planning Strategies for Shareholders and Corporations," *Practical Tax Strategies*, October 2003.

ISSUES FOR CLOSELY HELD CORPORATIONS

Section 542(a)(2) defines a **closely held corporation** as one that has five or fewer individuals who own 50 percent or more of the value of a corporation's outstanding stock at any time during the last half of the tax year. A practical definition for tax avoidance purposes is one in which one or several of the shareholders acting together can prevail on the corporation to act in a way that reflects their will. Nothing is intrinsically wrong with this, but closely held corporations come under particular scrutiny by the IRS to ensure that transactions are not designed to avoid taxes.

Constructive Dividends

Even with the reduction in the dividend tax rates for individuals, shareholders of closely held corporations may still try to avoid direct dividend payments and receive informal economic benefits as constructive dividends in a variety of forms, such as rents in excess of the property's fair rental value, the use of corporate property for personal purposes, a sale of property to a shareholder below its fair market value, loans to shareholders at low or no interest, and payment of a shareholder's personal expenses by a corporation. Shareholder-employees may also receive excessive compensation.

EXAMPLE 40

ABC Corporation rents office space from its majority shareholder. The office space normally rents for $5,400 per month but the corporation pays the shareholder $7,000 per month. The shareholder recognizes the $7,000 monthly rent as income, and the corporation deducts the full amount as rent expense. The IRS can reclassify the $1,600 in excess monthly rental payments as a constructive dividend, and the corporation would lose $1,600 per month in deductible expenses.

If a party related to the shareholder receives any of the benefits listed above because of the shareholder's relationship to the corporation, the benefit received by the related party can also be reclassified as a constructive dividend to the shareholder.

EXAMPLE 41

Continuing the previous example, assume the corporation also allows the shareholder's son to have a company vehicle solely for his personal use. The corporation deducts depreciation and other expenses for the vehicle. If the vehicle's rental value is $500 per month, this value can be reclassified as a constructive dividend to the shareholder, and the corporation loses all of the deductions for expenses related to the vehicle.

A reclassification as a constructive dividend is normally detrimental to the corporation but it may benefit the shareholder. If excess compensation or rental payments have already been included in the individual shareholder's ordinary income, their reclassification as dividends could reduce the tax rate to which they are subject to a maximum 20 percent (23.8 percent with the surtax) rate.[76] The loss of deductibility of an expense reclassified as a dividend, however, hits the corporation at its highest marginal tax rate and can subject the corporation to penalties and interest. If the corporation does not have positive earnings and profits, however, any value received by the shareholder cannot be taxed as a dividend, but would be treated as a return of capital by the shareholder and taxable only if the shareholder's stock basis is reduced to zero.

Penalty Taxes to Encourage Dividend Payments

When individual tax rates are higher than corporate rates, an incentive arises to leave earnings in a corporation so that the shareholders can profit from share price appreciation rather than from dividends. The personal holding company (PHC) tax and the accumulated earnings tax (AET) are penalty taxes designed to discourage corporations from retaining earnings. Prior to the 2003 Act, the penalty tax rate was the highest individual tax rate of 39.6 percent. As the purpose of the penalty tax is to

[76]The taxpayer would have to file an amended return to redetermine the tax if the return was filed prior to the reclassification.

encourage the payment of dividends, the 2003 Act changed the penalty tax rate to the individual 15 percent maximum tax rate for dividend income. The Taxpayer Relief Act of 2012 raised the tax rate to 20 percent to coincide with the increase in the dividend rate for higher income taxpayers to 20 percent. With the increase in the dividend tax rate for upper income individuals to a maximum of 20 percent (23.8% with the surtax), corporations may still be willing to pay dividends to avoid the tax. If, however, a corporation is subject to either penalty tax, the tax must be paid in addition to the regular corporate income tax. (If a corporation could be subject to both the AET and the PHC tax, only the PHC tax is imposed.) Paying sufficient dividends to shareholders avoids imposition of either of these penalty taxes.

Personal Holding Companies

A corporation is a **personal holding company** in any year it meets both ownership and income tests. The ownership test is met if (1) five or fewer individuals own more than 50 percent of the value of the corporation's outstanding stock at any time during the last half of the corporation's taxable year and (2) 60 percent or more of the corporation's adjusted ordinary gross income (AOGI) is personal holding company income (PHCI). The corporation meets the income test if PHCI/AOGI is greater than or equal to 60 percent.[77] A corporation whose stock is owned by nine or fewer individuals automatically meets the ownership test. Attribution rules under Section 544 are applied in determining ownership.[78]

Personal holding company income (PHCI) generally is passive income and includes dividends, interest, royalties, and annuities. Rental income, copyright royalties, software royalties, and royalties from mineral, oil, and gas rights are excluded if at least one-half of the corporation's income is from one of these sources and certain other requirements are met.[79]

If sufficient dividends are paid, the penalty can be avoided. The corporation self-assesses the 20 percent tax on adjusted taxable income less the dividends paid deduction to determine the PHC tax, paying this along with its regular corporate tax.

Accumulated Earnings Tax

The **accumulated earnings tax (AET)**, which is assessed by the IRS, applies only to corporations that are "formed or availed of for the purpose of avoiding income tax with respect to the shareholders."[80] No mechanical method can prove this intent, but a corporation that accumulates earnings beyond its reasonable needs or is an investment or holding company is deemed to meet the intent requirement.[81] Corporations with a balance in excess of $250,000 ($150,000 for a personal service corporation) in accumulated earnings and profits must prove that the accumulation is reasonable to avoid the 20 percent tax on excess accumulations.

The reasonable needs of the business include all current and reasonably anticipated future needs.[82] To be considered reasonably anticipated needs, the corporation must have plans that are "specific, definite, and feasible."[83] Thus, a corporation that has reserves for plant expansion that are approved by the board of directors and for which there is a definite timetable established is not subject to the tax. Other reasonable needs for which the corporation may accumulate earnings include liability losses, replacement of plant and equipment, retiring of debt, and working capital.

---

[77]S corporations, banks, and other financing companies, insurance companies, and foreign personal holding companies are exempt from this tax.

[78]These attribution rules are similar to those explained earlier for stock redemptions except that family is extended to include brothers, sisters, and all lineal ancestors and descendants.

[79]§ 543(a)(1). For example, rents are excluded if a large portion of the nonrental income is distributed as dividends.

[80]§ 532(a). As the law is written, the AET could apply to any corporation not just one that is closely held. Imposing the tax on a widely held corporation with no single person or related group controlling it is impractical because of the intent requirement.

[81]§ 533.

[82]§ 532(a)(1).

[83]Reg. § 1.537-1(b).

Factors cited as indicative of unreasonable accumulations include a poor dividend history, investments that are not related to the corporation's ongoing business, and loans to shareholders. Corporations are permitted to accumulate a maximum of $250,000 ($150,000 for a personal service corporation) of earnings as a credit without penalty.[84] Paying sufficient dividends prevents the IRS from imposing the AET.

Controlled Corporate Groups

To prevent taxpayers from establishing multiple corporations to benefit from the progressive corporate tax rates (and other favorable provisions), a controlled group of corporations can take advantage of the lower rates one time only. The lower rate can be apportioned to the controlled corporations in any manner the taxpayer chooses, but the corporations must calculate taxes as if they were one corporation.[85]

EXAMPLE 42

James owns 100 percent of the stock in Bee and Cee Corporations. Bee Corporation reports $300,000 of income and Cee Corporation reports only $10,000 of income. Corporation Cee calculates the tax on its $10,000 of income at the 15 percent tax rate. As a result, Bee Corporation can use the 15 percent tax rate to calculate tax on the first $40,000 ($50,000 – $10,000) of income only. The remaining rates apply to Bee in the usual manner.

Parent–subsidiary and brother–sister controlled groups are the two types of controlled corporate groups. A parent–subsidiary controlled group is one

1. that consists of two or more corporations, one of which is a common parent.
2. in which the common parent corporation directly owns 80 percent or more of the voting power *or* 80 percent or more of the total value of all classes of stock of a second corporation (the subsidiary).
3. that includes all other corporations, 80 percent or more of whose stock is owned jointly or separately by the parent and its subsidiary corporations, measured by voting power *or* total value of all classes of stock.

For purposes of apportioning the corporate tax brackets (as well as the accumulated earnings credit and the alternative minimum tax exemption amount), a brother–sister controlled group consists of two or more corporations with five or fewer individual shareholders who (1) own more than 50 percent of the total combined voting power *or* (2) more than 50 percent of the value of all shares of stock of the corporation with either percentage determined by taking into account only the lowest stock ownership percentage of each shareholder that is identical across each corporation. For all other purposes, the shareholders must own at least 80 percent of the combined voting power or value of the corporations *and* own more than 50 percent (voting or value) of the stock taking into account only the identical ownership by the shareholders across the corporations.[86]

EXAMPLE 43

	Ownership Percentage by Shareholder			
Corporation	X	Y	Z	Totals
A	20%	40%	25%	85%
B	40	40	15	95
C	60	15	10	85
D	20	15	50	85
Lowest percentage ownership of each shareholder	20	15	10	Total lowest percentage ownership = 45

[84]The credit allowed is either the current year's earnings and profits net of capital gains (adjusted for taxes) that the corporation needs to retain to meet its reasonable needs or the minimum credit, whichever is greater.

[85]A controlled group of corporations is permitted only one accumulated earnings tax credit.

[86]§ 1563.

Although the three shareholders own over 80 percent of each corporation, the sum of the lowest percentage ownership in each corporation by the shareholders does not equal 50 percent or more. Therefore, the four corporations are not a brother–sister controlled group. If, however, only Corporations A, B, and D are considered, the total of the lowest common percentage ownership is 50% (A = 20%, B = 15%, D = 15%) and A, B, and D constitute a brother–sister controlled group.

Controlled groups of corporations remain a problem, however, because of the ease by which one corporation can be used to avoid taxes for the owners of another corporation in the group. For example, one or more corporations in the group could pay constructive dividends to the shareholders of a related corporation through excessive salaries or rents or bargain purchases.

Example 44

Corporations P and S are a parent and subsidiary, respectively. P has only two shareholders, J and K. J works for the subsidiary as an accounts payable manager with a salary of $400,000. Salaries for comparable work are only $50,000. As long as either P or S has earnings and profits, the excess salary is a constructive dividend taxable to J but no longer deductible by S.

One of the more common schemes using controlled corporations is having one corporation purchase the shares of another corporation from a shareholder (a back-door redemption). The IRS has been aware of these schemes for many years and has developed slightly altered applications of the substantially disproportionate redemption rules to apply to these corporations. Failure to meet these rules results in dividend treatment and the earnings and profits available for the dividend are not limited to the redeeming corporation's earnings and profits.[87]

Expanded Topics—Earnings and Profits

The balance in a corporation's earnings and profits account determines if a cash or property distribution to shareholders is considered a dividend or a return of capital. If the corporation cannot establish that a distribution is a return of capital, then any distribution to a shareholder that does not qualify as a redemption or liquidation will be considered a taxable dividend distribution (including any distribution classified as a constructive dividend). Although reduced tax rates on dividends make this less onerous, it is important to calculate and keep track of the corporation's earnings and profits and to understand how they determine which distributions are taxable.

Earnings and profits (E&P) attempts to measure how much a corporation can distribute as dividends and leave contributed capital intact. As taxable income includes a number of legislative exclusions and deductions, it bears little resemblance to an amount the corporation can distribute without impairing corporate capital. Thus, many of the exclusions and artificial deductions allowed in determining taxable income are disallowed in the E&P calculation.[88] Each year, the starting point for determining E&P is taxable income, to which a number of positive and negative adjustments must be made to determine that year's E&P. Table 9.3 is a partial list of these adjustments.[89]

Example 45

Judah Corporation has $400,000 of taxable income on which it pays $136,000 of federal income tax. In arriving at taxable income, the corporation has the following:

[87] See §304 and the related regulations for a further discussion of redemptions by related corporations.

[88] Earnings and profits more closely resemble an economic concept of income or the financial accounting concept of retained earnings than it does taxable income.

[89] §312.

$10,000 dividend received deduction	$4,000 excess capital loss
$2,000 tax-exempt income	$5,000 nondeductible fines
$20,000 Section 179 expense	$6,000 NOL carryover

The corporation's E&P for the current year is determined as follows:

	$400,000	Taxable income
Minus	136,000	Federal income tax
Plus	10,000	Dividend received deduction
Plus	2,000	Tax-exempt income
Minus	5,000	Nondeductible fines
Minus	4,000	Excess capital loss
Plus	16,000	Excess of §179 expense (20% allowed)
Plus	6,000	NOL carryover
Equals	$289,000	Earnings and profits for the current year

The E&P determined above is more accurately called ***current* earnings and profits (CE&P)**. CE&P is the amount calculated from the current year's taxable income with the appropriate adjustments. This is distinguished from ***accumulated* earnings and profits (AE&P)**, the accumulation of CE&P for all prior years that has not been distributed as dividends.

At the end of each tax year, CE&P is calculated. Dividend distributions made during the tax year reduce this value. Assuming the dividend value does not exceed CE&P, the remaining CE&P is added to the balance in AE&P from all prior years.[91]

TABLE
9.3 ADJUSTMENTS TO TAXABLE INCOME TO CALCULATE CURRENT EARNINGS AND PROFITS

POSITIVE ADJUSTMENTS	NEGATIVE ADJUSTMENTS
Federal income tax refunds	Federal income taxes paid
Dividends received deductions	Capital losses in excess of capital gains
Proceeds of life insurance policies	Premiums on life insurance policies
Excess of a current year's installment gain over portion recognized	Installment sale gain from a prior year's installment sale
Percentage depletion in excess of cost depletion	Nondeductible fines and bribes
Depreciation expense in excess of allowable E&P depreciation	Disallowed losses on sales to related parties
Charitable contribution carryovers	Charitable contributions in excess of 10% limit
NOL carryovers	20% of cost of Section 179 expensed item
Capital loss carryovers	
Section 179 expense in excess of allowable depreciation[90]	

[90]For earnings and profits, 20 percent of the expensed amount is deducted in each of the current and four succeeding years.

[91]The calculation of CE&P can result in a negative number. If CE&P is negative, it can cause the balance in AE&P to be negative as well. Dividend distributions *cannot*, however, create or increase a negative balance in either CE&P or AE&P.

EXAMPLE 46

Corn Corporation has taxable income of $40,000 for the year, its CE&P prior to dividend distributions is $56,000, and it has a balance of $23,000 in AE&P. It distributes a $27,000 dividend to its shareholders during the year. The dividend distribution reduces Corn's positive CE&P balance to $29,000 ($56,000 – $27,000); this $29,000 then increases its AE&P balance to $52,000 ($23,000 + $29,000) at the beginning of the next year.

Most corporate distributions do not exceed CE&P. If they do, however, the distributions remain fully taxable as long as both current and accumulated E&P are not exceeded. If the distributions exceed both CE&P and AE&P, both CE&P and AE&P must be allocated to the shareholders, with any excess distribution identified by the corporation as a return of corporate capital.

When a distribution exceeds both CE&P and AE&P but only *one* dividend distribution is made during the year, both CE&P and AE&P are allocated to the shareholders according to their percentage stock ownership. If there is more than one dividend distribution and there is any type of ownership change between distributions, then specific allocation procedures must be followed. CE&P is allocated on a pro rata basis to all distributions regardless of when during the year they were made. AE&P, however, must be allocated to the earliest distributions first until AE&P is exhausted. These allocations of CE&P and AE&P are then reapportioned at each distribution date to each of the shareholders based on his or her percentage stock ownership on that date.

EXAMPLE 47

CBC Corporation has $1,400 in CE&P and $3,000 in AE&P. It makes a $2,000 distribution on June 30, a $3,000 distribution on September 1 and a final $2,000 distribution on December 31. CE&P is allocated on a pro rata basis over all distributions as follows: $400 ($2,000/$7,000 × $1,400) to June 1; $600 to September 1 ($3,000/$7,000 × $1,400) and $400 to December 31. AE&P is then allocated chronogically to the distributions as follows: $1,600 to June 1; $1,400 ($3,000 – $1,600 allocated to June 1) to September 1; AE&P is now exhausted and there is none remaining for the December 31 distribution. Thus, June 1 shareholders will have their entire distribution classified as dividend; $2,000 of the $3,000 distributed on September 1 is dividend and will be apportioned to the shareholders based on their percentage ownership on September 1; the remaining $1,000 is a return of capital; only $400 of the December distribution is dividend (to be apportioned to the shareholders on December 1) and $1,600 is return of capital.

Shareholders who receive a distribution identified as a return of capital must reduce their basis in the stock.

EXAMPLE 48

Corporation J has CE&P of $40,000 and AE&P of $20,000. It makes a $70,000 distribution to its shareholders. Only $60,000 is taxed as a dividend, $40,000 from CE&P and $20,000 from AE&P. The remaining $10,000 is a return of capital that reduces shareholders' stock bases.

A shareholder's basis cannot be reduced below zero, however. If the distribution also exceeds the shareholder's basis, the shareholder is treated as selling the stock for the excess and generally recognizes capital gain.

EXAMPLE 49

Tango Corporation has $5,000 in CE&P and $1,000 in AE&P when it makes a distribution of $15,000 to its sole shareholder, Tim. Tim has a basis in his stock of $7,000. The first $6,000 of the distribution is a taxable dividend from the corporation's CE&P and AE&P. The next $7,000 is a nontaxable recovery of Tim's $7,000 investment in the corporation and reduces his basis to zero. The remaining $2,000 ($15,000 – $6,000 – $7,000) of the distribution is treated as a gain on the sale of his stock, and he recognizes $2,000 of capital gain.

Revisiting the Introductory Case

The corporation has four potential investors: the chief engineer, the supplier, John's father-in-law, and John's brother. It would be advantageous to have each of the investors accept bonds instead of stock. The interest payments are deductible, and John's total control of the corporation is preserved.

The supplier is the one least likely to accept bonds. As a corporation, receiving dividends is far more desirable due to the dividend received deduction. The desired 20 percent voting stock to preserve its status as a supplier allows the supplier to take an 80 percent dividend received deduction but doesn't negate John's control of the corporation. John might consider issuing a second class of voting common stock so that dividends do not have to be paid on all common stock at one time.

John's father-in-law is the ideal candidate for corporate bonds. The corporation should issue bonds with a minimum of 6 percent annual interest and a maturity of 10 years to meet the father-in-law's income requirements. The interest is deductible by the corporation, reducing its after-tax cost.

John's brother wants an annual return on his investment. Yet he wants to be able to leave his investment to his heirs, most likely because he wants to take advantage of the step up in basis upon his death. Neither bonds nor preferred stock have significant appreciation potential, but John's brother might be agreeable to long-term bonds that have a conversion feature allowing them to be converted to common stock after some extended period of time (for example, 10 to 20 years). Bonds will provide current interest income that is deductible by the corporation. Preferred stock is a second, less desirable alternative as preferred stock dividends are not guaranteed and they are not deductible by the corporation.

It is a real advantage for the corporation to pay part of the engineer's salary in stock. The value of the stock is considered income to the engineer, and it is deductible by the corporation. The corporation conserves its cash by not having to pay the salary, and the deduction reduces its taxes. The issuance of incentive stock options, however, normally has no tax consequences. Thus, it may be best for the company to work out a combination of stock and stock options as compensation for the engineer. John may want to set an upper limit on the amount of stock the engineer can receive, however, to ensure that he maintains control. Alternatively, John could use the second class of voting stock. The corporation can declare a dividend on this stock to satisfy the supplier and the engineer without having to pay a dividend to John.

As an employee, John can take a reasonable salary from the corporation, but he can further extract money from the corporation on a before-tax basis by employing his wife and his college-age sons. His wife, with her recent computer education, should be able to command a substantial salary without causing any constructive dividend problems. The two sons can work part-time in suitable positions at appropriate salaries. John should also consider employing the other two children as soon as they are old enough to take on appropriate jobs.

Summary

A corporation has a number of advantages and disadvantages when compared to other forms in which to operate a business. Its principal advantages are limited liability, unlimited life, free transferability of its stock, the ease of raising additional capital, and the ability of shareholders to enjoy the benefits of employee status. Disadvantages include the double taxation of income and the costs of establishing and maintaining a corporate charter.

Corporations are subject to tax on their income as determined under the rules of tax accounting. These rules have numerous differences from the rules the corporation follows in calculating financial accounting income under GAAP. A corporation's net capital gains are taxed at its regular corporate tax rates. Its net capital losses can only be carried to years in which it had net capital gains. A corporation's shareholders are taxed a second time on corporate income when it is distributed in the form of dividends. Corporate shareholders are permitted a dividends received deduction to alleviate some of the effects of double taxation.

Corporations can make distributions to shareholders as part of qualifying redemptions, partial liquidations, or complete liquidations. The shareholders recognize gain or loss on the receipt of cash or property in exchange for their stock. The corporation recognizes gain on the distribution of appreciated property. It can only recognize loss on the distribution of depreciated property if it is distributed as part of a complete liquidation.

Shareholders who control a corporation or a group of controlled corporations may attempt to extract income from the corporation in such a way as to avoid dividend classification. Excess salary and rents, bargain purchases, low-interest loans, and personal use of corporate property are ways a shareholder could benefit from a constructive dividend. If the IRS reclassifies a benefit as a dividend, the corporation loses the deduction.

If a corporation fails to pay dividends to its shareholders, the IRS can levy one of two penalty taxes in addition to the regular corporate tax. The personal holding company tax is self-assessed if the corporation meets specific numerical guidelines as a personal holding company and fails to distribute sufficient dividends. The IRS asserts the accumulated earnings tax when a corporation accumulates earnings beyond its reasonable needs.

The corporation maintains two accounts: current earnings and profits and accumulated earnings and profits. Current earnings and profits is calculated starting with net income to which specific items are added or subtracted. This calculated current earnings and profits is the amount that a corporation could distribute from its current operations as a dividend. Accumulated earnings and profits is the sum of prior undistributed current earnings and profits less dividends from accumulated earnings and profits. Together, these accounts determine whether a corporate distribution is wholly taxable as a dividend or if all or part of the distribution is a tax-free return of corporate capital.

KEY TERMS

Accumulated earnings and profits (AE&P) 417
Accumulated earnings tax (AET) 414
Affiliated group 404
Alternative minimum tax (AMT) 401
AMT adjustments 402
Charitable contribution deduction limitation 394
Closely held corporation 413
Common stock 392
Consolidated return 404
Corporate income tax 397
Corporate tax rate 397
Corporate tax return 398
Current earnings and profits (CE&P) 417
Debt 391
Disqualified person 430
Dividend 406
Dividend received deduction 393
Earnings and profits (E&P) 406
Equity 391
Estimated taxes 403
Exempt organization 429
Form 1120 398
Franchise tax 431
General business credit 400
Net operating loss (NOL) 396
Net unrelated business income 430
Nexus 432
Parent corporation 404
Partial liquidation 410
Personal holding company 414
Preferred stock 392
Private foundations 430
Redemption 408
Schedule L 398
Schedule M-1 398
Schedule M-2 399
Schedule M-3 400
Stock dividend 407
Stock rights 407
Subsidiary 404
Taxable net income 392
Unrelated business income tax (UBIT) 429
Use tax 433

TEST YOURSELF

ANSWERS APPEAR AFTER THE PROBLEM ASSIGNMENTS

1. The Chester Corporation has $250,000 of taxable income. It distributes $100,000 of that income as a dividend to its sole shareholder who has $490,000 of other taxable income that places him in the 39.6 percent marginal tax bracket. What is the effective tax rate on the corporation's $250,000 of taxable income?

- **a.** 34 percent
- **b.** 35 percent
- **c.** 41.8 percent
- **d.** 47.7 percent

2. The Glass Corporation has $156,000 of income from operations. It has a $21,000 capital loss and a net operating loss from the prior year of $36,000. What is its income tax liability for the year?

- **a.** $53,040
- **b.** $44,090
- **c.** $30,050
- **d.** $21,910

3. Walter Corporation reports $500,000 of taxable income in the current year. Determine its book income if tax depreciation was $15,000 more than book depreciation, its deductible meals and entertainment expenses were $40,000, and it had $10,000 of tax-exempt income.

- **a.** $500,000
- **b.** $485,000
- **c.** $315,000
- **d.** $285,000

4. Beggin Corporation has $100,000 of regular taxable income. It has $40,000 of positive adjustments and a $50,000 preference item. What is the corporation's alternative minimum tax liability?

- **a.** $38,000
- **b.** $30,000
- **c.** $9,750
- **d.** $0

5. The Little D Corporation has $150 in current earnings and profits and $100 in accumulated earnings and profits. It makes a $400 distribution to its sole shareholder whose stock basis is $100. What are the shareholder's tax consequences?

- **a.** $250 dividend
- **b.** $250 dividend; $50 capital gain
- **c.** $250 dividend; $100 capital gain
- **d.** $400 dividend

PROBLEM ASSIGNMENTS

CHECK YOUR UNDERSTANDING

1. Explain how a corporation's income is subject to double taxation.

2. List five desirable characteristics of the corporate form of business.

1. Limited liability for owners
2. Ease of raising capital
3. Ease of selling ownership interest (shares)
4. Ability of owner-shareholder to recieve a salary deductible as an expence by the corporation;
5. Ability of owner-shareholder to participate in corporate fringe benefits

3. What is a dividend received deduction? What are the percentages and when do they apply? When is the dividend received deduction limited to a percentage of net income?

4. What is a corporation's overall charitable contribution deduction limitation?

5. What are the carryover periods for corporate net operating losses?

6. List three items that increase book income and three items that reduce book income when reconciling book to taxable income.

7. What is the purpose of the alternative minimum tax? What is the alternative minimum tax rate for corporations?

8. What is the unextended due date for the income tax return of a corporation whose fiscal year ends on February 28? What is its extended due date? In what months must it make estimated payments for the next tax year?

9. What is the purpose of corporate earnings and profits? Why isn't taxable income used to determine if a distribution is a dividend?

10. Why are corporations permitted to file consolidated returns?

11. What are the ownership requirements for a group of corporations to file a consolidated return? Illustrate.

12. What is a corporate redemption? What are the tax consequences to the shareholder in a qualifying redemption? What are they if it is not a qualifying redemption?

13. What is a corporate liquidation? What are the tax consequences for a corporation that distributes property as part of a complete liquidation? What are the tax consequences to the shareholders?

14. What are the two types of controlled groups?

15. What are five positive and five negative adjustments to taxable income to determine current earnings and profits?

CRUNCH THE NUMBERS

16. A corporation's taxable income is $1,500,000. If it distributes its after-tax income to its shareholders whose dividend tax rate is 15 percent, what are the total tax and the combined effective tax rate on corporate income?

17. The Crane Corporation issues $1,500,000 in bonds with a 7.5 percent interest rate. If its marginal tax rate is 35 percent, what is its after-tax cost of the debt?

18. A corporation has gross revenue from sales of $289,000, cost of sales of $98,000, a Section 179 deduction of $20,000 (financial depreciation = $5,000), operating expenses of $122,000, and a Section 1231 gain of $21,000 on the sale of some machinery (the gain is only $14,000 for financial accounting).

    a. What is the corporation's taxable income?

    b. What is the corporation's pretax financial accounting income?

19. The Jingle Corporation has income from operations of $459,000. It has dividend income of $68,000 from a corporation in which it owns 5 percent.

    a. What is the corporation's taxable income?

    b. How would your answer change if Jingle owns 35 percent of the corporation paying the dividend?

20. Velvet Corporation has revenues of $340,000 and deductible expenses of $350,000. It also received a $40,000 dividend from a corporation in which it owns 10 percent. What is the corporation's taxable income?

21. What is a corporation's income tax if its income is

a. $70,000?

b. $280,000?

c. $900,000?

d. $2,250,000?

e. $14,000,000?

22. What is the tax on WW Corporation's taxable income of $825,000 if

a. it is a regular corporation?

b. it is a personal service corporation?

23. Whitlaw Corporation has $150,000 of gross profit on sales, operating expenses of $60,000 (excluding cost recovery), $4,000 dividend income from a one percent owned corporation, a $10,000 capital gain and $15,000 capital loss, a $15,000 Section 179 deduction, additional tax depreciation of $25,000 (total financial accounting depreciation is $22,000), a $5,000 charitable contribution, and a net operating loss carryover from the prior year of $10,000.

a. What is Whitlaw's taxable income?

b. What is Whitlaw's income tax?

c. Complete a Schedule M-1 or a facsimile for the corporation.

24. Gordon Corporation had $102,000 of retained earnings at the beginning of the year. It had $87,000 of financial accounting income and paid $45,000 in dividends. What is the corporation's ending retained earnings balance?

25. Donut Corporation has $400,000 of taxable income. What is its net tax liability if it has a $120,000 general business credit available?

26. Mondial Corporation's financial accounting records show it had gross revenue of $980,000, cost of goods sold of $420,000, operating expenses of $380,000, and $4,000 of dividends received from a 40% owned company. Its operating expenses included the following:

$6,000 of life insurance premiums on which it was the beneficiary

$22,000 of meals and entertainment expenses

$30,000 of charitable contributions

a. Determine Mondial Corporation's taxable income.

b. Determine Mondial Corporation's income tax liability.

c. Determine Mondial Corporation's income tax liability if book depreciation is $15,000 less than tax depreciation.

27. Palmdale Corporation has a regular tax liability of $94,000. It is eligible for a $54,000 general business credit for the current year and has a $30,000 general business credit carryover from the prior year. What is Palmdale's allowable general business credit for the current year? What is its credit carryover, if any, to future years?

28. The Falcon Corporation has $68,000 in taxable income. Its accountant uncovered $87,000 in net positive adjustments and $2,000 of preference items in determining its alternative minimum taxable income. What are the corporation's AMTI and AMT?

29. Jenkins Corporation had $675,000 of taxable income last year and $575,000 this year. What is the minimum amount that it must submit for each estimated quarterly tax payment to avoid any penalty for underpayment?

30. The Caribe Corporation has $668,000 of taxable income for the current year. In determining this income the accountant listed the following items:

$45,000 in dividends from a 30 percent owned corporation
$40,000 net operating loss carryover from the prior year
$68,000 disallowed loss on a sale to its sole shareholder
$40,000 capital loss in excess of capital gains
$23,000 in excess charitable contributions
Determine Caribe's current earnings and profits.

31. The Amble Corporation has $4,000 in current earnings and profits and $23,000 in accumulated earnings and profits. It makes a $6,000 dividend distribution at the end of the year to its shareholders. How is this distribution taxed, and what is the corporation's balance in CE&P and AE&P at the beginning of the next year?

32. Vanguard Corporation has excess land that it distributes to its shareholders as a dividend. Each of the four shareholders gets a portion of the land valued at $23,000 ($92,000 total value). The corporation's basis for the land is $68,000. What are the consequences to the corporation and the shareholders as a result of this distribution?

33. Carrie received 10 shares of Collie common stock as a 10 percent dividend on the 100 common shares she currently owns. She paid $4,400 for the original shares. If she sells the 10 shares that she just received for $800, what is her gain or loss on the sale?

34. Jo received one stock right for each share of the 10 shares of stock that she owns in Bill Corporation, which she purchased three years ago for $5 a share. Each stock right allows her to purchase one share of stock for $10. The stock is currently selling for $13 per share. What is her basis in the stock rights?

35. Sheri owns 800 of the 1,500 outstanding shares of Carney Corporation, which she bought a number of years ago for $20 each. She needs money for her daughter's tuition but does not want to sell all of her shares in the corporation. Carney has $200,000 in earnings and profits.

a. What are the tax consequences if the corporation buys 150 of her shares for $15,000?

b. What are the tax consequences if the corporation buys 300 of her shares for $30,000?

c. If Sheri's father owns the other 700 shares of the corporation, what are the tax consequences of each of the sales?

36. Beacon Corporation had operated a chain of restaurants for 15 years and owned a small trucking company for 10 years. It decided to sell all the assets of the trucking company (Section 1231 assets) for $1,500,000. The assets had a basis of $900,000 and the corporation is in the 34 percent marginal tax bracket. The company invested half of the after-tax sale proceeds to update some of its restaurants, and distributed the remaining half to its shareholders in exchange for 10,000 shares of their stock in Beacon.

a. If the shareholders' average bases in their shares are $45 per share, what are the tax consequences to the shareholders and the corporation from this distribution?

b. How would your answers change if Beacon received only $600,000 for the assets of the trucking business?

37. Loser Corporation decides to liquidate and files a plan of liquidation with the IRS. It is unable to sell its assets, so it distributes them to its sole shareholder, Bummer. There are only three assets: inventory (fair market value = $4,000; basis = $3,500), building (fair market value = $56,000; basis = $67,000), and machines (fair market value = $38,000; basis = $29,500). Bummer surrenders all of his stock with a basis of $187,000 in exchange for the property. What are the tax consequences to Loser and to Bummer as a result of this liquidation?

38. P Corporation owns 90 percent of the stock of S1 Corporation. S1 Corporation owns 45 percent of S2 Corporation and 86 percent of S3 Corporation. S3 Corporation owns 40 percent of S2 Corporation and 70 percent of S4. S4 owns 100 percent of S5. Identify the consolidated group of corporations.

39. A corporation has 10 shareholders. Nine of the shareholders own 9 percent each of the stock. The tenth shareholder owns the remaining stock. Does the corporation meet the shareholder test as a personal holding company? Explain.

40. The Green Corporation has only six shareholders. In the current year, it has AOGI of $540,000 and personal holding company income of $390,000. Its adjusted taxable income is $460,000. What is its personal holding company income tax?

41. The Prosperity Corporation has accumulated $200,000 of earnings beyond the reasonable needs of the business. The corporation's regular taxable income is $165,000. Its adjusted taxable income for determining the accumulated earnings tax is $178,000. What is the total amount of taxes that the corporation must pay?

42. General Corporation has $900,000 of service revenue, a $15,000 capital loss, a $20,000 casualty loss, operating expenses of $685,000, and a charitable contribution of $25,000.

a. Determine General's separate taxable income.

b. What items must be determined on a consolidated basis?

43. Identify the brother–sister corporations given the following ownership percentages by four individuals:

Individual/Corporation	A	B	C	D
James	20%	40%	15%	15%
Carol	25%	10%	20%	20%
Joan	20%	40%	40%	20%
Wallace	10%	10%	20%	25%

THINK OUTSIDE THE TEXT

These questions require answers that are beyond the material that is covered in this chapter.

44. List at least 10 differences between taxable income and accounting income.

45. Bob and Jane, brother and sister, are equal partners in a family partnership that owns 400 shares of the Sibling Corporation. Their grandfather owns the remaining 100 shares of Sibling Corporation. How many shares of stock are owned directly and indirectly by Bob?

46. The Blanton Corporation had a deficit in its current earnings and profits of $36,500 for the current year. It has $75,000 in accumulated earnings and profits. It made two distributions to its shareholders. On April 30, it distributed $40,000, and on November 30, it distributed $20,000. When the corporation sends out its 1099-DIV forms to its shareholders, how much of the distribution will be taxable to the shareholders as dividends?

47. Why do you think Congress requires the recognition of gain on the distribution of appreciated property but does not allow the recognition of loss on depreciated property in a nonliquidating distribution? Why do you think both gain and loss are recognized on liquidating distributions?

48. Explain how a parent–subsidiary controlled group differs from an affiliated controlled group. Develop examples of each to illustrate the differences.

49. Waltjohn Corporation has $5,000 in CE&P and $10,000 in AE&P. It has two shareholders, Walter and John. On April 1 of the current year, Walter received a $10,000 distribution from the corporation on his Class A common stock. On July 1, John received a $10,000 distribution on his Class B common stock. How will the corporation identify these distributions on the shareholders' Forms 1099-DIV?

IDENTIFY THE ISSUES

Identify the issues or problems suggested by the following situations. State each issue as a question.

50. Seth and Jacob are brothers who own all of Marboro Corporation's 2,000 shares of outstanding common stock. Seth owns 1,100 shares to Jacob's 900 shares, and this has caused many problems over the years. They have not spoken to each other except through their secretaries for more than 10 years, and they have consistently fought over the running of the company. Seth has come upon some hard times, however, and needs cash for some overdue bills. He has the corporation redeem exactly 200 of his shares for $50,000 so that Jacob does not get the controlling interest in the corporation.

51. The Cabot Corporation has had financial problems for several years. The two shareholders have discussed liquidating the corporation, but they are concerned that they will have to pay a large tax bill because of the corporation's low basis in its assets and their high fair market value due to their uniqueness. Each shareholder owns some other depreciated business properties that they could give to the corporation as a contribution to capital approximately 20 months before they formally develop their plan of liquidation and liquidate the corporation.

52. Seven years ago, the Bonnet Corporation redeemed all of Joe Bonnet's stock as a complete termination of interest. At the time, Joe signed a waiver of family attribution rules because his three sons retained all their stock. As part of this arrangement, Joe agreed to notify the IRS if he acquired a forbidden interest in the corporation. Recently, the corporation acquired a contract with a defense contractor to build a machine to produce specialized instruments for jet planes. Joe had been the company's chief engineer prior to his retirement from the company. The sons asked Joe to come back as a consultant for a short period to get this project up and running.

53. The owner of a corporation used corporate funds to pay for his home, all the home's expenses, and numerous other personal expenses. This went on for a number of years until the corporation was audited. The IRS asserted that the use of the corporate funds for personal purposes was a constructive dividend. At the time the corporation was audited, the corporation had only $2,000 in earnings and profits.

54. Sweeney was the chairman of Sweeney, Inc., a large hardware and lumber store. When Sweeney became ill, his son took over the business but sold the property and all the inventory of lumber valued at $2,000,000 within a year. Shortly thereafter, Sweeney recovered and took control of the corporation. The corporation purchased a new building and started a new hardware store. This store, although slightly larger than the original store, did not carry any lumber. Sweeney changed the name of the corporation, and the board authorized a plan of partial liquidation. Pursuant to that plan, the original shares of the corporation were replaced, and Sweeney distributed almost $2,000,000 to the shareholders as part of the partial liquidation. Each shareholder received $5,000 and one share of stock for every two of the old corporation that was owned.

DEVELOP RESEARCH SKILLS

55. Locate and read Section 385 of the Internal Revenue Code and develop a comprehensive list of factors that indicate legitimate debt. What is the status of the regulations that are to expand on this Code section?

56. Several years ago, Congress repealed the General Utilities Doctrine. Locate and read *General Utilities & Operating Co. v. Helvering*, 296 US 200 (1935). Summarize this case. What was the General Utilities Doctrine, and how did its repeal affect current transactions?

57. Locate and read Internal Revenue Code Sections 267, 318, and 544. Compare the definition of family in each of these sections.

58. June owned all the stock of Corporation A. Over the years, the corporation had been very successful but had never paid any dividends, although it had substantial earnings and profits. June wanted to expand into another line of business as a sole proprietor but did not have the cash to do so. June decided to form B, a new corporation. She contributed all the stock of A to B. B borrowed $100,000 from a bank using A stock as collateral. B then distributed all of its stock and the $100,000 to June. How should June treat the distribution of the stock and the $100,000?

SEARCH THE INTERNET

59. Go to the IRS Web site (*www.irs.gov*) and locate instructions for Form 1120. If a corporation has less than $250,000 of total receipts and total assets at the end of the tax year, which schedules included with Form 1120 can it omit?

60. Go to the IRS Web site (*www.irs.gov*), print the first page of Form 1120, and enter the following information. Then determine Chelsea Corporation's tax owed or refund due if it made estimated tax payments of $15,000.

Chelsea Corporation (34 Chelsea Drive, Sarasota, Florida, 33456) is a calendar-year corporation; its EIN is 78–9999999 and it was incorporated on June 15, 2002. It reported the following for the current year:

Sales = $1,450,000	Pension Contributions = $28,000
Cost of Sales = $625,000	Meals and Entertainment = $12,000
Officers Compensation = $187,000	Utilities = $21,000
Salary and Wages = $266,000	Repairs and Maintenance = $14,000
Rent Expense = $48,000	Vehicle Expenses = $34,000
Taxes = $87,000	Insurance = $30,000
Depreciation = $34,000	Employee Benefit Plans = $17,000

61. Go to the IRS Web site (*www.irs.gov*) and locate Publication 538: *Accounting Periods and Methods*. How does a corporation make an election to use a 52-53-week tax year?

DEVELOP PLANNING SKILLS

62. The Cooper Corporation is trying to do some year-end tax planning due to a large bond issue that is coming due. To meet this debt payment, Cooper already has sold $4,000,000 of business assets at a gain of

$2,000,000. It is considering the sale of one of two assets: land valued at $3,000,000 with a basis of $1,250,000 or a building valued at $3,000,000 with a basis of $3,300,000. Its operating income for the current year is $2,000,000 without any asset sales. Due to prior profitable years, Cooper is subject to the alternative minimum tax and it has $4,500,000 of positive adjustments and preferences in determining its alternative minimum taxable income. Which asset do you recommend the corporation sell? Explain your reasoning.

63. One of Corbett Corporation's shareholders, Gene, is having severe financial problems due to extensive medical expenses. He has approached the company for a loan, but the other shareholders on the board of directors refuse to approve it. Gene owns 25 percent of the corporate stock with a basis of $100,000 and his brother owns 10 percent of the stock. Gene is not related to any of the other shareholders. One percent of the stock is worth $10,000. Gene needs $100,000 to pay off his current medical bills. The corporation has $100,000 in its accumulated earnings and profits account. What alternatives can you suggest to Gene and the corporation that would provide Gene the money he needs while minimizing taxes?

64. The Barnard Corporation needs additional cash to improve its facilities. It can borrow $2,000,000 from a bank at 9 percent interest for 10 years, with a balloon payment of the entire principal at the end of the 10-year period. It can issue $2,000,000 in 10-year corporate bonds paying 7.5 percent interest, but it will incur underwriting costs related to issuing the bonds of $200,000. Its third alternative is to issue $2,000,000 in preferred stock that will require annual dividend payments of 5 percent. The stock will be callable at the end of 10 years at 102. The costs of issuing the preferred stock will only be $50,000. Which alternative should the corporation choose? The corporation's effective tax rate is expected to be 30 percent for all relevant years, and the corporation uses a 6 percent discount rate for all of its financial analyses.

65. The Overseas Corporation has taxable income of $250,000 before either a deduction for foreign taxes paid or the foreign tax credit. It paid foreign taxes of $75,000 on foreign income of $300,000. Assuming the corporation cannot carry the foreign tax credit back to any prior year, and the availability of carryforwards is uncertain, should the corporation take the deduction or the credit for the foreign taxes paid?

ANSWERS TO TEST YOURSELF

1. c. **41.8 percent**. The corporate tax on $250,000 of income is $80,750 [($150,000 × 39%) + $22,250]. The shareholder's tax on the $100,000 distribution is $23,800. ($80,750 + $23,800)/$250,000 = 41.82%.

2. c. **$30,050**. Taxable income = $120,000 ($156,000 – $36,000). Tax = [($20,000 × 39%) + $22,250] = $30,050. Capital loss can only offset capital gain.

3. c. **$315,000**. $500,000 taxable income – $170,000 income tax + $15,000 excess tax depreciation – $40,000 additional meals and entertainment expense + $10,000 tax-exempt income.

4. c. **$9,750**. AMTI is $160,000 ($190,000 – the exemption of $30,000). Regular tax on $100,000 of income = $22,250. Tentative AMT = $32,000 ($160,000 × 20%); AMT = $9,750 ($32,000 – $22,250).

5. b. **$250 dividend; $50 capital gain.**

Appendix 9A Exempt Organizations

Organizations whose purpose is to serve the public are classified as tax-exempt (or simply *exempt*) organizations. An **exempt organization** does not pay tax on its income, and persons who donate to such organizations may be permitted a charitable contribution deduction.[92] To be completely free from tax, the corporation must be an exempt organization as specified in Section 501(c), and it must meet all requirements for tax-exempt status.[93] If it fails to meet these requirements on a continuing basis, it may either lose its status, or it may be assessed an income or excise tax.

Some of the more common organizations qualifying for exempt status are

1. Organizations operated exclusively for religious, charitable, scientific, literary, educational, and testing-for-public-safety purposes, as well as those operated to facilitate national and international amateur sports competitions (for example, churches, schools, Consumers' Union, and Olympics).
2. Civic leagues operated exclusively to promote social welfare (garden clubs and athletic little leagues).
3. Fraternal associations operating under the lodge system (Elks Club and Moose Lodges).
4. Credit unions and cooperative telephone and electric companies.
5. Trusts established to pay supplemental unemployment benefits.

Exempt organizations normally operate as corporations (incorporated under the laws of one of the states) or as trusts. All but churches must notify the IRS that they are applying for tax-exempt status.[94] The organization's purpose must be to serve the good of the public at large (for example, a tax-exempt hospital) or for the social welfare of a segment of society (an exempt society benefiting AIDs sufferers). The organization must continue its exempt purpose, or it forfeits exempt status.

Example 9A.1

Wilbur formed a tax-exempt organization that solicited grants and public funds to purchase land for a large garden. The organization's volunteers raised vegetables for donation to the various food banks around the city for six years. In the seventh year, Wilbur took over all the gardening and sold the produce to local groceries. Because the organization has abandoned its exempt purpose, it loses its tax-exempt status.

A tax-exempt organization can be assessed taxes when it engages in prohibited transactions. The two most common activities are engaging in unrelated businesses and transactions that benefit disqualified persons.[95] If the organization engages in an unrelated business, it can be assessed an unrelated business income tax. Transactions with disqualified persons are subject to punitive excise taxes.

Unrelated Business Income Tax

An exempt organization is assessed the **unrelated business income tax (UBIT)** if it regularly carries on a trade or business that is substantially unrelated to the organization's exempt purpose, except for organizations in which

1. volunteers perform substantially all the work (the local literary guild has a retail bookstore open to the general public).
2. the business sells primarily donated merchandise (Goodwill stores).
3. its activities are of a religious, charitable, educational, scientific, or literary nature and the business primarily benefits members, clients, students, or patients (college bookstores, hospital flower shops).

A business is substantially unrelated to the exempt purpose of an organization if the sales of goods or services do not make a significant contribution to its exempt purpose.[96]

Example 9A.2

The local art museum rents out its gallery space for weddings and receptions when it is normally closed. Renting this space does not contribute to the general public's ability to learn about and enjoy art at the museum.

UBIT is assessed when the exempt organization regularly carries on a business that competes with for-profit businesses. If it is not taxed on this income, its operating costs are lower, putting the for-profit business at an economic disadvantage. Factors considered in determining if an activity is regularly carried on include the frequency and manner in which the activity is pursued.[97] Sales of cookies by

[92]Many tax-exempt organizations are qualified charities, but numerous exclusions apply; for example, the NFL and a city's chamber of commerce do not qualify.

[93]Qualified pension, profit sharing, and stock bonus plans, as well as qualified state tuition programs, are also tax-exempt organizations.

[94]Other exempt organizations with gross receipts not exceeding $5,000 do not have to notify the IRS.

[95]Lobbying expenditures are generally disallowed and may cause loss of exempt status. §504.

[96]§511 and 513. Income from bingo games is not UBIT if the games of exempt entities are legal, even though the games sponsored by for-profit entities are not.

[97]§512(a)(1) and Reg. §1.513-1(c).

Girl Scouts and of candy by baseball teams are examples of occasional sales exempt from the UBIT.

UBIT is assessed on the exempt organization's **net unrelated business income**, the business's gross income reduced for all deductible expenses incurred in operating the business as if it were a regular corporation. It is then subject to certain positive and negative modifications. Unrelated business income (UBI) is modified for charitable contributions, certain payments from an 80 percent controlled organization and net passive income (dividends and interest, net of related expenses).[98] The organization also has a $1,000 exemption. The tax is assessed on the organization's unrelated business income at the regular corporate tax rates.

	Gross unrelated business income
Less	Deductions
Plus or minus	Modifications
Less	$1,000 exemption
Equals	Unrelated business income
Times	Corporate tax rate
Equals	Unrelated business income tax

EXAMPLE 9A.3

The Tree Planting Civic Organization, an exempt organization, has $5,500 of gross unrelated business income. It has $3,200 of deductions related to the earning of this income. It has no modifications. Tree Planting has $1,300 of UBI after its $1,000 exemption ($5,500 – $3,200 – $1,000). It pays a tax of $195 ($1,300 × 15%) on this income.

Exempt organizations normally file Form 990: *Return of Organizations Exempt from Income Tax*, which is due on the 15th day of the 5th month after the close of the organization's tax year. If it is required to pay UBIT, then it must also file Form 990-T: *Exempt Organization's Business Income Tax Return*.[99]

Excise Taxes on Certain Transactions

An excise tax is levied on any excess benefit transaction in which a disqualified person participates, such as a bargain purchase or personal use of the organization's assets. A **disqualified person** is anyone who can substantially influence the activities of an exempt organization. The excise tax is levied on the disqualified person and any exempt organization manager who also participates and knows the transaction is tainted.

The excise tax is 25 percent of the excess benefit (up to a maximum of $10,000) for the disqualified person and 10 percent for the manager. A 200 percent excise can also be assessed if the disqualified person fails to correct the transaction.[100]

EXAMPLE 9A.4

John, a friend of the exempt organization's controller, buys some property valued at $2,000 for $500 from the exempt organization. John's excess benefit is $1,500. He can be assessed an excise tax of $375 ($1,500 × 25%), and the controller can be assessed an excise tax of $150 ($1,500 × 10%). If John fails to pay the additional $1,500 or return the property, he could have an additional excise tax of $3,000.

Private Foundations

Exempt organizations are classified as **private foundations** if they are not supported by or operated for the general public as a whole but have a more narrow focus for their activities.

EXAMPLE 9A.5

The Fletcher family established a corporation in the name of a deceased relative who had been a math educator. The purpose of the corporation was to solicit money primarily from family members to provide scholarships for women who are studying to become high school math teachers. Fletcher Corporation is a private foundation.

A private foundation excludes 501(c)(3) organizations that receive a major part of their support from the public or governmental units such as churches, schools, hospitals, and related entities. To be excluded from the private foundation category, an exempt organization must meet an external support test and an internal support test. The external support test requires the organization to receive more than one-third of its annual support from the general public, governments, or other exempt organizations. Support includes membership fees, contributions, and grants. The internal support test limits interest, dividends, rent, royalty, and unrelated business income (net of tax) to one-third of the corporation's total support.

EXAMPLE 9A.6

Wilton, Incorporated is an exempt organization that has the following revenues:

Interest and dividend income	$50,000
Contributions	20,000
Membership dues	60,000
Total	$130,000

External support = $80,000/$130,000 = 62 percent
Internal support = $50,000/$130,000 = 38 percent

Wilton meets the external support test but fails the internal support test because internal support exceeds one-third of its total revenue. Thus, Wilton is a private foundation.

[98]§ 512.

[99]Churches and exempt organizations with annual gross receipts not exceeding $25,000 are not required to file Form 990. If they exceed $1,000 in gross UBI, however, they must file the 990-T. Since 2008, small tax-exempt organizations whose gross receipts are $25,000 or less may be required to electronically file Form 990-N, also known as the e-Postcard.

[100]§ 4958.

A private foundation is subject to taxes on its investment income, for failure to distribute its income, for excess business holdings, for investing in speculative assets, and for participating in transactions with disqualified persons. The excise tax on investment income is only 2 percent, but the initial excise taxes on the other activities range from 5 to 15 percent. A second round of excise taxes of up to 200 percent can be imposed if corrective actions are not taken.[101]

EXAMPLE 9A.7

Boone, Inc., a private foundation, failed to distribute $20,000 of unexpected income at the end of the year. Boone is assessed an excise tax of $3,000 ($20,000 × 15%). If it fails to distribute the $20,000 when the excise tax is assessed, it can be assessed an additional investment income excise tax of $20,000 ($20,000 × 100%).

PROBLEM ASSIGNMENTS

CHECK YOUR UNDERSTANDING

1. What can cause an exempt organization to lose its exempt status?
2. What alternatives does the federal government have when an exempt organization engages in a prohibited transaction?
3. Why is an exempt organization taxed on its unrelated business income?
4. Distinguish between an unrelated business and a related business for an exempt organization. Suggest examples.
5. What are at least three examples of prohibited transactions?
6. What distinguishes a private foundation from other tax-exempt organizations?
7. How does a private foundation reduce the excise tax on a prohibited transaction?

APPENDIX 9B

MULTISTATE ISSUES

This text focuses on federal taxation but an awareness of the principal state tax issues is important for a more complete understanding of how corporations are taxed in the United States. The principal state taxes relevant to corporations are income and sales taxes, particularly if the corporation does business in several states.[102] The increasing importance of these taxes is reflected in the growth of state and local tax (SALT) practices in public accounting.

Income Taxes

Forty-five states assess some type of income tax on corporations.[103] Rates typically range from 4 to 10 percent. In place of the income tax, some states impose a franchise tax. A **franchise tax** is an excise tax based on the right to do business or own property in the state. Whether the tax is called an income tax or a franchise tax, the tax is usually determined based on corporate income.[104]

Most states piggyback on the federal system by beginning their computation of state taxable income with the corporation's federal taxable income. Piggybacking on the federal system is particularly disadvantageous, however, when Congress amends the Internal Revenue Code and reduces taxable income (for example, by increasing or accelerating deductions). To minimize the immediate impact on state tax revenues, many states adopt a fixed version of federal tax law by defining state taxable income computed under the Internal Revenue Code in effect as of a specific date. This allows state legislatures time to study the impact of changes on state revenue before adopting them. Although most states eventually adopt the changes to the Internal Revenue Code, considerable delays are common. Tax practitioners cannot assume that any recent changes to the Internal Revenue Code automatically apply to the determination of state taxes.

State taxable income is determined by modifying federal taxable income. Although modifications differ from state to state, common adjustments include the following:

- *State and local income taxes*—Deductible when computing federal taxable income; usually not deductible in computing state taxable income.
- *Interest income earned on state and local bonds*—Some states tax all income from municipal bonds, while others tax only other states' obligations, exempting their own obligations.
- *Interest income on federal notes or bonds*—States imposing direct income taxes usually exclude this income; states imposing a franchise tax usually include it.
- *Dividend received deduction*—Most states allow a dividend received deduction, but it usually differs from the federal deduction.

[101]§§4940–4945.

[102]Corporations are also subject to tangible (operating assets and inventory) and intangible (accounts receivable and securities) property taxes in most states.

[103]The states that do not impose some type of corporate income tax are Nevada, South Dakota, Texas, Wyoming, and Washington. A few states impose a gross receipts tax on corporations instead of an income tax such as the franchise margin tax imposed by Texas and the commercial activity tax imposed in Ohio. Michigan imposes both a business income tax and a modified gross receipts tax.

[104]A few states impose their franchise tax on a corporation's stock value or net worth, either in addition to or instead of a tax on corporate income if it results in a higher tax.

- *Net operating losses*—Some states disallow loss carrybacks; the carryforward period may be shorter than the federal carryforward in other states.

A corporation is subject to income tax in the state in which it is organized and in any other state in which it does sufficient business to create nexus. **Nexus** is the connection between a state and the business that the state is seeking to tax. This connection can be established through physical presence of corporate property in the state or the presence of employees in the state.

EXAMPLE 9B.1

Brickell Corporation sells its products nationwide through mail order catalogs and the Internet. Brickell's corporate headquarters and principal production facilities are located in Florida. It also has production facilities and warehouses in Texas and Oregon. Brickell Corporation has nexus with Florida, Texas, and Oregon. Assuming that Brickell has no physical presence in other states, Florida, Texas, and Oregon are the only states that can assess an income tax against it.

When a corporation has nexus in several states, each state can tax only the percentage of the corporation's income based on the business allocated to that state. Although the computation differs from state to state, most states use the three-factor allocation formula of sales, payroll costs, and tangible property. Some states place more weight on the sales factor, while others weigh these factors equally.[105]

EXAMPLE 9B.2

Southeastern Corporation does business and has nexus in States X and Y. Its sales, payroll costs, and tangible property located in each state are as follows:

	SALES	PAYROLL	PROPERTY
State X	$800,000	$315,000	$540,000
State Y	$800,000	$135,000	$360,000
Total	$1,600,000	$450,000	$900,000

Based on the above dollar figures, the percentages for the three factors are as follows:[106]

	SALES	PAYROLL	PROPERTY	TOTAL
State X	50%	70%	60%	180%
State Y	50%	30%	40%	120%
Total	100%	100%	100%	

If each factor is weighted equally, the apportionment formula computes the average of the three factors so that the apportionment percentage for State X is 60 percent (180%/3) and the apportionment percentage for State Y is 40 percent (120%/3). Southeastern Corporation allocates 60 percent of its income to State X and 40 percent to State Y.

Nonbusiness income, such as interest, dividends, rent and royalties, is taxed in one state only. Nonbusiness income is usually taxed by the state where the corporation is domiciled or the state where the underlying property is located or used.[107]

Income tax planning for multistate corporations usually involves shifting income from high-tax states to low-tax states by outsourcing some functions to eliminate nexus in a state or by shifting assets from one state to another. Businesses considering expanding or relocating facilities should measure the impact this will have on the amount of income apportioned to the state. For example, a corporation planning to expand should avoid a state whose apportionment formula weighs property and payroll factors heavily. The expansion of plant and employees can increase the percentage of total income subject to tax in that state.

If payroll is a major factor, replacing employees with independent contractors may reduce this factor in a high-tax state if independent contractors are excluded from the payroll factor. An accurate recordkeeping system that carefully tracks the location to which goods are shipped can also assist in reducing the overall sales taxed. For example, a business ships goods to a customer that has locations in two different states, one in which the business is taxed and one in which it is not. Carefully tracking goods shipped to the nontax state and shipping as many goods as possible to this location can significantly reduce taxes.

If a business has only a limited connection with a high-tax state, it may be possible to eliminate nexus. For example, assume providing tangible business assets to a sales representative in a high-tax state creates nexus; the business may be able to eliminate its connection with that state if the sales representative purchases the assets and the business simply reimburses him or her for the business-related use of the asset.

S corporations also need to consider whether the state recognizes S status. Most states recognize flow-through entities and tax the individual owner.[108] A

[105]Because of the variation in allocation formulas between states, some corporations may have more than 100 percent of their total taxable income subject to state income taxes.

[106]The percentage for each factor is determined by dividing the dollar amount of the item attributable to that state by the total dollar amount for that factor. For example, payroll for State X is $315,000. Dividing $315,000 by the total payroll costs of $450,000 means 70 percent of all payroll costs were incurred in State X.

[107]The corporation's domicile is not always the state of incorporation. The domicile is the principal place from which the business is managed or directed.

[108]Not all states have individual income taxes, so income from flow-through entities in those states may go untaxed. Alaska, Florida, Nevada, South Dakota, Texas, Washington, and Wyoming do not impose individual income taxes. Additionally, New Hampshire and Tennessee only tax certain types of interest and dividend income.

few states, however, subject S corporations to corporate income tax.[109]

Sales Taxes

Forty-five states charge sales taxes that typically range from 3 to 7 percent.[110] In addition, many local governments (cities and counties) impose local sales taxes. As a result, the United States has more than 7,400 different taxing jurisdictions. Sales taxes are imposed on gross receipts from retail sales or leases of tangible personalty. The retailer is responsible for collecting and remitting sales taxes to the appropriate state and local tax authority.

Some retail sales are exempt from sales tax. Exempt items typically include food, prescription drugs, real property, intangible property, and most services; however, the determination of items subject to sales tax varies greatly from state to state. Multistate retailers must determine not only the appropriate sales tax rates (which may vary within a zip code due to local sales taxes) but also determine which items are subject to tax in each location.

Nexus is as important a concept for application of the sales tax as it is for income tax. A state can require an out-of-state business to collect sales tax only if it has nexus with the state. The exact definition for sales tax nexus may differ from that of income tax nexus; a business could have nexus in a state for sales tax and not for income tax or vice versa. For example, the presence of employees soliciting sales within a state may create sales tax nexus but not income tax nexus.

Each state that imposes a sales tax also imposes a companion use tax. A **use tax** is imposed on the use of property brought into a state when sales tax was not paid in the state of purchase. A use tax is self-assessed and usually has the same rate as the sales tax. Without a use tax, purchasers would have an incentive to make purchases from out-of-state businesses to the detriment of in-state businesses.

Example 9B.3

JX Corporation operates in a state that imposes a 6 percent sales and use tax. JX purchases office supplies over the Internet from an out-of-state supplier for $2,000. JX pays no sales tax. If JX had purchased its supplies from the local office supply store, it would have been charged a sales tax of $120 ($2,000 × 6%). JX should file a use tax return, paying the $120 use tax to its state because the supplies will be used within the state.

Most states have difficulty collecting use taxes from individuals (except for automobiles that require registration with the state). Collection from businesses is much easier to enforce because most states regularly audit businesses in their state for compliance with sales and use tax laws.

PROBLEM ASSIGNMENTS

CHECK YOUR UNDERSTANDING

1. The partner from your local public accounting firm tells you the firm has a growing SALT practice. What is a SALT practice?
2. The 2010 Tax Relief Act amended the Internal Revenue Code by allowing a 100 percent bonus depreciation deduction for certain qualifying acquisitions. Does this mean that states immediately adopted this depreciation provision for computing taxable income for their state? Explain.
3. What is nexus?
4. Suntan Corporation sells its products nationwide over the Internet. It has production facilities, warehouses, and offices only in the state of Florida. It has sales in excess of $600,000 for the year to customers in Arizona. It has no physical presence in Arizona. Can Arizona assess state income tax on Suntan Corporation for the sales made to Arizona customers?
5. When a corporation has nexus in several states, can each state tax 100 percent of the corporation's income? Explain.
6. What is a use tax?

[109] S corporations may be subject to some form of corporate income or business tax in California, Michigan, New Hampshire, New Jersey, Tennessee, Texas, and Washington.

[110] The states that do not impose a statewide general sales tax are Alaska, Delaware, Montana, New Hampshire, and Oregon. Of these, Alaska and Montana allow localities to charge local sales taxes. New Mexico imposes a gross receipts tax that is passed through to the consumer so that it resembles a sales tax. States that do not have a general sales tax may still impose a limited form of sales tax. For example, Oregon imposes a sales tax on lodging, Montana imposes a sales tax on lodging and rental vehicles, and New Hampshire imposes a sales tax on meals, lodging, and rental vehicles.

chapter

10 Sole Proprietorships and Flow-Through Entities

CHAPTER OUTLINE

This chapter examines the operations of sole proprietorships, partnerships, and S corporations. Each of these entities has advantages and disadvantages, and the taxpayer must sort through these issues to determine which entity best meets the taxpayer's needs.

Although each of these entities passes its income through to the owners for taxation rather than being taxed directly, significant differences exist. The owners' liability exposure, their ability to deduct losses that the entity passes through, and the tax treatment should the entity dissolve all differ for these entities.

Variations of the partnership form include general partnerships, limited partnerships, professional limited partnerships, limited liability companies, and professional limited liability companies. Each has its own advantages and disadvantages.

Certain corporations meeting specific corporate and shareholder restrictions can elect S corporation status. S corporations pass their income through to their shareholders for taxation similar to partnerships. S corporations retain several of the characteristics of regular C corporations but also have their own unique features.

At the end of this chapter, the basic picture of formation, operation, income distribution, and dissolution should emerge for the sole proprietorship, partnership, S corporation, and C corporation. When this information is fully integrated with the taxation of owners, taxpayers can make decisions that will minimize taxes and maximize wealth.

KEY CONCEPTS

- ★ Sole proprietorships, partnerships, and S corporations all have the advantage of one level of tax on business income.
- ★ The tax laws consider a sole proprietorship and the sole proprietor as one taxpayer.
- ★ Partners' and S corporation shareholders' bases increase for income items flowing through to them and are reduced for loss items. Liabilities undertaken by a partnership increase the basis of some or all of the partners; liabilities undertaken by an S corporation do not increase shareholder basis.
- ★ The deductibility of losses by partners in partnerships and S corporation shareholders is limited to their bases and amounts at risk. The passive loss rules further limit partners' or S corporation shareholders' deductions for their passive losses unless they have an equal amount of passive income or they have disposed of the activity.
- ★ Partners in a partnership and S corporation shareholders can withdraw income on which they have been taxed, with no additional tax consequences, as long as they have bases in their partnership interests or S corporation stock.

SETTING THE STAGE—AN INTRODUCTORY CASE

For eight years, Robert Winesap has operated Sparkling Cleaners, a dry cleaning business, as a sole proprietorship in St. Paul, Minnesota. During this time, he expanded his initial store to include two satellite stores, but all clothes are cleaned at the original location. He cannot expand further as the cleaning capacity at his original store is stretched to the limit. He would like to build a larger cleaning plant and establish additional store locations, but due to the recent illness of one of his children, he has no cash available and his personal debt is at its maximum.

Recently, James Buchman, the controlling shareholder of Crystal Cleaners, Inc. in Minneapolis, approached Robert to join him in a business arrangement that would allow Sparkling to build a new plant and add stores in underserved parts of St. Paul. Robert does not want to become a subsidiary of Crystal Cleaners because he wants to maintain control of day-to-day operations. Robert also found out that Crystal has two other shareholders besides James. One shareholder is James's brother, and the other is an investor who is a British citizen and resides in London. Robert is wary that at some point James could sell his controlling interest in the merged corporation to someone who would not agree with Robert's dedication to providing the best cleaning services available.

After several weeks of continuous discussions, Robert and James have agreed to form a new entity that will maintain the Sparkling Cleaners name if the form in which the business operates can meet the following conditions:

1. The formation of the new entity will have no tax consequences to Robert.
2. Robert will control the new entity; that is, he will continue to train the employees in his unique cleaning methods and to oversee the general operations so as to maintain the business's reputation.
3. Because he is worried about potential liability for past operations of Crystal Cleaners, Robert wants to be sure he is insulated from these liabilities.
4. If he so chooses, Robert wants to be able to dispose of his controlling interest in the cleaners with the least possible tax cost when he retires in approximately 12 years.

James is willing to accept the conditions that Robert has set out, but in addition he wants to be able to maintain control of his original Crystal Cleaners stores and keep them separate from Sparkling Cleaners. What factors should be considered in selecting the form of business entity for Sparkling Cleaners? At the end of this chapter we will return to this case.

INTRODUCTION TO FLOW-THROUGH BUSINESS ENTITIES

A **flow-through business entity** is an operating business whose net income (and certain other items) passes directly to the owners of the business, who then pay taxes on this net income along with their other taxable items. For example, a person who is a 50 percent partner in a partnership that reports $10,000 of net income would report $5,000 ($10,000 × 50%) of net income on his or her individual income tax return. This single level of tax has great appeal to many taxpayers.

A variety of flow-through business forms are available from which to choose, each with its own individual characteristics, from both legal and tax standpoints. They include general partnerships, limited partnerships, limited liability companies (LLCs), limited liability partnerships (LLPs), S corporations, and the most common flow-through entity, the sole proprietorship. Besides the advantage of a single level of tax on net income, each flow-through entity has certain characteristics that may make it more or less desirable than another type for a particular taxpayer. For example, both a general partnership and a limited liability company pass their income through to their owners in a similar manner for a single level of tax, but the general partners have no protection from personal liability—a benefit the members of an LLC enjoy. State laws related to flow-through entities are not consistent across all 50 states. Thus, it is important to consider state tax factors as well as nontax characteristics in selecting the form of entity. In addition, it is important to consider all factors from formation through operation and dissolution in making the choice of entity.

The Sole Proprietorship

The simplest flow-though business is the **sole proprietorship**, a business that has only one individual as the owner. Although it may have a name different from that of the sole proprietor and may receive a separate taxpayer identification number (TIN), the sole proprietorship has no identity separate from that of the owner for federal income tax purposes. (The Small Business and Work Opportunity Act of 2007 permits a partnership owned jointly by a husband and wife who file a joint return to elect to have the partnership treated as two sole proprietorships with each spouse reporting 50 percent of the business's income, gains, losses, and expenses on separate Schedule Cs.)

The owner **(sole proprietor)** has unlimited liability for the business operations; that is, the owner's personal assets are all at risk for the liabilities of the business. In spite of this, there are many sole proprietorships due to the ease with which they are formed. Legal requirements for formation are minimal, often limited to publishing a fictitious name and obtaining a business occupation license.[1] Many "casual" businesses are formed with no legal requirements at all. The number of businesses in which an individual can be involved is not restricted. Any person who is an employee has a trade or business by virtue of this employment, but many employees also have businesses on the side; for example, a chef employed by a restaurant has a separate business catering private parties on his or her days off.

Although usually small, a sole proprietorship is not limited in size. It simply must be an unincorporated business owned by one individual. Theoretically, if Bill Gates bought back all the outstanding stock of Microsoft, cancelled the stock, and surrendered the corporate charter, Microsoft could function as a sole proprietorship.

Forming the Sole Proprietorship

A sole proprietorship is formed whenever an individual starts a business with him or herself as the sole owner and chooses no other business form in which to operate. The sole proprietorship cannot be separated from the sole proprietor, however, and all of the results of the business operations are included with the sole proprietor's income tax return along with his or her other tax-related personal items.[2] In addition, the business must have the same tax year as the owner (most likely, the calendar year). The sole proprietor must apply to the IRS for permission to change his or her own tax year if he or she wants to change the tax year of the business.

The taxpayer may use either the cash or accrual method of accounting for the business. If, however, there are no separate accounting records, the business must use the cash method. It must maintain an inventory account if inventory is a material income-producing factor, but it may select its inventory valuation method. The business may select any allowable depreciation method and make the immediate expensing election, but the limit on immediate expensing first applies to the business and then to the sole proprietor. If the person has more than one sole proprietorship, he or she may make separate determinations for the method of accounting, inventory valuation, and other elective provisions.

Unlike other business forms, a sole proprietor has no capital account or tax basis in the business as a whole. He or she simply has basis in the separate business assets.

---

[1]A business uses a fictitious name when it does business under a name other than that of the owner.

[2]A separate schedule, Schedule C: *Profit or Loss from Business (Sole Proprietorship)* (or Schedule C-EZ,), part of Form 1040, includes the results of the sole proprietorship's operations.

Many sole proprietors convert some of their personal assets to business use in addition to purchasing additional assets specifically for business use. The conversion of personal-use assets to business use has no tax consequences, but their adjusted basis for cost recovery deductions is the lesser of their basis as personal-use assets or fair market value at the date of conversion.[3]

Operating the Sole Proprietorship

One of the principal stumbling blocks facing a sole proprietor is establishing that the business is a legitimate business and not a hobby. To be considered a legitimate business, the owner must have a profit motive.[4] Although this does not mean that the sole proprietorship must show a profit, the business must be carried on in a manner that indicates that profit (not the conversion of personal expenses to deductible "business" expenses) is the primary objective.

EXAMPLE 1

Carrie and Colleen are sisters who grew up riding and showing thoroughbred horses in hunter-jumper competitions. Both are now married with young families. Carrie owns two horses that she keeps on her property. She is teaching her children to ride and occasionally gives riding lessons to her neighbors' children for a modest fee. She seldom enters competitions anymore at other than the local level. Colleen, on the other hand, purchased a small stable in an affluent subdivision. She boards horses for their owners along with her own horses that she uses for riding lessons and breeding. Colleen has a regular schedule of lessons for children and adults. She also trains horses for their owners. Her students regularly enter local and regional competitions for which she earns substantial fees. She runs her own competitions for her students and other riders in the area and she continues to compete at the national level to enhance her prestige and gain additional clients. Carrie's activities would be considered a hobby while Colleen's rise to the level of a profit-motivated business.

TAX PLANNING

If the business shows a profit in three of five years, (seven years for horse-related businesses), the burden of proof shifts to the IRS to show that the business lacks profit motive and is a hobby. Selection of depreciation and inventory methods that minimize cost of goods sold and cost recovery deductions can help the owner realize a profit in three of five years to ward off an IRS challenge that the business is a hobby.

Once the taxpayer establishes the sole proprietorship as a legitimate business, all reasonable, necessary, and ordinary expenses of the business are deductible from the income of the business unless limited or excluded by a specific provision.[5] The sole proprietor uses Schedule C (or C-EZ) of his or her Form 1040 to report proprietorship income and expenses.[6] (Refer to the sample filled-in tax returns in Appendix C.) Business expenses include cost of goods sold, employee wages, depreciation, rent, supplies, and interest expense paid on funds borrowed for business activities of the sole proprietorship only. The sole proprietorship cannot be used to deduct otherwise personal expenses, nor are the results of most property transactions included on Schedule C. Investment income and expenses, charitable contributions, capital gains

---

[3]If fair market value is less than basis (the usual case) two cost recovery schedules should be maintained; on a subsequent sale, gain will be determined on basis less cost recovery, but loss will be determined on fair market value less cost recovery.

[4]Chapter 5 has a more extensive discussion of the requirements to establish a profit motive.

[5]§ 162. The at-risk and passive loss limitations discussed later also apply to the sole proprietor.

[6]A Schedule C-EZ: *Net Profit from Business* may not be used if the business has more than $5,000 of expenses, must file a Form 4562: *Depreciation and Amortization*, maintains inventory, has employees, has more than one sole proprietorship, or takes deductions for business use of the home.

and losses, and Section 1231 gains and losses[7] are reported on schedules included with the individual's tax return and not on Schedule C.

EXAMPLE 2

Joanna operates a cleaning store in the local mall. During the current year, she has revenues of $210,000 and the following expenses: employee wages, $54,000; dry cleaning supplies, $21,000; equipment repairs, $4,000; rent, $36,000; utility and telephone expenses, $6,000; depreciation, $3,000; and insurance expense, $16,000. In addition, Joanna sold her old dry cleaning machine when she purchased new ones at a loss of $1,000 and made a $500 charitable contribution to the United Way from business funds. Joanna will report $70,000 ($210,000 – $54,000 – $21,000 – $4,000 –$36,000 – $6,000 – $3,000 – $16,000) of net income from the business on Schedule C. She will report the loss on the equipment on Form 4797 rather than Schedule C, and will report the $500 charitable contribution with all of her personal charitable contributions as an itemized deduction on Schedule A.

Many sole proprietors use a part of their home as an office from which to operate their business. To take a deduction for space allotted to the home office, the area must be used *exclusively* and on a regular basis as an office. Expenses allocated to the qualifying home office space qualify as business expenses, but this deduction is limited to the taxable income from the business after deducting all other business expenses. Thus, expenses of a home office cannot be used to create or increase a loss. The sole proprietor must report these expenses separately on Form 8829: *Expenses for Business Use of Your Home*. Eligible sole proprietors should maintain documentation to substantiate these home office expenses and be prepared to justify the need for and exclusive use of the home office space in the event the return is audited.

EXAMPLE 3

Carol sells Mary Ray Cosmetics from her home. She uses her den solely to store her inventory of cosmetics, to make phone calls to her customers, and to do all the paperwork necessary for the business. The den occupies one-fifth of the total area of the house. Her mortgage interest is $8,000, taxes $2,500, and insurance $750; her allowable depreciation expense is $400. She has not had a very good year and her net income prior to deducting her home office expenses is only $2,200. Carol's allocated home office expenses are $1,600 interest, $500 taxes, and $150 insurance. She can deduct the interest and the taxes and $100 of the insurance. The remaining expenses can be carried forward and deducted in a year in which there is sufficient income.

TAX PLANNING

If the taxpayer has assets such as a computer within the home office space, the computer must be dedicated solely to the business. Using the computer for nonbusiness use will negate the solely business use for that portion of the home. The taxpayer should have a second computer for personal use or locate the computer in another part of the home. To take a deduction for any of the computer use, the taxpayer should keep a written record of the time spent on the computer for business versus personal use.

Because the proprietor and the sole proprietorship are a single taxable entity, the proprietor cannot be an employee of the business. As a result, the proprietor cannot receive a salary or participate in tax-free fringe benefits provided employees and the business cannot take a deduction for such payments made on behalf of the owner. Paying a salary or the proprietor's personal expenses is viewed as a cash withdrawal by the owner. It simply moves cash from the owner's business account to the owner's personal account and has no tax consequences to either the owner or the business.

[7]When the proprietor disposes of assets used in the business, the gains and losses are reported on Form 4797: *Sale of Business Property*. As discussed in Chapter 7, depreciation recapture on equipment sold at a gain is ordinary income with the balance Section 1231 gain.

EXAMPLE 4

Barbara operates a medical transcription business as a sole proprietorship. She has three typists who transcribe on a full-time basis and who are eligible to participate in the business-paid health insurance plan in which Barbara also participates. Barbara's net profit from the business is $100,000 before considering the following items: health insurance premium for Barbara and her three employees of $1,500 per person per year; stock sold by the business that resulted in a $4,000 long-term capital gain; interest income of $1,000; and charitable contributions of $1,500. In addition, Barbara withdrew a salary of $40,000 from the business and paid $20,000 of her personal expenses from the business cash account.

The business cannot deduct Barbara's salary, personal expenses, or health insurance premium as business expenses. The business can only deduct the health insurance premiums for her employees, reducing the net profit of the business to $95,500 ($100,000 – $4,500). Barbara will be taxed on the $95,500 income from the proprietorship, deducting the $1,500 for her own health insurance premiums for AGI. The $4,000 long-term capital gain will be reported with Barbara's other capital gains and the interest income will be reported with her other interest income. The $1,500 charitable contribution will be included with her other charitable contributions as an itemized deduction.

TAX PLANNING

A sole proprietor may be able to participate indirectly in some fringe benefits by hiring his or her spouse as an employee of the sole proprietorship. The spouse would have to meet any requirements set up by the business for employee participation in benefits, however.[8] The sole proprietor may also be able to reduce the taxable income of the business by employing his or her children. This strategy allows the proprietorship to deduct the child's wages as a business expense. If the child's earned income is less than the standard deduction ($6,100 in 2013), the child pays no income tax, making the transfer completely tax free. An additional benefit of operating as a sole proprietorship is that the owner's child under 18 is not subject to FICA taxes.

A sale of business property is viewed as a sale by the sole proprietor. The details of the sales are reported on the appropriate schedule (not Schedule C) and the net result is included on the owner's Form 1040. The sole proprietor must pay any taxes owing on gains along with the tax on net income reported by the business. A loss on property used solely by the business is recognized and deducted by the sole proprietor. If the sole proprietorship has a net operating loss for the year, the loss can offset other business income.[9] Any net operating loss that is not deductible in the current year can be carried back two years and forward 20 years.

The cash flow from property sales or business operations belongs solely to the sole proprietor. Any funds flowing to the owner from the business are tax free as he or she is taxed on the net income of the business annually regardless of cash withdrawals.

Property distributed to the sole proprietor is treated the same as cash; that is, neither the business nor the owner have any tax consequences, and the property basis carries over to the owner. If, however, the owner subsequently sells the property the owner will recognize gain or loss as long as the property has not been converted to personal use. If the property has been converted to personal use, the owner can no longer recognize any loss on the sale. If the distributed property was used for both business and personal purposes prior to the distribution, loss may be recognized on the business portion only.

[8]These fringe benefits would not be available to spouses if this were a partnership owned by both husband and wife but treated as a sole proprietorship.

[9]The net operating loss (NOL) provisions apply only to business-related losses; certain adjustments must be made for capital losses and nonbusiness deductions. For example, personal and dependency exemptions are not business expenses and are added back when computing an individual's NOL. For further discussion, refer to Chapter 11.

Self-Employment Taxes

Self-employed individuals (sole proprietors, general partners, and managing members of LLCs) must pay **self-employment taxes** on their net income from self-employment.[10] Self-employment taxes replace the employee and the employer portions of FICA (Social Security and Medicare) taxes. A self-employed individual is often surprised by the amount of self-employment taxes that are due. The taxpayer pays these taxes along with his or her income tax and may be required to adjust his or her estimated tax payments or withholding on other sources of income to cover this tax.

A separate deduction *for* AGI (a deduction taken before calculating AGI) is permitted for the employer portion of the self-employment taxes. This deduction applies not only to sole proprietors but also to partners and LLC members who are individuals and who pay self-employment taxes on income from these flow-through entities.

EXAMPLE 5

Cleo has $15,000 in net income from her sole proprietorship in 2013. Cleo's self-employment taxes are $2,119 ($15,000 × 92.35% × 15.3%). Cleo reports $15,000 in income from her sole proprietorship and deducts $1,060 ($15,000 × 92.35% x 15.3% x 1/2) *for* AGI for the employer's half of self-employment taxes [11] Cleo's AGI is $13,940. She must pay $2,119 in self-employment taxes in addition to the regular income tax on her taxable income.

PARTNERSHIPS

Businesses taxed as **partnerships** can take many forms and have a variety of owners. The Code defines a partnership as a "business, financial operation or venture . . . which is not . . . a corporation or a trust or estate."[12] From a legal standpoint, two or more persons who join together to operate a business for profit form a partnership. No formal agreement or legal process is necessary to form a partnership.

Partnerships are one of the more common business forms, partly because of this ease of entry and their flexibility. A partnership can have two or hundreds of partners. No restrictions apply to the individuals or other entities that may be partners in a partnership. Corporations, other partnerships, LLCs, and all individuals (including nonresident aliens) may be partners in a partnership.

Even though partnerships may have a broad range of appearances, the federal income tax laws treat them similarly. In addition, most LLCs are partnerships for tax purposes. Because the Code treats entities that are designated as partnerships uniformly regardless of their appearance, the information that follows regarding the tax treatment of partners and their partnerships applies equally to an LLC and its members if the LLC is taxed as a partnership. Each state, however, may define its own characteristics for partnerships and LLCs. Thus, on legal matters, state statutes should be consulted if particular characteristics are of significance.

Types of Partnerships

The two oldest forms of partnerships are general and limited partnerships. A **general partnership** is one that has only general partners. A **limited partnership** is one that

[10]Guaranteed payments to a partner, net income passed through to a general partner, and income passed through to the managing member of an LLC are generally subject to self-employment taxes.

[11]The reduction in the employee portion of self-employment taxes for self-employed individuals by the 2010 Tax Relief Act for the 2011 and 2012 tax years was not extended to 2013 by the Tax Relief Act of 2012. For a detailed discussion of self-employment taxes, refer to Chapter 4.

[12]§761(a) and §7701(a)(2).

has at least one limited partner and at least one general partner. General partners are those who are personally liable for all the debts of the partnership. A limited partner is one whose liability is limited to the full amount of his or her actual or agreed upon invested capital. A general partner has an active role in the management of a partnership and may bind the partnership with respect to third parties. A limited partner is denied these privileges. Limited partnerships are used extensively as investment vehicles, particularly for real estate development, because of their ability to pass deductible losses through to the limited partners while limiting their risk of investment loss.

The **limited liability partnership (LLP)** is a general partnership that conducts a business providing professional services. This entity protects partners from liability for the malpractice of other partners, but all partners remain liable for the general debts of the partnership.

A relatively new and very popular entity that limits owner's liability is the **limited liability company (LLC)**. All 50 states now have provisions for the creation and recognition of these entities. In many respects, the LLC looks like a corporation, as it is an entity that is separate and distinct from its owners. Its owners, called *members*, have the same type of limited liability afforded corporate shareholders. From a tax standpoint, no other business structure provides the flexibility of the LLC. Since 1997, LLCs can choose to be taxed as partnerships or corporations, for federal tax purposes. If the LLC does not elect to be taxed as a corporation, its tax status defaults to that of a partnership.[13] An operating agreement that meets the statutes of the state in which it is formed governs an LLC. The members generally can amend the operating agreement at will. The ownership structure is also flexible, allowing different classes of ownership carrying different rights to vote on management questions and to share in the entity's profits and losses. Only a few states, however, allow an LLC to have only one member. If the LLC has only one member, it cannot be taxed as a partnership.[14] Most states also permit professional service organizations to operate as LLCs designated as **professional limited liability companies (PLLCs)**. PLLCs also protect members from liability for malpractice of another member. In addition, they protect the members from the general liabilities of the business in much the same manner as corporate shareholders are protected.

Advantages and Disadvantages of Partnerships and LLCs

The primary advantage of selecting the partnership form and electing partnership treatment for an LLC is that the earnings of the entity are taxed only once—at the investor/owner level.[15] This avoids the double tax faced by corporations. Partnership and LLC earnings flow through to the owners regardless of any actual distributions they may receive. Thus, they have to pay taxes on business income, even if they receive nothing from the business with which to pay the taxes. Losses also flow through to the owners and may offset their other income, subject to the at-risk and passive activity loss rules.[16] The rules for the allocation of profits and losses are very flexible, allowing owners to make special allocations, as long as these allocations reflect economic reality.

Forming a partnership is much simpler and less costly than incorporation. No formal agreement is required for partnership formation, but the partners should have a clearly written formal agreement that spells out the details of formation, profit and loss sharing, operating policies, distribution treatment, withdrawal of a partner, sale

[13]Few LLCs elect to be taxed as corporations; however, if they do make this election they will have the advantage of allowing owners to be treated as employees for fringe benefits.

[14]Unless the corporate election is made, a single member LLC owned by an individual is taxed as a sole proprietorship; if owned by a corporation, it is treated as a corporate branch.

[15]If the investor/owner is a corporation, the earnings flow through to the corporation and are taxed along with the corporation's other taxable income.

[16]The passive activity and at-risk rules are discussed later in this chapter.

of a partnership interest, and, finally, dissolution of the partnership. The completion of the desired document may require the services of both an accountant and an attorney.

A major disadvantage of a partnership is that the general partners have unlimited liability for debts of the partnership. All general partners participate in the management of the partnership, and this may make it more difficult to carry on business in an orderly manner. The transfer of partnership interests can be very complex and may affect partnership operations long after the transfer dates. Finally, several events may trigger an unexpected termination of the partnership, such as the bankruptcy of a general partner.

Forming an LLC requires a much more formal process because it is an entity created under state law. The LLC must file some form of articles of organization and an operating agreement with the state of formation, and the costs associated with this are similar to those incurred to form a corporation. Even though an LLC elects tax treatment as a partnership, not all states recognize this election, and some may treat the LLC as a corporation for state tax purposes.

A partnership's general partners and the managing and other active members of an LLC must pay self-employment taxes on the net income passed through to them. Limited partners and LLC members who are only investors in the LLC do not pay self-employment taxes. All partners and LLC members, however, avoid the payment of self-employment taxes if the partnership or LLC activity is limited solely to rental real estate.

TAX PLANNING

Partners and LLC members cannot be employees of these entities, and they cannot participate in most tax-free fringe benefits available to employees. Payments by the partnership or LLC for fringe benefits such as medical or life insurance are either guaranteed payments or distributions to the partners. They are not deductible expenses of the entity. If the partner's (or member's) spouse is legitimately employed by the partnership (LLC), the business may pay for some fringe benefits through the spousal relationship (similar to the sole proprietorship).

Entity versus Aggregate Concepts

Two opposing concepts allow for the flexibility and complexity for which the partnership form is noted. The **entity concept** views the partnership as separate from the partners and allows a partner to sell property to the partnership and recognize gain or loss on the sale. The **aggregate or conduit concept** views the partnership as an extension of the partners and is the reason partners are liable for the debts of the partnership and share gains and losses from operations. These concepts should be kept in mind when examining the formation, operation, and dissolution of a partnership.

Partnership Operations

The general rules for determining the tax effects of operating a partnership apply to general and limited partnerships and to limited liability companies taxed as partnerships.[17] A partnership that is an electing large partnership may aggregate a number of the items that are normally separately stated to simplify the reporting of these partnership operations at the partner level.[18]

Partner's Basis and Capital Account

For tax purposes, a partner will have basis in the partnership interest based on the tax rules. In addition, the partner will also have a capital account for accounting purposes. Similarly, the partnership will maintain separate records for tax and financial accounting purposes. When property is contributed to a partnership, the tax records and the

---

[17]§761(a).

[18]An electing large partnership is one that has at least 100 partners at the end of its preceding tax year and elects to use the simplified reporting procedures.

partner's basis in the partnership will reflect the basis of the property contributed as discussed in Chapter 8. The partner's capital account and the partnership's financial records, however, will be based on the fair market value of the property contributed. Thus, each partner's capital account will show the partner's claim on the net book value of the partnership assets. The difference between the partner's capital account and the partner's tax basis is due to the unrecognized (deferred) gain or loss on the contributed property.[19]

Partner's Interests

A partner has a proportionate interest in the partnership's assets and a right to share in a percentage of the partnership's profits and losses, as set forth in the partnership agreement. The profit and loss sharing percentages may differ, and neither has to be the same as the partner's interest in the capital (assets) of the partnership. Unless the partners agree otherwise, profit and loss interests will be equal, and this interest will be the same as the partners' interests in the capital of the partnership. This is the assumption upon which the discussion of partnership operations is based.

Selection of a Partnership Tax Year

Profits and losses flow through to the partners on the last day of the partnership's tax year. The partners must report their share of profit or loss on their income tax returns in the year with which or within which the partnership tax year ends. If the partner's tax year is different from the partnership's tax year, the partner's tax on some portion of the partnership's income is deferred. Due to this potential deferral, Section 706(b) requires the partnership to use one of the following:

1. The tax year of its partner(s) who own a majority interest.
2. If the majority-interest partners do not have the same tax year, the tax year of all the principal partners (partners with at least a 5 percent interest in the partnership).
3. If neither 1 nor 2 applies, the month that provides the least aggregate deferral of income must be the tax year-end.[20]

Alternatively, a partnership also may choose a tax year that satisfies the requirement of the IRS that the tax year selected has a legitimate business purpose, is a natural business tax year, or allows no more than a three-month deferral of flow-through items from the required tax year.[21]

EXAMPLE 6

Bob and J Corporation are partners in the BJ Partnership. Bob is a calendar-year individual; both J Corporation and the partnership have January 31 fiscal year-ends that coincide with their natural business years. For the tax year ended January 31, year 2, the partnership reports $20,000 of income. J includes its share of income on its return for the tax year ending on January 31, year 2, which is due April 15, year 2. Bob reports his share of income on his year-2 calendar year tax return,which is due April 15, year 3.

---

[19]If the contributed property is later sold at fair market value, the gain or loss recognized is allocated to the contributing partner to the extent of the deferred precontribution gain or loss. Gain or loss in excess of the precontribution gain or loss is allocated to all partners in their profit and loss ratio. For accounting purposes, gain or loss will be allocated to the partners' capital accounts only if the selling price differs from the fair market value when contributed.

[20]This method uses a calculation, weighted by each partner's profits percentage, to determine the year-end that will result in the least deferral of flow-through items to the partners as a whole.

[21]In this latter case, the taxpayer must agree to a prepaid noninterest-bearing deposit of estimated deferred taxes.

Partnership Operating Results

A partnership files only an information return, **Form 1065**: *U.S. Partnership Return of Income.*[22] This return includes a **Schedule K**: *Partners' Shares of Income, Credits, Deductions, Etc.*, which reflects the aggregate of all the partnership's separately stated items and its aggregate income or loss for the year, and a separate **Schedule K-1**: *Partner's Share of Income, Credits, Deductions, Etc.* for each partner in the partnership, which reflects each partner's share of these separately stated items and aggregate income for the year.[23] The partnership never pays taxes with this return.[24]

Separately stated items are those items that cannot be aggregated into net income because they are subject to some form of special treatment, such as netting, limitation, or restriction at the partner level (for example, the limit on charitable contributions to 50 percent of an individual's adjusted gross income). **Partnership net income** or bottom-line income is the aggregate of all items that are *not* separately stated. Separately stated items include the following:

- Capital gains and losses—both short-term and long-term
- Section 1231 gains and losses[25]
- Dividends and interest and their related expenses
- Section 179 deductions
- Charitable contributions
- Medical and dental expenses paid by the partnership for partners
- Passive income
- AMT preferences and adjustment items
- Self-employment income

EXAMPLE 7

JOED Partnership (owned by individuals Joe and Ned) reports the following items of income and expense for the current tax year:

Fee income	$40,000
Tax-exempt interest income	3,000
Rent expense	10,000
Depreciation expense	12,000
Section 179 expense	16,000
Charitable contribution	3,000

The tax-exempt interest, Section 179 expense, and the charitable contribution are separately stated items. Net income is $18,000 ($40,000 – $10,000 – $12,000). On their individual tax returns, Joe and Ned each report $9,000 of net income from the partnership, $1,500 of tax-exempt interest, $8,000 of Section 179 expense, and a $1,500 charitable contribution.

TAX PLANNING

Partners must report their share of partnership items even if they receive no distributions from income with which to pay taxes. Partners who may need money with which to pay taxes on income that is passed through should see to it that the partnership agreement permits withdrawals of cash from the partnership for this purpose.

[22] Sample filled-in forms are in Appendix C.

[23] When a partner contributes appreciated or depreciated property to the partnership, §704(c) requires special allocations of depreciation expense and of gain or loss on disposition to the contributing partner.

[24] A partnership may be assessed certain penalties and interest for failing to file its return on a timely basis.

[25] Depreciation recapture is included with aggregate income, however.

Partner's Basis Account

A partner establishes outside basis at the formation of the partnership or other acquisition of the partnership interest.[26] According to the aggregate concept, every transaction that occurs at the partnership level is deemed to occur at the partner level. Their combined effects are summarized and allocated to each partner on the last day of the partnership tax year. The partner increases his or her partnership interest basis for the share of taxable gains and income that flows through and reduces basis by the share of deductible expenses and losses.[27] Basis also increases for a partner's share of any tax-exempt income earned by a partnership and decreases for "expenditures of the partnership not deductible in computing its taxable income and not properly chargeable to the capital account."[28]

EXAMPLE 8

Water Corporation is a 40 percent partner of BATH Partnership, both on a calendar-year basis. Water has a basis in its partnership interest of $100,000 before BATH reported the following items of income and loss.

	PARTNERSHIP TOTAL	PARTNER'S 40% SHARE
Ordinary income	$200,000	$80,000
Long-term capital gain	80,000	32,000
Charitable contributions	10,000	4,000
Tax-exempt interest	15,000	6,000

Water's basis in its interest in BATH is $214,000 (beginning basis of $100,000 + $80,000 income + $32,000 long-term capital gain + $6,000 tax-exempt interest – $4,000 charitable contributions) at the end of the year.

Effects of Liabilities

The amount and composition of liabilities held by the partnership affect a partner's basis in the partnership interest. The aggregate concept treats these liabilities as liabilities of the partners. Section 752 recognizes the risk that a partner assumes as a result of these liabilities by increasing a partner's basis for a proportionate share of liabilities of the partnership or any partnership liabilities assumed by the partner and decreases a partner's basis when these liabilities are discharged.[29] To prevent a negative basis, a partner must recognize gain equal to the amount that the decrease in the partner's share of the liability exceeds his or her basis.

EXAMPLE 9

Ray is a 40 percent partner in the NCCL Partnership. When Ray's basis in his partnership interest is $18,000, NCCL borrows $50,000 for its business operations. Ray's share of this debt is $20,000 ($50,000 × 40%), and his basis increases to $38,000.

NCCL then retires the $50,000 obligation when Ray's basis in his partnership interest is only $14,000. Ray must recognize $6,000 gain because his share of the liability discharged, $20,000, exceeds his $14,000 basis in the partnership interest by $6,000.

[26] Outside basis is a partner's basis in his or her partnership interest. Partnership formation and basis determination at formation are discussed in Chapter 8.

[27] § 705(a).

[28] § 705(a) also provides special rules for the treatment of depletion.

[29] § 752(a) and (b). The partner is assumed to contribute money to the partnership equal to a proportionate share of the liability of the partnership or the liability assumed. The partner is assumed to withdraw money from the partnership to pay the liabilities.

The mechanics of basis adjustment are relatively straightforward, but the precise effect of liabilities on a partner's basis depends on two factors: (1) the type of liability the partnership undertakes, whether recourse or nonrecourse and (2) the type of partner, general or limited.

Recourse debts are those for which the creditor can look not only to all the assets of the partnership for repayment but ultimately to the assets of all the general partners if the partnership does not satisfy its obligations. Because only general partners are responsible for recourse debt, only their partnership interest bases are increased for a proportionate share of increased debt, usually based on their loss-sharing ratio.[30] A limited partner's basis neither increases nor decreases for the partnership's recourse liabilities.

Nonrecourse debts are those for which the creditor can look only to the collateral for repayment of the debt on default by the debtor; that is, the creditor has no recourse against any of the partners for liabilities greater than the value of the property that secures the debt. Because the partnership must pay this debt with partnership profits, with neither general nor limited partners being held personally liable, a nonrecourse liability increases both types of partners' bases using their profit-sharing ratios.[31]

EXAMPLE 10

The Bad Dog Partnership has one general partner, BD, and two limited partners, AC and EF. BD's basis prior to incurring any debt is $13,000. AC and EF have bases of $30,000 each. The three are equal partners, each with a one-third profit- and loss-sharing ratio. To facilitate the development of some land, the partnership obtains a nonrecourse loan of $120,000 secured by the land and a $50,000 recourse loan for working capital needs. Only BD increases his basis for the $50,000 recourse loan as the limited partners are not held liable for this debt. Each partner, however, increases his or her basis by $40,000 for the one-third share of the nonrecourse debt that must be paid from partnership profits. Thus, BD has a basis of $103,000 ($13,000 + $50,000 + $40,000), and AC and EF will have bases of $70,000 ($30,000 + $40,000) as a result of these debts.

Loss Limitation Rules

The amount of loss that a partner can deduct on his or her individual tax return is directly tied to the partner's basis in the partnership interest. The at-risk and passive loss rules, enacted to remedy some of the abuses arising from tax shelters, further restrict the deductibility of losses for partners who are individuals or closely held corporations.

General Loss Rules

The **general loss limitation** provisions of Section 704(d) limit the loss that any partner can deduct on his or her tax return to the basis that the partner has in the partnership interest. A partner deducts losses only after all other adjustments are made to the partner's basis for gains, income, and distributions.[32] Losses that are disallowed due to insufficient basis carry forward until such time as the partner has sufficient positive basis resulting from other events, such as contributions to capital or flow through of income. Because debt increases partners' bases, partnerships that finance their operations with substantial amounts of debt allow greater loss deductions by the partners.

[30] The actual allocation of recourse liabilities uses a hypothetical liquidation scenario under which all liabilities become payable in full and all assets (other than property contributed to secure a liability) are considered worthless. Recourse liabilities are allocated to the partners to the extent they would be required to contribute cash to restore a capital account deficit.

[31] Some nonrecourse debt allocation involves two steps before an allocation according to the profit-sharing ratio. A more detailed discussion of these allocations is beyond the scope of this introductory material.

[32] Reg. §1.704-1(d)(2).

EXAMPLE 11

Juan invests $10,000 cash in Risky Ventures Partnership for a 10 percent limited partnership interest. Risky Ventures takes out $1,000,000 in nonrecourse financing and incurs $400,000 in losses its first year. Juan's share of the partnership liabilities increases his basis to $110,000 [$10,000 cash investment + ($1,000,000 × 10%)]. Juan's share of first-year loss is $40,000 ($400,000 × 10%), all of which may be currently deductible as he has sufficient basis due to the partnership debt. If Juan is in the 39.6 percent marginal tax bracket, he could save $15,840 ($40,000 × 39.6%) by deducting this loss. This would generate a positive cash flow of $5,840 ($15,840 tax savings–$10,000 initial cash investment) the first year. If additional losses are incurred in future years, he will still have $70,000 basis remaining ($110,000 basis – $40,000 first-year loss) against which he can deduct these losses.

At-Risk Rules

In the late 1960s and early 1970s, many taxpayers invested in tax shelters with losses that they deducted against profits from their other forms of income, including salaries and investment income. In 1976, Congress reacted to this abusive use of these tax shelters by instituting a set of **at-risk rules** to limit the deductibility of losses. These rules, which apply to individuals or closely held corporations who are partners and S corporation shareholders, limit the deduction by these particular entity owners to those amounts for which they are "at risk." That is, the debt must be satisfied with the owner's personal assets for the owner to be at risk. Thus, regardless of the effect of a nonrecourse debt on a partner's basis in his or her partnership interest, the partner does not have to satisfy the debt with any personal assets and is not at risk for the debt. The at-risk rules limit the deductibility of losses to partners' bases *reduced* by their share of any nonrecourse debt.[33] Similar to the general loss limitation provision, any loss not deductible because of the at-risk provision carries over until the partner is again at risk.

EXAMPLE 12

Refer to the information in the previous example. Juan's basis increased to $110,000 due to the partnership's $1,000,000 nonrecourse loan. Although Juan has sufficient basis to deduct the $40,000 loss, the at-risk rules now prevent him from deducting more than $10,000 of his loss. As a limited partner, he is at risk for his initial investment of $10,000 only.

Passive Loss Rules

Neither the basis nor at-risk rules eliminated what Congress perceived as abusive deductions from real estate and other tax shelter activities, so it enacted Section 469. This provision includes a complex set of limitations affecting the deductibility of **passive losses**, losses from passive activities in which the parties have limited participation. These rules, aimed only at individual taxpayers and closely held corporations,[34] are designed to prevent loss deductions by taxpayers who are primarily investors in a business, such as limited partners. These rules prevent the affected taxpayers from deducting losses from passive activities against active income (salaries, wages, and income from businesses in which the taxpayer materially participates) and portfolio income (interest and dividends). They can deduct passive losses only against income from other passive investments. *Expanded Topics* at the end of this

[33]§465(b)(6). The at-risk rules do not apply to nonrecourse debt secured by real property used in the partnership's real estate activity and made by a qualified lender or a government body; that is, the partner is considered at risk for a share of this type of nonrecourse debt.

[34]§469(a)(2). Closely held corporations are allowed to offset net passive losses against portfolio income. For passive loss purposes, a corporation is considered closely held if five or fewer shareholders own 50 percent or more of its stock at any time during the last half of the tax year.

chapter provides an introduction to the passive loss rules that primarily affect individual taxpayers who are owners of flow-through entities.

Partnership Distributions

Guaranteed and Nonguaranteed Payments

A partner who is working in the partnership may require payments similar to a salary to pay for living expenses. A partner who has invested in a partnership may also require partnership distributions for the use of the assets invested. **Guaranteed payments** are distributions a partnership is obligated to make to a partner for the performance of services or for the use of capital. These payments must be required regardless of the partnership results of operations and are accounted for as if they are salary or interest payments. If the payments are dependent upon partnership operations, they are not guaranteed payments. The partnership agreement should include provisions for guaranteed payments, if such payments are expected to be made. A partnership agreement can be amended as necessary, however, to add, change, or delete guaranteed payments.

EXAMPLE 13

June, Jim, and Jerry are equal partners in a partnership. June works full time in the business and is guaranteed a payment of $30,000 annually for this work. Jim invested a significant amount of money in the partnership and is paid an amount equal to 5 percent of his beginning capital balance each year. Jerry, who is the manager of the partnership, receives a payment of 25 percent of the net accounting profit after all expenses and the payments to June and Jim are made. In the current year, the partnership's accounting profit prior to June and Jim's payments is $125,000. Jim's beginning capital balance is $300,000 and he is due a payment of $15,000. The partnership's accounting net income is $80,000 ($125,000 – $30,000 – $15,000). Jerry then receives a payment of $20,000 ($80,000 × 25%). The partners will then share the remaining $60,000 equally, with each allocated $20,000 of the remaining income. If the partnership had no net income or a loss, Jerry would receive nothing. Regardless of other factors, June will receive her $30,000 and Jim his $15,000 as they are guaranteed payments. Jerry's payment is dependent on partnership income and is not guaranteed.

Although these payments may be made during the year, they are all accounted for at year-end and included in the income of the partner along with the other results of operations at that time. In the example above, June would include a total of $50,000 in income, Jim a total of $35,000, and Jerry a total of $40,000.

When the partner is allocated a guaranteed payment, this allocation increases the partner's basis in the partnership. The actual payment of the guaranteed payment then reduces the partner's basis. Thus, the net effect of a guaranteed payment on a partner's basis is zero. If, however, the partnership fails to make the actual payment, the partner must still take the guaranteed payment into income, increasing basis for this amount. Basis is reduced only for the actual amount received. (This is alternatively viewed as the full payment being made with the partner contributing to capital the amount he or she did not receive.)

Nonliquidating Distributions

When a distribution is made that is not a guaranteed payment, basis is a critical factor. If the partnership distributes cash (with or without any additional distribution of property) and the cash distributed *exceeds* the partner's basis in his or her partnership interest, gain is recognized to the extent this cash distribution exceeds this basis. Any property received in addition to the cash takes a zero basis in the partner's hands. If both cash and property are distributed but the cash is *less than* the partner's partnership interest basis, the cash received first reduces basis with any remaining basis allocated to the property up to the amount of the property's basis to the partnership.

If only property is received (no cash) and the partnership interest basis exceeds the total bases of the property received, the partner takes a carryover basis in the property equal to its basis in the partnership's hands. If the partnership interest basis is less than the total bases of the property received, the partnership interest basis must be apportioned to the property received according to their relative bases. On a **nonliquidating distribution**, a partner never recognizes loss regardless of how much money or property the partnership distributes.[35]

EXAMPLE 14

George receives $50,000 cash and a car valued at $20,000 as a distribution from a partnership when his basis is only $34,000. Amy receives a piece of land from the partnership that has a value of $50,000 but a basis of $40,000. Her basis in her partnership interest is $52,000. These are nonliquidating distributions. George is required to recognize a gain of $16,000 on the receipt of the money in excess of his basis, his basis in his partnership interest is reduced to zero, and his basis in the car is also zero, deferring recognition of any additional gain until the car is sold. Amy reduces her basis in the partnership interest to $12,000 ($52,000 – $40,000) and will have a $40,000 basis for the land; she recognizes no income. If Amy's partnership basis had been only $27,000, she would reduce her basis in the partnership interest to zero and would have a $27,000 basis for the land, deferring any gain until she sells the land.

If a partner receives income-producing property (for example, inventory) as part of a distribution, after allocating basis to any money received, basis is allocated to this property before it is allocated to any other property.[36]

Liquidating Distributions

Liquidating distributions are similar to nonliquidating distributions, but there is one significant difference—a partner may recognize loss if the total basis of the cash and ordinary income property received is less than his or her partnership basis.[37] If a partner receives any other property, the partner allocates basis remaining in the partnership interest to that property.[38] In this manner, any loss that the partner has is postponed until such time as the properties are disposed of.[39] In many instances, this property is no longer business property in the hands of the partner (it becomes personal-use property) and the loss is never recognized.

EXAMPLE 15

Walter receives a liquidating distribution from a partnership of $4,000 in cash, inventory valued at $7,000 with a basis of $5,000, and land worth $10,000 with an $8,000 basis. At the time of the distribution, Walter's basis in his partnership interest is $45,000. Walter allocates the first $4,000 of his basis to the cash, the next $5,000 of basis to the inventory, and the remaining $36,000 to the land. If he sells the land without using it for personal use, he will recognize loss on the difference between this $36,000 basis and its selling price. If he converts the land to personal use, the opportunity to recognize the loss will be lost.

TAX PLANNING

Similar to nonliquidating distributions, a partner recognizes gain only if the cash received exceeds the basis of the partner's partnership interest. The remaining basis is allocated to ordinary income property and then to all other property. Distributions of property, other than money, can effectively postpone gain recognition and may be desirable, but property distributions can also postpone or prevent loss recognition when a partnership liquidates. Partners should carefully plan whether to distribute or sell assets (distributing the cash received) on a partnership liquidation to obtain the optimum tax consequences.

[35]A nonliquidating distribution reduces but does not eliminate a partner's partnership interest.

[36]Complex allocation formulas require allocation adjustments for any property whose basis is more than its fair market value.

[37]A liquidating distribution liquidates a partner's entire partnership interest so he or she ceases to be a partner.

[38]If several properties are received with total basis less than the partnership basis, a complex allocation is required to apportion the basis among the various properties.

[39]This treatment recognizes the aggregate theory of the partnership.

If a partnership makes disproportionate distributions to its shareholders, the tax treatment of these distributions becomes far more complex. A disproportionate distribution is one in which ordinary income assets and other assets are distributed in different proportions to the partners. To determine the tax effect, a disproportionate distribution requires the partnership to first assume that it makes a proportionate distribution to the partners followed by an exchange of assets between partners and the partnership to achieve the disproportion. This procedure can result in additional tax consequences to the partners, the partnership, or both. Further discussion of this complexity is beyond the scope of this introductory text.

Selling a Partnership Interest

Normally, a partnership interest is a capital asset, and any gain or loss recognized on the sale of a partnership interest is a capital gain or loss. The aggregate theory that assumes each partner owns a share of each of the partnership's assets causes the tax result to be more complex than a simple sale of a capital asset. If the partnership owns ordinary income assets including inventory and unrealized receivables (so-called *hot assets*), the sale must be partitioned between the hot assets and all other assets to prevent the partner from converting gain on the sale of ordinary income assets to capital gain through the sale of the partnership interest. Unrealized receivables include the receivables of a cash-basis taxpayer and depreciation recapture.[40] Inventory as used in this regard includes all partnership property except money, capital assets, and Section 1231 assets.[41]

EXAMPLE 16

Helen sells her 25 percent partnership interest to Hal for $20,000 when her basis in her partnership interest is $15,000. The partnership has the following assets: $10,000 cash; inventory with a basis of $30,000 and a fair market value of $60,000; investment land with a basis of $20,000 and a fair market value of $10,000. Overall, Helen would appear to have a $5,000 gain on the sale, but the $20,000 received must be apportioned across Helen's one-quarter interest in each of the assets.

Asset	Adjusted Basis	FMV	Amount Received	Gain or Loss
Cash	$2,500	$2,500	$ 2,500	-0-
Inventory	7,500	15,000	15,000	$ 7,500
Land	5,000	2,500	2,500	(2,500)

Due to the apportionment requirement, Helen will actually have to recognize ordinary income of $7,500 on the inventory ($15,000 – $7,500) and a capital loss of $2,500 ($2,500 – $5,000) on the sale of the land. Although she still has a net $5,000 gain, the type of gain and loss recognized may significantly affect her tax consequences.

There are several other considerations when disposing of a partnership interest. First, when the partner sells an interest, the partnership allocates income up to the date of sale only to the selling partner. The partnership allocates the income from that point on to the purchasing partner. In addition, the partnership's tax year closes with respect to the selling partner; thus, all items pass through to him or her as of the date of sale. To further complicate a sale, the selling partner no longer has a share of liabilities of the partnership. This reduction in liabilities is treated as additional cash received on the sale of the partnership interest and must be included in the determination of gain or loss. The purchasing partner then becomes liable for the selling partner's share of liabilities and will include this in his or her basis in the partnership interest purchased.

[40] §751(a)(1).

[41] §751(d). The term *inventory* as used here is broad enough to include unrealized receivables, too.

EXAMPLE 17

The ABC Partnership owns only one asset, a building with a basis of $500,000 and a fair market value of $600,000. The building is encumbered by a $300,000 mortgage. Wally sells his one-third interest in the partnership with an outside basis of $175,000 for $100,000 in cash. Wally receives a total of $200,000 for his partnership interest, however—the $100,000 cash plus $100,000 (1/3 × $300,000) debt reduction. He recognizes a $25,000 gain on the sale ($200,000 - $175,000). The new owner of the partnership interest has a basis of $200,000 in the interest—$100,000 cash plus the assumption of the $100,000 one-third interest in the mortgage.

S CORPORATION CHARACTERISTICS

An **S corporation** is truly a unique business entity. It is formed under state law in the same manner as a C corporation, and the requirements for a nontaxable formation are identical. The S corporation does not veer from its path as a regular corporation until the shareholders elect to be treated as an S corporation. If the S election is made, the corporation becomes a flow-through entity, passing its income and losses through to its shareholders for taxation at the shareholder level. Thus, an S corporation appears to have the best of all worlds. It is a regular corporation from a legal standpoint and its shareholders enjoy limited liability. For tax purposes, it avoids the double taxation of a C corporation.

Unlike the partnership, an S corporation may, under certain circumstances, have to pay an income tax. It also continues to have some characteristics of a C corporation because it must follow the Code provisions for C corporations for redemptions and liquidations. The treatment of its cash and property distributions is unique to an S corporation, however.

Eligibility Requirements for S Status

To elect S status, a corporation must meet a number of restrictions on its operating characteristics and shareholders, and the corporation must continue to meet these restrictions throughout its life; if it fails to do so, the S election terminates.

Corporate Restrictions

An S corporation must be an eligible **domestic corporation**, that is, one that is formed in one of the 50 states of the United States. It cannot be a foreign corporation. Financial institutions using the reserve method for bad debt, insurance companies (taxed under Section L of the Code), and Puerto Rican and possession corporations are not eligible corporations.[42]

TAX PLANNING

The corporation can have only one class of stock issued and outstanding, although it can have more than one class of stock authorized.[43] More than one type of common stock may be issued if the only difference is in the voting rights attached to the stock.[44] The difference in voting rights allows one group of shareholders to retain voting control over the corporation while permitting other shareholders to benefit on an equal basis from corporate earnings.

An S corporation must pay attention to the terms of any debt instruments, as the reclassification of debt into a second class of stock can cause termination of an S election. Under the safe harbor provision for debt, loans should have a specific maturity date and required interest payments, should not be convertible into stock, and should be held by an individual.[45] Shareholder debt held in the same proportion as stock and

[42] § 1361(b).
[43] § 1361(b)(1)(D).
[44] § 1361(c)(4).
[45] § 1361(c)(5).

shareholder loans of up to $10,000 are exempt from reclassification as a second class of stock.

Shareholder Restrictions

Only individuals, estates, and certain trusts and not-for-profit organizations may be shareholders of an S corporation.[46] Individuals must be either residents or citizens of the United States.[47] Nonresident aliens are not allowed to own stock in an S corporation.[48]

The corporation can have no more than 100 shareholders (75 for years prior to 2005), but family members owning stock may elect to be counted as only one shareholder. When a shareholder dies, the deceased shareholder's family members and the estate are still one shareholder for meeting the 100-shareholder requirement. Although few S corporations have more than several shareholders, a corporation close to the 100-shareholder limit must closely watch sales to multiple shareholders or unrelated heirs inheriting stock from a deceased shareholder.[49]

TAX PLANNING

To prevent taxpayers from circumventing the 100-shareholder limit, a partnership or C corporation cannot own S corporation stock, but an S corporation can own a partnership interest or own stock in a C corporation. Thus, if two S corporations together own 100 percent of a partnership or a C corporation, more than 100 persons can effectively own an operating business through S corporations.

Making the S Election

An eligible corporation makes the **S election** on Form 2553: *Election by a Small Business Corporation* by the 15th day of the third month of the year for which the election is to be effective. Thus, a calendar-year corporation must file its election by March 15, 2013, to be effective for 2013 (a retroactive election), and it must have been an eligible corporation from the beginning of the year. If the corporation fails to meet that deadline, the election is effective at the beginning of 2014 (a prospective election). A prospective election (effective for the following tax year) can be made any time during the current tax year. The IRS has authority, however, to accept a late filing of an S election if the corporation can show reasonable cause for the delay in filing the election.[50]

The shareholders of the S corporation must give written consent to the S election. If the corporation has just formed, the forming shareholders sign the consent form. If the corporation is an existing corporation, a retroactive election requires that all the shareholders who would be affected by the election must consent to it.[51] Persons who become shareholders after the filing of the election do not have to consent. They are presumed to consent to the S election, or they would not have become shareholders.

Terminating the S Election

An S election can terminate by a positive election, or it can terminate by violating one of the S corporation requirements—either deliberately or inadvertently.

Termination Election

To affirmatively revoke an S election, shareholders holding more than 50 percent of the voting rights of the stock must vote to revoke the election. The revocation may be

[46] Tax-exempt organizations described in Sections 401(a), 501(c)(3), and 501(a) are eligible shareholders.

[47] § 1361(c).

[48] § 1361(b)(1)(C).

[49] For tax years ending prior to 2005, S corporations were allowed to have only 75 shareholders with husband and wife only allowed to be considered one shareholder. The American Jobs Creation Act of 2004 increased the number of permitted shareholders to 100 and allows relatives within 6 generations to elect to be treated as one shareholder. In addition, former spouses may also continue to be counted as one shareholder.

[50] § 1362(b). The IRS can also ignore an error in filing of the S election if the error was inadvertent, the corporation acted as an S corporation, and it would have qualified except for the error.

[51] § 1362(a)(2).

retroactive or prospective. To be retroactive, the **revocation** must be made by the 15th day of the third month of the tax year (March 15 for a calendar-year corporation), and it must not specify a later effective date. If this requirement is met, the revocation is effective from the beginning of the tax year.[52] A prospective revocation request may specify and be effective for any date on or after the date the request is filed.[53] If no date is specified, the revocation is effective as of the first day of the next tax year.

Example 18

BH Corporation, a calendar-year S corporation, has three shareholders, each holding one-third of the corporate stock. The corporation's shareholders decide that an S election is no longer advantageous. Only two of the shareholders are required to sign the revocation request that is filed by March 15 for the revocation to be effective as of the first of the year. If the request is filed after March 15 but no other date is specified, it will be effective at the beginning of the next tax year. If a revocation request is filed on May 31, to be effective July 1, the corporation will no longer be an S corporation as of July. It will file a short-period return as an S corporation for the period of January 1 through June 30 and a short-period return as a C corporation from July 1 through December 31.

Terminating Events

If a corporation fails to meet one of the requirements for being an S corporation (such as exceeding the 100-shareholder limit), its S election terminates as of the day before the **terminating event**.[54] If the corporation can show that the terminating event is inadvertent and corrects the defect as soon as possible after its discovery, the IRS can allow the S election to continue as if the event never occurred.

An S corporation's election terminates at the beginning of the fourth year if it is assessed a passive income tax for three years in a row and it has earnings and profits from a C corporation tax year.[55] The S corporation passive income tax is briefly addressed later.

S Corporation Operations

When accounting for the operations of an S corporation for tax purposes, there are few differences between an S corporation and a partnership. The S corporation separates its income, gain, loss, and expense items into those items that are aggregated to form net income and into separately stated items. The separately stated items are almost identical to those of partnerships. S corporation net income passed through to its shareholders is not subject to self-employment taxes, however. If the shareholders are also employees of the corporation, they and the corporation are subject to FICA (Social Security and Medicare) taxes on their salaries.

The S corporation files a **Form 1120S**: *U.S. Income Tax Return for an S Corporation* to report its operations. It also prepares a Schedule K: *Shareholders' Shares of Income, Credits, Deductions, Etc.* and a Schedule K-1: *Shareholder's Share of Income, Credits, Deductions, Etc.* for each of the shareholders to report net income and separately stated items in total and each shareholder's share, respectively. A comparison of the Form 1120S and Form 1065 and their respective Schedule Ks and K-1s illustrates how similar these reports of their operations to shareholders and the taxing authorities are.[56] S corporations' tax years are generally restricted to the calendar year to prevent deferral of income by the individual shareholders.[57] S corporation income and loss allocations are based solely on the number of days and the percentage ownership of each shareholder. To make the allocations, the S corporation prorates all income and loss items to

[52]§ 1362(d).
[53]§ 1362(d)(1)(D).
[54]§ 1362(d)(2).
[55]§ 1362(d)(3).
[56]Sample filled-in tax forms are in Appendix C.
[57]Similar to the partnership, the S corporation can make a Section 444 election that allows up to a three-month deferral of income, but a deposit to cover the income on the deferred taxes is required.

each day of the tax year, then multiplies the daily figure by the number of days held and the percentage ownership of the shareholder.[58]

EXAMPLE 19

John and Amy are currently 40 percent and 60 percent shareholders, respectively, in JA Corporation, an S corporation. At the beginning of the year, each was a 50 percent owner, but on January 31, Amy purchased a 10 percent interest from John. During the past tax year of 365 days, the corporation had net income of $36,500 and separately stated Section 1231 gains of $7,300. JA Corporation first allocates $100 of net income and $20 of Section 1231 gain to each of the days of the year. It then allocates $14,910 ([$100 × 31 × 50%] + [$100 × 334 × 40%]) of net income and $2,982 ([$20 × 31 × 50%] + [$20 × 334 × 40%]) of Section 1231 gain to John.[59] It allocates $21,590 ([$100 × 31 × 50%] + [$100 × 334 × 60%]) of net income and $4,318 ([$20 × 31 × 50%] + [$20 × 334 × 60%]) of Section 1231 gain to Amy. Thus, John will report ordinary business income from the S corporation of $14,910 and $2,982 of Section 1231 gain and Amy will report $21,590 of income and $4,318 of Section 1231 gain on their individual tax returns.

A shareholder of an S corporation can receive a salary as an employee, and both the employee and the corporation must pay their share of FICA taxes on the salary. S corporation shareholders do not pay self-employment taxes on the net income of the corporation that flows through to them. Shareholders owning more than 2 percent of the stock may not participate in most tax-free employee fringe benefits, such as medical insurance and group term life insurance.[60] If a greater than 2 percent shareholder receives these fringe benefits from the corporation, the corporation cannot deduct the cost of the fringe benefit unless the shareholder treats the value of the fringe benefit as additional compensation.

An S corporation must pay reasonable compensation to shareholder-employees. Unlike a regular corporation in which shareholder-employees try to receive very large salaries in lieu of dividends, an S corporation's incentive is to pay low salaries and then make nontaxable distributions to shareholder-employees. It is particularly important in both personal service corporations and family-held corporations for employee-shareholders to receive appropriate salaries because of the risk that the IRS will reclassify nontaxable distributions as salary (resulting in additional payroll taxes).

Loss Limitations

The same limitations apply to the shareholders of an S corporation as apply to partners in a partnership when determining if the losses flowing through to them are deductible currently:

1. The shareholder must have basis in the corporate interest.
2. He or she must be at risk.
3. If the losses are passive, the shareholder must have other passive income against which to offset the losses, or the activity generating the losses must have been disposed of in the reporting year.[61]

There is a striking difference here between a partnership and an S corporation, however. An S corporation shareholder is not allocated any basis due to recourse or nonrecourse debt undertaken by the S corporation. To be able to deduct losses in excess of basis in the corporate stock, the shareholder must have lent money directly

[58]If there is a significant ownership change, the shareholders may elect to use the interim closing of the books method to allocate income and loss.

[59]With an S corporation sale, the day of sale is attributed to the seller.

[60]This is the same as the treatment of partners in a partnership.

[61]Like partnerships, the shareholder must first have basis before the at-risk rules are encountered, and both apply before the passive loss limitation rules. The *Expanded Topics* section at the end of the chapter explains the passive loss deduction rules.

to the S corporation. The shareholder can then deduct losses to the extent he or she has basis in this debt.[62] The tax advantage of a current deduction must be weighed against the opportunity cost of lending the money, however. When debt basis has been reduced due to losses, income in a subsequent year first reinstates the basis of the debt before the stock basis is increased. If the corporation pays off the debt before basis has been restored, the shareholder has gain to the extent the payments exceed debt basis.

EXAMPLE 20

Jason owns 50 percent of the Beach Corporation, an S corporation. Due to prior losses, his stock basis is now only \$4,000. The company forecasts another loss of \$24,000, \$12,000 of which will be allocated to Jason, for the current year. Jason can deduct only \$4,000 of the loss unless he lends the company money to create debt basis. If Jason lends \$8,000 to the company (creating \$8,000 of debt basis), he will be able to deduct the remaining loss against this basis, and he will have a zero basis in both his stock and the debt. If Jason is in the 25 percent tax bracket, the additional \$8,000 loss deduction will reduce his taxes by \$2,000. If he must borrow the money at 9 percent interest and the corporation will pay him only 5 percent interest on the loan, lending the corporation money will cost him \$320 [\$8,000 × (9% – 5%)] annually.[63] (When Beach has income, Jason's basis in the debt will be restored before his stock basis.)

If the shareholder expects a lower marginal tax rate in future years, he should consider contributing capital or loaning funds to the corporation before year-end so he can get the tax benefit from the loss now. Conversely, if the shareholder expects a higher marginal tax rate in future years, deferring the tax benefit of the loss to a future year may be beneficial.

TAX PLANNING

Basis Adjustments

Each shareholder must keep track of his or her stock basis similar to the tracking of partnership interest basis by a partner. The shareholder's basis begins with the original contribution to capital or the purchase price of the stock. Any subsequent contributions to capital and all separately and nonseparately stated items of income and gain (including tax-exempt income) increase basis, while all nontaxable distributions and all separately and nonseparately stated deductions and losses (including nondeductible items) reduce basis, but never below zero. In a manner similar to partnerships, income items increase stock basis at year-end before distributions, then loss items reduce basis.

A distribution of cash or property or both from an S corporation to its shareholders is normally a nontaxable event, as long as it is a distribution of income that has already been taxed to the shareholder and the fair market value of the cash and property received does not exceed shareholders' bases in their stock. The fair market value of any distribution that exceeds a shareholder's basis is taxed as gain on the sale of the shareholder's stock.

EXAMPLE 21

Bob has a basis of \$1,300 in his S corporation stock after he adjusts it for the flow through of net income of \$600. He then receives a \$400 distribution from the corporation. The \$400 is a tax-free return of income that has already been taxed, and he simply is required to reduce his stock basis to \$900 (\$1,300 – \$400). If, instead, he receives a \$1,500 distribution, only \$1,300 of the distribution is tax free because that reduces his basis to zero. The remaining \$200 is taxable as gain as if he had sold his stock.

[62]The stock basis and at-risk amount are usually the same for S corporation shareholders.

[63]Additional factors such as the future income potential of the corporation and its ability to pay back the loan must also be considered before a final decision can be made.

The Accumulated Adjustments Account

The **accumulated adjustments account (AAA)** is a corporate-level account that tracks a corporation's undistributed, but previously taxed, earnings that are available for distribution to shareholders without additional tax. Adjustments to this account are similar to the adjustments to the shareholders' basis accounts, except that they reflect income and loss items in the aggregate whereas each shareholder must track his or her basis individually. Unlike the basis account, however, the accumulated adjustments account may have a negative value if loss (and expense) items exceed income and gain items. Distributions, however, may neither create nor increase a negative amount in the AAA.

EXAMPLE 22

Jim received a distribution of $1,000 from his S corporation. His basis in his stock is $40,000. The corporation's AAA account before the distribution is $2,000. The corporation has income items for the year of $8,000 and loss items of $6,000. The AAA is first increased to $10,000 for the income items and reduced to $4,000 for the loss items ($2,000 + $8,000 – $6,000). Jim's $1,000 will be tax free and will further reduce the AAA to $3,000 ($4,000 – $1,000).

The taxability of shareholder distributions for a corporation incorporated after 1982 that never operated as a C corporation is determined solely by the shareholder's basis account. If the shareholder has basis in his or her stock, the distribution is not taxable. If an S corporation has earnings and profits from C corporation years or S corporation years prior to 1983, the AAA determines the extent a distribution is tax free rather than taxable as a distribution of corporate earnings and profits.[64]

TAX PLANNING

An S corporation with no earnings and profits still needs to track AAA. It can be difficult to reconstruct AAA if at some point in the future the S corporation acquires earnings and profits through the acquisition of a C corporation. When an S corporation's election terminates (and it reverts to a C corporation), the balance in the AAA at the date of conversion determines the amount of cash that the corporation can distribute to its shareholders as tax-free return of income that has already been taxed during the post-termination period.[65] Without AAA to provide this information, cash distributions would be treated as taxable dividends to the extent the corporation now has earnings and profits.

Property Distributions

A shareholder receiving a property distribution from an S corporation uses fair market value for basis in the property distributed, similar to regular C corporation dividend distributions. The corporation recognizes gain on the distribution of appreciated property but cannot deduct any loss on depreciated property. Shareholders increase the basis in their stock for the recognized gains passed through to them on the distribution of appreciated property. They then reduce the bases in their stock by the fair market value of the distribution. Thus, this gain is taxed only once at the shareholder level. Although the corporation cannot deduct losses on the distribution of depreciated property (and no loss flows through), the shareholders must still reduce their bases for the unrecognized loss. Thus, it is highly disadvantageous to distribute loss property.[66]

---

[64]The interplay between AAA, shareholder basis, earnings and profits, and distributions of appreciated property can become quite problematic, particularly where there are multiple shareholders and distributions are nonpro rata. These complications and a complete discussion of AAA are beyond the scope of this introductory material.

[65]The post-termination period is a period of at least one year during which time the corporation can still make cash distributions of income that has already been taxed to the shareholders.

[66]Property distributions during the post-termination period are taxable as dividends to the extent the now C corporation has earnings and profits; only cash can be distributed tax-free during the post-termination period from income that has been previously taxed.

EXAMPLE 23

JJ Corporation, an S corporation, distributes property valued at $10,000 with a basis of $5,000 to it sole shareholder JoJo. JoJo's stock basis is $15,000 and the corporate AAA is $10,000. The corporation recognizes the $5,000 gain ($10,000 fair market value – $5,000 basis) on the distribution and increases its AAA to $15,000. It then reduces AAA to $5,000 for the fair market value of the tax-free property distribution. JoJo's stock basis also increases to $20,000 for the $5,000 gain and is reduced to $10,000 for the fair market value of the property received. If the property's basis had been $15,000 (fair market value = $10,000), a $5,000 loss on the distribution would not have been recognized by the corporation nor would it have passed through to JoJo. Nevertheless, the corporation and JoJo would have been required to reduce AAA and basis, respectively, by $15,000—$5,000 for the unrecognized loss and $10,000 for the fair market value of the distributed property.

The S Corporation Schedules M-1, M-2, and M-3

The S corporation's Schedule M-1: *Reconciliation of Income (Loss) per Books with Income (Loss) per Return*[67] looks quite similar to a C corporation's M-1, except that the S corporation generally pays no taxes and has no contribution carryovers, so those lines are missing. The M-1 reconciles book income to net income adjusted for separately stated items passing through to shareholders. In most cases, an S corporation is not a publicly traded corporation and is not required to prepare financial statements according to generally accepted accounting principles (GAAP). Thus, few reconciling entries may be required. If the statements are prepared according to GAAP, reconciling items are similar to those explained for C corporations.

Schedule M-2: *Analysis of Accumulated Adjustments Account, Other Adjustments Account, and Shareholders' Undistributed Taxable Income Previously Taxed* reconciles the AAA account at the beginning of the tax year to the balance at the end of the year. Additional columns are provided to reconcile the other adjustments account (OAA) and previously taxed income (PTI) from pre-1983 S corporation years.[68] OAA items are those that do not affect the AAA, such as tax-exempt income and any related expenses. The net adjustments to the AAA and OAA reported on Schedule M-2 generally will equal the change in retained earnings as reported on Schedule L: *Balance Sheets per Books*, the beginning and ending financial accounting balance sheet.[69]

Similar to C corporations, S corporations that have total assets of $10 million or more must file Schedule M-3. Schedule M-3 requires a more detailed reconciliation between financial accounting net income and taxable income than reported on Schedule M-1.

S Corporation Taxes

Under normal circumstances, an S corporation does not pay taxes. Three special taxes may be imposed on an S corporation, however, if the S corporation converted from a C corporation.[70] The three taxes are the built-in-gains (BIG) tax, the excess passive investment income tax, and the LIFO recapture tax. The tax rate that is imposed on the taxable amount in all three cases is the maximum regular corporate tax rate (excluding surcharges) and is currently 35 percent.

The Built-in-Gains Tax

The **built-in-gains** or **BIG tax** is applicable to an S corporation if, at the time of its conversion from a C corporation, the total fair market value of all its assets exceeded

[67]Sample filled-in forms are in Appendix C.

[68]This discussion of S corporations excludes pre-1983 S corporations.

[69]The IRS has developed a Schedule M-3 for S corporations similar to the Schedule M-3 for regular corporations.

[70]If an S corporation acquires another corporation with C corporation earnings and profits, the excess passive income tax could apply even though the acquiring corporation has always been an S corporation.

the total bases of these assets. The excess of fair market value over total bases is the built-in gain. If, the corporation subsequently sells any of those assets at a gain, a BIG tax would be assessed unless the actual holding period exceeded the required holding period called the recognition period. To stimulate investment in new assets, the American Recovery and Reinvestment Act lowered the recognition period to seven tax years for appreciated property sold in 2009 or 2010 on which there was a built-in gain at the time of conversion to an S Corporation. Thus, the sale would have to take place in no less than the eighth year as an S corporation. The 2010 Small Business Jobs Act further reduced the recognition period to five years for 2011 and the Taxpayer Relief Act of 2012 extended this five-year period through sales taking place in 2012 and 2013. Thus, sales taking place in at least the sixth tax year after conversion to an S Corporation avoid the BIG tax in 2011through 2013. For sales prior to 2009, the built-in gains tax recognition period is 10 years, and will revert to 10 years for sales after 2013 unless Congress again extends the five-year period. The corporation applies the current maximum corporate tax rate to the built-in gain to determine the BIG tax. The tax, however, reduces the gain passed through to the corporation's shareholders.

EXAMPLE 24

M Corporation became an S corporation January 1, 2008. It had only one asset with a fair market value not equal to its basis. This asset was valued at $40,000 but had a basis of only $20,000. This asset is sold in 2012 (only the fifth tax year after the conversion) for $35,000. M's built-in gain on the date of conversion was $20,000 ($40,000 - $20,000). It's realized gain on the sale was only $15,000 ($35,000 - $20,000). Only the $15,000 realized gain is subject to the 35% corporate tax rate. The corporation pays a tax of $5,250 on the gain but the gain passed through to the shareholders is only $9,750 ($15,000 - $5,250). If the corporation sells the asset in 2013, it is no longer subject to the BIG tax as the 5-year holding period applies in 2013. If the asset is not sold until 2014, it could again be subject to the BIG tax as the 10-year recognition period could now apply. If it holds the asset until 2018 (the eleventh tax year after the conversion) it would not have to pay the BIG tax.

The Excess Net Passive Investment Income Tax

The excess net passive investment income tax only applies to an S corporation that has earnings and profits from a prior C corporation year. Passive investment income includes gross receipts from dividends, interest, annuities, passive rents, royalties, and the disposition of stocks and securities, and the net gain only from the sale of capital assets, excluding stocks and securities. The tax applies to excess net passive investment income.[71] The tax rate is the maximum corporate tax rate. The tax paid flows through to the shareholders and reduces other income passing through to them.[72]

TAX PLANNING

The S corporation needs to be particularly careful in those years in which the corporation's gross receipts are reduced despite significant asset sales, for example, when a business is contracting. Not only can the corporation be subject to this tax, but its S election terminates if it is subject to this tax three years in a row.[73]

LIFO Recapture Tax

Another tax a C corporation that maintains its inventory on the LIFO basis must consider at conversion to an S corporation is the LIFO recapture tax. This tax

[71]§ 1362(d)(3). Excess net passive investment income is passive investment income that exceeds 25 percent of the corporation's total gross receipts for the year (excess passive income) adjusted for related expenses by the ratio of net passive income to total passive income for the year (excess net passive investment income); it is limited to an S corporation's taxable income determined as if it were a regular C corporation. §§ 1374(d)(4) and 1375(a)(b).

[72]Shareholders can elect to treat a distribution first as a taxable distribution of accumulated earnings and profits rather than a nontaxable distribution from AAA to eliminate earnings and profits.

[73]The S election is terminated at the beginning of the fourth year.

applies to the LIFO recapture amount, which is the difference in the value of the inventory under FIFO and the LIFO value at the date of conversion. The rate applied is the highest corporate tax rate and is paid in four installments. The first installment is due with the corporation's final tax return as a C corporation; the next three installments are due with the tax return for each of the corporation's next three S corporation tax years.

Redemptions and Liquidations by S Corporations

The S corporation provisions contain no special rules for stock redemptions by and liquidation of an S corporation. For these provisions, the regular C corporation provisions apply. For example, a redemption is simply treated as a sale of stock by the shareholder back to the corporation. As the S corporation normally has no potential for dividend income, the complex rules designed to prevent the conversion of dividend income into capital gain are unnecessary. If the S corporation redeems the shareholder's stock for property rather than cash, the S corporation recognizes gain on appreciated property but is not permitted to recognize loss on depreciated property. (These are the same rules that apply to property distributions.) The recognized gain flows through to the shareholders who are taxed on the gain, increasing the bases in their stock.

A liquidation of S corporation stock also follows C corporation liquidation provisions; that is, the S corporation may either sell the property and distribute the proceeds to the shareholders in exchange for their stock, or the corporation may distribute its property to the shareholders. In either case, the corporation generally recognizes both gains and losses on the property it sells or distributes to the shareholders. The gains and losses flow through to the shareholders whose bases are then increased or decreased for the net gain or loss that flows through. The shareholder recognizes gain or loss on the surrender of his or her stock based on this adjusted basis. In this manner, the S corporation shareholders pay only one level of tax on liquidation.

Example 25

The Regal Corporation's sole shareholder, Peter, decides to liquidate the business due to ill health. Regal has been an S corporation since its founding 18 years ago, and Peter's basis in his stock prior to the sale or distribution of any assets is $50,000. The corporation has only two assets: One is a building with a $100,000 fair market value and a basis of $50,000; the other is land valued at $75,000 with a basis of $90,000. The corporation sells the land for $75,000 and distributes the building directly to Peter. The corporation recognizes a $15,000 loss on the sale of the land and a $50,000 gain on the distribution of the building that pass through to Peter and increase his stock basis to $85,000 ($50,000 + $50,000 gain – $15,000 loss). Peter includes this gain and loss on his own return, in addition to a gain of $90,000 ($100,000 + $75,000 – $85,000 basis) on the liquidation of his stock. Thus, in total, Peter recognizes a net gain of $125,000 ($50,000 – $15,000 + $90,000) on the liquidation, the same as the difference between the fair market value of the assets ($175,000) and his original $50,000 stock basis.

Table 10.1 summarizes various entity characteristics for C corporations, S corporations, partnerships, and sole proprietorships.

The U.S. Production Activities Deduction

The deduction of a business taxpayer's qualified production activities income was made specifically allocable to sole proprietorships as well as partnerships and S corporations by the American Jobs Creation Act of 2004. The definition of a qualifying business and the percentage deduction (3 percent in 2005 and 2006, 6 percent for 2007 through 2009, and 9 percent after 2009) are identical to the provisions outlined for regular corporations in Chapter 9. The production activities deduction is determined at the owner level, however, based on the owner's share of the corporation's qualifying production activities income and W-2 wages necessary to calculate the production activities deduction. This information is provided on each owner's Schedule K-1.

TABLE
10.1 A SUMMARY OF ENTITY CHARACTERISTICS

Characteristic	C Corporation	S Corporation	Partnership	Sole Proprietorship
Formed under provisions of state law	Yes	Yes	No	No
Tax-free formation (excluding services)	Yes, if 80% control met	Yes, if 80% control met	Yes	Yes
Operating income taxed at entity level	Yes	No, except for certain penalty type taxes	No	No
Owners receive a salary subject to FICA and Medicare taxes	Yes	Yes	No	No
Owners pay self-employment taxes	No	No	Yes, on all guaranteed payments and residual income except limited partners	Yes
Owners may participate in tax-free employee fringe benefit programs	Yes	No, if over a 2% shareholder	No	No
Distributions of entity income are tax free	No	Yes	Yes	Yes
Gain/loss recognized on nonliquidating property distributions to owners	Gain only	Gain only	Gain only if cash distributed is greater than basis	No
Gain recognized on entity liquidation	Yes	Yes	No, unless cash distributed is greater than basis	No
Loss recognized on entity liquidation	Yes	Yes	Yes, if only money and ordinary income property distributed	No

Because owners of sole proprietorships and partnerships cannot be employees for purposes of determining W-2 wages eligible for the deduction, these entities should consider converting to S corporations. If the owners take salaries from the S corporations, their salaries would be included in determining the limitation based on wages.

TAX PLANNING

COMPARISON OF TOTAL TAX BURDEN BY ENTITY

The following example compares the total taxes (income and employment taxes) paid by the entity and its owners for a C corporation, S corporation, partnership, and sole proprietorship. The entity has $500,000 of operating income before deducting salaries (or guaranteed payments). The owners of the entity are a husband and wife who own equal shares of the entity (except for the sole proprietorship that is owned by one spouse with the other spouse as an employee). The husband and wife take individual salaries (or guaranteed payments) of $125,000, with the balance of the profits distributed to the owners. The husband and wife have no other source of income, file a joint return, and take the standard deduction.

Entity Level	C Corporation	S Corporation	Partnership	Sole Proprietorship
Operating income	$500,000	$500,000	$500,000	$500,000
Less: salary expense	(250,000)	(250,000)		(125,000)
Less: unemployment taxes[74]	(840)	(840)		(420)
Less: employer FICA taxes[75]	(17,724)	(17,724)		(8,862)
Business net income	$231,436	$231,436	$500,000	$365,718
Less: corporate income tax	73,510			
Available for distribution	$157,926	$231,436	$500,000	$365,718
Individual Owner Level				
Dividend income	$157,926			
Flow-through income		$231,436	$500,000[76]	$365,718
Salary income	250,000	250,000		125,000
Less: self-employment tax deduction[77]			(20,794)	(11,946)
Adjusted gross income	$407,926	$481,436	$479,206	$478,772
Less: standard deduction plus allowable exemption[78]	$13,136	$12,200	$12,200	$12,200
Taxable Income	$394,700	$469,236	$467,006	$466,572
Individual income tax[79]	$84,168	$133,464	$134,830	$134,575

[74]Federal unemployment tax is assessed at 6% on the first $7,000 of employee wages in 2013, paid only by the employer. Refer to Chapter 4 for details on employment taxes.

[75]The Social Security portion of FICA is assessed on only the first $113,700 at a 6.2% rate for both employees and employers ($110,100 in 2012 at a rate of only 4.2% on employees only); all employer and employee earnings are subject to the Medicare tax at a 1.45% rate for 2013.

[76]Income from the partnership consists of a $125,000 guaranteed payment to each partner with the $250,000 balance of the partnership earnings also taxed to the owners. All of these earnings are subject to self-employment taxes.

[77]Self-employed individuals are allowed a deduction for AGI for the employer's portion of their self-employment tax [($113,700 Social Security limit per individual for 2013 x 6.2%) + (all self-employment income x 92.35% x 1.45%)].

[78]Standard deduction is $12,200 for all taxpayers; only corporate shareholders can deduct $936 (12% of $7,800) of their personal exemptions.

[79]Income tax for corporate shareholders = $54,478 (regular tax on $236,864) + $23,689 (15% tax on $157,026 dividends) + $6,001 (3.8% Medicare NII surtax on $157,926 dividends). Income tax on S corporation shareholders = $133,464 tax on $469,236 flow-through income. Income tax on Partners = $132,580 on $467,006 flow-through income + $2,250 (0.9% Medicare surtax on self-employment income in excess of $250,000). Income tax on sole proprietors = $132,409 tax on flow-through and salary income + $2,166 (0.9% Medicare surtax on self-employment income and salary in excess of $250,000).

Total Tax Burden				
Corporate income tax	$73,510			
Individual income tax	$84,168	$133,464	$134,830	$134,575
Unemployment tax	840	840		420
Employer's FICA tax	$17,724	17,724		8,862
Employee's FICA tax	17,724	17,724		8,862
Self-employment tax[80]			41,031	23,893
Total taxes	$193,966	$169,752	$175,861	$176,612
Effective tax rate[81]	39.79%	33.95%	35.17%	35.32%

This example does not consider the tax savings that may be achieved through use of tax-free employee fringe benefits. Employees of a C corporation and the spouse who is an employee of the sole proprietorship are eligible for the tax-free benefits discussed in Chapter 4. Partners, greater than 2 percent shareholders of an S corporation, and sole proprietors are not eligible for most of these benefits.

Expanded Topics—The Passive Deduction Limitations

When the basis and at-risk loss limitation rules failed to discourage investment in tax shelters, Congress enacted the passive loss limitation rules. These rules, which limited the deductibility of losses meeting the definition of passive, were developed to remove the incentive to invest in activities with little economic benefit other than the creation of tax deductible losses and to refocus investment on profit-making activities. Although the passive loss rules are very complex, a basic understanding of them and their relationship to flow-through entities is necessary as the majority of owners of flow-through entities are individual taxpayers, at whom these rules are primarily directed.

The **passive activity loss rules** deny deductions to taxpayers who are allocated losses from real estate activities, S corporations, and partnership operations in which they have no participation other than as investors by defining such investments as passive activities.[82] In addition, Congress defined all limited partnership interests as passive. Originally, all rental activities were also included in the definition of passive activities, but Congress later modified the definition of rental activities to exempt persons who are in the real property business. It also provided a limited deduction for taxpayers with moderate adjusted gross incomes who actively manage their rental properties.

Example 26

Dian and two 49 percent limited partners purchased a rental apartment house for $400,000. After spending $100,000 for improvements, they rented out the apartments for a total of $9,000 per month. The cash inflow from rent is $108,000 per year. Dian is paid $5,000 by the partnership to manage the building. The partnership also pays $65,000 in mortgage interest, $19,000 in taxes, and $6,000 in insurance. The depreciation deduction is $18,000. Total deductible expenses are $113,000, but the cash outflow is only $95,000. Thus, there is a net positive cash inflow of $18,000 but a deductible loss of $5,000. (Mortgage principal payments are ignored.) Each limited partner is allocated 49 percent of the loss or $2,450. Because they are limited partners, the passive loss rules prevent them from deducting these losses against nonpassive income. Dian is also allocated $100 of this loss (2 percent) and may meet the exception for rental property in which a taxpayer actively participates, allowing her to deduct all or part of this loss (as discussed later).

[80]Self-employment tax is assessed on 92.35% of earnings from self-employment income. The Social Security rate is 12.4% on the first $113,700 per individual and the Medicare tax is 2.9% on all self-employment earnings for 2013.

[81]The effective tax rate is calculated by dividing the total tax by $500,000.

[82]The passive loss rules apply to individual shareholders in an S corporation, partners in a partnership, and sole proprietors who do not meet the participation requirements.

If a taxpayer materially participates in the activity, it is not passive and losses are currently deductible against other forms of income. The general definition of **material participation** requires involvement by a taxpayer (and his or her spouse) that is "regular, continuous and substantial."[83] Two sets of rules provide bright line tests—one based on current activities and the other based on prior activities. A taxpayer may also qualify under the general standard of regular, continuous, and substantial activity, but this can be a difficult standard to meet. To be exempt from the passive loss limits, individuals and closely held corporations must meet one of the following standards for material participation:

1. Current Activity Level
   a. Taxpayer has 500 hours or more of participation during the tax year.
   b. Taxpayer's participation constitutes substantially all the activity by all persons.
   c. Taxpayer participates at least 100 hours, but no other person's participation exceeds that of the taxpayer.
   d. Taxpayer has at least 100 hours participation in more than one activity such that the aggregate participation in all qualifying activities exceeds 500 hours.
2. Prior Activity Level
   a. Taxpayer participated materially in any 5 of the 10 preceding years.
   b. Taxpayer materially participated in any three prior years, and the business is classified as a personal service activity.

A taxpayer with investments in multiple passive activities generating both profits and losses must follow several steps to determine loss treatment because only net losses from passive activities are not deductible.[84] The taxpayer first determines the income and losses from all passive activities and then nets losses against gains. If gains exceed losses, all income is included and all losses deducted. If the losses exceed gains, losses equal to gains are deductible but the excess loss is disallowed (unless subject to the rental activities exception as explained later). The disallowed loss is allocated on a pro rata basis to each loss activity, with a portion of the loss carried forward by each loss activity. The taxpayer can only deduct the losses when he or she has passive income or the activity is disposed of completely.

EXAMPLE 27

Jo has income from passive activity F of $4,000 and a loss of $6,000 from passive activity B. Jo nets the $4,000 gain against the $6,000 loss for a net passive loss of $2,000. Although Jo includes the $4,000 of passive income on her tax return, her deduction for passive losses is limited to $4,000. (These, in effect, cancel out each other, and the net effect on her income is zero.) Jo carries forward a passive loss of $2,000 for activity B.

In the next year, Jo has a loss from F of $4,000 and a loss from B of $5,000 prior to disposing of B at a $1,000 gain. She has a net loss of $8,000 [$1,000 – ($4,000 + $5,000)]. Jo deducts a loss of $6,000—B's net $4,000 loss for the current year and its $2,000 loss carryover from the prior year—as she completely disposes of B this year. Jo must carry forward F's $4,000 loss until there is passive income or F is disposed of completely.

Disallowed losses may be carried forward indefinitely. The disadvantage to the taxpayer is the timing of the loss deduction. Because of the time value of money, the longer the loss deduction is postponed, the less value it has from a tax reduction

[83] § 469(h)(1). Both spouses' activities are considered in determining if the requirements for material participation are met.

[84] The loss limitations are applied in a specific order. First, the taxpayer must consider if there is basis against which to deduct the loss. If there is basis, the taxpayer must then consider if he or she is at risk. If the taxpayer is also at risk for the loss, then and only then are the passive loss rules considered.

standpoint. There are only two ways to deduct these losses in the current tax year: (1) to have gains from other passive activities or (2) to completely dispose of the activity. If the activity is a continuing loser, it may be difficult to find a buyer for the activity at almost any selling price. It may be possible to invest in a PIG, a passive income generator, but an excessive price may have to be paid for this type of investment because of its income producing value. (In addition, there may be little guarantee that a current PIG will continue to generate income.)

TAX PLANNING

It is the taxpayer's responsibility to maintain adequate records of the time spent in an activity to establish whether the activity is active or passive. A taxpayer may want a business that is producing income to be passive so that income from that activity can offset losses from other passive activities. A taxpayer must also keep records of basis and at-risk amounts, as any loss disallowed because of these limits cannot be deducted as a passive loss regardless of the amount of passive income.

Rental Relief for Middle-Income Taxpayers

Taxpayers with adjusted gross incomes of $150,000 or less may qualify for a limited deduction for rental real estate losses even though the rental activity is passive. To be eligible for this relief, the taxpayer must own at least 10 percent of the rental activity; the owner must not be a limited partner; and the taxpayer must "actively" participate in the activity. Although **active participation** requires less time and effort than material participation under the passive loss rules, the taxpayer must still participate in the management of the property, such as setting rents, qualifying renters, and approving repairs.

Section 469 permits a deduction of up to $25,000 for losses from rental properties by qualified individuals. For the full $25,000 deduction, the taxpayer's AGI must not exceed $100,000. For every dollar that the taxpayer's AGI exceeds $100,000, the taxpayer loses 50 cents of the deduction. When the taxpayer's AGI reaches $150,000, the entire $25,000 deduction is lost.

EXAMPLE 28

Gerry is the sole owner of an apartment building and owns a 25 percent interest as a limited partner in a partnership that owns a strip mall. During the current year, he has a $10,000 loss from the limited partnership and a loss of $16,000 on the apartment building. Gerry's AGI from all sources excluding these property interests is $120,000. He is not a real estate professional and has no other passive income sources. The $10,000 loss from the limited partnership does not qualify for deduction under this limited relief provision, but Gerry can deduct $15,000 of the $16,000 loss from the apartment building. The $25,000 special deduction must be reduced by $10,000, which is 50 percent of the $20,000 his AGI exceeds $100,000. He can carry over the remaining loss to a future year.

Real Property Business Exception

When the passive activity rules were first enacted, passive rental activities included the long-term rental of property that did not require the taxpayer to provide substantial additional services; thus, this definition included most residential and commercial rental properties.[85] Many real estate professionals spend a great amount of time acquiring, renovating, and renting residential and commercial real estate properties, and they have income that often fluctuates between large gains in some years and losses in others. Thus, Congress enacted a mitigating provision for taxpayers in the real property business that allows them to deduct losses currently. To qualify, taxpayers must spend more than half their time in **real property businesses** in which they materially participate, and the time spent must equal or exceed 750 hours. This provision generally

[85]See Reg. §1.469-1T(e)(3). Only rental properties for which substantial additional services had to be provided or for which the rental periods were generally short term (for example, hotels, motels, golf courses, and car rentals) were excluded.

(but not always) eliminates persons who hold full-time positions in other occupations but who dabble on the side in real estate.[86]

EXAMPLE 29

Bob retired two years ago as a carpenter. Since then, he has acquired several rundown properties that he has renovated and rented. In the first year following retirement, he spent 400 hours overseeing and working on renovating only one property. In the second year, he bought two more properties and spent 900 hours on renovations. That year the first building was rented out completely, but many units in the other two buildings stood empty. Thus, Bob had a $13,500 loss in year 2 on all the rental properties. In year 1, Bob did not qualify as a real estate professional in the real property business. In year 2, he meets the real property business exception to the passive loss rules and can deduct his $13,500 loss.

REVISITING THE INTRODUCTORY CASE

As a sole proprietorship, Robert personally owns all the assets of his cleaning operation. To maintain control, Robert should contribute these assets to the business in exchange for at least a 51 percent interest in the new entity. Crystal Corporation will contribute cash and/or property for the balance of the contributed capital to the new entity. To meet the requirement of formation without tax consequences, they could form a regular corporation, a partnership, or an LLC that elected either partnership or corporate treatment. They cannot form an S corporation because Crystal Corporation cannot be an S corporation shareholder. (If James joined in the enterprise with Robert instead of Crystal Corporation, an S corporation could be used.) In any of these forms, Robert's business assets and Robert will be insulated from Crystal's liabilities, as it is a separate entity. (Unfortunately, any interest in the new entity that is owned by Crystal is an asset and could be seized to satisfy Crystal's debts.)

If Robert and Crystal Corporation form a C corporation or an LLC electing corporate status, they must be sure to transfer sufficient cash and property to satisfy the 80 percent control requirement to avoid gain recognition on appreciated assets transferred. If they incorporate, Robert could receive all the voting common stock, and Crystal could receive nonvoting common or preferred stock. Either option would ensure Robert's control of the entity.

If they form a partnership, the partnership agreement would have to specify that Robert has the controlling interest. The partnership form, however, cannot insulate Robert from partnership liabilities, as he must be a general partner to control the day-to-day operations of the business. (Crystal could be a limited partner to limit its liability.)

An LLC operating agreement also would have to spell out Robert's position as a controlling member. A detailed operating agreement could be written to limit Crystal Corporation's ability to dispose of its interest to someone not approved by Robert. Other than including a right of first refusal, it could be very difficult for Robert to prevent Crystal from selling its interest in the new entity to an undesirable person. Electing either corporate or partnership status for the LLC would limit Robert's liability exposure.

A significant consideration in selecting a regular corporation or an LLC (taxed as a partnership) is the double taxation of income. Although Robert may be able to take out a significant amount of the entity's earnings as salary, any distributions to him or to Crystal would be taxed as dividends. This could be particularly undesirable to Crystal because the new entity would not be a subsidiary eligible for a 100 percent dividend received deduction; thus, part (20 percent or 30 percent) of any dividend distribution to Crystal would be subject to a third round of taxes as part of Crystal's income. If, however, they leave any excess income in the entity beyond Robert's salary, then double taxation is avoided as long as it is retained in the business. The

[86]Unlike the general material participation requirements, the individual alone must perform the 750 hours for a real property business. A spouse's time is not included.

partnership LLC would allow Robert to take tax-free distributions in excess of any guaranteed payments as long as he has basis in the interest. The partnership form of LLC would also allow Crystal to take guaranteed payments for the use of the equity that it is investing in the business. The principal disadvantage of this LLC form is that all income will be taxed to Robert and Crystal as it is earned by the new entity.

Finally, Robert would like to be able to dispose of his controlling interest in 12 years with minimal tax cost. Robert would have to meet some relatively complex rules to ensure capital gain treatment on a redemption of his corporate stock in the event he could not find a buyer for all or part of his interest. It would be likely that any redemption that does not eliminate his entire interest would result in dividend income. As long as the maximum dividend tax rate remains below the ordinary income tax rate, however, this would not be as punitive as prior dividend treatment.

If he liquidates his interest in the LLC, he would be able to take cash distributions from the LLC (partnership). To the extent the LLC has ordinary income assets (also referred to as hot assets), however, he would have ordinary income rather than capital gain. If he takes property other than cash, he would be able to postpone gain recognition until disposition of the property.

As can be seen from the above discussion, the choice between the corporate form and an LLC operating as a partnership is not simple. As in many tax situations, one option will not satisfy all the desired characteristics of the taxpayer. In this case, we do not have the relative tax rates of Robert and Crystal, nor do we have information on Crystal's plans for the future. It would be essential in an actual situation like this to become far better acquainted with the relevant parties to make a more informed recommendation. While it may appear that either the LLC (partnership) or the corporate form will meet most needs, it may become clear in talking to the taxpayers that certain traits are far more desirable than others, leading the way to a decision between these two entities.

SUMMARY

Many forms of business entities are available to taxpayers. The entities examined in this chapter—the sole proprietorship, the partnership, and the S corporation—all have one level of tax on their income due to the pass-through nature of these entities. The limited partnership, PLLP, LLC, and PLLC are all variations of the general partnership for tax purposes. The income and losses that flow through these entities increase and decrease the bases of the equity interest that partners have in partnerships and that shareholders have in S corporations. It is the owners' responsibility to maintain the balances in their basis accounts.

Depending on the type of partner and the type of liability, partners in a partnership increase their bases proportionately for liabilities of the partnership. For both partnerships and S corporations, the bases that their owners have in their equity interests limit the deduction for losses passed through by the entity.

The at-risk and passive loss rules also apply to partners and shareholders to determine the deductibility of losses. The at-risk rules prevent partners from deducting some losses even if they have bases. Passive losses of an individual or a closely held corporation are deductible to the extent the taxpayer has passive income; however, all passive losses become deductible when the taxpayer completely disposes of the activity.

Nonliquidating distributions of cash or property from partnerships generally have no tax consequences to the partnership or the partner. If the partner receives cash in excess of his or her partnership interest basis, the partner recognizes gain only. There is limited gain or loss recognition on the distribution of assets by a partnership in liquidation as the gain or loss is postponed until the partners dispose of the assets received in the distribution.

An S corporation must be incorporated in one of the 50 states, have only one class of outstanding stock, and have no more than 100 shareholders. Only individuals, estates, and certain trusts can be S corporation shareholders. Individuals must be either citizens or residents of the United States.

An S corporation recognizes gain on the distribution of appreciated assets to S corporation shareholders if the distribution is either liquidating or nonliquidating. Loss on the distribution of depreciated property is recognized only if it is a liquidating distribution. These gains and losses flow through to the shareholders and must be taken into account in the shareholders' bases before any shareholder's gain or loss can be determined on the surrender of the stock.

KEY TERMS

TEST YOURSELF

ANSWERS APPEAR AFTER THE PROBLEM ASSIGNMENTS

1. Lauren Cooper had a beauty shop in the basement of her home. During the current year, she had gross receipts of $32,000. She spent $3,500 for supplies, paid an assistant $4,200, incurred allocated utility expenses of $800, depreciation expense of $1,200, a Section 1231 gain of $800, and a charitable contribution of $500. What is the net income that she will report on her Schedule C?
   a. $22,600
   b. $22,300
   c. $21,800
   d. $21,600
2. Refer to the information in question 1 and assume the entity is an S corporation. What is the corporation's net income excluding separately stated items?
   a. $22,600
   b. $22,300
   c. $21,800
   d. $21,600
3. William and Joan form a partnership with William having a 30 percent interest and Joan the remaining 70 percent. Joan contributed $80,000 cash and services valued at $4,000. William contributed $6,000 cash and property

valued at $30,000 that has a basis of $20,000. At the end of the year, the partnership reports the following:

Ordinary income (excluding guaranteed payments)	$90,000
Tax-exempt bond interest	2,000
Capital loss	4,000
Guaranteed payment to Joan	30,000
Cash distribution to Joan	25,000
3-year note on land	15,000

What is William's basis in his partnership interest at year-end?

a. $43,400
b. $45,800
c. $47,900
d. $45,900

4. Using the information in question 3, what is Joan's basis in her partnership interest at year-end?
   a. $140,100
   b. $120,600
   c. $110,100
   d. $99,600

5. William and Joan form an S corporation with William owning 30 percent of the stock and Joan the remaining 70 percent. Joan contributed $80,000 cash and services valued at $4,000. William contributed $6,000 cash and property valued at $30,000 that has a basis of $20,000. At the end of the year, the S corporation reports the following:

Ordinary income (excluding salary)	$90,000
Tax-exempt bond interest	2,000
Capital loss	4,000
Salary to Joan	30,000
Cash distribution to Joan	25,000
3-year note on land	15,000

What is Williams's basis in his S corporation interest at year-end?

a. $43,400
b. $45,800
c. $47,900
d. $45,900

PROBLEM ASSIGNMENTS

CHECK YOUR UNDERSTANDING

1. Which entities discussed in this chapter insulate the owners from the general liabilities of the entity?
2. Explain the principal difference between an LLP and an LLC.
3. The Gem Company, a sole proprietorship, provides health insurance for its owner and two employees. The cost per person is $200 per month. Explain how the Gem Company and its sole proprietor will treat this expense.

4. Compare an owner's personal liability for debts of a business organized as a sole proprietorship, general partnership, limited partnership, LLP, LLC, and S corporation.

5. Explain how an increase or decrease in partnership liabilities can affect the basis of a general partner and a limited partner.

6. Do liabilities of an S corporation affect the basis of a shareholder's stock in the same manner as partnership liabilities affect the basis of a partner's partnership interest? Explain.

7. Although partners can generally deduct their share of losses from a partnership, what three things can limit their ability to deduct these losses on their current year's tax return?

8. Why are partnerships and S corporations required to separately state certain items on their Schedule K rather than combining these items with the organization's operating profit or loss? Provide examples of the items that must be separately stated.

9. How is income allocated to S corporation shareholders? Develop an example to illustrate this procedure.

10. What are the corporate and shareholder restrictions on making an S corporation election?

11. What is the difference between a prospective S election and a retroactive S election?

12. What is a terminating event in relation to an S corporation?

13. Why do the basis and at-risk rules usually prevent the same amount of losses from passing through to shareholders of S corporations?

14. What is the purpose of the accumulated adjustments account if the S corporation has always been an S corporation?

15. What types of taxes may an S corporation have to pay and under what circumstances?

CRUNCH THE NUMBERS

16. John Mason operates a consulting business, Mason Enterprises, as a sole proprietorship. He had to transfer $100,000 of stocks and securities into Mason Enterprises's name to show financial viability for the business. During the current year, the business had the following income and expenses from operations:

Consulting revenue	$125,000
Travel expenses	40,000
Transportation	3,000
Advertising	7,000
Office expense	3,000
Telephone	1,000
Dividend income	5,000
Interest income	2,000
Charitable contribution	1,000
Political contribution	6,000

Determine the Schedule C net income. How are items not included in the Schedule C net income reported?

17. Refer to the information in the preceding problem, except that John and his wife Mary are equal partners in Mason Enterprises, which operates as a partnership. How would they report the income and loss items from partnership operations?

18. Refer to the information in problem 16, except that John operates Mason Enterprises as an S corporation. How would John report the income and loss items from S corporation operations?

19. Maggie Brown is a transcriptionist for several doctors in her town and works from her home. She spends three to four hours per day transcribing medical notes for the doctors. During the year, she earned $13,200 from the business. She had automobile expense of $800, phone expense of $150, and child care expense related to the job of $1,100. Explain how she will report her income and expenses. Calculate her income from the business and her self-employment taxes if she has no other income in 2013.

20. Julie transferred a personal-use computer to her sole proprietorship. The computer originally cost her $3,000. At the date of transfer, the computer had a fair market value of $1,000. Explain how both Julie and the sole proprietorship will treat this for tax purposes.

21. Jim and Angie form the JAZ Partnership with Zoe by contributing $75,000 each to partnership equity. Zoe, the third partner, contributes property with a basis of $50,000 and fair market value of $75,000. The three are equal partners in the partnership.

a. Determine the tax consequences to Zoe for the contribution of property to the partnership.

b. What are the partnership's tax consequences?

c. What is each partner's basis in the partnership interest?

d. What is the partnership's basis in the property?

22. George and Georgenne formed the GG Partnership as equal partners. Each partner contributed cash and property with a value of $100,000 for partnership operations. As a result of these contributions, George had a basis of $80,000 and Georgenne a basis of $60,000 in their partnership interests. At the end of their first year of operations, they had the following results:

Gross sales	$150,000
Cost of goods sold	95,000
Rent expense	15,000
Salaries to employees	15,000
Utilities	4,000
Charitable contribution	1,000
Section 1231 gain	2,000

a. What is the net income, excluding separately stated items that each partner is required to report at the end of the year?

b. How is each of the separately stated items treated on the partners' tax returns?

c. What is each partner's basis at year-end?

23. Refer to the information in the preceding problem, except that George and Georgenne are equal shareholders in an S corporation.

a. What is the net income, excluding separately stated items, that each shareholder is required to report at the end of the year?

b. How is each of the separately stated items treated on the shareholders' tax returns?

c. What is each shareholder's basis at year-end?

24. Bob is a 50 percent owner of Barco Enterprises. During 2013, Barco earned $80,000 in net income after subtracting Bob's $50,000 salary. Bob also withdrew $20,000 from Barco during the year. Bob would like to know the amount of the FICA taxes and by whom they would be paid if

a. Barco is a general partnership.

b. Barco is an S corporation.

25. Alpha, Beta, and Gamma form the ABG partnership by transferring the following to the partnership:

Alpha	$10,000 cash and machinery valued at $20,000 with a basis of $15,000.
Beta	Land valued at $30,000 with a basis of $35,000.
Gamma	Cash of $20,000 and services valued at $10,000.

a. Determine the tax consequences of these transfers to Alpha, Beta, and Gamma.

b. Identify each of their bases in their partnership interests.

c. What basis does the partnership have in each of the properties transferred to it?

26. Refer to the information in the preceding problem. If the partnership sells the land for $27,000 after holding it for three years, what are the tax consequences to Alpha, Beta, and Gamma?

27. Explain the difference in recourse and nonrecourse liabilities when distinguishing between general and limited partners. Assume the partnership has $100,000 of recourse liabilities and $60,000 of nonrecourse liabilities. It has one general partner, Matt, who has a 20 percent interest in income and loss, and two limited partners, each of whom has a 40 percent interest in income and loss. Illustrate the difference in allocation of liabilities to these three partners.

28. CCC Partnership borrowed $100,000 on a five-year recourse note from a local bank. It also purchased land for $60,000, putting $10,000 down and signing a qualified nonrecourse loan secured by the land for the balance. The partners' interests in partnership profits and losses are as follows:

Partner	Loss	Profit
Carol (general partner)	25%	50%
Charles (limited partner)	40%	25%
Charlotte (limited partner)	35%	25%

a. How is the $100,000 recourse note allocated to the partners' bases?

b. How is the $50,000 nonrecourse note allocated to the partners' bases?

c. How would your answers change if Carol, Charles, and Charlotte were all general partners?

29. Luis and Jennifer formed the JL Partnership as equal partners. Each partner contributed cash and property with a value of $80,000 for partnership operations. As a result of these contributions, Luis had a basis of $80,000 and Jennifer a basis of $60,000 in their partnership interests. At the end of their first year of operations, they had the following results:

Gross sales	$110,000
Cost of goods sold	75,000
Rent expense	18,000
Employees' salaries	20,000
Utilities	3,000
Charitable contribution	500
Section 1231 gain	1,000
Tax-exempt interest income	2,000

a. What is the net income, excluding separately stated items, that each partner is required to report at the end of the year?

b. How is each of the separately stated items treated on the partners' tax returns?

c. What is each partner's basis at year-end?

d. Explain how Luis and Jennifer's initial bases could differ if they both contributed cash and property valued at $80,000.

30. In year 1, Sally invested $45,000 for a 10 percent interest in a limited partnership. This is Sally's only passive investment. The limited partnership has $100,000 of nonrecourse debt. (The debt is not secured by real property.) At the end of years 1 through 5, the partnership passed income and losses through to Sally as follows:

Year	Income (Loss)
1	($31,000)
2	$21,000
3	$4,000
4	$8,000
5	($22,000)

At the beginning of year 6, Sally sells her interest in the partnership for $40,000. For each of the years, determine Sally's deductible and nondeductible (suspended) losses. Explain the reason for the nondeductibility of any losses. What are the results of the sale of her interest?

31. Partner X, a 1/3 partner in XYZ Partnership, needs a distribution from the partnership for some unexpected bills. The partnership, however, does not have any extra cash to distribute. It will distribute land to the partner that has a value of $30,000 and a basis of $25,000 to the partnership. X's basis in his partnership interest is $45,000.

How will this distribution be treated for tax purposes?

a. Assume alternatively, that the partnership sells the land for its fair market value and distributes the cash to Partner X. What are the tax consequences of the sale and distribution?

b. Which alternative would you recommend to the partnership? Explain.

32. Maria, a 25 percent partner in MARS Partnership, needs a distribution from the partnership for some unexpected bills. The partnership, however, does not have any extra cash to distribute. It will distribute land to Maria that has a value of $27,000 and a basis to the partnership of $50,000. Maria's basis in her partnership interest is $55,000.

a. How will this distribution be treated for tax purposes?

b. Assume alternatively, that the partnership sells the land for its fair market value and distributes the cash to Maria. What are the tax consequences of the sale and distribution?

c. Which alternative would you recommend to Maria? Explain.

33. Charles owns a 25 percent interest in Cal Corporation, an S corporation. The corporation has run into some difficulties recently and Charles lent it $10,000. At the beginning of the year, Charles's basis in his stock was $16,000.

a. What is Charles's basis in his stock and debt at the end of the year if the corporation reports losses of $60,000?

b. What is Charles's basis in his stock and debt at the end of the year if the corporation reports losses of $90,000?

c. What is Charles's basis in his stock and debt at the end of the year if the corporation reports losses of $120,000?

34. Is there any tax advantage to a 100 percent shareholder-employee of an S corporation compared to a shareholder-employee of a C corporation under the following circumstances: shareholder-employee salary is $75,000; the corporate income before the $75,000 salary and any related employment expense is $100,000? The corporation also distributes $15,000 to the shareholder. The shareholder is single, has no dependents, and uses the standard deduction.

35. At the beginning of year 1, Lisa and Marie were equal shareholders in LM Corporation, an S corporation. On April 30, year 1, Lisa sold half of her interest to Shelley. On August 8, year 1, Marie sold her entire interest to George. On December 31, year 1, the corporation reported net income of $50,000. How is this income allocated to Lisa, Marie, Shelley, and George? (Year 1 is not a leap year, and the date of sale is allocated to the seller.)

36. During the current year, Biggie, Inc., a delivery company operating as an S corporation, reported the following results from operations:

Revenue	$280,000
Salaries	130,000
Truck expense	30,000
Taxes	18,000
Section 1231 loss	8,000
Traffic fines	1,200
Interest on truck loans	2,000
Interest income (bonds)	500

What are the corporation's net income and its separately reported items?

37. Crow Corporation, an S corporation from the date of its incorporation, is in the process of liquidating. During the current year, it reports gross receipts of only $40,000; it has passive investment income of $25,000 from the money it invested after the sale of a large portion of its operating assets. It has expenses related to this income of $1,000. Is the corporation liable for the passive investment income tax?

38. The Jane Corporation, an S corporation, makes several property distributions to its two equal shareholders, A and B, during the year. The distributions are as follows:

	A	B
Cash	$5,000	$5,000
Land (Basis=$5,000)	$10,000(FMV)	
Equipment (Basis=$15,000)		$10,000(FMV)

At the beginning of the year, the corporation's accumulated adjustments account is $35,000; A's basis in his shares is $24,000; and B's basis is

$32,000. The corporation reports net income of $6,000 for the year, excluding any effect of the distributions. Determine the basis in A and B's shares and the balance in the corporation's AAA at the end of the year.

39. PA Corporation, an S corporation, has two equal shareholders, P and A. Prior to the end of the current year, PA decides to liquidate and sell its three remaining assets distributing the cash received to P and A. Asset 1 has a basis of $10,000 and is sold for $6,000. Asset 2 has a basis of $4,000 and is sold for $12,000. Asset 3 has a basis of $9,000 and is sold for $10,000. Shareholder P has a basis of $4,000 in her shares, and A has a basis of $20,000. The corporation has a net loss (excluding the sales of the assets) of $2,500. Detail the tax consequences to PA Corporation and its two shareholders on the liquidation of the corporation.

40. The operating results for Peep Corporation, an S corporation, for last year were as follows:

Revenues	
Gross sales	$2,000,000
Tax-exempt bond interest	2,000
Dividend income	8,000
Section 1231 gain (land)	10,000
Expenses	
Cost of goods sold	$900,000
Salaries	600,000
Rent	200,000
Utilities	60,000
Depreciation	40,000
Charitable contribution	12,000
Section 179 expense	20,000

a. Determine the corporation's net income and its separately stated items.

b. Determine the corporation's financial accounting income if the gain on the sale of the land is only $6,000 and depreciation is $32,000 under financial accounting rules.

c. Complete a Schedule M-1 for the corporation. You can obtain forms from the IRS Web site *(www.irs.gov)*. Sample filled-in forms are in Appendix C of this text.

41. **Comprehensive Problem**. On March 15, 2011, James Smith formed a business to rent and service vending machines providing healthy snack alternatives and juices to the local middle and high schools. He operates the business as a sole proprietorship from his home, turning the den into an office from which he manages the business. The den contains 400 of the home's total 1,800 square feet. In addition, he rents additional space in a warehouse complex where he stores his inventory.

When he formed the business, he converted his Ford pick-up truck solely to business use to deliver machines and products to the schools. When converted, the truck had a basis of $18,250 and a fair market value of $12,500. He purchased a small car for his personal use.

During 2013, the business reported the following:

Rental income	$ 20,000
Sales of products	288,000
Cost of sales	121,000
Truck expense (excl. depreciation)	14,000

Telephone	600
Rent expense	2,400
Part-time delivery person	25,000
Machine repairs	5,500
Meals and entertainment	4,000
Charitable contributions	10,000
Liability insurance	12,000

In April of 2011, James bought 20 vending machines for $60,000; in April of 2012, he bought 20 more machines for $65,000; in June of the current year, he purchased 10 more vending machines for $35,000. All vending machines have a seven-year life and are depreciated under MACRS. James did not elect Section 179 expensing or bonus depreciation in any year. James's expenses related to his home are

Rent	$24,000
Utilities	600

In December, James sold the original truck for $5,000 and purchased a new truck for $24,000.

Determine James's income or loss from the business. Do not include in this figure items that would not be included on his Schedule C but detail those items separately. Calculate James's self-employment taxes assuming he has no other income subject to FICA taxes.

THINK OUTSIDE THE TEXT

These questions require answers that are beyond the material that is covered in this chapter.

42. What do you believe led to the conclusion that a sole proprietorship should report its results on the owner's tax return?

43. Why do you think Congress passed the law that allows an LLC to elect to be treated as a corporation or a partnership?

44. Why do you think services are excluded from the definition of property when a partner receives a partnership interest in exchange for property?

45. Why do you think an S corporation is limited to having common stock with no differences other than voting rights?

46. Compare the treatment of distributions of depreciated and appreciated property by an S corporation to that of a partnership.

IDENTIFY THE ISSUES

Identify the issues or problems suggested by the following situations. State each issue as a question.

47. Craig is a 20 percent shareholder in an S corporation and works an average of 20 hours per week in the business. His wife, Lynn, is a full-time employee of the corporation. The corporation provides fully paid health and life insurance benefits for herself, Craig, and their children.

48. The Gemini Corporation, an S corporation, wants to expand its lines of business. To do so quickly, it acquires 85 percent of the stock of Trojan Corporation, a regular C corporation.

49. ABCD partnership, a calendar-year partnership, has four owners: A owns a 20 percent interest; B a 25 percent interest; C a 40 percent interest; and D the remaining 15 percent interest. Some of the partners have been having difficulty working with each other, so, with partnership agreement,

D sells his 15 percent interest to F on October 20, year 1; B sells her interest to G on January 15, year2; and C sells his interest to H on December 1, year 1.

50. Shana is a 20 percent limited partner in the STU partnership. Her basis in her partnership interest is $40,000 when she decides to abandon her partnership interest. The partnership's balance sheet is as follows:

Net Assets	$203,000	Liabilities	$200,000
		Shana-Capital	1,000
		Tom-Capital	1,000
		Urban-Capital	1,000

51. Carol and her husband own 35 percent each of a land development partnership. Carol owns a piece of land purchased six years ago for $60,000 that has been declining in value. The partnership wants to buy the land for development but is only willing to pay $40,000.

DEVELOP RESEARCH SKILLS

52. Locate a recent appellate court case that has reversed a Tax Court decision regarding a partnership or S corporation tax issue.

- **a.** Summarize the facts, issues, and conclusions of the case.
- **b.** Explain why the appellate court reversed the Tax Court.
- **c.** Explain the impact this decision has on tax planning for clients.

53. Roberta Wynn has been a partner in the Cato Partnership for a number of years. With the permission of the other partners, she sells her partnership interest to a third party. At the time of sale, her basis in her partnership is only $100. For the portion of the year to the date of sale, she is allocated a partnership loss of $2,100. If she receives $10,000 for her partnership interest, what are the tax consequences of the sale and the results of partnership operations in her final year?

54. The partners of JPG Partnership want to change the form of entity from a partnership to a corporation. The corporation can be formed in several ways: The partnership can distribute the assets to the partners who then contribute the assets to the corporation. The partnership can transfer the assets directly to the corporation. The partners can transfer their partnership interests to the corporation. Write a memo outlining the tax effects of the various methods of forming the corporation.

SEARCH THE INTERNET

55. Go to the IRS Web site *(www.irs.gov)* and print out copies of Schedule C for Form 1040, Schedule SE, Form 4562, Form 4797, and the first page of Form 1040. Using the information in comprehensive problem 41, complete these schedules and forms to the extent possible from the information given.

56. Refer to the information in problems 22 and 23.

- **a.** Go to the IRS Web site *(www.irs.gov)* and print out the first page and Schedule K for Form 1065. Use the information in problem 22 to complete these two forms to the extent possible with the information given.
- **b.** Go the IRS Web site *(www.irs.gov)* and print out the first page and Schedule K for Form 1120S. Use the information in problems 22 and 23 to complete these two forms to the extent possible with the information given.

57. Go to *www.taxsites.com/state-links.html* and locate your state. Find and read your state's filing requirements for forming an LLC and write a one-paragraph summary of these requirements. Does your state recognize a single member LLC?

58. In addition to the federal income tax, an entity is subject to the laws of the state in which it is organized. Use the Internet to locate sources of tax law that govern the tax treatment of partnerships, LLCs, and S corporations for your state. Write a brief description regarding how each of those entities is treated for tax purposes in your state.

59. Go to the IRS Web site *(www.irs.gov)* and locate the form that a corporation uses to make an S election and its related instructions. Summarize the information required on the form. Do the instructions include information on how to obtain an extension of time for filing the S election? If so, summarize this information. If not, is this information available elsewhere on this Web site?

DEVELOP PLANNING SKILLS

60. An S corporation shareholder is currently in the 28 percent tax bracket. His S corporation is going to pass a very large loss through to him that would otherwise offset other income, except for the fact that he lacks sufficient stock basis to absorb the loss. The shareholder is coming to your office tomorrow to discuss the situation. Make a list of questions you will ask before you will advise him on possible alternatives.

61. Cynthia needs your advice regarding which form of business entity to choose for her new business. She expects the new business will have losses of approximately $80,000 in each of the first two years but anticipates profits that will grow steadily thereafter. Cynthia has no cash to contribute to the business but plans to work 50 or more hours per week managing the day-to-day operations of the new business. Four individuals will contribute $50,000 each to start the business. To fund growth, Cynthia anticipates that additional funding will be needed in three years. Cynthia wants to meet with you next week to discuss your analysis and preliminary recommendations.

- **a.** Based on this information only, what would you recommend?
- **b.** Before meeting with Cynthia, prepare a list of questions you would like to ask to obtain the additional information you would need to make a more thorough analysis.

62. Prior to BJ Corporation's year-end, its sole shareholder comes to you for advice. BJ is an established S corporation that was profitable until two years ago when the economy faltered. Due to distributions and losses passed through in prior years, the shareholder's basis in the S corporation is only $10,000. He anticipates that the corporation will have a loss of $50,000 in the current year. His previous accountant, who retired this year, had mentioned something to him about losses not being deductible if he did not have stock basis. What are the shareholder's alternatives? Make a list of questions you would ask the shareholder to assist you in selecting between alternatives.

63. Clare and Cora have been making wedding cakes in their homes for several years. The Health Department just learned about this and now requires them to shut down or find a commercial kitchen that can be subject to the proper inspections. Clare and Cora located a suitable small restaurant they can rent for $1,000 per month or purchase for $100,000.

Their monthly payments would be $1,000 per month for interest and taxes and $100 per month for the principal on a commercial mortgage if they put $10,000 down. Clara and Cora each have $10,000 in savings they can put into the business. Their husbands are also employed and would be able to provide some support during the start-up period. Both families are in the 28 percent marginal tax bracket. The women know that the first several years will be difficult, as they will need to build the business by more than word of mouth. As a result, their business plan shows losses of $5,000 in the first year, $4,000 in the second year, and $2,000 in the third year, but the fourth year and beyond show profits. These losses do not include either the rent or the mortgage payment. How do you suggest they set up their business? Should they buy or rent the building?

ANSWERS TO TEST YOURSELF

1. b. **$22,300**. The Section 1231 gain and the charitable contributions are reported separately.
2. b. **$22,300**. The Section 1231 gain and the charitable contributions are reported separately.
3. c. **$47,900**. $26,000 beginning basis + $18,000 net income + $600 tax-exempt income – $1,200 capital loss + $4,500 share of liability.
4. a. **$140,100**. $84,000 beginning basis + $30,000 guaranteed payment + $42,000 net income + $1,400 tax-exempt income – $2,800 capital loss + $10,500 share of liability – $25,000 cash withdrawal.
5. a. **$43,400**. $26,000 beginning basis + $18,000 net income + $600 tax-exempt income – $1,200 capital loss.

pa

V

TAXATION OF INDIVIDUALS

CHAPTER 11
INCOME TAXATIO
OF INDIVIDUALS

CHAPTER 12
WEALTH TRA
TAXES

chapter 11

Income Taxation of Individuals

CHAPTER OUTLINE

The individual tax model differs significantly from the corporate tax model due to the intermediate income concept of adjusted gross income. A number of unique features are also applicable to the determination of an individual's gross tax liability. These include the taxpayer's filing status, personal and dependency exemptions, the standard deduction, deductions for adjusted gross income, and deductions from adjusted gross income. Because many of the taxpayer's deductions are for personal expenses, the deductions may be limited to amounts that exceed specific minimums. Other deductions cannot exceed certain maximums.

Higher-income taxpayers face increases in their effective tax rates due to the income limitations affecting certain other deductions and credits. Examples include the income phaseout rules that reduce or eliminate the deduction for student loan interest and reduce or eliminate the child tax credit and the credits for undergraduate and graduate education.

A taxpayer's filing status determines the allowable standard deduction and the tax rate schedule or table used to determine the gross tax liability. After the taxpayer determines the gross tax liability, tax credits are subtracted and additional taxes are added. Many of the tax credits and additions to tax are also unique to individual taxpayers. Individuals who take excessive advantage of provisions that reduce taxes may be subject to the alternative minimum tax, as are corporations, but the rates for individuals are higher than for corporations.

Individuals are also required to make prepayments of their tax liability. Most prepayments are through withholding on wages and salaries, but estimated payments may also be required of certain taxpayers with income not subject to withholding. If the tax prepayments exceed the tax liability after all credits and additions, the taxpayer has a refund due. If the prepayments are less than the net tax liability, the taxpayer owes additional taxes.

KEY CONCEPTS

- ★ Individuals have two sets of deductions—one *for* adjusted gross income and the other *from* adjusted gross income in determining taxable income.
- ★ Individuals have two unique deductions from adjusted gross income, the greater of their standard deduction or itemized deductions and their exemptions, both personal and dependency.
- ★ To be deductible, medical expenses, casualty losses, and miscellaneous itemized deductions must exceed a certain minimum based on adjusted gross income (AGI). Deductions for allowable interest expense and taxes are not limited by AGI.
- ★ An individual's standard deduction and the tax rate tables or schedules used to determine the gross tax liability are dependent on the taxpayer's filing status. The five filing statuses are (1) married filing jointly, (2) married filing separately, (3) surviving spouse (qualifying widow or widower), (4) head of household, and (5) single.
- ★ The taxpayer's net tax due or refund expected is the mathematical sum of the taxpayer's gross tax liability less tax credits plus additions to their taxes less tax prepayments. A positive sum is the tax due; a negative sum is the expected refund.

Setting the Stage—An Introductory Case

Amy and Steve, a married couple who file a joint tax return, have just signed a contract to purchase their first home. They have never itemized their deductions and are looking forward to all the tax savings their real estate agent told them they would realize from their home mortgage interest and real property tax deductions. The interest on their home acquisition mortgage (principal amount of $315,000) is expected to be about $12,000 per year, and their real property taxes are about $2,500. Friends told them that their tax savings would be even greater because of other expenses they have not been able to deduct due to claiming the standard deduction. These other expenses include $5,500 of unreimbursed medical expenses, $1,400 in unreimbursed employee business expenses, and $2,400 in charitable contributions. Their adjusted gross income is $105,000, and they are in the 25 percent marginal tax bracket. They expect to be able to deduct an additional $23,800 due to these expenses and save $5,950 ($23,800 × 25%) in taxes. Their mortgage company also told them that they will be required to pay $1,500 in points at the closing. The mortgage company told them they have the option of closing during either the fourth week of December or the first week of January. Assuming their other expenses remain the same for both the current and the next year, when should they schedule the closing? At the end of this chapter we will return to this case.

The Individual Tax Model

This chapter concentrates on the taxation of individuals. The basic tax model for individuals, presented in Figure 11.1, begins with the concept of gross income and ends with the taxpayer's net tax due. The tax model is the basic format in which individuals report their tax liability.

Chapter 1 provided an overview of the individual model. This chapter provides a more detailed discussion of those components that have not been discussed in other chapters.

Income

Earlier chapters discussed the inclusions in and exclusions from gross income. Figure 11.2 shows the income section of Form 1040: *U.S. Individual Tax Return*.[1] Most of these different sources of income were discussed in Chapters 3 or 4. Salary and wages, interest, dividends, tax refunds, and alimony payments are reported on lines 7 through 11. Gains and losses from property transactions (discussed in Chapter 7) are reported on lines 13 and 14, and retirement plan distributions (discussed in Chapter 4) are reported on lines 15 and 16.

FIGURE 11.1 **THE INDIVIDUAL TAX MODEL**

	Gross income
Less	Deductions for adjusted gross income
Equals	Adjusted gross income (AGI)
Less	Itemized deductions or standard deduction
Less	Personal and dependency exemptions
Equals	Taxable income
Times	Applicable tax rates
Equals	Gross income tax liability
Less	Tax credits
Plus	Additional taxes
Less	Tax prepayments
Equals	Net tax due or tax refund

[1]Sample filled-in tax forms are included in Appendix C at the end of this textbook.

FIGURE
11.2 INCOME SECTION OF FORM 1040

Income

Attach Form(s) W-2 here. Also attach Forms W-2G and 1099-R if tax was withheld.

If you did not get a W-2, see instructions.

Enclose, but do not attach, any payment. Also, please use **Form 1040-V.**

7	Wages, salaries, tips, etc. Attach Form(s) W-2		7	
8a	**Taxable** interest. Attach Schedule B if required		8a	
b	**Tax-exempt** interest. **Do not** include on line 8a	8b		
9a	Ordinary dividends. Attach Schedule B if required		9a	
b	Qualified dividends	9b		
10	Taxable refunds, credits, or offsets of state and local income taxes		10	
11	Alimony received		11	
12	Business income or (loss). Attach Schedule C or C-EZ		12	
13	Capital gain or (loss). Attach Schedule D if required. If not required, check here ▶ ☐		13	
14	Other gains or (losses). Attach Form 4797		14	
15a	IRA distributions	15a	**b** Taxable amount 15b	
16a	Pensions and annuities	16a	**b** Taxable amount 16b	
17	Rental real estate, royalties, partnerships, S corporations, trusts, etc. Attach Schedule E		17	
18	Farm income or (loss). Attach Schedule F		18	
19	Unemployment compensation		19	
20a	Social security benefits	20a	**b** Taxable amount 20b	
21	Other income. List type and amount		21	
22	Combine the amounts in the far right column for lines 7 through 21. This is your **total income** ▶		22	

Included in Gross Income:
Salary and wages
Interest
Dividends
Tax refunds
Alimony received
Business Income (sole prop.)
Gains and losses on property transaction
Retirement plan distributions
Rental real estate, royalties, partnerships, S-corps, trusts
Unemployment
Social Security
Other (hobby, prizes, awards, jury duty fees, gambling, etc.)

Most excluded income items are not reported on an individual's tax return, except for tax-exempt interest (used to determine the taxable portion of Social Security) and the nontaxable portions of retirement plan distributions and Social Security benefits. Table 11.1 lists some of the more common exclusions (most discussed in Chapters 3 and 4).

Income and expenses from a sole proprietorship (discussed in Chapter 10) are reported on Schedule C with net income included on line 12. If the individual has ownership interests in partnerships or S corporations (discussed in Chapter 10), the profits and losses (reported first on Schedule E) are aggregated along with income from rental real estate (discussed in Chapter 5), royalties, and trusts, and reported on line 17 of Form 1040. Other income is reported on line 21; examples include income from a hobby (discussed in Chapter 5), prizes (discussed in Chapter 3), awards, gambling winnings, jury duty fees, and reimbursements for expenses deducted in an earlier year (to the extent a tax benefit was received).

TABLE
11.1 EXCLUSIONS FROM GROSS INCOME

Tax-exempt interest income	Scholarships
Nontaxable stock dividends and stock rights	Gifts and inheritances
Nontaxable portion of pension distributions	Proceeds of life insurance policies
Nontaxable portion of Social Security benefits	Welfare benefits
Qualified employee fringe benefits	Damages awarded for physical injury
Tax refunds to the extent no prior benefit	Gains and losses on property transactions subject to disallowance or nonrecognition provisions including up to $250,000 gain on the sale of personal residence ($500,000 if married filing jointly)
Combat pay for members of the Armed Forces	

Deductions for Adjusted Gross Income

Individuals are allowed a special category of deductions aptly called **deductions for adjusted gross income** because they are deducted prior to arriving at the subtotal of adjusted gross income (AGI). These deductions reduce an individual's AGI and taxable income regardless of whether the individual chooses to itemize or take the standard deduction. In addition, deductions for AGI are not subject to the general phase-out rules imposed on itemized deductions for higher-income taxpayers. Figure 11.3 shows this section of Form 1040. Most of these deductions have been discussed in previous chapters; only those not previously discussed are addressed here.[2]

Educator Expenses

The Job Creation and Worker Assistance Act of 2002 added a deduction for teachers who spent their personal funds for classroom supplies. Because these expenses seldom exceeded the 2 percent of AGI floor that applies to unreimbursed employee expenses, teachers received no tax benefit. This provision permits kindergarten through 12th-grade teachers to deduct up to $250 of unreimbursed expenses for books, supplies, computer equipment, software, and other supplementary materials they used in the classroom. This deduction expires at the end of 2013 but Congress may extend it.

Student Loan Interest Deduction

Since 1998, taxpayers have been able to deduct up to $2,500 of interest annually on qualified student loans. As the taxpayer's modified AGI increases from $60,000 to $75,000 ($125,000 to $155,000 for married persons filing jointly), the deduction is phased out proportionately over the phaseout range.[3]

EXAMPLE 1

Laura has $2,300 of qualifying student loan interest in 2013. She is single and her modified AGI is $69,000. Her AGI exceeds $60,000 by $9,000. Thus, 60 percent ($9,000/$15,000 phaseout range) of the allowable deduction is phased out. She can only deduct $920 [$2,300 × (1 – .60)] of her $2,300 interest.

The loans must have been incurred for eligible education expenses including tuition, fees, room, and board incurred for education at postsecondary educational institutions or certain vocational schools. Eligible education expenses must be reduced for tax-exempt scholarships, fellowships or grants, and for education tax credits.[4]

FIGURE 11.3 DEDUCTIONS FOR ADJUSTED GROSS INCOME

Adjusted Gross Income

23	Educator expenses	23			
24	Certain business expenses of reservists, performing artists, and fee-basis government officials. Attach Form 2106 or 2106-EZ	24			
25	Health savings account deduction. Attach Form 8889 .	25			
26	Moving expenses. Attach Form 3903	26			
27	Deductible part of self-employment tax. Attach Schedule SE .	27			
28	Self-employed SEP, SIMPLE, and qualified plans . .	28			
29	Self-employed health insurance deduction	29			
30	Penalty on early withdrawal of savings	30			
31a	Alimony paid b Recipient's SSN ▶	31a			
32	IRA deduction	32			
33	Student loan interest deduction	33			
34	Tuition and fees. Attach Form 8917	34			
35	Domestic production activities deduction. Attach Form 8903	35			
36	Add lines 23 through 35			36	
37	Subtract line 36 from line 22. This is your **adjusted gross income** . . . . . ▶			37	

[2]Deductions for IRA and other retirement plan contributions, moving expenses, self-employment tax, and self-employed health insurance premiums are discussed in Chapter 4. Alimony is discussed in Chapter 3. The domestic production activities deduction is discussed in Chapters 9 and 10.

[3]See § 221(b)(2)(C) for the definition of modified AGI. For 2012, the deduction phaseout range was the same as for 2013. For 2010 and 2011, the deduction phaseout range was $60,000 to $75,000 and $120,000 to $150,000 MFJ.

[4]These education credits are discussed later in this chapter.

EXAMPLE 2

John incurred $20,000 of qualifying educational expenses but obtained a $25,000 student loan. He begins payments on the loan on July 1, 2013 and makes payments totaling $1,300 by the end of 2013, of which $1,000 is interest and $300 principal. John may deduct only $800 of this interest *for* AGI [($20,000/$25,000) × $1,000].

TAX PLANNING

To claim the student loan interest deduction, a taxpayer must have a legal obligation to make the interest payments under the terms of the loan and may not be claimed as a dependent by another taxpayer. Once a student is no longer a dependent, he or she is allowed a deduction for interest on a loan in his or her name even if someone else makes the payments. For example, if a parent or grandparent who is not legally obligated to make interest payments makes them on behalf of the student, the payment will be treated as a gift to the student who then makes the deductible interest payment.

Tuition and Fees Deduction

The Economic Growth and Tax Relief Reconciliation Act of 2001 introduced a deduction for qualified higher-education expenses. The deduction is $4,000 for singles with modified adjusted gross incomes below $65,000 ($130,000 if married filing jointly).[5] Single taxpayers with incomes between $65,000 and $80,000 (between $130,000 and $160,000 if married filing jointly) are allowed to deduct $2,000 of qualifying expenses. Taxpayers who exceed the income limits, who are claimed as a dependent on another's return, or who are married but file a separate return, cannot take this deduction.[6]

Qualified expenses included tuition and fees for the taxpayer, the taxpayer's spouse, or any dependent for whom the taxpayer could claim a dependency exemption. If an expense is deductible under any other provision, it is not deductible under this provision. In addition, the deduction cannot be claimed in the same year as an education tax credit for the same student. (These credits are discussed later.) This is another deduction that is scheduled to expire at the end of the 2013 tax year but may be extended by Congress.

EXAMPLE 3

Julian, a single individual with income of $60,000, paid $6,000 for his own graduate school tuition in 2013. Julian can take a $4,000 deduction for AGI for his tuition expense.

Shelley and Ted, a married couple with income of $132,000, paid college tuition of $10,000 for their two children in 2013. Because their income is above $130,000, the maximum deduction they can take is $2,000. If their income had been over $160,000, they would not be allowed any deduction.

Health Savings Accounts

Taxpayers who are covered only by high-deductible medical insurance plans may put aside a specific amount of money in a health savings account (HSA) on a tax-deferred basis. Earnings on amounts held in an HSA grow tax free and neither contributions nor earnings are taxed when withdrawn to pay for qualified medical expenses. Distributions not spent on qualifying medical expenses are included in gross income and are subject to a 20 percent penalty.

To qualify as a high-deductible medical policy for 2013, the insurance must have an annual deductible of at least $1,250 for individual coverage and at least $2,500 for family coverage. Additionally, in 2013 the maximum annual out-of-pocket expenses

[5]Modified adjusted gross income is adjusted gross income before taking into account the tuition and fees deduction or any domestic production activities deduction but after adding back any foreign earned income exclusion or foreign housing exclusion.

[6]§ 222(d)(4). If a tuition waiver granted an employee of an educational institution is included in the employee's income, the employee is deemed to have paid the tuition and the payment may be eligible for the tuition deduction.

(other than for premiums) for covered benefits cannot exceed $6,250 for individual coverage and $12,500 for family coverage.

Contributions to HSAs are deductible *for* AGI as long as total contributions do not exceed $3,250 for individual coverage and $6,450 for family coverage in 2013.[7] Employees can deduct the premiums paid for their insurance policies as medical expenses, if they itemize. As discussed in Chapter 4, self-employed individuals are allowed to deduct their medical insurance premiums *for* AGI.

EXAMPLE 4

Ellen is a single employee and has a high deductible medical policy for herself with a $3,300 deductible. Ellen can contribute $3,250 to an HSA for 2013. Ellen can deduct the HSA contribution *for* AGI but can deduct the medical insurance premiums only if she itemizes.

Jonah is married and owns a sole proprietorship. He has a high deductible medical policy for himself and his family with a $4,500 deductible. Jonah can contribute $6,450 to an HSA. Jonah can deduct both the HSA contribution and the premiums he pays for the medical insurance *for* AGI.

TAX PLANNING

HSAs may be attractive to individuals who are considering switching from a low-deductible health plan to a less expensive high-deductible plan. They can then use a portion of the savings from the reduced premiums to make contributions to an HSA to accumulate funds on a tax-free basis to pay the medical expenses that will no longer be covered due to the increased deductible. Additionally, HSAs are portable so employees who switch jobs can take their HSAs with them.

Taxpayers also have the option of contributing to the more restrictive Archer medical savings account (MSA). These accounts are similar to HSAs but their deductibles must be between $2,150 and $3,200 for self-only plans or $4,300 and $6,450 for family plans. MSA contributions are limited to 65 percent of the policy deductible for individuals or 75 percent for families. Distributions from MSAs not used to pay for qualifying medical expenses are included in income and are subject to a 20 percent penalty.

Penalty on Early Withdrawals of Savings

If taxpayers make premature withdrawals from certificates of deposits or other savings accounts, they are normally assessed a penalty by the bank. Gross interest income, unreduced by the penalty, is included in income as taxable interest. The penalty is deducted for AGI to ensure that only the net interest income is included in taxable income.

Other Deductions for AGI

Due to space limitations, several unrelated deductions for AGI are combined and reported on line 24. These deductions are:

- Military Reserve and National Guard Travel Expenses: The Military Family Tax Relief Act passed in 2003 added a deduction for taxpayers who incur nonreimbursed travel expenses to attend U.S. Armed Forces Reserve or National Guard meetings that are more than 100 miles from home. The maximum allowable deduction is the per diem rate for that area.[8]
- Expenses of Performing Artists: Performing artists who work for two or more employers during the year may deduct their business expenses for AGI if these expenses exceed 10 percent of their gross income and their AGI does not exceed $16,000.

[7] Similar to the catch-up contributions allowed for IRAs, individuals who are at least age 55 are allowed additional contributions of $1,000 to an HSA. Once individuals are enrolled in Medicare, however, they are no longer eligible to make HSA contributions.

[8] The per diem rates can be found at *http://www.gsa.gov*. Travel expenses in excess of the per diem rate may be deducted as miscellaneous itemized deductions (subject to the 2% floor).

- Expenses of Fee-Basis Government Officials: A deduction is allowed for AGI for expenses of officials employed by a state or local government, such as court reporters, who are compensated on a fee basis (rather than a salary) for their services.

Congress has provided deductions for certain other less frequently claimed expenses for AGI without a specific line on Form 1040 on which to report them. For example, the American Jobs Creation Act of 2004 created a new deduction for AGI for legal fees paid from court awards or settlements from discrimination suits. This and other deductions for AGI for which no line is provided are simply included in the total on line 36 with an appropriate schedule providing the details.[9]

Adjusted Gross Income

Adjusted gross income (AGI) is the subtotal, unique to individual taxpayers, that is determined by deducting only the deductions *for* AGI from the taxpayer's total income. It is a very important concept within federal tax law, because of its use as a limiting factor for many of the deductions *from* AGI that follow. For example, medical expenses and casualty losses are deductible only to the extent they exceed 10 percent of AGI while the charitable contribution deduction cannot exceed 50 percent of AGI.

Deductions from Adjusted Gross Income

Individual taxpayers have a second category of deductions, **deductions from AGI**, of two types:

1. The greater of the taxpayer's itemized deductions or the taxpayer's standard deduction
2. The deduction for personal and dependency exemptions

For the first, the taxpayer compares the automatic standard deduction (determined by the taxpayer's filing status; for example, the standard deduction is $6,100 for a single individual in 2013) to the itemized deduction total and deducts the greater of the two. A taxpayer cannot deduct both. Itemized deductions are those personal expenses allowed as deductions by the Internal Revenue Code, such as medical expenses, home mortgage interest, property taxes, charitable contributions, and personal casualty losses. The second deduction subtracted from AGI is for the taxpayer's personal exemption as well as a dependency exemption for each of the taxpayer's dependents (for 2013, each exemption is $3,900). If the person is self-supporting, he or she claims a personal exemption. If an individual supports another, the individual providing the support claims a dependency exemption for the one supported. Itemized deductions, the standard deduction, and exemptions are discussed in greater detail later.

EXAMPLE 5

For 2013, Janice (a single individual) has gross income of $90,000, deductions for adjusted gross income of $2,000, and itemized deductions of $18,000. Because her itemized deductions are greater than her allowable standard deduction, she itemizes her deductions. She can also deduct $3,900 for her personal exemption because she is self-supporting. Her taxable income is $66,100, computed as follows:

Gross income	$90,000
Deductions for adjusted gross income	(2,000)
Adjusted gross income (AGI)	$88,000
Itemized deductions	(18,000)
Personal exemption	(3,900)
Taxable income	$66,100

[9]Repayments of items previously included in income would also be deducted here, such as the repayment of excess supplemental unemployment insurance benefits or jury duty fees remitted to an employer.

Determining the Tax Liability

After determining their taxable income, taxpayers compute their gross tax liability, the income tax liability before tax credits, prepayments, or additional taxes. The taxpayer uses the appropriate tax rate table or tax schedule based on filing status to determine the tax. The computation of the gross tax liability can be complicated, however, if the taxpayer has dividend income or one or more of the types of capital gain taxed at special rates.[10] Taxpayers then reduce the gross tax liability by their allowable tax credits, such as the child tax credit, the American opportunity and lifetime learning education credits, the earned income credit, and the dependent care credit. Tax credits are a direct dollar-for-dollar reduction in a taxpayer's gross tax liability. In contrast, a tax deduction only reduces the tax base (taxable income).

EXAMPLE 6

Susan is single and has taxable income of $51,000. She is in the 25 percent marginal tax bracket. If her deductions increase by $1,000, her taxable income decreases to $50,000. Her tax liability is reduced $250 ($1,000 × 25%). This $250 is the tax credit equivalent of her tax deduction; that is, a $250 tax credit reduces her tax liability the same as the $1,000 tax deduction.

Marie, single with taxable income of $201,000, is in the 33 percent marginal tax bracket. An additional $1,000 deduction reduces her taxable income to $200,000 and reduces her tax liability by $330 ($1,000 × 33%), the credit equivalent of her $1,000 deduction.

In addition to the gross tax on taxable income, taxpayers are subject to "add-on" taxes. The principal additional taxes are the self-employment tax, the penalty tax on premature distributions from pension plans and IRAs, the alternative minimum tax, and the Medicare surtax.

After subtracting credits and adding additional taxes, taxpayers subtract their prepayments to determine their net tax liability or the refund owed them. Prepayments include income tax withholding from salaries and wages and estimated tax payments. Self-employed taxpayers and taxpayers with income not subject to withholding may be required to make estimated tax payments directly to the IRS. If these prepayments exceed the net tax liability, the taxpayer has a refund due; if the payments are less than the net tax liability, the taxpayer must pay the difference. Finally, the taxpayer signs, dates, and files the tax return. Most individuals' tax returns are due by April 15 of the year following the end of the tax year; however, extensions to file of up to six months are available.

PERSONAL AND DEPENDENCY EXEMPTIONS

A taxpayer is allowed a **personal exemption** deduction of $3,900 in 2013 ($3,800 in 2012) for himself or herself (and one personal exemption for a spouse if filing a joint return). Additional exemptions of $3,900 are allowed for each qualifying dependent.

EXAMPLE 7

George and Imelda are married and have three dependent children. They claim five exemptions on their joint tax return. They have two personal exemptions for themselves and three dependency exemptions for their children. The total deduction for exemptions is $19,500 (5 × $3,900).

Taxpayers can only claim **dependency exemptions** for an individual who is either a qualifying child or other qualifying relative. A qualifying child must meet four tests and other qualifying relatives must meet three similar tests. In addition, a dependent cannot file a joint return with a spouse and must be a citizen or national of the United

[10]Long-term capital gains are typically taxed at a 15 percent rate (except for individuals in the 39.6 percent marginal tax bracket who generally use a 20 percent rate) but lower income taxpayers' rates can be as low as zero or 10 percent. For a more detailed discussion, see Chapter 7.

States or a resident of the United States, Canada, or Mexico.[11] Figure 11.4 shows the exemption section of Form 1040.

Qualifying Child

A qualifying child must satisfy each of these four tests to be claimed as a dependent:[12]

1. a residency test,
2. a relationship test,
3. an age test, and
4. a support test.

To satisfy the residency test, the child must have the same principal place of abode as the taxpayer for more than one-half of the year. Temporary absences for educational purposes, vacations, illness, business, or military service, are ignored for purposes of this test.

To meet the relationship test, the child must be the taxpayer's son, daughter, brother, sister, or descendant of any of these individuals (for example, a grandchild).[13]

To satisfy the age test, the child must be under age 19 (or under age 24 if a full-time student during at least 5 calendar months of the tax year). Additionally, the child must be younger than the taxpayer. There is no age limit for individuals who are totally and permanently disabled.

If a child provides more than one-half of his or her own support during the year the support test cannot be met. Additionally, a child cannot be a qualifying child if he or she files a joint return, unless the return was filed only to claim a refund.

Special tie-breaking rules apply if the child could be a qualifying child of more than one individual (for example, a child who lives with his or her mother and grandmother in the same home). In this case, a parent would take precedence over other relatives. If both parents want to claim the child, and they do not file a joint return, then the child is deemed a qualifying child of the parent with whom the child resides for the longer period of time. If the child resides with both parents for an equal amount of time, then the child will be considered a qualifying child of the parent with the higher adjusted gross income. If the child's parents do not claim the child, then the child can be claimed by another qualifying relative with the highest adjusted

FIGURE 11.4 EXEMPTION SECTION OF FORM 1040

Exemptions

6a ☐ **Yourself.** If someone can claim you as a dependent, **do not** check box 6a

b ☐ **Spouse**

c **Dependents:**

(1) First name Last name	(2) Dependent's social security number	(3) Dependent's relationship to you	(4) ✓ if child under age 17 qualifying for child tax credit (see instructions)
			☐
			☐
			☐
			☐

If more than four dependents, see instructions and check here ▶ ☐

d Total number of exemptions claimed

Boxes checked on 6a and 6b

No. of children on 6c who:
• lived with you
• did not live with you due to divorce or separation (see instructions)

Dependents on 6c not entered above

Add numbers on lines above ▶

---

[11]An adopted child who is a nonresident alien will qualify as a dependent as long as the taxpayer is a citizen or national of the United States, the taxpayer and the child have the same principal place of abode, and the child is a member of the taxpayer's household for the taxable year. §152(b)(c).

[12]§152(c). The definition of qualifying child also applies to the child tax credit (if the child is under age 17), the earned income credit, the dependent care credit (if the child is under age 13 or disabled), and for the head-of-household filing status.

[13]A child includes a legally adopted child or stepchild and a stepbrother or stepsister; a foster child must live in the home the entire year. §152(c) and (f).

gross income (if that person's adjusted gross income is higher than the highest adjusted gross income of either parent of the child).

For children of divorced or legally separated parents, a custodial parent may release his or her claim to the dependency exemption to the noncustodial parent.[14] If the custodial and noncustodial parents have different marginal tax rates, they can both benefit by bargaining for the dependency exemption.

TAX PLANNING

EXAMPLE 8

John is in the 39.6 percent marginal tax bracket and his ex-wife, Sarah, who has custody of their child, is in the 15 percent marginal tax bracket. The dependency exemption is only worth \$585 (\$3,900 × 15%) in reduced taxes to Sarah. If John is permitted the exemption, it will reduce his taxes by \$1,544 (\$3,900 × 39.6%). If Sarah releases the exemption to John in exchange for an additional \$1,000 in child support, John is \$544 (\$1,544 – \$1,000) better off, and Sarah is \$415 (\$1,000 – \$585) better off.

Qualifying Relatives

If the individual is not a qualifying child, then he or she must pass three tests to be a dependent:

1. a relationship test,
2. a support test, and
3. a gross income test.

Under the relationship test, the dependent must either be a qualifying relative of the taxpayer or a resident in the taxpayer's household for the entire year.[15]

Qualifying relatives do not have to reside in the taxpayer's household.[16] Qualifying relatives include the following:

- Parents, grandparents, and other direct ancestors.
- Children, grandchildren, and other lineal descendants. Children include stepchildren, adopted children, and foster children who live with the taxpayer for the entire year.
- Sisters and brothers, including stepbrothers and stepsisters.
- Sisters and brothers of the taxpayer's parents.
- Children of brothers and sisters.
- In-laws including brothers and sisters-in-law, sons-in-law, daughters-in-law, mothers-in-law, and fathers-in-law.

Cousins are not qualifying relatives, but a cousin can be claimed as a dependent if he or she meets the member of household test. In addition, only nieces, nephews, aunts, and uncles by blood are qualifying relatives. Relationships established by marriage do not end with divorce or death, however.

EXAMPLE 9

Mary and John are married and have two children who live with them. In addition, Mary's cousin lived with them the entire year. Mary and John also support John's aged father who lives in a nursing home. Assuming the other dependency tests are met, Mary and John may claim four dependency exemptions on their joint tax return: their two children, Mary's cousin, and John's father. The cousin lived with them the

---

[14] To transfer the exemption to the noncustodial parent, the custodial parent completes Form 8332: *Release of Claim to Exemption for Child of Divorced or Separated Parents*.

[15] The relationship cannot be in violation of local or state law. If a man and woman live together in violation of local or state law, no dependency relationship exists. If the state declares them common law husband and wife, they could file a joint tax return.

[16] In most cases, however, the dependent's failure to live in the taxpayer's household for more than half the year would prevent the taxpayer from claiming head of household status, unless otherwise qualified.

entire year and qualifies as a member of the household. John's father is a qualifying relative and does not need to live in the same household as Mary and John.

Support Test

The taxpayer must provide more than half the support for an individual to claim a dependency exemption; that is, the taxpayer must provide more support for the potential dependent than all other support providers, including the potential dependent. Support includes amounts spent for food, clothing, shelter, medical and dental care, recreational items, summer camp, and education.[17] Support also includes capital expenditures made solely on behalf of the dependent, such as a car purchased by the taxpayer for the dependent. Support excludes the value of services provided the individual and scholarships.[18] The source of the funds is irrelevant; thus, nontaxable income used for support must be included in the support determination.

Example 10

John and Martha provide $15,000 support to their 25-year-old daughter, Ann, a full-time student at the state university, and help support John's mother, who lives in a separate apartment. His mother spent $10,000 of her Social Security payments for clothes, utilities, and groceries. John and Martha only paid the $700 monthly rent on the apartment ($8,400 in total). Ann attends the university on a swimming scholarship that pays her annual tuition of $15,000. John and Martha can claim Ann as a dependent on their joint tax return because the scholarship does not count as support, assuming the other dependency tests are met. They cannot claim his mother, however, because she provided more than half of her support. The fact that she provided it from tax-exempt Social Security income is irrelevant.

Multiple support agreements are an exception to the rule that the taxpayer must provide more than half the support of a potential dependent. The **multiple support agreement** allows *one* of the group of support providers to claim the dependency exemption as long as that person provides more than 10 percent of the support of the dependent, the group as a whole provides more than 50 percent of the dependent's support, and the other members of the group who also provide more than 10 percent agree to grant the exemption to that person.[19]

Example 11

Ted, Sue, and Barbara together provide more than half the support for their mother, Alice, whose only income is $12,000 of tax-exempt Social Security. Ted provides 40 percent, Sue provides 30 percent, and Barbara provides 20 percent. Alice provides the remaining 10 percent of her own support. If the other two agree, any one of the children may claim Alice as a dependent.

The multiple support agreement is an annual agreement, and the person claiming the exemption can vary from year to year.[20] The exemption does not automatically go to the one providing the greatest percentage of support (unless that percentage exceeds 50 percent). Even Barbara could claim her mother as a dependent, as long as Ted and Sue agree to let her do so. Note that all other dependency tests must be met; for example, the dependent must be a qualifying relative or member of the taxpayer's household and have gross (taxable) income less than the exemption amount. Claiming a dependent under a multiple support agreement, however, does not qualify the taxpayer to file as head of household.

TAX PLANNING

A multiple support agreement presents another chance to create a "market" for the dependency exemption. The high-tax-bracket person may wish to "buy" the exemption from the low-tax-bracket person.

[17] Reg. §1.152-1(a)(2).

[18] §152(d).

[19] §152(c).

[20] The multiple support agreement is executed with a Form 2120: *Multiple Support Declaration*.

EXAMPLE 12

Ken and Barbie together provide more than half their mother's support; neither separately provides more than half, but each provides more than 10 percent. Ken is in the 33 percent marginal tax bracket, while Barbie is in the 15 percent tax bracket. If the dependency exemption is $3,900, the deduction reduces Ken's tax by $1,287 ($3,900 × 33%). The exemption deduction reduces Barbie's tax by only $585 ($3,900 × 15%). Ken should be willing to pay between $585 and $1,287 to "buy" the exemption from Barbie. If Ken reimburses Barbie $800 for amounts spent to support their mother, Barbie will sign a multiple support declaration and let Ken claim his mother as a dependent. Barbie is $215 better off ($800 – $585), and Ken is $487 better off ($1,287 – $800) than if Barbie had claimed her mother as a dependent.

Gross Income Test

A potential dependent's gross income subject to taxation must be less than the exemption amount for the year ($3,900 for 2013).

EXAMPLE 13

Jack provides more than half the support for his elderly mother, whose only income is $12,000 of Social Security and $3,000 of interest on state and local bonds. Because Jack's mother has no gross income under tax law (as all her income is from sources that are excluded from gross income), Jack can claim her as a dependent if all other tests for the dependency exemption are met. Jack also provides more than half the support of his 26-year-old brother, whose income for the year consists of $4,000 from a part-time job. Because income earned from the part-time job is included in the brother's gross income and it exceeds the exemption amount for the year, Jack cannot claim his brother as a dependent.

Table 11.2 compares the dependency requirements for a qualifying child with the requirements for a qualifying relative.

If an individual is claimed as a dependent on another person's tax return, he or she cannot take a personal exemption when computing his or her own tax liability. This loss of personal exemption applies to any taxpayer claimed as a dependent on another's return, regardless of their relationship.

EXAMPLE 14

Robert provides more than half the support for his mother, whose only income is Social Security of $6,000 and taxable interest of $2,000. Robert is allowed a dependency exemption deduction for his mother in computing his own taxable income. His mother is not allowed to take a personal exemption on her own tax return, however.

Phaseout of Exemptions for High-Income Taxpayers

High-income taxpayers whose AGI exceeds a threshold amount, may be required to phase out their personal and dependency exemptions. The AGI thresholds for reducing exemptions vary based on the taxpayer's filing status and are adjusted each year for inflation.[21] Table 11.3 shows the AGI at which the calculation of the phaseout for personal and dependency exemptions begins and the AGI at which the maximum phaseout is reached for 2013. These same phaseout thresholds apply to itemized deductions (discussed later in this chapter). The introduction of the phaseout of personal and dependency exemptions and itemized deductions is a method of increasing the taxes on higher-income taxpayers without expressly approving an increase in tax

[21]For 2009, the last year of the phaseout prior to its reinstatement in 2013, the AGI phaseout thresholds began at: $166,800 for single individuals, $208,500 for head of household, $250,200 for married filing jointly and surviving spouse, and $125,100 for married filing separately. Exemptions were phased out at the rate of 2 percent for each $2,500 (or fraction thereof) that AGI exceeded the threshold amount. For 2006 and 2007, two-thirds of the exemption amount could be eliminated; for 2008 and 2009, one-third of the exemption amount could be eliminated). For 2010-2012, the exemption phaseout rules did not apply so taxpayers were entitled to their full exemption amount regardless of their AGI. §151(2)(3)(E).

TABLE
11.2 DEPENDENCY REQUIREMENTS

TEST	QUALIFYING CHILD	QUALIFYING RELATIVE
Residence	Lives with taxpayer for more than half of the year (temporary absences for education, vacation, illness, business, or military service are ignored for this test)	Not applicable
Relationship	Taxpayer's child, stepchild, foster child, brother, sister, half-brother, half-sister, or a descendant of any of these relatives.	Taxpayer's descendant or ancestor, brother or sister, stepmother or stepfather, stepbrother or stepsister, niece, nephew, aunt, uncle, in-law, or any individual (except a spouse) who lives with the taxpayer for the entire year.
Age	Child must be under age 19 or a full-time student under age 24 and younger than the taxpayer claiming the child. No age limit for individuals who are totally and permanently disabled.	Not applicable.
Support	Child must not provide more than half of his or her own support.	Taxpayer must provide more than half of the support for the qualifying relative (except if claiming under a multiple support agreement).
Gross income	Not applicable.	Gross income must be less than exemption amount ($3,900 for 2013).

TABLE
11.3 2013 PHASEOUT RANGE FOR PERSONAL AND DEPENDENCY EXEMPTIONS

FILING STATUS	BEGINNING AGI THRESHOLD	AGI AT MAXIMUM PHASEOUT
Single (Unmarried)	$250,000	$372,500
Head of Household	$275,000	$397,500
Married Filing a Joint Return	$300,000	$422,500
Surviving Spouse	$300,000	$422,500
Married Filing a Separate Return	$150,000	$211,250

rates. The current phaseout of exemptions is a reinstatement of the phaseout that existed prior to 2010, but had been eliminated for 2010 through 2012.

Determining the allowable exemption deduction within the phaseout range is a multistep process:

1. (AGI – Threshold AGI)/$2,500 = Phaseout Factor (rounded up to the next whole number)
2. Phaseout Factor × 2 = Phaseout Percentage (cannot exceed 100%)
3. Phaseout Percentage × Exemption Amount = Exemption Reduction
4. Exemption Amount – Exemption Reduction = Allowable Exemption Deduction

This formula applies to all taxpayers, except married persons filing a separate return. They substitute $1,250 for $2,500 in the denominator of (1). Taxpayers who are required to phase out their exemptions, generally have part of their itemized deductions phased out as well. The two phaseouts often occur simultaneously.

EXAMPLE 15

Bill and Sue, married with two dependent children, have AGI of $383,000 on their 2013 joint return. Their 2013 exemption amount before phaseouts is $15,600 ($3,900 × 4). Their reduced exemption amount is computed as follows:

1. ($383,000 – $300,000)/$2,500 = 33.2 (rounded up to 34)
2. 34 × 2 = 68%
3. 68% × $15,600 = $10,608
4. $15,600 – $10,608 = $4,992 allowable exemption

FILING STATUS

To file a return, taxpayers must select their filing status from the five categories available: married filing jointly, married filing separately, surviving spouse (also referred to as qualifying widow or widower), head of household, and single. Taxpayers indicate their filing status on the first page of Form 1040 as shown in Figure 11.5. The taxpayer's standard deduction depends on the filing status for which he or she qualifies. Filing status also determines which tax rate schedule the taxpayer must use.

Married Filing Jointly

Couples who are legally married on the last day of the tax year are married for the entire year for federal tax purposes. If you divorce on December 31, you are single for the entire year. A separation from your spouse does not qualify you as single. You are considered married until the divorce becomes final.[22]

Most married couples file a joint return because this filing status generally provides the lowest tax liability for a given amount of taxable income, particularly when

FIGURE 11.5 FILING STATUS SECTION OF FORM 1040

Filing Status

Check only one box.

1 ☐ Single
2 ☐ Married filing jointly (even if only one had income)
3 ☐ Married filing separately. Enter spouse's SSN above and full name here. ▶
4 ☐ Head of household (with qualifying person). (See instructions.) If the qualifying person is a child but not your dependent, enter this child's name here. ▶
5 ☐ Qualifying widow(er) with dependent child

[22] The determination of whether a couple is legally married is a question of state law. If a state recognizes common law marriages, then the two individuals are recognized as husband and wife under federal tax law as well.

the spouses have differing income levels. The averaging effect of combining the two incomes can effectively keep the income in a lower tax bracket. The joint return rate schedule is more favorable than any other rate schedule.

TAX PLANNING

In addition to being married at the end of the year, both spouses must be U.S. citizens or residents of the United States to file a joint return.[23] If one of the spouses is a nonresident alien, a joint return can be filed only if the nonresident spouse agrees to include his or her worldwide income in the joint U.S. tax return. If a joint return is not filed, each must file a married filing separately return. In this case, however, the nonresident spouse is taxed on U.S. source income only. If the nonresident spouse has little U.S. source income but a significant amount of foreign-source income, it may be advantageous for the couple to file separate returns.

If one spouse dies during the year, marital status is determined on the date of death of the decedent. As long as the surviving spouse has not remarried prior to the end of the year, the surviving spouse is still considered married to the decedent spouse for tax purposes. In such cases, the surviving spouse may file a joint return for the year of death, and two personal exemptions are allowed. The widow or widower may also qualify for some relief as a surviving spouse in subsequent years, if certain conditions are met.

Surviving Spouse

A **surviving spouse** (qualifying widow or widower with a dependent child) may claim the standard deduction for married filing jointly and may use the joint tax rate schedule for a limited period after the spouse's death. Congress recognized that the death of a spouse can cause a particular hardship for the surviving spouse when a dependent child is still living at home. To provide temporary relief, a surviving widow or widower who does not remarry and has at least one dependent child in the home for the entire year, for whom he or she pays more than one-half the cost of maintaining the home, may continue to use the joint tax rate schedule and standard deduction for the two years following the year in which the spouse dies. At the end of this two-year period, the surviving spouse may qualify as head of household. For the two years that surviving spouse status is claimed, no personal exemption is allowed for the decedent spouse.

EXAMPLE 16

Mark and Mindy are married and have two dependent children living with them. Mark dies in year 1. Mindy remains unmarried and the two children continue to live with her. A joint return is filed in year 1 with two personal and two dependency exemptions. For years 2 and 3, Mindy files as a surviving spouse (qualifying widow) with one personal and two dependency exemptions, uses the favorable joint tax return rate table or schedule, and may claim the standard deduction available for joint returns. Beginning in year 4 she can file as head of household.

A widow or widower who does not have a dependent child living with him or her does not qualify as a surviving spouse. Instead, he or she would file as a single individual or, if qualified, as head of household.

Married Filing Separately

Taxpayers who are married but elect not to file a joint return generally must file returns as married filing separately. They are not allowed to file as "single" individuals. The tax rate schedule for married filing separate returns is the harshest of all the rate schedules, and is based on one-half of the rate schedule for married couples filing joint returns. Using the married filing separately tax rate schedule results in a higher tax liability than the liability computed using the rate schedule for single individuals when taxpayers have taxable income in excess of $73,200 in 2013.

[23] § 6013(a)(1).

When a nonresident alien is married to a U.S. citizen or resident alien, and both have taxable income, they normally must file as married persons filing separately. The nonresident alien can, however, elect to be taxed as a resident alien if both spouses agree to be taxed on their worldwide income and provide all information necessary to determine their tax liability.[24] This election permits a nonresident alien to file a joint tax return with his or her spouse to take advantage of the more favorable tax rates applicable to joint returns.

Married persons filing separately face a number of other limiting factors when filing separate tax returns. For example, married persons filing separately may claim neither the earned income credit nor the child and dependent care credit.

In spite of the disadvantages, filing separately may have some benefits. First, if the married couple is contemplating a separation or divorce, filing separately relieves one spouse of any liability for taxes, penalties, and interest arising from the other spouse's return. If they file jointly, they are both fully liable for the taxes, penalties, and interest arising from the joint return. Although it may cost the couple extra tax dollars, lack of trust or animosity between the couple may dictate separate returns. If problems are resolved, the couple may file an amended joint return within the time allowed for amended returns. On the other hand, once the due date has passed for filing a joint return, separate amended returns may not be filed.

TAX PLANNING

In some unusual situations, the couple could save tax dollars by filing separately. If one spouse has the majority of itemized deductions but a lower AGI, he or she may be able to claim a greater percentage of itemized deductions due to the lower thresholds based on AGI. If they file jointly, their thresholds based on their combined AGI could wipe out many of their itemized deductions. If the couple files separately, however, both must either itemize deductions or use their standard deduction.

Example 17

Jill has \$7,600 of qualified medical expenses. Jill's AGI is \$15,000, and her husband Jack's AGI is \$60,000. Medical expenses are deductible only to the extent they exceed 10 percent of AGI. If they file a joint return, only \$100 of the medical expenses [\$7,600 – (\$75,000 joint AGI × 10%)] is deductible. If they file separately, Jill can deduct \$6,100 for medical expenses [\$7,600 – (\$15,000 × 10%)].

Head of Household

To file as **head of household**, an individual must meet two principal tests:

1. He or she must be single at the end of the year, unless qualifying as an *abandoned spouse*.
2. He or she must pay more than half the costs of maintaining a home in which a *qualifying child* or other relative claimed as a dependent lives for more than half the tax year.[25] A qualifying child (as defined in the section on dependency exemptions) does not have to be a dependent of the taxpayer. This exception protects a parent who has custody of a child who is claimed as a dependent by the noncustodial spouse. The parent with custody can still claim head of household filing status, as long as he or she provides more than one-half the cost of maintaining the household. Also, temporary absences for school, vacation, or medical care count as time lived in the home.

Generally, a dependent relative must live in the home with the taxpayer; however, a dependent *parent* does not have to live in the home with the taxpayer. This allows a single taxpayer to claim head of household status if he or she pays more than

[24] §6013(g).

[25] Qualifying household costs include real property taxes, mortgage interest, rent, utility bills, repairs and maintenance, property insurance, and the cost of food consumed in the household. Qualifying household costs do not include clothing, education, or medical expenses. Reg. §1.2-2(d).

one-half the costs of a dependent parent's household, such as a separate apartment or a nursing home.

EXAMPLE 18

Phillip is single and supports his elderly father, who lives in another city. Phillip provides more than one-half of the costs of maintaining the apartment and claims his father as his dependent on his tax return. Because he can claim his father as a dependent and he provides more than one-half the cost of his father's apartment, Phillip can file as head of household.

Table 11.4 summarizes the types of qualifying relatives that would enable a taxpayer to claim the head of household status.

If a taxpayer qualifies as a head of household, the tax rate schedule is more favorable than that of a single individual but less favorable than that of married couples who file joint returns.

The abandoned spouse classification is an exception to the rule that the taxpayer claiming the head of household status must be single at the end of the year. An **abandoned spouse** is a person who is married at year-end but who has

- lived apart from his or her spouse at all times during the *last six months* of the tax year *and*
- paid more than one-half the cost of maintaining a home in which the taxpayer and a dependent child lived for more than half the tax year.[26]

Without this provision, a married, but abandoned taxpayer would have to file as married filing separately, unless the taxpayer files a joint return with the spouse. More

TABLE 11.4 RELATIVES QUALIFYING TAXPAYER FOR HEAD OF HOUSEHOLD STATUS

TYPE OF RELATIVE	DEPENDENCY STATUS	HOUSEHOLD REQUIREMENTS
Qualifying child who lived with taxpayer for more than half the year	Child does not need to be dependent of taxpayer	Taxpayer must pay more than half of the costs of maintaining a home in which the qualifying child lives for more than half the tax year
Taxpayer's mother or father	Mother or father must be a dependent of the taxpayer	Taxpayer must pay more than half of the costs of maintaining the home in which the mother or father lives for more than half the tax year (but can live apart from the taxpayer)
Qualifying relative (other than mother or father) who lives with the taxpayer for more than half the year	Qualifying relative must be a dependent of the taxpayer	Taxpayer must pay more than half of the costs of maintaining the home in which the qualifying relative lives for more than half the tax year.

[26] § 2(c).

likely, the spouse cannot be found or refuses to file a joint return. If the taxpayer does not meet the specific requirements for abandoned spouse relief and does not file a joint return, the taxpayer must file as married filing separately, a filing status with the harshest tax rate schedule.

EXAMPLE 19

Kelly and Jerry are married. Jerry left town and has not been heard from in two years. Kelly has two dependent children living in her home all year. Kelly provides more than half the cost of maintaining the home. Based on these facts, Kelly can file as head of household under the abandoned spouse provision.

Single (Unmarried) Individual

Taxpayers who do not qualify for one of the other filing statuses must file as single individuals. Thus, a single taxpayer who cannot file as head of household or as a surviving spouse must use the single (unmarried) filing status. A taxpayer is single if he or she is unmarried on the last day of the tax year.[27]

STANDARD DEDUCTION

Basic Standard Deduction

Taxpayers are allowed to deduct the greater of their **standard deduction** or their itemized deductions in determining their taxable income. The standard deduction is adjusted annually for inflation. Table 11.5 shows the standard deduction amounts for 2013.[28]

Taxpayers compare their standard deduction to their itemized deductions to determine the greater benefit. If their standard deduction equals or exceeds their itemized deductions, they take their standard deduction.[29] (Unlike exemptions and itemized deductions, standard deductions are never subject to any phaseout.)

TABLE 11.5 **STANDARD DEDUCTIONS FOR 2013**

FILING STATUS	BASIC	ADDITIONAL*
Single (Unmarried)	$6,100	$1,500
Head of Household	$8,950	$1,500
Married Filing a Joint Return	$12,200	$1,200
Surviving Spouse	$12,200	$1,200
Married Filing a Separate Return	$6,100	$1,200
Dependent	$1,000 (or if larger, earned income plus $350)	

**Additional amount for each instance of blindness or age (65 or older) of the taxpayer (or taxpayer and spouse if a joint return is filed).*

[27]§6013.

[28]For 2012, the standard deductions amounts were $5,950 for single individuals and married filing separately, $8,700 for head of household; and $11,900 for married filing a joint return. The additional amounts for elderly or blind taxpayers were $1,450 for unmarried taxpayers and $1,150 for married taxpayers.

[29]Two specific individuals are not permitted to use the standard deduction: a married individual filing a separate return if his or her spouse itemized deductions and a nonresident alien.

EXAMPLE 20

Jerry and Elaine, married filing jointly, have AGI of $75,000. Their itemized deductions are only $9,870, They should, however, claim their standard deduction of $12,200 for 2013, as it exceeds their itemized deduction total.

Additional Standard Deduction for Age or Blindness

Taxpayers who are age 65 or older at the end of the year, or who are blind, are allowed additional standard deductions.[30] For taxpayers who file as single taxpayers or as heads of household, the additional standard deduction for age 65 or older or for blindness is $1,500 each in 2013. In 2013, single taxpayers (or heads of household) may add a total of $3,000 to their basic standard deduction if they are both blind and age 65 or older. The additional standard deduction for married taxpayers in 2013 for age 65 or older or for blindness is $1,200 each. The maximum additional standard deduction on a joint return if both the taxpayer and spouse are at least age 65 and blind would be $4,800 (4 × $1,200). The additional standard deduction is adjusted periodically (in $50 or $100 increments) for inflation.

There is no additional standard deduction allowed for dependents who are blind or over 65. This additional amount can only be claimed on the taxpayer's own return. For example, if a taxpayer claims her 68-year-old grandmother as her dependent, the taxpayer is allowed no additional standard deduction because of her grandmother's age.

After adding the additional standard deduction to the basic standard deduction, a taxpayer compares this total to itemized deductions and deducts the greater of those two amounts from AGI in determining taxable income.

EXAMPLE 21

Newton and Betsy, a married couple, are both 68 years old. Newton is legally blind. The couple's 2013 total standard deduction is $15,800: the sum of their basic standard deduction of $12,200 plus three additional standard deductions of $1,200 each. If their itemized deductions are less than $15,800, they will use their standard deduction in computing taxable income. If their itemized deductions exceed $15,800, they will elect to claim their itemized deductions instead.

To provide temporary relief for taxpayers prior to 2010, Congress allowed taxpayers who claimed the standard deduction (rather than itemizing) to increase their standard deduction for three specific items previously only allowed as itemized deductions. The three targeted areas, which were all subject to certain limitations, were real property taxes, sales taxes for purchasing new qualifying vehicles, and personal casualty losses resulting from certain disasters. All of these expired at the end of 2009.

Standard Deduction for Dependents

In addition to the loss of the personal exemption, for 2013 the standard deduction for individuals claimed as dependents on another's tax return is limited to the *greater* of $1,000 ($950 in 2012) or their earned income for the year plus $350 ($300 in 2012) up to their otherwise allowable standard deduction. Earned income includes salaries, wages, tips, and net business income, but it does not include net rental income, interest, dividends, or capital gains.

EXAMPLE 22

Johnny, age 12, has $3,000 of dividend income for the year from stock that was a gift from his uncle several years ago. This is Johnny's only source of income, and he is claimed as a dependent on his parents' tax return. Johnny has neither itemized deductions nor earned income; thus, his standard deduction is

[30]§63(c)(3). Blindness is defined in §63(f)(4) as vision not exceeding 20/200 in the better eye with correcting lenses or a field of vision of 20 degrees or less.

limited to $1,000 for 2013. Johnny's taxable income is $2,000: his $3,000 dividend income less his standard deduction of $1,000.

If Johnny has $1,200 income from a newspaper route in addition to his $3,000 dividend income, Johnny's gross income is $4,200, and his standard deduction is $1,550 ($1,200 earned income + $350). His taxable income is $2,650 ($4,200 – $1,550).

The standard deduction for a dependent cannot exceed the standard deduction allowed a taxpayer in that filing status.[31] As many single children are dependents, they are limited to a standard deduction of $6,100 if their earned income exceeds $5,750.

Example 23

Susie, age 17, is claimed as a dependent on her parents' tax return. She earns $6,450 from modeling during 2013. She has no itemized deductions. Her standard deduction is limited to $6,100 (the maximum basic standard deduction for a single individual), and she is allowed no personal exemption. Susie's taxable income is $350: her earned income of $6,450 less her standard deduction of $6,100.

Taxpayers can maximize the use of their standard deductions and itemized deductions by timing certain deductible payments.

TAX PLANNING

Example 24

Trudy is single; assume her standard deductions in years 1 and 2 are both $6,100. In late December, year 1, she receives a $12,000 cash gift from her rich uncle. Trudy plans to donate the entire sum to her church. This charitable contribution will be her only itemized deduction. If she donates $6,000 in December, year 1, and $6,000 in January, year 2, she will obtain no tax benefit from either of the donations because they do not exceed her standard deduction. If, however, she donates the entire $12,000 in year 1, she can deduct it from AGI in computing her year 1 taxable income. She can then deduct the $6,100 standard deduction in year 2. This provides Trudy with total deductions from AGI over the two years of $18,100 ($12,000 + $6,100), an increase of $5,900 ($18,100 – $6,100 – $6,100) over her standard deductions for the two years. By timing deductible expenditures, taxpayers can often generate deductions over two years that are greater than the sum of their standard deductions.

Itemized Deductions

Itemizing deductions is an alternative to the individual's standard deduction. Under the guise of tax simplification, Congress imposed limitations on itemized deductions, reducing the number of taxpayers who itemize their deductions. The deductibility of certain **itemized deductions** (medical expenses, casualty losses, and miscellaneous itemized deductions) is restricted to the amounts, if any, by which they exceed specified floors based on the taxpayer's AGI.[32] Deductions for charitable contributions are limited by a ceiling based on various percentages of adjusted gross income.[33] Table 11.6 summarizes the various statutory provisions that serve to limit otherwise deductible itemized deductions.

Medical Expenses

Section 213 allows taxpayers to deduct expenditures paid for medical care for the following:

- Diagnosis, cure, mitigation, treatment, or prevention of disease or for the purpose of affecting any structure or function of the body.

[31]The limit on the standard deduction for dependents applies only to their basic standard deduction. Any additional standard deductions for age and blindness are added in full to the reduced basic standard deduction on their own tax returns.

[32]The floors, or thresholds, are the minimum expense that the taxpayer must incur before a deduction can be obtained.

[33]A ceiling is the maximum deduction that can be claimed in any one year.

TABLE 11.6 LIMITATIONS APPLIED TO ITEMIZED DEDUCTIONS

DEDUCTION	LIMITATION TYPE	LIMIT DESCRIBED
Medical expenses	Floor	10% of AGI*
Taxes	None	None
Home acquisition mortgage interest	Ceiling	Interest on up to $1,000,000 of debt principal
Home equity interest	Ceiling	Interest on up to $100,000 of debt principal
Investment interest	Ceiling	Interest up to amount of net investment income
Charitable contributions	Ceiling	50% of AGI
Charitable contributions of long-term capital gain property	Ceiling	30% of AGI
Casualty and theft losses	Floor	$100 plus 10% of AGI
Miscellaneous itemized deductions, including unreimbursed employee expenses	Floor	2% of AGI

**For individuals age 65 or older, the threshold is 7.5% of AGI.*

- Transportation primarily for and essential to medical care.[34]
- Insurance for medical care. [35]

Medical and dental expenses qualify as itemized deductions when incurred for the benefit of taxpayers and their dependents, including costs incurred for cosmetic surgery to correct a deformity resulting from a congenital abnormality, personal injury, or disease. Amounts incurred for elective cosmetic surgery, however, are not deductible.[36] Apparently, Congress felt that the tax system should not subsidize the costs of hair transplants, facelifts, liposuction, and other medical procedures that are undertaken for the sake of vanity.

Only expenditures for prescription drugs and insulin are deductible. Nonprescription drugs, except insulin, are not deductible even if recommended by a doctor. Other specialized medical products, such as wheelchairs, eyeglasses, contact lenses, crutches, false teeth, hearing aids, and artificial limbs, are deductible. Their

[34]The mileage rate for using a car to get medical care is 24 cents per mile for 2013 and was 23 cents per mile for 2012, 19 cents per mile for 1/1/11-6/30/11 and 23.5 cents per mile for 7/1/11 – 12/31/11. Notice 2012-72, 2012-50 IRB 673.

[35]Beginning in 2014, most U.S. citizens and residents will be required to maintain minimum essential health care coverage. Individuals who do not maintain this coverage will be subject to penalties starting in 2014 equal to the greater of $95 or 1% of household income in excess of the tax return filing threshold. The penalty increases to $325 or 2% of income in 2015 and $695 or 2.5% of income in 2016. The penalty for an uninsured dependent under age 18 is half of the penalty for an adult. A refundable tax credit will be available for individuals with household incomes of up to 400% of the federal poverty level to assist them in the cost of purchasing health insurance through an exchange.

[36]§ 213(d)(9)(A) and (B).

cost is deducted when purchased, even though the item may have an extended life. The cost of meals is deductible if provided by a hospital or similar care facility as a necessary part of a patient's medical care.

Health insurance premiums for taxpayers and their dependents are a deductible medical expense only if paid from the taxpayer's after-tax income. Thus, health insurance premiums paid through an employer-sponsored cafeteria plan (flexible spending account) are not deductible.[37] Such plans allow participants to purchase medical insurance with before-tax income. Taxpayers should use their employer's cafeteria plans to purchase medical insurance and to pay for medical expenses not covered by insurance, if available, because the tax savings from the exclusion is greater than a deduction as a medical expense.

TAX PLANNING

Premiums for disability insurance and insurance for the loss of life, limb, or income are not deductible insurance premiums. Premiums for long-term-care insurance qualify for the medical expense deduction, subject to limits based on the taxpayer's age.[38] The limits are adjusted annually for inflation.[39]

The taxpayer's qualifying unreimbursed medical expenses are deductible to the extent their total exceeds 10 percent of the taxpayer's AGI. Prior to 2013, medical expenses were deductible to the extent their total exceeded 7.5 percent of AGI. (It remains 7.5 percent for individuals age 65 or over.)[40]

EXAMPLE 25

Mario, age 50, has AGI of $75,000 for 2013. During the year, he incurred $12,000 of medical expenses and was reimbursed $4,000 for these expenses. Mario's allowable deduction for medical expenses is $500, computed as follows:

Medical expenses	$12,000
Less: reimbursements	(4,000)
Unreimbursed expenses	8,000
Less: $75,000 AGI × 10%	(7,500)
Allowed deduction	$500

Medical expenses that are charged on a credit card are deemed paid when charged, not when the credit card bill is paid.[41] Medical expenses paid in advance are not deductible until the year treatment is received unless prepayment is required as a condition of receiving medical care.[42] When medical expenses are paid in one tax year and reimbursed in a subsequent year, the tax benefit rule requires that the reimbursement be included in the taxpayer's income to the extent the prior deduction resulted in a tax benefit.

Taxes

Deductions are allowed for income and property taxes paid to state and local governments; however, no deduction is allowed for most taxes paid to the federal government.[43]

Section 164 identifies the following taxes as deductible:

1. State, local, and foreign real property taxes.
2. State and local personal property taxes.

[37]Cafeteria plans and flexible spending accounts are discussed in Chapter 4.

[38]§ 213(d)(1)(D).

[39]For 2013, deductible premiums are limited by age as follows: not more than age 40, $360 ($350 for 2012); more than age 40 but not more than age 50, $680 ($660 for 2012); more than age 50 but not more than age 60, $1,360 ($1,310 for 2012); more than age 60 but not more than age 70, $3,640 ($3,500 for 2012); over age 70, $4,550 ($4,370 for 2012).

[40]§ 213(d). In 2013, the 7.5% of AGI floor increased to 10% of AGI; however, the floor remains at 7.5% through 2016 for individuals age 65 or older and their spouses.

[41]Rev. Rul. 78-38, 1978-1 CB 67.

[42]Rev. Rul. 75-303, 1975-2 CB 87.

[43]§ 164.

3. State, local, and foreign income, war profits, and excess profits taxes.
4. Federal generation-skipping transfer tax on income distributions.
5. Federal environmental tax imposed on corporations that produce hazardous substances.
6. Other state, local, and foreign taxes that are incurred in the context of a trade or business or other income-producing activity.

TAX PLANNING

In October 2004, less than one month before the presidential and congressional elections, Congress modified Section 164 by adding a provision intended to benefit states that depend on sales taxes rather than income taxes (such as Florida and Texas), to raise revenue at the state and local level. Taxpayers could elect to deduct state and local general sales taxes *instead* of state and local income taxes as itemized deductions. The taxpayers who were subject to state income taxes compared both deductions, taking the higher of the two. Congress extended this alternative deduction through 2013.

To determine the allowable sales tax deduction, taxpayers can use the actual sales taxes paid (documented by accumulating receipts) or IRS-published tables that are based on average consumption (considering the taxpayer's income, number of exemptions, and sales tax rates). Taxpayers who elect to use the tables can add actual sales taxes paid for major purchases, such as a car or boat, to the table amount.[44]

Any payment to a government not listed in Section 164 is not deductible as a tax. Nondeductible taxes commonly incurred by individuals in addition to federal income taxes include federal and state excise taxes on the purchase of tires, motor fuels, tobacco, and alcohol; federal excise taxes on commercial airline tickets; and employee's share of federal payroll taxes.

A taxpayer must be careful to differentiate between taxes and fines and penalties imposed by a governmental unit. Section 162(f) specifically prohibits the deduction of any fine or penalty.

Income Taxes

Most state, local, and foreign income taxes are deductible as an itemized deduction in the year in which they are paid or accrued. Cash-basis taxpayers deduct taxes in the year they are actually paid. The refund of a cash-basis taxpayer's overpayment of income taxes from a prior year is included in income only to the extent that the deduction for the original tax payment produced a tax benefit.

EXAMPLE 26

Nick, a single taxpayer, reported 2013 adjusted gross income of $60,000 and total allowable itemized deductions of $6,250, including $3,500 for state income taxes. Nick receives a $1,100 state income tax refund in May of 2014. Nick must include $150 of the $1,100 refund in his 2014 gross income. His $1,100 overpayment of 2013 state income taxes reduced his tax base by only $150. He was entitled to a $6,100 standard deduction in 2013 without regard to his itemized deductions ($6,250 total itemized deductions − $6,100 standard deduction allowable = $150 benefit from itemizing deductions).

TAX PLANNING

Foreign income taxes are deductible as an itemized deduction only if the taxpayer foregoes the foreign tax credit for the amount of tax paid. In most circumstances, the

[44] The American Recovery and Reinvestment Act of 2009 added a new deduction for state and local sales taxes paid on new cars, light trucks, motor homes and motorcycles purchased after February 16, 2009 and before January 1, 2010. The deduction was limited to the tax on up to $49,500 of the purchase price of an eligible vehicle and was phased out for taxpayers with modified AGI between $125,000 and $135,000 ($250,000 and $260,000 if married filing a joint return). This deduction was available for taxpayers who claimed the standard deduction as an addition to the standard deduction. Taxpayers who itemized could elect to take the sale tax deduction in lieu of the deduction for state income taxes and would then include this in their sales tax deduction (i.e., it could not also be claimed as a standard deduction) to prevent a double deduction for sales tax on the vehicle.

taxpayer receives a greater tax benefit by electing the foreign tax credit than by deducting foreign income taxes.

Real Property Taxes

State and local personal property taxes and state, local, and foreign real property taxes are deductible when paid with respect to property that the taxpayer owns. Taxpayers must distinguish between the payment of real property taxes and the payment of assessments that fund improvements specifically benefiting the taxpayer's property. Assessments generally are not deductible as they usually are levied for improvements to the taxpayer's property and increase the property's basis accordingly. If, however, the assessments are for maintenance, repairs, or current interest due to financing improvements, they are deductible.

Interest Expense

The deductibility of any interest paid or incurred by an individual taxpayer is determined by the nature of the underlying debt; that is, taxpayers must trace the use of borrowed funds to determine their end use and their deductibility.[45] Nonbusiness indebtedness for individual taxpayers falls into one of four general categories: interest on student loans (deductible *for* AGI as discussed earlier); investment interest; qualified residence interest; and nondeductible personal interest, such as interest on credit cards, automobile loans, and other personal debts. Investment interest and qualified residence interest are itemized deductions.

Investment Interest

Investment interest includes interest on loans to acquire or hold investment property and margin interest paid to a broker to borrow against a brokerage account. The deductibility of investment interest is limited to a taxpayer's net investment income for the tax year.[46] Without this limitation, taxpayers could deduct interest paid to carry investments that produce little or no current income and whose income is deferred at the discretion of the taxpayer. Interest incurred to acquire investments that produce nontaxable income (for example, interest on municipal bonds) is not investment interest and is not deductible.[47]

Net investment income is the excess of gross investment income over deductible investment expenses (excluding interest) directly connected with the production of investment income, such as safe deposit box rental fees, investment counseling fees, and brokerage account maintenance fees. Investment income includes interest, annuity payments, and net short-term capital gains from the sale of investment property. Investment income does not include net long-term capital gains from the sale of investment property or dividend income unless the taxpayer elects to forego the favorable tax rate that may apply to such income.[48] Investment interest not currently deductible because of this limitation is carried forward indefinitely.

TAX PLANNING

Before electing to forego the favorable rates for long-term capital gains and dividend income, taxpayers should calculate the tax savings from the investment interest expense deduction to ensure that this provides a greater after-tax benefit than the reduced tax rate on the dividend income and capital gains. In making this comparison, individuals should take into account the time value of money and the marginal tax brackets for the current year and any future year to which the investment interest would be carried forward and deducted.

Because miscellaneous itemized deductions are deductible only to the extent that, in aggregate, they exceed 2 percent of the taxpayer's adjusted gross income,

---

[45] Temp. Reg. §1.163-8T.

[46] §163(d)(1).

[47] §163(h).

[48] §163(d)(4)(B). Investment income and expenses from economic activities that are passive activities under Section 469 are also excluded from the determination of net investment income.

the maximum amount of investment expenses that the taxpayer is allowed to deduct from gross investment income to determine net investment income is the lesser of the following:

1. The total of such investment-related expenses, or
2. Net miscellaneous itemized deductions that are deductible after reduction for the 2 percent of AGI floor.

EXAMPLE 27

Craig incurs interest expense of $9,400 attributable to his investment in stocks and bonds. He has gross investment income of $7,400, and his adjusted gross income, including his investment income, is $60,000. Craig incurs a $150 brokerage account maintenance fee and a $500 certified financial planner's counseling fee, both of which qualify as miscellaneous itemized deductions. He also has $1,000 of other qualifying miscellaneous itemized deductions. Craig's net miscellaneous itemized deduction is $450 [$150 + $500 + $1,000 – ($60,000 × 2%)]. Craig deducts investment interest to the extent of his net investment income of $6,950 ($7,400 – $450). The remaining investment interest expense of $2,450 ($9,400 – $6,950) is carried forward and treated as paid in the next tax year. The $450 of miscellaneous investment expense included in the determination of net investment income is the lesser of Craig's total miscellaneous investment expense ($650) and his net deduction for all miscellaneous expenses after reduction for the 2 percent floor. Note that Craig deducts the $6,950 of investment interest expense in the interest section of Schedule A: *Itemized Deductions* but the other investment expenses are deducted as miscellaneous itemized deductions.

Qualified Residence Interest

The interest expense paid on a home mortgage is not considered investment interest because the purchase of a personal residence (as a personal-use asset) does not qualify as an investment. Congress, however, decided it was important to encourage home ownership with a deduction for home mortgage interest. Since 1986, however, the deduction for home mortgage interest has been restricted to qualified residence interest, which includes interest both on acquisition debt and home equity loans within limits.

Debt secured by the taxpayer's residence to acquire, construct, or substantially improve such residence is defined as acquisition indebtedness. Interest on acquisition debt principal up to $1,000,000 is deductible as an itemized deduction. There is no carry forward of any amount in excess of the $1,000,000 limit.[49] The acquisition indebtedness on the taxpayer's principal residence can be combined with the acquisition indebtedness on one additional residence, however, to reach the $1,000,000 debt principal limit. If the second residence is rented out for part of the year, then the taxpayer's personal use of it must exceed the greater of 14 days or 10 percent of the rental days for any of the interest expense to qualify as acquisition debt.

EXAMPLE 28

Donna and Carl own three homes. The principal amount of the acquisition debt on their principal residence is $800,000 and the principal amount of the acquisition debt on their vacation home in the Florida Keys is $150,000. They also own a condo in Breckenridge, Colorado that is used by them for 10 days and rented out for 6 months during the year; the principal amount of this mortgage is $200,000. In the current year, they paid $30,000 in interest on the mortgage for their principal residence, $6,750 for interest on their Florida vacation home mortgage, and $9,800 for interest on the mortgage for their Colorado condo. They do not meet the minimum personal-use requirement for the Colorado rental home to qualify as a personal residence. Only the interest on the $950,000 of total acquisition debt for their principal residence and Florida

[49]Interest paid on acquisition indebtedness incurred prior to October 13, 1987, is not subject to any limitation on deductibility. The $1,000,000 debt principal limitation for liabilities incurred after October 13, 1987, is reduced, however, for any preexisting acquisition indebtedness the taxpayer may have. For taxpayers who are married filing separately, the limit is $500,000. Additionally, when there are multiple owners for a single property, the $1,000,000 for that property must be divided between the owners.

vacation home is deductible. They can deduct $36,750 ($30,000 + $6,750) mortgage interest expense as an itemized deduction. (As discussed in Chapter 5, they may also be able to deduct the interest and other expenses for the Colorado condo from their rental income reported on Schedule E.)

Assume the same facts as above except that the principal amount of the acquisition debt on their principal residence is $1,250,000 on which they paid interest of $46,875 on this mortgage. They can deduct only $37,500 of the interest expense [($1,000,000/$1,250,000) × $46,875] on the principal residence as acquisition debt. The interest expense for the Florida Keys vacation home cannot qualify as acquisition debt because they have exceeded the $1 million limit with the debt on the principal residence. They may, however, be able to deduct interest on an additional $100,000 in loan principal as a home equity loan as discussed below.

A taxpayer may also deduct interest on debt that uses the equity in a taxpayer's personal residence as loan security (a home equity loan). The equity in an individual's qualified residence is the difference between its fair market value and the amount of mortgage debt associated with the residence. Interest on such loans is deductible to the extent the principal amount does not exceed the lesser of $100,000 or the value of the taxpayer's home reduced by any acquisition indebtedness. Interest on home equity loans is deductible regardless of the use of the loan proceeds. Homeowners who borrow against the equity in their principal residence or qualified second home can effectively avoid the disallowance of the deduction for personal interest.

EXAMPLE 29

Dave owns a home worth $325,000. The principal remaining on his home acquisition mortgage is $250,000, giving him $75,000 of equity in his home. Dave borrows $30,000 to purchase a new personal-use automobile using his home equity as security. All the interest on the home equity loan is deductible, even though the loan proceeds are used to purchase the car and the interest on a personal loan using the new car as the security would not be deductible.

KEY RULING

An individual purchased a principal residence for its fair market value of $1,500,000 paying $300,000 cash and borrowing $1,200,000 through a mortgage that was secured by the home. The taxpayer had no other debt secured by the residence. The IRS ruled that the taxpayer could deduct the interest on $1,000,000 of the loan as acquisition debt and the interest on $100,000 as home equity debt.[50]

EXAMPLE 30

Refer to the information in example 28 in which Donna and Carl have $1,250,000 acquistion debt on their principal residence. If Donna and Carl purchased their principal residence for $1,350,000 with $100,000 as a down payment, they would have $100,000 of equity in their principal residence and would be able to consider $100,000 of the loan as home equity debt, deducting the related interest. Alternatively, if they purchased the Florida vacation home for at least $100,000 more than their acquisition indebtedness, they would have $100,000 of equity in that home and would be able to consider $100,000 of that loan as home equity debt and deduct the related interest.

TAX PLANNING

Because interest on home equity loans of up to $100,000 is deductible regardless of how the loan proceeds are used, a taxpayer who has the ability to borrow against his home equity should consider doing this to retire consumer debt on which the interest is nondeductible. When a taxpayer has the ability to retire debt early, he should first retire the debt with the highest after-tax interest cost.

Mortgage companies typically charge fees to borrowers for finding, placing, or processing their loans. These fees, called points or loan origination fees, are usually expressed as a percentage of the amount borrowed. Payment of points is considered

[50] Rev. Rul. 2010-25, 2010-44 IRB 571.

to be the equivalent of the prepayment of interest to the extent that such fees do not represent service charges for real estate appraisals, title searches, or other legal work. When such fees are paid in connection with borrowing to purchase or improve a taxpayer's primary personal residence, they are deductible from adjusted gross income in the year paid.[51] If incurred to refinance an existing home mortgage, points and other prepaid interest must be capitalized and amortized over the duration of the loan.

EXAMPLE 31

Richard and Helen purchase a $100,000 home with $20,000 of their own money and the proceeds of an $80,000 acquisition mortgage. The mortgage company charges two points ($1,600) for originating the loan. Richard and Helen paid the points at closing. Richard and Helen deduct the points as an interest payment in the tax year in which they are paid.

Three years later Richard and Helen refinance their mortgage to obtain a lower interest rate. They pay points in the amount of $1,500 to refinance their mortgage with a 30-year fixed-rate mortgage. Richard and Helen must amortize the points over the 30-year life of the mortgage ($50 per year). If Richard and Helen pay off their mortgage early, the unamortized balance of their points is deducted then.

Charitable Contributions

Section 170 allows taxpayers to deduct gifts made to qualified charitable organizations operated for religious, charitable, scientific, literary, or educational purposes based in the United States, as well as for gifts to U.S. federal, state, or local governments.[52] Contributions must be made through qualified organizations and not directly to individuals, regardless of the person's financial needs. In addition, contributions to organizations are not deductible to the extent any part of the donation is used for political lobbying purposes.[53]

If a taxpayer receives goods or services in return for a contribution, only the portion of the contribution in excess of the value of the goods or services received is deductible.[54]

EXAMPLE 32

Lynn and Dave, a married couple who file a joint tax return, contributed $3,000 to the Zoological Society, a qualified charity, in return for a one-year membership at the sponsor level. Sponsors receive free admission to all zoo exhibits, free cocktail party receptions for all exhibit openings, and a 10 percent discount at the zoo gift shop. The collective value of all sponsor member benefits is $1,000. Lynn and Dave have made a $2,000 contribution to the zoo. They are considered to have purchased member benefits valued at $1,000.

[51]§461(g)(2). For 2007-2013, an itemized deduction is available for the cost of mortgage insurance premiums paid on the purchase of a qualified residence. (Note that this deduction does not apply to homeowner's insurance that insures against perils such as fire and theft.) Taxpayers qualify for this deduction if they purchased a home with a low or no down payment and were required by the lender to buy mortgage insurance (such as PMI). These mortgage insurance premiums are classified as deductible mortgage interest if they were paid in connection with qualified acquisition debt. The deduction is gradually phased out at the rate of 10% for each $1,000 (or fraction thereof) of AGI over $100,000 so that no deduction is permitted once AGI exceeded $109,000. For married taxpayers filing separately, the phase-out rate is 10% for each $500 in excess of $50,000 AGI.

[52]§170(c). Contributions to assist international disasters such as the earthquakes in Haiti and Chili were deductible if made through qualified charitable organizations. Cash-basis taxpayers can usually deduct a contribution only on the tax return for the year the contribution is made; however, Congress created exceptions to encourage relief for certain disasters. For example, cash contributions made by April 15, 2010 to assist relief efforts for earthquakes in Haiti and Chili could be deducted on the taxpayer's 2009 tax return.

[53]§170(c)(2)(D).

[54]Under de minimis rules, contributions will be fully deductible in 2013 if the donor makes a minimum payment of $51 ($49.50 in 2012) and receives benefits that cost no more than $10.20 ($9.90 in 2012). Additionally, the contribution is fully deductible if the benefit is no more than the lesser of $102 ($99 in 2012) or 2% of the amount contributed.

Contributors to universities who receive preferred rights to purchase tickets for university athletic events may deduct 80 percent of the amount of their contribution, regardless of the value of their preferred ticket rights, however.[55]

EXAMPLE 33

Jim donated $3,500 to become a Hurricane Club contributor to the athletic department at the University of Miami. His membership gives him the right to purchase preferred seats to all home games. The value of this preferred right is $800. During the year, Jim purchased a total of 10 tickets at a cost of $100 each. Jim may deduct 80 percent of the amount of his Hurricane Club contribution, or $2,800. He may not deduct the actual cost of tickets as a charitable contribution.

Deductible charitable contributions may be made in cash or with property. No deduction is allowed, however, for a contribution of services or rent-free use of a taxpayer's property, as the owner simply has foregone income—income that is not subject to tax. Unreimbursed expenses related to the performance of charitable services, such as transportation and supplies, are deductible.[56] Total charitable contributions are deductible up to a limit of 50 percent of adjusted gross income. Excess contributions can be carried forward for up to five years.

Contributions of Property

Property contributions may be subject to different limitations and valuations depending on the type of property donated and the type of qualifying organization that receives the property. The donation value of property other than capital assets is the lesser of the property's fair market value or basis. The value of long-term capital gain property (property that would produce a long-term capital gain if sold) is the property's fair market value; thus, the capital gain element in the property escapes income taxation.[57] The ceiling limit is reduced, however, in exchange for this favorable valuation. Contributions of long-term capital gain property valued at fair market value are deductible up to a ceiling limit of only 30 percent of adjusted gross income, and this property is deductible only after other contributions (subject to the 50 percent limitation) are considered first.[58]

EXAMPLE 34

Jason contributes $25,000 to his favorite charity. The contribution consists of $10,000 cash and XYZ stock with a fair market value of $15,000. Jason acquired the XYZ stock four years ago for $4,000. Jason's adjusted gross income is $40,000. The overall deduction limit on contributions for the year is 50 percent of AGI, which equals $20,000 ($40,000 × 50%). The long-term capital gain property (stock) is subject to the 30 percent of AGI limit, so the maximum current deduction for the contributed stock is $12,000 ($40,000 × 30%). The cash contribution of $10,000 (subject only to the 50 percent limit) must be deducted from the overall limit before the long-term capital gain property; thus, only $10,000 of the stock contribution is deductible currently ($20,000 overall AGI limit – $10,000 cash contribution = $10,000 remaining current limit available for stock). The remaining $5,000 deduction for the stock ($15,000 FMV of stock – $10,000 current deduction) is carried forward to the next year and is subject to the 30 percent limitation in the future year.

[55]§ 170(l).

[56]A statutory standard mileage rate deduction of 14 cents per mile is provided in § 170(i) for an automobile used in a charitable activity.

[57]Capital assets are discussed in Chapter 7 and include investment assets (such as stock) and personal-use assets. Assets must be owned for more than one year to be considered long-term capital assets. § 170(b)(1)(C)(iv) expands the definition of donated long-term capital gain property to include Section 1231 gain property used by a taxpayer in a trade or business activity. The value of long-term capital gain property that is donated to a private nonoperating foundation generally is its adjusted basis, except for marketable securities held more than 12 months. § 170(e).

[58]The 30% of AGI limit also applies to contributions of cash and ordinary income property given to a private nonoperating foundation. The deduction for contributions of capital gain property to these private charities is limited to 20% of AGI.

If *tangible personalty* that is long-term capital gain property is donated to a public charity but the organization fails to use the property in its tax-exempt activity (unrelated-use property), the value of the contribution is reduced to the donor's basis (but the 50 percent of AGI limit now applies). This reduction does not apply to real estate or to *intangible* long-term capital gain property, such as marketable securities. A contributor of property should verify that the charitable organization plans to *use* tangible personalty before such a gift is made to ensure the maximum tax deduction is attained.

The charitable deduction for capital assets other than long-term capital gain property (such as short-term capital gain property or capital loss property) and ordinary income property is limited to the lesser of fair market value or the donor's adjusted basis.

Maximizing the Tax Benefit from Contributions

TAX PLANNING

Long-term capital gain property makes excellent charitable gifts. The owner not only gets a charitable deduction but avoids income tax on the appreciation element in the property. Appreciated stock makes an excellent contribution because the charity usually can sell the stock easily if it does not wish to hold it and the sale does not affect the contribution deduction.

The deduction for appreciated stock is limited to 30 percent of AGI, however. Even though any contribution in excess of 30 percent of AGI can be carried forward for five years, the longer the deduction is deferred, the lower the present value of the deduction. Donors should try to limit contributions of appreciated stock to no more than 30 percent of their AGI in any one year.

A taxpayer can elect to value long-term capital gain property under the alternative valuation rules (that is, value equal to the lesser of basis or fair market value) and avoid the 30 percent contribution limit.[59] If this election is made, the contribution is subject only to the 50 percent contribution limit. This election can prove to be beneficial if there is only a small amount of appreciation and the additional deduction at fair market value is not worth the cost of having a portion of the contribution deferred to a future tax year. It can also be advantageous if the 30 percent limitation greatly limits the taxpayer's allowable contribution deduction and little tax benefit is expected to be derived from carrying the unused contribution forward.

EXAMPLE 35

Walter, a single taxpayer, donated his collection of Mexican primitive art to the Metropolitan Museum last year. Walter's gift was valued at \$800,000, and his basis was \$500,000. Walter unexpectedly dies after making this charitable contribution. Walter's adjusted gross income is \$1,000,000 in the year of his death. Unless Walter's personal representative makes the alternative valuation election, Walter's contribution deduction on his final income tax return is limited to 30 percent of \$1,000,000, or \$300,000. The \$500,000 (\$800,000 – \$300,000) unused portion of his contribution is lost because there are no future tax years in which to use the contribution carryforward. Electing to value the contribution at \$500,000 (the lesser of fair market value or adjusted basis), allows all \$500,000 to fall within the 50 percent ceiling limit (\$1,000,000 AGI × 50%).

Stocks that have declined in value should be sold so that the loss can be claimed; the proceeds from the sale can be donated. This preserves the loss deduction that would otherwise be lost as the deduction is limited to the lower fair market value.

TAX PLANNING

A taxpayer with charitable contribution carryovers that are expiring may be able to use them by increasing current period income through acceleration of income recognition and the deferral of deductions.

The burden of proof is always on the taxpayer to substantiate the value of property donated to charity. Taxpayers should keep a contemporaneous record of their charitable contributions, but the IRS imposes specific recordkeeping requirements.

[59] § 170(b)(1)(C)(iii).

Since 2007, to deduct *any* charitable donation of money, the individual must have a bank record (such as a canceled check, bank statement, or credit card statement) or a written communication from the charity showing the name of the charity and the date and amount of the contribution. Bank statements should show the name of the charity and the date and amount paid; credit card statements should show the name of the charity and the transaction posting date. For contributions by phone or text message, a phone bill showing the name of the charity, the date, and amount contributed will satisfy this requirement. For payroll deductions, retain a pay stub, Form W-2 wage statement or other document furnished by an employer showing the total amount withheld for charity, along with the pledge card showing the name of the charity. These requirements effectively make taxpayers write checks to preserve the tax deduction rather than dropping cash in a church collection plate or the Salvation Army Christmas buckets.

Donations of clothing and household items (such as furniture, appliances, and electronics) made to charities after August 17, 2006, must be in "good used condition" or better to claim a deduction for their value. IRS has not defined what it means by good used condition but taking a photo might help substantiate that the items were in good condition when donated. This good-condition requirement can be avoided on a single item valued at no more than $500 by including a qualified appraisal with the tax return. Any single donation valued at $250 or more requires written substantiation from the charitable organization. If the value of the donation is between $500 and $5,000, the donor is required to furnish additional information. If a noncash donation exceeds $5,000, the taxpayer must obtain a qualified appraisal for the property. Failure to follow these requirements may result in the loss of the charitable contribution deduction. Fees incurred for professional third-party appraisals of donated property may be deducted as a miscellaneous itemized deduction as part of the cost of determining one's tax liability.

More stringent rules apply to donated vehicles (including cars, boats, and airplanes) to close a loophole that allowed charities to sell the items for only a fraction of the value that the contributors claimed as a charitable contribution deduction. Taxpayers must now obtain a qualified appraisal for any vehicle valued at more than $500 (excluding inventory). If the charity does not use the vehicle in its regular charitable activities but instead sells it, the charitable contribution deduction cannot exceed the gross sales proceeds. No deduction is allowed unless substantiated by a contemporaneous (within 30 days) written receipt from the charity including the taxpayer's identification number and the vehicle's identification number. Charities intending to use donated vehicles (for example, to deliver food to the needy) must provide a certification of the intended use, the intended duration of its use, and certify that the vehicle will not be sold or transferred before completion of that use.

TAX PLANNING

Congress made certain retirees eligible for a charitable-giving tax incentive, even if they did not itemize. After age 70½, retirees must begin taking minimum distributions each year from traditional IRAs, resulting in taxable income. This charitable-giving incentive allows an eligible retiree to withdraw up to $100,000 from an IRA without recognizing taxable income as long as the money is donated *directly* to a qualified charity. This direct contribution from an IRA to a charity counts toward the retiree's required minimum distribution but is not included in income. There is no double benefit, however, as no charitable contribution deduction is allowed for the donated amount since the IRA distribution is not included in adjusted gross income. With this reduced AGI, taxpayers can get other tax benefits, such as lower taxes on Social Security benefits or a higher deduction for medical expenses. This provision expires at the end of 2013 unless be extended by Congress.

Casualty and Theft Losses

A deduction is allowed for casualty and theft losses on property held for personal use.[60] The value of the loss is the lesser of the asset's tax basis or the decline in fair

---

[60]§ 165(h).

market value from the casualty, less any insurance proceeds. The deduction is limited by two provisions: each separate casualty is first limited to the amount in excess of a $100 floor; then the total of all casualties (in excess of the floor) is deductible only by the amount that exceeds 10 percent of the taxpayer's AGI for the year.[61] The loss amount, after applying these limitations, is the itemized deduction. The $100 loss reduction per event removes small losses from deductibility for individuals. The 10 percent threshold for all losses requires the net loss to be fairly large relative to income for a portion to be deducted. These deductions are discussed in Chapter 8.

EXAMPLE 36

Melissa's home was damaged in a flood. Its fair market value prior to the storm was $200,000 and after the storm was $120,000. She received only $60,000 from her flood insurance due to a large deductible that applies to flood related losses. She purchased the home 8 years earlier at a cost of $155,000. If her adjusted gross income is $50,000, her deductible casualty loss is only $14,900 computed as follows. Melissa starts with the lesser of the home's decline in value ($200,000 – $120,000 = $80,000) or her basis ($155,000 cost); she then subtracts her insurance recovery ($60,000) resulting in a $20,000 loss. This $20,000 loss must be reduced first by the $100 floor and then by 10 percent of her $50,000 AGI ($5,000) resulting in a deductible loss of only $14,900.

Miscellaneous Itemized Deductions

Miscellaneous itemized deductions include most employment-related and investment expenses and are subject to a 2 percent of AGI floor limitation.[62] Qualifying expenses include the costs of job hunting for employment in the same occupation, hobby expenses, and expenses related to the determination, collection, or refund of any tax. The latter category includes tax return preparation fees, appraisal fees to document the value of property donated to a charity, accounting and legal fees for representation in a tax audit, and accounting fees for tax planning advice. Figure 11.6 shows the miscellaneous itemized deduction section from Schedule A, Form 1040.

TAX PLANNING

An employee is usually better off negotiating lower compensation with expense reimbursements than higher compensation with no expense reimbursement. The 2 percent of AGI floor prevents most individuals from benefiting from a net deduction for employee business expenses.

FIGURE 11.6 MISCELLANEOUS DEDUCTIONS SECTION OF SCHEDULE A ITEMIZED DEDUCTIONS FOR FORM 1040

Job Expenses and Certain Miscellaneous Deductions	21	Unreimbursed employee expenses—job travel, union dues, job education, etc. Attach Form 2106 or 2106-EZ if required. (See instructions.) ▶	21	
	22	Tax preparation fees	22	
	23	Other expenses—investment, safe deposit box, etc. List type and amount ▶	23	
	24	Add lines 21 through 23	24	
	25	Enter amount from Form 1040, line 38 [25]		
	26	Multiply line 25 by 2% (.02)	26	
	27	Subtract line 26 from line 24. If line 26 is more than line 24, enter -0-		27

[61]The floor was $100 for 2008 (and prior years), $500 for 2009, and reverted to $100 for years after 2009. For losses in federal disaster areas in 2008 and 2009, the 10 percent threshold did not apply.

[62]Two categories of expenses are not subject to the 2 percent of AGI floor; these are gambling losses (deductible to the extent of gambling winnings) and impairment-related work expenses that are incurred by a disabled person, such as a reader for a blind person.

EXAMPLE 37

Carlos, who is 44 and single with no dependents, has AGI of $100,000 for the year. His itemized deductions (before AGI limits) are as follows:

Medical expenses (unreimbursed)	$ 6,000
Interest on home mortgage (acquisition debt with a principal amount of $320,000)	12,000
Real property taxes	4,000
Charitable contributions	10,000
Miscellaneous employee expenses	3,000
Casualty loss (after $100 floor)	12,000

The medical expenses are not deductible because they are less than 10 percent of AGI. Only $1,000 of the miscellaneous employee expenses are deductible because that is the amount by which they exceed 2 percent of Carlos's AGI. Only $2,000 of the casualty loss is deductible because that is the amount by which the casualty loss exceeds 10 percent of Carlos's AGI. Carlos's taxable income, before considering his personal exemption, is as follows:

Adjusted gross income		$100,000
Less itemized deductions:		
Mortgage interest	$12,000	
Property taxes	4,000	
Charitable contributions	10,000	
Casualty loss	2,000	
Miscellaneous employee expenses	1,000	29,000
Taxable income (before personal exemption)		$71,000

Phaseout of Itemized Deductions for High-Income Taxpayers

High-income taxpayers must reduce certain itemized deductions if their AGI exceeds a specific threshold. These thresholds are the same as those used for the phaseout of personal and dependency exemptions presented earlier in this chapter in Table 11.3. The threshold is $250,000 for 2013 for single individuals, $275,000 for heads of household, $300,000 for married persons filing a joint return, and $150,000 for married persons filing separately. The affected itemized deductions are reduced by three percent of the taxpayer's AGI over the threshold AGI up to a maximum of 80 percent of affected itemized deductions.[63] For most taxpayers, only their charitable contributions, home mortgage interest, and taxes are subject to this phaseout. Medical expenses, casualty losses, and investment interest are not subject to reduction by the phaseout.[64] There was no phaseout for 2010-2012 (after several years of partial phaseouts); however, the phaseout was reinstated in 2013 as a compromise measure to increase taxes on higher-income taxpayers.

EXAMPLE 38

Art, who is single, has AGI of $320,000 in 2013. He also has the following itemized deductions, before any AGI limits or phaseouts:

Medical expenses (unreimbursed)	$10,000
Taxes	20,000
Charitable contributions	5,000
Investment interest expense	15,000

[63]§68(f). For 2006 and 2007, the phaseout could not exceed two-thirds of 3% of excess AGI or 80% of affected itemized deductions, if smaller. For 2008 and 2009 this phaseout could not exceed one-third of the lesser of three percent of this excess AGI or 80 percent of affected itemized deductions.

[64]Additionally, gambling losses (which are deductible only to the extent of gambling winnings) are not affected by the phaseout.

The medical expenses are not deductible because they are less than 10 percent of AGI. The remaining deductions totaled $40,000, which are then reduced by $2,100. The $2,100 reduction is the *lesser* of:

[3% ($320,000 AGI − $250,000 Threshold AGI)] = $2,100

or

[80% ($20,000 taxes + $5,000 charitable contributions)] = $20,000

Art can only deduct itemized deductions of $37,900 ($40,000 − $2,100) on his Schedule A: *Itemized Deductions.*

The phaseout of itemized deductions and exemptions increases the effective tax rate for higher income taxpayers without a "formal" increase in the published tax rates.

NET OPERATING LOSS

If a corporation's expenses exceed its operating income, it has a **net operating loss (NOL)** that it can carry back two years (filing a claim for refund of taxes) or forward up to 20 years. If an individual's expenses exceed his or her income, a negative taxable income does not necessarily mean that the individual has an NOL. Individuals must make several adjustments to arrive at a potential NOL because an NOL can only be the result of business losses—for example, from an S corporation, a partnership or a sole proprietorship. Employee wages and salary, however, are considered business income and will effectively reduce any business losses in determining the NOL.

In computing an NOL, individuals cannot deduct any personal or dependency exemptions; nonbusiness capital losses can only offset nonbusiness capital gains (excess capital losses cannot increase an NOL); and nonbusiness deductions (such as most itemized deductions) can only offset nonbusiness income (such as interest and dividends).

EXAMPLE 39

Jim has a $25,000 loss from his sole proprietorship, $10,000 in wages from a part-time job, and $500 of interest income. His AGI is a negative $14,500. After he deducts $9,000 of itemized deductions ($5,000 home mortgage interest and $4,000 real property taxes) and his $3,900 personal exemption, he has negative taxable income of $27,400.

To compute his NOL, Jim must add back his $3,900 personal exemption and the $8,500 excess of his nonbusiness deductions ($9,000 itemized deductions) over his nonbusiness income ($500 interest income). This reduces his NOL to $15,000—the same number reached by offsetting his $25,000 sole proprietorship loss with his $10,000 in wages. Jim can carry this $15,000 NOL back two years (filing a claim for refund of taxes) or forward up to 20 years.

COMPUTING THE TAX

After determining taxable income, individuals compute their gross income tax liability. The complete tax rate schedules for individual taxpayers for 2013 are shown in Table 11.7. Individuals use one of these schedules to determine their tax liability based on their filing status.

The tax rate schedules illustrate the progressive nature of the federal income tax; that is, as a taxpayer's taxable income increases, his or her marginal tax rate also increases. For example, Schedule X shows that a single taxpayer with taxable income of $100,000 is in the 28 percent marginal tax bracket; that is, the next dollar of income is taxed at 28 percent.

TABLE
11.7 TAX RATE SCHEDULES FOR 2013

SCHEDULE X—*SINGLE*

If taxable income is:	The tax is:
Not over $8,925	10% of taxable income
Over $8,925 but not over $36,250	$892.50, plus 15% of the excess over $8,925
Over $36,250 but not over $87,850	$4,991.25, plus 25% of the excess over $36,250
Over $87,850 but not over $183,250	$17,891.25, plus 28% of the excess over $87,850
Over $183,250 but not over $398,350	$44,603.25, plus 33% of the excess over $183,250
Over $398,350 but not over $400,000	$115,586.25, plus 35% of the excess over $398,350
Over $400,000	$116,163.75, plus 39.6% of the excess over $400,000

SCHEDULE Y-1—*MARRIED FILING A JOINT RETURN AND SURVIVING SPOUSES*

If taxable income is:	The tax is:
Not over $17,850	10% of taxable income
Over $17,850 but not over $72,500	$1,785, plus 15% of the excess over $17,850
Over $72,500 but not over $146,400	$9,982.50, plus 25% of the excess over $72,500
Over $146,400 but not over $223,050	$28,457.50, plus 28% of the excess over $146,400
Over $223,050 but not over $398,350	$49,919.50, plus 33% of the excess over $223,050
Over $398,350 but not over $450,000	$107,768.50, plus 35% of the excess over $398,350
Over $450,000	$125,846, plus 39.6% of the excess over $450,000

SCHEDULE Y-2—*MARRIED FILING SEPARATELY*

If taxable income is:	The tax is:
Not over $8,925	10% of taxable income
Over $8,925 but not over $36,250	$892.50, plus 15% of the excess over $8,925
Over $36,250 but not over $73,200	$4,991.25, plus 25% of the excess over $36,250
Over $73,200 but not over $111,525	$14,228.75, plus 28% of the excess over $73,200
Over $111,525 but not over $199,175	$24,959.75, plus 33% of the excess over $111,525
Over $199,175 but not over $225,000	$53,884.25, plus 35% of the excess over $199,175
Over $225,000	$62,923, plus 39.6% of the excess over $225,000

SCHEDULE Z—*HEAD OF HOUSEHOLD*

If taxable income is:	The tax is:
Not over $12,750	10% of taxable income
Over $12,750 but not over $48,600	$1,275, plus 15% of the excess over $12,750
Over $48,600 but not over $125,450	$6,652.50, plus 25% of the excess over $48,600
Over $125,450 but not over $203,150	$25,865, plus 28% of the excess over $125,450
Over $203,150 but not over $398,350	$47,621, plus 33% of the excess over $203,150
Over $398,350 but not over $425,000	$112,037, plus 35% of the excess over $398,350
Over $425,000	$121,364.50, plus 39.6% of the excess over $425,000

EXAMPLE 40

Jennie, single with a dependent child in her home, files as head of household. Her taxable income for 2013 is $58,000. Using Schedule Z, her gross income tax liability is $6,562.50, computed as follows:

$6,652.50 + 25% ($58,000 – $48,600)
= $6,652.50 + 25% ($9,400)
= $6,652.50 + $2,350
= $9,002.50

If Jennie qualifies as a surviving spouse (qualifying widow) and uses Schedule Y-1 for joint return filers, her tax liability is $6,307.50 computed as follows:

$1,785 + 15% ($58,000 – $17,850)
= $1,785 + 15% ($40,150)
= $1,785 + $6,022.50
= $7,807.50

When Jennie files as a surviving spouse, her tax liability is lower than if she files as head of household, because she did not reach the 25 percent tax bracket. The married filing a joint return schedule (also used by surviving spouses) provides the lowest tax liability for any given amount of taxable income. When a higher income husband and wife each earn approximately the same income, however, their combined incomes are taxed at higher rates on their joint return than they would be if they could each report their separate income as single individuals on single returns. This *marriage penalty* occurs because the bracket widths for the 25 percent, 28 percent and 33 percent brackets on joint returns are less than twice the bracket widths at those tax levels for single-filer returns.

EXAMPLE 41

Barbara is single and has taxable income of $77,500 in 2013. As a single individual, she will pay taxes of $15,303.75. Shelly and John are married and have $155,000 in taxable income, one-half earned equally by each of them. They pay $30,865.50 in taxes. This is $258.50 [$30,865.50 – (2 × $15,303.50)] more than they would pay if each of them was taxed separately as a single individual. The $258.50 is their marriage penalty.

Tax calculations in the previous sections implicitly assumed that the taxpayer had no dividends or net long-term capital gains as part of taxable income for the year. As explained in Chapter 7, when an individual has a net long-term capital gain from sales of capital assets, he or she files a Schedule D: *Capital Gains and Losses* to separately report these gains and losses. The instructions for this schedule include a worksheet for determining the total tax liability if there are taxable long-term capital gains included in the taxpayer's taxable income.

EXAMPLE 42

George is single and has $45,000 of taxable income, excluding a $10,000 long-term capital gain that is eligible for the 15 percent tax rate. George's tax on his $45,000 of ordinary income is $7,178.75 [$4,991.25 + 25% ($45,000 – $36,250)]. His tax on the capital gains is $1,500 ($10,000 × 15%). His total tax liability is $8,678.75. The alternate capital gains rate saves George $1,000 [$10,000 × (25% – 15%)].

Similarly, as explained in Chapter 3, qualifying dividend income is taxed at a maximum 15 percent rate (20 percent for taxpayers in the 39.6 percent top marginal bracket). A worksheet is used to determine the tax due on dividend income. Table 11.8 summarizes the rates that apply to long-term capital gains and dividend income.

Congress limits the tax savings that can be achieved through asset transfers to children by taxing unearned income of certain children at their parents' marginal tax rate. This is generally referred to as the kiddie tax and applies to children under age 19 and full-time students under age 24. This special tax calculation applies only to the

TABLE 11.8 **TAX RATES FOR ORDINARY INCOME, LONG-TERM CAPITAL GAINS, AND DIVIDENDS**

TAXABLE INCOME BRACKET FOR SINGLE INDIVIDUALS	TAXABLE INCOME BRACKET FOR MARRIED FILING JOINT RETURNS	TAX RATES FOR ORDINARY INCOME	TAX RATES FOR LONG-TERM CAPITAL GAINS* AND DIVIDEND INCOME
\$0-\$8,925	\$0-\$17,850	10%	0
\$8,926-\$36,250	\$17,851-\$72,500	15%	0
\$36,251-\$87,850	\$72,501-\$146,400	25%	15%
\$87,851-\$183,250	\$146,401-\$223,050	28%	15%
\$183,251-\$398,350	\$223,050-\$398,350	33%	15%
\$398,351-\$400,000	\$398,351-\$450,000	35%	15%
\$400,001 and above	\$450,001 and above	39.6%	20%

**Rate can be as high as 28% for collectibles and 25% for unrecaptured §1250 gain as discussed in Chapter 7. (These rates exclude the Medicare surtaxes discussed at the end of this chapter.)*

child's net unearned income (including dividend income and net capital gains) that exceeds $2,000. The kiddie tax does not apply to earned income (such as salaries and wages) or to children whose net unearned income is $2,000 or less. The kiddie tax is discussed in more detail in Chapter 12.

Tax Credits

Credits versus Deductions

After determining the gross income tax liability, the taxpayer reduces it by any allowable tax credits. Credits are a direct dollar-for-dollar reduction in the tax liability. When considering tax policy, the advantage of a credit is that the tax relief or benefit is equal for taxpayers in different marginal tax brackets when compared to that of a deduction. A $1,300 tax credit provides the same tax savings to a person in the 15 percent marginal tax bracket as it does a taxpayer in the 39.6 percent marginal tax bracket. The foreign tax credit is discussed in Chapter 4. Most of the other common credits available to individual taxpayers are summarized in the following sections.

Child Tax Credit

A $1,000 tax credit is available for each qualifying child of the taxpayer under age 17.[65] The child tax credit is a flat dollar amount (no calculation is required) but is phased out at the rate of $50 for every $1,000 (or part thereof) of AGI in excess of $110,000 for married taxpayers filing jointly ($55,000 if filing separately) and $75,000 for single individuals and heads of household.

[65] See previous discussion of a "qualifying child" under the section on dependency exemptions. The 2003 Act increased the child tax credit (originally $600) to $1,000. A taxpayer who is a dependent cannot claim the child tax credit.

EXAMPLE 43

Carol and John are married and have two dependent children under age 17. They have AGI of $124,000. They must reduce their $2,000 child tax credit by $700 [($124,000 – $110,000)/1,000 × $50] to $1,300.

Some or all of the child tax credit may be treated as a refundable credit. The credit is refundable to the extent of the greater of: (1) 15 percent of the taxpayer's earned income in excess of $3,000 or (2) for a taxpayer with three or more qualifying children, the excess of the taxpayer's social security taxes over his or her earned income credit.

EXAMPLE 44

Joseph is a single parent with two children for whom he is eligible to claim a $2,000 child tax credit. His income for 2013 is only $16,000. Because his income does not exceed his standard deduction and personal and dependency exemptions, he owes no income tax. Without the refundability provision, he would get no benefit from the credit. The provision allows him to receive a refund of $1,950 [($16,000 – $3,000) × 15%] for the child tax credit.

A credit of $12,970 in 2013 ($12,650 in 2012) is allowed for expenses incurred to adopt an eligible child. Qualified adoption expenses include reasonable adoption fees, attorney fees, court costs, and other expenses that are directly related to the legal adoption of an eligible child.[66] This credit is claimed in the year the adoption is finalized.

Education Credits

Two elective tax credits are available to assist taxpayers with the cost of undergraduate or graduate education or vocational training. The American opportunity credit (an expanded version of the previous Hope scholarship credit) provides a tax credit equal to 100 percent of the first $2,000 and 25 percent of the next $2,000 for qualifying expenses for each year of postsecondary education pursued on at least a half-time basis.[67] The maximum $2,500 American opportunity credit may be claimed for no more than four years for each student

The lifetime learning credit provides a credit equal to 20 percent of up to $10,000 of qualifying expenses for part-time or full-time undergraduate, graduate, or professional degree programs. The maximum lifetime learning credit is $2,000 per year per taxpayer (that is, the lifetime learning credit is fixed and does not vary with the number of students in the taxpayer's family).[68] The lifetime learning credit is available for an unlimited number of years, however.[69]

Both credits are available for the taxpayer, the taxpayer's spouse, or the taxpayer's dependents. A student who is claimed as a dependent on another's return, however, cannot claim either credit. In this case, any qualified tuition or related expenses paid by the child during the year are treated as if paid by the parent.[70]

Qualifying expenses for the American opportunity credit include the tuition and fees an individual is required to pay to enroll at or attend an eligible institution as well as required course materials such as textbooks. Thus, book, supplies, and equipment do not need to be purchased from the educational institution to qualify for this credit. Expenses qualifying for the lifetime learning credit include tuition and fees but exclude textbooks and other course materials (unless the individual is required to pay

[66]§ 23. An eligible child is a child under the age of 18 at the time the adoption expense is paid (or someone who is incapable of caring for himself or herself, regardless of age). This credit is phased out for taxpayers with modified adjusted gross income in excess of $194,580 for 2013 ($189,710 for 2012).

[67]For 2009 and 2010, the maximum American opportunity credit was also $2,500 per student. The previous Hope scholarship credit (that the American opportunity credit replaced) could be claimed for only the first two years of higher education for each student.

[68]For 2009 and 2010, the maximum lifetime learning credit was also $2,000 per taxpayer.

[69]§ 25A(c)(1).

[70]§ 25A(g)(3).

the institution for the course-related books, supplies, and equipment). Charges and fees associated with room, board, student activities, athletics, insurance, transportation, and similar personal, living, or family expenses do not qualify for either credit. Costs for courses or other education involving sports, games, or hobbies are not eligible for any credit, unless they are part of the student's degree program.[71]

Only the student's out-of-pocket expenses may be taken into account in calculating the credit. Expenses paid with a Pell grant, a tax-free scholarship, or a tax-free employer-provided educational assistance plan are not out-of-pocket expenses.[72] Thus, the student's expenses must be paid with income, loans, gifts, inheritances, or personal savings. If a taxpayer claims the American opportunity credit for qualifying expenses of a particular student, none of that student's additional qualifying expenses for the year may be applied toward the lifetime learning credit. In addition, any expenses that are paid for with distributions from a Coverdell educational savings account (educational IRA) are not eligible for either the American opportunity or lifetime learning credit (although expenses in excess of those paid for with Coverdell distributions may qualify for the credit). When a taxpayer claims either the American opportunity or lifetime learning credit, no deduction is permitted for any of that student's other education expenses.

Both the American opportunity and lifetime learning credits are targeted to low and middle-income taxpayers and are subject to phaseout based on income. The allowable American opportunity credit phases out over modified adjusted gross income ranges of $80,000 to $90,000 for single taxpayers ($160,000 to $180,000 for married taxpayers filing a joint return). Modified adjusted gross income is adjusted gross income increased by any excluded foreign earned income.[73] The credit reduction is stated as a percentage determined by dividing the amount modified AGI exceeds the $80,000 ($160,000 for joint return filers) threshold by the $10,000 ($20,000 for joint return filers) phaseout range. Thus, single taxpayers with $90,000 and joint filers with $180,000 of modified adjusted gross income are not eligible to claim the American opportunity credit.

EXAMPLE 45

Ricardo and Lucy have AGI of $175,000 for 2013 and file a joint tax return. They have two sons, Ricky and Billy, who are full-time students at State University in 2013. Ricky is a freshman and Billy is a junior. Ricardo and Lucy pay $4,000 in qualified tuition annually for each son. If their AGI was less than $160,000, they would be allowed to claim an American opportunity credit of $5,000 ($2,500 for each son). Because their AGI exceeds $160,000, their tentative credit of $2,500 per student is partially phased out. Ricardo and Lucy may only claim an American opportunity credit of $1,250 ($625 for each son) computed as follows:

($175,000 – $160,000)/$20,000 = 75%
75% × $2,500 tentative credit = $1,875 phaseout
$2,500 tentative credit – $1,875 phaseout = $625 allowable credit for each student

The lifetime learning credit is also subject to a proportionate phaseout, but over a modified AGI range of $53,000 to $63,000 for single taxpayers ($107,000 to $127,000 for joint return filers).[74] Similar to the American opportunity credit, the taxpayer's lifetime learning credit is reduced by a percentage determined by dividing the taxpayer's modified AGI in excess of the $53,000 ($107,000 for joint filers) AGI threshold by the $10,000 ($20,000 for joint returns) phaseout range. Taxpayers with modified adjusted

[71] § 25A(f).

[72] § 25A(g)(2).

[73] § 25A(d). The American opportunity credit is partially refundable (up to 40 percent); if, however, the taxpayer is subject to the kiddie tax (discussed in Chapter 12), the credit is not refundable. Additionally, the American opportunity credit may be used to offset a taxpayer's alternative minimum tax liability. The lifetime learning credit is neither refundable nor can it offset an alternative minimum tax liability.

[74] The phaseout range for the lifetime learning credit for 2012 was $52,000 to $62,000 for single taxpayers and $104,000 to $124,000 for joint return filers.

gross incomes exceeding $63,000 ($127,000 for joint filers) may not claim the lifetime learning credit.

EXAMPLE 46

Mason is a single taxpayer with modified AGI of $57,000. During the current year, he pays $7,000 in tuition for MBA courses in management. Mason is eligible for a tentative lifetime learning credit of $1,400 ($7,000 × 20%). Because his modified AGI exceeds the threshold amount for single taxpayers by $4,000 or 40 percent of the phaseout range [($57,000 AGI – $53,000 threshold AGI)/$10,000 income in phaseout range], his $1,400 tentative lifetime learning credit is reduced by $560 ($1,400 × 40%) to $840. Alternatively, Mason could claim the $4,000 tuition deduction for AGI.

Table 11.9 compares the American opportunity and the lifetime learning credits. Employment-related tax-free tuition benefits that employers can provide to employees and their family members are discussed in Chapter 4.

TAX PLANNING

For both credits, qualified tuition and fees generally include only out-of-pocket expenses and do not include any expenses covered by employer-provided educational assistance programs or scholarships if none of the payments are included in gross income. When an education institution provides a reduction in tuition to an employee (or to the spouse or dependent child of an employee) and the amount of the tuition reduction is included in the employee's gross income, that amount may qualify for an education credit. For purposes of computing either credit, the employee is treated as receiving a payment equal to the tuition reduction and then paying that amount to the educational institution.

The lifetime learning credit is a nonrefundable credit (that is, it may only offset a tax liability), but forty percent or $1,000 (40% of $2,500 = $1,000) of the American opportunity credit is refundable and will result in a payment to the taxpayer with no offsetting tax liability.

TABLE
11.9 COMPARISON OF EDUCATION CREDITS

PROVISION	MAXIMUM BENEFIT	PHASE-OUT RANGE	QUALIFYING EXPENSES
American Opportunity Credit	Maximum $2,500 credit per year per student	Phase-out range $80,000 to $90,000 AGI ($160,000 to $180,000 if MFJ)	Tuition, fees and course materials for only the first four years (course-related books, supplies and equipment do not need to be purchased from the institution to qualify)
Lifetime Learning Credit	Maximum $2,000 credit per year per taxpayer	Phase-out range $53,000 to $63,000 AGI ($107,000 to $127,000 if MFJ)	Tuition and fees (only includes course-related books, supplies and equipment if required to be paid to the institution)

Dependent Care Credit

Taxpayers who must pay for child or dependent care to be gainfully employed are eligible for a dependent care credit regardless of their income. The credit percentage, however, varies from 20 to 35 percent of qualifying expenditures up to certain limits based on the taxpayer's AGI. The credit percentage is 35 percent for taxpayers whose AGI does not exceed $15,000. The rate is gradually reduced to 20 percent at the rate of 1 percent for each $2,000 (or fraction thereof) that AGI exceeds $15,000. Taxpayers with AGIs exceeding $43,000 are allowed a credit of only 20 percent of qualifying expenses. Qualifying expenses include amounts paid for babysitting, cooking, and housekeeping, but do not include expenses for a gardener, chauffeur, or an overnight camp. The maximum expenditures qualifying for the credit are limited to $3,000 for one qualifying child and $6,000 in total for two or more qualifying children (however divided between the children) under the age of 13.[75]

EXAMPLE 47

Celina is a single attorney with AGI of $50,000. Celina's four-year-old daughter is in day care while Celina works. Celina spends $6,000 for child care during the year. Only $3,000 qualifies for the credit. Celina's child care credit is $600 ($3,000 × 20%). If she had spent only $2,000 on child care, her credit would have been $400 ($2,000 × 20%). If Celine also has an eleven year old daughter for whom she paid $400 in childcare in addition to the $6,000 for the younger child, she could base her credit on the maximum $6,000 even though she only spent $400 for the older child's care.

The child care credit is a nonrefundable credit; that is, if the computed credit exceeds the tax liability, the excess credit is simply lost. It is not refunded and cannot be carried to other tax years.

Earned Income Credit

The standard deduction and personal and dependency exemptions shelter many low-income individuals from paying income tax, but they do nothing to minimize the effect of payroll taxes. The earned income credit was added to the tax law to reduce the impact of payroll taxes through a refundable credit.[76] This credit, available to low-income taxpayers, is equal to a certain percentage of the taxpayer's earned income below a creditable maximum amount.[77] The credit percentage varies depending on whether the taxpayer has one, two or more, or no children in the home. Earned income includes salary, wages, tips, and net self-employment income.

In 2013, the maximum earned income credit for a taxpayer with one qualifying child is $3,250 ($9,560 × 34%), $5,372 ($13,430 × 40%) for a taxpayer with two or more qualifying children, and $6,044 ($13,430 × 45%) for three or more qualifying children. To the extent that the greater of AGI or earned income exceeds $22,870 for married taxpayers filing a joint return ($17,530 for others), the credit is gradually phased out.

A smaller credit is available to taxpayers without children. This credit is only available to working taxpayers ages 25 through 64 who are not eligible to be claimed as

[75] § 21. There is no age limit for disabled dependents. The maximum qualifying expense cannot exceed the individual's earned income. For married couples, the limitation applies to the earned income of the spouse with the lower income. A spouse who is a full-time student or is incapacitated is considered to have earned income of at least $250 per month for purposes of computing the credit. § 21(d)(2).

[76] Another credit available to low-income individuals is the § 22 credit for elderly or disabled. This credit is equal to 15 percent of the sum of a $5,000 base amount ($7,500 if MFJ) less reductions for Social Security and other nontaxable benefits and one-half of AGI in excess of $7,500 ($10,000 if MFJ). This credit is nonrefundable. Most elderly or disabled individuals are ineligible for this credit because they receive Social Security benefits in excess of the limit or they have AGI in excess of the limit.

[77] § 32. In 2012, the maximum amount of earned income on which the earned income tax credit was computed was $6,210 for taxpayers with no qualifying children, $9,320 for taxpayers with one qualifying child, and $13,090 for taxpayers with two or more qualifying children.

a dependent on another's tax return. For 2013, this credit is computed on a maximum earned income of \$6,370 times 7.65 percent (resulting in a credit of \$487) and gradually phases out when income exceeds \$13,310 for married taxpayers filing a joint return and \$7,970 for others. The American Recovery and Reinvestment Act of 2009 increased the credit percentage for families with three or more qualifying children to 45 percent. Taxpayers do not have to calculate this credit, however; the IRS provides simplified tables showing the amount of credit for all qualifying income levels and family size.[78] Because the earned income credit is a refundable credit, the amount of the credit that is greater than the taxpayer's income tax liability is refunded to the taxpayer. If the taxpayer has \$3,300 or more of investment income (unearned income) in 2013 (\$3,200 in 2012), however, the taxpayer may not claim this credit.

EXAMPLE 48

Emily has a gross income tax liability of \$600. She has an earned income credit of \$1,000. The credit completely eliminates her tax liability and creates a \$400 refund for her.

Most credits are listed in the credits section of Form 1040 on page 2, just below the income tax liability calculation. The earned income credit, however, is listed in the payments section of Form 1040, along with taxes withheld and estimated tax payments. This affords it the same treatment as overwithheld taxes, and like these, it can create a refund.

Excess Payroll Tax Withheld

If an individual works for more than one employer during the year and earnings exceed the Social Security ceiling (\$113,700 for 2013), generally too much Social Security tax (6.2 percent FICA tax) will have been withheld.[79] Each employer performs its payroll tax calculations independent of any other job the employee may have had during the year. The employee is allowed a credit for any excess Social Security taxes withheld.

EXAMPLE 49

Tim worked for Alpha Company for the first seven months of 2013, earning \$80,000 from which Alpha withheld \$6,120 (\$80,000 × 7.65%) for payroll taxes. In August, Tim accepted a job with Baker Company. During the last five months of the year he earned \$60,000 from which Baker withheld \$4,590 (\$60,000 × 7.65%) for payroll taxes. While the 1.45 percent Medicare portion of the tax is owed on Tim's entire \$140,000 (\$80,000 + \$60,000) earned in 2013, the 6.2 percent Social Security portion of the tax is due only on the first \$113,700 of salary. Therefore, Baker Company withheld \$1,630.60 excess payroll taxes from Tim computed as follows:

Payroll taxes withheld:		
Alpha Company (\$80,000 × 7.65%)		\$6,120.00
Baker Company (\$60,000 × 7.65%)		4,590.00
Total payroll taxes withheld		\$10,710.00
Tim's 2013 payroll tax:		
\$140,000 total wages × 1.45% Medicare tax	\$2,030.00	
\$113,700 Social Security ceiling × 6.2%	7,049.40	
Total payroll taxes		9,079.40
Excess withheld		\$1,630.60

Tim can claim a \$1,630.60 tax credit for the excess payroll tax withheld. This credit has no effect on Tim's employers, however, as they are not entitled to a refund of any excess employer's payroll tax.

[78] Refer to the instructions for Schedule EIC for the table.

[79] For 2011 and 2012, the employee's rate for Social Security was reduced from 6.2 percent to 4.2 percent on employee wages up to \$106,800 and \$110,100, respectively, while the employer's rate remained at 6.2 percent.

Retirement Contributions by Low-Income Wage Earners

Few low-income wage earners contribute to retirement plans because they spend almost all their disposable income. To encourage greater participation, the 2001 Tax Act added a saver's tax credit for low-income employees' elective contributions of up to $2,000 to employer plans or IRAs.[80] The maximum credit is 50 percent of the individual's qualifying contribution. This effectively provides a refund of part of their retirement contributions in the form of an income tax credit of up to $1,000. This credit is over and above any other deduction or exclusion that applies to the contribution. The credit rates (50, 20, or 10 percent) depend on the taxpayer's filing status and AGI.

Joint filers with AGIs up to $35,500 ($17,750 for single individuals) get a 50 percent credit. For joint filers, the credit drops to 20 percent for AGIs of $35,500 to $38,500 ($17,750 to $19,250 for single persons) and to 10 percent for AGIs of $38,500 to $59,000 ($19,250 to $29,500 for single persons). Joint filers receive no credit if AGI is above $59,000 ($29,500 for single individuals). An individual who can be claimed as a dependent on another's return, who is a full-time student, or who is not at least age 18, is not eligible for the credit.

EXAMPLE 50

Carla, a single individual, has AGI of $18,000 in 2013. She contributes $2,000 to a Roth IRA. She is eligible for a tax credit of $400 ($2,000 × 20%). If she had instead contributed to a traditional IRA, she would also be allowed to deduct the $2,000 contribution to the traditional IRA in addition to taking the tax credit.

Health Coverage Tax Credit

The health coverage tax credit (HCTC) is a refundable credit created to help persons who lost their jobs as a result of increased imports and retirees whose pensions were taken over the by the Pension Benefit Guaranty Corporation. The HCTC makes health coverage more affordable for these groups through a refundable credit equal to 72.5 percent of the premiums paid by the eligible taxpayer.[81] Qualified taxpayers can claim the credit on Form 8885 or have IRS make advance monthly payments directly to their health plan administrator. The HCTC also covers the spouse and dependents of eligible taxpayerss.

Credits to Encourage Energy Efficiency

Individuals are allowed a *nonrefundable* credit if they made improvements to residential property that made it more energy efficient such as new windows and exterior doors, insulation, heat pumps, furnaces, central air conditioners, and water heaters. The credit is 10 percent of the cost of qualified energy efficiency improvements up to a maximum lifetime credit of $500 per taxpayer.[82] The taxpayer's basis in the property must be reduced by the amount of the credit. The improvements must have been made on the taxpayer's principal residence; thus, improvements to rental property and vacation homes are not eligible for the credit.

A similar credit is allowed for expenditures for solar hot water heaters, solar electric property, fuel cell property, wind property and geothermal heat pumps installed on the taxpayers' principal residence by December 31, 2016. This credit is 30 percent of the cost of eligible property including installation costs. It, however, is not subject to the $500 limit.[83]

[80]§25B. Eligible retirement plans include Roth IRAs, traditional IRAs, 401(k) plans, and 403(b) plans.

[81]§35. The HCTC was 65% prior to May 2009 and then increased to 80% for eligible coverage months beginning before February 13, 2011 when it declined to the current 72.5%.

[82]§25C. This credit is scheduled to expire at the end of 2013.

[83]§25D.

There are several nonrefundable credits that encourage taxpayers to invest in alternative vehicles. For example, taxpayers who purchase plug-in electric drive vehicles can qualify for a credit. The full credit will be available until 60,000 eligible vehicles are sold and will be followed by a phase-out period. Many of the credits that were previously available for purchasing hybrid vehicles have gradually phased out because the automobile manufacturers have sold the allotted 60,000 qualifying vehicles.

Pre-2011 Homebuyer Credit and Recapture

In response to the surplus of unsold homes, Congress passed a first-time homebuyer tax credit (FTHTC) for qualifying taxpayers who purchased a principal residence after April 8, 2008 and before May 1, 2010. The amount of the credit depended on the date the home was purchased. For homes purchased in 2008, the maximum credit was $7,500; for homes purchased from January 1, 2009 through November 30, 2009, the credit was 10 percent of the purchase price with the maximum credit $8,000 ($4,000 if married filing separately).[84] The credit was refundable and was phased out for modified AGI between $75,000 and $95,000 ($150,000 and $170,000 for married couples filing a joint return).[85]

The Worker, Homeownership, and Business Assistance Act of 2009 extended the $8,000 credit for first-time homebuyers to homes purchased prior to May 1, 2010. It also expanded this provision to include a new $6,500 ($3,250 married filing separately) credit for any taxpayer who had owned and used the same home as his or her primary residence for five out the last eight years (a long-time resident) and purchased a new primary residence after November 6, 2009 and before May 1, 2010. For purchases after November 6, 2009, the phaseout ranges for the credit were increased to modified AGIs of $125,000 to $145,000 for individuals and $225,000 to $245,000 for married persons filing jointly. The credit could not be claimed for any home with a purchase price exceeding $800,000.

The credit for homes purchased in 2008 was effectively a 15-year interest-free loan from the government because it has to be repaid over a 15-year recapture period beginning two years after the year of purchase. In addition, if the home is sold before the 15-year recapture period is complete, the unrecaptured balance is due in the year of sale. The recaptured amount cannot exceed the gain the taxpayer realizes on the sale, however.[86]

EXAMPLE 51

Michael, a single first-time homebuyer with AGI of $70,000, purchased a home for $100,000 in 2008 and claimed a $7,500 credit on his 2008 tax return. Beginning in 2010, Michael must include an additional tax of $500 ($7,500 × 1/15) for each of the next 15 years to recapture the credit. If Michael sells his home in 2013 for $115,000, he must recapture the $6,000 balance of the credit ($7,500 – $1,500 recaptured in 2010, 2011, and 2012). On his 2013 tax return, Michael will report the gain on the sale of his home of $15,000 ($115,000-$100,000) but will only increase his 2013 tax liability by the $6,000 recaptured credit. He will not have to pay a tax on the gain on this sale as it qualifies for the $250,000 exclusion on the sale of a personal residence.

The credit for a home purchased in 2009 or 2010 is not subject to recapture or repayment unless the home ceases to be the taxpayer's principal residence within 36 months after the purchase date. In this case, the lesser of the entire $8,000 credit ($6,500 alternative credit for long-term residents) or gain realized on the sale must be recaptured. No recapture is required upon the taxpayer's death or after completion of the required 36 months as the primary residence.

---

[84] § 36(a) and (b).

[85] § 36(b)(2).

[86] § 36(f)(1) and (7). The recapture amount does not qualify for the § 121 exclusion discussed in Chapter 7.

EXAMPLE 52

Maria and Juan are married and file a joint return. In April 2010 they purchased their first home and claimed an $8,000 credit. They must repay the credit if they sell the home prior to April 2013. The repayment of the the credit must be included on their tax return for the year of sale (up to any gain on the sale). If they live in the home for more than 36 months, then none of the credit has to be repaid.

PAYMENT OF INCOME TAX

To determine the net tax due or the expected refund, the individual now subtracts income tax prepayments (withholding on salaries and wages and estimated payments) from the tax liability adjusted for credits and additions. Estimated payments are the tax prepayments of persons with large amounts of income from sources other than salaries or wages for which there is no withholding (for example, self-employed individuals). It is a form of self-withholding. Generally, taxpayers must pay estimated taxes in equal quarterly installments, unless sufficient taxes have been withheld from wages earned. The required quarterly payments are based on the total estimated taxes owed for the current year. Some taxpayers, however, may base their current year's estimates on their previous year's tax liability. A calendar-year individual's quarterly estimated tax payments are due on April 15, June 15, and September 15 of the current year, and January 15 of the following year.

If an installment payment is not made, or if total payments are less than 90 percent of the tax liability, a penalty may be imposed on the shortfall.[87] This penalty is not imposed if the total shortfall for the year is less than $1,000. The penalty rate is determined by the IRS on a quarterly basis and is computed as simple interest based on each quarter's underpayment. Thus, a different penalty rate could apply to each quarter's underpayment. The penalty may be reduced or eliminated by using a special annualization method that essentially matches the required quarterly payments to the pattern in which income is received.

After subtracting the prepayments, the taxpayer has completed the determination of his or her net tax due or the tax refund expected, as the case may be. After signing and dating, the taxpayer is ready to file the tax return.

TAX PLANNING

Assuming the underpayment penalty can be avoided, it is usually better to underpay taxes rather than to receive a refund for an overpayment. The IRS pays no interest if it issues the refund within 45 days from the later of the filing date or due date of the return.[88] In effect, an overpayment is an interest-free loan to the government. If a taxpayer has unusually large deductions, then additional withholding allowances may be claimed on Form W-4 to avoid an overpayment of taxes.

Who Must File a Return?

A taxpayer with sufficient gross income, generally gross income exceeding the sum of the applicable basic standard deduction (plus the addition for age) and personal exemption(s), must file a tax return on or before April 15 following the end of the tax year.[89] The taxpayer cannot consider any exemptions for dependents in determining the gross income threshold for filing, nor could nonitemizers consider any of the

[87]The penalty is not assessed if the tax prepayment is equal to at least 100 percent of the previous year's tax liability if AGI is $150,000 or less, or 110 percent if AGI is over $150,000. §6654(d)(1). Since 2009, the required annual payment for individuals with small businesses is the lesser of 90 percent of the tax for the current year or 90 percent of the previous year's tax liability if AGI on the preceding year's return is less than $500,000 ($250,000 if married filing separately) and at least 50 percent of that gross income was from a business that employed no more than 500 people on average during the preceding year.

[88]§6611(e).

[89]§6012(a)(1). Taxpayers can file a Form 1040 (long form), a Form 1040A (short form), or an even shorter form, 1040EZ. Taxpayers may qualify for an automatic extension of time to file of 6 months, as discussed in Chapter 2.

temporary deductions from AGI for property taxes, automobile sales taxes, or casualty losses in prior years.

If the taxpayer's gross income is less than the sum of the basic standard deduction and personal exemption, no tax liability is owed even if the taxpayer has no other deductions. Filing a return would create an unnecessary administrative and compliance burden on both the taxpayer and the IRS. Despite this gross income threshold, the taxpayer must file a tax return to obtain any expected tax refund. The IRS does not send a refund of taxes to a taxpayer without receiving a tax return.

EXAMPLE 53

Bill, single and age 32, has no dependents. His 2013 gross income is $9,000, and his employer withheld $400 of income taxes from his salary. Because Bill's gross income is less than $10,000 ($6,100 standard deduction + $3,900 personal exemption), he is not required to file a tax return for 2013. Bill's taxable income is zero, and he has no gross income tax liability. Although Bill is not required to file a tax return, he must file a return to claim a refund of the $400 tax his employer withheld.

There are, however, certain exceptions to the gross income threshold that may necessitate the taxpayer's filing a return. The four principal exceptions are as follows:

1. Self-employed individuals must file a tax return, regardless of their gross income, if their net earnings from self-employment exceed $400 for the year.
2. Taxpayers who are age 65 or older may only add their additional standard deduction of $1,200 (married taxpayers) or $1,500 (single or head of household) for age in determining their gross income filing requirements. They may not take into account the additional standard deduction for blindness.
3. Taxpayers claimed as dependents on another taxpayer's return are subject to a complex set of filing rules. The most common of these are for children who are claimed as dependents on their parents' returns. The gross income threshold for such taxpayers is the greater of $1,000 or their earned income plus $350. Thus, a child with *only* investment income must file a return if that investment income exceeds $1,000.
4. Married persons filing separate returns must file a return if their gross income equals or exceeds their personal exemption. Therefore, for 2013, the gross income filing threshold is only $3,900.

EXPANDED TOPICS—ADDITIONAL TAXES

Individuals may be subject to certain add-on taxes in addition to the regular tax, such as the self-employment tax, employment taxes for household employees, the 10 percent penalty for premature withdrawal from retirement accounts, Medicare surtaxes, and the alternative minimum tax. Employment taxes and the penalty tax for premature withdrawals are discussed in Chapter 4. The alternative minimum tax is discussed here as are the Medicare surtaxes.

Alternative Minimum Tax

To ensure that high-income taxpayers pay their "fair share" of taxes, they are required to compute an alternative taxable income and an alternative tax on this income. In computing alternative taxable income, certain deductions are reduced or disallowed and certain exempt income items are subject to the alternative tax. This alternative income is called **alternative minimum taxable income (AMTI)**, and the tax is called the **alternative minimum tax (AMT)**. If the AMT is greater than the regular tax, taxpayers pay the larger amount.[90] This is similar to the AMT for corporations discussed in Chapter 9.

[90] § 55.

The AMT is intended for taxpayers whose true economic income diverges significantly from taxable income, due to what is considered excessive use of tax reduction provisions; unfortunately, it can also apply to middle-income taxpayers who have not planned wisely. The AMT is paid only when it exceeds the regular tax liability.

The characteristics most likely to cause AMT liability for individuals include the following:

- Nontaxable interest income from private activity bonds[91]
- Numerous personal and dependency exemptions
- Large amounts of state and local taxes and miscellaneous itemized deductions
- The bargain element of incentive stock options

To compute the AMT, taxpayers generally start with regular taxable income, add or subtract certain adjustments, add tax preferences, and subtract the allowable exemption amount. The tentative minimum tax (TMT) is then calculated using the following AMT schedule for individuals:

AMTI	Tentative Minimum Tax
0–$179,500	26% × AMTI
Over $179,500	$46,670 + 28% (AMTI – $179,500)[92]

The TMT is then compared to the regular tax. If the TMT exceeds the regular tax, the difference, called the alternative minimum tax (AMT), is added to the regular tax on page 2 of Form 1040. The AMT can only be positive. If the TMT is less than the regular tax, the AMT is simply zero. Figure 11.7 illustrates the AMT model.

Example 54

An individual taxpayer has AMTI of $775,000. His TMT is $213,500, computed as follows:

$$\$46{,}670 + 28\%\ (\$775{,}000 - \$179{,}500) = \$213{,}410$$

If the taxpayer's regular tax is $100,000, his AMT is $113,410. This amount is added to his regular tax. The total income tax equals $213,410 (which equals the TMT). If the taxpayer's regular tax is $220,000, there is no AMT liability because the TMT is less than the regular tax. The taxpayer's total income tax is $220,000.

If the taxpayer's AMTI is below a certain level, a portion of the income may be exempt from the alternative tax. The exemption is based on the filing status of the

FIGURE 11.7 THE AMT MODEL

	Taxable Income
Plus/Minus	Adjustments to Taxable Income
Plus	Tax Preferences
Less	Allowable Exemption
Equals	Alternative Minimum Taxable Income (AMTI)
Times	AMT Tax Rates
Equals	Tentative Minimum Tax (TMT)
Less	Regular Income Tax
Equals	AMT

[91]Private activity bonds issued in 2009 and 2010 were not considered a tax preference item.

[92]Individuals who qualify for the 15 percent capital gains rate for regular income tax can also use the 15 percent rate for AMT. §55(b)(3).

individual and is indexed for inflation. If the taxpayer's AMTI before the exemption exceeds a phaseout threshold, the exemption is phased out at a rate of 25 cents for each dollar the AMTI exceeds the threshold. The exemption is completely phased out when AMTI is equal to the threshold at which the exemption phaseout begins plus (4 × exemption amount). Table 11.10 shows the exemptions for 2012 and 2013 along with the 2013 phaseout threshold.[93]

Adjustments can be positive or negative, but most result in a reduction or disallowance of something that can be deducted in computing the regular income tax. For example, the standard deduction and personal and dependency exemptions are not allowed in computing AMTI. Additionally, many itemized deductions are limited or disallowed. Table 11.11 compares the deductibility of itemized deductions for the regular income tax and for the AMT. The deductions allowed for medical expenses (in excess of the 10% of AGI floor), interest on home acquisition mortgages, investment interest, charitable contributions, and casualty losses are the same for both regular taxable income and AMTI.

EXAMPLE 55

Samantha, single person and age 45, reports 2013 adjusted gross income of $216,150 and has the following itemized deductions before applicable limitations:

TABLE
11.10 AMT EXEMPTIONS

FILING STATUS	2012 EXEMPTION	2013 EXEMPTION	2013 PHASEOUT BEGINS AT
Married Filing a Joint Return	$78,750	$80,800	$153,900
Married Filing Separately	$39,375	$40,400	$76,950
Head of Household	$50,600	$51,900	$115,400
Single	$50,600	$51,900	$115,400

TABLE
11.11 TABLE 11.11 ITEMIZED DEDUCTIONS DISALLOWED FOR AMT

DEDUCTION	REGULAR INCOME TAX	AMT
Taxes	No limit	No deduction allowed
Home equity interest	Interest on up to $100,000 of debt principal	No deduction allowed
Miscellaneous itemized deductions, including unreimbursed employee expenses	Expenses in excess of 2% of AGI allowed	No deduction allowed

[93] § 55(d).

Medical expenses	\$19,200
Interest on home acquisition mortgage (\$720,000 principal amount)	27,000
Interest on home equity loan (\$75,000 principal amount)	3,000
Taxes	15,000
Charitable contributions	5,000
Miscellaneous itemized deductions (subject to 2% of AGI floor)	9,300
Total	\$78,500

In computing her regular taxable income, she cannot deduct any medical expenses because they do not exceed the 10% of AGI floor (10% × \$216,150 = \$21,615) and she can deduct only \$4,977 [\$9,300 – (2% × \$216,150)] for miscellaneous itemized deductions. This reduces her total itemized deductions from \$78,500 to \$54,977.

For purposes of computing Samantha's alternative minimum tax liability, her itemized deductions are reduced even further. The following deductions remain under AMT rules:

Qualified residence interest	\$27,000
Charitable contributions	5,000
Total	\$32,000

Samantha loses all her deductions for home equity interest, taxes, and miscellaneous itemized deductions.

TAX PLANNING

Taxpayers who expect to be subject to the alternative minimum tax in a given tax year should attempt to shift their itemized deductions to a future tax year in which the AMT is not applicable. If, however, the taxpayer is in the 33 percent or above regular tax bracket in a year when the alternative minimum tax applies, accelerating income into that year can save taxes. The additional income will be subject to the 28 percent alternative minimum tax; income can be added until the point at which the recalculated regular tax with the additional income equals the tentative minimum tax, also including the income.

Tax preferences are only positive additions to AMTI. Most preferences are somewhat obscure, so only the nontaxable interest on private activity bonds and the bargain element of stock options are considered here.[94]

The interest on bonds issued by a state or local government is fully taxable to the bond holders if the proceeds are used for private business operations rather than for certain specified exempt activities. If, however, the proceeds of the private activity bonds are used to construct exempt facilities such as airports, hazardous waste facilities, or water and sewage treatment facilities, the interest is exempt from regular income tax, but the tax-exempt interest on these private activity bonds is a tax preference item that is added to regular taxable income to determine alternative minimum taxable income.[95]

EXAMPLE 56

Samir has taxable income of \$175,000 and tax-exempt private activity bond interest of \$800,000. Although this interest is exempt from regular taxation, his regular taxable income must be increased by \$800,000 to determine AMTI.

Taxpayers who receive incentive stock options (ISOs) from their employers pay no regular income tax when the options are exercised. They may be subject to the AMT, however, because the bargain element (the difference between the exercise price and the fair market value on the exercise date) is a tax preference item. Exercising the stock option when the fair market value of the stock is low can minimize the employee's AMT.

[94] A portion of the excluded gain on the sale of small business stock is another preference item.§ 57(a)(7).

[95] § 142. The American Recovery and Reinvestment Act of 2009 provided that interest on private activity bonds issued in 2009 and 2010 would not be treated as a tax preference.

EXAMPLE 57

In January year 1, RapidGrowth Corporation granted its employee, Ken, 25,000 ISOs with an exercise price of $10 per share. On January 5, year 3, Ken exercises all of the ISOs when the fair market value of the stock is $30 per share because the shares have been appreciating significantly over the past several months. Ken recognizes no gain on the appreciation of the stock for regular tax purposes until the year he sells the stock acquired with the ISO. At that time, he will have long-term capital gain. For AMT purposes, however, Ken's year-3 income tax return will show an AMT adjustment of $500,000 [($30 fair market value at exercise date – $10 exercise price) × 25,000 shares]. When Ken sells his shares, his long-term capital gain for AMTI will be measured from this $30, however. Assume that Ken waits until December to exercise his options when the fair market value of the stock is $50 per share. Now his year-3 income tax return will show an AMT adjustment of $1,000,000 [($50 fair market value at exercise date – $10 exercise price) × 25,000 shares].

The basis for regular tax purposes is the exercise price, whereas the basis for AMT purposes is the fair market value of the stock on the exercise date. The difference in the capital gain recognized for regular tax and AMT purposes results from this difference.

EXAMPLE 58

Continuing the previous example, on November 10, year 5, Ken sells his stock for $70 per share. He will have $1.5 million long-term capital gain [($70 – $10) × 25,000] for regular tax determination. If he exercised the option when the price was $30, Ken would have a $1 million [($70 – $30) × 25,000] AMT long-term capital gain. If he exercised the option when the price was $50, he would have a $500,000 [($70 – $50) × 25,000] AMT long-term capital gain.

TAX PLANNING

Ken's AMTI and AMT are significantly lower when he exercises his ISOs at the lower fair market value. His lower stock value resulted in a decrease in the AMT adjustment and a corresponding decrease in the AMT due. Ken traded AMT ordinary income, which is taxed at 26 to 28 percent for AMT long-term capital gain income, which is generally taxed at 15 percent (maximum 20 percent excluding the Medicare surtax). Ken also deferred payment of the tax because AMT ordinary income is a year-3 income tax liability, while the AMT long-term capital gain tax from the subsequent sale of the stock is deferred until year 5.

Medicare Surtax

To pay for expanded health care coverage, the Patient Protection and Affordable Care Act expands the Medicare tax in two ways beginning in 2013. First, an additional 0.9 percent Medicare tax applies to the earned income of employees and self-employed persons with earnings and wages in excess of $200,000 ($250,000 if married filing a joint return); this new rate applies only to individuals and a matching amount will not be assessed on businesses. Self-employed individuals will pay the same additional 0.9% rate as employees and there is no deduction for this additional tax. This tax was discussed in Chapter 4.

Second, a new Medicare tax is levied on unearned income including taxable interest, dividends, capital gains, annuities, royalties, certain rents of individuals, and income from passive investments (such as a limited partnership interest). The new 3.8% tax on unearned income is imposed on the lesser of (a) net investment income or (b) the excess of modified adjusted gross income (AGI) over a threshold amount of $250,000 for married couples filing joint returns, $125,000 for married individuals filing separately, and $200,000 for all other individuals. This tax was discussed in Chapter 3.

EXAMPLE 59

Julie and Kevin, a married couple filing a joint return, have modified AGI of $320,000 in 2013 which includes $300,000 from wages and $20,000 net investment income. In 2013, they will pay a Medicare surtax on wages of $450 [($300,000 wages – $250,000 threshold) × 0.9%] and $760 ($20,000 × 3.8%) for the Medicare surtax on their net investment income.

Tim, a single individual, has modified AGI of $225,000 in 2013 which includes $190,000 of self-employment income and $35,000 net investment income. Tim will pay a Medicare surtax on net investment income of $950 [($225,000 AGI – $200,000 threshold) × 3.8%] but will pay no additional Medicare surtax on his self-employment income because that income is less than $200,000.

REVISITING THE INTRODUCTORY CASE

Amy and Steve should schedule the closing for January. They need to consider that in itemizing their deductions they give up the standard deduction, and floors now apply to some categories of itemized deductions. Medical expenses are only deductible to the extent they exceed 10 percent of AGI ($105,000 × 10% = $10,500), so none of their medical expenses are deductible. The unreimbursed employee expenses are only deductible to the extent they are greater than 2 percent of AGI ($105,000 × 2% = $2,100), so none of their unreimbursed employee expenses are deductible. In years after 2013, Amy and Steve will be able to deduct the full amount of their mortgage interest ($12,000), property taxes ($2,500), and charitable contributions ($2,400), resulting in total itemized deductions of $16,900 for a full tax year. If they close the last week of December in 2013, the deductible mortgage interest and property taxes for that year will be reduced to only $231 (1/52 × ($12,000) for mortgage interest and $48 (1/52 × $2,500) for taxes). Thus, their itemized deduction for 2013 would be $231 mortgage interest, $48 taxes, $2,400 charitable contributions, and $1,500 for points (interest) on the mortgage, for a total of $4,179. Because this is less than their $12,200 standard deduction, they would get no benefit from itemizing in 2013. In 2014, they should benefit from itemizing because they will now have a full year's mortgage interest and taxes; their itemized deductions will be $12,000 mortgage interest + $2,500 taxes + $2,400 charitable contributions, for a total $16,900, which should be more than their indexed standard deduction in 2014. Waiting until January to close, will allow them to add the points on the purchase in 2013, increasing their itemized deductions to $18,400 ($16,900 + $1,500 for points).

In estimating their potential tax savings of $5,950 from itemizing their deductions, they forgot to consider that their tax benefit comes only from the incremental deductions that are in excess of the standard deduction. Based on the 2013 standard deduction, the $18,400 itemized deductions are only $6,200 greater than the $12,200 standard deduction, so their maximum additional tax savings are only $1,550 ($6,200 × 25%). They may still be slightly better off itemizing their deductions in future years, but certainly will not save as much in taxes as they had hoped.

SUMMARY

The individual taxpayer's tax model is significantly different from the corporate model. Although most income items and business deductions are similar, the individual has two sets of personal deductions: deductions *for* adjusted gross income and deductions *from* adjusted gross income. Adjusted gross income, an intermediate income subtotal, limits most of the taxpayer's deductions from adjusted gross income except taxes and interest, although other limits may apply to the interest deductions. AGI does not limit any of the deductions for adjusted gross income.

To compute their taxes, individuals must determine their filing status and their personal and dependency exemptions. These items are also unique to individual taxpayers. Taxpayers have a choice of five filing statuses: married filing jointly, married filing separately, surviving spouse, head of household, and single. The determination of filing status is based on marital status, the year a spouse died, if deceased, and whether or not the taxpayer provides a home for a qualifying relative. The filing status is used to determine the taxpayer's basic standard deduction and the rate table or schedule that must be used to determine the gross tax liability. If the taxpayer's itemized deductions are less than the standard deduction, the taxpayer claims the standard deduction as their deduction from adjusted gross income.

Taxpayers are permitted a personal exemption for themselves on their own tax return. They are also allowed dependency exemptions for qualifying children and other persons for whom they provide more than half the support. The person must also meet relationship and gross income tests to be claimed as a dependent. An exception to the support requirement is made for the multiple support agreement. A person who is claimed as a dependent on another taxpayer's return may not claim a personal exemption on his or her own tax return.

In determining their final tax, taxpayers subtract their allowable credits, such as the child tax credit, the earned income credit for low-income taxpayers, and the dependent care credit. The taxpayer also may be subject to additional employment taxes and the alternative minimum tax, which increase the tax due. After these adjustments to the tax liability, the taxpayer subtracts any prepayments of tax to determine the tax due or the refund expected.

KEY TERMS

Abandoned spouse 496
Adjusted gross income (AGI) 486
Alternative minimum tax (AMT) 524
Alternative minimum taxable income (AMTI) 524
Deductions for adjusted gross income 483
Deductions from AGI 486
Dependency exemptions 487
Head of household 495
Itemized deductions 499
Multiple support agreement 490
Net operating loss (NOL) 512
Personal exemption 487
Standard deduction 497
Surviving spouse 494

TEST YOURSELF

ANSWERS APPEAR AFTER THE PROBLEM ASSIGNMENTS

1. Tony and Anita are married and file a joint tax return. They provide more than half the support for their daughter (age 16) who had gross income of $4,000 and their nephew (Tony's deceased brother's child who is 17 and lives with them) who had gross income of $3,400. Both the daughter and the nephew are full-time students. What is the total number of exemptions Tony and Anita can claim on their tax return?

a. 4
b. 3
c. 2
d. 1

2. Maria, age 12, is claimed as a dependent on her parents' tax return. She has gross income consisting solely of taxable dividends of $2,800. What is Maria's taxable income?

a. $2,800
b. $1,850
c. $1,800
d. $0

3. George and Laura, a married couple with an adjusted gross income of $100,000, made the following contributions to qualified charitable organizations:

- Cash of $8,000 given to State University.
- Used personal clothing donated to Goodwill. The clothing was acquired two years ago at a cost of $6,000. Its current fair market value is $2,000.

- Apex stock donated to their church. The stock was acquired in 1990 at a cost of $30,000. Its current fair market value is $15,000.
- Microsoft stock donated to the Red Cross. The stock was acquired in 1993 at a cost of $4,000. Its current fair market value is $11,000.
- Laura provided free services to the local charity that provides free food to homeless people. The fair value of the services she donated was $7,000.

How much can George and Laura deduct for these charitable contributions on their current year's tax return?

a. $8,000
b. $10,000
c. $25,000
d. $36,000
e. $50,000

4. Lynn and Dave, a married couple with a dependent child age 16, have AGI of $300,000 in 2013 and report the following itemized deductions before deducting any floors that may apply:

Home acquisition mortgage ($900,000 principal amount) interest	$40,000
Taxes	13,000
Charitable contributions	15,000
Medical expenses	11,000
Miscellaneous itemized deductions	2,000

What is the amount of their taxable income for 2013?

a. $232,000
b. $220,300
c. $219,000
d. $207,900

5. Donna, a single individual with no dependents, reports AGI of $100,000. She also reports the following itemized deductions:

Medical expenses in excess of 10% AGI	$ 1,000
Interest on home acquisition mortgage ($250,000 principal amount)	10,000
Property taxes on principal residence	3,000
State income taxes	6,000
Qualified charitable contributions	5,000
Miscellaneous itemized deductions in excess of 2% AGI	3,000

What amount of these deductions is allowed in the determination of Donna's alternative minimum taxable income (AMTI)?

a. $10,000
b. $16,000
c. $18,000
d. $28,000

PROBLEM ASSIGNMENTS

CHECK YOUR UNDERSTANDING

1. Briefly explain two deductions that an individual has for adjusted gross income.

2. What is the purpose of adjusted gross income?
3. What are the filing statuses available to unmarried taxpayers? Which statuses are available only to married taxpayers?
4. What are the requirements to file as head of household?
5. Distinguish the personal exemption from the dependency exemption.
6. What is the purpose of the abandoned spouse provision?
7. Who are qualifying relatives for purposes of the dependency exemption? Which relatives do not qualify?
8. What is the purpose of a multiple support agreement?
9. Explain the gross income test for the dependency deduction.
10. When would a taxpayer itemize his or her deductions?
11. What itemized deductions must exceed a basic minimum (floor) before the taxpayer's taxable income is reduced for the excess amounts expended?
12. What is qualified residence interest?
13. What is the overall charitable contribution deduction limitation?
14. Collin pledged a $5,000 gift to his church for its building fund. He has 125 shares of stock that he purchased six years ago for $100 per share. It is currently worth $40 per share. Collin wants to give the stock to the church to satisfy his pledge. What advice do you have for Collin?
15. If an individual has a negative taxable income does that mean that he or she has an NOL? Explain.
16. What is the difference between a tax credit and a tax deduction?
17. What is the difference between a refundable and a nonrefundable credit? Provide examples of each.
18. What is the purpose of the alternative minimum tax for an individual?

CRUNCH THE NUMBERS

19. Cecilia is married and files a joint return with her husband, Steve. They have modified adjusted gross income of $130,000. Cecilia paid $2,700 in student loan interest this year. What is her deduction for the interest paid?
20. Ashley is single and owns a sole proprietorship. She pays an annual premium of $2,600 for a high-deductible medical policy for herself with a $2,300 deductible. How much can Ashley set aside in an HSA? How much can she deduct for AGI?
21. Joseph provides $12,000 of support for his mother, Miriam, who lives in his house. Miriam is a U.S. citizen and single. Miriam's only income is Social Security of $5,000 and taxable pension income of $4,000. Miriam uses the Social Security income for support but puts all of the pension income into her savings account. Joseph also provides $6,000 of support for his 22-year-old son, Mike, who is a full-time student attending college on a basketball scholarship. The balance of Mike's support comes from the scholarship that pays Mike's $10,000 tuition and fees for the year. How many dependents can Joseph claim on his tax return?
22. Harry and Silvia, a married couple, are both age 67 and legally blind. What is their standard deduction for 2013?

23. Lynn is an unmarried individual who has a dependent grandchild who lives with her. Lynn is age 66. What is Lynn's standard deduction for 2013?

24. Scott is 15 years old and qualifies as a dependent on his parents' tax return. During 2013 he earns $2,500 from a part-time job and also receives $800 of dividend income on stock given to him by his aunt. What is Scott's taxable income?

25. Michael's adjusted gross income for 2013 is $90,000. He is age 30 and single with no dependents. What is Michael's taxable income?

26. What is the total deduction for personal and dependency exemptions for the following taxpayers in 2013 if their AGI is $350,500?

a. Married filing jointly with three dependents

b. Single with no dependents

27. Daniel's adjusted gross income is $90,000. During the year he incurred $14,000 of medical expenses and was reimbursed for $3,000 of these expenses. What is his allowable medical expense deduction if he is age 45 and itemizes? How would your answer change if Daniel is 70 years old?

28. In 2013, Rebecca and Gregory, a married couple filing a joint return, reported adjusted gross income of $70,000 and total allowable itemized deductions of $12,800, which included state income taxes paid of $3,100. They received a $900 refund of state income taxes in April 2014. How much of the state income tax refund must they include in income and in which year do they include it?

29. Edward, a single individual with a 25 percent marginal tax rate, incurs interest expense of $10,000 attributable to his investment in stocks and bonds. His gross investment income is $6,200 ($1,000 of which is from long-term capital gains and dividend income), and his adjusted gross income, including his investment income, is $68,000. Edward incurs a $100 brokerage account maintenance fee and a $300 certified financial planner's counseling fee. He also has $1,200 of other qualifying miscellaneous itemized deductions.

a. How much can Edward deduct for miscellaneous itemized deductions?

b. What are Edward's options in determining his deduction for investment interest expense? Explain.

c. What happens to the investment interest expense that he cannot deduct in the current year?

30. Pablo and Adriana, a married couple who file a joint return, purchase a $190,000 home by paying $38,000 cash down and taking a mortgage for the balance of the purchase price. The mortgage company charges them $3,000 in points for originating the loan that they pay at closing. They pay $7,000 in interest on the mortgage this year. They also purchase a new car this year for $28,000 by taking out a car loan from their credit union. They paid $975 in interest on the car loan this year. How much can Pablo and Adriana deduct for interest expense this year if they itemize their deductions?

31. Arnold, a single individual, has adjusted gross income of $65,000 in the current year. Arnold donates the following items to his favorite qualified charities:

- $5,000 cash to the athletic department booster club at State University. This contribution gives him the right to purchase preferred seats to all home games. The value of this preferred right is $900.

- ABC stock acquired six years ago at a cost of $6,000. Its fair market value at the date of contribution was $22,000.
- Personal clothing items purchased two years ago at a cost of $1,000. Their fair market value at the date of contribution was $400.

How much can Arnold deduct for his charitable contributions in the current year?

32. Mark and Patricia report adjusted gross income of $380,500 and itemized deductions of $64,000 (interest on home acquisition mortgage with a principal amount of $890,000, taxes, and charitable contributions). They file a joint income tax return and claim their four children as dependents. What is their taxable income for 2013?

33. Jennifer, a single individual, has a $20,000 loss from an S corporation, $11,000 salary from a part-time job, and $2,000 of interest income. Her itemized deductions include $4,000 interest on the $100,000 principal on her home acquisition mortgage, $2,800 in taxes, and $500 in charitable contributions. Compute Jennifer's net operating loss.

34. Cindy files as head of household and has three dependent children ages 12, 14, and 16. Her AGI is $80,000. How much can Cindy claim for the child tax credit?

35. Greg and Barbara, a married couple with an AGI of $80,000, have three children who are full-time college students. They pay $6,000 for tuition annually for each child. They have one son who is a sophomore in college and another son who is a senior. Their daughter is a graduate student. How much can Greg and Barbara claim for education credits for 2013?

36. Doris is a single individual with modified AGI of $54,000. During the year, she pays $11,000 for tuition for a master's in taxation program. How much can Doris claim for the lifetime learning credit?

37. June is a single individual with AGI of $45,000. June has a five-year-old son who is in day care while she works.

a. How much can she claim for the dependent care credit if she spends $5,000 for child care during the year?

b. How much can she claim for the dependent care credit if she spends $2,000 for child care during the year?

38. Roland worked for Sorbonne Company for the first four months of 2013 and earned $40,000 from which his employer withheld $3,060 for payroll taxes. In May, Roland accepted a job with Lyon Company. During the last eight months of the year, Roland earned $84,000 from which Lyon withheld $6,426 for payroll taxes. How much credit can Roland claim for excess payroll taxes withheld?

39. Juan and Celina are married, file a joint return, and have AGI of $148,000. On April 1, 2010 they purchased their first home for $118,000 and claimed the homebuyer credit on their 2010 tax return.

a. If they sold their home on March 20, 2013 for $128,000, how does this affect the first-time homebuyer credit?

b. How would your answer change if they had purchased the home on April 15, 2008 (claiming the credit on their 2008 return) and sold their home on April 15, 2013 for $128,000?

40. Which of the following individuals must file a tax return in 2013?

a. Carolyn is single and age 66. She receives $2,000 of interest income, $3,000 of dividend income, and $6,000 in Social Security benefits.

b. Tim is single, age 18, and a full-time student. He is claimed as a dependent on his parents' tax return. Tim earned $2,000 from a part-time job and $400 in interest income.

c. Justin is single, age 25, and a full-time graduate student. He earned $8,750 from a part-time job.

41. Diana, a single individual, has regular taxable income of $220,000 and alternative minimum taxable income of $350,000.

a. What is Diana's tentative minimum tax?

b. What is Diana's AMT?

42. Michelle, a single individual, reports 2013 adjusted gross income of $280,000 and has the following itemized deductions before applicable limitations:

Medical expenses	$14,000
Interest on home acquisition mortgage with a principal amount of $650,000	25,000
Interest on home equity loan with a principal amount of $95,000	6,000
Taxes	18,000
Charitable contributions	7,000
Miscellaneous itemized deductions	8,800

a. What are Michelle's itemized deductions for regular tax purposes?

b. What are Michelle's itemized deductions for AMT purposes?

43. Jason and Lynn are married and file a joint tax return for 2013. Lynn has salary income of $270,000 and Jason has salary income of $380,000. They also have the following additional types of income: $59,000 net long-term capital gain on sale of stock, $9,000 dividend income, $7,000 interest income from corporate bonds, and $6,000 interest income from tax-exempt municipal bonds. Compute their Medicare surtax(es).

44. Miguel, single, earned $210,000 net income from his sole proprietorship in 2013. He also had the following additional types of income: $30,000 net short-term capital gain on sale of stock, $8,000 dividend income, and $7,000 interest income from corporate bonds. Miguel also had $3,000 of deductible investment expenses. Compute Miguel's Medicare surtax(es).

45. Heather, a head of household, received a salary of $198,000 in 2013. She also had following additional types of income: $20,000 net long-term capital gain from the sale of stock, $4,000 dividend income, $5,000 interest income from corporate bonds, and $3,000 interest income from tax-exempt municipal bonds. Compute Heather's Medicare surtax(es).

46. Kelly is single; her dependent child, Barbara, lives with her. After her divorce, Kelly was awarded permanent custody of Barbara and has not agreed to waive her right to claim Barbara as a dependent. Kelly has the following items of income and expense:

INCOME:	
Salary	$ 60,000
Cash dividends	3,000
Interest income on City of New York bonds	5,000
Interest income on U.S. Treasury bills	4,000
Net rental income	3,500
Alimony received from ex-husband	2,500
Child support received from ex-husband	3,500

SALES OF CAPITAL ASSETS:	
Stock held for 3 months (basis is $12,000) sold for	18,000
Investment land held 5 years (basis is $30,000) sold for	14,000
Life insurance proceeds received on the death of her mother	100,000
EXPENSES:	
Interest on the $150,000 principal from her home acquisition mortgage	6,000
Real property taxes on the home	2,000
Charitable contributions	7,000
Qualifying child care expense	3,700
Federal income tax withheld	7,000

Compute Kelly's taxable income and her net tax due or refund expected for 2013.

THINK OUTSIDE THE TEXT

These questions require answers that are beyond the material that is covered in this chapter.

47. Discuss the factors to consider when evaluating the choice between taking the child and dependent care credit versus participating in an employer-sponsored qualified dependent care assistance program.

48. Prior to 1986, all consumer interest expense was deductible. In 1986, Congress eliminated the deduction for consumer interest expense, including interest paid on car loans and credit card balances. Why do you think Congress made this change?

49. Select one of the expenses that is deductible *for* adjusted gross income. Present an argument about why you think that expense is misclassified and should be classified instead as a deduction *from* adjusted gross income.

50. Select one of the expenses that is deductible *from* adjusted gross income. Present an argument about why you think that expense is misclassified and should be classified instead as a deduction *for* adjusted gross income.

51. If a modification to the tax law was proposed to allow taxpayers who do not have dependent children to claim a $500 dependency deduction per pet (up to a maximum of two pets) if the taxpayer spends at least $2,000 per year for maintaining each animal, would you be in favor of this proposal or against it? Present your argument either in favor of or against this proposal.

IDENTIFY THE ISSUES

Identify the issues or problems suggested by the following situations. State each issue as a question.

52. Last year, after a very bad argument, Holly's husband moved out and has not been seen since. Holly's eight-year-old daughter lives with her.

53. Carla is single and provides more than 50 percent of the support for her mother who lives in a nursing home. Her mother received $2,000 in interest income from State of Florida bonds, $3,000 in dividend income, and $8,000 in Social Security benefits.

54. Jose is single and a U.S. citizen living in Texas. Jose provides all of the support for his parents who are citizens and residents of Argentina. Jose's parents are considering moving to and becoming residents of Mexico.

55. Jessica invites a 16-year-old foreign exchange student to live in her home for the academic school year. Jessica provides all of the student's support for that period of time. The student is not related to Jessica.

56. Liza pays $5,000 for extensive liposuction surgery. Her medical insurance does not cover this expense.

57. Barry has a chronic back problem that requires that he receive regular therapy in a swimming pool. He purchased a new home with a larger backyard so that he could install a swimming pool. The purchase price of the home was $180,000. The cost of installing the pool was $12,000, and the real estate appraiser said that it increased the value of the home by $7,000. The pool is used only for Barry's therapy workouts.

58. In March, Helen purchased a new home for $140,000. She paid $28,000 cash down and financed the balance with a mortgage. She also paid $1,800 in closing costs and $1,100 in points to obtain the mortgage. The interest paid on the mortgage for the year is $5,300.

59. Gillian and Paul are married and have a son who is a sophomore at the local university. In the current year, they paid $5,000 for tuition and $3,000 for room and board for their son. Their adjusted gross income is $95,000, and they are in the 25 percent marginal tax bracket.

DEVELOP RESEARCH SKILLS

60. Don has a very painful terminal disease. He has learned that marijuana may assist in mitigating his pain. Don lives in a state in which it is legal to use the drug if its use is under the direction of a medical doctor. Can Don deduct the cost of the marijuana as a medical expense?

61. Charlene provides 100 percent of the support for her elderly handicapped mother, Amanda. Amanda insists on living alone in her own apartment even though she has a severe hearing impairment. Amanda has always liked cats, so Charlene purchased a cat that is registered as a hearing assistance animal with the county animal control division. The cat is trained to respond to unusual sounds in an instantaneous and directional manner, alerting Amanda to possible dangers. Charlene paid $800 for the cat and an additional $1,000 for special training. The maintenance costs for the cat are $15 a week. Charlene would like to know if any of these costs qualify as deductible expenses.

62. Howard is a single parent with an 11-year-old dependent son. The son currently attends sixth grade at public school. Howard accepts a temporary foreign assignment from his employer, which is expected to last from August through December. Because of the unstable political environment in the foreign country, Howard is uncomfortable taking his son with him. Therefore, Howard decides to send his son to a boarding school for the fall term at a cost of $5,000, of which $3,000 is for tuition and $2,000 is for room, board, and care. Will the $5,000 qualify for the dependent care credit?

63. Sarah pays $800 per month for her five-year-old daughter to attend a private kindergarten from 8:30 A.M. until 2:30 P.M. and after-school care until 5:30 P.M. The price of the kindergarten without the after-school care is $500 per month. Assuming Sarah pays $800 each month of the year, how much will qualify for the dependent care credit?

SEARCH THE INTERNET

64. Go to the IRS Web site *(www.irs.gov)* and locate Publication 502: *Medical and Dental Expenses*. What expenses qualify for impairment-related work expenses? How do employees deduct these expenses, and does an AGI floor (percentage) limit apply to them?

65. Go to the IRS Web site *(www.irs.gov)* and locate Publication 501: *Exemptions, Standard Deduction, and Filing Information*. What documentation is necessary for a taxpayer with impaired vision to qualify for the additional standard deduction for blindness?

66. Go to the IRS Web site *(www.irs.gov)* and print Form 1040. Using the information in problem 46, complete this form to the extent possible.

67. Go to the IRS Web site *(www.irs.gov)* and print Schedule A: *Itemized Deductions*. Using the following information, complete this form for Simon and Ellen, a married couple filing jointly, who have adjusted gross income of $60,000. They paid the following unreimbursed expenses during the year:

Prescription drugs	$ 600
Doctor bills	4,600
Contact lenses	300
Dentist bills	900
State income tax withheld from salary	1,800
Real property taxes	3,000
Interest on a home acquisition mortgage with a principal amount of $160,000 (reported on Form 1098)	6,000
Cash charitable contributions	1,400
Employee business expenses	1,300
Tax return preparation	150
Safe deposit box (for storing investment documents)	120

DEVELOP PLANNING SKILLS

68. Larry wants to purchase a new car for personal use. He anticipates financing $40,000 of the purchase price. The car dealer is offering a special 3.5 percent interest rate on new cars. Alternatively, Larry could use a home equity loan with an interest rate of 5 percent. Larry is in the 33 percent marginal tax bracket. Should Larry finance the car through the dealer or through a home equity loan?

69. Which one of the following assets should Manuel contribute to his favorite charity and why?

a. Stock acquired five years ago at a cost of $13,000. The current fair market value is $10,000.

b. Stock acquired six months ago at a cost of $4,000. The current fair market value is $10,000.

c. Inventory items acquired last year for Manuel's sole proprietorship. Their cost was $12,000, and their current fair market value is $10,000.

d. $10,000 in cash.

70. Martin, a single man, contributes a painting to an art museum in the current year. The museum is thrilled to get the painting because it fits perfectly into its Impressionist collection. Martin purchased the painting 10 years ago for $50,000. At the time of the donation, the painting is worth $60,000. Martin's adjusted gross income this year is $100,000 and his only other itemized deduction is his annual $2,000 for property taxes. Martin plans to retire next year. A significant portion of his income will be from tax-exempt bonds so he expects his AGI in future years will be only $15,000. Martin wants to know what his options are regarding his charitable contribution deduction and how much he should claim as a deduction this year. Compute the present value of each alternative using a 6 percent discount rate, assuming his allowable standard deduction remains unchanged. What do you recommend?

71. Sharon has not worked outside the home since her first child was born five years ago. Now that the younger of her two children has reached age three, she thinks they are old enough to go to a day care center and she can return to work. Sharon received two job offers. Mahalo Company offered to pay her a salary of $19,000 and also provide free on-site child care facilities as an employee fringe benefit. Ohana Company offered to pay her a salary of $26,000 but offers no employee fringe benefits. There is a day care facility across the street from Ohana Company that would cost $525 per month. Sharon files a joint tax return with her husband, Tom. Their current taxable income, without Sharon's salary, is $75,000. Sharon and Tom would like to know which job provides the greater after-tax cash flow.

72. Laura and Bryan's daughter, Lillian, will start college in a few months. They would like to know what tax issues they should consider when they pay for Lillian's college tuition and related expenses.

73. Eileen files as head of household and earns a salary of $75,000. She has a 4-year-old dependent daughter for whom she pays $5,000 in annual day care expenses so that she can work. Eileen's employer offers a dependent care flexible spending arrangement (FSA) in which she could contribute up to $5,000 on a pre-tax (before income tax and FICA tax) basis. If she does not participate in the FSA, Eileen can claim a dependent care credit for these expenses. Eileen has no other income or deductions. Compute the tax savings of these two alternatives and make a recommendation to Eileen.

74. Two years ago, Micro Corporation granted its employee, Alisa, 20,000 incentive stock options with an exercise price of $15 per share. The stock is currently trading at $40 per share, but Alisa expects that it will continue to increase. She wants to exercise her options this year and can either exercise them now or wait until later in the year when she believes the stock will be trading at $55 per share. Regardless of when she exercises the options, she expects to hold onto the stock for at least a year before selling it at an expected price of $100 per share. Alisa wants to know if it makes any difference when she exercises the options. She also wants to know what the tax implications will be when she sells the stock.

ANSWERS TO TEST YOURSELF

1. **a.** 4. Tony and Anita are allowed two personal exemptions for themselves, plus one exemption each for their daughter and Tony's nephew. Under the dependency definition, the nephew is a qualifying child and the gross income test is waived for qualifying children under age 19 or full-time students under the age of 24. The gross income test is waived for both the daughter and the nephew.

2. **c. $1,800**. Because the child is a dependent on her parents' tax return, she is allowed no personal exemption and her standard deduction is limited to $1,000. Her taxable income is $1,800 ($2,800 – $1,000).

3. **d. $36,000**. They can deduct the $8,000 cash, $2,000 FMV of clothing, $15,000 FMV of Apex stock, and $11,000 FMV of Microsoft stock. No deduction is allowed for the value of the donated services.

4. b. **$220,300**. $300,000 less $40,000 mortgage interest less $13,000 taxes less $15,000 charitable contributions less ($3,900 x 3 exemptions) = $220,300. Medical expenses do not exceed the 10% of AGI floor and miscellaneous itemized deductions do not exceed the 2% of AGI floor so they are not deductible, but their AGI does not exceed the threshold for phaseout of the remaining itemized deductions or exemptions. Their income is above the phaseout limit for the child tax credit so they are not eligible for the credit.

5. b. **$16,000**. Only the medical expenses, mortgage interest, and charitable contribution deductions are allowed for AMT purposes. Miscellaneous itemized deductions and taxes are not deductible.

Wealth Transfer Taxes

chapter 12

The federal transfer tax system consists of the gift tax, the estate tax, and a third lesser-known tax called the generation-skipping transfer tax. Transfer taxes are assessed on the transferor of the property. The recipient receives the property free of taxes.

A number of provisions exclude all or a portion of gifts and inheritances from transfer taxation. They include the annual gift exclusion (currently $14,000 per donee), a lifetime exclusion (currently $5.25 million), the charitable contribution deduction, and the unlimited marital deduction. By the wise use of these exclusions, most individuals can transfer their wealth without paying transfer taxes.

One of the major dilemmas facing very wealthy individuals is whether to make lifetime gifts or hold property until their death. Making lifetime gifts removes both income and appreciation subsequently realized on the transferred assets from the donor's estate and transfers the taxation of income to the donee. If, however, the heirs receive appreciated assets as testamentary transfers, the assets normally take their fair market values as bases; thus, the heirs recognize less gain and have reduced income taxes, when they dispose of them. Their inclusion of these assets in the taxable estate increases estate taxes, however. Family tax planning involves finding the best solution to this dilemma that both minimizes taxes and meets other family objectives. Through proper planning, both wealth transfer taxes and income taxes can be minimized.

Trusts are a vehicle that allows a grantor to transfer the benefit derived from asset ownership to another without transferring actual property ownership. Trusts must be set up properly if one of the objectives is to transfer the taxation of income from trust property to beneficiaries. Transfers in trust and other transfers to minor and certain adult children need special consideration to avoid having the child's income taxed at the parents' marginal income tax rates.

Trusts and estates are both taxable persons, referred to as *fiduciaries*. The income taxation of trusts and estates has many similarities to individual taxation, but there are certain rules that apply specifically to them. These rules must be understood to comply with the requirements for filing a fiduciary income tax return.

KEY CONCEPTS

- ★ The federal gift and estate taxes are assessed on the transferor of property while the recipient receives the property free of tax. The transfer tax is assessed on the fair market value of property transferred.
- ★ The annual gift exclusion allows a donor to give each donee property valued at $14,000 annually without being subject to the gift tax. The lifetime exclusion amount provides an additional exemption from transfer taxes for property transferred in excess of the annual gift exclusion.
- ★ The gift and estate taxes are integrated so that the total taxable gifts of an individual during his or her lifetime increase the amount on which the estate tax is assessed at death prior to any exclusions or credits.

CHAPTER OUTLINE

- ★ The marital deduction allows one spouse to give or bequeath an unlimited amount of property to the other spouse free of transfer taxes.
- ★ The kiddie tax can cause unearned income of children under age 24 to be taxed at their parents' marginal income tax rates.
- ★ Trusts and estates must file their own separate income tax returns and pay income tax on income that is not distributed to their beneficiaries.

SETTING THE STAGE—AN INTRODUCTORY CASE

Sarah, a 70-year-old widow, owns more than $10 million in assets. Sarah's son, Kevin, has two children, ages 11 and 13. Her daughter, Lisa, also has two children, ages 8 and 12. Sarah has decided that she wants to begin giving her assets to her grandchildren so she can minimize the size of her estate. She specifically wants to provide for her four grandchildren's college education. What planning opportunities can you suggest so that Sarah can provide for her grandchildren's education while minimizing any transfer taxes? At the end of this chapter we will return to this case.

OVERVIEW OF WEALTH TRANSFER TAXATION

Since 1916, the United States has imposed an **estate tax**, an excise tax based on the value of property transferred at the owner's death. This was enacted as a way to redistribute some of the wealth accumulated by the richest families in the nation. Without some form of transfer tax applicable to gifts during an individual's lifetime, however, individuals could avoid estate taxes by making lifetime gifts. Therefore, the **gift tax** was imposed in 1932 on donors who make lifetime gifts. The recipients are not subject to income tax on the receipt of a gift or inheritance, so there is no second income tax assessed on the property transferred.[1] Individuals who have accumulated substantial assets need to develop strategies to minimize transfer taxes and maximize the wealth available to pass to the desired recipients.

The Unified Transfer Tax

Prior to the Tax Reform Act of 1976 (1976 Act), the federal gift tax was imposed separately from the estate tax. Gift tax rates were about three-fourths of the estate tax rates for the same dollar value of property transferred. By making lifetime gifts, individuals and families were able to avoid paying substantial amounts of estate transfer taxes. This removed the property and any future appreciation in its value (as well as any gift taxes paid) from the donor's estate. This phenomenon led Congress to enact the unified transfer tax system in 1976, the primary features of which remain in place today (although a modified gift and estate tax provision was hastily enacted at the end of 2010). The gift tax is calculated separately from the estate tax, but the two taxes have a significant relationship due to the lifetime exclusion, and the single progressive tax rate schedule applicable to both taxable gifts and estates which removed the inequity in tax rates prior to the 1976 Act. Essentially, a transfer made through the estate at death (a testamentary transfer) is viewed as a final gift.

After 1976, the next major change to the taxation of gifts and estates was made by the Economic Growth and Tax Relief Reconciliation Act of 2001 (2001 Act), enacted at a time when there was a budget surplus. This surplus allowed Congress to pay for the provisions included in the 2001 Act that would dramatically reduce the estate tax over the next several years and ultimately repeal it in 2010. First, the top rate for the

---

[1]It can be argued, however, that double federal taxation is the result of the transferor paying a federal income tax when the assets were acquired and now having to pay a tax on their transfer. Minimizing this second federal tax is the objective of good transfer tax planning.

unified estate and gift tax was gradually reduced from a high of 55 percent to 45 percent in 2007. Second, it gradually increased the estate tax exclusion from $1 million to $3.5 million in 2009 but left the equivalent gift tax exclusion at just $1 million. Third, it contained a provision that repealed the estate tax entirely in 2010 (but with modified basis carryover rules) while retaining the gift tax with a $1 million exclusion.[2] Gifts, however, would only be taxed at a rate equal to the top individual income tax rate in 2010 (35 percent) above the $1 million exclusion. Because the changes in the estate and gift tax provisions were not revenue neutral in years beyond 2010, Congress created a sunset provision that automatically reinstated the pre-2001 Act tax law in 2011.[3] This meant that after one year of no estate taxes in 2010, the top estate tax rate would revert to 55 percent and the $1 million exclusion amount would be reinstated for both gifts and estates in 2011 unless Congress could find the funds to pay for an extension or permanent repeal.

Given the budget deficits, many persons believed that there would be a revision of the estate tax in 2010 (or at least an extension of the law in effect for 2009) and that adjustments would be made for years beyond 2010. Congress, however, failed to act on the expiration of the estate tax until well after the 2010 mid-term elections when they finally enacted the Tax Relief, Unemployment Insurance Reauthorization, and Job Creation Act of 2010 (2010 Relief Act). This act temporarily revised the estate tax for 2010 through 2012 by providing a $5.12 million lifetime exclusion amount in 2012 ($5 million in 2010 and 2011) and a 35 percent maximum estate and gift tax rate. This had the effect of retroactively reinstating the estate tax for decedent's dying in 2010. The act did, however, give the fiduciary for a decedent dying in 2010 the option of following this new tax law (with the maximum 35 percent tax rate and $5 million exclusion) or electing the earlier provision that repealed the estate tax but imposed a limited basis carryover.[4] For 2010, the gift tax exclusion amount was left at $1 million but with a top gift tax rate at 35 percent. For 2011 and 2012, the gift tax was fully reintegrated with the estate tax by increasing the lifetime exclusion to $5 million (2011), indexed for inflation in 2012 to $5.12 million, and kept at the maximum tax rate of 35 percent. The American Taxpayer Relief Act of 2012 increased the maximum tax rate to 40 percent with the lifetime exclusion amount increased to $5.25 million after the inflation adjustment for 2013. Estate planning beyond 2012 had been impossible until the beginning of 2013 when Congress finally passed the American Taxpayer Relief Act making the changes permanent.

The unified rate schedule under Section 2001(c) continues to be applicable to both gift and testamentary transfers, only now with a 40 percent top rate (35 percent prior to 2013). The unified rate schedule applicable in 2013 is reproduced in Table 12.1.[5]

---

[2]The gift tax was retained to discourage income tax avoidance by taxpayers shifting income-producing property through gifts to family members in lower income tax brackets.

[3]The Congressional Budget Act of 1974 contains a provision that requires any tax cut not paid for by permanent spending cuts to sunset after 10 years unless 60 or more senators vote to waive this requirement. Although the tax bill passed, there was not enough support to waive the sunset rule. This meant that after the repeal of the estate tax effective January 1, 2010, the estate tax would be reinstated on January 1, 2011, with a 55 percent top rate and a $1 million exclusion amount.

[4]When an estate is subject to the estate tax, the beneficiaries inherit property using rules that allow them to use fair market value for the inherited assets' bases. This usually reduces the gain on which the beneficiaries will pay income tax when they dispose of appreciated inherited property. If an estate instead elects to apply the 2010 provision that repealed the estate tax, it will need to follow modified carry over basis rules (as explained later in the section on the alternative estate provision for 2010). This increases the possibility that the beneficiaries will have to pay more income tax when they dispose of appreciated inherited property.

[5] For 2010 through 2012, the maximum estate tax rate was 35% on estates in excess of $500,000. The 35 percent maximum tax rate effective in 2010 eliminated the five rates in excess of 35 percent from the rate schedule in effect prior to 2010. These rates were as follows: $500,000 - $750,000: 37%; $750,000 - $1,000,000: 39%; $1,000,000 - $1,250,000: 41%; $1,250,000 - $1,500,000: 43%; and 45% over $1,500,000. Prior to passage of the 2010 Act, the cumulative nature of the gift and estate tax applied higher marginal tax rates to taxable gifts given in later years and taxable estates.

TABLE
12.1 UNIFIED TRANSFER TAX RATES FOR 2013

AMOUNT OF TAXABLE TRANSFER	TAX RATE
Up to $10,000	18%
$10,001–$20,000	$1,800 + 20% of excess over $10,000
$20,001–$40,000	$3,800 + 22% of excess over $20,000
$40,001–$60,000	$8,200 + 24% of excess over $40,000
$60,001–$80,000	$13,000 + 26% of excess over $60,000
$80,001–$100,000	$18,200 + 28% of excess over $80,000
$100,001–$150,000	$23,800 + 30% of excess over $100,000
$150,001–$250,000	$38,800 + 32% of excess over $150,000
$250,001–$500,000	$70,800 + 34% of excess over $250,000
$500,001–$750,000	$155,800 + 37% of excess over $500,000
$750,000–$1,000,000	$248,300 + 39% of excess over $750,000
Over $1,000,000	$345,800 + 40% of the excess over $1,000,000

Although the rates are progressive in nature, the exclusion amount of $5.25 million is applied in the form of a credit (as explained later) and offsets taxes applied at the lower rates effectively resulting in a flat tax of 40 percent on transfers in excess of $5.25 million.

EXAMPLE 1

Phyllis gave her first *taxable* gift of $90,000 (after her *annual* exclusion) in 2013. Her tax, before consideration of her *lifetime exclusion amount*, is $21,000 [$18,200 + 28% ($90,000 – $80,000)]. She owes no tax, however, due to her lifetime exclusion amount.

Features of the Unified Transfer Tax

There are many basic features of this unified transfer tax system that distinguish it from the federal income tax system.

- The tax is assessed on the transferor rather than the recipient of the property. The giver of the gift pays the gift tax, not the recipient, and the estate pays the estate tax, not the beneficiaries or heirs. The tax base for levying both gift and estate taxes is the fair market value of property transferred.
- A single transfer tax rate schedule applies to gifts and estates. As of 2013, the maximum tax rate is 40% for gifts and estates.
- All individuals are permitted to transfer a certain base amount of wealth by lifetime gifts and transfers at death without tax through use of the lifetime exclusion amount (currently $5.25 million).
- Although the gift tax is computed on an annual basis and it is cumulative in nature; the tax due in any year is based on the current year's taxable gifts combined with total taxable gifts from prior years. The donor, however, would not owe any tax until the lifetime exclusion amount (currently $5.25 million) is exceeded.
- The gift and estate taxes are also integrated so that all or part of a decedent's estate escapes taxation unless his or her total lifetime taxable gifts and taxable testamentary transfers exceed the lifetime exclusion amount (currently $5.25 million).

The basic procedures for calculating the estate tax have not changed over the years; only the rates and exclusions amounts have varied. It should also be noted, that many states levy a death tax on property owned by a decedent. An understanding of the federal estate tax will aid in understanding death taxes at the state level.

Major Exclusions

Two exclusions, the annual gift tax exclusion and a lifetime gift and estate exclusion amount prevent most taxpayers from being subject to transfer taxes.

Annual Gift Tax Exclusion

Theoretically, gifts of any value could be subject to gift taxes, including holiday, wedding, and birthday gifts. To eliminate the reporting and administrative burden for taxpayers and the IRS with respect to small gifts, Congress enacted the Section 2503(b) annual exclusion. This section exempts the value of most gifts up to $14,000 ($13,000 in 2012) *per donee* (gift recipient) annually from reporting and taxation.[6] If the value of property given to any donee in any one year does not exceed the annual exclusion, no gift tax or gift return is required. Unused annual exclusion amounts do not carry over.

EXAMPLE 2

David gave $14,000 to each of his ten grandchildren this year. Although David gave away a total of $140,000 this year, none of the gifts exceeded the annual exclusion per donee so they are free of any gift tax. No gift tax return is required.

Lifetime Transfer Tax Exemption—The Unified Credit

If the value of property transferred during a year exceeds the annual gift exclusion, the excess is a taxable gift. The donor still may not pay any tax on the transfer, however, as the lifetime gift and estate exclusion amount allows up to $5.25 million in cumulative gifts to escape taxation in 2013.[7] The $14,000 annual gift exclusion does not affect the lifetime exclusion allowance; only gifts in excess of the gift annual exclusion are considered taxable gifts and reduce the lifetime exclusion amount. Table 12.2 shows the exclusion amounts along with the top marginal transfer tax rates for 2001 through the present.

As the gift tax is imposed on cumulative gifts, gifts made in prior years increase the total subject to gift taxes in later years. Any lifetime exclusion amount remaining at death reduces the estate tax liability.

EXAMPLE 3

Clarice gave a taxable gift (after her annual exclusion) of a home valued at $950,000 to her son in 2010. In 2013, she gave her son taxable gifts of stocks valued at $6.4 million (after her annual exclusion). She paid no tax in 2010 because her $1 million lifetime gift exclusion offset the $950,000 value of the house. In 2013, she has made cumulative taxable gifts of $7,350,000 and must now pay a gift tax on the $2,100,000 in gifts in excess of her $5.25 million lifetime exclusion ($7,350,000 – $5,250,000).

[6]Gifts in excess of the annual exclusion must be reported but may not be taxed due to the lifetime exclusion. The $1 million gift tax exclusion amount in place since 2002 remained at $1 million for 2010 but was increased to $5 million for 2011 and $5.12 million in 2012 to equal the estate exclusion amount after 2010.

[7]The credit equivalent of the $5.25 million exclusion amount can be determined from Table 12-1 (using the 40% maximum tax rate that applies to gifts and estates exceeding $1,000,000) as follows: $345,800 + (.40 × $4,250,000) = $2,045,800.

TABLE
12.2 GIFT AND ESTATE TAX EXCLUSION AMOUNTS AND TOP MARGINAL TAX RATES BY YEAR

YEAR OF TRANSFER	TOP MARGINAL TAX RATE	GIFT TAX EXCLUSION AMOUNTS	ESTATE TAX EXCLUSION AMOUNTS
2001	55%	$675,000	$675,000
2002	50%	$1,000,000	$1,000,000
2003	49%	$1,000,000	$1,000,000
2004	48%	$1,000,000	$1,500,000
2005	47%	$1,000,000	$1,500,000
2006	46%	$1,000,000	$2,000,000
2007 and 2008	45%	$1,000,000	$2,000,000
2009	45%	$1,000,000	$3,500,000
2010	35%	$1,000,000	$5,000,000
2011	35%	$5,000,000	$5,000,000
2012	35%	$5,120,000	$5,120,000
2013	40%	$5,250,000	$5,250,000

The taxpayer does not apply the lifetime exclusion amount directly to taxable gifts to determine the tax on net gifts, however. In practice, the lifetime exclusion amount has always been equated to a lifetime unified credit equivalent. Cumulative taxable gifts are first determined; the tax is then determined from the tax rate schedule on cumulative taxable gifts; finally, the unified credit that is the equivalent of the tax on the lifetime exclusion amount is then applied to the tax to determine if any gift tax is due.

EXAMPLE 4

Continuing example 3, Clarice determines the tax due on her 2013 taxable gifts (using the rates in Table 12.1) as follows:

1. Cumulative taxable gifts: $950,000 + $6,400,000 = $7,350,000
2. Tax on $7,350,000: $345,800 + .40($7,350,000 – $1,000,000) = $2,885,800
3. Credit equivalent of tax on $5,250,000: $345,800 + .40($5,250,000 – $1,000,000) = $2,045,800 unified credit
4. Net tax after credit equivalent applied: $2,885,800 – $2,045,800 credit = $840,000 tax liability

This is the same tax that would be determined by multiplying her $2,100,000 in gifts in excess of her lifetime exclusion amount by the flat 40 percent tax rate [($7,350,000 – $5,250,000) × . 40] = $840,000). A similar procedure is used to determine the estate tax of a decedent that has made prior taxable gifts. Prior taxable gifts are added to the value of the taxable estate. The estate tax is determined from the tax rate schedule and the credit equivalent of the tax on $5,250,000 ($2,045,800 for 2013) is deducted from the tax due. The credit equivalents for years 2009 through 2013 are shown in Table 12.3. These credit equivalents are based on the exclusion amounts in effect in each year shown.

TABLE
12.3 CREDIT EQUIVALENTS FOR EXCLUSION AMOUNTS

YEAR OF TRANSFER	GIFT TAX EXCLUSION AMOUNTS	GIFT TAX CREDIT EQUIVALENT	ESTATE TAX EXCLUSION AMOUNTS	ESTATE TAX CREDIT EQUIVALENT
2009	$1,000,000	$345,800	$3,500,000	$1,455,800
2010	1,000,000	330,800	5,000,000	1,730,800
2011	5,000,000	1,730,800	5,000,000	1,730,800
2012	5,120,000	1,772,800	5,120,000	1,772,800
2013	5,250,000	2,045,800	5,250,000	2,045,800

EXAMPLE 5

Assume the same facts in example 4 except that instead of making a 2013 gift Clarice dies in 2013 leaving a $6,400,000 taxable estate to her son. The tax result would be the same as in example 4. The estate would be liable for an estate tax of $840,000 on the cumulative taxable gifts and taxable estate of $7,350,000.

Exclusion Amount Portability

Under the 2010 Tax Relief Act, the surviving spouse of a decedent dying in 2011 or 2012 could "inherit" any unused portion of the decedent's lifetime exclusion. Thus, the surviving spouse would not only have available his or her own $5 million exclusion amount, but all of the decedent's unused exclusion amount. Only the surviving spouse, no other relative, could "inherit" this exclusion amount. The surviving spouse, however, could use the "inherited" exclusion amount to offset gift taxes currently as well as estate taxes upon death. This portability feature was made permanent by the American Taxpayer Relief Act.

EXAMPLE 6

Walter died in early 2013 and his estate used only $2 million of his $5.25 million lifetime exclusion amount on his taxable estate. Wilma, his wife and executor of Walter's estate, elects to add his unused $3.25 million exclusion amount to her $5.25 million lifetime exclusion amount (assuming that she has not had any prior taxable gifts). Wilma now has an $8.50 million exclusion amount to offset any taxes due on current gifts and her estate (if she dies in 2013).

The executor of the estate must make an irrevocable election to pass the unused exclusion amount to the surviving spouse and show the calculations for the amount transferred. In addition, the surviving spouse can only add the unused portion of the most recently deceased spouse to his or her exclusion amount and combined exemptions can never exceed $10 million for any decedent.

EXAMPLE 7

Refer to example 6. Wilma marries Howard three months after Walter's death. In late-2013, Howard dies, but he had used $4.5 million of his lifetime exclusion amount in 2012 on gifts to his children. Because Howard is the most recently deceased spouse, Wilma loses the $3.25 exemption amount carried over from Walter's estate and now has only $750,000 from Howard's estate plus her basic $5.25 million exclusion amount available in 2013.

The Federal Gift Tax

Transfers Subject to Gift Tax

Only gratuitous lifetime transfers of property or property interests are subject to gift taxes. The value of services performed gratuitously is not taxable as a gift because of the difficulty of measuring the value. Because the gift tax is meant to apply broadly, the gift tax is levied on transfers of property whether real or personal, tangible or intangible, made directly or indirectly, or in trust.[8]

Example 8

John is very wealthy and likes to share his good fortune with friends and family. He gave each of his children \$100,000 in stock; he put \$2,000,000 in a trust fund for the care of his elderly parents; he gave his Saab convertible to a friend who had admired it earlier in the year; he gave his devoted secretary \$15,000 for unusual medical expenses that she had been unable to pay; and he took three months off from running his company to head the United Way Campaign. These are all potentially taxable gifts, except for the services to the United Way Campaign.

Transfers for Insufficient Consideration

Sales, exchanges, and other dispositions can be treated as gifts if the transferor receives insufficient consideration for the property transferred.[9]

Example 9

Eileen sells land worth \$180,000 to her son for \$60,000. Because Eileen receives less than a fair market value price for the land, she has made a gift valued at \$120,000 (\$180,000 – \$60,000).

A sale, exchange, or other transfer of property made in a bona fide business transaction with no donative intent is not a gift.[10] Thus, a business forced to sell inventory items at a substantial discount does not make gifts. Normally, transactions that result from free bargaining between nonrelated parties have no gift implications.

Any item that cannot be valued in money or money's worth (such as love and affection) cannot be treated as consideration in an exchange.[11] Thus, a transfer made in exchange for something not reducible to a monetary value avoids valuation problems by treating the item as a gift.

Example 10

Sam promises his daughter, Sarah, \$50,000 if she graduates from college with a nursing degree. When she graduates with this degree, Sam gives her the \$50,000. The money is a gift because the act of graduating with the nursing degree cannot be valued in monetary terms.

Joint Property Transfers

When one party places funds into a joint bank account in his or her name and the name of one or more other persons, no gift results because the donor can withdraw the funds and terminate the joint ownership at will. Instead a gift is made when one of the other persons withdraws funds, ending the donor's control over the funds withdrawn.[12]

---

[8]The gift tax applies to all gifts made by U.S. citizens or residents and to gifts of tangible property situated within the United States by a nonresident alien.

[9]Reg. §25.2512-8.

[10]Ibid.

[11]Ibid.

[12]Reg. §25.2511-1(h)(4).

EXAMPLE 11

George places $30,000 into a joint savings account in his and his son's names. Two years later, the son withdraws $14,000. George does not make a gift until the son withdraws the $14,000.

When an individual purchases property (such as stock and realty) with his or her own funds but titles the property (when purchased or at a later date) with one or more other individuals as joint tenants with the right of survivorship, the purchaser makes a gift equal to the value of the other individuals' interests.[13] The donor no longer controls the interests transferred to the other individuals after the transfer.

EXAMPLE 12

Shannet purchases land for $300,000 but enters both her name and Jason's name on the title as joint tenants with right of survivorship. Shannet makes a gift to Jason of $150,000, one-half the value of the property, at the date she puts his name on the title.

Life Insurance Transfers

When an individual irrevocably assigns all rights of ownership in an insurance policy to another, the assignor makes a gift equal to the cost to purchase a comparable policy on the date of the gift.[14] Ownership rights include the right to borrow against the policy, cash the policy in for its cash surrender value, and change the beneficiary. Paying the premium on an insurance policy that is owned by another person is also considered a gift to the policy's owner; the gift is valued at the amount of the premium paid. Naming someone as beneficiary of a life insurance policy is not a gift because the owner of the policy can change the beneficiary at any time in the future.

EXAMPLE 13

On October 12, year 1, Samuel transfers his ownership rights in a $500,000 life insurance policy on his life to his brother, Tony. Samuel makes a gift to Tony equal to the cost of a comparable policy at the date of the gift. In year 2, Samuel pays the $2,000 annual premium on the policy now owned by Tony. The premium payment is also a gift from Samuel to Tony.

Transfers to a Trust

The creation of a trust may be a gift subject to a gift tax. A **trust** is a legal arrangement involving three parties:

1. **grantor**—transfers assets that become the **corpus** or principal of the trust
2. **trustee**—holds title to the assets, makes investment decisions, files tax returns, and makes distributions according to the trust document[15]
3. **beneficiary**—has the legal right to receive the income or the assets (The beneficiary's rights are defined by state law and by the trust document.)

In some situations, fewer than three persons may be involved in a trust. For example, a parent who wants to transfer assets to a minor child might use a Uniform Transfers to Minors Act (UTMA) account.[16] The grantor parent can also be the trustee and maintain control over the property.

[13]In a joint tenancy with right of survivorship, if one owner dies, the others automatically receive the decedent's interest. A joint tenancy between husband and wife is a tenancy by entirety.

[14]Reg. §25.2511-1(h)(8).

[15]A trustee can be an individual or a corporation, such as a bank. Many banks have trust departments that manage trust assets for a fee.

[16]Under the Uniform Transfer to Minors Act (also known as Uniform Gifts to Minors Act), parents can give assets to their children and maintain control over the income by retaining custodial authority over the property. To the extent that income from property in a custodial account is used for support of the minor, the income will be taxed to the parent.

The grantor of a trust gives the beneficiary or beneficiaries rights designed to accomplish the goals of the trust. An **income beneficiary** has the right to receive income generated by the trust assets. A beneficiary called the *remainderman* has the right to receive the trust assets upon termination of the trust. He or she has a **remainder interest**.

A trust may be established for a specific number of years (a term certain) or until a specific event occurs. For example, the length of a trust might be established as follows:

1. for the life of the income beneficiary (a life tenant)
2. for the life of some other individual
3. until the beneficiary reaches the age of majority
4. until the beneficiary reaches some specified age or marries

Cessation of Donor's Control

A gift must be an unconditional, gratuitous transfer of property, or an interest in property. If the donor retains an interest in the transferred property or control over the use or disposition of the transferred interest, the transfer is not a gift and a gift tax is not assessed.

EXAMPLE 14

Andy transfers property into a trust with the income payable to Sandy for 10 years but retains the right to designate who will receive the remainder interest. Andy has made a gift of the income interest only, as he still controls who will receive the remainder.

The transfer of assets into an irrevocable trust is considered a gift by the grantor. A trust is **irrevocable** when the grantor gives up all future control.[17] A trust that the grantor can rescind is a **revocable** trust and is not a gift because the grantor has not given up control of the trust property.[18] Similarly, a trust in which the grantor retains an unlimited right to change trust beneficiaries or to decide how much the beneficiaries of a trust will receive is not a completed gift. When trust income is transferred to the beneficiaries, however, the donor has made a gift of the income transferred even though the donor has retained control or the right to revoke. Transferring the income to the beneficiary ends the donor's control and the donor makes a gift at that time.

EXAMPLE 15

Ken transfers property into a revocable trust for the benefit of David and Mary. The transfer is not a gift. During the current year, however, $18,000 of trust income is paid to David, and $17,000 to Mary. These amounts are gifts to David and Mary when paid from the trust.

If a donor merely reserves the power to change the manner or timing of a donee's enjoyment of a property interest, a gift is made because the donee will ultimately get the property interest, free of the donor's control.

EXAMPLE 16

Ray transfers property into a trust for the benefit of his son. Ray can decide whether to transfer the income to his son or to add the income to the trust principal. Ray has made a gift, as he controls only the timing of the payments.

---

[17]Reg. §25.2511-2(c) indicates there is no gift if the donor can revoke the transfer or can otherwise control trust property.

[18]A grantor trust is also ignored for gift and income tax purposes. This is a trust in which the grantor retains beneficial enjoyment or the power to dispose of trust income without approval or consent of an adverse party. §§672 and 674.

Transfers Excluded from Gift Taxes

Congress has eliminated certain gratuitous transfers from the gift category to limit taxpayer–IRS controversies over the taxability of certain transfers and to recognize that certain transfers represent support of another individual rather than gifts.

Transfers of Marital Property Pursuant to a Divorce

Property transfers from one ex-spouse to the other to satisfy a support obligation or to carry out a court decree are not gifts. Property transferred to an ex-spouse pursuant to a property settlement that is not part of an enforceable court decree could be a gift, however, because agreeing to a divorce is not reducible to money terms. To provide relief, Section 2516 provides that any property transferred to an ex-spouse as part of a property settlement agreement entered into within one year before or two years after a divorce is not a taxable gift.

EXAMPLE 17

Michael and Jennifer divorced on November 5, year 1. On January 31, year 2, they entered into an agreement whereby Michael would transfer the Key Largo condo to Jennifer as a condition of the divorce. When he transfers the Key Largo condo to Jennifer, he does not make a taxable gift.

Other Exclusions

Meeting support obligations is not subject to gift tax with state law determining what constitutes an obligation for support. The payment of medical expenses and school tuition for minors is normally a support obligation under state law and not a gift. These payments could be treated as gifts if they are made for adults (even elderly parents) and no legal support obligation exists. Yet, many individuals regard these payments as a form of support. To avoid any confusion and inequity surrounding this issue, Section 2503(e) provides an unlimited exclusion for the *direct* payment of the qualified medical expenses and tuition and fees of another regardless of the relationship to the donor.[19]

EXAMPLE 18

Alisha paid $15,000 of uninsured medical expenses directly to the hospital and doctors for her Aunt Mary. She also paid $10,000 directly to the college for her grandson's tuition. Neither of these payments is a taxable gift.

Transfers of money and property to political organizations such as national, state, or local political parties for their political purposes are not considered taxable gifts.[20]

Valuation of Gift Property

The value of a gift is its fair market value at the date of the gift.[21] Fair market value is a price that a willing buyer and willing seller would arrive at in an arm's-length agreement where neither is under a compulsion to buy or sell and both are aware of the relevant facts.[22] Fair market value is not a distressed sale price or a wholesale value.

EXAMPLE 19

Ken gave his nephew a Toyota Camry. Its trade-in value is $14,000, but dealers normally sell that car for $16,700. The value of the gift is $16,700.

---

[19]The exclusion is not allowed to the extent medical expenses are reimbursed by the donee's insurance.

[20]§ 2501(a)(5).

[21]Reg. § 25.2512-1.

[22]Reg. § 20.2031-1(b).

If the gift property is stock or securities sold on an established securities market, fair market value is the mean between the high and low price on the date of the gift.

EXAMPLE 20

Ken gave 10,000 shares of XYZ stock to Silvia on August 31 when the highest selling price for the stock was $60 per share and the lowest selling price was $50. The stock is valued at $550,000 [10,000 × (($60 + $50)/2)].

If an income interest is given to one individual and a remainder interest is given to a different individual, the total value of the property must be allocated between the two gifts.[23]

Special Rules Affecting the Annual Gift Tax Exclusion

Certain gifts are not eligible for the annual gift tax exclusion, currently $14,000 per donee per year.

Present versus Future Interests

The annual gift tax exclusion only applies to gifts to which the donee has an immediate and unrestricted right to benefit from and enjoy; thus, only gifts of present interests qualify for the exclusion. A **present interest** is an "unrestricted right to the immediate use, possession or enjoyment of property or the income from property."[24] Outright transfers and transfers of life estates (the right to the income from or enjoyment of property for the donee's life) or term certain interests (the right to income for a specified time period) are present interests. The exclusion is not allowed for gifts of future interests. A future interest is an interest that does not begin immediately or that restricts the use or benefits of the property. Remainder interests (interests that take effect after termination of a life estate or term-certain interest) or *reversions* (the donor retakes the property) are future interests.

EXAMPLE 21

Darla transfers property into a trust, giving a life estate worth $17,000 to Nancy and the remainder worth $25,000 to her grandchildren. The annual exclusion only offsets the life estate, reducing its gift value to $3,000 ($17,000 – $14,000). The gift of the $25,000 remainder interest does not qualify for the annual gift tax exclusion because it is a gift of a future interest.

Gifts to Minors

Many donors are reluctant to give minors the immediate use of or control over gifted property or the income from it; thus, gifts to minors that are restricted would not be eligible for the annual exclusion because they are not gifts of present interests. To permit exclusion, Congress enacted Section 2503(c), which allows an annual exclusion for gifts made into Section 2503(c) minor's trusts. To qualify, two conditions must be met:

1. Before the beneficiary reaches age 21, the trustee may pay the income and/or trust assets to or for the benefit of the beneficiary.
2. Any income and remaining assets must be distributed to the minor once he or she reaches age 21 or to his or her estate or intended beneficiaries if the minor dies before reaching age 21.

If the trust instrument contains these provisions, the gift is not considered a gift of a future interest. This allows a trustee to accumulate income on behalf of a minor while preserving the annual exclusion. The income will be taxed to the trust unless it is distributed (and taxed) to the minor.

---

[23]The value depends on the projected income from the property and the term or life expectancy of the income beneficiary.

[24]Reg. §25.2503-3(b).

A Crummey trust also qualifies for the annual exclusion because it provides for a present interest. A **Crummey trust** is similar to a 2503(c) minor trust, except it is more flexible.[25] It has an annual demand provision usually equal to the annual exclusion that expires if not exercised. The donor typically tries to persuade the beneficiary not to exercise his or her right to withdraw current year contributions (such as by tying future contributions to the beneficiary's agreement not to withdraw current contributions). A Crummey trust does not require a distribution of assets when the beneficiary reaches age 21.

EXAMPLE 22

Simon funds two $500,000 irrevocable trusts and names the local bank as trustee. The first trust is for the benefit of his 16-year-old son, Sam. The trustee may distribute income or principal to Sam until he reaches age 21. At age 21, all income and assets are to be distributed to Sam. If Sam dies before age 21, the trust assets are payable to whomever Sam appoints in his will or to his estate if he dies without a will. The second trust is for the benefit of Sarah, Simon's 20-year-old daughter. The trustee may pay income or principal to Sarah until she reaches age 30, when she will receive the trust assets. Sarah may demand by December 31 of each year that the trustee pay her the lesser of $14,000 or the amount transferred to the trust that year. Sam's is a 2503(c) trust, and Sarah's is a Crummey trust. Amounts contributed annually to both trusts qualify for the annual exclusion.

TAX PLANNING

Gifts to Coverdell education savings accounts and qualified tuition programs (Section 529 plans) are also considered gifts of a present interest.[26] These plans allow parents to save for their children's education with the earnings exempt from income tax.[27] Gifts to Section 529 plans also qualify for a special election that allows a gift in excess of the annual exclusion to be spread equally over five years for purposes of the annual gift tax exclusion; thus, a lump sum of up to $70,000 can be transferred into a Section 529 account plan free of gift consequences at one time.[28] The election may be filed only once every five years for each donee. Any gift in excess of the sum of the annual exclusions for the five-year period is treated as a taxable gift in the first year.

EXAMPLE 23

Carolyn contributes $75,000 to a Section 529 plan in year 1 with her son, Barry, as the beneficiary. Carolyn may elect to treat the gift as covered by annual gift exclusions of $14,000 each year for years 1 through 5. The $5,000 excess [$75,000 – ($14,000 × 5 years)] is a taxable gift in year 1.

Gift Splitting

When married persons in community property states make gifts of community property, each spouse is treated as giving only his or her one-half share of the gifted property.[29] The gift splitting provision of the gift tax equalizes the treatment of married persons in common law states with those in community property states. The election to split gifts allows married couples to elect to treat the value of any gift made by either spouse as if one-half of each gift's value is made by each spouse, allowing both of them to use their combined annual exclusions on gifts to each donee.[30] As a

[25]Crummey trusts derive their name from the case (*Crummey*, 22 AFTR 2d 6023) that was the first to allow an annual exclusion to apply to this type of trust.

[26]§ 530. These education IRAs were renamed in 2001 after Senator Paul Coverdell, who was a leading proponent of many of the improvements made to these education IRAs.

[27]The income tax consequences of these plans are discussed later in this chapter.

[28]§ 529(c)(2)(B). The gift cannot be spread over less than five years; the period must be five years only.

[29]States with community property rules include Arizona, California, Idaho, Louisiana, Nevada, New Mexico, Texas, Washington, and Wisconsin.

[30]§ 2513. If gift splitting is elected, it applies to all gifts made by either spouse during the tax year.

result, gift splitting allows two annual exclusions per donee to apply to gifts for which gift splitting is elected.[31]

EXAMPLE 24

Clem gives $28,000 to each of his 10 grandchildren for $280,000 in total gifts. If gift splitting is not elected, Clem can apply only his $14,000 annual exclusion to each $28,000 gift, leaving a $14,000 taxable gift to each donee, a potential total of $140,000 in taxable gifts. Alternatively, if he and his wife elect gift splitting, Clem and his wife are each treated as having made gifts of $14,000 (1/2 of $28,000) to each of the 10 grandchildren. Each is now allowed to use their $14,000 annual exclusion to reduce taxable gifts to $0. Thus, through the use of gift splitting and the annual exclusion, Clem and his wife can give away $280,000 (10 × $28,000) free of gift tax, rather than having $140,000 of taxable gifts.

EXAMPLE 25

Len and Rita are married. Len gives a cash gift of $30,000 to his nephew to purchase a car. If Len does not elect gift splitting, he has made a taxable gift of $16,000 ($30,000 – $14,000 annual exclusion) to his nephew. If the couple elects to gift split, Len and Rita are each deemed to give a gift of $15,000 (1/2 of $30,000) to the nephew. Each can now take advantage of the $14,000 annual exclusion for this gift. They have $1,000 each in taxable gifts remaining ($15,000 – $14,000). As a family, Len and Rita together have total taxable gifts of $2,000. By gift splitting, the two have each removed $14,000 from transfer taxation.

TAX PLANNING

In most situations, electing gift splitting reduces the overall gift tax. Gift splitting should not be elected, however, if one spouse has used all of his or her unified credit and owes gift taxes on any current gifts as this could increase the gift tax.

Gift Tax Deductions

The Internal Revenue Code allows unlimited deductions for gifts to qualified charitable organizations and for gifts made to the taxpayer's spouse.

Charitable Deduction

To encourage gifts to charitable organizations, Section 2522 provides a deduction for transfers of property or money to a qualified charitable organization. A similar deduction is allowed to estates for charitable transfers. Qualifying charities include U.S. federal, state, and local governments and qualifying charities organized for charitable, scientific, literary, or educational purposes or to foster sports competition, foster the encouragement of art, or to prevent cruelty to children. Because the annual exclusion also applies to a charitable gift, the actual charitable deduction is calculated as the value of the money or property transferred less the annual exclusion.

EXAMPLE 26

Mary transferred $16,000 of property to United Church, a qualified charity. Her charitable deduction is $2,000 ($16,000 – $14,000 annual exclusion) for gift tax purposes.

Marital Deduction

Before the marital deduction was enacted, one spouse giving part ownership in property to the other spouse (so that they jointly owned the property) would be assessed gift taxes if they lived in a common law state. Couples living in a community property state accomplished this division free of gift taxes, however. This inequity was corrected through the Section 2523 unlimited marital deduction for property transferred to one's spouse (including gifts of community property). The marital deduction is also calculated as the value of the transferred property less the annual exclusion.[32]

---

[31]In the actual gift tax calculation formula, the spouse making the gift subtracts one-half of the gift from total gifts and the other spouse adds one-half of the gift to total gifts.

[32]For gifts made to noncitizen spouses, only $143,000 can be excluded for 2013 ($139,000 for 2012).

Example 27

Bill gave 100 shares of IBM stock worth $25,000 to his wife. The gift tax marital deduction is $11,000 ($25,000 – $14,000 annual exclusion).

A similar unlimited marital deduction is allowed estates as well. Thus, if someone leaves his or her entire estate to the surviving spouse, no estate tax is owed.

Tax Consequences for Donees

TAX PLANNING

The donor's adjusted basis (and holding period) in gifted property carries over to the donee.[33] Using a carryover basis shifts unrealized appreciation from the donor to the donee. Income and appreciation on the asset is then taxed at the donee's rates. Although a dependent's standard deduction is limited to $1,000 (or earned income plus $350, if greater), shifting income-producing assets to dependents can save a significant amount of taxes for the family.

Example 28

Larry, who is 25, single, and an intern at Johns Hopkins, receives stock worth $24,000 as a gift from his parents. His parents purchased the stock four years ago for $10,000 and elected to gift split, so no gift tax is owed on the transfer. Larry's basis in the stock is $10,000 as both the basis and holding period carry over from his parents. During the year, Larry receives $1,800 in dividend income. He sells the stock at the end of the year for $25,000, resulting in a $15,000 long-term capital gain ($25,000 – $10,000). Larry's other income for the year as an intern is $9,100, which is $900 less than his combined standard deduction ($6,100) and personal exemption ($3,900) amounts. Because his parents are in the 28 percent marginal tax bracket, the gift results in a tax savings of $2,520. Following is a comparison of Larry's tax on the dividends and capital gain with the tax cost to his parents if they had not made the gift:

	Larry	Parents
Tax on dividends for Larry [($1,800 – $900 remaining deduction/exemption) × 0%]	$0	
Tax on dividends for parents ($1,800 × 15%)		$270
Tax on capital gain for Larry ($15,000 × 0%)	0	
Tax on capital gain for parents ($15,000 × 15%)		2,250
Total tax	$0	$2,520
Tax savings		$2,520

Additional savings can be achieved if Larry continues to hold the stock for several more years, collecting additional dividends taxed at his lower tax rate, before selling the stock.

This example demonstrates why many parents want to transfer income-producing assets to their children. Transfers to young children that allow parents to manage the assets have been particularly popular, but may not offer the same level of tax benefit as gifts to adult children.

Kiddie Tax

Congress limits the tax savings that can be achieved on asset transfers to many children by imposition of the **kiddie tax**, which taxes unearned income of certain children at their parents' marginal tax rate. Prior to 2008, the kiddie tax applied only to children under age 18. With the reduction in dividend and capital gains rates for

[33] § 1015. See the basis discussion in Chapter 6.

low income taxpayers to zero percent, the age at which these provisions apply was raised to children under 19 or, if a full-time student, under age 24.[34] This special tax calculation applies to the net unearned income that exceeds $2,000 if the child is under age 19 (24, if a full-time student) at year-end.[35] Unearned income includes taxable interest, dividends, and net capital gains on property owned directly by the child, as well as income received as a beneficiary of a trust.[36] The child's earned income (wages, tips, and salaries) and the first $2,000 of unearned income are subject to normal income tax rules. The kiddie tax does not apply to children whose net unearned income is $2,000 or less. This allows a child to earn a small amount of unearned income on wages that were saved or invested. Examples of the tax calculations are included in the *Expanded Topics* section later in this chapter.

Special Education Savings Plans

Parents whose children are subject to the kiddie tax, may wish to consider two special vehicles to save for their children's education. Both are free of income tax consequences:

- Section 529 qualified tuition programs
- Coverdell education savings accounts (previously known as education IRAs)

Under either plan, income on the funds contributed is not taxed currently. In addition, income from these plans that is used to pay for a beneficiary's eligible education expenses is never subject to income tax.[37] There is no annual limit on contributions to Section 529 plans.[38] The maximum contribution to a Coverdell education savings accounts is $2,000 per year (but is phased out gradually as modified adjusted gross income increases from $95,000 to $110,000 for single individuals or $190,000 to $220,000 for married couples). A donor can make contributions to both a Section 529 plan and a Coverdell plan for the same child in the same year. Multiple donors, such as grandparents or other relatives, who want to contribute to the child's education, can also contribute in the same year to these plans.

Another advantage of Section 529 plans is the ability to change the beneficiary.[39] If, for example, a grandchild does not use the entire balance in the Section 529 account for his or her education, the grandparent can change the beneficiary to another grandchild or a great grandchild with no adverse tax consequences as the donor is considered the owner of the plan. Whether the donor can change the beneficiary for a Coverdell account depends on the terms of that particular account.

TAX PLANNING

Both of these education accounts may be preferable to a UTMA account because, in addition to kiddie tax issues, the assets from a UTMA account may not be used to pay for college expenses in some states. Moreover, the donor to a Section 529 plan can redirect funds to another beneficiary or cash out the account, pay the income tax (and an additional 10 percent penalty tax), and use the remainder as the donor chooses.

---

[34]§ 1(g). Legislation in 2007 raised the age at which a child's unearned income could be taxed at the parent's rate to under 19 or under 24, if a full-time student, effective for tax years beginning after May 17, 2007. This provision does not apply if both parents are deceased, if the child is married filing a joint return, or the child's earned income exceeds one-half of his or her support.

[35]This $2,000 consists of $1,000 offset by the child's standard deduction and $1,000 taxed at the child's regular tax rates; so only $1,000 of *taxable* unearned income is taxed at the child's rates.

[36]The source of the assets is not important. Thus, income from assets transferred from grandparents or others can be taxed at the parents' rates.

[37]Under Section 529 plans, qualified higher education expenses include tuition, fees, books, supplies, and equipment at eligible institutions. Subject to limitation, room and board costs may also qualify. Additionally, Coverdell funds can be used for qualified elementary and secondary school expenses.

[38]In some states, contributions are limited to the cost of four years of college at the most expensive institution in the state.

[39]§ 529(c)(3)(C).

The Taxable Estate

An **estate** is the entity created upon the death of an individual to own and manage the property of the **decedent** (the person who died) until ownership of the property is transferred to the decedent's beneficiaries or heirs.[40] Estate taxes are levied on the value of all property owned by a decedent and transferred to heirs or beneficiaries at the decedent's death.[41] The estate pays the estate taxes. There are three basic steps to compute the decedent's taxable estate:

1. Identify and value the assets included in the gross estate.
2. Identify the deductible claims against the gross estate and deductible expenses of estate administration.
3. Identify any deductible bequests.

Identifying the Gross Estate

The **gross estate** includes all property and property interests of the decedent.[42] This is similar to the all-inclusive definition of gross income contained in Section 61, which states that everything is included in taxable income unless it is specifically excluded.

Probate is the state law process by which a will is declared legally valid and governs the transfer of property by will to the beneficiaries. The probate estate includes the property governed only by the will or by the state's intestacy laws if there is no valid will. It does not include property transferred by operation of law, such as property held in joint tenancy with right of survivorship. The gross estate includes property that transfers both by will and by operation of law. Thus the decedent's gross estate is usually larger than the decedent's probate estate.

Example 29

Gillian owns a car and a bank account in her own name. Her only other asset is her house, owned with her husband as joint tenants with right of survivorship. Upon her death, her gross estate includes the car, the bank account, and half the house. Her probate estate includes only the car and the bank account. The house passes outside of probate directly to her husband, the surviving joint tenant.

TAX PLANNING

One strategy for avoiding probate costs is to use a living trust that holds title to all an individual's assets.[43] The trust document specifies how these assets are transferred when the individual dies. The taxpayer's will only has to designate the treatment of any assets not included in the trust. Unlike a will, a living trust is not a public document available for anyone to inspect. Thus, a living trust has the dual advantages of removing assets from the probate estate and maintaining privacy for the decedent's heirs. Placing property in a living trust does not exclude it from the decedent's gross estate, however.

The estate tax is not a tax on the property the decedent owned but a tax on the transfer of property due to the decedent's death. Thus, the gross estate may include some items not actually owned by the decedent at death. Taxpayers may give their property away while living, but they continue to benefit from or enjoy the property. Such gifts with *strings attached* may have been complete for gift tax purposes but will still be included in the gross estate because the transfer does not take place until the donor's death. If the decedent retained the right to income from or the right to designate who may possess or enjoy property, the value of the property transferred during life is included in the gross estate.

[40]Beneficiaries refer to persons named in a will; heirs refer to beneficiaries of property of a decedent who dies intestate (without a will).

[41]The estate tax applies to decedents who were U.S. citizens or residents at death. Nonresident aliens may be taxed on the value of property located in the United States. §2511(a).

[42]§§ 2031, 2033, and 2034.

[43]As the grantor is usually the trustee, the trust is ignored for income tax purposes.

EXAMPLE 30

Jason transfers a rental apartment building to his daughter, Sarah, but retains the right to collect all the rental income from the building for his life (a life estate). When Jason dies, the value of the building is included in his gross estate because he retained an interest in the property.

If at death the decedent possessed the right to alter, amend, revoke, or terminate the terms of the transfer, the value of property transferred during life is also included in the gross estate.

EXAMPLE 31

Robert creates a trust naming his local bank as trustee. Robert's four children are to receive the income for their lives. Robert's grandson is to receive a remainder interest upon the death of the children. Robert reserves the right to designate annually the portion of income to be paid to each income beneficiary. Upon Robert's death, the value of the trust assets is included in his gross estate because he kept control over the income flow. If he had ***cut the strings*** and surrendered his right to designate the income to be paid each year, the property would not be included in his gross estate.

An important part of estate planning involves ensuring that the estate has sufficient funds to pay the estate tax liability. Otherwise, the estate may be forced to sell assets to pay the tax. Life insurance is one of the simplest means to ensure estate liquidity. Life insurance proceeds (which do not come into existence until the decedent's death) are included in the gross estate if (1) the decedent's estate is the beneficiary or (2) the decedent possessed any incidents of ownership at his or her death.[44] Incidents of ownership include the power to change the beneficiary, surrender or cancel the policy, assign the policy, revoke an assignment, pledge the policy for a loan, or obtain a loan from the insurer against the surrender value of the policy. Payment of premiums is not an incident of ownership. If the decedent retains any incidents of ownership or the estate is the beneficiary of the policy, the policy will be included in the taxable estate and up to 40 percent of the life insurance proceeds may be wasted on additional taxes.

EXAMPLE 32

James purchased a \$2 million life insurance policy on his own life five years ago and named his daughter, Rebecca, as the sole beneficiary. He retained the right to change the beneficiary and to cancel the policy. When James dies, the insurance proceeds are included in his gross estate because he retained incidents of ownership. Assuming James's estate is large enough to be taxed at the 40% flat rate for 2013, including the insurance policy in his estate results in an additional \$800,000 (\$2,000,000 × 40%) in estate taxes.

TAX PLANNING

If James had transferred ownership of the policy to his daughter when it was obtained, and had retained no incidents of ownership, the proceeds would not have been included in the estate. Rebecca could have paid the premiums on the policy by having James make an annual gift to her for the appropriate amount.

Before the estate and gift taxes were unified, gifts made within three years of a decedent's death, commonly referred to as deathbed gifts, were automatically included in the decedent's gross estate unless it could be shown the gifts were not made in contemplation of death. This rule prevented a decedent from circumventing the then higher estate tax rates by transferring assets as gifts shortly before death. Although gifts within three years of death are no longer automatically pulled back into the estate, a limited version of this provision remains. Any gift tax paid on gifts made within three years of death, and certain property interests transferred

[44]Insurance is deemed payable to the estate if proceeds are required to be used for the payment of the insured's debts.

within three years of death that would have been included in the gross estate had the gift not occurred, are brought back into the estate.[45] Under these rules, if a decedent gives away an insurance policy within three years of death, the value of the policy must be included in the gross estate, as if the transfer had not occurred during those three years.

EXAMPLE 33

Two years before his death, Alex gave an insurance policy on his own life to his son, Mike. When gifted, this whole life policy had a cash surrender value of $120,000. Upon Alex's death, the policy paid Mike the face amount of $800,000. Alex's gross estate includes the $800,000 value of the insurance policy because it was given away within three years of his death.[46]

Valuation Issues

Normally, the value of the gross estate includes the value of all property, real or personal, tangible or intangible, regardless of location, as of the date of death.[47] Section 2032 allows an **alternative valuation date** of six months after the decedent's date of death, if the executor makes an irrevocable election on the estate tax return and the gross estate and estate tax are both reduced by using this alternate date. If the alternate valuation date is elected, it must be applied to all estate assets. If any assets are sold prior to the valuation date, they are valued at their date of sale.[48] The legislative intent of the alternate valuation date is to protect estates against sudden declines in value.

EXAMPLE 34

When Godfrey died, his assets were valued as follows:

Asset	Date of Death Valuation	Alternate Valuation Date
Stocks	$1,100,000	$1,000,000
Bonds	3,000,000	3,100,000
Home	4,000,000	3,800,000
Total	$8,100,000	$7,900,000

If the executor elects the alternate valuation date, then all assets are valued as of six months after death. Because the value of the gross estate at the alternate valuation date is $200,000 less than the date of death valuation and the estate taxes will be reduced, the alternative valuation date may be elected.

Three methods of valuation are commonly used: market price, actuarial valuations, and capitalization of earnings. The market price method is used for such items as stocks, bonds, and real estate. Stocks traded on a stock exchange are valued at the average of their high and low selling prices as of the valuation date. Actuarial valuation must be used for annuities, life estates, terms certain, and remainder interests in property. Capitalization of earnings is appropriate when valuing going businesses, particularly those that are closely held.

[45]If a decedent relinquishes the right or control that causes a gift to be included within the estate (§ 2036 transfers with a retained life estate, § 2037 transfers taking effect at death, or § 2038 revocable transfers), exercises a general power of appointment (§ 2041), or gives away an insurance policy (§ 2042) within three years of death, the property will be brought back into the estate under § 2035.

[46]Any gift tax paid would also be included in the gross estate, but the $120,000 value of the policy when gifted would be excluded in the determination of total taxable transfers.

[47]Sec. 2031(a).

[48]If property is distributed to heirs prior to the alternate valuation date, the fair market value on the date of distribution is used.

EXAMPLE 35

At the time of his death, Ken owned 1,000 shares of XYZ stock and a three-bedroom house. On the date of death, the highest selling price for the stock was $60 per share, and the lowest selling price was $50. The stock is valued at $55,000 [1,000 × (($60 + $50)/2)]. The house was appraised at $350,000 on the valuation date. Ken's gross estate is valued at $405,000 ($55,000 + $350,000).

Estate Deductions

The gross estate is reduced by outstanding debts of the decedent, the decedent's funeral expenses, and any administrative costs of settling the estate. Casualty and theft losses incurred during the administration of the estate are also deducted for estate tax purposes as well as any state death taxes. The taxable estate is reduced by bequests to charitable organizations and by the property transferred to the decedent's surviving spouse.[49] The unlimited marital deduction allows the estate tax on the wealth accumulated by a married couple to be deferred until both spouses are deceased. The taxable estate is the amount remaining after all deductions are taken.

TAX PLANNING

To maximize the benefits of the marital deduction and the lifetime exclusion, a decedent's will should specify that taxable bequests should be limited to his or her remaining portion of the $5.25 million lifetime exclusion after consideration of prior taxable gifts. The remaining assets can be left tax free to the surviving spouse and the estate can avoid paying any estate taxes.

EXAMPLE 36

Mr. Moneybags died in 2013 and was survived by his wife and their only child, Cherie. All of Mr. Moneybags's lifetime gifts were for amounts less than the annual gift tax exclusion, so he had used none of his unified credit. Mr. Moneybags's will contained two specific bequests: the Lowe Art Museum received his art collection, and Cherie received marketable securities with a value equal to Mr. Moneybags's lifetime transfer tax exclusion of $5,250,000. The remainder of his estate went to Mrs. Moneybags. No transfer tax will be owed by Mr. Moneybags's estate.

If the decedent's spouse and children do not have compatible interests (for example, the decedent's children are from a prior marriage), the decedent may be reluctant to maximize the marital deduction. In this case, the decedent can leave the property in trust with all income to be distributed to the surviving spouse for the rest of his or her life and the remainder interest to be transferred to the decedent's children upon the spouse's death. This type of trust, known as a **qualified terminal interest property (QTIP)** trust, allows the decedent to exclude the value of the property transferred in trust from his or her estate, while still guaranteeing the eventual transfer of property to the designated beneficiaries.[50]

Alternate Estate Provision for 2010

The 2010 Tax Relief Act provided two potential alternatives for the estates of decedents dying in 2010. The first alternative that was in place at the beginning of 2010 repealed the estate tax for 2010 but allowed only a limited step-up in basis for estate property. The other imposed an estate tax at a rate of 35 percent on the taxable estates of decedents that exceeded the $5,000,000 lifetime exemption amount. For most decedents dying in 2010, the $5 million lifetime exemption precluded their estates from having to pay any estate taxes while providing a normal step-up in basis for property included in the estate. For decedents with taxable estates exceeding the $5,000,000 exemption amount, there was no simple answer.

[49]Property passing to a surviving spouse who is not a U.S. citizen is not eligible for the marital deduction unless the surviving spouse becomes a U.S. citizen before the estate tax return is filed. §2056(d)(4).
[50]§2056(b)(7).

The 2001 Act that repealed the estate tax in 2010 included a carryover basis rule for inherited property that was similar to the carryover basis for gifts. Fortunately, two exceptions permitted limited basis increases and reduced taxes on subsequent sales of inherited property by the beneficiaries of many estates. These were as follows:

1. $1.3 million of basis could be added to certain assets
2. $3 million of basis could be added to assets transferred to a surviving spouse[51]

The basis increase allocated to a piece of property could not exceed the excess of the property's fair market value over the decedent's basis. Not all property was eligible for a basis increase, however.[52] These carryover basis rules required extensive basis records for assets that had been in a family for many generations. A prior attempt at using carryover bases for inherited property was promptly repealed as being too complicated.

If the estate property was not highly appreciated so that the $4.3 million of allowable basis increase would bring most or all of the property up to its fair market value (and records were available to verify basis), then electing the alternate estate provision that imposed no estate tax made perfect sense. If, however, the estate assets had extremely low bases (or no bases could be established) and the heirs were highly likely to sell the assets in the near future, the more likely that the estate taxes paid currently would be less than the taxes on the taxable gains on the asset dispositions.

Generation-Skipping Transfer Taxes

The generation-skipping transfer tax, the final transfer tax, is discussed only briefly here. Before 1986, many wealthy taxpayers avoided transfer taxes by using generation-skipping trusts. These trusts were set up so that only a life estate was left to each successive generation. When the life estate holder died, the life estate also ended so that none of the trust's value was included in the decedent's gross estate. The complex generation-skipping transfer tax (GSTT) eliminates this tax benefit by applying a separate flat tax at 40 percent, the highest transfer tax rate in 2013, whenever a transfer skips a generation (whether in trust or otherwise). For example, a direct transfer from a grandparent to a grandchild is a generation skip (unless the grandchild's parent on the transferor's side of the family is deceased).

As part of the 2010 Tax Relief Act, the GSTT exclusion amount was increased from $3,500,000 in 2009 to $5,000,000 for 2010 and 2011, $5,120,000 for 2012, and $5,250,000 in 2013 by the American Taxpayer Relief Act.[53] At the same time, the GSTT transfer tax rate was reduced from 45 percent to 35 percent for 2011 and 2012. It was subsequently increased to 40 percent by the American Taxpayer Relief Act and is now imposed at a 40 percent flat rate tax on qualifying transfers in excess of $5,250,000 in 2013. Because a number of transfers taking place after 2009 and prior to the enactment of the 2010 Tax Relief Act had been made under the assumption that the GSTT had been repealed for 2010, Congress imposed a zero percent tax rate on GSTT transfers in 2010, effectively repealing this tax for the year.

EXAMPLE 37

Grandfather died in 1985 with a taxable estate of $8 million, leaving $5 million to his son, Ronald, and $3 million to his grandson, Bill. This year Ronald died, leaving his $5 million estate to his son, Bill. If Grandfather had left the entire $8 million to his son, Ronald, and Ronald then left the entire $8 million estate to Bill, Ronald's taxable estate would have been $8 million. By skipping Ronald and leaving $3 million directly to grandson Bill, Grandfather allowed the family to avoid estate tax at Ronald's level on this $3 million.

---

[51]§ 1022(b)(3).

[52]See §§ 1022(c) and (d) for details on excluded property.

[53]The GSTT exclusion amount became the exclusion amount applicable to the federal estate tax in 2004. Although the 2010 Tax Relief Act retroactively reintroduced an estate tax and the GSTT in 2010, the rate for the GSTT was set at zero percent. In 2013, the exclusion amount increased to $5,250,000 as adjusted for inflation as provided in the 2010 Act.

TAX PLANNING

The GSTT is best avoided by structuring transactions that take advantage of the GSTT exclusion amount along with the $14,000 annual gift exclusion.

Transfer Tax Planning

Selecting the Right Property to Give

A gift of property can provide income tax benefits, transfer tax benefits, or both. The transfer of investment property (such as bonds) allows a family to shift income to lower-bracket family members but offers few transfer tax benefits if there are relatively small differences between the current and future value of the transferred assets. In contrast, a gift of growth stock or appreciating land provides potentially significant transfer tax savings but may shift little income to the donee. By comparison, the transfer of an equity interest in a flow-through entity offers both current income tax and future transfer tax benefits. The donor can retain control by giving the donee a minority interest, a nonvoting interest, or a limited partnership interest in the business.

Example 38

Elizabeth and Phillip (husband and wife) are the sole shareholders of an S corporation. On January 1 of the current year, when the corporation's net worth is $2,800,000, they give 1 percent of the outstanding stock to each of the children, Harry and Diana, both of whom are married and have modest incomes. The corporation's taxable income for the year is $700,000. The gifts to Harry and Diana are each worth $28,000 ($2,800,000 × 1%) and are offset by the annual gift tax exclusion using gift splitting. Any future appreciation in the gifted stock accrues to the children and is not subject to either gift or estate tax. Each child is taxed on $7,000 ($700,000 × 1%) of income, but at a much lower rate than the parent's. Elizabeth and Phillip have successfully shifted $14,000 of income to their children and removed any future appreciation on 2 percent of the stock from their estate. This process can be repeated annually, transferring corporate stock equal to the annual gift tax exclusion to the children and removing it from the parent's estate with no gift tax consequences. The corporation can distribute sufficient cash to the children to pay the taxes on the income passed through without additional tax consequences to the children.

If the donor is concerned about an unexpected sale of the interest, a buy–sell agreement can guarantee the donor the right to buy the property back if the donee decides to dispose of the asset. The agreement should provide for repurchase at the fair market value to ensure that the original gift is not disregarded and that any income generated by the property is taxed to the donee, not shifted back to the donor.

A gift-leaseback arrangement may be an attractive alternative if a donor wishes to continue using property after giving it away. This arrangement allows the donor to give property to the donee and then lease it back at a fair market value rent. If the donor uses the property for a legitimate business purpose, this arrangement is usually effective at shifting the property's income from the donor to the donee.[54]

Example 39

Howard is a dentist. Five years ago, he purchased the building in which his office is located for $400,000. Howard transfers ownership of the building to his son, Bryan, signing a leaseback agreement stipulating that Howard is to pay annual rent of $40,000 for the use of the building. Assuming that $40,000 is a reasonable rent, Howard can deduct the $40,000 payment from the income for his dental practice and Bryan reports the same amount as rental income. This arrangement shifts $40,000 income each year from Howard to Bryan.

[54] Mathews, 61 TC 12 (1973) rev'd 35 AFTR 2d 75-4965 (CA-5, 1975), cert. denied 424 US 957 (1976).

Advantages of Making Lifetime Gifts

Although the enactment of the unified transfer tax system reduced some of the advantages of making gifts during one's lifetime, it certainly did not eliminate them. In many cases the advantages of making lifetime gifts still outweigh the disadvantages. A discussion of some of the more common advantages and disadvantages follows.

Shielding of Post-Gift Appreciation from Estate Taxes

Gifts that are subject to transfer taxes are taxed at their date of gift value. Any later appreciation in value of the gifted property is shielded from any further transfer taxation with respect to the donor. Therefore, everything else being equal, a donor with multiple properties should give away those with the highest appreciation potential during his or her lifetime.

EXAMPLE 40

Maury gave some land near the city limits to his grandchildren many years ago when the land was worth \$100,000. Maury, however, expected the city to grow and the value of the land to increase tremendously. The property is now valued at \$2,000,000. Because he made a gift of the property when it was worth only \$100,000, Maury shielded \$1,900,000 (\$2,000,000 – \$100,000) from estate taxation. If he has at least \$5.25 million of other property that would be part of his taxable estate upon his death, this action will have saved his estate \$760,000 (\$1,900,000 × 40%) in transfer taxes (ignoring present value) if he dies in 2013.

The increase in the lifetime exclusion amount for gifts from \$1,000,000 in 2010 to \$5,000,000 in 2011 (\$5,120,000 in 2012 and \$5,250,000 in 2013), an unprecedented increase, provides an opportunity for persons who have planned to transfer a majority of their wealth through testamentary transfers to make transfers currently to take advantage of the increased lifetime exclusion amount for gifts. This would be particularly true for appreciating property as it can be transferred now at a lower value than its potential future value, using less of the lifetime exclusion amount.

Property that has declined in value should neither be gifted nor held until death. Instead, this property should be sold and any allowable losses deducted for income tax purposes. When a donee or heir receives property that has declined in value, the donor's basis is limited to the fair market value on the date of the gift. This prevents a donor from shifting a tax loss through a gift or bequest.

Using the Annual Exclusion and Gift Splitting

A significant amount of an individual's estate can be removed by making gifts qualifying for the annual per donee gift tax exclusion. Gifts of \$14,000 or less to each of several donees, such as children and grandchildren, repeated annually can remove thousands, if not hundreds of thousands of dollars from the transfer tax base of the donor at no tax cost. Even a terminally ill person can still make a significant reduction in his or her estate. In addition, the income from the gifted properties is shielded from transfer taxes and may even be subject to lower marginal income tax rates in the hands of the donees rather than the donor.

EXAMPLE 41

Charles made ten annual gifts of \$10,000 bonds to each of his six grandchildren over the past 10 years. As a result, he has transferred \$600,000 (6 × 10 × \$10,000) of property free of any transfer taxes and removed a like amount from his estate. Additionally, all interest income from the bonds has been transferred from Charles to the grandchildren, further reducing his estate and possibly reducing income taxes on the interest.

Through gift splitting, married couples can each take advantage of the annual exclusion on the gifts for each donee, effectively doubling the transfer tax savings from the annual exclusion and reducing the potential tax applicable to transfers.

Example 42

Assume the same facts as the previous example, except that Charles made gifts of $20,000 to each of the six grandchildren but he and his wife elected to split gifts in each of the years. As a result, $1,200,000 of property has been transferred free of any transfer taxes to the grandchildren.

Noncash assets, such as real estate, can be transferred as fractional interests over time using a series of gifts. As an alternative to transferring a fractional interest each year, the taxpayer could sell the real estate under the installment method, making the annual principal and interest installments no more than $14,000 (or $28,000 if gift splitting). The taxpayer then forgives the payments as each annual installment is due. Care must be taken when this sale approach is used so that the IRS does not recharacterize the entire transfer as a gift in the year of sale by arguing substance over form.[55]

The portability of the lifetime exclusion amount from a deceased spouse to the surviving spouse provides another reason generally to claim gift splitting on all or at least a major part of taxable gifts. Using gift splitting will ensure that the amount of the unused lifetime exclusion amount "inherited" by the surviving spouse will be relatively equal regardless of which spouse dies first.

Nontax Advantages of Trusts

Trusts can be used for a variety of nontax reasons. A trust can be used to protect property from creditors or others who may bring future claims against the beneficiary (such as a doctor concerned about malpractice claims) or to shield the assets of well-known individuals from public scrutiny (such as a politician placing assets in a blind trust). Trusts are commonly formed to hold property for the benefit of a minor child or an adult beneficiary who does not wish to or is unable to manage the property. Trusts are also frequently used for the transfer of property for the benefit of multiple beneficiaries, allowing them to share the benefits of property ownership while management responsibility stays in the hands of a single trustee. This minimizes the potential for disputes over the management or division of the trust income. Trusts can also be used to transfer interests sequentially with an income interest going to one beneficiary and a remainder interest to a different beneficiary.

Disadvantages of Lifetime Gifts

A number of disadvantages are associated with the making of lifetime gifts, however. Two of the more common disadvantages are the basis carryover and the acceleration of transfer taxes.

Carryover Basis on Gift Property

In deciding whether to make lifetime gifts of property, donors should recognize that appreciated property will have a carryover basis (the donor's adjusted basis plus the applicable gift tax adjustment) if given, but the same appreciated property will get a basis stepped up to fair market value if retained until death.

Example 43

Dena owns land worth $400,000. She paid $60,000 for the land several years ago. If she gives the land to her son now, the son will have an income tax basis of $60,000 plus any gift tax adjustment. If Dena keeps the property until she dies, the property will have a basis of $400,000 or more (assuming its value does not decrease). By keeping the property until her death, $340,000 or more of potentially taxable gain is never recognized, resulting in substantial income tax savings to the family. Dena's gross estate and estate taxes could be higher, however, if her estate now exceeds her lifetime exclusion.

[55]Rev. Rul. 77-299, 1977-2 CB 343.

When property is expected to significantly appreciate, the potential income tax savings to the donee (due to the step-up in basis) when the transfer is made at death may be greater than the transfer tax savings from making a current gift (when the tax is assessed on its pre-appreciation value). If the donee expects to keep the property rather than sell it, however, the carryover basis may be of little importance. Thus, a current gift removes the appreciation from the estate.

Early Payment of Transfer Taxes

Any gift taxes paid as a result of making taxable gifts are a form of prepayment or early payment of the transfer taxes due on an estate. If no taxable gifts are made, transfer tax payments may be postponed for many years.

The lifetime gift tax exclusion amount increased from $675,000 in 2001 to $1 million in 2002 and remained there through 2010, when it increased to $5,000,000 for 2011, $5,120,000 in 2012, and $5,250,000 in 2013. The estate tax exclusion amount also increased from $675,000 to $1 million in 2002 and then gradually increased to $3.5 million in 2009 before finally rising to $5,000,000 for 2010-2011, $5,120,000 for 2012, and $5,250,000 in 2013. Since the changes in the estate and gift tax provisions were made permanent by the American Taxpayer Relief Act, future estate planning will be much more readily accomplished. In addition, the portability feature of the decedent's remaining lifetime exclusion amount increases the surviving spouses lifetime exclusion amount; this increase could be used to offset gifts of the surviving spouse preserving the surviving spouse's own $5,250,000 lifetime exclusion amount.

Fiduciary Income Tax Issues

The Decedent's Final Tax Return

A federal income tax return is due for the period from the beginning of the tax year up to the date of death for the decedent. The return is due on the decedent's regular income tax due date as if death had not occurred. If the decedent used the cash method of accounting, only income actually or constructively received up to the date of death is included on the final tax return. Income earned by a cash-basis decedent but not received prior to death is called **income in respect of a decedent (IRD)**. Examples of IRD include unpaid salary, interest, dividends, retirement plan income, and unrecognized gains on installment sales.

IRD is included on the income tax return of the estate or beneficiary who is entitled to and actually receives the payment.[56] This has significant income tax consequences to the recipient of the IRD and may result in an income tax liability much greater than any estate tax liability. Unlike other inherited property, there is no step-up in basis; that is, the decedent's basis carries over to the recipient (estate or beneficiary).[57] The recipient of the income recognizes gain (or loss) on the difference between the amount realized and the adjusted basis of the IRD. The character is the same as it would have been to the decedent.

Deductions in respect of a decedent (DRD) are expenses or liabilities incurred by a cash-basis decedent prior to death, which are not paid until after death (such as property taxes and state individual income taxes). The party legally required to pay these expenses (usually the estate) can deduct them.

Example 44

Roland died on September 18 of the current year. On October 1, his estate received a $1,000 check from Roland's former employer for the last pay period of his life. On October 15, Roland's estate received a $50,000 distribution for Roland's 401(k) plan. Both of these amounts are included as IRD taxable as ordinary income. If any deductible items were withheld from the payment, such as state income taxes, they would be deductible as DRD.

---

[56]§691(a) and Reg. §1.691(a)-2.

[57]Typically, as unrecognized income, the decedent's basis in IRD is zero.

Income Tax Consequences of Inherited Property

Beneficiaries use fair market value for their basis in inherited property, except for property inherited from certain decedents dying in 2010.[58] This results in a stepped-up basis for appreciated property (or a stepped-down basis for property that has depreciated).[59] Using fair market value as basis eliminates income tax gain (and loss) on property at the date of death.[60]

EXAMPLE 45

Sam inherits land from his mother who died in early 2013. When she died, the land was worth $500,000. She purchased the land 15 years ago for $40,000. Sam's basis for the land is $500,000. If Sam sells the land for $500,000, he will have no taxable gain and pay no income tax. The $460,000 appreciation is not subject to income tax; instead the $500,000 value is subject to the estate transfer tax.

Appreciated property that is inherited will have a higher basis than property received as a gift. The differences in bases between appreciated property that is inherited (fair market value at date of death) and property received by gift (carryover basis from the donor) forms one of the major considerations for persons wishing to reduce the total tax burden when passing property to their children or grandchildren. If the property is gifted, the donee will pay income tax on all the appreciation if sold (while owned by both the donor and the donee), but the property is removed from the donor's estate, reducing potential estate taxes. If it is inherited, the heir has the higher fair market value as basis in the property, reducing taxable gain on a future sale. Potential estate taxes will be higher, however, as the asset's fair market value is included in the decedent's estate.

The enactment of the 2010 Tax Relief Act in December 2010 came so late in the year that Congress decided it needed to provide an alternative to retroactively imposing the estate tax on those who had died before the tax was reinstated. As a result, the personal representative for decedents dying in 2010 prior to the enactment of the 2010 Relief Act could elect to apply the 2001 Act law, which repealed the estate tax in 2010 but included a modified carryover basis rule that allowed limited increases in bases of $1.3 million for certain assets and $3 million for assets transferred to a surviving spouse. It was expected that there would be a limited number of these elections as they required extensive records to establish the bases for the assets transferred.

Income Taxation of Trusts and Estates

Subchapter J of the Internal Revenue Code (Sections 641–692) contains the rules for income taxation of fiduciary entities (estates and trusts). These provisions create a modified conduit approach that taxes an estate or trust only on the income that it retains, not on income that it distributes to the beneficiaries. The recipient beneficiaries are taxed on any distributed income.[61] The character of all income is determined at the fiduciary level and the income retains this character when distributed to a beneficiary; for example, tax-exempt income received by the estate is tax-exempt income when distributed to the beneficiary.

There is little incentive for a fiduciary to retain income within a trust, as the tax rate structure is highly progressive. The maximum marginal rate of 39.6 percent is reached at taxable income of only $11,950. The tax rate structure is deliberately

---

[58]§ 1014. Fiduciaries for decedents dying in 2010 only could elect to apply the law in effect prior to the 2010 Tax Relief Act that repealed the estate tax but limited the step-up in basis to $1.3 million for certain property and $3 million for property transferred to the surviving spouse.

[59]The only property that does not get a basis step-up is IRD, except for the property of decedents dying in 2010 for which the repealed estate provisions were elected.

[60]Or alternate valuation date, if elected by the executor.

[61]An individual taxpayer reports the income that is received as the beneficiary of a trust or estate on Schedule E: *Supplemental Income and Loss* of Form 1040.

designed to ensure that a fiduciary entity distributes its income to the beneficiaries. The tax rates for 2013 are shown in Table 12.4.[62]

Table 12.5 compares the marginal income tax brackets for various entities with taxable income of $25,000.

Distributing income annually usually results in lower overall taxes because the beneficiaries typically are in lower marginal tax brackets.

TAX PLANNING

The grantor must be careful in designing the trust to ensure that it is recognized for tax purposes. If the donor retains some incidents of ownership, such as a reversionary interest, the trust will be considered a **grantor trust** with the income taxed to the grantor. It is possible for only a portion of the trust to be treated as a grantor trust, with the remainder treated as a separate trust.

EXAMPLE 46

Dorothy created a trust 10 years ago for the benefit of her children. In the current year, when the value of the trust assets is $800,000, Dorothy transfers additional rental property valued at $400,000 into the trust. Because Dorothy is concerned that she might need some income in a future year if her investments do not perform well, she retains the right to receive the income from this rental property in any year in which her gross income falls below a specified amount. The $400,000 transfer into the trust is not recognized for tax purposes. Dorothy will be taxed on the portion of the trust's income generated by the $400,000 rental property, even if the income is distributed to her children. Income from the trust's original assets continues to be taxed to the trust or the beneficiaries.

TABLE 12.4 INCOME TAX RATES FOR TRUSTS AND ESTATES FOR 2013

TAXABLE INCOME	TAX RATE
0–$2,450	15%
$2,451–$5,700	25%
$5,701–$8,750	28%
$8,751–$11,950	33%
Over $11,950	39.6%

TABLE 12.5 MARGINAL INCOME TAX RATES IN 2013

ENTITY	TAXABLE INCOME	TAX RATE
Single Individual	$25,000	15%
C Corporation	$25,000	15%
Trust or Estate	$25,000	39.6%

[62]If capital gains are allocated to principal, they qualify for the preferential capital gains rates available to individuals.

Expanded Topics—The Tax Calculations

Computing the Gift Tax

Section 2502 provides that the gift tax in any given year is based on the taxable gifts made in that year as well as previous taxable gifts. Thus, the gift tax is determined on a cumulative basis as follows:

	Includible gifts made during the current period
Plus	One-half of gifts made by taxpayer's spouse for which gift splitting is elected
Less	One-half of gifts made by the taxpayer for which gift splitting is elected with the spouse
Less	Annual exclusions
Less	Charitable deduction
Less	Marital deduction
Equals	Taxable gifts for the current period
Plus	Taxable gifts in previous periods
Equals	Cumulative taxable gifts

Determination of gift tax payable:

	Gift tax on cumulative taxable gifts
Less	Current period unified credit
Less	Credit for taxes paid on prior taxable transfers (based on current tax rates but prior year's unified credit)
Equals	Gift taxes payable on current period's gifts

Example 47

Charles made a taxable gift of $15,028,000 to his son in 2013 and he and his wife Emma elected to split gifts. This the only gift made by either of them in 2013. In 2009, Charles made an adjustable taxable gift of $2,500,000 paying $660,000 [($500,000 × .45) + $780,800 - $345,800 credit for 2009] in gift taxes for this gift. The net gift tax liability is $1,198,000 determined as follows:

	Includible gifts made during the current period	$15,028,000
Plus	One-half of gifts made by taxpayer's spouse for which gift splitting is elected	0
Less	One-half of gifts made by the taxpayer for which gift splitting is elected with the spouse	(7,514,000)
Less	Annual exclusions	(14,000)
Less	Charitable deduction	0
Less	Marital deduction	0
Equals	Taxable gifts for the current period	$7,500,000
Plus	Taxable gifts in previous periods	2,500,000
Equals	Cumulative taxable gifts	$10,000,000

Determination of gift tax payable:

	Gift tax on cumulative taxable gifts (1)	$3,945,800
Less	Current period unified credit (2)	(2,045,800)
Less	Credit for taxes paid on prior taxable transfers (based on current tax rates but gift year's unified credit) (3)	(600,000)
Equals	Gift taxes payable on current period's gifts (4)	$1,300,000

(1) [($9,000,000 × .40) + $345,800] = $3,945,800

(2) [($4,250,000 × .40) +$345,800] = $2,045,800

(3) Tax on prior gifts using 2013 rates and 2009 unified credit: [($1,500,000 × .40) + $345,800 – $345,800 unified credit for 2009 = $600,000]

(4) This is the same as a 40% tax on total gifts in excess of $5,250,000 ($1,900,000) less credit at current rates for prior gift taxes ($600,000).

The federal gift tax return, Form 709: *United States Gift (and Generation-Skipping Transfer) Tax Return*, must be filed for a calendar year in which the following types of transfers were made:

1. Transfers of present interests in excess of the $14,000 annual exclusion or transfers of future interests.
2. Transfers to charitable organizations in excess of the annual exclusion.
3. Transfers for which married couples elect gift splitting.

The return is due by April 15 of the following year with an additional six-month extension available by filing the same extension form used for the individual income tax return.[63]

Computing the Estate Tax

The taxable estate (the gross estate less allowable deductions) is added to the total amount of the decedent's adjusted taxable gifts (taxable gifts made after 1976). The transfer tax rates are then applied to the sum of the taxable estate plus adjusted taxable gifts. The tentative tax is then reduced by the current unified credit and a credit on prior taxable gifts determined using the current rate structure and the current credit available for taxable gifts. Because of the changing rates and unified credit, this can result in little or no credit for prior taxable gifts on which a tax had actually been paid. This amount is further reduced by any other credits, including the credit for death taxes imposed by a foreign government.

The tax base for the federal estate tax is defined in Section 2501 and is calculated as follows:

	Gross estate
Less	Deductible expenses, debts, taxes, and losses
Less	Charitable deduction
Less	Marital deduction
Equals	Taxable estate
Plus	Adjusted taxable gifts from previous periods
Equals	Tax base
	Gross estate tax
Less	Unified credit
Less	Credit for taxes on prior taxable gifts using current rates and current unified credit
Less	Other allowable credits
Equals	Net estate tax liability

Example 48

Charlene died in 2013. In 2009, she had made $2,500,000 in taxable gifts, paying $660,000 [($500,000 × .45) + $780,800 - $345,800 credit] in gift taxes for these gifts (using tax rates and credit in effect in 2009). When she died, she had a gross estate of $4,000,000. Funeral and administrative expenses were $80,000. Under her will, she directed that $100,000 be given to State College, a qualifying charity. Her will also provided the transfer of $400,000 to a QTIP trust benefiting her husband, with her remaining property left to her son. The net estate tax liability is $268,000, determined as follows:

	Gross estate	$4,000,000
Less	Funeral and administrative expenses	(80,000)
Less	Charitable deduction	(100,000)
Less	Marital deduction	(400,000)
Equals	Taxable estate	$3,420,000
Plus	Adjusted taxable gifts	2,500,000
Equals	Tax base	$5,920,000

[63]The tax must be paid by April 15 to avoid interest and penalties for late payment.

	Gross estate tax (1)	$2,313,800
Less	Unified credit	($2,045,800)
Less	Credit for prior transfers (2)	(0)
Equals	Net estate tax liability (3)	$268,000

(1) [($4,920,000 × .40) + $345,800]

(2) Using the 2013 (date of death) tax rates and credit amount, there will be no credit for prior transfers determined as follows: The tax on $2,500,000 = [($1,500,000 × .40) + $345,800 - $2,045,800] is less than zero, so no credit is allowed.

(3) This is the same as a 40% tax on total transfers in excess of $5,250,000 ($670,000 × .40 = $268,000)

The estate tax return, Form 706, is due nine months after the date of the decedent's death, and the tax is due with the return. An extension of up to six months to file the return can be obtained.[64]

Computing the Kiddie Tax

The kiddie tax is a special calculation that taxes unearned income of children under age 19 (24 if a full-time student) at their parents' marginal tax rate. Prior to 2008, the kiddie tax only applied to children under 18. Because taxes on dividends and long-term capital gains were reduced to zero percent in 2008 for lower income taxpayers, Congress passed legislation increasing the age to make it more difficult to minimize the tax savings from income shifting. Unearned income subject to this tax includes taxable interest, dividends, and net capital gains on property owned directly by the child, as well as income received as a beneficiary of a trust. The child's earned income (wages, tips, and salaries) and the first $2,000 of unearned income are subject to normal income tax rules.

The tax calculation is a four-step process:

1. Determine the child's taxable income; if the child is claimed as a dependent, the child is allowed no personal exemption and the standard deduction is limited to the greater of $1,000 ($950 in 2012) or earned income plus $350 ($300 in 2012).
2. Calculate the tax on the child's net unearned income in excess of $2,000 at the parents' marginal tax rate.[65]
3. The child's remaining taxable income is taxed at the child's normal tax rates (for a single individual).
4. The taxes determined in (2) and (3) are summed to determine the child's gross income tax liability.[66]

The tax calculated is then compared to the tax that would be paid if all of the child's income were reported on his or her own return. The greater of these two amounts is the tax that must be paid. It is unlikely that the child's tax would exceed that determined under the kiddie tax rules, as that would require the child's income to fall into a higher tax bracket than that of the parents'.

EXAMPLE 49

Mary, age 13, has $3,800 interest income from a trust established by her grandparents; this is her only source of income for the year. She has no itemized deductions. Mary's parents are in the 33 percent marginal tax bracket. Mary's net unearned income is $1,800, the excess of her interest income over $2,000. Her taxable income is $2,800 ($3,800 – $1,000 standard deduction). Mary's tax on her unearned income

[64]For decedents dying in 2010, the estate tax return was not due until nine months after the date of enactment of the 2010 Tax Relief Act. §6075(a).

[65]Parents calculate this tax by adding the child's net unearned income to their taxable income and determining the hypothetical increase in their tax. In certain situations, the parents may also elect to include the child's unearned income in their own tax return by filing Form 8814: *Parents' Election to Report Child's Interest and Dividends.*

[66]The kiddie tax is calculated on Form 8615. The tax is included on page 2 of Form 1040.

at the parents' marginal tax rate is \$594 (\$1,800 × 33%). The remaining \$1,000 income (\$2,800 taxable income – \$1,800 taxed at parents' rates) is taxed at the child's regular rates resulting in \$100 of tax (\$1,000 × 10%). The total tax owed is \$694 (\$594 + \$100).

The kiddie tax does not apply to a child age 19 or older, unless that child is a full-time student; it will not apply to *any* child age 24 or older regardless of student status. Age is determined at the end of the year under current law.

EXAMPLE 50

Assume the same facts as the preceding example, except that Mary is 24 years old so she is no longer subject to the kiddie tax. As a dependent on her parents' tax return, she still is denied a personal exemption and her standard deduction is limited to \$1,000. Her taxable income remains \$2,800, all taxed at 10 percent. Her tax is \$280 (\$2,800 × 10%).

TAX PLANNING

Families can minimize the impact of the kiddie tax by transferring assets that defer income until the child is age 19 (or 24 for students). For example, taxable income from U.S. government series EE savings bonds can be deferred until they are redeemed. Transferring growth company stock that pays little or no dividends or land expected to appreciate facilitates deferring capital gains until the child reaches the age at which the kiddie tax no longer applies.

Computing the Fiduciary Income Tax

Income taxation of fiduciary entities uses a modified conduit approach that taxes the estate or trust on income it retains but taxes the beneficiaries on the income that is distributed to them.

Two types of trusts are defined for tax purposes: simple and complex. A **simple trust** must distribute all of its accounting income annually to its beneficiaries.[67] Normally, the trustee is not required to distribute capital gains, as they are usually allocated to principal and are excluded from accounting income. [68] **A complex trust** is any trust that is not a simple trust. Complex trusts are not required to distribute all their accounting income each year, thus allowing trust principal to accumulate. Complex trusts can make charitable contributions and take tax deductions for doing so. Estates are considered complex trusts.

Fiduciary gross income is computed using rules similar to individual income taxation. For example, if the fiduciary earns tax-exempt income, the income is excluded and no deduction is allowed for expenses related to the exempt income. Deductions are allowed for expenses of producing taxable income, depreciation, administrative expenses, and charitable contributions.[69] Simple trusts are allowed a personal exemption of \$300, a complex trust a \$100 exemption, and estates a \$600 exemption. Finally, taxable income is reduced by the distribution deduction.

Distributable net income (DNI) is the current increase in value available for distribution to income beneficiaries.[70] DNI determines the fiduciary's maximum distribution deduction and the beneficiary's maximum taxable income from the trust. Thus, if the fiduciary distributes more than the current year's taxable income (by distributing prior year's earnings), the excess distributions are not taxable to the beneficiaries. Additionally,

---

[67] Additionally, simple trusts are not allowed to make charitable contributions.

[68] The trust document controls which items of income and expense are part of trust accounting income and which are allocated to trust principal. If the trust document is silent, state law controls. Most states have adopted the Uniform Principal and Income Act that allocates to principal capital gains and losses, casualty gains and losses, capital improvements, and taxes levied on items allocated to principal. For an estate, if the decedent's will specifies an allocation of estate income between income and principal beneficiaries, that allocation will be followed in computing estate accounting income.

[69] Administrative expenses for an estate can be claimed on the estate's transfer tax return or its income tax return but not both. The executor can choose to allocate the expenses in whatever way is most beneficial.

[70] DNI is calculated by starting with taxable income and adding back the personal exemption, subtracting capital gains and adding capital losses allocated to principal, adding tax-exempt interest, and subtracting expenses allocated to tax-exempt interest. §643.

if a distribution is made up of both taxable and tax-exempt income, the beneficiaries do not pay tax on tax-exempt income as income retains its character when distributed.

EXAMPLE 51

Simple Trust has two equal income beneficiaries, Steven and Elisa. Simple has trust accounting income of \$50,000 for the year and DNI of \$48,000. Included in DNI is \$12,000 of net tax-exempt income, so the trust distribution deduction is limited to \$36,000 (the taxable portion of DNI). Steven and Elisa are each entitled to receive a distribution of \$25,000 (50 percent of \$50,000 accounting income) of which only \$18,000 (50 percent of the \$36,000 trust distribution deduction) is taxable. The remaining \$7,000 (\$25,000 – \$18,000) distributed to Steven and Elisa is not taxed. Their share of tax-exempt income is \$6,000, which remains tax exempt when distributed; the remaining \$1,000 represents income retained and taxed to the trust in a previous year. It is not taxed a second time when distributed to the beneficiaries.

All trusts must use a calendar year, eliminating any potential for deferral by adopting a trust tax year that differs from that of the beneficiaries. A trust is required to file a Form 1041: *United States Income Tax Return for Estates and Trusts* by April 15 of the following year if it has gross income of \$600 or more or if it has any taxable income. Estates may use either a fiscal or a calendar year. Any estate with gross income of \$600 or more is required to file a Form 1041 by the 15th day of the fourth month following the close of the estate's taxable year.[71] Beneficiaries report their share of income based on the fiduciary's year that ends within the beneficiary's tax year.

EXAMPLE 52

In April of year 1, Samantha becomes the beneficiary of a new calendar-year trust. At the same time, Samantha also becomes the beneficiary of an estate that elects a January 31 fiscal year-end. During year 1, Samantha receives income distributions of \$10,000 from the trust and \$15,000 from the estate. Samantha must report the \$10,000 distributed in year 1 on her year-1 Form 1040 because the trust's December 31 year-end falls within her tax year. Samantha will not be taxed on the \$15,000 distributed from the estate until year 2 because the distribution is not considered to be allocated to her until January 31, year 2 (the end of the estate's fiscal year).

When property is distributed to trust beneficiaries, generally no gain or loss is recognized by the trust for any difference between the asset's fair market value and its basis, and the beneficiaries take the trust's adjusted basis for the asset acquired. If, however, the property is distributed to satisfy a required income distribution, the distribution deduction is limited to the lesser of the property's basis or its fair market value on the distribution date.[72] The beneficiary still uses the trust's adjusted basis for the property, however.[73]

TAX PLANNING

The trustee can elect to recognize gain on the distribution of appreciated property and may choose to do so if it is capital gain property and the trust has unused capital losses to net against the gain. If this election is made, the beneficiary's basis is the higher fair market value.[74]

REVISITING THE INTRODUCTORY CASE

Sarah can contribute up to \$70,000 per grandchild to a Section 529 plan, electing to spread the gift over five years. In this manner, she can give \$280,000 (\$70,000 × 4 grandchildren) in the current year but cannot claim any subsequent annual exclusion for gifts to these grandchildren for five years. When her grandchildren are ready for college, at least a portion of their expenses can be paid by distributions from the Section 529 plan to gain the maximum tax benefits from the plan. By then, Sarah has removed \$280,000 (and the future appreciation on those assets) from her estate, assuming she lives at least five years. Additionally, the funds can be redirected to another beneficiary if the grandchildren do not need all of the funds in the Section 529 account.

[71] § 6012(a).

[72] § 643(d).

[73] The beneficiary's holding period includes the trust's holding period.

[74] The holding period begins on the date of distribution.

Alternatively, Sarah can make $14,000 annual gifts to each of her grandchildren, either in trust or in a UTMA account. Over five years, she can make nontaxable gifts totaling $280,000 (assuming the annual exclusion remains at $14,000). In addition, Sarah may then pay the tuition expenses for her grandchildren as they attend college. This will allow her to transfer a larger amount tax free, but she also must live until her grandchildren are in college to equalize the benefit.

Sarah could also use a portion or all of her unified credit to establish an irrevocable trust for her grandchildren to fund expenses that are not eligible to be paid from a Section 529 plan.

SUMMARY

The transfer tax system consists of the gift tax, the estate tax, and the generation-skipping transfer tax. Transfer taxes are assessed on the transferor of the property, not the recipient. The value of properties transferred by gift and inheritance is measured by their fair market values.

Gifts of a present interest in property are eligible for an annual gift exclusion of $14,000 per donee. An unlimited marital deduction and a charitable contribution deduction make lifetime and testamentary transfers to a spouse or charity tax free. The tax on lifetime gifts and estates is determined on a cumulative basis; thus, taxable gifts cause the estate to be taxed at higher marginal tax rates, and earlier gifts force later gifts into a higher marginal tax bracket. To provide relief for persons with moderate wealth, a unified credit applies to the tax determined on the taxable gifts and estate of an individual.

Trusts provide a method for persons to bestow the benefits of property on one or more other persons without transferring outright property ownership to the transferee. Minor and Crummey trusts allow the transferor to circumvent the present interest rule and still claim the annual gift exclusion. Trust beneficiaries or the trust itself are normally taxed on trust income, unless the grantor fails to relinquish all control over the trust property. Transfers of income producing assets to children under age 24 require special consideration to avoid the kiddie tax, which cause most of the child's income to be taxed at the parents' marginal income tax rate.

Trusts and estates are taxable persons and must file income tax returns if more than a minimal amount of income is earned. Income produced by trust or estate properties should be distributed to the beneficiaries each year to avoid the high income tax rates that apply to a fiduciary.

A good family tax plan involves multiple strategies. It allows the family to shift income, and income tax liability, to younger family members. It balances the income tax consequences of property dispositions with the benefits of giving lifetime gifts or providing testamentary transfers. Giving appreciating assets to the younger family members avoids the inclusion of these assets and their appreciation in the taxable estate of the donor. As a person ages, the original tax plan should be examined and modified to take advantage of any changes in the tax laws and to ensure the plan still meets the person's goals.

KEY TERMS

Alternative valuation date 559
Beneficiary 549
Complex trust 571
Corpus 549
Crummey trust 453
Decedent 557
Deductions in respect of a decedent (DRD) 565
Distributable net income (DNI) 571
Estate 557
Estate tax 542
Gift tax 542
Grantor 549
Grantor trust 567
Gross estate 557
Income beneficiary 550
Income in respect of a decedent (IRD) 565
Irrevocable 550
Kiddie tax 555
Present interest 552
Probate 557
Qualified terminal interest property (QTIP) 560
Remainder interest 550
Revocable 550
Simple trust 571
Trust 549
Trustee 549

TEST YOURSELF

ANSWERS APPEAR AFTER THE PROBLEM ASSIGNMENTS

1. Marta placed $50,000 into a savings account in her name and the name of her son. Later this year, the son withdraws $16,000 from the account. Marta made no other gifts to her son this year. Marta has made a taxable gift of
   a. $2,000
   b. $11,000
   c. $16,000
   d. $25,000
   e. $36,000
2. Which of the following transfers is considered a taxable gift?
   a. Alex sold land to an unrelated party for less than its fair market value because he needed cash in a hurry.
   b. After a friend's death, Nicole wrote a check to the university to pay the college tuition for the friend's son.
   c. Melissa wrote a check to the landlord to pay her aunt's rent for two months when her aunt was unemployed.
   d. Howard wrote a check to the doctor to pay a friend's medical bill when he had surgery.
3. Which of the following transactions is a taxable gift?
   a. Mack transfers $5,000 to his favorite political organization.
   b. Sonia gives $25,000 in stocks to her church.
   c. Veronica gives $25,000 to her husband, Jose.
   d. Carla transfers $30,000 into an irrevocable trust for the benefit of her two children.
4. According to the provisions of the decedent's will, the following disbursements were made by the estate's executor:
   1. Payment of the decedent's funeral expenses
   2. Payment of a charitable bequest to a local charity

   What is deductible in determining the decedent's taxable estate?
   a. 1 only
   b. 2 only
   c. Both 1 and 2
   d. Neither 1 nor 2
5. Lorraine created a trust by transferring $500,000 of stock and bonds into it on January 1, year 1. The trust is to provide her mother with income for her lifetime, with the remainder interest going to Lorraine's son. Lorraine retained the power to revoke both the income interest and the remainder interest. Who is taxed on the trust's year 1 income?
   a. Lorraine's son
   b. Lorraine's mother
   c. Lorraine
   d. The trust

PROBLEM ASSIGNMENTS

CHECK YOUR UNDERSTANDING

1. Discount Auto Company sold an automobile at a $2,000 discount to an unrelated customer. Is this a gift?

2. Sharon transferred property into an irrevocable trust, but she retained the right to change the beneficiaries. What circumstances are required for this transfer to be a completed gift?

3. What is the gift tax annual exclusion and why was it enacted?

4. What is a present interest and how is it distinguished from a future interest?

5. Under what circumstances will a gift made in trust for a minor child qualify for the annual exclusion?

6. Under what circumstances is the face value of life insurance on the decedent's life included in the decedent's gross estate?

7. Five years before his death, Troy purchased a $5 million whole life insurance policy on his life and named his son, Don, the beneficiary. Shortly after purchase, Troy transferred the policy to an irrevocable trust, naming his son as trustee. Troy retained no incidents of ownership.
   a. Has Troy made a gift?
   b. Is the $5 million in proceeds included in Troy's gross estate?

8. How is estate property valued and what is the alternate valuation date?

9. What is the lifetime unified credit amount for 2013 and its related exclusion equivalent?

10. If the generation-skipping transfer tax did not exist, what type of planning would maximize the preservation of a family's wealth?

11. Sidney is a psychiatrist. Four years ago, he purchased the building in which his office is located for $375,000. Sidney transfers ownership of the building to his daughter, Nora, and signs a leaseback agreement stipulating that he pay annual rent of $35,000 to Nora for the use of the building for his practice. What family tax-planning goal has this transaction achieved?

12. What is income in respect of a decedent, and how is it taxed?

13. How do the estate income tax rules encourage a quick distribution of estate assets?

14. What are adjusted taxable gifts, and how do they affect the calculation of a decedent's estate tax?

15. What distinguishes a simple trust from a complex trust?

16. What purpose is served by the distributable net income of a trust or estate?

CRUNCH THE NUMBERS

17. Which of the following are completed gifts, and what is the value of each gift (before any exclusions)?
   a. Hughlene sold stock worth $90,000 to her son for $30,000.
   b. Ken deposits $15,000 into a savings account in his name and his daughter's name as joint owners.
   c. Jim transferred $800,000 into a revocable trust that will pay income to his daughter for her life and the remainder to his granddaughter.

18. Determine the taxable gift for each of the following.
   a. In February, Cynthia transferred $200,000 into a revocable trust. In October, the trustee distributes $18,000 of income to the beneficiary, Eileen.

b. Carrie prepared the tax returns at no charge for the elderly in a volunteer program sponsored by a local charity.
c. Ted gave his cousin $15,000 to pay medical expenses.
d. Vera paid her nephew's college tuition of $20,000 by writing a check directly to the university.

19. Which of the following are completed gifts, and what is the value of each gift (before any exclusions)?

a. In March, Stephanie deposits $30,000 cash into a joint checking account for herself and her boyfriend, Michael, who deposits nothing in the account. In July, Michael withdraws $15,000 from the account.
b. Jennie pays $16,000 of her neighbor's medical expenses directly to the hospital.
c. Jane pays her sister's $20,000 tuition directly to the university.
d. Miriam transfers the title of investment land (valued at $85,000) to her son, Kevin.
e. Miguel deposits $180,000 into a revocable trust in February. In November, the trustee distributes $20,000 of income to the beneficiary, Juan.

20. Edward gave 15,000 shares of ABC stock to Valerie on July 15. On July 15, the highest selling price for the stock was $40 per share, and the lowest selling price was $36 per share. What is the value of this gift (before any exclusions)?

21. John gave $30,000 to each of his 10 grandchildren this year. Lisa, his wife, made no gifts during the year.

a. How much are John's taxable gifts if gift splitting is not elected?
b. How much are John's taxable gifts if gift splitting is elected?

22. Ginny made the following gifts during the current year. Her husband, Ken, made no gifts during the year.

- Gift of land valued at $250,000 to her husband
- Gift of $20,000 in stock to her daughter
- Gift of $32,000 to her sister to pay for medical expenses

a. How much are Ginny's taxable gifts if gift splitting is not elected?
b. How much are Ginny's taxable gifts if gift splitting is elected?

23. In the current year, Marah gives $20,000 cash to Sam, $60,000 of stock to Craig, and $100,000 of bonds to Lynn. In the same year, Marah's husband, Bryan, gives $120,000 of land to Jerry.

a. What are Marah and Bryan's taxable gifts if they do not elect gift splitting?
b. What are the couple's taxable gifts assuming the couple elects gift splitting?

24. During the current year, Cherie gives $30,000 cash to her daughter, Helen, and a remainder interest in investment land to her sister, Silvia. The remainder interest is valued at $40,000. In the current year, John, Cherie's husband, also gives Dan $18,000 in marketable securities. What is the total dollar amount of the annual gift tax exclusions available to Cherie and John for the current year if they elect gift splitting?

25. Determine whether each of the following situations involves the transfer of a present interest or a future interest.

a. A trust is established for the donor's 8-year-old daughter. The trustee can decide how much income to pay the daughter each year. At age 21, the daughter will receive all of the accumulated income and principal.

b. A trust is established by transferring $10,000 each year for each of three beneficiaries who are given 30 days after receiving notice of the transfer to demand payment of the $10,000.

c. All rights to a life insurance policy are given to the donor's son.

26. On January 15 of the current year, Eileen, age 24, receives stock worth $28,000 as a gift from her parents. Her parents jointly purchased the stock six years ago for $12,000. During the year, Eileen receives $2,100 dividend income on the stock. In December, she sells the stock for $39,000.

a. Assuming this is Eileen's only income for the year, and her parents are in the 33 percent marginal tax bracket, how much income tax does the family save as a result of this gift?

b. Are there any transfer taxes as a result of this gift? Explain.

27. Which of the following items are included in the decedent's gross estate?

a. A life estate in a trust that pays the decedent $25,000 per year until he dies

b. A remainder interest in a trust worth $60,000 owned by the decedent

c. A one-half interest in investment land valued at $100,000 owned as joint tenants with right of survivorship

28. Five years ago, Jason purchased a $400,000 life insurance policy on his life. For each of the following, indicate how much of the $400,000 policy proceeds are included in his gross estate.

a. The proceeds are payable to his estate.

b. The proceeds were paid to his daughter, but Jason retained the right to change beneficiaries.

c. $100,000 of the proceeds will be used to pay debts of his estate with the balance paid to his daughter. Jason retained no rights in the policy.

29. Laura transferred property valued at $120,000 into an irrevocable trust. Laura is to receive one-half of the income each year for the balance of her life. The other half of the income and the remainder interest are to go to Robert. One year before her death, Laura gave up her right to receive her half of the income, so all the income is payable to Robert. The property is worth $160,000 when Laura dies. How much is includible in Laura's gross estate?

30. When Ben died, his executor elected the alternate valuation date. What value is included in the gross estate for each of the following properties?

a. Marketable securities valued at $80,000 at date of death, valued at $89,000 six months after death, and sold for $92,000 by the estate 10 months after death.

b. Investment land valued at $100,000 at date of death, valued at $102,000 when it was distributed to a beneficiary four months later, and valued at $110,000 six months after death.

31. Samson's gross estate was valued at $1 million when he died. Determine the value of his taxable estate before any credits using the following information:

- The executor's fees were $16,000.
- His funeral expenses were $15,000.
- A cash donation of $110,000 was given to San Jose State University.

- Real estate worth $700,000 was transferred to his surviving spouse, Delilah.
- Samson had promised to give stock worth $24,000 to his nephew, but he never did.

32. Jessica owns investment land currently worth $500,000. She paid $80,000 for the land 10 years ago. She expects that the land will probably increase in value to at least $800,000 before she dies. She has not previously given any taxable gifts.

a. If Jessica gives the land to her son now, what basis will he use for determining gain when he sells the land?

b. If Jessica dies in 2013 and bequeaths the land to her son, what basis will he use for determining gain when he sells the land?

c. If Jessica's son plans to keep the land instead of selling it, should she give it to him now or bequeath it to him? Explain the reason for your choice.

33. George transfers investment securities worth $200,000 with a tax basis of $130,000 to a trust, naming himself as trustee. The terms of the trust agreement require the trustee to pay all dividends and interest to George's brother, Mark. George has the right to revoke the trust at any time and take back title to the securities. During the trust's first year, George, as trustee, distributes $20,000 in dividends and $10,000 interest from the securities to Mark. None of the income was tax exempt.

a. How much gross income does Mark recognize from the payments?

b. How much gross income does George recognize from the above?

34. Glen transferred corporate stock worth $300,000 with a tax basis of $160,000 to an irrevocable trust. No gift taxes are paid. The terms of the trust require the independent trustee to distribute the trust income annually to Glen's sister, Barbara. Any capital gain or loss is charged to trust corpus. Upon Barbara's death, the trust corpus is to be distributed to Barbara's children on a pro rata basis. During the first year of the trust, the trustee distributes $23,000 in dividend income to Barbara. The trust also has capital gains of $20,000.

a. What is the trust's tax basis in the securities transferred to it by Glen?

b. Who is taxed on the dividend income?

c. Who is taxed on the capital gains?

35. Thomas died on August 15 of the current year. On September 2, his estate received a check for $2,000 from Thomas's former employer for his final pay period. On September 18, Thomas's estate received a $70,000 distribution from his employer's retirement plan. Both Thomas and the estate are cash-basis, calendar-year taxpayers. How much income must the estate report as a result of receiving these items?

36. Wayne created a trust six years ago for the benefit of his children. In the current year, when the value of the trust assets is $1,000,000, Wayne transfers additional property valued at $300,000 into the trust. Because Wayne is concerned that he might need some income in a future year if his investments do not perform well, he retains the right to receive the income from this latter property in any year in which his gross income falls below a specified amount. The trust received $100,000 in income this year: $30,000 from the newly transferred assets and $70,000 from the original assets. The entire $100,000 income is distributed directly to Wayne's children before the end of the year. Who is taxed on the income?

37. In June of year 1, Angelina (a calendar-year taxpayer) becomes the beneficiary of a new calendar-year trust. At the same time, Angelina also becomes the beneficiary of an estate that elects a March 31 fiscal year-end. During year 1, Angelina receives income distributions of $12,000 from the trust and $18,000 from the estate.

a. In which year does Angelina report the income from the trust?

b. In which year does Angelina report the income from the estate?

38. Carolyn has made no previous taxable gifts. Determine her gift tax (before her lifetime exclusion amount) if she makes $2,650,000 in taxable gifts (after all annual exclusions) in the current year.

39. Benjamin has made no previous taxable gifts. Determine his gift tax if he makes $14,000,000 (after annual exclusions) in taxable gifts in 2013.

40. Steven had a taxable estate of $8,850,000 when he died in 2013. If he had no prior taxable gifts, what is his net estate tax liability?

41. Cherry's widowed mother, Nancy, had to quit working for health reasons and now her only income is $1,100 per month from Social Security. Cherry recently became partner of a law firm and has moved into the 33% marginal tax bracket. Cherry's mother steadfastly insists on living independently so Cherry gave her mother $200,000 in 9% corporate bonds to supplement her income.

a. How much of her lifetime unified credit and related exclusion amount must Cherry use to avoid paying a gift tax?

b. How much income taxes are saved by the transfer of the bonds by Cherry to her mother?

42. Sondra and Jason, a wealthy married couple, won $96 million in a 2013 Powerball drawing. They decided to share some of this new wealth immediately with some of their friends and family. They paid $1,800,000 on a new home for Sondra's parents, titling the home jointly in the parents' names; bought a condominium on Captiva Island for Jason's widowed mother for $950,000; gave $1 million to a local charity that provides homes and job training for homeless families; sent $150,000 to Stanford University to be used for their nephews college tuition for his next 4 years in school; gave $500,000 each to Sondra's sister and Jason's brother for new homes; gave $750,000 to the best man at their wedding last year to defray the costs of a needed kidney transplant; and finally donated $250,000 to their church to build a wedding chapel. The only taxable gift previously made by either Sondra or Jason was a $200,000 gift in 2011 by Jason to the widow of an employee who had been killed in an auto accident. This gift was made prior to their marriage. Sondra and Jason elect gift splitting. Determine their separate total taxable gifts and the gift taxes they will owe after applying each of their lifetime unified credits.

43. Julie had a gross estate of $7 million when she died in 2013. Her funeral expenses were $26,000; her administrative expenses were $30,000; her charitable deduction was $350,000; and her marital deduction was $600,000. She made no prior taxable gifts. What is her net estate tax liability?

44. Lenny, age 12, has $3,500 interest income from a trust established by his uncle. This is Lenny's only source of income for the year. Lenny's parents are in the 33 percent marginal tax bracket.

a. What is Lenny's taxable income and how much income tax does he owe?

b. How would your answers change if Lenny were age 24?

THINK OUTSIDE THE TEXT

These questions require answers that are beyond the material that is covered in this chapter.

45. In 2010, Congress chose to repeal the estate tax for that year, but retained the gift tax. Why do you think they did that?

46. Beginning in 2012, Congress increased the top estate and gift tax rate to 40 percent and permanently increased the unified credit with inflation indexing. What (if any) changes do you think Congress might make in this area in the future?

47. Mark's father, Michael, loaned Mark $300,000 interest free for five years to invest in securities that yield a 10 percent annual return. At the end of the five years, Mark sells the securities to repay his father. Unfortunately, the market declined and Mark was able to sell the securities for only $280,000. Michael accepted the $280,000 as payment in full on the loan. How do you think this transaction will be treated for tax purposes?

48. Why do you think Congress enacted the kiddie tax? Do you think it is achieving its goal? Can you think of a better way to achieve this goal?

49. Myron's will specified that his entire $10 million estate was to pass to his girlfriend, leaving nothing to his wife, Ellen. Do you think Myron can prevent his wife from inheriting any of his assets? What do you think Ellen can do?

IDENTIFY THE ISSUES

Identify the issues or problems suggested by the following situations. State each issue as a question.

50. Martha provides the sole support for her son, David, who lives at home while he attends school. Martha gives David a $40,000 automobile for his 18th birthday.

51. When Chet died on March 12, 2013, he owned $900,000 in stock of ABC Corporation and $100,000 in City of Omaha bonds. The ABC Corporation declared a cash dividend on March 1 that was payable to shareholders of record on March 15. In early April, the executor of Chet's estate received the following: ABC Corporation dividend of $6,000 and interest of $3,200 ($200 accrued since March 12) on the City of Omaha bonds.

52. Ten years ago, Carolyn created a revocable trust using marketable securities valued at $500,000. The trust department at the local bank is the trustee. Under the terms of the trust, Carolyn retained a life estate with a remainder interest for her grandchildren. Last year, when the trust assets were valued at $900,000, Carolyn released her right to revoke the trust, making it irrevocable. Carolyn dies in the current year when the trust assets are valued at $1 million.

53. At the time of Frank's death, he had received $6,000 in credit card bills that had not been paid.

54. In year 1, Loren and Tim enter into a property settlement agreement under which Tim agrees to pay $600,000 to Loren in return for the release of her marital rights. The payment is to be made in three annual installments of $200,000 each. Loren and Tim divorce in year 2, but Tim dies late in the year before the second and third installments can be paid. In year 3, Tim's executor pays Loren the $400,000 balance due.

55. Jorge is a resident and citizen of Spain. He invests $500,000 in Miami Beach real estate. When Jorge died in 2013, he owned $1,000,000 in assets in Spain in addition to the Miami Beach real estate.

56. Jennifer plans to establish a trust in which she will place all her income-producing investments. She will be the income beneficiary for the balance of her life, with her son having a remainder interest. She plans to name herself as trustee.

57. The Lincoln Trust is a simple trust whose only investments are in corporate bonds producing interest income. The trustee is thinking about moving some of the investments into municipal bonds.

DEVELOP RESEARCH SKILLS

58. Two years ago, Herbert, a widower, made a gift of marketable securities to his 35-year-old daughter, Sabrina, on which he paid a federal gift tax of $3 million. When Herbert died in 2013, his estate had been greatly reduced in value due to his having given away most of his assets over his lifetime. Herbert's executor filed an estate tax return that showed an estate tax liability attributable to the gift to Sabrina. The estate tax was not paid because the estate had no liquid assets. The IRS assesses the portion of the estate tax related to this gift that Sabrina previously received against Sabrina under the rules relating to transferee liability. Is Sabrina liable for the estate tax?

59. Samantha is a single parent providing the sole support for her six-year-old daughter, Hillary. They live in an area of Oakland where the public school is known to have problems with drugs and other crimes. Samantha wants to send Hillary to a private school to avoid these problems and provide a better environment for Hillary's educational development. Eight years ago, Samantha set up two trusts to manage the securities she inherited from her grandfather. Samantha is the sole beneficiary of Trust A from which she receives bimonthly distributions each made after approval by the trustee. Hillary is the sole beneficiary of Trust B and all distributions from this trust must be approved by its trustee. If Samantha convinces the trustee to pay for Hillary's tuition, writing a check out of the Trust B funds to the school, are there any income tax consequences to Samantha?

SEARCH THE INTERNET

60. Go to the IRS Web site *(www.irs.gov)* and locate the instructions for Form 706-NA for the estate of a nonresident alien.

a. What is the definition of a nonresident alien decedent?

b. Under what circumstances must the executor for a nonresident alien decedent file a Form 706-NA?

61. Go to the IRS Web site *(www.irs.gov)* and locate the instructions for Form 709. Can spouses who elect to gift split file a joint gift tax return? Explain how they must file.

DEVELOP PLANNING SKILLS

62. When Godfrey died in 2013, his assets were valued as follows:

ASSET	DATE OF DEATH VALUATION	VALUATION SIX MONTHS LATER
Stocks	$2,220,000	$2,180,000
Bonds	4,600,000	4,620,000
Home	800,000	780,000
Total	$7,620,000	$7,580,000

The executor sold the stock two months after the decedent's death for $2,200,000. The bonds were sold seven months after the decedent's death for $4,630,000. What valuation should be used for the gross estate?

63. Oscar (age 70) and Maggie (age 60) were married and jointly owned a personal residence valued at $3,800,000 when Oscar died in 2013. Oscar also owned stocks valued at $4,700,000; an art collection valued at $1,400,000; a retirement account valued at $900,000 (contributions were entirely from pretax income); $800,000 in cash; and $1,000,000 in other miscellaneous assets. Oscar's will specified that when he died his half of the personal residence would go to Maggie but that all his other assets would pass to his four children because Maggie has sufficient income from a trust fund she inherited from her grandfather. Oscar made no previous taxable gifts.

a. What was Oscar's estate tax liability when he died in 2013?

b. Each of Oscar's four children has three children (total of 12 grandchildren). If Oscar had begun transferring assets to his children and grandchildren in years 2009 through 2013, how much could he have removed in value from his estate over those five years through gift splitting and making annual transfers equal to the gift exclusion?

64. Your client, Ted, would like your assistance in selecting one of the following assets to give to his 16-year-old daughter.

ASSET	FAIR MARKET VALUE	ADJUSTED BASIS
Cash	$13,000	$13,000
Corporate stock	13,000	6,000
10 percent of the outstanding shares of Ted's wholly owned S corporation	13,000	8,000
Limited partnership interest	13,000	3,000

The corporate stock pays only $100 in dividend income each year but has doubled in value since Ted purchased it three years ago. The S corporation has generated a profit of $80,000 each year for the past three years and is expected to perform even better in the future. The limited partnership has generated losses for the past three years and is expected to do so for at least the next several years.

a. Discuss the advantages and disadvantages from both transfer and income tax perspectives for each asset as a potential gift.

b. Which asset do you recommend Ted choose and why?

65. You are the trustee for the Steadman Trust. The trust has $50,000 of interest income, all of which it plans to distribute to its beneficiaries in the current year. The trust also has $14,000 in net capital losses for the year that are allocated to corpus. The trust distributes some investment land to one of its beneficiaries. The land was acquired eight years ago and has an adjusted basis of $40,000 and a fair market value of $55,000. The beneficiary plans to sell the land.

a. What would be the impact on the trust and the beneficiary if an election is made to recognize gain on the land?

b. What is the impact on the trust and the beneficiary if the election is not made?

c. What you do recommend?

ANSWERS TO TEST YOURSELF

1. a. **$2,000.** ($16,000 – $14,000 exclusion).
2. c. **Melissa wrote a check to the landlord to pay her aunt's rent for two months when her aunt was unemployed.**
3. d. **Carla transfers $30,000 into an irrevocable trust for the benefit of her two children.**
4. c. **Both 1 and 2.**
5. c. **Lorraine.**

APPENDIX A

TAX RESEARCH USING CHECKPOINT®

This appendix includes basic instructions for locating primary sources of authority using Checkpoint®. Students at schools that do not subscribe to Checkpoint® can use this appendix to gain a general understanding of how to research using a subscription-only tax service.

To get started, go to ***http://checkpoint.riag.com/*** and enter your User Name and Password. Click on "Login."

A. Getting acquainted with the Home screen

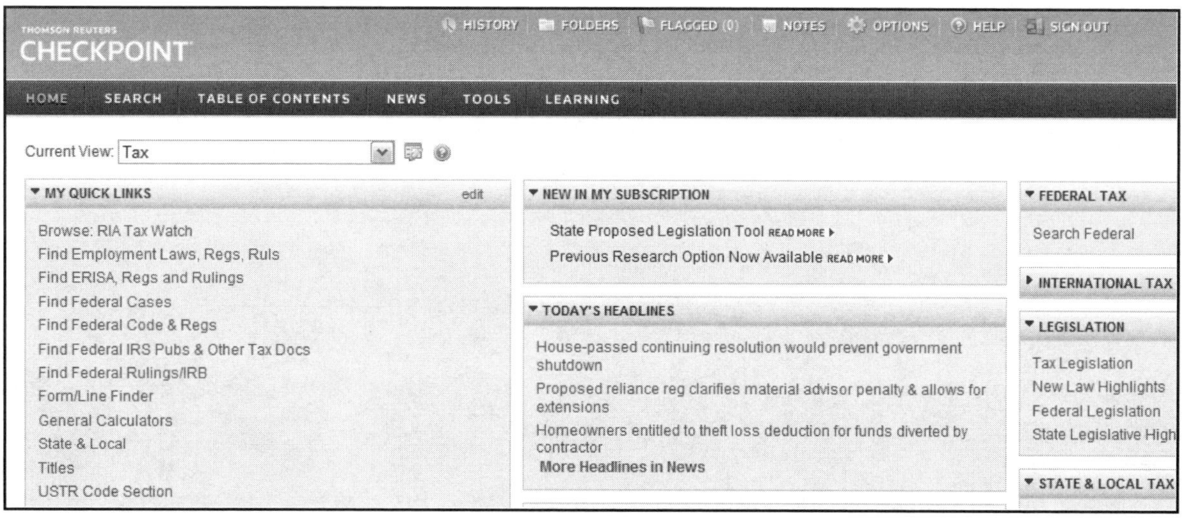

My Quick Links take you directly to templates for locating authorities.

User Guides are located at the bottom of the Home screen under Training and Support.

Clicking on the Search tab at the top of the screen takes you to the Search screen where you will usually begin your research.

B. Getting acquainted with the Search screen

Anytime you are researching in Checkpoint, you can return to this Search screen by clicking on "Search" near the top left of the screen.

The left panel of the screen allows you to choose the method for searching. You can choose to do a Keyword Search, Find by Citation, use an Index (under Go To), or use the USTR Code Section (also under Go To) approach to locating authorities.

The middle of the screen is used for keyword searching.

You can access the Table of Contents from the top of the screen

You will first learn how to search when you know the citation; then you will learn how to use an index, the USTR code section approach, and keyword searching. Finally you will see how to browse through the Table of Contents.

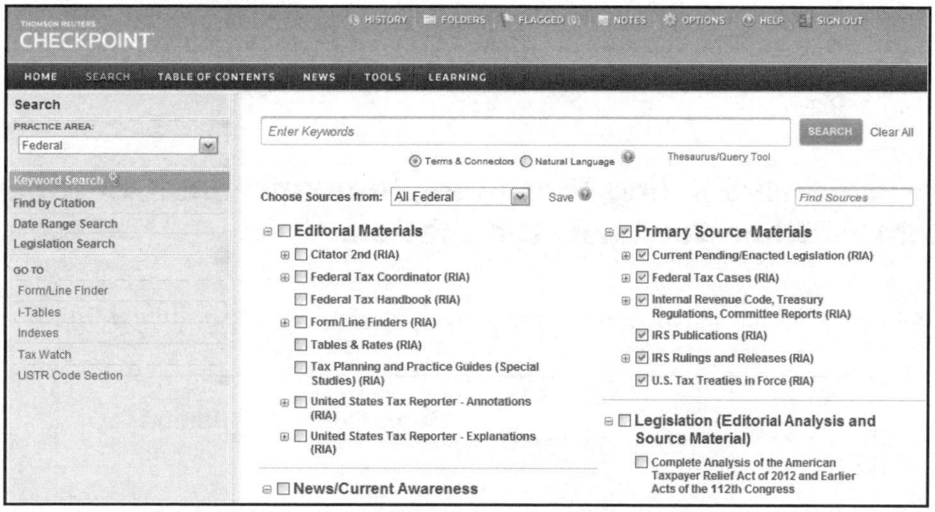

C. How to retrieve Internal Revenue Code or Regulations Sections when you know the citation

In the left panel of the Search screen, select Find by Citation, and then click on "Code & Regs."

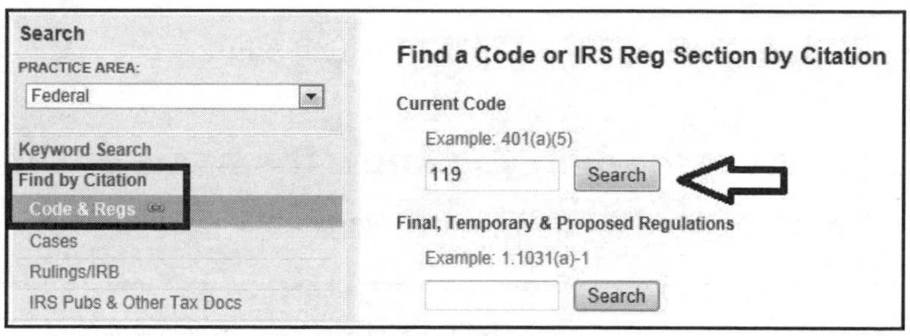

Enter the Section number in the appropriate box and click on the [Search] button.

The full text of the Code Section will appear on the screen.

There are several buttons at the top of the screen above the Code Section number that can be used to go directly to related materials. [Expl] goes to U.S. Tax Reporter editorial explanations; [Annot] goes to annotations that are short summaries of cases or rulings; [FTC] goes to Federal Tax Coordinator editorial explanations; [Regs] goes to the related Regulations; [Com Rpts] goes to the related Committee Reports; [Hist] retrieves the history for the Code Section, allowing you to trace changes in that area of law over time; and [New Law Analysis] goes to analysis of recent relevant legislation.

D. How to retrieve an IRS Ruling, Procedure, Announcement, or other IRS pronouncement when you know the citation

Select Find by Citation in the left panel of the main Search screen. Click on "Rulings/IRB."

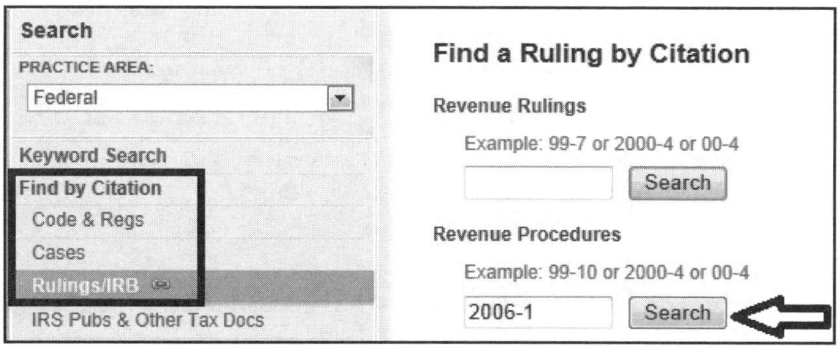

Enter the citation in the appropriate box and click on the [Search] button.

E. How to retrieve a court case when you know the name or the citation

Select Find by Citation in the left panel of the main Search screen. Click on "Cases."

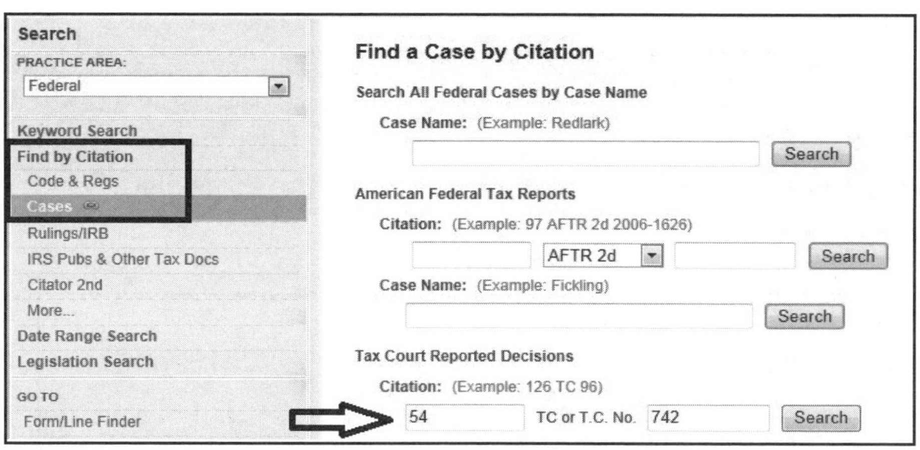

Enter the name or citation in the appropriate box and click on the [Search] button.

F. Using a Topical Index to Access Editorial Materials

In the left panel of the main Search screen under GO TO, select "Indexes."

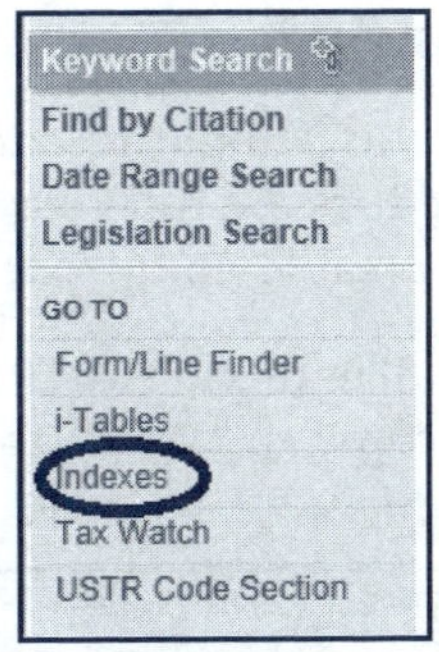

A list of available indexes will be displayed.

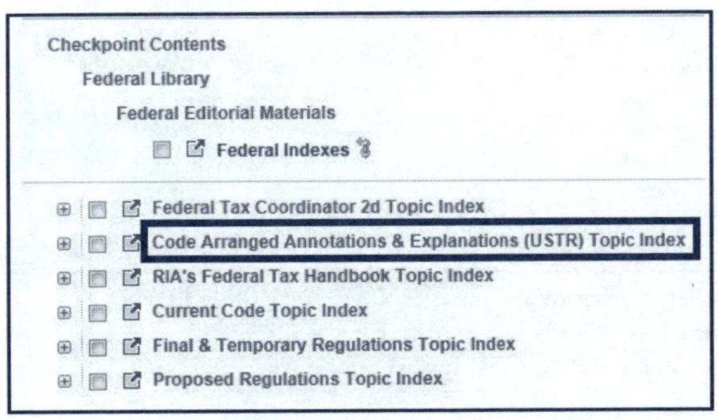

Click on the second index, "Code Arranged Annotations & Explanations (USTR) Topic Index," to locate an editorial summary of the law along with relevant cases and rulings.

An alphabetical listing will be displayed. Select the letter of the index to locate your topic.

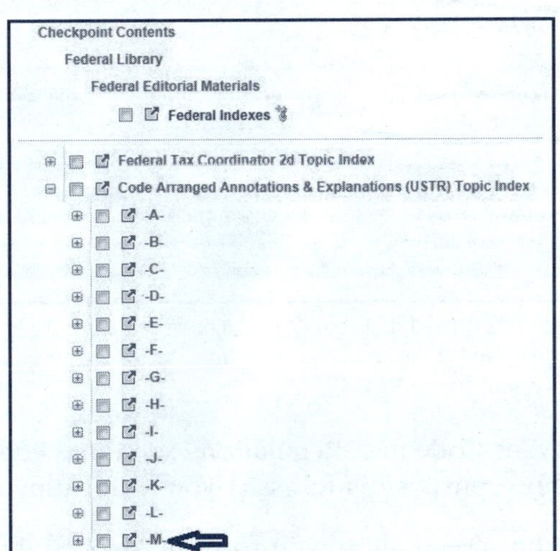

G. Example Starting with Topical Index

For this example, you will use the facts from the sample research problem in the Chapter 2 appendix. Your client, a casino hotel, wants to know if it can deduct the full cost of meals furnished to its employees in its cafeteria without the value of the meals treated as taxable compensation to the employees

Look in the "Code Arranged Annotations & Explanations (USTR) Topic Index" for Meals (under the letter M). Scroll through the list of documents until you come to "Meals, incidental expenses, and lodging." Click on it.

Meals, incidental expenses, and lodging
Annotation & Explanations (Code Arranged - USTR) Topic Index

Navig

. .employee eating facilities, employer operated	1324.06 ; 2744.01
. . . nondiscrimination rules	1324.06
. .employer-furnished, foreign earned income exclusion	9114.02
. .exclusion of value from employee income, in general	1194.01
. .expenses, deductibility of	2625.01(17) ; 2625.01(20) ; 2625.01(50) ;
. .50% of cost rule	2744 ; 2744.01
. . . exceptions to	2744.01
. .fishermen	1625.147(20)
. .flight training and private airplanes	1625.149
. .foreign conventions	2744.04
. .foreign earned income exclusion	9114.02
. .foreign employment	
. . . hardship camps	1194.05
. .free meals in company cafeterias (See Cafeterias, company)	
. .gaming corporation free meals	1195.02(90)

Scanning the topical list, you see a reference to *employee eating facilities, employer operated* and paragraph 1324.06 next to it. Click on the paragraph number.

Explanation ¶1324.06 contains a general editorial summary of the rules on employer-operated eating facilities.

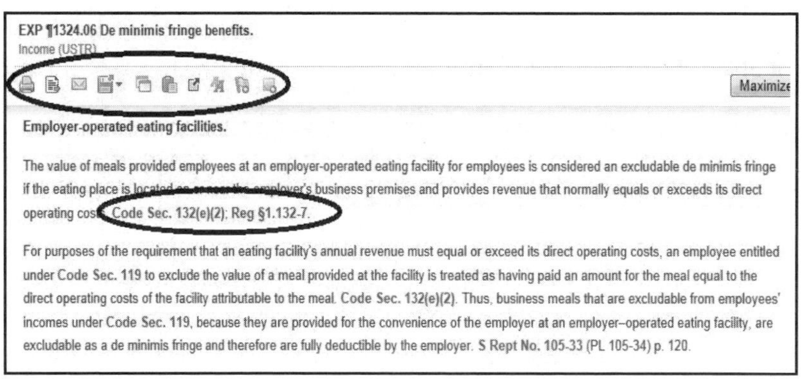

EXP ¶1324.06 De minimis fringe benefits.
Income (USTR)

Maximize

Employer-operated eating facilities.

The value of meals provided employees at an employer-operated eating facility for employees is considered an excludable de minimis fringe if the eating place is located on or near the employer's business premises and provides revenue that normally equals or exceeds its direct operating costs. Code Sec. 132(e)(2); Reg §1.132-7.

For purposes of the requirement that an eating facility's annual revenue must equal or exceed its direct operating costs, an employee entitled under Code Sec. 119 to exclude the value of a meal provided at the facility is treated as having paid an amount for the meal equal to the direct operating costs of the facility attributable to the meal. Code Sec. 132(e)(2). Thus, business meals that are excludable from employees' incomes under Code Sec. 119, because they are provided for the convenience of the employer at an employer–operated eating facility, are excludable as a de minimis fringe and therefore are fully deductible by the employer. S Rept No. 105-33 (PL 105-34) p. 120.

Hyperlinks are included to the relevant Code and Regulations sections. Remember that any editorial explanation is only secondary authority whose purpose is to assist you in locating relevant primary authority.

The document tool icons at top of the screen allow you to print, export, e-mail, save, flag this document, and add a note.

Return to the topical list and then examine the other interesting references such as *gaming corporation free meals* at ¶1195.02(90) by clicking on that paragraph number.

Annotation ¶1195.02(90) includes a short summary of a relevant court case, *Boyd Gaming Corp.*

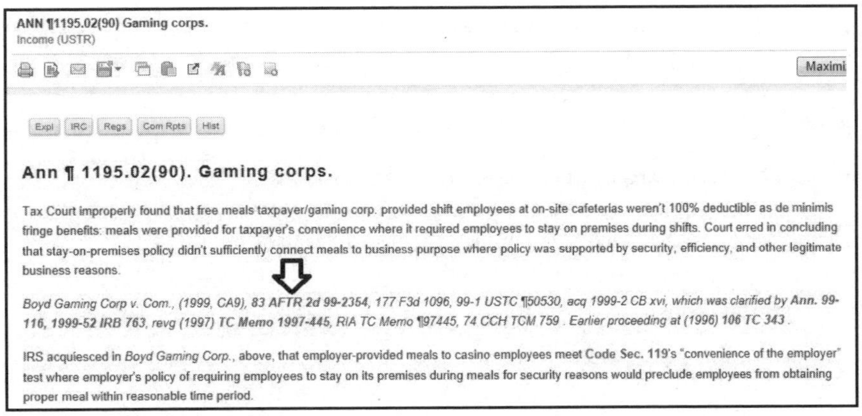

ANN ¶1195.02(90) Gaming corps.
Income (USTR)

Maximi

Expl IRC Regs Com Rpts Hist

Ann ¶ 1195.02(90). Gaming corps.

Tax Court improperly found that free meals taxpayer/gaming corp. provided shift employees at on-site cafeterias weren't 100% deductible as de minimis fringe benefits: meals were provided for taxpayer's convenience where it required employees to stay on premises during shifts. Court erred in concluding that stay-on-premises policy didn't sufficiently connect meals to business purpose where policy was supported by security, efficiency, and other legitimate business reasons.

Boyd Gaming Corp v. Com., (1999, CA9), 83 ***AFTR 2d 99-2354****, 177 F3d 1096, 99-1 USTC ¶50530, acq 1999-2 CB xvi, which was clarified by* ***Ann. 99-116, 1999-52 IRB 763****, revg (1997) TC* ***Memo 1997-445****, RIA TC Memo ¶97445, 74 CCH TCM 759 . Earlier proceeding at (1996)* ***106 TC 343*** *.*

IRS acquiesced in *Boyd Gaming Corp.*, above, that employer-provided meals to casino employees meet Code Sec. 119's "convenience of the employer" test where employer's policy of requiring employees to stay on its premises during meals for security reasons would preclude employees from obtaining proper meal within reasonable time period.

Click on the hyperlink for the case citation to retrieve the full text of the case.

The full text of the case is displayed.

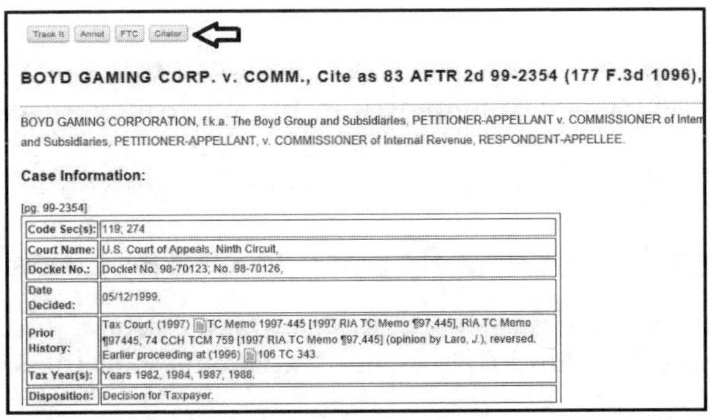

Track It Annot FTC Citator

BOYD GAMING CORP. v. COMM., Cite as 83 AFTR 2d 99-2354 (177 F.3d 1096),

BOYD GAMING CORPORATION, f.k.a. The Boyd Group and Subsidiaries, PETITIONER-APPELLANT v. COMMISSIONER of Inter
and Subsidiaries, PETITIONER-APPELLANT, v. COMMISSIONER of Internal Revenue, RESPONDENT-APPELLEE.

Case Information:

[pg. 99-2354]

Code Sec(s):	119; 274
Court Name:	U.S. Court of Appeals, Ninth Circuit,
Docket No.:	Docket No. 98-70123; No. 98-70126,
Date Decided:	05/12/1999.
Prior History:	Tax Court, (1997) TC Memo 1997-445 [1997 RIA TC Memo ¶97,445], RIA TC Memo ¶97445, 74 CCH TCM 759 [1997 RIA TC Memo ¶97,445] (opinion by Laro, J.), reversed. Earlier proceeding at (1996) 106 TC 343.
Tax Year(s):	Years 1982, 1984, 1987, 1988.
Disposition:	Decision for Taxpayer.

Scroll down through the case until you come to the headnote. The headnote includes a summary of the case.

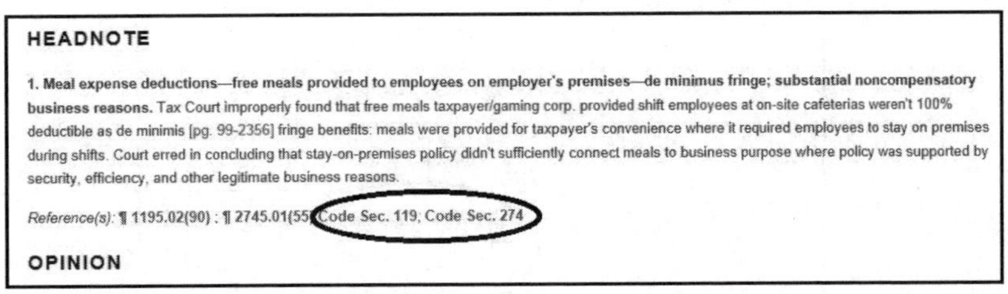

HEADNOTE

1. Meal expense deductions—free meals provided to employees on employer's premises—de minimus fringe; substantial noncompensatory business reasons. Tax Court improperly found that free meals taxpayer/gaming corp. provided shift employees at on-site cafeterias weren't 100% deductible as de minimis [pg. 99-2356] fringe benefits: meals were provided for taxpayer's convenience where it required employees to stay on premises during shifts. Court erred in concluding that stay-on-premises policy didn't sufficiently connect meals to business purpose where policy was supported by security, efficiency, and other legitimate business reasons.

Reference(s): ¶ 1195.02(90) ; ¶ 2745.01(55) Code Sec. 119; Code Sec. 274

OPINION

When you skim through the headnote, you determine that this case appears to be on point. You cannot reach a conclusion based on the headnote; you must read the entire opinion.

Hyperlinks are included to relevant Code Sections and other authorities. Clicking on these links takes you to the full text of that document.

Scroll back up to the top of the screen and click on the [Citator] button above the case name. Click on the citation for the appellate case you just viewed (83 AFTR 2d 99-2354).

A pop-up window displays the Citator listing for the case.

The Citator shows the judicial history of the case and also lists other cases or rulings that have cited it. The validity of a decision may be assessed by examining how the subsequent cases viewed the cited decision. Cases that have cited it favorably generally agree with the decision. If the cases had disagreed with the decision, then it would not be as strong an authority. Clicking on a hyperlink takes you to the full text of that document.

H. Searching by United States Tax Reporter (USTR) Code Section

Searching by USTR provides an easy way to retrieve a Code Section, the related Regulations, Committee Reports, annotations of relevant cases and rulings, and explanations at the same time.

Return to the main Search screen. In the left panel under the GO TO heading, select "USTR Code Section."

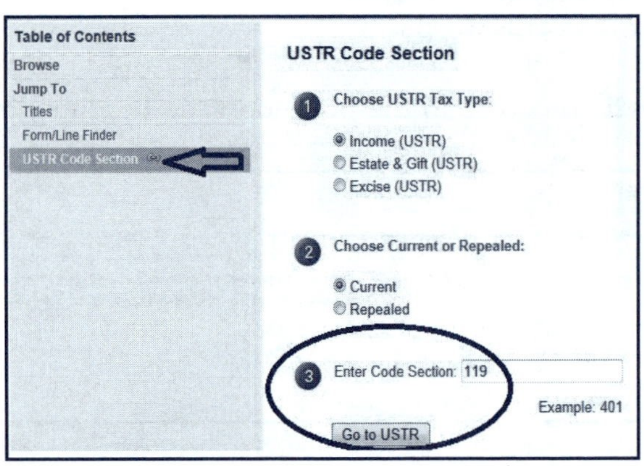

You can also access the USTR search template from the Table of Contents screen by clicking on the link under the Jump To heading in the left panel.

1. Select Income (USTR)
2. Choose Current.
3. Enter the Code Section number in the box. Click on the [Go to USTR] button.

The results include links to the full text of the Code Section, the related committee reports, the related Regulations, editorial explanations, and annotations.

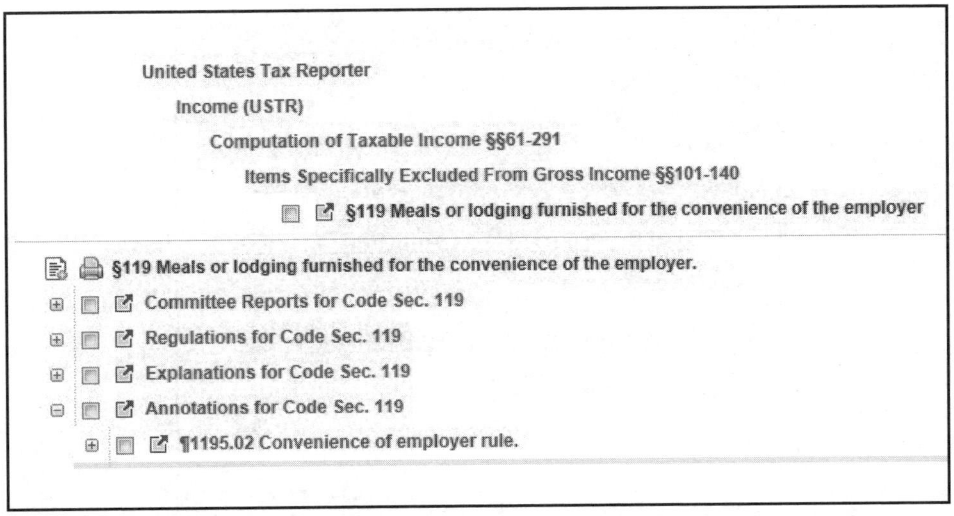

Clicking on the plus (+) in front of *Annotations for Code Section 119*, displays the next level of documents containing short summaries of relevant cases or rulings. Click on the paragraph number to retrieve the summaries for that topic with hyperlinks to the full text of the cases and rulings.

I. Keyword Searching

In the main Search screen, enter your keyword in the box and check the sources you wish to search.

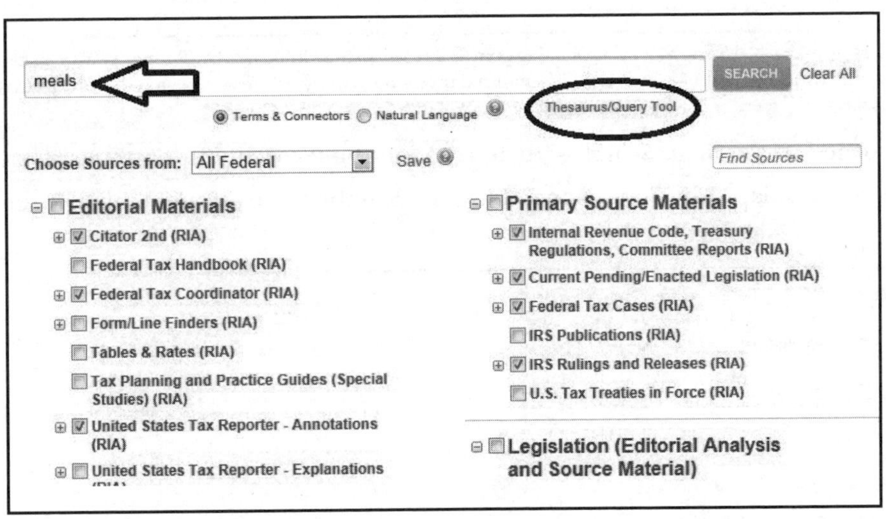

A Natural Language search lets you use conversational phrasing to state your query as a simple question. A Terms & Connectors search lets you perform a more advanced search by selecting connectors to string together your keywords usually resulting in a more focused search. Click on "Thesaurus/Query Tool" to select connectors.

You can add keywords by highlighting the desired connector, clicking on the [Append] button, and entering the additional keyword in the Current Query box.

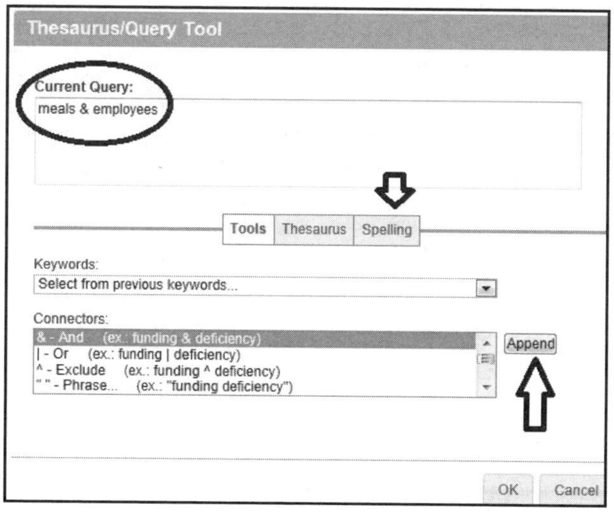

Clicking on the [Spelling] button allows you to check the spelling of your keyword. If Checkpoint recognizes any spelling errors, alternate suggestions for the word will be displayed in the Select Alternative box.

Click on the [OK] button and return to the main Search screen.

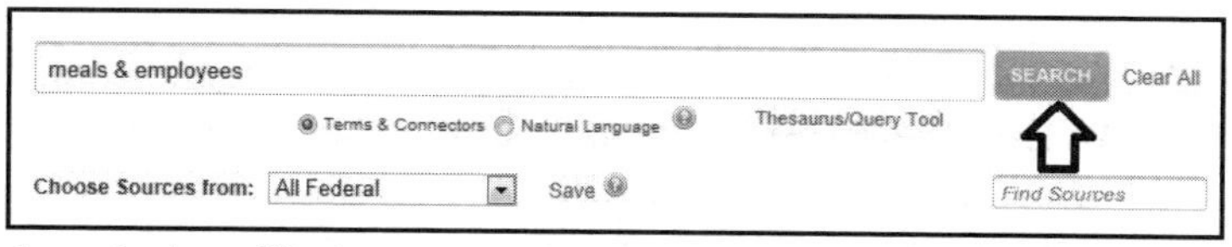

When you have returned to the main Search screen, click on the [Search] button to start your keyword search. Your search results are displayed by source and show the number of documents that include your keywords.

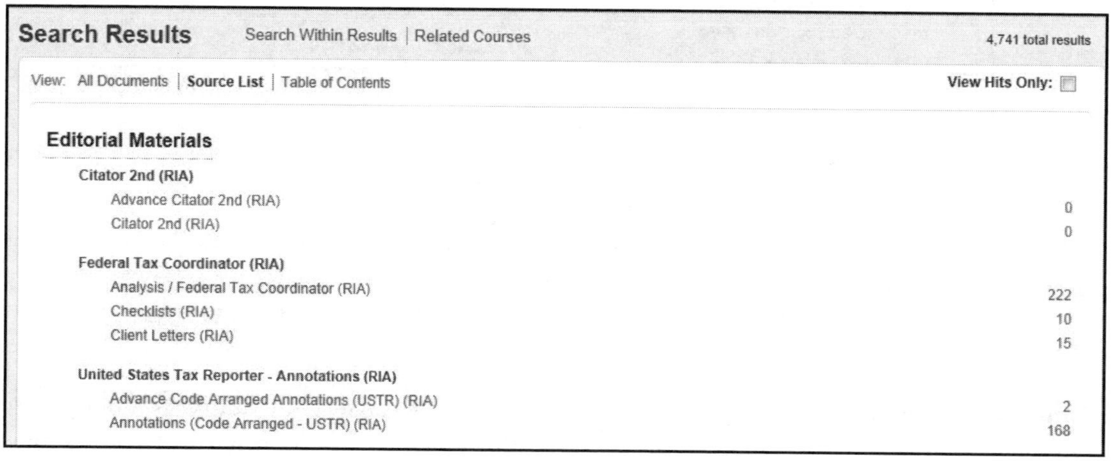

Click on any of the links to review the documents retrieved.

J. Table of Contents

To browse the table of contents for any editorial or source materials, click on "Table of Contents" near the top of the screen.

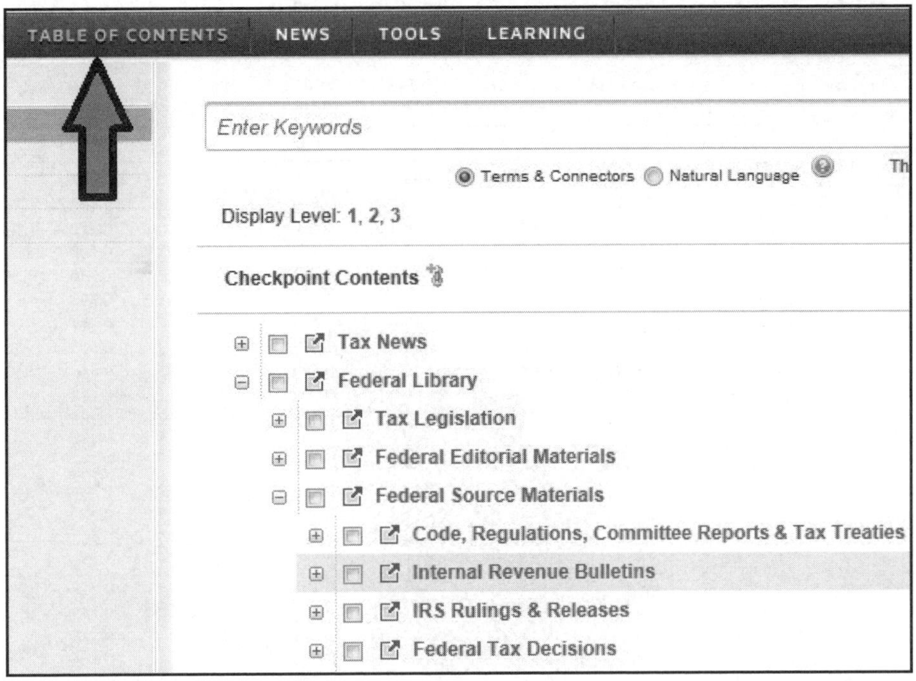

You can drill down through the contents by clicking on the plus (+) sign to display the next level for each heading. Click on a subheading to go to the full text of that document.

K. The Top Toolbar

The Top Toolbar is available at the top on every screen.

Click on "History" to access your recent searches and documents viewed.

You can use "Folders" to save and later retrieve documents.

Click "Flagged" to view a list of recently flagged documents.

Click on "Options" to set your preferences for interacting with Checkpoint.

Click on "Help" to learn more about using Checkpoint features.

When you have finished your research, click on "Sign Out."

APPENDIX B

PRESENT VALUE AND FUTURE VALUE TABLES

Present Value of $1

Periods	4%	5%	6%	7%	8%	9%	10%	12%
1	0.962	0.952	0.943	0.935	0.926	0.917	0.909	0.893
2	0.925	0.907	0.890	0.873	0.857	0.842	0.826	0.797
3	0.889	0.864	0.840	0.816	0.794	0.772	0.751	0.712
4	0.855	0.823	0.792	0.763	0.735	0.708	0.683	0.636
5	0.822	0.784	0.747	0.713	0.681	0.650	0.621	0.567
6	0.790	0.746	0.705	0.666	0.630	0.596	0.564	0.507
7	0.760	0.711	0.665	0.623	0.583	0.547	0.513	0.452
8	0.731	0.677	0.627	0.582	0.540	0.502	0.467	0.404
9	0.703	0.645	0.592	0.544	0.500	0.460	0.424	0.361
10	0.676	0.614	0.558	0.508	0.463	0.422	0.386	0.322
11	0.650	0.585	0.527	0.475	0.429	0.388	0.350	0.287
12	0.625	0.557	0.497	0.444	0.397	0.356	0.319	0.257
13	0.601	0.530	0.469	0.415	0.368	0.326	0.290	0.229
14	0.577	0.505	0.442	0.388	0.340	0.299	0.263	0.205
15	0.555	0.481	0.417	0.362	0.315	0.275	0.239	0.183
16	0.534	0.458	0.394	0.339	0.292	0.252	0.218	0.163
17	0.513	0.436	0.371	0.317	0.270	0.231	0.198	0.146
18	0.494	0.416	0.350	0.296	0.250	0.212	0.180	0.130
19	0.475	0.396	0.331	0.277	0.232	0.194	0.164	0.116
20	0.456	0.377	0.312	0.258	0.215	0.178	0.149	0.104
21	0.439	0.359	0.294	0.242	0.199	0.164	0.135	0.093
22	0.422	0.342	0.278	0.226	0.184	0.150	0.123	0.083
23	0.406	0.326	0.262	0.211	0.170	0.138	0.112	0.074
24	0.390	0.310	0.247	0.197	0.158	0.126	0.102	0.066
25	0.375	0.295	0.233	0.184	0.146	0.116	0.092	0.059
30	0.308	0.231	0.174	0.131	0.099	0.075	0.057	0.033
40	0.208	0.142	0.097	0.067	0.046	0.032	0.022	0.011

Present Value of Annuity of $1

Periods	4%	5%	6%	7%	8%	9%	10%	12%
1	0.962	0.952	0.943	0.935	0.926	0.917	0.909	0.893
2	1.886	1.859	1.833	1.808	1.783	1.759	1.736	1.690
3	2.775	2.723	2.673	2.624	2.577	2.531	2.487	2.402
4	3.630	3.546	3.465	3.387	3.312	3.240	3.170	3.037
5	4.452	4.329	4.212	4.100	3.993	3.890	3.791	3.605
6	5.242	5.076	4.917	4.767	4.623	4.486	4.355	4.111
7	6.002	5.786	5.582	5.389	5.206	5.033	4.868	4.564
8	6.733	6.463	6.210	5.971	5.747	5.535	5.335	4.968
9	7.435	7.108	6.802	6.515	6.247	5.995	5.759	5.328
10	8.111	7.722	7.360	7.024	6.710	6.418	6.145	5.650
11	8.760	8.306	7.887	7.499	7.139	6.805	6.495	5.938
12	9.385	8.863	8.384	7.943	7.536	7.161	6.814	6.194
13	9.986	9.394	8.853	8.358	7.904	7.487	7.103	6.424
14	10.563	9.899	9.295	8.745	8.244	7.786	7.367	6.628
15	11.118	10.380	9.712	9.108	8.559	8.061	7.606	6.811
16	11.652	10.838	10.106	9.447	8.851	8.313	7.824	6.974
17	12.166	11.274	10.477	9.763	9.122	8.544	8.022	7.120
18	12.659	11.690	10.828	10.059	9.372	8.756	8.201	7.250
19	13.134	12.085	11.158	10.336	9.604	8.950	8.365	7.366
20	13.590	12.462	11.470	10.594	9.818	9.129	8.514	7.469
21	14.029	12.821	11.764	10.836	10.017	9.292	8.649	7.562
22	14.451	13.163	12.042	11.061	10.201	9.442	8.772	7.645
23	14.857	13.489	12.303	11.272	10.371	9.580	8.883	7.718
24	15.247	13.799	12.550	11.469	10.529	9.707	8.985	7.784
25	15.622	14.094	12.783	11.654	10.675	9.823	9.077	7.843
30	17.292	15.373	13.765	12.409	11.258	10.274	9.427	8.055
40	19.793	17.159	15.046	13.332	11.925	10.757	9.779	8.244

Future Value of $1

Periods	4%	5%	6%	7%	8%	9%	10%	12%
1	1.040	1.050	1.060	1.070	1.080	1.090	1.100	1.120
2	1.082	1.103	1.124	1.145	1.166	1.188	1.210	1.254
3	1.125	1.158	1.191	1.225	1.260	1.295	1.331	1.405
4	1.170	1.216	1.262	1.311	1.360	1.412	1.464	1.574
5	1.217	1.276	1.338	1.403	1.469	1.539	1.611	1.762
6	1.265	1.340	1.419	1.501	1.587	1.677	1.772	1.974
7	1.316	1.407	1.504	1.606	1.714	1.828	1.949	2.211
8	1.369	1.477	1.594	1.718	1.851	1.993	2.144	2.476
9	1.423	1.551	1.689	1.838	1.999	2.172	2.358	2.773
10	1.480	1.629	1.791	1.967	2.159	2.367	2.594	3.106
11	1.539	1.710	1.898	2.105	2.332	2.580	2.853	3.479
12	1.601	1.796	2.012	2.252	2.518	2.813	3.138	3.896
13	1.665	1.886	2.133	2.410	2.720	3.066	3.452	4.363
14	1.732	1.980	2.261	2.579	2.937	3.342	3.798	4.887
15	1.801	2.079	2.397	2.759	3.172	3.642	4.177	5.474
16	1.873	2.183	2.540	2.952	3.426	3.970	4.595	6.130
17	1.948	2.292	2.693	3.159	3.700	4.328	5.054	6.866
18	2.026	2.407	2.854	3.380	3.996	4.717	5.560	7.690
19	2.107	2.527	3.026	3.617	4.316	5.142	6.116	8.613
20	2.191	2.653	3.207	3.870	4.661	5.604	6.728	9.646
21	2.279	2.786	3.400	4.141	5.034	6.109	7.400	10.80
22	2.370	2.925	3.604	4.430	5.437	6.659	8.140	12.10
23	2.465	3.072	3.820	4.741	5.871	7.258	8.954	13.55
24	2.563	3.225	4.049	5.072	6.341	7.911	9.850	15.18
25	2.666	3.386	4.292	5.427	6.848	8.623	10.83	17.00
30	3.243	4.322	5.743	7.612	10.06	13.27	17.45	29.96
40	4.801	7.040	10.29	14.97	21.72	31.41	45.26	93.05

Future Value of Annuity of $1

Periods	4%	5%	6%	7%	8%	9%	10%	12%
1	1.000	1.000	1.000	1.000	1.000	1.000	1.000	1.000
2	2.040	2.050	2.060	2.070	2.080	2.090	2.100	2.120
3	3.122	3.153	3.184	3.215	3.246	3.278	3.310	3.374
4	4.246	4.310	4.375	4.440	4.506	4.573	4.641	4.779
5	5.416	5.526	5.637	5.751	5.867	5.985	6.105	6.353
6	6.633	6.802	6.975	7.153	7.336	7.523	7.716	8.115
7	7.898	8.142	8.394	8.654	8.923	9.200	9.487	10.09
8	9.214	9.549	9.897	10.26	10.64	11.03	11.44	12.30
9	10.58	11.03	11.49	11.98	12.49	13.02	13.58	14.78
10	12.01	12.58	13.18	13.82	14.49	15.19	15.94	17.55
11	13.49	14.21	14.97	15.78	16.65	17.56	18.53	20.65
12	15.03	15.92	16.87	17.89	18.98	20.14	21.38	24.13
13	16.63	17.71	18.88	20.14	21.50	22.95	24.52	28.03
14	18.29	19.60	21.02	22.55	24.21	26.02	27.98	32.39
15	20.02	21.58	23.28	25.13	27.15	29.36	31.77	37.28
16	21.82	23.66	25.67	27.89	30.32	33.00	35.95	42.75
17	23.70	25.84	28.21	30.84	33.75	36.97	40.54	48.88
18	25.65	28.13	30.91	34.00	37.45	41.30	45.60	55.75
19	27.67	30.54	33.76	37.38	41.45	46.02	51.16	63.44
20	29.78	33.07	36.79	41.00	45.76	51.16	57.28	72.05
21	31.97	35.72	39.99	44.87	50.42	56.76	64.00	81.70
22	34.25	38.51	43.39	49.01	55.46	62.87	71.40	92.50
23	36.62	41.43	47.00	53.44	60.89	69.53	79.54	104.6
24	39.08	44.50	50.82	58.18	66.76	76.79	88.50	118.2
25	41.65	47.73	54.86	63.25	73.11	84.70	98.35	133.3
30	56.08	66.44	79.06	94.46	113.3	136.3	164.5	241.3
40	95.03	120.8	154.8	199.6	259.1	337.9	442.6	767.1

APPENDIX C

SAMPLE FILLED-IN TAX RETURNS

SAMPLE RETURN 1 (SR1)

INFORMATION FOR CORPORATE TAX RETURN

Facts

William Spicer (SS# 123-45-6789) owns 80 percent of the stock in Bill's Market, an accrual-basis gourmet food market operating as a corporation. It is located at 387 Spring Street, Raleigh, NC 29288. William's wife, June (SS# 987-65-4321), owns the other 20 percent of the outstanding stock of the corporation but she is not active in the business. The Market's EIN is 79-7979797 and its business code is 445290. It was incorporated on July 15, 2003. During the last tax year, the Market had the following results from its operations:

Gross Sales ($1,300,000 from credit card sales)	$2,700,000
Merchandise Purchases	1,980,000
Expenses:	
Advertising	$40,000
Charitable Contributions	2,000
Cleaning/Maintenance	12,000
Depreciation (MACRS pre-2012 purchases)	3,000
Section 179 Expense (2/1/12 display case)	5,000
Payroll Taxes (excluding FICA on William's salary)	18,000
FICA on William's Salary	9,726
William's Salary	200,000
Health Insurance	15,000*
Insurance (excludes health)	18,000
Interest	1,000
Licenses/Fees	4,000
Meals/Entertainment	1,000
Office Expenses	14,000
Rent	120,000
Salary/Wages	210,000
Travel	8,000
Utilities	16,000

**Includes $3,000 for health insurance for William and his family.*

The Market sold a unique piece of equipment for $13,000. It had originally cost $5,000 when purchased on March 5, 2010; it had an adjusted basis of $3,000 when sold on August 15, 2012. The Market also sold a display case for $1,000 on December 12, 2012, that had cost $12,000 when purchased on June 6, 2008; it had an adjusted basis of $4,000 when sold. The gains or losses on these asset sales are the same for tax and financial accounting. The business complies with all Form 1099 requirements.

Information specific to the corporate form: The corporation made estimated payments for its own taxes of $10,000 and withheld $45,000 from William's salary for income taxes. For financial accounting, the corporation does not expense the new display case but deducts $1,000 of depreciation expense. It has a beginning balance of $200,000 in its retained earnings account and made a $25,000 dividend distribution to its shareholders on December 31, 2012.

The corporation's beginning and ending accrual-basis balance sheets for 2012 are shown below:

	January 1, 2012		December 31, 2012	
Assets:				
Cash		$62,000		$50,174
Accounts Receivable		37,500		37,500
Inventory		340,000		340,000
Tax Refund				5,399
Plant, Property, and Equipment	$80,000		$68,000	
Less: Accumulated Depreciation	62,000	18,000	59,000	9,000
Total Assets		$457,500		$442,073
Liabilities and Equities:				
Accounts Payable		$20,000		
Deferred Tax Liability		0		$600
Note Payable		12,500		12,500
Common Stock		225,000		225,000
Retained Earnings		200,000		203,973
Total Liabilities and Equities		$457,500		$442,073

Explanation

The completion of the Form 1120 for the corporation is straightforward. The income and expense items are reported on Form 1120 except for the following items: Form 1125-A is used to report cost of goods sold. Form 4797 is used to report the asset sales including the depreciation recapture. In completing Form 4797, the equipment subject to recapture is entered in Part III. The net Section 1231 gain is determined in Part I and the $2,000 recapture is transferred to Part II. The recapture is then included directly in corporate income on line 9, Form 1120. The $5,000 Section 1231 net gain is entered on line 11, Schedule D, and also becomes part of the corporate taxable income on line 8. Form 4562 includes the depreciation expense and the Section 179 expense. These items are combined and deducted from corporate income. The FICA taxes on William's salary of $200,000 are determined ($9,726) and deducted from taxable income along with the other deductible corporate expenses. (The schedule of other deductions appears below.) The corporation deducts the health insurance paid for William and his family as he is an employee. The deduction for the charitable contribution is not limited as it does not exceed 10 percent of corporate net income. The corporation pays an income tax of $4,616 on its taxable income of $30,774. The overpayment of $5,384 is refunded to the corporation.

Form 1120 and Related Forms and Schedules

Form 1120: *U.S. Corporate Income Tax Return*
Schedule D: *Capital Gains and Losses*
Schedule G: *Information on Certain Persons Owning the Corporation's Voting Stock*
Form 1125-A: *Cost of Good Sold*
Form 4562: *Depreciation and Amortization*
Form 4797: *Sales of Business Property*
(Form 1125-E is not required as it duplicates information provided elsewhere.)

Schedule of Other Deductions:

Bill's Market EIN: 79-7979797
Form 1120
Page 1, Line 26, Other deductions:

Meals/Entertainment @ 50%	$500
Office Expense	14,000
Travel	8,000
Insurance	18,000
Utilities	16,000
	$56,500

Schedule of Other Assets:

Form 1120, Page 4, Line 6
Tax refund due = $5,384

Schedule of Other Liabilities:

Form 1120, Page 4, Line 21
Deferred taxes = $600

Determining Book Income and the Tax Provision:

Book Income:	
Taxable income	$30,774
Subtract nondeductible portion of meals (permanent difference)	500
Book income before temporary differences	$30,274
Add depreciation difference	4,000
Book income before tax	$34,274

Tax Provision:
Tax liability: $30,774 × .15 = $4,616
Permanent difference: $500 nondeductible meals
Temporary differences: $4,000 depreciation
Deferred tax liability: $4,000 × .15 = $600
Book tax expense: $4,616 current tax liability + $600 deferred tax liability = $5,216

Adjusting entry to books for book tax expense and tax provision:

	Debit	Credit
Tax Expense	5,216	
Deferred Tax Liability		600
Taxes Payable		4,616

Book income after tax: $34,274 – $5,216 = $29,058
$10,000 estimated payments – $4,616 taxes payable = $5,384 refund due

SAMPLE RETURN 2 (SR2)

Information for Partnership Tax Return

Facts

The facts for the partnership tax return are the same as those for the corporate tax return (SR1) with the following exceptions:

1. William is an 80 percent partner and his wife is a 20 percent general partner.
2. William has a guaranteed payment of $200,000 from the partnership instead of a salary (and the partnership withholds no FICA for William).
3. William takes drawings during the year equal to his guaranteed payment.
4. The partnership balance sheet that follows reflects the full Section 179 expense in accumulated depreciation.

	January 1, 2012		December 31, 2012	
Assets:				
Cash		$62,000		$95,000
Accounts Receivable		37,500		37,500
Inventory		340,000		340,000
Plant, Property, and Equipment	$80,000		$68,000	
Less: Accum. Depreciation	62,000	18,000	63,000	5,000
Total Assets		$457,500		$477,500

	January 1, 2012	December 31, 2012
Liabilities and Equities		
Accounts Payable	$20,000	
Note Payable	12,500	12,500
Capital–William	340,000	372,000
Capital–June	85,000	93,000
Total Liabilities and Equities	$457,500	$477,500

Explanation

Note: Forms 1125-A, 4562, and 4797 are the same as those completed for the corporate problem except for minor differences related to the type of entity.

To complete Form 1065, the partnership's separately stated items of income and expense must be segregated from the balance of the income and expense items that constitute ordinary or "bottom line" income. The separately stated expense items are the charitable contributions and the Section 179 expense. The health insurance premium paid by the partnership for William and his family is considered a guaranteed payment to William. The net Section 1231 gain is also a separately stated item. Note, however, that the Section 1245 recapture is an element of ordinary income for the partnership. It does not require separate reporting for partnership purposes and is included in partnership ordinary income ($42,500).

To complete the partnership tax return, cost of goods sold is calculated separately on Form 1125-A; the Section 1231 gain and loss and the Section 1245 recapture are both entered on Form 4797; only the Section 1231 net gain is separately reported on Schedule K (Form 1065), line 10. The $2,000 depreciation recapture is reported on line 6, Form 1065. The partnership's Form 4562 is used to report both the Section 179 expense and depreciation expense. The Section 179 expense is reported as a separate item on line 12 of the Schedule K, however. The annual limitation on the Section 179 expense applies at both the partnership and partner level. The charitable contribution is subject to limitation at the partner level and is separately reported on line 13a, Schedule K.

The $3,000 payment for health insurance by the partnership for William is reported as part of the guaranteed payment ($203,000) on line 10, p. 1, Form 1065. The guaranteed payment is also reported on line 4, Schedule K.

To complete Schedule K, the earnings from self-employment are reported on line 14(a). These earnings include ordinary income ($42,500) plus guaranteed payments ($203,000) less the $2,000 Section 1245 income and equal $243,500. William's guaranteed payments plus share of ordinary income (as adjusted) ($203,000 + $34,000 – $1,600 = $235,400) are subject to self-employment taxes. Because June is a general partner, her income ($8,500 – $400) is also subject to self-employment taxes even though she no longer works actively in the business. If she were a limited partner, she would not be subject to self-employment taxes on this income. Finally, the $500 of nondeductible meals/entertainment expense is reported on line 18(c), Schedule K. This item must be reported because it reduces the partners' outside bases in their partnership interests. (Note: The interest expense is not reported separately; it is from accounts payable rather than interest incurred for investment purposes.)

The partnership then completes Schedules K-1 for William and June that include their share of each of the items reported on Schedule K. These forms tie directly to the items reported on Schedule K. Thus, William's 80 percent and June's 20 percent shares of net ordinary income are reported on line 1, the Section 1231 gain on line 10, the charitable contribution on line 13(a), the Section 179 expense on line 12, and the nondeductible expense on line 18(c). The guaranteed payment (including the health insurance premium) is reported only on William's line 4 and the appropriate self-employment income is included on line 14(a). William's self-employment income includes not only his share of the partnership ordinary income but includes the guaranteed payment.

Form 1065 and Related Forms and Schedules

Form 1065: *U.S. Return of Partnership Income*
Schedule B-1: *Information on Partners Owning 50% or More of the Partnership*
Schedule K-1: *Partner's Share of Income* (One each for June and William)
Forms 1125-A, 4562, and 4797 are essentially the same as those included with the corporate solution. These forms are not repeated here.

Schedule of Other Deductions:

Bill's Market EIN: 79-7979797

Form 1065

Page 1, Line 20, Other deductions:

Advertising	$40,000
Interest	1,000
Meals/Entertainment @ 50%	500
Office Expense	14,000
Travel	8,000
Insurance	18,000
Utilities	16,000
	$97,500

SAMPLE RETURN 3 (SR3)

Information for S Corporation Tax Return

Facts

The facts for the S corporation tax return are the same as those for the corporate tax return (SR1) with the following exceptions:

1. The FICA tax on William's salary is $9,769.70 as the health insurance premium paid by the company is subject to the FICA tax.
2. The S corporation withholds $45,000 from William's salary for income taxes.
3. The corporation has a beginning balance of $200,000 in its accumulated adjustments account and makes a $25,000 distribution to the shareholders on December 31, 2012.
4. The corporation's beginning and ending accrual-basis balance sheets for 2012 follow:

	January 1, 2012		December 31, 2012	
Assets:				
Cash		$62,000		$60,230
Accounts Receivable		37,500		37,500
Inventory		340,000		340,000
Plant, Prop. and Equipment,	$80,000		$68,000	
Less: Accum. Depreciation	62,000	18,000	59,000	9,000
Total Assets		$457,500		$446,730
Liabilities and Equities:				
Accounts Payable		$20,000		
Note Payable		12,500		$12,500
Common Stock		225,000		225,000
Retained Earnings		200,000		209,230
Total Liabilities and Equities		$457,500		$446,730

Explanation

Note: Forms 1125-A, 4562, and 4797 are essentially the same as those completed for the corporate problem and are not repeated here.

The completion of the Form 1120S resembles the Form 1065 with the exception of the treatment of the salary and FICA taxes for William. Because he is a more-than 2 percent shareholder, the payment of the health insurance by the company is treated as additional income to William and is subject to FICA taxes. The corporation also has to treat the charitable contributions, the Section 179 expense deduction, and the $5,000 net Section 1231 gain as separately stated items. The remaining items constitute the corporation's ordinary income.

In completing the return, the recapture is included on line 4, Form 1120S. The $3,000 depreciation expense is deducted from the corporation's income, but the Section 179 expense is passed through separately.

The corporation's ordinary income is $32,730, and this along with the other separately stated items are entered on the Schedule K and allocated to William and June in their 80 percent, 20 percent ownership percentages, respectively.

Form 1120S and Related Forms and Schedules

Form 1120S: *U.S. Income Tax Return for an S Corporation*

Schedule K-1: *Shareholder's Share of Income* (One each for William and June)

Forms 1125-A, 4562, and 4797 are the same as those included with the corporate solution.

Schedule of Other Deductions – Line 19	
Meals/Entertainment	$500
Insurance	18,000
Office Expense	14,000
Travel	8,000
Utilities	16,000
Total Other Deductions	$56,500

SAMPLE RETURN 4 (SR4)

Information for Individual Tax Return with Sole Proprietorship

Facts

William and June Spicer have two dependent children, Sophie age 9 and Carl age 7, both of whom live at home. (Additional personal data are provided directly on Form 1040.) William operates a gourmet market in Raleigh, Bill's Market, as an accrual-basis sole proprietorship. The information on gross market sales, expenses, and property transactions is the same as provided for the regular corporate tax return (Sample Return 1) except that William receives no salary and there is no related FICA tax.

William is also a 10 percent shareholder in Imagineers Corporation, an S corporation, but takes no active role in the business. He received a Schedule K-1 from this S corporation reporting $1,800 in ordinary business income. June is a general partner in The Bridal Shop Partnership. She worked 3 days a week at the shop and received a Schedule K-1 reporting a $12,000 guaranteed payment and $8,000 in ordinary business income. June paid $3,800 for after-school and summer child care while she worked.

The following information pertains to the completion of the Spicers' personal tax return:

Interest Income	$500
Dividend Income (all qualified)	1,300
Unreimbursed Doctor's Bills	8,000
Unreimbursed Hospital Bills	9,000
Dental Bills	2,000
Mortgage Interest	14,000
Real Estate Taxes	3,000
Contributions to their Church	1,500

The Spicers sold 10,000 shares of ABC stock on February 2, 2012 for $4,000. They had purchased the stock on August 1, 2005 for $18,000. During 2012, the Spicers paid $300 with their 2011 North Carolina state income tax return and made $4,600 in estimated payments for 2012. This amount exceeds their alternate state sales tax deduction. June is a volunteer at the children's school two days a week tutoring at-risk students. Her total mileage for her trips to and from the school was 1,200 miles. She also had unreimbursed out-of-pocket expenses for teaching materials of $232. Additionally, the Spicers contribute $3,000 each to regular IRAs. The Spicers made quarterly estimated tax payments of $17,500 each quarter. All payments were made when due. Any refund that the Spicers have for 2012 is to be applied to their 2013 estimated taxes.

Form 1040 and Related Forms and Schedules

Form 1040: *U.S. Individual Income Tax Return*
Schedule A: *Itemized Deductions*
Schedule C: *Profit or Loss From Business*
Schedule D: *Capital Gains and Losses*
Schedule E: *Supplemental Income and Loss*
Schedule SE: *Self-Employment Tax (2)*
Form 2441: *Child and Dependent Care Expenses*
Form 4562: *Depreciation and Amortization*
Form 4797: *Sales of Business Property*
Form 8949: *Sales and Other Disposition of Capital Assets*

The Spicers will prepare only one tax return, their Form 1040, along with all the required schedules and forms including the Schedule C where the income and expenses for the business are reported. A Form 4797 is completed for the business property dispositions; the sale of the stock is entered on the Form 8949; the net gain on the equipment disposition and the loss on the stock are both included on the Spicers' Schedule D. The $2,000 depreciation recapture is also entered on Form 4797 but is transferred directly to the Spicers' Form 1040. Two other items are not included on the Schedule C—the health insurance for William and his family (which is deducted on page 1 of the Form 1040 as a deduction for AGI) and the charitable contribution (which is included with the Spicers' personal charitable deductions on their Schedule A). June is allowed to deduct 14 cents per mile for the 1,200 miles driven ($168) for her volunteer work along with her out-of-pocket expenses of $232.

Their total itemized deductions are $26,750 and their exemptions are $15,200 (4 × $3,800). They are not able to benefit from the child tax credit as their AGI exceeds the allowable limit for claiming all or part of this credit, but they are allowed a $760 credit for June's child care expenses. Their dividend income is taxed at 15 percent while the rest of the income is taxed at the regular rates.

SAMPLE RETURN 1 (SR1)

Form **1120** Department of the Treasury Internal Revenue Service

U.S. Corporation Income Tax Return

For calendar year 2012 or tax year beginning ________, 2012, ending ________, 20 ___

▶ Information about Form 1120 and its separate instructions is at *www.irs.gov/form1120.*

OMB No. 1545-0123

2012

A Check if:
1a Consolidated return (attach Form 851) ☐
b Life/nonlife consolidated return ☐
2 Personal holding co. (attach Sch. PH) ☐
3 Personal service corp. (see instructions) ☐
4 Schedule M-3 attached ☐

TYPE OR PRINT

Name: Bill's Market
Number, street, and room or suite no. If a P.O. box, see instructions.: 387 Spring Street
City or town, state, and ZIP code: Raleigh, NS 29288

B Employer identification number: 79-7979797
C Date incorporated: 7/15/03
D Total assets (see instructions): $ 442,158

E Check if: (1) ☐ Initial return (2) ☐ Final return (3) ☐ Name change (4) ☐ Address change

Income	1a	Gross receipts or sales	1a	2,700,000		
	b	Returns and allowances	1b	0		
	c	Balance. Subtract line 1b from line 1a			1c	2,700,000
	2	Cost of goods sold (attach Form 1125-A)			2	1,980,000
	3	Gross profit. Subtract line 2 from line 1c			3	720,000
	4	Dividends (Schedule C, line 19)			4	
	5	Interest			5	
	6	Gross rents			6	
	7	Gross royalties			7	
	8	Capital gain net income (attach Schedule D (Form 1120))			8	5,000
	9	Net gain or (loss) from Form 4797, Part II, line 17 (attach Form 4797)			9	2,000
	10	Other income (see instructions—attach statement)			10	
	11	**Total income.** Add lines 3 through 10 ▶			11	727,000
Deductions (See instructions for limitations on deductions.)	12	Compensation of officers (see instructions—attach Form 1125-E) ▶			12	200,000
	13	Salaries and wages (less employment credits)			13	210,000
	14	Repairs and maintenance			14	12,000
	15	Bad debts			15	
	16	Rents			16	120,000
	17	Taxes and licenses			17	31,726
	18	Interest			18	1,000
	19	Charitable contributions			19	2,000
	20	Depreciation from Form 4562 not claimed on Form 1125-A or elsewhere on return (attach Form 4562)			20	8,000
	21	Depletion			21	
	22	Advertising			22	40,000
	23	Pension, profit-sharing, etc., plans			23	
	24	Employee benefit programs			24	15,000
	25	Domestic production activities deduction (attach Form 8903)			25	
	26	Other deductions (attach statement)			26	56,500
	27	**Total deductions.** Add lines 12 through 26 ▶			27	696,226
	28	Taxable income before net operating loss deduction and special deductions. Subtract line 27 from line 11.			28	30,774
	29a	Net operating loss deduction (see instructions)	29a			
	b	Special deductions (Schedule C, line 20)	29b			
	c	Add lines 29a and 29b			29c	0
Tax, Refundable Credits, and Payments	30	**Taxable income.** Subtract line 29c from line 28 (see instructions)			30	30,774
	31	Total tax (Schedule J, Part I, line 11)			31	4,616
	32	Total payments and refundable credits (Schedule J, Part II, line 21)			32	10,000
	33	Estimated tax penalty (see instructions). Check if Form 2220 is attached ▶ ☐			33	
	34	**Amount owed.** If line 32 is smaller than the total of lines 31 and 33, enter amount owed			34	
	35	**Overpayment.** If line 32 is larger than the total of lines 31 and 33, enter amount overpaid			35	5,384
	36	Enter amount from line 35 you want: **Credited to 2013 estimated tax** ▶		Refunded ▶	36	5,384

Sign Here

Under penalties of perjury, I declare that I have examined this return, including accompanying schedules and statements, and to the best of my knowledge and belief, it is true, correct, and complete. Declaration of preparer (other than taxpayer) is based on all information of which preparer has any knowledge.

▶ Signature of officer | Date | ▶ Title

May the IRS discuss this return with the preparer shown below (see instructions)? ☐ Yes ☐ No

Paid Preparer Use Only

Print/Type preparer's name	Preparer's signature	Date	Check ☐ if self-employed	PTIN

Firm's name ▶ | Firm's EIN ▶
Firm's address ▶ | Phone no.

For Paperwork Reduction Act Notice, see separate instructions. Cat. No. 11450Q Form **1120** (2012)

Form 1120 (2012) Page 2

Schedule C **Dividends and Special Deductions** (see instructions)

		(a) Dividends received	(b) %	(c) Special deductions (a) × (b)
1	Dividends from less-than-20%-owned domestic corporations (other than debt-financed stock)		70	
2	Dividends from 20%-or-more-owned domestic corporations (other than debt-financed stock)		80	
3	Dividends on debt-financed stock of domestic and foreign corporations		see instructions	
4	Dividends on certain preferred stock of less-than-20%-owned public utilities		42	
5	Dividends on certain preferred stock of 20%-or-more-owned public utilities		48	
6	Dividends from less-than-20%-owned foreign corporations and certain FSCs		70	
7	Dividends from 20%-or-more-owned foreign corporations and certain FSCs		80	
8	Dividends from wholly owned foreign subsidiaries		100	
9	**Total.** Add lines 1 through 8. See instructions for limitation			
10	Dividends from domestic corporations received by a small business investment company operating under the Small Business Investment Act of 1958		100	
11	Dividends from affiliated group members		100	
12	Dividends from certain FSCs		100	
13	Dividends from foreign corporations not included on lines 3, 6, 7, 8, 11, or 12			
14	Income from controlled foreign corporations under subpart F (attach Form(s) 5471)			
15	Foreign dividend gross-up			
16	IC-DISC and former DISC dividends not included on lines 1, 2, or 3			
17	Other dividends			
18	Deduction for dividends paid on certain preferred stock of public utilities			
19	**Total dividends.** Add lines 1 through 17. Enter here and on page 1, line 4 ▶			
20	**Total special deductions.** Add lines 9, 10, 11, 12, and 18. Enter here and on page 1, line 29b ▶			

Form **1120** (2012)

Schedule J Tax Computation and Payment (see instructions)

Part I–Tax Computation

1	Check if the corporation is a member of a controlled group (attach Schedule O (Form 1120)) ▶ ☐				
2	Income tax. Check if a qualified personal service corporation (see instructions) ▶ ☐			2	4,616
3	Alternative minimum tax (attach Form 4626)			3	0
4	Add lines 2 and 3			4	4,616
5a	Foreign tax credit (attach Form 1118)	5a			
b	Credit from Form 8834, line 30 (attach Form 8834)	5b			
c	General business credit (attach Form 3800)	5c			
d	Credit for prior year minimum tax (attach Form 8827)	5d			
e	Bond credits from Form 8912	5e			
6	**Total credits.** Add lines 5a through 5e			6	0
7	Subtract line 6 from line 4			7	4,616
8	Personal holding company tax (attach Schedule PH (Form 1120))			8	0
9a	Recapture of investment credit (attach Form 4255)	9a			
b	Recapture of low-income housing credit (attach Form 8611)	9b			
c	Interest due under the look-back method—completed long-term contracts (attach Form 8697)	9c			
d	Interest due under the look-back method—income forecast method (attach Form 8866)	9d			
e	Alternative tax on qualifying shipping activities (attach Form 8902)	9e			
f	Other (see instructions—attach statement)	9f			
10	**Total.** Add lines 9a through 9f			10	0
11	**Total tax.** Add lines 7, 8, and 10. Enter here and on page 1, line 31			11	4,616

Part II–Payments and Refundable Credits

12	2011 overpayment credited to 2012			12	
13	2012 estimated tax payments			13	10,000
14	2012 refund applied for on Form 4466			14	( )
15	Combine lines 12, 13, and 14			15	
16	Tax deposited with Form 7004			16	
17	Withholding (see instructions)			17	
18	**Total payments.** Add lines 15, 16, and 17			18	10,000
19	Refundable credits from:				
a	Form 2439	19a			
b	Form 4136	19b			
c	Form 8827, line 8c	19c			
d	Other (attach statement—see instructions)	19d			
20	**Total credits.** Add lines 19a through 19d			20	0
21	**Total payments and credits.** Add lines 18 and 20. Enter here and on page 1, line 32			21	10,000

Schedule K Other Information (see instructions)

		Yes	No
1	Check accounting method: a ☐ Cash b ☐ Accrual c ☐ Other (specify) ▶		
2	See the instructions and enter the:		
a	Business activity code no. ▶		
b	Business activity ▶		
c	Product or service ▶		
3	Is the corporation a subsidiary in an affiliated group or a parent-subsidiary controlled group? If "Yes," enter name and EIN of the parent corporation ▶		✓
4	At the end of the tax year:		
a	Did any foreign or domestic corporation, partnership (including any entity treated as a partnership), trust, or tax-exempt organization own directly 20% or more, or own, directly or indirectly, 50% or more of the total voting power of all classes of the corporation's stock entitled to vote? If "Yes," complete Part I of Schedule G (Form 1120) (attach Schedule G)		✓
b	Did any individual or estate own directly 20% or more, or own, directly or indirectly, 50% or more of the total voting power of all classes of the corporation's stock entitled to vote? If "Yes," complete Part II of Schedule G (Form 1120) (attach Schedule G)	✓	

Form 1120 (2012) Page **4**

Schedule K Other Information *continued* (see instructions)

		Yes	No
5	At the end of the tax year, did the corporation:		
a	Own directly 20% or more, or own, directly or indirectly, 50% or more of the total voting power of all classes of stock entitled to vote of any foreign or domestic corporation not included on **Form 851,** Affiliations Schedule? For rules of constructive ownership, see instructions. If "Yes," complete (i) through (iv) below.		✓

(i) Name of Corporation	**(ii)** Employer Identification Number (if any)	**(iii)** Country of Incorporation	**(iv)** Percentage Owned in Voting Stock

		Yes	No
b	Own directly an interest of 20% or more, or own, directly or indirectly, an interest of 50% or more in any foreign or domestic partnership (including an entity treated as a partnership) or in the beneficial interest of a trust? For rules of constructive ownership, see instructions. If "Yes," complete (i) through (iv) below.		✓

(i) Name of Entity	**(ii)** Employer Identification Number (if any)	**(iii)** Country of Organization	**(iv)** Maximum Percentage Owned in Profit, Loss, or Capital

		Yes	No
6	During this tax year, did the corporation pay dividends (other than stock dividends and distributions in exchange for stock) in excess of the corporation's current and accumulated earnings and profits? (See sections 301 and 316.)		✓
	If "Yes," file **Form 5452,** Corporate Report of Nondividend Distributions. If this is a consolidated return, answer here for the parent corporation and on Form 851 for each subsidiary.		
7	At any time during the tax year, did one foreign person own, directly or indirectly, at least 25% of **(a)** the total voting power of all classes of the corporation's stock entitled to vote or **(b)** the total value of all classes of the corporation's stock?		✓
	For rules of attribution, see section 318. If "Yes," enter: **(i)** Percentage owned ▶ ________ and **(ii)** Owner's country ▶ ________		
	(c) The corporation may have to file **Form 5472,** Information Return of a 25% Foreign-Owned U.S. Corporation or a Foreign Corporation Engaged in a U.S. Trade or Business. Enter the number of Forms 5472 attached ▶ ________		
8	Check this box if the corporation issued publicly offered debt instruments with original issue discount . . . . ▶ ☐ If checked, the corporation may have to file **Form 8281,** Information Return for Publicly Offered Original Issue Discount Instruments.		
9	Enter the amount of tax-exempt interest received or accrued during the tax year ▶ $ ________		
10	Enter the number of shareholders at the end of the tax year (if 100 or fewer) ▶ ________		
11	If the corporation has an NOL for the tax year and is electing to forego the carryback period, check here . . . . . . ▶ ☐ If the corporation is filing a consolidated return, the statement required by Regulations section 1.1502-21(b)(3) must be attached or the election will not be valid.		
12	Enter the available NOL carryover from prior tax years (do not reduce it by any deduction on line 29a.) ▶ $ ________		
13	Are the corporation's total receipts (line 1c plus lines 4 through 10 on page 1) for the tax year **and** its total assets at the end of the tax year less than $250,000?		✓
	If "Yes," the corporation is not required to complete Schedules L, M-1, and M-2 on page 5. Instead, enter the total amount of cash distributions and the book value of property distributions (other than cash) made during the tax year ▶ $ ________		
14	Is the corporation required to file Schedule UTP (Form 1120), Uncertain Tax Position Statement (see instructions)? . . . . If "Yes," complete and attach Schedule UTP.		✓
15a	Did the corporation make any payments in 2012 that would require it to file Form(s) 1099?	✓	
b	If "Yes," did or will the corporation file required Forms 1099?	✓	
16	During this tax year, did the corporation have an 80% or more change in ownership, including a change due to redemption of its own stock?		✓
17	During or subsequent to this tax year, but before the filing of this return, did the corporation dispose of more than 65% (by value) of its assets in a taxable, non-taxable, or tax deferred transaction?		✓
18	Did the corporation receive assets in a section 351 transfer in which any of the transferred assets had a fair market basis or fair market value of more than $1 million?		✓

Form 1120 (2012) Page 5

Schedule L Balance Sheets per Books

Assets	Beginning of tax year (a)	(b)	End of tax year (c)	(d)
1 Cash		62,000		50,274
2a Trade notes and accounts receivable	37,500		37,500	
b Less allowance for bad debts	(0)	37,500	(0)	37,500
3 Inventories		340,000		340,000
4 U.S. government obligations				
5 Tax-exempt securities (see instructions)				
6 Other current assets (attach statement)				5,384
7 Loans to shareholders				
8 Mortgage and real estate loans				
9 Other investments (attach statement)				
10a Buildings and other depreciable assets	80,000		68,000	
b Less accumulated depreciation	(62,000)	18,000	(59,000)	9,000
11a Depletable assets				
b Less accumulated depletion	( )		( )	
12 Land (net of any amortization)				
13a Intangible assets (amortizable only)				
b Less accumulated amortization	( )		( )	
14 Other assets (attach statement)				
15 Total assets		457,500		442,158
Liabilities and Shareholders' Equity				
16 Accounts payable		20,000		
17 Mortgages, notes, bonds payable in less than 1 year				
18 Other current liabilities (attach statement)				
19 Loans from shareholders				
20 Mortgages, notes, bonds payable in 1 year or more		12,500		12,500
21 Other liabilities (attach statement)				600
22 Capital stock: a Preferred stock				
b Common stock	225,000	225,000	225,000	225,000
23 Additional paid-in capital				
24 Retained earnings—Appropriated (attach statement)				
25 Retained earnings—Unappropriated		200,000		204,058
26 Adjustments to shareholders' equity (attach statement)				
27 Less cost of treasury stock		( )		( )
28 Total liabilities and shareholders' equity		457,500		442,158

Schedule M-1 Reconciliation of Income (Loss) per Books With Income per Return

Note: Schedule M-3 required instead of Schedule M-1 if total assets are $10 million or more—see instructions

1 Net income (loss) per books	29,058	7 Income recorded on books this year not included on this return (itemize): Tax-exempt interest $	0
2 Federal income tax per books	5,216	8 Deductions on this return not charged against book income this year (itemize):	
3 Excess of capital losses over capital gains		a Depreciation . . $ 4,000	
4 Income subject to tax not recorded on books this year (itemize):		b Charitable contributions $	4,000
5 Expenses recorded on books this year not deducted on this return (itemize): a Depreciation $ b Charitable contributions $ c Travel and entertainment $	500	9 Add lines 7 and 8	4,000
6 Add lines 1 through 5	34,774	10 Income (page 1, line 28)—line 6 less line 9	30,774

Schedule M-2 Analysis of Unappropriated Retained Earnings per Books (Line 25, Schedule L)

1 Balance at beginning of year	200,000	5 Distributions: a Cash	25,000
2 Net income (loss) per books	29,058	b Stock	
3 Other increases (itemize):		c Property	
		6 Other decreases (itemize):	
		7 Add lines 5 and 6	25,000
4 Add lines 1, 2, and 3	229,058	8 Balance at end of year (line 4 less line 7)	204,058

Form **1120** (2012)

SCHEDULE D (Form 1120)
Department of the Treasury
Internal Revenue Service

Capital Gains and Losses

▶ Attach to Form 1120, 1120-C, 1120-F, 1120-FSC, 1120-H, 1120-IC-DISC, 1120-L, 1120-ND, 1120-PC, 1120-POL, 1120-REIT, 1120-RIC, 1120-SF, or certain Forms 990-T.
▶ Information about Schedule D (Form 1120) and its separate instructions is at *www.irs.gov/form1120.*

OMB No. 1545-0123
2012

Name	Employer identification number
Bill's Market	79-7979797

Part I Short-Term Capital Gains and Losses—Assets Held One Year or Less

Complete Form 8949 before completing line 1, 2, or 3. This form may be easier to complete if you round off cents to whole dollars.	**(d)** Proceeds (sales price) from Form(s) 8949, Part I, line 2, column (d)	**(e)** Cost or other basis from Form(s) 8949, Part I, line 2, column (e)	**(g)** Adjustments to gain or loss from Form(s) 8949, Part I, line 2, column (g)	**(h) Gain or (loss).** Subtract column (e) from column (d) and combine the result with column (g)
1 Short-term totals from all Forms 8949 with **box A** checked in **Part I.**				
2 Short-term totals from all Forms 8949 with **box B** checked in **Part I.**				
3 Short-term totals from all Forms 8949 with **box C** checked in **Part I.**				

4 Short-term capital gain from installment sales from Form 6252, line 26 or 37	4	
5 Short-term capital gain or (loss) from like-kind exchanges from Form 8824	5	
6 Unused capital loss carryover (attach computation)	6	( )
7 Net short-term capital gain or (loss). Combine lines 1 through 6 in column h.	7	

Part II Long-Term Capital Gains and Losses—Assets Held More Than One Year

Complete Form 8949 before completing line 8, 9, or 10. This form may be easier to complete if you round off cents to whole dollars.	**(d)** Proceeds (sales price) from Form(s) 8949, Part II, line 4, column (d)	**(e)** Cost or other basis from Form(s) 8949, Part II, line 4, column (e)	**(g)** Adjustments to gain or loss from Form(s) 8949, Part II, line 4, column (g)	**(h) Gain or (loss).** Subtract column (e) from column (d) and combine the result with column (g)
8 Long-term totals from all Forms 8949 with **box A** checked in **Part II.**				
9 Long-term totals from all Forms 8949 with **box B** checked in **Part II.**				
10 Long-term totals from all Forms 8949 with **box C** checked in **Part II.**				

11 Enter gain from Form 4797, line 7 or 9	11	5,000
12 Long-term capital gain from installment sales from Form 6252, line 26 or 37	12	
13 Long-term capital gain or (loss) from like-kind exchanges from Form 8824	13	
14 Capital gain distributions (see instructions)	14	
15 Net long-term capital gain or (loss). Combine lines 8 through 14 in column h	15	5,000

Part III Summary of Parts I and II

16 Enter excess of net short-term capital gain (line 7) over net long-term capital loss (line 15)	16	
17 Net capital gain. Enter excess of net long-term capital gain (line 15) over net short-term capital loss (line 7)	17	5,000
18 Add lines 16 and 17. Enter here and on Form 1120, page 1, line 8, or the proper line on other returns	18	5,000

Note. *If losses exceed gains, see* ***Capital losses*** *in the instructions.*

For Paperwork Reduction Act Notice, see the Instructions for Form 1120. Cat. No. 11460M **Schedule D (Form 1120) (2012)**

SCHEDULE G
(Form 1120)
(Rev. December 2011)
Department of the Treasury
Internal Revenue Service

Information on Certain Persons Owning the Corporation's Voting Stock

▶ Attach to Form 1120.
▶ See instructions on page 2.

OMB No. 1545-0123

Name	Employer identification number (EIN)
Bill's Market	79-7979797

Part I **Certain Entities Owning the Corporation's Voting Stock.** (Form 1120, Schedule K, Question 4a). Complete columns (i) through (v) below for any foreign or domestic corporation, partnership (including any entity treated as a partnership), trust, or tax-exempt organization that owns directly 20% or more, or owns, directly or indirectly, 50% or more of the total voting power of all classes of the corporation's stock entitled to vote (see instructions).

(i) Name of Entity	(ii) Employer Identification Number (if any)	(iii) Type of Entity	(iv) Country of Organization	(v) Percentage Owned in Voting Stock

Part II **Certain Individuals and Estates Owning the Corporation's Voting Stock.** (Form 1120, Schedule K, Question 4b). Complete columns (i) through (iv) below for any individual or estate that owns directly 20% or more, or owns, directly or indirectly, 50% or more of the total voting power of all classes of the corporation's stock entitled to vote (see instructions).

(i) Name of Individual or Estate	(ii) Identifying Number (if any)	(iii) Country of Citizenship (see instructions)	(iv) Percentage Owned in Voting Stock
William Spicer	123-45-6789	USA	100
June Spicer	987-65-4321	USA	100

For Paperwork Reduction Act Notice, see the Instructions for Form 1120. Cat. No. 52684S **Schedule G (Form 1120) (Rev. 12-2011)**

Form **1125-A** (Rev. December 2012) Department of the Treasury Internal Revenue Service

Cost of Goods Sold

▶ Attach to Form 1120, 1120-C, 1120-F, 1120S, 1065, or 1065-B.
▶ Information about Form 1125-A and its instructions is at *www.irs.gov/form1125a*.

OMB No. 1545-2225

Name: **Bill's Market**

Employer identification number: 79-7979797

1	Inventory at beginning of year	1	340,000
2	Purchases	2	1,980,000
3	Cost of labor	3	
4	Additional section 263A costs (attach schedule)	4	
5	Other costs (attach schedule)	5	
6	**Total.** Add lines 1 through 5	6	2,320,000
7	Inventory at end of year	7	340,000
8	**Cost of goods sold.** Subtract line 7 from line 6. Enter here and on Form 1120, page 1, line 2 or the appropriate line of your tax return (see instructions)	8	1,980,000

9a Check all methods used for valuing closing inventory:
- *(i)* ☑ Cost
- *(ii)* ☐ Lower of cost or market
- *(iii)* ☐ Other (Specify method used and attach explanation.) ▶

b Check if there was a writedown of subnormal goods ▶ ☐

c Check if the LIFO inventory method was adopted this tax year for any goods (if checked, attach Form 970) ▶ ☐

d If the LIFO inventory method was used for this tax year, enter amount of closing inventory computed under LIFO — 9d

e If property is produced or acquired for resale, do the rules of section 263A apply to the entity (see instructions)? ☐ Yes ☑ No

f Was there any change in determining quantities, cost, or valuations between opening and closing inventory? If "Yes," attach explanation ☐ Yes ☑ No

Section references are to the Internal Revenue Code unless otherwise noted.

General Instructions

Purpose of Form

Use Form 1125-A to calculate and deduct cost of goods sold for certain entities.

Who Must File

Filers of Form 1120, 1120-C, 1120-F, 1120S, 1065, or 1065-B, must complete and attach Form 1125-A if the applicable entity reports a deduction for cost of goods sold.

Inventories

Generally, inventories are required at the beginning and end of each tax year if the production, purchase, or sale of merchandise is an income-producing factor. See Regulations section 1.471-1. If inventories are required, you generally must use an accrual method of accounting for sales and purchases of inventory items.

Exception for certain taxpayers. If you are a qualifying taxpayer or a qualifying small business taxpayer (defined below), you can adopt or change your accounting method to account for inventoriable items in the same manner as materials and supplies that are not incidental.

Under this accounting method, inventory costs for raw materials purchased for use in producing finished goods and merchandise purchased for resale are deductible in the year the finished goods or merchandise are sold (but not before the year you paid for the raw materials or merchandise, if you are also using the cash method).

If you account for inventoriable items in the same manner as materials and supplies that are not incidental, you can currently deduct expenditures for direct labor and all indirect costs that would otherwise be included in inventory costs. See the instructions for lines 2 and 7.

For additional guidance on this method of accounting, see Pub. 538, Accounting Periods and Methods. For guidance on adopting or changing to this method of accounting, see Form 3115, Application for Change in Accounting Method, and its instructions.

Qualifying taxpayer. A qualifying taxpayer is a taxpayer that, (a) for each prior tax year ending after December 16, 1998, has average annual gross receipts of $1 million or less for the 3 prior tax years and (b) its business is not a tax shelter (as defined in section 448(d)(3)). See Rev. Proc. 2001-10, 2001-2 I.R.B. 272.

Qualifying small business taxpayer. A qualifying small business taxpayer is a taxpayer that, (a) for each prior tax year ending on or after December 31, 2000, has average annual gross receipts of $10 million or less for the 3 prior tax years, (b) whose principal business activity is not an ineligible activity, and (c) whose business is not a tax shelter (as defined in section 448 (d)(3)). See Rev. Proc. 2002-28, 2002-18 I.R.B. 815.

Uniform capitalization rules. The uniform capitalization rules of section 263A generally require you to capitalize, or include in inventory, certain costs incurred in connection with the following.

- The production of real property and tangible personal property held in inventory or held for sale in the ordinary course of business.
- Real property or personal property (tangible and intangible) acquired for resale.
- The production of real property and tangible personal property by a corporation for use in its trade or business or in an activity engaged in for profit.

See the discussion on section 263A uniform capitalization rules in the instructions for your tax return before completing Form 1125-A. Also see Regulations sections 1.263A-1 through 1.263A-3. See Regulations section 1.263A-4 for rules for property produced in a farming business.

Form **4562** Department of the Treasury Internal Revenue Service (99)

Depreciation and Amortization (Including Information on Listed Property)

▶ See separate instructions. ▶ Attach to your tax return.

OMB No. 1545-0172 **2012** Attachment Sequence No. 179

Name(s) shown on return	Business or activity to which this form relates	Identifying number
Bill's Market	Retail Food Sales	79-7979797

Part I Election To Expense Certain Property Under Section 179

Note: *If you have any listed property, complete Part V before you complete Part I.*

1	Maximum amount (see instructions)	1	500,000
2	Total cost of section 179 property placed in service (see instructions)	2	5,000
3	Threshold cost of section 179 property before reduction in limitation (see instructions)	3	2,000,000
4	Reduction in limitation. Subtract line 3 from line 2. If zero or less, enter -0-	4	0
5	Dollar limitation for tax year. Subtract line 4 from line 1. If zero or less, enter -0-. If married filing separately, see instructions	5	500,000

6 (a) Description of property	(b) Cost (business use only)	(c) Elected cost
Display Case	5,000	5,000
7 Listed property. Enter the amount from line 29	7	

8	Total elected cost of section 179 property. Add amounts in column (c), lines 6 and 7	8	5,000
9	Tentative deduction. Enter the **smaller** of line 5 or line 8	9	5,000
10	Carryover of disallowed deduction from line 13 of your 2011 Form 4562	10	0
11	Business income limitation. Enter the smaller of business income (not less than zero) or line 5 (see instructions)	11	30,674
12	Section 179 expense deduction. Add lines 9 and 10, but do not enter more than line 11	12	5,000
13	Carryover of disallowed deduction to 2013. Add lines 9 and 10, less line 12 ▶	13	

Note: *Do not use Part II or Part III below for listed property. Instead, use Part V.*

Part II Special Depreciation Allowance and Other Depreciation (Do not include listed property.) (See instructions.)

14	Special depreciation allowance for qualified property (other than listed property) placed in service during the tax year (see instructions)	14	
15	Property subject to section 168(f)(1) election	15	
16	Other depreciation (including ACRS)	16	

Part III MACRS Depreciation (Do not include listed property.) (See instructions.)

Section A

17	MACRS deductions for assets placed in service in tax years beginning before 2012	17	3,000
18	If you are electing to group any assets placed in service during the tax year into one or more general asset accounts, check here ▶ ☐		

Section B—Assets Placed in Service During 2012 Tax Year Using the General Depreciation System

(a) Classification of property	(b) Month and year placed in service	(c) Basis for depreciation (business/investment use only—see instructions)	(d) Recovery period	(e) Convention	(f) Method	(g) Depreciation deduction
19a 3-year property						
b 5-year property						
c 7-year property						
d 10-year property						
e 15-year property						
f 20-year property						
g 25-year property			25 yrs.		S/L	
h Residential rental property			27.5 yrs.	MM	S/L	
			27.5 yrs.	MM	S/L	
i Nonresidential real property			39 yrs.	MM	S/L	
				MM	S/L	

Section C—Assets Placed in Service During 2012 Tax Year Using the Alternative Depreciation System

(a) Classification of property	(b)	(c)	(d)	(e)	(f)	(g)
20a Class life					S/L	
b 12-year			12 yrs.		S/L	
c 40-year			40 yrs.	MM	S/L	

Part IV Summary (See instructions.)

21	Listed property. Enter amount from line 28	21	
22	**Total.** Add amounts from line 12, lines 14 through 17, lines 19 and 20 in column (g), and line 21. Enter here and on the appropriate lines of your return. Partnerships and S corporations—see instructions	22	8,000
23	For assets shown above and placed in service during the current year, enter the portion of the basis attributable to section 263A costs	23	

For Paperwork Reduction Act Notice, see separate instructions. Cat. No. 12906N Form **4562** (2012)

Form **4797**

Department of the Treasury
Internal Revenue Service

Sales of Business Property

(Also Involuntary Conversions and Recapture Amounts Under Sections 179 and 280F(b)(2))

► Attach to your tax return.

► Information about Form 4797 and its separate instructions is at *www.irs.gov/form4797.*

OMB No. 1545-0184

2012

Attachment Sequence No. 27

Name(s) shown on return	Identifying number
Bill's Market	79-7979797

1	Enter the gross proceeds from sales or exchanges reported to you for 2012 on Form(s) 1099-B or 1099-S (or substitute statement) that you are including on line 2, 10, or 20 (see instructions)	1	13,000

Part I **Sales or Exchanges of Property Used in a Trade or Business and Involuntary Conversions From Other Than Casualty or Theft—Most Property Held More Than 1 Year** (see instructions)

2 (a) Description of property	(b) Date acquired (mo., day, yr.)	(c) Date sold (mo., day, yr.)	(d) Gross sales price	(e) Depreciation allowed or allowable since acquisition	(f) Cost or other basis, plus improvements and expense of sale	(g) Gain or (loss) Subtract (f) from the sum of (d) and (e)
Display Case	6-6-08	12-12-12	1,000	8,000	12,000	(3,000)

3	Gain, if any, from Form 4684, line 39	3	
4	Section 1231 gain from installment sales from Form 6252, line 26 or 37	4	
5	Section 1231 gain or (loss) from like-kind exchanges from Form 8824	5	
6	Gain, if any, from line 32, from other than casualty or theft	6	8,000
7	Combine lines 2 through 6. Enter the gain or (loss) here and on the appropriate line as follows:	7	5,000
	Partnerships (except electing large partnerships) and S corporations. Report the gain or (loss) following the instructions for Form 1065, Schedule K, line 10, or Form 1120S, Schedule K, line 9. Skip lines 8, 9, 11, and 12 below.		
	Individuals, partners, S corporation shareholders, and all others. If line 7 is zero or a loss, enter the amount from line 7 on line 11 below and skip lines 8 and 9. If line 7 is a gain and you did not have any prior year section 1231 losses, or they were recaptured in an earlier year, enter the gain from line 7 as a long-term capital gain on the Schedule D filed with your return and skip lines 8, 9, 11, and 12 below.		
8	Nonrecaptured net section 1231 losses from prior years (see instructions)	8	0
9	Subtract line 8 from line 7. If zero or less, enter -0-. If line 9 is zero, enter the gain from line 7 on line 12 below. If line 9 is more than zero, enter the amount from line 8 on line 12 below and enter the gain from line 9 as a long-term capital gain on the Schedule D filed with your return (see instructions)	9	5,000

Part II **Ordinary Gains and Losses** (see instructions)

10 Ordinary gains and losses not included on lines 11 through 16 (include property held 1 year or less):

11	Loss, if any, from line 7	11	( )
12	Gain, if any, from line 7 or amount from line 8, if applicable	12	
13	Gain, if any, from line 31	13	2,000
14	Net gain or (loss) from Form 4684, lines 31 and 38a	14	
15	Ordinary gain from installment sales from Form 6252, line 25 or 36	15	
16	Ordinary gain or (loss) from like-kind exchanges from Form 8824	16	
17	Combine lines 10 through 16	17	2,000
18	For all except individual returns, enter the amount from line 17 on the appropriate line of your return and skip lines a and b below. For individual returns, complete lines a and b below:		
a	If the loss on line 11 includes a loss from Form 4684, line 35, column (b)(ii), enter that part of the loss here. Enter the part of the loss from income-producing property on Schedule A (Form 1040), line 28, and the part of the loss from property used as an employee on Schedule A (Form 1040), line 23. Identify as from "Form 4797, line 18a." See instructions	18a	
b	Redetermine the gain or (loss) on line 17 excluding the loss, if any, on line 18a. Enter here and on Form 1040, line 14	18b	

Part III Gain From Disposition of Property Under Sections 1245, 1250, 1252, 1254, and 1255 (see instructions)

19 (a) Description of section 1245, 1250, 1252, 1254, or 1255 property:	(b) Date acquired (mo., day, yr.)	(c) Date sold (mo., day, yr.)
A Equipment	3-5-10	8-15-12
B		
C		
D		

These columns relate to the properties on lines 19A through 19D. ▶		Property A	Property B	Property C	Property D
20 Gross sales price (**Note:** *See line 1 before completing.*)	20	13,000			
21 Cost or other basis plus expense of sale	21	5,000			
22 Depreciation (or depletion) allowed or allowable	22	2,000			
23 Adjusted basis. Subtract line 22 from line 21	23	3,000			
24 Total gain. Subtract line 23 from line 20	24	10,000			
25 **If section 1245 property:**					
a Depreciation allowed or allowable from line 22	25a	2,000			
b Enter the **smaller** of line 24 or 25a	25b	2,000			
26 **If section 1250 property:** If straight line depreciation was used, enter -0- on line 26g, except for a corporation subject to section 291.					
a Additional depreciation after 1975 (see instructions)	26a				
b Applicable percentage multiplied by the **smaller** of line 24 or line 26a (see instructions)	26b				
c Subtract line 26a from line 24. If residential rental property **or** line 24 is not more than line 26a, skip lines 26d and 26e	26c				
d Additional depreciation after 1969 and before 1976	26d				
e Enter the **smaller** of line 26c or 26d	26e				
f Section 291 amount (corporations only)	26f				
g Add lines 26b, 26e, and 26f	26g				
27 **If section 1252 property:** Skip this section if you did not dispose of farmland or if this form is being completed for a partnership (other than an electing large partnership).					
a Soil, water, and land clearing expenses	27a				
b Line 27a multiplied by applicable percentage (see instructions)	27b				
c Enter the **smaller** of line 24 or 27b	27c				
28 **If section 1254 property:**					
a Intangible drilling and development costs, expenditures for development of mines and other natural deposits, mining exploration costs, and depletion (see instructions)	28a				
b Enter the **smaller** of line 24 or 28a	28b				
29 **If section 1255 property:**					
a Applicable percentage of payments excluded from income under section 126 (see instructions)	29a				
b Enter the **smaller** of line 24 or 29a (see instructions)	29b				

Summary of Part III Gains. Complete property columns A through D through line 29b before going to line 30.

30 Total gains for all properties. Add property columns A through D, line 24	30	10,000
31 Add property columns A through D, lines 25b, 26g, 27c, 28b, and 29b. Enter here and on line 13	31	2,000
32 Subtract line 31 from line 30. Enter the portion from casualty or theft on Form 4684, line 33. Enter the portion from other than casualty or theft on Form 4797, line 6	32	8,000

Part IV Recapture Amounts Under Sections 179 and 280F(b)(2) When Business Use Drops to 50% or Less (see instructions)

		(a) Section 179	(b) Section 280F(b)(2)
33 Section 179 expense deduction or depreciation allowable in prior years	33		
34 Recomputed depreciation (see instructions)	34		
35 Recapture amount. Subtract line 34 from line 33. See the instructions for where to report	35		

SAMPLE RETURN 2 (SR2)

Form **1065** Department of the Treasury Internal Revenue Service

U.S. Return of Partnership Income

For calendar year 2012, or tax year beginning ________, 2012, ending ________, 20____.
▶ Information about Form 1065 and its separate instructions is at *www.irs.gov/form1065.*

OMB No. 1545-0099

2012

A Principal business activity Retail Food Sales	Print or type.	Name of partnership Bill's Market	D Employer identification number 79-7979797
B Principal product or service Gourmet Foods		Number, street, and room or suite no. If a P.O. box, see the instructions. 387 Spring Street	E Date business started 7/15/03
C Business code number 445290		City or town, state, and ZIP code Raleigh, NC 29288	F Total assets (see the instructions) $ 477,500

G Check applicable boxes: (1) ☐ Initial return (2) ☐ Final return (3) ☐ Name change (4) ☐ Address change (5) ☐ Amended return
(6) ☐ Technical termination - also check (1) or (2)

H Check accounting method: (1) ☐ Cash (2) ☑ Accrual (3) ☐ Other (specify) ▶

I Number of Schedules K-1. Attach one for each person who was a partner at any time during the tax year ▶ 2

J Check if Schedules C and M-3 are attached ☐

Caution. *Include **only** trade or business income and expenses on lines 1a through 22 below. See the instructions for more information.*

Income	1a	Gross receipts or sales	1a	2,700,000		
	b	Returns and allowances	1b	0		
	c	Balance. Subtract line 1b from line 1a			1c	2,700,000
	2	Cost of goods sold (attach Form 1125-A)			2	1,980,000
	3	Gross profit. Subtract line 2 from line 1c			3	720,000
	4	Ordinary income (loss) from other partnerships, estates, and trusts (attach statement)			4	
	5	Net farm profit (loss) (attach Schedule F (Form 1040))			5	
	6	Net gain (loss) from Form 4797, Part II, line 17 (attach Form 4797)			6	2,000
	7	Other income (loss) (attach statement)			7	
	8	**Total income (loss).** Combine lines 3 through 7			8	722,000
Deductions (see the instructions for limitations)	9	Salaries and wages (other than to partners) (less employment credits)			9	210,000
	10	Guaranteed payments to partners			10	203,000
	11	Repairs and maintenance			11	12,000
	12	Bad debts			12	
	13	Rent			13	120,000
	14	Taxes and licenses			14	22,000
	15	Interest			15	
	16a	Depreciation (if required, attach Form 4562)	16a	3,000		
	b	Less depreciation reported on Form 1125-A and elsewhere on return	16b		16c	3,000
	17	Depletion **(Do not deduct oil and gas depletion.)**			17	
	18	Retirement plans, etc.			18	
	19	Employee benefit programs			19	12,000
	20	Other deductions (attach statement)			20	97,500
	21	**Total deductions.** Add the amounts shown in the far right column for lines 9 through 20			21	679,500
	22	**Ordinary business income (loss).** Subtract line 21 from line 8			22	42,500

Sign Here

Under penalties of perjury, I declare that I have examined this return, including accompanying schedules and statements, and to the best of my knowledge and belief, it is true, correct, and complete. Declaration of preparer (other than general partner or limited liability company member manager) is based on all information of which preparer has any knowledge.

▶ Signature of general partner or limited liability company member manager ▶ Date

May the IRS discuss this return with the preparer shown below (see instructions)? ☐ Yes ☐ No

Paid Preparer Use Only

Print/Type preparer's name	Preparer's signature	Date	Check ☐ if self- employed	PTIN
Firm's name ▶			Firm's EIN ▶	
Firm's address ▶			Phone no.	

For Paperwork Reduction Act Notice, see separate instructions. Cat. No. 11390Z Form **1065** (2012)

Form 1065 (2012) Page 2

Schedule B Other Information

		Yes	No
1	What type of entity is filing this return? Check the applicable box: a ☑ Domestic general partnership b ☐ Domestic limited partnership c ☐ Domestic limited liability company d ☐ Domestic limited liability partnership e ☐ Foreign partnership f ☐ Other ▶		
2	At any time during the tax year, was any partner in the partnership a disregarded entity, a partnership (including an entity treated as a partnership), a trust, an S corporation, an estate (other than an estate of a deceased partner), or a nominee or similar person?		✓
3	At the end of the tax year:		
a	Did any foreign or domestic corporation, partnership (including any entity treated as a partnership), trust, or tax-exempt organization, or any foreign government own, directly or indirectly, an interest of 50% or more in the profit, loss, or capital of the partnership? For rules of constructive ownership, see instructions. If "Yes," attach Schedule B-1, Information on Partners Owning 50% or More of the Partnership		✓
b	Did any individual or estate own, directly or indirectly, an interest of 50% or more in the profit, loss, or capital of the partnership? For rules of constructive ownership, see instructions. If "Yes," attach Schedule B-1, Information on Partners Owning 50% or More of the Partnership	✓	
4	At the end of the tax year, did the partnership:		
a	Own directly 20% or more, or own, directly or indirectly, 50% or more of the total voting power of all classes of stock entitled to vote of any foreign or domestic corporation? For rules of constructive ownership, see instructions. If "Yes," complete (i) through (iv) below		✓

(i) Name of Corporation	(ii) Employer Identification Number (if any)	(iii) Country of Incorporation	(iv) Percentage Owned in Voting Stock

		Yes	No
b	Own directly an interest of 20% or more, or own, directly or indirectly, an interest of 50% or more in the profit, loss, or capital in any foreign or domestic partnership (including an entity treated as a partnership) or in the beneficial interest of a trust? For rules of constructive ownership, see instructions. If "Yes," complete (i) through (v) below		✓

(i) Name of Entity	(ii) Employer Identification Number (if any)	(iii) Type of Entity	(iv) Country of Organization	(v) Maximum Percentage Owned in Profit, Loss, or Capital

		Yes	No
5	Did the partnership file Form 8893, Election of Partnership Level Tax Treatment, or an election statement under section 6231(a)(1)(B)(ii) for partnership-level tax treatment, that is in effect for this tax year? See Form 8893 for more details		✓
6	Does the partnership satisfy **all four** of the following conditions?		
a	The partnership's total receipts for the tax year were less than $250,000.		
b	The partnership's total assets at the end of the tax year were less than $1 million.		
c	Schedules K-1 are filed with the return and furnished to the partners on or before the due date (including extensions) for the partnership return.		
d	The partnership is not filing and is not required to file Schedule M-3		✓
	If "Yes," the partnership is not required to complete Schedules L, M-1, and M-2; Item F on page 1 of Form 1065; or Item L on Schedule K-1.		
7	Is this partnership a publicly traded partnership as defined in section 469(k)(2)?		✓
8	During the tax year, did the partnership have any debt that was cancelled, was forgiven, or had the terms modified so as to reduce the principal amount of the debt?		✓
9	Has this partnership filed, or is it required to file, Form 8918, Material Advisor Disclosure Statement, to provide information on any reportable transaction?		✓
10	At any time during calendar year 2012, did the partnership have an interest in or a signature or other authority over a financial account in a foreign country (such as a bank account, securities account, or other financial account)? See the instructions for exceptions and filing requirements for Form TD F 90-22.1, Report of Foreign Bank and Financial Accounts. If "Yes," enter the name of the foreign country. ▶		✓

Form **1065** (2012)

Form 1065 (2012) Page **3**

Schedule B Other Information *(continued)*

		Yes	No
11	At any time during the tax year, did the partnership receive a distribution from, or was it the grantor of, or transferor to, a foreign trust? If "Yes," the partnership may have to file Form 3520, Annual Return To Report Transactions With Foreign Trusts and Receipt of Certain Foreign Gifts. See instructions		✓
12a	Is the partnership making, or had it previously made (and not revoked), a section 754 election? See instructions for details regarding a section 754 election.		
b	Did the partnership make for this tax year an optional basis adjustment under section 743(b) or 734(b)? If "Yes," attach a statement showing the computation and allocation of the basis adjustment. See instructions		✓
c	Is the partnership required to adjust the basis of partnership assets under section 743(b) or 734(b) because of a substantial built-in loss (as defined under section 743(d)) or substantial basis reduction (as defined under section 734(d))? If "Yes," attach a statement showing the computation and allocation of the basis adjustment. See instructions.		✓
13	Check this box if, during the current or prior tax year, the partnership distributed any property received in a like-kind exchange or contributed such property to another entity (other than disregarded entities wholly-owned by the partnership throughout the tax year) ▶ ☐		
14	At any time during the tax year, did the partnership distribute to any partner a tenancy-in-common or other undivided interest in partnership property?		✓
15	If the partnership is required to file Form 8858, Information Return of U.S. Persons With Respect To Foreign Disregarded Entities, enter the number of Forms 8858 attached. See instructions ▶		
16	Does the partnership have any foreign partners? If "Yes," enter the number of Forms 8805, Foreign Partner's Information Statement of Section 1446 Withholding Tax, filed for this partnership. ▶		✓
17	Enter the number of Forms 8865, Return of U.S. Persons With Respect to Certain Foreign Partnerships, attached to this return. ▶		
18a	Did you make any payments in 2012 that would require you to file Form(s) 1099? See instructions	✓	
b	If "Yes," did you or will you file required Form(s) 1099?	✓	
19	Enter the number of Form(s) 5471, Information Return of U.S. Persons With Respect To Certain Foreign Corporations, attached to this return. ▶		
20	Enter the number of partners that are foreign governments under section 892. ▶		

Designation of Tax Matters Partner (see instructions)

Enter below the general partner or member-manager designated as the tax matters partner (TMP) for the tax year of this return:

Name of designated TMP ▶		Identifying number of TMP ▶	
If the TMP is an entity, name of TMP representative ▶		Phone number of TMP ▶	
Address of designated TMP ▶			

Form **1065** (2012)

Form 1065 (2012) Page 4

Schedule K		Partners' Distributive Share Items		Total amount
Income (Loss)	1	Ordinary business income (loss) (page 1, line 22)	1	42,500
	2	Net rental real estate income (loss) (attach Form 8825)	2	
	3a	Other gross rental income (loss) 3a		
	b	Expenses from other rental activities (attach statement) 3b		
	c	Other net rental income (loss). Subtract line 3b from line 3a	3c	
	4	Guaranteed payments	4	203,000
	5	Interest income	5	
	6	Dividends: a Ordinary dividends	6a	
		b Qualified dividends 6b		
	7	Royalties	7	
	8	Net short-term capital gain (loss) (attach Schedule D (Form 1065))	8	
	9a	Net long-term capital gain (loss) (attach Schedule D (Form 1065))	9a	
	b	Collectibles (28%) gain (loss) 9b		
	c	Unrecaptured section 1250 gain (attach statement) 9c		
	10	Net section 1231 gain (loss) (attach Form 4797)	10	5,000
	11	Other income (loss) (see instructions) Type ▶	11	
Deductions	12	Section 179 deduction (attach Form 4562)	12	5,000
	13a	Contributions	13a	2,000
	b	Investment interest expense	13b	
	c	Section 59(e)(2) expenditures: (1) Type ▶ (2) Amount ▶	13c(2)	
	d	Other deductions (see instructions) Type ▶	13d	
Self-Employment	14a	Net earnings (loss) from self-employment	14a	243,500
	b	Gross farming or fishing income	14b	
	c	Gross nonfarm income	14c	
Credits	15a	Low-income housing credit (section 42(j)(5))	15a	
	b	Low-income housing credit (other)	15b	
	c	Qualified rehabilitation expenditures (rental real estate) (attach Form 3468)	15c	
	d	Other rental real estate credits (see instructions) Type ▶	15d	
	e	Other rental credits (see instructions) Type ▶	15e	
	f	Other credits (see instructions) Type ▶	15f	
Foreign Transactions	16a	Name of country or U.S. possession ▶		
	b	Gross income from all sources	16b	
	c	Gross income sourced at partner level	16c	
		Foreign gross income sourced at partnership level		
	d	Passive category ▶ e General category ▶ f Other ▶	16f	
		Deductions allocated and apportioned at partner level		
	g	Interest expense ▶ h Other ▶	16h	
		Deductions allocated and apportioned at partnership level to foreign source income		
	i	Passive category ▶ j General category ▶ k Other ▶	16k	
	l	Total foreign taxes (check one): ▶ Paid ☐ Accrued ☐	16l	
	m	Reduction in taxes available for credit (attach statement)	16m	
	n	Other foreign tax information (attach statement)		
Alternative Minimum Tax (AMT) Items	17a	Post-1986 depreciation adjustment	17a	
	b	Adjusted gain or loss	17b	
	c	Depletion (other than oil and gas)	17c	
	d	Oil, gas, and geothermal properties—gross income	17d	
	e	Oil, gas, and geothermal properties—deductions	17e	
	f	Other AMT items (attach statement)	17f	
Other Information	18a	Tax-exempt interest income	18a	
	b	Other tax-exempt income	18b	
	c	Nondeductible expenses	18c	500
	19a	Distributions of cash and marketable securities	19a	203,000
	b	Distributions of other property	19b	
	20a	Investment income	20a	
	b	Investment expenses	20b	
	c	Other items and amounts (attach statement)		

Form 1065 (2012) Page **5**

Analysis of Net Income (Loss)

1	Net income (loss). Combine Schedule K, lines 1 through 11. From the result, subtract the sum of Schedule K, lines 12 through 13d, and 16l	1	243,500

2 Analysis by partner type:	(i) Corporate	(ii) Individual (active)	(iii) Individual (passive)	(iv) Partnership	(v) Exempt organization	(vi) Nominee/Other
a General partners		243,500				
b Limited partners						

Schedule L Balance Sheets per Books

Assets	Beginning of tax year (a)	(b)	End of tax year (c)	(d)
1 Cash		62,000		95,000
2a Trade notes and accounts receivable	37,500		37,500	
b Less allowance for bad debts	0	37,500	0	37,500
3 Inventories		340,000		340,000
4 U.S. government obligations				
5 Tax-exempt securities				
6 Other current assets (attach statement)				
7a Loans to partners (or persons related to partners)				
b Mortgage and real estate loans				
8 Other investments (attach statement)				
9a Buildings and other depreciable assets	80,000		68,000	
b Less accumulated depreciation	62,000	18,000	63,000	5,000
10a Depletable assets				
b Less accumulated depletion				
11 Land (net of any amortization)				
12a Intangible assets (amortizable only)				
b Less accumulated amortization				
13 Other assets (attach statement)		457,500		477,500
14 Total assets				
Liabilities and Capital				
15 Accounts payable		20,000		
16 Mortgages, notes, bonds payable in less than 1 year				
17 Other current liabilities (attach statement)				
18 All nonrecourse loans				
19a Loans from partners (or persons related to partners)				
b Mortgages, notes, bonds payable in 1 year or more		12,500		12,500
20 Other liabilities (attach statement)				
21 Partners' capital accounts		425,000		465,000
22 Total liabilities and capital		457,500		477,500

Schedule M-1 Reconciliation of Income (Loss) per Books With Income (Loss) per Return

Note. Schedule M-3 may be required instead of Schedule M-1 (see instructions).

1	Net income (loss) per books	243,000	6	Income recorded on books this year not included on Schedule K, lines 1 through 11 (itemize): a Tax-exempt interest $	
2	Income included on Schedule K, lines 1, 2, 3c, 5, 6a, 7, 8, 9a, 10, and 11, not recorded on books this year (itemize):				
3	Guaranteed payments (other than health insurance)		7	Deductions included on Schedule K, lines 1 through 13d, and 16l, not charged against book income this year (itemize): a Depreciation $	
4	Expenses recorded on books this year not included on Schedule K, lines 1 through 13d, and 16l (itemize): a Depreciation $ b Travel and entertainment $ 500	500	8	Add lines 6 and 7	
5	Add lines 1 through 4	243,500	9	Income (loss) (Analysis of Net Income (Loss), line 1). Subtract line 8 from line 5	243,500

Schedule M-2 Analysis of Partners' Capital Accounts

1	Balance at beginning of year	425,000	6	Distributions: a Cash	203,000
2	Capital contributed: a Cash			b Property	
	b Property		7	Other decreases (itemize):	
3	Net income (loss) per books	243,000			
4	Other increases (itemize):		8	Add lines 6 and 7	203,000
5	Add lines 1 through 4	668,000	9	Balance at end of year. Subtract line 8 from line 5	465,000

Form **1065** (2012)

SCHEDULE B-1 (Form 1065)
(Rev. December 2011)
Department of the Treasury
Internal Revenue Service

Information on Partners Owning 50% or More of the Partnership

▶ Attach to Form 1065. See instructions on back.

OMB No. 1545-0099

Name of partnership	Employer identification number (EIN)
Bill's Market	79-7979797

Part I Entities Owning 50% or More of the Partnership (Form 1065, Schedule B, Question 3a)

Complete columns (i) through (v) below for any foreign or domestic corporation, partnership (including any entity treated as a partnership), trust, tax-exempt organization, or any foreign government that owns, directly or indirectly, an interest of 50% or more in the profit, loss, or capital of the partnership (see instructions).

(i) Name of Entity	(ii) Employer Identification Number (if any)	(iii) Type of Entity	(iv) Country of Organization	(v) Maximum Percentage Owned in Profit, Loss, or Capital

Part II Individuals or Estates Owning 50% or More of the Partnership (Form 1065, Schedule B, Question 3b)

Complete columns (i) through (iv) below for any individual or estate that owns, directly or indirectly, an interest of 50% or more in the profit, loss, or capital of the partnership (see instructions).

(i) Name of Individual or Estate	(ii) Identifying Number (if any)	(iii) Country of Citizenship (see instructions)	(iv) Maximum Percentage Owned in Profit, Loss, or Capital
William Spicer	123-45-6789	USA	100
June Spicer	987-65-4321	USA	100

651112

☐ Final K-1 ☐ Amended K-1 OMB No. 1545-0099

Schedule K-1 (Form 1065) **2012**

Department of the Treasury
Internal Revenue Service

For calendar year 2012, or tax year beginning ________, 2012 ending ________, 20____

Partner's Share of Income, Deductions, Credits, etc.

► See back of form and separate instructions.

Part I Information About the Partnership

A Partnership's employer identification number
79-7979797

B Partnership's name, address, city, state, and ZIP code
Bill's Market
387 Spring Street
Raleigh, NC 29288

C IRS Center where partnership filed return
Cincinnati, OH

D ☐ Check if this is a publicly traded partnership (PTP)

Part II Information About the Partner

E Partner's identifying number
123-45-6789

F Partner's name, address, city, state, and ZIP code
William Spicer
2345 Carolina Street
Durham, NC 29212

G ☒ General partner or LLC member-manager ☐ Limited partner or other LLC member

H ☒ Domestic partner ☐ Foreign partner

I1 What type of entity is this partner? (see instructions) Individual

I2 If this partner is a retirement plan (IRA/SEP/Keogh/etc.), check here (see instructions) ☐

J Partner's share of profit, loss, and capital (see instructions):

	Beginning	Ending
Profit	80 %	80 %
Loss	80 %	80 %
Capital	80 %	80 %

K Partner's share of liabilities at year end:

Nonrecourse	$
Qualified nonrecourse financing	$
Recourse	$ 10,000

L Partner's capital account analysis:

Beginning capital account	$ 340,000
Capital contributed during the year	$
Current year increase (decrease)	$ 235,000
Withdrawals & distributions	$ (203,000)
Ending capital account	$ 372,000

☒ Tax basis ☐ GAAP ☐ Section 704(b) book
☐ Other (explain)

M Did the partner contribute property with a built-in gain or loss?
☐ Yes ☒ No
If "Yes," attach statement (see instructions)

Part III Partner's Share of Current Year Income, Deductions, Credits, and Other Items

1	Ordinary business income (loss)	34,000
2	Net rental real estate income (loss)	
3	Other net rental income (loss)	
4	Guaranteed payments	203,000
5	Interest income	
6a	Ordinary dividends	
6b	Qualified dividends	
7	Royalties	
8	Net short-term capital gain (loss)	
9a	Net long-term capital gain (loss)	
9b	Collectibles (28%) gain (loss)	
9c	Unrecaptured section 1250 gain	
10	Net section 1231 gain (loss)	4,000
11	Other income (loss)	
12	Section 179 deduction	4,000
13	Other deductions	
a		1,600
14	Self-employment earnings (loss)	
a		235,400
15	Credits	
16	Foreign transactions	
17	Alternative minimum tax (AMT) items	
18	Tax-exempt income and nondeductible expenses	
c		400
19	Distributions	
a		203,000
20	Other information	

*See attached statement for additional information.

For IRS Use Only

651112

☐ Final K-1 ☐ Amended K-1 OMB No. 1545-0099

Schedule K-1 (Form 1065) **2012**

Department of the Treasury
Internal Revenue Service

For calendar year 2012, or tax year beginning ________, 2012 ending ________, 20____

Partner's Share of Income, Deductions, Credits, etc.

▶ See back of form and separate instructions.

Part I Information About the Partnership

A Partnership's employer identification number
79-7979797

B Partnership's name, address, city, state, and ZIP code
Bill's Market
387 Spring Street
Raleigh, NC 29288

C IRS Center where partnership filed return
Cincinnati, OH

D ☐ Check if this is a publicly traded partnership (PTP)

Part II Information About the Partner

E Partner's identifying number
987-65-4321

F Partner's name, address, city, state, and ZIP code
June Spicer
2345 Carolina Street
Durham, NC 29212

G ☒ General partner or LLC member-manager ☐ Limited partner or other LLC member

H ☒ Domestic partner ☐ Foreign partner

I1 What type of entity is this partner? (see instructions) Individual

I2 If this partner is a retirement plan (IRA/SEP/Keogh/etc.), check here (see instructions) ☐

J Partner's share of profit, loss, and capital (see instructions):

	Beginning	Ending
Profit	20 %	20 %
Loss	20 %	20 %
Capital	20 %	20 %

K Partner's share of liabilities at year end:

Nonrecourse	$
Qualified nonrecourse financing	$
Recourse	$ 2,500

L Partner's capital account analysis:

Beginning capital account	$ 85,000
Capital contributed during the year	$
Current year increase (decrease)	$ 8,000
Withdrawals & distributions	$ ( )
Ending capital account	$ 93,000

☒ Tax basis ☐ GAAP ☐ Section 704(b) book
☐ Other (explain)

M Did the partner contribute property with a built-in gain or loss?
☐ **Yes** ☒ **No**
If "Yes," attach statement (see instructions)

Part III Partner's Share of Current Year Income, Deductions, Credits, and Other Items

1	Ordinary business income (loss)	8,500
2	Net rental real estate income (loss)	
3	Other net rental income (loss)	
4	Guaranteed payments	
5	Interest income	
6a	Ordinary dividends	
6b	Qualified dividends	
7	Royalties	
8	Net short-term capital gain (loss)	
9a	Net long-term capital gain (loss)	
9b	Collectibles (28%) gain (loss)	
9c	Unrecaptured section 1250 gain	
10	Net section 1231 gain (loss)	1,000
11	Other income (loss)	
12	Section 179 deduction	1,000
13	Other deductions	a 400
14	Self-employment earnings (loss)	a 8,100
15	Credits	
16	Foreign transactions	
17	Alternative minimum tax (AMT) items	
18	Tax-exempt income and nondeductible expenses	c 100
19	Distributions	
20	Other information	

*See attached statement for additional information.

For IRS Use Only

For Paperwork Reduction Act Notice, see Instructions for Form 1065. IRS.gov/form1065 Cat. No. 11394R **Schedule K-1 (Form 1065) 2012**

SAMPLE RETURN 3 (SR3)

Form **1120S**

Department of the Treasury
Internal Revenue Service

U.S. Income Tax Return for an S Corporation

▶ Do not file this form unless the corporation has filed or is attaching Form 2553 to elect to be an S corporation.
▶ Information about Form 1120S and its separate instructions is at *www.irs.gov/form1120s.*

OMB No. 1545-0130

2012

For calendar year 2012 or tax year beginning , 2012, ending , 20

A S election effective date: 7-15-03	Name: Bill's Market	**D** Employer identification number: 79-7979797
B Business activity code number (see instructions): 445290	TYPE OR PRINT — Number, street, and room or suite no. If a P.O. box, see instructions.: 387 Spring Street	**E** Date incorporated: 7-15-03
C Check if Sch. M-3 attached ☐	City or town, state, and ZIP code: Raleigh, NC 29288	**F** Total assets (see instructions): $ 446,730

G Is the corporation electing to be an S corporation beginning with this tax year? ☐ Yes ☐ No If "Yes," attach Form 2553 if not already filed

H Check if: **(1)** ☐ Final return **(2)** ☐ Name change **(3)** ☐ Address change **(4)** ☐ Amended return **(5)** ☐ S election termination or revocation

I Enter the number of shareholders who were shareholders during any part of the tax year ▶ 2

Caution. Include **only** trade or business income and expenses on lines 1a through 21. See the instructions for more information.

Income	1a	Gross receipts or sales	1a	2,700,000		
	b	Returns and allowances	1b	0		
	c	Balance. Subtract line 1b from line 1a			1c	2,700,000
	2	Cost of goods sold (attach Form 1125-A)			2	1,980,000
	3	Gross profit. Subtract line 2 from line 1c			3	720,000
	4	Net gain (loss) from Form 4797, line 17 (attach Form 4797)			4	2,000
	5	Other income (loss) (see instructions—attach statement)			5	
	6	**Total income (loss).** Add lines 3 through 5 ▶			6	722,000
Deductions (see instructions for limitations)	7	Compensation of officers			7	203,000
	8	Salaries and wages (less employment credits)			8	210,000
	9	Repairs and maintenance			9	12,000
	10	Bad debts			10	
	11	Rents			11	120,000
	12	Taxes and licenses			12	31,770
	13	Interest			13	1,000
	14	Depreciation not claimed on Form 1125-A or elsewhere on return (attach Form 4562)			14	3,000
	15	Depletion **(Do not deduct oil and gas depletion.)**			15	
	16	Advertising			16	40,000
	17	Pension, profit-sharing, etc., plans			17	
	18	Employee benefit programs			18	12,000
	19	Other deductions (attach statement)			19	56,500
	20	**Total deductions.** Add lines 7 through 19 ▶			20	689,270
	21	**Ordinary business income (loss).** Subtract line 20 from line 6			21	32,730
Tax and Payments	22a	Excess net passive income or LIFO recapture tax (see instructions)	22a			
	b	Tax from Schedule D (Form 1120S)	22b			
	c	Add lines 22a and 22b (see instructions for additional taxes)			22c	
	23a	2012 estimated tax payments and 2011 overpayment credited to 2012	23a			
	b	Tax deposited with Form 7004	23b			
	c	Credit for federal tax paid on fuels (attach Form 4136)	23c			
	d	Add lines 23a through 23c			23d	
	24	Estimated tax penalty (see instructions). Check if Form 2220 is attached ▶ ☐			24	
	25	**Amount owed.** If line 23d is smaller than the total of lines 22c and 24, enter amount owed			25	
	26	**Overpayment.** If line 23d is larger than the total of lines 22c and 24, enter amount overpaid			26	
	27	Enter amount from line 26 **Credited to 2013 estimated tax** ▶	Refunded ▶		27	

Sign Here

Under penalties of perjury, I declare that I have examined this return, including accompanying schedules and statements, and to the best of my knowledge and belief, it is true, correct, and complete. Declaration of preparer (other than taxpayer) is based on all information of which preparer has any knowledge.

▶ Signature of officer Date ▶ Title

May the IRS discuss this return with the preparer shown below (see instructions)? ☐ Yes ☐ No

Paid Preparer Use Only

Print/Type preparer's name	Preparer's signature	Date	Check ☐ if self-employed	PTIN
Firm's name ▶			Firm's EIN ▶	
Firm's address ▶			Phone no.	

For Paperwork Reduction Act Notice, see separate instructions. Cat. No. 11510H Form **1120S** (2012)

Form 1120S (2012) Page 2

Schedule B Other Information (see instructions)

		Yes	No
1	Check accounting method: a ☐ Cash b ☑ Accrual c ☐ Other (specify) ▶		
2	See the instructions and enter the: a Business activity ▶ **Retail Food Sales** b Product or service ▶ **Gourmet Foods**		
3	At any time during the tax year, was any shareholder of the corporation a disregarded entity, a trust, an estate, or a nominee or similar person?		✓
4	At the end of the tax year, did the corporation:		
a	Own directly 20% or more, or own, directly or indirectly, 50% or more of the total stock issued and outstanding of any foreign or domestic corporation? For rules of constructive ownership, see instructions. If "Yes," complete (i) through (v) below		✓

(i) Name of Corporation	(ii) Employer Identification Number (if any)	(iii) Country of Incorporation	(iv) Percentage of Stock Owned	(v) If Percentage in (iv) is 100%, Enter the Date (if any) a Qualified Subchapter S Subsidiary Election Was Made

		Yes	No
b	Own directly an interest of 20% or more, or own, directly or indirectly, an interest of 50% or more in the profit, loss, or capital in any foreign or domestic partnership (including an entity treated as a partnership) or in the beneficial interest of a trust? For rules of constructive ownership, see instructions. If "Yes," complete (i) through (v) below		✓

(i) Name of Entity	(ii) Employer Identification Number (if any)	(iii) Type of Entity	(iv) Country of Organization	(v) Maximum Percentage Owned in Profit, Loss, or Capital

		Yes	No
5 a	At the end of the tax year, did the corporation have any outstanding shares of restricted stock?		✓
	If "Yes," complete lines (i) and (ii) below. (i) Total shares of restricted stock ▶ (ii) Total shares of non-restricted stock ▶		
b	At the end of the tax year, did the corporation have any outstanding stock options, warrants, or similar instruments?		✓
	If "Yes," complete lines (i) and (ii) below. (i) Total shares of stock outstanding at the end of the tax year ▶ (ii) Total shares of stock outstanding if all instruments were executed ▶		
6	Has this corporation filed, or is it required to file, **Form 8918,** Material Advisor Disclosure Statement, to provide information on any reportable transaction?		✓
7	Check this box if the corporation issued publicly offered debt instruments with original issue discount ▶ ☐ If checked, the corporation may have to file **Form 8281,** Information Return for Publicly Offered Original Issue Discount Instruments.		
8	If the corporation: **(a)** was a C corporation before it elected to be an S corporation **or** the corporation acquired an asset with a basis determined by reference to the basis of the asset (or the basis of any other property) in the hands of a C corporation **and (b)** has net unrealized built-in gain in excess of the net recognized built-in gain from prior years, enter the net unrealized built-in gain reduced by net recognized built-in gain from prior years (see instructions) ▶ $		
9	Enter the accumulated earnings and profits of the corporation at the end of the tax year. $		
10	Does the corporation satisfy **both** of the following conditions?		
a	The corporation's total receipts (see instructions) for the tax year were less than $250,000		
b	The corporation's total assets at the end of the tax year were less than $250,000		✓
	If "Yes," the corporation is not required to complete Schedules L and M-1.		
11	During the tax year, did the corporation have any non-shareholder debt that was canceled, was forgiven, or had the terms modified so as to reduce the principal amount of the debt?		✓
	If "Yes," enter the amount of principal reduction $		
12	During the tax year, was a qualified subchapter S subsidiary election terminated or revoked? If "Yes," see instructions		✓
13a	Did the corporation make any payments in 2012 that would require it to file Form(s) 1099?	✓	
b	If "Yes," did the corporation file or will it file required Forms 1099?	✓	

Form **1120S** (2012)

Form 1120S (2012) Page 3

Schedule K		Shareholders' Pro Rata Share Items			Total amount
Income (Loss)	1	Ordinary business income (loss) (page 1, line 21)		1	32,730
	2	Net rental real estate income (loss) (attach Form 8825)		2	
	3a	Other gross rental income (loss)	3a		
	b	Expenses from other rental activities (attach statement)	3b		
	c	Other net rental income (loss). Subtract line 3b from line 3a		3c	
	4	Interest income		4	
	5	Dividends: **a** Ordinary dividends		5a	
		b Qualified dividends	5b		
	6	Royalties		6	
	7	Net short-term capital gain (loss) (attach Schedule D (Form 1120S))		7	
	8a	Net long-term capital gain (loss) (attach Schedule D (Form 1120S))		8a	
	b	Collectibles (28%) gain (loss)	8b		
	c	Unrecaptured section 1250 gain (attach statement)	8c		
	9	Net section 1231 gain (loss) (attach Form 4797)		9	5,000
	10	Other income (loss) (see instructions) Type ▶		10	
Deductions	11	Section 179 deduction (attach Form 4562)		11	5,000
	12a	Charitable contributions		12a	2,000
	b	Investment interest expense		12b	
	c	Section 59(e)(2) expenditures **(1)** Type ▶ **(2)** Amount ▶		12c(2)	
	d	Other deductions (see instructions) Type ▶		12d	
Credits	13a	Low-income housing credit (section 42(j)(5))		13a	
	b	Low-income housing credit (other)		13b	
	c	Qualified rehabilitation expenditures (rental real estate) (attach Form 3468)		13c	
	d	Other rental real estate credits (see instructions) Type ▶		13d	
	e	Other rental credits (see instructions) Type ▶		13e	
	f	Alcohol and cellulosic biofuel fuels credit (attach Form 6478)		13f	
	g	Other credits (see instructions) Type ▶		13g	
Foreign Transactions	14a	Name of country or U.S. possession ▶			
	b	Gross income from all sources		14b	
	c	Gross income sourced at shareholder level		14c	
		Foreign gross income sourced at corporate level			
	d	Passive category		14d	
	e	General category		14e	
	f	Other (attach statement)		14f	
		Deductions allocated and apportioned at shareholder level			
	g	Interest expense		14g	
	h	Other		14h	
		Deductions allocated and apportioned at corporate level to foreign source income			
	i	Passive category		14i	
	j	General category		14j	
	k	Other (attach statement)		14k	
		Other information			
	l	Total foreign taxes (check one): ▶ ☐ Paid ☐ Accrued		14l	
	m	Reduction in taxes available for credit (attach statement)		14m	
	n	Other foreign tax information (attach statement)			
Alternative Minimum Tax (AMT) Items	15a	Post-1986 depreciation adjustment		15a	
	b	Adjusted gain or loss		15b	
	c	Depletion (other than oil and gas)		15c	
	d	Oil, gas, and geothermal properties—gross income		15d	
	e	Oil, gas, and geothermal properties—deductions		15e	
	f	Other AMT items (attach statement)		15f	
Items Affecting Shareholder Basis	16a	Tax-exempt interest income		16a	
	b	Other tax-exempt income		16b	
	c	Nondeductible expenses		16c	500
	d	Distributions (attach statement if required) (see instructions)		16d	25,000
	e	Repayment of loans from shareholders		16e	

Form **1120S** (2012)

Form 1120S (2012) Page 4

Schedule K **Shareholders' Pro Rata Share Items** (continued)

				Total amount
Other Information	17a	Investment income	17a	
	b	Investment expenses	17b	
	c	Dividend distributions paid from accumulated earnings and profits	17c	
	d	Other items and amounts (attach statement)		
Recon-ciliation	18	**Income/loss reconciliation.** Combine the amounts on lines 1 through 10 in the far right column. From the result, subtract the sum of the amounts on lines 11 through 12d and 14l	18	30,730

Schedule L **Balance Sheets per Books**

	Assets	Beginning of tax year (a)	(b)	End of tax year (c)	(d)
1	Cash		62,000		60,230
2a	Trade notes and accounts receivable	37,500		37,500	
b	Less allowance for bad debts	(0)	37,500	(0)	37,500
3	Inventories		340,000		340,000
4	U.S. government obligations				
5	Tax-exempt securities (see instructions)				
6	Other current assets (attach statement)				
7	Loans to shareholders				
8	Mortgage and real estate loans				
9	Other investments (attach statement)				
10a	Buildings and other depreciable assets	80,000		68,000	
b	Less accumulated depreciation	(62,000)	18,000	(59,000)	9,000
11a	Depletable assets				
b	Less accumulated depletion	( )		( )	
12	Land (net of any amortization)				
13a	Intangible assets (amortizable only)				
b	Less accumulated amortization	( )		( )	
14	Other assets (attach statement)				
15	Total assets		457,500		446,730
	Liabilities and Shareholders' Equity				
16	Accounts payable		20,000		0
17	Mortgages, notes, bonds payable in less than 1 year				
18	Other current liabilities (attach statement)				
19	Loans from shareholders				
20	Mortgages, notes, bonds payable in 1 year or more		12,500		12.500
21	Other liabilities (attach statement)				
22	Capital stock		225,000		225,000
23	Additional paid-in capital				
24	Retained earnings		200,000		209,230
25	Adjustments to shareholders' equity (attach statement)				
26	Less cost of treasury stock		( )		( )
27	Total liabilities and shareholders' equity		457,500		446,730

Form **1120S** (2012)

Form 1120S (2012) Page **5**

Schedule M-1 Reconciliation of Income (Loss) per Books With Income (Loss) per Return

Note. Schedule M-3 required instead of Schedule M-1 if total assets are $10 million or more—see instructions

1	Net income (loss) per books	34,230	5	Income recorded on books this year not included on Schedule K, lines 1 through 10 (itemize):	
2	Income included on Schedule K, lines 1, 2, 3c, 4, 5a, 6, 7, 8a, 9, and 10, not recorded on books this year (itemize)		a	Tax-exempt interest $	
3	Expenses recorded on books this year not included on Schedule K, lines 1 through 12 and 14l (itemize):		6	Deductions included on Schedule K, lines 1 through 12 and 14l, not charged against book income this year (itemize):	
a	Depreciation $		a	Depreciation $ 4,000	
b	Travel and entertainment $ 500	500	7	Add lines 5 and 6	4,000
4	Add lines 1 through 3	34,730	8	Income (loss) (Schedule K, line 18). Line 4 less line 7	30,730

Schedule M-2 Analysis of Accumulated Adjustments Account, Other Adjustments Account, and Shareholders' Undistributed Taxable Income Previously Taxed (see instructions)

		(a) Accumulated adjustments account	(b) Other adjustments account	(c) Shareholders' undistributed taxable income previously taxed
1	Balance at beginning of tax year	200,000		
2	Ordinary income from page 1, line 21	32,730		
3	Other additions	5,000		
4	Loss from page 1, line 21	( )		
5	Other reductions	(7,500)	( )	
6	Combine lines 1 through 5	230,230		
7	Distributions other than dividend distributions	25,000		
8	Balance at end of tax year. Subtract line 7 from line 6	205,230		

Form **1120S** (2012)

671112

☐ Final K-1 ☐ Amended K-1 OMB No. 1545-0130

Schedule K-1 (Form 1120S) **2012**
Department of the Treasury
Internal Revenue Service

For calendar year 2012, or tax year beginning ____________, 2012 ending ____________, 20____

Shareholder's Share of Income, Deductions, Credits, etc.

▶ See back of form and separate instructions.

Part I Information About the Corporation

A Corporation's employer identification number
79-7979797

B Corporation's name, address, city, state, and ZIP code
Bill's Market
387 Spring Street
Raleigh, NC 29288

C IRS Center where corporation filed return
Cincinnati, OH

Part II Information About the Shareholder

D Shareholder's identifying number
123-45-6789

E Shareholder's name, address, city, state, and ZIP code
William Spicer
2345 Carolina Avenue
Durham, NC 29212

F Shareholder's percentage of stock ownership for tax year . . . . 80 %

For IRS Use Only

Part III Shareholder's Share of Current Year Income, Deductions, Credits, and Other Items

1	Ordinary business income (loss) 26,184	13	Credits	
2	Net rental real estate income (loss)			
3	Other net rental income (loss)			
4	Interest income			
5a	Ordinary dividends			
5b	Qualified dividends	14	Foreign transactions	
6	Royalties			
7	Net short-term capital gain (loss)			
8a	Net long-term capital gain (loss)			
8b	Collectibles (28%) gain (loss)			
8c	Unrecaptured section 1250 gain			
9	Net section 1231 gain (loss) 4,000			
10	Other income (loss)	15	Alternative minimum tax (AMT) items	
11	Section 179 deduction 4,000	16	Items affecting shareholder basis	
12	Other deductions	c		400
a	1,600	d		20,000
		17	Other information	

* See attached statement for additional information.

671112

☐ Final K-1 ☐ Amended K-1 OMB No. 1545-0130

Schedule K-1 (Form 1120S) **2012**
Department of the Treasury
Internal Revenue Service

For calendar year 2012, or tax year beginning __________, 2012 ending __________, 20____

Shareholder's Share of Income, Deductions, Credits, etc.

▶ See back of form and separate instructions.

Part I Information About the Corporation

A Corporation's employer identification number
79-7979797

B Corporation's name, address, city, state, and ZIP code
Bill's Market
387 Spring Street
Raleigh, NC 29288

C IRS Center where corporation filed return
Cincinnati, OH

Part II Information About the Shareholder

D Shareholder's identifying number
987-65-4321

E Shareholder's name, address, city, state, and ZIP code
June Spicer
2345 Carolina Avenue
Durham, NC 29212

F Shareholder's percentage of stock ownership for tax year . . . . 20 %

For IRS Use Only

Part III Shareholder's Share of Current Year Income, Deductions, Credits, and Other Items

1	Ordinary business income (loss) 6,456	13	Credits	
2	Net rental real estate income (loss)			
3	Other net rental income (loss)			
4	Interest income			
5a	Ordinary dividends			
5b	Qualified dividends	14	Foreign transactions	
6	Royalties			
7	Net short-term capital gain (loss)			
8a	Net long-term capital gain (loss)			
8b	Collectibles (28%) gain (loss)			
8c	Unrecaptured section 1250 gain			
9	Net section 1231 gain (loss) 1,000			
10	Other income (loss)	15	Alternative minimum tax (AMT) items	
11	Section 179 deduction 1,000	16	Items affecting shareholder basis	
12	Other deductions	c		100
a	400	d		5,000
		17	Other information	

* See attached statement for additional information.

For Paperwork Reduction Act Notice, see Instructions for Form 1120S. IRS.gov/form1120s Cat. No. 11520D **Schedule K-1 (Form 1120S) 2012**

SAMPLE RETURN 4 (SR4)

Form 1040 Department of the Treasury—Internal Revenue Service (99) U.S. Individual Income Tax Return 2012

OMB No. 1545-0074 | IRS Use Only—Do not write or staple in this space.

For the year Jan. 1–Dec. 31, 2012, or other tax year beginning , 2012, ending , 20 | See separate instructions.

Your first name and initial	Last name	Your social security number
William	Spicer	123-45-6789
If a joint return, spouse's first name and initial	Last name	Spouse's social security number
June	Spicer	987-65-4321

Home address (number and street). If you have a P.O. box, see instructions. Apt. no.
2345 Carolina Avenue

▲ Make sure the SSN(s) above and on line 6c are correct.

City, town or post office, state, and ZIP code. If you have a foreign address, also complete spaces below (see instructions).
durham, NC 29212

Foreign country name | Foreign province/state/county | Foreign postal code

Presidential Election Campaign
Check here if you, or your spouse if filing jointly, want $3 to go to this fund. Checking a box below will not change your tax or refund. ☐ You ☐ Spouse

Filing Status

Check only one box.

1 ☐ Single
2 ☑ Married filing jointly (even if only one had income)
3 ☐ Married filing separately. Enter spouse's SSN above and full name here. ▶
4 ☐ Head of household (with qualifying person). (See instructions.) If the qualifying person is a child but not your dependent, enter this child's name here. ▶
5 ☐ Qualifying widow(er) with dependent child

Exemptions

6a ☑ **Yourself.** If someone can claim you as a dependent, **do not** check box 6a — Boxes checked on 6a and 6b: 2
b ☑ **Spouse**

c **Dependents:**

(1) First name Last name	(2) Dependent's social security number	(3) Dependent's relationship to you	(4) ✓ if child under age 17 qualifying for child tax credit (see instructions)
Sophie Spicer	333-33-3333	Daughter	☑
Carl Spicer	444-44-4444	Son	☑
			☐
			☐

If more than four dependents, see instructions and check here ▶ ☐

No. of children on 6c who: • lived with you: 2
• did not live with you due to divorce or separation (see instructions):
Dependents on 6c not entered above:

d Total number of exemptions claimed — Add numbers on lines above ▶ 4

Income

Attach Form(s) W-2 here. Also attach Forms W-2G and 1099-R if tax was withheld.

If you did not get a W-2, see instructions.

Enclose, but do not attach, any payment. Also, please use **Form 1040-V.**

7	Wages, salaries, tips, etc. Attach Form(s) W-2		
8a	**Taxable** interest. Attach Schedule B if required		500
b	**Tax-exempt** interest. **Do not** include on line 8a	8b	
9a	Ordinary dividends. Attach Schedule B if required		1,300
b	Qualified dividends	9b 1,300	
10	Taxable refunds, credits, or offsets of state and local income taxes		
11	Alimony received		
12	Business income or (loss). Attach Schedule C or C-EZ		238,500
13	Capital gain or (loss). Attach Schedule D if required. If not required, check here ▶ ☐		(3,000)
14	Other gains or (losses). Attach Form 4797		2,000
15a	IRA distributions	15a	b Taxable amount 15b
16a	Pensions and annuities	16a	b Taxable amount 16b
17	Rental real estate, royalties, partnerships, S corporations, trusts, etc. Attach Schedule E		21,800
18	Farm income or (loss). Attach Schedule F		
19	Unemployment compensation		
20a	Social security benefits	20a	b Taxable amount 20b
21	Other income. List type and amount		
22	Combine the amounts in the far right column for lines 7 through 21. This is your **total income** ▶		261,100

Adjusted Gross Income

23	Educator expenses		
24	Certain business expenses of reservists, performing artists, and fee-basis government officials. Attach Form 2106 or 2106-EZ		
25	Health savings account deduction. Attach Form 8889		
26	Moving expenses. Attach Form 3903		
27	Deductible part of self-employment tax. Attach Schedule SE	11,432	
28	Self-employed SEP, SIMPLE, and qualified plans		
29	Self-employed health insurance deduction	3,000	
30	Penalty on early withdrawal of savings		
31a	Alimony paid b Recipient's SSN ▶		
32	IRA deduction	6,000	
33	Student loan interest deduction		
34	Tuition and fees. Attach Form 8917		
35	Domestic production activities deduction. Attach Form 8903		
36	Add lines 23 through 35		20,432
37	Subtract line 36 from line 22. This is your **adjusted gross income** ▶		240,668

For Disclosure, Privacy Act, and Paperwork Reduction Act Notice, see separate instructions. Cat. No. 11320B Form **1040** (2012)

Form 1040 (2012) Page 2

Tax and Credits	38	Amount from line 37 (adjusted gross income)			38	240,668
	39a	Check if: ☐ **You** were born before January 2, 1948, ☐ Blind. ☐ **Spouse** was born before January 2, 1948, ☐ Blind. **Total boxes checked ▶ 39a** ☐				
	b	If your spouse itemizes on a separate return or you were a dual-status alien, check here ▶ 39b ☐				
	40	**Itemized deductions** (from Schedule A) **or** your **standard deduction** (see left margin)			40	26,750
	41	Subtract line 40 from line 38			41	213,918
	42	**Exemptions.** Multiply $3,800 by the number on line 6d			42	15,200
	43	**Taxable income.** Subtract line 42 from line 41. If line 42 is more than line 41, enter -0-			43	198,718
	44	**Tax** (see instructions). Check if any from: **a** ☐ Form(s) 8814 **b** ☐ Form 4972 **c** ☐ 962 election			44	43,251
	45	**Alternative minimum tax** (see instructions). Attach Form 6251			45	0
	46	Add lines 44 and 45 ▶			46	43,251
	47	Foreign tax credit. Attach Form 1116 if required	47			
	48	Credit for child and dependent care expenses. Attach Form 2441	48	760		
	49	Education credits from Form 8863, line 19	49			
	50	Retirement savings contributions credit. Attach Form 8880	50			
	51	Child tax credit. Attach Schedule 8812, if required	51			
	52	Residential energy credits. Attach Form 5695	52			
	53	Other credits from Form: **a** ☐ 3800 **b** ☐ 8801 **c** ☐	53			
	54	Add lines 47 through 53. These are your **total credits**			54	760
	55	Subtract line 54 from line 46. If line 54 is more than line 46, enter -0- ▶			55	42,491
Other Taxes	56	Self-employment tax. Attach Schedule SE			56	20,295
	57	Unreported social security and Medicare tax from Form: **a** ☐ 4137 **b** ☐ 8919			57	
	58	Additional tax on IRAs, other qualified retirement plans, etc. Attach Form 5329 if required			58	
	59a	Household employment taxes from Schedule H			59a	
	b	First-time homebuyer credit repayment. Attach Form 5405 if required			59b	
	60	Other taxes. Enter code(s) from instructions			60	
	61	Add lines 55 through 60. This is your **total tax** ▶			61	62,786
Payments	62	Federal income tax withheld from Forms W-2 and 1099	62			
	63	2012 estimated tax payments and amount applied from 2011 return	63	70,000		
	64a	**Earned income credit (EIC)**	64a			
	b	Nontaxable combat pay election 64b				
	65	Additional child tax credit. Attach Schedule 8812	65			
	66	American opportunity credit from Form 8863, line 8	66			
	67	Reserved	67			
	68	Amount paid with request for extension to file	68			
	69	Excess social security and tier 1 RRTA tax withheld	69			
	70	Credit for federal tax on fuels. Attach Form 4136	70			
	71	Credits from Form: **a** ☐ 2439 **b** Reserved **c** ☐ 8801 **d** ☐ 8885	71			
	72	Add lines 62, 63, 64a, and 65 through 71. These are your **total payments** ▶			72	70,000
Refund	73	If line 72 is more than line 61, subtract line 61 from line 72. This is the amount you **overpaid**			73	7,214
	74a	Amount of line 73 you want **refunded to you.** If Form 8888 is attached, check here ▶ ☐			74a	
	▶ b	Routing number ▶ **c** Type: ☐ Checking ☐ Savings				
	▶ d	Account number				
	75	Amount of line 73 you want **applied to your 2013 estimated tax** ▶	75	7,214		
Amount You Owe	76	**Amount you owe.** Subtract line 72 from line 61. For details on how to pay, see instructions ▶			76	
	77	Estimated tax penalty (see instructions)	77			

Standard Deduction for—
- People who check any box on line 39a or 39b **or** who can be claimed as a dependent, see instructions.
- All others:

Single or Married filing separately, $5,950

Married filing jointly or Qualifying widow(er), $11,900

Head of household, $8,700

If you have a qualifying child, attach Schedule EIC.

Direct deposit? See instructions.

Third Party Designee Do you want to allow another person to discuss this return with the IRS (see instructions)? ☐ **Yes.** Complete below. ☐ **No**

Designee's name ▶ Phone no. ▶ Personal identification number (PIN) ▶

Sign Here Under penalties of perjury, I declare that I have examined this return and accompanying schedules and statements, and to the best of my knowledge and belief, they are true, correct, and complete. Declaration of preparer (other than taxpayer) is based on all information of which preparer has any knowledge.

Joint return? See instructions. Keep a copy for your records.

Your signature	Date	Your occupation	Daytime phone number
Spouse's signature. If a joint return, **both** must sign.	Date	Spouse's occupation	If the IRS sent you an Identity Protection PIN, enter it here (see inst.)

Paid Preparer Use Only

Print/Type preparer's name	Preparer's signature	Date	Check ☐ if self-employed	PTIN
Firm's name ▶		Firm's EIN ▶		
Firm's address ▶		Phone no.		

Form **1040** (2012)

SCHEDULE A (Form 1040)

Department of the Treasury Internal Revenue Service (99)

Itemized Deductions

▶ Information about Schedule A and its separate instructions is at *www.irs.gov/form1040*.

▶ Attach to Form 1040.

OMB No. 1545-0074

2012

Attachment Sequence No. **07**

Name(s) shown on Form 1040: William and June Spicer

Your social security number: 123-45-6789

Medical and Dental Expenses		**Caution.** Do not include expenses reimbursed or paid by others.				
	1	Medical and dental expenses (see instructions)	1	19,000		
	2	Enter amount from Form 1040, line 38 [2] 240,668				
	3	Multiply line 2 by 7.5% (.075)	3	18,050		
	4	Subtract line 3 from line 1. If line 3 is more than line 1, enter -0-			4	950
Taxes You Paid	5	State and local **(check only one box):** a ☑ Income taxes, **or** b ☐ General sales taxes	5	4,900		
	6	Real estate taxes (see instructions)	6	3,000		
	7	Personal property taxes	7			
	8	Other taxes. List type and amount ▶	8			
	9	Add lines 5 through 8			9	7,900
Interest You Paid	10	Home mortgage interest and points reported to you on Form 1098	10	14,000		
Note. Your mortgage interest deduction may be limited (see instructions).	11	Home mortgage interest not reported to you on Form 1098. If paid to the person from whom you bought the home, see instructions and show that person's name, identifying no., and address ▶	11			
	12	Points not reported to you on Form 1098. See instructions for special rules	12			
	13	Mortgage insurance premiums (see instructions)	13			
	14	Investment interest. Attach Form 4952 if required. (See instructions.)	14			
	15	Add lines 10 through 14			15	14,000
Gifts to Charity	16	Gifts by cash or check. If you made any gift of $250 or more, see instructions	16	3,500		
If you made a gift and got a benefit for it, see instructions.	17	Other than by cash or check. If any gift of $250 or more, see instructions. You **must** attach Form 8283 if over $500	17	400		
	18	Carryover from prior year	18			
	19	Add lines 16 through 18			19	
Casualty and Theft Losses	20	Casualty or theft loss(es). Attach Form 4684. (See instructions.)			20	3,900
Job Expenses and Certain Miscellaneous Deductions	21	Unreimbursed employee expenses—job travel, union dues, job education, etc. Attach Form 2106 or 2106-EZ if required. (See instructions.) ▶	21			
	22	Tax preparation fees	22			
	23	Other expenses—investment, safe deposit box, etc. List type and amount ▶	23			
	24	Add lines 21 through 23	24			
	25	Enter amount from Form 1040, line 38 [25]				
	26	Multiply line 25 by 2% (.02)	26			
	27	Subtract line 26 from line 24. If line 26 is more than line 24, enter -0-			27	
Other Miscellaneous Deductions	28	Other—from list in instructions. List type and amount ▶			28	
Total Itemized Deductions	29	Add the amounts in the far right column for lines 4 through 28. Also, enter this amount on Form 1040, line 40			29	26,750
	30	If you elect to itemize deductions even though they are less than your standard deduction, check here ▶ ☐				

For Paperwork Reduction Act Notice, see Form 1040 instructions. Cat. No. 17145C **Schedule A (Form 1040) 2012**

SCHEDULE C (Form 1040)

Department of the Treasury
Internal Revenue Service (99)

Profit or Loss From Business

(Sole Proprietorship)

▶ For information on Schedule C and its instructions, go to *www.irs.gov/schedulec.*

▶ Attach to Form 1040, 1040NR, or 1041; partnerships generally must file Form 1065.

OMB No. 1545-0074

2012

Attachment Sequence No. 09

Name of proprietor	Social security number (SSN)
William Spicer	123-45-6789

A	Principal business or profession, including product or service (see instructions): Retail Food Sales - Gourmet Foods	B Enter code from instructions ▶ 4 4 5 9 2 0
C	Business name. If no separate business name, leave blank. Bill's Market	D Employer ID number (EIN), (see instr.) 7 9 7 9 7 9 7 9 7
E	Business address (including suite or room no.) ▶ 387 Spring Street	
	City, town or post office, state, and ZIP code: Raleigh, NC 29288	
F	Accounting method: (1) ☐ Cash (2) ☐ Accrual (3) ☐ Other (specify) ▶	
G	Did you "materially participate" in the operation of this business during 2012? If "No," see instructions for limit on losses	☑ Yes ☐ No
H	If you started or acquired this business during 2012, check here ▶	☐
I	Did you make any payments in 2012 that would require you to file Form(s) 1099? (see instructions)	☐ Yes ☑ No
J	If "Yes," did you or will you file required Forms 1099?	☐ Yes ☐ No

Part I Income

1	Gross receipts or sales. See instructions for line 1 and check the box if this income was reported to you on Form W-2 and the "Statutory employee" box on that form was checked ▶ ☐	1	2,700,000
2	Returns and allowances (see instructions)	2	0
3	Subtract line 2 from line 1	3	2,700,000
4	Cost of goods sold (from line 42)	4	1,980,000
5	**Gross profit.** Subtract line 4 from line 3	5	720,000
6	Other income, including federal and state gasoline or fuel tax credit or refund (see instructions)	6	
7	**Gross income.** Add lines 5 and 6 ▶	7	720,000

Part II Expenses

Enter expenses for business use of your home only on line 30.

8	Advertising	8	40,000	18	Office expense (see instructions)	18	14,000
9	Car and truck expenses (see instructions)	9		19	Pension and profit-sharing plans	19	
10	Commissions and fees	10		20	Rent or lease (see instructions):		
11	Contract labor (see instructions)	11		a	Vehicles, machinery, and equipment	20a	
12	Depletion	12		b	Other business property	20b	120,000
13	Depreciation and section 179 expense deduction (not included in Part III) (see instructions)	13	8,000	21	Repairs and maintenance	21	12,000
				22	Supplies (not included in Part III)	22	
				23	Taxes and licenses	23	22,000
				24	Travel, meals, and entertainment:		
14	Employee benefit programs (other than on line 19)	14	12,000	a	Travel	24a	8,000
15	Insurance (other than health)	15	18,000	b	Deductible meals and entertainment (see instructions)	24b	500
16	Interest:			25	Utilities	25	16,000
a	Mortgage (paid to banks, etc.)	16a		26	Wages (less employment credits)	26	210,000
b	Other	16b	1,000	27a	Other expenses (from line 48)	27a	
17	Legal and professional services	17		b	**Reserved for future use**	27b	

28	**Total expenses** before expenses for business use of home. Add lines 8 through 27a ▶	28	481,500
29	Tentative profit or (loss). Subtract line 28 from line 7	29	238,500
30	Expenses for business use of your home. Attach **Form 8829.** Do **not** report such expenses elsewhere	30	0
31	**Net profit or (loss).** Subtract line 30 from line 29. • If a profit, enter on both **Form 1040, line 12** (or **Form 1040NR, line 13**) and on **Schedule SE, line 2.** (If you checked the box on line 1, see instructions). Estates and trusts, enter on **Form 1041, line 3.** • If a loss, you **must** go to line 32.	31	238,500

32 If you have a loss, check the box that describes your investment in this activity (see instructions).

- If you checked 32a, enter the loss on both **Form 1040, line 12,** (or **Form 1040NR, line 13**) and on **Schedule SE, line 2.** (If you checked the box on line 1, see the line 31 instructions). Estates and trusts, enter on **Form 1041, line 3.**
- If you checked 32b, you **must** attach **Form 6198.** Your loss may be limited.

32a ☑ All investment is at risk.
32b ☐ Some investment is not at risk.

Schedule C (Form 1040) 2012 Page 2

Part III Cost of Goods Sold (see instructions)

33 Method(s) used to value closing inventory: a ☑ Cost b ☐ Lower of cost or market c ☐ Other (attach explanation)

34 Was there any change in determining quantities, costs, or valuations between opening and closing inventory? If "Yes," attach explanation . . . ☐ Yes ☐ No

35	Inventory at beginning of year. If different from last year's closing inventory, attach explanation . . .	35	340,000
36	Purchases less cost of items withdrawn for personal use . . .	36	1,980,000
37	Cost of labor. Do not include any amounts paid to yourself . . .	37	
38	Materials and supplies . . .	38	
39	Other costs . . .	39	
40	Add lines 35 through 39 . . .	40	2,320,000
41	Inventory at end of year . . .	41	340,000
42	**Cost of goods sold.** Subtract line 41 from line 40. Enter the result here and on line 4 . . .	42	1,980,000

Part IV Information on Your Vehicle.

Complete this part **only** if you are claiming car or truck expenses on line 9 and are not required to file Form 4562 for this business. See the instructions for line 13 to find out if you must file Form 4562.

43 When did you place your vehicle in service for business purposes? (month, day, year) ▶ ____ / ____ / ____

44 Of the total number of miles you drove your vehicle during 2012, enter the number of miles you used your vehicle for:

a Business ____________ b Commuting (see instructions) ____________ c Other ____________

45 Was your vehicle available for personal use during off-duty hours? . . . ☐ Yes ☐ No

46 Do you (or your spouse) have another vehicle available for personal use?. . . ☐ Yes ☐ No

47a Do you have evidence to support your deduction? . . . ☐ Yes ☐ No

b If "Yes," is the evidence written? . . . ☐ Yes ☐ No

Part V Other Expenses.

List below business expenses not included on lines 8–26 or line 30.

48 **Total other expenses.** Enter here and on line 27a . . . 48	

Schedule C (Form 1040) 2012

SCHEDULE D (Form 1040)

Department of the Treasury Internal Revenue Service (99)

Capital Gains and Losses

▶ Attach to Form 1040 or Form 1040NR.
▶ Information about Schedule D and its separate instructions is at *www.irs.gov/form1040*.
▶ Use Form 8949 to list your transactions for lines 1, 2, 3, 8, 9, and 10.

OMB No. 1545-0074

2012

Attachment Sequence No. 12

Name(s) shown on return: William and June Spicer

Your social security number: 123-45-6789

Part I Short-Term Capital Gains and Losses—Assets Held One Year or Less

Complete Form 8949 before completing line 1, 2, or 3. This form may be easier to complete if you round off cents to whole dollars.	(d) Proceeds (sales price) from Form(s) 8949, Part I, line 2, column (d)	(e) Cost or other basis from Form(s) 8949, Part I, line 2, column (e)	(g) Adjustments to gain or loss from Form(s) 8949, Part I, line 2, column (g)	(h) Gain or (loss) Subtract column (e) from column (d) and combine the result with column (g)
1 Short-term totals from all Forms 8949 with **box A** checked in **Part I**				
2 Short-term totals from all Forms 8949 with **box B** checked in **Part I**				
3 Short-term totals from all Forms 8949 with **box C** checked in **Part I**				

	Line	Amount
4 Short-term gain from Form 6252 and short-term gain or (loss) from Forms 4684, 6781, and 8824	4	
5 Net short-term gain or (loss) from partnerships, S corporations, estates, and trusts from Schedule(s) K-1	5	
6 Short-term capital loss carryover. Enter the amount, if any, from line 8 of your **Capital Loss Carryover Worksheet** in the instructions	6	( )
7 **Net short-term capital gain or (loss).** Combine lines 1 through 6 in column (h). If you have any long-term capital gains or losses, go to Part II below. Otherwise, go to Part III on the back	7	

Part II Long-Term Capital Gains and Losses—Assets Held More Than One Year

Complete Form 8949 before completing line 8, 9, or 10. This form may be easier to complete if you round off cents to whole dollars.	(d) Proceeds (sales price) from Form(s) 8949, Part II, line 4, column (d)	(e) Cost or other basis from Form(s) 8949, Part II, line 4, column (e)	(g) Adjustments to gain or loss from Form(s) 8949, Part II, line 4, column (g)	(h) Gain or (loss) Subtract column (e) from column (d) and combine the result with column (g)
8 Long-term totals from all Forms 8949 with **box A** checked in **Part II**	4,000	18,000	0	(14,000)
9 Long-term totals from all Forms 8949 with **box B** checked in **Part II**				
10 Long-term totals from all Forms 8949 with **box C** checked in **Part II**				

	Line	Amount
11 Gain from Form 4797, Part I; long-term gain from Forms 2439 and 6252; and long-term gain or (loss) from Forms 4684, 6781, and 8824	11	5,000
12 Net long-term gain or (loss) from partnerships, S corporations, estates, and trusts from Schedule(s) K-1	12	
13 Capital gain distributions. See the instructions	13	
14 Long-term capital loss carryover. Enter the amount, if any, from line 13 of your **Capital Loss Carryover Worksheet** in the instructions	14	( )
15 **Net long-term capital gain or (loss).** Combine lines 8 through 14 in column (h). Then go to Part III on the back	15	(9,000)

Part III **Summary**

16 Combine lines 7 and 15 and enter the result **16** (9,000)

- If line 16 is a **gain**, enter the amount from line 16 on Form 1040, line 13, or Form 1040NR, line 14. Then go to line 17 below.
- If line 16 is a **loss**, skip lines 17 through 20 below. Then go to line 21. Also be sure to complete line 22.
- If line 16 is **zero**, skip lines 17 through 21 below and enter -0- on Form 1040, line 13, or Form 1040NR, line 14. Then go to line 22.

17 Are lines 15 and 16 **both** gains?

☐ **Yes.** Go to line 18.

☑ **No.** Skip lines 18 through 21, and go to line 22.

18 Enter the amount, if any, from line 7 of the **28% Rate Gain Worksheet** in the instructions . . ▶ **18**

19 Enter the amount, if any, from line 18 of the **Unrecaptured Section 1250 Gain Worksheet** in the instructions . . . . ▶ **19**

20 Are lines 18 and 19 **both** zero or blank?

☐ **Yes.** Complete the **Qualified Dividends and Capital Gain Tax Worksheet** in the instructions for Form 1040, line 44 (or in the instructions for Form 1040NR, line 42). **Do not** complete lines 21 and 22 below.

☐ **No.** Complete the **Schedule D Tax Worksheet** in the instructions. **Do not** complete lines 21 and 22 below.

21 If line 16 is a loss, enter here and on Form 1040, line 13, or Form 1040NR, line 14, the **smaller** of:

- The loss on line 16 or
- ($3,000), or if married filing separately, ($1,500)

} **21** (3,000)

Note. When figuring which amount is smaller, treat both amounts as positive numbers.

22 Do you have qualified dividends on Form 1040, line 9b, or Form 1040NR, line 10b?

☑ **Yes.** Complete the **Qualified Dividends and Capital Gain Tax Worksheet** in the instructions for Form 1040, line 44 (or in the instructions for Form 1040NR, line 42).

☐ **No.** Complete the rest of Form 1040 or Form 1040NR.

Schedule E (Form 1040) 2012 Attachment Sequence No. **13** Page **2**

Name(s) shown on return. Do not enter name and social security number if shown on other side.	Your social security number
William and June Spicer	123-45-6789

Caution. The IRS compares amounts reported on your tax return with amounts shown on Schedule(s) K-1.

Part II Income or Loss From Partnerships and S Corporations

Note. If you report a loss from an at-risk activity for which **any** amount is **not** at risk, you **must** check the box in column **(e)** on line 28 and attach **Form 6198.** See instructions.

27 Are you reporting any loss not allowed in a prior year due to the at-risk or basis limitations, a prior year unallowed loss from a passive activity (if that loss was not reported on Form 8582), or unreimbursed partnership expenses? If you answered "Yes," see instructions before completing this section. ☐ **Yes** ☑ **No**

28	(a) Name	(b) Enter P for partnership; S for S corporation	(c) Check if foreign partnership	(d) Employer identification number	(e) Check if any amount is not at risk
A	The Bridal Shop Partnership	P	☐	64-7654321	☐
B	Imagineers Corporations	S	☐	59-7654321	☐
C			☐		☐
D			☐		☐

	Passive Income and Loss		Nonpassive Income and Loss		
	(f) Passive loss allowed (attach Form 8582 if required)	(g) Passive income from Schedule K-1	(h) Nonpassive loss from Schedule K-1	(i) Section 179 expense deduction from Form 4562	(j) Nonpassive income from Schedule K-1
A					20,000
B		1,800			
C					
D					
29a Totals		1,800			20,000
b Totals					

30	Add columns (g) and (j) of line 29a	30	21,800
31	Add columns (f), (h), and (i) of line 29b	31	( )
32	**Total partnership and S corporation income or (loss).** Combine lines 30 and 31. Enter the result here and include in the total on line 41 below	32	21,800

Part III Income or Loss From Estates and Trusts

33	(a) Name	(b) Employer identification number
A		
B		

	Passive Income and Loss		Nonpassive Income and Loss	
	(c) Passive deduction or loss allowed (attach Form 8582 if required)	(d) Passive income from Schedule K-1	(e) Deduction or loss from Schedule K-1	(f) Other income from Schedule K-1
A				
B				
34a Totals				
b Totals				

35	Add columns (d) and (f) of line 34a	35	
36	Add columns (c) and (e) of line 34b	36	( )
37	**Total estate and trust income or (loss).** Combine lines 35 and 36. Enter the result here and include in the total on line 41 below	37	

Part IV Income or Loss From Real Estate Mortgage Investment Conduits (REMICs)—Residual Holder

38 (a) Name	(b) Employer identification number	(c) Excess inclusion from **Schedules Q,** line 2c (see instructions)	(d) Taxable income (net loss) from **Schedules Q,** line 1b	(e) Income from **Schedules Q,** line 3b

39	Combine columns (d) and (e) only. Enter the result here and include in the total on line 41 below	39	

Part V Summary

40	Net farm rental income or (loss) from **Form 4835.** Also, complete line 42 below	40	
41	**Total income or (loss).** Combine lines 26, 32, 37, 39, and 40. Enter the result here and on Form 1040, line 17, or Form 1040NR, line 18 ▶	41	21,800
42	**Reconciliation of farming and fishing income.** Enter your **gross** farming and fishing income reported on Form 4835, line 7; Schedule K-1 (Form 1065), box 14, code B; Schedule K-1 (Form 1120S), box 17, code U; and Schedule K-1 (Form 1041), box 14, code F (see instructions)	42	
43	**Reconciliation for real estate professionals.** If you were a real estate professional (see instructions), enter the net income or (loss) you reported anywhere on Form 1040 or Form 1040NR from all rental real estate activities in which you materially participated under the passive activity loss rules	43	

Schedule E (Form 1040) 2012

SCHEDULE SE (Form 1040)

Department of the Treasury
Internal Revenue Service (99)

Self-Employment Tax

▶ Information about Schedule SE and its separate instructions is at *www.irs.gov/form1040.*
▶ Attach to Form 1040 or Form 1040NR.

OMB No. 1545-0074
2012
Attachment Sequence No. **17**

Name of person with **self-employment** income (as shown on Form 1040)	Social security number of person with **self-employment** income ▶
William Spicer	123-45-6789

Before you begin: To determine if you must file Schedule SE, see the instructions.

May I Use Short Schedule SE or Must I Use Long Schedule SE?

Note. Use this flowchart **only if** you must file Schedule SE. If unsure, see *Who Must File Schedule SE* in the instructions.

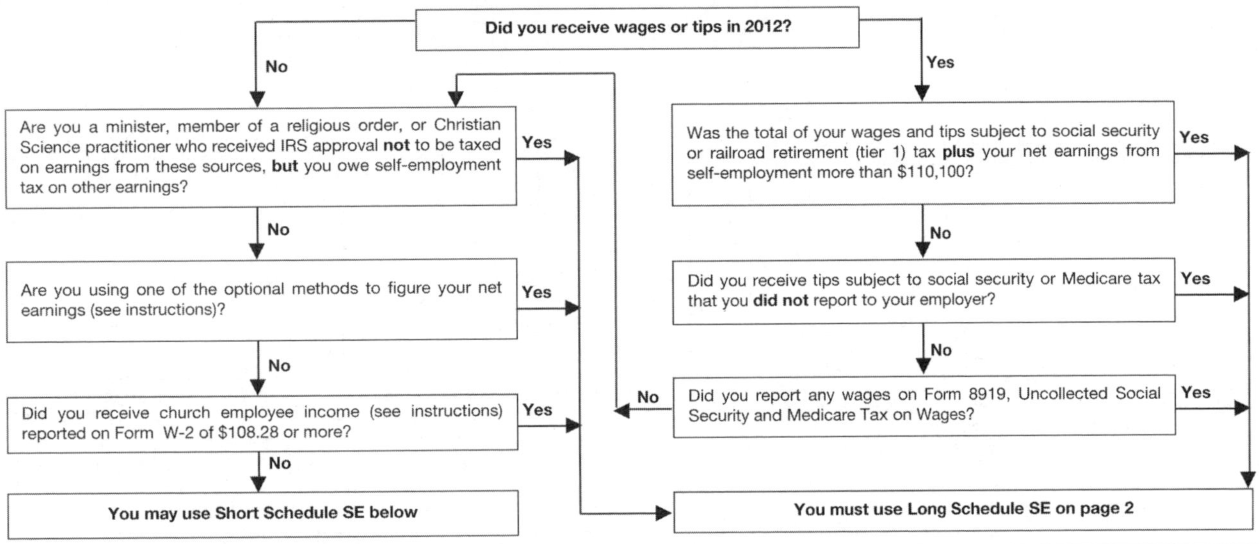

Section A—Short Schedule SE. Caution. Read above to see if you can use Short Schedule SE.

1a	Net farm profit or (loss) from Schedule F, line 34, and farm partnerships, Schedule K-1 (Form 1065), box 14, code A	**1a**	
b	If you received social security retirement or disability benefits, enter the amount of Conservation Reserve Program payments included on Schedule F, line 4b, or listed on Schedule K-1 (Form 1065), box 20, code Y	**1b**	( )
2	Net profit or (loss) from Schedule C, line 31; Schedule C-EZ, line 3; Schedule K-1 (Form 1065), box 14, code A (other than farming); and Schedule K-1 (Form 1065-B), box 9, code J1. Ministers and members of religious orders, see instructions for types of income to report on this line. See instructions for other income to report	**2**	238,500
3	Combine lines 1a, 1b, and 2	**3**	238,500
4	Multiply line 3 by 92.35% (.9235). If less than $400, you do not owe self-employment tax; **do not** file this schedule unless you have an amount on line 1b . . . . . ▶	**4**	220,255
	Note. If line 4 is less than $400 due to Conservation Reserve Program payments on line 1b, see instructions.		
5	**Self-employment tax.** If the amount on line 4 is: • $110,100 or less, multiply line 4 by 13.3% (.133). Enter the result here and on **Form 1040, line 56,** or **Form 1040NR, line 54** • More than $110,100, multiply line 4 by 2.9% (.029). Then, add $11,450.40 to the result. Enter the total here and on **Form 1040, line 56,** or **Form 1040NR, line 54**	**5**	17,838
6	**Deduction for employer-equivalent portion of self-employment tax.** If the amount on line 5 is: • $14,643.30 or less, multiply line 5 by 57.51% (.5751) • More than $14,643.30, multiply line 5 by 50% (.50) and add $1,100 to the result. Enter the result here and on **Form 1040, line 27,** or **Form 1040NR, line 27** **6** 10,019		

SCHEDULE SE (Form 1040)

Department of the Treasury
Internal Revenue Service (99)

Self-Employment Tax

▶ Information about Schedule SE and its separate instructions is at *www.irs.gov/form1040.*

▶ **Attach to Form 1040 or Form 1040NR.**

OMB No. 1545-0074

2012

Attachment Sequence No. **17**

Name of person with **self-employment** income (as shown on Form 1040)	Social security number of person with **self-employment** income ▶
June Spicer	987-65-4321

Before you begin: To determine if you must file Schedule SE, see the instructions.

May I Use Short Schedule SE or Must I Use Long Schedule SE?

Note. Use this flowchart **only if** you must file Schedule SE. If unsure, see *Who Must File Schedule SE* in the instructions.

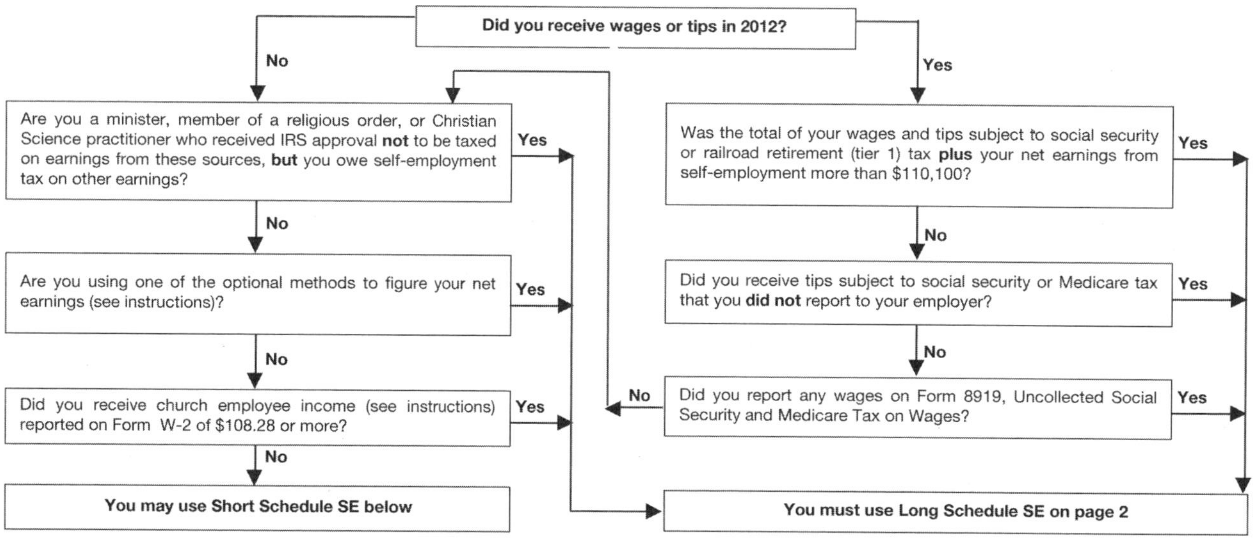

Section A—Short Schedule SE. Caution. Read above to see if you can use Short Schedule SE.

1a	Net farm profit or (loss) from Schedule F, line 34, and farm partnerships, Schedule K-1 (Form 1065), box 14, code A	1a	
b	If you received social security retirement or disability benefits, enter the amount of Conservation Reserve Program payments included on Schedule F, line 4b, or listed on Schedule K-1 (Form 1065), box 20, code Y	1b	( )
2	Net profit or (loss) from Schedule C, line 31; Schedule C-EZ, line 3; Schedule K-1 (Form 1065), box 14, code A (other than farming); and Schedule K-1 (Form 1065-B), box 9, code J1. Ministers and members of religious orders, see instructions for types of income to report on this line. See instructions for other income to report	2	20,000
3	Combine lines 1a, 1b, and 2	3	20,000
4	Multiply line 3 by 92.35% (.9235). If less than $400, you do not owe self-employment tax; **do not** file this schedule unless you have an amount on line 1b ▶	4	18,470
	Note. If line 4 is less than $400 due to Conservation Reserve Program payments on line 1b, see instructions.		
5	**Self-employment tax.** If the amount on line 4 is: • $110,100 or less, multiply line 4 by 13.3% (.133). Enter the result here and on **Form 1040, line 56,** or **Form 1040NR, line 54** • More than $110,100, multiply line 4 by 2.9% (.029). Then, add $11,450.40 to the result. Enter the total here and on **Form 1040, line 56,** or **Form 1040NR, line 54**	5	2,457
6	**Deduction for employer-equivalent portion of self-employment tax.** If the amount on line 5 is: • $14,643.30 or less, multiply line 5 by 57.51% (.5751) • More than $14,643.30, multiply line 5 by 50% (.50) and add $1,100 to the result. Enter the result here and on **Form 1040, line 27,** or **Form 1040NR, line 27**	6	1,413

Form **2441**

Department of the Treasury
Internal Revenue Service (99)

Child and Dependent Care Expenses

▶ Attach to Form 1040, Form 1040A, or Form 1040NR.

▶ Information about Form 2441 and its separate instructions is at *www.irs.gov/form2441*.

1040 / 1040A / 1040NR / 2441

OMB No. 1545-0074

2012

Attachment Sequence No. 21

Name(s) shown on return	Your social security number
William and June Spicer	123-45-6789

Part I **Persons or Organizations Who Provided the Care—**You **must** complete this part.
(If you have more than two care providers, see the instructions.)

1 (a) Care provider's name	(b) Address (number, street, apt. no., city, state, and ZIP code)	(c) Identifying number (SSN or EIN)	(d) Amount paid (see instructions)
Country Club Day Care	111 Main Street Durham, NC	59-1122333	3,800

Did you receive **dependent care benefits?**
No ▶ Complete only Part II below.
Yes ▶ Complete Part III on the back next.

Caution. If the care was provided in your home, you may owe employment taxes. If you do, you cannot file Form 1040A. For details, see the instructions for Form 1040, line 59a, or Form 1040NR, line 58a.

Part II **Credit for Child and Dependent Care Expenses**

2 Information about your **qualifying person(s).** If you have more than two qualifying persons, see the instructions.

(a) Qualifying person's name — First	Last	(b) Qualifying person's social security number	(c) **Qualified expenses** you incurred and paid in 2012 for the person listed in column (a)
Sophie	Spicer	333-33-3333	1,900
Carl	Spicer	444-44-4444	1,900

3 Add the amounts in column (c) of line 2. **Do not** enter more than $3,000 for one qualifying person or $6,000 for two or more persons. If you completed Part III, enter the amount from line 31 . . . . . **3** 3,800

4 Enter your **earned income.** See instructions **4** 228,481

5 If married filing jointly, enter your spouse's earned income (if your spouse was a student or was disabled, see the instructions); **all others**, enter the amount from line 4 . . . . **5** 18,587

6 Enter the **smallest** of line 3, 4, or 5 . . . . . **6** 3,800

7 Enter the amount from Form 1040, line 38; Form 1040A, line 22; or Form 1040NR, line 37. . . . . **7** 240,668

8 Enter on line 8 the decimal amount shown below that applies to the amount on line 7

If line 7 is: Over	But not over	Decimal amount is	If line 7 is: Over	But not over	Decimal amount is
$0	15,000	.35	$29,000	31,000	.27
15,000	17,000	.34	31,000	33,000	.26
17,000	19,000	.33	33,000	35,000	.25
19,000	21,000	.32	35,000	37,000	.24
21,000	23,000	.31	37,000	39,000	.23
23,000	25,000	.30	39,000	41,000	.22
25,000	27,000	.29	41,000	43,000	.21
27,000	29,000	.28	43,000	No limit	.20

8 X. 20

9 Multiply line 6 by the decimal amount on line 8. If you paid 2011 expenses in 2012, see the instructions **9** 760

10 Tax liability limit. Enter the amount from the Credit Limit Worksheet in the instructions. **10**

11 **Credit for child and dependent care expenses.** Enter the **smaller** of line 9 or line 10 here and on Form 1040, line 48; Form 1040A, line 29; or Form 1040NR, line 46 . . . . **11** 760

For Paperwork Reduction Act Notice, see your tax return instructions. Cat. No. 11862M Form **2441** (2012)

Form **4562** Department of the Treasury Internal Revenue Service (99)

Depreciation and Amortization (Including Information on Listed Property)

▶ See separate instructions. ▶ Attach to your tax return.

OMB No. 1545-0172 **2012** Attachment Sequence No. 179

Name(s) shown on return	Business or activity to which this form relates	Identifying number
William Spicer	Retail Food Sales	123-45-6789

Part I Election To Expense Certain Property Under Section 179

Note: *If you have any listed property, complete Part V before you complete Part I.*

1	Maximum amount (see instructions)	1	500,000
2	Total cost of section 179 property placed in service (see instructions)	2	5,000
3	Threshold cost of section 179 property before reduction in limitation (see instructions)	3	2,000,000
4	Reduction in limitation. Subtract line 3 from line 2. If zero or less, enter -0-	4	0
5	Dollar limitation for tax year. Subtract line 4 from line 1. If zero or less, enter -0-. If married filing separately, see instructions	5	500,000

6 (a) Description of property	(b) Cost (business use only)	(c) Elected cost
Display case	5,000	5,000
7 Listed property. Enter the amount from line 29	7	

8	Total elected cost of section 179 property. Add amounts in column (c), lines 6 and 7	8	5,000
9	Tentative deduction. Enter the **smaller** of line 5 or line 8	9	5,000
10	Carryover of disallowed deduction from line 13 of your 2011 Form 4562	10	0
11	Business income limitation. Enter the smaller of business income (not less than zero) or line 5 (see instructions)	11	238,500
12	Section 179 expense deduction. Add lines 9 and 10, but do not enter more than line 11	12	5,000
13	Carryover of disallowed deduction to 2013. Add lines 9 and 10, less line 12 ▶	13	

Note: *Do not use Part II or Part III below for listed property. Instead, use Part V.*

Part II Special Depreciation Allowance and Other Depreciation (Do not include listed property.) (See instructions.)

14	Special depreciation allowance for qualified property (other than listed property) placed in service during the tax year (see instructions)	14	
15	Property subject to section 168(f)(1) election	15	
16	Other depreciation (including ACRS)	16	3,000

Part III MACRS Depreciation (Do not include listed property.) (See instructions.)

Section A

17	MACRS deductions for assets placed in service in tax years beginning before 2012	17	
18	If you are electing to group any assets placed in service during the tax year into one or more general asset accounts, check here ▶ ☐		

Section B—Assets Placed in Service During 2012 Tax Year Using the General Depreciation System

(a) Classification of property	(b) Month and year placed in service	(c) Basis for depreciation (business/investment use only—see instructions)	(d) Recovery period	(e) Convention	(f) Method	(g) Depreciation deduction
19a 3-year property						
b 5-year property						
c 7-year property						
d 10-year property						
e 15-year property						
f 20-year property						
g 25-year property			25 yrs.		S/L	
h Residential rental property			27.5 yrs.	MM	S/L	
			27.5 yrs.	MM	S/L	
i Nonresidential real property			39 yrs.	MM	S/L	
				MM	S/L	

Section C—Assets Placed in Service During 2012 Tax Year Using the Alternative Depreciation System

(a) Classification of property	(b)	(c)	(d)	(e)	(f)	(g)
20a Class life					S/L	
b 12-year			12 yrs.		S/L	
c 40-year			40 yrs.	MM	S/L	

Part IV Summary (See instructions.)

21	Listed property. Enter amount from line 28	21	
22	**Total.** Add amounts from line 12, lines 14 through 17, lines 19 and 20 in column (g), and line 21. Enter here and on the appropriate lines of your return. Partnerships and S corporations—see instructions	22	8,000
23	For assets shown above and placed in service during the current year, enter the portion of the basis attributable to section 263A costs	23	

For Paperwork Reduction Act Notice, see separate instructions. Cat. No. 12906N Form **4562** (2012)

Form **4797**

Department of the Treasury
Internal Revenue Service

Sales of Business Property

(Also Involuntary Conversions and Recapture Amounts Under Sections 179 and 280F(b)(2))

▶ Attach to your tax return.

▶ Information about Form 4797 and its separate instructions is at *www.irs.gov/form4797.*

OMB No. 1545-0184

2012

Attachment Sequence No. 27

Name(s) shown on return: William and June Spicer

Identifying number: 123-45-6789

1	Enter the gross proceeds from sales or exchanges reported to you for 2012 on Form(s) 1099-B or 1099-S (or substitute statement) that you are including on line 2, 10, or 20 (see instructions)	1	13,000

Part I Sales or Exchanges of Property Used in a Trade or Business and Involuntary Conversions From Other Than Casualty or Theft—Most Property Held More Than 1 Year (see instructions)

2 (a) Description of property	(b) Date acquired (mo., day, yr.)	(c) Date sold (mo., day, yr.)	(d) Gross sales price	(e) Depreciation allowed or allowable since acquisition	(f) Cost or other basis, plus improvements and expense of sale	(g) Gain or (loss) Subtract (f) from the sum of (d) and (e)
Display Case	6-6-08	12-12-12	1,000	8,000	12,000	(3,000)

3	Gain, if any, from Form 4684, line 39	3	
4	Section 1231 gain from installment sales from Form 6252, line 26 or 37	4	
5	Section 1231 gain or (loss) from like-kind exchanges from Form 8824	5	
6	Gain, if any, from line 32, from other than casualty or theft	6	8,000
7	Combine lines 2 through 6. Enter the gain or (loss) here and on the appropriate line as follows:	7	5,000
	Partnerships (except electing large partnerships) and S corporations. Report the gain or (loss) following the instructions for Form 1065, Schedule K, line 10, or Form 1120S, Schedule K, line 9. Skip lines 8, 9, 11, and 12 below.		
	Individuals, partners, S corporation shareholders, and all others. If line 7 is zero or a loss, enter the amount from line 7 on line 11 below and skip lines 8 and 9. If line 7 is a gain and you did not have any prior year section 1231 losses, or they were recaptured in an earlier year, enter the gain from line 7 as a long-term capital gain on the Schedule D filed with your return and skip lines 8, 9, 11, and 12 below.		
8	Nonrecaptured net section 1231 losses from prior years (see instructions)	8	
9	Subtract line 8 from line 7. If zero or less, enter -0-. If line 9 is zero, enter the gain from line 7 on line 12 below. If line 9 is more than zero, enter the amount from line 8 on line 12 below and enter the gain from line 9 as a long-term capital gain on the Schedule D filed with your return (see instructions)	9	

Part II Ordinary Gains and Losses (see instructions)

10 Ordinary gains and losses not included on lines 11 through 16 (include property held 1 year or less):

11	Loss, if any, from line 7	11	( )
12	Gain, if any, from line 7 or amount from line 8, if applicable	12	
13	Gain, if any, from line 31	13	2,000
14	Net gain or (loss) from Form 4684, lines 31 and 38a	14	
15	Ordinary gain from installment sales from Form 6252, line 25 or 36	15	
16	Ordinary gain or (loss) from like-kind exchanges from Form 8824	16	
17	Combine lines 10 through 16	17	2,000
18	For all except individual returns, enter the amount from line 17 on the appropriate line of your return and skip lines a and b below. For individual returns, complete lines a and b below:		
a	If the loss on line 11 includes a loss from Form 4684, line 35, column (b)(ii), enter that part of the loss here. Enter the part of the loss from income-producing property on Schedule A (Form 1040), line 28, and the part of the loss from property used as an employee on Schedule A (Form 1040), line 23. Identify as from "Form 4797, line 18a." See instructions	18a	
b	Redetermine the gain or (loss) on line 17 excluding the loss, if any, on line 18a. Enter here and on Form 1040, line 14	18b	2,000

For Paperwork Reduction Act Notice, see separate instructions. Cat. No. 13086I Form **4797** (2012)

Form 4797 (2012) Page 2

Part III Gain From Disposition of Property Under Sections 1245, 1250, 1252, 1254, and 1255 (see instructions)

19 (a) Description of section 1245, 1250, 1252, 1254, or 1255 property:	(b) Date acquired (mo., day, yr.)	(c) Date sold (mo., day, yr.)
A Equipment	3-5-10	8-15-12
B		
C		
D		

These columns relate to the properties on lines 19A through 19D. ▶		Property A	Property B	Property C	Property D
20 Gross sales price (**Note:** *See line 1 before completing.*)	20	13,000			
21 Cost or other basis plus expense of sale	21	5,000			
22 Depreciation (or depletion) allowed or allowable	22	2,000			
23 Adjusted basis. Subtract line 22 from line 21	23	3,000			
24 Total gain. Subtract line 23 from line 20	24	10,000			
25 **If section 1245 property:**					
a Depreciation allowed or allowable from line 22	25a	2,000			
b Enter the **smaller** of line 24 or 25a	25b	2,000			
26 **If section 1250 property:** If straight line depreciation was used, enter -0- on line 26g, except for a corporation subject to section 291.					
a Additional depreciation after 1975 (see instructions)	26a				
b Applicable percentage multiplied by the **smaller** of line 24 or line 26a (see instructions)	26b				
c Subtract line 26a from line 24. If residential rental property **or** line 24 is not more than line 26a, skip lines 26d and 26e	26c				
d Additional depreciation after 1969 and before 1976	26d				
e Enter the **smaller** of line 26c or 26d	26e				
f Section 291 amount (corporations only)	26f				
g Add lines 26b, 26e, and 26f	26g				
27 **If section 1252 property:** Skip this section if you did not dispose of farmland or if this form is being completed for a partnership (other than an electing large partnership).					
a Soil, water, and land clearing expenses	27a				
b Line 27a multiplied by applicable percentage (see instructions)	27b				
c Enter the **smaller** of line 24 or 27b	27c				
28 **If section 1254 property:**					
a Intangible drilling and development costs, expenditures for development of mines and other natural deposits, mining exploration costs, and depletion (see instructions)	28a				
b Enter the **smaller** of line 24 or 28a	28b				
29 **If section 1255 property:**					
a Applicable percentage of payments excluded from income under section 126 (see instructions)	29a				
b Enter the **smaller** of line 24 or 29a (see instructions)	29b				

Summary of Part III Gains. Complete property columns A through D through line 29b before going to line 30.

30 Total gains for all properties. Add property columns A through D, line 24	30	10,000
31 Add property columns A through D, lines 25b, 26g, 27c, 28b, and 29b. Enter here and on line 13	31	2,000
32 Subtract line 31 from line 30. Enter the portion from casualty or theft on Form 4684, line 33. Enter the portion from other than casualty or theft on Form 4797, line 6	32	8,000

Part IV Recapture Amounts Under Sections 179 and 280F(b)(2) When Business Use Drops to 50% or Less (see instructions)

		(a) Section 179	(b) Section 280F(b)(2)
33 Section 179 expense deduction or depreciation allowable in prior years	33		
34 Recomputed depreciation (see instructions)	34		
35 Recapture amount. Subtract line 34 from line 33. See the instructions for where to report	35		

Form 4797 (2012)

Form 8949 (2012) Attachment Sequence No. **12A** Page **2**

Name(s) shown on return. (Name and SSN or taxpayer identification no. not required if shown on other side.)	**Social security number or taxpayer identification number**
William and June Spicer	**123-45-6789**

Most brokers issue their own substitute statement instead of using Form 1099-B. They also may provide basis information (usually your cost) to you on the statement even if it is not reported to the IRS. Before you check Box A, B, or C below, determine whether you received any statement(s) and, if so, the transactions for which basis was reported to the IRS. Brokers are required to report basis to the IRS for most stock you bought in 2011 or later.

Part II **Long-Term.** Transactions involving capital assets you held more than one year are long term. For short-term transactions, see page 1.

You *must* check Box A, B, *or* C below. Check only one box. If more than one box applies for your long-term transactions, complete a separate Form 8949, page 2, for each applicable box. If you have more long-term transactions than will fit on this page for one or more of the boxes, complete as many forms with the same box checked as you need.

- ☑ **(A)** Long-term transactions reported on Form(s) 1099-B showing basis **was** reported to the IRS
- ☐ **(B)** Long-term transactions reported on Form(s) 1099-B showing basis was **not** reported to the IRS
- ☐ **(C)** Long-term transactions not reported to you on Form 1099-B

3 (a) Description of property (Example: 100 sh. XYZ Co.)	(b) Date acquired (Mo., day, yr.)	(c) Date sold or disposed (Mo., day, yr.)	(d) Proceeds (sales price) (see instructions)	(e) Cost or other basis. See the **Note** below and see *Column (e)* in the separate instructions	**Adjustment, if any, to gain or loss.** If you enter an amount in column (g), enter a code in column (f). **See the separate instructions.** (f) Code(s) from instructions	(g) Amount of adjustment	(h) **Gain or (loss).** Subtract column (e) from column (d) and combine the result with column (g)
ABC stock - 10,000 shares	8-1-05	2-2-12	4,000	18,000			
4 Totals. Add the amounts in columns (d), (e), (g), and (h) (subtract negative amounts). Enter each total here and include on your Schedule D, **line 8** (if **Box A** above is checked), **line 9** (if **Box B** above is checked), or **line 10** (if **Box C** above is checked) ▶			4,000	18,000			

Note. If you checked Box A above but the basis reported to the IRS was incorrect, enter in column (e) the basis as reported to the IRS, and enter an adjustment in column (g) to correct the basis. See *Column (g)* in the separate instructions for how to figure the amount of the adjustment.

APPENDIX D

TAX RETURN PROBLEMS

TAX RETURN PROBLEM 1 (TRP 1)

CORPORATE TAX RETURN PROBLEM

The Snap-It-Open Corporation incorporated and began operations on January 15 of the current year. Its address is 3701 Commerce Drive, Baltimore, MD 23239. Its employer identification number is 69-7414447. It elects to file its initial tax return as a calendar-year corporation and uses the accrual method of accounting. It elects the FIFO method of inventory valuation.

Jason Sprull (SSN 333-33-3333) and Martin Winsock (SSN 555-55-5555) formed the business. They each contributed $250,000 cash for 50 percent of the 100,000 shares of $1 par value stock issued and outstanding.

The company was formed to assemble and market a unique, compact, snap-open umbrella and its business activity code is 339900. These umbrellas are sold to a variety of organizations as premiums. The company purchases the umbrella frames and several types of waterproof fabric for the umbrella material and covers from various manufacturers. It prints the organizations' advertising logos or other designs on the umbrella material and covers. It then assembles these on the umbrella frames for delivery to the customer along with the covers.

On January 16, the company placed in service two new machines that they had purchased for $250,000 each for printing and cutting the fabric for the umbrellas and two used umbrella assembly machines purchased for $200,000 each. The company obtained a bank loan of $750,000 secured by the machines. Jason and Martin were required to personally guarantee this loan that has an 8 percent annual interest rate on the unpaid balance. The first principal and interest payment of $160,000 is not due until January 16 of next year.

During the year, the company purchased $150,000 of fabric and $210,000 of umbrella frames. It returned one order of frames valued at $5,000 because of a defect in the snap-open mechanism and received a cash refund for that amount.

Both Jason and Martin worked full-time in the business. Jason was the salesperson for the company and Martin managed the office and the printing and assembly operations. Each received a salary of $60,000 for the year. They had six employees with the following incomes for the year: $45,000 for an accountant; $21,000 for a receptionist; $28,000 for each of two print machine operators; and $25,000 for each of two assembly machine operators. There are no accrued salaries or taxes as of the end of the current year. FUTA taxes are assessed on the first $7,000 of wages at a rate of 6.0 percent.

During the year, the company had $1,535,000 in umbrella sales and collected $1,180,000 on these sales. They also paid the following expenses in cash:

Rent	$240,000
Repairs and Maintenance	20,000
Utilities	80,000
Taxes and Licenses (excluding FICA and FUTA taxes)	10,000
Health Insurance	16,000
Advertising	40,000
Travel (excluding meals)	20,000
Meals and Entertainment	15,000
Group Term Life Insurance	2,000

As an accrual-basis taxpayer, the company recognized $57,500 in interest expense on the note ($750,000 × .08 × 11.5/12) and established an allowance account for bad debts equal to two percent of sales.

They recognized depreciation expense for financial accounting equal to 10 percent of the purchase price for the new printing machines and 12.5 percent of the purchase price for the used assembly machines.

Their inventory at year-end consisted of $15,000 of fabric and $18,000 of umbrella frames based on the FIFO inventory method. (For simplicity, you are only required to allocate the factory salaries to the calculation of cost of goods sold.)

The company made estimated tax payments of $40,000 for the year.

Required

Part a. Prepare a financial accounting income statement (before income tax) and balance sheet for Snap-It-Open Corporation for the current year. (Do not forget to compute FICA and FUTA taxes for all employees.)

Part b. Complete a Form 1120 and Form 4562 for Snap-It-Open Corporation using the following additional information. The corporation wrote off no bad debts for the year and it maximized its cost recovery deductions on the four machines purchased. Use the latest available tax forms from the IRS Web site at *www.irs.gov*.

TAX RETURN PROBLEM 2 (TRP 2)

PARTNERSHIP TAX RETURN PROBLEM

The Rite-Way Plumbing Company began business three years ago as of March 1 of the current tax year in Sarasota. Its business address is 124 Division Lane, Sarasota, FL 33645. Its employer identification number is 69-3456789. Its principal business activity is residential plumbing repairs and maintenance; its business code is 238220. It files its income tax returns on the calendar-year basis.

The business was formed as a limited partnership by two brothers, John Henry (SSN 555-55-5555) and James Henry (SSN 666-66-6666), who work full-time in the business, and their father Tom Henry (SSN 888-88-8888), the limited partner. The brothers each have a 25 percent interest in the income, loss, and capital of the business while their father owns a 50 percent interest in income, loss, and capital, but takes no active interest in the business other than as that of an investor.

At the end of the current year, its operations showed cash gross receipts of $1,240,000 and the following cash expenditure items:

Salaries and wages (excluding John and James)	$378,000
Repairs and Maintenance	2,000
Rent	28,000
Taxes and Licenses	38,000
Advertising	3,000
Pension Plans (excluding John and James)	15,000
Health/Dental Insurance	16,000
Material Purchases	220,000
Truck Expense	45,000
Insurance (excluding health/dental)	65,000
Legal/Professional Fees	3,000
Office Expenses	6,000
Utilities/Telephone	8,000
Meals/Entertainment	4,000
Draw—John	75,000
Draw—James	60,000
Total Cash Expenditures	$966,000

John and James each receive a guaranteed payment of $75,000 in addition to the payment of their health and dental insurance premiums, which are $3,000 each for the current year (included in the $16,000 total for health/dental insurance). The other insurance payments include the $1,500 premiums for $200,000 term life insurance policies each on John and James that name the partnership as beneficiary.

Although the company maintains a certain level of plumbing supplies for its business, inventory is not a material income producing factor; thus, material purchases are expensed. The partnership uses the cash method of accounting for revenue and expenses.

The company purchased the following items for use solely in the business during the current year: a new truck (weighing over 6,000 pounds) that cost $21,250 (June 21); a new computer system costing $3,200 (August 17); additional new office furniture costing $2,500 (December 4).

At the beginning of the current year, the company owned the following items that were all purchased the month the company began business. In that year, the company claimed only basic MACRS depreciation (that is, it elected no bonus depreciation or Section 179 expensing if available) for any of its trucks, equipment, or furniture purchases:

Asset	Cost Basis
Trucks	$78,000
Plumbing equipment (7-year property)	23,000
Office Furniture	16,000
Computer system	4,000

On March 12, it sold one of its old trucks for $6,000 that had cost $17,000 originally. It also was able to sell its old computer system on September 12 for $250. It donated two pieces of its old office furniture to Goodwill Industries. This furniture had cost $1,500 and had a current value of $600.

Required

Prepare Form 1065 to the extent possible for the Rite-Way Plumbing Company along with the Schedule K-1s for each of the three partners and any other required forms. The partnership wants to maximize its cost recovery deductions for the current year for tax purposes. Use the latest available tax forms from the IRS Web site at *www.irs.gov*.

TAX RETURN PROBLEM 3 (TRP 3)

S Corporation Tax Return Problem

John Forsythe (SSN 555-55-5555) began a custom cabinet manufacturing business, John's Cabinets (EIN 86-1122334 and Business Code 321000), four years ago as of July 1 of the current tax year. John incorporated the business, and the corporation made a timely election to be taxed as an S corporation. The business has been highly successful, but to bring in additional capital for expansion, it sold 10,000 shares of previously unissued stock to John's friend, Tom Jones (SSN 666-66-6666), on March 1 of the current year for $80,000. John continues to hold his original 15,000 shares that were issued at incorporation for his contribution of money and property valued at $120,000.

The business used the additional capital to purchase $20,000 of new woodworking machines (7-year property) on October 15 and $60,000 as a down payment on the purchase of a new building for its manufacturing and office operations located at 7620 N. Commerce Place, Beavercreek, OH 45440. The business claimed only the basic MACRS depreciation deductions for these acquisitions. The total cost of the building was $320,000 and the S corporation began using it on October 1.

In the month the business began, the S corporation purchased $60,000 of used woodworking machinery. It elected to use ADS for cost recovery on the 7-year property to reduce any potential losses in the first years of the business. On September 15 of the current year, the business sold one of the old machines that had cost $10,000 originally for $5,000. When moving to the new building, a second machine that had cost $5,000 originally fell off the truck used to move it and was a total loss. The loss was not covered by insurance.

John works full-time in the business and takes a salary of $9,000 per month. Wages for his seven employees were $220,000. (None of those employees made less than $7,000 or more than the FICA maximum.)

Additional data for the completion of the S corporation tax return are

Sales revenue	$850,000
Sales returns	12,000
Purchases	335,000
Rent	36,000
Repairs	4,000
Insurance*	21,000
Truck rental	3,000
Taxes and licenses**	14,000
Advertising	2,000
Interest expense	4,000
Charitable contribution	10,000
Meals and entertainment	1,000
Fines for improper permitting	2,000
Beginning inventory (at cost)	25,000
Ending inventory (at cost)	30,000

**Includes $500 for John's group term life insurance of $200,000 and $3,000 for medical and dental insurance premiums for him and his family. The balance is for insurance for other employees.*
***Excludes Social Security and FUTA taxes (calculated at 6% for the year) for John and the other employees.*

For its books prepared for banks and other creditors, the company shows $2,000 as an addition to its allowance for bad debt for the current year, depreciation of $8,200, a gain on the sale of the machine of $1,500, and a loss of $2,500 on the destruction of the machine.

The corporation is a calendar-year S corporation and uses the hybrid method of accounting, recording all but its sales and cost of goods sold on the cash method of accounting. It has a balance of $35,700 in it accumulated adjustments account at the beginning of the year.

John's home address is 100 Main Street, Kettering, OH 45435 and Tom's home address is 222 Williams Street, Fairborn, OH 45422.

Required

Prepare Form 1120S for this corporation, excluding Schedule L. Complete the schedule K-1s for John and Tom as well as any other required forms. Assume that the Section 263A rules do not apply and that you do not have to apportion any other costs to inventory. Use the latest available tax forms from the IRS Web site at *www.irs.gov.*

TAX RETURN PROBLEM 4 (TRP 4)

Simple Individual Tax Return Problem

Janice Morgan is 17 and in her senior year of high school. She lives with her parents at 7829 Dowry Lane, Boston, MA 02112, and they are her primary source of support and claim her as a dependent on their tax return. Her Social Security number is 988-77-6543. She elects to contribute to the Presidential Election Campaign fund.

From January through May of the current tax year, Janice took care of two children on weekends and earned $1,600. Her employer did not withhold any federal income tax but did withhold the proper amount of FICA taxes. During the summer, she then worked full-time at a fast-food restaurant and during the remainder of the year she worked part-time. Her earnings totaled $5,580 from which the employer withheld $255 for federal income taxes along with her FICA taxes. Janice's only other income was $210 in interest on her savings account.

Required

Complete a Form 1040EZ for Janice using the latest year form available on the IRS Web site at *www.irs.gov*.

TAX RETURN PROBLEM 5 (TRP 5)

Individual Tax Return Problem

Cletus and Josepha Mayor have been married for twelve years and currently live at 2907 Seven Oaks Lane, Columbia, SC 29210. Their Social Security numbers are 223-34-4444 and 322-32-2222, respectively. They have two daughters, Sheena, age 10, (SSN 344-44-1234) and Carletta, age 7, (SSN 566-55-6543) who live with them and are fully supported by them.

Cletus is a manager for a local building contractor and earned a salary of $59,800 for the current tax year. He had $7,600 withheld for federal income taxes and $1,300 for state income taxes. Josepha is an elementary school teacher and earned $31,950. She had $3,280 withheld for federal income taxes and $700 for state income taxes.

On July 20 they purchased a new home for $210,000. The last five years they have lived in rented homes or apartments because they moved frequently for Cletus's job before settling in Columbia. They paid total mortgage interest on their new home of $7,250 for the period of time they owned the home, all of which was reported to them on Form 1098. Points incurred on the purchase of the new home were $1,800 (also reported on Form 1098).

Cletus contributed $2,000 to his Roth IRA and Josepha contributed $1,000 to hers.

They paid $1,200 in premiums for medical and dental insurance, had $2,800 in unreimbursed doctor and dentist bills, and paid $300 for an unreimbursed hospital bill.

They paid property taxes of $1,825 on the new home, which was properly allocated between them and seller on their closing statement.

In June, they renewed the license plates on their two cars paying a total of $265. This amount includes a flat fee of $40 per auto plus one percent based on the value of the autos. They also paid a total of $1,100 in state general sales taxes during the year.

Josepha spent $1,120 on materials for use in her classroom and spent $1,400 on tuition and fees for two courses leading to her master's degree in education at a local college. Cletus took two continuing education courses to maintain his general contractor's license. These courses cost $300 and were not reimbursed by his employer.

Just prior to moving to the new home, the Mayor's had a party for the neighbors to say "goodbye." During the party, Josepha took off her diamond ring while she was working in the kitchen. When she went to get the ring later, it was gone. It was established that the ring had been stolen and could not be recovered. The ring cost $3,700 when purchased a number of years before. Because Josepha had replacement value insurance on the ring, she received $5,000 from the insurance company to acquire a substantially similar ring. She decided not to purchase a replacement.

Josepha paid $2,300 in after-school child care expenses ($1,150 for each daughter) to Dawn-to-Dusk Care, 18 Elk Grove Street, Columbia, SC 29210, EIN 59-12345678.

The couple earned $90 in interest on their savings and checking accounts with the First National Bank of South Carolina and $220 in interest on the Teacher's Union money market fund.

Required

Complete Form 1040 (married filing jointly) and any required related forms and schedules for the Mayors using the latest forms available on the IRS Web site at *www.irs.gov*.

TAX RETURN PROBLEM 6 (TRP 6)

Individual Tax Return Problem

Jose (SSN 123-45-6789) and Rosanna (SSN 123-45-7890) Martinez are a married couple who reside at 1234 University Drive in Coral Gables, FL 33146. They have two children: Carmen, age 19 (SSN 234-65-4321), and Greg, age 10 (SSN 234-65-5432). Carmen is a full-time student at the local university; she lives at home and commutes to school.

Jose is an architect for Deco Design Architects and is covered by his employer's defined benefit pension plan. His Form W-2 for 2012 reported the following information:

Wages	$65,000	Federal Tax W/H	$9,100.00
Soc Sec Wages	$65,000	Soc Sec Tax W/H	$2,730.00
Medicare Wages	$65,000	Medicare Tax W/H	$942.50

Rosanna was a loan officer at BankOne until October of the current year. Her Form W-2 for 2012 reported the following information:

Wages	$43,000	Federal Tax W/H	$4,000.00
Soc Sec Wages	$43,000	Soc Sec Tax W/H	$1,806.00
Medicare Wages	$43,000	Medicare Tax W/H	$623.50

Rosanna's employer does not provide any retirement plan for its employees.

Jose and Rosanna received interest income from BankOne in the amount of $3,500 and qualified dividend income on Microserf stock of $130. On November 10, they sold 1,000 shares of Dotcom stock for $925. They had purchased the Dotcom stock last year on October 2 for $4,900. On September 12, they sold 800 shares of Microserf stock for $3,800. They had purchased the Microserf stock three years ago on April 22 for $3,050. The proceeds from these sales were reported on the Form 1099-B they received from their broker but basis was not reported.

Rosanna received $45 in jury duty pay in May.

The Martinez family has medical insurance that they purchase through the cafeteria plan offered by Jose's employer (on a pre-tax basis). The annual cost of this medical insurance for the entire family was $3,600. Martinez family also paid $9,100 for qualified medical expenses for which they received no insurance reimbursements.

The Martinez family paid $9,400 in interest on their home mortgage (which Overnight Mortgage Company reported to them on Form 1098). The Martinez family also owns a vacation home in Breckenridge, Colorado, for which they paid $4,100 of mortgage interest. (This is qualified mortgage interest for a second home.) Other interest paid by Jose and Rosanna includes $1,100 for a loan on their personal automobile and $400 on credit cards.

The Martinez family paid real estate taxes on their principal residence in the amount of $3,500. An additional $2,000 of real estate taxes was paid on their vacation home. Total sales taxes paid are $3,200.

The vacation home in Breckenridge was rented out for 120 days during the year for which they received $10,000 in rental income. Jose and Rosanna made significant decisions such as approving new tenants while a local management company handled the day-to-day needs. The Martinez family used it for 30 days for personal vacation use during the year. Expenses for this vacation home (other than the interest and taxes mentioned above) include: $700 for real estate management fees paid to a local agent who handles the rental of the property, insurance expense $2,200, repairs expense $500, and utilities expense $1,800. They purchased this home in 2003 and use the IRS formula for allocating interest and taxes. Depreciation expense for the rental portion of the home is $400.

Rosanna was a 20 percent shareholder in Simply Smart Corporation (TIN is 59-7654321) an S corporation. She materially participated in the activities of this corporation. She received a Schedule K-1 reporting $722 in ordinary business income on line 1.

The Martinez family has the necessary documentation for the following contributions made to qualified charitable organizations:

1. Cash of $2,500 given to their church.
2. Ford stock purchased 6 years ago on March 16, at a cost of $750 was given to United Way (a qualified charitable organization) on February 22 when it had a fair market value of $1,650 (the average stock price on the date of donation).

Jose had the following employment-related expenses that were not reimbursed by his employer:

1. Jose drove his Volvo (which he purchased four years ago on November 18) a total of 11,000 miles during the year. He drove 4,700 miles while conducting business during the first half of the year. In July, the firm purchased several hybrid autos that the architects were then required to use for all business travel rather than their personal autos. These autos were kept at the firm's offices. Jose used his personal auto for the three mile commute to his office, a total of 1,500 miles for the entire year.
2. Jose attended the AIA Architects conference in Salt Lake City. He paid a registration fee of $200 and incurred costs of $400 for transportation, $325 for lodging, and $160 for meals. He was not reimbursed for these expenses.

Jose and Rosanna incurred the following miscellaneous expenditures during the year:

1. Fees for preparation of last year's tax return of $220 that were paid in April of the current year.
2. Safe deposit box rental fee of $50 (for storage of investment securities).

Jose and Rosanna paid $8,000 for Carmen's tuition and $750 for books while she attended the local university where she is a sophomore. They want to maximize any tax benefits they can receive from the expenses they paid for Carmen's education.

In October, Rosanna quit her job with the bank and began a consulting business. The business code is 541990. She is operating the business under her own name and rented a small office at 1234 Coral Way, Coral Gables, FL 33146. Since Rosanna began her business so late in the year, her consulting income was only $5,900. She incurred the following expenses: $475 supplies, $210 telephone, $2,200 office rent, and $325 advertising. In addition, Rosanna drove her two-year old Lexus on business a total of 750 miles during this time to visit prospective and current clients.

Rosanna contributed $2,000 to a traditional individual retirement account on December 5. This is the first time she has contributed to an IRA.

Other information: Both Jose and Rosanna want $3 to go to the Presidential Election Campaign. Jose was born on April 1, 1974; Rosanna was born April 1, 1975.

Required

a. Based on the information presented above, prepare a Form 1040 (married filing jointly) and any required related forms and schedules for the Martinezes for 2012 using the forms available on the IRS Web site at *www.irs.gov*.

b. What will be different for tax year 2013?

Index

D

E

F

J

K

L

Q

R

T

U

V

W

Y

Z

Chapter 2

1. The Internal Revenue Service is NOT part of the Justice Department.

2. All of the following are primary sources of tax law: Internal Revenue Code, Treasury regulations, Report of the House Ways and Means Committee, Supreme Courts Decisions

3. Which of the following types of returns does not have an un-extended due date of the 15th
day of the 4th month after the end of the tax year? S corporations

4. The Statute of limitations for a return that inadvertently overstates expenses by 30 percent of gross revenues is: 3 years (the 6 year limit only applies when income is omitted)

5. Eduardo filed his 2012 tax return on March 15, 2013. Eduardo accidentally omitted 10,000 of income from his individual tax return. The total gross income shown on the tax return was $35,000, when will the statute of limitations expire for Eduardo's 2012 tax return? April 15, 2019

6. Timing Issues

Kimo Corporation, a cash basis calendar-year taxpayer, is in the 25 percent marginal tax bracket this year. Kimo owes a 15,000 expense that it may pay before the end of this year or in January of next year.

a. MTR 25% next year, should it pay this year or next? (7% discount factor)

Kimo should pay the expense in this year. Because Kimo's marginal tax rate is expected to be the same, the only consideration is the time value of money. If Kimo chooses to pay expense this year, it will have an after-tax savings of $3,750 (15,000 × 25%). If Kimo defers payment of the expense, its net present value of the after-tax savings will be 3,506 (15,000 × 25% × .935 PV factor). Therefore, Kimo should pay the expense this year since it will result in a $244 greater after-tax savings (3,750 − 3,506).

b. How would your answer change if Kimo's expected marginal tax rate next year is only 15%? Kimo should pay the expense this year. If Kimo's marginal tax rate is expected to decrease to 15%, Kimo will have a lower after-tax savings next year. The net present value of Kimo's after-tax savings would be $2,104 (15,000 × 15% × .935 PV factor). Kimo should pay the expense this year since it will result in a $1,646 greater after-tax savings (3,750 − 2,104).

c. How would your answer change if Kimo's expected marginal tax rate next year is 34%? Kimo should wait and pay the expense next year. If Kimo's marginal tax rate is expected to increase to 34%, Kimo will have a greater after-tax saving next year.
The NPV of Kimo's after-tax savings would be 4769 (15000 × 34% × .935 PV factor). Kimo should wait and pay the expense next year since it will result in a $1,019 greater after-tax savings (4,769 − 3,750).

7. Penalties

Robert decided not to file his return on April 15 because he knew that he could not pay the balance due. Robert files his return on August 3, paying the full 4,000 balance. How much can Robert expect to be charged for late payment/late-filing penalties?

He will be charged $860. Robert's return and tax payment is 1 partial and 3 full months late. He will be assessed a late filing penalty of 18% (4.5% × 4 × 4,000 = 720, which is greater than the minimum $135 penalty) and a late payment penalty of 2% (.5% × 4 × $4,000 = $80) for a total of 20% of the $4,000 balance due. He will be charged a total of $800 (20% × $4,000).

Chapter 3

When income is taxed in a different period than it is accrued for fin. acct. there is a timing difference.

All of the following result in nontaxable income except: a. stock dividend b. interest on municipal bonds c. Capital gain distribution reinvested in the mutual fund d. Distribution identified as a return of capital

In 1988, when Sherry was 55 years old w/ an additional life expectancy of 20 years, she purchased a single life annuity for 200,000 that was to pay her 15,000 per year for life starting in 1991. Sherry just received her 15,000 payment for 2012. How much of the 15,000 must Sherry include in income? 15,000, she recovered her entire investment.

Which of the following is not included in income? 5% interest on NYC general revenue bonds.

Chapter 4

A single employee who is not covered by an employer's retirement plan may always contribute at least 5,500 of earned income to his or her IRA.

George is allowed to buy fringe benefits equal to 10% of his annual salary of 75,000. Which of the following would be taxable if selected? $1,500 country club membership

Elizabeth received the following benefits from her employer this year:

- 5,000 year-end bonus for exceeding sales expectations
- 400 cash as a length-of-service award
- 2,400 for insurance premiums paid by her employer for a disability income policy
- 5,100 for tuition paid by her employer for courses related to her job under an educational assistance plan

How much must Elizabeth include in gross income? 5,400

Mary, a taxpayer in the 33% marg. tax bracket borrows $500,000 at 10% interest to invest in 7% tax-exempt municipal bonds. The annual interest expense on the loan is 50,000. Mary earns 35,000 interest income on the bonds. What is Mary's interest expense deduction? Mary is allowed no interest deduction because the loan proceeds were used to invest in tax-exempt

3. Interest Deduction

When Kelley couldn't make several monthly payments on a business loan, her brother Mike made 3 of the monthly payments of 700 each, a total of 2,100 (1950 for i.e and 150 for the principal).

a. What is Mike's deduction for i.e? Can't deduct anything b/c it's not a loan.

b. What is Kelley's deduction for i.e? 5,850 i.e for the 9 monthly payments that should be made.

c. What could they have done to preserve the tax deductions? Mike should have given (or loaned) the money to Kelley and let Kelley make the loan payments. That way, Kelley could take a deduction for the 7,800 interest paid that year.

An accrual-basis taxpayer does **not** recognize an expense when the cash is paid even if the service for which the money is paid has not been rendered.

1. Sales taxes on supplies, property taxes on real property, FICA taxes on employees' wages are deductible by a business.

2. Claudia went to the west coast to attend several meetings with prospective clients for her business. She flew out on Wednesday afternoon, spent all day Thursday, Friday, Monday and Tuesday attending meetings, and then spent the rest of the week touring the area, returning home on Saturday. She spent $800 on airfare, $1600 on hotels (10 nights at $160 per night), 400 for a rental car ($40 per day from Wednesday night through Saturday of the following week), and $360 for meals ($30 per day Thursday through the following Friday and $15 on each of her travel days), what is her allowable deduction for travel away from home? 2,305

800 + (7 × 160) + (4 × 40) + .5 (6 × 30) + .5 (2 × 15) = 2,305

3. Waldo bought 2 tickets for a Packers game on Ebay for $400. The tickets had a face value of $50 each. He took a client to the game and they had dinner afterwards where they discussed business. The cost of the dinner was $70. What is Waldo's deduction for these expenses? $85

[.5 (70 + 50 + 50)]

Chapter 6

22. Joe started a new business year. He had purchased a computer 2 years ago for $4,000 and decided to use it in his business until he could afford a new system. He could purchase a new computer with the same specifications for $1,800, but his used computer is worth only $1,100. What is his computer's basis for depreciation? 1,100

Chapter 7

1. Wesley sold a piece of property for 30,000 cash paying a $3,000 sales commission the buyer assumed Wesley's $13,000 mortgage on the property. Wesley had purchased the property for $15,000 and had invested an additional $6,000 in it. What is Wesley's realized gain on the sale? 19,000

(30,000 − 3,000 + 13,000) − 21,000 = 19,000

aldwell Corporation sold a factory building for 300,000. The building originally cost $600,000 d had an adjusted basis of $200,000 due to the $400,000 depreciation taken when it was id. What is Caldwell's Section 1231 gain on the sale of property? 80,000

300,000 - 200,000 = 100,000 total gain; 100,000 × .2 = 20,000 Section 291 recapture;

80,000 = Section 1231 gain

n March 17, a calendar-year taxpayer sells a machine used in its usiness for $9,500. The machine was purchased sixteen months earlier for $9,000 nd depreciation deductions of $1,800 have been taken. What is the amount nd type of gain recognized on the sale? $1,800 section 1245 recapture; $500 Section 1231 gain

9,000 - (8,500 - 1,800) = 2,300

1,800 = Section 1245 recapture

500 = Section 1231 gain

hich of the following is a capital asset? Personal auto

dna had 20,000 of ordinary income. In addition, she had a $1500 short term pital gain on one stock and a 4,900 long-term capital loss on another. What is r net income before any deductions? 17,000

LTCL 4,900 - STCG 1,500 = 3,400 LTCL; current deduction limited to 3,000

During the current tax year, the Feckel Company has the following gains and losses om property transactions:

$12,000 Section 1231 gain
$23,000 long-term capital gain
$21,000 Section 1231 loss
$4,000 Section 1231 gain

What is the amount and type of gain or loss reported by Feckel for the year?

(5,000 net Section 1231 loss; 23,000 capital gain

12,000 Section 1231 gain + 4000 Sec. 1231 gain - 21,000 Sec 1231 loss = 5,000 net Sec 1231 loss that is deducted currently

23,000 LTCG included in income

Bobsy Company has a $14,000 net Section 1231 gain for the current tax year from its only property transaction. In the previous year, it had a $7,000 net Section 1231 loss. For the current year, the net Section 1231 gain will be taxed as: A 7,000 ordinary income and a $7,000 long term capital gain

Ginger sold stock that she had purchased five years ago for 15,000 to her brother, Carl, for $12,000. Next month, Carl sold the stock for $11,000. What is the amount and type of gain or loss included in Carl's income from this sale?

1,000 short-term capital loss

9. Wally (who is in the 25% tax bracket) has a $5,000 short-term capital loss on some bonds, a $6,000 long-term capital loss on collectibles, $15,000 Section 1202 gain, and a net $4,000 long term capital gain from an investment. What is amount and type of gain(s) an tax rate(s) applied? $4000 gain @ 28%; 4000 long term capital gain @ 15
The 6000 collectible loss and 5,000 STCL loss offset 11,000 of the 15,000 section 1202 gain; the remaining gain 4,000 is taxed at 28%; the [illegible] LTCG is taxed at 15%

10. Donza company has unrecaptured Section 1231 losses from the two previous years totaling $25,000 and a $32,000 Section 1231 gain in the current year. Based on this information, all of the following statements concerning Donza's taxable income for the current year are correct except:

Unrecaptured Section 1231 losses are taxable as capital gain

Correct

- Taxable ordinary income is $25,000
- Taxable capital gain is $7,000
- The amount taxable as ordinary income is lesser of the unrecaptured losses or the current Section 1231 gain

11. Justin, who is single, sells his principal residence that he has owned and occupied for the past five years. His adjusted basis for the residence is $90,000. He incurred selling expenses of $10,000. How much gain must Justin recognize if sells the residence for $390,000? $40,000

(390,000 - 10,000 - 90,000 - 250,000 exclusion)

Capital 1. Gain on sale of stock by an individual

1231 & Section 1250 2. Gain on the sale of a building used for 15 years by a corporation

1245 3. Gain on the sale of a machine used by a business for 4 years sold at a price less than its original cost

Capital 4. Gain on the sale of a personal residence

Ordinary 5. Gain on the sale of inventory

1231 6. Loss on the sale of equipment used in a business for 3 years.

Capital 7. Loss on the sale of municipal bonds by a corporation

ordinary 8. Gain on sale of a machine used by a business for 11 months.

ordinary 9. Loss on the factoring of recievables.

1231 10. Gain on sale of a building used by a partnership for 8 years in excess of its original cost.

Chapter 2

Merced Company has invested 200,000 in a project. It had before tax net income of 100,000 in year 1, 150,000 in year 2, and 125,000 in year 3. What is the net present value of this project's after-tax net cash flow if Merced's discount rate is 8% and its marginal tax rate is 34% in all years? 11,464

1 - .34 = .66

100,000 × .926 × .66 = 61116

150,000 × .857 × .66 = 84,843

125,000 × .794 × .66 = 65,505

+

211,464 - 200,000 = 11,464

Chapter 6

1. Bangor Company incurred 70,000 of research costs in year 1. In May of year 2, it began to sell the products developed through this research. Which of the following is correct regarding these expenditures? Bangor can deduct 9,333 in year 2.

$\left(70,000 \times \frac{8}{60}\right)$ ← May - Dec

↖ 5 years × 12 months

Chapter 5

1. Andrew's hobby is painting. During the current year, Andrew sold three of his paintings for a total of \$2,200. His related expenses include \$800 utilities, \$1,200 supplies, and \$400 in depreciation. Of these expenses incurred, how much can Andrew deduct in the current year? \$2,200

it's a hobby so you can't go more than total income

Chapter 4

Henry, age 45, is an employee of Argus corporation. His fringe benefits for the current year included:

Don't include

- 2,500 contributed by Argus to his qualified deferred compensation retirement plan. This year, the retirement plan earned \$600 in interest and dividend income. Henry received no distributions from this plan.
- A 100,000 face value group term life insurance policy for which Argus paid premiums of \$650. Henry is a key employee and it is a discriminatory plan. ← include amount paid because it's discriminatory
- The use of a company-owned automobile. The annual lease value of this car is \$15,000. Henry used it 70% of the time (and miles) for personal use and 30% for business use.
- Free parking in the company parking lot valued at \$100 per month)

How much must Henry include in gross income? 11,150

(650 + (15,000 × 70%))

23.) [c]

Schedule M-1:

Net income per books = 150,000 gross profit -60,000 operating expenses + 4,000 dividend income + 10,000 capital gain - 15,000 capital loss - 22,000 financial depreciation - 5,000 charitable contribution - 5,520 income tax = $56,480 net income per books

56,480 net income per books + 5,520 income tax + 5,000 (15,000 capital loss - 10,000 capital gain) excess capital loss + 600 (5,000 - 4,400) excess charitable contributions - 18,000 (15,000 Section 179 expensing - 22,000 financial depreciation) excess tax depreciation + 25,000 additional tax depreciation - $22,000 financial depreciation) excess tax depreciation = 49,600 taxable income before special deductions

1. Net income	56,480	7. Income recorded	
2. Federal income	5,520	Tax-exempt interest	
3. Excess of capital losses	5,000	8. Deductions	
4. Income subject to tax		a. Depreciation	18,000
		b. Charitable	
			18,000
5. Expenses			
a. Depreciation			
b. Charitable 600			
c. Travel	600	9. Add lines 7 and 8	18,000
6. Add line 1 through 5	69,600	10. Income	49,600

36,800 taxable income + 10,000 NOL + 2,800 DRD = 49,600 taxable income before special deductions